POST WALL
POST SQUARE

Also by Kristina Spohr

Germany and the Baltic Problem after the Cold War:
The Development of a New Ostpolitik, 1989–2000

Building Sustainable and Effective Military Capabilities:
A Systemic Comparison of Professional and Conscript Forces (editor)

At the Crossroads of Past and Present: 'Contemporary' History and
the Historical Discipline (co-editor, with Jan Palmowski)

The Global Chancellor: Helmut Schmidt and the Reshaping of the
International Order

Helmut Schmidt: Der Weltkanzler

Transcending the Cold War: Summits, Statecraft, and the Dissolution of
Bipolarity in Europe, 1970–1990 (co-editor, with David Reynolds)

Open Door: NATO and Euro-Atlantic Security after the Cold War
(co-editor, with Daniel S. Hamilton)

Exiting the Cold War, Entering a New World
(co-editor, with Daniel S. Hamilton)

Wendezeit: Die Neuordnung der Welt nach 1989

POST WALL
POST SQUARE

*How Bush, Gorbachev,
Kohl, and Deng Shaped
the World after 1989*

Kristina Spohr

Yale
UNIVERSITY
PRESS
NEW HAVEN AND LONDON

For my godchildren

Anna Lisa (*1997)
Daniel (*2004)
James (*2007)
Clio (*2013)

born into the post-Wall world

Contents

Maps

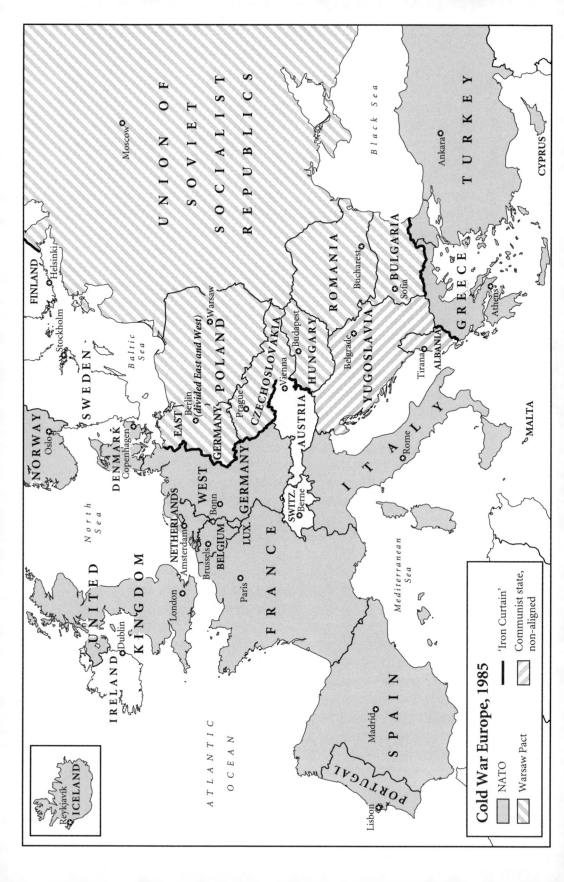

Cold War Europe, 1985

'Iron Curtain'

NATO

Warsaw Pact

Communist state, non-aligned

UNION OF SOVIET SOCIALIST REPUBLICS

Moscow ✦

Black Sea

FINLAND
Helsinki ✦

NORWAY
Oslo ✦

SWEDEN
Stockholm ✦

Baltic Sea

DENMARK
Copenhagen ✦

POLAND
Warsaw ✦

EAST GERMANY
Berlin *(divided East and West)*

CZECHOSLOVAKIA
Prague ✦

ROMANIA
Bucharest ✦

BULGARIA
Sofia ✦

TURKEY
Ankara ✦

CYPRUS

HUNGARY
Budapest ✦

Vienna ✦
AUSTRIA

YUGOSLAVIA
Belgrade ✦

ALBANIA
Tirana ✦

GREECE
Athens ✦

WEST GERMANY
Bonn ✦

LUX.

SWITZ.
Berne ✦

North Sea

NETHERLANDS
Amsterdam ✦

BELGIUM
Brussels ✦

UNITED KINGDOM
London ✦

IRELAND
Dublin ✦

FRANCE
Paris ✦

ITALY
Rome ✦

Mediterranean Sea

MALTA

SPAIN
Madrid ✦

PORTUGAL
Lisbon ✦

ATLANTIC OCEAN

ICELAND
Reykjavik ✦

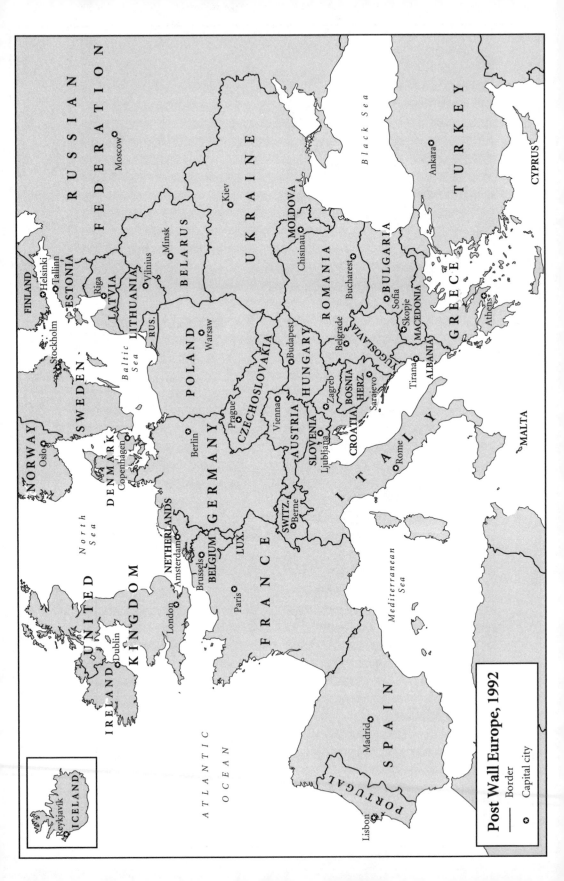

Post Wall Europe, 1992

— Border
⊕ Capital city

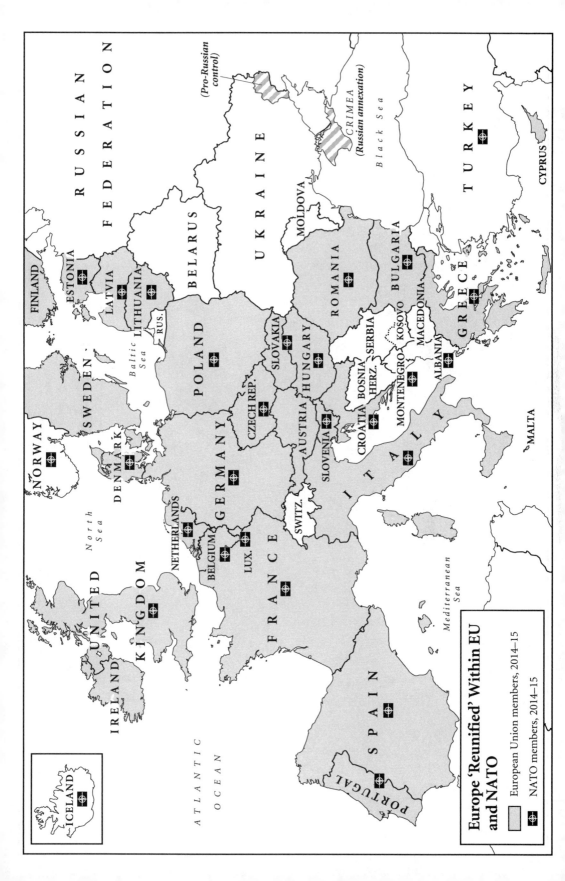

Europe 'Reunified' Within EU and NATO

European Union members, 2014–15

NATO members, 2014–15

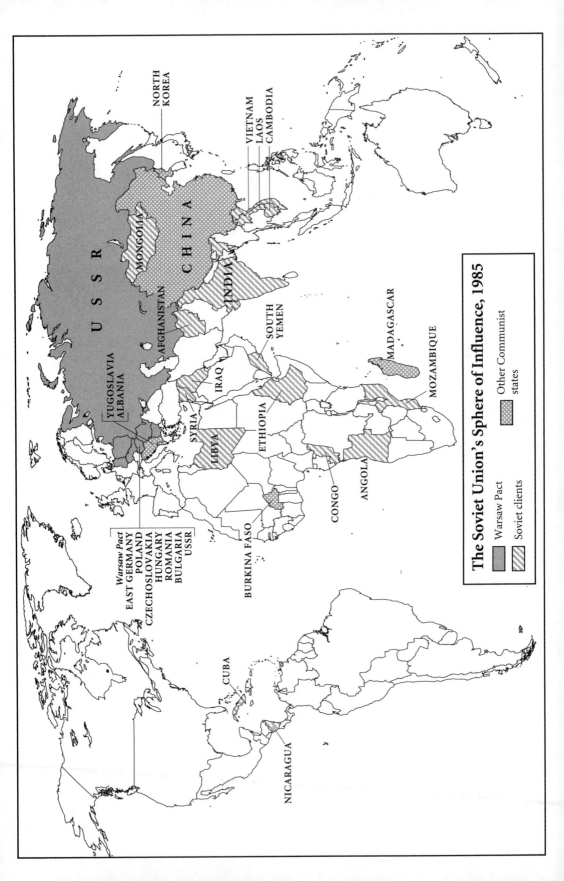

The Soviet Union's Sphere of Influence, 1985

Warsaw Pact
EAST GERMANY
POLAND
CZECHOSLOVAKIA
HUNGARY
ROMANIA
BULGARIA
USSR

YUGOSLAVIA
ALBANIA

U S S R

MONGOLIA

AFGHANISTAN

C H I N A

NORTH KOREA

VIETNAM
LAOS
CAMBODIA

INDIA

SYRIA

IRAQ

SOUTH YEMEN

LIBYA

ETHIOPIA

BURKINA FASO

CONGO

ANGOLA

MADAGASCAR

MOZAMBIQUE

CUBA

NICARAGUA

Warsaw Pact

Soviet clients

Other Communist states

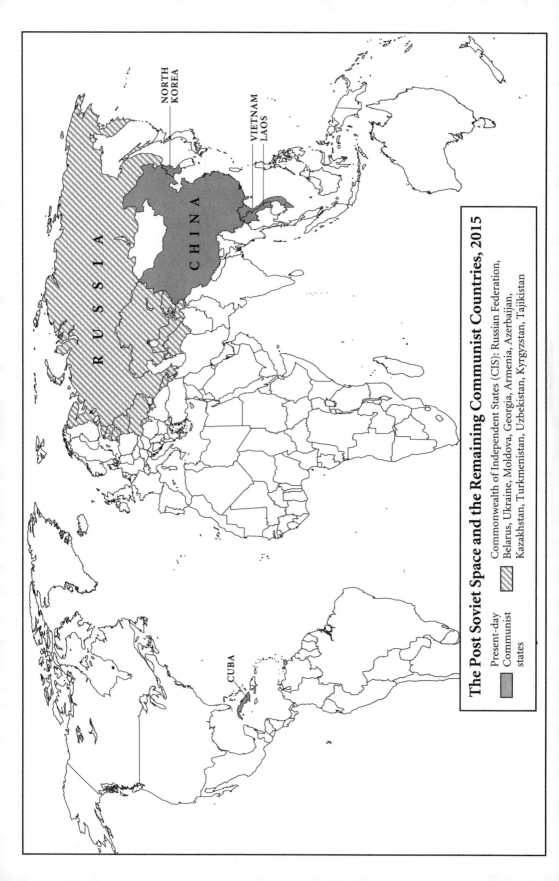

The Post Soviet Space and the Remaining Communist Countries, 2015

Commonwealth of Independent States (CIS): Russian Federation, Belarus, Ukraine, Moldova, Georgia, Armenia, Azerbaijan, Kazakhstan, Turkmenistan, Uzbekistan, Kyrgyzstan, Tajikistan

Present-day Communist states

RUSSIA

CHINA

NORTH KOREA

VIETNAM
LAOS

CUBA

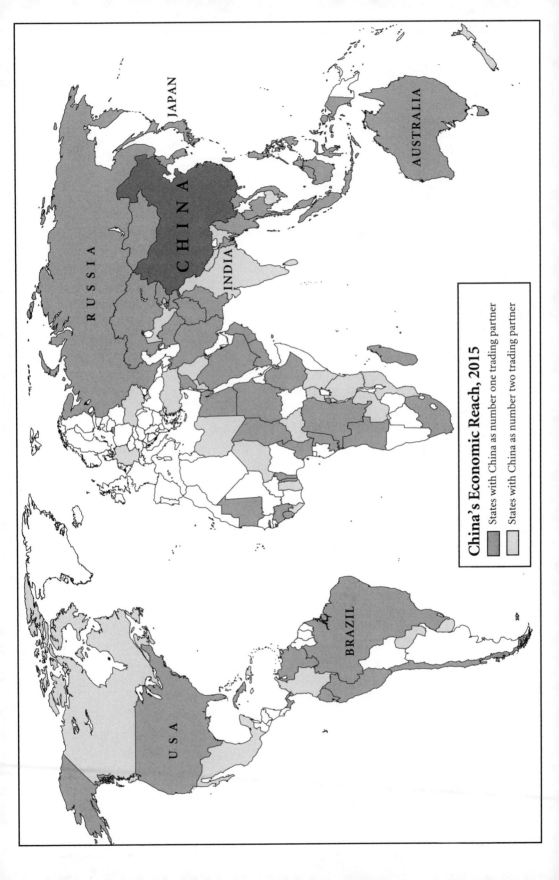

China's Economic Reach, 2015

☐ States with China as number one trading partner
☐ States with China as number two trading partner

If 1989 was the year of sweeping away, 1990 must become the year of building anew.

James A. Baker, 1990

We don't care what others say about us. The only thing we really care about is a good environment for developing ourselves. So long as history eventually proves the superiority of the Chinese socialist system, that's enough.

Deng Xiaoping, 1989

France is our homeland, Europe is our future.

François Mitterrand, 1987

Peace is not unity in similarity but unity in diversity, in the comparison and conciliation of differences.

Mikhail Gorbachev, 1991

Politics needs a sense of the possible, also of what is acceptable to others.

Helmut Kohl, 2009

Introduction

Economic crisis in the Soviet Union ... War in the Gulf ... Chaos in Yugoslavia ... A Stalinist coup against Soviet leader Mikhail Gorbachev ... Mobilisation across the whole Eastern bloc ... Soviet invasion of the Balkans ... The West calls up reservists and puts civil defence on highest alert ...

At dawn on 24 February 1989, thousands of Warsaw Pact tanks begin rolling into West Germany, from the Baltic right down to the border with Czechoslovakia. The main attack comes across the North German Plain, with a secondary strike toward Frankfurt. At first Western armoured forces manage to keep the enemy in check, despite a tidal wave of refugees. But then the Kremlin resorts to the use of poison gas against Great Britain and northern Germany. On 5 March, Allied forces start to break and NATO authorises the first use of tactical nuclear weapons. Undeterred, the Soviets press home their attacks, so NATO moves to a second and this time massive nuclear strike on 9 March with twenty-five nuclear bombs and missiles, a third of which are launched from West Germany. The Soviet leadership reciprocates in kind. An atomic firestorm engulfs most of West and East Germany. The radiation spreads across Poland, Czechoslovakia and Hungary ...[1]

Of course this was not what really happened. It was the storyline for NATO's biennial 'Wintex' war game. In the 1989 scenario Germany became the theatre of a 'limited nuclear war', which meant instant obliteration for hundreds of thousands of Germans, and radioactive contamination across the historic heartland of Europe condemning millions more to a lingering, agonising death. Worse, the spectre loomed that localised nuclear conflict might ignite the Third World War.

Even before the war game had begun, the Wintex 89 drill narrative had been leaked to the press and then sensationalised in the German and Soviet media. So appalling was the prospect sketched out in the simulation that Waldemar Schreckenberger – the man from the Chancellery chosen to play commander-in-chief (*Bundeskanzler übung-shalber*) during the exercise while the real chancellor was busy conducting West Germany's normal government business – refused to launch the second strike in an effort to curtail the human tragedy. As a result, Wintex 89 was prematurely aborted. There would be no more NATO Wintex drills in the future.

At the beginning of 1989 the Western defence establishment still took seriously the prospect that the long superpower confrontation might climax in a global nuclear holocaust. Only a few months later, however, the European future looked radically different. The Cold War did indeed come to an end in a rapid and unexpected fashion – but not with the nuclear 'big bang' for which the two armed camps had spent so much time, money and ingenuity rehearsing.

The war between East and West never did take place; the Cold War denouement was a largely peaceful process, out of which a new global order was created through international agreements negotiated in an unprecedented spirit of cooperation. The two chief catalysts of change were a new Russian leader, with a new political vision, and popular protest in the streets of Eastern Europe. People power was explosive, but not in the military sense – the demonstrators of 1989 demanded democracy and reform, they disarmed governments that had seemed impregnable and, in a human tide of travellers and migrants, they broke open the once-impenetrable Iron Curtain. The symbolic moment that captured the drama of those months was the fall of the Berlin Wall on the night of 9 November.

In 1989, everything seemed in flux. Currents of revolutionary change surged up from below, while the wielders of power attempted political reform at the top.[2] The Marxist–Leninist ideology of Soviet communism, once the mental architecture of the Soviet bloc, haemorrhaged credibility and rapidly lost grip. Liberal capitalist democracy now seemed like the wave of the future: while the 'East' embarked on a 'catch-up' transformation in Western Europe's image, the world appeared set on a path of convergence around American values. There was talk of 'the end of history'.[3]

Nothing had prepared international leaders for such swift and all-encompassing change. For decades they had played war games like

Wintex 89. They had never formulated a scenario for a *peaceful* exit from the Cold War; at worst they just had a fictive military strategy for surviving nuclear Armageddon or, at best, diplomatic tactics for managing a muddled competitive coexistence between two adversarial blocs. They could scarcely have been less prepared for the actual ending that came in 1989–91. This book explores why a durable and apparently stable world order collapsed in 1989 and then examines the process by which a new order was improvised out of its ruins.[4]

In order to understand the paths they took and the decisions they made, I peer over the shoulders of key statesmen, watching them struggle to understand and control the new forces at work in their world. These men (and one woman) explored a range of often-conflicting options in an effort to manage events, impose stability and avoid war. Lacking road maps or shared blueprints for a future world order, they adopted an essentially cautious approach to the challenge of radical change – using and adapting principles and institutions that had proved successful in the West during the Cold War. This was undoubtedly a diplomatic revolution, but conducted – paradoxically perhaps – in a conservative manner.

The leaders involved were a small, interconnected group. In Europe, the triangle that particularly mattered was formed by the Soviet Union, the United States and the Federal Republic of Germany: on one level, the political leaders – Mikhail Gorbachev, George H. W. Bush and Helmut Kohl;[5] on another their foreign ministers – Eduard Shevardnadze, James Baker and Hans-Dietrich Genscher.[6] It was within these fields of force that post-Cold War Europe was shaped. On the margins were two potent but increasingly isolated figures: Margaret Thatcher in Britain, who opposed the rapid unification of Germany, and the French president François Mitterrand, who reluctantly participated on the condition that a united Germany must be deeply embedded in Europe.[7] Their interactions with Kohl, especially over the project of European integration, formed a further power-political triangle.[8]

Yet it is a central assertion of my book that we cannot understand post-Wall Europe without taking account of what happened in 1989 on the other side of the world. Under Deng Xiaoping, the People's Republic of China experienced a dramatically different exit from the Cold War – forever synonymous with the bloodshed in Tiananmen Square on 4 June.[9] China's gradual entry into the global capitalist economy was therefore counterbalanced by Deng's determination to maintain the dominance of the Communist Party. This balancing act – so different from

Gorbachev's complete loss of control – moved his country into another orbit. The people power that had played such a central role in Eastern Europe had no analogue here. Deng's 'success' in suppressing it had vast implications that are still being played out in today's world. So, the European story has to be framed within another, global triangle – itself a continuation of the Sino-Soviet-American 'tripolarity' that was emerging in the later stages of the Cold War.[10]

Taken as a whole, these managers of change formed a cohort largely from the same generation, born between 1924 and 1931, with the exceptions of Mitterrand (b.1916) and Deng (b.1904). All of them were marked by the memory of a world at war between 1937 and 1945 and thus shared an acute awareness of the fragility of peace. It is noteworthy that most of them (Kohl and Mitterrand were exceptions) also lost power in 1990–2, so they were never obliged to confront in a sustained way – as political leaders – with the fallout from their actions.

My first three chapters deal with the headline-grabbing upheavals of 1989 – the cutting of Hungary's Iron Curtain with Austria, the bloodbath in Tiananmen Square, the accidental fall of the Berlin Wall. But the main focus is on what happened in the exhilarating yet alarming era that followed: the era of the post-Wall and the post-Square. The hope that humankind was entering a new age of freedom and sustained peace competed with the dawning recognition that the bipolar stability of the Cold War era was already giving way to something less binary and more dangerous.[11]

The core of the book traces the story of how in 1990–1 the world was reshaped by conservative diplomacy – adapting the institutions of the Cold War to a new era. Although this was led by the West, and particularly by US president George Bush, the Soviet leader Mikhail Gorbachev was also willing to buy into the process as part of an effort to reorient the Soviet Union's official ideology towards the 'common' values Soviet citizens shared with the West.[12] The resulting rapprochement culminated in a brief era of unprecedented cooperation between the US and the USSR. Their collaborative approach to Iraq's invasion of Kuwait in 1990 was to serve as the centrepiece of what the American president described as the 'new world order'. Confrontational bipolarity appeared to be metamorphosing into a two-pillar approach to global security, rooted in superpower cooperation within the United Nations and guided by international law.[13]

Both Bush and Gorbachev hoped that this new modus vivendi could serve as the foundation for post-Cold War international relations. America was clearly the senior partner but the cooperation was real. The partnership worked, but it was fragile, precisely because it was overly focused on the relationship between the two men at the apex of their respective states. Bush, Kohl and other Western leaders all clung to Mikhail Gorbachev rather than engaging with the deeper problems of the unravelling Soviet Union. At the end of 1991, the USSR totally disintegrated, forcing Bush to take seriously the man at the helm of post-Soviet Russia, Boris Yeltsin – who was struggling to confront the immense challenge of his country's transition to capitalist democracy.[14] This new upheaval in global geopolitics, affecting not only Europe but also Asia, obliged Bush to rethink his two-pillar approach.

With the Soviet Union gone and bipolarity a thing of the past, the United States was now pressing with fresh urgency for a truly global US-led free-trading system. Intended to replace the almost moribund 1947 General Agreement on Tariffs and Trade (GATT) which no longer seemed adequate to the dynamics of an increasingly globalised world economy, a new World Trade Organisation should embrace the big players Russia and China as they moved out of their respective command economies or 'Plans', and offer more support to the developing countries. Yet the US was not alone in seeking to reposition itself in the global economic power play. Japan, with its prodigious economy, was touted as the coming hegemon of the 'Pacific Century', whose economic weight would fill the geopolitical vacuum created by the collapse of the Soviet Union. The leadership of communist China had its own ambitions. The Chinese regime survived 'the Tiananmen Incident', consolidated its hold on the country and prospered post-Square; over time this would prove far more important, both economically and geo-strategically, than the false dawn of the Rising Sun.[15]

In Europe, too, the peace and stability of the post-war era were starting to fray in 1991 when Yugoslavia became engulfed by a genocidal war. A once firm Balkan polity fractured into warring statelets, triggering massive movements of refugees. These new Balkan wars did not ignite a European or global conflagration, as in 1914, but international leaders struggled to put out the flames.[16]

The splintering of Yugoslavia also raised fears of what Gorbachev himself called the 'Balkanisation' of the Soviet Union in 1991.[17] For a while Moscow's power struggle with Kiev over territory in Ukraine and Crimea seemed even to teeter on the edge of war. Disputes and clashes erupted during 1992 about ownership of the Black Sea Fleet and strategic ports, Russian basing rights and the use of Ukrainian military facilities. And Washington was particularly anxious about the fate of the Soviet nuclear arsenal – now scattered between Russia and three other newly independent post-Soviet republics.

The collapse of Soviet power allowed former clients around the world to assert themselves as 'renegade' states. Even after the Kuwait War of 1990–1, the problem of Saddam Hussein's Iraq remained unresolved, and Kim Il-sung's North Korea, with its secret nuclear weapons programme, now became a particular headache.[18] This is why the last two chapters of *Post Wall, Post Square* are devoted to global events in 1992 – a year largely ignored in most accounts of the end of the Cold War, in which problems were spawned that are still with us in the twenty-first century. Notwithstanding the premature triumphalism of some commentators, the Cold War did not end with the simple victory of the United States over the Soviet Union, and the world was not remade in America's image.[19]

Nowhere did international diplomacy produce swifter and more impressive results than in the unification of Germany. The German question posed a huge challenge because of the country's problematic place in Europe, its centrality to the origins of two world wars and its subsequent position as the cockpit of the Cold War. In the process of managing German unification, two key alliances of the West during the Cold War – NATO and the European Community – were conserved, modified and eventually enlarged to encompass the states of Central and Eastern Europe.[20]

The measures adopted to stabilise post-Wall Europe were thus essentially conservative in character, in the sense that they made use of pre-existing, Western institutions and structures, rather than custom-designing new ones to meet the exigencies of a new era. Despite the efforts of some European statesmen – notably Genscher, Gorbachev and Mitterrand – in 1989–91, no new pan-European architecture was created to embrace the two halves of the continent and incorporate Russia into a shared security structure. The Helsinki 1975 Conference on Security and Cooperation in Europe (CSCE) possessed the potential to become such a structure, but it was never converted into an operative security organisation. The post-Wall political reality – with America set to remain a 'European power' – conspired against such pan-European paths. And the attractions of a Europe reunified under the aegis of an ever-closer

European Union and secured by a reinvented NATO were simply too strong.[21]

Consequently, the West–East asymmetry increased over time, as the jumbled fragments of what had been the Cold War order were re-formed within an ever-larger Western-dominated framework. The resulting imbalance would become intolerable for Gorbachev's successors, Boris Yeltsin and Vladimir Putin. A marginalised – though still powerful and status-conscious Russian rump state – was left to lick its wounds on the periphery of the new Europe. We are still grappling with the consequences.[22]

This rereading of the period 1989–92 draws on archival material in various languages from both sides of the former Iron Curtain. *Post Wall, Post Square* relies heavily on recently declassified or neglected documents – ranging from memoranda to memcons, from personal letters to intelligence reports – in the national, presidential and Foreign Ministry archives of the United States, the Soviet Union (Russia), Germany, Britain, France and Estonia. Other important resources include the National Security Archive, the Woodrow Wilson Center Digital Archive and the associated Cold War International History Project in Washington DC – with their abundance of electronic briefing books and published documentary collections from the West, Eastern Europe, Russia and China (including party and Politburo materials). Further primary sources include diaries and private papers by the leaders and their advisers and numerous memoirs by the major actors.[23]

Post Wall, Post Square combines the granular reconstruction of key episodes with the synoptic study of macro-historical change. To comprehend properly this era of transitions requires us to adopt an artificial vantage point 'above' the confusion of events. But a successful analysis must also find space for the narratives with which leading protagonists made sense of their world and justified their actions. After all, the story of what happened in those years was 'co-written' by the chief actors. They were never just players in someone else's tale, but powerful, if flawed, makers of history in their own right.

In 1995 German president Roman Herzog characterised his era as 'a time that as yet has no name'.[24] Twenty-five years later, his aphorism has lost little of its poignancy, because the distinguishing features of the post-Cold War era remain difficult to discern or understand. Some may say, as 1989 recedes into the past, that the overarching narrative must be economic – taking us from the collapse of the Bretton Woods financial system in the 1970s to the financial crash of 2008.[25] But I argue that a deeper analysis of these crucial 'hinge years' of 1989–92 helps to make sense of the underlying geopolitical order in which the upheavals of global capitalism take their place. And it is this order that is now under threat.

The achievements of the conservative managers were impressive: above all, they stabilised Central Europe during a period of rapid geopolitical change. But the (mainly American) confidence that the world would henceforth converge towards US values in an increasingly Washington-centred global order has not stood the test of time. The notion that an aggrieved but resurgent Russia[26] or the People's Republic of China – always following its own compass[27] – would accept subordinate status in a unipolar world now appears hopelessly naive.[28] And the Europe of the Maastricht Treaty failed to generate the vision and energy to create a continent that was whole, free and dynamic. It was cramped by its adherence to dogmas forged after 1945 and hobbled by its chronic lack of independent political and military power.

This new European Union of 1992 co-opted the logic of the West German state's post-war trajectory. The Federal Republic had long renounced Germany's historical pretensions as a military power. European integration was conceived in the 1950s as a German–French peace project built around economic prosperity and social welfare. As the EU sought to reap the post-Cold War peace dividend in the 1990s, it saw itself in German mode as a beacon of 'civilian power'[29] – not of military might.

This represented a linear reading of the post-Wall future, extrapolating the peaceful unification of Germany onto the European plane. But the plausibility of this eirenic dream has been called into question by the rise in the 2010s of populism, nationalism and illiberalism – with 'Brexit' shaking the core belief that the European integration project is irreversible and US President Donald Trump undermining the presumed indestructibility of the transatlantic alliance. The American vision of a 'global community of nations'[30] – an order based on international law, liberal values, the limited use of force and a legitimate international arbitrating authority – now looks utopian.[31] The old great power rivalry is back with a vengeance and the traditional Western verities of democracy and free trade are being challenged around the world – especially by Russia and China, but also by America itself.

The deficiencies of the international settlement that ended the Cold

War are now obvious. Frozen conflicts, the unravelling of arms-control agreements, the sclerosis of international institutions, the emergence of powerful authoritarian regimes and the proliferating threat of weapons of mass destruction (WMD) – these are just some of the unforeseen consequences of design flaws in the new order improvised with such haste and ingenuity by the shapers of world affairs in 1989–92.[32] That is why – now more than ever – we need to understand its origins and troubled birth.

Chapter 1

Reinventing Communism: Russia and China

The 7th of December 1988. Manhattan was abuzz that evening. Thousands of New Yorkers and tourists lined the streets, cheering, waving and giving thumbs-up signs behind the police barricades as Mikhail Gorbachev rode down Broadway in a forty-seven-car motorcade.

Gorbymania in Manhattan

Suddenly, in front of the Winter Garden Theater where the musical *Cats* was playing, Gorbachev ordered his stretch limo to halt. Smiling, he and his wife Raisa jumped out and had their pictures taken. The Soviet leader was photographed beneath a huge neon Coca-Cola sign, raising his clenched fists in triumph – like Robert 'Rocky' Balboa.

Gorbachev was really soaking up American adulation. A block south, in the middle of Times Square – the Mecca of world capitalism – the electronic billboard was flashing a red hammer and sickle with the message 'Welcome, General Secretary Gorbachev'. He might still have been a communist at heart and the leader of America's rival superpower, but that night in New York, 'Gorby' was a superstar, hailed above all as a peacemaker. Indeed most of his time in Manhattan the Soviet leader was mixing with celebs, billionaires and high society, rather than rubbing shoulders with the American proletariat.[1]

One of the visits tentatively scheduled was to Trump Tower. Real-estate developer Donald Trump could not wait to take Mrs Gorbachev around the glitzy shops in his tower's marble atrium. He was also dying to show off to the Gorbachevs a suite on the sixtieth floor with a swimming pool that he claimed was 'virtually regulation size, within the confines of an apartment' and, of course, his own opulent $19 million domicile on the sixty-eighth floor. He said he wanted them to get 'a good shot of what New York and the United States are about' and he hoped that they would 'find it special'. In the end, Gorbachev's itinerary was altered and Trump Tower slipped off the list. That after-noon, however, when a Gorbachev lookalike was seen strolling past Tiffany's and down Fifth Avenue followed by a horde of film crews drawing huge crowds, Trump and his bodyguards rushed down from his office thinking that the Soviet leader had changed his mind and was now keen to view his temple of consumerism. Squeezing on to the sidewalk, the tycoon enthusiastically pumped the fake Gorbachev's hand.

The real Gorbachev was actually sequestered inside the Soviet mission. Caught out, Trump assured journalists he had seen through the stunt, declaring 'I looked into the back of his limo and saw four attractive women. I knew that his society had not come that far yet in terms of capitalist decadence.' Mikhail Gorbachev certainly did not share Donald Trump's ideal of decadence. Nevertheless, he was clearly fascinated by the market economy. Bystander Joe Peters reckoned that Gorbachev was 'going to learn all our tricks of capitalism and become the Donald Trump-ski of the Soviet Union'.[2]

The sense of anticipation was palpable. That very morning Gorbachev achieved perhaps his greatest international triumph so far. At the United Nations he had delivered a truly astounding address, one that would become pivotal for future Soviet foreign policy and for the course of world politics. Gorbachev's intention was to deliver 'the exact opposite' of Winston Churchill's notorious Iron Curtain speech of 1946.

Over the course of one hour, the Soviet leader dropped a succession of bombshells on specific policy issues. Most striking, he declared the termination of the international class struggle, insisting that 'the use or threat of force no longer can or must be an instrument of foreign policy'. Instead, he urged the world to embrace 'the supremacy of the universal human idea' and lauded the significance of the 1948 UN Universal Declaration of Human Rights which had been adopted, almost to the day, forty years before.[3]

These were amazing words from any Moscow policymaker, let alone the general secretary of the Communist Party of the Soviet Union. On the eve of 1989 Gorbachev stood before the world as the master of reform, apparently in control of events.

In reality, he would unleash a revolution that swept everything before it – eventually even himself. And the Western leader who would have to cope with the fallout was a cautious new American president who felt considerable scepticism about his magnetic Soviet counterpart and was wary about the true intentions behind Russia's headline-grabbing reforms. George H. W. Bush had been vice president for all eight years of Ronald Reagan's presidency (1981–9). He would enter the White House determined to take stock of US–Soviet relations and rethink his priorities as he started building a new agenda that would distinguish him politically from the Reagan administration.[4] In fact, his main concern in early 1989 was how to handle the 'reinvention' of communism that was under way not in Europe but in Asia.

*

Mikhail Sergeyevich Gorbachev was not a 'normal' Soviet leader. Born in 1931 in Privolnoye, a small village near Stavropol in the north Caucasus, he grew up witnessing his family's suffering under Stalin's collectivisation drive and later the Great Purge. When Gorbachev was ten, his father was drafted into the army and did not return for five years. Privolnoye was spared destruction during the Great Patriotic War but Stavropol was occupied by the Germans for five months in 1942–3, so Gorbachev experienced the ravages of war close-up and did not forget. Academically gifted and interested in politics, he shone at school and was cultivated from an early age by the local leaders of the Communist Party. Thanks to their patronage, he was sent to the prestigious Moscow State University (MGU) to study law; in order to gain entry he wrote an essay entitled 'Stalin is our battle glory, Stalin is the Flight of our Youth' – evidence that his political views then were still 'straight Stalinist, like everyone else at the time', as his best friend at university put it. At a third-year ball he met Raisa Maximovna Titarenko, a chic and clever philosophy student. A year later, in 1954, they were married.

Sent back to Stavropol, Gorbachev rose steadily through the Soviet *nomenklatura* system in the usual way, while Raisa taught Marxism at the local polytechnic and studied for a PhD on the peasantry in the region's collective farms. Gorbachev's youthful Stalinism was shaken by First Secretary Nikita Khrushchev's 1956 'secret speech' which denounced his predecessor Stalin's monstrous crimes and laid bare the endemic problems of Russian industry and agriculture. Henceforth Gorbachev, though continuing to believe faithfully in communist ideology, recognised how flawed it had become in Soviet practice. Through his travels with Raisa to France, Italy and Sweden from the 1960s onwards, he encountered the West and glimpsed an alternative future. Meanwhile, his political career accelerated. In 1967, he became the regional party boss, aged only thirty-five; twelve years later he was put in charge of Soviet agriculture, moving to the centre of power in Moscow, while Raisa was given a teaching post at MGU. One of his leading patrons was KGB chief Yuri Andropov, who succeeded Leonid Brezhnev as general secretary in November 1982.[5]

Although nearing fifty, Gorbachev was almost a spring chicken by the standards of the Soviet Politburo. Andropov, nearly seventeen years his senior, suffered from acute kidney failure and died in February 1984. His successor Konstantin Chernenko was two decades senior to Gorbachev: afflicted with heart and lung problems, he expired in March 1985. Finally the old men of the Kremlin decided to jump a generation and opt for Gorbachev. Justifying to Raisa why he was taking the job, Mikhail said 'all those years ... it's been impossible to achieve anything substantial, anything on a large scale. It's like coming up against a wall. But life demands it. We can't go on like this.'[6] Yet what should be done instead was much harder to determine. First Gorbachev tried an anti-alcohol campaign; after that failed he looked for deeper remedies and new slogans, espousing first 'uskorenie' (acceleration), then 'perestroika' (restructuring) and 'glasnost' (transparency). But these did not entail revolutionary changes: Gorbachev was still a party man and wanted to re-form the Soviet system to make it more viable and competitive: his motto was 'Back to Lenin'.

His frequent invocations of Lenin were in part to justify to the party his policies of innovation and restructuring, which so sharply deviated from the Stalinist and Brezhnevite practice that in Gorbachev's opinion had perverted 'socialism'. But more than that, he identified his own view of fundamental reform of the Soviet system under the auspices of perestroika with Lenin's 1920s ideas of a New Economic Policy: a guided and limited system of free enterprise. His goal at this stage was not a turn to capitalism or to social democracy. For him Lenin remained the source of legitimacy for policy changes within the Communist Party of the Soviet Union (CPSU) – the pure font of Soviet doctrine. He wanted to restructure the traditional Soviet sociopolitical order 'within the system', which is why under glasnost he also advocated 'socialist pluralism' ahead of full 'political pluralism' – all this to reinvigorate the Soviet Union.[7]

To achieve reform and rejuvenation, Gorbachev had to reduce the burden of the military-industrial complex on the Soviet economy, intensified during the 1980s by the war in Afghanistan and the spiralling arms race with America.

To be sure, the Soviet command economy was performing poorly simply for structural reasons – a fact masked by the global oil price rise of the 1970s and the country's vast Siberian reserves which fuelled a GDP growth rate of 2–3.5% between 1971 and 1980. But when the oil price dropped in the next decade, national income fell sharply. Indeed, in 1980–5 the USSR found itself at near zero growth. The increasing dissatisfaction of Soviet consumers was exacerbated by declining living standards and limited access to high-tech civilian goods. This was due in part to the inflexibility of the planned economy and the lack of industrial modernisation, but the root problem was that perhaps up to a quarter of GDP was being gobbled up by the military sector to the detriment of the civilian production.[8]

In order to galvanise the economy at home while slowly opening it up to the outside world, Gorbachev needed to foster a stable international environment and also to address the USSR's 'imperial overstretch' in Eastern Europe and the developing world. This meant reducing US hostility (disengaging from the arms race) and making compromises in the Third World (including ideological recognition of the right to self-determination). So domestic policy was inextricably bound up with foreign policy. Seeking a less confrontational relationship with the United States, Gorbachev was keen to talk with his American opposite number.[9]

At first glance, however, US president Ronald Reagan seemed an unlikely partner. Born in 1911, and so the same age as the man Gorbachev had just replaced, Reagan was a vehement anti-communist who had intensified the arms race once he came to power in 1981. He was notorious for his denunciation of the USSR as an 'evil empire' and for his prediction that the 'march of freedom and democracy' would 'leave Marxism–Leninism on the ash heap of history'.[10] This all-out ideological competition, he believed, justified the military build-up of his early years. But there was another side to Reagan – the would-be peacemaker, who saw military power as a basis for diplomacy to secure 'peace through strength'. Even more surprising, this hard-headed realist cherished a utopian belief in a nuclear-free world.[11]

During his first term, Reagan had been unable to initiate dialogue with the sick old men of the Kremlin. But with the accession of Gorbachev, not merely dialogue but negotiation suddenly became possible. Over the course of four summits between Geneva in November 1985 and Moscow in May/June 1988 the discussions were often heated but the two leaders gradually forged a relationship based on personal trust and even affection. Gorbachev's radical nuclear arms-reduction proposals at Reykjavik in October 1986 – six months after the horrendous Chernobyl accident – almost carried Reagan along with him, to the horror of some die-hard advisers. By the time of their Washington meeting in December 1987 they had moved on to first-name terms. There was also substance in the new relationship. At Washington, Reagan and Gorbachev signed away a whole category of nuclear weapons in the Intermediate Nuclear Forces Treaty – the first time the superpowers had ever agreed to *reduce* their nuclear arsenals. Here was a significant step in defusing the Cold War, making it less likely that a nuclear conflict would break out. Atomic scientists put back their celebrated 'Doomsday Clock' to six minutes before midnight, instead of three. And on 31 May 1988, when Reagan was asked in Red Square whether he still felt the USSR was an 'evil empire', he replied 'I was talking about another time, another era.'[12]

Reagan was moving on – and so was Gorbachev. Six months later, the dramatic address at the UN on the morning of 7 December was for the Soviet leader a 'watershed' moment. He wanted to present himself as a shaper of international affairs but, unlike Churchill, moving the world *out* of the Cold War. And he was keen to wrong-foot the Americans, especially at a time of transition between presidents when their foreign policy would be in limbo. 'The Americans are scared that we might do something as in the spirit of Reykjavik.' He had been preparing the speech for months, ever since Reagan's visit, and it went through many drafts, being tweaked right up to the last minute. Gorbachev was determined to use the occasion to show the world his belief in the bright future of the rejuvenated Soviet Union and to confirm his credentials as a visionary peacemaker. And he hoped that by setting out his new political thinking in such an eye-catching way he would secure Western credits and economic assistance.[13]

By the time Gorbachev arrived at the UN, the vast General Assembly Hall was totally packed, with all 1,800 seats occupied. There was a buzz of excited chatter. Expectations were high. Gorbachev stepped up to the podium, dressed in a dark, well-tailored suit, white shirt and burgundy-coloured tie. At the start of his address, he spoke slowly and deliberately but then gathered pace, with increasing sweep and authority. In doing so, he set out his ideological blueprint for how Marxism–Leninism should evolve and how the world should extricate itself from the Cold War.[14]

He began with remarks that drew together Western and Eastern European history around the revolutionary idea: 'Two great revolutions, the French Revolution of 1789 and the Russian Revolution of 1917, have exerted a powerful influence on the actual nature of the historical process and radically changed the course of world events. Both of them, each in its own way, have given a gigantic impetus to man's progress.' Having detoxified revolution and established common ground across the divided continent, Gorbachev expatiated on the universality of human experience – 'today we have entered an era when progress will be based on the interests of all mankind' – and insisted that further progress was possible only through a truly global consensus, in a movement towards what he called 'a new world order'. If that were so, he added, 'then it is also worth agreeing on the fundamental and truly universal prerequisites and principles for such activities. It is evident, for example, that force and the threat of force can no longer be, and should not be, instruments of foreign policy.' Here was an explicit renunciation of the 'Brezhnev Doctrine' – Moscow's claimed right to deploy the Red Army within its own sphere of influence to save a fellow communist state – that in 1968 had justified the use of tanks to crush the Prague Spring. Instead, considering the 'variety of sociopolitical structures', he declared 'freedom of choice' to be a 'universal principle' that knows 'no exception'.[15]

So Gorbachev was thinking big, way beyond the conventional bipolarities of East versus West. After more than forty years of Cold War, he was explicitly advocating the 'de-ideologisation of interstate relations' and thereby declaring an end to Third World interventionism. Indeed, with the world as a whole now seriously tackling hunger, disease, illiteracy and 'other mass ills', he argued for recognising 'the primacy of the *universal* human idea'. Nevertheless, he did not intend to abandon Soviet values: 'The fundamental fact remains that the formation of the peaceful period will take place in conditions of the existence and rivalry of various socio-economic and political systems.' However, he went on, 'the meaning of our international efforts, and one of the key tenets of the new thinking, is precisely to impart to this rivalry the quality of sensible competition in conditions of respect for freedom of choice and a balance of interests'. So the two systems would not blur into each other, but their relationship would become one of peaceful 'co-development'. In this way, working together, the superpowers would be able to 'eliminate the nuclear threat and militarism' whose eradication was essential for world development and the survival of the human race.

In addition to his grand vision, Gorbachev made specific proposals, especially terminating the nine-year intervention in Afghanistan, the USSR's equivalent of America's Vietnam, and on disarmament, which he called 'the most important topic, without which no problem of the coming century can be resolved'. He spoke of the need for a new strategic arms-reduction treaty (START), reducing each superpower's arsenal by 50%. And, to put pressure on the United States, he unveiled a unilateral proposal to cut the Soviet troop strength in Europe by half a million men over the next two years. In this way Gorbachev sought to initiate a shift from the 'economy of armament' to an 'economy of disarmament'.

Such a conversion had become absolutely essential to underpin his project of a 'profound renewal' of the entire socialist society – a project that had grown vastly in scope since 1985 as he developed his big ideas of perestroika and glasnost. Indeed, Gorbachev explained, 'under the sign of democratisation, perestroika has now spread to politics, the economy, intellectual life and ideology'. Soviet democracy would be 'placed on a solid normative base' including 'laws on the freedom of conscience, glasnost, public associations and organisations'. Nevertheless, in order not to tempt anybody to 'encroach on the security' of the Soviet

Union and its allies while the Kremlin undertook the much-needed 'bold revolutionary transformations', Gorbachev was adamant that the USSR's defence capability should be maintained at what he termed a level of 'reasonable and reliable sufficiency'. Such language was a marked change from the pursuit of 'superiority' that had dominated East–West relations for most of the Cold War. Serious differences still existed, he admitted, and tough problems had to be resolved between the superpowers but the Soviet leader was essentially upbeat about the future as he looked around the hall: 'We have already graduated from the primary school of learning to understand each other and seek solutions in both our own and common interests.'[16]

Near the end of his speech he acknowledged the work of President Reagan and his Secretary of State, George Shultz, in forging agreements. 'All this', he said, 'is capital that has been invested in a joint undertaking of historic importance. It must not be wasted or left out of circulation. The future US administration headed by newly elected President George Bush will find in us a partner, ready – without long pauses and backward movements – to continue the dialogue in a spirit of realism, openness, and goodwill, and with a striving for concrete results, over an agenda encompassing the key issues of Soviet–US relations and international politics.'[17] Bush was not in the audience – he watched the speech on television – but he could not have missed the message. As Gorbachev had told the Politburo before leaving Moscow, with his diplomatic offensive there would be 'nowhere for Bush to turn'.[18]

Gorbachev's aide Anatoly Chernyaev was in the audience. Having helped write the speech, he had expected it would make an impression but was not prepared for the reaction that morning. 'For over an hour nobody stirred. And then the audience erupted in ovations, and they would not let [Gorbachev] go for a long time. He even had to get up and bow as if he were on stage.'[19] Gorbachev, a great showman, lapped it all up. Much of the press reaction was also positive. The *New York Times* editorialised, 'Perhaps not since Woodrow Wilson presented his Fourteen Points in 1918 or since Franklin Roosevelt and Winston Churchill promulgated the Atlantic Charter in 1941 has a world figure demonstrated the vision Mikhail Gorbachev displayed.'[20] But others looked behind the occasion and the rhetoric. The *Christian Science Monitor*, for instance, drew attention to what Gorbachev did *not* say. There was no suggestion that the Kremlin intended to pull back fully from its farthest positions of strategic influence gained in the Second World War – in East Germany and in East Asia. Indeed the speech said virtually nothing about Asia. Armed forces in Soviet Asia would be reduced, he promised, and 'a major portion' of Soviet troops temporarily stationed in the Mongolian People's Republic would 'return home'. But there was no mention of the bases in Vietnam, the *Monitor* complained, and not a word about the four northern Japanese islands seized by Stalin in 1945 whose disputed status had blocked a peace treaty between Japan and the USSR to formally end the Second World War.[21] The newspaper had a point – Gorbachev's post-Cold War vision *was* selective – but the UN speech made clear that for him the cockpit of the Cold War lay in Europe. It was there that the tension had to be defused.

As soon as his show at the United Nations was over,[22] Gorbachev turned his mind to the next event in his packed New York schedule: a meeting with President Reagan and Vice President Bush on Governors Island, off the southern tip of Manhattan. Yet in the limo down to the pier at Battery Park, the Soviet leader had to take an urgent phone call from Moscow: a major earthquake had hit the Caucasus and the latest reports said that some 25,000 people in Armenia had died. Gorbachev decided to return home the next morning, without stopping over in Cuba and London as originally planned.[23] Controlling his anxieties, Gorbachev turned his mind during the short boat ride to what would be his fifth and farewell meeting with Reagan, the man he no longer considered an 'unreconstructed Cold Warrior' but instead with whom he had managed against the odds to develop a genuine fondness and friendship.[24]

As Bush watched the ferry coming towards him across the choppy waters of New York Harbor, he sensed a feeling of tense expectation among the waiting American and Soviet officials. He was certainly on edge himself. As president-elect, a few weeks away from inauguration and not yet in a position to set policy, he had to weigh his future role against his present status as merely Reagan's deputy. He knew Gorbachev would be anxious to know in which direction he intended to take relations with the Soviet Union, but Reagan was still the man in the Oval Office. On this particular day Bush wanted to avoid doing anything that could be interpreted as undermining the current president's authority or to circumscribe his own future freedom of action.[25]

Gorbachev walked off the boat – waving to the onlookers, a broad smile on his face – and an equally cheerful Reagan greeted him on the quayside. The two delegations were soon sitting in the commandant's residence on Governors Island. Conversation during their meeting was mostly light and nostalgic: it was not a 'negotiating session', as Gorbachev remarked to the media present. Yet it was in some way 'special', as Bush put it, because of his own double role, looking to the past and the future.[26]

After the journalists and photographers had left, Reagan and Gorbachev reminisced about their first encounter in Switzerland a mere three years before, and the president offered the Soviet leader a memento – a photo of the moment they met in the parking lot with Reagan's handwritten inscription that they had 'walked a long way together to clear a path to peace, Geneva 1985–New York 1988'. Gorbachev was touched and said how much he valued their 'personal rapport'. Reagan agreed. He felt proud of what they had 'accomplished together': two leaders who had the 'capability of creating the next world war' had decided 'to keep the world at peace'[27] and so they had laid a 'strong foundation for the future'. This was possible, he claimed, because they had always been 'direct and open' with each other. What Reagan did not mention – naturally, because this was a cosy wander down memory lane – was that their Moscow summit in May/June had failed to 'crown', as Gorbachev hoped, the procession of meetings with a treaty to reduce their strategic offensive weapons – START I. This, as Gorbachev emphasised in his UN speech, was significant unfinished business.[28]

Reagan asked Bush whether he wanted to add anything. The vice president chose to comment only on the symbolism of the photo. The two countries had come a long distance in the last three years, he said, going on to express the hope that in three years' time there would be 'another such picture with the same significance'. Bush said he wanted to build on what President Reagan had done, working with Gorbachev. Nothing that had been accomplished ought to be reversed. But he added that he would just need 'a little time to review the issues'. Gorbachev wanted assurances that Bush would follow the path laid down by Reagan. Yet the vice president would not be drawn, using the need to construct a new Cabinet as his excuse. His theory, he said, was to 'revitalise things by putting in new people'. He wanted to 'formulate prudent national security policies' but insisted that he didn't want to 'stall things' or 'set the clock back'. Bush was trying to keep the discussion loose and vague, using platitudes to keep his options open.[29]

There was, however, no let-up from the Soviet leader. His eyes firmly on the future, Gorbachev continued to probe Bush over lunch. He fished for substantive reactions to his UN speech. Shultz merely said the audience had been 'very attentive' and the final burst of applause was totally 'genuine'. Bush, apart from commenting that Gorbachev seemed to have had 'a full house, with every seat filled', stayed silent. Gorbachev stressed that he was committed to all that he had said at the UN about cooperation between their countries.[30] While admitting that there were 'real contradictions' between them, particularly on regional issues, he insisted that Washington should not be suspicious of the Soviet Union. Turning directly to Bush, he said that it was 'a good moment to make that point, with the vice president there'. The Soviet leader did a quick *tour d'horizon* of crisis hotspots around the world and then reprised his main theme about the cooperation he and the president had managed to build up. Glancing pointedly again at Bush as well as Reagan, he declared that 'continuity was the name of the game' and that 'we should therefore be able to work together on all regional problems in a constructive way'. There was still no reaction from Bush, so Gorbachev tried to put him on the spot. 'If the next president has studies under way, and has some remarks or suggestions on these issues I would like to hear from him.' Bush again declined to be drawn. In the end Gorbachev simply joked that 'the important thing was to make life easier for the next president'.[31]

Throughout the meeting, Bush remained buttoned up and stayed on the margins – sometimes, according to journalist Steven V. Roberts, edging 'awkwardly into the picture'.

George H. W. Bush – The marginal man

Speaking to the press later that day in Washington, the vice president stuck to this non-committal tone: 'I made clear to the general secretary that I certainly wanted to continue the progress that's been made in the Reagan administration with the Soviets, and I also made clear that we needed some time, and he understood that.'[32]

*

George H. W. Bush was inaugurated on 20 January 1989 as forty-first president of the United States. He was the first serving vice president to be elected to the White House since Martin Van Buren in 1836. To many, in fact, George Bush had always seemed in the anteroom of history, doing useful jobs but on the edge of greatness: ambassador to the United Nations, US envoy to China and head of the CIA in the 1970s. And when he finally stuck out his neck in 1980, by running for the Republican nomination to the presidency, Bush had been outclassed by the telegenic Reagan – a product of Hollywood – whose financial policies Bush denigrated as 'voodoo economics'.[33]

Reagan initially hoped to enlist former president Gerald Ford as his running mate, but after negotiations broke down less than twenty-four hours before the ticket was to be announced, he offered the position to Bush who, despite the bruising campaign for the nomination, immediately accepted. He was a loyalist and team player. His diary entries included comments such as 'I am not going to be building my own constituency or doing things like background conferences to show that I am doing a good job', and also 'the president must know that he can have the vice president for him and he must not think that he has to look over his shoulder'.[34]

In Reagan's second term, when Bush started to plan his own campaign, such loyalty was sometimes held against him – as evidence of his perpetual readiness to play second fiddle.[35] And when pressed to articulate his own agenda, he reportedly exclaimed 'Oh, the vision thing!' – a phrase often cited against him.[36] Did Bush have the backbone and self-confidence to take that final big step into the Oval Office?[37] He also lacked Reagan's carefully crafted homespun eloquence and, although his speech accepting the Republican nomination in July 1988 won praise, it also contained the pledge 'Read my lips: no new taxes.' Bush slipped this in to appease the Republican right, to whom he looked unacceptably centrist compared with Reagan. In due course those words would come back to haunt him, but at the time they typified the thrust of his bid for the presidency, which concentrated on economic and social issues, rather than foreign affairs.[38] During a highly personalised, at times truly ugly, campaign the Republicans lambasted their Democratic opponent Michael Dukakis, former governor of Massachusetts, as an effete Harvard liberal who was weak on crime and profligate on spending. On 8 November 1988, number two finally became number one, chalking up a landslide victory by winning forty of the fifty states and 80% of the electoral college vote.[39]

Many people assumed that Bush would largely continue the policies of the outgoing administration, both at home and abroad, but the new president was determined not to be the stand-in for a Reagan third term. In fact the two men had never been particularly close and Bush privately held Reagan in fairly low esteem, as someone who was 'kind of foolish and simplistic on many issues'. So the handover was really a 'takeover', albeit friendly. And, contrary to impressions during the campaign, foreign policy would not take a back seat. What's more, in diplomacy Bush had a different style and agenda from his predecessor. It was here that the 'real' George Bush would step out of Reagan's shadow.[40]

This fresh approach to foreign affairs was mapped out during the interregnum from November to January. Bush's two key advisers were James A. Baker III, the new Secretary of State, and Brent Scowcroft, who became national security adviser. Their close relations with the president created a kind of constructive tension, as they acted out different roles in Bush's diplomacy. Both men agreed that Washington had a strong hand to play in dealing with the Kremlin, but they differed significantly on how to use it.[41]

Baker was a long-time Texan sidekick (born in Houston in 1930, he was six years younger than Bush). The two had been close friends for over thirty years: Baker was almost like a younger brother. He had been a US Marine in his youth, then a successful attorney, before becoming a Washington insider. He went on to organise the election campaigns of Gerald Ford in 1976 and Ronald Reagan in 1984, and served right through Reagan's two terms as White House chief of staff and then Treasury Secretary. In the view of Dennis Ross, a Washington veteran who was appointed director of the State Department policy planning staff, Baker was a superb instinctive negotiator, with a natural flair for dealing with people and a rare talent for identifying priorities. As regards the Soviet Union, Baker favoured continued and intensive diplomatic engagement. He wanted to test Gorbachev's sincerity and encourage the Soviet leader into further reforms at home and abroad.[42]

Scowcroft served as the focus for a second group of advisers who were much more sceptical of Gorbachev and his plans, fearing that they might be intended to revitalise Soviet power. Moscow, Scowcroft warned, might 'smother the West with kindness' and thus weaken NATO's resolve and cohesion. For this reason he firmly opposed an early summit meeting between Bush and Gorbachev in 1989, lest it would simply feed into Soviet propaganda. As he reflected later: unless there were substantive accomplishments, such as in arms control, the Soviets would be able to capitalise on the one outcome left – the good feelings generated by the meeting. They would use the resulting euphoria to undermine Western resolve, and a sense of complacency would encourage some to believe the United States could relax its vigilance. The Soviets in general and Gorbachev in particular were masters at creating these enervatingly cosy atmospheres. Gorbachev's UN speech had established, largely with rhetorical flourish, a mood of heady optimism. He could exploit an early meeting with a new president as evidence to declare the Cold War over without providing substantive actions from a 'new' Soviet Union.[43]

Scowcroft and Bush were almost the same age: they had both been airmen but Bush's service was confined to the Pacific War whereas Scowcroft was a career officer in the post-war US Air Force from 1947 until he joined the Nixon White House in 1972, before becoming Ford's national security adviser (1975–7). It was during the Ford years that he became closely acquainted with Bush, who was US envoy to China and then director of the CIA. They shared the same world view, one defined by the Second World War, the Cold War and Vietnam. Both believed in US leadership in the world, the centrality of the transatlantic alliance, and the necessity of using force decisively if and when it had to be employed. And both believed in the efficacy of personal diplomacy and the paramount importance of good intelligence. Bush trusted Scowcroft completely. He called him 'the closest friend in all things' – on the golf course as much as in the Oval Office.[44] Scowcroft saw his role as the president's personal adviser and also an honest broker, being free – unlike Baker – from having to represent the interests of a particular government department. And as national security adviser, he was also the nodal point of Bush's security and foreign policy. Now in the post for a second time, Scowcroft developed his own 'system', a highly effective decision-making process. Its hallmarks were regular consultation among the NSC staff, and ruthless discouragement of leaks, with everything channelled through Scowcroft to the president. But, unlike the NSC under Henry Kissinger or Zbigniew Brzezinski in the 1970s, the atmosphere was essentially collegial rather than conspiratorial. And Scowcroft and Baker, despite their inevitable frictions, managed to work productively together.[45]

Taken as a whole, therefore, the Bush administration possessed great expertise in foreign policy, and the president himself cared deeply about these issues. He enjoyed reading briefing papers and memos and, unlike his three immediate predecessors – Ford, Carter and Reagan – brought to the job extensive experience in international affairs. In addition to the posts he held in the 1970s, he had served eight years as vice president, during which he got to know many foreign officials and most heads of government. In terms of personality, Bush was unassuming and cautious but also highly ambitious and self-assured. Though he may not have been a strategic visionary, his statecraft was guided by a clear set of basic convictions and goals. A stable world order needed leadership and, in spite of much pessimism in the 1980s, Bush had no doubt that the United States alone could provide it; he did not see America as being in 'decline'.

To be sure, in some American circles the narrative of 'decline' combined with gloomy talk about a dawning 'Pacific century' (with Japan in the vanguard due to its prodigious economic growth) and a potential 'Fortress Europe' (an ever more closely economically and politically integrated and protectionist European Community). But the Bush White House focused on what it perceived as the rising popularity and spread of America's liberal values across the world and on pushing for the creation of a new, truly global trading system (led by the United States) – one that would replace the dying 1947 GATT agreement and include the Soviet Union, China and the Third World.

Bush was confident that the US was actually entering a new era of ascendancy; the twenty-first century would be America's. The United States, Bush declared expansively in November 1988, just before his election, had 'set in motion the major changes under way in the world today – the growth of democracy, the spread of free enterprise, the creation of a world market in goods and ideas. For the foreseeable future, no other nation, or group of nations, will step forward to assume leadership.'[46]

These themes of global change and American opportunity were developed more fully in his inaugural address on 20 January, looking out from the West Front of the Capitol across the Mall to the Lincoln Memorial. After the customary invocations of the deity and American history, Bush positioned himself on the cusp of a new era, as yet ill-defined. 'There are times when the future seems thick as a fog; you sit and wait, hoping the mists will lift and reveal the right path. But this is a time when the future seems a door you can walk right through into a room called tomorrow.' And Bush was ready to do so. 'We live in a peaceful, prosperous time, but we can make it better. For a new breeze is blowing, and a world refreshed by freedom seems reborn. For in man's heart, if not in fact, the day of the dictator is over.' The new president made no direct reference to the amazing transformations under way in the Soviet bloc and in communist China, but no one could have been in any doubt of what he meant. 'The totalitarian era is passing, its old ideas blown away like leaves from an ancient, lifeless tree … Great nations of the world are moving toward democracy through the door to freedom.' And America was the gatekeeper. 'We know what works: freedom works. We know what's right: freedom is right.' The president set out the country's mission: 'America is never wholly herself unless she is engaged in high moral principle. We as a people have such a purpose today. It is to make kinder the face of the Nation and gentler the face of the world. My friends, we have work to do.'[47] This was America's moment and he wanted to seize it.

But where should the work begin? One might have expected that Bush would have opened the door towards Moscow: after Gorbachev's watershed speech at the UN and with the political transformation under way in Poland and Hungary, much of the world was fixated on the changes in the Soviet Union and the ferment in Eastern Europe. Yet, guided by the scepticism of Scowcroft and also keen to break from Reagan's cosy relations with Gorbachev, Bush's presidency began with a deliberate 'pause' in superpower diplomacy.[48] With few active agenda items left by the Reagan White House – START I being the notable exception – Bush decided to order a set of studies 're-examining existing policy and goals by region, with reviews of arms control as well'. Working out how to deal with Moscow was 'obviously our first priority', Scowcroft would later recall, but the reports would take a while to produce. Indeed, the NSC review on the Soviet Union (NSR 3) did not land on the president's desk until 14 March, the reviews on Eastern (NSR 4) and Western Europe (NSR 5, focused on closer union by 1992) two weeks after that.[49]

Meanwhile, Bush had not only opened the China door but strode right through it. On 25–6 February he met with the Communist Party in Beijing. It was the first time in American history that a new US president had travelled to Asia before going to Europe.[50]

*

Bush, who considered himself an expert on China, was keen to bring Beijing into a 'Trans-Pacific Partnership'. 'The importance of China is very clear to me,' Bush told Brzezinski two weeks after his election. 'I'd love to return to China before Deng leaves office entirely. I feel I have a special relationship there.'[51] Deng Xiaoping was the mastermind of China's policies of 'reform and opening up' – the drive after Mao Zedong's death in 1976 to abandon the autarkic planned economy and cautiously enter the global market. By 1989 the diminutive Deng was eighty-four and Bush was anxious to exploit their unusually long-standing personal relationship, which dated back to Bush's quasi-ambassadorship to China in 1974–5. For Bush, China meant Deng. The president's fascination with China had less to do with the country per se (its language, landscape or culture) than with its social and economic potential that Deng was in the process of unleashing into the global capitalist economy. Conversely, the Chinese referred to Bush as a *lao pengyou* – their term for a really trusted 'old friend' who is committed to building positive relations and acting as interlocutor between the People's Republic of China (PRC) and the wider world but who also enjoys a special confidence that permits plain speaking. Those Americans before Bush who had earned such a distinction included Nixon and Kissinger; but neither Carter nor Reagan were considered a *lao pengyou*.[52]

China's new course, promoted by Deng from 1978, was one of the transitional moments of the twentieth century. Under his leadership Beijing promoted rapid modernisation through greater engagement in an increasingly interdependent world, particularly with technologically advanced Western Europe and America. Domestically, measures were introduced to make policy more responsive to economic incentives. These included the decollectivisation of agriculture, allowing farmers to make profits; rewards for especially efficient industrial performance; and the promotion of small-scale private business. With an eye on both the global economy and the international power balance, Deng gradually relaxed controls on foreign investment and trade and sought membership of global financial institutions. His stated aim was to accomplish before the end of the century a total socio-economic transformation of his country, which in the 1980s ranked among the poorest third of states in the world. By the time Bush was elected president Deng's gamble was already paying off. In just over one decade of reform, China's GDP more than doubled from $150 billion in 1978 to over $310 billion in 1988.[53]

The world's most populous country was in the throes of an economic revolution which, unlike Soviet Russia under Gorbachev, was very tightly managed by the Chinese Communist Party (CCP) and which also advanced step by step. Not only did Gorbachev's economic liberalisation begin much later, in 1985 rather 1978, but the concomitant political reforms, which gradually dismantled the Soviet Communist Party's monopoly on power, amounted to nothing less than a new system of governance. This process in turn stirred up destructive ethnic conflicts in what was a much less homogeneous society than China's. Whereas in the PRC the process of economic reform was controlled from above, in the USSR perestroika combined with glasnost would eventually undermine the Soviet state.[54]

In the course of this Chinese revolution, the United States played a major role. Although Deng was initially keen to engage with Western Europe, America represented his ultimate model, especially after his eye-opening visit in early 1979 to mark the opening of full diplomatic relations: 'what he saw in the United States was what he wanted for China in the future'. During a week's whirlwind tour from Washington DC to Seattle, America's factories and farms simply 'bowled him over'. So impressive was US technology and productivity that, by his own admission, Deng could not sleep for several weeks.[55]

The Carter administration was keen for Deng's reforms to succeed; it also wanted to pull China closer to the USA at a time when détente was eroding and the relationship with Moscow had slipped into a deep freeze amid the 'New Cold War'. Not only did Carter normalise diplomatic relations with China but he granted 'most favoured nation' (MFN) status twelve months later – a crucial precondition for expanded bilateral trade. The PRC joined the World Bank in April 1980, the same month that it took over from Taiwan China's place on the IMF. Accelerating the momentum, in September 1980 the Carter administration concluded four commercial agreements: on aviation, shipping, textiles and expanded consular representation. Announcing these, Carter called the Sino-American relationship 'a new and vital force for peace and stability in the international scene' which held 'a promise of ever-increasing benefits in trade and other exchanges' for both countries.[56]

Reagan took up Carter's policy and pursued it with even greater vigour. One of the priorities of his new 'global strategy' was the integration of the Pacific Rim into the world economy. Within that enlarged market, China was potentially the biggest player, so its successful opening up would offer exceptional opportunities for US trade and investment. There was also a strategic dimension. The drive for economic modernisation would align China with the capitalist order and make it a more robust bulwark against the Soviet Union. In this vein, the Reagan administration offered Deng in 1981 a 'strategic association' with the USA – effectively a de facto alliance. So at a time when Cold War tensions ratcheted up, Sino-American security cooperation expanded. Beijing got US weapons technology, while coordinating with the American anti-communist campaigns in Afghanistan, Angola and Cambodia.[57] Although Reagan himself visited China in 1984, he was happy to make as much use as possible of his vice president's old-friend status with the Chinese. Bush paid two week-long visits to Beijing in May 1982 and October 1985. On the second occasion he was particularly bullish about Sino-American trade: 'The sky's the limit, the door's wide open,' he told a news conference, adding that he found 'much more openness' now than three years before. Of course, continued progress depended on the Paramount Leader, now eighty-one. Observers were keenly aware that, in the interval between Bush's first and second trips to China, three gerontocrats had passed from the scene in the Kremlin. But Bush cheerfully told the press of Deng's words to him: 'The vital organs of my body are functioning very well.'[58]

The evolving Sino-American relationship was proving a win-win situation. In 1983, the Reagan administration had taken the crucial step of liberalising Cold War controls on trade, technology and investment, allowing the private sector to engage with China at minimal cost to the American taxpayer. Deng, for his part, was desperate to tap every kind of American know-how. Between 1982 and 1984 export licences doubled and sales of high-tech goods such as computers, semiconductors, hydro-turbines and equipment for the petrochemical industry rose seven-fold from $144 million in 1982 to $1 billion in 1986.[59] Out of this grew American joint ventures with China, in areas such as energy exploration, transport and electronics. Consumer goods were another important sector for collaboration, with Coke and Pepsi, Heinz, AT&T, Bell South, American Express and Eastman Kodak among the high-profile US corporations represented.[60] In all these ways the US government acted as low-cost facilitator and gatekeeper for American private enterprise, using natural market forces to try to draw China out of its old shell during the course of the 1980s. In a dozen years of reform. Beijing and Washington became significant trading partners: US–China bilateral trade grew from $374 million in 1977 to nearly $18 billion in 1989.[61]

By the end of the Reagan administration Washington viewed Beijing with almost a sense of triumph. Secretary of State George Shultz described China's 'long march to the market' as a 'truly historic event – a great nation throwing off outmoded economic doctrines and liberating the energies of 1 billion talented people'. When Bush took office, therefore, it seemed axiomatic that Deng's economic reforms were fully embedded and would go from strength to strength. The question now in Washington was how soon economic change would generate political change – akin to the transformations in the Soviet bloc under Gorbachev. Like a succession of American leaders since the era of Franklin Roosevelt and Cordell Hull, Bush tended to assume that one form of change would lead to the other: democratisation in China therefore seemed not a question of whether but when.[62]

Yet the consequences of Deng's economic reforms were double-edged. They stirred popular desire for a more open society but also provoked mounting discontent by the late 1980s. During Mao's Cultural Revolution a whole generation had lost out on higher education, and when Deng set China on course to catch up with the developed and developing world, frustrated radicals turned Beijing, Shanghai, Wuhan and other university cities into hotbeds of dissent. This occurred just when inflation hit unprecedented levels (8.8% in 1985) as the command economy was eased. The regime embarked on cautious political reforms and allowed intellectuals and academics a freer rein. Fang Lizhi, astrophysicist and vice chancellor of the University of Science and Technology in Hefei, became celebrated in the West for his advocacy of human rights and his support of student protest. And journalist Liu Binyan gained notoriety after he famously stated that 'the economic reform is a very long leg in China, while the political reform is a very short one. One can't proceed without being tripped up by the other.' By way of explanation, he added: 'The student movement [...] exploded because political reform had hardly begun.'[63]

China's leadership was not ready for democracy. Spasms of political openness were followed by harsh crackdowns when protests got out of hand. The problem wasn't simply in the streets or on the campuses, it was also eating away at the party itself in a battle between hardliners and reformers. In a backlash against 'bourgeois liberalisation', conservative elders forced out the reformist party general secretary, Hu Yaobang, in January 1987.[64] There was a further challenge. The ageing Deng knew he had to hand over soon to the next generation. He ensured that Hu was replaced by another moderate, Zhao Zhiang, who in the autumn, at the CCP Congress, pushed through a watered-down programme of political reform. This resulted in the retirement of nearly half the Central Committee members – a major step in rejuvenating the party. Retirees included Deng himself who retained only the crucial post of chairman of the Military Affairs Committee. A temporary calm was established between the rival factions of the CCP and the Politburo's vital Standing Committee, which hung in uneasy balance between reformists led by Zhao and conservatives headed by Li Peng.[65]

During 1988 the inflation rate rose to an unprecedented 18.5%[66] and student protests at price hikes, overcrowding and corruption hit new heights. Things got even worse in 1989. Media reports and images of the political transformation under way in the Soviet satellite states galvanised the protestors, and the impending seventieth anniversary of China's fabled student uprising against the humiliations imposed on the country by the Versailles Treaty in 1919 – the Fourth of May Movement – also loomed large.[67] Deng – revealing that he worried more about the contagion of the Eastern European and Soviet reforms than Western political ideas – stated in a speech on 25 April 1989: 'This is not an ordinary student movement but a turmoil ... Those influenced by Yugoslav, Polish, Hungarian, and Soviet liberalism have destabilised our society with the objective of overthrowing the Communist leadership, which will endanger the future of our country and our nation.' The CCP still had no intention of loosening its grip on society or allowing political pluralism in the manner of Gorbachev.[68]

This, however, did not seem to bother George Bush. He had faith in Deng as a progressive leader, whereas Gorbachev was still an unknown quantity and the Soviet Union much more of an existential threat to America and NATO. So, once he became president, there seemed no reason for any kind of 'pause' in Sino-American relations. On the contrary Bush, as he had told Brzezinski in November 1988, was keen to consolidate and advance his 'special relationship' with Deng and China as soon as possible.

There was also another pressing concern on Bush's mind. Nothing about China could ever be considered without taking Sino-Soviet relations into account. Washington, Moscow and Beijing formed a strategic triangle whose dynamics were always in flux. Bush was well aware that, a year before he assumed office, Mikhail Gorbachev had already formally proposed a summit meeting with the Chinese leadership – the first since Khrushchev and Mao had met in 1959 on the brink of the Sino-Soviet split that brought the two countries to the verge of war ten years later.

Gorbachev's overture reflected his desire for normal relations between the world's two largest communist nations but it was also driven by the need for international stability so as to concentrate on reforms at home. Deng, in turn, had always been clear about China's conditions for such a summit: 1) that Moscow reduce its military presence along the Sino-Soviet border; 2) that the Soviets withdraw their troops from Afghanistan; and 3) that the Kremlin end support for the Vietnamese occupation of Cambodia. By the end of 1988 the Chinese were sufficiently satisfied with Soviet concessions to issue a formal invitation for Gorbachev to come to Beijing in May 1989 for summit talks with Deng. The visit was intended to symbolise Sino-Soviet rapprochement after three decades of estrangement and even antagonism.[69]

Gorbachev did not know Deng personally. He had never been to China and was certainly not a *lao pengyou*. Twenty-seven years Deng's junior, Gorbachev had few memories of Sino-Soviet relations before the split, which had occurred when he was only in his twenties. Nevertheless, like Bush, he had prioritised a breakthrough with China ever since becoming general secretary. Yet Deng was wary. Although he welcomed closer economic links with the USSR, he did not appreciate Gorbachev's enthusiasm for political reforms and even spoke of him as an 'idiot' for putting politics before economics.[70] For his part, Gorbachev remained sceptical of China's reform programme in the absence of a major political overhaul, which to his mind was required for a full and successful perestroika. And so he kept downplaying Chinese reforms and indeed prophesied their failure. He also dismissed the Chinese as mere imitators. 'They all now claim they started perestroika before us,' he scoffed. 'They are adopting our approaches.' Gorbachev's lofty attitude reflected both a traditionally dismissive Soviet stereotyping of the PRC and also his own competitive, almost messianic, ambition that perestroika – as proclaimed on the title page of his book *Perestroika* – was not just 'for our country' but 'for the entire world'.[71]

In fact Gorbachev appeared to see himself as the new Lenin. He claimed that his country was the leading state of the socialist system and, as his aide Georgy Shakhnazarov put it, one of the 'greatest powers or super-powers of the modern world, upon which depends the fate of the world'. From this perspective, predominant among Kremlin policymakers and especially Gorbachev's own entourage, China was still a secondary power, despite its remarkable recent rise from poverty and backwardness. Moscow itself had always craved recognition from the West to which it looked, at times neurotically, as the sole benchmark against which to measure its own successes. And in this bigger quest for international status, it was almost necessary to deride China's experience and achievements.[72]

This was not, of course, the way the relationship was viewed in Beijing. Deng was adamant that China not be seen as Moscow's 'younger brother' – as Stalin cynically treated Mao. And with a view to resetting Sino-Soviet relations, Gorbachev was at pains to assure the Chinese he did not harbour any such views: China, he said, had outgrown such a role. Their mutual edginess, however, was a reminder that thirty years of alienation could not be transcended overnight. And the Chinese leaders were quietly watching and drawing conclusions from what seemed to them an utterly chaotic Soviet situation.[73]

So Sino-Soviet relations were at a particularly delicate moment at the beginning of 1989, with the Gorbachev–Deng summit scheduled for May. In Washington, on the third point of the triangle, Bush and Scowcroft were keen to get to Beijing ahead of the Soviets. Even though the Cold War was on the wane, the old verities of Nixon-era competitive triangularity remained a strategic imperative. Bush and his advisers feared that the smooth-talking Gorbachev would be able to charm the Chinese, as he had done in Europe, ending conflict on their joint borders and burying the ideological hatchet. As Scowcroft put it: 'We anticipated that he might attempt a rapprochement between Moscow and Beijing, and would have liked to be certain it did not come at our expense. There was no way, however, to justify a trip to China in the first quarter of the first year of the president's term.'[74]

Then fate came to Bush's aid. Hirohito, the emperor of Japan, died on 7 January 1989.

*

The president's attendance at Hirohito's funeral in Tokyo on 24 February meant a great deal to the Japanese. Not only was Bush the head of state of Japan's great ally and protector, he was also a veteran of the Pacific War in which Hirohito had been the official leader of one of America's Axis enemies. The visit therefore symbolised the remarkable reconciliation between their two states since 1945. Yet it also mattered in other ways. The presence of the US president prompted other world dignitaries to come as well, further raising the profile of the occasion, and it gave Bush the chance to engage in funeral diplomacy. He held over twenty one-to-one meetings on the margins of the ceremonies, with figures such as François Mitterrand and Richard von Weizsäcker, the presidents of France and West Germany. Tokyo was a perfect opportunity for Bush to take the temperature of world politics without becoming entangled in the paraphernalia of high-profile summitry.[75]

Above all, the unforeseen trip to Japan offered an ideal pretext to visit China. As soon as Bush was inaugurated, Scowcroft met with Chinese ambassador Han Xu to start detailed planning. Time was too short to set up a full-dress state visit, so instead a 'working visit' was arranged – a trip without any specific agenda except for the president to reconnect with China's senior leaders and to reaffirm his commitment to the Asia-Pacific region.[76] Just before Bush flew from Tokyo to Beijing, he and Japan's prime minister Noboru Takeshita compared notes. It was 'important for the US and Japan to help the modernisation of China', Takeshita told Bush. And he stressed that improved Sino-Soviet relations were not expected to 'pose any threat to Japan'. The president, for his part, sought to reassure Japan by emphasising that, when he eventually unveiled his policies on the USSR and arms control, they would not have any detrimental effect on Japan or China. Overall, Bush's main message was: don't worry, we remain a staunch ally of Japan.[77]

Happy returns: George and Barbara in the Forbidden City

On arriving in Beijing on the evening of 25 February, Bush was warmly received at the Great Hall of the People by Chinese president Yang Shangkun, who again highlighted Bush's special stature as a *lao pengyou*. In a cordial forty-five-minute chat, Yang called Bush's first presidential visit to Beijing (and his fifth trip to China since his serving as US envoy in 1974-5) 'very significant'. There was plenty of personal flattery, of the sort that Chinese leaders lavished on their 'special friends'. President Yang threw in lines like 'you've made great contributions to the development of Sino-US relations and to cooperation between our two countries ... I think this shows that you, Mr President, pay much attention to our bilateral relationship ... Personally, as I have told Ambassador Lord many times, if I could vote, I would vote for Bush.'[78]

But behind all the sweet talk there was substance as well. Both sides made clear their commitment to deepening the bilateral relationship in and for itself – not just to counterbalance Soviet power. 'I feel the relationship we have now is not based on some facet of Soviet relations,' Bush declared, 'but on its own merits. For example, we now have cultural, educational and trade relations. It is not just based on worry about the Soviets, although we still do to a degree.' Yang agreed: 'We are two big countries, located on opposite sides of the Pacific Ocean. So the friendly cooperation between our two countries will promote cooperation in the Pacific region and in the world as well. This is most important for the maintenance of world peace, stability and security.'[79]

All this was a curtain-raiser to the meeting that Bush really wanted, with China's diminutive Paramount Leader.[80] He talked with Deng for an hour on the morning of 26 February in a room off the Great Hall of the People. Bush was at pains to offer assurances that he had not rushed to Beijing in order to steal a march on Gorbachev, but the two leaders spent much of their time circling around the great imponderable of where the Soviet Union was going. Deng spoke at length about history, emphasising that the two countries which had caused China the most suffering and 'humiliation' over the last century and a half had been Japan and Russia. Even though Japan cost China 'tens of millions of lives' and 'incalculable' financial damage, the Soviet impact had been much more profound because they acquired 3 million square kilometres of Chinese territory. Given that background, Deng wondered, even if his summit with Gorbachev proved successful and relations were normalised, what would follow? 'Personally, I think it is still an unknown quantity,' he said.

'The fact is there are many accumulated problems. What's more they have deep historical roots.'[81]

Bush echoed Deng's feeling that one man could not change history. 'Gorbachev is a charming man, and the Soviet Union is in a state of change. But the byword for the US is caution ... Our experience tells us that you cannot make broad foreign policy decisions based on the personality or aspirations of one man. You need to consider the trend of the whole society and country.'[82]

At the end, Deng brought this point much closer to home. 'With regard to the problems confronting China, let me say to you that the overwhelming need is to maintain stability. Without stability, everything will be gone; even accomplishments will be ruined.' Looking hard at Bush, he added: 'We hope our friends abroad can understand this point.' Bush did not blink: 'We do.' Deng's message was clear. Whatever one thought about perestroika and glasnost, about freedom of choice in Eastern Europe and grand proclamations about universal values, there would be no Gorbachevs in China. Human rights and political reform were not appropriate subjects for discussion, even with a *lao pengyou*. Bush got the message and had no intention of challenging it. The two leaders understood each other. 'All right,' said Deng, 'let's go to lunch.'[83]

Bush left Beijing optimistic that important groundwork had been laid for what he called a 'productive period' in diplomatic relations, despite the turbulence in China's domestic affairs. The president remembered appreciatively 'the warm and genuine handshakes between old friends'. But more pragmatically he also felt that he had been able to speak frankly with the Chinese leadership[84] and that the two sides could develop a practical working relationship based on a 'real level of trust'. Bush had no illusions that anything would be easy with Beijing and therefore lobbied for good communication on all issues, but he recognised that criticism should not be expressed in public, particularly about human rights. 'I understood that strong words and direct views were best exchanged between us privately, as in this visit, not in press statements and angry speeches.'[85]

Returning to Washington from his first foreign trip as president, Bush reflected on what he had learned. Back at Andrews Air Force Base on 27 February he told the assembled press that his whirlwind tour of Japan, China and South Korea had underscored for him America's stature as a present and future 'Pacific power'. From those four days of intensive discussions, what stuck in his mind was that 'the world looks to America for leadership'. This, he asserted, was 'not just because we're militarily strong, not just because we have the world's largest economy, but because the ideas we have championed are now dominant. Freedom and democracy, openness, and the prosperity that derives from individual initiatives in the free marketplace – these ideas, once thought to be strictly American, have now become the goals of mankind all over Asia.'[86]

This was a striking ideological clarion call from a man who was not a natural rhetorician. Less than three months after Gorbachev's grandstanding performance at the UN, the new US president was putting down his own markers. The Soviet leader liked to present his new socialism as the answer not only for Russia but also for the whole world. Now Bush was making a counterclaim for American values, almost as if the ideological Cold War was still raging. Although that February evening at Andrews he talked particularly about the USA in Asia, by the middle of April he was also speaking in similar tones about Eastern Europe.

*

The president had already made clear to Weizsäcker in Tokyo on 24 February 'we don't want Gorbachev to win a propaganda offensive'. As Atlantic allies 'we must stay together'.[87] Six weeks later, on 12 April, he developed his thinking when talking with NATO secretary general Manfred Wörner. He said he intended to strengthen the Alliance's solidarity by taking a leading role. He was worried that 'Gorbachev had dominated the headlines in Europe, causing strains over NATO defense issues' – in particular undermining support in West Germany for short-range nuclear missiles. Now was the time, said the president, to ensure that NATO would not 'unravel'. Wörner agreed: he saw the upcoming NATO summit in late May as a 'unique opportunity' in a truly 'historic' situation. The challenge was that 'although we are successful, public perception is that Gorbachev is driving history'. It was up to Bush to 'turn this public perception around'. NATO should not just challenge Moscow on arms control but 'stress the political battleground', pushing for 'a Europe of self-determination and freedom, free of the Berlin Wall and the Brezhnev Doctrine'. In this endeavour NATO looked for American 'ideas, concepts and cooperation' because the other allies would not be able to 'deliver much'. Bush concurred. Gorbachev had, 'like a kind of surfer, caught a wave of public support'. It would be important at the upcoming NATO summit to find 'agreement on a broad vision of our own'.[88]

The president was now ready for 'the vision thing'. In a carefully planned series of major speeches during April and May, he gradually unveiled his grand scenario for a Europe emerging from the Cold War. The first speech was deliberately staged in Hamtramck, a predominantly Polish–American suburb of Detroit, on 17 April – twelve days after Poland had unveiled major constitutional reforms: the creation of the Senate and the office of the president, as well legalisation of the free trade union Solidarity. These major structural changes were the result of two months of round-table talks between the opposition movement and the communist regime under General Wojciech Jaruzelski. Democratic elections would follow later in the summer. The 'ideas of democracy', as Bush put it, were clearly 'returning with renewed force in Europe', with Poland in the vanguard – hence the otherwise unlikely venue of Hamtramck.

Picking up themes from his inaugural address, Bush reflected on the passing of totalitarianism, the spread of freedom and the right to self-determination. 'The West can now be bold in proposing a vision of the European future,' he declared. 'We dream of the day when there will be no barriers to the free movement of peoples, goods, and ideas. We dream of the day when Eastern European peoples will be free to choose their system of government and to vote for the party of their choice in regular, free, contested elections ... And we envision an Eastern Europe in which the Soviet Union has renounced military intervention as an instrument of its policy.' Bush's refrain about 'dreams' and 'visions' fleshed out his comments five days earlier to Wörner. He was driven by a growing conviction that America, as the leader of the West, now had an unprecedented opportunity to apply its statecraft to the reshaping of Europe. 'What has brought us to this opening?' he asked. 'The unity and strength of the democracies, yes, and something else: the bold, new thinking in the Soviet Union, the innate desire for freedom in the hearts of all men.' The president proclaimed that 'if we're wise, united, and ready to seize the moment, we will be remembered as the generation that made all Europe free'.[89]

Scowcroft called the Hamtramck speech the administration's 'first major step on Eastern Europe'. Although he admitted that it received 'scarcely a glance' in the US, Bush's words attracted much greater attention in Europe and the USSR, where *Pravda* was indeed rather favourable, singling out the president's positive evaluation of Soviet reforms and the prospects for better superpower relations.[90]

By May the administration's sluggish review of Soviet policy was finally gathering pace. On the 12th Bush used the commencement ceremonies at Texas A&M University in his adopted home state to publicise something of the new strategy for superpower relations, which he summed up in the key concept 'Beyond Containment'. In other words, the president wanted to transcend the defensive posture that had characterised US policy at the height of the Cold War. Here was a more assertive Bush: the cautious bystander on the margins of the Reagan and Gorbachev summit at Governors Island the previous December now had a clear sense of where *he* wanted to go:

> We are approaching the conclusion of an historic post-war struggle between two visions: one of tyranny and conflict and one of democracy and freedom. The review of US–Soviet relations that my administration has just completed outlines a new path toward resolving this struggle ... Our review indicates that forty years of perseverance have brought us a precious opportunity, and now it is time to move beyond containment to a new policy for the 1990s – one that recognises the full scope of change taking place around the world and in the Soviet Union itself. In sum, the United States now has as its goal much more than simply containing Soviet expansionism. We seek the integration of the Soviet Union into the community of nations.

Bush also set out the terms on which the USSR would be welcomed back 'into the world order'. Fine rhetoric from Gorbachev was not sufficient – 'promises are never enough'. The Kremlin must take some concrete 'positive steps'. Top of the list were to reduce Soviet forces (proportionate to legitimate security needs), provide support for self-determination, 'tear down the Iron Curtain' and find diplomatic solutions with the West to resolve regional disputes around the world, such as in Afghanistan, Angola and Nicaragua. Taking these steps would make possible a qualitatively new relationship between the two superpowers.[91]

And yet, as Bush admitted, Soviet military capabilities remained 'awesome'. So deterrence still remained vital and this demanded a strong NATO – the theme of Bush's speech on 24 May in New London, Connecticut, to the US Coast Guard Academy. There he outlined future US military strategy and arms-control policy for the next decade. 'Our policy is to seize every – and I mean every – opportunity to build a better, more stable relationship with the Soviet Union, just as it is our policy to defend American interests in light of the enduring reality of Soviet military power.' He acknowledged that, 'amidst the many challenges we'll face, there will be risks. But let me assure you, we'll find more than our share of opportunities ... There's an opportunity before us to shape a new world.'

A new world was possible because 'we are witnessing the end of an idea: the final chapter of the communist experiment. Communism is now recognised ... as a failed system ... But the eclipse of communism is only one half of the story of our time. The other is the ascendancy of the democratic idea' – evident across the world from trade unionists in Warsaw to students in Beijing. 'Even as we speak today,' he told the young American graduands, 'the world is transfixed by the dramatic events in Tiananmen Square. Everywhere, those voices are speaking the language of democracy and freedom.'[92]

The Coast Guard speech completed Bush's public exposition of his administration's new strategy toward the European cockpit of East–West relations ahead of the NATO summit in Brussels on 30 May.[93] His visionary statements about peace and freedom, about global free markets and a community of democracies, give the lie to later claims that his foreign policy was aimless, merely reactive and 'too unwilling to move in untested waters'. Above all, he was repeatedly emphasising the place of US leadership in the world and asserting what the administration regularly referred to as the 'common values of the West'.[94] As Bush had said in that scene-setting cameo on Governors Island, he intended to take his time and act prudently in an era when the fundamentals of international relations had been shaken as never before since 1945. 'Prudence' would indeed remain a watchword of Bush's diplomacy but this did not preclude vision and hope. Those speeches of April and May 1989 – often neglected by commentators amid the dramas of the second half of the year – make the ambition of his foreign policy abundantly clear.

But converting ambition into achievement was a different challenge. And his first test was particularly demanding. The NATO summit in Brussels was unusually high profile because it coincided with the fortieth anniversary of the Atlantic Alliance and because it was imperative to come up with an eye-catching response to the potpourri of dramatic arms-reduction proposals Gorbachev had tossed out in his UN speech.

To make matters worse, NATO governments had been unable to agree in advance on a joint position, mainly because of fundamental disputes about short-range nuclear forces (SNFs) – those with a range of less than 500 kilometres. And, at a less visible level, the arguments surrounding the NATO summit may be seen as marking a subtle but significant shift in America's alliance priorities in Western Europe – away from Great Britain and towards West Germany.[95]

Britain, represented by Prime Minister Margaret Thatcher – the notorious 'Iron Lady' – demanded rapid implementation of a 1985 NATO agreement to modernise its SNFs (eighty-eight Lance missile launchers and some 700 warheads). Her fixation was with their deterrent value and NATO's defensibility. The coalition government of West Germany, where most of these missiles were stationed, instead pressed the USA to pursue negotiations on SNF reduction with the Soviet Union, building on the success of the superpower 1987 treaty to eliminate all their intermediate nuclear forces (INFs) worldwide. Foreign Minister Hans-Dietrich Genscher – leader of the junior coalition partner the Free Democrats (FDP) – even lobbied, like Gorbachev, for the total abolition of SNFs. This was known as the 'third zero' – building on the 'double zero' agreement for the abolition of INFs in Europe and Asia. For Thatcher, relatively secure in her island kingdom, these weapons were an instrument of military strategy but for Genscher and for the German left they were a matter of life or death, because Germany would be the inevitable epicentre of a European war. Kohl considered Genscher's position as far too extreme but he not only needed to appease his coalition partner and calm the domestic public mood by supporting some kind of arms-reduction talks, he also had to navigate around 'that woman', as he called Thatcher, and keep the Alliance strong.[96]

Both the British and the Germans had been manoeuvring ahead of the summit. Thatcher met Gorbachev on 6 April in London. On a human level, the two of them had got on famously ever since their first encounter in December 1984, before he became general secretary, when she proclaimed that Gorbachev was a man with whom she could 'do business'.[97] At their meeting in 1989 the personal chemistry was equally evident but so were their fundamental differences on nuclear policy. Gorbachev launched into a passionate speech in favour of nuclear abolition and 'a nuclear-free Europe' – which Thatcher totally rejected – and he vented his frustrations with Bush for not responding more positively to his disarmament initiatives. The prime minister, playing her preferred role as elder stateswoman, was at pains to reassure him: 'Bush is a very different person from Reagan. Reagan was an idealist who firmly defended his convictions ... Bush is a more balanced person, he gives more attention to detail than Reagan did. But as a whole, he will continue the Reagan line, including on Soviet–American relations. He will strive to achieve agreements that are in our common interest.'

Gorbachev jumped on those last words: 'That is the question – in our common interests or in your Western interests?' The reply came back: 'I am convinced in the common interest.' Her subtext was clearly that she was the one who could broker the relationship between the two superpowers.[98]

Privately, however, Thatcher was worried about the new US president. She had developed a close, if sometimes manipulative, rapport with 'Ronnie' and had felt secure about the centrality of the much-vaunted Anglo-American 'special relationship' in US foreign policy.[99] With Bush, the situation was less clear. It appeared that the new administration's 'pause' also entailed a review of relations with Britain. And she felt that the State Department under Baker was biased against her and inclined to favour Bonn rather than London.[100] Her suspicions were not unfounded. Bush, a pragmatist, disliked Thatcher's dogmatism and certainly did not intend to let her run the Alliance. Both he and Baker found her difficult to get on with, whereas Kohl seemed an agreeable partner.[101]

The problem in Bonn was not on the personal level but the political, because of the deep rift within the coalition. In several phone conversations during April and May, Kohl tried to reassure Bush of his loyalty to the transatlantic partnership and that he would not let the SNF issue ruin the summit. His language was almost desperate – a point not concealed even in the official American 'telcon' record of their talks. 'He wanted the summit to be successful ... He wanted the president to have a success. It would be the president's first trip to Europe as president. The president was a proven friend of Europeans and, in particular, of the Germans.'[102]

The pre-summit bickering in Europe did not faze Bush. He knew that Kohl's aim was 'a strong NATO' and that the chancellor had 'linked his political existence to this goal'.[103] But the prognostications before the summit were distinctly bleak. 'Bush Arrives for Talks With a Divided NATO', the *New York Times* headlined on 29 May. The paper claimed that Bonn's insistence on reducing the threat of SNFs to German territory raised fears in Washington, London and Paris of nothing less than the 'denuclearisation' of NATO's central front. Such was the gulf, the news-paper noted, that no communiqué had been agreed in advance, which meant that NATO's sixteen leaders would 'have to thrash it out themselves' at the summit. One NATO delegate confessed, 'I honestly don't know if a compromise is possible.'[104]

The president, however, had something up his sleeve when he arrived in Brussels. He presented his allies with a radical arms-reduction proposal not on SNFs but on conventional forces in Europe. This had not been easy to hammer out in Washington but fear of an alliance crisis in Brussels enabled Bush to bang heads together. What the president dubbed his 'conventional parity initiative' of 275,000 troops on each side would mean the withdrawal of about 30,000 Americans from Western Europe and about 325,000 Soviet soldiers from Eastern Europe. This was to be agreed between the superpowers within six to twelve months. Bush's initiative was intended to probe Gorbachev's longer-term readiness to accept disproportionate cuts that would eliminate the Red Army superiority in Eastern Europe on which Soviet domination of their satellite states had always depended. But more immediately, according to the *New York Times*, it was meant to 'bring about a dramatic shift in the summit agenda', thereby 'swamping the missile discussion'. And this indeed proved to be the case. After nine hours of intense debate the allies accepted Bush's proposals on cuts to conventional forces in Europe and especially his accelerated timetable. In return, the United States committed itself to 'enter into negotiations to achieve a partial reduction of American and Soviet land-based nuclear missile forces' as soon as the implementation of a conventional-arms accord was 'under way'. This deal kept the Genscherites happy because of the prospect of rapid SNF negotiations, while Thatcher and Mitterrand – representing the two European nuclear powers – were gratified that there had been no further erosion of the principles of NATO's nuclear deterrence per se. And it also suited Bush: keen to lower the conventional-warfare threat in Europe, he had been adamant that on the issue of nukes there should be 'no third zero'.[105]

So the NATO summit that had seemed so precarious ended up as a resounding success. 'An almost euphoric atmosphere' surrounded the final press conference. Kohl declared ebulliently that he now perceived 'a historic chance' for 'realistic and significant' progress on arms control. He could not resist poking fun at his bête noire, Thatcher, who, he said, had come to Brussels taking a very hard line against any SNF negotiations and fiercely opposing concessions to the Germans. 'Margaret Thatcher stood up for her interests, in her temperamental way,' the chancellor remarked. 'We have different temperaments. She is a woman and I'm not.'[106]

The remarkably harmonious outcome of the Brussels meeting – 'we were all winners', proclaimed Kohl[107] – was a big boost for NATO at forty. Indeed, he felt it was the 'best kind of a birthday present' the Alliance could have.[108] But it was also a huge boon for Bush, who had been under attack at home for failing to give leadership to the Alliance and for surrendering the diplomatic initiative to Gorbachev. Now, however, with his compromise package he had turned the entire situation around. As Scowcroft reflected with satisfaction, after this 'fantastic result' the press 'never returned to their theme of the spring – that we had no vision and no strategy'.[109] Brussels, stated an American reporter, was 'Bush's hour'.[110]

As soon as the NATO press conference was over, the president travelled on to a sunlit evening in Bonn, basking in the warm glow of his success.[111] At a state dinner that night in a grand eighteenth-century restaurant, the president toasted another fortieth anniversary – that of the Federal Republic itself. 'In 1989,' he declared expansively, 'we are nearer our goals of peace and European reconciliation than at any time since the founding of NATO and the Federal Republic.' He added: 'I don't believe German–American relations have ever been better.'[112]

The following morning, 31 May, the Bush–Kohl caravan sailed on down the Rhine to the picture-book city of Mainz, capital of the Rhineland-Palatinate, Kohl's home state.[113] 'The United States and the Federal Republic have always been firm friends and allies,' the president announced, 'but today we share an added role: partners in leadership.'[114]

This was a striking phrase, testimony to the maturation of the American–West German relationship over the previous forty years – made ever sharper by the downgrading at the summit of Thatcher and by implication of London's 'special relationship'. To speak about Bonn as Washington's 'partner in leadership' definitely stuck in her gullet: as she sadly admitted, it 'confirmed the way American thinking about Europe was going'.[115]

Whereas Thatcher fixated on the partnership aspect of what Bush was saying, in his Mainz speech the president focused much more on what it meant to lead. 'Leadership', he declared, 'has a constant companion: responsibility. And our responsibility is to look ahead and grasp the promise of the future … For forty years, the seeds of democracy in Eastern Europe lay dormant, buried under the frozen tundra of the Cold War … But the passion for freedom cannot be denied forever. The world

has waited long enough. The time is right. Let Europe be whole and free
… Let Berlin be next – let Berlin be next!'[116]

Two years before, Bush's predecessor Ronald Reagan had stood before
the Brandenburg Gate and called on the Soviet leader, 'Mr Gorbachev,
tear down this wall.'[117] Now in June 1989 a new US president was throwing
down the gauntlet once again, mounting a new propaganda offensive
against the charismatic Soviet leader. 'Let Berlin be next' was in one way
headline-grabbing rhetoric, but it revealed that the administration was
already beginning to grapple with the issue of German unification. As
Bush said in his Mainz speech, 'the frontier of barbed wire and minefields
between Hungary and Austria is being removed, foot by foot, mile by
mile. Just as the barriers are coming down in Hungary, so must they fall
throughout all of Eastern Europe.' Nowhere was the East–West divide
starker than in Berlin. 'There this brutal wall cuts neighbour from neighbour, brother from brother. And that wall stands as a monument to the
failure of communism. It must come down.'

Despite his emphasis on Germany, Bush's vision remained much
broader. The will for freedom and democracy, he insisted yet again, was
a truly global phenomenon. 'This one idea is sweeping across Eurasia.
This one idea is why the communist world, from Budapest to Beijing, is
in ferment.'[118] By June 1989, Hungary was undoubtedly on the move but
here change was occurring peacefully. On the other side of the world,
however, the forces of democratic protest and communist oppression
collided violently and with dramatic global consequences in China's
Forbidden City.

*

On 15 May, just before noon, Mikhail Gorbachev landed at Beijing's
airport to begin a historic four-day trip to China. Descending the steps
of his blue-and-white Aeroflot jet, he was greeted by the Chinese president Yang Shangkun. The two men then walked past an honour guard
of several hundred Chinese troops in olive-green uniforms and white
gloves. A twenty-one-gun salute boomed in the background.

The long awaited Sino-Soviet summit showed that relations between
the two countries were returning to something like 'normal' after three
decades of ideological rifts, military confrontation and regional rivalries.
The Soviet leader certainly viewed his visit as a 'watershed'. In a written
statement issued to reporters at the airport, he remarked: 'We have come

to China in the springtime … All over the world people associate this season with renewal and hope. This is consonant with our mood.' Indeed, it was anticipated that Gorbachev's visit could seal the reconciliation of the two largest communist nations at a time when both were struggling through profound economic and political changes. 'We have a great deal to say to each other as communist parties, even in practical terms,' observed Yevgeny Primakov, a leading Soviet expert on Asia, ahead of the meeting. 'This normalisation comes at a time when we are both studying how socialist countries should approach capitalism. Before, we both thought that socialism could be spread only by revolution. Today,' he added, 'we both stress evolution.' There were fears in Asia and America that this summit meeting might even presage a new Sino-Soviet axis, after years when the United States had been able to capitalise on the rift between Moscow and Beijing.[119]

Gorbachev arrived in a city gripped by political upheaval. For over a month students from across China, but especially from Beijing, had been on the streets. Their frustrations against the authorities had been simmering for several years but the immediate trigger was the death of Hu Yaobang, former general secretary of the Chinese Communist Party (1982–7) – the man who in 1986 had dared to suggest that Deng was 'old-fashioned' and should retire. Instead Deng and the hardliners had forced out Hu in 1987, who was then lauded by the students as a champion of reform. In the weeks after Hu died on 15 April 1989, more than a million people turned out to protest in Beijing – denouncing growing social inequality, nepotism and corruption and demanding democracy as an all-purpose panacea. What started out as law-abiding protest quickly swelled into a radical movement. And the stakes rose even higher for both sides, after the party newspaper the *People's Daily*, in an editorial on 26 April, characterised the demonstrations as nothing less than 'turmoil' and denounced the students as 'rioters' with a 'well-planned plot' to cause anarchy. They were accused of displaying unpatriotic behaviour, of 'attacking' and even 'rejecting' the Chinese Communist Party and the socialist system.[120]

On 13 May, two days before Gorbachev's arrival in the capital, a thousand students began a hunger strike in Tiananmen Square, bedding down on quilts and newspapers close to the monument honouring the nation's heroes. The Soviet leader's visit was a pivotal moment for the young Chinese protestors, for it offered an unprecedented opportunity to air their grievances while the eyes of the world were upon them. They carried banners in Russian, English and Chinese. One read 'Welcome to a real reformer'; another 'Democracy is our common dream'.[121] Gorbachev – a household name from the media – represented to them everything the Chinese leaders were not: a democrat, a reformer and a changemaker. Their aim was to take their case straight to him – over the heads of the regime – while embarrassing their leaders into making concessions. The students delivered a letter with 6,000 signatures to the Soviet embassy asking to meet with Gorbachev. The response was cautious. The embassy announced that the general secretary would talk with members of the public but it gave no details about who and when.[122]

New dawn for China?

The CCP leadership was caught in a cleft stick. For weeks the summit talks had been meticulously prepared: the Chinese government wanted everything to unfold without a hitch. Instead, the centre of their capital had been turned into a sea of demonstrators chanting to the world media 'You have Gorbachev. And who do we have?'[123] The massive student protests were therefore a major embarrassment, especially considering the presence of no less than 1,200 foreign journalists, there to cover the summit but now taking every opportunity to interview protestors and broadcast live pictures of the chaos into which Beijing had descended. And the government could do nothing to stop them, for fear that repression would be beamed around the world. It was, as Deng tersely admitted, a 'mess'. He told insiders: 'Tiananmen is the symbol of the People's Republic of China. The Square has to be in order when Gorbachev comes. We have to maintain our international image.'[124]

On Sunday 14 May, the day before the summit talks, the students made clear that they had no intention of complying with appeals to their patriotism by the Chinese authorities, who had called on them to clear the Square. On the contrary, some 10,000 held a vigil in the middle of Tiananmen; by daylight on Monday the crowd had swollen to an estimated 250,000. Top party officials spoke repeatedly with student leaders, promising to meet their demands for dialogue and warning of grave international embarrassment for China if they did not desist. All this was to no avail. In fact, the students' obduracy forced a last-minute shift in Chinese protocol – changing the whole dynamic of the summit.[125]

The grand red-carpet entrée for Gorbachev up the sweeping steps of the Great Hall of the People that faces Tiananmen Square had to be abandoned. Instead there was a hastily arranged welcome ceremony at Beijing's old airport and an incognito drive through backstreets and alleyways to enter the National People's Congress building by a side door. Only when safely inside would Gorbachev enjoy a lavish state banquet hosted by President Yang.[126]

The situation was equally delicate for Gorbachev. The only appropriate response, it seemed, was to keep completely out of China's internal politics and pretend that everything was running normally. But privately the Soviet delegation was shocked. Largely in the dark, they wondered whether China was falling apart. Maybe the country was in the midst of a wholesale 'revolution', perhaps on its political last legs? Gorbachev tried to act with appropriate 'reserve and judiciousness', as he put it later, but as soon as he saw the situation first-hand he felt they should leave for home as quickly as possible.[127] Obliged to speak to the press once during his visit, he offered only vague answers. He dodged questions about the protests – admitting he had seen the demonstrators with their banners demanding Deng's resignation but saying that he would not himself assume 'the role of a judge' or even 'deliver assessments' about what was going on.[128] Of course, he said, he was personally for glasnost, perestroika and political dialogue but China was in a different situation and he was in no position to be 'China's Gorbachev'. Indeed, he had told his own staff on arriving that he was not keen to take the Chinese road, he did not want Red Square to look like Tiananmen Square.[129]

Conversely, the Chinese leadership did not want Beijing to go the way of Budapest or Warsaw. The visit of the prime champion of communist reform provoked intense debate within the CCP. On 13 May Deng had made clear his dogmatic hard-line position to the politically reformist Zhao Ziyang. 'We must not give an inch on the basic principle of upholding Communist Party rule and rejecting a Western multiparty system.' Zhao was not convinced: 'When we allow some democracy, things might look chaotic on the surface; but these little "troubles" are normal inside a democratic and legal framework. They prevent major upheavals and actually make for stability and peace in the long run.'[130]

Prime Minister Li Peng took a position similar to Deng, with a preconceived and highly negative view of the man from the Kremlin and his reform agenda: 'Gorbachev shouts a lot and does little,' Li wrote in his diary. And by eroding the party monopoly on power he had 'created an opposition to himself', whereas the CCP had kept sole control and thereby 'united the great majority of officials'. Li also blamed glasnost for triggering ethnic unrest inside the USSR, especially the Caucasus, and for stirring up the political upheavals in Eastern Europe. He warned that such recklessness might lead to the total break-up of the Soviet empire and spread this contagion to China itself. Deng and Li spoke for most of the inner circle, which was extremely wary of their Soviet visitor – especially given the inspirational effect he clearly had on his youthful Chinese fan club.[131]

Like Bush three months earlier, on 15 and 16 May Gorbachev met with China's senior figures. But unlike Bush's experience, there were no warm recollections of past times together; no intimacy or small talk. In fact, even though Yang and Li had lived for a while in the USSR as students and spoke Russian quite well, there was no personal connection between

Gorbachev and his Chinese interlocutors. But, as with Bush, it was the encounter with Deng that really mattered to Gorbachev.

'Gorbachev 58, Deng 85'* read some of the banners in the streets, contrasting the youthfulness and dynamism of the Russian leader and the conservatism of his 'elderly' Chinese counterpart, who would be 85 in August. Gorbachev was keen to make a good impression on Deng: trying to be tactful and deferential – for once, inclined to listen rather than talk. To let the older man speak, he reasoned, 'is valued in the East'. The Chinese were equally sensitive to style and symbolism. They wanted to avoid all bear hugs or smooching of the sort that communist leaders so often lavished on each other. Instead they were keen to see the 'new' Sino-Soviet relationship, symbolised by a respectful handshake. This would be appropriate to international norms and also underline the formal equality now being established between Beijing and Moscow.[132]

A friendly grip? Deng with Mikhail and Raisa

---

*   The elegant symmetry 58/85 gives rise to a small puzzle: by Western reckoning Deng was 84 years old in May 1989. Chinese reckoning adds one year for the period of pregnancy and sets the threshold not at the actual date of birth but at the Chinese New Year. By that reckoning Deng was already 86 at the time of Gorbachev's visit. For the students, presumably, near enough was good enough.

Deng and Gorbachev met for two hours in the Great Hall of the People on 16 May. The first few minutes were televised live so they could announce to the world the official normalisation of their relations. The catalyst, Deng said, had been when Gorbachev assumed power in 1985 and began to reassess Soviet foreign policy, moving away from the Cold War with the West and conflicts with other countries. He particularly praised Gorbachev's speech at Vladivostok in July 1986, when the Soviet leader had made a major overture to China. 'Comrade Gorbachev, all the people of the world, and I myself, saw new content in the political thinking of the Soviet Union. I saw that there might be a turning point in your relations with the United States and it might be possible to find a way out of the confrontation and transform the situation into one of dialogue.' Since then, he added, Gorbachev had gradually removed or reduced the three big obstacles: Afghanistan, the Sino-Soviet border disputes, and then the war in Cambodia. As a result they had been able to normalise both state and party relations between the USSR and PRC.[133]

In public, therefore, all was sweetness and light. But once the TV cameras had left, Deng changed his tone. 'I would like to say a few words about Marxism and Leninism. We have studied it for many years.' Much of what had been said in the past thirty years had 'turned out to be empty', he observed. The world had moved on from the days of Marx, and Marxist doctrine must move as well. Gorbachev remarked that 'Thirty years did not pass in vain ... by contrast, we rose to a new level of comprehension of socialism' and, he added, 'now we study Lenin's legacy more attentively'. But, Deng interjected, Leninism also had to move with the times, not least because 'the situation in the world is constantly changing ... he who cannot develop Marxism–Leninism taking into consideration the new conditions is not a real Communist'. Deng's thrust seemed to be that ideology had to evolve in the light of changing national and international circumstances – 'there is no ready-made model of any kind' – but that a socialist ideological framework remained essential to avoid the chaos of pragmatism and mere experimentation.[134]

Here was a coded but clear critique of Gorbachev's approach to reform in the 'construction of socialism', but the Soviet leader – seeking to remain deferential – chose to ignore it, agreeing instead with his Chinese counterpart that they 'must now draw a line under the past, turning one's sights to the future'. Yes, said Deng, 'but it would be incorrect if I did not say anything today about the past'. Each side, he added, had 'the right to express their own point of view' and he would start the ball rolling. 'Fine,' said Gorbachev, only to be on the receiving end of a long and rambling monologue by the aged Chinese leader about the damage and indignities inflicted on his country over the course of the twentieth century. Deng listed in turn the territorial depredations by Britain, Portugal, Japan, tsarist Russia and then the USSR under Stalin and Khrushchev – and especially, after the Sino-Soviet split, the Soviet military threat along China's own border. Though dismissing the ideological quarrels of the past, Deng conceded 'We were also wrong.' But he clearly laid overwhelming blame for their bilateral tensions at the Kremlin's door: 'the Soviet Union incorrectly perceived China's place in the world … the essence of all problems was that we were in an unequal situation, that we were slighted and oppressed'.[135]

Eventually Gorbachev got his chance for a few words. He said that he saw things differently but did accept 'a certain culpability and responsibility on our part' for the very recent past. All the rest – especially the territorial shifts of the early twentieth century – belonged already to history. 'How many states have disappeared, and new ones have appeared? … History cannot be rewritten; it cannot be remade anew. If we took the road of restoring past borders on the basis of how things were in the past, which people lived in which territory, then, in essence, we'd have to redraw the entire world. That would lead to a worldwide scuffle.' Gorbachev stressed his belief in geopolitical 'realities' – the 'principle of the inviolability of borders gives stability to the world' – and reminded Deng that his own generation had grown up 'in the spirit of friendship with China.'

These mollifying words seemed to snap the old man out of his historical reverie. 'This was just a narrative,' Deng muttered. 'Let us consider that the past is over with.' 'Good,' replied Gorbachev. 'Let's put an end to this.' After some final vague words about the 'development' of their relations, the meeting came to a conclusion. It was as if they had settled the past, but without any clear sense of the future.[136]

This was indeed the case. When Gorbachev had tried to discuss Sino-Soviet trade and joint economic projects with Li Peng, he had made no progress. He could offer the USSR's usual export staples – oil and gas – but the Chinese were not particularly interested. When asked for Soviet investment, Gorbachev was in no position to provide anything. And as for advanced technology, especially IT, Li made clear that China looked to the United States and also Japan. There were no other substantive talks.[137] In fact, on his last day in Beijing Gorbachev was largely marooned in a guest house on the outskirts – unable, as originally scheduled, to reach the Forbidden City or attend the opera because of the protests. After a short visit to Shanghai, he returned home on 19 May with very mixed feelings about the whole trip: real satisfaction about the normalisation of relations – 'a watershed event' of 'epoch-making significance' – but also profound uncertainty about the future not only of Sino-Soviet relations but of the People's Republic itself.[138]

The moment Gorbachev had left Beijing, Deng turned his mind to sorting out the students. Their brazen refusal to leave Tiananmen voluntarily had humiliated the Paramount Leader but, while his Soviet guest was around, Deng's hands had been tied. Now his anger boiled over. The Chinese capital had become virtually paralysed with over a million protestors sitting in the Square and marching down the boulevards. The students had been joined by workers, shopkeepers, civil servants, teachers, peasants – even recruits from Beijing's police academy dressed in their uniforms.[139] Order was crumbling; the regime itself seemed in danger.

Over the weekend of 20 May, Deng declared martial law in Beijing. The government brought in thousands of troops armed with machine guns and backed by tanks, tear gas and water cannons.[140] It imposed tight media censorship and forced out Zhao, the liberal chief of the party, because of his conciliatory approach to the protestors. The hardliners were now in charge. But it would take another two weeks of heightened tension before the crisis was resolved. The mere presence on the streets of the People's Liberation Army was not enough: the men had in any case been briefed not to cause bloodshed. The students, certainly, were not cowed and they used techniques of non-violence to keep the troops at bay. Even though their numbers had diminished by late May to perhaps 100,000, they continued to hold the Chinese communist leadership hostage, both politically and ideologically.[141]

State power and human vulnerability

What the protestors stood for was summed up, at least for the global media, in the 'Goddess of Democracy'. This ten-metre-high white pâpier-mâché and styrofoam statue resembling New York's Statue of Liberty was erected on 29 May at the heart of the Square in front of the Imperial Palace. Press photographs showed it as if eyeing defiantly the great picture of Mao. Democracy – on the US model – had become the celebrated symbol of the demonstrators' demands. The Chinese government issued an official statement ordering the statue to be taken down, calling it an 'abomination' and declaring 'this is China, not America'.[142]

Beside himself with frustration, Deng finally ordered the military to use force on those who, he said, were trying to subvert the nation. His justification was that China needed a peaceful and stable environment to continue along its reform path, to modernise and open up to the capitalist world. But reform, he insisted, did not mean doing away with four key principles: upholding socialism, maintaining the CCP's leadership and party monopoly, supporting the 'people's democracy', and adhering to Marxist–Leninist–Maoist philosophy. Pure ideology, enforced by autocratic party rule, was there to stay.[143]

At dawn on Sunday 4 June, tens of thousands of Chinese soldiers flooded Tiananmen Square and the surrounding streets, firing their sub-machine guns into crowds of men and women who refused to move out of the way. Scores of students and workers were killed and wounded. Several thousand on the edge of the mayhem left the Square peacefully, though still defiantly waving their university banners. Their encampment was then destroyed: armoured personnel carriers ran over the tents, ruthlessly driving over individuals who had chosen to stay put. When some of the protestors retaliated by toppling army vehicles and stoning the Great Hall of the People, the soldiers used tear gas and truncheons. Soon the city's hospitals were inundated. 'As doctors, we often see deaths,' said one medic at the Tongren Hospital. 'But we've never seen such a tragedy like this. Every room in the hospital is covered with blood.'[144]

The precise death toll remains impossible to establish: estimates vary from 300 to 2,600. Chinese state news on 4 June exulted in the crushing of a 'counter-revolutionary rebellion' and highlighted the casualties among police and troops. The demonstrators were soon airbrushed out of China's official history. But what really mattered was that the country's brief and traumatic battle for democracy had been immortalised by the world's media. In addition to the reports of the carnage and the civilian deaths, images emerged of the crackdown that became truly iconic – fetishised by reformers around the world as symbols of China's lost 1989. The two most notable icons were the photo of a lone man apparently defying a line of tanks, whose fate remains tantalisingly unknown. He would become the classic emblem of global 1989 – the power of the people. And the Goddess of Democracy captured in an eye-catching way what the protestors had struggled for. On the morning of 4 June the statue was quickly reduced to shards and then washed out of the Square by the clean-up troops amid the debris of a failed revolution. But the world would not forget.[145]

Tiananmen – The tanks take over

And so China reinvented communism – by force. In the process, as the tragedy was played out in real time on TV, the students became identified in the Cold War context with Western ideals of freedom, democracy and human rights. The Chinese government's use of tanks against unarmed students also evoked memories of 1968, not just student protests around the world but the suppression of the Prague Spring by the Red Army – which had shaken European communism to its core. Deng was now widely seen as the villainous enemy of freedom and many asked whether Gorbachev would stay true to his UN speech, when he had renounced the Brezhnev Doctrine and championed 'freedom of choice'. With unrest mounting in the Soviet bloc and the USSR itself, would Gorbachev go the way of Deng? Would the tanks now roll in Eastern Europe?

*

Five days later Moscow issued a limp statement of 'regret' over the bloodshed and expressed the 'hope' that common sense and continued reform would prevail in the PRC. Soviet government spokesman Gennady Gerasimov admitted that Soviet officials were surprised at the brutality with which the Chinese leaders put down the student demonstrators. 'We hadn't expected this.'[146] Privately, Gorbachev told Kohl that he was 'dismayed' by developments in China, but did not elaborate further.[147] For him the stand-off in Beijing corroborated his long-held view that Deng's approach to reform was bound to create tensions and that political liberalisation was the only way to resolve such tensions without spilling blood. So the Soviet leader became ever more convinced that *his* strategy, aimed at avoiding violence and building a 'mixed economy' without the extremes of capitalist privatisation and social inequality, was the only sensible way forward. In short, for Gorbachev economic reform had to be complemented by political reform – whatever that would mean.[148]

Others in the Soviet Union wanted Gorbachev to openly condemn the Chinese government. The radical politician Boris Yeltsin and the human-rights advocate Andrei Sakharov decried Deng's actions as 'a crime against the people' and drew parallels between the Chinese crackdown and the Soviet military's 'repression' of demonstrations in Tbilisi, Georgia, in April, only weeks before Gorbachev went to Beijing. (Interestingly, Deng had cited that incident to his own people as an example of good discipline.) But Gorbachev had no intention of emulating Yeltsin and Sakharov. He was not about to sacrifice the hard-won gains of his personal diplomacy for the sake of abstract principles.[149] China was too important to the USSR to risk alienating Deng by what both sides would have agreed was 'interference in internal affairs'.

Bush's reaction to Tiananmen was similarly cautious. The Americans had not been surprised by the turn of events – James Lilley, the new US ambassador in Beijing, had been predicting a crackdown for weeks and the president himself had been careful not to make any encouraging noises to the demonstrators to avoid inflaming passions.[150] He told reporters on 30 May: 'I'm old enough to remember Hungary in 1956, and I would want to do nothing in terms of statement or exhortation that would encourage a repeat of that.'[151]

In private the president had sent Deng a letter three days earlier appealing to him frankly as an old friend and warning against 'violence, repression and bloodshed', lest this damage Sino-American relations.[152] Deng took no notice. On 4 June Bush tried to reach him by phone but Deng simply refused to take the call. It was a blatant snub: even a *lao pengyou* had no clout when it didn't suit China.[153]

Deng clearly believed he could risk the crackdown. He predicted that the West would soon forget, and in any case they knew that trade with China was too important to sever relations altogether. Indeed, Deng had been careful to reassure Washington about his deep concern for their mutual relations. The Chinese leader was not wrong in his assumptions. The signals from Washington were mixed. On the one hand, Bush 'deplored' Deng's decision to use force against peaceful demonstrators[154] and suspended military sales and high-level official contacts with China. He also offered humanitarian and medical assistance to anyone who had been injured in the Tiananmen tragedy. But, on the other hand, he had no intention of severing diplomatic relations or pressing for tough sanctions, from which only ordinary people would suffer. Given his personal bond with Deng and his faith in the magnetic attraction of capitalism, Bush sought to avoid any confrontation that would jeopardise a blossoming Sino-American relationship in the long run. China in Bush's eyes had come such a long way. If he acted too harshly, he might feed the anti-reformist, hard-line elements in Beijing and set the clock back – something he wanted to avoid at all costs. But if he was seen as acting too softly, the communist regimes in Eastern Europe including the USSR might feel encouraged to use force against their political opponents. The problem was that his room for manoeuvre was severely limited – especially at home where Congress was calling for stricter sanctions and the human-rights lobby wanted to punish the 'butchers of Tiananmen' and denounced Bush as the 'appeaser' of Beijing.[155]

Juggling these various pressures, and having publicly defended presidential pre-eminence in foreign policy against congressional encroachment, on 21 June Bush tried again to reach out to Deng. This time he sent a handwritten letter composed, he said, 'with a heavy heart'. He appealed to their 'genuine friendship', stressed his respect for Deng personally, and even trumpeted his own 'great reverence for Chinese history, culture and tradition'. He made it clear that he would not dictate or interfere but appealed to Deng not to 'let the aftermath of the tragic recent events undermine a vital relationship patiently built over the past seventeen years'. Mindful of the 4 June snub, the president added, 'I would of course welcome a personal reply to this letter. This matter is too important to be left to our bureaucracies.'[156]

This time personal diplomacy worked. Bush got a reply within twenty-four hours – sufficiently positive that at the beginning of July Bush asked Scowcroft to smuggle himself into China for talks with Deng and Li. It was an epic adventure story reminiscent of Kissinger's Marco Polo visit to Beijing in July 1971. They set off at 5 a.m. on 30 June 1989 from Andrews Air Force Base, travelling on a C-141 military cargo plane 'in which had been installed what was euphemistically called a portable "comfort pallet", a huge box containing bunks and place to sit'. The aircraft could be refuelled in the air, avoiding the need to land anywhere en route, and their official destination was Okinawa but that was amended on the way. All USAF markings had been removed and the crew started in military uniforms but changed to civilian clothes before arriving in Beijing. The mission was so secret that Chinese military air defence had not been informed. Fortunately, when they saw an unidentified aircraft entering Chinese airspace near Shanghai and asked whether they should shoot it down, the call went right through to President Yang Shangkun who told them to hold their fire. The American party landed safely at lunchtime on 1 July and spent the rest of the day recovering from their ordeal at the State Guest House.[157]

Scowcroft's conversation with Deng on 2 July in the Great Hall of the People set the parameters for future policy on both sides – so much so that it's worth setting out their positions in detail.[158] Deng started by saying that he had 'chosen' Bush as a special friend because, ever since they first met, he had found him 'trustworthy'. Of course, the problems in Sino-US relations could not be 'solved by two persons from the perspective of being friends', the Chinese leader said. So Deng was pleased that Bush had sent Scowcroft 'as his emissary'. It showed that Bush understood the complexities of the situation. He had taken 'a wise and cool-headed action – an action well received by us'. And so, 'it seems there is still hope to maintain our originally good relations'.[159]

Nevertheless, in Deng's view, the blunt truth was that 'on a large scale the United States has impugned Chinese interests' and 'hurt Chinese dignity'. That for him was the 'crux of the matter'. Some Americans who were keen for the PRC and its socialist system to be overthrown had helped stir up 'counter-revolutionary rebellion'. And because the US had tied the knot, to borrow from a Chinese proverb, Deng insisted 'our hope is that in its future course of action the United States will seek to untie the knot'. In other words, it was up to Bush to remedy the situation.

His government, Deng added, was determined to put down 'the counter-revolutionary leaders' in line with 'Chinese laws'. And he insisted that 'China will by no means waver in its resolution'. Otherwise, he asked rhetorically, 'how can the PRC continue to exist?' Deng left Scowcroft in no doubt that any interference in China's internal affairs would not be tolerated and he warned Congress and the US media not to add more fuel to the fire. Indeed, he expected Washington to find a 'feasible way and method' to settle their differences regarding the events of Tiananmen.[160]

Scowcroft responded with the studied courtesy that always mattered in America's relations with China. He spoke at length about the personal bond between Bush and China and his own depth of feeling for the country. He tried to underline the strong US investment in the steady 'deepening' of its relations with Beijing since 1972, from which both sides had benefited strategically and economically, as well as on a human level. He also stressed the significance of his visit. 'Our presence here after a trip of thousands of kilometres, in confidence so as not to imply anything but an attempt to communicate, is symbolic of the importance President Bush places on this relationship and the efforts he is prepared to take to preserve it.'[161]

Having echoed Deng's emphasis on the importance of personal friendship, Scowcroft then inserted the irreducible American agenda. 'It is into this bilateral climate of deepening cooperation and growing sympathy that the events of Tiananmen Square have imposed themselves.' He explained that the president had to cope with his electorate's emotional reaction. This was America's 'internal affair' – touching on its people's fundamental values which Bush in turn shared to a significant degree. In other words, the president stood by his commitment to 'freedom' and 'democracy' that he had enunciated in his inaugural address. And, by thereby defending America's stance on human rights, he could not be seen to visit Beijing in person because that would confer a legitimacy on Deng's regime which the bloodshed in Tiananmen had removed. But, Scowcroft told Deng, Bush wanted to 'manage events in a way which will assure a healthy relationship over time'. And he was 'very sensitive to Chinese concerns'. Back-channel diplomacy was therefore the only way to 'restore, preserve and strengthen' the bilateral relationship.[162]

Deng did not reply directly. Instead, he emphasised three maxims that drove China. First, 'I think one must understand history,' Deng said. China had fought a twenty-two-year war costing 20 million lives – a conflict waged by the Chinese people under the leadership of the Communist Party. Indeed, he told Scowcroft, 'if one should add the three-year war to assist Korea against US aggression then it would be a twenty-five-year effort'. Second, he underlined the sanctity of China's independence: a country that would not allow itself to be directed by another nation 'no matter what kind of difficulties should crop up in our way'. China would follow its own course for development regardless of the 'macro international climate'. As for the third fundamental: there existed 'no other force' except the Chinese Communist Party that could represent China. This had been proved over 'several decades'.[163]

Scowcroft had a similar discussion with Li. Reflecting later, he sensed a deep rift and a 'clash of cultures'[164] which could not at the moment be bridged, but the clandestine trip had served its main purpose: to maintain channels of communication and thus quietly preserve economic ties. Bush noted in his diary, 'I kept the door open.'[165]

The Kremlin and the White House therefore reacted cautiously to Tiananmen. But behind the scenes their thinking was now in flux. In different ways Gorbachev and Bush had focused on relations with China in the early months of 1989 – both making high-profile visits to Beijing – but there was little that could be done, at least for the foreseeable future, in view of the Chinese communist leaders' hard-line response to revolution.[166] In mid-1989 Gorbachev and Bush were both recalibrating their policies.

The Soviet leader, it must be said, was still inclined to look east. Discussing Tiananmen with the Indian prime minister, Rajiv Gandhi, in Moscow on 15 July 1989, Gorbachev brushed aside emotive talk about the death toll, remarking 'politicians have to be careful in these matters. Especially when we are talking about a country like China. About a country with a population higher than 1 billion people. This is a whole civilisation!' Looking for positives, he even felt that China's estrangement amidst world outrage about the 'Tiananmen massacre' had a silver lining: Beijing now needed friends and this might give Moscow and New Delhi a real opportunity at a time when Deng had become really fed up with

Bush's procrastination. 'The Americans want everything to go badly here, or even worse than that. So we need to put hope mainly in ourselves.' And also, he mused, perhaps in other sympathetic countries undergoing the tribulations of modernisation and development. 'Yesterday we spoke to the minister of science and technology of the PRC. We talked about cooperation. He is well disposed.' Gorbachev reminded Gandhi about their previous talks about 'the triangle' – a new framework of trilateral cooperation between the Soviet Union, India and China. 'Perhaps now is the exact moment when they are truly interested in ties with you and with us?'[167]

Gorbachev's musings were symptomatic of the uncertainties of the international scene in the confusing summer of 1989. Yet others in his entourage viewed Tiananmen in the light of more immediate challenges in Europe. Vladimir Lukin, the head of Gorbachev's planning staff, warned that the events of 4 June showed that the PRC leadership was drifting 'more and more obviously towards the group of socialist countries with traditional ideology' – meaning East Germany, Cuba, Romania and North Korea – 'and, at the same time, treats with fear and suspicion those countries which are reforming the administrative-bureaucratic system' – in other words Poland and Hungary. This, said Lukin, 'of course is an unpleasant fact but it would be incorrect not to take it into account in our contacts with the Chinese'. Rather than trying to build an overt Asian axis, he advocated a posture of 'well-wishing reserve' towards Beijing, devoid of any flamboyant gestures. Such a policy would allow the Soviet Union 'to pass through the current difficult period without spoiling relations with official Beijing'. And it would have the additional advantage of securing 'the respect of the most advanced sections of the Chinese people' who, he predicted, would doubtless play a role during the 'not so distant period after Deng' and would support 'our forward movement in the "Western direction" of our foreign-policy activity'. This was a striking admonition. Lukin not only warned that China had now aligned itself firmly with the rearguard not the vanguard of communist re-invention – though he clearly thought the Deng era was coming to an end – but he also explicitly saw Russia's future as lying not in Asia but with Europe and the Western world.[168]

Amid all the furore about Tiananmen, it is easy to forget that 4 June was not just a landmark moment for China. That was the day when Solidarity came to power in Poland. So democracy was also on the march in Eastern Europe. Quite literally, indeed, because it was just four weeks earlier that Hungary's communist government had taken the fateful step of cutting open its barbed-wire border with Austria. That breach offered a loophole to the West, particularly for East Germans who had the right of citizenship in the Federal Republic. At a time when China was walling itself into a new hybrid model – communist-controlled embryonic capitalism – the Iron Curtain was coming apart in Europe. This was a challenge to the Cold War order as a whole – and one that only the two superpowers could address. After pussyfooting around Mikhail Gorbachev for half a year, George H. W. Bush had no choice but to engage.

Chapter 2

Toppling Communism: Poland and Hungary

The 4th of June 1989. That Sunday was not just a turning point in China's modern history but also a landmark date for Poland and for Eastern Europe's evolution out of the Cold War. Many observers proclaimed it as the day of Poland's first 'free' and democratic elections since the Second World War.

Yet that wasn't quite right: Poland's exit from communist dictatorship began with a rigged vote gone wrong. The Polish Communist Party – locked since 1980 in an enervating power struggle with the Solidarity trade union movement – conceded the demand for elections in the hope of controlling the process of reform. This was intended to be the reinvention of communism, Polish-style. As US reporter John Tagliabue observed, General Wojciech Jaruzelski, the party leader, wanted to 'use the vote to sweep reform-minded leaders into key posts' and 'sweep away apparatchiks resistant to change so that new blood can be pumped into the party' – as Gorbachev had tried to do in the USSR.[1] The regime's resort to democracy was largely a facade. All one hundred seats of the upper house, or Senate, were openly contested, but this was the case for only 161 (35%) of the 460 seats in the all-important lower house (Sejm). The rest were reserved for the communists (38%) and fellow-traveller parties (27%). What's more, thirty-five seats of the communists' quota were allotted to prominent government and party officials. These candidates faced no challengers and were put on a special, separate 'national list'. The only 'choice' open to voters was to cross out as many names from the various lists as they wished. The regime knew some people would do so but did not expect this on a large scale: hence its requirement as regards the special 'national list' that each candidate gain the support of 50% of voters. On the face of it, then, there was no reason to believe that the Polish Communist Party's monopoly on power would be threatened by this tepid experiment in democracy.[2]

In fact, many people that Sunday had their eyes on what was happening to 'democracy' on the other side of the world: a story not of ballots but of bullets. Press and TV were full of Tiananmen, six hours ahead of Warsaw and twelve in advance of Washington. British journalist and commentator Timothy Garton Ash, in the Polish capital to cover the elections, sat that morning in the makeshift offices of the recently founded opposition daily *Gazeta Wyborcza* (motto '*Nie ma wolności bez Solidarności*', 'There's no freedom without Solidarity'). But he and his Polish friends became mesmerised by footage of dead or wounded Chinese protestors being carried out of the Forbidden City.[3] The *New York Times* that morning featured a front-page banner headline 'TROOPS ATTACK AND CRUSH BEIJING PROTEST; THOUSANDS FIGHT BACK, SCORES ARE KILLED'. Tucked away at the bottom of the page, a small box entitled 'The Polish Vote' noted: 'Some say that, four years hence, the opposition will be in control.'[4]

In fact, change in Poland was only hours away. Although official results were not expected until a few days later, it was clear by that evening that the opposition would win virtually all the seats in the Senate. What's more, in the elections for the Sejm, millions of voters defied the government by crossing out huge numbers of names on the official list, so that dozens of key party functionaries – including the prime minister, the defence minister and the minister of internal affairs – failed to get over the 50% hurdle. This was a stunning outcome: Solidarity had outpolled the communists. Not only was the election a slap in the face for the party, it also undermined the foundations of effective government. The regime had lost control of its reinvention of communism. The people were taking over.

And yet the mood across Poland was not exuberant on that sunny evening. The populace appeared unsettled. Solidarity leader Lech Wałęsa expressed anxiety about the implications of what seemed like a landslide for his trade union movement: 'I think that too big a percentage of our people getting through would be disturbing.' After a decade of bruising struggle with the regime, he was wary of how the Jaruzelski government would react. Party spokesman Jan Bisztyga warned: 'If feelings of triumph and adventurism cause anarchy in Poland, democracy and social peace will be seriously threatened.' He added darkly, 'Authorities, the coalition and the opposition cannot allow such a situation.'[5]

Garton Ash witnessed how the Solidarity leaders 'plunged into fevered discussions, tortuous negotiations, and late-night cabals' – their reaction to the polls 'a curious mixture of exaltation, incredulity, and alarm. Alarm at the new responsibilities that now faced them – indeed the problems of success – but also a sneaking fear that things could not continue to go so well.'[6] That fear, of course, was heightened by the news from China. Both Solidarity and reform communist leaders had been suddenly and painfully reminded of what could happen if violence broke out – not least given the presence of some 55,000 Red Army troops on Polish soil.[7] And so they did everything possible to avoid it.

The Solidarity leadership now realised that it must dare to engage in national politics – to move beyond its original role of 'the opposition' and take on the responsibilities that came with electoral success. The government, too, was stunned by the results. It had solicited a qualified vote of confidence from the people, who instead had delivered a damning verdict on more than four decades of communist rule sustained by the external force of Soviet military power. With Poland entering uncharted waters, both sides were being forced to work together – fearful of risking another Tiananmen if they did not. Solidarity and the communists were seemingly bound in a community of fate – incapable of acting for Poland without each other.

In Moscow, Gorbachev and his advisers were shocked by the news from Warsaw. They had expected that perestroika-style reforms would be met with gratitude in the satellite states, enabling reform communists to stay in charge. The Soviet leadership put the result down to Polish peculiarities. After all, as aide Andrei Grachev remarked, the Poles were the 'weak link' in the Soviet bloc. What happened in Poland would most likely stay there.[8] Gorbachev, therefore, stuck to the principles he had enunciated before the UN. The Brezhnev Doctrine was dead; 'freedom of choice' was now paramount. The Polish people had spoken. So be it – as long as Poland remained a member of the Warsaw Pact.[9]

No one foresaw the cascade of falling dominoes that would follow Poland's electoral revolution. But the problems had been gestating for years.

*

In retrospect, the whole Soviet bloc seems like a house of cards. First, because it was rooted in the presence of the Red Army ever since the end of the Second World War. Soviet control of these territories had developed incrementally – rapidly in the Polish case, more slowly, for instance, in Czechoslovakia – but single-party communist regimes tied to Moscow were essentially imposed by force. In 1955 that iron fist was covered with a thin velvet glove in the form of an international alliance among independent states, ostensibly mirroring NATO and colloquially known in the West as the Warsaw Pact, but this was in fact a convenient cover for Soviet dominance. In 1956 the pact backed up the Red Army when it put down the anti-communist protests in Budapest; in 1968 it did the same to crush the Prague Spring. Ultimately the bloc was held together by fear of the tank. Of course, the United States was the unquestioned hegemon of NATO, essential provider of nuclear security and using bases on Allied soil. But, if Western Europe was part of an American 'empire', this was empire both by 'invitation' and by 'integration'. In Eastern Europe, however, the Soviet bloc was always 'empire by imposition'.[10]

What also held the satellite states together (under the umbrella of Comecon, the Council of Mutual Economic Assistance, founded in 1949) was common adherence to concepts of economic planning that emanated from Moscow. 'The Plan' set government targets for total production, for performance within each industry and indeed each factory and farm, thereby eliminating market forces but also personal incentives. Building on wholesale nationalisation programmes pushed through after 1945, the Plan promoted rapid industrialisation and urbanisation of hitherto largely agrarian societies and initially led to a sharp growth of living standards and welfare provision for much of the population. But these gains were soon exhausted and by the 1970s the inflexibilities of the command economies became palpable. Resentment grew about the paucity and poverty of consumer goods. Because the bloc was intended to be autarkic, it was also largely sealed from Western imports, even during the détente years of the 1970s. By then the system was surviving to a great extent thanks to infusions of Western credits and the subsidised price of Soviet oil. A decade later, as the West's IT revolution was taking off, the inefficiencies of Comecon and the fragility of the Soviet bloc generally seemed transparent.[11]

These grave structural flaws notwithstanding, the 'revolution of 1989' was in no way preordained. Neither CIA analysts nor international relations theorists predicted the bloc's sudden disintegration in 1989.[12] The turmoil of that year was not simply the culmination of popular discontent and protest in the streets: transformation was instigated in part by national leaders, in struggles between reformers and conservatives. There was 'revolution from above' as much as 'revolution from below'. Moreover, national leaders operated in an international context – responding to signals initially from Gorbachev and later from the West. In view of this lateral dynamic we might even speak of a 'revolution from across'. And one of the most crucial 'across' factors that would determine the success or failure of reform would be the actions of the Red Army – because the Soviet military presence was the *fons et origo* of the bloc as a whole.

Yet 1989 was not just simply a bloc-wide uprising against the Soviet 'empire by imposition'. Change resulted from specific circumstances in individual states, with their different societies, cultures and religions. The catalysts occurred at different times and unfolded at different speeds, driven by diverse national and local circumstances. Many of their roots lay in long-simmering grievances; and many of the historical reference points came from earlier revolutions, not just in the communist era (Berlin, 1953; Poznan, 1956; Budapest, 1956; Prague, 1968) but also going back, say, to 1848 or 1918.

In the case of Poland[13] nationalist resentment against alien rule was channelled through the Catholic Church, which held a unique position of authority there compared with anywhere else in the bloc. For centuries the church had embodied Polish values against both Russian Orthodoxy and Prussian Protestantism, especially at times when Poland had been erased from the map during various periods of partition. In the communist era, it successfully retained its independence from the state and ruling party and functioned as almost an alternative ideology. The election of the charismatic cardinal Karol Józef Wojtyła in October 1978 as the first Polish pope (John Paul II), and his triumphal visit to his homeland the following June, elevated him into an alternative leader who championed human rights and freedom of speech yet who, by virtue of his office, was now resident in the West. Such were his authority and aura that the regime was left virtually impotent as the people discovered a surrogate voice.[14]

Poland also had another well-organised force capable of standing up to the state. Solidarity, the independent trade union, had been formed in 1980 during a rash of strikes that spread along the Baltic coast of Poland from Gdańsk north to Gdynia and then west to Szczecin in response to massive price rises imposed by the government. The crucible of the movement was the Lenin Shipyard in Gdańsk, Poland's leading port, where some 20,000 workers and their families formed a significant and cohesive force of resistance, and the leader who emerged was Lech

Wałęsa, a forceful and feisty workers' organiser, who became an international icon with his big, bushy moustache. After months of unrest, the regime – now led by General Wojciech Jaruzelski who, unlike his predecessor, had Moscow's full backing – eventually imposed martial law in December 1981. It was a crackdown Polish-style, but at least there was no Warsaw Pact intervention akin to Prague 1968. Political deadlock ensued. The authorities were unable to eliminate Solidarity, but the outlawed union was in no position to overthrow the government either.[15]

The Polish economy continued in spiralling decline until another round of price hikes in winter 1988 as part of what the government described as a broad programme of economic and political change. But while retail prices jumped 45% in the first quarter of 1988, in the case of household fuel going up 200%, much of the programme ground to a halt almost as soon as it had begun.[16] During the spring and summer strikes and protests spread across the country, enveloping all branches of industry – from the shipyards to the buses, from steelworks to coal mines – at a time when Gorbachev was encouraging reform from Moscow and spurring Jaruzelski into further 'socialist renewal'. When a new wave of strikes in August paralysed Poland's key export industries, especially coal and steel, the government's facade of self-confidence began to crack. 'A very powerful thing came out of the last strike,' said Wieslaw Wojtas, the leader at Stalowa Wola, the heart of Poland's steel industry and epicentre of the 1988 strikes. He and his fellow workers had had the audacity to end the August strike by marching through the city, together with 30,000 of the city's 70,000 residents, to the local Catholic church. 'We broke the barriers of fear,' he declared proudly. 'And I think the authorities realised we won.'[17]

Wojtas was right. Now that the fear of the tank had dissipated, the Poles could no longer be forced into silent submission. Jaruzelski agreed to discuss economic, social and political reforms. Round-table talks opened in February 1989 with Solidarity, the church and communists sitting as equals around the same bagel-shaped table.[18] On 5 April they reached an agreement that would amend the 1952 constitution and take the Polish polity a long way towards representative government, including a restored upper house to complement the Sejm. What's more the former would be chosen entirely by free elections, thereby paving the way for the legalisation of Solidarity and the election of 4 June.

Poland – Refolution at the round table

Wałęsa had called off the strikes in September 1988, in return for Jaruzelski's commitment to round table discussions.[19] Popular protests would never be repeated on such a large scale. From the autumn of 1988 what happened in Poland was 'entirely an elite-managed crisis, with the masses only stepping onto the political stage to cast their votes, on June 4 and 18, 1989', bringing to an end the communist monopoly on power.[20] Indeed this was an elite affair on both sides, with the deals largely hammered out between ruling and opposition leaders. Hence commentator Timothy Garton Ash's neologism 'refolution', signifying reform from above prompted by revolutionary pressure from below.[21]

In Hungary in 1988–9, the dynamic was similar though the logic and pace of the narrative were different. There was no rash of strikes to act as a catalyst, and no trade union movement or rallying around the church; instead the crucial trigger was a power struggle within the party elite. In May 1988 the ailing János Kádár, now in his mid-seventies, who had held power since his installation by the Kremlin in 1956, was finally toppled. His departure opened the door for a new generation of communists, all of them in their forties or fifties and mostly reformers.[22] Their outlook was defined by the complex legacy of November 1956, when Soviet tanks had rumbled into the capital, Budapest, to put down popular demonstrations against Russian oppression and to overthrow a reformist communist government that had committed itself to free elections and the country's withdrawal from the Warsaw Pact. In the bloody crackdown, an estimated 2,700 Hungarians died and 20,000 were injured.[23]

After the Soviet tanks rolled in, the Kremlin expected its puppet Kádár to sort out the mess. His first move was to send some 20,000 people to prison and execute 230, including the ringleaders of the 'counter-revolution' (the Soviet bloc's official description of this popular insurrection). Imre Nagy, his predecessor, was tried in secret, hanged in the prison yard, and then buried face down in an unmarked grave with his hands and feet tied by barbed wire. Although no mourning or commemoration was allowed in Hungary, Nagy became a cult figure for Hungarians and in the West.[24]

Kádár, having proved his loyalty to Moscow, gradually and quietly jettisoned Marxist dogma and allowed a measure of free enterprise. The command economy was loosened to free many goods from price controls and to introduce a new programme for agricultural collectivisation, including revised household plot regulations that permitted people to grow food for the market on private land.[25] This was the origin of Hungary's so-called 'goulash economy' of the 1960s – officially termed the 'New Economic Mechanism'.[26] Kádár's economic and political reforms made possible rising living standards and a relatively relaxed ideological climate. He also cautiously opened up Hungary socially; Western radio broadcasts were no longer jammed and the restrictions on travel across the Iron Curtain were relaxed. In 1963, 120,000 Hungarians travelled to the West, four times more than in 1958. All this made the country one of the most prosperous and tolerant states in the Soviet bloc.[27] Kádár became a popular figure – at least for the moment.

By the mid-1980s, however, overshadowed by Gorbachev, the aged Hungarian leader had passed his sell-by date. Certainly that was the view of the younger generation of his party who were keen to embrace the new ideas and dynamism emanating from the Kremlin. Kádár had lost the appetite for change, rather like the Moscow gerontocrats from the Brezhnev era in the early 1980s. During 1987 Kádár tried to shore up his own position as party secretary by appointing to the premiership Károly Grósz, a party functionary with conservative credentials. But Grósz defied Kádár and sided with the reform faction, whittling down state controls and subsidies and encouraging private entreprise. In a climate of slackening financial discipline Hungary acquired the highest per capita debt in Eastern Europe.[28]

Amid the deepening crisis, dissidents grew in confidence, creating with the acquiescence of the party a profusion of opposition groups. It was these new political forces that increasingly set the political agenda. In response, communist reformers defeated the conservatives and replaced Kádár as party general secretary with Grósz at a special party conference in May 1988; the young economist Miklós Németh took over as prime minister from Grósz in the autumn. The strategy of the reformers – like that of their Polish counterparts – was for the party to retreat and renew itself without relinquishing control. As in Poland, these hopes would prove illusory. Hungary would become the bloc's second domino.

By February 1989 the government's attempt to co-opt the opposition had failed. What emerged was a kind of competitive cooperation. Many of the opposition groups had evolved into political parties and the Communist Party felt obliged to declare its support in principle for Hungary's transition to a multiparty democracy. Indeed the party soon abandoned the formal Leninist principle of 'democratic centralism', which had legitimised its monopoly on power. Within this fraught political process, historical memory also played a part.[29] The 15th March was traditionally Hungary's national day – commemorating the outbreak of the abortive nationalist revolt of 1848 against the Austrian empire, which had eventually been crushed by troops of its ally, the Russian tsar Nicholas I. During the communist era, all celebration of that day had been banned for fear of generating anti-Russian protests, but in 1989 the reformist government – hoping to appease the opposition through a collective commemoration and thereby garner credit for its current political course – declared that 15 March would again be a national holiday. However, the government-sponsored event on the steps of the National Museum was dwarfed by a throng of no less than 100,000 people who took to the streets that morning to re-enact 1848.[30]

In this heady atmosphere the regime's opponents felt emboldened to form an opposition round table (ORT). Eight of these came together, seeking to unify around a clear negotiating strategy in the face of the regime's own reform agenda. This seemed essential in order to give Hungary's opposition the same kind of weight and influence as Solidarity had achieved in Poland. After some weeks of haggling about how to conduct the talks, negotiations between the ORT and the government began in earnest on 13 June, and then in secret (again unlike Poland).[31]

Three days later, on 16 June – the thirty-first anniversary of Imre Nagy's execution – the opposition disinterred his remains and finally gave him and several other prominent figures of the 1956 revolution a public funeral in Heroes Square in the centre of Budapest, amid crowds that even the government admitted topped 200,000. The whole funeral was screened on state television, and was attended by four reformist members of the ruling Communist Party, led by Prime Minister Németh. Not that it did them any good. A twenty-six-year-old spokesman for the 'Federation of Young Democrats' by the name of Viktor Orbán paid tribute to Nagy as a man who, though a communist, 'identified himself with the wishes of the Hungarian nation to put an end to the communist taboos, blind obedience to the Russian empire [sic] and the dictatorship of a single party'. Gesturing at the four communist leaders present, he continued scathingly, 'we cannot understand that those who were eager to slander the revolution and its prime minister have suddenly changed into great supporters and followers of Imre Nagy. Nor can we understand that the party leaders, who made us study from books that falsified the revolution, now rush to touch the coffins as if they were charms of good luck.' A note of malice had crept into the proceedings: Orbán's remarks signalled a sharp rejection of the reform-communist narrative of managed transformation and national reconciliation, and it anticipated the spirit of resentment and the purge mentality that would come to suffuse Hungarian politics.[32]

Nagy's reburial catalysed strong anti-Soviet, anti-communist nationalism at the grass roots – rather like the papal visit to Poland, but in this case through memory politics instead of religious fervour. Both of these political transformations were largely shaped by specific national experiences, and were also contained within national boundaries. Yet they occurred at much the same time and each fed on and into the other. What was happening in both Poland and Hungary represented extrication from dictatorship through the creation of new institutional structures for new regimes. In addition, there was also a wider diffusion of revolutionary ideas,[33] even beyond Eastern Europe. Indeed it is telling that the conservative hardliners in Beijing likened this to a contagion emanating from Poland and Hungary.[34] In due course the 'disease' of economic reform combined with political democratisation[35] would spread as the year went on, infecting the bloc from Estonia on the Baltic coast to Bulgaria on the shores of the Black Sea.

But contagion affecting a plethora of communist states was not the only dynamic of 1989. In one of these countries, Hungary, reform had the power to act as a solvent for the whole Soviet bloc and indeed for Cold War Europe itself.

*

This became clear on 27 June 1989, in a graphic image that rapidly made its way around the globe: two men, smartly dressed in business suits but standing in open country, wielded bolt cutters to nip holes in a rusty barbed-wire fence. The duo – Hungarian foreign minister Gyula Horn and his Austrian counterpart Alois Mock had travelled specially to the Austria–Hungary border to send a deliberate signal. Side by side, cutting through the wire fence, they seemed to be conveying the good news that the division of post-war Europe was coming to an end.

Horn and Mock cut the Iron Curtain

It was, of course, something of a public-relations stunt. When Horn proposed the fence-cutting ceremony, Németh jokingly replied: 'Gyula, do it, but hurry up – there isn't much barbed wire left.'[36] In reality, the two governments had started to remove the border installations, including watchtowers and alarm system, on 2 May and the actual decision to do so dated back to the end of 1988 when Németh, as part of his package of reforms, had scrapped the budget for the maintenance of the whole decrepit system. The alarm was still going off – around 4,000 times a year, but mostly caused by rabbits, deer, pheasants and the occasional drunk. The bankrupt government did not have the money to repair it and, in any case, earlier that year travel restrictions for Hungarians had been lifted entirely: twelve months on, by the end of 1988 6 million Hungarian tourists had travelled abroad, mostly to the West.[37]

Németh checked his decision to take down the iron fencing around his country with Gorbachev when visiting Moscow on 3 March and the Soviet leader raised no objection: 'We have a strict regime on our borders, but we are also becoming more open.' But, as Németh admitted to Gorbachev, the situation was more complex for Budapest, because the only remaining purpose of the fence was to catch citizens from East Germany who were trying to escape illegally to the West via Hungary. 'Of course,' he therefore added, 'we will have to talk to the comrades from the GDR.'[38]

The East German regime, led by Erich Honecker since 1971, received the news of the border opening with a mixture of anger and anxiety. Anger, because the Hungarians had done it alone – with Gorbachev's blessing but without consulting the rest of the Warsaw Pact allies. And real anxiety because any East German with valid travel documents to Hungary could conceivably escape the bloc into Austria and then on to automatic citizenship in West Germany. In other words, Hungary would become a fatal loophole in the Iron Curtain that the GDR had struggled so long to preserve in order to maintain its political existence.

Nevertheless, when Hungary began the removal in early May the East German defence minister General Heinz Kessler appears to have still been relatively unstressed. He told Honecker that his Hungarian counterpart General Ferenc Kárpáti had assured him that the dismantling was being done 'entirely for financial reasons' and that Hungary would obviously continue to secure the border through more watchtowers and 'intensified patrols' with sniffer dogs. Kárpáti, of course, was following instructions from Németh who had told him to play for time and keep things vague with East Berlin. 'If we start to explain the full situation we'll give ourselves away and get into even worse trouble.' Crucially, Kessler took Kárpáti at his word and dutifully reported to Honecker that the dismantling of the 260-kilometre border fence was intended as a gradual process that would last until the end of 1990, at a rate of about four kilometres a week, and starting in the vicinity of four of the eight border crossings. Hungary, he explained, was undertaking this 'cosmetic venture' in a timely manner to advance good neighbourly relations with Austria and as part of a general relaxation of tensions in Europe.[39]

With barbed wire disappearing every day, however, East Berlin remained on edge. Honecker sent his foreign minister Oskar Fischer to Moscow to complain, only to be told by Shevardnadze that the GDR had to resolve this matter directly with Hungary.[40] And so East Germany found itself alone, without any support from Moscow – sandwiched between a reforming Poland in the East, its capitalist German rival in the West and an ever more liberal and open Hungary further south.

Initially, as Kárpáti had promised, Hungarian border guards did detain East German 'fugitives' at those first de-fenced sections near border checkpoints. The Iron Curtain seemed to be holding. But, as news got out and especially after seeing the images of Horn and Mock on 27 June, people felt increasingly emboldened. And so, as the weeks wore on, the so-called 'green border' (the dismantled sections farther away from the crossings and therefore less thoroughly patrolled) offered better opportunities for escapees. By August some 1,600 East Germans had successfully taken this route to reach the West.[41]

The Honecker regime did its level best to keep all this out of the papers and off the TV. But it was too late. East Germans had got the message: Hungary was their gateway to freedom.

*

Hungary's simmering international crisis was also the top item on the agenda when Gorbachev met Kohl in Bonn on 12 June 1989 for his first state visit to the FRG since he took office.[42] 'We are watching the developments in Hungary with great interest,' the chancellor declared. 'I told Bush that as far as Hungary is concerned, we are acting on the basis of an old German proverb: let the church remain in the village. It means that the Hungarians should decide themselves what they want, but nobody should interfere in their affairs.' Gorbachev agreed: 'We have a similar proverb: you do not go to somebody's monastery with your charter.' They both laughed. 'Beautiful folk wisdom,' exclaimed Kohl.

Then the Soviet leader became more sombre. 'I am telling you honestly – there are serious shifts under way in the socialist countries. Their direction originates from concrete situations in each country. The West should not be concerned about it. Everything moves in the direction of a strengthening of the democratic basis.' Here was Gorbachev's endorsement of socialist renewal on a national level. But he also issued a guarded warning to Kohl, mindful of pressures on the chancellor to offer financial support to opposition groups in the Soviet bloc. 'Every country decides on its own how it does it. It is their internal affair. I think you would agree with me that you should not stick a pole into an anthill. The consequences of such an act could be absolutely unpredictable.'

Rather than get into that argument, Kohl simply said that there was 'a common opinion' in the USSR, the USA and the FRG that 'we should not interfere with anybody's development'. But Gorbachev wanted to underline his point. If anyone tried to destabilise the situation, he said, 'it would disrupt the process of building trust between the West and the East, and destroy everything that has been achieved so far.' [43] Next day, 13 June, he and Kohl signed no less than eleven agreements expanding economic, technological and cultural ties and a joint declaration affirming the right of peoples and states to self-determination – a significant step, especially from the German perspective.[44]

Yet the 'Bonn Declaration' was much more. It was the centrepiece of a state visit whose primary importance for the West Germans was the symbolic reconciliation of two nations whose brutal struggle had left Germany and Europe divided. It defined what both deemed to be a new and more promising phase in Soviet–West German relations. This was reflected in the conclusion expressing 'the deep, long-cherished yearning' of the two peoples 'to heal the wounds of the past through understanding and reconciliation and to build jointly a better future.'[45]

Gorbachev and Kohl: A toast to peace and understanding

Buoyed up by the achievement and the atmosphere, the two men really bonded over the course of three days. They talked in private on a total of three separate occasions. And in contrast to the usually stilted meetings between a Western leader and a communist, they developed the confidence to exchange very candid assessments of their 'mutual friends'. Both of them respected Jaruzelski; both were keen to support Poland's transformation under his leadership and also Hungary's reform course, as long as the latter was not spinning out of control. Each of them had problems with the diehard socialist regime of Erich Honecker, and neither could stand Nicolae Ceaușescu. In Kohl's opinion the old dictator had plunged his country into 'darkness and stagnation'; Gorbachev called Romania 'a primitive phenomenon', akin to North Korea, 'in the centre of civilised Europe'.[46]

As human beings they also developed a real closeness, sharing childhood memories and reflecting on their families' wartime sufferings: 'There is not a single family' in either country, said Kohl quietly, 'whom the war did not touch'.[47] He told Gorbachev that his government saw the visit as marking nothing less than 'the end of hostilities between Russians and Germans, as the beginning of a period of genuinely friendly, good neighbourly relations'. He added that 'these are words supported by the will of all the people, by the will of the people who greet you in the streets and squares'. Without doubt, this was another striking feature of the visit. Gorbachev had been welcomed ecstatically in West Germany – the little Rhineland towns, as much as the Ruhr steelworks he visited, were all mobbed with people shouting 'Gorby, Gorby.' The conversation between the leaders became increasingly intimate. 'I like your policy, and I like you as a person,' confessed Kohl; 'let's communicate more often, let's call each other on the phone. I think we could accomplish many things ourselves without delegating to the bureaucracies.' Gorbachev agreed: he felt that mutual trust was growing 'with every meeting'.[48]

On their last evening, after a long and relaxed dinner in the Chancellery bungalow, Kohl and Gorbachev, with only a translator in tow, wandered into the park and down the steps to the Rhine. There they sat on a low wall, chatting occasionally to passers-by, and gazing at the Siebengebirge hills beyond. Kohl never forgot this moment. The two men imagined a comprehensive reordering of Soviet–German relations to be codified in a 'Grand Treaty'[49] that would open new perspectives for the future. But Kohl warned that it was impossible as long as Germany remained divided.

Gorbachev was unmoved: 'The division is the result of a logical historical development.' Kohl did not let go. On that balmy night, in a haze of wine and goodwill, he sensed a not-to-be-missed opportunity. Pointing to the broad, steadily flowing Rhine, the chancellor mused: 'The river symbolises history. It's nothing static. Technically you can build a dam ... But then the river will overflow and find another way to the sea. Thus it is with German unity. You can try to prevent unification, in which case we won't experience this in our lifetimes. But as certainly as the Rhine flows towards the sea, as certainly German unity will come – and also European unity.'

Gorbachev listened and this time he did not demur. That evening on the bank of the Rhine, so Kohl thought looking back, was truly a turning point in Gorbachev's thinking and also in their whole relationship. As they parted the two men hugged each other. An unlikely combination, perhaps: the stocky Kremlin leader and the massive, six-foot four, 250-pound chancellor. But the feeling was real: a political friendship had been born. What's more, for Gorbachev West Germany had become what he called Moscow's 'major foreign partner' – after the United States – and was therefore playing nothing less than a 'global role'.[50]

Kohl could now bask in the glow of hugely successful state visits in quick succession from each of the superpower leaders – Bush and Gorbachev. He told the press exultantly: 'within three weeks the two most powerful men from two different systems visited Germany. This new era brings new responsibilities to Germany', and also, he added, 'for peace'.[51]

Gorbachev's evaluation of the summit was also warm and positive. 'I think we have come out of a period of Cold War, even if there are still some chills and drafts,' he announced before leaving. 'We are simply bound to a new stage of relations, one I would call the peaceful period in the development of international relations.' He even suggested that the Berlin Wall could 'disappear when those conditions that created it fall away. I don't see a major problem here.' This was a scarcely veiled snub to the Honecker regime. And, alluding to the division of Germany itself, he stated 'we hope that time will resolve this'. But while speculating about the end of one great geopolitical barrier, Gorbachev also aired his fears of a new, 'impenetrable wall across Europe' – referring to the European Community's plans for a totally integrated single market by 1992. 'So far we have not heard the economic or political arguments

convincing enough to dispell such apprehensions.' Here is a reminder
that in June 1989 the process of 'European integration' seemed like a
way of deepening the division between the two halves of the continent,
rather than a unifying force of the sort that Gorbachev envisaged when
he spoke of a 'Common European Home' stretching from the Atlantic
to the Urals.[52]

For Gorbachev, Bonn was part of a series of visits around Europe in
mid-1989 during which – like Bush with his speaking tour in the spring
– the Soviet leader presented his evolving ideas about the new Eastern
Europe that was emerging through his programme of political and
economic restructuring.

In Paris three weeks later, he developed the line taken with Kohl on
Poland and Hungary, insisting that communist countries 'now in transition' would 'find a new quality of life within a socialist system, a socialist
democracy' as the 'process of democratisation' ultimately transformed
all of Eastern Europe. In other words, what was going on within the
Soviet bloc was reconstruction not deconstruction. Yet, pointing to the
historical connections between 1789 and 1917, he declared that perestroika
was also a 'revolution'. Speaking to a packed and eager audience of
professors, writers and students in the Sorbonne – a venue he had specially
requested – Gorbachev felt like the intellectual that he yearned to be. He
philosophised about the fundamentally 'new global problems facing
mankind at the end of the twentieth century' to which his 'new thinking'
provided answers. He warned the West not to expect Eastern Europe's
'return to the capitalist fold' or to cherish 'the illusion that only bourgeois
society represents eternal values'.[53]

Lurking beneath these comments was Gorbachev's real irritation with
those addresses Bush had delivered in April and May. He did not see
any 'realism' or a 'constructive line' in those statements and in fact found
them 'quite unpleasant', he told Kohl in Bonn. 'Frankly speaking, those
statements reminded us of Reagan's statements about the "crusade"
against socialism.' Like Reagan, Bush 'appealed to the forces of freedom,
called for the end to the "status quo", and for "pushing socialism back".
And all this', Gorbachev fumed, 'at a time when we are calling for the
de-ideologisation of relations. Unwillingly, questions come to mind –
where is Bush genuine, and where is Bush rhetorical?'[54]

When the topic came up between Mitterrand and Gorbachev on 5
July in the Elysée Palace, the French president did not mince words about
his own quite different views. 'George Bush would conduct a very

moderate policy even without congressional constraint because he is conservative.' In fact, he added, Bush 'has a very big drawback – he lacks original thinking altogether'. Mitterrand's frustration about his own lack of influence and France's diminished status in global affairs was palpable. He also felt sidelined by the active European diplomacy of Bush and Kohl – a theme to which I will return in chapters four and five. Conversely, the Soviet leader must have relished the Frenchman's dig at the foot-dragging US president as much as he appreciated Mitterrand's profession of 'faith in the success of perestroika'.[55]

Nevertheless, determined to take the initiative from the 'crusading' Bush and regain the moral high ground, the Soviet leader pulled out the stops when speaking to the Council of Europe in Strasbourg. Declaring that 'the post-war period and the Cold War are becoming a thing of the past', Gorbachev offered an eye-catching disarmament package, proposing cuts in Soviet short-range nuclear missiles 'without delay' if NATO agreed, and the ultimate goal of eliminating all these weapons. Mindful of recent Alliance arguments over the 'third zero', he mischievously claimed that the USSR was holding fast to its 'non-nuclear ideals', while the West was clinging on to its dated concept of 'minimum deterrence'.

The Soviet leader also elaborated on his vision of a Common European Home. This ruled out 'the very possibility of the use or threat of force' and postulated 'a doctrine of restraint to replace the doctrine of deterrence'. He envisaged, as the Soviet Union moved towards a 'more open economy', the eventual 'emergence of a vast economic space' right across the continent in which the 'eastern and western parts would be strongly interlocked'. He continued to believe in the 'competition between different types of society' and saw these kinds of tensions as 'creating better material and spiritual conditions of life for people'. But he was looking forward to the day when 'the only battlefield would be markets open for trade and minds open to ideas'.

Admitting that he had 'no finished blueprint' in his pocket for the Common European Home, he reminded his listeners of the work of the 1975 Helsinki Conference on Security and Cooperation in Europe (CSCE), when thirty-five nations had agreed common principles and values. It was now time, he declared, for the present generations of leaders in Europe and North America 'to discuss, in addition to the most immediate issues, how they contemplate future stages of progress towards a European Community of the twenty-first century'. At the cornerstone of Helsinki 1975 were the two superpowers and, Gorbachev believed, that situation had not changed. 'The realities of today and the prospects for the foreseeable future are obvious: the Soviet Union and the United States are a natural part of the European international and political structure. Their involvement in its evolution is not only justified, but also historically conditioned. No other approach is acceptable.'[56]

Gorbachev returned home via Romania, where he led a Warsaw Pact meeting that formally and publicly renounced the Brezhnev Doctrine – in other words cementing his statements in New York and more recently Strasbourg that force would not be used to control the development of individual socialist states. Combined with Gorbachev's PR offensive of drastic, unilateral Soviet force reductions in Eastern Europe and his express desire for the Warsaw Pact states to make progress with NATO countries on producing a conventional arms accord by 1992,[57] this was another deeply worrying moment for Honecker and the other hardliners in the bloc – Ceauşescu and Miloš Jakeš of Czechoslovakia – especially considering that they had used the summit to lobby vehemently for Warsaw Pact military intervention in Hungary. Champions of repression and intransigence, they must have felt that the Kremlin was abandoning them.[58] Gorbachev certainly left his fellow communist leaders in no doubt what he thought about the dinosaurs among them. He stressed that 'new changes in the party and in the economy are needed ... Even V. I. Lenin said that new policies need new people. And this does not depend on subjective wishes any more. The very process of democratisation demands it.'[59]

The Soviet leader left Bucharest on 9 July, just as the president of the United States was arriving in Warsaw. Each superpower was putting down markers on a Europe in turmoil.

*

Bush had been alarmed by the Soviet leader's peace offensive around Europe, not least because America's NATO allies appeared to be in the grip of some kind of 'Gorbymania' which made them susceptible to Soviet blandishments about arms reduction. His own European tour – to Poland and Hungary ahead of the G7 meeting in France – had been planned in May but it was now all the more imperative, in order to 'offset the appeal' of Gorbachev's message.[60]

Indeed, before even setting off for Europe, Bush made a point of quickly and strongly rebuffing Gorbachev's Paris proposals: 'I see no reason to stand here and try to change a collective decision taken by NATO,' he declared, and reiterated that there would be no talks on SNFs until agreement had been reached in Vienna on reducing conventional forces in Europe, an area in which the USSR was vastly superior. He wrote sarcastically in his memoirs about Gorbachev's attempt to persuade the West that it 'need not wait for concrete actions by the Soviet Union before lowering its guard and military preparedness'.[61]

That said, Bush did not want his European trip to be about scoring points off Gorbachev. The president had already laid down his own ideological principles in the spring and, far from wishing to mount a 'crusade', he was sensitive both to the volatile situation in Eastern Europe and to Gorbachev's delicate political position at home. He did not intend to 'back off' from his own values of freedom and democracy but was acutely conscious that 'hot rhetoric would needlessly antagonise the militant elements within the Soviet Union and the Pact'. He even worried about the impact of his own presence, regardless of what he said. While wanting to be what he called a 'responsible catalyst, where possible, for democratic change in Eastern Europe', he did not want to be a stimulus for unrest: 'If massive crowds gathered, intent on showing their opposition to Soviet dominance, things could get out of control. An enthusiastic reception could erupt into a violent riot.' Although he and Gorbachev were jockeying for position, the two leaders agreed on the importance of stability within a bloc that was in flux.[62]

Bush and his entourage arrived at Warsaw's military airport around 10 p.m. on 9 July. It was a humid summer evening as they descended from Air Force One to be greeted by a large official welcoming party. Jaruzelski was in the forefront but, for the first time ever during a state visit, representatives of Solidarity were also present. No spectators were allowed near the plane, but en route from the airport to the government guest house in the city centre, where George and Barbara Bush would be staying, thousands of people lined the streets, three or four deep, waving flags and giving the Solidarity 'V' for victory symbol. Others leant from the balconies of their apartments, throwing down flowers onto the passing motorcade. The mood, contrary to Bush's fears, was that of a friendly welcome, not a political demonstration.[63] In fact, this was typical of the whole trip. There were no massed throngs cheering in adulation – nothing like Pope John Paul II in 1979 or

Kennedy in Berlin in 1963. The public mood seemed uncertain, characterised by what American journalist Maureen Dowd called a mixture
of 'urgency and tentativeness' as Poles contemplated a strange future
in which the 'jailors' and those they had jailed would now have to try
to govern together.[64]

Bush and Jaruzelski managed to turn their scheduled 'ten-minute
cup of coffee' in the morning of 10 July into an extended and frank
conversation that lasted almost an hour. Their *tour d'horizon* spanned
Polish politics and economic reforms, US financial aid, superpower
relations, the German question and Bush's vision of 'a united Europe
without foreign troops'.[65] The president's meeting with Prime Minister
Mieczysław Rakowski – a veteran communist journalist until he was
suddenly appointed premier the previous September – was similarly
businesslike and also opened up some of the complexities underlying
the glib word 'reform'. Poland's 'chief problem', Rakowski explained,
was to 'introduce reforms while avoiding serious unrest'. Privatisation
would be an important step but he warned it would take 'a full generation' before Poles accepted the Western-style 'stratification of wealth'
that would necessarily follow. What Polish people did not need, he
added, was an American 'blank check' – in other words 'untied credits'
from the West. Instead he hoped Bush could encourage the World
Bank and IMF to display flexibility about the staggering of debt repayments. Rakowski conceded his party's 'economic errors of the past'
but insisted that these 'constitute a closed chapter' and that Polish
leaders now understood the need to turn the page. Bush promised that
the West would help but stated that he had no intention of supporting
the radical, indeed frankly utopian, demands by the labour unions
that would 'break the Treasury'. In that way Bush stood closer to the
aims of Polish communist reformers including Jaruzelski and Rakowski,
who sought managed economic cooperation with the USA and the
West, than to Wałęsa and the opposition, who wanted immediate and
large-scale direct aid to ease the pain of transition and thus maintain
popular support.[66]

The president did talk about economic aid when he addressed the
Polish parliament on the afternoon of the 10th, but what was grandly
described as his 'Six-Point Plan' received a mixed reception. To be sure,
the need was clear: Poland's debt to Western creditors in summer 1989
stood at around $40 billion, with the country's growth rate barely above
1% while inflation was running at almost 60%. But although Bush

promised to ask the US Congress for a $100 million enterprise fund to invigorate Poland's private sector, he hoped that the rest of the aid package he proposed ($325 million in fresh loans and a debt rescheduling of $5 billion) would come from the World Bank, the Paris Club, the G7 and other Western institutions.[67] It was all a bit vague and certainly nothing like the $10 billion that Wałęsa, for one, had requested. Nor did it even come close to the $740 million in aid that Reagan, at the height of the Cold War, had offered the communist government before martial law was declared in December 1981.[68] That, of course, was prior to the USA's foreign debt going through the roof as a result of Reaganomics – from $500 billion in 1981 to $1.7 trillion in 1989.[69] Certainly the public reaction in Poland was almost openly critical. 'Very little concrete material', a government spokesman complained, and 'too much repeated emphasis on the need for further sacrifices by the Polish people'. So much for popular hopes in Poland of a 'mini-Marshall Plan'. While Bush saw himself as being 'prudent', Scowcroft told journalists defensively that the value of the aid was 'political and psychological' as much as 'substantive'.[70]

Next day Bush flew to Gdańsk to meet Wałęsa for lunch at his modest but cosy two-storey stucco house on the outskirts of the city. This was a deliberately informal, down-home affair. George and Barbara chatted with Lech and Danuta as 'private citizens', because the Solidarity leader had not stood for election and therefore had no official political role now. Looking around the rooms, the president was struck by the 'lack of modern appliances and furnishings that most American families take for granted'. 'Stylish waiters' borrowed from a nearby hotel and a 'fancy' Baltic meal served on silver salvers did not cover up those realities. After more of what Bush described as Wałęsa's 'uncertain and unrealistic' financial requests, backed by lurid warnings of 'a second Tiananmen in the middle of Europe' if Polish economic reforms failed, the president was happy to escape from their uneasy get-together and drive to the Lenin Shipyard to address 25,000 dockworkers. He considered standing outside the factory gate in front of the monument commemorating the forty-five workers killed by the security forces during the 1970 strikes – three anchors nailed to giant steel crosses – the 'emotional peak' of his Polish trip. Bush felt 'heart and soul, emotionally involved' as he spoke, with a 'heady sense' that he was 'witnessing history being made on the spot'.[71]

Trumping Lenin in Gdańsk – Bush with Wałęsa

His trip to Poland had been brief (9–11 July) but it underlined the magnitude of the political and economic problems that had to be surmounted. One presidential adviser told the press, it would 'take hundreds of millions of dollars, from us and lots of other people, and even that won't guarantee success'.[72]

That evening Bush arrived in Budapest during a heavy thunderstorm. He and Barbara were driven straight to Kossuth Square – named for the leader of Hungary's failed revolution of 1848 and one of the centres of the 1956 uprising against Soviet rule. As the motorcade pulled into the square in front of the Parliament building it was greeted by a huge mass of people, some 100,000 strong – a crowd in an ebullient mood, full of expectation, despite being drenched by the rain. Bush, too, was very excited. It was the first ever visit of an American president to Hungary.[73]

The rain continued to fall while Hungary's president Bruno Straub droned on for a full quarter-hour of plodding introductions. When Bush finally got a chance to speak, he waved away an umbrella, dispensed with his notecards and made a few extempore remarks 'from the heart' on the changes taking place in Hungary and on its reform-minded leadership. Just as he finished, the evening sun broke through the dark clouds. There was another special moment. Out of the corner of his eye, Bush noticed an elderly lady near the podium who was soaked to the skin. He took off his raincoat (which actually belonged to one of his security agents) and put it round her shoulders. The spectators roared with approval. Then Bush plunged into their midst, shaking their hands and shouting good wishes. Scowcroft noted: 'The empathy between him and the crowd was total'.[74]

Next day, 12 July, Bush followed a similar script to his Warsaw visit. He was careful not to be seen associating with any opposition-party officials too closely. Indeed his meetings with both opposition and Communist Party figures were behind closed doors while in public he expressed his support for the communist reformers who now ran the government. Still, the difference in overall atmospherics between Budapest and Warsaw was clear: Hungary had enjoyed for two decades 'more political freedom – nightclubs feature biting satirical sketches about the government – and more economic energy, with food markets piled high with fruits and vegetables, than the other Warsaw Pact countries'.[75]

In his talks with Bush, Prime Minister Miklós Németh emphasised his firm belief that the Hungarian Socialist Workers' Party (HSWP) could 'renew itself and will be able to, through electoral means, gain a dominant position in the coalition. The danger is that if the HSWP is defeated, the opposition is not yet ready to rule.' Bush agreed. As regards the 'political system for Hungary', the president stated that 'the principles articulated by the prime minister are ones that Americans support' and promised that he would 'do nothing to complicate the process of reform'. Being inclined toward stability, Bush believed that it was the reform communists who were uniquely equipped to successfully engineer a gradual exit from Moscow's orbit.[76]

In Hungary – unlike Poland where the political situation was rather precarious in the wake of the elections – the question was not whether reform would proceed but how fast and on whose terms. Currently the reform communists were driving the transformation, and they did so with confidence. Internationally Hungary had more room for manoeuvre than Poland, a strategically more pivotal country for the Soviet Union. And Budapest also knew that it benefited from following in Warsaw's slipstream. Poland had clearly managed to get away with its reform course by staying within the Warsaw Pact, and the Hungarian reformers also saw this as the best path – especially after Gorbachev had held firm to his non-interventionist position in the Bucharest summit. (Leaving the Warsaw Pact had been the step too far by Hungary in 1956.)

Understanding the new rules of the game, Hungarians were also willing to test the limits of the possible. In fact, they had done so already with the dismantling of the barbed wire. As Imre Pozsgay – effectively Hungary's deputy prime minister under Németh – explained to Bush, there were only two situations that might attract Soviet intervention: 'the emergence of civil war' or 'a Hungarian declaration of neutrality'. The former he deemed unlikely: he was sure Hungary would undergo a 'peaceful' transformation. And the latter was simply 'not possible' for Hungary: as in Poland's case, Hungary's Warsaw Pact membership was non-negotiable to avoid provoking the Kremlin. Bush entirely agreed that Hungarians should not have to choose between East and West. What was important, he declared, was 'for Soviet reforms to go forward' while the United States did not 'exacerbate Gorbachev's situation or make the Hungarian course more difficult'.[77]

Bush found the reformers' buzz and energy infectious. Quite contrary to a Poland that had seemed drab, subdued and worried about its new political pluralism, Hungary, opening rapidly towards the West, seemed really full of vitality. And Bush conveyed this in his speech at Karl Marx

University on the afternoon of 12 July. 'I see people in motion,' he said. 'I see colour, creativity, experimentation. The very atmosphere of Budapest is electric, alive with optimism.' Bush wanted his words to act as an accelerator of the process of change ahead of the multiparty elections, so the country would not get stuck in half-measures. 'The United States will offer assistance not to prop up the status quo but to propel reform,' he declared, before reminding his audience that here, as in Poland and across the bloc, simple solutions did not exist: 'There are remnants of the Stalinist economy – huge, inefficient industrial plants and a bewildering price system that is hard for anyone to understand, and the massive subsidies that cloud economic decisions.' But, he added, 'the Hungarian government is increasingly leaving the business of running the shops to the shopkeepers, the farms to the farmers. And the creative drive of the people, once unleashed, will create momentum of its own. And this will ... give each of you control over your own destiny – a Hungarian destiny.'[78]

In spite of this passionate rhetoric, as in Warsaw the president offered relatively meagre economic aid: $25 million for a private-enterprise fund; $5 million for a regional environmental centre; the promise of 'most favoured nation' status as soon as Hungary liberalised its emigration laws. He also made much about sending a delegation of Peace Corps volunteers to teach Hungarians English.[79]

His audience listened quietly but intently throughout the address. The most emotional moment was Bush's comments on 'the ugly symbol of Europe's division and Hungary's isolation' – the barbed-wire fences that, he said, were being 'rolled and stacked into bales'. Bush declared grandly: 'For the first time, the Iron Curtain has begun to part ... And Hungary, your great country, is leading the way.' What's more, with the Soviet Union withdrawing troops, he promised, 'I am determined that we will work together to move beyond containment, beyond the Cold War.' He ended ringingly with the invocation: 'Let us have history write of us that we were the generation that made Europe whole and free.' It won him a standing ovation.[80]

*

On Thursday 13 July, as Bush flew from Budapest to Paris for the G7 summit, he and Scowcroft reflected on the 'new Europe being born'. During the flight the president also shared his impressions with members of the press corps, huddled around him on Air Force One. He said he had come away with 'this real acute sense' of the change that was taking place in Eastern Europe – a change he described as 'absolutely amazing', 'vibrant' and 'vital'. He declared his determination to 'play a constructive role' in that process of change. The meetings, especially with the Hungarian leaders, had been 'very good, very frank'. Warming up, Bush added, 'I mean it was with emotion, and it wasn't your traditional "I'll read my cards, and you read your cards" kind of diplomacy.' There had been 'an intensity to it, a fervour to it' that, he said, 'moved me very much'.[81]

The president had no idea what lay ahead and so he remained cautious, but he was certainly encouraged by what he had seen. 'I am firmly convinced that this wave of freedom, if you will, is the wave of the future,' said Bush buoyantly. To some, it seemed that he was too cautious and overly sympathetic to the communist old guard. Yet others, including his deputy national security adviser Robert Gates, argued that the president was playing a more complex game. While preaching democratic freedoms and national independence to the crowds, he talked the language of pragmatism and conciliation to the old-guard leaders – in a deliberate attempt to 'grease their path out of power'.[82]

Certainly, the challenge faced by his administration was to encourage reform in Eastern Europe without going so far and fast as to provoke turmoil and then a backlash. A fraught economic transition could easily result in inflation, unemployment and food shortages – all of which would force reform-oriented leaders to reverse course. Above all, Bush wanted to be sure to avoid triggering a Soviet reaction – possibly a crackdown in the style of 1953, 1956 and 1968. The key to successful change in the Soviet bloc was Soviet acquiescence, and Bush was keen to make it easy for Gorbachev to provide this. 'We're not there to poke a stick in the eye of Mr Gorbachev,' he told the reporters. 'Just the opposite – to encourage the very kind of reforms that he is championing and more reforms.'[83]

Fresh from witnessing revolutionary change, Bush arrived in a city obsessed with commemorating revolution. 14 July 1989 would mark the bicentenary of the fall of the Bastille, the starting point of France's quarter-century roller coaster of demotic politics and imperial autocracy. French president François Mitterrand was determined to impress his international guests with an extravagant celebration of French grandeur – and his own quasi-regal position. Yet, given the dramatic upheavals in

Eastern Europe, France's historical pageant had particular resonance in July 1989.

As soon as Bush arrived, he was whisked off to the Place du Trocadéro opposite the Eiffel Tower. He sat with the six other leaders of the major industrialised nations, together with over twenty leaders from developing countries in Africa, Asia and the Americas, for a ceremony to commemorate the 1789 Declaration of the Rights of Man. Actors read excerpts from the declaration and quotations from the revolutionary leaders, wreaths were laid at a stone inscription of the document and 500 doves were released into the blue Paris sky. Mitterrand's intent was clear: France's pioneering revolution was to be remembered not for the blood in the gutters but for its enduring values: *liberté, fraternité, égalité*. Then followed an evening at the brand-new, gleaming mammoth Opera House in the Place de la Bastille, on the site of the once-dreaded royal prison. On this occasion too Mitterrand's special twenty guests were present, together with the leaders of the G7 – as they were for the Bastille Day Parade the next morning, when the French president put on a massive display of France's 'world class' military prowess down the Champs-Elysées. Nobody could mistake the implicit message: the Fifth Republic was still a power with global reach. Watching 300 tanks, 5,000 troops and a mobile nuclear missile unit go by along Paris's grand boulevard, Scowcroft couldn't help being reminded of 'a Soviet May Day parade'.[84]

Mitterrand's friends from the Third World really irritated the Americans. After all, the Paris G7 economic summit had been prepared especially to deal with the pressing issues of debt relief and the global environment. But the US delegation emphatically did not want to get the G7 meeting conflated with an impromptu North–South gathering on the margins of the French national celebrations, especially after the debtor countries had already seized the spotlight in Paris to appeal for relief from the developing world's $1.3 trillion debt. The White House worried about the risk that in such an *ex tempore* meeting between creditors and debtors, as advocated by France, the 'South' as a bloc would dress up their demands to the 'North' as 'reparations' for years of colonial 'exploitation', laced with Marxist–Leninist-inspired rhetoric. And generally, the US strongly opposed collective debtor action. In its view, debt problems should be resolved country by country and in this vein the Americans announced a $1–2 billion short-term loan to neighbouring Mexico and then picked up the case of Poland.[85]

Given the G7 summit's central focus on debt relief, General Jaruzelski saw his opportunity and appealed to the Big Seven for a two-year, multi-billion-dollar rescue programme on 13 July. Published in all major Polish party newspapers, his six-point programme included seeking $1 billion to reorganise food supplies, $2 billion in new credits, as well as a reduction and rescheduling of Poland's debt of roughly $40 billion, plus financing for an assortment of specific projects. Significantly, the Solidarity movement endorsed Jaruzelski's appeal; indeed, Wałęsa had just come out in support of an approved Communist Party candidate for the presidency, which made General Jaruzelski's victory much more likely – thus helping to end the political deadlock of the post-election weeks.[86]

Still elated by his recent visits, Bush was happy to use Jaruzelski's financial demands to put Eastern Europe on the top of the summit agenda, wresting the initiative away from Mitterrand and his supporting cast of global little leaguers. But if support for democratic change were to be the centrepiece of the meeting, this meant the summit also had to engage with a less palatable issue for the Americans: the crushed revolution in China. And so the Paris G7 came to be dominated by two burning *political* issues of the moment – problems that potentially threatened global order.

As soon as the summit got under way on the afternoon of Friday 14 July – in the new glass pyramid entrance of the Louvre – the leaders started by arguing over how far they should go in condemning China. Most Europeans, led by the French president, wanted to punish the PRC with exemplary sanctions, but Bush (as well as Prime Minister Thatcher, who was worried about the fate of Hong Kong[87]) urged them to be prudent. The US president wanted as little damage as possible to the Sino-American relationship that was so important to world peace. Yet he was going out on a limb in Paris, because the US Senate voted that very day by eighty-one to ten to impose more stringent US sanctions against the PRC.

Japan's prime minister Sosuke Uno, Asia's sole voice among the G7, also urged caution. Tokyo did not want to see Beijing isolated and by default pushed into Moscow's arms. Moreover, given Japan's long history of invading China, it lacked the moral high ground to punish Beijing. Japan saw itself in a unique position. If it could keep channels to China open while using its position as America's key Pacific ally, it might be able to broker the restoration of Sino-American cooperation. Seeing real benefits in this, Bush worked hard with Uno to soften the language on China in the summit communiqué. In the end, the leaders issued a strong condemnation of the PRC's 'violent repression' but they did not announce any additional sanctions and merely urged the Chinese to 'create conditions which enable them to avoid isolation'.[88]

With the prickly topic of China out of the way, on Saturday the G7 moved quickly to achieve agreement on Poland and Hungary. Their 'Declaration on East–West Relations' stated: 'We recognise that the political changes taking place in these countries will be difficult to sustain without economic progress.'[89] In order to facilitate this progress, they agreed to impose somewhat easier conditions than on a normal IMF loan, by allowing Poland to postpone its $5 billion tranche of foreign debt repayment due in 1989. They also agreed to consider an array of economic aid options for Poland and Hungary (investments, joint ventures, professional training and an infusion of skilled managers), as well as emergency food supplies.

None of this was particularly surprising. What was much more noteworthy and eventually significant was the decision that the economic and food aid for Eastern bloc countries would be coordinated by the European Community – a striking novelty in international politics.[90] Bush got what he wanted. Enlisting support for Eastern Europe endowed his largely symbolic visit to Warsaw, Gdańsk and Budapest with real substance. But he had never intended to bear the burden alone. The G7 had readily bought his concept of 'concerted Western action' in support of Poland and Hungary which, Bush hoped, would lift Western engagement with Eastern Europe out of the superpower domain, spread the burden and make possible a larger, more synchronised and less competitive Western effort. The White House also believed that, couched within this broader multilateral framework, US action would look less threatening to the Soviets. Working with and through allies would become a hallmark of Bush's diplomatic style.

It was Chancellor Kohl who proposed, with prompt agreement from the others, to ask the European Commission to head a group of donor countries to provide assistance to Poland and Hungary. This eventually became the G24: twenty-four industrialised states both from within the EC and outside it. Commission president Jacques Delors – always keen to assume a larger role for himself at the head of this supranational body – was very ready to oversee what was effectively a 'clearing house for aid'. After all, in 1988 the EC had already established loose links with the Comecon as a trading bloc and Hungary had intimated its desire to work towards an association agreement. So, while the USA was content to take a back seat, the EC gained a position of leadership that signalled its growing political power.

The Eastern European aid package was the first time the European Community had been chosen as a follow-up agency for a G7 decision. It was a harbinger of things to come. Just three weeks earlier in Madrid on 26-7 June the EC had agreed to consummate a closer union – both political and economic – in 1992. And it was no accident that the specific blueprint for tighter economic and monetary union had been mapped out by Delors himself.[91]

Delors had been propelled into the presidency of the European Commission in 1984, following a strikingly effective three-year stint under Mitterrand as France's finance minister which highlighted his skills as a political broker. He had successfully persuaded his notoriously obstinate boss to temper his socialist Keynesianism with a policy of austerity and fiscal consolidation. This shored up the failing franc and enabled France to remain within the European Monetary System. On the back of these achievements, moving on to Brussels as Commission president, Delors deftly steered the twelve often divergent members of the European Community towards the signing of the Single European Act in 1986, which embodied a firm commitment to move towards full economic and monetary union (EMU). Delors undoubtedly saw EMU as a way to advance the cause of European integration but he was not an avid federalist, passionate about a United States of Europe. His objections, both pragmatic and philosophical, to European federalism also help to explain his caution about highly centralised approaches to decision-making when developing the embryonic 'Euro Area'. In 1988, at the EC Council meeting in Hanover, European leaders authorised Delors to chair a committee of central-bank governors and other experts to propose concrete stages towards EMU. Here, again, he showed his ability to forge compromises between proponents of different economic approaches, in particular building bridges between France and Germany.[92]

And so at Madrid in June 1989 it was agreed by the leaders of the EC 12 to launch the following year the first stage of EMU – completion of the single market by 1992. This would involve abolition of all foreign-exchange controls, a free market in financial services and strengthening of competition policy – which entailed a radical reduction in state subsidies. The other prong of this policy was the reinforcement of social cohesion, which involved freedom of movement between states and guaranteed workers' rights. Achieving the single market with enhanced cohesion was top priority for this new and exciting chapter in the history of the Community. And with it came a visibly greater role in international affairs for the EC – and its Commission president. This was evident when Bush made a point of meeting Delors in Washington in June, two weeks before Madrid and five weeks ahead of the G7.

The meeting was intended to signal that the United States took seriously the Community and the 'EC 92' project (US shorthand for the transformation of the EC into the EU). [93] Keen to head off the danger of an economically protectionist Fortress Europe, Bush and Baker made it quite clear that America wanted to see the completion of the single European market linked with real progress in the so-called Uruguay Round negotiatiations on a new agreement about global tariffs and trade – one that would replace the crumbling Cold War GATT system. Delors agreed that the EC 92 and global trade talks had to run together: if the Uruguay Round were not successful, it would not be possible for the Community to meet its EC 92 objectives. In fact, he emphasised, 'it would be a contradiction for the Uruguay Round to fail and EC 92 to go forward'. The sticking points on all this, however, were French agriculture, because of the country's entrenched farm lobby, and Japan, with its strong export economy but heavily protected domestic market. Delors hoped that 'in the future the US, EC, and Canada could jointly put pressure on the Japanese'.[94]

Although apparently emerging as an independent actor, the EC always relied for its effectiveness on the key member states. Delors, for all his ambition, never forgot this. And the most significant economic power in the EC was the Federal Republic, so it was vital to work closely with Kohl. Bush, of course, knew this; and he also understood well that the German–American axis was one way of engaging with the West European engine. After all, the chancellor was genuinely supportive of EMU: as Delors told Bush, 'Kohl reinforces the goals of the European Community.' Of course, there was now a danger in the summer of 1989 that further Western European integration might be derailed by the incipient disintegration of Eastern Europe. Yet here again Germany was pivotal.

This became clear during the Paris G7 summit over the question of how to channel aid to Poland and Hungary. It was Kohl who sponsored the idea of the EC as the conduit for Western financial assistance. For the chancellor – ever mindful of the German question – this route offered several advantages. First, West Germany (like America) was keen to maintain the momentum of change within the Eastern bloc but he wanted to keep the process peaceful and avoid bloodshed. A concerted Western economic initiative could prevent anarchy and forestall Soviet military intervention. Second, if the FRG sheltered under the EC umbrella, nobody could blame Kohl going it alone – edging away from West, cosying up to the East and even asserting German power in ways that raised the spectre of the Kaiser and the Führer.

What's more, unlike Bush, Kohl was ready to put a substantial sum of money on the table. He had already told Bush on 28 June that he intended to offer Hungary an additional DM 1 billion (nearly $500 million) of 'fresh money', on top of a loan without conditions of the same amount that he had granted in 1987. Even if the fine print made clear that this funding was actually loans and credits for buying German goods and services rather than direct aid, the sum involved was forty times more than what the president himself had offered Budapest. The chancellor was also very keen to help Poland bilaterally, but this was currently on ice because the aid question was entangled with the position of the German minority in Poland – a sensitive matter for the Poles and for the political right in the FRG. This controversy, rooted in unsettled territorial legacies of the Second World War, was another reminder of the FRG's limits as an independent international actor. The deadlock over a deal also frustrated Kohl's aspiration to go to Warsaw. Initially planned for the summer to follow on the heels of Mitterrand and Bush, his state visit to Poland would not take place until 9 November.[95]

Delors and the G24 moved fast because Warsaw and Budapest feared that economic collapse might undermine democratic reform. Officials made a distinction between Hungary and Poland, however, since only the latter had requested short-term food aid to combat severe shortages. Hungary's twenty-four-page wish list concentrated on better terms of trade with the industrialised world and the liberalisation of foreign investment. The Poles, of course, would come in for similar consideration once their immediate food crisis was resolved. On 18 August, as part of a $120 million package including meat, cereals, citrus fruit and olive oil, the EC announced its first delivery of 10,000 tons of beef to Poland, to arrive in early September. A further shipment of 200,000 tons of wheat stored in Germany, as well as 75,000 tons of barley from France and 25,000 tons from Belgium, were soon to follow – with 500,000 more in the pipeline. The idea was that the Polish government would sell the free food to the people and then reinvest the profits in their economies, especially the private farm sector. This arrangement was formalised in a counterpart fund agreement the G24 negotiated. The role played by EC/ G24 in the late summer of 1989 would provide a template for further Eastern aid packages in the future.[96]

So, in the end, it was Brussels, not Washington, which oversaw Western support for change in Central and Eastern Europe. This somewhat undercut Bush's claims that it was he and the United States who were 'propelling' reform in Poland and Hungary. Although his rhetoric had grown bolder since the spring, Bush's actions revealed his preference for evolution over revolution, privileging stability and order, backed by a deliberate policy of burden-sharing with allies.[97] A mild recession in the USA and a legacy of debt from the Reagan years that had dramatically increased the federal budget deficit reinforced Bush's apprehensions about the dangers of anarchy in a Europe that might become a bottomless pit for US dollars. The president was therefore pleased with the outcome of the G7 summit. What worried him most was a letter that Mitterrand read out on Bastille Day at the very start of their meeting.

*

The letter came from Gorbachev – it was the first time that a Soviet leader had written officially to the G7. And, it was also the first time the USSR had proposed not only expanded economic cooperation but even direct Soviet participation in such efforts.

'The formation of a cohesive world economy implies that the multi-lateral economic partnership be placed on a qualitatively new level,' Gorbachev wrote. 'Multilateral East–West cooperation on global economic problems is far behind the development of bilateral ties. This state of things does not appear justified, taking account of the weight that our countries have in the world economy.' That, he said, was the logical extension of his programme of domestic economic restructuring. 'Our perestroika is inseparable from a policy aiming at our full participation in the world economy,' he stated. 'The world can only gain from the opening up of a market as big as the Soviet Union.'[98]

As with all of Gorbachev's words, the rhetoric was impressive, even compelling. There was no mistaking the Soviet leader's keenness to join the G7. But Bush was wary about the Soviets. Their reforms had not yet advanced far enough to warrant full membership in the top club of free-market economies.[99] And he could see that Soviet involvement would mostly be of benefit to Moscow. Yet Gorbachev's letter, widely quoted in the international press, was impossible to ignore. The absence of the Soviet leader was felt throughout the summit, just as it had been during Bush's visits to Warsaw and Budapest. Tiananmen was another ghost at the feast – an ugly reminder of what could happen if democratic reform went wrong.

After the summit ended on Sunday morning, 16 July, Bush chatted with Baker and Scowcroft on the steps of the Paris embassy overlooking the garden; they discussed their impressions and experiences of the past few days. Suddenly the president announced that the time had come for him to meet at long last with Gorbachev – speaking, as Scowcroft later recalled, 'in that way he has when his mind is made up. Neither Baker nor I remonstrated with him. Baker had never been as negative as I about an early Gorbachev meeting, and I no longer felt so strongly about it.'[100]

It looked like a spontaneous impulse, but in fact Bush had been mulling over this for several weeks. Particular impetus came from the West Germans. On 6 June, in the Oval Office, FRG president Richard von Weizsäcker had warned Bush about the implications of the recent turbulence in Poland and Hungary. 'It would be useful if the US had quiet talks with Moscow about the future of Eastern Europe,' he said. The West European allies would do the same based, as he put it, 'on the values of the Atlantic Alliance' and the FRG would act within this framework to avoid any impression of an independent Ostpolitik.* Weizsäcker returned to the same point later in the conversation, warning Bush more bluntly that 'in their foreign relations, the Soviets are approaching a time that is totally unknown to them, and they are legitimately worried'. He added firmly: 'The West needs to talk to Moscow to alleviate these fears.' The US president did not respond directly but segued to China, observing that he 'had the feeling that the Soviets are saying "there but for the grace of God go I". They may be worrying that reform could affect them in the same way.'[101]

The impressions gleaned from this conversation were reinforced on 15 June when Chancellor Kohl – immediately after his talks with Gorbachev in Bonn – called Bush on the phone to convey his impressions. The Soviet leader, he said, had been in 'good shape' and relatively

---

* *Neue Ostpolitik* (new eastern policy), or *Ostpolitik* for short, was the normalisation of relations between the FRG and Eastern Europe, particularly the USSR and GDR beginning in the 1960s. This policy of détente with the Soviet-bloc countries was initiated by Willy Brandt as foreign minister and then chancellor.

'optimistic', showing himself keen to support Polish and Hungarian reform efforts. But Kohl kept coming back to one issue: Gorbachev was 'seeking ways of establishing personal contact with the president'. Laying it on thick, the chancellor claimed that he and Gorbachev had 'talked for quite some time about the president'. It was clear, said Kohl, that Gorbachev had a 'general suspicion towards the United States' but also that he had 'greater hope for establishing good contact with Bush than he had with President Reagan.' At an intellectual level, Kohl insisted, Gorbachev saw 'eye to eye with the president' and wanted to 'deepen contacts with the US and Bush personally.' Kohl urged sending direct and personal messages to Gorbachev from time to time. This, he declared, would 'signal the president's confidence, which is a key word for Gorbachev, who places a high premium on "personal chemistry"'. Bush probably took it all with a pinch of salt – at the end, to quote the official US record, he merely 'thanked the chancellor for his debrief and said he had listened very carefully' – but the main point clearly registered.[102]

At the weekend Bush had a chance to reflect on the week's events. On 18 June, three days after talking with Kohl, he wrote in his diary: 'I'm thinking in the back of my mind what we should do about meeting with Gorbachev. I want to do it; but I don't want to get bogged down on arms control.' Bush hoped that 'some cataclysmic world event' might occur to give him and Gorbachev the chance to 'do something that shows cooperation' and in the process 'talk quietly' without raising expectations of some dramatic breakthrough on arms control. In short, the president wanted a chat not a summit.[103]

Bush's visits to Poland and Hungary sharpened his awareness that reform might easily get out of hand and turn violent. He could not forget those images of Tiananmen Square, nor could he ignore Eastern Europe's 'traumatic uprisings' of the past. If Eastern Europe was now in transition, this had to be managed by the superpowers: 'to put off a meeting with Gorbachev was becoming dangerous'.[104] And Mitterrand had rammed this very point home on 13 July, the eve of the G7, dismissing Bush's concerns about finding a pretext without raising expectations. The French president said the two of them could 'simply meet as presidents who had not yet met – to exchange views'.[105]

The pressure from his European allies had become intense but Bush was both stubborn and circumspect: he had to make up his own mind in his own time. By mid-July 1989 he had finally done so. Seven months after his inauguration – having grown into the role of president and with his initial China opening now stalled – his focus was firmly on Europe and he had consolidated his own leadership position at the NATO summit in May and the recent G7. Bush had come a long way from that halting bit-part role on Governors Island in the wake of Gorbachev's barnstorming performance in Manhattan. He now felt psychologically prepared to tangle with the Kremlin seducer.

This slow and deliberate approach to decision-making was characteristic of the Bush style, so different from that of Reagan, who had been nicknamed 'the Great Communicator' and 'the Cowboy President'. There was no flamboyance or fireworks. Bush's approach was more measured and pragmatic, based on long experience of government. Some commentators mistook Bush's understated manner and preference for consultation as signs of weakness – an intimation, even, that America's power was on the wane. But Bush understood cooperation, collegiality and persuasion to be the hallmarks of leadership and these required personal contact and the building of trust. By the time the G7 was over, Bush knew that these techniques had worked with his Western partners and he felt ready and able to try them out on his superpower counterpart, quietly confident that he could handle Gorbachev's unsettling mixture of sweet talk and 'one-upmanship'. Gorbachev had told Reagan that it took two to tango. Bush was now willing to join the dance.[106]

On Air Force One, flying home from Europe, the president drafted a personal letter to Gorbachev to explain how, as he put it, 'my thinking is changing'. Previously, he explained, he had felt that a meeting between them would have to produce major agreements, especially on arms control – not least because of the hopes of the 'watching world'. But now, after seeing the Soviet bloc first-hand, holding 'fascinating conversations' with other world leaders in Paris, and learning about Gorbachev's recent visits to France and West Germany, he felt it was vital for the two of them to develop a personal relationship, so as to 'reduce the chances that there could be misunderstandings between us'.

The president thus proposed an informal, no-agenda encounter, 'without thousands of assistants hovering over our shoulders, without the ever-present briefing papers and certainly without the press yelling at us every 5 minutes about "who's winning"' and whether or not the meeting was a success or failure. In fact, Bush added firmly 'it would be best to avoid the word "summit"' altogether. He hoped they could meet very soon but he did not want to put Gorbachev under any undue pressure.

By early August, to Bush's satisfaction, Gorbachev had replied affirm-atively to his proposal. But it would still take several weeks to sort out schedules and location.[107]

*

Meanwhile, change in the once glacial Eastern Europe continued at an astonishing pace. As before, Poland was in the vanguard. The logjam over the new post of president suddenly broke. On 18 July Jaruzelski announced that he would actually be a candidate. Next day the combined houses of parliament met and voted in the general unopposed, albeit after a good deal of arm-twisting of recalcitrant Solidarity parliamentar-ians by their leaders. Jaruzelski promised to be a 'president of consensus, a representative of all Poles'. It was, of course, bitterly ironic that this diehard communist and decade-long suppressor of the trade union move-ment was now appointed Poland's president in the guise of a 'reformer' through a genuinely free vote essentially by those he had previously imprisoned. Many of the Solidarity rank and file were livid. But their political leadership argued that this was the best possible result in order to advance freedom while preserving stability. At the same time Jaruzelski's narrowest of victories (he gained the necessary majority by one vote) showed who had the real legitimacy and political strength in the land: the freed workers, Solidarity.[108]

The next step was to replace the caretaker government under Prime Minister Rakowski. According to the round-table agreement, Solidarity was meant to stay in opposition while a new communist-led government ran the country. But the dramatic election results of 4 June had made a mockery of that original springtime arrangement. In consequence, the communists now sought a grand coalition with Solidarity (not least to try to shrug off some of the responsibility for the deepening economic crisis). But Solidarity was split over this course; most of their members did not want to participate in a government in which Communists would rule. And in any case, they believed that the June election results had actually given them the mandate to govern the country.

In the event, on 2 August Jaruzelski nominated his fellow communist General Czesław Kiszczak as prime minister. But the latter failed to form a Cabinet – because the Communist Party's allies, the Peasant Party and Democratic Alliance, refused to cooperate. And so it was Lech Wałęsa who announced that he would put together a Cabinet under the Solidarity banner. With this daring move Wałęsa went way beyond the round-table agreement. What was now a highly volatile political situation was compounded by growing instability in the first weeks of August, amid a new wave of strikes against rampant inflation and food shortages in the industrial south around Katowice and in the Baltic shipyards.

Jaruzelski was in a bind. Should he cave in and accept the accelerating pace of the political transition? Or should he stand firm and dissolve the legislature? New and unconstrained elections would undoubtedly spell total disaster for the communists. The US ambassador in Warsaw warned that Poland was now 'right on the brink'. If the situation escalated, how long would 'the decaying power elite fail to defend itself'? How to prevent a conservative backlash? Or even civil war?[109]

Jaruzelski agonised for several days. What tipped him against a hard line was the prospect of political and economic chaos and also quiet but firm pressure from Gorbachev and the Kremlin. Wałęsa also made crucial concessions – promising that Poland would remain within the Warsaw Pact and offering the communists the key ministries of Defence and the Interior, in other words control of the army and the police. Both of these were important gestures to Moscow – or at least to the Moscow of 1956 and 1968, just in case that Cold War past was not as dead as Gorbachev claimed. Under these conditions Jaruzelski decided to take the step that would push Poland's political system beyond anything being attempted elsewhere in the Eastern bloc – a 'partnerlike cooperation' between party and movement. The communist president accepted a Solidarity prime minister.[110]

The editor of the opposition newspaper *Gazeta Wyborcza* – applying the 'one for us and one for them' rule – had a month earlier also proposed this solution in an opinion piece he entitled 'Your president, our prime minister'. And so the chalice passed to Tadeusz Mazowiecki, a journalist and prominent Catholic layman since the 1950s. From the early days of Solidarity he had been a vital link between the progressive intelligentsia and the militant workers, and had worked as editor of *Tygodnik Solidarność*, the new Solidarity weekly, before being interned for a year under martial law. In 1988–9 he helped negotiate the end of the mass strikes and the construction of the round-table accords.[111]

On 24 August, Mazowiecki was confirmed prime minister by the Sejm, including the votes of most of the communist deputies, who thus indicated their willingness in principle to serve under him. He had become the first non-communist head of government in Eastern Europe since the early post-war years, yet nobody in the West was too jubilant. 'A historic step,' said a US State Department official, but 'there is no sense of gloating here' considering the immense economic challenges Mazowiecki faced.[112] In fact, the new Polish leader did not deny this, admitting 'Nobody has previously taken the road that leads from socialism to capitalism.'[113]

On the plus side, it took only three weeks for the new Polish PM to present his government to parliament – where it was approved unanimously by 402 votes to nil, with thirteen abstentions. Yet it was perhaps symbolic that the sixty-two-year-old Mazowiecki suffered a dizzy spell while delivering his opening speech on 12 September, which forced him to take a break for nearly an hour. When he returned to the stage, to thunderous applause, he joked: 'Excuse me, but I have reached the same state as the Polish economy.' After the laughter had died down, he added 'I have recovered – and I hope the economy will recover too.' At the end, Mazowiecki stood at the prime minister's bench 'as a man of Solidarity', arms raised in triumph, flashing the two-fingered Solidarity victory sign.[114]

Having fought each other for nearly a decade, Solidarity and communists were now working in uneasy collaboration, while most of the government bureaucracy simply remained in situ, adapting, often eagerly, to new goals and a fresh ethos. In place of the deadlocked triangle of Party–Solidarity–Church the country was now run by a novel configuration of forces: government, parliament and president, with Solidarity's leading figurehead and strategist Lech Wałęsa looking on – effectively as president-in-waiting.

Although Poland's ravaged economy had hardly begun to move from the Plan to the market, the first and crucial phase of political transition – guided but not defined by the round-table pact – had been concluded without conflict. There had been no civil war and no Soviet military intervention. This peaceful 'refolution' had a dynamic effect not only in Poland but also in other communist-ruled countries, signalling that the once inconceivable was now possible.

As events in Poland unfolded, the superpowers looked on as bystanders. To be sure, the State Department favoured a more adventurous and openly supportive policy. But the White House remained more guarded – placing the onus firmly on Warsaw. 'Only the Poles can see that they succeed,' Scowcroft told CNN when asked why the president was not rushing to offer the Poles more aid. 'We can help, but we can only help if money goes into structures which can make it used properly.' His message was clear: let's wait and see. Bush felt it 'important to act carefully and to avoid pouring money down a rat-hole'.[115]

As for the USSR, Gorbachev appeared to cling to the illusion that the 'democratising socialism' of Poland and Hungary had a future. Be that as it may, the Kremlin had neither the will nor the resources to police Eastern Europe in the style of Stalin, Khrushchev or Brezhnev. In any case, Gorbachev was being severely challenged just to hold on to power at home and keep the Soviet Union together. He was now operating within a very different political system, the consequence of the USSR's first free election since 1917. Having persuaded the Communist Party to abolish the Supreme Soviet and create a functioning parliament, the Congress of People's Deputies, in March 1989, he found that this triumph of perestroika created a more independent body that gradually undermined his power. As biographer William Taubman observed, he was 'replacing the old political "game", at which he excelled, with a new one that he never really mastered'. In the process new nationalist, even secessionist, energies were set loose as more and more power was devolved to the republics. These centrifugal forces emerged dramatically in Georgia – prompting the intervention of the Red Army in Tbilisi in April, when twenty-one people were killed – and became even more visible as far as Europe was concerned in the Baltic States on the USSR's western rim.[116]

On 23 August, the day before Mazowiecki was confirmed as Poland's premier, an estimated 2 million people formed a human chain some 400 miles right across Estonia, Latvia and Lithuania to commemorate the fiftieth anniversary of Stalin's pact with Hitler in 1939 that assigned these three Baltic States, independent since 1918, to the Soviet Union. The 'Baltic Chain' or 'Chain of Freedom' was a graphic reminder that the USSR and the Soviet empire had been held together by force. Both the Polish Assembly and the Polish Communist Party publicly condemned the Pact, as had Gorbachev himself just a few days before. But none of them was, as yet, willing to grapple with the logical implication of their words. The Pact had pulled not only the Baltic States within the USSR but also much of eastern Poland. Denouncing Stalinist policies was therefore not simply a political act; it was another sign that the Soviet bloc's burgeoning revolution was also opening up buried questions about European geopolitics – questions that affected basic relations between the superpowers.[117]

And so Poland served almost as the icebreaker of the Cold War in the summer of 1989. Hungary followed in its wake, pursuing its own round-table talks for the reform of the electoral process and the governmental structure. In this case, though, the table was not round but triangular – as befitted the more pointed configuration of Hungarian politics in which the key players were the communists, the opposition parties and the non-party organisations. Having started on 13 June, the three groupings reached agreement on 18 September on the transition to a multiparty parliamentary democracy via fully-free national elections. The plan was that, before the elections, a president would be elected by the old, existing parliament – indeed, there was a certain understanding that Imre Pozsgay was the most likely candidate. Yet, as soon as that idea was aired, the Free Democrats, Young Democrats and Independent Trade Unions broke the consensus, refusing to sign the agreement. Quickly Hungary's triangular politics began to fragment. The opposition parties started to feud among themselves, while on 7 October the Communist Party (in other words, the Hungarian Socialist Workers' Party) voted to dissolve and then rebrand itself as the Hungarian Socialist Party led by Rezső Nyers. This proved a fatal move, because the public saw through the cosmetic change. Over the following months, in the run-up to the elections, the 'new-old party' would fail to grow in membership, unlike its opposition rivals. Meanwhile some communists around Grósz formed, under the old name, their own 'new-old' splinter party which was to become even more marginal in Hungarian political life.[118]

These dramatic shifts left Hungarian politics totally up for grabs. On 18 October the parliament went ahead and passed the constitutional amendments agreed by the national round table, not least renaming the country the 'Hungarian Republic' – dropping the word 'People's'. Free elections were scheduled for 25 March 1990 and the presidential election for the summer. So Hungary had moved to multiparty politics before becoming a democracy. And for longer than in Poland an old – albeit now reform-oriented – government led by the renamed communists would continue to run political affairs. Whereas in Poland, the 4 June elections were the decisive turning point in the exit from communism, the emotional and symbolic roots of Hungary's renewal as a nation were dramatised on 16 June, with the reburial of Nagy and the renunciation of 1956.

So the Poles were in the vanguard of democratisation. But this was a process that took place within the boundaries of a single state, just as in the Soviet republics of Estonia, Latvia and Lithuania. It was in Hungary that Europe's Iron Curtain would be lifted.

*

August was the continent's main holiday month. Paris almost closed down. Italians cooled off in the coastal resorts of the Mediterranean and the Adriatic. West Germans disappeared to the mountains of Bavaria or to the North Sea coast. In the communist East, sunseekers headed to Bulgaria's Black Sea beaches or relaxed by the Baltic Sea, while large numbers of East Germans piled into their little, candy-coloured Trabants and drove off to Hungary. The shores of Lake Balaton were a particularly popular destination for those who loved camping. But this year, many campers were planning a one-way trip, having read or seen news reports about the end of Hungary's barbed-wire border. They glimpsed the chance of slipping into the West. As historian Mary Sarotte has pointed out, the East German secret police, the Stasi, wrote up a 'surprisingly honest internal summary' of their citizens' motives for wanting out of the GDR: lack of consumer goods, inadequate services, poor medical care, limited opportunities for travel, bad workplace conditions, the relentlessly bureaucratic attitude of the state, and the lack of a free media.[119]

Material reasons aside, there was another more political cause for flight. Inspired by the amazing political transformations in Poland and Hungary – countries they knew well and had visited in their hundreds of thousands – many East Germans saw Honecker, by contrast, as an immovable obstacle to progress in their own country. He was 'giving yesterday's answers to today's questions'. Resentment first broke into the open in May when local elections, which many East Germans hoped would be held in the spirit of the USSR's democratisation, had in fact been as tightly controlled as ever by the party. At the polling station everyone was merely expected to approve the list of candidates put forward by the ruling party. There was no opposition and no choice – other than rejecting candidates, which many did. Those who 'forgot' to vote were promptly visited with a helpful reminder from the Stasi. When on election night, 7 May 1989, the results were announced, 98.85% had voted for the official lists. Everything was 'in order': that's at least what state election director Egon Krenz proclaimed.[120]

The election was a travesty and the result obviously bore no relation to the real mood of GDR citizens. They felt conned by this charade of democracy. One of the few protest posters read sarcastically 'Always on board for election fraud' (*Nie genug vom Wahlbetrug*). It was as if East Germans were being treated as children in a playpen, whereas the Poles and Hungarians were allowed to behave like adults – free to voice independent political views and help shape political change for themselves.

'Many people can no longer tolerate the kindergarten atmosphere, or being constantly led by the nose on all fronts,' said Reinhard Schult, a leading East German activist. 'People are leaving East Germany because they have lost all hope of change.'[121] In 1988 a total of 29,000 people from the GDR had legally exited west. In just the first six months of 1989, 37,000 had been granted permission to do so.[122]

Economic prospects and political despair were the 'push' factors. On the 'pull' side, Hungary's increasingly porous border with Austria was obviously significant. Yet that in itself was not sufficient because, if people got caught 'preparing' or 'trying' to run away illegally, the Hungarian authorities were obliged to send them back to the GDR under a secret protocol to a 1969 bilateral treaty. But on 12 June 1989 there was a new legal twist when the Hungarian government started to adhere to the 1951 UN Geneva Convention on Refugees – honouring a commitment it had made in March. This striking substitution of political principles suggested that Hungary might no longer force East Germans back to the GDR: to borrow Gorbachev's language, the government now placed allegiance to universal values above any obligations to fellow communist states. Rather than being illegal defectors, East German escapees could now hope to obtain the status of 'political refugee' in international law and thereby give legitimacy to their flight.[123]

The situation on the ground, however, was still somewhat opaque. The Hungarian bureaucracy had so far not decided on the status of GDR citizens: they argued that those desiring to leave (*ausreisewillige DDR-Bürger*) were not in the same category as those deemed to be politically persecuted (*politisch Verfolgte*) under the UN convention. But even if Hungarian border officials were still hindering escape attempts by East Germans, sometimes with firearms as happened on 21 August, the number of those being returned to the GDR security forces or even just notified by name to East Berlin as attempted escapees was dwindling. Clearly close cooperation between the Stasi and the Hungarian security forces (and also those in Poland) was a thing of the past; this was another sign that the bloc was beginning to crumble.[124]

By late August an estimated 150,000–200,000 East Germans were vacationing in Hungary, mostly near Lake Balaton. Campsites were full and roads were jammed. Many GDR visitors had overstayed their originally planned and officially approved two- or three-week holidays. Some were simply hanging around in the hope of dramatic new political developments; others were watching for the right moment to slip through the increasing number of open stretches of border fences through quiet fields or secluded woodland. Hundreds more tried a different route to freedom, squatting in the grounds of the West German embassy in Budapest where they hoped to claim their automatic right to citizenship in the Federal Republic. Whatever their route, the East Germans were becoming a serious refugee problem for Hungary.[125]

The 19th of August would prove a pivotal moment. The MEP Otto von Habsburg – eldest son of the last Austro-Hungarian emperor – together with human-rights activists and the opposition Hungarian Democratic Forum, had planned a party to say 'farewell to the Iron Curtain'. What became known as the 'Pan-European Picnic' was intended as a jolly gathering of Austrians and Hungarians to celebrate freedom on a sunny summer afternoon in meadows near a border crossing on the road from Sopron (Hungary) to Sankt Margarethen im Burgenland (Austria). This was where, several weeks earlier, foreign ministers Horn and Mock had cut open the barbed-wire fence between East and West.[126]

But these modest, local festivities turned into something much more political when, at the last minute, Imre Pozsgay got in on the act as the party's co-sponsor. He arranged with his old friend István Horváth, the reformist interior minister, as well as Prime Minister Németh, that as a symbolic gesture the border gate would be open for three hours that afternoon. Border guards were instructed to carry no weapons and not to take any action. While the picnic posed no particular legal issues for Hungarian and Austrian citizens, who had permission to travel between their countries, the situation was different for East Germans. Leaflets publicising the event were printed in German and distributed beforehand; these included maps guiding people to the picnic spot and to where they could 'clip off part of the Iron Curtain'. As a result the little border town of Sopron filled up with some 9,000 people camping or staying in B&Bs, and the West German Foreign Ministry had even dispatched extra consular staff there to 'assist fellow Germans'. All this added to the pressure on the Hungarian border guards who were now, in effect, being observed by Western diplomats.[127]

Nevertheless most of the East Germans who toyed with escaping were really scared. They did not know about the orders given to the Hungarian soldiers. But then the picnic began. A brass band played, the beer flowed and folk dancers in traditional Hungarian and Burgenlandish attire mingled with the crowd. Some 660 East Germans who attended the picnic took heart that day. As soon as the wooden gate was opened, there was a stampede. They rushed through and, unhindered by the border guards, they entered Austria – surprised and elated. It was the largest mass escape of East Germans since the Berlin Wall went up in 1961. Another 320 managed to cross to freedom elsewhere that weekend.[128]

Such numbers were not in themselves spectacular. Thousands more East Germans stayed behind, hesitating. Over the next few days the Hungarian government increased the number of guards patrolling its western border, which resulted in far fewer refugees reaching the West. Nevertheless, every day more East Germans poured into Hungary. Behind the scenes the FRG government kept pressing the Hungarian authorities to clarify the UN refugee status of the East Germans. But Bonn's aim was not to turn the flow into a flood – far from it: the FRG was desperate to avoid disorder and instability. Frantic efforts were made to prevent the media getting their hands on an escapee crossing the border or an embassy-occupier (*Festsetzer*) lest such publicity would fan East German hopes of an easy exit at a time when the FRG had agreed nothing formally with either Hungary or the GDR. And the historic shadow of the Red Army also still loomed in the background. What if the situation suddenly got out of hand? What if a crowd of refugees rioted or some soldiers or secret police panicked and started shooting? Would the Soviets suddenly get drawn in? It was in this edgy atmosphere that the transnational migration crisis gathered momentum. Alarmingly, there was still no international solution.[129]

In the end, however, what forced matters to a head was not the toing and froing on Hungary's borders but the humanitarian crisis in Budapest. The Németh government realised that it could no longer sit on its hands and watch events unfold: before its eyes the crowd of GDR refugees outside the German embassy was growing every day. Some 800 were now camped out near the building. There were also 181 in the embassy grounds and the mission itself had been forced to close to the public on 13 August. Several emergency reception camps were then created in the vicinity by the Red Cross, the Order of Malta and other aid agencies: in the Budapest suburbs of Zugliget (capacity 600 people) and Csillebérc (2,200 people) and later around Lake Balaton for another 2,000 or so. In all the camps food and water were desperately short. There were not enough toilets and showers, let alone sleeping bags, pillows, clothing and toiletries.[130]

In the intense glare of the world media, Bonn was desperate to alleviate the distress of the East Germans and contain the international crisis. But the two German governments were deadlocked about how to deal with these people. The Honecker regime was obsessed with holding on to communist orthodoxy and not letting the GDR drift into 'the bourgeois camp'. It took no fewer than six conversations between 11 and 31 August 1989 before East Berlin grudgingly promised Bonn that it would not 'persecute' embassy-occupiers and would process applications for exit – but without any commitment to give a positive response for immediate permanent emigration. Meanwhile in East Berlin the pressure for such permits was mounting almost exponentially day by day, because of the GDR's bureaucracy's restrictive practices and its citizenry's alienation in the light of Poland and Hungary's liberalisation.[131]

To resolve the crisis, the West German leadership took the initiative to deal with matters at the highest level, both with East Berlin and Budapest.[132] Normally East German leavers or escapees – being a German–German matter rather than an issue of 'foreign' relations – came under the aegis of the Chancellery. But most refugees were in third countries, moreover in or around FRG embassies, so the Foreign Ministry had to be involved. It was run by the forceful Hans-Dietrich Genscher – a man with his own agenda. Born in 1927 in Halle – a town that became East German after 1945 – Genscher felt he had a personal interest, almost a mission, to sort out this issue, going far beyond the call of duty. What's more, Kohl headed a coalition government, formed by his own Christian Democrats and the liberal Free Democrats (FDP), whose party leader was Genscher. This made the foreign minister also the political 'kingmaker' on whom the chancellor depended for his working majority in the Bundestag. So Kohl had to tolerate a certain amount of independence by Genscher in the handling of this deeply national and highly emotional problem, and their relationship was certainly not devoid of rivalry. The result was something like a dual-track policy as the FRG responded to the refugee crisis in the summer and autumn of 1989. The Foreign Ministry handled Budapest and Gyula Horn (as well as Warsaw and Prague), while the Chancellery dealt with East Berlin and Erich Honecker.[133]

But the German–German track was not much use that summer. The West German mission (or 'permanent representation') in East Berlin had also been obliged to close, in part because of the crush of would-be escapees. What's more, Honecker himself was seriously ill with what proved to be cancer and was largely out of active politics for three months from July to late September, as party underlings began to jockey for power.[134]

So the onus fell on the Hungarian government, amid all the other political and economic problems on its plate, to try to square the diplomatic circle as a human drama unfolded in the muddy, squalid camps. It was obliged now to deal in totally novel ways with the FRG in order to address the crisis at the heart of Budapest. Yet, at the same time, the government had no desire to break entirely and openly with the GDR: Horn did not want to repudiate Hungary's bilateral secret treaty of 1969 about how to deal with 'criminal offenders' who got caught planning or attempting 'desertion from the Republic'. And he also kept resisting West German pressure to recognise the East Germans officially as 'refugees' under international law and to call in the UNHCR to deal with them. In short, his government was in a kind of no man's land between one international order and another. At the end of his tether, Horn told one of Genscher's staff: 'Hungary is in a precarious situation.'[135]

Whatever the protocols of Bonn's informal dual track, it would take the intervention of Chancellor Kohl to force matters to a head – engaging directly with his counterpart in Budapest, Prime Minister Németh. On 25 August Németh and Horn travelled secretly to Bonn to meet with Kohl and Genscher at Schloss Gymnich, a restored castle and government guest house. In a two-and-a-half-hour meeting followed by lunch, Hungarians and West Germans sought to resolve the matter irrespective of what the East Germans wanted.[136]

Kohl and Genscher convinced their Hungarian visitors that the most sensible way forward was to cooperate wholeheartedly with the West on the issue of East German refugees. It was an emotional moment. Németh assured Kohl that 'deportations' back to the GDR were 'out of the question' and added 'we will open the border' by mid-September. 'If no military or political force from the outside compels us to act differently, we will keep the border open for East German citizens' as an exit route. Taking in these words, Kohl had difficulty in containing his emotions. Indeed he was moved to tears.[137]

Németh then went on to agree with Kohl that, such was the severity of Hungary's economic crisis, he would need the help of the West to get on top of it. By contrast, the GDR could do nothing for Hungary; nor could Gorbachev because of his 'difficult position' at home, though Németh said it was important to do everything possible to 'ensure the success of Gorbachev's policies' because that was the only way to keep peace in the bloc. In short, by doing as Bonn wanted with regard to the touchstone issue of the East Germans, Németh seems to have hoped to encourage both Bonn and also Washington to offer Hungary financial support and to develop more extensive trade relations. Kohl did not make any commitments then, but promised to speak to West German bankers (and to Bush). A substantive DM 1 billion financial support package duly followed for Hungary's democratisation and market reforms – comprising a 500 million credit guarantee by Bavaria and Baden-Württemberg and 500 million from the Federal German government. By the end of the visit Németh had made a fateful decision: Hungary would fully open its border to the West for GDR citizens in return for Kohl's DM to help his country emerge from the bloc into the Western world.[138]

It was a sign of the times that this deal was struck before Budapest officially informed the Kremlin of its border decision. An intense few days of 'travel diplomacy' ensued. But once Horn spoke to Shevardnadze, it was clear that the Soviets were willing to grant the Hungarians a free hand in their actions.[139] And Kohl's telephone conversation with Gorbachev himself also produced a green light, with the Soviet leader's laconic, even banal, observation 'the Hungarians are good people'.[140]

The Hungarians were, however, much less successful in sorting out arrangements with the GDR. In East Berlin on 31 August Horn told Foreign Minister Oskar Fischer he was willing to send the East Germans home if the GDR pledged it would grant the escapees immunity from prosecution and guaranteed their right to emigrate legally. Yet Fischer offered only immunity and kept insisting that upon their return these East Germans would have to 'pursue their individual exit visas' with legal assistance but with no promise that permanent exit permits would be automatically granted. He also demanded that Hungary close its borders for East Germans, which Horn rejected. East Berlin also tried to convene a meeting of Warsaw Pact foreign ministers to put pressure on Budapest – but Soviet, Polish and Hungarian officials all objected, arguing that the Pact was not an appropriate forum to deal with the matter. So by 5 September the SED Politburo was reduced to old-fashioned communist bluster, accusing Hungary of 'doing the bidding of Bonn' and 'betraying socialism'.[141]

On 10 September Horn made his public announcement that the Hungarian government would allow East Germans to cross freely into Austria, from where they could continue to the Federal Republic. Hungary, Horn declared, did not want to become 'a country of refugee camps' and was determined to 'resolve the situation on humanitarian gounds'. His deputy Ferenc Somogyi told the international press – carefully choosing his words, delivered in English. 'We want to open up and diversify relations with Western Europe and the West in general.' In this vein, Somogyi said, Hungary had accepted a general European attitude and thereby moved 'closer to the West', placing 'absolute primacy on universal humanitarian values'. What's more, he added approvingly, 'similar considerations' now also characterised Soviet policy.[142]

The drama then unfolded on TV screens across the world. From the early hours of 11 September a mass exodus ensued. The East Germans, many of them young people in their twenties and thirties (mainly craftsmen such as bricklayers and masons, plumbers and electricians), poured across the Austrian border in cars, buses and trains. Austrian Interior Ministry officials said that by late that evening 8,100 East Germans had entered Austria en route to West Germany and that the flow was increasing steadily. And with this stream of people, Craig Whitney of the *New York Times* remarked that the 'German question', that 'dream, or fear, of German reunification, also came alive with them'. He quoted a senior US diplomat: 'It's still not going to happen any time soon, but there's beginning to be serious thought about it. It's not just a pious platitude any more.'[143]

On 12 September Kohl sent Németh a telegram thanking him for this 'generous act of humanity'. The same day, the chancellor exploited the euphoric mood in West Germany to full effect at his party convention in Bremen where some Christian Democrats were trying to overthrow him. He declared that it could never be the policy of responsible West German officials to urge East Germans to flee. But 'it is a matter of course that everyone who comes to us from East Germany will be greeted by us as a German among Germans'. Appealing to national sentiments and presenting himself as a true patriot chancellor, Kohl managed to fend off the leadership challenge and secure reconfirmation as party leader. Not for the first or last time in these turbulent years, international politics reverberated in domestic affairs.[144]

By the end of September, between 30,000 and 40,000 people – far more than even informed circles had ever anticipated – had gone West via this route.[145] The Honecker regime was furious but East Germany was now diplomatically isolated in the Warsaw Pact. Crucially, Moscow hardly protested at all. On the contrary, Gennady Gerasimov, the Foreign Ministry spokesman, merely said that the border opening was 'a very unusual and unexpected step' but that it did not affect the USSR directly. That the Soviet Union went along with the Hungarian decision, thereby distancing the Kremlin even further from East Berlin, was a serious blow to the Honecker regime's morale. There were even question marks over Gorbachev's much-anticipated attendance at the upcoming fortieth-anniversary celebrations of the GDR's foundation on 7 October. It was no secret that Gorbachev deeply disliked the 'scumbag' (*mudak*) Honecker, as he told Chernyaev. And the Soviet leader certainly did not want to be seen as supporting Honecker's hard-line position against more reform-minded East German communists. Indeed, after his triumphant trip to Bonn, he had explained to Honecker in no uncertain terms that the USSR was changing. 'This is the destiny of the Soviet Union,' he declared, 'but not only its destiny; it is also our common destiny.' Nor was he keen to jeopardise his budding political friendship with Kohl: like Németh, Gorbachev's policy towards the GDR was now being framed against hopes of West German financial injections, which the chancellor had promised during the Soviet leader's June visit in Bonn.[146]

Unable to mobilise the Warsaw Pact in its support, the East German government used its own powers to the utmost. During September it imposed severe restrictions on GDR citizens travelling to Hungary. Although many still managed to get through, this policy simply had the effect of diverting the human traffic towards the West German embassies in Warsaw and Prague. By 27 September there were 500 East Germans seeking refuge at the Warsaw embassy and 1,300 in the Prague mission.[147]

Camp out for freedom – East Germans besiege the FRG Embassy in Prague

Prague was particularly hard hit because Czechoslovakia was in any case the transit route for East Germans hoping to head West via Hungary. And the moment East Berlin denied permission to travel to Hungary, GDR emigrants simply stayed in Czechoslovakia rather than returning home. These were people who had so far neither applied for a permanent exit visa to West Germany nor did they have adequate papers to enter Hungary. For fear of being picked up by the Czechoslovak authorities and then deported to the GDR, they hoped to achieve their goal of getting to the West by sitting it out in the grounds of the West German embassy – an eighteenth-century palace in the centre of Prague, whose beautiful park became a squalid and unsanitary refugee camp.

By the end of the month, more than 3,000 people lived in and around the main embassy building, 800 of whom were children. They had four toilets between them. The women and children bedded down at night on foam-rubber pads, while the men slept in shifts in tents spread out incongruously under black baroque statues of goddesses in the once-elegant gardens. Food was at best simple: coffee, tea, bread and jam for breakfast, and a thick soup that the Germans call 'one-pot' (*Eintopf*) for the other meals – served from field kitchens that steamed and smoked behind the wrought-iron garden gates. 'There's an occasional orange for every two or three children, for vitamins,' a young mother said bleakly.[148]

Bonn was desperate to negotiate a deal to release these GDR squatters to the West, and the UN General Assembly on 27–9 September in New York offered Genscher the perfect opportunity. On the margins of the conference he was able to discuss the matter quietly with his Soviet, Czechoslovak and East German counterparts.[149] As a result of Genscher's pleas, it appears, Shevardnadze pressed East Berlin to 'do something' and Honecker, with approval of the Politburo on the 29th, offered Bonn a one-off deal: the embassy-occupiers' could go West as long as their 'exit' to the FRG would be presented as their 'expulsion' from East Germany. Honecker would thereby be able to demonstrate that he remained in control by seeming to oust these traitors from his state. To further show that he was orchestrating the whole business, the East German leader insisted that the refugees travel on sealed trains from Prague back to the GDR before being transported to West Germany. Honecker wanted to use the train journey to record the identities of the escapees, so that GDR authorities could confiscate their property. Sealed trains had, of course, a dark historical connotation, summoning up images of Nazi Germany's transports to the concentration camps. There were also fears that the trains could be stopped in the GDR. Still, the Kohl government agreed to Honecker's offer because this was at least an arrangement under which the East German escapees were being treated as legal emigrants rather than illegal fugitives – part of the general effort to bring the crisis within the domain of international law and universal humanitarian values.[150]

As soon as Genscher got back to Bonn from New York at dawn on 30 September, he found himself on a mission to implement the plan. With a small team of officials he headed for Prague. Other FRG diplomats set out on a similar mission to Warsaw. Both groups had the daunting task of overseeing an orderly exodus and ensuring that the GDR honoured its grudging concessions. Genscher landed in the Czechoslovak capital in the afternoon, only to learn that – contrary to earlier understandings – he would not be allowed to accompany the refugees on their freedom train. Honecker had now decided that only lower-level West German officials could travel: he did not want the added publicity from the foreign minister's presence with the freedom riders.[151]

Undeterred, Genscher hurried to the West German embassy. There, an air of excitement had been building up over the course of the day. Suddenly, just after dusk and without any fanfare, Genscher stepped onto the baroque balcony and looked out at the huge crowd beneath him. Visibly moved, he announced 'Dear fellow Germans, we have come to you to inform you that today your departure to West Germany has been approved.' That magic word 'departure' was enough: the rest of his sentence was drowned in cries of jubilation.[152]

'It was unbelievable,' exclaimed a man from Leipzig. 'Genscher was there like the incarnation of freedom.' The people at the Prague embassy, some of whom had been there for eleven weeks, began hastily packing. It's 'like Christmas and Easter in one shot', a young man told a journalist before he hurriedly boarded a bus to the train station with his wife and infant child in tow.[153]

For Hans-Dietrich Genscher, this was a hugely emotional moment. The fate of Germans in the GDR was a gut issue for him, in a way it could never have been for Kohl, a man from the Franco-German border-lands of the Rhineland-Palatinate, because Genscher had once literally been an East German refugee himself – he had fled to West Germany in 1952. Genscher had never lost his distinctive Saxon accent. Having started his legal studies in the GDR, he completed them in Hamburg before moving into West German politics.[154] These personal roots explain Genscher's profound commitment to German unification and also his belief that this should be done through legal agreements as a peaceful embrace of the Soviet bloc. Hence his passion for West Germany's Ostpolitik, and for the principles outlined in the Conference on Security and Cooperation in Europe, which were enshrined in the Helsinki Final Act of 1975, affirming both the borders of Cold War Europe and also the shared values of universal human rights. His grand ambition was to transcend the Cold War and German division not by unilateral Western actions but by consensual pan-European solutions. Therefore it was an added bonus that he was the one who commanded the show at the Prague embassy, not his ally-rival Chancellor Kohl. Little wonder that Genscher a few days later described that moment on the balcony as 'the most moving hour in my political career'. The wheel was coming full circle for him, as he encountered the escapees of a younger generation who wanted to take the same path. 'You can see what people will go through so that they can live like we do,' he added, 'not in the material sense, but to have the right to decide for themselves what to do with their lives.'[155]

And so on that night of 30 September, Prague police rerouted normal traffic to allow more than a dozen buses to evacuate the West German embassy. At Prague-Liben train station, just out of town, the throng of exuberant East Germans waiting for their trains grew ever larger. Applause rippled through the crowd at the arrival of West Germany's ambassador to Czecholsovakia, Hermann Huber. Faces glowed with excitement, they pressed close, hugging and kissing him, even handing their children for a kind of benediction. A knot of Czechoslovak police officers stood at a distance, observing but not interfering. After many delays, six trains finally rolled out of Prague, in the company of a few token West German officials, who hoped to keep people calm.[156]

The trains had to travel for seven hours along the circuitous route from Prague through Schönau, Reichenbach, Dresden, Karl-Marx-Stadt (Chemnitz), Plauen, Zwickau and Gutenfürst. The tensest moments occurred inside the GDR when East German security officials got on the trains. No one could be sure that they wouldn't try to force the passengers to disembark and end their journey to freedom. But nothing worse happened than recording the names of those leaving and collecting their official identity cards. These moments passed without incident. The train stopped in Dresden and Karl-Marx-Stadt, where more émigrés managed to clamber aboard – without impediment or punishment. Other East Germans gathered along the track to wave as the special trains of the Deutsche Bahn sped past.[157]

When the trains reached FRG territory at Hof in north-eastern Bavaria, hundreds of West Germans packed the station, cheering and waving as each train pulled in. They had stacked up mounds of used clothing, shoes, toys and prams for the newcomers. Some pressed cash into the hands of exhausted parents or gave their children candy bars. For others, it was all too much: they stood silent, weighed down by emotions they could not put into words. In the minds of many older bystanders in this border town, the scene evoked memories of the time they – like Genscher – had gathered up their few belongings after the war to begin new lives in the West.

Although not allowed to participate in the exodus itself, Genscher sensed history in the making and relished his personal role in it. That moment on the embassy balcony in Prague had got him into the limelight of the unfolding unification drama ahead of Kohl, who also coveted a place in history. 'What has happened shows that we are in a historical period of change which cannot be reversed and will continue,' Genscher told the press. 'I hope that the East German leadership realises this and will not isolate itself by refusing to change. Gorbachev is coming and I hope he will convince East Germany that reform lies in its best interests, that reform means more, not less stability.'[158]

But the very opposite happened: Honecker, ill and out of his depth, chose to box himself in. Just days before East Germany's grand fortieth-birthday celebrations, he felt humiliated, even threatened. The stark images now flickering incessantly across TV screens of innumerable East Germans clambering over fences, besieging trains, overrunning embassies and finally clenching their fists in triumph on West German soil were a glaring indictment of his government.[159]

On 3 October Honecker sealed off all of East Germany from the outside world, even the rest of the Warsaw Pact. This was an unprecedented act. Now, for the first time, the crossing of *any* of the GDR's borders required both a passport, possessed by only a minority of citizens, and a specific permit for each trip – documentation that in the current circumstances was highly unlikely to be issued.[160] East Germans were really angry. With the autumn school holidays just around the corner, thousands of East Germans had booked trips either to or through Czechoslovakia. Now with passport- and visa-free travel suspended, they were stuck at the GDR–Czechoslovak border in Saxony. Consequently it was here that demonstrations became the largest anywhere in the GDR. And as the last vents closed, the East German state was turning into a pressure cooker.[161]

Ironically, between 1 and 3 October, yet another 6,000 East Germans had poured into the West German Prague embassy. In all, some 10,000 to 11,000 would-be escapees were in limbo in and around Prague. On a smaller scale similar scenes occurred in Warsaw. And so another series of sealed trains was hastily arranged – whose departure was followed avidly by a multitude of local and foreign TV companies as well as the international press. It took eight trains from Prague to Hof to clear the backlog in Czechoslovakia; two more, carrying 1,445 people, left Warsaw for Hanover.[162] During this latest transit operation, thousands of East Germans – now feeling like prisoners in their own state – flocked to the tracks and stations to watch what became known as 'the last trains to freedom'. Many hoped to sneak aboard. The situation in Dresden became so fraught that police had use force to clear the station and tracks – overrun by some 2,500 people – and the doors of trains were sealed from the outside. It took until the early hours of 5 October to get three of the trains through Dresden Hauptbahnhof. The rest had to be rerouted through other cities.[163]

Meanwhile, a mob of some 20,000 angry people were left milling around outside on Dresden's Lenin-Platz (now Wiener Platz) and in the adjoining streets. Police and troops went in hard with rubber truncheons and water cannons to disperse the crowd; the demonstrators fought back, hurling paving stones at the police, in what observers called the worst outbreak of civil disobedience since 1953.[164]

The East German security forces did their rough stuff under the watchful eye of officials from Dresden's outpost of the Soviet KGB. It may well be that one of them was a young special officer by the name of Vladimir Vladimirovich Putin. As a KGB man, Putin sympathised with Honecker and his crackdown on state-traitors. What most disturbed him – as we know from later statements – was the deafening silence from his political superiors in Moscow. The call from the Kremlin never came: not one soldier of the Red Army was deployed to help the East German comrades reimpose order. The truth was that Gorbachev despised the ailing Honecker and his Stalinist henchmen; totally committed to his mission as a reformer, the Soviet leader abandoned this atrophied country that had no intention of renewing itself. His aide Anatoly Chernyaev lamented in his diary the 'terrible scenes' of violence damaging the East German and Soviet regimes alike. The brutal scenes in Dresden, played out in the media, only worsened the split between Honecker and Gorbachev, between East Berlin and its Soviet patron.[165]

By contrast, Honecker – fed up with the man in the Kremlin – turned to another communist ally: the People's Republic of China. In June his regime expressed effusive support for Beijing's use of force. The way Deng Xiaoping's China had simply crushed the 'counter-revolutionary unrest' in Tiananmen Square was in Honecker's mind an example to the whole bloc and a ray of hope for the future of real socialism, given Gorbachev's failure to slap down protest and subversion.[166] The summer had shown how, as a direct result of the USSR stepping back, the Polish and Hungarian contagion of liberalisation was spreading across Eastern Europe. It had infected the GDR itself, causing first a haemorrhage of people and now, as Dresden demonstrated, unrest on the streets in the once-secure police state. Amid this domestic upheaval, the GDR was determined to shore up the international image of communism. That's why Honecker sent Egon Krenz, his number two, on a high-profile week-long visit to Beijing, to celebrate the PRC's fortieth anniversary on 1 October 1989, just days before the GDR's own fortieth-birthday party. This was definitely a time for solidarity among true communists.

Throughout his trip, Krenz was eager to learn from the Chinese communist leadership about how to deal with protestors and reinforce the status quo.[167] Talking with party secretary Jiang Zemin on 26 September, Krenz expressed his pleasure in visiting an 'impenetrable bastion of socialism in Asia' where 'under the leadership of the Communist Party, the most populous country in the world was freed from its half-colonial chains'. Jiang and Krenz agreed that the events of June 1989 had revealed the true hostile intent behind the Western strategy of 'so-called peaceful evolution' in relations with China, exposing it as 'an aggressive programme of undermining socialism'.[168] Qiao Shi, another top CCP Politburo member and a key figure in implementing martial law, impressed on Krenz how closely he and his colleagues were following events in Europe, especially 'developments in Poland and Hungary'. While these were a source of alarm, Qiao voiced great satisfaction at the East German refusal to take the same path and his resolve to 'hold on to socialism'. After all, 'we are all communists, our life consists of struggle' – in 'politics, ideology and the economy'.[169] The Paramount Leader Deng Xiaoping told Krenz emphatically 'We defend socialism together – you in the GDR, we in the People's Republic of China.'[170] Krenz in turn declared: 'In the struggles of our time, the GDR and China stand side by side.'[171] They saw themselves as two beacons of socialism, shining out in a darkening and hostile world.

Krenz was one of very few VIPs on the strikingly meagre official list of foreigners to grace the PRC's fortieth-anniversary festivities. The rest were minor figures from relatively marginal countries – a Czechoslovak Politburo member, a Cuban Communist Party official and Cabinet ministers from Ecuador and Mongolia. The Soviet Union was represented by the deputy chairman of the Soviet–Chinese Friendship Society. Largely because of international outrage about the 4 June events, no heads of government had come to take part. Even many ambassadors – from the United States, Canada, Western Europe and Japan – stayed away. Krenz, as deputy to the head of a major communist state in Europe, together with his North Korean counterpart Vice President Li Jong-ok, was the most senior foreign friend to sit with the ageing Chinese elite on the rostrum as they looked out over the restored tranquillity of Tiananmen Square. As Deng told Li, 'When you go home, please tell President Kim Il-sung that China's social order has returned to normal ... What happened in Beijing not long ago was bad, but in the final analysis it is beneficial to us, because it made us more sober-minded.' Li replied, 'I am sure President Kim will be very happy about this.'[172]

The foreign dignitaries were treated to a massive fireworks display and a performance of colourful dances by 100,000 flowers of communist youth. Their mood, however, seemed more 'languid' than 'joyous'. And instead of a huge military parade as five years earlier, only a token group of forty-five soldiers goose-stepped in front of the stage to symbolise the power of the state. Given the stiff security, ordinary Chinese could not get within a mile of the birthday party for their 'People's Republic'. What's more, martial law remained in force in Beijing, almost three months since it was imposed at the height of student demonstrations. And so soldiers armed with machine guns continued to patrol the city centre. The tone of the PRC at forty was not, then, one of jubilation; indeed until recently the plans had been for something very low-key and even austere. Yet by October the party, with regained inner confidence, wanted to show and celebrate the fact that it was fully in control. 'National Day this year is of unusual significance,' stated Li Ruihuan, a senior politburo member in charge of propaganda. Because, he added, 'we have just won a victory in curbing the turmoil and quelling the counter-revolutionary rebellion'.[173]

*

Whereas communist China marked its fortieth birthday with what might be called a muted certainty, still shaken by 4 June but discerning a clear path ahead, its German comrades had been planning a grand jamboree for months, only to be faced at the last moment with mounting social upheaval that threatened their political control. The intention was that 6–7 October in East Berlin would be a huge media extravaganza, with parades of the military and party youth, lavish banquets in the glittering Palace of the Republic and endless self-congratulatory speeches. In further contrast to Beijing, most of the leading figures of global communism would be in attendance, above all China's vice premier Yao Yilin and Gorbachev himself. For Honecker this was to be a huge event, the pinnacle of almost two decades at the top and further recognition of the GDR's status in the communist world. To ensure that everything went to plan, visits from West Berliners were curtailed for the period of the celebrations while a precisely 'organised and coordinated' operation of intelligence sharing and security enforcement was launched to ensure that any attempt at protest was put down immediately. His model, in short, was Beijing not Moscow.[174]

At first all seemed to go according to plan. When Gorbachev arrived at Berlin's Schönefeld airport on 6 October, he and Honecker put on a public diplay of socialist brotherhood for the cameras. They embraced sweetly before driving into a city 'festooned with banners and glowing under crisscrossing beams of light' where they stood shoulder to shoulder late into the night reviewing the massive torchlight parade of 100,000 members of the German communist youth organisation (FDJ). All evening GDR television showed the two leaders smiling and waving at the youthful throng as it flowed down Unter den Linden holding high their flags and torches. Occasionally the Soviet leader drew cheers and chants of 'Gorby, Gorby!' from some admiring young Germans. Then to Gorbachev's astonishment some 300 FDJ members started chanting 'Gorby help us! Gorby save us!' – almost as a code word for the reforms they were demanding from their unyielding government. Honecker must have been infuriated at this turn of events, but it was still a minor aberration from an otherwise perfectly orchestrated event in which the two leaders showed themselves in total harmony.[175]

Next morning, however, the atmosphere was very different. Gorbachev again stood beside Honecker, this time on the VIP stand on Karl-Marx-Allee as they watched a military parade – an annual affair which on this occasion was considerably smaller, to demonstrate the Warsaw Pact's commitment to disarmament. But the Soviet leader now appeared 'distracted and impatient' as line upon line of troops marched past: the contrived festivities seemed to be taking their toll on him.[176]

Happy birthday or last rites? East Berlin, 7 October 1989

After the parade, 'Gorby' and 'Honni' met for almost three hours alone and then with the whole SED Politburo. Little went to plan; in fact Honecker and Gorbachev were simply not on the same page. They ended up talking past each other. Gorbachev, in a typical big-picture performance, enthused about his new thinking and the current 'revolution within a revolution' (in other words, not negating October 1917) while also underlining communism's ongoing historical competition with capitalism, albeit in a changing world. Honecker, on the other hand, heaped praise on the GDR as one of the world's great economies. Fifteen billion Ostmark had been invested in the microchip industry, including the great state conglomerates Mikroelektronik Erfurt, Carl Zeiss Jena and Robotron Dresden. Systems had been automated and production raised by 300–700%. He left nobody in doubt that he was determined to stick to the old form of state socialism. 'We will solve our problems ourselves with socialist means,' he insisted.

Their speeches to the Politburo followed similarly divergent courses. But by now Gorbachev had heard enough. He told his East German audience a story about miners in Donetsk who 'taught a good lesson' to the secretary of the regional party: 'we often see that some leaders cannot pull the cart any more, but we don't replace them, we are afraid to offend them'. As he looked knowingly around the SED Politburo members, no one could be under any illusions that here was a direct reference to the seventy-seven-year-old hardliner Honecker. 'If we lag behind, life will punish us straight away,' he concluded pithily. Later, before the world media, his press spokesman Gerassimov condensed this into what became a celebrated aphorism: 'Life punishes those who come too late!'[177]

The clock is ticking, Erich! Gorbachev with Honecker

It had been twenty-four hours of mixed messages. Having eventually decided to attend the GDR's festivities, Gorbachev clearly intended to offer the Soviet Union's most prized Cold War ally a measured show of solidarity. After the extraordinary images of the recent exodus and escalating popular demands for reform and democracy across the cities of East Germany, Gorbachev's primary mission was to soothe the frazzled nerves in East Berlin and to help prevent a combination of social frustration and political paralysis from increasing to the point where it could destabilise the East German state. At the same time, however, Gorbachev made clear that Moscow would not interfere in East Germany's problems – problems, as he put it, that were not merely about 'sausage and bread' but about the need for 'more oxygen in society' which demanded a totally new approach by the GDR. Ultimately Honecker himself would have to have the courage to undertake political reform. Gorbachev was no longer prepared to prop him up.[178]

As regards the international situation, however, standing on the Cold War front line in the heart of Europe, the Soviet leader was defiant. In his speech during the gala dinner on the 6th, he rebutted accusations that Moscow bore sole responsibility for the continent's post-war division and he took issue with West Germany for seizing on his reforms to 'reanimate' dreams of a German Reich 'within the boundaries of 1937'. He also specifically rejected demands that Moscow dismantle the Berlin Wall – a call made by Reagan in 1987 and again by Bush in 1989. 'We are constantly called on to liquidate this or that division,' Gorbachev complained. 'We often have to hear, "Let the USSR get rid of the Berlin Wall, then we'll believe in its peaceful intentions."' He was adamant that 'we don't idealise the order that has settled on Europe. But the fact is that until now the recognition of the post-war reality has insured peace on the continent. Every time the West has tried to reshape the post-war map of Europe it has meant a worsening of the international situation.' Gorbachev wanted his socialist comrades to embrace renewal, but he had no intention of dismantling the Warsaw Pact or abruptly dissolving the Cold War borders that had given stability to the continent for the last forty years.[179]

And so, each in his own way, these two communist leaders were hanging on to the past. Gorbachev adhered to existing geopolitical realities, despite the cracks opening up in the Iron Curtain. Honecker clung to the illusion that East Germany remained a socialist nation, united by adherence to the doctrines of the party.

The intransigence of the GDR regime during the celebrations, and the growing social unrest of recent weeks, made for a potentially explosive mix. Within less than two weeks Honecker had been ousted. And only a month after the GDR's fortieth-birthday party, on 9 November, the Berlin Wall fell without a fight. The Wall had been the prime symbol of the Cold War, the barrier that contained the East German population and the structure that held the whole bloc together. The party of 7 October proved to be a theatre of illusions. Yet there was nothing inevitable about what came next.

Chapter 3

Reuniting Germany, Dissolving Eastern Europe

The 9th of November 1989. Helmut Kohl was beside himself. Here he was, sitting at a grand banquet in the Radziwill Palace in Warsaw with the new leaders of Poland – Mazowiecki, Jaruzelski and Wałęsa – in a wonderfully festive atmosphere, together with a delegation of seventy, including Foreign Minister Hans-Dietrich Genscher and six other ministers of his Cabinet. But all around him people were murmuring '*Die Mauer ist gefallen!*' ('The Wall has fallen!'). Throughout that Thursday evening, as the chancellor tried to make polite chit-chat with his hosts, he kept being interrupted – receiving updates on little slips of paper and being called out to take phone calls from Bonn. All the while Kohl was desperately trying to think.[1] He was in the wrong place at the right time – the most dramatic moment of his chancellorship, perhaps of his whole life. What should he do?

Moment of reconciliation: Kohl, Mazowiecki and Genscher in Warsaw

Kohl's mood had been very different when the dinner started. His five-day visit, in the planning for months, was intended as a milestone in West Germany's relations with one of its most sensitive neighbours. History hung heavy in 1989. This was fifty years after Hitler's brutal invasion of Poland, beginning a war that led to the extermination of 6 million Polish citizens (half of them Jewish), the obliteration of the city of Warsaw after the abortive rising of 1944, and the absorption of Poland into the Soviet bloc in 1945. Germany had a lot to answer for, and the process of reconciliation by Bonn had been long and painful. It had been an SPD chancellor, Willy Brandt, who made the first and more dramatic move in December 1970, dropping to his knees in silent remorse at the memorial to the Warsaw Ghetto. Kohl's trip was the first time a Christian Democrat chancellor had visited Poland. But he was not simply catching up with his political rivals and trying to redress the past; he also wanted to make a statement about the future, about the Federal Republic's commitment to Poland's resurrection as a free country in its post-communist incarnation. So the German chancellor had been delighted to sit down at the banquet that evening. Delighted, that is, until he got the news from Berlin.[2]

As soon as the dinner was over, the Germans held a crisis meeting over coffee. The situation was extremely delicate. The Polish leadership wanted to stop Kohl from going to Berlin, warning that this would be taken as a blatant snub. Horst Teltschik, the chancellor's top foreign-policy adviser, was also hesitant. 'Too much has been invested in this trip to Warsaw,' he warned, 'too much hangs on it for the future of German–Polish relations.' Among the events on Kohl's itinerary were a visit to Auschwitz – as an act of penitence for the Holocaust, preceded only once, by Chancellor Helmut Schmidt (also SPD) in 1977 – and a bilingual Catholic Mass in Lower Silesia shared with Mazowiecki, set up as an act of reconciliation with the Poles. The mass was to be held in a place – the Kreisau estate of Graf von Moltke, one of the July 1944 Christian conservative plotters against Hitler – that symbolised a 'better Germany in the darkest part of our history', as the chancellor later put it. Kohl giving the kiss of peace to Mazowiecki linked up with his other iconic act of reconciliation: holding hands with Mitterrand at Verdun in 1984. But this gesture in Silesia was also intended to speak, at home, to the *Vertriebene* – the ever-prickly members on the right of his own party who had been expelled from the eastern German territories when these were absorbed into the new Poland (and the Soviet Union) after 1945.[3]

Upon leaving the Radziwill Palace, Kohl rushed to the city's Marriott Hotel, where the West German press corps was staying, to answer their questions. And he remained for several hours because only in a Western hotel was it possible to see the news on German TV and to access a sufficient number of international phone lines. At midnight, when he spoke once more to the Chancellery, staff there confirmed that the crossing points in Berlin were opened. They also conveyed a sense of the massive flows of people and the joyous atmosphere in the once-divided city. Putting down the phone, the chancellor – pumped up with adrenalin – told the journalists that 'world history is being written … the wheel of history is spinning faster'.[4]

Kohl decided to return to Bonn as soon as diplomatically feasible. 'We cannot abort the trip,' he observed, 'but an interruption is possible.' Next morning, 10 November, he placated his Polish hosts with a Brandt-style visit to the Warsaw Ghetto and a promise that he would be back within twenty-four hours. By the time he left Poland together with Genscher and a handful of journalists at 2.30 p.m., his destination had changed. While at the Ghetto Memorial, Kohl had received more disturbing news. Walter Momper, the SPD mayor of West Berlin, was organising a major press event, featuring his fellow socialist and former chancellor Willy Brandt, on the steps of the city hall (Schöneberger Rathaus) at 4.30 p.m. that very day. Brandt – the mayor of West Berlin when the Wall went up in August 1961 and then the celebrated chancellor of Ostpolitik – was now going to hog the limelight as the Wall came down. With barely a year to go before the next Federal elections, Kohl could not afford to be upstaged – especially when an earlier CDU chancellor, Konrad Adenauer, had been conspicuously absent from Berlin during those fateful days in 1961 when the eastern half of the city was walled in.

It was all very well to want to go to Berlin. But getting there in November 1989 was no simple business. West German aircraft were not permitted to fly across GDR territory or land in West Berlin because of the Allied four-power rights – another legacy of Hitler's war. So Kohl and Genscher flew circuitously through Swedish and Danish airspace to Hamburg before boarding a plane specially provided by the US Air Force for the flight to Berlin. Both men used the journey to frantically scribble their speeches. As much as they were partners, they were in the end also political rivals jockeying for position. After this humiliating diversion, they landed at Tempelhof, right in the centre of the city, just as the celebration at the Schöneberger Rathaus was about to begin.

Sharing the spotlight with Brandt, they addressed a crowd of 20,000 and world media on the very steps from which, in 1963, President John F. Kennedy had declared 'Ich bin ein Berliner.'[5]

That evening, three key figures of FRG politics each put his own spin on the momentous events of the last twenty-four hours. Brandt, in keeping with his Ostpolitik strategy of 'small steps', talked of the 'moving together of the German states', emphasising that 'no one should act as if he knows in which concrete form the people in these two states will find a new relationship'. Genscher opened his address by emotionally recalling his roots in East Germany, from which he fled after the war: 'My most hearty greetings go to the people of my homeland.' He was much more emphatic than Brandt about the underlying fact of national unity. 'What we are witnessing in the streets of Berlin in these hours is that forty years of division have not created two nations out of one. There is no capitalist and there is no socialist Germany, but only one German nation in unity and peace.' But, as foreign minister, he was anxious to reassure Germany's neighbours, not least the Poles. 'No people on this earth, no people in Europe have to fear if the gates are opened now between East and West.'[6]

Chancellor Kohl spoke last. While the sea of Berlin lefties had cheered Brandt and Genscher, they had no patience with the bulky conservative Catholic politico from the Rhineland. Here party enmity, regional pride and explosive emotions combined; the spectators tried to drown out every word of Kohl's speech with boos, catcalls and whistling. The chancellor felt his anger rise at the behaviour of what he called contemptuously the 'leftist plebs' (linker Pöbel). Suppressing his fury, he ploughed on doggedly. Mindful of the upcoming election, Brandt's iconic place in the history of Deutschlandpolitik and the way that Genscher had grabbed his moment on the balcony in Prague, Kohl ignored the crowd in front of him and spoke to millions of TV viewers, especially in the GDR. He sought to present himself as the man who was really in control, the true leader and statesman. He urged East Germans to stay put and to stay calm. He reassured them: 'We're on your side, we are and remain one nation. We belong together.' And the chancellor made a particular point of thanking 'our friends' the Western allies for their enduring support and ended by playing the European card: 'Long live a free German fatherland! Long live a united Europe!'[7]

For many – at home and abroad – Kohl's expression of nationalism went too far. An ominous phone message from Gorbachev was received during the rally. He warned that the Bonn government's declarations could fan 'emotions and passions' and went on to stress the existence of two sovereign German states. Whoever denied these realities had only one aim – that of destabilising the GDR. He had also heard rumours that a furious German mob had plans to storm Soviet military facilities. 'Is this true?' he asked. Gorbachev urged Kohl to avoid any measures that 'could create a chaotic situation with unpredictable consequences'. [8]

Gorbachev's message summed up the turmoil of the past couple of days, and it also did not appear to bode well for the future. Kohl sent a reply assuring the Soviet leader that he need not worry: the atmosphere in Berlin was like a family feast and nobody was about to start a revolt against the USSR.[9] But, with a profound sense of risk in the air, these were fraught and uncertain times for the chancellor. Would his three Western allies react as negatively as Gorbachev? As soon as he got back to his Bonn office later that evening, despite his exhaustion, he tried to arrange phone calls with Thatcher, Bush and Mitterrand.

He rang Thatcher first, at 10 p.m., because he thought that conversation would be 'the most difficult'.[10] On the face of it, however, it went well. The prime minister, who had been watching events on television, said that the scenes in Berlin were 'some of the most historic which she had ever seen'. She stressed the need to build a true democracy in East Germany and the two of them agreed to keep in close touch: Thatcher even suggested coming over for a half-day meeting before the upcoming European Council in Strasbourg early in December. Throughout the conversation, there was no mention of the word 'unity', but the chancellor clearly sensed that she felt 'unease' at the implications of the situation.[11]

He was able to extricate himself in less than half an hour, ready for what promised to be a more agreeable chat at 10.30 p.m. with George Bush. Kohl started with a survey of his trip to Warsaw and the economic predicament of Poland, but the president wasn't interested. Cutting in, Bush said he wanted to hear all about the GDR. Kohl admitted the scale of the refugee problem and expressed scepticism about Krenz as a reformer. He also let off steam about those 'leftist plebs' who had tried to spoil his speech. But his assessment, overall, was very positive: the general mood in Berlin was 'incredible' and 'optimistic' – like 'witnessing an enormous fair' – and he told Bush that 'without the US this day would not have been possible'. The chancellor could not stress enough: 'This is a dramatic thing; an historic hour.' At the end Bush was extremely enthusiastic: 'Take care, good luck,' he told Kohl. 'I'm proud of the way you're handling an extraordinarily difficult problem.' But he also remarked 'my meeting with Gorbachev in early December has become even more important'. Bush was right, the long-awaited tête-à-tête between him and the Soviet leader – only recently scheduled to take place in Malta on 2–3 December – could now not come soon enough.[12]

It was not possible to talk with Mitterrand that night. When they did speak at 9.15 the next morning Kohl took the same line but with an appropriately different spin. Not forgetting that 1989 was the bicentenary of the start of the French Revolution, the chancellor likened the mood on the Kurfürstendamm (West Berlin's main shopping street) to the Champs-Elysées on Bastille Day. But, he added, the process in Germany was 'not revolutionary but evolutionary'. Responding in similar vein, the French president hailed events in Berlin as 'a great historical moment ... the hour of the people'. And, he continued, 'we now have the chance that this movement would flow into the development of Europe'. All very positive, of course, but perhaps also a reminder of traditional French concerns to see a strong Germany firmly anchored in the European integration project. Kohl had no problem with this and he was happy that both of them emphasised the strength of the Franco-German friendship.[13]

After talking to Mitterrand, Kohl took a call from Krenz – who had been pressing for a conversation. The two spoke for nine minutes – politely but insistently on both sides. Krenz was emphatic that 'currently reunification was not on the political agenda'. Kohl said that their views were fundamentally different because his position was rooted in the FRG's Basic Law of 1949, which affirmed the principle of German unity. But, he added, this was not the topic that should concern them both at the moment. Rather, he was interested in 'getting to decent relations between ourselves'. He looked forward to coming to East Germany for an early personal meeting with the new leadership. Yet, he wanted to do so 'outside East Berlin' – the familiar FRG concern to avoid any hint of recognition of the GDR's putative capital.[14]

The last of Kohl's big calls – and the most sensitive of all – was with Gorbachev, before lunch on 11 November. Kohl set out some of the grave economic and social problems now facing the GDR, but stressed the positive mood in Berlin. Gorbachev was less testy than in his initial message to Kohl the previous day and expressed his confidence in the chancellor's 'political influence'. These were, he said, 'historical changes in the direction of new relations and a new world'. But he emphasised the need above all for 'stability'. Kohl firmly agreed and, according to

Teltschik, ended the conversation looking visibly relieved. *'De Bärn is gschält'* ('The pear has been peeled') he told his aide in a thick Palatinate accent with a broad smile: it was clear that Gorbachev would not meddle in internal East German affairs, as the Kremlin had done in June 1953.[15]

Kohl could now feel reassured about his allies and the Russians, yet these were not his only worries. As he got off the phone he must have reflected on his own Deutschlandpolitik – its future direction and the responsibilities that now weighed heavily on him. All the more so, given what he had learned in Cabinet that morning about just how unstable the situation really was.

So far that year, according to the Interior Ministry, 243,000 East Germans had arrived in West Germany, as well as 300,000 ethnic Germans (*Aussiedler*) who could claim FRG citizenship: in other words, well over half a million immigrants in ten months. And this was before the fall of the Wall. The economic costs were also escalating. According to the Finance Ministry, DM 500 million had to be added to the budget in 1990 just to provide emergency shelters for the recent influx of GDR refugees. And an additional DM 10 billion a year for the next ten years might be required to build permanent housing and provide social benefits and unemployment payments. Moreover, the FRG was already subsidising the GDR economy to the tune of several billion a year. And far more would clearly be needed if the GDR were to be propped up sufficiently to stem the haemorrhage of people. But for how long could it be sustained? And what would happen if Germany unified? Revolution was certainly turning the East upside down, but life for West Germans was evidently changing as well – and not all those changes were welcome.[16]

Even if, in the short term, such spending on the GDR and on the migrants was economically feasible, any talk of raising taxes to cover the costs was politically impossible for Kohl and his coalition partners in an election year. The recent rise in the FRG of the Republikaner (the radical right's new party) reflected growing resentment at the immigrant crisis and dismay at the financial burden to be carried by West German citizens.[17]

Although Kohl had talked about 'stability' to Gorbachev and to his Western allies, as he flew back to Warsaw on the afternoon of 11 November to pick up the threads of his Polish visit, he must have seen how difficult it would be to keep the GDR functioning. But, of course, he had no real desire to do so in the longer run. The 'stability' he was now beginning to contemplate was how to facilitate a peaceful and consensual transition to a unified German state – a project that had been inconceivable just two days before.[18]

*

How had this Rubicon been reached, only five weeks after the grand celebrations to mark the fortieth anniversary of the East German state?

In reality the big party on 7 October was a facade, to paper over the huge and growing cracks in the communist state. As soon as Gorbachev left East Berlin for Moscow, demonstrations erupted across the city and elsewhere in the GDR and the authorities now cracked down hard. The 7th was the day of what had become a monthly protest against the May election fraud. Nevertheless, while those who had fled the country amounted to tens of thousands, the number of dissidents and those openly antagonistic to the regime was still relatively small, especially outside the big cities of Dresden, Leipzig and East Berlin. Protests and demonstrations were quite contained, involving no more than several hundred people. Formal opposition groups had only just been created since the opening of the Austro-Hungarian border: by the beginning of October some 10,000 people belonged to Neues Forum as well as Demokratie Jetzt, Demokratischer Aufbruch, SDP (SozialDemokratische Partei in der DDR) and Vereinigte Linke. These smaller groupings were mostly associated with Neues Forum. Millions of GDR citizens remained passive and hundreds of thousands were still willing to defend the state.[19]

The atmosphere in those days was tense and uncertain – the rumour mill was in overdrive about what might happen next. At the top, Erich Honecker envisaged a 'Chinese solution' to counter the mounting protests over the anniversary weekend (6–9 October),[20] prefigured in East Berlin when Stasi boss Erich Mielke jumped out of his bulletproof limo on the evening of 7 October screaming to police '*Haut sie doch zusammen, die Schweine!*' ('Club those pigs into submission!').[21] That night in and around Prenzlauer Berg near the Gethsemane church, police officers, plain-clothes security forces and volunteer militia attacked some 6,000 demonstrators who shouted 'Freedom', 'No violence' and 'We want to stay', as well as bystanders, with dogs and water cannons – beating and kicking peaceful citizens and throwing hundreds into jail. Women and girls were stripped naked; people were not allowed to use the toilets and told to piss or shit in their pants. Those who asked where they would be taken were told: '*Auf eine Müllkippe*' ('To the landfill').[22]

Unlike similar scenes in other East German cities, where foreign journalists were banned, the images from East Berlin that weekend soon went around the world. And when those arrested were released and talked to the press, what they told the cameras about merciless brutality by the riot police and abuse at the hands of the Stasi interrogators was both really shocking and also entirely believable. Because many of them were simply ordinary citizens, some even SED members, not militant protestors or hardcore dissidents.[23]

Matters came to a head on Monday 9 October in Leipzig, which had been the epicentre of people-protest for the past few weeks. In fact the Monday night demo there had become a weekly feature since the first gathering by a few hundred in early September, spilling out spontaneously – as numbers grew exponentially – from the evening prayers for peace (*Friedensgebet*) in the Nikolaikirche in the city centre to a big rally along the inner ring road. On the night of 25 September, the fourth such occasion, 5,000 people had come together; a week later there were already 15,000, calling for '*Demokratie – jetzt oder nie*' ('Democracy – now or never'), and '*Freiheit, Gleichheit, Brüderlichkeit*' ('Freedom, equality, fraternity'). On the march, they chanted defiantly '*Wir bleiben hier*' ('We stay here'), as opposed to the earlier '*Wir wollen raus*' ('We want out'), while demanding '*Erich laß die Faxen sein, laß die Perestroika rein*' ('Erich [Honecker] stop fooling around, let the perestroika in'). Each week, Leipzigers became more daring in their activities and more vehement in their demands.[24]

The 9th of October was expected to be the largest ever protest – facing off against the regime's full display of force. With this in mind, the Leipzig opposition groups and churches had disseminated appeals for prudence and non-violence. The world-renowned conductor Kurt Masur of the Gewandhaus orchestra, together with two other local celebrities, enlisted the support of three leading SED functionaries of the city government, and issued a public call for peaceful action: 'We all need free dialogue and exchanges of views about further development of socialism in our country.' What's more, they argued, dialogue should not only be conducted in Leipzig but also with the government in East Berlin. This so-called 'Appeal of the Six' was read aloud, as well as being broadcast via loud-speakers across the city during the evening church vigils.[25]

Honecker, for his part, was determined to make an example of Leipzig. The state media replayed footage of Tiananmen and endlessly repeated the government's solidarity with their comrades in Beijing.[26] When

Honecker met Yao Yilin, China's deputy premier, on the morning of the 9th, the two men announced that there was 'evidence of a particularly anti-socialist action by imperialist class opponents with the aim of reversing socialist development. In this respect there is a fundamental lesson to be learned from the counter-revolutionary unrest in Beijing and the present campaign' in East Germany. Honecker himself was positively bombastic: 'Any attempt by imperialism to destabilise socialist construction or slander its achievements is now and in the future nothing more than Don Quixote's futile running against the steadily turning sails of a windmill.'[27]

As darkness fell that evening, 9 October, with memories fresh of horrors from Berlin, many expected a total bloodbath in Leipzig. Honecker had pontificated that riots should be 'choked off in advance'. Some 1,500 soldiers, 3,000 police and 600 paramilitary backed by hundreds of Stasi agents were ready. 'It is either them or us,' police were told by their superiors. 'Fight them with no compromises,' the interior minister ordered. The army had been given live ammunition and gas masks; the Stasi were briefed by Mielke in person; and paramilitaries and police were also called up in readiness.[28] Around 6 p.m., after prayers at the Nikolaikirche and neighbouring churches, the crowd struggled out into the streets. With more people joining the march all the time, an estimated 70,000 slowly pushed their way out onto the ring road.[29]

Marching for democracy on the Leipziger Innenstadtring

Yet the dreaded confrontation never took place. The local party was unwilling to make a move without detailed instructions from the leadership in East Berlin. The army and police were not prepared for the size of the crowd, double what they had expected. Above all, Honecker's word was no longer law. An intense power struggle was now under way in East Berlin. Egon Krenz – twenty-five years Honecker's junior – had been plotting a coup for some time. But, despite his recent 'fraternal' visit to Beijing, he did not wish to be saddled by Honecker with the opprobrium of a Tiananmen solution at home, because that would stain his own hands with German blood while allowing the elderly leader to blame him for the violence. This left the party paralysed between hardliners, ditherers and reformers. And, with no clear word that night from Berlin, the local party chief did a volte-face. Heeding the Appeal of the Six, he ordered his men to act only in self-defence. Meanwhile, the Kremlin had issued a directive to General Boris Snetkov, commander of the Western Group of Soviet Forces with his HQ in Wünsdorf near Berlin, not to intervene in East German events. The Red Army troops on East German soil were to stay in their garrisons.

So the 'Chinese card' was never played. Not because of a deliberate decision by the SED at the top, growing out of a change of heart, but because of the distinct absence of any decision. Time passed. The masses kept marching. There was no violence. The repressive state apparatus that Mielke had pulled together was not confronted with fearsome 'enemies of the state' or anarchic 'rowdies' but by well-disciplined ordinary citizens bearing candles and speaking the language of non-violence. What they wanted was recognition by the governing party of their legitimate quest for basic freedoms and political reform: their slogan was '*Wir sind das Volk*' ('We are the people').[30]

New facts on the ground had been created. And a new demonstration culture had emerged – spilling out from the church vigils into the squares and the streets. The regime's loss of nerve that night dispelled the omnipresent climate of fear. This would change the face of the GDR. The civil rights activists and the mass of protestors were beginning to merge.

It was a huge victory for the peaceful demonstrators and an epic defeat for the regime. '*Die Lage ist so beschissen, wie sie noch nie in der SED war*' ('The situation is so shitty, like it never was in the SED'), summed up one Politburo member on 17 October.[31] Next day Honecker resigned – officially on health grounds – and Krenz took over as party boss.[32] But that did not improve the public mood: the people interpreted the power transfer as the result of their pressure from below rather than as the outcome of party machinations and manoeuvrings going on ever since Honecker was taken seriously ill during the Warsaw Pact meeting in Bucharest in July.[33]

Egon Krenz at the Volkskammer as the
New Party Secretary of the SED in East Berlin

Krenz promised the Party Central Committee on 18 October that he would initiate a 'turn' (*Wende*). He committed himself to open 'dialogue' with the opposition on two conditions: first, 'to continue building up socialism in the GDR ... without giving up any of our common achievements' and second, to preserve East Germany as a 'sovereign state'. As a result, Krenz's *Wende* amounted to little more than a rhetorical tweak of the party's standard dogma. And, in similar vein, the personnel changes he made among the leadership were largely cosmetic. There was, in short, little genuine 'renewal' in the offing: clearly *Wende* did not mean *Umbruch* (rupture and radical change).[34]

Not only did Krenz's accession to power leave more reformist elements in the SED frustrated; worse, he personally appeared clueless in judging the true nature of the public mood. After his election to the post of SED general secretary, he asked the Protestant church leaders when 'those demonstrations finally would come to end'. After all, continued Krenz obtusely, 'one can't spend every day on the streets'.[35] Little did he know.

In any case, Krenz was not a credible leader. Rumours were rife about his health and his alcohol problems. And 'long-tooth' Krenz, as he was nicknamed – a party hack for more than thirty years – had no plausibility as a 'reformer'. So, rather than stabilising SED rule, his takeover actually served to fuel popular displeasure with the party and accelerated the erosion of its monopoly on power. What's more, when the Krenz regime renounced the open use of force, that token concession only emboldened the masses to demand ever more fundamental change. They now felt they were pushing at an open door: 'street power' was shaking 'the tower'.[36]

After the fall of Honecker on 18 October, anti-government protest – in the form of peace prayers, mass demonstrations and public discussions – spread right across the country. In the process various currents of criticism flowed together into a surging tide. Long-time dissidents from the churches; writers and intellectuals from the alternative left; critics of the SED from within the party; and the mass public spilling out onto the streets: all these fused in what might be called an independent public sphere. They spoke in unison for people's sovereignty. Discontent was now open. The long spell of silence had been broken.

On 23 October in Leipzig, 300,000 participated in the Monday march around the ring road. In Schwerin on the Baltic, the 'reliable forces' who were meant to come out for the regime ended up in large swathes joining the parallel demo by Neues Forum. Next day the protests returned to East Berlin, whose squares had remained quiet since the brutal crackdown of 7 and 8 October. Overall, there were 145 anti-government events in the GDR in the last week of the month, and a further 210 in the first week of November. Not only were these protests growing, the demands were becoming both more diverse and also more pointed:

> *Die führende Rolle dem Volk* ('The leading role to the people', 16 October)
> *Egon, leit Reformen ein, sonst wirst Du der nächste sein!* ('Egon, introduce reforms, or else you'll be next!', 23 October)
> *Visafrei bis Hawaii!* ('Visa-free travel to Hawaii!', 23 October)
> *Demokratie statt Machtmonopol der SED* ('Democracy instead of the SED's monopoly on power', 30 October)

Conversely, the SED leadership appeared lost for words. Increasingly unable to win the argument, the Krenz Politburo hid behind traditional orthodoxy.[37] In particular, the party was totally unwilling to give up its constitutionally entrenched 'leading role' (*Führungsanspruch*) – which was the principal demand of all those who wanted liberalisation and democratisation.[38] To make matters worse, while seeking to reinstate its authority, the regime showed itself bewildered and helpless in the face of the GDR's deteriorating economic situation. Discussions in the Politburo revolved around how to get consumers more tyres, more children's anoraks, more furniture, cheaper Walkmen and how to mass-produce PCs and 1 MB chips – not the structural flaws of the economy.[39]

Only on 31 October were the stark realities finally laid bare in an official report to the Politburo by the chief planner, Gerhard Schürer, on the economic state of the GDR. The country's productivity was 40% lower than that of the Federal Republic. The system of state planning had proved totally unfit for purpose. And the GDR was close to national insolvency. Indebtedness to the West had risen from 2 billion Valutamarks in 1970 to 49 billion in 1989.* Merely halting further indebtedness would entail a lowering of the East Germans' living standards by 25–30% in order to service the existing debt. And any default on debt repayments would risk opening the country to an IMF diktat for a market economy under conditions of acute austerity. For the SED, this was ideologically untenable. In May, Krenz had declared that economic policy and social policy were an entwined unit, and had to be continued as such because this was the essence of socialism in the GDR. So the regime was trapped in a vicious circle: socialism depended on the Plan, and the survival of the planned economy required external credits on a scale that now made East Germany totally dependent on the capitalist West, especially the FRG.[40]

Straight after this fateful Politburo meeting, Krenz flew to Moscow for his first visit to the Kremlin as the GDR's secretary general. There on 1 November he admitted the economic home truths to Gorbachev himself. The Soviet leader was unsympathetic. He coldly informed Krenz that the USSR had been aware of East Berlin's predicament all along; that was why he had kept pressing Honecker for reforms. Even so, when Gorbachev heard the precise figures – Krenz said the GDR needed $4.5 billion in credits simply to pay off the interest on its debts – the Soviet leader was, for a moment, speechless – a rare occurrence. The Kremlin was in no position to help, so Gorbachev could only advise Krenz to tell his people the truth. And, for a country that had already haemorrhaged over 200,000 alienated citizens since the start of 1989, this was not a happy prospect.[41]

Afterwards, Krenz tried to put the best face on things in a seventy-

---

*   The Valutamark was an East German currency unit used exclusively for calculating
    the value of economic exchanges between the GDR and non-socialist economies.

minute meeting with the foreign press, presenting himself as an 'intimate friend' of Gorbachev and no hardliner. But the media were not convinced. When Krenz talked policy, he sounded just like Honecker, his political mentor, and he flatly rejected any talk of reunification with West Germany or the removal of the Berlin Wall. 'This question is not on the table,' Krenz insisted. 'There is nothing to reunify because socialism and capitalism have never stood together on German soil.' Krenz also put a positive spin on the mass protests. 'Many people are out on the streets to show that they want better socialism and the renovation of society,' he said. 'This is a good sign, an indication that we are at a turning point.' He added that the SED would seriously consider the demands of the protestors. The first steps, he said, would be taken at a party meeting the following week.[42]

In truth, the SED had its back to the wall. Desperate, it decided to give ground to the protestors on the question of travel restrictions – to allow an appearance of freedom. So on 1 November the GDR reopened its borders with Czechoslovakia. The result was no surprise, except perhaps to the Politburo itself. Once again the people voted with their feet: some 8,000 left their *Heimat* on the first day. On 3 November, Miloš Jakeš, leader of the Czech communists in Prague – having secured Krenz's approval – formally opened Czechoslovakia's borders to the FRG, thereby granting East Germans a legal transit route to the West. But instead of this halting the frenzied flight, the exodus only continued to grow: 23,000 East Germans arrived in the Federal Republic on the weekend of 4–5 November, and by the 8th the total number of émigrés had reached 50,000.[43]

On his return home Krenz pleaded with East Germans in a televised address. To those who thought of emigrating, he said: 'Put trust in our policy of renewal. Your place is here. We need you.'[44] That last sentence was true: the mass flight that autumn had already caused a serious labour shortage in the economy, especially in the health sector. Hospitals and clinics had reported losing as many as 30% of their staff as doctors and nurses had succumbed to the lure of freedom, much better pay and a more high-tech work environment in the West.[45]

By this stage, few were listening to the SED leader. On 4 November half a million attended a 'rally for change' in East Berlin, organised by the official Union of Actors. For the first time since the fortieth-anniversary weekend, there was no police interference in the capital. Indeed, the rally – which included party officials, actors, opposition leaders, clergy, writers and various prominent figures – was broadcast live on GDR media. Speakers from the government were shouted down, with chants of 'Krenz Xiaoping, no thanks'. Others, such as the novelist Christa Wolf, drew cheers as she announced her dislike for the party's language of 'change of course'. She said she preferred to talk of a 'revolution from below' and 'revolutionary renewal'.

Wolf was one of thousands of opposition activists who desired a better, genuinely democratic and independent GDR. Quite definitely they did not see the Federal Republic as the ideal. They did not want their country to be gobbled up by the dominant, larger western half of Germany – in a cheap sell-out to capitalism. People like Wolf and Bärbel Bohley, the artist founder of Neues Forum, had stuck with the GDR despite all its frustrations; in their minds, running away was the soft option. So they now wanted to reap the fruit of their hard work as dissidents. They were idealists who aspired to a democratic socialism, and saw the autumn of 1989 as their chance to turn dreams into reality.

But Ingrid Stahmer, the deputy mayor of West Berlin, had a different perspective. With GDR citizens now freely flooding out of the country through its Warsaw Pact neighbours, she remarked that the Wall was soon going to become history. 'It's just going to be superfluous.'[46]

On Monday 6 November, close to a million people in eight cities across the GDR –some 400,000 in Leipzig and 300,000 in Dresden – marched to demand free elections and free travel. They denounced as totally inadequate the latest loosening of the travel law, published that morning in the state daily *Neues Deutschland*, because it limited foreign travel to thirty days. And there was a further question: how much currency would East Germans be allowed to change into Western money at home? The Ostmark was not freely convertible, and up to now East Germans had been allowed once a year to exchange just fifteen Ostmarks into DMs – about $8 at the official exchange rate – hardly enough for a meal, let alone an extended trip.[47]

So the pressure was intense when the SED Central Committee gathered on 8 November for its three-day meeting. Right at the start, the entire Politburo resigned and a new one – reduced in size from twenty-one members to eleven – was elected, to create the appearance of change. In the event, six members retained their seats, while five new ones were named. Three of Krenz's preferred new Politburo candidates were rejected and the party gave the position of prime minister to Hans Modrow, the SED chief in Dresden – a genuine reformer. As a result, the party elite was now visibly split. What's more, on the outside of the party headquarters, 5,000 SED members protested openly against their leaders.[48]

Next day, 9 November, the party struggled to think up responses to people's demands in the streets. In late afternoon the Central Committee came back to the problematic travel regulations. A short memo was drawn up and passed to the secretary of the Central Committee, Günter Schabowski, who had been appointed that morning as the SED's media spokesman but did not attend that part of the discussions. At 6 p.m. Schabowski briefed the world media on the day's deliberations, in a press conference broadcast live on GDR TV.[49]

It was a long and boring meeting. Near the end Schabowski was asked by one journalist about the alterations in the GDR travel law. He offered a rather incoherent summary and then, under pressure, hastily read out parts of the press statement he had been given earlier. Distracted by further questions he omitted the passages regarding the grounds for denying applications both for private travel and permanent exit applications. His omissions, however, only added to the confusion. Had the Central Committee radically changed its course? A now panicky Schabowski talked of a decision to allow citizens to emigrate permanently. The press room grew restless. The media started to get their teeth into the issue.

What about holidays? Short trips to the West? Visits to West Berlin? Which border crossings? When would the new arrangements come into effect? A seriously rattled Schabowski simply muttered 'According to my knowledge ... immediately, right away.' Because they had not been given any formal written statement, the incredulous press corps hung on Schabowski's every word, squeezing all they could out of them.[50]

Finally someone asked the fatal question: 'Mr Schabowski, what is going to happen to the *Berlin Wall* now?'

Schabowski: It has been brought to my attention that it is 7 p.m. That has to be the last question. Thank you for your understanding.

Um ... What will happen to the Berlin Wall? Information has already been provided in connection with travel activities. Um, the issue of travel, um, the ability to cross the Wall from our side ... hasn't been answered yet and exclusively the question in the sense ... so this, I'll put it this way, fortified state border of the GDR ... um, we have always said that there have to be several other factors, um, taken into consideration. And they deal with the complex of questions that Comrade Krenz, in his talk in the – addressed in view of the relations between the GDR and the FRG, in ditto light of the, um, necessity of continuing the process of assuring peace with new initiatives.

And, um, surely the debate about these questions, um, will be positively influenced if the FRG and NATO also agree to and implement disarmament measures in a similar manner to that of the GDR and other socialist countries. Thank you very much.

The media was left to make what they wanted of his incoherence. The press room emptied within seconds. The news went viral on the wire services and soon made its way via TV and radio into living rooms and streets of Berlin. 'Leaving via all GDR checkpoints immediately possible' Reuters reported at 7.02 p.m., 'GDR opens its borders', echoed Associated Press three minutes later. At 8 p.m. on West German TV, the evening news *Tagesschau* – which millions of East Germans could watch – led with the same message. Correct in substance, these headlines were, of course, in formulation much balder, bolder and far-reaching than the small print of the actual East German *Reiseregelung*, or the reality on the ground.[51]

But during the course of this damp and very cold November evening, reality soon caught up – and with a vengeance.

Over the next few hours, thousands of East Berliners converged on the various checkpoints at the Wall, especially in the centre of the city – to see for themselves if and when they could cross. They were not put off by East German state television or the police telling them to come back next morning at eight o'clock when the bureaucracy would be all ready. Instead they kept shouting: *'Tor auf!'* ('Open the gate!'). At Bornholmer Strasse, some sixty armed border guards – commanded by Lieutenant Colonel Harald Jäger, who had been doing the job since 1964 – sat in their tiny checkpoint huts, totally outnumbered, and without any instructions from on high. Both the Central Committee and the military top brass, locked away in meetings, were unreachable. So the men on the front line had to make their own decisions. At around 9 p.m. they began to let people through: first as a trickle, one by one, meticulously stamping each person's identity card – the idea being these exiters would not later be let back in. Then, at around 10.30 p.m., they lifted the barriers in both directions and gave up trying to check credentials. It was as if the floodgates had been opened. People poured across into West Berlin. No East or West German politicians were present, nor any representatives of the four occupying powers. There were just a few baffled East German men in uniform, soon reduced to tears as they were overcome by the emotion of this historic moment.[52]

Within thirty minutes, several thousand people had squeezed their way to the other side. Somewhere in the chaos a young East German quantum chemist called Angela Merkel was swept along by the crowd. After a quiet sauna evening with her friends, she just wanted to experience for herself German history in the making. Once on the western side of the Wall, she phoned her aunt in Hamburg and joined the celebrations before heading back home – wondering what 9 November would mean for her.[53]

By midnight – after twenty-eight years of sealed borders – all the crossings in Berlin were open; likewise, as news spread, any other transit point along the border between the two Germanies. Neither the GDR security forces nor the Red Army did anything to prevent this. Not a single shot was fired, and no Soviet soldier left his barracks. Now, thousands of East Berliners – of all ages, from every walk of life – were making their way on foot, bike or car into the western half of the city – a forbidden place hitherto only glimpsed from afar. At Checkpoint Charlie, where Allied and Soviet tanks had been locked in a tense face-off in August 1961 as the Berlin Wall went up, the jubilant horde of visitors was greeted by cheering, flag-waving West Germans, plying them with flowers and sparkling wine.

'I don't know what we're going to do, just drive around and see what's going on,' said one thirty-four-year-old East Berliner as he sat at the wheel of his orange Trabant chugging down the glittering Kurfürstendamm. 'We're here for the first time. I'll go home in a few hours. My wife and kids are waiting for me. But I wasn't going to miss this.'[54]

At the Brandenburg Gate, the most prominent landmark of the city's division, hundreds of people chanted on the western side 'The Wall must go!' Then some climbed on top of the Wall and danced on it; others clambered over and headed right through the historic arch that for so long had been inaccessible to Berliners from either side. These were utterly unbelievable pictures – captured gleefully by American TV film crews for their prime-time news bulletins back home.[55]

All through the night and over the next few days, East Berliners continued to flood into West Berlin in vast numbers – 3 million in three days, most of whom came back.

The open Wall: Potsdamer Platz, 12 November 1989

They saw the promised land – and were being bribed to savour it. While in the East, banks and travel agents lacked sufficient foreign (DM) currency reserves to exchange for every traveller even the permitted maximum of fifteen Ostmarks, in the West long lines of East Berliners formed in front of the West Berlin banks to pick up the DM 100 'Welcome Money' – about $55 – that the FRG had always given East Germans on their first time in the West. Spending their own, free DMs in the shiny emporia of the consumer society, they filled up their plastic bags with precious goods – often as simple as bananas, oranges or children's toys – and carried them back into the grey streets of the socialist utopia.[56]

It was in those days that all the talk about revolution and renewal in the GDR totally evaporated as a credible political project.[57] Not for opposition intellectuals, of course – for the idealist alternative left and the earnest socialist reformers such as Bohley and Wolf – or even for the new echelon of younger SED functionaries. They denounced all talk of reunification as reactionary *Heim ins Reich* patriotism, derided capitalist culture as materialist trash and condemned consumption and foreign travel as the new opium of the masses.[58] But most of the 'masses' took no notice. For them, the idea of reforming the GDR and of pursuing a 'third way'[59] between SED-state socialism and Western capitalism was now dead. That was the true revolution: popular rejection of the old regime and no affirmation of any new socialist-democratic vision of society. Why stay in a broken communist state when you could start a new life amid the temples of capitalism? Or even demand the merger of East Germany with the West?

*

How was it that the GDR experience turned out so differently from that of Poland and Hungary? In part because in the GDR the transition from communism began much later and developed much faster. Poland and Hungary had entered the process of political transformation in earnest in the summer of 1988; in the GDR the first rumblings of protest did not occur till May 1989 and street demonstrations only began in September. In part, too, because the Polish and Hungarian economies were in a far worse state than East Germany's, so their tortuous navigation out of a command economy towards the market offered little attraction in the GDR. Indeed, the politico-economic transition produced more shortages and hardship than the people had bargained for. But it was also because the East German party state had failed, despite forty years of assiduous effort, to inculcate a sense of GDR patriotism. In Hungary and Poland the changes were rooted in national unity; this was not so in the GDR, where unity became *all*-German, not *East* German.

The GDR regime was also much more hard-line and unreconstructed for much longer. Only in East Berlin was a 'Chinese solution' seriously considered – and not just because Tiananmen happened after Polish and Hungarian reforms had got into their stride. Honecker was locked in the past, totally wedded to his state and his version of real socialism. Yet while the GDR might have been the technologically most advanced country in the Eastern bloc, it was also more dependent on the USSR than its neighbours because of the size of the Red Army presence and because the GDR was an artificial polity, created and sustained by Moscow. As Brezhnev had told Honecker back in 1970, 'Erich, I tell you frankly, don't ever forget this: the GDR cannot exist without us, without the Soviet Union, its power and strength. Without us there is no GDR.' Honecker's problem in 1989 was that Gorbachev was definitely not Brezhnev. He wanted radical reforms and, furthermore, had renounced the use of force. For Honecker, that would spell the end of his rule – and indeed of the SED itself.

Out of this face-off between East Berlin and the Kremlin came domestic political paralysis. There was no Chinese-style crackdown in Leipzig on 9 October to crush the protests, no transfer of the Tiananmen 'contagion' to Europe. This indicated a fundamental divide between the Asian and European transitions from the Cold War – between the use of repression and a consensus on non-violence. And the GDR's policy paralysis did not go away even after Honecker was toppled, because Krenz refused to allow any breach in the SED's monopoly on power until after the 'fall of the Wall'.

In fact, the reforms in Poland and Hungary had little effect on developments in the GDR. Where Hungary did matter was as an exit rather than an exemplar. It was the opening of the Hungarian border with Austria and the ensuing exodus of East Germans that proved the real catalyst for change within the GDR. The impact was intensified by the opening of Czechoslovakia's frontier with West Germany, and ultimately by the collapse of the inner German border as well. Once East Germans started to move en masse, the 'German question' was back in people's minds. That's why the moment of political convergence with Poland and Hungary was so brief – a matter of three weeks or so before the fall of the Wall and then Kohl's policy offensive undermined the aspirations of Neues Forum and its allies for a reformed socialism. It also made nonsense of the efforts of Hans Modrow – hailed by many in the GDR as the 'German Gorbachev' – to form a new and stable government and to negotiate in a Polish-style round-table process with the opposition. Before round-table talks even began, the SED disintegrated at all levels, amid corruption scandals and a string of resignations, and in early December it was renamed the PDS (Partei des Demokratischen Sozialismus) and its monopoly deleted from the constitution. The brief 'Krenz era' was history.

Similarly, Neues Forum and other opposition groups such as Demokratischer Aufbruch were undermined by the 'post-Wall' divergence between political activists and the general mass of GDR citizens. Just when the opposition's dream of realising a democratic and reformed socialist GDR seemed finally within reach – as commentator Timothy Garton Ash wrote, putting the 'D for Democratic' into the GDR – the whole idea was stillborn. The round-table talks were set for 7 December, but over the previous four weeks 130,000 more people emigrated to the FRG. In the Leipzig Monday demonstrations the slogan '*Deutschland einig Vaterland*' ('Germany the united fatherland') was heard for the first time as early as 13 November; a week later '*Wir sind das Volk*' had transmuted into '*Wir sind ein Volk*' ('We are one people'). In contrast to Hungary and Poland, it was the GDR's opening to the West and the prospect of unification that made the crucial difference. Hungarians and Poles had to imagine an alternative future for themselves at home; East Germans could look to the reality of an existing alternative on their own doorstep: a prosperous, functioning West German state, run by compatriots. And they did. As Garton Ash also observed, it was at once a chance and a tragedy for East Germany that 'the boundaries of social self-determination and national self-determination were not the same'.[60]

Significantly, Germany's national story had wider repercussions. When we talk today about the fall of the Wall, what comes into our minds is the image of the Brandenburg Gate and people dancing on the Wall. But in fact the Gate was in no man's land; it was not a crossing point and, after the extraordinary night of 9 November, it would remain closed for another six weeks. Not until 22 December was the Wall opened at the

Gate. This is a reminder that the media was at once a catalyst, a shaper and a multiplier of events. Even in one day, the headlines shifted from 'The GDR Opens its Borders to the Federal Republic' (10 November) to 'Wall and Barbed Wire Do Not Divide Anymore' (11 November). A local moment full of contingency was quickly transformed into an event of universal significance. As an experience of liberty through the overcoming of physical separation, the end of the Wall had a meaning and resonance which spread fast and far beyond Berlin.

In the process, the focus of the story rapidly shifted away from the politicians (especially Schabowski and his botched press conference) making history through blunders and happenstance to a narrative of ordinary people bringing about revolutionary change. And then, even more abstractly, as GDR politicians and Western journalists who drove events that night were edited out of the story, 'the fall of the Wall' became a magical and highly symbolic moment in history. The dancers on the Wall at the Brandenburg Gate became the ultimate symbol of freedom for 1989 – rather like the way, at the other end of the spectrum, the man in front of the tank near Tiananmen Square became the year's ultimate symbol of repression.[61]

*

The fall of the Wall had certainly not been Kohl's moment. And he was struggling to catch up for the next three weeks. But then he would seize the initiative with a vengeance.

Most of November was spent responding to the demands of others, rather than working out his own agenda. On the 9th, that momentous night for Germany, he had not even been in the country. When he finally escaped from Poland and got to Berlin next day, he had been shouted down by the crowds. Soon he had to rush back again to Warsaw to wrap up the interrupted visit. But the Poles were harder to placate – because it was no longer just a matter of burying the past but alleviating fears about the future. After the three culture-focused days of reconciliation – at Auschwitz and in Silesia – the trip was rounded off by a carefully calibrated finale. Kohl announced an aid package amounting to $2.2 billion – the largest by far from any Western government (Bush had offered $100 million when he was in Poland in early July). And the chancellor wrote off $400 million in West German loans since the 1970s. With these measures he wanted to forestall any fresh talk about a peace treaty for the Second World War, which would raise the unhappy issues of reparations and the Oder–Neisse border with Poland. So in the press conference, when finally asked about the elephant in the room – 'reunification' – the chancellor replied 'We do not speak about reunification but about self-determination.'[62]

Moment of penitence: Kohl at Auschwitz

Kohl was clearly careful how he spoke publicly about unity, preferring to argue his case around the strict legal principles of the East Germans' right to self-determination and the provision in the FRG's Basic Law that unity should be attained through the exercise of the Germans' free will. Kohl, of course, assumed that when East Germans had the opportunity to choose, they would opt for unification. He had made this point in his state-of-the-nation address on 8 November, before the Wall was breached, and reiterated it at greater length, again in the Bundestag, on 16 November.

'Our compatriots in the GDR must be able to decide for themselves which way they want to go in the future,' the chancellor declared. 'Of course we will respect every decision that is being made by the people of the GDR in free self-determination.' On the question of economic assistance, he added that this would be useless 'unless there is an irreversible reform of the economic system, an end to a bureaucratic planned economy and the introduction of a market economy'. In other words, self-determination was in principle entirely free but was also susceptible to a little bribery.

In his speech Kohl made a deliberate nod towards Bonn's Western allies and their suppressed concerns about a resurgence of German nationalism. 'We are and remain a part of the Western system of values,' he insisted, adding that it would be a 'fatal error' to slow the process of European integration.[63]

His cryptic statement about 'Europe' was, however, insufficient to allay all fears. This became evident when Kohl travelled to Paris for a special dinner of European Community heads of government on 18 November. Mitterrand, then holding the rotating position of president of the EC, had invited his colleagues to the Elysée Palace at very short notice – keen to ensure that the EC 12 would be an active partner for the reforming states of Central and Eastern Europe but without allowing the Community to be deflected from the already ongoing processes of deeper economic and political integration. In particular, the French president worried that, after the drama in Berlin, plans for economic and monetary union (EMU) might no longer take centre stage at the upcoming EC Council meeting in Strasbourg on 8–9 December. He believed that those plans were all the more urgent precisely because of the great transformation sweeping across the Soviet bloc. And he wanted the EC to make this position public well before the Bush–Gorbachev summit talks in Malta on 2–3 December.[64]

Mitterrand therefore had a clear agenda when speaking for 'Europe'. But, as the leader of France, he was acutely nervous about where Germany was now going. He and Kohl had not met since that epoch-making night of 9 November and he wanted to use the gathering in Paris to talk face-to-face with his German counterpart. They did so, according to Kohl's memoirs, in a short tête-à-tête before the dinner. Mitterrand avoided mentioning the issue of reunification but Kohl – conscious of what was in the air – raised it himself. 'I talk to you as a German and as chancellor,' he said, and then solemnly pledged his active commitment to building Europe. More reflectively, he added: 'I see two causes for the developments in the East: that the alliance [i.e. NATO] stayed firm thanks to the dual-track decision[65] and the fact that the European Community has evolved in such dynamic fashion.' Thus, succinctly, he underlined Bonn's intertwined loyalty to the Western alliance and the European project.[66]

Having put his own cards on the table, Kohl joined Mitterrand for dinner with the other EC leaders. The meal, in one of the opulent salons of the Elysée, went smoothly. Not even a word was 'whispered' about unification, Kohl would later recall. Instead Mitterrand went on about the need to support the democratisation processes in the East at large. He argued for constant prudence and against anything that might destabilise Gorbachev. Yet the German question was clearly hanging there, unspoken.

Finally Margaret Thatcher could contain herself no longer. Over dessert she exploded to Kohl: There could be 'no question of changing Europe's borders', which had been confirmed in the Helsinki Final Act. 'Any attempt to raise this or the issue of German reunification would risk undermining Mr Gorbachev's position,' she warned, and would 'open the Pandora's box of border claims right through Central Europe'. Kohl was visibly taken aback at her outburst, which upset the whole mood of the dinner. Struggling to respond, he cited a 1970 NATO summit declaration, in which the allies had expressed their continued support on the issue of German unity. Thatcher retorted that this endorsement happened at a time when nobody seriously believed that reunification would ever take place. But Kohl dug in. Be that as may, he said coldly, NATO agreed on this declaration and the decision still stood. Even Thatcher would not be able to stop the German people in their tracks: they now held their fate in their own hands. Sitting back, his ample girth filling the chair, he looked the British prime minister in the eye. Angrily, she stamped her feet several times and shouted: 'That's the way *you* see it, *you* see it!'[67]

To Kohl it was quite clear that the Iron Lady was determined to uphold the status quo. For her, borders were immutable; even their peaceful change was simply not on the agenda. This also applied to the inner German frontier, which he – like most Germans – did not consider as an international border, never mind the Oder–Neisse frontier with Poland.

Although shaken by Thatcher's diatribe, Kohl was conscious that her rooted antipathy to the European project meant that she was an outsider in the EC's decision-making. And she could not play the American card because Kohl was already certain that Bush supported the principle of German unification. What worried Kohl much more was that Mitterrand just sat there quietly, seeming to approve of Thatcher's words. Had he egged her on? Was this an Anglo-French axis in the making? The chancellor began to wonder whether the French leader was playing a double game.[68]

Only two weeks earlier, Mitterrand had told Kohl in Bonn that he did not fear German reunification. On the other hand, at the end the French president entered the caveat that he would have to consider what in practice worked best in the interests of France and of Europe. There was, in other words, an ambiguity in the French position: Mitterrand thought plenty of time should be allowed for German unification ('la nécessaire durée du processus'), while, simultaneously, the process of creating an ever-closer European union should be speeded up. This double dynamic of largo and accelerando was evidently something that mattered to the Frenchman. And it made the chancellor just a little bit uneasy. But he placed his trust in their history of partnership and cooperation going back to 1982.[69]

Kohl was beginning to realise that the EC, or certainly one of its leading members, was going to demand something in return for going along with his talk about a united Germany. Piecing together their discussions in Bonn and then Paris, he recognised that it was essential to convince Mitterrand of the FRG's continued commitment to completing European monetary and political union – and not just as a fellow traveller but as a fellow shaper using the power of the Franco-German tandem. This mattered even more because Kohl had no illusions about the coolness felt towards German unification by many Europeans, not least the Italians and the Dutch.

The chancellor decided to confront the issue head-on in Strasbourg on 22 November at a special meeting of the European Parliament, convened to discuss recent events in Eastern Europe. In his address, he issued a clarion call that the division of both Europe and Germany be ended. Not only London, Rome, Dublin and Paris belonged to Europe, he declared, but also Warsaw and Budapest, Prague and Sofia. And, of course, Berlin, Leipzig and Dresden. German unity could only be achieved within this larger, pan-European process of unification: 'In a free and united Europe, a free and united Germany.' 'Deutschlandpolitik' and 'Europapolitik' were, Kohl said, 'two sides of the same coin'.[70]

Kohl had made a point of asking Mitterrand to attend his speech. When the president did so, it was taken as a clear endorsement of what the chancellor was saying. For Kohl, Strasbourg proved a great success. At the end the European Parliament passed an almost unanimous resolution (only two MEPs out of 518 voting against) saying that East Germans had the right to 'to be part of a united Germany and a united Europe'.[71]

The German chancellor had spoken to Europe and gained its approval.

And with Bush not particularly fazed about the matter, leaving the initiative to Kohl, there was hope that at a later point even Thatcher might be brought into line with the help of the Americans, if not the French and the EC. None of this, however, could obscure the fact that at home pressure was mounting on Kohl to spell out clearly and openly how he intended to achieve German unification – because so far the chancellor had been distinctly circumspect about the specifics. And he was being buffeted from all sides.

Among the many voices who demanded that the chancellor come out strongly for unification was Rudolf Augstein, editor of *Der Spiegel*. In his magazine on 20 November he wrote a column entitled '*Sagen, was ist*' ('To say what's what'). Augstein could barely conceal his impatience. Rather than hiding behind talk about *European* unity, he argued, the Kohl government should face up to the truly popular desire for *German* unity. The question that should be addressed was not if, but how, unification could be made to happen.[72]

Similarly outspoken for unity was Alfred Herrhausen, head of Deutsche Bank, an advocate of European economic integration and also an adviser to the chancellor. In an interview he pointed out the reality that as soon as foreign investment was allowed in the GDR, the West German economy would very quickly swallow up that of the East. Referring to an idea currently being floated about possible GDR membership in the EC, Herrhausen said that, as a banker, he thought it desirable in the short term but, speaking as a German citizen, he would definitely not want to forgo the historic opportunity for unity. That, for him, seemed to supersede everything else.[73]

Yet Kohl was also under pressure from those who did not believe in unification.

Günter Grass, the leftist author and public intellectual, came out strongly against the idea of 'a conglomeration of power' in the heart of Europe, calling instead for 'a confederation of two states that have to redefine themselves'. In other words, he wanted a 'settlement' between West and East. The past was dead, he insisted. 'There is no point in looking back to the German Reich, be it within the borders of 1945 or 1937; that's all gone. We have to define ourselves anew.'[74]

Oskar Lafontaine of the SPD, Kohl's direct rival for the chancellorship, also took a diametrically opposite position from the chancellor. Amid the turmoil before the fall of the Wall, he had warned of the 'spectre of a strong fourth German Reich' that was 'scaring our Western and no less our Eastern neighbours'.[75] And on 8 November, after Kohl lauded unity through self-determination, Lafontaine blasted the goal of a unified nation state as 'wrong and anachronistic'.[76] Once the borders were open Lafontaine denigrated the heady, almost delirious, atmosphere as 'national drunkenness' and, hard-nosed, asked whether it was right that all East German citizens who came west should simply get access to the FRG's social security benefits. Mindful of the impending Federal elections, he was trying to play on the anxieties of West Germans – who, according to Gallup polls, were prepared to help East Germany financially but without tax rises for themselves.[77]

Particularly striking was the denunciation of unification from Egon Bahr, who in the 1960s had designed Neue Ostpolitik based on the idea that 'change through rapprochement' would pave the way to unity. Before 9 November he had said that people should stop 'dreaming or nattering on about unity'.[78] And he had rejected the priority given to the 'lie' of unification – spluttering that it was 'poisoning' the atmosphere and causing 'political pollution'. Afterwards he took a cautious line, keener on a slower approach to unification and hiding behind Lafontaine.[79]

Within the SPD, only Willy Brandt, Bahr's old patron, spoke out for unity. It would be inconceivable, he declared, to 'batten down the hatches in the West'.[80] German unity was now only a question of time and it should not come only after Europe's unity had already been achieved. In this way Brandt distanced himself from the Lafontaine–Bahr line in his own party but, more generally, those on the left who privileged a pan-European framework, or Gorbachev's 'Common European Home', within which Germany could unite.[81] He also set himself apart from Genscher's 'Europa-Plan', tossed out in October, which airily suggested that the East Europeans, including the GDR, would be integrated into the EC, at the same time as Brussels kept marching towards monetary and political union.[82]

And so, ironically on the issue of German unity, the position taken by Lafontaine and Bahr was closer to that of the GDR's political opposition (and even reformers within the SED) than to the stance of their own Federal government in Bonn. Indeed, the writers and clergy representing the opposition in East Berlin called on 26 November for the independent self-sufficiency of the GDR, believing that they still had the chance, as 'equal neighbours to all European states to develop a socialist alternative to the FRG'.[83]

Kohl and Teltschik were particularly troubled by a statement from the East German prime minister, Hans Modrow, in his first 'government declaration' on 17 November. He promised secret multiparty elections for 1990 as well as a root-and-branch overhaul of the command economy, but not an outright shift to the market. Modrow said he was confident that decisive change in East Germany would end 'unrealistic and dangerous speculation about reunification'. He proposed that a stabilised GDR was a prime condition for wider stability in Central Europe, even across Europe as a whole. In this vein, looking to Bonn, he declared that his government was 'ready for talks' to put relations with West Germany 'on a new level'. His aim was a 'treaty union' which would build on the complex of political and economic treaties of Ostpolitik and Osthandel that had been signed by the two states over the previous few decades.[84]

Modrow had made the first official statement from either the FRG or the GDR on how to move forward on relations between the two Germanies. He had beaten Kohl to it and, furthermore, clearly sought to stall the drive towards unification. West German criticism of the chancellor became more strident. The editor of *Die Welt* asked on 19 November, 'Are we letting others dictate the blueprint for unity?'[85] And the co-founder of the extreme-right Die Republikaner party Franz Schönhuber saw in Kohl's silence the chance to raise his party's profile, putting top of the list in his election programme 'reunification' and 'regaining' the Eastern territories.[86]

Yet Kohl still held back. On Monday 20 November a worried Teltschik noted in his diary: 'international as much as domestic discussion over the chances of German unity has fully erupted and can no longer be stopped. We are more and more conscious of this, but the chancellor's directive remains the same: to exercise restraint in the public discourse. Neither within the coalition, and therefore domestically, nor on the foreign plane, does he want to open himself to attack.'

Teltschik saw this as a decisive moment for Kohl, at home and abroad. Chewing things over with Kohl's inner circle that evening, with an eye on the 'election marathon', they concluded: 'The high international reputation of the chancellor should be used more in domestic politics, and the German question could serve as a bridge to improve his image.' The opposition should be confronted 'head-on'.[87]

With all this still swirling around in Teltschik's head, next day in the early-morning briefing with Kohl, they took in the implications of

Monday's mass demonstrations across East Germany with the unmis-
sable new slogan '*Wir sind ein Volk*'. 'The spark has ignited,' he thought.
He was also turning over in his mind a line from Augstein's column,
echoing a famous phrase from Adenauer, '*der Schlüssel liegt im Kreml*'
– the key to unity lies in the Kremlin.[88]

The first big item on his diary that day, 21 November, was a meeting
at 10.30 a.m. with Nikolai Portugalov, on the staff of the Central
Committee of the CPSU, with whom he had meetings fairly frequently.
Although finding Portugalov rather foxy, even slimy, Teltschik respected
his intellect and grasp of the German scene and always relished such
opportunities to get news directly from Moscow and not via arch rival
Genscher's Foreign Ministry. On this occasion, however, Portugalov's
manner was unusually grave. He said he was conveying a message for
the chancellor himself and then handed over a set of handwritten pages
about Soviet thinking on the German question.

One paper was entitled 'Official Position'. This mostly reaffirmed the
pledges made by Kohl to Gorbachev about non-interference in GDR
affairs, and included references to their 12 June summit. For now, it
stressed, there ought to be a modus vivendi between the two German
states, and envisaged Modrow's proposal of a treaty union as the way
forward. Otherwise the GDR would find itself existentially threatened. Significantly, the paper also declared bluntly that an all-European
peace order was an 'absolute prerequisite' for resolving the German
question.[89] Such a peace order would, of course, take years to establish
but the document showed some signs of movement. It indicated that the
idea of German–German rapprochement through a confederation was
something the Soviets were already discussing at the Politburo level and
were prepared to accept in principle. Indeed it echoed a message received
in Bonn from the Moscow embassy that Shevardnadze, in utterances on
17 November, had rejected unilateral changes of the status quo but
approved the idea of mutual peaceful changes within 'an all-European
consensus'.[90]

What really grabbed Teltschik's attention, however, was the document
headed 'Unofficial Position'. This began, rather theatrically: 'The hour has
now come to free both West and East Germany from the relics of the
past.' After a few generalities about the immediate situation, Teltschik
was struck by an almost languid proposition: 'Let's ask purely theoretically: if the Federal government envisaged pushing the question of
"reunification" or "new unification" into practical politics ...' Developing

this hypothesis, the paper said it would be necessary among other things to discuss the future alliance membership of both German states and, more specifically, how to extract West Germany from both NATO and the European Community. And, on the other side, what would be the consequences of a future German confederation within the EC? This, pondered the paper, could become the germ of a pan-European integration project, but, then, how could the Soviet Union conduct its trade within East Germany via Brussels and cope with EC import taxes and other regulations? The paper stated bluntly that, 'in the context of the German question, the Soviet Union was already thinking about all possible alternatives, effectively thinking the "unthinkable"'. The paper ended by saying that Moscow could 'in the medium term' give a 'green light' to a German confederation, providing it was completely free from foreign nuclear weapons on its soil.[91]

Teltschik was electrified by what he read. This combination of blue-sky thinking and diplomatic flexibility was unprecedented and sensational. How to balance the 'official' and 'unofficial' papers was difficult but they clearly revealed that what Moscow was saying publicly was not necessarily a guide to what it might be willing to do. Rushing out of the meeting with Portugalov, Teltschik managed to have a word with Kohl before the chancellor's next appointment. Their conversation was only brief but Teltschik had sown the seed in Kohl's mind that, in view of the signals from Moscow, this was an opportune time to go onto the offensive. Kohl was reinforced in this opinion during the afternoon when his head of Chancellery, Rudolf Seiters, returned from a trip to East Berlin, full of news about the reforms under way and the talk about treaty union. Before he left for his trip to Strasbourg – to square François Mitterrand and the EC – Kohl told Teltschik to have something ready for his return. For the first time the chancellor talked about taking a 'step by step' approach on the German question. An overall political strategy was finally beginning to germinate.[92]

While Kohl was away, Teltschik was alarmed to learn, first, that Mitterrand was going to visit East Germany before Christmas and also intended to meet Gorbachev in Kiev on 6 December. Even more disconcerting, Paris had not informed Bonn in advance, before the news appeared on the wire services. What, Teltschik wondered, were the French and Soviets plotting? Yet news from Genscher, visiting Washington, was much more encouraging: the foreign minister had stressed the momentum of 'unification from below' and warned against any attempt at interference by the four victor powers. To his delight, at the State Department Baker had simply responded by stating America's full support for German unity without any caveats. And so, with a green light from Washington, positive signals from Moscow, and endorsement in Strasbourg from Mitterrand and the EC, Teltschik found himself frantically planning a speech for Kohl – what would be a ten-point programme.[93]

In their evening meeting on Thursday 23 November, Kohl agreed with Teltschik that Deutschlandpolitik was the boss's job (*Chefsache*) and that it was now time to lead opinion formation both in Germany during an election year and with regard to the Four Powers (i.e. the US, the USSR, France and the UK as Allied victors of the Second World War). Otherwise his government would be faced with a diktat.[94] It was also decided then that Kohl would present his proposals for achieving German unity at the earliest suitable opportunity, which would be five days later, on 28 November, during the Bundestag's scheduled debate on the budget. So a small team of eight, led by Teltschik, worked around the clock in utmost secrecy to prepare a draft of the speech. On the afternoon of Saturday 25th this was taken by car from Bonn to the chancellor, who was at his home in Oggersheim.[95]

So obsessed was Kohl about possible leaks, or even being talked out of the speech by his coalition partner or his NATO allies, that everybody in the know was sworn to total silence. For the rest of the weekend, he worked over the draft with a handful of trusted friends and his wife Hannelore, scribbling corrections and queries on the draft and periodically calling Teltschik on the phone. Then, on Sunday night, he asked Hannelore to type up an amended version on her portable typewriter.[96]

As he finalised the draft, several key concerns were in Kohl's mind. In the run-up to the Federal elections, he was keen to position himself as a true German patriot and the chancellor of unity – ahead of the Liberal Genscher who had been promoting his own 'Europa-Plan' and who, on the Prague balcony, had stolen the show from Kohl once before. Nor did he want to be overshadowed by the SPD's great figurehead, the *Altkanzler* Brandt, who had nearly eclipsed Kohl in Berlin on 10 November and was now presenting unification as the culmination of his own Ostpolitik. It was also for electoral reasons that the chancellor decided to omit any mention of the Oder–Neisse line, even though he personally accepted it as Germany's eastern border. After all, to remove the final obstacle in the way of his Warsaw trip he had supported the 8 November Bundestag resolution assuring the inviolability of Poland's post-war borders.[97] But Kohl was cautious not to rub things in further with the expellees. He could not be sure that these traditionally CDU voters might not be seduced by Schönhuber's Republikaner propaganda for the restoration of Germany's 1937 borders.

Another of Kohl's concerns was the language regarding the various stages of German rapprochement and merger on the way to a unified state. Instead of picking up on the Modrow term 'confederation', Kohl preferred the phrase 'confederative structures' so that nobody in the CDU should have reason to accuse him of setting in stone a *Zweistaatlichkeit* of two sovereign German states, as was apparently envisaged by Lafontaine, Bahr and other SPD rivals. At the same time, his own, looser phrase was intended to placate the Soviets and East German officials as well as GDR opposition groups, all of whom feared an overt *Anschluss* on the lines of 1938: the socialist GDR swallowed up by the capitalist FRG. In the long run, of course, Kohl did aspire to a full *Bundestaat* or 'federation', in other words a unified state. But he did not have any clear idea yet what this new Deutschland might look like, though he was sure it should be a *Bundestaat*, not the *Staatenbund* or 'confederation' that East German political elites imagined. And so, Kohl thought, by talking of eventual 'unity' his speech could both reflect and amplify the public mood in East Germany – the still diffuse but increasingly vocal yearning for unity expressed in recent protest slogans such as '*Deutschland, einig Vaterland*' and '*Wir sind ein Volk*'. Indeed, offering *Einheit* ('unity') as the ultimate destination in his speech, he could present 'from above' a vision for East Germans 'below' that would make them look west.

There were so many 'what ifs' to keep in mind. Kohl could barely grasp all the implications. At this stage, he envisaged that the whole intricate process of rapprochement, closer cooperation and eventual unification would take a decade at least. But he was clear about the basic point. That weekend in Oggersheim, he was psyching himself up for a surprise offensive – to put German unity unequivocally on the international agenda.[98]

The eagle arises: Kohl presents his 10 Points to the Bundestag in Bonn

On Tuesday 28 November at 10 a.m. Helmut Kohl addressed the Bundestag. Instead of droning on, as expected, about the budget, Kohl dropped his bombshell of a 'ten-point programme for overcoming the division of Germany and Europe'.⁹⁹ Kohl first talked about 'immediate measures' to deal with the 'tide of refugees' and the 'new scale of tourist traffic'. Second, he promised further cooperation with the GDR in economic, scientific, technological and cultural affairs, and also, third, greatly expanded financial assistance if the GDR 'definitively' and 'irreversibly' embarked on a fundamental transformation of its political and economic system. To this end, he demanded that the SED give up its monopoly on power and pass a new law for 'free, equal and secret elections'. Because the East German people clearly wanted economic and political freedom, he said he was unwilling to 'stabilise conditions that have become untenable'. This was not so much negotiation; more like an ultimatum.

At the core of the speech (points four to eight), the chancellor presented his road map to unity – namely to 'develop confederative structures between both states in Germany ... with the aim of creating a federation'. All this would be done in conformity with the principles of the 1975 Helsinki Final Act, as part of a larger pan-European process: 'The future architecture of Germany must fit in the future architecture of Europe.' Kohl noted that his plan also accorded with Gorbachev's idea of a Common European Home, as well as the Soviet leader's concept of 'freedom of choice', in the sense of the 'people's right to self-determination' as set out in the Final Act. In fact, Kohl reminded the Bundestag, he and Gorbachev had already expressed their agreement on these issues in their Joint Declaration of June 1989. But in the dramatically new circumstances of November the chancellor wanted to go further. He argued that the European Community should now reach out to the reform-oriented states of the Eastern bloc, including the GDR. 'The EC must not end at the Elbe,' he proclaimed. Opening up to the East would allow for 'truly comprehensive European unification'. With this he neutralised and effectively absorbed Genscher's 'Europa-Plan'.

The central theme of Kohl's speech was working towards a 'condition of peace in Europe' within which Germans could regain their unity. This, he made clear at the end, could not be separated from wider questions of international order. 'Linking the German question to the development of Europe as a whole and to West–East relations', he declared, 'takes into account the interests of everyone involved' and 'paves the way for a peaceful and free development in Europe'. Speedy steps would be required towards disarmament and arms control. Here the West German chancellor was appealing directly to the superpowers and to his European allies.

What Kohl did not say is as revealing as what he did say. He omitted the Polish border, and he also made no reference to Germany's membership of NATO, present or future, or to the Reserved Rights of the Allied powers on German soil. Even on his ultimate goal – German unity – Kohl was circumspect. 'No one knows today what a reunified Germany will ultimately look like.' But he kept affirming the German people's 'right' to unity, and he stated emphatically: 'That unity will come, however, when the people of Germany want it – of this, I am certain.' The chancellor pointed expansively to the pattern of 'growing together' that was part of 'the continuity of German history'. State organisation in Germany, he added 'has almost always meant a confederation or a federation. We can certainly draw on these historical experiences.' Kohl may have been looking back to the Bismarck era (the Norddeutscher Bund of 1867 and the Reich of 1871), but he was surely drawing on his own lifetime – the model of the post-war Federal Republic.[100]

The chancellor was relieved to have delivered the speech and exhilarated by its reception. In the lunch break he told aides that the reaction of MPs had been 'almost ecstatic'. What about Genscher, Teltschik asked mischievously – aware that the foreign minister had been totally out of the loop. Kohl grinned. 'Genscher came over to me and said: "Helmut, this was a great speech."'[101]

For the first time Kohl's plan started to clarify the relationship between the processes of German unification and European integration as being interwoven but separate. Neither should impede the other and they could take place at different speeds. German unification must be effected within the framework of the EC but the specific evolution and form of future inner German relations was up to the Germans to decide for themselves.

In sum, Kohl had proposed a blueprint for that new relationship between the two Germanies, and one clearly based on Bonn's terms. Reflecting 'the greater political self-assurance' of the Federal Republic – 'already widely recognised as a weighty economic power', as Vernon Walters, the US ambassador to the FRG, put it – Kohl had presented the world with a fait accompli and set the agenda.[102] And as East Germany unravelled, far more rapidly than anybody had expected, other leaders now had to respond to what the chancellor had put on the table. Coming from a man who had been in essentially reactive mode for the previous three weeks, it was an extremely skilful demonstration of political leadership.

*

What's striking in retrospect is the lack of public attention devoted to Kohl's speech internationally. This was, however, hardly surprising at the time given the drama that was beginning to unfold across Czechoslovakia. On the day Kohl addressed the Bundestag, the front page of the *New York Times* ran as its main headline 'Millions of Czechoslovaks Increase Pressure on Party With 2-Hour General Strike'. A foretaste of Kohl's speech was buried on page 14 stating that he would 'call for a form of confederation', mainly to dispel criticism that his reaction to the 'tumultuous changes taking place in East Germany' had been 'passive and grounded in West German party politics'.[103] On Wednesday 29 November, Czechoslovakia was again the main news with a banner headline across the paper's front page 'Prague Party to Yield Some Cabinet Posts and Drop Insistence on Primacy in Society'. Kohl and his 'confederation outline' got a small box lower down the page.[104] Thereafter Germany disappeared from the *Times*'s front page for the rest of week, with Prague continuing to dominate the news, together with the weekend's Soviet–American summit in Malta. Even in the Federal Republic, the story was seen as an essentially domestic issue. In any case from Thursday, all other news was eclipsed by the latest act of Baader–Meinhof terrorism, the shock killing of Kohl intimate, Alfred Herrhausen.[105]

Despite the lack of immediate public reaction, however, the 'Ten Point' plan was a ticking time bomb. Whatever Kohl might have hoped, his speech naturally opened him up to comment, mostly critical, from all the major powers. Because in his vision, as Ambassador Walters put it, 'the German states, virtually alone, would plan their future'.[106] Now that the chancellor had gone out on a limb, he had to gear up for another round of international diplomacy to rebuff the criticism, and secure, if not acceptance, at least tolerance for his blueprint for German self-determination. This round would go on until the middle of December.

The first and most important person to be kept happy was Bush. The chancellor had sent the president a pre-emptive letter on the morning of his speech – the only advance warning he sent out. Kohl couched it as a steer on how the US president should handle Gorbachev at Malta

but his lengthy missive offered a wide-ranging analysis of the revolutionary processes in Europe, the situation in the Soviet Union and the
imperatives for arms reduction, both strategic and conventional. This
was all a prelude to what was really on his mind, namely how Bush
should discuss the German question at Malta. Kohl made a point of
linking Gorbachev's 'freedom-of-choice policy' in 1989 with America's
grand design in 1776 for 'life, liberty and the pursuit of happiness'. He
stressed that the current bid for emancipation was coming from the
people themselves – Poles, Hungarians, Czechs as well as East Germans
– and that this was no simple turn to the West but a historically significant movement for reform emanating from within each nation and its
distinctive culture. With this statement he sought a neat way out of any
Western 'victory' rhetoric while at the same time giving weight to the
core theme of his letter, 'self-determination': so crucial for his approach
to resolving the German question. Only then did the chancellor discuss
unification – the longest element in his message – setting out his Ten
Points. With an eye on the upcoming summit, Kohl explicitly asked Bush
for his support, insisting that the superpowers must not simply sort out
Germany over his head, like Roosevelt and Stalin in 1945. There should
not, he told Bush, be 'any parallel between Yalta and Malta'.[107]

Interestingly Egon Krenz also wrote to Bush about Kohl's speech – a
striking sign of the times in that he clearly realised that Moscow's support
would no longer be sufficient to ensure the GDR's survival. Krenz warned
of 'nationalism' and 'a revival of Nazi ideas' – clearly pointing the finger
at Bonn – and asked the president to support the status quo, in other
words the two German states as members of 'different alliances'. Krenz
never got a reply. Bush knew he was a nobody whose days in office were
numbered.[108]

But the president picked up the phone next morning to talk to Kohl.
The White House had immediately grasped the implications of the
Ten-Point Plan, seeing it as a strategic move in international politics
rather than a mere tactical game on the domestic plane. Scowcroft was
concerned about Kohl's bold, unilateral step but Bush, though surprised,
was not particularly worried. He knew that the chancellor could not
pursue unification on his own and doubted that Kohl would want to
alienate his closest ally. 'I was certain he would consult us before going
further,' Bush reflected later. 'He needed us.'[109]

On 29 November president and chancellor talked for thirty minutes.
First, they discussed arrangements for a meeting as 'personal friends'

straight after Malta, from which it was agreed to exclude Genscher. Kohl would bring only his unification mastermind Teltschik – a decision that once more underlined the institutional and personal rivalry between the Chancellery and the Foreign Ministry. Then Kohl explained in more detail how he hoped to proceed towards unification. Despite the display of solidarity at Strasbourg a week before, the chancellor remained concerned about the extent of Mitterrand's support. He also made clear his reliance on the United States. 'History left us with good cards in our hands,' he told Bush. 'I hope with the cooperation of our American friends we can play them well.' The president, as usual, did not waste words. 'I am very supportive of your general approach. I note your stress on stability. We feel the same way. Stability is the key word. We have tried to do nothing that would force a reaction by the USSR.' Bush went on to amplify this latter point. He recognised that the Soviet economy was doing much worse than he had previously realised, yet Shevardnadze had stated proudly that the Soviets did not want America to 'bail us out'. So help would have to be offered 'in a sensitive way'. But Bush and Kohl agreed that Western aid would be needed because 'we want him to succeed'. The chancellor was gratified by the conversation, thanking Bush for his 'good words' – 'Germans East and West are listening very carefully. Every word of sympathy for self-determination and unity is very important now.'[110]

Commenting on the phone call to the press straight afterwards, Bush said: 'I feel comfortable. I think we're on track.' Having been mocked when vice president for his reluctance to indulge in what he had called the 'vision thing', he was asked about how he saw Europe's future over the next five or ten years.[111] The president was now sufficiently relaxed to joke: 'In terms of the "vision thing", the aspirations, I spelled it out in little-noted speeches last spring and summer, which I would like everyone to go back and reread. And I'll have a quiz on it.' When the laughter died down, Bush continued, 'You'll see in there some of the "vision thing" – a Europe whole and free.' And, he added, 'I think a Europe whole and free is less vision than perhaps reality.' But the president had to admit: 'How we get there and what that means and when the German question is resolved and all of these things – I can't answer more definitely.'[112]

The mood was much less positive in Moscow. Kohl was moving too fast and planning Europe's future 'without taking the view of the other Germany at all into account', declared Vadim Zagladin, one of Gorbachev's advisers. The Soviet leader – on a state visit in Rome – told Italian premier

Giulio Andreotti bluntly that 'two Germanies remained the reality' and that 'the reunification of FRG and GDR was no topical issue'. Kohl, he said, was 'playing the revanchist tune for the forthcoming elections'. Later in the press conference, Gorbachev added, 'Let history decide. It is not necessary to initiate something or push forward half-baked processes.'[113] There was also a backlash in West European capitals. Thatcher let Kohl know in no uncertain terms that unification was 'not on the agenda' and French diplomats publicly expressed strong reservations about the chancellor's 'precipitate' action.[114]

Kohl, it seemed, had unleashed a firestorm and the man who had to do the firefighting was Genscher. The foreign minister had been totally blindsided just a few days before when the chancellor dropped his 'Ten Point' bombshell. Obliged to grin and bear it, Genscher congratulated Kohl through gritted teeth in the Bundestag and then told the world that the policy laid out in the Ten Points represented nothing less than 'the continuity of our foreign, security and Deutschland policies'. Of course, Genscher resented that he had been sidelined as Kohl's coalition partner.[115] Yet he had done the same to Kohl on the Prague balcony a few months before. And they had different instincts about how unification should be achieved – Kohl favouring the Adenauer line of *Westbindung*, drawing East Germany into the Federal Republic and into the Western alliance, whereas Genscher was more inclined to extending Ostpolitik into a full pan-European architecture. But despite their rivalry, despite their differences on means, the two men fundamentally agreed on ends, namely German unity. For Genscher, this was a matter of both head and heart. That's why, swallowing his pride, he was willing to play firefighter and try to bring London, Paris and Moscow onside.

Technically, of course, the foreign minister did not have responsibility for Deutschlandpolitik because inner-German relations did not constitute 'foreign' policy. Nevertheless, Genscher was now drawn fully into the unification issue because of the external complications it engendered – relations with the FRG's neighbours, Four Powers' rights, the prerogatives of the superpowers, the domain of international organisations as well as questions of territory and security. As Genscher saw things, it was his duty to build international consensus and pave the way to unity.

Moscow would obviously be the most problematic obstacle, requiring the greatest amount of persuasion. What's more, the Soviets held strong cards: they were a nuclear superpower, one of the Four Powers and had more than half a million troops and dependants stationed in the GDR.

This gave the Kremlin several options. It could press for a pan-European structure. Or offer Germany unity for neutrality, as Stalin tried in 1952. It could simply say *nyet* to unity, or decide to use force to hold the GDR in place. But were things really secure in the Kremlin? Would perestroika be reversed? What about the deteriorating economy? Could secessionist demands from the republics be contained? Might there even be a coup?

And so, a week later, on 5 December Genscher flew into the Soviet capital – on a dark, gloomy afternoon in the middle of a snowstorm. As his motorcade crawled into the city, it passed another heading in the opposite direction towards the airport. This was Krenz, Modrow and other SED dignitaries who had just finished their own business in the Kremlin. Genscher speculated wryly that the Soviets had orchestrated events so as to avoid an awkward German–German encounter in the airport.[116]

Tension was therefore already in the air. And what followed proved to be the 'most disagreeable encounter' with the Soviets that Genscher could ever remember. So ill-tempered was his meeting with Gorbachev that he later asked the German notetaker to write up the meeting in a somewhat more emollient tone.[117] 'Never before and never afterwards have I experienced Gorbachev so upset and so bitter,' Genscher remarked in his memoirs. The Soviet leader was unable to restrain his anger at Kohl's lack of consultation. According to Chernyaev he had been fuming for days, though this may have been due to pressures at home as well as the worsening situation in Eastern Europe at large. Whatever was going on in Gorbachev's mind, Genscher was a convenient target for his wrath. In fact, Genscher felt, at times Gorbachev was so furious that it was simply impossible to discuss important issues with any seriousness.[118]

Genscher, however, was not flustered and loyally defended the chancellor's policies. He underlined that Germany would never 'go it alone', that the Federal Republic was firmly tied into the EC and CSCE (i.e. the Helsinki Final Act), and that the 'growing together of the two German states' would have to be fitted into these frameworks. He also affirmed Bonn's *Politik der Verantwortung* ('politics of responsibility') and that the FRG adhered to its treaty commitments, not least on the Polish border. This, he said, was important to stress in the light of Germany's 'history, its geopolitical position and the size of its population'. Gorbachev let him say his piece but then retorted angrily that Kohl's Ten Points were wholly 'irresponsible' and a grave 'political mistake' which presented an 'ultimatum' to the East German government; Kohl was trying to prescribe a particular 'internal order' for the GDR, a sovereign state. 'Even Hitler didn't allow himself anything like that!' Shevardnadze piped up.

By now seething, Gorbachev denounced Kohl's programme as 'genuine revanchism', delivered as an 'address to subjects' and nothing less than a 'funeral' of the European process. He was getting into his stride. The Ten Points were 'irresponsible'. German policy was in a total 'mess' (*Wirrwarr*). 'The Germans are such an emotional people.' Don't forget, he added, 'where headless politics had led in the past'.

Genscher cut in: 'We know our historic mistakes and have no intention of repeating them.'

'You,' said Gorbachev, 'had a direct role in developing Ostpolitik. Now you are endangering all this,' just for the sake of 'election battles'. He kept criticising Kohl for 'running around' and 'taking hasty actions' which 'undermined the pan-European process that had been laboriously developed'.

Gorbachev also tried to drive a wedge between Genscher and Kohl. 'By the way, Herr Genscher, it seems to me that you only found out about the Ten Points in the Bundestag speech.'

Genscher admitted that this was true but added 'It's our internal affair. We resolve this ourselves.'

Well, said Gorbachev drily, 'you can see for yourself that your "internal affairs" has annoyed everybody else'.

The Soviet leader ended with something like an olive branch. 'Don't take everything I said personally, Herr Genscher. You know that we have a different relationship to you than to others.' The implication seemed clear: Genscher was not Kohl. The foreign minister was getting it in the neck because the chancellor was not present. Gorbachev felt frankly betrayed by Kohl. It was a far cry from their balmy June evening on the banks of the Rhine. Relations would clearly take time and effort to repair.[119]

Although Gorbachev and the Soviet Union were the main problem, Kohl and Genscher faced problems on their Western front as well. And in London there was a leader as fiery as Gorbachev and at least as critical of any moves towards German unification – not least because Margaret Thatcher was hung up on history. Born in 1925 and raised in the provincial Lincolnshire town of Grantham, she had come of age during Hitler's war, amid the mythology of Britain's 'finest hour'. This permanently coloured her view of post-war Germany. Trained first as a research chemist and as a barrister, she had entered Parliament as a Tory MP in 1959 at the height of the Cold War and became prime minister twenty years later, just as détente was freezing over. Since then, her decade in power had been marked by a radical programme of economic liberalisation and a forceful nationalism for which she gained (and relished) the nickname 'Iron Lady'.

Her foreign policy was traditional, built around ideas of a balance of power. Thatcher was passionate about the 'special relationship', assiduously cultivating Ronald Reagan. She was equally ardent about nuclear deterrence, advocating the modernisation of NATO's theatre nuclear forces and pushing through the deployment of cruise missiles despite fierce opposition from the left. She was as convinced as Reagan that communism was an ideology of the past and therefore endorsed Gorbachev's reform policies, though keeping a wary eye on their consequences for Soviet power. Within Europe she was a ferocious critic of deeper economic and political integration, especially the Delors Plan, although she did sign up enthusiastically to the single market in 1986. And as the Soviet bloc crumbled in 1989, her biggest fear was that a new German hegemon could destroy the European equilibrium, painfully constructed over four decades. The combination of a single currency and a unified, sovereign Germany in the centre of Europe would be simply 'intolerable', she told Mitterrand on 1 September. She had, she said, 'read much on the history of Germany during her vacation and was very disturbed'.[120] Three weeks later, in similar vein, she informed Gorbachev that 'although NATO traditionally made statements supporting Germany's aspirations to be reunited, in practice we would not welcome it at all'.[121] In other words, even before the Wall had fallen, she was clearly 'on the warpath' against German unity.[122]

Thatcher seemed to object to pretty much everything, and didn't hide it. Yet she had little to offer in the way of practical alternatives. She longed to see the end of communism but dreaded the effect this might have on the European power balance. When Genscher visited her on the day after Kohl's speech, she worried about Gorbachev's fate. If Germany unified, the Soviet leader fell and the Warsaw Pact disintegrated, what then? It was imperative, she lectured Genscher, to first develop democratic structures in Eastern Europe. She insisted that political freedom in Eastern Europe would only be sustainable if economic liberalisation were properly implemented, and blamed Gorbachev for being too fixated with repairing socialism rather than ditching it. The changes now under way in Eastern Europe, geared towards freedom and democracy, must take place against a 'stable background'. In other words, she said, 'one should leave the other things as they are'. History had shown that Central Europe's problems always started with minority issues; if one tinkered with borders, everything would unravel. That was how the First World War had broken out. Ten days ago in Paris, she asserted, unification and borders had not been on the table; now Kohl's speech had shaken all the foundations.

Genscher tried to calm her down by refocusing on the topic of conventional arms-reduction talks to stabilise the heart of Europe. He, of course, wanted to persuade the Soviets to withdraw their troops from eastern Germany. But Thatcher jumped on that. She didn't want Soviet troop withdrawals if that meant the Americans would pull out as well. For her, it was not just a question of strategic balance or European security, the troop question was also about keeping the Germans under control.[123]

Britain's Foreign Secretary Douglas Hurd sat in on the whole meeting, but hardly said a word. He had little opportunity whenever Thatcher went on the rampage. But the Foreign and Commonwealth Office (FCO) was genuinely concerned about the line Thatcher was taking.[124] An internal FCO memo on the day of Genscher's visit acknowledged that Germans 'see our position as being outside the mainstream'. As indeed did Washington: the president was 'taking his distance from us on the Warsaw Pact and on German reunification'. As for Thatcher's obsession with Gorbachev's political fragility, the FCO considered this greatly exaggerated because Gorbachev himself was 'not intervening to stop communism being swept away in Eastern Europe'. So there was a real danger that 'we are being *plus royaliste que le roi*'. And they warned against a status quo policy and being left behind by not being seen to share Bush's vision of a Europe 'whole and free'. If, *in extremis*, the PM decided to block German unification by asserting Britain's position as one of the four victor powers, 'we should not count on carrying anyone else with us'.[125]

Thatcher was simply not on the same page as her diplomats. Not only was she blunt with Genscher, she did not hesitate to speak out against Kohl, whom she disliked personally – a fat, sausage-munching, Teutonic stereotype – as well as resenting him as the embodiment of the colossus of Europe.[126]

The British prime minister was the most outspoken Western critic of the Ten Points but Genscher also had difficulties with the French president. Mitterrand was shocked at being left in the dark by Kohl – especially after their intense discussions throughout November, in Bonn, Paris and Strasbourg. Kohl had even written to him at length on the 27th about the future of economic and monetary union without dropping a hint of what he would announce next day about unification. Nevertheless, biting his tongue, Mitterrand told the press in Athens where he was on a state visit, that although he expected the Four Powers to be kept in the loop by Bonn, the German desire for unity was 'legitimate' and that he had no intention of opposing their aspirations. What's more, he said, he trusted the Germans to make sure that the other European peoples would not be confronted by German faits accomplis made in secret.[127]

When Mitterrand met Genscher in the Elysée Palace, their forty-five-minute encounter was polite but rather distant. Invited to speak first, Genscher highlighted his credentials as a European. He insisted that the FRG was fully committed to EC integration and willing to engage with the East. He believed that the destiny of Germany must be tied to the destiny of Europe. European reunification could not happen without German reunification. Nor did he want the dynamism of the EC's integration process to be left behind because of the energy devoted to reshaping East–West relations. And NATO, too, should get engaged – not least because America's presence in Europe and on German soil was an 'existential necessity'.[128]

Mitterrand heard him out but then delivered his own lecture, expressed with mounting intensity, as he reflected on his personal odyssey through two world wars. Born in 1916 – the year of the Franco-German slaughterhouse at Verdun – Mitterrand was himself a veteran of 1940. Like any patriotic Frenchman, he had historical obsessions about Germany. But, like most of France's post-war leadership, especially since the Adenauer–de Gaulle entente of 1963, he was deeply committed to Franco-German reconciliation, to fostering the 'special relationship' between Paris and Bonn and to the leading role of their two countries in European integration.[129] Although a socialist and therefore ideologically at odds with the Christian Democrat chancellor, he and Kohl had become good friends – famously standing hand in hand in 1984 at the Verdun memorial. Despite such public displays of friendship, however, Mitterrand remained ambivalent about the German state.[130]

German unity looked fine as long as it remained a distant prospect.

Mitterrand had told Thatcher in September that he was less alarmed than she, not only because he believed that the EC, and specifically the single currency, would act as a restraint, but also because he did not envisage German unification happening quickly. Gorbachev, he told her confidently, would never accept a united Germany in NATO and Washington would never tolerate the FRG leaving the Alliance: '*Alors, ne nous inquiétons pas: disons qu'elle se fera quand les Allemands le décideront, mais en sachant que les deux Grands nous en protégeront*' ('So let's not worry: let's say it will happen when the Germans decide, but in the knowledge that the two superpowers will protect us from them').[131]

But now, Mitterrand told Genscher, things had clearly moved on. With Europe in flux, old territorial questions had been awakened. One could not even rule out a return to 1913, and a world on the brink of war. It was imperative that unification, whenever it occurred, should be caught in the safety net of an even more consolidated European Community. If that integration process was disrupted he feared that the continent might return to days of alliance politics. And he made clear to Genscher that he saw Kohl as being disruptive, acting as the 'brake' on EMU. Up to now, he added, the Federal Republic had always been a motor in the European unification project. Now it was stalling. And if Germany and France did not see eye to eye at the Strasbourg summit in December, others would profit. Thatcher would not only block any progress on Europe but would also gang up with others against German unity.

Unlike Thatcher, Mitterrand accepted that German unity was unstoppable and, indeed, justifiable. But he insisted that this unstoppable process must be properly integrated within the EC project. 'Europe' not only helped absorb his ingrained suspicions of the Germans, he also felt it gave him leverage over Bonn: that was the benefit of subsuming the Deutschmark in the single currency. Whereas Thatcher, who was far more Germanophobe, had no such weapons in her armoury: she loathed the European project and abhorred a single currency. Indeed she was increasingly on the margins of European politics. Not that this worried the British prime minister. Indeed she seemed to love it when she was in a minority, convinced of her own rectitude.[132]

'Helmut! Can we start?' – 'I'm coming, I'm coming!':
Priorities at the European Council in Strasbourg

This was the atmosphere in which the EC leaders gathered in Strasbourg on 8–9 December. Now Kohl, not Genscher, had to face the music – and he didn't enjoy it. As he wrote later in his memoirs, he could not remember such a 'tense' and 'unfriendly' meeting. It was like being in court.[133] Unification was on everyone's mind. Long-standing colleagues who had appeared so trusting of the FRG's European-ness, now seemed terrified that Bonn would go its own way – like a train that was suddenly moving faster and faster and might go in a totally different direction from what anyone had expected. Kohl felt that the room was full of questions: was he still trustworthy? Was the FRG still a reliable partner? Would the Germans remain loyal to the West? Only the leaders of Spain and Ireland embraced the idea of German unification wholeheartedly. Kohl felt Belgium and Luxembourg would not cause problems. But everyone else had their fears and did not conceal them. Giulio Andreotti of Italy openly warned of 'pan-Germanism'; even Kohl's fellow Christian Democrat, Ruud Lubbers of the Netherlands, could not hide his distaste for Germany's unification ambitions.[134]

But it was Thatcher who really got under Kohl's skin. Her hobby horse throughout the two days was 'inviolability of borders'. She brought it up in the first working meeting, and Kohl was greatly irritated because he sensed that her target was not Poland's western border but the divide between East and West Germany. Over dinner that evening, haggling over the wording of the summit communiqué, Thatcher even threatened to veto the whole thing if the CSCE principle of 'inviolability of borders' was not explicitly spelled out. Kohl again lost his temper, angrily reminding her that EC heads of government had on numerous occasions affirmed what she was now questioning: German unification through self-determination according to the Helsinki Final Act. Thatcher erupted: 'We have beaten the Germans twice! And now they're back again!' Kohl bit his lip. He knew she was saying blatantly what many others around the table thought.[135]

He was particularly sensitive because he knew Thatcher and Mitterrand had held their own tête-à-tête earlier in the day. What he did not know was that during the meeting, she pulled out of her famous handbag two maps showing Germany's borders in 1937 and 1945. She pointed to Silesia, Pomerania and East Prussia: 'They will take all of this, and Czechoslovakia.' Mitterrand played along with her at times – for instance saying that 'we must create special relations between France and Great Britain just as in 1913 and 1938' – but he also stated calmly that unification could not be prevented, adding 'we must discuss with the Germans and respect the treaties' that had affirmed the principle of unification. But Thatcher would have none of it: 'If Germany controls events, she will get Eastern Europe in her power, just as Japan has done in the Pacific, and that will be unacceptable from our point of view. The others must join together to avoid it.'[136]

But they didn't. When the communiqué was published it was clear that France and Germany had stuck together, firmly committed to both monetary union and German unification. What's more, the others who had griped were all now on board.

On monetary union, the EC 12 ignored vehement objections from Thatcher, and took a new and important step towards creating a central bank and a common currency. They agreed to call a special intergovernmental conference in December 1990 – after completing closer coordination of economic policies under the Delors Report's stage 1, scheduled for July, and getting through the FRG elections (to satisfy Kohl). Clearly the recent upheavals in Eastern Europe had added impetus to economic integration. Mitterrand argued that the Community needed to be strengthened to face the challenge of helping the 'emerging democracies of Eastern Europe as they move toward greater freedom and to handle the growing prospect of German reunification'. This French-led consensus left Thatcher in her familiar position as the sole opponent of accelerated integration, extending also to her refusal to sign a Community Charter of Social Rights that everyone else happily approved. Its broad endorsement of labour, welfare and other workers' rights was supported as an important counterweight to the strongly pro-business orientation of much of the integration agenda.[137]

In a separate statement, EC leaders also formally endorsed the idea of a single German state, but they attached some conditions which were intended to ensure that German unity did not cause European instability. 'We seek the strengthening of the state of peace in Europe in which the German people will regain its unity through free self-determination. This process should take place peacefully and democratically, in full respect of the relevant agreements and treaties and of all the principles defined by the Helsinki Final Act, in a context of dialogue and East–West cooperation. It also has to be placed in the perspective of European integration.' In other words, Western integration and pan-European security, underwritten by the United States, were integral to any process of German unification.

The EC statement did not ignore their 'common responsibility' for closer cooperation with the USSR and Eastern Europe in what was called 'this decisive phase in the history of Europe'. In particular, it stressed the EC's determination to support economic reform in these countries. There was also an affirmation of the European Community's future role: 'It remains the cornerstone of a new European architecture and, in its will to openness, a mooring for a future European equilibrium.'[138]

Kohl was enormously relieved. Despite all the arguments, his Ten Point gamble had paid off. With Europe and America fully behind him,[139] it seemed that he was now free to develop Deutschlandpolitik in the way he wanted.

*

As soon as he got back to Bonn, Kohl started planning the details of his meeting with Hans Modrow in Dresden, which was scheduled for 19 December. But no West German chancellor could take anything for granted. That seemed to be the lesson of forty years of history – with the FRG always beholden to the occupying powers, always bearing the burden of the Hitler era, always edgy about its lack of sovereignty.

One worry was the French announcement on 22 November that

Mitterrand would visit the GDR on 20 December. Why now? Ostensibly his trip was simply to reciprocate Honecker's visit to Paris in January 1988 but Kohl was aggrieved that he – the most interested party – was being upstaged. At a deeper level, he felt that the French president was being two-faced – professing support for Kohl and the drive for unity yet apparently cultivating a failing state for France's own benefit. Moreover, on 6 December Mitterrand had met Gorbachev in Kiev to talk over Germany and Eastern Europe. Getting to the GDR ahead of Mitterrand was therefore the main reason for fixing the Kohl–Modrow meeting for the day before.[140]

On 8 December, there was another bombshell. Kohl learned that the ambassadors of the Four Powers were going to meet in Berlin to discuss the current situation. And not merely in Berlin but in the Allied Kommandatura – notorious to Germans as the centre of the occupation regime of the 1940s and a venue not used since 1971 when the Quadripartite Agreement on access to the city had been signed. The Soviets, apparently taking advantage of the EC summit, called for the discussion to be held on 11 December, just three days later. Asked if Bonn would be displeased about the meeting, a senior French official retorted: 'That is the point of holding it.' The Kohl government was indeed furious; its anger subsided only when the Americans promised to make sure that the agenda was limited to Berlin rather than straddling the German question as a whole. On the day itself, robust diplomacy by the Americans was required to kill off this rather crude Russian ploy to give the Four Powers a formalised role in deciding the German question.[141]

Coming just a few days after Gorbachev's explosion to Genscher, the Soviet powerplay at the Kommandatura persuaded the chancellor that he had to make a determined effort to explain his Ten Points to Gorbachev and disarm Soviet criticism. He instructed Teltschik to draft a personal letter to the Soviet leader, eventually running to eleven typescript pages laying out a very carefully constructed argument.

In it Kohl explained that his motivation for the Ten Points had been to stop reacting and running after events, and instead to begin shaping future policies. But he also insisted that his speech was couched, and must be understood, within the wider international context. He referred specifically to the 'parallel and mutually reinforcing' process of East–West rapprochement as evidenced at Malta, closer EC integration as agreed in Strasbourg, and the likely shifts of the existing military alliances into more political forms and what he hoped would be the evolution of the CSCE process via a follow-up conference (Helsinki II). In these various processes, the chancellor emphasised, his pathway to unity would be embedded. He added that there was no 'strict timetable', nor had he set out any preconditions – as Gorbachev wrongly alleged. Rather the speech gave the GDR options and presented a gradual, step-by-step approach that offered a way to weave together a multitude of political processes. Kohl then summarised the ten points in detail before stating at the end of the letter that he sought to overcome the division of both Germany and Europe 'organically'. There was no reason, he insisted, for Gorbachev to fear any German attempts at 'going it alone' (*Alleingänge*) or 'special paths' (*Sonderwege*), nor any 'backward-looking nationalism'. In sum, declared Kohl, 'the future of all Germans is Europe'. He argued that they were now at a 'historical turning point for Europe and the whole world in which political leaders would be tested as to whether and how they had cooperatively addressed the problems'. In this spirit, he proposed that the two of them should discuss the situation face-to-face, and offered to meet Gorbachev wherever he wanted.[142]

This weighty letter, however, appeared to have no effect. On 18 December, the evening before his visit to Dresden, the chancellor received a letter from Gorbachev. Kohl assumed this would be a reply but Gorbachev addressed other issues.[143] In a brusque two pages the Soviet leader referred only to the Genscher visit and reiterated the USSR's view that the Ten Points were virtually an 'ultimatum'. Like the GDR, he said, the Soviets viewed this approach as 'unacceptable' and a violation of the Helsinki accords and also of agreements made in the current year. Finally, referring to his speech to the Central Committee on 9 December, Gorbachev highlighted the GDR's Warsaw Pact membership and East Berlin's status as a 'strategic ally' of the USSR, and he asserted that the Soviet Union would do anything to 'neutralise' all interference in East German affairs.[144]

Having heard much of this already via Genscher, Kohl was not seriously put out. What the letter seemed to show, he felt, was that Gorbachev was under the spell of Hans Modrow's visit to Moscow on 4–5 December. Having not himself visited East Germany since the 7 October celebrations, the Soviet leader had no first-hand feeling of the situation or the popular mood. Taking his cue from Modrow – with his talk of reformed communism, continued East German independence, and a treaty community with the FRG – perhaps the Soviet leader was anxious to demonstrate his commitment to the GDR. That, at any rate, was the most positive reading of Gorbachev's letter. A more pessimistic take was to focus on the Kremlin leadership's rejection of the 'tempo and finality' of the German–German march toward unity and Gorbachev's evident concern for 'the geopolitical and strategic repercussions of this process for the Soviet Union itself'.[145]

The battle of the letters strengthened Kohl's determination to exploit the window of opportunity before Christmas – to take the measure of Modrow and, at last, to immerse himself in East Germany's revolution. Ironically, the West German chancellor had since the fall of the Wall travelled to West Berlin, Poland, France and most recently Hungary – but not to the GDR itself. This omission was finally rectified on the morning of 19 December when Kohl, Teltschik and a small entourage from the Chancellery landed in Dresden. Foreign Minister Genscher was not on board.

Kohl was a tactile politician, with keen antennae for public moods. He may have talked with passion about German unity to the Bundestag in Bonn but – as he admitted in his memoirs – it was when he encountered the cheering crowd at Dresden airport on that icy Tuesday morning that he really got the point. 'There were thousands of people waiting amid a sea of black, red, and gold flags,' Kohl recalled. 'It suddenly became clear to me: this regime is finished. Unification is coming!' As they descended the stairs onto the tarmac, there was another telltale sign: an ashen-faced Modrow gazing up at them with a 'strained' expression. Kohl turned round and murmured: 'That's it. It's in the bag.'[146]

The leaders of the two Germanies sat next to each other in the car as they were driven at a snail's pace into the city. They made small talk about their upbringing: Modrow, unmoving and self-conscious, went on about his working-class background and how he had risen from being a trained locksmith to completing an economics degree at the Humboldt University in Berlin. But Kohl was not really listening. His eyes were on the crowd lining the streets. He could barely believe what he saw. Nor could Teltschik, who captured the scenes in his diary: 'whole workforces had come out of their factories – still wearing their blue overalls, women, children, entire school classes, amazingly many young people. They were clapping, waving big white cloths, laughing, thoroughly enjoying themselves. Some were simply standing there, crying. Joy, hope, expectation radiated from their faces – but also worry, uncertainty, doubt.' In front of the Hotel Bellevue, where the formal talks were to take place, thousands more young people had congregated shouting 'Helmut! Helmut!' Some held banners proclaiming *Keine Gewalt* ('No violence').[147]

Kohl and his aides felt exhilarated. During a brief pit stop in the hotel everyone had to unburden their feelings. They knew it was a 'great day', a 'historical day', an 'experience that cannot be repeated'. After all that, the formal meetings were something of an anticlimax. The East German premier – stressed out, eyes down – went through his party piece about the need for economic aid and the reality of two German states – none of which particularly moved Kohl. When Modrow proposed that the Germanies first create a 'community of treaties' and then talk about what to do next 'in about one or two years', Kohl was incredulous. Demanding a frank and realistic talk about cooperation, he told Modrow there was no way he was coming up with DM 15 billion, nor would he allow any money, of whatever sum, to be designated by the historically loaded term '*Lastenausgleich*' ('compensation').

By the end of the forty-five minutes a shaken Modrow realised that he had to operate on Kohl's terms. That meant dropping his demand that the Joint Declaration they were going to sign should refer to a 'treaty community originated by two sovereign states'. The chancellor totally rejected the language of 'two states' because that risked cementing the status quo and propping up the mere shell of an East German state. Instead, he focused on the German people and their exercise of the right to self-determination. By now Kohl was quite clear in his mind about what East Germans wanted: a single, unified Deutschland.[148]

Who's boss? Kohl with Modrow in Dresden

After a rather stiff lunch and a press conference with journalists, the chancellor walked to the ruins of the Frauenkirche – destroyed in the Allied firebombing in 1945. In his memoirs Kohl claimed he had spoken to the crowd spontaneously, but in fact a speech had been prepared very carefully with Teltschik the night before. Amid the blackened stones of the eighteenth-century church – which had become a 'memorial against war' and a prime site in 1989 for anti-regime protests – Kohl climbed on a temporary wooden podium in the darkening winter evening. He looked out at a crowd of some 10,000. Many were waving banners and placards proclaiming such slogans as '*Kohl, Kanzler der Deutschen*' ('Kohl, Chancellor of the Germans'), '*Wir sind ein Volk*' ('We are one people') and '*Einheit jetzt*' ('Unity now').[149] But, presumably, blending into the mass of people were operatives of the Stasi and the Soviet security services – maybe even the KGB's special agent in Dresden, Vladimir Putin.

His throat tight with emotion, the chancellor began slowly, feeling the weight of expectation. He conveyed warm regards to the people of Dresden from their fellow citizens in the Federal Republic. Exultant cheers. He gestured to show he had more to say. It got very quiet. Kohl then talked about peace, self-determination and free elections. He said a bit about his meeting with Modrow and talked of future economic cooperation and the development of confederative structures, and then moved to his climax. 'Let me also say on this square, which is so rich in history, that my goal – should the historical hour permit it – remains the unity of our nation.' Thunderous applause. 'And, dear friends, I know that we can achieve this goal and that the hour will come when we will work together towards it, provided that we do it with reason and sound judgement and a sense for what is possible.'

Trying to calm the surging emotions, Kohl proceeded to speak matter-of-factly about the long and difficult path to this common future, echoing lines he had used in West Berlin the day after the fall of the Wall. 'We, the Germans, do not live alone in Europe and in the world. One look at a map will show that everything that changes here will have an effect on all of our neighbours, those in the East and those in the West ... The house of Germany, our house, must be built under a European roof. That must be the goal of our policies.' He concluded: 'Christmas is the festival of the family and friends. Particularly now, in these days, we are beginning to see ourselves again as a German family ... From here in Dresden, I send my greetings to all our compatriots in the GDR and the Federal Republic of Germany ... God bless our German fatherland!'

By the time Kohl ended, the people felt serene – mesmerised by the moment. No one made any move to leave the square. Then an elderly woman climbed onto the podium, embraced him and, starting to cry, said quietly: 'We all thank you!'[150]

That night and next morning Kohl talked with Protestant and Catholic clergy from the GDR and leaders of the newly formed opposition parties.[151] All his meetings in Dresden simply proved to Kohl that the GDR elites were in denial about the desires of the broader public. The crowds in Dresden did not want a modernised GDR standing alone, as touted by the opposition, or an update of the old regime, led by Modrow and the renamed communists (PDS) in some kind of confederation with the FRG. Twenty-four hours amid the people of Dresden convinced the West German chancellor that his Ten-Point Plan was already becoming out of date. In what was now a race against time, those 'new confederative structures' he had been advocating were too ponderous and would take too long. The chancellor no longer had any inclination to support the Modrow government – clearly a flimsy, transitional operation that lacked any kind of democratic legitimacy and was merely trying to save a sinking ship from going under fast.[152]

Kohl could suddenly see a window of opportunity opening up in the midst of crisis. The cheers of the East German crowds spurred him on and served as the justification for dramatic action. As would-be driver of the unification train, he was now ready to move the acceleration lever up several notches. And he was also energised by the overwhelmingly positive reception in the media for his Dresden visit – both at home and abroad. The common theme next day was that a West German chancellor had laid the foundation for unification, and had done so on East German soil.[153]

Dresden was the beginning of a veritable sea change in public perceptions of Kohl. He had bonded with the people. He had addressed the East Germans repeatedly as 'dear friends'. He had clearly relished being bathed in the adulation of the masses. The chants of 'Helmut! Helmut!' revealed the familiarity East Germans had suddenly come to feel for the West German leader. With all this shown live on TV in both Germanies, the chancellor and this mood of exuberant patriotism flooded into German living rooms from Berlin to Cologne, from Rostock to Munich.[154]

There were, of course, similar cheers for Willy Brandt at an SDP rally in the GDR city of Magdeburg on the same day. Hans-Dietrich Genscher was also greeted enthusiastically when he returned to East Germany to speak in his home town, Halle, and in Leipzig on 17 December.[155] But Kohl in Dresden outshone both of them by miles. Rarely had the chancellor – often the butt of ridicule as a clumsy provincial – experienced such an ecstatic reaction in his own West Germany. With national elections in the FRG now less than a year away and German unity looming as the dominant issue, Dresden was the best public-relations coup that the chancellor could have dreamed of.

Nor was there much international competition. On 19 December, the same day Kohl spoke in Dresden, Eduard Shevardnadze became the first Soviet foreign minister to enter the precincts of NATO[156] – another symbolic occasion in the endgame of the Cold War. On the 20th François Mitterrand became the first leader of the Western allies to pay an official state visit to the East German capital – another bridging moment across the crumbling Wall.[157] But both of these were almost noises off compared with Kohl's big bang. What's more, these initiatives were striking mainly by reference to the past, whereas the chancellor was looking to the future and everyone now knew it.[158]

What made that point transparently clear was the brief instant on 22 December – a rainy Friday afternoon just before the Christmas holiday – when Kohl and Modrow formally opened crossing points at the Brandenburg Gate. Watching the people celebrating the unity of their city, Kohl exclaimed: 'This is one of the happiest hours of my life.' For the chancellor at the end of that momentous year – less than a month after his Ten Point speech – Dresden and Berlin were indeed memories to savour.[159]

*

The end of 1989 was not happy for everyone, of course. As the Western world ate its Christmas dinner, TV screens were full of the final moments of Nicolae and Elena Ceauşescu. The absolute ruler of Romania for twenty-four years and his wife were executed by soldiers of the army that, until just a few days before, he had commanded.

Romania was the last country in the Soviet bloc to experience revolutionary change. And it was the only one to suffer large-scale violence in 1989: according to official figures 1,104 people were killed and 3,352 injured.[160] Here alone tanks rolled, as in China, and firing squads took their revenge. This reflected the nature of Ceauşescu's highly personal and arbitrary dictatorship – the most gruesome in Eastern Europe. Having gone off on his own from Moscow since the mid-1960s, Ceauşescu had also stood apart from Gorbachev's reformist agenda and peaceful approach to change.

So why, in this repressive police state, had rebellion broken out? Unlike the rest of the bloc, Ceauşescu had managed to pay off almost all of Romania's foreign debts – but at huge cost to his people: cutting domestic consumption so brutally that shops were left with empty shelves, homes had no heat and electricity was rationed to a few hours a day. Meanwhile, Nicolae and Elena lived in grotesque pomp.

Despite such appalling repression, their fall was triggered not by social protest but by ethnic tensions. Romania had a substantial Hungarian minority, some 2 million out of a population of 23 million, who were treated as second-class citizens. The flashpoint was the western town of Timişoara where the local pastor and human-rights activist László Tőkés was to be evicted. Over the weekend of 17–18 December some 10,000 people demonstrated in his support, shouting 'Freedom', 'Romanians rise up', 'Down with Ceauşescu!' The regime's security forces (the Securitate) and army units responded with water cannons, tear gas and gunfire. Sixty unarmed civilians were killed.[161]

Protest now spread through the country as people took to the streets, emboldened by the examples of Poland, Hungary and East Germany. The regime hit back and there were lurid reports of perhaps 2,000 deaths. On 19 December, the day Kohl was in Dresden, Washington and Moscow independently condemned the 'brutal violence'.[162]

In Bucharest, Ceauşescu, totally out of touch with reality, sought to quell the chaos through a big address to a mass crowd on 21 December, which was also relayed to his country and the world on television. But his show of defiance was hollow. On the balcony of the presidential palace, the great dictator, now seventy-one, looked old, frail, perplexed, rattled – indeed suddenly fallible. Sensing this, the crowd interrupted his halting speech with catcalls, boos and whistles – at one point silencing him for three minutes. The spell had clearly been broken. As soldiers and even some of the Securitate men fraternised with the protestors in the streets, the regime began to implode. Next morning the Ceauşescus were whisked away from the palace roof by helicopter, but they were soon caught, tried by a kangaroo court and shot – or rather, mown down in a fusillade of more than a hundred bullets. Their blood-soaked bodies were then displayed to the eager cameramen.[163]

But Romania was 1989's exception. Everywhere else, regime change had occurred in a remarkably peaceful way. In neighbouring Bulgaria, Todor Zhivkov – who boasted thirty-five years in power, longer than anyone else in the bloc – had been toppled on 10 November. Yet the world hardly seemed to notice because the media was mesmerised by the fall of the Wall the night before. In any case, this was simply a palace coup: Zhivkov was replaced by his foreign minister Petar Mladenov. It was only gradually that people power made itself felt. The first street demonstrations in the capital, Sofia, began more than a week later on 18 November, with demands for democracy and free elections. On 7 December, the disparate opposition groups congealed as the so-called Union of Democratic Forces. Under pressure, the authorities decided to make further concessions: Mladenov announced on the 11th that the Communist Party would abandon its monopoly on power and multiparty elections would be held the following spring. Yet the sudden ousting of Zhivkov did not produce any fundamental transfer of power to the people, as in Poland, or a radical reform programme, as in Hungary. Hence the preferred Bulgarian term for 1989: 'The Change' (*promianata*). In a few weeks, the veritable dinosaur of the Warsaw Pact had been quietly consigned to history.[164]

Most emblematic of the national revolutions of 1989 was Czechoslovakia. The Czechs witnessed the GDR's collapse first-hand, as the candy-coloured Trabis chugged through their countryside and the refugees flooded into Prague.

Driving to freedom: Trabis in Czechoslovakia

But their own communist elite had an uncompromisingly hardline reputation and so change came late to Czechoslovakia. Indeed, Miloš Jakeš, the party leader, had rejected any moves for reform from above, as in Hungary and Poland. Yet there was context. Memories of 1968 – only two decades earlier – were still vivid and painful. But then they were galvanised by the scenes at the Berlin Wall on 9–10 November. A week later, on the 17th, the commemoration for a Czech student murdered by the Nazis fifty years before, rapidly escalated into a demonstration against the regime which the police broke up with force. This was the spark. Every day for the next week, the student protests mushroomed – drawing in intellectuals, dissidents and workers and spreading across the country. By the 19th the opposition groups in Prague had formed a 'Civic Forum' (in Bratislava, the capital of Slovakia, the movement was called 'Public against Violence') and by the 24th they were in talks with the communist government – which was now dominated by moderates after the old guard around Jakeš had resigned. The two key opposition figures – each in his own way deeply symbolic – were the writer Václav Havel, recently released from imprisonment for dissident activities as a key member of the Charter 77 organisation – and the Slovak Alexander Dubček, leader of the Prague Spring in 1968. The formal round-table negotiations took place on 8 and 9 December. The following day President Gustáv Husák appointed the first largely non-communis government in Czechoslovakia since 1948, and then stepped down.[165]

The pace of change had been breathtaking. On the evening of 23 November Timothy Garton Ash – who had witnessed Poland's upheavals in June and then the start of Czechoslovakia's revolution – was chatting to Havel over a beer in the basement of Havel's favourite pub. The British journalist joked: 'In Poland it took ten years, in Hungary ten months, in East Germany ten weeks; perhaps in Czechoslovakia it will take ten days!' Havel grasped his hand, smiling that famous winning smile, summoned a video team who happened to be drinking in the corner, and asked Garton Ash to say it again, on camera. 'It would be fabulous, if it could be so,' sighed Havel.[166] His scepticism was not unwarranted. Admittedly the revolution took twenty-four days not ten, but on 29 December Václav Havel was elected president of Czechoslovakia by the Federal Assembly in the hallowed halls of Prague Castle.

The playwright becomes president: Václav Havel and the
Velvet Revolution in Prague

Although this was for the moment a transitional government – free
elections would not be held until June 1990 – the transformation was
truly profound. This had been a 'Velvet Revolution': smooth and swift,
on occasion even merry. By comparison with Poland, Hungary and GDR,
opposition politics in Prague had been improvised by amateurs – but

they had been able to learn from the mistakes of the others, as well as from their successes. And what's more, revolution in Czechoslovakia came without the pain of deepening economic crisis, with which the new governments in Warsaw and Budapest had to grapple. And so by the New Year, Czechoslovakia found itself firmly on the road towards political democracy and a market economy.[167]

So much had changed in only two months. At the start of November 1989, it was still possible in Eastern Europe to imagine a future for communism, albeit in a reformed state. But within weeks no one could doubt that it was in irreversible decline. And by the end of the year 'those who had come too late', as Gorbachev put it in East Berlin, had most certainly been punished (Ceauşescu, Zhivkov and Honecker), while those who had never let themselves be silenced (notably Havel and Mazowiecki) had now replaced the leaders they previously denounced.

The fact that Gorbachev presided over these variegated national exits from communism without intervening also allowed Kohl more leeway and gave hope for his mission in 1990: to bring the two Germanies closer to unity. The chancellor set the tone in his New Year message, expressing the aspiration that the coming decade would be 'the happiest of this century' for his people – offering 'the chance of a free and united Germany in a free and united Europe'. That, he said, 'depended critically on our contribution'. In other words, he was reminding his fellow Germans – so long weighed down by the burden of the past – that they had now been given the opportunity to shape the future.[168]

But the new architecture could not be constructed by Germans alone. With the communist glacier in retreat – indeed melting before one's eyes – and the ascendant Western Europe opening out, the stark, two-bloc structure of Cold War Europe had cracked asunder. The pieces would now have to be put together in a new mosaic and this would require not merely the consent but also the creative engagement of the superpowers.

In other words, Kohl might have had his problems with Mitterrand and especially Thatcher, but they were mere stumbling blocks. When it came to building a new order around a unifying Germany, this could be achieved only by working with Bush and Gorbachev. Yet both these leaders were deeply preoccupied in late 1989 with their own problems: how belatedly, to create an effective personal rapport after their slow, at times frosty, start. And, more than that, how to manage the delicate business of moving beyond the Cold War in the heart of Europe.

Chapter 4

Securing Germany in the Post-Wall World

The 3rd of December 1989. It was almost incredible. George Bush and Mikhail Gorbachev, the leaders of the United States and the Soviet Union, sitting together in Malta, relaxed and joking, in a joint press conference at the end of their summit meeting. This was a month after the fall of Wall and barely a week after Kohl's surprise announcement of his Ten-Point Plan in the Bundestag.

Happy days: Bush and Gorbachev on the *Maxim Gorky*

'We stand at the threshold of a brand-new era of US–Soviet relations,' Bush declared. 'And it is within our grasp to contribute, each in our own way, to overcoming the division of Europe and ending military confrontation there.' The president was optimistic that together they could 'realise a lasting peace and transform East–West relations to one of enduring cooperation'. This, said Bush, was 'the future that Chairman Gorbachev and I began right here in Malta'.[1]

The Soviet leader fully agreed. 'We stated, both of us, that the world leaves one epoch of Cold War and enters another epoch. This is just the beginning. We're just at the very beginning of our long road to a long-lasting peaceful period.' Looking ahead he stated bluntly: 'the new era calls for a new approach ... many things that were characteristic of the Cold War should be abandoned'. Among them 'force, the arms race, mistrust, psychological and ideological struggle ... All that should be things of the past.'[2]

At Malta, there were no new treaties, not even a communiqué. But the message of the summit was clear – symbolised in this first ever *joint* press conference of superpower leaders. The Cold War, which had defined international relations for over forty years, seemed to be a thing of the past.

*

A full year had elapsed since these two men last met, at Governors Island, New York, in 1988 when Reagan was still president. Then Bush had assured Gorbachev that he hoped to build on what had been achieved in US–Soviet relations but would need 'a little time' to review the issues. That 'little time' had turned into twelve months, during which the world had been turned on its head.[3]

Bush's initial diplomatic priority had been to pursue an opening with China, but this was much more difficult post-Tiananmen. It was only after his European tour – the NATO summit in May and his trips to Poland and Hungary in July – that the president really began to grasp the magnitude of change in Europe. With the language of revolution ringing in his ears as he witnessed the bicentennial celebrations of 1789 during the G7 summit in Paris, he decided it was finally time to propose a meeting with Gorbachev to develop a personal relationship in order to manage the growing turmoil. This was a veritable 'change of heart' – indeed, as Bush would later admit in Malta, a turn of '180 degrees'.[4]

The Soviet leader, of course, had always been keen to meet, but it was not possible to agree firmly on date and place until 1 November. And by the time they actually met one month later, the Iron Curtain was a thing of the past: East Germany was dissolving, a palace coup had taken place in Bulgaria, and Czechoslovakia's Velvet Revolution was in full swing. Bush worried that political leaders might not be able to control this remarkable revolutionary upsurge. In particular, he feared that Gorbachev could still be pushed into using force to hang on to the bloc and shore up Soviet power. That is why the president resisted the temptation to celebrate the triumph of democracy – to the puzzlement of many Americans, especially in politics and the press. Bush felt it was in the American national interest, first, to help Gorbachev stay in power, given his continued commitment to reform and, second, to keep US troops in Europe to maintain American influence over the continent. With the geopolitical map in flux, a meeting of minds between the superpowers had become vital for the peaceful management of events. That is why he and Gorbachev needed to talk, even if they had no agreements to sign.

Ten days before their encounter, on 22 November, Bush cabled the Soviet leader: 'I want this meeting to be useful in advancing our mutual understanding and in laying the groundwork for a good relationship.' More, 'I want the meeting to be seen as a success.' He insisted: 'Success does not mean deals signed, in my view. It means that you and I are frank enough with each other so that our two great countries will not have tensions that arise because we don't know each other's innermost thinking.'[5]

The two sides had already agreed that it would be a 'no agenda' meeting, but the president wanted Gorbachev to have a general idea of what he had in mind. He listed six key topics: Eastern Europe; regional differences (from Central America to Asia); defence spending; visions of the world for the next century; human rights; and arms control. 'Of course,' Bush added, 'you will have your own priorities.'[6]

The president clearly sought the freedom to improvise in Malta. This horrified Scowcroft and the NSC staff who had never wanted a summit with no agenda. They feared another Reykjavik, when – so they believed – Reagan had got seduced by Gorbachev. In their eyes it was imperative to save Bush from falling for the Kremlin's smooth talker who with sweet words like 'peace', 'disarmament', and 'cooperation' had gained a huge cult following in the West. Most of the president's entourage believed that if Bush could be persuaded to work from a firm agenda based on 'a package of initiatives on every subject', that would put Gorbachev on the defensive. And it would help them to keep the president on a tight leash and minimise the dangers – at such a pivotal moment in history – of ill-advised American concessions.[7]

Bush and Gorbachev flew to Valletta with their foreign ministers and a few key advisers. Their weekend of talks, held on Saturday and Sunday 2–3 December 1989, were originally intended to move to and fro between an American and a Soviet battle-cruiser. But a massive storm blew up and so the venue was moved to the huge Soviet passenger liner *Maxim Gorky*, safely moored in Valletta's great harbour. Even so, the Saturday afternoon and evening sessions had to be cancelled. Bush jotted down in his diary: 'It's the damnedest weather you've ever seen ... the highest seas that they've ever had, and it screwed everything up ... The ship is rolling like mad ... Here we are, the two superpower leaders, several hundred yards apart, and we can't talk because of the weather.' Scowcroft recalled: 'Gorbachev could not reach the *Belknap* [i.e. the US cruiser] for dinner that evening, so we ate a marvellous meal meant for him – swordfish, lobster, and so forth.'[8]

But in spite of the stormy weather, president and general secretary managed to spend most of the two days in calm and fruitful discussion. They clicked right from the start. Bush even approved of Gorbachev's taste in clothes, noting in his diary: 'He wore a dark blue pinstripe suit, a cream-coloured white shirt (like the ones I like), a red tie (almost like the one out of the London firm with a sword).' And, the president added, he had a 'nice smile'.[9]

In the first plenary the Soviet leader proposed that they should develop 'a dialogue commensurate with the pace of change' and predicted that, although Malta was officially just the prelude to a full-scale summit the following summer, it would have 'an importance of its own'. Bush agreed, but he then tried to cut through the standard Gorby grandiloquence. Getting down to brass tacks, he spelled out the specific 'positive initiatives' by which he hoped to 'move forward' into the 1990 summit.[10]

The president assured Gorbachev that he believed the world would be 'a better place if perestroika succeeds'. To this end, he said he would like to waive the Jackson–Vanik amendment, which since 1974–5 had prohibited open economic relations with the Soviet bloc. Trade negotiations combined with export credits would, he declared, enable the USSR to import the modern technology that it needed. 'I am not making these suggestions as a bailing out', Bush insisted, but in a genuine spirit of 'cooperation'.[11]

In similar vein, the president was now ready to act openly as an advocate for Soviet 'observer status' in the GATT, 'so that we can learn together'. He promised to support Moscow's aspiration, after completion of the latest round of multilateral trade renegotiations – the so-called Uruguay Round – between the 123 contracting members. Joking that the prospect of early Soviet association might even serve as an 'incentive' to EC countries to end their 'fighting' between themselves and with the USA over the vexed theme of 'agriculture', he recommended that meanwhile the Kremlin 'move toward market prices at wholesale level, so that Eastern and Western economies become somewhat more compatible'. At this point Bush hoped the Uruguay Round would be completed in less than a year.[12]

Gorbachev, equally optimistic about his country's prospects to speedily join in global trade, was keen to 'get involved in the international financial institutions'. He stressed: 'We must learn to take the world economy into perestroika.' And he truly appreciated US 'willingness to help' the Soviet Union to open out. But he was also adamant that the Americans should stop suspecting the Soviets of wanting to 'politicise' these organisations. Times had changed, he said, averring that both sides had abolished 'ideology', so now they should 'work on new criteria' together.[13]

It wasn't all sweetness and light, however. The president touched on human rights (and the issue of divided families) before turning to the Cold War hotspots of Cuba and Nicaragua. He told Gorbachev to stop giving Fidel Castro cash and arms. The Cuban leader was 'exporting revolution' and exacerbating tensions in Central America, particularly Nicaragua, El Salvador and Panama. Prodding Gorbachev, he said that ordinary Americans were asking how the Soviets could 'put all this money into Cuba and still want credits?' Finally, Bush moved to the area of arms control, emphasising his hopes for a chemical-weapons agreement, the completion of a conventional forces in Europe (CFE) treaty and strategic arms-reduction treaty (START) in 1990.[14]

Gorbachev answered with a *tour d'horizon* of his own. He stated that 'all of us feel we are at a historic watershed': international politics is shifting from a 'bipolar' to a 'multipolar' world, while the whole human race is facing truly global challenges such as climate change. Specifically, the American and Soviet peoples were following a strong desire to 'move toward each other'; governments, however, were lagging behind. Gorbachev strongly objected to the Cold War triumphalism he felt was present in US government circles. Acknowledging that Bush had shown he was different, Gorbachev now sought in a formal way the respect of the United States. He was emphatic that he did not wish to be lectured or put under pressure by the Americans. What he wanted was to 'build bridges across rivers rather than parallel to them'; he looked for new approaches and new 'patterns of cooperation' that befitted the 'new realities'. He also referred back to the productive, cooperative relationship he had eventually managed to establish with Ronald Reagan despite 'times of impasse'. He still wanted arms control but, furthermore, he wanted the USSR to get involved in the world economy at large. This was surprising talk coming from a Soviet leader.[15]

A lot of the first plenary session was the usual for-the-record mutual positioning and ideological point-scoring that occurred at the start of any superpower meeting. But behind their rhetoric were already hints of something more personal and significant. Bush deliberately reached out to Gorbachev. 'I hope you have noticed that as dynamic change has accelerated in recent months, we have not responded with flamboyance or arrogance ... I have conducted myself in ways not to complicate your life.' That's why, he added, 'I have not jumped up and down on the Berlin Wall.'[16] Gorbachev appreciated Bush's refusal to inflame passions. He made an equally striking observation: 'The US and the USSR are doomed to cooperate for a long time,' but, in order to cooperate fruitfully, 'we have to abandon the vestiges of images of an enemy'.[17] 'Doomed to cooperate' was a striking phrase. Here was an echo of Reykjavik 1986, when Gorbachev had stated: 'As difficult as it is to conduct business with the United States, we are doomed to it. We have no choice.'[18] It betrayed a negative-positive approach to relations, reflecting the abiding Russian angst about whether assertion against the West or integration within the world was the key to national identity and international status.

The two leaders really got down to business in their one-on-one meeting – held with only an adviser and an interpreter from each side, after a short break. What exercised Gorbachev above all were Washington's operations in its Latin American backyard. He made the provocative suggestion that Cuba and the US should normalise relations, and then complained about US intervention in 'independent countries'. Bush tried to brush all this aside, waxing eloquent about America's war on drugs in Panama and Colombia and reminding the Soviet leader that it was a *democratic* government in Manila that had asked America for help against Filipino rebels. Carrying on the tit-for-tat, Gorbachev retaliated: 'in the Soviet Union some are saying the Brezhnev Doctrine is being replaced by the Bush Doctrine'. He stressed that he was an advocate of 'peaceful change' and 'non-interference' (as exemplified by his conduct in Eastern Europe). This new Soviet attitude, he insisted to Bush, was 'bringing us closer'.[19]

Having spent most of the session jousting about the global Cold War, Gorbachev finally zeroed in on Germany. 'Mr Kohl is too much in a hurry on the German question,' Gorbachev exclaimed. 'This is not good.' He insisted that German unification was not something the USSR would endorse. 'There are two states, mandated by history.' Nor did the Soviet leader want to speculate about Germany's future within or outside alliances such as NATO. Such talk was 'premature', he declared: 'let history decide what happens. We need an understanding on this.' Vehemently, Gorbachev urged Bush to help restrain the enthusiasm for rapid unification that the German chancellor had unleashed through his Ten-Point Plan the week before.[20]

Such an outburst was typical of every Gorbachev summit. Bush tried to calm things down, saying that Kohl's rhetoric was understandably 'emotional' given recent events. He promised the Soviet leader 'we will do nothing to recklessly try to speed up reunification'. At this point, both men were in agreement that there would be no quick fix for the German question, nor would it be fixed by the Germans alone. They were united in seeing this as a time of both 'great opportunity' and also 'great responsibility' for all concerned. This dualism of opportunity and responsibility would be a continuing theme of their relationship as superpower leaders.[21]

Gorbachev was equally concerned about ideological rivalry. He wanted Bush to change his outlook and his entire rhetoric about Soviet–American relations. Perestroika and glasnost were intended to rejuvenate the USSR while placing its continued competition with the USA on a peaceful footing. His long-term aim was to bring Soviet society in line with the rest of Europe and integrate it into the global community. He envisaged a modernised, 'socialist democratic' Soviet Union for the twenty-first century. But this transformation, he insisted, required the West to abandon its rooted view of the Soviets, and indeed tsarist Russia, as alien from the West. Gorbachev vehemently protested that the USSR was being falsely blamed for 'exporting ideology:' he told Bush flatly that he had renounced revolution. And he totally dismissed the idea of 'some US politicians' – though 'not you', he assured the president – who say that the 'unity of Europe should occur on the basis of Western values'. Germany and values were really hot topics, to which they would return the following day.[22]

The Saturday afternoon and evening sessions had to be cancelled because of rough seas and gales. By Sunday morning, however, the weather had improved and the two men resumed on schedule. Bush recalled in his memoirs: 'He was very jovial and once again direct – another relaxed meeting ... I felt we were on the same wavelength as we talked.'[23] Yet they didn't pull their punches. At the start of a one-hour tête-à-tête, Bush immediately confronted Gorbachev with the USSR's nationalities problem, going 'straight for the Baltics'. Gorbachev admitted this was a sensitive issue but explained that he intended to deal with it 'through greater autonomy'. He conceded rather lamely that if separatism became 'dominant', that would be 'dramatic'. Bush warned that the use of force would 'create a firestorm'. Closing off the conversation, Gorbachev stated: 'We are committed to a democratic process and we hope you understand.' In other words: please don't push me on this one.[24]

After lunch, in the final plenary session, they grappled with the big questions of East–West relations that had challenged their predecessors throughout the Cold War. Gorbachev's opener was striking. 'The Soviet Union will under no circumstances start a war – that is very important.' He also declared that the United States was no longer 'an adversary' and called their relationship 'cooperative'. This was remarkable language for a Soviet leader.[25]

Although reassured, Bush wanted something more concrete. 'How do you see beyond the status quo?' he asked. Gorbachev replied that the Warsaw Pact and the Atlantic Alliance remained essential pillars as Europe moved forward – these, he said, were 'the instruments that have maintained the balance' – but insisted that these organisations should 'change to a more political than military nature'. Gorbachev's approach to revolutionary turmoil, like Bush's, was cautious, indeed conservative.

He also rejected any attempt by the Americans to dictate the rules of international affairs. As he presented it, Eastern Europe was changing 'to respect universal human values' and was 'moving closer to the economic arrangements of the world economy'. Evoking the first pan-European Conference on Security and Cooperation in Helsinki in 1975, when thirty-five nations from East and West had signed the famous Final Act, he advocated a 'Helsinki II summit to develop new criteria for this new phase'. For the Soviet leader, the dynamic was one of East and West drawing closer together and becoming more compatible. This he called an 'objective process'.[26]

The president would not let this go by. He argued that it was distinctly 'Western' values – such as 'lively debate, pluralism and openness', as well as 'free markets' – that had taken root over a long period in the countries of the Atlantic Alliance and the wider world. But Bush was careful not to rub this in with 'chauvinistic pride'. He and his advisers were looking for a mode of discourse that allowed Gorbachev, as he tried to integrate the Soviet Union into the world, to espouse these values without losing face. For the United States it was imperative that Europe should be transformed peacefully and that, to a large extent, would depend on Gorbachev. A magnanimous attitude, combined with a bit of fudging about words, were therefore tactically necessary for the Americans. But, in the process, both sides would benefit.[27]

The fudge was most evident on German unification. Bush declared that he could not 'disapprove' of this happening. Secretary of State James Baker added that it was surely best for Germany to be unified on the basis of mutually acceptable 'common' or 'democratic values' – namely self-determination, openness and pluralism. Gorbachev agreed; it was evident that he did not relish the prospect but would tolerate it. Nowadays, he said, every country in Eastern Europe had the right 'to make its own choices'. The Brezhnev Doctrine was clearly torn up. With the threat of the tank gone and with an amber light from Moscow for German unification, both sides felt that a 'new relationship was beginning' between East and West.[28]

The give-and-take atmosphere of the final plenary was symptomatic of Malta as a whole. The effort of the two leaders to find a common language was not merely rhetorical, but reflected a genuine wish to establish common ground. It is crucial to understand that Bush and Gorbachev were both inclined to approach this superpower encounter as a win-win situation. They were working towards an outcome that was mutually beneficial, rather than being a victory for one side or the other. Although holding stronger cards, Bush knew that, to ensure evolution without conflict in Europe, he as much as Gorbachev had to be willing to compromise. Both perceived themselves as the managers trying to channel societal forces, prevent outbreaks of violence, and stabilise international politics in order to re-establish some kind of predictability. They were acutely conscious of what Gorbachev called their 'special responsibility' as leaders of the only two superpowers for shaping a more peaceful future.

Malta also epitomised the larger attraction of personal summitry. As Gorbachev stated during the joint Q&A after the meeting, 'the personal contacts are a very important element in the relations between leaders of state'. He said that they 'help us implement our responsibilities and help us better interact' in the interests of both nations and the entire world. Bush, in turn, spoke warmly about 'regular contacts' to build on the 'good personal relationship' that they had established. Neither man expected to totally convert the other but they had been able to talk constructively about their differences 'without rancour' and 'as frankly as possible'. The president continued: 'if we hadn't sat here and talked we might not have understood how each other feels on these important questions'. So, he concluded, 'I couldn't have asked for a better result out of this non-summit summit.' That last phrase provoked general laughter but it captured what Bush really wanted: an informal, unscripted face-to-face, without any pressure to produce specific results.[29]

In his diary, Gorbachev's foreign-policy adviser Anatoly Chernyaev nicely captured the mood of Malta. 'Despite the sensational nature of the event,' he reflected, 'it seemed like a regular normal affair.' Gorbachev 'acted like he and Bush were old pals – frank and simple, openly well-intentioned'. Above all, he added, 'the USSR and US are no longer enemies. This was the most important thing.'[30] Chernyaev was right. The break-through at Malta *was* remarkable. Yet, translating friendly noises into a truly new framework for European security would require sustained and careful diplomacy. And the biggest challenge was how to handle Germany.

*

The president flew out of Valletta at 6 p.m. on 3 December. Three hours later he was dining with Chancellor Kohl at the elegant Château Stuyvenberg in Laeken near Brussels. It was the eve of the NATO Council meeting and this meal in Belgium was their first personal encounter since the Wall had fallen. Given that Kohl had exploded his Ten Points bombshell just days before Malta and the NATO summit, the US president might have been angry. But this was not the case. He appreciated Kohl's explanatory letter and now appeared very happy, as Teltschik noted, albeit tired – which was understandable after eight hours of intense discussions with Gorbachev.[31]

Bush was firmly supportive of German reunification. For that, Kohl was grateful. But, the president warned the chancellor, 'Gorbachev said you are in too much of a hurry.' Kohl promised, 'I will not do anything reckless.' He made clear that he saw West Germany as an integral part of Europe and that the country's position in NATO and the EC was totally firm. He envisaged a gradual process of unification which might take up to ten years or so. There was, he said, so much 'nonsense' written in newspapers – even Henry Kissinger had recently speculated on German TV about reunification within two years. 'It is not possible,' Kohl exclaimed, 'the economic imbalance is too great.'[32]

The chancellor said nothing, however, about a future unified Germany's NATO membership or about the construction of any alternative European security system. He only expressed his dedication to further European integration – a process on which he was working closely with Mitterrand and also a 'precondition' for successful reform in Eastern Europe. Bush then returned to the issue of Gorbachev's unease over German affairs: 'We need a formulation which doesn't scare him, but moves forward.' Kohl did appreciate the sensitivities involved – 'I don't want Gorbachev to feel cornered' – and he had a solution up his sleeve: 'The CSCE says borders can be changed by peaceful means.' Bush shared this view. 'I think the answer is self-determination.' Once that was agreed, he said, 'then let things work.'[33]

All in all, it was a successful dinner. Scowcroft noted that this meeting between Bush and Kohl 'marked a turning point'. They had achieved, he said, 'a perfect conjunction of the minds on reunification' and 'the atmosphere of comradeship in a great venture was palpable to me'.[34] In fact, 3 December had been a very good day for George Bush. He now had his main adversary onside and had also reined in his most important yet challenging ally. Thanks to Malta and Laeken, Bush was confident that he could use the NATO Council to get the United States back into the driving seat and shape Western policy.

Next morning, 4 December, Bush spoke to his European partners at the Alliance headquarters in Brussels. Above all, he wanted to reassure them 'there was to be no US–Soviet condominium, no Yalta-style deal on Eastern Europe'. Looking right back to the origins of the Alliance in 1949, he reminded the council that NATO had been established 'to provide the basis for precisely the extraordinary evolution which is occurring in Eastern Europe today'. Only a healthy, strong and unified NATO could act as a 'reliable guarantor of peace in Europe' – supporting 'both moves toward greater unity within Western Europe as well as the dissolution of barriers with the East'. He looked forward to creating 'a new Europe and a new Atlanticism, where self-determination and individual freedom everywhere replace coercion and tyranny, where economic liberty everywhere replaces economic controls and stagnation, and where lasting peace is reinforced everywhere by common respect for the rights of man'. Ultimately, however, it would all depend on the actions 'we take, as governments and individuals, to offer leadership, protection, and encouragement for this process of peaceful transformation'.[35]

In front of the press Bush affirmed that 'the United States will remain a European power' and that Washington would continue to 'maintain significant military forces in Europe as long as our allies desire our presence as part of a common defence effort'.[36] With this he laid down a marker for future US policy. And, crucially, he was not willing to declare publicly that the East–West conflict was over. Challenged to say as much by an American reporter, he was evasive and rambling: 'We're fooling around with semantics here. I don't want to give you a headline. I've told you the areas where I think we have progress. Why do we resort to these code words that send different signals to different people? I'm not going to answer it.' Eventually he rephrased the question: 'Is the Cold War the same – I mean, is it raging like it was before in the times of the Berlin blockade? Absolutely not. Things have moved dramatically. But if I signal to you there's no Cold War, then it's "What are you doing with troops in Europe?" I mean, come on.'[37]

With the two alliances still facing off across a Germany in turmoil, Bush felt in no position to announce the end of the Cold War. Yet, as he said, superpower relations were in a very different state from the late 1940s. Soviet military intervention in Europe – let alone a Third World War – seemed highly unlikely. The nuclear arms race had been wound down and the ideological competition was also being defused. Most important, the tenor of personal relations between the leaders was now fundamentally different. Nevertheless, when it came to Germany – the flashpoint of two previous world wars – Bush firmly believed that this needed firm yet delicate handling; a process in which Washington must take the lead.

In his press conference, the president read out four principles that together summed up the American position on German reunification:

Self-determination must be pursued without prejudice to its outcome, and we should not at this time endorse any particular vision.

Secondly, unification should occur in the context of Germany's continued commitment to NATO and an increasingly integrated European Community, and with due regard for the legal role and responsibilities of the allied powers.

Third, in the interest of general European stability, moves toward unification must be peaceful, gradual, and part of a step-by-step basis.

And lastly, on the question of borders, we should reiterate our support for the principles of the Helsinki Final Act.[38]

It was the second principle that was the Americans' prime concern. Germany as a unified country had to be kept inside NATO. And it was clearly axiomatic for Washington that NATO should play a key role in Europe's post-Cold War security order.

On 4 December Bush was actually repeating what Baker had first presented on 29 November – done off-the-cuff in an answer to press questions about Kohl's Ten-Point Plan the day before.[39] In fact, however, the Four Principles were the result of weeks of grappling with the German crisis at the highest levels of the State Department that had started even before the Wall came down. And these ideas would feed into a major speech that Baker would give in Berlin on 12 December.

*

Like everyone, US policymakers were struggling to make sense of what had happened in Europe over the past few weeks and what it all portended. Sometime in October 1989 Baker had scribbled on top of a State Department document about the superpowers a headline that their relations were moving 'From <u>confrontation</u> to <u>dialogue</u>, Now to: <u>cooperation</u>.' The paper asserted that a good relationship was 'critical for world affairs' and that, to ensure global stability, it was obviously in America's interest to see 'perestroika succeed'. For the sake of 'predictability' at a time of 'fundamental change', Baker considered it imperative that Washington did not frame its policy in isolation from events in the Soviet Union. The objective was therefore to 'stay engaged across broader agenda' and be '<u>creative</u> about finding points of mutual advantage'.

Since nobody could be certain that Gorbachev would pull off his reform programme, the State Department saw all the more reason to 'take advantage' of what was seen as 'a favourable situation' for both the United States and NATO, especially when it came to making progress in arms control. And in order to create an enduring basis for European security, the focus should be on concluding the CFE treaty – because, so Baker thought, it was the massive Soviet superiority in conventional forces that 'make war thinkable and cast a shadow over Europe politically'. If the Americans could move ahead with Gorbachev on the CFE – all the while not losing sight of their own defence programme – he believed that they were effectively reducing military options for future Soviet leaders who might be less open to cooperation than Gorbachev.[40]

Around the same time as Baker was jotting down these thoughts, one of his key advisers, Robert Zoellick, engaged in blue-sky thinking of his own in a paper dated 17 October, full of underlinings for emphasis. He argued that the US was facing a situation 'analogous to [the] task after 1945 – devising a new world order for changed circumstances'. The main task was to 'manage change effectively to serve US interests'. A 'new type of US leadership' was needed, one that would 'use diplomatic brains as well as economic brawn'. Especially required was 'skill in managing multilateral processes' (akin to the 'G7 for international economic management'). To this end, not only was it necessary to work towards strengthening or even institutionalising America's connections with the European Community, even perhaps through a full-scale treaty, in parallel with the EC's anticipated transformation by 1992 into the European Union (EU). Zoellick also argued that, with the 'old anti-Soviet glue of post-war alliances weakening', NATO ties had to be re-established on a 'new basis' resting on 'shared political and economic values'. This, he noted, was why the Americans kept emphasising 'Western values'.[41]

By 27 November 1989, after the fall of the Wall but before Kohl's Ten-Point Plan, thinking in the State Department was starting to crystallise. Zoellick typed up some 'Points for Consultations with European leaders', with his usual underlinings, which Baker then annotated by hand with his equally characteristic thick felt pen. (These amendments are shown in italics.) The result is a fascinating insight into State Department thinking ahead of the Malta summit.

Overview Theme: Cold War not over yet, but moving into final stage (*structure of peace*). There's a view in the U.S. that we win the war and then lose the peace. As we move into this ~~final stage of the Cold War~~

post-postwar era, we must concentrate on building a new age of peace, democracy, and economic liberty: A New Atlanticism and a New Europe that reaches further East.

S[oviet Union] will remain a European partner

Possible Points to Explore

General: Architecture of the New Atlanticism and New Europe should not try to develop one overarching structure. Instead, it will rely on a number of complementary institutions that will be mutually reinforcing – NATO, EC, CSCE, WEU, Council of Europe.[42]

The Secretary of State had no doubt that a turning point in history had been reached. The world was moving into what he called in that striking phrase the 'post-postwar era' – one in which Moscow would 'remain' in Europe but now as a 'partner'. These annotations revealed that Baker was one of the first policymakers to articulate the idea of transcending not merely the Cold War but also the era that had begun in 1945.[43]

Yet, despite the new thinking, here again we see an essentially conservative approach to the future – in particular the idea of using existing international organisations to shape the new structure of Europe. Indeed, on the German question itself, while not endorsing Kohl's 'whole programme' as set out in the Ten Points, Baker noted 'we share his view that the key institutions that promote and protect Western values, like the EC and the Alliance, will be the foundation stones for German unity'.[44]

This brainstorming by Baker and Zoellick had fed into the Malta and Brussels summits. After the president's dramatic meetings on 2–4 December with Gorbachev, Kohl and the NATO allies, Baker developed his earlier inchoate ideas into a fuller blueprint for future US policy. This took the form of the 12 December speech, drafted by Zoellick from material from State Department specialists, which the Secretary of State delivered to the Berlin Press Club.

I spy with my little eye

The speech was scheduled for lunchtime on the 12th. Earlier that morning, after breakfast with Kohl and a brief meeting with the mayor of West Berlin, Baker joined Hans-Dietrich Genscher for a walk along the Wall near the ruined Reichstag building. It was the Secretary of State's first visit to an undivided Berlin and therefore a moment to savour. He 'peered through a crack in the wall' and glimpsed what he called 'the high-resolution drabness' that characterised the eastern part of the city. Clad in his beige mac on a 'foggy, overcast day', Baker felt 'like a character in a John le Carré novel', surreptitiously watching the banalities of life behind the Iron Curtain. But he was also impressed. 'I realised that the ordinary men and women of East Germany, peacefully and persistently, had taken matters into their own hands. This was their revolution, and it was the job of men like me to help them to secure the freedom they were working so hard to win.'[45] In other words, Baker sensed the historical force of people power, but equally the obligation it placed on men at the top, particularly Americans. This sense of duty and opportunity was highly personal: he, James A. Baker III, had to channel and convert the molten energies of the masses into a new and stable European structure, built from the ruins of the Wall and the Cold War.

The visit to the Wall fired him up for his speech to the Press Club. Evoking the current feeling of epic novelty, Baker told his audience that the Western world needed nothing less than a new 'architecture for a new era'. This, he said, should be built around 'a new Atlanticism' in which 'America's security remains linked to European security' and 'a new Europe that reaches further east', once division had been overcome. NATO would have to transform itself from 'a military organisation' into a 'political alliance'. Irrespective of the Warsaw Pact's fate, Baker made clear that NATO and the European Community would be fixities of this new Europe. Furthermore, he insisted that, whatever new German state might emerge, it would have to remain committed to both these organisations.[46]

The Bush administration was therefore the first government to propose keeping a unified Germany anchored in Western institutions. By perpetuating NATO the president would also ensure America's continued military presence in Europe. And as the EC 12 was about to metamorphose into the European Union, Washington was keen to tighten links with the organisation that it saw as the future core of the new Europe. The EU would help anchor unified Germany in the Western camp. And American observers also predicted that it would serve as a powerful 'magnet' drawing Eastern Europe toward 'the free world'. The EU, unlike NATO, was not under the American aegis, and was potentially an economic rival to the United States, so Washington hoped its support for further integration would allow it to gain more of a foothold within the organisation.[47]

Baker's speech in Berlin, said the *New York Times,* was the 'most comprehensive and detailed set of ideas to emerge from the Bush administration to deal with the upheavals that are reshaping Europe's political landscape'.[48] In fact, the talk exemplified the role Baker frequently played in shaping US foreign policy. He was the one to conceptualise the president's looser ideas, especially about the post-Cold War future. And, he could do so because, as Bush's long-time friend, he had the president's ear and enjoyed his trust.

Yet the impact of what Baker said in the morning seemed to be undercut – at least in the short run – by what he did in the afternoon. Because what grabbed the headlines was his impromptu meeting (arranged just the night before) with East German prime minister Hans Modrow and several opposition politicians. This, as it happened, took place in Potsdam – near where Churchill, Stalin and Truman had met in 1945 to conclude the war in Europe and plan Germany's post-war occupation. Indeed Baker had written about the conference in his senior thesis at Princeton in 1952.[49]

As soon as his Press Club speech was over, Baker slipped away and was taken in a Mercedes limousine to Brandenburg on what was the first (and last) visit of an American Secretary of State to the German Democratic Republic. 'The drive to Potsdam turned out to be one of the most surreal trips I took as Secretary of State,' Baker recalled. 'Beginning at twilight, we crossed into the south-east corner of West Berlin and approached the Glienicke Bridge' – a stark rusty steel structure 'famous as a scene of numerous spy swaps'. As they drove over the bridge, in true le Carré fashion, the West German police gave way, 'much like a caterpillar shedding its cocoon', to their East German counterparts. Crossing from West to East, said one of Baker's staff, was like 'going from color to black and white'.[50]

It seemed even worse when they got to Potsdam. Here the faded grandeur of eighteenth-century Prussia blurred through the drizzle into the bombastic concrete of GDR modernism. As they neared Potsdam's Inter-Hotel, 'everything was gray: the clothing, the buildings, the people, the mood. The roads were empty, except for a few tiny Trabants with very dim lights that scurried about like roaches on a dark, unclean kitchen floor.' Baker had never been a fan of West Berlin – 'not the most colourful of cities', as he politely put it – but, faced with monochrome Potsdam, 'it seemed like Times Square or Piccadilly Circus'.[51]

When he met the East Germans in the hotel, Baker emphasised 'non-violence', 'peaceful reforms', free elections and 'stability' but the details of their conversation were of no great significance.[52] Memories of meeting Modrow were 'as fleeting as Modrow's regime itself', Baker later noted. What mattered was the fact of the meeting itself. Mitterrand was due in East Berlin the following week. Baker had got there first, to demonstrate US leadership on the German question. But there was a downside. Some of the press interpreted Baker's visit to Potsdam as an attempt to 'shore up' the GDR government and put the brakes on Bonn's push for rapid unification. They did so by linking Baker's Potsdam jaunt to the meeting of the ambassadors from the Four Powers in the Allied Kommandatura the day before – which had so offended Kohl.[53]

What made things worse, while the Big Four were talking, the chancellor was addressing his party leadership about the future of Germany. Seeking to mollify the victors, all of whom except the USA were on edge about his Ten Points, Kohl went out of his way to declare that he did not want to 'establish an over-powerful Germany' and that he would not 'move without consulting' the Four Powers.[54] But then, it seemed, the allies had cavalierly gone over his head and, to add insult to injury, the Secretary of State had acted on his own – unilaterally, publicly and unprecedentedly – to talk with the East Germans. With stories like this circulating in the world press, Baker's whole trip to Berlin became widely seen as a total PR disaster. He later wrote a deeply apologetic note to the German chancellor.[55] The ideas in his Press Club speech would take time to be appreciated.

On 16 December, returning from Europe, Baker caught up with Bush and Scowcroft on the island of Saint Martin, in the French West Indies, to join in talks with François Mitterrand and his foreign minister Roland Dumas. Meeting in 'casual clothes under a striped tent' on the beach of a luxury resort, they relaxed and chatted for an hour over a lunch of 'lobster, goat cheese, Chassagne-Montrachet wine and chocolate tarts'. For Baker the sunny skies and balmy breeze were a delight after the cold and damp of Berlin. After the meal, they continued their discussions as the two presidents walked on the powdery sand. Everything was conducted in English, without a translator – which enhanced the informality and closeness of the occasion. This was all the more valuable since France was a notoriously prickly ally.[56]

The conversation ranged broadly across the future of Europe. Little was said directly about Germany, but it was clear that the Americans were using the mini-summit to get the French onside. This was particularly important because, as Kohl had drily put it during his dinner with the president in Brussels, Thatcher was 'rather reticent' on unification. Bush hooted with laughter: 'That is the understatement of the year.'[57] Mitterrand had come to the same realisation a week before at Strasbourg when Thatcher pulled out her maps of wartime Europe and declared 'We have to place some limits on the Germans.'[58]

By this time, of course, Mitterrand was resigned to German unity but he warned Bush 'it could cause a diplomatic crisis if it goes too fast. It would have the wrong effect and would complicate East–West relations at a time when the West is winning hands down.' Like the Americans, he feared anarchy in the GDR and therefore believed 'developments in Germany must be linked to developments in NATO and the EC'. Mitterrand insisted to Bush, as he had to Kohl, 'we must move on arms control, on EC integration, on European monetary union, and on US–EC cooperation all at the same time in order to create a new Europe. Otherwise, we will be back in 1913 and we could lose everything.' If Germany was allowed to unify and then behaved like a loose cannon, Europe might be teetering on the brink of another Great War. History loomed large in the Frenchman's mind – but, as a believer in the European project, he saw a way to move on from the darkness of the past.[59]

At their joint news conference, Mitterrand went public about Germany. 'I often made this comparison, including with President Bush: if the horses of the team don't move at the same speed, there will be an accident. And we have to deal with the German problem, in particular, and that of Eastern Europe at a pace which must be harmonious, must be in step with that of European construction.'[60] Mitterrand's line about the 'horses of the team' was nicely ambiguous. It could signify the EC as a whole or the Four Powers in particular. Whatever he meant, the canny French president was clearly aligning himself with American policy at a time when Thatcher's mordant suspicion of the Germans was pushing Britain to the sidelines. Whereas she had been a special partner for

Reagan over relations with the USSR, Bush saw more value in a close relationship with Mitterrand, as well as Kohl, over Europe and the German question.

At the end of 1989, Bush's and Baker's actions were still predicated on the assumption that East Germany remained a viable state, at least in the immediate future, and that change could be managed gradually from above by the Allied powers, in conjunction with Kohl. Even if Thatcher proved recalcitrant, the general consensus that the president had forged with Gorbachev and Mitterrand would be sufficient to coerce her. Bush saw America's role as the lead partner in what he later described as 'a careful dance'. In particular, he had to avoid stepping on Gorbachev's toes. 'I knew', he wrote, 'that if we were to see progress on reunification, it would be our role to work with Moscow as an equal on the issue, to show Gorbachev without a doubt we understood the enormous problems that a united Germany could cause to the Soviet Union.'[61]

*

Although Bush did not yet know it, Gorbachev was slowly beginning to come round. On 4 December 1989 – the same day that Bush addressed his NATO allies in Brussels – Gorbachev put his own spin on the Malta summit to the leaders of the Warsaw Pact in Moscow. Echoing his refrain at the summit about a mutual convergence, he claimed that Bush had agreed that *both* alliances should serve as the basis of stability and security in Europe. He also denounced the 1968 invasion of Czechoslovakia. And on the German question he said Bush had conceded that Britain and France shared Soviet reservations about German unification.[62] What's more, with growing nationalist unrest in Georgia, Azerbaijan and the Baltic States, the Soviet leader was coming under mounting pressure domestically for failing to hold the bloc together – which helps explain his outbursts to Genscher on the 5th. Four days after that, at a meeting of the CPSU Central Committee, he was criticised by several participants for running foreign policy without reference to the party. Gorbachev lost patience and offered to resign. It took time to calm the meeting and, in the circumstances, he chose to make no reference to the Malta summit. It was clear that Gorbachev could not translate success abroad into support at home. Ending the Cold War – so popular in the West – was arousing growing resentment in Moscow itself.[63]

His underlying problem was that he had little control over events, especially in Germany. By the New Year it was becoming evident that the GDR's days were numbered: with the economy in free fall, the state no longer viable and Kohl fast-forwarding a total merger.

By now the chancellor had revised his estimate of the likely timescale for unification, judging that it might take less than five years, maybe only two or three.[64] His optimism was rooted in a new confidence that Mitterrand was fully on board. Kohl's frissons of anxiety in December about the French leader's trips to Kiev and East Berlin – was the Franco-German tandem being secretly compromised by some sinister Franco-Soviet entente? – were dispelled by a day together on 4 January at Mitterrand's holiday home at Latché, near Biarritz on the Atlantic coast. Walking and talking along the beach helped clear the air and, Kohl felt, finally convinced Mitterrand that the chancellor was really serious about the indissolubility of Germany and Europe.[65]

That was a great relief to Kohl. But he also took seriously what Mitterrand kept saying about Gorbachev – his concern that 'resolving the German problem should not end in a Russian tragedy'. The growing fear was that if Gorbachev fell and a hardliner came to power, everything would become much more difficult. Yet Mitterrand turned it around, telling Kohl that 'Gorbachev's fate depends more on you' than on what the hardliners might do. 'And Gorbachev knows this,' Kohl added. The Federal Republic was already the major donor of aid to Eastern Europe, potentially also for the USSR given Bush's financial reticence, and was likely to have the most influence in preventing the dissolution of East Germany becoming a full-blown crisis in the heart of Europe. Kohl could see ever more clearly that he enjoyed real political leverage through the power of the Deutschmark. But after Gorbachev's explosions in December he knew he had to use that power judiciously and without seeming in too much of a hurry.[66]

Kohl no longer had any doubt that East Germany was totally unravelling. On 11 January Modrow had announced a plan to relaunch in modified form the Stasi operations, renamed as the Office of the Protection of the Constitution. This was a flagrant breach of earlier promises in the round-table talks to eradicate the Stasi. In response to what seemed like counter-revolution, huge strikes and protests broke out in East Berlin and other cities. Neues Forum called for a demonstration on the 15th outside the Stasi's central HQ, and this got completely out of hand as protestors stormed and ransacked the building. Three weeks later the Council of Ministers established a committee to implement the root-and-branch dismantling of the whole internal security apparatus. The Stasi had been the cement of the GDR state, through both the fear it generated and also the jobs it provided (employment for nearly 1.2% of the population). Moreover, Modrow's government had now lost all legitimacy. Even though he now brought the elections forward to 18 March and came up with a new half-baked plan for German unification ('*Deutschland einig Vaterland*'), it was obvious that his days and those of his party were numbered.

Indeed, the GDR haemorrhaged a further 58,000 young citizens in January alone without any diminution of the flow in sight; the renamed communist SED-PDS lost some 1.6 million of its 2.3 million party members; and soon the West CDU like all other big West German parties (SPD, FDP and Greens) were funding and therefore shaping the election campaigns of their sister parties or aligned lists. It was Kohl, Brandt and Genscher who became the political icons for many East Germans. When on the margins of the Davos World Economic Forum Modrow begged Kohl yet again for DM 15 billion, this time just to survive until the elections, the chancellor not only said no but boldly stated that the only option going forward was rapid economic union founded on the Deutschmark. Modrow had no choice but to agree.[67]

The dramatic turn of events in East Berlin inevitably had an impact in Moscow. Meeting with senior advisers on 26 January, shortly after a fraught trip to renegade Lithuania where calls for independence grew louder by the day, Gorbachev made plain that he now believed German unity to be ultimately inescapable – despite the fact that it would take 'several years' for the FRG to 'economically gobble up the GDR'. Fixated on preparing well for the 'all-European summit' and on the CSCE process at large, Gorbachev made his top tactical priority no longer blocking unification but slowing it down. He remained emphatic, however, that 'no one should expect unified Germany to join NATO'. The USSR's best leverage, in his view, derived from its Allied occupation rights and the Red Army presence in the GDR – even though he said it was axiomatic that 'there will be no action by our forces'. Like the Americans, he wanted to deal with German issues through talks among the Allied powers, but he was willing to include the FRG and maybe the GDR in what he called the 'Five' or 'Six'. All this was, nevertheless, his private position: he was not yet ready *in public* to give a green light to unification.[68]

In the New Year of 1990, therefore, the Soviet leadership was essentially still optimistic that time was on its side to shape both German unification and European geopolitics. They believed the USSR could forestall any erosion of Soviet security interests and the Warsaw Pact was going to survive the revolutions of 1989. This latter idea was not completely ridiculous because opinion in Eastern Europe was divided. Hungary and Czechoslovakia pressed for total Soviet troop withdrawal, which the Kremlin agreed in February would be completed by July 1991. But Poland, despite its historic antagonism towards Russia, was even more fearful of a resurgent, unified Germany and its possible territorial ambitions; at this point it actually wanted to consolidate the Warsaw Pact. Indeed, at the Pact's meeting on 29 January in Moscow, the Mazowiecki government demanded the continued presence of at least 275,000 Soviet troops in the GDR and Poland. This was also intended as a bargaining chip, to extract final German recognition of the Oder–Neisse border.[69]

On the American side in January the Bush administration concentrated on follow-up from Malta and on preparing a full-scale summit in Washington in late spring. Their aim was to sign arms-control treaties on strategic nuclear weapons (START) and conventional forces in Europe (CFE). In particular, the White House wanted to encourage more withdrawals of Soviet troops from Eastern Europe – both to further defuse the Cold War in general and also to reduce the danger of another 'Tiananmen'. Since Red Army forces were far more numerous than America's, any negotiated reductions to parity would require far larger cuts on the Soviet side, as well as having the additional benefit of legitimising the continued US military presence in Europe. Bush envisaged a figure of 195,000 on either side in the Central Zone and planned to feature this new CFE initiative in his upcoming State of the Union address at the end of the month.[70]

Concerned to explain this in advance to Thatcher, Mitterrand and Kohl – lest they fear signs of a possible US withdrawal from Europe – Bush sent Deputy Secretary of State Lawrence Eagleburger and Deputy National Security Adviser Robert Gates on a whirlwind tour of Western Europe. This was a tried-and-tested double act, nicknamed in Washington 'Tweedledum and Tweedledee'.[71] Their most instructive European conversation was with Kohl because, for the first time, he began to reveal his attitude to unified Germany's relations with NATO. The president's emissaries explained that Bush hoped the USSR would go along with the CFE proposal because thereby Gorbachev could save face at home and abroad by being able to announce Soviet troop withdrawals as part of arms-control negotiations rather than as the result of pressure from East European post-communist governments.

The chancellor backed the American plan. He said he was keen to keep the United States coupled to Europe. By doing so he hoped to reassure the White House and counter US scepticism about holding a CSCE summit on Europe's future later in 1990. What's more, as he saw it, the US plan could have distinct benefits for Germany. A cutback to 195,000 on each side implied the withdrawal of up to half the Soviet troops stationed in the GDR (currently 380,000). Such a move would greatly enhance the FRG's security.[72]

With his European allies fully on board, Bush went public with his CFE troop-reduction plan in his speech on Capitol Hill on the evening of 31 January. He packaged it within a grand vision of where Europe and the world were going. 'There are singular moments in history, dates that divide all that goes before from all that comes after,' he told Congress. '1945 provided the common frame of reference, the compass points of the post-war era we've relied upon to understand ourselves. And that was our world, until now. The events of the year just ended, the revolution of '89, have been a chain reaction, changes so striking that it marks the beginning of a new era in the world's affairs.'[73]

Earlier that day in Bavaria, however, Hans-Dietrich Genscher had set out his own distinctive view of the future in an address at the Evangelische Akademie in Tutzing. This was where twenty-seven years earlier Egon Bahr had delivered his celebrated lecture about a Neue Ostpolitik. In contrast with Bush's and Baker's emphasis on NATO as a framing agent, the West German foreign minister wanted to transcend the Cold War and German division by consensual pan-European solutions. Instead of reworking an institution from one side of the Iron Curtain, he hoped to create something new, to which both sides contributed equally. His benchmark was therefore not NATO but the Conference on Security and Cooperation in Europe convened for the first time in Helsinki in 1975. This détente-era process would, in his view, provide a genuinely 'all-European' exit strategy from the Cold War.[74]

Here was a very different approach from the one set out by Baker to the Berlin Press Club, seven weeks earlier. The contrast was not surprising. The two foreign ministers came at the German question from opposite directions. Baker had peered through the Wall on 12 December at what was left of East Germany from a deeply American perspective, tinged with incredulity. His German counterpart, standing beside him, was still the man from Halle, who saw and felt a homeland lost and, now, perhaps to be regained.

Although Genscher had become a titan of West German politics, these emotional roots in an East German *Heimat*, as much as his ambition for a place in history, account for his deep and outspoken support for German unification. And his professional background helps to explain his belief that the process should be accomplished through legal agreements, as a peaceful embrace of the Soviet bloc. For Genscher, therefore, transcending the division of Germany was an issue of both heart and head. Despite their differences of perspective, Genscher and Baker had in common that they were lawyers who sought orderly solutions in a disorderly world. And whereas their leaders were men of instinct and impulse, the two foreign ministers focused on principles and institutions – seeking architectural frameworks for a new order. In their memoirs both used this figure of speech: Baker referred to 'Diplomacy as Architecture'; Genscher wrote about 'Rebuilding a House Divided'.[75]

Genscher's proposed structure was profoundly at odds with the rough designs of his own chancellor. Exacerbating the tension, Genscher felt jealous of his own prerogative as foreign minister while Kohl insisted that Deutschlandpolitik was a matter for the boss (*Chefsache*). Genscher had stolen the show on the balcony in Prague in September 1989, telling the East Germans they could come West. Then Kohl hit back with his Ten-Point Plan in November, about which Genscher had no prior notice, and trumped him again in December with that performance in Dresden. So the foreign minister's Tutzing speech – deliberately not cleared with the Chancellery – may be seen as the next round in this battle between West Germany's big beasts. Kohl had spoken only in private, and then in hints, about how he saw the security architecture for a unified Germany. Tutzing provided Genscher with the opportunity to step in and make his mark. Like an insect, he was also putting out feelers to get a response and gauge the international climate.[76]

Sensitive to how things looked from the other side of the crumbling Iron Curtain, Genscher used his speech to address Moscow's anxieties. Following the bouleversement in Eastern Europe in 1989, he insisted that 'it was necessary to give special attention to the security interests of the Soviet Union' and to avoid interfering in the affairs of the Warsaw Pact. He argued that NATO should declare unequivocally that 'whatever happens in the Warsaw Pact there will be no expansion of NATO territory eastwards, that is to say, any closer to the borders of the Soviet Union. This security guarantee is important for the Soviet Union and its conduct.' What's more, he warned that rapprochement between the two Germanies would be blocked by the USSR if the West proposed 'incorporating the part of Germany at present forming the GDR within NATO's military structures'. He envisaged that the two military alliances would continue for the moment but would in time 'move away from confrontation to cooperation' and eventually become 'elements' of what he called a new 'cooperative security structure throughout Europe'.[77]

Genscher did not go into great detail at Tutzing – his speech raised as many questions as it answered – but it seems that the German foreign minister favoured the ultimate dissolution of both NATO and the Warsaw Pact into a pan-European security structure under the aegis of the CSCE. This conflicted, of course, with Bush's and Baker's scenario for a new Atlanticism. Yet Genscher's ideas held considerable attractions for Gorbachev. At Malta the Soviet leader had talked about a 'Helsinki II' summit in pursuit of his own concept of a 'Common European Home' and advocated the transformation of NATO and the Warsaw Pact into 'more political than military' alliances.[78]

The Tutzing speech of 31 January therefore represented a potential provocation for the Bush administration and, when Genscher visited Washington on 2 February, he was pressed by Baker to clarify his position. How exactly the conversation unfolded is unclear, because no minutes appear to exist on either side. But some light is shed on the sensitive nature of this conversation by a report from Baker cabled on the 3rd to the US ambassador in Bonn, Vernon Walters, with the express instruction to 'review the substance' and then discuss 'with Teltschik in order to ensure the Chancellery and Foreign Ministry is fully up to date on the state of our dialogue on these issues'.

The two men talked for two hours: 'German unification is a fast-moving train', said Genscher, 'only the rapid prospect of unification can stabilise a rapidly deteriorating situation in the GDR' and stem the tide of emigrants 'from East to West'. He confirmed that 'neutrality' for a united Germany was 'out of the question' and that the new German state would 'remain in NATO' because the Alliance 'was an essential building block to a new Europe'. In this context he reiterated his Tutzing view of there being a 'need to assure the Soviets that NATO would not extend its territorial coverage to the area of the GDR nor anywhere else in Eastern

Europe for that matter'. But Genscher's subsequent emphasis – and 'he spent a lot of time elaborating on his recent speech' – lay on the 'CSCE process' for the wider European architecture of unification. Not only would it help 'the Soviets to "save face"', in the long run CSCE would supersede all other security arrangements, making them effectively transitional. This was because ultimately, according to his vision of the future, it was the CSCE that would be 'the vehicle to new security arrangements in all of Europe'. Genscher wanted this pan-European forum to be institutionalised via two CSCE summits in 1990 (in Paris) and 1992 (in Helsinki). Baker, however, would not go that far, suggesting that he did not think that the CSCE alone would 'satisfy the need of the Soviets to feel involved'. The Secretary of State did not really engage further and left the CSCE idea hanging.[79]

Afterwards the two foreign ministers informed the world media that, as regards Germany in NATO, they were 'in full agreement'. Genscher stated once more that there was 'no intention to extend the NATO area of defence and security toward the east'. But when journalists demanded more details, he specified 'no halfway membership this way or that'.[80] In other words, NATO membership would be enjoyed by all of unified Germany (rooted in Articles 5 and 6 of the North Atlantic Treaty), but former GDR territory would not be used for NATO troops and materiel. Genscher was trying to make a legalistic distinction between 'political' NATO and 'military' NATO. It should be noted that expansion of the Alliance beyond Germany itself was not mentioned in public, nor did this seem of major political concern at the time when the Warsaw Pact was still intact.[81] Nevertheless, on 2 February Genscher had managed to somewhat sharpen his Tutzing concept and it appeared that he and Baker were now more on the same page. In doing so, however, the Secretary of State acted off his own bat, without instruction from the White House, just as the German foreign minister often pursued his own line without special directive from the Chancellery.[82]

Moreover, practicalities were largely unaddressed. And on process, one further key difference did emerge. Baker pressed for a 2 + 4 structure involving the two Germanies and the Four Powers as the framework within which to negotiate Germany's new security arrangements. Genscher, with his fixation on the CSCE, according to Baker's cable, 'seemed not to have thought along these lines', but 'was open to the idea'. For him the guiding maxim was that nothing should be done 'that makes the Soviets feel discriminated against'.[83]

A week later, on 9 and 10 February, first Baker and then Kohl visited Moscow – as a deliberate sign that the Americans and Germans were indeed 'partners in leadership'. They made progress on the question of unification but not on the overarching security structure.

Baker's visit was intended to prepare the ground for a Bush–Gorbachev summit that would develop the understandings reached in Malta. The outline agenda he discussed with Gorbachev and Shevardnadze covered the usual range of Cold War issues. Baker urged progress on CFE and START. The Russians pushed back strongly when he criticised continued Soviet support for the Nazibullah regime in Afghanistan. Gorbachev went for him over the recent US military intervention in Panama. On Nicaragua, Baker conceded that the USA would recognise the Sandinista government if elections there were conducted fairly. Then they got on to the question they could not avoid: Germany.

The 2 + 4 formula did not take long. Shevardnadze favoured the CSCE process but Baker called that 'too unwieldy' and appealed to a sense of shared history. 'We fought a war together to bring peace to Europe. We didn't do so well handling the peace in the Cold War. And now we are faced with rapid and fundamental change. And we are in a better position to cooperate in preserving peace.' Gorbachev agreed with Baker. '4 + 2 or 2 + 4, assuming it relies on an international legal basis, is suitable for the situation.' Baker, as he put it, 'pocketed' Gorbachev's assent 'quietly and quickly', while noting later that this was the first time he had seen Shevardnadze 'in denial on an issue that Gorbachev was facing head-on'. Here, although the Secretary of State did not know it, was a straw in the wind.[84]

Baker then moved on to explain that Washington, like Bonn, rejected the idea of German neutrality – the Kremlin's demand for a unified Germany outside NATO and the Warsaw Pact. He argued that neutrality would not prevent possible German remilitarisation; on the contrary, a Germany unbound might feel encouraged to acquire its own nuclear weapons. Following on from this, he said, America's West European partners and several East Europeans had in fact asked for a continued US presence on the continent. But of course, if the allies demanded US withdrawal, Washington would comply. 'If US forces stayed in Germany, within the framework of NATO', he promised that 'neither the jurisdiction nor the military presence of NATO would extend one inch to the east'. In effect, Baker was conveying Genscher's ideas on Germany and NATO in the guise of presenting America's own thoughts on these issues.[85]

His phraseology was more specific than Genscher's Tutzing formula: 'no expansion of NATO territory eastwards'. But greater specificity did not enhance the clarity. Did Baker mean not crossing the inner-German border, or also the frontier with Poland? What exactly did he intend to signify by 'jurisdiction' and 'military presence'. Troops? Conventional forces? Nuclear weapons?

Baker had talked almost uninterrupted for several minutes. Gorbachev responded vaguely, 'I want to say that by and large we share this kind of thinking.' Then he came out with his most unequivocal statement to date. There was nothing 'terrible' in the prospect of a unified Germany. Britain and France might have their concerns but this was not the case for the Soviets and the Americans. 'We are big countries and have our own weight.' The NATO issue remained unresolved, however, so Baker returned to it at the end of the meeting, posing a precise question. He asked whether Gorbachev preferred an unbound, united Germany without US troops on German soil, or a united Germany in NATO with the guarantee of non-extension of NATO jurisdiction or NATO forces beyond the current line and into eastern Germany. Gorbachev stated that the Soviets intended to contemplate all options. But, he added, 'obviously an extension of the NATO zone is unacceptable'. Baker replied, 'I agree.'[86] And yet, Gorbachev judged, it was too early now to come to any conclusion. Remaining non-committal, he did not appear to feel any particular urge or time pressure to resolve the big security questions on this occasion.

The following day, 10 February, Kohl secured his own reassurances about German unity in the Kremlin. The mood in the two-and-a-half-hour meeting was 'cool' and 'focused' – as the chancellor put it. Gorbachev, so angry about the Ten-Point Plan in December, did not utter a word of criticism of Kohl or his policies. The Soviet leader explicitly mentioned the economic benefits of unification for Moscow and told the chancellor that the decision about whether or not to unify rested with the Germans themselves. According to the Soviet minutes of the meeting, Gorbachev specified that 'it surely could be said that between the Soviet Union, the Federal Republic and the GDR are no differences of opinion on the question of the unity of the German nation and the Germans shall decide this issue themselves. In short, on the most important point of departure exists agreement: the Germans themselves have to make their choice. And they ought to know this very position of ours.'

'The Germans know that. You want to say, that the issue of unity is the choice of the Germans themselves.'

'But in the context of the realities.'

'I agree with that,' Kohl concluded.[87]

To date, the chancellor had heard only second-hand talk about 'self-de-termination'. Now he was getting it from the horse's mouth. Almost tearful with delight, Kohl assured Gorbachev that only peace would arise from German soil, gesturing to his aide Horst Teltschik to write everything down. 'This is the breakthrough,' Teltschik noted in his diary. 'A sensation. No demand for a price and no pressure. What a meeting!'[88]

The news was revealed to the world's press at 10 p.m. after a convivial Kremlin banquet. 'This is a good day for Germany and a happy day for me personally,' the chancellor declared. 'The general secretary has prom-ised me uncontrovertibly that the Soviet Union will respect the decision of the Germans to live in one state and that it is up to the Germans to decide on the timing and route to unity.'[89] The Soviet news agency *TASS* published the declaration and emphasised the 'personal trust' between Kohl and Gorbachev. The German newspaper *Süddeutsche Zeitung* spoke of Gorbachev offering Kohl the 'key to resolving the German question'.[90] In the course of two days the Americans and the Germans had returned from Moscow with effectively a 'green light' for German unification. How this was to be squared with the security of Europe was still to be deter-mined. But on that issue, Bush would call the shots.

*

The president had reacted differently from Baker to the ideas that Genscher had floated at Tutzing and refined in Washington on 2 February. After listening to his national security staff, the president set out his own thinking to Kohl in a letter on 9 February. He explained that the continued presence of US forces on German soil and the continuation of nuclear deterrence were both 'critical to assuring stability in this time of change and uncertainty'. And so he suggested to Kohl that a component of a united Germany's NATO membership could be what he called a '*special military status* for what is now the territory of the GDR'.[91]

This approach differed from those of Genscher and Baker in that, as Scowcroft put it, '*all* of a united Germany would be inside NATO terri-tory and jurisdiction and thus covered by NATO's security guarantee'. And this status would be accompanied by 'substantial, perhaps ultimately total, Soviet troop withdrawals from Central and Eastern Europe'. The implication was that, because the whole of unified Germany would be within NATO, the Red Army would have to pull out completely from the former GDR. This, said Scowcroft, was 'a critical correction' in order to 'prevent Gorbachev from tying us in knots with the Genscher idea'. The president was, however, conscious – as were Genscher and Baker in their own ways – of the need to make NATO more palatable to Gorbachev. He proposed again that the Alliance should have 'a changing mission, with more emphasis on its political role'.[92]

Baker's and Genscher's phraseology had the effect of limiting the options – seeming to rule out any kind of military expansion by NATO – whereas Bush's language of special military status potentially ruled every option in as far Germany was concerned. This wasn't just hair-splitting about words. It represented a significant change in policy, from a defensive American stance to something more assertive.

The White House had now clearly decided that unification was to be achieved unequivocally on Western, indeed US, terms. NATO should not only survive but serve as the vehicle to perpetuate America's leading role in European security after the Cold War. This geopolitical perspective was underscored by the current NATO secretary general, Manfred Wörner – a former CDU politician for whom Bush had considerable respect. 'This is a unique opportunity. This is a decisive moment,' he told the president at Camp David on 24 February. 'We must avoid the classic German temptation: to float freely and bargain with both East and West … That is your historic task.'[93] The Bush administration saw the Atlantic Alliance as a 'force of stability' which, 'along with other multilateral institutions such as the EC and the CSCE', should 'overlap to provide a common security and policy framework to complement the role of economic and political groupings'.[94] As Baker put it, 'if history is a guide, then continued US presence & influence would be constructive'.[95]

The pace of American diplomacy was quickening. At the first meeting of NATO and Warsaw Pact foreign ministers since the fall of the Wall, held in Ottawa on 11–12 February, Baker had persuaded his colleagues to accept the 2 + 4 framework. He and Genscher dealt briskly with protests from minor powers such as Italy and Poland and from those who had imagined a grand peace conference – somehow completing the unfinished business from Potsdam in 1945.[96] That hurdle surmounted, Bush invited Kohl to come over for a personal discussion on the principle and parameters of Germany's NATO membership. This was the crunch issue now.[97] The White House feared that in an election year the

Germans might succumb to nationalist-pacifist thinking. Bush therefore considered it imperative to 'get Kohl to agree that a united Germany would be a full member of NATO and a participant in its integrated military structure', unlike France since the days of de Gaulle. Equally important, he wanted Kohl to 'state that publicly' during their meeting at Camp David – the presidential retreat in rural Maryland – scheduled for 24–5 February.[98]

On the morning of Kohl's arrival, Bush phoned Canadian prime minister Brian Mulroney – with whom he had a close relationship – using him as a sounding board on how to handle the chancellor. In confidence, Bush revealed nagging fears about German power and his underlying tensions with Baker. 'I do not think we can stand in the way of unification. Helmut has a deep emotional commitment to the fatherland. I talked to Jim Baker. He wants us to let the Soviets stay in East Germany. It gives me heartburn ... That is what we have been against all these years.' Mulroney agreed: 'I don't see how, in fairness, we can accept that. The minimum price for German unity should be full membership of Germany in NATO and full membership in all the Western organisations and full support for American leadership of the Alliance.' The Canadian premier became emotional: 'I will tell you: we are not renting our seat in Europe. We paid for it. If people want to know how Canada paid for its seat in Europe, they should check out the graves in Belgium and France. We were there in two wars, and paid an enormous cost. It is not unreasonable to say that change comes about, but NATO got us this far. Solidarity of the Alliance will get us further.' Bush was greatly reassured. He noted in his memoirs: 'Brian was right on target.'[99]

The president was particularly struck by one line from Mulroney: 'you are the only one to lead this alliance – you must do it'. This message was further amplified when Wörner, Bush's guest over lunch, insisted: 'An American president who wants a Europe whole and free cannot accept neutralization of a united Germany.' Neutrality would not allow for a security framework within the EC because that organisation only had a 'small security role'. As for the Western European Union (WEU), it was 'pure discussion, no hardware', and the 'CSCE is all talk.' For this reason, Wörner told Bush, 'I think *you* have to maintain the strong position that Germany must be a member of NATO. There can be no ambiguity. There can be no "association" with NATO.' Indeed, stressed Wörner, '*you* and Germany have to agree now on German unity within NATO and sell this to the Russians'.

Musing on Mulroney's and Wörner's words while waiting for the chancellor, Bush reflected that 'I think we have a disproportionate role for stability. We've got strong willed players – large and small in Europe – but only the United States can do this.' It would not be easy, of course. 'I've got to look after the US interest in all of this without reverting to a kind of isolationistic or peacenik view on where we stand in the world.' And he also had to think about America's role in a confusing new world. 'Who's the enemy? I keep getting asked' – because it was no longer the 'evil empire'. 'It's apathy; it's the inability to predict accurately; it's dramatic change that can't be foreseen; and it's events that can't be predicted.' That, for Bush, was the great new challenge: 'There are all kinds of events that we can't foresee that require a strong NATO, and there's all kinds of potential instability that requires a strong US presence.'[100]

His reverie was interrupted by the sound of the helicopter bringing Kohl and his wife Hannelore from Dulles airport in Washington on a bleak and cloudy morning. It was freezing – an icy wind blowing across the mountaintop and hard snow on the ground. The German visitors were accompanied by Scowcroft and Baker – the latter 'resplendent in red flannel shirt, cowboy boots and hat' – as Bush noted. This was the first time in the forty-year history of the FRG that a West German chancellor had been accorded the privilege of a stay at the presidential hideaway.

Equally significant, Genscher had been deliberately excluded by both Kohl and Bush. After changing into casual clothes and enjoying a 'lively lunch', the statesmen moved to the large wood-panelled living room of the main cottage for their talks.[101]

A cosy chat: Kohl, Bush and Baker at Camp David

Kohl categorically ruled out the possibility that Soviet troops should remain on German soil. But he recognised that an orderly, phased withdrawal would take time. At least during that interim period, he argued, no Western forces, even from the Bundeswehr (the German army), should be moved onto former GDR soil. Bush, like Kohl, was confident that eventually Gorbachev would not be able to hold out against all-German membership of NATO. The chancellor laid particular responsibility here on the president, because so much of 'Gorbachev's prestige was at stake over the German question and Bush was the only equal negotiating partner'. The onus was therefore on the upcoming superpower Washington summit, not the 2 + 4 process. On the other hand, Kohl believed that talking would not be enough. 'This may end up as a matter of cash,' he told the Americans. 'They need money.' Bush batted this back at Kohl: 'You have deep pockets.'

Summing up, the president said:

> On US–Soviet relations, we want to see Gorbachev succeed. We want a successful US–Soviet summit which will give him a boost at home. We want a CFE agreement signed. A CSCE Summit. A START accord this year. Having said that, the Soviets are not in a position to dictate Germany's relationship with NATO. What worries me is talk that Germany must not stay in NATO. To hell with that. We prevailed and they didn't. We can't let the Soviets clutch victory from the jaws of defeat.[102]

The two leaders had seen eye to eye, which was made abundantly clear in a joint press conference at the end of the talks. Bush stated:

> We share a common belief that a unified Germany should remain a full member of the North Atlantic Treaty Organisation, including participation in its military structure. We agreed that US military forces should remain stationed in the united Germany and elsewhere in Europe as a continuing guarantor of stability. The chancellor and I are also in agreement that in a unified state the former territory of the GDR should have a special military status, that it would take into account the legitimate security interests of all interested countries, including those of the Soviet Union.

Kohl echoed his sentiments: 'the security link between North America and Europe is and continues to be today and in future for us Germans

– that is to say also for a united Germany – of vital importance. That is why we need the presence of our American friends in Europe, in Germany – and that includes the presence of American forces.' It was obvious that Kohl had now adopted Bush's policy and language, in other words that the Genscher line had been abandoned.[103]

But Genscher did not capitulate straight away. Although now accepting the NATO framework for German unification, he did not give up on the CSCE as the architecture for the unity of Europe as well. On 21 March, a month after Kohl and Bush met at Camp David, Genscher took the opportunity of meeting Baker and Shevardnadze at Namibia's independence ceremonies in Windhoek to discuss future options for the new free Europe and the dangers of 'Balkanisation'.[104] From their chat, Baker gathered that Genscher was committed to the Atlantic Alliance but envisaged that the CSCE would 'supplement NATO, not replace it'.[105] Genscher highlighted his worries about an emerging power vacuum between the USSR and NATO, if and when all of Germany joined the Alliance and the Warsaw Pact started falling apart. He and Baker agreed that, to avoid antagonising the Russians, East European desires for closer ties with the Alliance should be deflected.[106]

Nevertheless, their discussion shows that Western leaders were sensing that NATO might be seen as a viable solution to security dilemmas not only by Germans but also by countries further east. Genscher hoped of course that in the long run his pan-European visions would render obsolete any East European interest in NATO.[107] Emboldened by his talks in Windhoek, he went public two days later in a speech in Luxembourg on 23 March. He dwelt at length on his dream of institutionalising the CSCE and of eventually dissolving the Warsaw Pact and NATO into a new European 'association of common collective security' (*Verbund gemeinsamer kollektiver Sicherheit*). NATO, he implied, 'with its present forms and functions would be needed only for a transitional phase of unspecified duration'.[108]

These ideas may have been a typical Genscherite fudge, but the speech itself was seen as an overt provocation to the Chancellery. Indeed it was probably motivated by Genscher's exclusion from Camp David – the latest round in their tit-for-tat rivalry. Certainly Kohl was absolutely incensed. On the same day that the speech was delivered, he wrote an angry letter to his foreign minister stating that 'with all formality, I want to let you know that I neither share nor support your views'. He particularly rejected the idea of an 'ultimate merger' (*aufgehen*) of the two alliances in a new European structure. And, he added, 'I am not prepared to accept that you predetermine the position of the Federal government on these questions without consultation.' In other words, Kohl insisted on a single policy for the German government and on his prerogative as chancellor to make it.[109]

Kohl's rebuke clearly had the desired effect. Thereafter Genscher stayed silent, at least in public, and Washington and Bonn started working towards the goals agreed at Camp David. The other two Western members of the Four Powers were onside: despite some underlying misgivings about German unification, both France and Britain considered NATO membership as both a satisfactory framework to restrain Germany and also a kind of insurance policy against the USSR.[110] The task was now to gain Moscow's consent to unified Germany's NATO membership, given that the USSR was about to lose its most prized Warsaw Pact ally, the GDR, to the other side.

*

When he had met Baker in Moscow in February, Gorbachev had declared 'an extension of the NATO zone' to be 'unacceptable'. Nevertheless, he also stated that he would explore all options. Among other models floating around was the concept of a security arrangement based on a new part-nership between the USSR and the West that would allow for a European peace order without NATO and the Warsaw Pact. This was an idea touted by Egon Bahr, the Social Democrat architect of the party's celebrated Ostpolitik. Bahr stated on 27 February, when in Moscow, that nobody in Germany except within the CDU/CSU wanted rapid unification. So the best strategy to ensure peace and stability was indeed to build a 'Common European Home' founded on a Central European security zone consisting of Denmark, the Benelux states, the two Germanies, Poland, Czechoslovakia and Hungary as well as the USA and USSR, equipped with a 'European Security Council' and with all national armed forces placed under an integrated command.[111]

Throughout the winter and spring, Gorbachev and Shevardnadze continued to speak out, in public and in private, against full German NATO membership. They played with a variety of possible solutions to the German security question without plumping for any one of them. As Bush had rightly said, the big new enemy was unpredictability.

At least the situation in East Germany was no longer the major issue after the 18 March elections. Kohl's sister party the CDU-Ost had won a landslide victory as part of the Wahlbündnis Allianz für Deutschland, putting the chancellor in clear control of the trajectory of unification within Germany as a whole. This meant economic and monetary union, scheduled for 1 July, and the absorption of the GDR state into the FRG. Both these outcomes were the result of clever tactical moves ahead of the GDR vote, not least to stem the chronic migratory flow from East to West. Regarding monetary union, Kohl had in midwinter – over the heads of the Bundesbank bosses – promised East Germans the Deutschmark as a response to their ever-louder street chants, including the jocular threat: 'Kommt die D-Mark bleiben wir. Kommt sie nicht, gehen wir zu ihr' ('If the Deutschmark comes, we'll stay. If it doesn't come, we'll go to it'). As for unifying the two states, Kohl's actions reflected his conviction of the need for the speediest and least complicated method. This was to be done – not, as Oskar Lafontaine's SPD preferred, via Article 146 of the Basic Law which envisaged the joining of two equal halves to form a new entity – but through Article 23, whereby the East German states (Länder) would simply accede to the Federal Republic. In other words, they would take on the constitution, penal code, political system and currency of the FRG in the winding down of the GDR – pending a final decision on the shape of the post-Wall European security order.[112]

The really incalculable element in resolving the conundrum of European security was now the USSR itself. Gorbachev's privatisation policies were failing: productivity was negligible and inflation rampant, while salaries and rents remained fixed. The Soviet leader was desperate to conclude a trade agreement with the United States. And food was so scarce that he had to consider begging the West for donations. On this, he looked to Kohl in particular and the chancellor had responded with DM 220 million in aid for food and clothing.[113] In Soviet politics, the increasing devolution of power to the republics and the innovation of free multiparty parliamentary elections began to create what Gorbachev called 'a parade of sovereignties' – with Lithuania in the vanguard. None of this made for coherent policymaking in international affairs.

Whereas Bush and his Western partners had been able to close ranks over Germany's alliance membership, Moscow was deeply divided. For example, at Windhoek in his conversation with Genscher, Shevardnadze had postulated four possible options:

- first, a unified Germany in NATO;
- second, a neutral unified Germany;
- third, a revision of the Potsdam agreements of 1945 – in other words, a full peace treaty to draw a final line under the Second World War, arranged under the aegis of the CSCE;
- fourth, the simultaneous destruction of both alliances and the establishment of a pan-European security structure.[114]

Other possibilities thrown up by the Kremlin included a demilitarised zone in Germany or even German 'double membership' of the two alliances – meaning NATO troops in the territory of former West Germany and Soviet troops in the former GDR.

Moscow's policy vacillations reflected differences in personal outlook and tactical calculation and, at a deeper level, the increasing rift between reformists and hardliners. Gorbachev's closest advisers, Anatoly Chernyaev and Georgy Shakhnazarov, were amenable to unified Germany's NATO membership, but the German experts in the Soviet Foreign Ministry and CPSU Central Committee around Valentin Falin were vehemently opposed.[115] Indeed, the latter group had only grudgingly tolerated Gorbachev's earlier consent to unification via self-determination. Fixated on traditional concepts of the USSR's geopolitical and security interests, they insisted that the new Germany must be totally neutral.[116]

As April turned to May and still no coherent line emerged on the Soviet side, Western policymakers grew increasingly optimistic. They read the debate in Russia as evidence of flexibility in the Soviet position.[117] On the other hand, there were underlying worries concerning the pressures Gorbachev was under at home – politically and economically. Thatcher was particularly anxious about 'keeping Gorbachev in the saddle'. She had told Bush back in late March that she was 'deeply worried': Gorbachev had been 'somber, pessimistic, and felt he was under attack'.[118]

Washington and Bonn agreed that the West must help the Soviet leader. Kohl and Genscher discussed this with Bush and Baker when visiting the White House on 17 May. They focused on trying to remove 'the demonic image' (*Entdämonisierung*) of the Western Alliance in Soviet eyes. By now the German foreign minister was firmly on message, with no more talk about NATO's dissolution, and the mood on the German side had become really urgent: 'We have to push unification – bring in the harvest.' Bonn was mindful of Shevardnadze's haunting question at Windhoek: 'what if perestroika is halted and a dictator comes to power?'[119]

If agreement were not reached quickly on German unification, then the resolution of all the wider issues of European security would be delayed. This would be bad for the West and the USSR. 'It is important to stress the role of the US and the Western Alliance for stability,' Genscher told Bush, because in Eastern Europe there were 'still a lot of national difficulties'. Ominously he added, 'It reminds us of 1913.' That's why NATO, besides its military function, had 'an enormous political purpose'. He urged the president when Gorbachev visited in a couple of weeks to 'underscore the importance of concluding 2 + 4' and thereby tie up the Alliance question. That should all be signed and sealed before a CSCE summit in the autumn. In other words, Bonn first wanted to resolve the German question, both internal and external, before turning to the larger orbit of Europe. These two questions were to be addressed sequentially not simultaneously.[120]

How, then, to sell to the Soviets the idea of embedding a unified Germany in NATO? Kohl focused on financial inducements. As Bush had said at Camp David, the chancellor indeed had 'deep pockets' – thanks to what Kohl liked to call his country's 'brilliant' economic situation after eight years of continuous growth. In early 1990 inflation was running at 2.3%, growth for the whole year was predicted at possibly 4% and there was an export surplus of DM 36.9 billion ($21.5 billion). In contrast, the US inflation rate was over 5% and growth under 2%, while exports were running a deficit of $88.53 billion. In short, Kohl had ample Deutschmarks to use as leverage in Moscow.[121] He confided to Bush the 'surprising talks' that had recently taken place between Gorbachev and Teltschik, especially the Soviet leader's secret request for DM 5 billion with an FRG government guarantee and for $10–15 billion from other banks including some in the USA, to purchase American wheat. What this revealed, said Kohl, was Gorbachev's 'enormous problems with his credit line', both short and medium term, which opened up real options for bargaining by the West. Kohl was keen to engage in this kind of chequebook diplomacy, as long as it was 'low-profile in public'.[122]

Genscher, however, wanted to appeal to the Soviets on grounds of principle. He was adamant that the Helsinki Final Act already enshrined the 'rights of countries to join and leave alliances'. Everybody seemed to focus on the idea of East Europeans having the right to *leave* the Warsaw Pact, but that was the wrong way to present the German case to Gorbachev. Instead Genscher believed the West should simply say to the Soviets, who were themselves signatories of the Helsinki agreement, that the Federal Republic was only asking for the right to 'remain' in an alliance. Genscher was trying to exploit an agreed principle – the right to self-determination – and one which Gorbachev had already conceded. The tactic had worked before. First in Malta in December 1989 when the Soviet leader had accepted the right of the German people to self-determination. And then in Moscow in February 1990, when he granted the Germans the right to unify if they so wished.[123]

So when Gorbachev came to Washington at the end of May Bush was primed to try this approach again. He may have been helped by Mitterrand's visit to Moscow on 25 May, when the French leader disabused the Kremlin of any hope that France would block German membership of NATO.[124] But the key ally for Bush was Germany. Communiction between Washington and Bonn was particularly intense around this time. The chancellor wanted to ensure that the president was on message, as he saw it; Bush wanted to placate Kohl but he now clearly regarded the chancellor as a valued sounding board.

On 30 May, the day the Washington summit commenced, Kohl called Bush first thing in the morning. Having gone through the necessary courtesies – 'I acknowledge very much what you have done for us and appreciate your friendship and reliability' – the chancellor launched into a list of his key concerns. 'One thing that is very important for Gorbachev to understand is that irrespective of developments, we will stand side by side. And one sign of this cooperation are the links between us by future membership of a united Germany in NATO without any limitations.' Kohl was pulling no punches: 'You should make this clear to him, but in a friendly way, and also make it clear that is the view I hold. There should be no doubt about that.' Then he came back to the money question: 'We can find a sensible economic arrangement with him. He needs help very much. He should also know that we have no intention of profiting from his weakness.' More cryptically, the chancellor raised a final point: 'It is of immense importance that we make further progress in disarmament.' What he had in mind was reducing the size of the Bundeswehr as a quid pro quo for the Red Army's withdrawal from eastern Germany and for this reduction to be enshrined in the new agreement on the reduction of conventional forces in Europe, in order that Germany not be treated as a special case.[125]

Bush replied with equal forthrightness. He said he did not expect any 'breakthrough' on Germany in his talks with Gorbachev, but promised that there would be 'no new constraints on German sovereignty' after

Four Powers rights had been terminated. 'On the economic side', he recalled their previous conversation but said that the Lithuania problem remained. Nevertheless he promised to heed Kohl's 'advice' about Gorbachev. After all, 'I don't want him to think we are taking advantage of him because of his weakness. We will move the arms-control agenda forward, but he must realise that on conventional forces, those are Alliance decisions.' On the Bundeswehr ceilings, therefore, this should be dealt with in the context of setting the force levels of all countries in the two military alliances. It was a decision for the NATO summit; not one for America or for the reunification talks. That's fine, Kohl responded: everything was up for discussion. But, he told Bush, '*we* have to agree' first, before any general agreement could be reached involving the allies.[126]

A little bit of back-seat driving from Kohl was all very well, but Bush did not find it easy going when he met the Soviet leader head-on in the White House on 31 May.[127]

In their afternoon meeting, Baker sought to soften the ground by highlighting for Gorbachev how the administration had tried to 'take the interests of the Soviet Union into account to the fullest extent'. He alluded to 'strengthening the political component' of NATO, limiting the Bundeswehr, and also suggested a transitional period in which there would be no NATO troops 'in the GDR', while Soviet troops would be allowed to stay there 'for a short period of time'.[128]

Shevardnadze then went off on a collective security line, talking about the two blocs 'moving closer together'.

The president cut in sharply: 'NATO is the anchor of stability.'

'Two anchors are better,' Gorbachev replied with a smile. 'As a seaman, you should be able to understand that.'

'And where will we find the second anchor?' the president asked.

'In the East. Let our ministers think about what it would be concretely.'

This was a typical Gorbachev manoeuvre, trying to play for time. He suggested the option of united Germany having simultaneous member-ship in the Warsaw Pact and NATO because, he claimed portentously, 'if we want to put an end to the split of the continent once and for all, the military-political structures should be synchronised in accordance with the unifying tendencies of the all-European process'.

Bush reiterated that a CSCE-style mechanism was 'too ponderous to expect any fast and concrete result'. Given the 'exceptional pace' of events in Germany, he said they 'could only rely on NATO'.

The two leaders circled around these questions for several minutes, becoming gradually more exercised.

'If you don't break your psychological stereotype,' Bush asserted, 'it will be difficult for us to come to an agreement.'

'We do not have fear of anybody,' Gorbachev shot back – 'not the US, not Germany.' And he added pugnaciously: 'I hope nobody here believes in the nonsense that one of the sides won the Cold War.'

The Soviet leader tried to regain the initiative. 'Now about trust. You assert that we do not trust the Germans. But then why would we give the green light to their unification aspirations? We could have given them the red light, we had requisite mechanisms. However, we gave them the opportunity to make their choice by democratic means. You, on the other hand, are saying that you trust the FRG, but you are pulling her into NATO, not allowing her to determine her future on her own after the final settlement. Let her decide on her own what alliance she wants to belong to.'

'I fully agree with that,' the president responded. 'But the Germans have already made their choice quite clear.'

'No, you are just trying to put them under your control ... If Germany does not want to stay in NATO, it has a right to choose a different path. This is what the Final Act says too.'[129]

At last they had got to Helsinki. The American memoirs suggest that the president quickly and adroitly drew the Soviet leader into his net. In fact, the transcript shows there had been a longish discussion, ebbing to and fro, before Gorbachev himself raised the self-determination issue by talking of united Germany being allowed to 'determine her future on her own' and deciding 'what alliance she wants to belong to'. Only then was Bush able to nail him on Helsinki.[130]

Gorbachev suggested that they make a 'public statement' on the issue. He wanted to say they agreed that, after unification, the new Germany 'would decide on its own which alliance she would be a member of'.

Bush proposed a different form of words: 'The United States is unequivocally in favour of united Germany's membership in NATO; however, if it makes a different choice, we would not contest it, we will respect it.'

Gorbachev replied: 'I agree. I accept your formulation.'[131]

At these words there was evident agitation in the Soviet camp. Gorbachev's military adviser Marshal Sergey Akhromeyev's eyes flashed angrily as he talked in loud whispers with Valentin Falin. Gorbachev indicated that the latter should speak up, whereupon Falin proceeded to reiterate the original Soviet position about the ultimate goal of a pan-European system, preceded by a German withdrawal from NATO.[132]

But Gorbachev had already given the game away and there was no going back.[133] In their joint press conference at the end of the summit on 3 June, Bush was able to make this clear without rubbing it in:

> On the matter of Germany's external alliances, I believe, as do Chancellor Kohl and members of the Alliance, that the united Germany should be a full member of NATO. President Gorbachev, frankly, does not hold that view. But we are in full agreement that the matter of Alliance membership is, in accordance with the Helsinki Final Act, a matter for the Germans to decide.[134]

Principle was one thing, practicalities quite another.[135] What really troubled Gorbachev was that the USSR had 380,000 troops and military personnel in East Germany, together with 164,000 dependants in over 1,000 locations. Taken together, these installations covered an area equivalent to the whole of the Saarland in West Germany. The equipment statistics were equally formidable: 4,100 tanks, 7,900 armoured vehicles, 3,500 artillery, 1,300 aircraft, and 800,000 tons of ammunition. If, as Kohl wanted, all this had to be withdrawn as a consequence of German unification, Gorbachev would have to relocate 10% of the Red Army manpower and 7.5% of its equipment back home to the USSR. A logistical nightmare, with grave social implications. And to withdraw all this would impose massive costs on a Soviet government teetering on the edge of bankruptcy.[136]

Aware of Gorbachev's predicament, in June Kohl started to dangle the prospect of West German money to ease the cost of the transition. But the chancellor's position was also delicate. He assumed that Moscow would drive a hard financial bargain as the price for its formal consent to a fully sovereign united Germany being a member of the Western Alliance. He told Bush on 8 June that 'if Germany is not in NATO, the US will leave and Great Britain and France will have a nuclear entente. Then the small powers will be left alone ... If we change the security situation now, it would have a catastrophic effect on the EC. There would be two nuclear powers, a neutral Germany, and the small powers with nowhere to go. Then begins a debate in Germany: why don't we have nuclear weapons?' Kohl was adamant that Germany in NATO was 'non-negotiable'. Otherwise 'forty years have been wasted. NATO would collapse and the US would withdraw from Europe'.[137]

Because the stakes were so high, Kohl had no doubt that a high price would have to be paid. 'They have the expectation that we will help – 20–25 billion'. Kohl was talking Deutschmarks but Baker remarked that he had been quoted the same figure in dollars – in other words almost double the amount. It was obvious, Kohl replied, that Gorbachev was 'playing poker', while he sought a 'deal based on reciprocity'. Bush took his usual line: 'our hands are tied on this question'. But Kohl's were not. He observed that Mitterrand had recently said 'Helmut, now you hold all the strings in your hand' – referring to the FRG's exceptional economic performance, compared even to the United States. As Bush wrote in his memoirs: 'We couldn't hand them the $20 billion of financing they wanted unless they made deep reforms – and even then we didn't have the money'.[138] Bush's message was clear: when it came to money for Moscow, Germany had to take the lead.[139]

Kohl, now ready and eager for a personal summit with the Soviet leader, started to drip-feed the Deutschmarks. First, in early June, DM 5 billion in credits from West German banks – an offer to which Gorbachev responded 'euphorically'.[140] On 11 June, he sent the long-awaited invitation for a meeting in mid-July.[141] Two weeks later the chancellor came up with another sweetener, offering a further DM 1.25 billion to cover 'stationing costs' for Soviet troops during the rest of 1990. Conscious that the East German mark was now worthless, he also allowed Soviet troops to exchange their field bank savings into Western Deutschmarks at a favourable rate after the German economic and currency union took effect on 1 July.[142]

These financial overtures came at a time of acute political sensitivity for Gorbachev. The 28th Party Congress would open on 2 July. He faced the challenge of gaining re-election as general secretary of the Communist Party of the Soviet Union (CPSU) in the face of a substantial body of delegates now intent on his overthrow. Hardliners attacked his feeble handling of the German question. General Albert Mashakov complained bitterly that 'the Soviet army is leaving the countries that our fathers liberated from fascism without a fight'. Gorbachev and Shevardnadze therefore desperately needed to show that German unification would not be a threat. Meeting with Baker on 23 June, the Soviet foreign minister repeatedly stressed the importance of the upcoming NATO summit. This, he said, must send out a signal that the Alliance was changing and a 'new Europe' was being born: it was necessary for Gorbachev's whole 'political position'.[143]

Baker took this conversation to heart, and brought the allies round.[144] The 'London Declaration on a Transformed North Atlantic Alliance' on 5 July spoke of NATO evolving into a more political alliance, with smaller military forces, reduced reliance on nuclear weapons, and 'regular diplomatic liaison' with the USSR and Eastern European states.[145] NATO secretary general Manfred Wörner proclaimed: 'The Cold War belongs to history. Our Alliance is moving from confrontation to cooperation. We look at the Soviet Union and the countries of Central and Eastern Europe as potential partners and friends.' But, Wörner added, 'Europe is not yet immune from future risk or danger.' NATO still had an essential role to play. 'This Alliance, which has contributed so much to overcoming Europe's painful division, must play its full part alongside other Western institutions in extending the stability and security we enjoy to all European nations.'[146] In other words, NATO was becoming less of a threat to the Soviet Union, but it was still essential for European stability.[147]

NATO's London Declaration helped Gorbachev get through the Party Congress without having his wings clipped. He was now free to concentrate on the upcoming meeting with Kohl.

The summit would start in Moscow on 15 July. In Bonn beforehand, Horst Teltschik and other key advisers were at pains to play down hopes of big developments, stressing larger goals such as a possible treaty of Soviet–German friendship. Just before getting on the plane Kohl gathered that this would be a highly personal affair, not merely a formal occasion in the Soviet capital. Gorbachev issued an invitation to visit the city of Stavropol, near his birthplace.[148]

Teltschik was thrilled: with such a personal gesture by the Soviet leader, the chances of this state visit ending in public failure seemed minimal. Surely, he reasoned, the Stavropol invitation could only be read as a signal that the Russians would not be negative about the 2 + 4 negotiations. Kohl, too, was excited. He considered Gorbachev's invitation as testimony to the 'good personal relations that had evolved over the past few months' between the two of them, and 'undoubtedly' a signal that German policy was on 'the right track'. However, the chancellor did not expect any major breakthroughs in Russia, and thought that the negotiations would drag on into 1991. Privately he feared that the Germany-in-NATO question would be like 'squaring the circle'.[149]

In fact, the chancellor's visit was one prong – albeit the most important

– of a Western charm offensive. The Soviet–German summit would take place immediately after Wörner visited the Kremlin. This was another remarkable moment, the first time the head of NATO – the Alliance seen in the Kremlin as its arch antagonist – had ever visited the Soviet Union.[150] And Kohl's visit came just before a trip by the president of the European Commission, Jacques Delors. In other words, the chancellor's mission should not be seen as a unilateral German act. It was embedded in a sequence of international initiatives by the key Western institutions into which Germany itself was bound.

Kohl arrived in Moscow late on the night of 14 July in a Boeing 707 of the Bundesluftwaffe. A second plane followed with a massive entourage of press and media. During the flight there was much speculation as to whether this was the chancellor's most important foreign trip to date. Whatever Teltschik had told the press officially, expectations were running sky-high.

*

The Soviet–German summit began on the morning of Sunday 15 July in Moscow. The venue was the Ministry of Foreign Affairs' main guest house – a grand neo-Gothic building, formerly the mansion of a Moscow textile magnate. Gorbachev and Kohl met with only one translator for each of them, plus their foreign-policy advisers Chernyaev and Teltschik.[151] Right from the start, Kohl was keen to get beyond the formalities to create a congenial atmosphere and highlight the momentousness of their meeting.

'These are historically significant years,' he declared. 'Such years come and go. The opportunities have to be used. If one does not act, they will pass by.' Citing Bismarck's famous phrase, he told Gorbachev, 'You have to grab the mantle of history.' Kohl was trying to convey a sense of the unique responsibility to shape the future that the two of them had to bear. He spoke of this as 'a special opportunity' of 'our generation' – a generation that had been 'too young in the Second World War to become personally guilty, but which, on the other hand, had been old enough to experience those years consciously'. Now, he said, it was their duty to use the opportunities before them to reshape the world. Gorbachev echoed Kohl's sentiments, saying that he wanted them to seize the 'great opportunities that had opened up', taking 'the notion of one world as the starting point'. He told the chancellor that cultivating Soviet–German relations was on a par for him with the ongoing 'normalisation of relations with the United States'. Kohl and Germany had been elevated, at least in Gorbachev's mind, to the position of an associate superpower.[152]

The meetings in the Kremlin were mostly ceremonial and atmospheric. The serious business would be done in the Caucasus. At a press conference before leaving Moscow, Kohl and Gorbachev radiated camaraderie. 'Smiling and bantering like old friends', to quote American commentator Serge Schmemann, they said they now 'expected major progress in their talks on lifting the last obstacles of German unity'. [153]

And so the summit caravan flew south to Stavropol. No other Western leader, not even the US president, had been accorded this unusual privilege by Gorbachev. As a gesture it was more personal than Bush hosting Kohl at Camp David – the official retreat of US presidents – because in this case the chancellor was actually being welcomed into the Soviet leader's *Heimat*. And by opening up to Kohl in this way, Gorbachev was laying to rest ghosts from the past. In a symbolic act of German–Soviet reconciliation, the two leaders placed wreaths on Stavropol's gigantic war memorial to the Red Army's fallen heroes, in a city that less than fifty years earlier had been under the Nazi jackboot. There they also met with Russian veterans of the war. This could have been an edgy moment, but Gorbachev told the old soldiers that, because he and Kohl had lived through the conflict, they had a responsibility to make peace with each other and secure Europe against any recurrence of that horror.[154]

Ending the war: Gorbachev and Kohl with Soviet veterans in Stavropol

Through these intimate gestures, the Soviet leader (and president since March) was underscoring the importance he ascribed to this summit with the man likely to become the first chancellor of a united Germany. Gorbachev waxed eloquent and emotional to journalists, noting that Stavropol lay at an altitude of 2,030 feet. He pointed to the Caucasus Mountains towering in the distance: 'We want to develop our relations further upward ... It will take time to reach the height of Mount Elbrus, but in our prospects we want to go even beyond that.'[155]

In the evening the leaders and their delegations were whisked off by helicopter to Gorbachev's mountain dacha near the resort village of Arkhyz. As soon as they arrived, they changed into informal clothes – Gorbachev in trainers, chinos and a comfy black jumper, while Kohl took off his tie and put on a big blue cardigan. Then, chatting amicably, they wandered through the grounds and into the dense forest, amid high grass, alpine flowers and tall fir trees – followed closely by a pack of Russian and German journalists.

On the edge: Kohl and Gorbachev in the Caucasus

Eventually they reached a rushing mountain stream, some twenty metres wide. Gorbachev clambered down the steep embankment to the very edge of the ice-cold torrent and then, holding out his hand, invited the portly chancellor to come and join him to look at the rapids. 'If you both fall in the water,' one German journalist joked, 'tomorrow's headline will read "Gorbachev fell. Pulled Kohl with him"'. Everyone laughed. The mood was relaxed. The cameras kept clicking. For the press, this was a perfect photo opportunity. But diplomatically it was also iconic: a moment of rare spontaneity for a summit, especially one held in the Soviet Union where all such events had previously been highly formal and meticulously staged.[156]

Soon the politicians ambled back to the dacha, a modern hunting lodge in the style of an old manor house, with a tower and inner court-yard. It was an eccentric mixture of old and new: facing you in the entrance hall stood a stuffed mountain goat next to a shoe-shining machine. The Russians and Germans ate informally in the rustic dining room, around a table that could seat twenty, sampling a variety of local dishes and drinks: blinis, caviar, shashlik and barbecued chicken thighs, followed by strawberry ice cream. This was washed down with Crimean and Georgian wines, Armenian cognac, Bavarian beer and the inevitable vodka.[157]

Next morning, 16 July, however, they got down to hard realities. It was time to square the proverbial circle. Around the table where they had dined convivially the night before, Kohl and Genscher were ranged against Gorbachev and his foreign minister Eduard Shevardnadze. And it would be tough going.[158]

The Germans wanted to hammer out the deals on the four key areas of national sovereignty, NATO membership, troop withdrawal and ma-terial aid. But the Russians dug in hard on each of these issues. Gorbachev said he would accept Germany's full sovereignty only if there was 'no extension of NATO's military structures to the territory of the present GDR'. Genscher countered that they had to end up with a document stating that Germany had 'the right to join the alliance of its choice'. By using the word 'right' he was trying to hold Gorbachev to the Helsinki principle of 'self-determination', which the Soviet leader had endorsed six weeks earlier in his summit with Bush. Obviously, Genscher added, 'Germany would choose NATO.'

Put on the spot, Gorbachev assented but immediately added that he preferred to see as little as possible in writing about an explicit German commitment to NATO. After they had debated the matter for some minutes, Kohl summed up the discussion: their deal was that, as a fully sovereign state, united Germany 'had the right to be a member of an alliance and that this membership meant NATO' – but NATO did not have to be explicitly mentioned in the concluding summit document. With that neat formulation, Gorbachev seemed happy to agree.[159]

They then spent much time haggling over the Red Army presence and the payback for early withdrawal. Kohl was certain that in Moscow the day before he and Gorbachev had agreed on a three- to four-year transition period for the withdrawal of the Soviet troops. But now in Arkhyz the Soviet leader suddenly toyed with five to seven years: after an initial pull-out, the USSR would keep a continued presence of some 195,000 Soviet soldiers for the rest of the time. Kohl pushed back, reminding Gorbachev of their Moscow discussion while stressing that it was actually in the Soviet soldiers' interest to be able to return home earlier rather than later, given the entirely changed economic environment including the shift to the Deutschmark that they would face in the (former) GDR. In his mind it was imperative that by 1994 every member of the Soviet Western Group of Forces and their dependants – some 600,000 people[160] – had been completely withdrawn. What mattered, as Genscher underlined, was not 'when the first soldier leaves, but when the last soldier has gone'. In any case, unified Germany's maintenance payments (which would now be paid in Deutschmarks) for the remaining Soviet troops beyond 1991 must under no circumstances be called 'stationing-costs'. In fact all that was to be regulated in a bilateral 'transition agreement'.[161]

This discussion was now deeply entangled with the issue of German financial support – always Gorbachev's top priority. The chancellor explained that he would not be able to help directly with housing for troops returning to the USSR – the Soviet side would have to do the construction work themselves – but Germany would be willing to help the Soviet building sector through its package of economic aid. In this context they discussed East German imports of Soviet gas and oil, which Kohl pledged to honour, if not increase. He also promised to lobby the EC and G7 for more Western aid.[162]

Kohl and Genscher now felt in a position to put on the table their detailed proposals for reducing the size of the Bundeswehr. They proposed a figure of 370,000 men by 1994, compared to a combined figure of 480,000 FRG military and 160,000 East German national army in 1990.

Their suggestion was to announce this German troop cut as soon as the ongoing negotiations about conventional arms reductions were concluded later that autumn. These were to culminate in what they called 'Vienna I': the signing of the treaty on conventional forces in Europe.[163]

Gorbachev agreed. He also gave in fairly quickly on the timetable for the Soviet troop withdrawal, commenting that he would talk to the German finance minister to work out an adequate compensatory package. But the Soviet leader was more concerned about the topic of NATO. In typical Soviet negotiating style, he resumed the offensive – reverting to issues that the Germans thought had already been agreed – in order to test the other side's resilience. As he ground on, it even seemed that he was pulling back from his earlier concession about Germany's NATO membership, asserting that he wanted 'the new sovereign Germany to declare that it understood the Soviet concerns and that no extension of NATO to the territory of the GDR would occur'. Shevardnadze jumped in on what he called this 'very serious question', adding his own twist about the bomb: 'One should not permit NATO structures to be extended to the GDR and nuclear weapons to be deployed there after the withdrawal of Soviet troops.'[164]

For almost four hours, the two sides went to and fro on these all-important word games on NATO. Sometimes Gorbachev gave ground to the Germans, only then to backtrack and reiterate old positions. Negotiating with such an interlocutor was extremely wearing and required great attention and skill from Kohl and Genscher, who had to hold their nerve and keep their focus. But this they did. The tactic that crystallised under pressure was that periodically Kohl would sum up the points of agreement in a matter-of-fact way (one, two, three) while temporarily ignoring the more controversial issues and the disputed formulations, only to return to them after making progress in other areas. For his part, Genscher tended to enter the discussions – often very effectively – by articulating statements of principle that the Soviets would find impossible to dispute.

Using this negotiating tactic and working together, the German tandem managed to accumulate agreement on enough small points to secure eventually the big deal that they desired for their country: full sovereignty upon unification, NATO membership, and total Red Army withdrawal within four years. It was also agreed that all external aspects of German unity should be settled ahead of the CSCE summit planned for November in Paris. In fact, Kohl and Genscher had conceded only on two points.

First, there would be no (NATO) foreign troops on East German soil while the Soviets were still there: only Bundeswehr and territorial defence forces that were not under NATO command could move in. And second, united Germany would, like the FRG in 1954,[165] renounce ever acquiring any atomic, biological or chemical weapons.[166]

Exhausted but elated, the Germans left that evening for the flight home.[167] Next morning, back in Bonn, Kohl held an upbeat press conference about the historic agreement, stressing the dual commitment to German unification and continued membership of NATO. With a necessary eye on Poland, the chancellor also stated that the new Germany would honour the existing borders of East and West Germany and include Berlin. And he also announced bilateral talks with Moscow about economic cooperation. In the words of one American journalist, the chancellor was 'smilingly self-confident and securely self-deprecatory' – pleased with what he had accomplished but careful not to rub it in because of the historical anxieties of Germany's neighbours. Kohl promised that a united Germany would regain its place at the heart of Europe peacefully, without once more becoming a threat. He emphasised as usual that a transformed Germany remained firmly committed to European integration and European ideals of democracy.[168]

In Washington, Bush publicly welcomed the bilateral deal in the Caucasus as being 'in the best interests of all the countries of Europe, including the Soviet Union'. And, with justification, he emphasised that the United States had been 'in the forefront' of negotiations on a unified Germany since the fall of the Wall. But privately, administration officials were intensely conscious of the symbolism: this was a deal worked out by Kohl and Gorbachev in the Caucasus with Bush over 5,000 miles away. And Baker had been totally out of the loop until he heard the news from the media when his plane stopped to refuel at Shannon airport in Ireland.[169]

Bush's political opponents exploited their opportunity. Congressman Lee Hamilton, a senior Democrat, stuck the knife in hard: 'This makes clearer than ever that the Germans are leading Western policy' towards the USSR. 'I am not saying that it is George Bush's fault,' Hamilton added coyly, 'and I am not saying that we have become a non-power' – but his implication was clear. Indeed, as one West European ambassador observed, 'not even a fig leaf was left' to conceal the fact that Bonn had negotiated German unification on its own terms. Even members of Bush's own political party acknowledged that the chancellor had transformed

Germany's international position. 'Kohl used to come here as a supplicant,' one Republican senator remarked, 'but now he comes into a room up here and senior people defer to him. He is polite and good-humored of course, but he dominates conversations.'[170]

In Moscow, the Soviet press accentuated the positives ('East and West have quit their path of war and taken the road of trust and cooperation' wrote *Izvestia*[171]) but in the Kremlin Gorbachev's feuding colleagues – many of them emerging as political opponents – were utterly aghast at what had unfolded: nothing less than the 'liquidation of the GDR', to quote Valentin Falin, head of the International Department of the Central Committee. They were furious at being told little more than was available in the Soviet papers. Falin complained in his memoirs that key memcons of meetings between Gorbachev and Shevardnadze with their Western colleagues were not being shared with the members of the Politburo. He resented being left on the margins. Similar complaints were voiced by KGB boss Vladimir Kryuchkov, Defence Minister Dmitry Yazov, as well as Nikolai Ryzhkov, chairman of the Council of Ministers. Such internal criticism and jockeying for position were confined for the moment to the corridors of the Kremlin, but it would become a growing problem for Gorbachev at home.[172]

For these conservative critics, Gorbachev was seen almost as a traitor who had squandered the great triumphs of the USSR in the Great Patriotic War – abandoning the hard-won Soviet sphere in Eastern Europe, selling out eastern Germany and throwing the USSR on to the charity of its Cold War foes.[173] All the more galling, therefore, was the international acclaim for Gorbachev as the great peacemaker, especially after the Arkhyz summit when he had 'brought an end to the war with the Germans'.[174]

This 'Gorbymania' reached a new pinnacle on 15 October with the announcement from Oslo that the Soviet leader was being awarded the 1990 Nobel Peace Prize for 'his leading role in the peace process which today characterises important parts of the international community'. Gorbachev was hailed by the Nobel committee as a man who had brought about sweeping political change in the Soviet Union and had revolution-ised the Kremlin's foreign policy since coming to power. He was praised for changing the fundamental nature of superpower relations and for his arms-control agreements. There was also mention of how he had extri-cated the Soviet Union from Afghanistan and allowed popular revolutions to topple hard-line Communist governments in Eastern Europe, paving the way for German unity. While, said the Nobel committee, there were many reasons for these historic changes, it was Gorbachev who had made decisive contributions to bring about greater openness and trust in international affairs. No leader of the Soviet Union had ever received a Nobel Peace Prize – or such a resounding international endorsement.[175]

*

Despite the plaudits for Gorbachev, Helmut Kohl had been the principal architect of the new Soviet–German détente – and also its main beneficiary. In the Caucasus summit – settled largely on his terms – he had indeed seized the mantle of history. And with this diplomatic coup, he was now virtually assured of becoming for posterity 'the chancellor of unity'. Through his bilateral dealings on almost equal footing with the two superpowers he had adroitly sidelined the British and French and made possible the emancipation of Germany as an international actor.

Not bad for nine months' hard work. It was time for a holiday.[176] Kohl (and Teltschik) took a whole month off, from mid-July to mid-August. It was left to the 2 + 4 delegations to write up the 'Treaty on Final Settlement with Respect to Germany'. Meanwhile, the two German bureaucracies had to complete the 'domestic' legal documents for unification through intensive inner-German negotiations. And the finance minister Theo Waigel was tasked with calculating the exact amount of Deutschmarks on the 'cheque' to the USSR for its permission to let the Germans go.

At the Paris 2 + 4 of foreign ministers on 17 July – the day after the German–Soviet summit – the news from the Caucasus was warmly welcomed by Baker, Hurd and Dumas. But the main topic was German borders and for this reason Poland, exceptionally, had been invited to take part. It was now clear to the Poles that, with German unity having Moscow's blessing, their own leverage on the matter had drastically diminished. On the other hand, the Four Powers declared in Paris that unified Germany's borders would be final and definitive. In this context, Polish foreign minister Krzysztof Skubiszewski agreed that two bilateral treaties – on the border and on cooperation and friendship – between Poland and a united Germany could be signed immediately after unification.[177] Later in the summer, on 23 August, the GDR government secured parliamentary approval for the GDR's accession to the FRG under Basic Law Article 23. A week later, the inter-German unity treaty was approved in both Bonn and East Berlin and the date for formal unification set for 3 October. This enabled Kohl, in a letter on 6 September, to invite Polish prime minister Tadeusz Mazowiecki to visit Germany later in the autumn, proposing an informal meeting in the Polish–German borderlands for 8 November. This was deliberately chosen as the eve of the first anniversary of the fall of the Wall and exactly one year after Kohl's reconciliatory visit to Warsaw. At this auspicious moment, they would agree on a pact to solve the border issue once and for all.[178]

Two days after the Caucasus meeting, on 18 July, Ryzhkov sent Bonn the Kremlin's list of demands in return for Gorbachev's concessions. He wanted cash on the barrel – more than DM 20 billion. The main items were funding for the upkeep in Germany of Soviet troops (4 billion), the cost of their transportation home (3 billion), and the bill for constructing 36,000 new homes in the USSR (11 billion). Ryzhkov believed that unified Germany should compensate the USSR for all possible economic disadvantages that might result from unification, and so he also proposed the establishment of a trilateral (Soviet–FRG–GDR) group to look at existing West and East German treaties with the USSR and how to update them for the post-unification era. Furthermore, he asked for negotiations about the consequences of the GDR's absorption into the EC and to establish the widest possible trade and economic relations between the USSR and unified Germany.[179] A week later Gorbachev followed up Ryzhkov's extensive wish list with a letter of his own to Kohl pressing for the start of discussions on a treaty entitled 'Soviet–German Cooperation, Good Neighbourliness and Friendship'.[180]

The chancellor did not reply until after his return from holiday, and when he did so – on 22 August – he simply said that the Finance Ministry would be handling all such negotiations.[181] What then ensued was a Moscow–Bonn face-off over the exact terms. In this, the United States played little part. Bush had already made clear that Washington was not offering any significant money to the USSR. Sorting out the small print of the Caucasus summit would be a test of the new Soviet–German relationship.

Meanwhile, to keep up the momentum for unification, Kohl – refreshed by his vacation in Austria – acted vigorously on several fronts. He made a deal with Jacques Delors of the European Commission that unification would in no way be linked to any rise in the EC budget. He did not want to give other Europeans the excuse to complain that they had lost out on European funds due to German greed.[182] With his mind on the forthcoming all-German Federal elections set for 2 December, Kohl was also keen to keep any speculation about the cost of unification out of the headlines. At this stage the chancellor talked privately about a likely bill of DM 30–40 billion in 1990 and another 60 billion in 1991.[183]

Kohl's principal objective was to secure unity by October – two months ahead of the elections. In consequence, the money was secondary. This meant that the 2 + 4 talks would have to be concluded at the meeting in Moscow scheduled for 12 September. In order to do so, Finance Minister Theo Waigel needed to agree with the Kremlin on the price tag. It was down to the art of the deal. And so he and Teltschik had to work against a very tight timetable. The biggest issue was the terms and conditions of the treaty on the Red Army's planned withdrawal. Talking with Ambassador Kvitsinsky on 28 August, Teltschik learned that Gorbachev was under great internal pressure. Shevardnadze was said to be in a state of 'open warfare' with the military top brass, who had dug in their heels. They argued that housing needed to be built for some 80,000 families from the GDR, at a time when another 80,000 families were also coming back from Hungary and Czechoslovakia. They warned that if Waigel did not cooperate there would be a 'revolution' in the Red Army. They also asserted that it was 'inconceivable' to withdraw all those troops in only four years. They had to stay in the GDR for longer.[184]

On 6 September, Waigel warned Kohl that the Soviet demands amounted to at least DM 18.5 billion. Yet he believed that paying even DM 6 billion would stretch the Federal budget to the limit.[185] The chancellor took matters in his own hands and phoned Gorbachev at ten o'clock the next morning. This was their first conversation since Arkhyz. Kohl opened with some lyrical words about their summit and its positive and constructive ambience. He also reiterated his general commitment to cooperation and specifically to the 'big treaty' between their two countries which he hoped to see signed soon after 3 October. Having warmed up the conversation, Kohl tackled the real bone of contention. He offered a maximum of DM 8 billion for troop withdrawal (2 billion more than Waigel said was feasible). To give himself some wriggle room, he also promised to use his voice in upcoming discussions with Western partners about multilateral aid to the USSR.[186]

Gorbachev would have none of this. Bonn, he said, was not short of cash. He insisted he was not 'begging' (clearly worried about loss of the USSR's status) but dismissed Kohl's 8 billion as a 'dead end' – it undermined everything they had achieved together – and said, rather whiningly, that he felt he had 'fallen into a trap'. Kohl rejected Gorbachev's accusation and said they could not talk like this: they had to stick with the realities. Unable to resolve matters in their forty-minute phone call, they agreed to talk the following week.[187] Over the weekend Kohl worked feverishly on his advisers, trying to squeeze out a bit more money.[188] On Monday 10th he haggled with Gorbachev again – offering 11–12 billion while Gorbachev demanded 15–16 billion. In the end they settled on DM 12 billion cash, plus an interest-free credit of 3 billion. 'I shake your hand,' said Gorbachev over the phone. And so the deal was done.[189]

This frenzied bargaining cleared the way for the signing of the 2 + 4 treaty in Moscow two days later, on 12 September. The agreement underlined the special status in perpetuity of the former East German terrain. It specified that no foreign armed forces and no nuclear weaponry must be stationed or deployed in the new Länder even after 1994.[190] As a result the day after that, Genscher and Shevardnadze were able to initial the German–Soviet 'good neighbour' pact. Bonn had been determined to complete this ahead of a similar agreement between the Soviet Union and France. The German pact banned mutual aggression, called for annual summits and expanded trade, travel and scientific cooperation. The details were not yet spelled out and the treaty was therefore largely symbolic. Both sides evidently wanted at this moment to promulgate it in conjunction with the 2 + 4 document, as well as to mark the thirty-fifth anniversary of the restoration of relations between the USSR and the FRG after the Second World War on 13 September 1955.

In other words, a new era was beginning and the two foreign ministers were beaming. 'The treaty leads both our countries into the twenty-first century marked by responsibility, trust and cooperation,' declared Genscher, while Shevardnadze called it a 'historic document in spirit and content'. He added: 'Now we can rightly say that the post-war era has ended. We are satisfied that the Federal Republic and we again appear as partners. This is a great thing.'[191]

In this vein on 1 October 1990 in New York – on the margins of the CSCE foreign ministers' meeting – the Four Powers formally declared the suspension of their Allied reserved rights and responsibilities over Germany and Berlin, leaving the two Germanies fully sovereign. They unified two days later. Genscher declared: 'We Germans are uniting in happiness and gratitude, not in nationalistic exuberance. On such an occasion the bright and dark chapters of our history are a cause for reflection, reflection on what was done in Germany's name. That will not be repeated. We commemorate all victims of the war and totalitarianism.'

Baker rounded that off by saying that the CSCE had brought humanity back to all Europeans and so now 'A new era begins – for Germany, Europe and the world.'[192]

In Berlin on 2–3 October a million people ecstatically greeted the moment of German unity. In terms of international diplomacy, however, the ceremonies were almost a non-event. Kohl had invited Gorbachev and Bush to attend but both had declined. They each had their own headaches at home and other, much bigger priorities abroad. In the Soviet Union, Gorbachev was grappling with an increasingly vocal communist-conservative backlash – especially after his perceived sell-out to Germany and the West – as well as nationalist protests on the rim of the USSR just as he was seeking to garner support for his reform programme. On the other side of the Atlantic, Bush was struggling with Congress over a budget deal, while simultaneously trying to form an international coalition to tackle the crisis in the Gulf. In fact, Kuwait was already becoming more important in defining the new post-Cold War order than Germany and Europe.[193] In the event the absence of Gorbachev and Bush from Berlin did not spoil Kohl's celebrations. Indeed, it allowed the new Germany to grace the stage on its own and jubilantly celebrate its birthday.[194]

Over the next couple of months, Germany tied up the international loose ends of unification with its Eastern neighbours. On 12 October, Bonn and Moscow signed the Treaty on Transitional Measures that codified the DM 15 billion contribution to the USSR, as well as the Treaty on the Conditions of Temporary Presence and the Terms of Planned Withdrawal of the Red Army from German soil.[195] Shortly afterwards Germans and Poles put to bed their border argument once and for all. Following a symbolic meeting of reconciliation on 8 November by Chancellor Kohl and Polish premier Mazowiecki at Frankfurt an der Oder and Slubice, on the frontier itself,[196] Genscher signed the Border Pact in Warsaw on 14 November in a low-key ceremony at a simple wooden table in the ballroom of a government building – very different from the high ceremony of the Polish–German meeting a year before. The treaty, which came into effect immediately, ended months of anxiety among Poles about the intentions of their Western neighbour.[197]

Reminding the world of the immense suffering Germany inflicted on Poland in the Second World War, Mazowiecki stated: 'The signing of this treaty closes the period when the problem of the border divided our two nations and created for us, the Poles, feelings of fear and threat.' But, in a spirit of reciprocity, he also asked for 'the forgiveness of the German nation for the sufferings which were caused by moving Poland from East to West' – alluding to the more than 7 million expellees who were driven west. 'Remember,' he declared, 'that in the counting of victims, arithmetics have no value and the sufferings will remain, regardless of who inflicted them.'[198]

Looking to the future, the treaty opened a new chapter in Polish–German relations in which the most important issues between the two nations would no longer be political but economic. Genscher – a man from the East, in fact with a wife from Silesia – acknowledged that the treaty was evidence of his nation's historic 'responsibility' for peace in Europe. But he knew that there could only be lasting peace if there was real prosperity: that was the lesson of European integration. And so he observed: 'Together we must ensure that the frontier does not become a watershed between rich and poor ... We fully support Poland's request for association with the European Community. The advantages that Western Europe can offer because of the large common market must also be shared by the nations of Central and Eastern Europe which have regained their freedom.'[199]

And so the Border Guarantee Treaty was more than a specific and bilateral matter. That is why, for Genscher, it was not just a painful moment when Germany renounced all claims on Silesia, eastern Brandenburg, Pomerania, Posen-Westpreussen, Danzig and Ostpreussen – heartland of the historic Prussian state – but a stepping stone on the road to European reunification.[200]

Even more significant was 9 November, when Gorbachev came to Bonn to sign the German–Soviet Treaty on Good-Neighbourliness, Partnership and Cooperation.[201] That day was the first anniversary of the fall of the Wall. Unlike in 1989, Kohl was now in the right place at the right time and Gorbachev on the right side of history – in marked contrast to when the Soviet leader participated in the grotesque charade of a fortieth birthday party for the dying East German state. What's more, Gorbachev – still popular and esteemed by ordinary Germans – became the first foreign leader to make a state visit to the reunited Germany.

Yet it was also clear that Gorbachev was not quite the same leader who had aroused those chants of 'Gorby! Gorby!' when he first visited Bonn in June 1989. In those days he was still undisputed master of the Soviet Union, with leverage over Germans in the East and in the West. In November 1990, however, his shaky standing at home was evident from the fact that he had to delay his visit by several days because of 'Soviet problems', and from his rather lame appeal to Germans to treat the Soviet soldiers remaining in the East of their new country with kindness – 'as a test of the ability to build relations among people truly on the basis of humanity and friendship'.

Perhaps sensitive to any echo of the infamous Hitler–Stalin Pact of 1939, Gorbachev seemed desperate to preclude any impression that the 'good neighbour' treaty created some kind of special relationship between Germany and the USSR. He declared that the new relationship with Germany was a product of the general improvement in Soviet relations with the other three wartime allies, especially the United States. 'The Soviet–German treaty is not aimed against anyone,' he continued; nor was it 'unique'. A similar pact had been signed with France, though it was noteworthy that the French had refused to sign a non-aggression clause. But the FRG could not escape carrying the burden of the Nazi past, including 28 million Soviet dead.

So they were in no position to argue. Indeed Kohl's tone was gracious: 'We Germans in particular acknowledge with deep gratitude your personal contribution to the propitious turning point in our history', he told Gorbachev in front of the clicking cameras at the state banquet. He promised that Germany would continue to help the Soviet Union 'with word and deed' (*mit Rat und Tat*) and act as Moscow's chief lobbyist with the EC, G7 and other financial bodies. Yet it was also becoming evident that the nature of German aid would change in the future. Henceforth, it would no longer be imperative to dig deep to buy unity, and German policy would be to solicit multilateral aid rather than bear the burden of assistance alone.[202]

Less than a month later Kohl experienced his own triumph and very personal moment in history. On 2 December he claimed his reward for accomplishing German unity – the goal that had eluded all his predecessors as Federal chancellor – with another huge victory for his ruling coalition. He won well over half the popular vote in the first free all-German elections for fifty-eight years – since 1932. Kohl had run a bold, in-your-face campaign: posters of the grinning *Kanzler für Deutschland* were everywhere. Kohl made only twenty-eight campaign appearances – his SPD rival Oskar Lafontaine about a hundred – because he did not need to run around the country. By making the headlines abroad, the chancellor was visible every night on the TV news, and this also enabled him to be seen as above grubby domestic politics: truly a world leader. In the Kohl landslide, the parties that had wavered or opposed unity – the SPD, Greens and PDS – all paid a price. The CDU– FDP coalition won 398 out of 662 Bundestag seats. Kohl was exultant, calling it 'a day of joy'. The six-foot four-inch, 250-pound 'chancellor of unity' towered over his aides and reporters as he stood beaming outside the CDU headquarters in Bonn, on an evening he would never forget.

Start of a new era: Merkel with Kohl and the rest of
unified Germany's first Cabinet

Over the Christmas period, he formed a new Cabinet that included a token trio of ministers from the former GDR. This underlined the essential continuity of the West German state – subsuming the former East in the virtually unchanged institutions of the Federal Republic. As a footnote to history in the making, it is interesting that the new minister for youth and women was the thirty-six-year-old former deputy spokes-woman of the last East German government. And so Angela Merkel moved from a shabby apartment in East Berlin to the green provincialism of Rhineland Bonn to place her foot on the first rung of the political ladder.[203]

Kohl, in tandem with Genscher, had won another four-year term in office. They could now work on completing the shotgun marriage between two very different halves of Germany. As the recent treaties showed, this had to be accomplished in harmony with Germany's still-wary neigh-bours. And that, in turn, had to be woven into an even larger tapestry – the ongoing process of building European institutions, by adapting existing organisations such as NATO, the EC and the CSCE to the exciting but unsettling realities of an undivided continent. The challenge now was how to move from the post-war world into what James Baker called the 'post-postwar' world.

Chapter 5

Building a Europe 'Whole and Free'

The 19th of November 1990. Six weeks after German unification thirty-four international leaders gathered at the Kléber International Conference Centre near the Arc de Triomphe in Paris. Top of the list were George Bush and Mikhail Gorbachev, but Kohl, Mitterrand and Thatcher were also there; likewise Havel from Czechoslovakia and Mazowiecki from Poland. All came with their foreign ministers or some other key advisers. They sat at a hexagonal table around three-foot-high cutout maps of North America and Eurasia that resembled pieces from a giant jigsaw puzzle. There were sixty-nine delegates in all – sixty-seven men and two female prime ministers: Margaret Thatcher of Britain and Gro Harlem Brundtland of Norway.

Post-Wall Europe around one table

Welcoming them as host, François Mitterrand underlined the significance of the moment. 'It is the first time in history that we witness a change in depth of the European landscape that is not the outcome of a war or a bloody revolution,' he declared. 'We do not have sitting here either victors or vanquished but free countries equal in dignity.'[1]

Such a pan-European summit meeting had not been seen since 1975 when the Helsinki Final Act was signed. The Paris gathering was billed as a kind of Helsinki II – at the end of which the Final Act was reaffirmed, upgraded and adapted to the post-Cold War era in the 'Charter of Paris for a New Europe'. Gorbachev had been pushing for such a summit since his talks with Bush in Malta and it was in deference to him that the date was brought forward from 1992.[2] The Soviet leader saw this new Conference on Security and Cooperation in Europe as essential to realise his vision of NATO and the Warsaw Pact gradually dissolving into a 'Common European Home'. He had made that phrase his own, but others were touting variants of the same idea: Mitterrand's 'European Confederation', and what Genscher called an 'All-European Security Architecture'.

There were, in fact, many scenarios for the new Europe. Kohl's centred on adapting the European Community, both by deepening integration and enlarging its membership to the East. That, after all, was what he had committed himself to as a condition of German unification.[3] For Bush what mattered above all was the perpetuation of NATO – albeit as more of a political alliance – both to help safeguard order on the continent and to ensure that the USA kept a foot in Europe. On this, Kohl also agreed.

During 1990–1 these competing visions – Common European Home, European Confederation, CSCE, EC and NATO – were played out amid a fast-changing European situation, as Germany embarked on the gamble of unification and the states of the former Soviet bloc asserted new independence but also urgent needs. As Baker declared in Prague, 'If 1989 was the year of sweeping away, 1990 must become the year of building anew'. But the architecture for a new Europe in this new era proved easier to imagine than to design and build.[4] Over Europe, just as over Germany, 1990 was a time for choices.

*

Among these visions of a new European order, Gorbachev's Common European Home was the most expansive and inclusive.

Ever since his UN speech in December 1988, the Soviet leader had believed that a reconfiguration of European security was both necessary and desirable – not just because of the diminishing strategic significance of the satellite states for Soviet security but also because of the ideological revolution underlying his foreign policy. Whatever his Leninist roots, Gorbachev acknowledged the economic vitality of the West and his inability to confront capitalism in a revolutionary struggle, not least because of the danger of nuclear annihilation. It became an article of faith for him that the best course lay in deepening cooperation with the West by defusing the nuclear arms race and developing a nexus of positive interaction ranging from trade to culture, from technology to the environment. Soviet foreign minister Eduard Shevardnadze underwrote this strategy when he declared that the Soviet Union's status as a 'civilised country' depended on its successful construction of a new 'law-ruled and democratic state' and its role in the 'creation of an integral European economic, legal, humanitarian, cultural and ecological space'.[5]

This inclusive approach to international politics, though global in implications, focused particularly on security and stability in Europe. Gorbachev's vision was in reality more Western than Soviet in inspiration, yet he liked to insist that it was based on 'universal' values. And he managed to offset his apparent limitations as a strategic thinker with displays of diplomatic virtuosity – taking the initiative and grabbing the limelight whenever possible.

So Gorbachev's policy concessions in 1989–90 were not simply a reflection of Soviet weakness but also clearly expressed his new political thinking and mirrored actual developments in European affairs. His language of 'mutual security', 'defensive defence' and 'reasonable sufficiency' in armaments had been embodied in the Intermediate Nuclear Forces Treaty of 1987 and would be expressed anew in the Treaty on Conventional Forces in Europe, signed in Paris at the same time as the Paris Charter. His slogans about 'freedom of choice' and the 'right to self-determination' were used to justify Soviet non-intervention in Eastern Europe in 1989 and also acceptance of German unification within NATO in 1990. Similarly, his dream of a Common European Home seemed to be realised in the decisions taken in Paris to institutionalise the CSCE through annual meetings of foreign ministers, a permanent headquarters staff in Prague, a conflict-prevention centre in Vienna and a 'parliamentary assembly' in Strasbourg.[6]

In retrospect, Gorbachev's high hopes for a totally new all-European system of 'collective security'[7] built around the CSCE may seem delusional. Yet, for quite a while, he was encouraged in his imaginings by authoritative voices from the West. At the end of 1989, Baker and Kohl had mentioned a new role for the CSCE within the European 'architecture' of the future. Genscher was even more engaged. On 31 January 1990, in his major speech in Tutzing, the West German foreign minister called for a cooperative 'pan-European security order'. This should be rooted in the CSCE, which would 'bring about more stability for the whole of Europe' while taking account of 'legitimate Soviet security interests'. He elaborated these ideas in other speeches, in Potsdam on 9 February and Luxembourg on 23 March. The new pan-European order, he said, would entail cooperation between the Warsaw Pact and NATO, as the two alliances were gradually 'absorbed' and then dissolved into a new European 'association of common collective security'. He talked about reinforcing the CSCE to 'create a framework of security and a network of stability'. And he declared that 'German unity will not be achieved without Europe, and European unity will not bypass the Germans'.[8]

Genscher touted these arguments for several months, in public and in private. But then in April, after a stern ticking-off from the chancellor whose sights were firmly set on rapid unification, he fell into line behind Bush and Kohl and adopted their focus on NATO and the EC.[9]

More encouraging for Gorbachev was the European vision of François Mitterrand. It was in his speech on 31 December 1989[10] that the French president called for a 'European Confederation'.[11] Devoting most of this televised address to the peaceful revolutions in Eastern Europe, he enfolded those events into the *longue durée* of the French Revolution – the fight for liberty, equality and fraternity – whose bicentenary had been celebrated with such éclat the previous summer. He praised the 'Velvet Revolutions' as a 'Victory of Democracy, 1789–1989' over 'Tyranny'. But Mitterrand did not fail to point out the darker side, which the bloody events in Romania had just illustrated. The Eastern Europeans would clearly need the help of the West after what he called 'such a long night'.[12]

In his speech, Mitterrand asserted that, having been dominated for half a century by the two superpowers, Europe would now experience 'a homecoming' and 'recover its own history and its own geography'. Struggling with the plasticity of borders and the resurgence of nationalism, he sketched out two alternative scenarios for Europe. On the one hand, the risk of disorder and instability, of a continent fragmenting and eventually blowing up as the 'Europe of 1919' had done. On the other,

'Europe will construct itself' – thereby facilitating the peaceful emergence of a new stable post-Cold War order. The latter, he explained, could happen in two stages. First, European Community structures ought to be 're-inforced'. This was necessary because, in Mitterrand's view, the EC had played a major role in the 'awakening' of the peoples of Eastern Europe and served as a magnet for the countries behind the Iron Curtain. The second stage had as yet to be 'invented', though he saw its basis as being the Helsinki Accords of 1975. Mitterrand predicted the creation during the 1990s of a European Confederation in the true sense of the word – one which would tie in 'all states of our continent in a common and permanent organisation for exchanges, peace and security'. As a precondition, of course, the Eastern European states would have to intro-duce political pluralism, free elections and representative government. But, he said, that day 'might not be too far off'.[13]

Mitterrand's New Year's Eve speech evoked a good deal of surprise – not just abroad but also within the president's inner circle, because he had not even discussed it with any of his Elysée staff. Still, since the speech clearly heralded a major initiative, most of them embraced the idea enthusiastically as France's distinctive intervention in the big debate opening up on the architecture of 'greater Europe' in the post-Cold War era.[14]

Yet the French president's motives for launching his *grand projet* were complicated. His ideas on how to construct the new Europe had fluctu-ated during the final weeks of 1989, that year of revolutions, as 'history was accelerating'.[15] For a while in October and November the CSCE had seemed an attractive option around which to structure a 'post-Yalta' pan-European order. That is why, when meeting Gorbachev in Kiev on 6 December, Mitterrand came out in support of the Soviet leader's proposal for a Helsinki II summit of all 35 members in 1990,* and for institutionalising the CSCE – not least as a vital framework within which to manage the German question. He told Gorbachev that Kohl's Ten Points had 'turned everything upside down'. 'We should not change the order of the processes, he declared. 'First and foremost among them should be European integration, the evolution of Eastern Europe, and the all-European process, the creation of a peaceful order in Europe'.[16] Behind Mitterrand's thinking was also, perhaps, the French calculation

---

* Until 1990, when the two Germanies became one, the CSCE was made up of 35 participating states all of whom had originally signed the Helsinki Final Act in 1975.

that with the two superpowers sharing the same 'conservatism of blocs', as the Malta summit had shown, the strengthening of the CSCE might serve to reduce any danger of the EC becoming too tightly bound into the new Atlanticism and thereby helping to perpetuate the two alliances.

Mitterrand's thinking soon shifted again – under the impact of the Strasbourg EC summit on 8 December 1989 and especially as the fragility of East Germany became evident during Kohl's and Mitterrand's visits to the GDR later in the month. The French president was still adamant that German unification should accompany, not precede, European transformation. But as it became clear that the two Germanies were inexorably and rapidly coming together, he urgently needed to speed up European construction. His problem was that he and Kohl did not exactly agree on what was the priority.[17]

Mitterrand focused on monetary union, whereas Kohl was keener on political union and EC enlargement. The latter approach was clearly articulated in point seven of the chancellor's Ten-Point Plan: 'the EC must not end at the Elbe; rather, it must also maintain openness towards the East. Only in this sense – for we have always understood the Europe of twelve to be only a part and not the whole – can the European Community serve as the foundation for a truly comprehensive European unification.'[18] Fearful of a 'dilution' of the EC/EMU project, the French Foreign Ministry argued that, while 'it is imperative to combine European construction with the opening to the East', enlargement could 'only take place after a strengthening' of the EC, and so one had to 'offer alternatives to membership' for the Eastern European countries.[19]

This conflict between 'enlarging' and 'deepening' was a major motivation behind Mitterrand's advocacy of a European Confederation – a concept which conveniently offered a variety of staging posts for the rest of Europe while the EC 12 moved on to closer union. This was what Jacques Delors had already called a Europe of 'concentric circles'.[20] Crucially, Delors' circles – EC, European Free Trade Area, Eastern Europe – excluded the Soviet Union, whereas Mitterrand's putative Confederation was both looser and more inclusive. It would start with a deepened Franco-German core, around which would be formed a second circle that included the rest of the EC, which was now moving towards EMU. Beyond that lay the last circle which included everybody else: the Soviet Union and its former satellites, plus northern and south-eastern Europe. Mitterrand did not envisage many of these states entering the second circle for ten or twenty years.[21]

Here, in embryo, was what might be considered a Western response to Gorbachev's Common European Home – one that paralleled Moscow's objectives for a political and security structure from Vancouver to Vladivostok. The Confederation idea seemed to offer Moscow a way towards political-economic inclusion within Europe, while protecting the Soviets from being completely shut out after deeper EC integration. Instead of a dividing line between two blocs – demarcated by walls, fences and an Iron Curtain – Europe's political geometry would be described in circles, within which a reformed USSR would somehow find a place.[22]

The language used by Gorbachev and Mitterrand to promote their visions of Europe was idealistic and vague. It seemed interchangeable, and therefore easily conflated into a common idea with minor differences that were bridgeable. Chernyaev, for instance, observed that Gorbachev and Mitterrand had 'strikingly similar views of world developments, at least on a "theoretical" level'.[23]

But the differences were real. For Gorbachev, the Common European Home – in other words a continent at peace with itself – was essentially a security structure, which would grow out of the CSCE. For Mitterrand, the European Confederation idea allowed the EC to deepen itself while keeping the rest of the continent, including the USSR, in a holding pattern, and America firmly out. It provided what the French called a *cadre de règlement*, a framework for stabilising the Community's Eastern neighbours while the new European Union of 1992 emerged. Yet the wily president was able to exploit the looseness of the two concepts for his own ends – encouraging Gorbachev to believe that the two of them were both on the same page – using elastic phrases such as 'European construction'.[24] For the same reason he was ready to host Gorbachev's cherished CSCE in Paris.[25]

Yet Mitterrand's Confederation was not merely a tactical expedient. It was a *grand projet* in at least two fundamental senses. First, there were the dark lessons of history: his recurrently expressed fear that the end of what the French liked to call 'Yalta Europe' should not precipitate turmoil akin to the first half of the twentieth century. Mitterrand's shorthand for this was the 'Europe of 1913' – about to tumble into the abyss. Or, even more sombrely, the 'Europe of Sarajevo'.[26] Secondly, the *grand projet* also looked forward. In a Europe that was finally open after half a century during which France had been a sulky subaltern of the United States, there seemed at last a chance to realise the elusive Gaullist vision. The Confederation could perhaps be a vehicle of a French-led Europe 'from the Atlantic to the Urals'. Like the general himself in the 1960s, Mitterrand envisaged the Atlantic border starting at Lisbon and not Washington. While not denying the importance of NATO in guaranteeing the balance of power on the continent, Mitterrand saw the Confederation as a new space within which Europe – France at the helm – could grow on its own.[27]

So there was a good deal going on behind Mitterrand's five-minute speech on New Year's Eve 1989. His Confederation scenario for the post-Cold War order was no casual aside. Little wonder that it proved a major topic of conversation when he and Kohl trod the beach at Latché a few days later, on 4 January 1990. The two leaders strode to and fro, struggling to make sense of the current situation, but what emerged were clear lines of argument on the relationship between the EC 12 and Eastern Europe.[28]

Fixated on a Eurocentric vision for the future, Mitterrand explained to Kohl that he currently saw two interconnected problems – the Russian and the German – but the one was not easily reconcilable with the other.

The 'Gorbachev experiment' would certainly continue for a while, the president said. 'But what would come after that, if he failed? Ultras!' A hard military dictatorship, because communism was dead. Everybody knew that. And also a resurgence of Russian nationalism. And if the military won, there would be bloodshed as they cracked down on seces-sionist republics in the Soviet Union. Kohl agreed. Indeed they both felt that Gorbachev provided them with a rare but delicate opportunity – if he fell and a hardliner came to power, everything would be much more difficult.

As regards the German question, Mitterrand added, fortunately for the first time in a thousand years there was now an answer available, namely 'the close tie between Germany, France and Europe'. Instead of an armed balance of power, there had finally emerged a peaceful equilibrium.[29]

Kohl, of course, had no problem about the need to anchor Germany in the EC. Quoting Adenauer he said, 'The German problem can only be resolved under a European roof.' At this stage he was still thinking about a transitional phase of German–German cooperation (each within its bloc), but he was clear that full unification would follow, and only then the completion of 'European integration'. This latter development should be open to states which wanted to join and, in order to do so, would give up some sovereignty to the Community. Citing his excellent personal relations with Mitterrand, he portrayed the two of them as the 'motor of Europe'. Historically, the evolution of the Community had depended on political personalities and their visions; he was sure that this would and should be true in the future.[30]

With a focus on anchoring a united Germany in a deepened EC, Kohl said that for states not currently eligible to join the EC – such as Hungary, Poland and Czechoslovakia, but also Austria and Turkey – one would have to find a special status and create appropriate structures. He envisaged a system of political treaties made with these states and perhaps also with the USSR. By 1995 he expected that the EC would have been sufficiently strengthened to engage with the East in this way. If the Soviet Union did not achieve the necessary level of democratisation, it would become isolated.[31]

Their conversation had been bracingly frank, to help clear the air. But in their press conference Mitterrand and Kohl fudged their differences and highlighted areas of agreement. The chancellor kept stressing his commitment to the Franco-German tandem and to Europe, repeating the Adenauer line on German and European unity. He said he agreed with Mitterrand that it was now important to move forward along the Community road, while offering East European neighbours some kind of outlook towards the future. 'The term Confederation', he said, 'is relevant for this development, whereas it is not for the inner-German situation.'[32]

In this way, Kohl offered Mitterrand endorsement for his elastic concept with regard to the USSR and its former satellites, while making absolutely clear its non-applicability to the German question. Now ready to move on with his Deutschlandpolitik, he was content, for the moment at least, to keep the Confederation in play with regard to Eastern Europe – if only to propitiate Mitterrand.

After Latché, Mitterrand started to canvass the key states of East Central Europe about the Confederation idea. Talking with the leaders of Hungary he explained that the EC could not 'expand indefinitely to all countries' and therefore proposed the Confederation as another kind of 'organic link with Western Europe'. The Hungarians reacted positively, as would later the Czechoslovaks.[33]

But over the next few weeks, the terms of debate changed fundamentally once Kohl imposed currency union,[34] the 2 + 4 process got started and the CSCE became merely a rubber stamp to ratify the outcome.[35] Assuming a pro-CDU result in the upcoming GDR elections, the road to German unification on Kohl's terms was now essentially a fait accompli.

Meanwhile it became apparent that the organisation providing the security order around Germany was not going to be the CSCE, let alone

Mitterrand's vague dream of a Confederation. Although Moscow kept insisting that united Germany must be neutral, the NATO–Warsaw Pact foreign ministers' 'Open Skies' conference in Ottawa in mid-February demonstrated the unanimity of the Western allies that the new Germany had to remain in NATO.[36] It is notable that Eastern Europeans, in part due to their own historical fears, were equally keen on the idea that NATO would serve as the binding agent of Germany. Otherwise, as Polish foreign minister Krzysztof Skubiszewski warned in Ottawa, the German nation might become 'a power or superpower on the European stage'.[37] Unification diplomacy and NATO perpetuation were of a higher game order than speculative designs for a new pan-European security architecture.

These wider developments in the early weeks of 1990 took much of the wind out of Mitterrand's sails, but he still ploughed on with the Confederation idea when meeting Kohl over dinner on 15 February.[38] The evident disintegration of the Warsaw Pact – both agreed it was becoming 'a fiction' – allowed Mitterrand to reiterate his argument. While insisting that further integration of the EC 12 should be accelerated, he noted that this would leave the states freeing themselves from the Soviet orbit feeling increasingly small and dispossessed. It would be 'a dangerous path' if some EC states sought to forge regional alliances – for example the Italians 'would want to form a federation with Yugolavia, Austria and Hungary'. So the Confederation would head off this danger by providing a loose umbrella, with few fixed obligations.[39]

Kohl did not dissent from all this but said – in a typical example of his conservative approach – what mattered was to relate this issue of future applicants to the 'existing institutions'. In any case, he saw the unification process as being tightly entwined with the EC integration process and in this way Germany would be a key shaper of EC affairs. Pushing back, Mitterrand reminded Kohl that Genscher had proposed that the CSCE would deal with the question of German unification and indeed all the other issues that the two of them had discussed over dinner. Kohl's rejoinder was blunt: in Bonn the chancellor set foreign policy, not the foreign minister. The CSCE's role would simply be to offer its consent to the conclusions of 2 + 4.[40]

By the end of the dinner, two things had become evident. The November 1990 CSCE summit and the Confederation idea remained on the international agenda when trying to frame the future of Europe as a whole. But it was also clear that Germany's accelerated drive towards unification, far from derailing the deepening of the EC, was actually pushing that whole process forward. On this, both Kohl and Mitterrand could agree. Yet what exactly the EC's closer union would mean now had to be worked out. With Kohl inclined to a political solution and Mitterrand fixated on monetary union, they emphatically did not see eye to eye. And their disagreements had to be resolved amid France's lingering worries about German unification.

*

Monetary union had been a central feature of the *relance européenne* mounted by Commission president Jacques Delors since 1985. France was particularly keen because it feared the growing dominance of the West German economy and the Bundesbank within the exchange-rate mechanism that had existed since 1979. Formal economic and monetary union would be a way to harness the strength of the German currency and economy and to defuse what the French called the 'atom bomb'[41] of the Deutschmark. Genscher, reflecting the economic liberalism of his FDP, welcomed the EMU idea, whereas reservations were expressed by CDU finance minister Gerhard Stoltenberg and other advocates of price stability, low inflation and the social market economy. Kohl initially inclined to Stoltenberg but then backed Genscher and Delors in setting up the so-called Delors Committee at the Hanover EC Council of June 1988.[42]

This committee of 'wise men', chaired by the Commission president himself, was charged with sketching out possible paths to monetary union. A key member was Otto Pöhl, the president of the Bundesbank. Sceptical from the outset, he feared losing the Bundesbank's autonomy and worried about the predominance of loose 'Latin' Keynesianism on the committee, which might prevail over the ingrained West German commitment to monetary stability. Kohl was keen to persuade Pöhl that politics must have primacy over economics, arguing that Franco-German relations 'went beyond the economic'. He also noted that Austria and the Nordic countries would surely apply soon to join the EC, thereby buttressing Bonn's view of economic imperatives.[43]

But, at a deeper level, the chancellor had reservations about the road to EMU. He regarded monetary union as the end result, not the starting point. What had to be achieved first was economic convergence among EC economies, and this would be a long process conditional on the opening up of markets and complete liberalisation of capital movements. His was also the view of the British, Danes and Dutch. But Delors – echoing the approach of France, Italy and Belgium – gave priority to creating a new monetary institution, claiming that this would push EC countries into 'a process of economic convergence by changing market behaviour'.[44]

The Delors Report was approved by the European Commission in April 1989. It set out three conditions for moving towards economic and monetary union: full and irreversible convertibility of currencies, free movement of capital, and irrevocably fixed exchange rates. They were unanimously accepted at the Madrid EC Council in June 1989. Even the Bundesbank considered this an 'optimal' outcome – initially preserving the system of national central banks, firmly committing to price stability and rejecting the idea of introducing a single currency before the three conditions had been achieved.[45]

There was, however, one serious caveat. Pöhl emphatically repudiated the idea of a European Central Bank (ECB). He deplored any transfer of monetary sovereignty away from the Bundesbank, historically regarded by most West Germans as the guarantor of the strong Deutschmark and thus of the country's post-war prosperity. Even to set the ECB as a long-term target would be a mistake. If West Germans got wind of the idea that their money would underpin EMU but their national bank would not control monetary policy, it could have a really damaging effect on public confidence.[46]

It is not surprising, therefore, that tensions arose between Paris and Bonn over the future shape of EMU. In the opinion of Mitterrand, who had been re-elected for another seven-year term in 1988, EMU was 'the pre-eminent goal' for the remainder of his presidency and he wanted the EC to convene an early intergovernmental conference (IGC) to implement the Delors Report. Mitterrand also held on to his belief that EMU should be ratified by late 1992. What he called 'other institutional questions', in other words further political integration, were only to be tackled when the negotiations on economic and monetary union had been completed. By contrast, Kohl hesitated to set a date for the IGC. In the autumn of 1989 he had wished to decouple EMU negotiations from the Federal elections in December 1990 and also hoped to link EMU with European political union (EPU). The chancellor did not want EMU to go ahead without parallel political reform of the EC's institutions. He wished the economic and political integration processes to be entwined, with the aim of securing ratification by every member state just before the European Parliament elections in 1994.[47]

On 27 November 1989 Kohl set out his concerns in a letter to Mitterrand. He argued that the process of economic convergence – meaning exchange-rate stability, low budget deficits and harmonisation of VAT rates – was not sufficiently advanced to move to the first stage of EMU by July 1990: the completion of the single market and the inclusion of all EC currencies within the exchange-rate mechanism. With his letter, he also sent Mitterrand a 'working schedule' which proposed a year's deferral of the actual decision to establish the IGC, from the Strasbourg summit in two weeks' time to late December 1990 when Italy would hold the presidency.[48]

Mitterrand regarded all this as politically motivated delaying tactics, and even a possible German ploy to escape EMU altogether. To make matters worse, Kohl's letter was delivered in Paris on 28 November, the very day he made his shock announcement to the Bundestag of the Ten Points. These did not contain any specific reference to EMU and IGC.

No wonder Mitterrand smelled a rat.

A difficult partnership: Mitterrand and Kohl

On 30 November, when Genscher was visiting Paris, Mitterrand told him in no uncertain terms that unification was 'an unstoppable thing', but that 'this unstoppable thing had to be integrated'. And, he added, 'in every phase of this evolution Germany and France should move forward together'. The president added, in his usual refrain, 'the first priority lay with European unity'.[49]

Next day, in a firm response to Kohl's letter, Mitterrand insisted on reaching and announcing at Strasbourg an unequivocal commitment that the EC would launch the EMU IGC twelve months later. He said he would reject any postponement and would not modify his view that the IGC should deal with political reform only after the treaty for monetary union had been agreed – sometime in early 1991.[50] Kohl's EC adviser Joachim Bitterlich suggested that monetary union was for Mitterrand clearly the essential complement to the single market – not least to counter French fears of the Deutschmark. What's more, noted Bitterlich, this 'necessary acceleration' of economic integration could be presented by Mitterrand at Strasbourg in a few days' time as the answer to the 'challenges from the East'.[51]

The implications of Mitterrand's thinking were stark. Monetary union was necessary to nip in the bud any German dreams of an independent Central European economic fiefdom and avoid a Deutschmark zone within the existing exchange-rate mechanism. Instead the Deutschmark should be subsumed into the new single European currency. Furthermore, through the IGC on monetary union, Mitterrand would ensure that the Delors Report would not suffer the fate of earlier abortive EC plans for economic union.

So EMU served three purposes for the French president: first, to prevent Germany from dominating not only Western Europe but also the emerging markets of the East. Second, to consolidate the core of the EC 12 and press on with this big symbolic project, in order to avoid the danger of the Community being distracted by all the heady talk about reuniting the continent as a whole. Third, to ensure a united Germany was truly integrated into European structures by locking it into a single European currency. The French saw this as a 'decisive test' for Germany to prove its 'willingness to reconcile German with European identity'. As a result, fixing a firm date for the IGC had become the touchstone of Mitterrand's strategy for the future, informed as usual by the lessons of the past.[52]

Mitterrand's scenario reflected the French public mood. Kohl's Ten

Point surprise on unification rang real alarm bells about the German past. The day of his speech, the Elysée switchboard was inundated with anxious calls. Had the president been informed in advance? Did Kohl's plan not sideline the interests of the EC as a whole? Was the chancellor offering any guarantees of his commitment to Europe? Almost overnight it became clear that any German wavering on EMU would be interpreted as a signal that Bonn was choosing the GDR over the EC. As a disgruntled Teltschik told a *Le Monde* journalist on 1 December, the situation was now such that Bonn 'would have to agree to practically every French initiative for Europe'.[53]

Kohl realised that he would have little room for manoeuvre in Strasbourg. So he wrote again to Mitterrand on 5 December, this time endorsing French policy for the European Council which was to move fast towards EMU by setting December 1990 as the date for the IGC and worrying about convergence later. In his letter the chancellor urged that the Council should give 'a clear political signal' that the EC would also 'decisively move on along the road towards political union'.[54] But little attention was paid to this qualification in Strasbourg. Instead, what Kohl got from the summit – in return for signing up to the acceleration of EMU on French terms – was an EC declaration in favour of German unity. There was no formal bargain but obviously an implicit linkage. This was not, however, the trade-off that Kohl had originally hoped for: an early EMU for progress towards European political union.[55]

So Mitterrand could consider the Strasbourg summit a real success. He had achieved his primary objective of kick-starting the Community's ambitious economic-integration agenda. The final declaration spelled out their agreement to call a special intergovernmental conference to launch EMU at the Rome Council in December 1990. It further claimed that 'at this time of profound and rapid change' the EC must act as 'a mooring for a future European equilibrium'. In short, 'the building of [the] European Union will permit the further development of a range of effective and harmonious relations with the other countries of Europe'.[56]

Fine words, to be sure, but in reality just papering over the cracks. France had extracted reassurance on Bonn's commitment to Europe and the single currency. Kohl had been given the green light to press on with German unification, which would give him new leverage over Mitterrand. And now that he had fully embraced the principle of monetary union, he intended to make Mitterrand pay a price in return: acceptance of European central-bank independence (on the Bundesbank model) and of political union with strong federalist characteristics.

For Kohl, his actions at Strasbourg had been governed by politics. Explaining his reasoning to Secretary of State James Baker, he said he was 'happy to grant France the glory of Strasbourg', but without him, he added wrily, 'the thing would not have happened'. He had taken this decision 'against German interests': even the Bundesbank president was opposed. But, said Kohl, it was 'politically important since Germany needs friends. There must be no mistrust towards us in Europe.' Of course, he added with a smile, the Federal Republic was already 'the number 1 economy in Europe' and, if 17 million more Germans were included, 'that was obviously for some a nightmare'. A genuine Europeanist, if not to say federalist, he had been declaring for many years that 'we need further European cooperation' and it was now more imperative than ever 'to anchor the FRG as firmly as possible in the Community'.[57]

For his part, Mitterrand was acutely aware that – despite his coup at Strasbourg – France's window of opportunity was limited. His aim was to make EMU irreversible before Germany was in a position to shape the debate in its own direction – or worse, decided to pull out of the whole process. Throughout the winter he still entertained hopes of somehow slowing down the German drive towards unification. As he confided to Baker on 16 December: 'German reunification must not go forward any faster than the EC.'[58] He also wanted to curb Kohl's federalist project for political union. Its security dimensions were anathema because of the threat posed to France's position as the sole continental nuclear power. And, following the French tradition, Mitterrand's conception of the EC was essentially intergovernmental, not supranational. For him, closer political union meant more power to the Council – in other words, the heads of government.[59]

Kohl had tried to calm Mitterrand's fears in private on the beach at Latché in January 1990. Realising he had to do so in public as well, he went out of his way to demonstrate his fidelity to the bilateral bond and to the European idea on 17 January when speaking in Paris to the French Institute of International Relations. 'The Federal Republic of Germany stands without hesitancy to its European responsibilities – because especially for us Germans it is valid to say: Europe is our fate!' To make clear this was a matter of choice not mere determinism, he proclaimed that the FRG 'is today inseparably fused with free and democratic Europe' and that there was no intention of going back to nineteenth-century nationalism. 'The "German challenge" was in reality a European challenge', one that Europeans would have to confront together 'with foresight and perseverance'.[60]

Mitterrand, however, was not appeased. Knowing that the chancellor would speak about reunification and a federal Europe, he deliberately boycotted the event in Paris and even declined to see him. As Mitterrand told Thatcher three days later, 'this was the first time for years that they had not met on such an occasion'. Blowing off steam, he said 'the sudden prospect of unification' had 'delivered a sort of mental shock' to the German people, turning them 'once again into the "bad" Germans they used to be'. They were behaving, he said, 'with a certain brutality and concentrating on reunification to the exclusion of everything else. It was difficult to maintain good relations with them in this sort of mood.' Although 'most affable and courtly', according to Thatcher's private secretary, Mitterrand did not mince his words: 'The Germans could not be allowed to throw their weight around like this.'[61]

Mitterrand was further irritated by another speech on 17 January, in this case one delivered by Jacques Delors at the European Parliament in Strasbourg. Presenting 'The Commission's Programme for 1990', Delors suggested that EMU should be accompanied by 'institutional strengthening'. With this coded phrase he relaunched the debate about a political Europe. Raising the thorny issue of what to do with East Germany, Delors reminded MEPs that the Treaties of Rome had long ago committed the EC to support eventual German unification. 'I would like to repeat clearly here today that there is a place for East Germany in the Community should it so wish, provided, as the Strasbourg European Council made quite clear, the German nation regains its unity through free self-determination, peacefully and democratically, in accordance with the principles of the Helsinki Final Act, in the context of an East–West dialogue and with an eye to European integration. But the form that it will take is, I repeat, a matter for the Germans themselves.' Delors indicated that in this way East Germany would be treated as a 'special case' and could not set a precedent for how to handle the rest of Eastern Europe. The concept of the GDR as a *Sonderfall* or 'exception' was much to the liking of Bonn.[62]

In both these respects – on European political union and on the GDR

– Delors' 17 January speech helped Kohl. But the Commission president's view of political union was not entirely to the chancellor's taste. At its heart would be an enhanced role for the European Commission itself, whereas Kohl particularly wanted to strengthen the power and authority of the European Parliament through direct elections to provide democratic legitimacy.

Despite these differences of approach, political union was firmly back on the table. This could, however, only be advanced through strong Franco-German cooperation to which Mitterrand – still cripplingly ambivalent about Germany – was at this stage unwilling to commit himself. He remained convinced that the principal way to deepen Europe was through monetary union, not least in order to deal with the German question. In this vein, he told Italian prime minister Giulio Andreotti on 13 February that 'the local train' (meaning Europe) had to speed up and catch up the 'express train' (Germany). He griped again about Kohl's propensity to go it alone, complaining bitterly that the chancellor had not consulted him at all over his plan for the German currency union before announcing it a week before – even though this might well have consequences for EMU.[63]

The same day, Delors weighed in with the idea of a 'special summit' of EC leaders to examine the consequences of German unification for the Community. In justifying this to MEPs he spoke in expansive terms. 'Some say that the Community's days are numbered because it was a product of the Cold War and because we now need to think in terms of a greater Europe.' But this, he said, was to ignore the efforts made for over thirty years to 'maintain what might be called a fraternal spirit'. He also warned against 'the risk of destroying a unique, a major, historical experiment' to create a 'Community' rather than merely 'an intergovernmental organisation'.[64]

The problems, Delors said, were that progress had been 'too slow' in building the Community and that its current dimensions were too limited. In the present circumstances, 'we must think in terms of a political Community. This was not the case a few years ago. The revitalisation programme for the Community proposed by the Commission in 1985 was an economic one. It was a response to a simple question: would our economies survive or decline? We found an answer to that question, but the problems facing us today are political. Unless we think in political terms, unless we give our Community an adequate institutional structure, how can we speak of a social dimension? The social dimension is meaningless without this political structure.' How, he asked – especially after 1989 – 'can we speak about "A People's Europe"?'[65]

Delors' proposal for an 'extraordinary' EC Council was picked up by Kohl during his dinner with Mitterrand on 15 February. The chancellor argued that the summit would be best held in the second half of April, after the GDR situation had been clarified by the elections there in March. In pushing this idea, the chancellor underlined his commitment to the Strasbourg decision to begin formal discussion of monetary union at the IGC in December – stressing that 'Germany would do everything imaginable to contribute to progress in integration'. But it is also likely that he was trying to get back into the driving seat in EC affairs because he assumed the summit would naturally be directed by the Franco-German tandem. Kohl said he wanted to work together with France, observing that the French would benefit from a united Germany's future economic strength.[66]

For his part, Mitterrand conceded that a unified Germany would not be a problem for the Community. He certainly found the idea of a bigger Germany more palatable than admitting the GDR as a thirteenth state. Yet he still could not throw off his lingering doubts. Of course Germany was in a very strong position because of its economy. So had been the Germany of Kaiser Wilhelm II. But, he added slyly, its leader had 'a bad foreign policy, which led to war'. Today, at least there was 'a democratic Germany that was bound into the European Community' and, to tighten that bond, he proposed bringing forward from December 1990 the IGC on monetary union. Kohl rejected this out of hand. He was not to be blackmailed by cheap historical analogies into an even speedier EMU timetable than had already been agreed. After all, it was in his personal as well as the FRG's interest to hold the IGC after the Federal German elections in early December.[67]

That dinner had been a real jousting match. Overall, however, the result was positive progress. France and Germany had committed themselves to a special EC summit within two months to define the future of the Community. The details still had to be sorted out, including the balance and interconnection between political and monetary union, but what Kohl had called 'the motor of Europe' was beginning to run again.

*

The Franco-German idea of a special EC summit was quickly endorsed by the rest of the Community. It would take place in Dublin in April, hosted by Irish premier Charles Haughey – the current president of the European Council. And France and Germany were now in a 'much more intensive' bilateral relationship, with constant interaction between officials.

The road to Dublin was not without its potholes.[68] But some French worries were definitely being ticked off the list. In mid-March the '2 + 4' negotiations got under way and the GDR elections delivered a resounding endorsement of Kohl's vision for rapid reunification. The fear of anarchy at the heart of Europe began to recede. Moreover, thanks to Kohl's proposed use of Article 23 of the Basic Law – the extension of West German state structures to the East – reunification no longer seemed a bureaucratic and political nightmare. It was certainly not going to get the EC into a fraught debate about enlargement, as happened in the 1980s over Greece, Spain and Portugal and was feared would recur over Eastern Europe.

Mitterrand was also coming round to some kind of political union. He recognised that, if he wanted to shape the outcome in his own way, he had to engage with what Delors and Kohl were proposing. Now convinced that the Germans would not block EMU, he was willing to consider institutional reform on its own merits. He was not opposed per se to an enhanced role of the European Parliament. But he wanted it to be balanced by intergovernmental cooperation through the Council of Ministers. Unlike Delors, Mitterrand believed the Council's role had to be increased – because the Commission, he said scathingly, was certainly 'not the government of Europe'.[69]

And there were other external pressures to get moving. On 22 March Belgium came forward with a proposal that the EC should convene an IGC specifically on institutional questions. This prodded Mitterrand, and indeed Kohl, to develop their own initiative for a political Europe.[70]

Keen now to dispel the impression of Franco-German bickering, Mitterrand declared on 25 March on French television that Germany was 'solidly anchored in European policy' and that he would 'demonstrate this with Kohl in the coming weeks'.[71] Three days later, during Haughey's visit to Bonn, Kohl suggested that the EC 12, when they met in Dublin on 28 April, should call for an IGC specially devoted to political union. Next day Mitterrand stated his agreement.

And so Kohl had retrieved the ground lost on EPU because of the distractions following the fall of the Wall. By the end of March he had managed to nest unification within his vision for closer European union. On this Delors had served as a valuable ally: his support was not only unequivocal but delivered an all-important French accent. In one of their exchanges, Kohl confided to Delors how much he appreciated the Community's welcoming attitude towards the East Germans, and said that he believed pushing on with political union in Dublin would be the best way to build trust and banish what he called the image of Germany as the 'steamroller' of the European continent.[72]

On 3 April, the chancellor gave the green light to his staff to begin reconciling with the Elysée 'elements of conclusions' for Dublin. Behind the bureaucratic jargon, this was an important instruction because it signalled that Kohl wanted an agreed outcome to emerge from the special summit and was willing to trade off with the French in order to get there. Paris, however, had still not abandoned its reservations about the form and character of political union and it proved difficult to pin down precise wording. Eventually, recognising that the clock was ticking to launch the Franco-German initiative ahead of the summit, Bonn accepted that it would have to settle for a general set of principles rather than a detailed blueprint.

And so, on 18 April, ten days before Dublin, Mitterrand and Kohl addressed a joint public letter to Haughey in his role as EC Council president. They stated that it was now 'necessary to accelerate the political construction of the Europe of the Twelve' with the aim that a treaty embodying both monetary and political union would come into force on 1 January 1993, after ratification by the national parliaments. To this end, they proposed the intensification of the preparatory work for the EMU IGC in December, and the creation of a separate, 'parallel' IGC on political union. The EPU IGC would have four specific goals: strengthening the democratic legitimacy of the union; rendering its institutions more efficient; ensuring 'unity and coherence' of the EC's 'political actions'; and defining and implementing a 'common foreign and security policy' (CFSP).[73]

Although proclaimed with due fanfare, this document was far less ambitious than Kohl had wanted. He had hoped to kick-start a process leading to an agreed constitution for a truly federal Europe that, like any state actor, could conduct a coherent foreign policy. In its stead he got some watered-down aspirations, formulated in non-committal language. Nor was there any categorical statement on the start date of the political

IGC. Compromise with the French resulted in a proposal that the foreign ministers should undertake preparatory work after the 28 April summit, now called Dublin I, and develop a first progress report for the regular EC Council in June (Dublin II). A final report would be prepared for discussion at the Rome Council meeting in December. The idea was that at Dublin II, the EC leaders should decide on convening the EPU IGC at the end of year.

Significantly, in this context, the French did not bring up their confederation idea; instead, they focused on how to 'deepen' the EC itself. They were fixated on the aspect of 'coherence' which, in their view, only the Council of Ministers could ensure. And considering that so far some measure of political unity had been achieved by the Council through the coordination of national foreign policies, it was also through this body that France hoped to develop a CFSP.

The areas of agreement underlying the Kohl–Mitterrand letter to Haughey were therefore quite limited and the initiative papered over unresolved differences in outlook and priorities. The media noted 'France and West Germany seem to agree more on method than substance' with Kohl speaking of the 'inevitability of "a federal Europe"' while French officials admitted in private 'we don't like the word federation'.[74]

Yet there could be no doubt that Bonn and Paris had jointly launched a new dynamic for a European revival. And so, three days before the Dublin I special summit, during the biannual Franco-German consultations on 25 April – the fifty-fifth of its kind – Kohl stated with satisfaction: 'European unity and German unity are being made together; this has always been the European dream ... we have to do this together.' Mitterrand agreed emphatically. After months of subterranean tensions, this, according to Teltschik, was a happy occasion for chancellor and president. Both men sensed that they were on the threshold of building a new Europe, acting on the lessons of history, with France and Germany finally in unison.[75]

Crucially, this willingness to converge was possible because the French were now thinking of their national interest as being fundamentally entwined with the destiny of Europe. A unifying Germany was being tamed not through a traditional balance of power (as advocated by Thatcher who was vocal in favouring a 'dispersed' over a 'federal' Europe)[76] but by its integration into an increasingly robust Community architecture. So Mitterrand's policy on Europe was not, then, animated solely by pragmatism – by economic necessity and the need to restrain German power. Rather he acted from the conviction that a closer economic, political and defence community in Europe would be to France's general advantage. Consequently, the 'future of Europe' became firmly 'a function of Franco-German cooperation' – which was total anathema to Thatcher.[77]

Amid this new mood, Dublin I concluded positively on 28 April. The EC leaders confirmed the Bonn–Paris agenda of a political relaunch, also under the Irish presidency, at Dublin II. And most of the Community partners rallied enthusiastically to the Franco-German goal of establishing a European 'Union' – though what exactly this would mean was left as yet undefined.[78]

The Germans also resolved some problems about unification that could have impeded European integration. The fact that the GDR would be absorbed into the FRG implied that the addition to the EC of the territory of the Eastern *Länder* would not involve any revision of existing EC treaties. And it would come at very little extra cost to the Community because Bonn made clear that it would not seek any regional development funding or agricultural subsidies. As Kohl put it, 'the Germans don't intend to stick their hand into the European Community wallet'. Indeed, he painted a glossy picture of transforming the dour command economy of East Germany into a free-market paradise in a mere five years. And because the introduction of the Deutschmark to the East would occur on 1 July 1990 – the same day as stage one of EMU was launched – it all looked beautifully neat. Even before political unification, the expanded German market would be fully included in the open economic space of the EC's single market.[79]

On top of this, the chancellor – conscious of his partners' sensitivities – went out of his way to squash all talk of an increase in German voting power in the EC. It was agreed that any adjustments that might be necessary in the balance of the Commission or Council of Ministers would be considered later, as part of the talks on institutional reform. Meanwhile, the Commission would develop a few 'transitional arrangements' for the Eastern *Länder* that would be 'confined to what is strictly necessary'.[80] For example, the GDR's trade treaties with the Comecon countries, including the USSR, would remain in effect, and the EC's regulatory regime – on issues ranging from food quality to environmental protection – would not be applied until at least the completion of its own internal market on 31 December 1992.

Further progress was made at the second Dublin Council of 25–6 June. Having long ago set the 13 December date for the EMU IGC, the EC 12 finally bit the bullet and resolved to launch the EPU IGC the day after, on 14 December. The mandate of this second IGC was to transform what was still a predominantly economic European Community into a political union with a common foreign and security policy of its own. Just how much sovereignty each country would have to surrender was left to be determined at the coming negotiations. For the moment, what mattered to Kohl was a momentous and hard-won decision of principle.[81]

Throughout these frantic months since the fall of the Wall and despite his twists and turns, the German chancellor had maintained a consistent perspective. Linking national and European interests not only served to secure German unification but also assisted his ambitious pro-integrationist agenda. This passion for Europe went way beyond what was demanded by the economic situation or political imperatives. The chancellor's aim was to help shape the architecture of post-Cold War Europe.

And that architecture was complex. It entailed economic and monetary integration which, through the Community's formalised new EMU, would anchor a large zone of monetary stability and thereby safeguard German economic interests vis-à-vis the dollar and the global economy at large. But it also included further federalisation through strengthening the parliament and a common foreign policy and, in the longer run, the 'EC 92' or EU opening to the East. In all these ways Kohl was far more interested than Mitterrand in giving new form to an 'ever closer union', as the founding fathers had imagined and the 1957 Treaties of Rome formally stated. For him, as for Adenauer, German unity and European unity were, as he liked to say, 'two sides of the same coin'. Kohl made the *Altkanzler's* maxim his own. But whereas Adenauer envisaged European integration as a means to achieve German unity, in 1990 Kohl used reunification as the impetus for deeper integration.[82]

Kohl even spoke of himself as the 'grandson' of Adenauer.[83] In so doing, he was alluding to both Adenauer's commitment to Franco-German reconciliation and his conviction that *Westbindung* (binding to the West) was also *Selbstbindung* (binding of the self) – tying the unruly German people into organisations that restrained their assertive tendencies. Being anchored into this 'institutional West' had served both West Germany and Western Europe well during the Cold War. Now, Kohl believed, it would serve united Germany equally well at a time when Europe was turning east. At root, for both chancellors, Europe constituted a question of war and peace. Kohl told the World Economic Forum in Davos on 3 February 1990 that in Western Europe there was 'no way back to the power-political rivalries of past times ... Human rights and human dignity; free self-determination; a free societal order; private initiative; market economy. These are the building blocks for a future European order of peace, which overcomes the division of Europe and the division of Germany.'[84]

So the push for European union was not a 'hasty' reaction to 'French dismay and frustration over developments in Germany', as has been suggested,[85] but the continuation of a long-running process of rapprochement and partnership. Building on this historical foundation, France and Germany became active shapers of the future of the continent.

Britain, by contrast, did not.

*

In fact, Margaret Thatcher managed to isolate herself altogether from the process of contructing the new Europe.[86] Journalist George Urban – one of her informal circle of foreign-policy advisers – recorded what he called 'a memorable lunch' at 10 Downing Street on 19 December 1989. '"You know George," she said coming quite close to me, "there are things that people of your generation and mine ought never to forget. We've been through the war and we know perfectly well what the Germans are like, and what dictators can do, and how national character doesn't basically change" ... She added that it was "now within the Germans' power to expand into an economically dominant empire, and what they could not attain through world wars they would try to achieve through economic imperialism. The whole of Eastern Europe is going to be their bailiwick; they are already taking over East Germany; all of which is going to create a menace for Britain."'[87]

On Germany, there was real tension between Number 10 and the FCO[88] – which expected to define British policy on this matter and intended to do so along the line that Britain had taken since the 1950s, namely to support the principle of eventual unification based on the right of self-determination. For British diplomats, the 2 + 4 process was an appropriate way of moving towards this goal in an orderly fashion. By contrast, on 4 December 1989 Thatcher categorically told her NATO partners – Kohl included – that 'reunification should not take place for ten or fifteen years'.[89] Six weeks later she insisted that 'East Germany must take its place in the queue for membership of the Community'.[90] Her relentless efforts – by phone and in person – to persuade Gorbachev and Mitterrand to join in opposing, or at least in delaying, German unification were entirely individual initiatives, with no support from Cabinet colleagues or the FCO.

The one notable exception was Charles Powell, Thatcher's private secretary for foreign affairs since 1983, who had become one of her most trusted advisers. As Scowcroft later remarked, 'I became thoroughly convinced that he was the only serious influence on Thatcher's views on foreign policy. He was close to her, had uncanny insights into her thinking, and, even given her powerful personality, could be very persuasive.' Powell clearly egged the prime minister on with his bold notes and memoranda, shrewdly composed to chime with her own hymn sheet. Thus he wrote, for example, ahead of her meeting with François Mitterrand in late January 1990:

> The FCO have prepared a complex of papers for your meeting ... The papers are distinguished essays, but perhaps a bit too cerebral and too complicated. We need to stand back a bit and consider the essentials.
>
> We have three worries. First, that arms reductions will get out of hand ... Second, that German unification will happen quickly and will create an economic and political monster (and could revert to the type of Germany we have witnessed twice this century). Third that Americans will lose interest in Europe, leaving us inadequately defended and face-to-face with the German Frankenstein.[91]

None of this language should surprise us. Thatcher herself never made any secret of her feelings about Germany, which were compounded by personal distaste for the chancellor himself.[92]

Mitterrand, of course, was also quite capable of blowing off steam about the Germans in private to Thatcher – as revealed in their explosive conversation about 1913 and 1938 at Strasbourg in December. When they met on 20 January 1990, the French president again aired his fears that Germany might not only reunify but also seek to 'regain other territories which it had lost as a result of the war'. He added dramatically: 'They might even make more ground than Hitler.'[93] But Mitterrand vented such comments mainly behind closed doors – unlike Thatcher. As Sir

Christopher Mallaby, the British ambassador in Bonn, ruefully admitted, although French doubts 'seem if anything stronger than ours', Mitterrand's government managed to 'maintain a more positive public image ... As the FRG's best friend and most important European partner, France can get away with a great deal ... The UK by contrast is at present seen as neither especially important nor as well disposed.'[94]

The French president not only held a stronger hand, he also played it more subtly. Whereas he tended to speak out of different sides of his mouth depending on who was his audience, Thatcher's line was relentlessly consistent and her tone almost invariably shrill. After ten years in power, she was impervious to contrary arguments and accustomed to getting her own way, especially on issues about which she was almost neurotic: Germany, the war, and the balance of power.

In short, she was ruling herself out of creative diplomacy – failing to engage in the deal-making that had begun to emerge from the confusion of 1989. The most immediate of these bargains was the European solution to the German question, now being forged by Bonn and Paris. And here Mitterrand, cunning as ever, may even have been baiting Thatcher into a public rant about reunification and thereby marginalising Britain, while he pursued his own European goals in tandem with Kohl. Be that as it may, the Iron Lady remained unwavering in her belief that 'the European construct will not bind Germany; it's rather the case that Germany will dominate the European construct'.[95]

Two months later, she was still on the warpath. She told French prime minister Michel Rocard on 26 March 1990 during their generally 'good-humoured' talks in London, that further European integration meant 'centralisation' – just as 'the Soviet Union and Eastern Europe', she exclaimed, were 'moving away from that'! Indeed, 'all over the world, the lesson was that greater prosperity and democracy came from devolving responsibility not trying to centralise power'. How could the Community choose this moment to 'move in the opposite direction'? It was better to maintain a degree of national independence, rather than giving away one's sovereignty to some 'amorphous amalgam' that would be ruled by Germany.[96]

On European monetary union, Thatcher was positively visceral – blasting Delors in her notorious Bruges speech of 20 September 1988: 'The lesson of the economic history of Europe in the 70s and 80s is that central planning and detailed control *do not* work ... We have not successfully rolled back the frontiers of the state in Britain, only to see them reimposed at a European level with a European super-state exercising a new dominance from Brussels.'[97] And she was equally opposed to bolstering the EC's political authority, especially that of the Commission. At Dublin I she told her European colleagues that her constituents feared that 'Brussels would take away their queen and make the Mother of Parliaments irrelevant'. She was adamant that political union must not mean giving up 'our legal or electoral systems, or our defence through NATO'. She even made the same point to the press, contemptuously dismissing her fellow leaders: 'they do not quite know what political union means ... It astounds me.'[98]

Battle of wills: Thatcher vs Delors

By the time they got to Dublin II in June, Thatcher was in a world of her own. She said she would attend the IGCs on EMU and EPU but made clear that she had no time for either. She was in principle 'quite prepared to join the exchange-rate mechanism' but definitely not to 'go for a single currency, that is, drop the pound sterling'. She allowed that 'one day, I don't know, in the long-distant future, there may be a single currency' but added: 'I don't think it is for our generation to take that decision.'[99]

Thatcher had not only managed to outmanoeuvre herself and her country from Euro-politics, she also ended up on the margin of the other big bargain that would shape the continent's future – hammered out between the United States and the Federal Republic – whereby Bush backed rapid German unification in return for Kohl's commitment that unified Germany would remain in NATO. Especially after Kohl's visit to Camp David in February 1990 this line was forcefully pursued – with Thatcher's acquiescence but little input on her part. The sidelining of Britain had been evident for more than a year. Kohl was the first foreign leader to visit Bush after his election victory – on 15 November 1988. And in May 1989 the president, in his Mainz speech about 'a Europe whole and free' had elevated Germany to the status of America's 'partner in leadership'. Given Bush's agenda and his desire to distance himself from Reagan, he felt that he need not defer to Thatcher or be seen to follow in her footsteps, especially with regard to Gorbachev.[100] As the *New York Times* headlined it on 10 December 1989: 'US Ties With West Germany Begin to Eclipse Relationship With Britain'.

Three's a crowd – George, Helmut and Maggie

Nevertheless, this was a sensitive moment for US diplomacy because Britain and America were two old friends, even though Germany was now on the up. As an administration source put it, Baker was 'trying very hard to avoid juggling the two ... The key is not to have to juggle. If you're juggling, you're in trouble.' In any case, Baker – after two years running the Treasury – was already predisposed to view Bonn and its Bundesbank as the real powerhouse of Europe. And with liberalisation taking hold amid chaotic conditions in Eastern Europe, West Germany was Washington's primary partner for managing change across the old

Soviet bloc – ceding to Bonn the lead role in both coordinating and financing the Western aid to Poland and Hungary, and indeed, after Dublin I, for the rest of Eastern Europe.[101]

Bush was not only supporting Kohl on strictly German issues, he also endorsed a European solution to the German question. This, too, caused friction with Thatcher. The administration's line, according to one senior official, was that the EC was 'clearly going to be the core of the future Europe, promoting greater European political and security integration' and Thatcher ought to recognise this. 'Instead of resisting that process, she should join it and shape it and not fear it. Back in the '60s when the British were arguing about whether to join the EEC, the proponents said the Americans won't take us seriously if we are just a small island off the continent. That argument was valid then,' the official added, 'and it is still valid today.'[102]

It is interesting to consider Thatcher and Mitterrand in parallel. Like her, he had exhibited an initial 'refusal to believe, a denial of what was happening in plain sight, because it flew in the face of everything that half a century of history had taught him.'[103] But then Mitterrand had come around to the idea of German unification once he accepted Kohl's assurances that a united Germany would be anchored in Europe. That also meant that France and Germany would drive the integration process forward together. For Thatcher, by contrast, a European solution to the German question was quite simply no solution. A transatlantic framework, however, did seem to offer an answer – and to that she gradually came round in the spring of 1990, as she took in Bush's insistence on, and Kohl's acceptance of, Germany in NATO. Binding the new Germany into the Western Alliance, and thereby taming it, was an adaptation of the old rationale for NATO – 'to keep the Americans in, the Russians out and the Germans down'. And it was also attractive to Thatcher[104] because the British had a privileged position in the Alliance as a founding member – present at the creation, unlike Britain's relationship with the EEC – and also as a nuclear power fully within NATO's integrated command system, unlike France since the days of de Gaulle. So Thatcher was reconciled by the Germany-in-NATO solution even though she would simply be a supporting figure, rather than the equal partner – which was Mitterrand's role in the Germany-in-Europe solution.

At the end of March, during the fortieth annual Anglo-German Königswinter Conference, held in Cambridge, Thatcher accepted Kohl's promises that the new Germany would remain part of the Atlantic

Alliance. Judged by the usual rather frosty standards of Kohl–Thatcher encounters, this one not only proved constructive but could reasonably be described as 'cordial' – even though it did not start well. Kohl had arrived in Britain in a huff – still seething at spiky comments about the Oder–Neisse border that Thatcher had made in a recent interview for *Der Spiegel*, the left-liberal weekly that he loathed. As a result he snubbed her when she went to meet him at Cambridge airport and refused to get in the same car to St Catharine's College. After that, it took quite a while for the evening to warm up. During the reception, the prime minister was mingling at one end, the chancellor at the other. At dinner in the college hall, Sir Oliver Wright – a former ambassador in both Bonn and Washington – had been carefully seated between them, to serve as a buffer. But as soon as the meal began, Thatcher, looking over to Kohl, made a teasing comment about the chancellor's habit of always draping his napkin across the full expanse of his ample belly. Kohl was up for a bit of banter as well: could she not see? This was his white flag, a symbol of surrender to the Iron Lady. Laughter all round – the ice had been broken. The atmosphere warmed further as Thatcher, so Kohl recalled, then proceeded to give a friendly speech, delivered in her most charming manner.[105]

Two weeks later, having made peace with Kohl, the prime minister had a productive and wide-ranging discussion with Bush in Bermuda on 13 April. The president was particularly solicitous: 'Let me make clear at the beginning how important I think it is that we stay on the same wavelength … I don't want us to stumble into accidental differences. Our relations are in good shape, but I want to keep it that way.' He emphasised to Thatcher that 'both of us see the need to have a united Germany remain a full member of the NATO Alliance, including its structures'. But the meeting with Mitterrand next week, he said, 'could be difficult because we are not on the same wavelength with France on NATO and some European issues'.[106]

The prime minister responded warmly to his overtures. 'In the area of European defence,' she insisted, 'all defence matters should be done through NATO, which has been fantastically successful.' This, she added waspishly, had been 'made a bit fuzzy' because France is not in 'the military side of NATO'.[107] They also discussed the future of the Alliance. NATO, the president said, 'represents our principal link to Europe. I think it is vital that the US maintain itself in Europe, but without a vigorous NATO, I don't see how this can be done.' Therefore, he insisted, 'as force reductions and an undivided Europe become real possibilities, and as the Warsaw Pact loses its cohesion', the Alliance would have to consider how to 'project a renewed Western vision for the future of Europe'. Bush was enthusiastic about the suggestion from Manfred Wörner, the Alliance's secretary general, for a NATO summit sometime in the summer, and so was she – as long as 'everyone was on board'. For her part, the prime minister welcomed what he called his 'main message' that America's 'commitment to keep nuclear weapons deployed in Europe, including in Germany, is strong'. And she particularly mentioned retaining the British Army of the Rhine, which was another of her hobby horses and further evidence of her residual distrust of the Germans.[108]

Knowing Bush was a strong supporter of the EC 92 integration project, she could not restrain herself from a few snide remarks on that topic even though Community politics were largely absent from their talks. To be sure, she was keen on an EC–US free-trade agreement. But 'on EC political union', she was scathing – 'the words come out with little meaning, and we, of course, have the oldest parliament on earth'. Instead she believed 'we need to enlarge the area of free trade' across the globe, 'rather than moving towards blocs'. Thatcher knew which notes to sound in order to get the president's ear. She was well aware of Bush's keenness to finally 'make the Uruguay Round a success', his desperate desire to see a compromise emerge on tariffs and his chronic frustration with the EC, especially the apparently endless dispute over French farming subsidies. 'We are all impure on this one, but need to get toward a more open market. It's a terribly important problem for us', he replied to her overture. Realising she could manoeuvre herself centre stage on the issue of re-inventing the regime of global trade, she even ventured the idea of perhaps giving 'a big internationalist, "Bruges II", speech'.[109]

Overall, then, the Bermuda summit was a success for both sides. At the end, Thatcher publicly affirmed that she and Bush 'both attach the greatest possible importance to preserving NATO as the heart of the West's defence and to keeping American forces and their nuclear weapons in Europe ... We'll be happy to see NATO play a bigger political role within the Atlantic community'. The president for his part stressed that 'These talks with Prime Minister Thatcher have been especially valuable to me. Our two countries have worked together for peace and freedom for many years now, and we've watched that cause prevail in many places and times ... The US–UK friendship is the kind that doesn't need the words to describe it. It's a special friendship that is evident from the way we share a common vision for the future of humanity.' Special! Here was the magic word that every British prime minister yearned to hear from a US president.[110]

Having ticked that box, Bush highlighted the agreement with Chancellor Kohl that 'Germany should remain a full member of NATO, including its military structures' – a view, he said, that 'the entire North Atlantic Alliance, and several of the countries in Eastern Europe' share as well, because it is 'in the genuine security interest of all European States'.[111] Teltschik noted with pleasure that at Bermuda was issued 'the first, unequivocal public pronouncement' from the British, as well as the Americans, on the goal of restoring full sovereignty to a united Germany.[112]

If Thatcher was reticent on the direction of EC Europe, and happy to support the US in constructing the continent's defence architecture around NATO, she really pushed Bush on the importance of the CSCE and its 'strengthening'. This issue also offered her an opportunity to act as an interlocutor for Gorbachev. For some weeks, she had been making positive noises about the CSCE as a framework to discuss European security, one that included both superpowers. 'Not only would this help avoid Soviet isolation,' she told Bush over the phone on 24 February, 'it would help balance German dominance in Europe.'[113] In doing so she partly echoed Shevardnadze's calls in Ottawa the week before that Europe must 'lock a greater Germany into a new "pan-European" political structure for its own safety'.[114] In Bermuda, Thatcher developed her argument face-to-face, stating that 'NATO would handle defence responsibilities' while the CSCE 'would be a political forum' – indeed 'the only big East–West forum where we meet with the East Europeans and Soviets'. Thus its role in Europe-wide dialogue should be heightened. And, on a larger plane, the CSCE was central for her approach to Gorbachev whom she considered a 'sensible politician' under immense domestic pressure. She even declared, 'I haven't given up the dream of using CSCE to help democratise the USSR.'[115]

Bush agreed that the CSCE could play 'a critical role in overcoming the division of Europe'. As did Baker, who said it was giving Gorbachev 'some cover at home'. This, he added, was 'one of the merits of a CSCE summit, if we can also sign a CFE agreement'. Bush, however, offered a qualification. 'It's OK,' he said, 'as long as it doesn't cut the other way and we don't get outvoted on Western security interests at a CSCE summit.' Hence, the Bush administration wanted to delay preparatory meetings about a summit until substantive issues about conventional forces had been resolved and a CFE treaty was ready for signature. Baker aired another American concern: 'We don't want all political functions in CSCE. We need to keep some political functions in NATO. We can't leave it all to the CSCE or NATO will look too military.' Recalibrating and rebranding NATO was an essential part of US policy.[116]

*

NATO was indeed changing, though only slowly. Here the eleventh leaders' summit – intended for the summer – would definitely help. But the Alliance and especially Washington also needed to work out how NATO would relate to those other putative security institutions for Europe, the EC and CSCE.[117] They were the subject of Bush's discussions with Mitterrand and Delors on 19 and 24 April – the first in Key Largo, the second in Washington – during which the president spelled out the American position. He made clear that, although the USA sought to 'retain its involvement' in Europe, it did not seek a 'thirteenth seat at the EC table'. Baker chipped in: 'We are not seeking a veto over EC decisions, but we do want to enhance US–EC institutional interaction.' As for the CSCE, that could not be 'a guarantor of security in Europe', said Bush. Rather 'we do see an expanded role for NATO' – this 'broader US presence' also being the only way to justify to the American people that US troops did not constitute 'a mercenary force'. The president spoke of NATO and the EC as 'complementary institutions' and since both had 'legitimate interests' in the CSCE they should discuss that issue in parallel. Looking at the whole European tableau, he said it was imperative that the United States remained involved with 'the overall security decisions' of the continent. Given these priorities, it was therefore natural they all agreed that NATO leaders should meet in advance of any CSCE summit.[118]

In Washington Delors told Bush that the EC Commission favoured a 'vigorous NATO'. He was conscious of the 'continuing danger' from the Soviet Union.[119] Mitterrand shared this view. He noted that the risk of war had decreased but felt that 'the Soviet Union is not reassuring: a great power which is in a weakened position is dangerous. The US should have a say in all issues that affect equilibrium in Europe.'[120] Delors also affirmed the centrality of the Atlantic Alliance. Even if the EC drive to political union included a 'security role for the EC', this would constitute 'a sort of European pillar of NATO ... Mr President you must take this political integration as reinforcing the Alliance.'[121] But Delors and Mitterrand disagreed about the CSCE and the EC's security role. Whereas the Commission president envisaged the CSCE as 'becoming a sort of matrix' for 'incorporating Eastern European countries', Mitterrand dismissed the organisation as, at best, marginally useful in dealing with the former Soviet satellites. It could only serve, he said, as a 'meeting place' during 'moments of international tension'.[122]

In Key Largo – as they talked in a lush private resort of palms and hibiscus at the ocean villa of a business friend of the president[123] – the French leader indulged in some crystal-ball-gazing about the future of European security and the transatlantic relationship. Anxious to reassure the Americans, despite France being out of the integrated command system, he insisted it would always be a full player in the Alliance. Mitterrand was more concerned about the states of Eastern Europe: 'alone, poor and humiliated'. What was needed, he said, was 'a place for these countries to do their work where they are respected and treated with dignity'. If admitted to the EC, they would 'come with their hats in hand like beggars'. The CSCE, of which they were already members since 1975, was not 'really appropriate' because it was not an institutionalised 'political entity'. As for Gorbachev's 'Common European Home', that was only a 'vision'. At this point Mitterrand again pulled from his bag of tricks the Confederation idea, arguing that new times required new institutions. He talked of it as a 'European Union' which, he admitted, would take 'a generation' to develop and would 'not happen in my time'. Such a Confederation might be 'visionary', he acknowledged, but it would 'build on' the EC 12, rather than 'replace' it. To mollify Bush, he specified that the European Confederation would 'not be designed to get rid of the United States'; that, he exclaimed, would be 'idiotic'. He envisaged a treaty or alliance between the Confederation and the United States but insisted, 'Europeans need to feel European.'[124]

Mitterrand's blue-sky thinking was a bizarre performance – delivered in several long monologues before and after lunch, which did not always hang together. What was going on? Bush pondered this a couple of weeks later in conversation with NATO secretary general Manfred Wörner. 'Maybe he's only telling us things to feel good,' the president opined. 'Or he may be leaving it to the French bureaucracy, who only wants to stiff us.' Wörner endeavoured to shed some light on the Gallic mind. 'I have recently visited France. They want to restrict NATO to being a military alliance with no real political decision-making role. NATO for them is an instrument of American influence.' Instead, 'they want political cooperation to be in the EC'. His recommendation was blunt: 'We should not let the French use the summit for those ends. We should reach a summit declaration that finishes the question of why NATO is necessary. NATO should not be questioned any longer.' Bush emphatically agreed.[125]

But it didn't prove as simple as that. At Dublin I on 28 April the EC 12 proposed that preparations should begin in July for the CSCE summit meeting that Gorbachev so keenly wanted. Paris was offered as the venue later in the year. EC leaders also pledged to work within the CSCE framework to help establish 'new political structures or agreements' for Europe, but emphasised that these would not replace the 'existing security arrangements' of member states. This last comment was a reminder of the variegated tapestry of European institutions: Ireland, for instance, as a neutral country, was not a member of NATO – unlike its other eleven EC partners. And the CSCE included not only NATO and EC states but also Warsaw Pact and non-aligned countries.[126]

A CSCE summit was not Bush's priority, or even his preference, but he had to go along with it. The Dublin I fait accompli did prod him into thinking and talking more concretely about NATO's new and 'different' role, not only in relation to Eastern Europe but also in its emerging 'political component'.[127]

The challenge of how to reinvent NATO had been on Bush's mind for several months: discussed with Kohl back at Camp David in February and aired more recently with Thatcher, Mitterrand and Wörner. This was now also the subject of a major NATO strategy review in Washington. The most urgent aspect, after the upheavals of 1989, was whether to proceed with the modernisation of America's short-range Lance nuclear missiles in Europe – the so-called 'follow-on to Lance' (FOTL). Kohl and Genscher were strongly against, and the US Congress was reluctant to fund procurement without strong NATO endorsement. And so FOTL was 'dead as a doornail', as Bush put it to Kohl, but his problem was how to bury it? There was general agreement that cancellation must not seem like capitulation to the current Soviet peace propaganda campaign. As a result FOTL's demise was packaged within a set of positive proposals for NATO, which were unveiled by Wörner on 3 May and fleshed out the following day by Bush in a major policy speech.[128]

In Brussels the NATO secretary general concluded a special meeting of foreign ministers by going public with the news that the Alliance would hold a full-scale summit of leaders in late June or early July. This would round off a series of ministerial meetings as NATO prepared for the future. Slipping in an announcement that America was not going ahead with FOTL, Wörner linked this with US plans for talks with Moscow about reducing SNFs in Europe as soon as a conventional-arms treaty had been signed. The foreign ministers also expressed NATO's support for a CSCE summit and adopted a package of proposals for transforming the Western Alliance into a more political organisation and for making unified Germany's membership in NATO acceptable to the Soviet Union.[129]

There had not been a major US address on the prospective security architecture of Europe since December 1989, when Baker spoke in Berlin. It was now important to speak out, to show leadership and shape the international agenda as the president had done so strikingly the previous spring, from Hamtramck to Mainz. All that, however, was long before the Wall came down. And by early summer 1990, the United States was expected to spearhead a visible, dramatic change in NATO's outlook and posture and to build a consensus on turning the CSCE into a complementary 'forum for political dialogue'. But to do so the president had to keep his allies happy and, at the same time, reassure Gorbachev. This was the delicate balancing act that Bush had to perform when he addressed the graduating class at Oklahoma State University, Stillwater, on 4 May.[130]

With the world entering what the president called 'a new Age of Freedom … a time of uncertainty, but great hope', he insisted in his speech that the United States must 'remain a European power in the broadest sense: politically, militarily, economically'. This, for him, was no mere regional issue: he referred to America's 'peaceful engagement in Europe' through NATO as 'part of our global responsibilities'. The president declared that, building on 'the longest uninterrupted period of international peace in the recorded history of that continent', the Alliance was now ready to 'craft a new Western strategy for new and changing times' – even 'for the next century'.

Bush identified 'four critical points' as the agenda for the NATO summit. First, 'the political role that NATO can play in Europe'. Second, on conventional forces, what the Alliance would need and its goals for arms control. Third, the role of US nuclear weapons and Western objectives in new superpower arms-control negotiations. And fourth, how to strengthen the CSCE, in order to 'reinforce NATO and help protect democratic values in a Europe that is whole and free'. The president spelled out each point in some detail, along the way making deft gestures to key protagonists. He singled out Thatcher as 'one of freedom's greatest champions of the last decade'. He made a coded reference to Mitterrand: 'We should consider whether new CSCE mechanisms can help mediate and settle disputes in Europe.' And there was also a signal to Gorbachev in Bush's phrase 'our enemy today is uncertainty and instability' – in other words, implicitly, not the evil empire. But his real message was for his own people, especially those who asserted that the waning Cold War justified a US retreat from transatlantic commitments. 'America's mission in Europe', he declared, 'can make a world of difference. The cry for freedom – in Eastern Europe, in South Africa, right here in our precious hemisphere to our south – was heard around the world in the revolution of 1989.' Today, he told the graduates, 'in this new Age of Freedom, add your voices to the thundering chorus'.[131]

The speech was bold, promising historic results on a very ambitious agenda. Conceptually, Bush offered a conservative defence for NATO as the continued focus of Europe's security and for the United States remaining the linchpin of the Alliance. And, by doing so two months before the summit, he was bucking conventional diplomatic wisdom about downplaying expectations in advance of international meetings. In fact, he was taking a big gamble. He needed to devise initiatives that would calm Moscow while re-energising the Alliance and commanding wide support in Western Europe. The US strategy depended on Western cohesion in uncertain times and equally on Gorbachev's reluctance to take any kind of decisive action. Only if German unity in a revivified NATO could be secured from the Soviets would a continued US foothold in Europe be guaranteed and the Alliance survive as the prime European security organisation. Meanwhile the CSCE could serve as a framework to give Eastern Europeans some sense of a stake in shaping the continent's future, at a time when they were renouncing the Warsaw Pact and eagerly awaiting the exit of the Red Army.[132]

These concerns were in the forefront of Bush's mind as he prepared for the NATO summit, working especially closely with the Alliance secretary general and the German chancellor. On 7 May he and Wörner fixed the summit for 5–6 July in London – thereby squeezing it in between Dublin II and the G7 in Houston. Both men wanted quick results. 'NATO must act', Wörner declared. 'We do not want to use the summit to open up questions for six or eight months in which NATO's role is being challenged ... We should not give a sense that we are studying these problems, drifting.' They further agreed that Gorbachev must be 'convinced NATO isn't dangerous in the new era' – what Wörner called 'partnership in a cooperative structure'. They were conscious of the likely antagonism of the Soviet military but Baker, who was sitting in, said that he for one was confident about NATO's power of persuasion over the Soviet leadership: 'They don't have any cards, only Four Powers rights. They have little leverage, so ultimately they will have to come along.' While not disagreeing, Bush and Wörner felt that sweeteners for Gorbachev were desirable. 'CSCE can help,' Baker remarked. And not just with the Eastern Europeans. 'We have to persuade the Soviets that the CSCE is a place for them too.'[133]

*

Talk of sweeteners missed the point, however. Bush faced a real diplomatic-strategic conundrum in trying to persuade Gorbachev to accept the perpetuation of NATO, including unified Germany, when he lacked effective leverage over the Kremlin because his hands were tied at home. First, a growing US budget crisis meant that the president was not in a position to offer significant financial inducements. Second, because Moscow's crackdown on Lithuania's bid for freedom was causing uproar in the US Congress and prejudicing any chance for Bush to secure 'most favoured nation' trade status for the USSR. These two problems threatened the success of the NATO summit in July.

On 18 April 1990 the Kremlin had imposed harsh economic sanctions against Lithuania – slashing gas supplies by 70% and halting the flow of crude oil – to force the defiant republic into rescinding its March declaration of independence. This placed Bush in a real bind. He wanted to support what Americans saw as a legitimate bid for self-determination: the USA had never formally recognised the 1940 Soviet annexation of any of the Baltic States. But Bush had to keep in mind the bigger international picture regarding the USSR and Germany. On 19 April, he spoke about his Lithuanian dilemma to the press: 'My reluctance stems from trying to keep open a dialogue and discussion that affects many, many countries. And I'm talking about arms control. I'm talking about solidifying the democracies in Eastern Europe.' He added: 'I am convinced that Mr Gorbachev knows that there are limits in terms of this matter.

I don't think that there is any danger that there will be a misunderstanding on this point. None at all.'[134]

Bush felt that encouraging negotiations between Lithuania and the USSR seemed the most practical solution – to defuse tension and remove the danger that the West might have to intervene. But he could not say so openly. He did not want to provoke Gorbachev, thereby straining the whole fabric of cooperative relations with Moscow. He was afraid of doing 'something imprudent', he told journalists on 24 April. 'I am concerned that we not do anything … that would set back the cause of freedom around the world.' Yet the president was equally concerned about inflaming Republican hardliners who 'seriously detest or suspect Gorbachev, and want to go after him in the name of human rights'. He mused in his diary, 'how do you preserve a relationship without condoning the very kind of behavior the Soviets are involved in?'[135]

So Bush simply sat on his hands, pondering America's options behind closed doors. By deferring any announcement about how to react against Moscow, he earned the wrath of Lithuania's leadership who complained about 'another Munich!'[136] Kohl and Mitterrand, by contrast, felt less constrained. Indeed they had strong reasons to act. The chancellor did not want anything that might derail unification; the French president was always keen to display his special ties with Gorbachev; and both of them saw an opportunity to show off the Franco-German tandem in action via a 'common Ostpolitik' initiative. On 26 April they sent a public letter to Vilnius asking the Lithuanian leadership to rescind its independence declaration in order to get substantive negotiations with the Kremlin under way. Their initiative was intended to ease relations with Moscow while not totally alienating Lithuania. It also served to take the pressure off Bush internationally.[137]

At home, though, criticism of the president's inaction escalated, especially after it was announced that US negotiators had reached agreement in principle with the Soviets on a pact that, once approved by Congress, would grant the USSR 'most favoured nation' tariff treatment. The agreement – to be signed at the upcoming superpower summit in Washington – would initially be for three years, automatically renewable for another three if neither side objected. Before the trade agreement could be signed, as per the Jackson-Vanik amendment of 1974, Bush kept insisting that Moscow would have to adopt a new emigration law – a demand that had prevented a similar trade pact signed in 1972 from coming into force. Yet, above all else it was the Baltic crisis that now put congressional approval in doubt. Indeed, on 1 May the Senate voted to withhold US trade benefits from Moscow until Lithuania's future was resolved.[138]

In this atmosphere, the president privately decided that all US 'economic initiatives' towards Moscow had to be suspended – a step short of sanctions, but including a halt to the trade-agreement talks and to the granting of MFN status. This seemed to him a 'measured, proportionate response', which, he hoped, would create incentives for the Kremlin to lift the energy embargo on Lithuania without America having to resort to threats that made it 'difficult for Gorbachev to relent without losing face at high political cost'. On 29 April he sent the Soviet leader a letter warning him that, far from getting preparations ready for the signing of a comprehensive economic deal at the summit, he was going to put everything on ice. 'I have no choice but to identify with our strongly held convictions about Lithuanian self-determination and the right to control its own destiny.' Still, he promised, 'I am determined to keep that meeting on track in spite of existing tensions. There is a lot at stake here.'[139]

Gorbachev's reaction was frosty, blaming Bush for 'escalation' and for meddling in the USSR's 'internal affairs'. The president, in turn, found this response 'disappointing'. He worried about a 'crackdown' by the Soviet military, whose position had hardened. In its view there should be no more concessions at home or abroad that might endanger the USSR's strategic position in Eastern Europe. And so the Lithuanian crisis cast a dark shadow over the whole US foreign-policy agenda: rapid German unification, the liberalisation of Central Europe and the succession of new-architecture summits.[140]

Bush aired his worries in his conversation with Kohl on 17 May, two weeks before the superpower summit. He didn't want Gorbachev to fail, but 'what we hear about the Soviet economy is very discouraging'. Without a guarantee from the Federal government, he said, US banks 'would not think the Soviet Union is a good risk'. And anyway 'I don't see it without reform. He sounds desperate.' Kohl was more optimistic. 'It's not a financial problem for us. As a debtor they have been good.' He also believed he could 'calm the Lithuanians'. Bush was much more worried about the impact of the Soviet sanctions on the Baltic, which cramped his room for manoeuvre. 'If only we could solve the Lithuania problem … We don't want the summit to be a failure … I am trying to keep the relationship on track' but 'we can't grant MFN now'.[141]

Bush had another concern on his mind. He wanted Kohl's 'honest view' about US troops remaining in Germany. 'I think I can convince Gorbachev' but 'I must know that Germany would want US troops.' The chancellor was unequivocal: 'If the US left, NATO would vanish and there might be only CSCE.' What's more, he added, even if the Red Army pulled out, the USSR was geographically and politically 'still in Europe. If the US withdraws, it is 6,000 kilometres away. That is a big difference.' In unambiguous fashion, Kohl summed it up: 'As I look at the future of Europe I see the US there. In the year 2000 it must be a matter of course to have the US there.'[142]

But, said Bush, 'we can't predict the political climate here or in Germany by then'. That's true, replied Kohl, 'but we can create facts'. With unified Germany in NATO, the Alliance would survive and therefore the United States would remain a European power. But, Kohl continued, 'if the Europeans allowed the Americans to leave, it would be the greatest defeat for us all. Remember Wilson in 1918.' Despite these assurances, Bush kept fussing. So Kohl laid it on the line. 'George, don't be worried about those in the FRG who make parallels between US forces in the FRG and Soviet forces in the GDR. We will push this through. We'll put our political existence at stake for NATO and the political commitment of the US in Europe.'[143]

They then discussed the next couple of months and the need for close coordination between them. 'Three dates are important in this context,' Kohl observed. 'The Gorbachev meeting, the NATO summit, and the Economic summit. Don't underestimate the last,' he added. 'These three will determine who is the leader of the West', and it must be 'the president of the United States of America'. Kohl might have had the coffers to fund chequebook diplomacy but in the larger scheme of things he had no doubt that it was the president who must 'give a sense of leadership'.[144]

Progress was eventually achieved on at least one problem during the superpower summit. On 31 May Gorbachev laid into Bush about economic relations. 'He told me that if we didn't have a trade agreement,' the president noted, 'it would be a disaster.' Gorbachev even said that the Soviets looked at MFN status as being 'equal with START': the outlines of this new strategic arms-reduction agreement were also to be signed at the summit. Bush insisted that he could do nothing until Gorbachev relented on Lithuania. Yet he pondered the issue much of the night.[145]

Early next morning, the public caught a glimpse of just how fractious relations were when Gorbachev – flanked by a dozen aides – held a one-hour televised meeting with a dozen Senate and House leaders. This took place in the ornate Gold Room of the Soviet embassy. Although the meeting was generally amicable, Gorbachev got testy on two points: the Baltic republics and MFN. 'What do we need to do so you will give us MFN?' he asked, adding sarcastically: 'Maybe we should introduce presidential rule in the Baltic republics and at least fire some rounds!' The Americans were unfazed. 'MFN's a possibility, but so is snow,' said Senate Republican leader Bob Dole drily. Gorbachev hit back: 'Why did you let your administration intervene in Panama if you love freedom so much?' – a reference to the toppling of the Noriega regime at the end of 1989. And, he stabbed: 'You have given "most favoured nation" [status] to China after Tiananmen.' Senate Democratic leader George Mitchell quickly reminded Gorbachev that many congressmen were also 'very much opposed' to this. The White House clearly had choppy waters to navigate with both the Kremlin and Congress.[146]

Overnight, however, Bush and Baker managed to come up with a compromise, so that, in the president's words, Gorbachev could 'go home with something tangible'. In what came as a shock to the assembled press, the trade agreement (a first step toward gaining MFN) was one of more than fifteen agreements that the two leaders signed in the East Room of the White House on 1 June. That way Gorbachev would not return to Moscow empty-handed. But at the same time Bush kept Capitol Hill happy by saying that he would neither send the agreement to Congress for approval nor waive the Jackson–Vanik amendment until Gorbachev had enacted a long-delayed emigration law. What the public did not know was the secret condition that Bush also attached, namely that nothing at all would happen until Moscow began negotiations with Vilnius and lifted the economic embargo.[147]

This was a convoluted strategy but it did bear fruit over the next month. Under pressure from the French and Germans, Lithuania froze its independence declaration and the USSR ended sanctions, mindful of US linkage to the trade agreement. So by July this particular Soviet–Lithuanian crisis was over and the Baltic independence struggle was effectively decoupled from the diplomacy surrounding Germany and Europe's security architecture.

On the crucial issue of Germany's membership of NATO, Bush tried to get across to Kohl in their phone call on 1 June that Gorbachev had now consented to Germany's 'right to choose its alliance' under the Helsinki Accords. To shore up this concession, he felt it 'vitally important' for the NATO summit to take steps to 'convince him that NATO <u>is</u> changing in ways that do <u>not</u> threaten Soviet security'. Kohl, focused on Germany's future, wanted a more categorical statement from Gorbachev. 'If a united Germany is not in NATO,' he told Bush, 'you and I know the US would not remain in Europe, because there would be no more NATO.' And, given the plans to expand the EC, 'destroying NATO would have disastrous consequences for unifying Europe'. While not sharing the chancellor's preoccupation about buying Soviet acceptance of Germany's membership of the Atlantic Alliance, Bush was profoundly concerned for the future of NATO in a changing and precarious world.[148]

*

NATO was, however, only one half of Europe's Cold War jigsaw. Despite the 1989 revolutions, the Warsaw Pact was still alive. Bush was brought up to speed on its internal deliberations when Lothar de Maizière, the GDR prime minister and the Pact's current chairman, visited the White House on 11 June 1990. He reported on the Pact's recent summit in Moscow which had issued a declaration that the dissolution of the two military blocs was 'becoming irreversible' and that the Pact would 'start its transformation into a treaty of sovereign states with equal rights, formed on a democratic basis'.[149]

But that was window-dressing, de Maizière told Bush: frankly, he said, 'the Pact won't survive very long'. It would, therefore, be essential to 'establish new structures' because, if individual countries felt isolated and marginalised, they would eventually seek to replicate the Warsaw Pact in some shape or form. Thus, he went on:

> it is important for Western Europe to open to Eastern Europe at all levels – economically, through the EC, and also building common security structures. All participants in the Moscow summit favoured the CSCE process – not in a way that CSCE should replace efforts at European unification made so far, but as a kind of umbrella. All made it clear that socialism as it has existed has failed and is now on the road to complete downfall. It has failed economically and as a method of administration, and its values have proved not bearable. This means defeat: all of [them] see that very clearly. But there is a danger of [the West] portraying this as a defeat for the other side.

Bush was receptive. 'We will have a NATO summit in early July, and we will be talking about steps to transform the Alliance. We have talked about a new political role and a changed threat. Out of that we want to develop a common position on CSCE. As we do, we hope it will be of some comfort to the other side, so they will not be suspicious of our intentions ... we believe the CSCE has a role to play in helping the countries of Central and Eastern Europe build free societies and giving the Soviets and the East Europeans a role in the new Europe.' Even if 'unwieldy', he added, the CSCE provided 'a home for a lot of countries, including the US'.[150]

In these ways Bush was becoming sensitised to what both the Germans and the Soviets needed in order to wrap up the Germany-in-NATO question and, around that, to construct a stable architecture for European security. Meanwhile a small working group from across the administration was refining the presidential four-point outline from 4 May in Oklahoma for presentation at the NATO summit in London on 5–6 July. The result was a twenty-two-paragraph policy statement about the Alliance's transformation. Although primarily intended as a face-saver for Moscow, it was too important a document to review with all the allies in the usual way, thereby risking a watered-down 'compromise package'. So Bush decided to bypass the bureacracy and send the draft to only a few key allied leaders. These included Wörner, Kohl, Thatcher and Mitterrand. The first two were enthusiastic but Thatcher and Mitterrand were more sceptical. Being nuclear powers, they were unhappy about issuing any declaration that nuclear forces were 'weapons of last resort' and they disliked the idea of closer liaison with the Warsaw Pact states – preferring NATO to remain dedicated to the security of the West.[151]

Bush did not intend to haggle over the small print. He said that the text would be finalised at the summit and sent the document out to the other members, appealing for Alliance solidarity. He also phoned a couple of colleagues among the smaller states to shore up support, winning over the Belgians, Danes and Dutch. 'The big thing from our standpoint', he told Ruud Lubbers, the Dutch premier, 'is that we demonstrate that this summit comes at a turning point in Alliance history and will have an important role in shaping the future of Europe. Our paper was worked out with that in mind.'[152]

On the morning of the summit itself, held in London's Lancaster House, Bush fine-tuned the choreography with Wörner. The president made clear that the NATO Declaration was an American draft – he wanted to highlight US leadership – and he had no intention of allowing lengthy argument. The foreign ministers would be given a few hours to iron out remaining details while their leaders delivered speeches and engaged in 'free discussion'. The declaration would be published to the world the next morning, 6 July. Wörner was on board. It was clear, he admitted, that the US going it alone had 'ruffled some feathers' but that was an 'old dilemma. Everybody wants US leadership, but they don't want to admit it.'[153]

The 'London Declaration' made an impact.[154] 'NATO Allies, After 40 Years, Proclaim End of Cold War' was the *New York Times* headline on 7 July, at the end of the summit. 'Nato Declares Peace on the Warsaw Pact' titled the *Independent* in London.[155] After some skilful negotiations a compromise final text had been agreed, which bore a close resemblance to the original American draft.[156]

The wording was deliberately intended to echo the ringing tone and historical resonance of the foundational North Atlantic Treaty in April 1949. 'Europe has entered a new, promising era. Central and Eastern Europe is liberating itself ... They are choosing peace. They are choosing a Europe whole and free.' But how to secure this new era? 'The North Atlantic Alliance has been the most successful defensive alliance in history. As our Alliance enters its fifth decade and looks ahead to a new century, it must continue to provide for the common defense.'[157]

Yet the declaration also stressed that 'our Alliance must be even more an agent of change'. In doing so, it could 'help build the structures of a more united continent'. This meant that 'the Atlantic Community must reach out to the countries of the East which were our adversaries in the Cold War, and extend to them the hand of friendship'. Among NATO's proposals for building 'new partnerships with all the nations of Europe' were a joint statement with the members of the Warsaw Pact that the era of mutually hostile blocs was over. The Alliance also envisaged NATO, the Warsaw Pact and other CSCE member states combining in a 'commitment to non-aggression'. They invited Gorbachev to travel to Brussels to speak at NATO headquarters, and the Warsaw Pact countries to 'establish regular diplomatic liaison' with the Alliance. And they proclaimed their support for making CSCE 'more prominent in Europe's future'.[158]

The declaration also outlined doctrinal changes for NATO itself. 'We reaffirm that security and stability do not lie solely in the military dimension, and we intend to enhance the political component of our Alliance as provided for by Article 2 of our Treaty.' This phraseology of adaptation was deliberately intended to imply historical evolution rather than a total break with the past. And while NATO's defence would continue to be built on a 'significant presence of North American conventional and US nuclear forces in Europe', which demonstrated 'the underlying political compact binding North America and the European democracies', Western leaders promised a new defensive strategy, modifying flexible response and moving away from forward defence. They proclaimed that 'we will never in any circumstance be the first to use force' and that nuclear forces should be 'truly weapons of last resort'. They also made a major concession to Soviet fears about a united Germany within NATO, promising to specify 'manpower levels' for post-unification German armed forces as soon as the CFE Treaty was signed later in 1990.[159]

The initial reaction from Moscow was favourable. Gorbachev told ABC News that he saw 'very constructive signs coming out of this summit' and said he was 'always ready to go' to Brussels to meet with the Western allies. Bush was delighted: he had engineered a landmark shift in the Alliance – and left his fingerprints all over it. At the news conference, the president explained that he thought the declaration would help Gorbachev and the members of the Warsaw Pact. 'The London Declaration transforms the Alliance's vision for the CSCE ... We know the CSCE process – bringing together North America and all of Europe – can provide a structure for Europe's continued political development; and that means new standards for free elections, the rule of law, economic liberty, and environmental cooperation.' And he waxed eloquent on the declaration's historical significance: 'For more than forty years, we've looked for this day – a day when we have already moved beyond containment, with unity on this continent overcoming division. And now that day is here, and all peoples from the Atlantic to the Urals, from the Baltic to the Adriatic, can share in its promise.' By this verbal echo of Winston Churchill's Fulton speech of 1946, the president was clearly implying that the Iron Curtain was a thing of the past.[160]

Kohl was equally content. Indeed, the US press commented that 'after the president, the leader who seemed most pleased by what had been accomplished in London was clearly Chancellor Kohl, who over the last two days has held his own background briefings, in his own hotel, in his own language, while the other leaders were content with common facilities provided by their British hosts'. The chancellor also frankly acknowledged that the declaration could not have been achieved without the US president. 'As far as I'm concerned, the chemistry is right with George Bush,' he said. 'The present American administration has a very clear view of things.'[161]

But on one issue the two men continued to disagree. Bush remained obdurately against giving direct American economic aid to the Soviet Union, which Gorbachev explicitly requested in a letter to Bush on 4 July.[162] The Soviet leader also wrote to Thatcher, as host of the NATO summit, setting out his concerns. Like NATO, he said, 'we share the view that stability in Europe is a vital prerequisite for its democratic development', but added that this 'in turn, is impossible without the success of perestroika' which he believed would have to be completed within 'the nearest two–three-year period'. To do so, he needed 'assistance' from the EC and G7 in two forms: first, 'urgent loans' to level the balance of payments and to purchase consumer goods; and second, 'finance' for specific programmes of investment cooperation with participation of international consortia. For all his pleas, however, aid to the Soviets was not a formal agenda item in London, and so the issue was left hanging to be discussed a few days later at the G7 in Texas.[163]

Asked in the press conference about Gorbachev's offensive to elicit financial aid, Bush said that the Alliance had not made any decision on the issue. But, he exclaimed, 'I have some big problems with that one' and 'I think the American people do'. One concern, he added, about the Soviets was that 'a great percentage of their gross national product is going into the military'. Another was their 'spending $5 billion a year on Cuba, for example, to sustain a totalitarian regime'. Asked whether he was opposed to other countries giving aid to the USSR, he replied 'If the Germans decide they want to do that, that's their business.'[164]

Baker elaborated on US anxieties in an interview for CNN. 'Before we spend taxpayer dollars on direct economic assistance to the Soviet Union, we ought to have some reasonable idea or some reasonable faith that the money is going to be well spent,' he said. 'Some countries here will want to go with direct economic assistance. Other countries, the United States included, will say we really ought to see some progress toward economic reform before we make the same mistake we made with respect to Poland in the 1970s.'[165]

Baker's comments were no mere casual aside. They came just a week after the president had made a fundamental shift in US fiscal policy, about which he had anguished for months. 'If I didn't have this budget deficit problem hanging over my head,' he noted in his diary, 'I would be loving this job.'[166] The budget issue had become purgatory for him. His core campaign promise of 1988 had been 'Read my lips: no new taxes.' But on 26 June 1990 he reluctantly issued a written statement, agreed with Democrat leaders on Capitol Hill, that in order to address the yawning budget deficit of $160 billion projected for 1991, he and Congress would work on a package of measures that include 'tax-revenue increases' and 'orderly reductions in defense expenditures'. This meant breaking his word, but the alternative, he had been warned, was to risk a serious recession.[167]

The *New York Times* featured this news on a revealing front page. Under the main title about Bush's tax increases, the paper also headlined 'Republicans Fear a Kiss of Death as Bush Moves His Big Lips on Taxes', and in a smaller box below, 'European Leaders Back Kohl's Plea to Aid Soviets'. Connoisseurs of the future will also appreciate another belt-tightening headline at the bottom right: 'Banks Approve Loans for Trump, But Take Control of His Finances'. The impoverished New York casino developer, the paper announced, 'must learn to live on $450,000 a month, and even less in future years'. Hard times for all.[168]

Bush did not mention the tax embarrassment in his reply to Gorbachev's request for financial aid, which he drafted on Air Force One from London en route to the Houston G7 summit. He also made no reference to the aid issue but instead laid out what had happened at the NATO summit and detailed how he believed the declaration addressed Soviet concerns. 'Mr President, we have important decisions before us as we work towards Europe's reconciliation ... I hope today's NATO declaration will persuade you that NATO can and will serve the security interests of Europe as a whole'. The letter was then transmitted in flight by radio to the US Embassy in Moscow and rushed to an embattled Gorbachev at the Congress of the CPSU. Chernyaev scanned it quickly and, despite seeing no mention of dollars, exclaimed 'This is indeed an important letter'. He passed it straight to his boss. Bush's commitment to the transformation of NATO helped Gorbachev appease the hardliners and ensure his re-election as Party Secretary by a three-to-one majority. This was good news for Bush.[169]

To some extent, the Houston G7 was a political opportunity for the president to celebrate recent progress on Germany and NATO and also to show off to world leaders his home town and that of Baker. On the evening of 8 July, before the formal proceedings began, he took some of them to a rodeo where they were entertained with a bizarre mix of armadillo racing, square dancing, bull riding and styrofoam cacti. 'We work real hard at being authentic,' said one window-glass salesman dressed up in a sombrero and bandana. 'A lot of these people from foreign countries think this is still the way the South is. That's what they expect to see so we might as well give it to them.' Entering into the kitsch, Canadian prime minister Brian Mulroney arrived in blue jeans, cowboy belt and Stetson, while his Japanese counterpart managed a colourful Hawaiian shirt. Mrs Thatcher wore a check suit with white handbag, more appropriate for a Tory garden party in Surrey. The German chancellor was in particularly high spirits after his country had defeated Argentina 2–1 in the football World Cup Final, discomforting President Mitterrand who had planned to make a dramatic late entrance on board the supersonic Concorde.[170]

The G7 rodeo: Toshiki Kaifu and Brian Mulroney in Texas

Next morning it was down to the serious business, in the spacious precincts of Rice University where the atmosphere was much less consensual than in London a few days earlier. The G7, unlike NATO, was not an American-led alliance, so Bush could not write the script. And because the central issues revolved around aid for the USSR and the global economy, Bush's fiscal crisis left him with a weaker hand. Compromise proved the order of the day. No big breakthroughs were featured in the final communiqué.

Despite vigorous lobbying by Kohl and Mitterrand for substantial credits to Moscow, the others were firmly opposed. Thatcher put it most bluntly: 'It was impossible for the summit seven to run a country of 280 million stretching from the Arctic to the Tropics with different religions and nationalities. The Soviet Union's economic managers knew neither their inputs nor outputs. They did not have clue what to do.' And so the G7 agreed to disagree.[171] 'Each country has different political imperatives,' an American official said. 'The president is happy to have each one help the Soviet Union in complementary ways.' Hubert Védrine, the French president's spokesman, was less diplomatic. Asked by a reporter whether Houston could be described as a summit of 'cordial misunderstanding', he responded, 'I will leave that to you.'[172]

To ensure that something positive could be stated in the communiqué, the leaders asked the IMF to begin – in conjunction with the World Bank, the Organisation for Economic Cooperation and Development and the new European Bank for Reconstruction and Development – a detailed study on the state of the Soviet economy, which would present its non-binding recommendations by the end of the year. This IMF study was to complement a similar report (due in October) requested by the EC Council at Dublin II from the European Commission services. The latter document was to provide an analysis of the possibility and desirability of extending short-term credits and longer-term support for structural reform in the Soviet Union as well as an exploration of how the USSR could be integrated into the world economy.[173]

Meanwhile negotiations to reduce global trade-and-tariff barriers remained paralysed because of the EC's commitment to high agricultural subsidies, jealously guarded by the French, which still absorbed the bulk of the EC's spending. This was particularly embarrassing now that the buzz was all about dissolving blocs and opening markets. 'Command economies have crumbled,' Thatcher proclaimed. 'We have an opportunity to make the 1990s a success. We have an opportunity to consolidate market democracies.' Success in the GATT round would also 'help the poorer nations' of the developing world, by allowing them to export more to richer nations. But while significant sacrifices needed to be made by the EC, Japan too would have to further liberalise its financial services and the US its defence procurement. Only these steps would ensure 'the freest possible trade over the widest possible area'.[174]

Little progress was made, however, on the GATT issue and leaks to journalists reported 'unusually bitter words' between Bush and Delors, representing the EC 12. 'They simply have not been engaged in the process,' complained Bush's agriculture secretary, Clayton Yeutter. His European counterpart, Guy Legras, retorted that if 'you cut subsidies' the result would be such price fluctuations that 'the farmers would go bust'.[175]

For Bush, this issue underlined the complexity of dealing with 'Europe'. Countries that had so recently in London proved reliable allies within the security framework of NATO behaved completely differently as members of the EC when it came to their economic interests. Even Kohl did little to change EC policy – retreating behind the argument that subsidies were a problem that Bush would have to sort out bilaterally with Mitterrand.

Bill Brock, a former special trade representative in the Reagan administration who came to Houston in an unofficial capacity, painted a dire picture for the US media, predicting a walkout from the trade talks not only by America but also by Third World countries if farm subsidies were not ended – because, he said, 'they have nothing else to sell but agricultural products'. The result of such a walkout, he prophesied, would be 'rampant protectionism and economic decline'. With the next GATT meeting due in Geneva two weeks later and the Uruguay Round expected to be completed in Brussels in December, the prospects for success looked slim. In fact, agriculture and the Uruguay Round would remain a headache for the rest of Bush's presidency. And a new World Trade Agreement would not be concluded until December 1993 – after eight years of bruising negotiations. Indeed, Robert Hutchings, who was the NSC's European Affairs director at that time, reflected later that these negotiations 'loomed at least as large as security matters in US–European relations after 1990'.[176]

But what helped to paper over the G7's various disagreements in Houston was a general sense of achievement about how the world had changed in the previous twelve months. 'With the West so near to final victory with respect to our struggles over the last forty years,' declared Gianni De Michelis, the Italian foreign minister, 'it would be a criminal form of stupidity to enhance West–West tensions now.' The Houston G7 ended on 11 July with a feeling of satisfaction.

Behind this mood music, some commentators detected a deeper pattern. The veteran American correspondent R. W. 'Johnny' Apple cited Bush's remarks at the conference welcoming ceremony that this economic summit 'was not of the post-war era', but the first of the 'post-postwar era'. With that Bush had made public what Baker had said in private after Malta. Apple also observed that Houston 'turned out to be a kind of coming-out party for Chancellor Helmut Kohl of West Germany, reflecting the new, more subtle balance of power in the world'. Even more than in London, he remarked, Kohl emerged 'as a dominant figure in these international deliberations' – 'the leader', as a French diplomat put it, 'of the richest, strategically best placed, most populous country in Europe, and acting every inch of the role'. Even Thatcher had to acknowledge that 'there are three regional groups at this summit, one based on the dollar, one based on the yen, one on the Deutschmark'.[177]

*

Midsummer 1990 was in many ways a decisive moment in Europe's exit from the Cold War. After two weeks of intensive summitry in the EC, NATO and G7, from Dublin via London to Houston, the future architecture of Europe had moved beyond the design stage. As soon as the G7 was over, Kohl returned to Bonn before jetting off again to Moscow and the Caucasus for two days of haggling over the politics of unification. There he hammered out with Gorbachev their epochal deal on German unification, Soviet troop withdrawal and economic assistance to the USSR, paving the way to unveil the fully sovereign united Germany on 3 October. And after the new FRG officially confirmed the Oder–Neisse line as its definite eastern frontier, the 'German question', with all its echoes of 1937 borders and the Hitler era, had been laid to rest.

As Bush put it, one of the most profound changes in European politics and security in the recent past had been 'accomplished without confrontation, without a shot fired, and with all Europe still on the best and most peaceful of terms'. Even the usually terse Scowcroft expressed delight about this moment: 'We had concluded the long process that had ended the superpower confrontation.' What is more, he and Bush had succeeded in what they considered the 'critical' aspect of the process, namely keeping united Germany within the Atlantic Alliance. This they had identified as the one area where 'we could and did exercise real, perhaps decisive, influence', and they exerted it through negotiations 'at the highest levels'. In short, declared Scowcroft, 'this was personal diplomacy in the finest sense of the term'. There was no vast and formal peace conference: 'Coalition-building, consensus, understanding, tolerance, and compromise had forged a new Europe ... There was no Versailles, no residual international bitterness.' Their rhetoric had carefully avoided the language of 'victory for "us" and defeat for "them".' Because, Scowcroft reflected, 'we had, perhaps, learned from the mistakes of the past. All had found their stake in the outcome. It was a shepherded victory for peace.'[178]

The deliberate inclusion of the power that had lost out – in this case the USSR – was indeed a marked difference from previous post-conflict settlements, notably Versailles. Nevertheless, big questions still remained. Germany was being reunited, while remaining within NATO and the EC. And each of these institutions was evolving: NATO was opening up as a political organisation; the EC was engaged in a process of deeper integration that would, under the Maastricht Treaty, transform the European Community into the European Union by the end of 1992.

But this was mostly about Western Europe. How would the countries of Eastern Europe, freeing themselves from the shackles of the Warsaw Pact, relate to this new 'institutional West'? And what could be made of the one Cold War institution that had managed to embrace both West and East – the CSCE? These were the questions still to be addressed about the 'New Europe' as 1990 neared its end.

The Soviet bloc orphans were now evolving rapidly, with 'Democracy', 'Markets' and 'Europe' as the headline slogans. In December 1989, the Polish parliament scrapped the command economy and abolished the 'leading role' of the Communist Party. Local elections in May 1990 were completely free, and at the end of the year Solidarity's Lech Wałęsa became the country's first freely elected president since the 1920s. Hungary's first post-war free parliamentary elections took place in March–April 1990. The ensuing coalition government was the first since the Second World War without communist participation. Similarly, Czechoslovakia held its first post-1945 free elections in June 1990, endowing democratic legitimacy on the government of President Havel and its agenda of rapid economic liberalisation.[179]

This agenda was, however, more easily stated than implemented – not only in Prague but thoughout the former Soviet bloc. Price liberalisation, privatisation of state entreprises, wage alignments and currency convertibility were very costly endeavours. And all these countries, albeit in different ways, looked for massive financial assistance from the West to shore up their fledgling democracies.

The Poles (38.5 million people) had $40 billion of foreign debt – $27 billion of which was owed to Western governments (the FRG being the largest creditor) and the rest to commercial banks. But by the spring of 1990 Poland was judged to have leapt ahead of other Eastern European countries thanks to its hard push to radically transform its economy – willing to inflict such bitter medicines as allowing workers to be laid off and enterprises to go bankrupt and also slashing subsidies to industry and consumers. Poland was therefore deemed by Western lenders to be an 'exceptional case' and became the first former Soviet satellite to receive loans. These amounted to $2.5 billion from the World Bank over the next three years, as well as an immediate credit of $723 million from the IMF. Furthermore, the Paris Club* decided to reschedule $9.4 billion of Poland's debt repayments on unsually lenient terms. Warsaw wanted greater generosity, including some of the official Polish debt to be written off, but the US government – which was owed only $80 million – was once again unwilling to take a lead.[180]

Hungary had $20.7 billion of foreign debt for a population of 10.5 million people – the highest per capita debt burden in Eastern Europe – but the head of the nation's central bank was against any debt rescheduling. In part this was because the country was already well ahead in the move toward a free market: more than 75% of prices in Hungary were no longer regulated, a stock market had been opened, and the privatisation of state industry was under way. 'The big bang in Poland just brings them to where we already were,' said Peter Bod, Hungary's industry minister. 'We cannot make very bold or theatrical declarations because we are already at the difficult stage where the decisions are not so political as they are a question of solving day-to-day problems.' That said, the government clearly did not want to take any bold decisions. In fact, it was only under pressure from the IMF to bring down a ballooning budget deficit that the Hungarian government consented to impose price hikes on cigarettes, alcohol and fuel.[181]

By the autumn of 1990 the consequent decline in living standards had become a political problem. So Prime Minister József Antall, visiting Washington, told Bush on 18 October that Hungary needed '$4 billion to sustain and operate our economy – of which we can raise only half. We will need to rely on aid and long-term loans.' Also of great importance, he added, was 'foreign capital, including US, which gives political

---

* The Paris Club, founded in 1956, is an informal group of creditor countries who seek to find coordinated and sustainable solutions to the payment difficulties of debtor states.

signals about your support'. Antall wanted an IMF agreement as soon as possible. Because 'if we fail, it will be a signal to the whole region. This would lead to the loss of hope and strengthen negative factors domestically'. And this, in the worst case, given the 'growing potential for unrest', might awaken old 'national tensions' in Central Europe, such as those between Czechs and Slovaks. Bush promised to find ways to help: 'your economic success is essential to us. We don't want the clock turned back.' But he added his customary rider, 'you know the constraints we have'.[182]

Czechoslovakia (population 15.6 million) had a relatively small foreign debt by comparison with its neighbours, at $6.1 billion, and it had also been much less aggressive in requesting American cash.[183] In the autumn, however, the Czechoslovak government did ask Washington for $3.5 billion to launch the transition to the market and to a convertible currency: 'we need just a first injection, so we could move without major jolts'. Like Budapest, Prague played up the complications of the current situation, stressing 'delays in oil supplies from the Soviet Union' and 'the collapse of markets' in the Comecon states with whom they had largely traded hitherto. 'What is at stake is not only economic, but also has a security aspect,' Havel told Bush. 'The worst thing would be if the newly emerging democracies are strangled. If the West contributed by providing some financial assistance, this would be a cheaper way of safeguarding security'.[184]

The Soviet orphans were not only shaking the begging bowl in the White House, they were also trying to work together as a group. This was noted by Baker as early as 7 February 1990 in a major speech at Charles University in Prague entitled 'From Revolution to Democracy'. He welcomed 'the first signs of coordination and association among the newly democratic states' – singling out recent discussions between Hungary, Poland and Czechoslovakia about a possible free-trade agreement. More broadbrush, he declared: 'The spirit of revolution needs to move from the streets into the government.' But, he emphasised, political reform and democratisation alone were not sufficient to consolidate 'people-power revolutions'. Without steps to promote 'economic vitality', Europe's stability would be undermined: this was 'one of the painful lessons of the interwar years'. Yet, as usual, the administration was wary about making any financial commitments, preferring to talk about the key role of private American capital and multilateral international bodies.[185]

The states of East Central Europe were indeed encouraged by the provision of Western funds. The G24 states, mostly European, gave food aid and financial assistance to much of the former Soviet bloc, channelled via the European Commission, while the new European Bank for Reconstruction and Development, headed by Mitterrand's chief adviser Jacques Attali, granted loans.[186] But the prospect of a formal engagement in continental institutions was more important. Mitterrand's 'European Confederation' had suggested Eastern Europe's inclusion in a looser circle around the EC 12, while Kohl's Ten-Point Plan even floated the idea of possible future membership of the Community. Nothing came in the end of France's grand design of a Confederation,[187] because the former Soviet satellites soon wanted nothing but EC membership. The precedent had already been set in February 1990 when it became clear that the GDR would be fast-forwarded into the EC 12.

At the time, to be sure, East Germany was very definitely ring-fenced as a special case. Other countries stood in front of Eastern Europe in the queue for the EC. Austria and Sweden, for instance, were developed market economies and thriving democracies, whose move straight into membership would pose no serious transition problems: they were already part of the European Free Trade Area. Post-communist suitors like Poland, Hungary and Czechoslovakia, for all their keenness to integrate into the EC, would have to wait until December 1991 even for association agreements. Yet all that was more attractive than being relegated to an amorphous 'Confederation'.

With regard to the other major Western institution, NATO, the Eastern European states felt encouraged by the London Declaration in July 1990. Hungary, which saw itself as 'a model for the region as a whole', was as keen on the Atlantic Alliance as on European integration, and had been the first former Soviet bloc state to appoint an ambassador to NATO.[188] Also seeking to come under the American security umbrella was Czechoslovakia, a Slavic nation with a distinctly Western culture now looking to reposition itself again in the centre of Europe, as a hinge between East and West. As Havel explained to Bush, the Czechoslovaks considered NATO 'a pillar that might be used in building a new European security structure' and envisaged an association agreement 'similar to the one we are negotiating with the EC'.[189]

But the London Declaration did not offer membership of the Western Alliance. Indeed it could not, because these countries were still members of the Warsaw Pact and had thousands of Red Army troops on their soil:

48,000 in Poland,[190] 75,000 in Czechoslovakia[191] and more than 20,000 in Hungary.[192] So the NATO door remained locked – at least for the moment.

Eastern Europe's immediate hopes therefore focused on the CSCE. A conference in Bonn in March–April 1990, instigated by the FRG, was intended to reach agreement on how to move from the Plan to the Market. The US delegation came with a list of ten principles linking 'political pluralism and market economies' which were adopted in the conference's final declaration. One commentator called this a 'Magna Carta of Free Enterprise'.[193] The Bonn conference was followed by another, held in Copenhagen in May, to discuss the human-rights aspects of entering the West, at which Baker delivered the keynote address. Picking up on the president's catchphrase, he said 'we are now closer than ever to realising CSCE's long-cherished vision of a Europe whole and free'. And he affirmed the organisation's centrality as 'the one forum where our nations can meet on common ground to channel our political will towards meeting these challenges for the entire continent'. Although admitting that the CSCE lacked 'military or political power', he said 'it can speak to Europe's collective concerns and interests. It can become, if you will, the conscience of the continent'.[194]

On 17 and 18 November 1990, just before the CSCE summit convened in Paris, Bush talked with Havel in Prague. For the president, this was an especially important trip. His eye-opening visit to East Central Europe in the middle of 1989 had been confined to Poland and Hungary. Indeed he was the first US president to come to Czechoslovakia while in office.

The visit was an intense combination of political theatre and personal diplomacy. As darkness descended on the afternoon of the 17th, Bush addressed a crowd of some 100,000 in Wenceslas Square. He drew loud cheers when announcing that he was returning to Prague a historic letter written in 1919 by Jan Masaryk, founder of the Czecholovak Republic, to President Woodrow Wilson outlining his country's declaration of independence and new constitution. And so, Bush proclaimed with a flourish, '1989 was the year that freedom came home to Czechoslovakia; 1990 will be the year your declaration of independence came home to the golden city of Prague.'

This emotional rally mixed up symbols from different cultures, nations and eras. Amid the tight presidential security, agents in orange vests prowled rooftops behind neon signs advertising both the original Czech

Budweiser beer and also Licensintorg, a now-defunct Soviet foreign trade agency. The president spoke from a spot between the statue of King Wenceslas, the Czechs' patron saint, and an equally iconic modern memorial, marking the place where in early 1969 the student Jan Palach set fire to himself in protest against the Soviet-led invasion of the previous year. This was now covered with flowers and candles in memory of both Palach and also the student march on 17 November 1989 whose violent suppression by the police triggered the final stages of the Velvet Revolution that overthrew the communist leadership.

Feeling the pulse of history, Bush spoke fervently about the future of Czechoslovakia. 'A year ago, the world saw you face down totalitarianism. We saw the peaceful crowds swell day by day in numbers and in resolve. We saw the few candles grow into a blaze. We saw this square become a beacon of hope for an entire nation as it gave birth to your new era of freedom.' He assured the crowds, 'We have not forgotten. The world will never forget what happened here in this square where the history of freedom was written.' But for all his grand words, he kept his wallet tightly closed – merely repeating an earlier pledge to try and get $5 billion in loans from the IMF.[195]

Bush also had three meetings with the Czechoslovak president. 'I felt in awe of Havel,' he admitted later. 'Here was a man who had been in jail only the year before. He had been beaten and driven to his knees, but refused to give up. I found him to be a very modest, close-to-shy man, completely unpretentious and straightforward.' The president was equally impressed, but in a totally different way, by the venue for their talks, another location steeped in history, the Hradčany Palace. The hilltop royal castle and now presidential palace had been, as Havel proudly boasted, 'one of the biggest seats of power in the world'.[196]

In their talks Havel unburdened himself to Bush about his country's latest crisis and the need, this time, for the West to deliver on its airy promises about freedom and democracy. 'With the collapse of communism in Czechoslovakia, Poland, Hungary and other countries, we may be facing a temporary vacuum as all the old links cease to exist. It could be a breeding ground for chaos and instability. Our democracies are just emerging. To fill this vacuum is not just our problem; it is also an obligation of the West. For years you helped assure the victory of freedom. Therefore it is not in the West's interest for a new threat to emerge.'

'We agree with that,' said Bush, anxious to sound reassuring. 'We think the CSCE offers a good structure, and you already have a toehold in NATO through your mission there.'

'Since the outset,' Havel went on, 'Czechoslovakia has placed high hopes in the CSCE process, as we see in CSCE a possible line for shaping the future European order and eliminating the vacuum.' In fact, he said, 'We want to institutionalise the CSCE. We hope the permanent secretariat might be in Prague.'

Bush was sympathetic about the secretariat. And emphatic that 'we don't want Poland, Hungary, or Czechoslovakia in a European no man's land'.[197]

*

The stage was therefore set for Paris on 19 November. The international media speculated that the CSCE summit in 1990 could be another Congress of Vienna, which in 1815 had ended the Napoleonic era and ushered in nearly half a century of peace in Europe.[198]

The conference opened under the sparkling chandeliers of the Elysée Palace on the fifth anniversary of Gorbachev's first encounter with Reagan at Geneva, from which had developed a remarkable succession of arms-control initiatives that began to demilitarise the armed heart of Europe. Under the INF Treaty signed in Washington in 1987 the two superpowers scrapped their intermediate-range nuclear forces on the continent. Now the CSCE was rounding off two years of painstaking bargaining in Vienna between NATO and the Warsaw Pact, embodied in a treaty signed by no fewer than twenty-two countries. The 160-page CFE agreement was the most ambitious arms-control agreement in history – pledging the signatories to destroy tens of thousands of tanks, howitzers and other non-nuclear weapons across a huge tract of Europe from the Atlantic to the Urals. 'What a long way the world has come!' Gorbachev exulted. Bush hailed the treaty as a sign of 'the new world order that is emerging'.

The result of the CFE was certainly not total disarmament. In future, the Atlantic Alliance and the Warsaw Pact would each be limited to 20,000 tanks, 20,000 artillery pieces, 30,000 armoured fighting vehicles, 6,800 combat aircraft and 2,000 attack helicopters – quite sufficient to cause massive devastation in the heart of Europe. But the cuts were significant, especially for the Warsaw Pact. To reach the new parity, the West would have to make only a tenth of the cuts needed to eliminate the Pact's long-standing edge in the number of conventional arms in Europe. Troops were not covered under the CFE treaty: limits for each nation would be negotiated later in Vienna, with a new treaty to be completed by the time of the next CSCE summit in 1992. But after the Kohl–Gorbachev Caucasus summit, the United States and Germany had already agreed ceilings outside the formal agreement – no more than 195,000 US soldiers in the 'central zone' of Europe and no more than 370,000 in the unified German armed forces. Yet the numbers being bandied around were paper figures, because neither superpower was likely to maintain in the region their full entitlement of troops. In the new era, large land armies seemed irrelevant. In this context it was therefore unsurprising that the leaders of both NATO and the Warsaw Pact also signed a declaration stating explicitly that they were 'no longer adversaries and will establish new relations of partnership and mutual friendship'.[199]

Building on this, the main function of the conference was to affirm the 'Charter of Paris for a New Europe', signed by thirty-four CSCE countries (the two Germanies now being one). The charter proclaimed that 'the era of confrontation and division of Europe has ended. We declare that henceforth, our relations will be founded on respect and cooperation. Europe is liberating itself from the legacy of the past' and entering 'a new era of peace, democracy and unity'.[200]

The supporting rhetoric was equally extravagant. Kohl spoke of building 'a Europe of eternal peace' – echoing the phrase of Immanuel Kant, an eighteenth-century apostle of European unity. He also urged his colleagues to cast their gaze back for inspiration to the French Revolution, the American Declaration of Independence and England's Magna Carta. The alternative, he said, was clear: in the last two centuries 'Europe, and my country in particular, became the epicentre of worldwide catastrophes'. His French host, looking to the future, proclaimed: 'For more than forty years, we have known stability without freedom. Henceforth, we want freedom in stability'.[201]

For all the Kohl–Mitterrand talk about historic European ideals, the rhetoric, one might say, was as asymmetrical as the force reductions. The values being underwritten in Paris were ones that the West had long espoused – democratic government, economic liberty, human rights, and other 'fundamental freedoms'. They had been endorsed, in name at least, by all CSCE members in 1975 and were now being patchily implemented in the former Soviet satellites of Eastern Europe. And Gorbachev, too, it appeared, was beginning to turn principles into practice within the Soviet Union itself.

In fact, the Paris charter was a particularly public example of Gorbachev's diplomatic alchemy. No previous Soviet leader would have dreamed of signing up to such an endorsement of pluralistic democracy and economic liberalism, but this great betrayal of Marxist–Leninist principles was presented by the Soviet leader as 'a turning point in the history of our age ... We are entering into a world of new dimensions, in which universal human values are acquiring the same meaning for all.' The whole process, he said at the Paris CSCE on 19 November, showed a new kind of 'international solidarity' based on 'the ability to meet each other halfway ... While remaining a great power our country has changed and will never be the same as it was before. We have opened up to the world and the world has opened up to us in response.'[202]

High-flown the rhetoric may have been, but it was also vague. A major function of the CSCE was now to ensure that the USSR and the new post-communist democracies of Eastern Europe were folded into the political and economic progress of the West.[203] Ultimately, however, the Paris CSCE Charter for a New Europe – just like the original Helsinki Final Act fifteen years earlier – was a piece of paper, asserting common values for Europe's 'conscience' but not building a viable institution for Europe's security. This sort of soft politics did not ultimately address the hard realities of the post-Cold War continent. The United States had no time for the persistent but ineffectual efforts of Gorbachev and Mitterrand to turn the CSCE into a security organisation. Real security, in Bush's view, could be provided only by the Atlantic Alliance. In his mind, the CSCE was useful mainly as a comfort blanket for those not inside Europe's inner circle of NATO and the EC. But those outside actually felt left, to quote Havel, in 'a political and security vacuum'. And that was because the 'main pillars of the new Europe' remained 'those of the old Western Europe'.[204]

Not surprisingly, therefore, the CFE and the charter, even though they hit the headlines, were not the issues that really preoccupied the leaders of the great powers during those glittering three days in the French capital.

For François Mitterrand, this was not the Peace of Paris that he had hoped for – drawing a line under the Cold War in the way Vienna 1815 had done for the era of Napoleon, and Versailles 1919 for the Kaiser's Germany. Instead, the crunch issue of German unification had already been resolved – by the 2 + 4 process and by Kohl's double diplomacy with Bush and Gorbachev and not, as Mitterrand had wished, by the CSCE. As the French presidential spokesperson Hubert Védrine later remarked, this was not 'the event of the century's end' that had figured in Mitterrand's imaginings.[205]

The realities of Paris were even starker for Margaret Thatcher. While she was away from London, the long-simmering resentments in her Cabinet had come to a head. Her prickly nationalism had managed to marginalise Britain on the big issues of German unification and European integration, to the despair of many colleagues. And, after more than a decade in power, the Iron Lady seemed distinctly rusty. The Conservative Party was ready for a change. In the middle of the Paris summit she received the devastating news that, on a ballot for re-election as party leader, she had won the support of only 55% of Tory Members of Parliament. Severely wounded, she returned home to Downing Street determined to fight on but was then dissuaded from contesting a second round. On 28 November, the Thatcher era came to an end.[206]

There was astonishment at this news, even in Moscow. The Soviet ambassador in London delivered a personal message to 'Margaret' from Gorbachev expressing 'consternation' at the turn of events. Apparently the Soviet leader had sent Shevardnadze out of a high-level meeting in the Kremlin to phone the London embassy and find out how such a thing could be 'conceivable'. The ambassador said he found it very hard to explain. Indeed it appeared rather ironic. 'Five years ago they had party coups in the Soviet Union and elections in Britain. Now it seemed to be the other way round.'[207]

During the Paris summit, Mikhail Gorbachev was also absorbed by problems at home – indeed the very cohesion of the USSR as a unitary state. The Baltic republics, having all made clear their intention to regain independence, had been invited by the French government to participate in the summit as observers but Gorbachev and Shevardnadze publicly blocked their admission to the conference hall. The continued presence in Paris of all three Baltic foreign ministers[208] was hugely embarrassing for a Soviet leadership that was at this very moment reaffirming the grand values of democracy and self-determination. Seeking to deflect the moral argument, Gorbachev warned that 'militant nationalism and mindless separatism can easily bring conflict and enmity, Balkanisation and even, what is worse, the Lebanonisation of different regions.' Invoking the dangers of ethnic strife and secessionism, he remarked that 'both could put a brake on European cooperation and contradict the European process'.[209]

And although supposedly focusing on Europe, George H. W. Bush spent most of his time at the CSCE summit on an even bigger question of war and peace – one far beyond the continent itself and raising grave questions about what the post-Wall era would mean for the world as a whole. Indeed, on 19 November, when Bush and Gorbachev got together for their only substantive one-on-one during the Paris summit, they hardly mentioned Europe at all. Instead the president focused on the Middle East, where the Iraqi leader Saddam Hussein had annexed Kuwait three months earlier. 'He is right up there with Hitler,' Bush told Gorbachev. 'This is why I am asking you to help me.' It was through the military operations Desert Shield and Desert Storm that the new 'post-postwar' relationship between the United States and the Soviet Union would be truly tested.[210]

Chapter 6

'A New World Order'

The 29th of January 1991: 'Members of the United States Congress ...' Bush's tone was sombre and measured, in contrast to the triumphalism of the State of the Union message he delivered a year before, when he spoke of communism crumbling and the beginning of a new era for the world. This January, however, Bush was the first president since the Vietnam era to address Americans while their country was at war.[1]

Airpower: USAF fighter jets above burning oil fields in Kuwait

'... we stand at a defining hour. Halfway around the world, we are engaged in a great struggle in the skies and on the seas and sands ... What is at stake is more than one small country; it is a big idea: a new world order, where diverse nations are drawn together in common cause to achieve the universal aspirations of mankind – peace and security, freedom, and the rule of law.'

Saddam Hussein's Iraqi armed forces had invaded the tiny emirate of

Kuwait on 2 August 1990. Within 48 hours he had brought the oil-rich sheikhdom brutally under his control. The border disputes and political rivalries between the two neighbours had a long and tortured history, but for Bush the invasion of Kuwait was a stark and simple issue of 'lawless aggression'. He reminded Congress in his State of the Union address: 'Saddam Hussein's unprovoked invasion – his ruthless, system-atic rape of a peaceful neighbour – violated everything the community of nations holds dear. The world has said this aggression would not stand, and it will not stand. Together, we have resisted the trap of appeasement, cynicism and isolation that gives temptation to tyrants.'

That was why Bush had not only mobilised American power but had also, more laboriously, pressed for months to construct an international coalition built on the UN. It was truly a remarkable alliance – twenty-eight countries from six continents, embracing traditional US allies such as Britain and Australia, more prickly partners like France, and even Saddam's fellow Arabs in Egypt, Syria and Saudi Arabia. 'The end of the Cold War', he declared, 'has been a victory for all humanity.'

Most striking of all was the cooperation between the United States and the Soviet Union – despite Saddam being a long-time Moscow client. This rested on the now warm personal accord between Bush and Gorbachev and on the community of 'universal values' that they had been professing since the Malta summit of December 1989. Bush went out of his way to praise this in his address to Congress. 'Our relationship to the Soviet Union is important, not only to us but to the world ... If it is possible, I want to continue to build a lasting basis for US–Soviet cooperation – for a more peaceful future for all mankind.'

'If it is possible ...' Behind the grand clarities of that evening on Capitol Hill, the picture was more complex. Moscow's recent violent crackdown in Lithuania cast a shadow over the gleaming rhetoric of freedom and independence. Bush was struggling to balance his principled assertion of democratic values within the USSR against his pragmatic need for Gorbachev's cooperation in the Gulf conflict and in building the new world order.[2]

Other tensions also contorted the simplicity of the evening. Public opinion in America clearly dreaded the prospect of war, fearing very heavy casualties. Would the post-Cold War nation be willing to 'bear any burden'[3] – as John F. Kennedy had put it – for the sake of the new order? Bush offered his answer: 'Any cost in lives – any cost – is beyond our power to measure. But the cost of closing our eyes to aggression is beyond mankind's power to imagine.' To reinforce that statement, he invoked the lessons of history. 'As Americans, we know that there are times when we must step forward and accept our responsibility to lead the world away from the dark chaos of dictators, toward the brighter promise of a better day. Almost fifty years ago we began a long struggle against aggressive totalitarianism. Now we face another defining hour for America and the world.'[4]

Not everyone believed that Kuwait was the *defining* challenge. 'As critical as the Gulf conflict is, the other business of the nation won't wait,' declared Democratic majority leader Senator George Mitchell. 'The president says he seeks a new world order. We ask him to join us in putting our own house in order. We have a crisis abroad but we also have a crisis here at home.' Mitchell was referring to the country's recent slide into recession, which mattered more to the majority of Americans than faraway conflicts in the desert sands or the icy Baltic. Bush's bluff assurance that 'we will get this recession behind us and return to growth – soon' did not paper over the cracks between White House and Capitol Hill about tax rises and the budget deficit. The power to lead abroad depended on the mobilisation of consent at home.

Like many American presidents, Bush therefore turned foreign policy into a moral issue. 'Yes, the United States bears a major share of leadership in this effort. Among the nations of the world, only the United States of America has both the moral standing and the means to back it up. We're the only nation on this earth that could assemble the forces of peace. This is the burden of leadership and the strength that has made America the beacon of freedom in a searching world.'[5] For Bush, Soviet cooperation was a necessary but not a sufficient condition for his project. Ultimately the new world order would hinge on sustained American power and decisive presidential leadership.[6]

*

How had the peace president become a war president – a leader who ended up going to war in the Middle East, on the old periphery of the Cold War, to secure a more peaceful new global order? It was 8.20 p.m. on Wednesday 1 August 1990 when Bush heard the fateful news. He was on the medical table in the White House basement, getting some treatment for his shoulders, having hit 'a bucket's worth of golf balls' that afternoon. Not exactly a hard day at the office. But then Scowcroft entered, face grave, and said, 'Mr President, it looks very bad. Iraq may be about to invade Kuwait.' The president got a briefing from his NSC Middle East expert, Richard Haass, who suggested he make a warning phone call to Saddam Hussein. But that idea was aborted when it was reported that Iraqi troops were already in Kuwait City.[7]

Within two days the emir of Kuwait and his family had fled and the whole country was under Iraqi occupation, enforced by some 140,000 troops and 1,800 tanks. In fact Saddam Hussein was keen to erase Kuwait from the map, making it the newest and clearly the richest part of Iraq, now labelled 'Province 19' and destined, according to Saddam's propaganda, to be part of Iraq for all eternity.[8] In little more than twenty-four hours the Iraqi leader had not only redrawn the borders but plunged the Gulf region into crisis, sending tremors of anxiety around the globe. Having annexed Kuwait, he was now in control of one-fifth of the world's known oil reserves. They were less than 250 miles of flat sand away from Saudi Arabia's primary oilfields, accounting for another fifth, and nobody could be sure about where and when Saddam intended to stop. Oil prices surged and the dollar rose, while most of the world's stock markets fell precipitously.[9]

Until then, it had been a good summer. Bush felt 'convinced we're on the right track in the big picture'.[10] He had achieved goals that really mattered to him: Germany was set for speedy reunification and continued full membership of NATO; Gorbachev had become a close partner, especially after his position had been reaffirmed at the CPSU Party Congress; the former Soviet satellites were moving steadily towards democracy and capitalism; and at the recent NATO summit America had confirmed its leadership of Europe for the post-Wall era. 'It's a challenging and very exciting time to be president of the United States,' Bush told magazine publishers on 17 July. 'Isn't it exciting when you think back a year and a half ago to where we stand today?'[11]

At home, too, things weren't too bad. Opinion-poll approval ratings held steady around 60% and 'as I drive around the country', Bush noted in his diary, 'there seems to be a warmth of feeling'.[12] What kept nagging at him, however, were the continued repercussions of his 26 June tax-rise bombshell to tackle the budget deficit problem. The ensuing negotiations between the White House and Congress soon became deadlocked. Many federal programmes were in danger of being cut, including defence spending which Bush was desperate to preserve after he had managed – against the isolationists – to keep US troops in Germany, Europe and beyond.

The president was still worrying about the budget on 1 August. 'My mind that evening was on things other than Iraq,' he admitted later in his memoirs. 'We were in the midst of a recession and an ugly, partisan budget battle.'[13] The challenge of hammering out a deal would keep diverting Bush from foreign policy for much of the autumn.

He was not exactly surprised at Saddam's blatant power grab. Over the previous year, the Iraqi dictator had adopted an increasingly aggressive tone fuelled by a volatile mix of strength and weakness – strength born of victory in the brutal war with Iran between 1980 and 1988, which had made Iraq the leading military power in the region, but also a state with crippling foreign debts and mounting domestic instability. After Iran, Saddam looked for opportunities elsewhere. He threatened to destroy Israel with chemical weapons but increasingly focused on Kuwait which he accused of trying to undermine Iraq by illicitly tapping Iraqi oilfields in the contested borderlands and flooding international markets with cheap fuel. When abuse and intimidation failed to elicit the response that Saddam wanted from the emir of Kuwait, he simply overpowered his prodigiously wealthy but militarily impotent little neighbour.[14]

Yet what seemed to have emboldened Saddam even more was his view of America. Distrustful of Bush's efforts at engagement, Saddam's suspicions only deepened as he witnessed Soviet decline which in his eyes left Washington as the world hegemon, free to pursue domination in the Middle East. Saddam alleged that not only was America inciting Israeli military action against Iraq and conspiring with dissidents to overthrow his regime, but that they were also masterminding what he saw as Kuwait's campaign of economic strangulation. 'Imperialist and Zionist circles', he claimed, were out to destroy Iraq. In July 1990 on the twenty-second anniversary of his Baath party's 1968 seizure of power, he warned his rich Arab neighbours, with Kuwait top of the list, that Iraqis 'will not forget the maxim that cutting necks is better than cutting the means of living. Oh, God Almighty, be witness that we have warned them.'[15]

To a leader with such an embattled mentality, a Blitz-style attack against Kuwait appealed as a quick-fix way of solving Iraq's economic problems and derailing the supposed American-led conspiracy against his regime. He also warned US ambassador April Glaspie on 25 July 'yours is a society which cannot accept 10,000 dead in a single battle' – a reference to the Vietnam syndrome and a prediction that Bush's America was too soft to fight. But in the same meeting he also promised not to strike as long as negotiations continued. 'We don't want war because we know what war means,' Saddam said. US policymakers were lulled into complacency; a week later when reality hit, 'improvisation was the order of the day', Haass later wrote. 'There was no playbook and no contingency plan for dealing with this scenario or anything like it.'[16]

Improvising or not, Bush did have an immediate gut sense that Saddam's military gamble represented a crucial moment in his presidency. It posed a fundamental challenge to his claims as world leader and to the way that he wanted international politics to evolve.[17] Although hopeful for a new era of peace as East–West tensions abated, Bush feared the emergence of new conflicts along what we might call the North–South divide. The increasing fluidity of global politics could easily dissolve into anarchy; and if the US acquiesced in Saddam's aggression, other despots might feel emboldened. As Scowcroft put it, if the US did nothing, 'we would be setting a terrible precedent – one that would only accelerate violent centrifugal tendencies – in this emerging post-Cold War era'.[18] So how the White House responded at this critical juncture would have a defining impact on the future.

The administration was in agreement that, whereas passivity meant decline into chaos, decisive action could help foster a very different global order. Seen in this light, the Gulf crisis also seemed like an opportunity. In a narrowly American sense, here was a chance to shape the future of the Middle East and secure US access to the region's oil. And, from a broader perspective, successful management of the conflict could assert US leadership in the post-Cold War environment, act as a catalyst for international cooperation against aggression, and lay the foundations for a new global system that was more stable and guided by shared values and laws.[19]

So Bush's reaction was immediate, forceful and public. Even though he said he was 'prepared to deal with the crisis unilaterally if necessary', before going to bed that night he phoned Tom Pickering, the US ambassador to the UN. Bush recalled, 'I wanted the United Nations involved as part of our first response, starting with a strong condemnation of Iraq's attack on a fellow member.' He believed that 'decisive UN action would be important in rallying international opposition to the invasion and reversing it'. He instructed Pickering to push for an emergency Security Council meeting as soon as possible, aware that 'this would be the first post-Cold War test' of the council in crisis. Like Truman in 1950 over the North Korean invasion of the South, he was mindful of 'what had happened in the 1930s when a weak and leaderless League of Nations had failed to stand up to Japanese, Italian, and German aggression'. Unlike Truman, Bush hoped that 'our improving relations with Moscow and our satisfactory ones with China offered the possibility that we could get their cooperation in forging international unity to oppose Iraq'.[20]

For Bush, the Soviets were key, 'first because they had veto power in the Security Council, but also because they could complete Iraq's political isolation'. Yet what he was trying to accomplish would run against rooted Soviet interests because they had long been Saddam's main military backer. 'My solid relationship with Gorbachev, and Jim's [i.e. Baker's] with Shevardnadze promised goodwill', Bush reflected later, 'but how far they would (or could) go with us was still to be seen.'[21] Over the next twenty-four hours, the president and his Secretary of State made the decisive moves – Bush in Washington and Baker in Russia – each of them crafting public statements that would define the next few months.

Bush got a few hours of sleep; his aides little or none. Just before 5 a.m. Scowcroft arrived in his bedroom, 'visibly exhausted', with the latest update. The president sent orders for an American naval task force in the Indian Ocean to sail to the Persian Gulf. He also signed an executive order freezing a total of $30 billion of Kuwaiti and Iraqi assets in the USA – primarily from the emirate to keep them out of Saddam's clutches – and declared a trade embargo against the Iraqi regime, exempting only informational materials and humanitarian supplies.[22]

Then good news came through from New York. By 6 a.m. of the 2nd, the fifteen-member UN Security Council voted 14–0 in favour of Resolution 660, condemning Iraq's aggression, calling for immediate and unconditional Iraqi withdrawal from Kuwait and demanding that the dispute be resolved by negotiations. Only Yemen abstained. Bush was pleased. Here was an early sign that the Soviets, as well as the Chinese, were inclined to support US policy: for him, that was 'step one in building opposition'.[23] Around 7.30 a.m., during his daily CIA briefing, he rang James Baker who was thousands of miles away in Ulan Bator, the capital of Mongolia, following an arms-control meeting with Shevardnadze in Irkutsk. There Baker had pressed his Soviet colleague to halt Russian arms shipments to its Iraqi client, and Shevardnadze flew back to Moscow to consult with Gorbachev. After talking with Bush, Baker changed his travel plans and also flew to Moscow for hastily arranged talks in order to formulate a joint US–Soviet statement.[24]

In Washington, meanwhile, at 8.05 a.m. Bush appeared in front of the media in the Cabinet Room of the White House to make an announcement. The president was firm yet judicious. He condemned the invasion in the strongest terms, declaring: 'There is no place for this sort of naked aggression in today's world.' And he urged the international community to 'act together to ensure that Iraqi forces depart Kuwait immediately'. But he did not want his 'first public comments to threaten the use of American military might'. So he said: 'We're not discussing intervention ... I'm not contemplating such action', though adding the caveat that 'I would not discuss any military options even if we'd agreed upon them'. In truth, as he admitted later, on 2 August he had 'no idea what our options were'. For now, he wanted to keep an open mind and learn all the facts. So he ended the Q&A by saying 'I'm sure there will be a lot of frenzied diplomatic activity. I plan to participate in some of that myself, because at this time, it is important to stay in touch with our many friends around the world, and it's important that we work in concert.'[25]

Of those 'many friends' it was Gorbachev who really mattered. Considering his strong and publicly stated opposition to the use of force in order to resolve international conflicts, but also considering Moscow's traditional ties with Baghdad, even his closest advisers were not entirely sure how their boss would react. Despite Bush's public reticence, the US position left open the option of future military action. Nevertheless, given the Soviet leader's domestic difficulties, his desperate need for Western technology, trade and aid, and his proclaimed devotion to democratic values – repeatedly asserted at summits since his UN speech in New York in 1988 – it would be difficult for him to rebuff American overtures.[26]

And so when Baker met Shevardnadze again at 7.30 p.m. on 3 August in the VIP area of Moscow's Vnukovo II airport, the waiting world media was in suspense. Could the two foreign ministers fabricate a joint statement? Would it be just a fudge? Baker began by explaining 'I've come here because I thought it important to demonstrate that we can and will act as partners facing new challenges to international security.' He insisted that Moscow and Washington must 'send a signal to the world and to the Iraqis' that 'US–Soviet partnership is real ... that together we have entered a new era' and intend to 'demonstrate that when a crisis develops, we're prepared to act swiftly and affirmatively in a meaningful way'. Shevardnadze agreed, explaining that both he and Gorbachev believed that a joint statement was 'right and correct'. After ninety minutes – sitting side by side on a sofa in the corner of a room with their interpreters –

they finalised the communiqué that aides had slowly concocted during that day.[27]

About 9 p.m. Baker and Shevardnadze each read out the text to the press in their own language. They denounced Saddam Hussein's brazen 'transgression of basic norms of civilised conduct' in his 'brutal and illegal invasion of Kuwait'. They declared that 'governments that engage in blatant aggression must know that the international community will not acquiesce in nor facilitate that aggression'. And they announced: 'Today, we take the unusual step of jointly calling upon the rest of the international community to join with us in an international cut-off of all arms supplies to Iraq'. The two foreign ministers then made a few ad hoc comments. For Baker, the joint declaration in that shabby, crowded airport lounge was a truly historic moment. In his memoirs, published five years later, he saw it as nothing less than the end of the Cold War.[28]

But that joint moment was also personal. Baker regarded Shevardnadze as both a representative of a rival power and as a diplomat whom he had come to admire, trust and even like. And he knew that his counterpart was under enormous pressure from hardliners in the Politburo and Arabists in his own ministry who warned there would be 'blood on his hands' if he went along with the Americans. But Shevardnadze stuck to his guns. 'This aggression', he stated in his impromptu remarks at the airport, 'is inconsistent with the principles of new political thinking and in fact with the civilised relations between nations.' That was another reason why Baker believed that 'history was made': for the first time since 1945 'the United States and the Soviet Union were allies on a matter of war'.[29]

Getting the Soviets onside had been a major achievement for the Secretary of State. Meanwhile Bush and his aides had been working around the clock putting together the larger diplomatic coalition to force the Iraqis out of Kuwait. As Baker put it, 'practically overnight, we went from trying to work with Saddam to likening him to Hitler'.[30]

The pace of events was frenetic. Soon after finishing his press conference on the morning of 2 August, Bush flew out to Aspen, Colorado to give a planned speech on post-Cold War security. He didn't want to cancel the trip lest this suggested he was rattled. The trip also allowed him not to miss a previously scheduled meeting with Thatcher, who was predictably supportive: 'He won't stop,' she said of Saddam. But 'it's got to be stopped. We must do everything possible.' The invasion, she told the assembled media afterwards, was 'totally unacceptable, and if it were allowed to endure, then there would be many other small countries that could never feel safe'. Bush used their shared stage in Aspen to clarify remarks he had made earlier that morning at the White House as regards the possible use of force: 'we're not ruling any options in, but we're not ruling any options out'. In other words, the military card was now definitely on the table.[31]

From his plane, Bush spoke on a secure line with two key Arab leaders – President Hosni Mubarak of Egypt and King Hussein of Jordan – who were both in Alexandria. Equally predictably, they wanted to play for time. 'I really implore you, sir, to keep calm,' said Hussein. 'We want to deal with this in an Arab context.' Bush was respectful but firm: 'We will try to remain calm but we cannot acquiesce in the status quo.' Mubarak added his voice: 'We are trying hard to solve this, to find a good solution for withdrawal and not throwing away the regime ... George, give us two days to find a solution.' The president was willing to do so. He knew that the coalition could not be forced. But he did not intend to wait for long.[32]

Bush found King Fahd of Saudi Arabia somewhat more receptive. Fahd was emotional and angry about Saddam who, he railed, was 'upsetting the world order. He seems to think only of himself. He is following Hitler.' Fahd told Bush bluntly, 'Nothing will work with Saddam but the use of force.' Yet he stayed silent when Bush offered US air support, and instead spoke of Saudi Arabia's plans with Mubarak to convene an Arab summit in two days' time. The president confided in his diary, 'I worry that somehow they'll try to buy a solution' because there was 'a historical Arab propensity to work out "deals"'.[33]

Bush got back to Washington at 2.30 in the morning of 3 August. After a few hours' sleep, he conferred with his National Security Council. The mood was distinctly hawkish. To 'accommodate Iraq should not be a policy option. There is too much at stake' (Scowcroft). 'With his new wealth he will ... be able to acquire new weapons, including nuclear weapons. The problem will get worse not better' (Dick Cheney, Secretary of State for Defense). 'If he succeeds, others may try the same thing. It would be a bad lesson' (Lawrence Eagleburger, Deputy Secretary of State). The president left the meeting reinforced in his determination to confront Iraq.[34]

Toughness was also the message from NATO leaders he phoned that afternoon. Mitterrand pushed Bush particularly hard. 'If we are talking about military measures, which military measures [?] ... If it remains just a Platonic threat, it will not have much effect. So, how far are you going in your own thinking?'[35] Also important was the conversation with President Turgut Özal of Turkey, significantly the leader of the only NATO state bordering Iraq and one with a largely Muslim population. Saddam 'should get his lesson', Özal told Bush. 'If he stays, the problem will pop up again.' And 'if Iraq pulls back and Kuwait pays, that is not a solution but another Munich ... We should not repeat the mistakes made at the beginning of World War Two.' Özal promised to talk with Syria and Iran.[36]

With support building, Bush phoned Prime Minister Toshiki Kaifu of Japan. He ran through the various talks he'd had with NATO leaders and emphasised the support of the USSR. Now he needed a key Asian ally to come on board, one that was a member of the G7 but also dependent on oil from the Gulf. 'Toshiki, I know Iraq is in debt to Japan, but I hope that this consideration will not prevent you from joining us in showing Baghdad, as soon as possible, that it faces worldwide opposition. We believe this situation is very serious. Saddam Hussein simply cannot get away with this. If he gets away with this, there is no telling what he will do with his oil and with his new-found power. The status quo really has to be reversed.' But the president didn't have to do much preaching. Kaifu made clear that Japan was totally on board about full-scale sanctions.[37]

Saudi Arabia was now his biggest worry. 'Trying to stiffen the spine of the Saudis,' the president noted in his diary. When Bush and key advisers gathered again for a two-and-a-half-hour meeting on Saturday morning, this time in Camp David, it was to discuss how to defend Saudi Arabia and how the US and its allies might enforce a full-scale economic embargo. The president was also still worried about the Mubarak–Hussein summit-initiative. 'Both of them are in the hand-wringing stage, and neither of them is being a constructive influence for positive action.'

The Americans had no intention of waiting while Saddam gained strength and planned his next move – most likely a strike against Saudi Arabia. So the Camp David meeting swiftly concluded that King Fahd would need US military reinforcements to protect his country. Indeed, the Americans wanted to deploy troops, and do so quickly, lest the kingdom's oil soon fall into Saddam's hands. Bush told the NSC that his worry was their 'lack of will'. (The Saudis were, of course, concerned about the reaction across the Muslim world to the presence of US soldiers in a country that was home to some of the most sacred sites of Islam.[38])

When the president called Riyadh straight after the meeting, King Fahd remained evasive. 'We need your view on a US force presence,'

Bush kept insisting. 'I am very concerned about a possible Iraqi move south across your border.' Still no response. Bush laid it on thick: 'I have great respect for your leadership. That is why we are prepared to make an enormous sacrifice on the US part and to support you in any way.' He told the king: 'The security of Saudi Arabia is vital – basically fundamental – to US interests and really to the interests of the Western world. And I am determined that Saddam will not get away with this infamy. When we work out a plan once we are there, we will stay until we are asked to leave. You have my solemn word on this. I am sick and tired of Saddam and his lying to other countries.' Bush ended by venting his frustration that the Arab summit, on which Hussein and Mubarak had placed such stock, had been cancelled because of divisions in the Arab ranks. 'I am not going to mention any names on this call,' the president complained. 'I understand that there is some pressure from Saddam Hussein on these countries.' His mind was particularly on Jordan, which had long ties to the West but more recently had become one of Saddam's strongest backers. King Hussein himself had said publicly that he had 'every confidence' that Saddam would 'live up to his word' on withdrawing his forces from Kuwait and warned against any military intervention by non-Arab countries, because that 'could set the whole area ablaze'. Persuading the Arabs to help themselves was clearly going to be no easy business.[39]

Blocked in his direct advances, Bush tried more circuitous tactics. The Turkish president Özal proved an invaluable middleman between the West and the Arab world. And Mulroney of Canada, also energetically working the phones, was someone in whom Bush often confided. 'We're sending a high-level mission to Saudi Arabia to flesh out the options,' Bush told Mulroney after talking to Fahd. 'They'll go tomorrow. That hasn't been made public.' Again he let off steam about Saddam: 'I'm determined that this man will not carry the day.'[40]

Despite Fahd's apparent intransigence, the failure of Arab mediation left him with few options. The mission that Bush mentioned was headed by Dick Cheney. And it was made a condition of their departure from Washington that Fahd privately had to promise that US troops would be welcome in Saudi Arabia. Once the Americans arrived, Fahd brushed aside the many sceptics in his government, telling Cheney: 'OK, we'll do it. Two conditions: one, you bring enough to do the job, and two, you will leave when it's over.'[41] On behalf of the president, Cheney accepted. By morning on Monday 6 August – after eighteen presidential phone calls with twelve leaders over five days, and a top-level US delegation – Saudi Arabia was finally ready to accept US troops. But the previous night, confident in his own judgement, the president had already authorised General Colin Powell, chair of the Joint Chiefs of Staff, to begin assembling the forces that would go to Saudi Arabia. Operation Desert Shield had been launched.[42]

As Bush flew back to the White House after his weekend at Camp David, he had time for a brief moment of reflection: 'Its been the most hectic forty-eight hours since I have been president,' he wrote in his diary. 'The enormity of Iraq is upon me now. I have been on the phone incessantly ... The bottom line is that the West is together.' And also Japan: that morning Bush had been buoyed up by another conversation with Kaifu, who had promised full support in imposing total economic sanctions. Sitting in the helicopter, Bush wrote that Iraq was 'the most serious problem I have faced as president because the downside is so enormous'. If the Saudis were invaded and the US had to fight a war of liberation, 'we would be really involved in something that could have the magnitude of a new world war'.[43]

With all this churning around in his mind, the president landed on the South Lawn of the White House and had to say a few words to the eager media. He delivered a brief factual statement, mostly describing the recent flurry of diplomatic activity. But then, when answering questions, his pent-up feelings came to the surface. 'I'm not going to discuss what we're doing in terms of moving of forces, anything of that nature. But I view it very seriously ... please believe me, there are an awful lot of countries that are in total accord with what I've just said, and I salute them. They are staunch friends and allies, and we will be working with them all for collective action. This will not stand. This will not stand, this aggression against Kuwait.'

It was a powerful punchline. But Bush didn't do political theatre in the Reagan style, so that wasn't his last word. 'I've got to go,' he told the press. 'I have to go to work. I've got to go to work.'[44]

Another dimension of that work was getting the United Nations onside.[45] On Monday the Security Council voted 13–0 in favour of total economic sanctions against Iraq – Resolution 661. Only Cuba and Yemen abstained. Bush had been anxious about China. Admittedly, the PRC had condemned the aggression (voting earlier for UN Resolution 660) and agreed to stop weapons sales to Iraq. But would Beijing back full-scale sanctions? Here Giulio Andreotti, Italian premier and current EC president, proved a useful channel of information. 'Are you sure about China?' Bush asked over the phone on Monday morning. Andreotti was confident: 'According to the last information I had, China would also take part in a general condemnation.' The president agreed: 'I think that is right, but I have no direct information.' In the event, Bush's worries about Beijing were unfounded – for the moment.[46]

Meanwhile Baker had taken care of the Soviets, ringing up Shevardnadze – albeit apologetically because his colleague was on vacation. But, said Baker, he felt 'it was important to call', to 'stay in close touch', because they needed to be 'in sync'. After explaining the situation with Iraq and filling in Shevardnadze about Dick Cheney's trip to Saudi Arabia, the Secretary of State came to the crux of his call: 'Let me assure you, as I did in Moscow, that we are not seeking an excuse to use force. But we do have vital interests, as you do too, in this area, and we will protect those interests. We want to work closely with you, but we will have to protect US interests.' He further stressed that 'we believe it is the primary responsibility of the international community to respond to the Iraqi aggression against Kuwait' and hoped that the US and Soviet Union would 'stand together' on this at the UN. Baker need not have worried. Shevardnadze informed him that, after an abortive last-minute attempt to convince Saddam to withdraw, Gorbachev was now ready to take action via the UN. And so the superpowers found themselves on the same page also in New York.[47]

That very day, NATO secretary general Manfred Wörner flew to Washington to discuss various ways in which the Alliance could support US actions. Thatcher, on her way home from Colorado, also joined in. Like Bush, the prime minister warmly applauded the UN vote – even though privately believing that the UN route tied American hands too much – and she was also ready to commit Britain to a de facto naval blockade in the Gulf to enforce the international sanctions regime. The president took the opportunity to parade Thatcher and Wörner with him on the White House lawn. 'I cannot remember a time when we had the world so strongly together against an action as now', Thatcher declared, 'and I hope that those sanctions will be properly and effectively enforced as a positive action against what we all totally and utterly condemn.' Wörner duly chimed in: 'My impression is that this is the moment for the West to show cohesion, determination and to make it clear what cannot be accepted in this world and to safeguard its own security interests.'

For Bush, these kinds of photo opportunities – even in the pouring rain that afternoon – were a godsend. As the *New York Times* noted, 'The administration is seeking to assemble as broad a coalition as possible against Iraq, both to isolate Baghdad and to ensure that efforts to restore Kuwait's independence will not turn into a symbolic duel.' Any hint of a face-off between Bush and Saddam 'might prompt many Arab countries to lean toward the Iraqi president'. Instead, practically overnight a multi-national military force was taking shape that included, crucially, Egypt and Morocco. What's more, even if behind the scenes Moscow tried to keep dialogue with erstwhile client Baghdad going, the sotto voce Kremlin decision to dispatch a destroyer and an anti-submarine ship to the Persian Gulf represented an unprecedented degree of coordination with America.[48]

The president now felt in a position to talk candidly to the American people. At 9 a.m. on Wednesday 8 August, he spoke from the Oval Office on TV to announce the US troop deployment to Saudi Arabia and the coalition he was building.[49] Appealing to Americans' patriotism, he declared: 'In the life of a nation we're called upon to define who we are and what we believe. Sometimes these choices are not easy. But today as president, I ask for your support in a decision I've made to stand up for what's right and condemn what's wrong, all in the cause of peace.' He then explained his action of sending key units of the air force and of the 82nd Airborne Division to the Arabian Peninsula: 'There is no justification whatsoever for this outrageous and brutal act of aggression. A puppet regime imposed from the outside is unacceptable. The acquisition of territory by force is unacceptable. No one, friend or foe, should doubt our desire for peace; and no one should underestimate our determination to confront aggression.'

But, Bush went on, 'we agree that this is not an American problem or a European problem or a Middle East problem: it is the world's problem.' And also a moment on the cusp of history. 'We succeeded in the struggle for freedom in Europe because we and our allies remain stalwart. Keeping the peace in the Middle East will require no less. We're beginning a new era. This new era can be full of promise, an age of freedom, a time of peace for all peoples. But if history teaches us anything, it is that we must resist aggression or it will destroy our freedoms. Appeasement does not work. As was the case in the 1930s, we see in Saddam Hussein an aggressive dictator threatening his neighbours.'

The peace president was gearing up for the possibility that he would now have to become a war president. As Bush told a press conference later that morning, 'We have sent forces to defend Saudi Arabia'. Though he also stressed, 'we're not in a war'. This was legally correct and administration officials were at pains to emphasise that the USA would greatly prefer it if sanctions – in the form of Turkey and Saudi Arabia closing Iraqi pipelines and thereby depriving Baghdad of its main source of foreign income – were successful in forcing Iraq out of Kuwait, rather than having to use American military might. In strategic terms, however, mobilising for a start some 50,000–100,000 US soldiers to be stationed in Saudi Arabia, backed by aircraft carriers, missiles, fighters, bombers, tanks and all sorts of other weapons, together with the embargo was an in-your-face display of US power – intended to make Saddam pull back. As Bush put it, 'A line has been drawn in the sand.'[50]

*

Global reaction to Bush's speech was positive. 'I saw you on CNN,' Özal told him on the phone, 'you were very good.'[51] Likewise Thatcher: 'I saw your broadcast on television. It was marvellous. It is getting very good press in the UK.' Bush reciprocated with thanks for her recent visit – 'It gave the whole situation an ecumenical look' – and he praised her 'leadership'. To which the reply was unusually obsequious: 'It was your leadership. I was just a chum.' Maggie was clearly on a charm offensive, seeing Iraq as a chance to put Anglo-American relations back on track after Bush's flirtations with Kohl over Germany and to remind the president that, when it came to the real issues of war and peace, only Britain was special.[52]

As well as old European allies, more tricky Arab nations openly offered their support – not only Egypt, Morocco and Syria but also Oman, Bahrain and the United Arab Emirates. A key development here was that on 10 August an ad hoc Arab League Summit voted narrowly but decisively (12 out of 21) in favour of sending troops to help the Saudis – with only Libya and the PLO (apart from Iraq itself) openly opposed. Even King Hussein of Jordan approved this resolution, intended to help Riyadh 'defend its lands and its regional security against foreign attack' – although he expressed some reservations. Anticipating the vote, Saddam made an emotional radio broadcast calling for the Arab masses to rise against foreign intervention and against the 'humiliation' of Muslim shrines in Saudi Arabia. Urging a 'holy war', he proclaimed: 'Your brothers in Iraq are determined to continue jihad without any hesitation or retreat and without any fear from the foreigner's power'. Despite some large

pro-Saddam demonstrations in Jordan and Yemen, Baghdad was generally isolated and within days the UN boycott of Iraqi oil was reported at
near 100%.[53]

International solidarity was consolidated by the daily news from
Kuwait. The Iraqi occupiers committed numerous atrocities against civilians and there were many stories of theft and pillage, even the blowing
up of banks. With Kuwait apparently descending into hell and no sign
of Saddam relenting, the US build-up gathered pace. By 19 August it was
reported '20,000-plus soldiers are in Saudi Arabia, about 35,000 more
are on 59 ships ringing the Saudi peninsula or bound there and up to
45,000 Marines are heading for the Persian Gulf.'[54] By November, Saudi
Arabia would be home to no less than a quarter of a million US troops,
including heavy mechanised forces.[55]

All this was made possible by major improvements in lift and logistics
in recent years, and thanks to a post-Cold War dividend. In summer
1990 the USA still had a Cold War-size military, but 100,000 active-duty
military personnel were scheduled to be redeployed or even demobilised
– half of them from Europe because of the end of the NATO–Warsaw
Pact stand-off. As a result Washington was free to shift manpower and
resources to a non-European theatre just as the Gulf crisis exploded,
specifically deploying the army's now redundant VII Corps from Europe
to Saudi Arabia. As Colin Powell later noted, 'We could now afford to
pull divisions out of Germany that had been there for the past forty years
to stop a Soviet offensive that was no longer coming.'[56]

In fact, within two weeks, while Congress was in summer recess, the
Bush administration had committed the United States to its broadest and
most hazardous overseas military venture since Vietnam. The strategy
was codified in National Security Directive NSD-45.[57] Policy had been
formulated by a very small circle – the president and a few top advisers,
notably Scowcroft, Cheney, Baker and Powell – which did prompt some
criticism of secretive White House decision-making. More generally,
there were private mutterings that Washington was paying the price for
its longer-term Iraq policy: Reagan had built up Saddam with weapons
in the mid-1980s to prevent his defeat by fundamentalist Iran. But in
public the mood was very much 'rally around the flag'. Thus far no one
on Capitol Hill had proposed congressional hearings. Indeed, most politicians scrambled to support the president's decision. 'I think we'll stand
it for a long period of time, as long as there are not casualties,' said
Arizona Republican senator John McCain, a Vietnam veteran who was

also a member of the Armed Services Committee. In similar vein, James Schlesinger, a former Secretary of State for Defense and CIA director from the Nixon–Ford era, stated that the American public would undoubtedly back Bush's commitment to Saudi Arabia, thereby safe-guarding US access to world oil production. But he did warn 'it is not clear that there is strong public support for a rollback in Kuwait, especially if it will require heavy American casualties.'[58]

At the moment, Bush was careful to talk about deterring war, not waging it.[59] And the multilateral nature of the military coalition also helped counter any criticism of America being out on its own. In fact, for Bush, multilateralism served many purposes. As he and Scowcroft later wrote, the UN 'could provide a cloak of acceptability to our efforts and mobilise world opinion behind the principles we wished to project'. The president's commitment to the ideal of a new world order was not feigned. But Bush and his inner circle felt it 'even more important to keep the strings of control tightly in our hands'.[60] Desert Shield was a protection for vital US interests, which only the White House could look after. Indeed, the ongoing operation also 'demonstrated the limits of European power', as a NATO official highlighted, because it showed that 'only the United States can play the role of global policeman'. Or, in the words of the British newspaper the *Independent*: 'Only the Americans can mount a swift military response to a challenge of this sort outside the NATO area.'[61]

Packaged in this way as assertive-consensual US leadership, multilat-eralism could serve as a force-multiplier in military terms. And also a cost-defrayer, because those countries that did not make military commit-ments were contributing financially. On 29 August, the media reported Pentagon estimates that US operations in the Persian Gulf would require $2.5 billion up to the end of September (above and beyond normal mili-tary operating costs). This was more than twice the $1.2 billion figure stated twelve days earlier. Officials cited higher charges for fuel, the expense of mobilising 200,000 reservists and increased shipping sched-ules by way of explanation. It was clear that expenditure would keep rising exponentially – especially if America had to fight. 'If you have a shooting war,' a congressional budget analyst told reporters, 'all bets are off. Then you consume ammunition, fuel, and hardware. You start to replace tanks and planes and missiles. You increase your presence, and the cost jumps, depending on how hot it gets.'

In short, the Middle East deployment jeopardised hopes of cutting the 1991 defence budget. Not only would some $50 billion in surplus funds currently sitting in various Pentagon accounts be swallowed up by Desert Shield, some Democrats on Capitol Hill were now calling for a special income-tax surcharge to help foot the bill. They were also insistent that countries not sending troops should contribute cash instead. 'The Japanese have a hell of a stake in this,' declared New Jersey Democrat senator Frank R. Lautenberg, 'and ought to pay a hell of share.'[62]

Burden-sharing was an essential part of Bush's policy. Financial aid from allies and friends could come in two main ways – through bearing some of the costs of the military deployment, or by disbursing financial assistance and humanitarian aid to countries especially hard hit by the trade embargo, such as Turkey and Egypt. In both these respects, Japan and West Germany – the world's second and third strongest economies by GDP – were particularly significant. And it became part of the administration's calculations to buy off domestic criticism by pressing above all for Deutschmarks and yen. After all, Washington reasoned, following their defeat in 1945, the FRG and Japan had been the prime beneficiaries of more than four decades of US support as protector power.[63]

On 13 August, Bush pitched hard in his opening phone call on the subject to Kaifu: 'I would like you to consider a direct Japan contribution to the multinational naval force.' Realising that this would be a watershed in the post-war history of Japan, he spoke of Tokyo showing that it was now a 'full participant in the Western alliance'. Bush had in mind Japanese minesweepers to patrol waters in the Gulf and transport ships that could carry equipment to Saudi Arabia. Kaifu, fully conscious of his country's heavy reliance on Gulf crude, promised cooperation but was firm on his government having to respect its 'constitutional constraints and Diet resolutions' – what he called 'almost a national policy' that made it 'next to unthinkable' to participate militarily. 'Well that's fine,' replied Bush. But 'my bottom line is that when this chapter of history is written, Japan and the US and a handful of other counties will have stood side by side as much as possible.'[64]

Two weeks later, on the 29th, Kaifu rang Bush back to say that 'we have considered all of the options open to us to see how we can help, with the exception of sending our self-defence forces, which has significant constitutional limitations'. He specified that Japan would assist US and multinational forces with transportation and housing, as well as medical supplies and personnel – aid worth an estimated $1 billion. And, he told Bush, 'we will also extend a substantial scale of economic support to the negatively affected states such as Jordan, Turkey and Egypt, as well as bearing substantial assistance for the flood of refugees'. The president expressed appreciation but privately he was disappointed. Resentment was also stirring in Congress, and many in the administration were 'very unhappy' that the Japanese were ducking a military role. As one official told the media sarcastically, 'If you look at the situation in the Middle East, we judge it to be basically a military situation. There's a limited number of Girl Scout cookies that can be used there.'[65]

Bush was also in contact with Kohl, who made clear on 22 August the limitations imposed by the FRG's 1949 constitution on the use of German troops outside its own borders. His own attention was moreover focused on the politics – and the costs – of German unification. But, he told the president, 'it is very important that solidarity be a two-way street. The US has always helped us, so we want to be able to help in any way we can.' He assured Bush of Bonn's 'full support' for the US position on Iraq, expressing the hope that a strong international showing would convince Saddam to withdraw.[66]

It took some weeks to sort out the nature of Germany's financial assistance, and the Senate Foreign Relations Committee singled out the FRG for special criticism for not pulling its weight. The crucial meeting did not occur until after the 2 + 4 treaty had been signed in Moscow on 12 September – but three days later in Kohl's home in Ludwigshafen the chancellor stepped up to the plate. He told Baker he was not going put up with the accusation that he was 'getting all the benefits' and 'not contributing' in return, let alone that he was 'being skimpy on the money'. It was agreed that the Federal Republic would provide assistance to the value of almost $2 billion – support equipment for US forces, increased military and economic aid to Turkey and ships to transport Egyptian armoured units and their tanks to the Gulf.[67]

Germany was the last stop in a whirlwind fundraising tour by Baker – nine countries in eleven days – which the US press dubbed his 'tin-cup trip'. The crucial stopover had been the first, in Riyadh, where Baker met King Fahd. The Saudi monarch was fulsome in his gratitude, saying that the United States was 'all that stood between peace and disaster' for his country. So Baker suggested that $15 billion would be an appropriate way of saying thank you. Fahd did not blink: he told Baker to sort it out with the Foreign Ministry. The latter's message was 'don't ask us for $15 billion unless you get $15 billion from the Kuwaitis'. And thus the Secretary of State moved on to the Sheraton in Taif where the emir of Kuwait resided in genteel Saudi exile. Described by Baker drily as 'a quiet man who grows roses and has taken thirteen wives', the emir readily agreed to pay up. All in all, Baker's two days in Saudi Arabia netted him $30 billion – which proved half the eventual cost of the Gulf operation.[68]

Despite all the benefits of multilateralism, however, what mattered most for the White House was its bilateral relationship with the Kremlin. In fact, it was surely because of Moscow's cooperation that a strong multilateral response to Saddam's invasion had become possible; and it was with the consent of Moscow, and also Beijing, that US Ambassador Pickering managed to win approval for a series of UN Security Council resolutions.[69]

As Desert Shield took shape, however, this post-Cold War entente was coming under strain. When Baker phoned Shevardnadze on 7 August, he found him in a distinctly gloomy mood. The Soviet foreign minister had gone out on a limb supporting Baker in their Moscow joint statement, and since then had come under sustained attack from Middle Eastern experts in his ministry. Worse, he now felt personally snubbed that Bush had gone ahead with military deployment. 'What am I being consulted about?' was his line. Shevardnadze felt that Iraq should have been given a chance to respond to Resolution 661 before the US acted unilaterally. He told Baker in no uncertain terms that the USSR considered Washington's action 'exceptional, extraordinary and temporary'. Military forces should leave Saudi Arabia 'as quickly as possible'.[70] This scenario was at odds with the one emerging from the Pentagon and Oval Office.[71] But over the phone Baker tried to reassure Shevardnadze that the Gulf build-up was considered 'an extraordinary matter'. In fact, 'no offensive actions were planned', he insisted. Desert Shield was 'strictly to deter'.[72]

Despite Baker's efforts, Moscow was unhappy that the Soviet Union was being excluded from US decision-making. And there were also troubling signs that Gorbachev and Shevardnadze were no longer fully in sync. The foreign minister was willing if necessary to increase the pressure on Saddam, sharing the American belief that ultimately the only way to deal with the Iraqi despot was by force. Gorbachev, however, was firmly against this. According to Chernyaev, his boss was positively 'repulsed by mass use of modern weapons and deeply concerned to keep casualties to a minimum'.[73] As Baker wrote to Bush 'Gorbachev's image of the new international order is such that he has a hard time reconciling the fact that we might need to use force in this initial test.'[74]

Gorbachev had spoken for several years about the wisdom of removing the use of military force from the conduct of international relations – starting well before Bush became president. And, since Malta, the two men had frequently talked about superpower diplomacy now operating under new rules. So the Soviet leader had no intention – still less the financial capability – to go to war in the Middle East.

What's more, he had to consider the Soviet Union's standing amid the intricacies of Gulf politics vis-à-vis a clear-cut and assertive USA. It was around this time that Gorbachev turned to Yevgeny Primakov – the Foreign Ministry's top Arabist, a long-time acquaintance, if not personal friend, of Saddam Hussein, and now a close adviser to the Soviet leader. In a move that infuriated Shevardnadze and would create a running sore between them, the Soviet leader made Primakov his personal envoy in the Gulf crisis. Primakov kept telling Gorbachev what the latter liked to hear; namely that it might be possible to talk Saddam out of Kuwait. Playing the independent Soviet peacemaker, Primakov proposed direct bilateral negotiations with Saddam. This would rescue the tattered Cold War patron–client relationship and promote Soviet interests in the region. By contrast, Primakov argued that supporting the USA outright risked stoking up discontent among the Muslim population in the USSR's already volatile Central Asian republics.[75]

Susceptible to Primakov's arguments, Gorbachev was willing to explore what became a two-track strategy – quietly pursuing a bilateral Soviet–Iraqi channel while continuing his public support of the US via the UN. In the latter vein on 25 August, after intense telephone diplomacy between Baker and Shevardnadze and Gorbachev's abortive appeal asking Saddam to observe Security Council calls to withdraw, the Soviets went along in supporting UN Resolution 665 outlawing all trade with Iraq by any means and authorising military enforcement of these sanctions, effectively by a naval blockade.[76]

Bush was relieved at the resolution's passage – not least because, after some toing and froing, China had also voted in favour. To be sure the Chinese envoy made the caveat that, in their view, 665 did 'not contain the concept of using force'. But surface unity had been preserved. It would have been intolerable for Bush if one of the five permanent members of the Security Council had vetoed the resolution. Beijing was clearly keen to resume its role as a big player in the world after its self-inflicted diplomatic isolation post-Tiananmen. To achieve this outcome the president had initiated a flurry of meetings between American and Chinese officials in both countries, as well as sending a presidential message to the Chinese leadership. He could therefore tell members of Congress on 29 August, 'we are seeing international cooperation that is truly historic ... The Soviets, the Chinese, our traditional allies, our friends in the Arab world – the cooperation is unprecedented.'[77]

The president was particularly anxious to maintain the momentum with Gorbachev – not least because he feared that, if the Kremlin became alienated over the Gulf, the USSR might at the last minute still throw a spanner in the works on German unity. To this end, Bush wrote to Gorbachev on 29 August, picking up on their Camp David meeting in June and their idea about 'getting together more frequently' and 'talking informally without an agenda'. He proposed 'one day of talks' about the Middle East in Switzerland or Finland which, he said, would 'send a good signal around the globe'. He also stated that he planned a major speech to the American people in the week of 10 September and therefore hoped they could meet before then. A later date was not possible because he would be entangled in 'domestic budget matters'. Bush apologised for the very short notice but stressed that he thought, because 'things dramatically change around the world', it was now essential for them to be 'in close contact'. Gorbachev welcomed the invitation and chose Helsinki for the venue.[78]

*

The Soviet–American summit was set for Sunday 9 September. Briefing papers prepared for the president revealed that the USSR was in dire economic straits, as well as highlighting Gorbachev's political problems. In a memo to the president Scowcroft suggested that Gorbachev's public 'authority, popularity and power' were now 'in precipitous decline' and the Communist Party 'had been irreparably weakened'. He had problems implementing the centre's decisions due to growing rifts in the Union and his tensions with republic leaders, especially Boris Yeltsin of the Russian Republic.*[79] Despite these domestic problems, the CIA assured Bush that superpower cooperation over conflicts in Afghanistan, Cambodia and especially Kuwait was sustaining the positive momentum in Moscow's 'growing relationship with the United States and the West'.

---

* The Russian Republic was officially called Russian Soviet Federative Socialist Republic (Rossiyskaya Sovetskaya Federativnaya Socialisticheskaya Respublika, RSFSR).

Scowcroft in turn reminded Bush, 'We have told the Soviets many times that we want to help them accelerate the integration of their economy in to the world market system and normalise our bilateral relationship. But access to our private capital markets and government-backed credit depends on Soviet good faith at the negotiating table.'[80]

The president approached the summit in an optimistic mood but told reporters en route to Helsinki that he had no plans to ask Moscow to send ground troops to the multinational force assembled in Saudi Arabia. The Soviets feared a military conflict a few hundred miles from their southern border, he said, because that would revive painful memories of their war in Afghanistan. He, like Scowcroft, also alluded to the USSR's internal tensions between Russians and the country's large Islamic minority.[81]

Landing at Vantaa airport just before noon on 8 September, Bush – attentive as usual to local detail – praised Helsinki as a frequent meeting place 'for nations seeking to advance the cause of peace' and applauded the Finns as a people 'resolute' in their 'commitment to liberty and independence'. (He did not add 'particularly against the USSR'.) The president also singled out Finland as a long-standing 'voice of peace and stability between nations in the councils of the CSCE' and currently as a member of the UN Security Council, 'upholding international law in [the] face of Iraq's unwarranted aggression'.[82]

Gorbachev arrived some seven hours later, and the two leaders got down to business on the 9th.

At the presidential palace, they first met alone with their closest advisers and interpreters. Simultaneously Baker and Shevardnadze held their own talks.[83] To Bush's relief, Gorbachev seemed 'relatively relaxed and even cheerful'. The president's hopes were high – even imagining that 'maybe this Helsinki trip with Gorbachev and the Iraq crisis will be the fulcrum that we need to lever a [budget] deal through the Congress'. Keen to move towards a public display of superpower partnership, he took the initiative. 'I think there is an opportunity to have develop out of this tragedy a new world order,' he told Gorbachev. But, he continued, the bottom line 'must be that Saddam Hussein cannot be allowed to profit from his aggression'. Bush was adamant that failure to implement the UN resolutions was not an option. 'I do not want this to escalate and I do not want to use force.' Yet, if Saddam did not withdraw, 'he must know the status quo is unacceptable'. The Americans were determined to prevail.[84]

Then Bush alluded to the traditional US policy of trying to contain

Soviet global influence. Looking Gorbachev in the eye, he said that this had now changed. 'The world order I see coming out of this is US and Soviet cooperation to solve not only this but other problems in the Middle East.' It had been a wonderful signal to the world that so far the two superpowers had been 'proceeding in concert in the Gulf ... I want to work with you as equal partners in dealing with this.' Mindful of his upcoming speech to Congress, Bush added: 'I want to go to the American people tomorrow night to close the book on the Cold War and offer them the vision of this new world order in which we will cooperate.'[85]

At this point Gorbachev handed Bush a Soviet cartoon showing the two of them as boxers, with a referee in between whose head was a globe. He held both men's arms up in victory as they towered over the 'Cold War' figure at their feet – vanquished and apparently melting. 'Knockout' (in Russian) read the caption. The two leaders laughed heartily – at which point Bush coyly asked if it was OK to call each other by first names. 'Fine, George,' said Mikhail, with a broad grin.[86]

Winners in Cold War boxing ring: Bush and Gorbachev in Helsinki

The initial bonhomie could not, however, conceal hard political realities. The two leaders simply did not agree on how to deal with Saddam's
aggression and there was a distinct edge to their dialogue. Gorbachev was
sceptical of US intentions. Seeking to offer reassurance, Bush promised
not to keep American troops in the Gulf 'on a permanent basis' and
declared that, even if Saddam were to remain in power, 'any mechanisms
developed to safeguard against the recurrence of aggression and the
possible use of nuclear weapons would not be American, but international'.

But America's unquestionable ability and will to project massive military power overseas spoke for itself, at a time when the Kremlin was
struggling with all the practical and psychological problems of the Red
Army in retreat from the heart of Europe. In truth the two superpowers
were not on the same footing – and, however much he squirmed,
Gorbachev knew it. 'I think this crisis is a test of the process we are going
through in world affairs and of the new US–Soviet relationship,' he said.
They would have to think in new ways – even though the price was high
– because 'in this new world US–Soviet Union cooperation is essential'.
The Soviet leader stressed that the USSR did also strictly abide by the
UN Security Council resolutions. But, he stated emphatically, there were
limits. Disputing Bush's rhetoric about a partnership of equals, Gorbachev
complained that it was 'difficult for us at first because you decided to
send forces' and only 'told us' after the fact, when US troops were 'already
in motion'. This lack of consultation was a point which Gorbachev particularly laboured – as is clear from the Soviet transcript, though omitted
from the American minutes.[87]

Bush dutifully ate humble pie. 'I accept your words as constructive
criticism. Evidently, I should have called you then. I want to assure you
that we did not intend to act behind your back.' Gorbachev mellowed
a bit. 'In general, we were able to work together, shoulder to shoulder.
We were able to mobilise the UN Security Council and virtually the
entire world community. And this was a huge achievement. In the light
of this, the US presence in the region is perceived differently.' Nevertheless,
Kuwait remained a country under occupation and it would not be easy
to get Saddam out. So Gorbachev acknowledged the need for decisive
action but warned against any unilateral military move by the United
States. Moscow would regard that as totally unacceptable. In addition,
he raised the spectre of domestically intolerable casualty levels, invoking
the ghosts of Vietnam and Afghanistan. And, he went on, who could
be sure that China's position would not change? After all, Beijing had

a veto power, so the 'unity of the Security Council could be disrupted'.[88]

Above all, Gorbachev did not want Saddam to be driven 'into a corner'. He preferred an option that would allow the Iraqi tyrant 'to save face' and therefore proposed a 'linkage' deal. Saddam would withdraw from Kuwait and restore the Kuwaiti government. In return the US would promise not to strike Iraq, its forces would be replaced by Arab UN peacekeepers and a grand international conference on the Middle East would soon follow, with an agenda that included not just Iraq but the perennial issues of Lebanon and Israel–Palestine.

Gorbachev took the line that Saddam would reject the plan and thereby be unmasked. But Bush totally disagreed. He believed the Iraqi leader would jump at such a proposal. In which case, he said, 'any agreement on a plan which left the Kuwait issue open would be a major defeat for collective action'. Worse, it would shift attention away from the Gulf to Israel and risk turning Saddam into a hero of the Arab world. Furthermore, once the USA left the Arabian Peninsula, the Iraqi leader could 'return to aggression' with his nuclear programme intact. Bush therefore wanted to act – and to do so rapidly.[89]

Gorbachev decided to humour Bush, urbanely expressing sympathy for his 'difficult' position at home. 'I understand it very well, maybe even better than some people in the US ... People expect quick victories from the president ... People want strong, decisive action.'[90] Reverting to his own case, Gorbachev read an extract from Saddam's speech the day before, in which he claimed that Kuwait was an unlawful product of 'British colonialism' to which Iraq had never agreed, and then ranted 'when the Americans invaded Panama, the UN Security Council and the Soviet Union were silent'. Whereas now, Saddam went on, when the matter was the business of the Arabs, 'everyone protests'.

'Bullshit!' So far Bush had kept his cool during Gorbachev's lengthy monologues in apparent defence of his Iraqi client. But now he exploded.[91] For the rest of the meeting the two leaders went round and round in circles talking past each other and blowing off steam. Eventually Gorbachev rephrased his essential point. 'If Saddam gets absolutely nothing and finds himself cornered, then we can expect very severe retribution ... Therefore we should not bring him to his knees. Nothing good will come of it.'[92]

'Do you think one could reach a compromise with Hitler?'

'I think these are disparate phenomena, there is no analogy,' Gorbachev countered.

'Saddam Hussein is not a global phenomenon,' Bush conceded, 'but they are comparable in terms of personal cruelty.' He reeled off what he considered the lessons of history. Dictators could not be appeased, and even less trusted. Insatiable, they responded only to force. A policy using carrots and linkage sent the wrong signals and was totally misguided. Saddam should not be allowed to get away with aggression. Appeasement had been the crucial mistake of the 1930s – a time when America had been isolationist – and one which Bush did not intend to repeat.[93]

After three long hours, much of the time going at each other hammer and tongs, the two leaders ended abruptly for lunch. It had been probably the most abrasive Gorbachev–Bush session to date, reminiscent of the Soviet leader's first meeting with Reagan in Geneva. As their staffs joined them for the afternoon session in Helsinki, seeking to concoct a mutually agreed statement for the press, nobody knew quite how the gulf could be bridged. Scowcroft, in particular, was filled with foreboding, suspecting that Gorbachev was under the influence of Primakov and seeing this as part of the bigger 'battle between Shevardnadze and Primakov for Gorbachev'. Scowcroft thought gloomily that it 'could not be happening at a worse time'. He even feared that Moscow was seeking a separate peace with Baghdad. 'We had to head that off.'[94]

In the event, however, the Bush administration's anxieties were unfounded. The joint statement was thrashed out fairly quickly, because Baker and Shevardnadze and their staffers – much less entrenched in their positions – had managed to find common ground during a very constructive meeting of their own. And they duly presented a draft in the post-lunch plenary. Gorbachev went through it line by line but, to Bush's surprise, he only asked for modest changes. Despite all his bombast in the morning, the final version said nothing explicit about a Middle East peace conference – making only vague references to cooperation in the region. On the other hand, an American demand for Saddam's unconditional withdrawal was also omitted. The final communiqué issued by Bush and Gorbachev was therefore fudged. But the Americans felt they had got 'a good bargain' – 'far more than half a loaf', said Baker. For Scowcroft, after the contretemps in the morning, this was 'an amazing – and exceedingly reassuring – turnabout'.[95]

Baker usually disliked 'constructive ambiguity' in the practice of diplomacy. 'For the most part, it's a dangerous tool, to be used sparingly. More often than not, absolute precision is the more preferable device.' He believed it generally better to leave meetings with 'a discordant air' rather than a 'misunderstanding' that only stored up bigger problems for later. On this occasion in Helsinki, however, he could live with the verbal fuzziness – not least because he felt that the US had got the better of the argument.[96]

Indeed, in spite of all the sweet talk about partnership and Gorbachev's private posturing, America's position of strength was now evident for all to see. This impression was accentuated when Gorbachev spent a long time spelling out his plans for economic reform, to be announced on 1 October, and talked of the political fallout he was clearly dreading. So far, he said, 'confrontation or civil conflict' in a country with such a 'complicated history' had been averted but the next three to five months would be 'critical'. His biggest problem in this necessary shift to the market was how to get goods on the shelves of Soviet shops. 'I hope Western countries can help. The numbers are not great.'

As always, Bush did not take the bait. He just trotted out his usual line: 'As you know, we don't have the cash for large economic assistance.' Instead he vaguely promised some technological help and more US investment. Regarding the trade agreement that Gorbachev coveted, Bush said it was up to the Soviets to get the emigration legislation approved before any talks on this could start. Airily he added that 'there is still some old thinking' in the USSR but expressed optimism as a result of this meeting arguing 'we are on common ground now'.[97]

And it was that 'common ground' which seemed most evident in the press conference that followed their seven hours together. In Finlandia Hall, the personal chemistry between the superpower leaders was perceptibly relaxed and even affectionate. 'The Two New Friends Come Smiling Through' was the headline of Maureen Dowd's report for the *New York Times*. Amid this world crisis, the dramatically improved relationship between Washington and Moscow had changed the whole dynamic of international affairs. With a strong joint statement pledging to act both 'individually and in concert' to reverse Iraq's conquest of Kuwait, they reaffirmed the Baker–Shevardnadze declaration of 3 August and their common support for UN resolutions to ensure Saddam's withdrawal from Kuwait. Gorbachev talked of the total reversal since 1967, when the two superpowers seemed on the brink of war when backing opposite sides in the Arab–Israeli Six Day War. Bush alluded to their recent summits – Malta, Washington, Camp David – 'as we enter upon a new peaceful period and as we emerge from the Cold War'. He celebrated their ability to collaborate and defend the same principles.[98]

Nevertheless, in front of the world media, their divergences were also evident, especially on the use of force. Bush did not conceal the ultimate threat of military action, whereas Gorbachev tried to distance himself from that option. Answering questions, he insisted convolutedly: 'I did not say that if Iraq does not withdraw peacefully we're going to have recourse to military methods. I did not state that. I do not state that. And moreover, in my view, that would draw us into consequences which we can't at this stage forecast.' Still, he had not rejected it categorically. The door was left marginally open.

He also responded acerbically to Bush's patronising comment: 'I think this remarkable cooperation that has been demonstrated by the Soviet Union at the United Nations gets me inclined to recommend as close cooperation in the economic field as possible'. Gorbachev shot back that it 'would be oversimplified and very superficial to judge that the Soviet Union could be bought for dollars'.[99]

This sharp exchange was revealing. In the last analysis, for Gorbachev the summit was a minor distraction. 'There is no great domestic pay-off for focusing on the crisis,' commented Maureen Dowd. 'The Soviet people are more interested in trying to buy bread and cigarettes' than in 'punishing' Saddam. The story was very different on the US side. With Americans facing a possible war, the way Bush handled the Gulf crisis would 'test his leadership' and 'help define his presidency'.[100] But even if the president was clearly in the ascendant, with a poll rating of 76%,[101] he was far from indifferent to Gorbachev's predicament. For the journalist R. W. Apple, the meeting 'underlined President Bush's determination to help his beleaguered Soviet friend to show himself a world statesman and his country a player on the world stage when everything is going so badly at home'. Apple spoke of it as possibly a 'sleeper summit' – one with greater significance than either leader yet discerned, perhaps marking 'the beginning of a common search for peace in the turbulent Middle East – a goal that has eluded world statesmen even longer than an end to the Cold War did'.[102]

Bush flew home from Helsinki in upbeat mood. Calling King Fahd, he was relieved to learn that the Arab reaction to the summit was positive.[103] For his part, Kohl was frankly effusive. 'It made an excellent impression. I spoke with Gorbachev yesterday on the telephone … He is very pleased.' Bush, too, expressed satisfaction. 'He came across with a stronger statement than we had anticipated. We got everything we wanted.'[104] All in all, Helsinki gave the president an ideal platform for his address to the Joint Session of Congress – with which he hoped to strengthen support for his approach in the Gulf and underscore what had been achieved at the summit.

In that speech on 11 September he began by reminding his listeners of the objectives he had earlier set out: 'Iraq must withdraw from Kuwait completely, immediately, and without condition. Kuwait's legitimate government must be restored. The security and stability of the Persian Gulf must be assured.' But he went on to depict the Gulf operation on a much wider canvas. 'Out of these troubled times,' he declared, 'a new world order can emerge ... an era in which the nations of the world, East and West, North and South, can prosper and live in harmony. A hundred generations have searched for this elusive path to peace, while a thousand wars raged across the span of human endeavour. Today that new world is struggling to be born, a world quite different from the one we've known. A world where the rule of law supplants the rule of the jungle. A world in which nations recognise the shared responsibility for freedom and justice. A world where the strong respect the rights of the weak. This is the vision that I shared with President Gorbachev in Helsinki.'

That September evening on Capitol Hill Bush revealed more fully than ever before his idea of a new international system. He faced what he judged to be a hinge moment in history. His address contained echoes – conscious or not – of the Fourteen Points speech in 1918, when Woodrow Wilson talked of a 'new world' based on 'the principle of justice to all peoples and nationalities, and their right to live on equal terms of liberty and safety with one another'. For Bush, his 'new world order' now seemed attainable because history appeared to be moving inexorably towards the dominance of democracy. But also because a multitude of nations – many of them bitter antagonists in the Cold War era – were now pulling in the same direction, above all the Soviet Union but also the People's Republic of China. This connected up his vision with that of another great Democratic president – Franklin Delano Roosevelt – who laboured all through the Second World War to bring the United Nations into being in 1945, only for it to be paralysed by the East–West conflict. With the Security Council now unlocked, the UN seemed at last to be coming into its own in 1990 – forty-five years after its inauguration. 'We're now in sight of a United Nations that performs as envisioned by its founders.' Bush painted a vivid picture of American soldiers 'serving together with Arabs, Europeans, Asians, and Africans in defence of principle and the dream of a new world order. That's why they sweat and toil in the sand and the heat and the sun.'[105]

The press response was enthusiastic. According to the *New York Times*, Bush had shown 'clear-eyed purpose' and had the 'right strategy' in what was 'perhaps the hardest-hitting and best-delivered speech' he had given since accepting his party's nomination over two years before. And in *US News and World Report* Mortimer B. Zuckerman stated 'George Bush has looked great so far. His leadership in establishing consensus was a major diplomatic triumph.' Most extravagant of all, on 24 September 1990 Bruce W. Nelan of *TIME* magazine declared 'No one, not even the president's most loyal supporters, would confuse a Bush speech and its delivery with a performance by Churchill. Last week, however, George Bush gave a speech – no, make that an oration – that riveted listeners and left absolutely no doubt he meant every word he uttered.'[106]

Bush himself had felt 'a charge of adrenalin' when addressing the Chamber. And at the end he was delighted by the warm reception of his words by the legislators who seemed to be cheering as much for him as for the troops in the desert. He now felt confident that there was broad support for his actions so far – though well aware that confrontation was brewing under the surface over whether to use force. Keen to secure political backing at every stage, Bush kept thinking about how President Lyndon B. Johnson had worked to garner a congressional vote of support over Vietnam in 1964. But, with LBJ again in mind, Bush also worried about the likely erosion of popular approval if the deterrent mission turned into overt military action and resulted in American casualties.[107]

Even at his most rhetorical, George H. W. Bush was no starry-eyed visionary. His 'new world order' was not totally new. He was talking of a world 'freer from the threat of terror, stronger in the pursuit of justice, and more secure in the quest for peace'. His was a conservative approach to global change and to crisis management. The president also had no doubt that, despite his talk of novel international cooperation, all depended – as in the Cold War – on the power and will of the United States. 'Recent events have surely proven that there is no substitute for American leadership.' But, he added, 'our ability to function effectively as a great power abroad depends on how we conduct ourselves at home ... This is never easy in democracies, for we govern only with the consent of the governed.' Acutely conscious that he was addressing a Democrat-controlled Congress, in which partisan animosities were intense, the president asked the lawmakers to remember those coalition soldiers in the desert sand. 'If they can come together under such adversity, if old adversaries like the Soviet Union and the United States can work in common cause, then surely we who are so fortunate to be in this great Chamber – Democrats, Republicans, liberals, conservatives – can come together to fulfil our responsibilities here.' What particularly concerned him was the still unresolved fiscal gridlock. 'To revitalise our leadership, our leadership capacity, we must address our budget deficit – not after election day, or next year, but now.'[108]

*

The Iraqi invasion of Kuwait, UN sanctions, Bush's deployments and the Helsinki summit had all generated new headlines, wiping domestic tax battles off America's front pages, but that issue had never gone away. Early in the summer the president had decided that, in order to tackle the budget deficit and get a deal, he would 'eat crow' if others did as well. He had been willing to backtrack on 'read my lips' but felt that, in return, Democrats would 'have to yield on some of their rhetoric on taxes and on entitlements'.[109] The government's fiscal year would end on 30 September – in three weeks – and without bipartisan agreement on a new budget, Bush would be obliged to shut down all non-essential federal offices. This was a truly humiliating situation: a president who was trying to wield a big stick abroad while his hands were tightly bound at home.

This contradiction was picked up by the US media. A *Newsweek* story suggested Bush was a 'bold world leader' but a 'modest domestic problem solver'. A veritable 'split personality' was detected by Paul A. Gigot of the *Wall Street Journal*: 'On foreign and domestic policy, Mr Bush can seem like two different men. The one is decisive and cool under pressure. The other is detached and quick to give in. Foreign Bush can be stubborn about China, deft toward Europe and Mikhail Gorbachev, gutsy in taking out Manuel Noriega. Domestic Bush trades his tax pledge for nothing.[110]

Despite all the plaudits about foreign policy, Bush's 11 September speech made no perceptible difference on the home front. Two weeks later the president noted in his diary, 'budget is getting down to the crunch'; he did not even know whether the Republicans would stay solid – because many did not forgive Bush for reneging on his 1988 campaign promise of 'no more taxes'. At the beginning of October the president had to shut down the federal government for several days. Indeed, on the 6th, having secured a budget compromise with congressional negotiators, the

Republican rank and file revolted and the deal was voted down. Bush noted that 'this week has been the most unpleasant, or tension-filled, of the presidency'. Other big decisions – such as going into Panama the year before or moving against Iraq in August – had been bipartisan. 'Here we are divided. There is name-calling, and accusations – and I don't like it.' Bush referred to a newspaper story claiming that he was 'more comfortable with foreign affairs' – an assertion about which he was not in the least apologetic. 'That is absolutely true. Because I don't like the deficiencies of the domestic, political scene. I hate the posturing on both sides ... putting their own selves ahead of the overall good ... It's the damnedest pounding I've ever seen, but I will just have to hang in there and do my best.' Bush rounded off his moan with a weary laugh: 'It's tough when you don't control the Congress ... If you want a friend in Washington, get a dog, and I sure have a good one.'[111]

The budget deadlock continued for much of October. 'I think this is the biggest challenge of my life – by far,' Bush exclaimed on the 17th.[112] A deal was finally hammered out on 25 October[113] and signed into law on 5 November – the day before the midterm elections. Congress agreed to raise taxes by more than $140 billion over the next five years, in the hope of reducing the federal deficit. The top rate of federal income tax was pushed up from 28% to 31% – another bitter pill for the president to swallow. And the eleventh-hour deal did Bush and his party no good with voters: the Republicans lost nine seats in the House and one in the Senate. The president's approval rating slumped to 57%. It was becoming clear that abandoning his 1988 pledge had been a real political misjudgement: it had sown confusion within his party, raised voter resentment and damaged the president's domestic credibility with a re-election campaign just two years away.[114]

For a few days Washington's infighting dominated the headlines almost completely. But on Friday 9 November press attention shifted once more after Bush announced his intention to send 150,000–200,000 additional ground, sea and air forces to the Persian Gulf, doubling the existing US troop presence and thereby providing 'an adequate offensive military option' to drive Iraqi troops from Kuwait. Immediately speculation was rife that this new build-up presaged the use of force. Defense Secretary Cheney added fuel to the flames by saying that the Pentagon no longer planned to rotate troops through Saudi Arabia and that both the forces in situ and those en route would serve for the duration of the crisis. Taken together, Bush's and Cheney's statements clearly signalled that Washington was upping the ante. The media considered that Bush now had only three choices left: keep Americans in the region indefinitely; feebly back down from his clear threat to use force; or bite the bullet and go to war.[115]

The president knew that playing it long was not an option. Inaction would soon sap troop morale and, in any case, the US embassy in Saudi Arabia had alerted him to looming time constraints. It warned that any fighting during March would be imprudent, because that was the month of Ramadan, when Muslims would be fasting. And assuming the USA would still be in build-up phase until early December, to reach adequate logistic and troop levels, the good-weather window would further limit the scope for military action to the months of January and February before the spring rains began. Regardless of this advice, Bush was now fired up for action by graphic stories of Iraqi atrocities. 'I've just read a horrible intelligence report on the brutal dismembering and dismantling of Kuwait,' he wrote in his diary on 22 September: 'Shooting citizens when they are stopped in their cars ... Brutalising the homes ... making an oasis into a wasteland.'[116] Reflecting later, Bush concluded that this was the point when 'I began to move from viewing Saddam's aggression exclusively as a dangerous strategic threat and an injustice to its reversal as a moral crusade.' In his deepening conviction of a struggle between good and evil, he felt strengthened by reading historian Martin Gilbert's study of the Second World War. 'I saw a direct analogy between what was occurring in Kuwait and what the Nazis had done, especially in Poland.' Seeing the Iraqi leader as another Hitler intensified Bush's determination: Saddam had become 'the epitome of evil'.[117]

As his own views hardened, the president was frustrated but not distracted by the attempted mediation efforts of some of his coalition partners. Historically, France had been Iraq's closest Western partner, and even after the crisis broke it tried to keep open lines of communication with Baghdad. What's more, Mitterrand wanted to avoid any commitment to restore the Kuwaiti royal family to power, envisaging a more democratic future for the emirate. But Bush believed that the US should not 'impose democracy on the Kuwaitis – rather it was something that should grow from within'.[118] Here was further evidence of Bush as a cautious manager in foreign policy. Unlike the hawks in his government, though toying with the idea, he was not hell-bent on wholesale regime change across the Middle East.

Bush could shrug off Paris's continued flirtation with the Arabs – the 'French are French' – but he did resent the way they seemed to be cosying up to the Kremlin and supporting Soviet peace overtures to Saddam. The president was seriously irritated by the Soviets. To be sure Shevardnadze seemed well disposed, affirming that 'if we are to speak of a new world order, US–Soviet relations will be the main support of that order.'[119] But over Iraq the foreign minister had become a marginal player because Gorbachev was using Primakov – behind Shevardnadze's back – as the main channel of Moscow's Middle Eastern policy. In a visit to Baghdad on 4–5 October, the Soviet envoy endeavoured to resurrect the Kremlin's former special relationship with Baghdad and offer concessions that would induce Saddam to leave Kuwait.[120] Bush, by contrast, was emphatic that Iraq had to make an unconditional withdrawal, without any sweeteners.

After talking with Mitterrand in Paris on the 29th,[121] Gorbachev blasted Saddam's 'adventurism' and warned him against gambling on a division of the multinational anti-Iraq coalition. At the same time, however, he declared publicly that it was 'unacceptable to have a military solution to this question'. He gave the impression of hoping against hope that Primakov's continued missions might bring about a diplomatic breakthrough. Mitterrand did not share that illusion and refrained from any public statement favouring a diplomatic rather than a military solution. Even more important for Washington, the French did not make a joint statement with Russia on the issue of Kuwait. Instead Mitterrand said it was essential to preserve the 'cohesion' of the international community and maintain the embargo of Iraq for as long as necessary. 'That doesn't mean that we do not prefer peace to armed conflict,' he went on. 'But peace is subject to law, and peace should be based on law.' In his own somewhat contorted way, Mitterrand had aligned himself with Bush.[122]

Yet, among Bush's major coalition partners, only Thatcher was ready to countenance early military action. 'The Brits are strong,' Bush noted in his diary. Indeed, he found Thatcher positively 'impatient' for military action. She deemed the existing UN resolutions sufficient to strike (under United Nations Charter Article 51) and, unlike Bush and especially Baker – who saw distinct political advantages to having a further UN resolution that would spell out the right to go to war – Thatcher had little interest in waiting for another Iraqi provocation that might serve as a pretext. She had warned Bush a few weeks earlier that this was not the time 'to go wobbly'. In her mind, going back to the UN meant risking amendments: 'I don't think we need an extra reason to go.'[123]

The White House did not, however, agree with her. Bush and Baker were mindful of the international stereotype of 'America's cowboy mentality' – recently reinforced by Reagan's 1983 intervention in Grenada and Bush's invasion of Panama in 1989. Doing it alone was diplomatically unwise as well as militarily imprudent.[124] To further prepare international and domestic opinion, on 29 October Baker delivered a major address to the Los Angeles World Affairs Council. He underscored America's resolve to end this 'story of barbarism in its most crude and evil form' and put Saddam on notice. 'Let no one doubt: we will not rule out a possible use of force if Iraq continues to occupy Kuwait.'[125]

Baker had initially been more cautious than Bush about using force but there was no stark difference of policy. The issue was more one of timing. While the president was always firmer in his willingness to confront Saddam militarily, until mid-October Baker had emphasised the need for patience. But by the time of his LA speech the Secretary of State had come round to the president's view, because Saddam remained utterly unrepentant and his troops were systematically destroying Kuwait. In a note to himself on the back of an envelope, Baker scribbled: 'New world order – have to be principled & stand up to aggression. Don't make same mistake as in 30s; *nor* same as in Vietnam – uncertain, tentative, etc. – if we go in we have to have *massive* force. At the same time we should go to the Congress and the UN to ask their support for possible use of force.'[126]

Baker agreed with Powell that the existing policy was 'drifting'. In which case, it was important to 'get ahead of [the] erosion of support'. The United States had to secure UN backing and not lose a UN Security Council vote. It was a fortunate coincidence that the US would hold the presidency of the Council (which rotates monthly) in November, before that position passed to Yemen – an Iraqi ally – in December, followed by Zaire and then Zimbabwe. In other words the diplomatic timetable was driven by the 'simple, unyielding reality', as Baker put it, that the best time to hold the vote on the use of force would be before the end of the month.[127]

The White House therefore turned to selling the idea of the 'offensive option'[128] abroad and securing UN authorisation to resolve the Kuwait crisis by military means as a prerequisite to war. As America's salesman-in-chief, Baker would spend eighteen days in twelve countries across three continents. On 3 November he set out for the Middle East and Europe. Officially the trip was to 'consult with our coalition partners about the general situation in the Gulf', but it was no secret among the

Washington press corps that the underlying goal was to 'assess the allies' feelings on when, how or whether to use force'.

During his travels Baker talked personally with all his Security Council colleagues in what he called 'an intricate process of cajoling, extracting, threatening and occasionally buying votes'. Such, he noted drily, 'are the politics of diplomacy'. He also met most members of the military coalition seeking three critical assurances in the event of war:

1. all combat operations would be under the firm control of US commanders;
2. they would not object to bombing Iraq;
3. they would remain with the US if Israel retaliated against a preceding attack by Iraq.[129]

Money talks: Baker with Saudi King Fahd during the Gulf crisis

Arab backing proved solid – with Fahd's Saudi Arabia particularly eager to hit Saddam and to do so sooner rather than later.[130] On the way from the Middle East to Moscow, Baker met – in the airport lounge in Cairo on 6 November – Chinese foreign minister Qian Qichen, himself en route to see Saddam.[131] Baker tried to convince Qian of the benefits of a use-of-force resolution. 'The best thing you can do to help a peaceful solution of this crisis is to tell Saddam that China will support this resolution.' But Qian was non-committal. He believed that sanctions were starting to bite and that talk of force was premature. War would alter the power balance in the Gulf and that, in the eyes of Beijing, had to be averted at all costs.

His line, said Baker, was that 'so long as there is a ray of hope for peace, China will do its best to strive for a peaceful settlement'.[132]

Underpinning Qian's views was the assumption that America was not acting out of principle but was pursuing the 'hegemonistic' goal of controlling Gulf oil resources. As part of its efforts at international rehabilitation after the Tiananmen massacre, the PRC leadership wanted China to play a higher-profile role among the five permanent members of the Security Council, while also representing itself as the Third World advocate of smaller Middle Eastern states. And, if it helped facilitate a peaceful outcome in the Gulf, this might strengthen Chinese pressure on the USA and the EC to lift post-Tiananmen sanctions.[133]

Despite all this, Qian recognised that a force resolution might offer a useful diplomatic lever for China. He sought to link Chinese support to an American pledge that Bush would visit the PRC, which the president had not done since February 1989. But Baker was having none of this. During their airport meeting, he made clear that neither such linkage nor a visit were acceptable to the USA. In fact, he reminded Qian that China was beholden to Bush for his non-response to Tiananmen and for keeping open the Scowcroft backchannel despite international sanctions. Baker rammed home that, if the PRC vetoed a use-of-force resolution at the UN, this would be disastrous for Sino-American relations: 'we don't hold it against our friends that they are not joining us ... But we *do* ask that they do not stand in the way.' Qian did not respond, but Baker flew on from Cairo in buoyant mood. He cabled the president 'I do not think we need a visit by me to obtain their support or acquiescence on the UN resolution.'[134]

Baker's odyssey took him on to the Kremlin, where on 8 November he spent four hours with Shevardnadze and two more with Gorbachev. The Secretary of State found Shevardnadze 'not enthusiastic' about military action but inclined to recognise that it 'would have to be used eventually'. The Soviet leader, however, was much more resistant. He observed to Baker that 'we want this era to be different from the Cold War and based on different kinds of norms'. Overall, Baker informed Bush, 'my own sense is that in the end they will go along with us' but 'he didn't want to be pushed into making a decision today'. Gorbachev promised to give the president an answer in eleven days, when they would meet in person at the CSCE summit in Paris.[135]

On 9 November – the first anniversary of the fall of the Wall – Baker flew to London where he found Thatcher increasingly out of step with

US policy. Again she expressed scepticism about needing the UN resolution, warning that setting a future date to begin combat operations
made an Iraqi chemical attack more likely. She also complained that
having to square minor states on the Security Council would constrain
the coalition's freedom of manoeuvre. And when Baker asked her for the
deployment of a full armoured division, on top of the land, naval and
air power already committed, the prime minister hesitated and her
Foreign Secretary Douglas Hurd 'winced visibly'. Thatcher explained that
Britain would need significant lift from the Americans in order to move
manpower and hardware to the Gulf, while warning that the extra deployments would leave Germany 'denuded' because few of the troops would
return there.[136]

Flying on to Paris, Baker was relieved to find that, unlike Thatcher,
Mitterrand's position on the next phase in the Gulf was 'remarkably
similar, indeed almost identical, to our own'. The French were primed
for war, and shared the American view that the UN Charter by itself was
insufficient to justify an attack. Furthermore, in his report to Bush, Baker
alluded to the French president's 'earlier-stated preference for an Arab
or Arab–Western committee to determine Kuwait's future government
(he clearly finds that lifestyle of the Gulf Arabs distasteful)'. But Baker
now found that this idea of regime change had been dropped. On the
question of troops, Mitterrand was clearly 'reluctant to discuss force
augmentation beyond their existing 6,000 men plus air and naval forces'.
So Baker merely transmitted an American request for one or two additional French divisions, believing that the French response would be
affirmative in due course, and told Mitterrand that he believed Bush
would be 'extraordinarily pleased' by Paris's support for a new UN resolution. Mindful of France's reputation as Europe's awkward customer,
Mitterrand replied that his country would certainly be doing more than
'some of your best friends' – explicitly mentioning Germany, Japan and
Italy.[137]

Baker returned home confident that the USA should be able to count
on the support of at least nine countries on the fifteen-member UN
Security Council. Further details were tied down by Bush on the margins
of the Paris CSCE on 19 November. At a breakfast meeting Thatcher told
him that she would indeed deploy a full British armoured division
(augmenting the existing single armoured brigade with a second, together
with support troops). Also valuable was Baker's meeting with Shevardnadze, when they agreed the language of a UN resolution text that the

USSR would be able to endorse. 'But we don't want to say this publicly,' Shevardnadze insisted. 'We want to talk to the Iraqis one more time.' And in Paris Gorbachev finally gave Bush his long-awaited answer. 'After comprehensive thinking and analysis, we came to the conclusion that we should agree to the passing of a UN Security Council resolution.'[138]

For both superpower leaders, this agreement was not just about the Gulf but had wider implications. 'Our two countries were opponents, but today we are working together,' Bush reflected. 'Thinking about how we want to build our relationship in the future, I believe that your support would serve as strong proof of our partnership. This is why I am asking you to help me. And not even me so much – who knows, in two years, somebody else could become president. I am asking you to help do what is just.' Gorbachev was responsive. 'If we do not prove now that we are capable, at this new stage of global development, of dealing with this kind of problem, it would mean that what we started does not mean all that much.' Therefore, 'we must find a solution to this problem'. He, too, wanted the Gulf conflict to be managed internationally through the United Nations – a forum, of course, in which the Kremlin had veto power. And he wanted the two superpowers to do this together. 'I have thought it all over,' he told Bush. 'This moment is exceptionally important not just for both of us, but also for everything that we started to do in the world.'[139]

Both Bush and Gorbachev also thought in terms of triangular power politics. While in Paris, Baker had gleaned from another phone conversation with Qian in Beijing that the Chinese were playing hardball. The foreign minister was unready to commit to a public statement that China would not veto the upcoming UN resolution on Iraq. As in Cairo he continued to insist on a US presidential visit as a condition for China not using its veto power. 'This wasn't our deal,' Baker crisply reminded him. But on the 19th, as an inducement, he invited Qian to Washington on 30 November, the day after the pivotal UN Security Council session in New York. Playing what he called his 'best chip', he said that the president would be leaving for Latin America the following day. Qian accepted the invitation, possibly believing he would get to meet Bush.[140]

Still uncertain about China, during their Paris meeting Gorbachev and Bush speculated about whether the PRC would eventually follow their lead. The president was optimistic. 'You know that we have problems with the Chinese,' he told Gorbachev, 'but we start from the assumption that the Chinese do not want to be in isolation.' Gorbachev suggested

America should lift the post-Tiananmen sanctions against the PRC. Bush agreed in principle, but pointed to 'legal' obstacles he was facing at home in 'our crazy system'. He had even been obliged to veto congressional resolutions directed against China. By the way, he added, 'if you are talking with the Chinese, tell them that our administration is persistently trying to normalise relations. Cooperation in the UN framework will allow us to do even more in this direction.' [141]

Multilateralism over the Gulf also offered the USA an opportunity to deal with Beijing on issues of mutual interest within a larger, less controversial context. This would help defuse probable domestic and international criticism when memories of 4 June 1989 were raw. At the same time, the administration made it plain that any Chinese opposition to the UN resolution would come at a price. In general, the Americans knew they could exploit the need of the Soviets, Chinese and others for good relations with the USA to ensure at least acquiescence over Kuwait. 'People want to stay close to us,' Baker said later. Beijing itself kept agitating for the Qian audience with Bush in Washington and for continuance of its 'most favoured nation' status.[142] But, as Bush had told Deng earlier in the autumn, 'more needs to be done on the Chinese side before I can guarantee a general improvement in our relations'.[143] In fact in the hostile post-Square climate Beijing's privileged trading status (annually renewed since 1980) was being sharply debated in Congress with renewal through 1991, as recommended by Bush, now very much in the balance.[144] And Bush was sure that 'MFN could fall apart if [China's] Iraq support erodes'.[145]

Nearing the crucial UN vote, Bush thought he had a deal: Chinese support at the UN in return for American trade concessions. But in the end this proved too optimistic. On 29 November UN Security Council Resolution 678 was passed by twelve votes to two, with China abstaining. This authorised 'all member states cooperating with the government of Kuwait' to use 'all necessary means' to evict Iraq from Kuwait if Iraq did not withdraw by 15 January 1991. 'The deadline', as Scowcroft noted, 'was set.' By giving Iraq 'respite of 47 days', the Security Council was offering what it called 'a pause of goodwill' – and this would be exploited by some of America's partners – but the historical magnitude of the resolution could not be missed. This was the first time since the Korean War began in 1950 that the United Nations had invoked its power to sanction the use of force in order to counter aggression by a member nation.[146] Baker had given an impassioned opening speech as chairman of the Security

Council session, reminding a packed chamber of the fatal failure of the international community in the 1930s to meet force with force. 'History has given us another chance,' he said. 'We must not let the United Nations go the way of the League of Nations.'[147]

Pin-stripe diplomacy: Saddam sits tight

With regard to China, Baker was enraged that Washington had been denied the full weight of global opinion which Bush desired, and wanted to cancel at the last minute Qian's visit to Washington. But the president was more philosophical: 'We do not need an international crisis in the wake of our UN success.'[148] Reminding his staff that an abstention was not a veto, the president felt that Beijing had done just about enough. The United States had managed to avoid any humiliation. And Bush also thought that granting the PRC foreign minister his coveted presidential meeting would boost the chance of future Chinese support if further resolutions on Iraq proved necessary.

Qian duly paid a courtesy call on Bush on 30 November. The White House stated that their meeting represented 'the highest official contact' between the two governments since June 1989. Facing congressional criticism that this was 'precisely the wrong message' to send, the president stressed that Beijing knew that 'we have some differences on this whole broad question of human rights'. But he also made much of the two governments' similar moral position over Iraq: 'China and the United

States have made common ground in terms of standing up against aggression.'[149]

In sum, Bush believed that his cautious China diplomacy since June 1989, however offensive to human-rights enthusiasts, had eventually paid unexpected dividends. Eighteen months before, the president had faced a furious Congress and global outrage after his relatively mild reactions to Tiananmen. US Ambassador Lilley remembered 'the terrible savaging' Bush had endured in 1989 but felt that now, 'when it came to collect the fee for that', the president was able to get his money's worth.'[150]

*

By late 1990, therefore, reversing Iraqi aggression had become the crucial test case for establishing a secure and just post-Cold War order. And, in the process, to project unquestionable American leadership and power. 'We cannot restore the status quo ante' in the Gulf, the State Department asserted: this had revolved around the regional power of Iraq. After Kuwait a new 'post-crisis security architecture' would have to be 'reinforced from the outside' and US military support for the Gulf states should be 'the cornerstone on which the other parts of the structure rest'.[151]

With Washington envisaging a long-term US commitment to the region, this made a military resolution to the present crisis more attractive. Even if their intention was not regime change – in other words to go after Saddam – it was expected that the multinational coalition would inflict devastating damage on the Iraqi military. This, it was hoped, would lead to the neutralisation of the Iraqi despot, if not his actual demise. As Bush had said only four days after the invasion of Kuwait, 'All will not be tranquil until Saddam Hussein is history'.[152]

And so, after the passage of UN Resolution 678, the administration did not want any further discussion of a negotiated settlement. The consequence, it feared, would simply be a 'diplomatic circus' in which a mixed bag of 'would-be mediators, peace advocates and serious diplomats' would be endlessly 'shuttling back and forth to Baghdad'.[153] And playing it long in this way would allow the Iraqis more time and opportunity for 'attempts to weaken the international coalition'.[154] A particular concern, given the importance of Arab solidarity with the USA, was that Saddam might draw Israel into conflict. The Americans had heard via the Soviets that 'if war begins' Iraq would 'attack Israel'.[155] Bush feared that if the

Israelis then retaliated, the Arab nations might abandon the coalition. The president told his Israeli counterpart Itzhak Shamir bluntly on 11 December that a 'pre-emptive strike by Israel would be very bad': fighting must be left to the coalition. 'If he attacks you, or if an attack becomes apparent, we have the capability to obliterate his military structure.' The president emphasised, however, that America had no intention of sacrificing Israel's vital interests: 'We have a beautifully planned operation, calculated to demoralise him forever.'[156]

Bush's Soviet partnership was also under strain. Gorbachev persisted in using Primakov to explore peace initiatives – in defiance of American preferences. And this bid for a more independent Soviet foreign policy also deepened the Soviet leader's rift with Shevardnadze who felt increasingly undermined. Differences over handling the Persian Gulf crisis were the immediate trigger for the foreign minister's sudden resignation just before Christmas, but he was also concerned about Gorbachev's growing reliance on communist hardliners in the hope of stabilising the domestic situation. This was deteriorating rapidly because of a collapsing economy and growing separatism, particularly in the Baltic and the Caucasus. Gorbachev's lurch to the right was dramatically illustrated by his autumn decision to set up an inner Cabinet of ministers, which included the defence minister Dmitry Yazov, KGB head Vladimir Kryuchkov and the new interior minister Boris Pugo. While courting these leading communist-conservative critics, Gorbachev quietly sidelined prominent reformers within his entourage. It was in this context that Shevardnadze dropped his political bombshell on 20 December: 'A dictatorship is on the way ... Nobody knows what kind of dictatorship it will be, who will come to power, what kind of dictator or what kind of order will be installed ... I am going into retirement ... Let this be my protest against the coming of dictatorship.'[157]

For weeks Washington had been closely monitoring what NSC aide Condoleezza Rice called the 'creeping crackdown' in the USSR. But it was particularly alarmed by Shevardnadze's abrupt departure. Scowcroft felt 'shocked and concerned' at the news; Bush wondered 'what it might mean for the crisis, the coalition, and the superpower relationship as a whole'.[158]

In any case, none of this changed the fact that the Kremlin had never intended to contribute any troops to Desert Shield. By the New Year the Soviet leadership had also informed the Americans that they would no longer provide transport to the Gulf for British helicopters. And on the

US side, there was, after the UN vote on 29 November, never any genuine consultation with Gorbachev about the course of action in the Gulf. Whatever the rhetoric about Soviet–American 'partnership', Washington talked mainly to its key NATO allies and to Saudi Arabia about the conduct of the war. Although Bush's new world order was designed around two pillars – the USA and the USSR – there were worrying signs that the Soviet pillar was starting to crumble.[159]

So the president now concentrated on achieving a military solution to the crisis – on US terms. In his eyes, any compromise would be equivalent to failure. 'We will prevail', he wrote in his diary on 28 November. 'Saddam Hussein will get out of Kuwait, and the United States will have been the catalyst and the key in getting this done, and that is important. Our role as world leader will once again have been reaffirmed.'[160] By the beginning of 1991 there would be in the Gulf some 415,000 US troops along with almost 120,000 motor vehicles, 12,000 tanks, and 520,000 tons of ammunition and supplies. With 108 navy vessels including six aircraft carriers and two battleships offshore and the region's largest air force based in Saudi Arabia (1,350 US warplanes and 1,700 helicopters), this American force was an amazing piece of power projection, both in size and in rapidity of deployment. Overall the international coalition comprised 680,000 troops – 45,000 from Britain, 10,000 from France, 35,000 from Egypt, Syria (20,000), Pakistan (10,000) and Kuwait (7,000), with several hundred warplanes and some twenty ships from other coalition members. They were pitted against an estimated 545,000 Iraqi troops dug into Kuwait and southern Iraq.[161]

In preparing for this conflict, Bush thoroughly absorbed what were deemed to be the lessons of America's last war. Vietnam still haunted the American imagination, both at the public level and in military circles. General Colin Powell, chairman of the Joint Chiefs of Staff, was – as Richard Haass put it – 'a reluctant warrior' having been scarred by his formative years fighting in Indochina. Later, in the 1980s, he served as military assistant to Reagan's defence secretary Caspar Weinberger. What was variously called the 'Powell Doctrine' or 'Weinberger Plus' stipulated that you must define the mission and then apply overwhelming force to carry it out. The aim was to rely on America's massive firepower and technological superiority to keep US casualties low. Powell advocated a long air campaign to degrade and demoralise the opposition forces before confronting them on the battlefield. Following that, a combination of air support and ground mobility would be deployed to overwhelm Saddam's troops. The war that Bush and Powell prepared to unleash in 1991 would not be a series of grinding attritional battles but a rapid blitzkrieg-style campaign with every effort made to minimise the American body count.[162]

Yet it was one thing to plan war on paper, much harder to persuade Congress and the American public – especially after Bush's budget fiasco on Capitol Hill. As soon as the creation of an offensive capability had been announced, congressional opposition stiffened. Having two months earlier sold – with considerable optimism – the sanctions package and blockade as the most devastating embargo in history which would coerce Saddam to withdraw, Bush now offered the alarming prospect of having to expend American lives in real combat. This appeared to many as an unacceptable reversal of policy. Four polls conducted between mid-August and November 1990 showed that the public was divided on the merits of going to war: 47% were in favour, and 43% were not, with 10% undecided. Yet after the passage of Security Council Resolution 678 on 29 November, effectively authorising the use of force, public opinion swung back to 53% in favour of war and 40% against.[163]

Conscious that ordinary Americans were deeply conflicted about the issue, Bush kept his eyes on both audiences – particularly evident in a dramatic statement to the press on 30 November. On the one hand he set out the case for war in ringing tones. 'We're in the Gulf because the world must not and cannot reward aggression. And we're there because our vital interests are at stake. And we're in the Gulf because of the brutality of Saddam Hussein. We're dealing with a dangerous dictator all too willing to use force who has weapons of mass destruction and is seeking new ones and who desires to control one of the world's key resources – all at a time in history when the rules of the post-Cold War world are being written ... And there's never been a clearer demonstration of a world united against appeasement and aggression.'

Bush told the press: 'I remain hopeful that we can achieve a peaceful solution to this crisis. But if force is required, we and the other twenty-six countries who have troops in the area will have enough power to get the job done.' He also countered those who raised the spectre of 'another' Vietnam. 'This will not be a protracted, drawn-out war. The forces arrayed are different. The opposition is different. The resupply of Saddam's military would be very different. The countries united against him in the United Nations are different. The topography of Kuwait is different ... We will not permit our troops to have their hands tied behind their backs.'

But after what seemed like a clarion call for war, Bush adroitly changed tack. Insisting that, even at this eleventh hour, 'I want peace, not war' he said that he was ready to 'go the extra mile for peace'. To this end he invited the Iraqi foreign minister Tariq Aziz to Washington and said he would send Baker to Baghdad for a 'last chance' meeting with Saddam. Prince Bandar, the Saudi ambassador in Washington, thought this idea was utterly crazy. 'To you,' he told Scowcroft, 'sending Baker is goodwill; to Saddam it suggests you're chicken.' Scowcroft said it had been a last-minute decision: the president felt he had to show Congress and the American public that he was exhausting every diplomatic avenue before choosing war. And Bush was proved right. A *Washington Post* poll showed that 90% of Americans approved of sending Baker to Baghdad. But the Pentagon was dismissive, as were Haass and Scowcroft of the NSC. Like Prince Bandar, they considered talks with Aziz 'a bad idea, since it looked as though we were searching to give Saddam a way out short of full compliance with the UN resolutions'. Worse still, it looked like 'we were blinking'.[164]

In spite of Bush's attempts at reassurance, another opinion poll on 2 December found that two-fifths of Americans thought it 'somewhat' or 'very likely' that war against Iraq would become a quagmire like Vietnam.[165] Many congressional Democrats and former military accused Bush of a rush to war that might cause thousands of casualties. Robert McNamara, who had been Secretary of State for Defense during the Vietnam War, predicted at least 30,000 casualties, while former senator George McGovern talked of up to 50,000 American deaths, painting a grisly picture of thousands of dismembered bodies.[166] At the other end of the spectrum, the Brookings Institution was notably less alarmist, predicting – with spurious precision – 'between 1,049 and 4,136 US fatalities after fifteen to twenty-one days of intense combat'. Even this smaller number spooked many influential figures, especially on Capitol Hill. Here several leading Democrats, stressing that the public was 'very, very strongly' opposed to casualties, increasingly pushed for a technowar air campaign of the sort Nixon had used in Cambodia. As a nation 'our reaction to wars is surprisingly consistent', Richard Morin of the *Washington Post* had aptly observed early in the crisis. 'Of all the complex variables governing public opinion, the single overwhelming fact is the casualty total.' [167]

Fuelling the public debate, Democrat Sam Nunn, chairman of the Senate Armed Services Committee, held televised hearings on Iraq. A parade of former defence VIPs testified that sanctions alone could succeed in forcing Saddam out of Kuwait. 'The issue is not whether an embargo will work but whether we have the patience to let it work,' said Admiral William J. Crowe Jr, Powell's immediate predecessor as chairman of the Joint Chiefs of Staff (JCS). 'In my judgement,' he added, 'we are selling our country short by jumping to the conclusion that we can't stare down our opponent.' General David Jones, JCS chair in 1978–82, worried that the troop build-up would drive policy, causing the US to go to war prematurely in the manner of Europe in 1914. On the other hand, former Secretary of State Henry Kissinger favoured moving steadily towards war: he warned that the international coalition would erode as time passed. As the debate on the Hill dragged on, most Democrats coalesced around the continuance of sanctions, while most Republicans supported allowing the president discretion to go to war if he deemed it necessary.[168]

Over the Christmas period, commentators drew breath, taking the opportunity to reflect on Bush's capacities as a leader. In the *New York Times*, R. W. Apple depicted a presidency 'poised between success and failure' in what was going to be 'a make-or-break year'. If the Middle East crisis turned into either 'a bloodbath' or 'a prolonged stalemate', Apple predicted it could 'prove as damaging to him as Vietnam proved to Lyndon B. Johnson'. Like LBJ, Bush could find it 'devilishly hard' to deliver the two things that 'matter most to the American electorate – peace and prosperity'.[169] Unpicking this duality, other pundits again noted the contrast between Bush abroad and at home. Indeed *TIME* magazine's ultimate accolade of 'Man of the Year' was conferred on 7 January 1991 in a remarkably double-edged way. It depicted on its cover an amiable but two-headed George H. W. Bush, who 'seemed like two presidents' during 1990: 'one displayed a commanding vision of the new world order; the other showed little vision for his own country'. Inside, one article talked of how on 1 August the president had promptly risen to the challenge of Saddam's invasion of Kuwait: 'This was the moment for which he had spent a lifetime preparing, the epochal event that would bear out his campaign slogan, "Ready to be a great President from Day 1"'. But, whereas Bush's foreign policy, *TIME* asserted, was 'a study in resoluteness and mastery', his 'domestic visage' was 'just as strongly masked by wavering and confusion'. The central element of the magazine's indictment was his 'flipping and flopping' during the October budget crisis, 'like a beached bluefish'.[170]

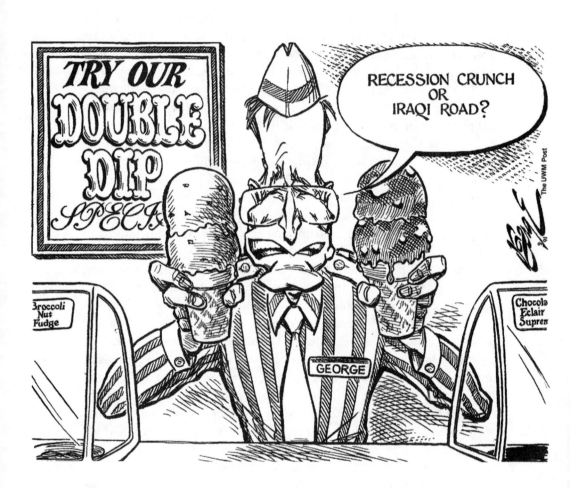

On 3 January 1991, the 102nd Congress convened. Judging that the mood on Capitol Hill was beginning to harden, the president decided to request its formal authorisation to employ force. His letter of 8 January was, however, crafted to avoid any suggestion that he was constitutionally required to obtain congressional approval. Instead, he asked legislators to 'adopt a Resolution stating that Congress supports the use of all necessary means to implement UN Security Council Resolution 678'. Such action, he said, 'would send the clearest possible message to Saddam Hussein that he must withdraw without condition or delay from Kuwait. Anything less would only encourage Iraqi intransigence; anything else would risk detracting from the international coalition arrayed against Iraq's aggression'. The letter itself made history, being the first such request by a president since the 1964 Gulf of Tonkin Resolution that had authorised the use of force in Vietnam.[171]

While the House and Senate debated his request, attention shifted to Geneva where on 9 January Baker finally met with Aziz, as the president had previously promised. The Secretary of State handed his Iraqi coun- terpart a sealed letter from Bush to Saddam. After reading a photocopy, Aziz said he would not take it to his leader, complaining that Bush had not used 'polite language'. Pushing the envelope into the middle of the table, he declared 'We accept war.' The letter, which Bush subsequently released, reiterated his demand that Saddam withdraw his forces from Kuwait and contained little that was new. But Aziz's rejection of the letter was taken to symbolise Iraq's unyielding stance and helped influence the debate on Capitol Hill. 'He stiffed us,' said Congressman John Murtha – a Democrat from Pennsylvania.[172]

At the same time there was unsettling news for the president from the Soviet Union. The Baltic republic of Lithuania was now determined to implement its independence declaration put on hold in 1990. Gorbachev visited the capital Vilnius on 10 January 1991 and demanded that Lithuania's leaders must restore the Soviet constitution. When they failed to comply, Soviet military units seized key government buildings and the TV tower on 12–13 January. More than a dozen civilians were killed – shot or crushed by tanks. There were cries of outrage in the West, not least in Congress, but Bush tried to play down the whole thing. He said he deplored this 'great tragedy' but avoided reprimanding Gorbachev publicly or even privately, merely telling the Soviet leader over the phone 'I really empathise with you this week

… We are so hopeful that the Baltic situation can be resolved peacefully. It would really complicate things.' The president was acutely conscious that if he made an issue of this matter it would threaten coalition unity in the run-up to war against Iraq. But the events in Lithuania were disconcerting: the EC openly condemned the attack and threatened to suspend $1 billion in economic aid to Moscow. Even though Gorbachev denied ordering the crackdown, Bush noted 'we could not help thinking that this was just what Shevardnadze had been predicting when he resigned three weeks earlier. It appeared that Gorbachev was losing control.'[173]

The impassioned debate on Capitol Hill concluded on 12 January with the passage of identical resolutions authorising Bush to 'use United States armed forces' to end Iraq's 'illegal occupation of, and brutal aggression against, Kuwait'. The Senate voted 52–47 in favour and the House 250–183 – largely along partisan lines. An alliance of Republicans, north-eastern liberals and conservative Democrats gave Bush his victory – albeit very narrowly in the upper house.[174]

Bush had followed the debate anxiously. 'Congress is in a turmoil, and I am more determined than ever to do what I have to do,' he wrote in his diary a few days earlier. But the president never intended the vote to sway him from his chosen course. 'If they are not going to bite the bullet, I am. They can file impeachment papers if they want to.' The possibility of being impeached weighed heavily on his mind, materialising in his diary five times between 12 December 1990 and 13 January 1991. Looking back, he said that 'even had Congress not passed the resolutions I would have acted and ordered our troops into combat. I know it would have caused an outcry but it was the right thing to do. I was comfortable in my own mind that I had the constitutional authority. It had to be done.'[175]

On 15 January, the day the UN deadline to Saddam ran out, the president made public National Security Directive 54, which mapped out his war aims to effect the unconditional withdrawal of Iraqi forces from Kuwait and ensure the security of Saudi Arabia and the Persian Gulf region. The military mission included destroying 'Iraq's chemical, biological, and nuclear capabilities' and its 'command, control, and communications' as well as eliminating the Republican Guard – the elite core of Saddam's armed forces. The die had been cast.[176]

At 9 p.m. on 16 January, the president spoke from the Oval Office, informing the nation and the world that Operation Desert Shield had now become Operation Desert Storm. 'Tonight, the battle has been joined ... As I report to you, air attacks are under way against military targets in Iraq.' Reprising the story of the previous half-year and reiterating yet again his case for war, Bush declared: 'This is an historic moment. We have in this past year made great progress in ending the long era of conflict and Cold War. We have before us the opportunity to forge for ourselves and for future generations a new world order – a world where the rule of law, not the law of the jungle, governs the conduct of nations. When we are successful – and we will be – we have a real chance at this new world order, an order in which a credible United Nations can use its peacekeeping role to fulfil the promise and vision of the UN's founders.' One of those contributing to the speech, Richard Haass, consciously had in mind President Harry Truman's address in July 1950 about why the United States had to resist aggression in another 'small country, thousands of miles away' at the height of the Cold War – South Korea.[177]

Bush's audience was huge. Indulging in some purple prose, one journalist tried to evoke this 'one long moment' across the whole nation. 'In split-level suburban homes on the East Coast where dinner was in the oven, in big-city restaurants in the Midwest where bars were jammed with the happy-hour crowd, and in the skyscraper offices on the West Coast where people were still at work, there was an odd mixture of apprehension, sadness and relief.' The reaction among military personnel was very different. Halfway around the world on an airbase in Saudi Arabia, a forty-four-year-old US colonel called the first airstrikes 'absolutely awesome. I mean the ground shook and you felt it ... We've been waiting here for five months; now we finally got to do what we were sent here to do. This is history in the making.'[178]

*

As the president spoke, waves of fighters, bombers and missiles had already been blasting strategic targets throughout Iraq for several hours. The military campaign had begun with a night of massive air strikes at targets deep in Iraq and Kuwait – inflicting grave damage at no cost to the Americans. The first onslaught included Tomahawk sea-launched cruise missiles and F-117 Stealth fighter bombers as well as a variety of other air force and navy hardware. The US warplanes were accompanied by British, Saudi and Kuwaiti combat aircraft. The aim was to damage Iraqi command and control centres, including those in Baghdad, and to establish air superiority by knocking out Iraqi air defences, airfields and Scud missile batteries and also destroying nuclear and chemical weapons production sites. The following morning General Colin Powell told a Pentagon news conference that there had been 'no air resistance'.[179]

On day two, however, Saddam struck back with Scud missile attacks against Saudi Arabia and Israel. These threatened to seriously complicate Washington's coalition strategy. But Baker persuaded the Israelis not to retaliate lest Saddam exploit that to turn the Gulf War into another Arab–Israeli conflict. US fighter bombers mounted retaliatory raids on the Iraqi Scud sites and Washington installed and manned Patriot anti-missile batteries in Israel to provide protection. This was the first time that Americans had been deployed in Israel to help defend that country. It was reported on 21 January that US and Israeli leaders had 'spoken as much in the last three days as in two years'.[180]

Virtually impotent in the air,[181] Saddam resorted to a scorched-earth policy on the ground. On 22 January his troops started to set Kuwait's oil installations ablaze. Thick black smoke poured into the sky, conjuring up images of Dante's *Inferno*, but once again the Iraqi threat was more apparent than real. The smoke and dust did not prevent Allied high-tech surveillance or the computer-guided precision bombing campaign, which went on relentlessly night and day for all six weeks of the conflict. By mid-February USAF staff claimed that they had destroyed 30% of Iraq's tanks and armoured vehicles and over 40% of artillery pieces, while reducing Iraqi front-line units to about half-strength.[182]

In Washington the air war quickly settled into a rhythm. There were daily Pentagon and CIA reports, full of estimates about what the bombing had accomplished. The president spoke publicly several times a week – helping to prepare for the transition from air campaign to ground warfare. There was also a plethora of statements to buttress coalition cohesion and domestic support.

The war and the diner: Cheney and Powell brief America

In terms of media management, none of this was particularly novel. But the media war itself was truly something different: a 24/7 barrage of news around the clock, with live footage in the ever-networked world. It was the first real-time war – with a speech by Saddam Hussein, a briefing in Washington, or even a Scud vs Patriot missile duel over Saudi Arabia visible for all to see. Yet the images and their interpretation were in fact tightly controlled by the Pentagon and the coalition command, headed by General Norman Schwarzkopf. 'Once actual fighting begins,'

Haass observed, 'the military takes the lead, and civilians in the government properly tend to take a back seat except when significant matters of policy arise.'[183]

Yet they did arise. Bush could never relax. The French did not participate in the initial bombing campaign on targets inside Iraq. Its defence minister made a point of saying that France would engage in hostilities only within Kuwait itself – as a way to show off his country's independence in world affairs.[184] Even worse in Bush's view, the Soviets were still rocking the boat. On 18 January, Gorbachev phoned Mitterrand to propose a joint political initiative. Then he spoke to Kohl – knowing that Genscher had supported several peace initiatives and that the German public was split over the Iraq War. The chancellor was not deflected, however, and pledged up to $6.7 billion towards the expenses of the US forces and a further $4.3 billion for those of other coalition states. The FRG also sent a token contingent of eighteen fighter planes to Turkey, with 270 pilots and maintenance workers. But that was as far as Kohl could go legally: German political consensus at the time was that the Basic Law forbade the sending of German soldiers to combat zones, especially outside the NATO area.[185]

Gorbachev also tried it on Bush, to no effect. But Jim Baker seemed to be wobbling. On 29 January, while Bush was preparing for his State of the Union address that evening, Scowcroft informed him of a surprise Soviet–American joint statement read out on camera by Alexander Bessmertnykh – recently appointed as Shevardnadze's successor after a great deal of dithering by Gorbachev – who had visited the State Department for talks. It included the sentence: 'The ministers continue to believe that a cessation of hostilities would be possible if Iraq would make an unequivocal commitment to withdraw from Kuwait' – backed by 'immediate, concrete steps leading to full compliance with the Security Council resolutions'. Scowcroft was 'dumbfounded' and Bush absolutely 'furious'. As soon as he arrived on Capitol Hill the president was interrogated about the statement, obliging the White House to move into damage-limitation mode just when it was expecting to command the headlines in the wake of Bush's speech. After a 'sleepless night', Baker made a fulsome apology to the president: it was a rare occasion when the hard-driving Secretary of State had taken his eye off the ball and failed to keep in step with the president. Bessmertnykh had taken full advantage of this lapse.[186]

Just before the ground war commenced, Bush had to fend off yet another diplomatic foray by Gorbachev.[187] In three phone calls over three days, the Soviet leader, who had sent Primakov yet again to Iraq on attempted deal-making, urged Bush to stop the bombing because they were, supposedly, on the brink of success. On 23 February, Gorbachev was in particularly assertive mood. 'After our talk yesterday, something has happened that changed the situation. In Baghdad, an official statement has been issued that agrees to full and unconditional withdrawal from Kuwait as specified in the UN resolution and that it will happen from Kuwait City within four days. That is to say we have a white flag from Saddam Hussein.' So, Gorbachev continued confidently, 'now we have a new situation that is new for both of us. And I believe that we must weigh carefully the entire situation and discuss what we must decide to do next.'

'Thank you sir,' Bush said coldly. At that eleventh hour, he was having none of this 'we' business. He reminded Gorbachev that there had been 'a bunch more oil wells set on fire overnight', despite Iraqi claims that Bush was lying when he made that charge, and that Saddam's troops were 'continuing to use a scorched-earth policy and stalling'. All this, he said, had 'made a profound impact on me and on other coalition partners'. He therefore discerned a basic divergence between Washington and Moscow. 'You think they have agreed to unconditional withdrawal and we and others with us do not agree. Let's not let this divide the US and the Soviet Union,' he warned Gorbachev. 'There are things far bigger than this conflagration which is going to be over very soon.'

'George, let's keep cool,' the Soviet leader responded. The two of them managed to finish their conversation more temperately, but Bush did not budge on his essential point. 'Mikhail, I appreciate that spirit but I don't want to leave a false impression that there is any more time.'[188]

The ground war was due to start next day, 24 February. Admitting that Saddam's 'fate has been determined', Gorbachev recalled Primakov from Baghdad. 'We're doomed to be friends with America,' groaned his aide Anatoly Chernyaev. 'Otherwise, we would face isolation and everything would go haywire again.' He told the president they should stop any further communication with Saddam. 'You're right! There's no point now,' Gorbachev exclaimed. 'It's a new era.'[189]

The devastating air campaign – so far 94,000 missions – had represented a clinical implementation of the Powell Doctrine: overwhelming force applied with the latest technology. And technowar took on added meaning when the ground forces went into action. This was no ponderous infantry slogging match. Central Command's war plan was built around synchronised operations across hundreds of miles of battlefield. While coalition forces engaged the main enemy forces in Kuwait, US Marines feigned an amphibious landing up the Kuwaiti coast and over a quarter of a million US, British and French troops, including most of the armoured units, mounted a massive left hook around the Iraqi rear to slice through Kuwait. Saddam had promised 'the mother of all battles' but within a couple of days of combat his army was falling apart – outfought by the coalition land forces and pulverised from above by wave upon wave of fighter-bombers. 'It was close to Armageddon,' said one US officer. Along what became known as the 'Highway of Death' between Kuwait City and Basra, 'burned-out, bombed-out vehicles of every description littered the highway, with charred Iraqi bodies everywhere, and booty ranging from television sets to brass door handles to bathtubs'.[190]

Images of the Highway of Death were relayed on TV all over the world. One phrase from an American journalist was picked up to encapsulate what was happening: 'a turkey shoot'. Bush himself was shaken by the images, and worried by the impression that the US was now slaughtering almost defenceless Arabs. On the morning of 27 February the president unburdened himself over the phone to Mitterrand. 'I think the fighting is almost over. The southern half of Kuwait is almost liberated. There is only one division left in a high state of competence and even that may not be combat effective.' Having just talked to Defense Secretary Dick Cheney, Bush told Mitterrand that he could probably stop the ground fighting after one more day. 'We control the battlefield, but I want to assure you that we want to end the shooting as soon as we can.'

Bush decided to delay any ceasefire until he was satisfied 'we had met all our military objectives and fulfilled the UN resolutions'. That afternoon, during the president's daily conference with key advisers, Powell spoke with Schwarzkopf in the Gulf who stated categorically 'we've accomplished our mission'. When Bush declared it was time to stop, there was no dissent in the room. They decided to formally end hostilities at midnight Washington time – which, someone then realised, would mean that the ground war had lasted exactly one hundred hours. 'Too cute by half,' Scowcroft reflected drily.[191]

Just after 9 p.m. Bush spoke to the nation again from the Oval Office. 'Kuwait is liberated. Iraq's army is defeated. Our military objectives are met. Kuwait is once more in the hands of Kuwaitis, in control of their own destiny.' But the president's tone was not triumphalist:

'No one country can claim this victory as its own. It was not only a victory for Kuwait but a victory for all the coalition partners. This is a victory for the United Nations, for all mankind, for the rule of law, and for what is right.'[192]

Although Bush talked in internationalist terms, his gut feelings were deeply national. 'It's a proud day for America,' he told conservative legislators on Capitol Hill. 'And, by God, we've kicked the Vietnam syndrome once and for all.' For Bush, that was hugely important. 'It's surprising how much I dwell on the end of the Vietnam syndrome,' he had written in his diary on the 26th. 'I felt the division in the country in the 60s and the 70s – I was in Congress.' He had still not forgotten the pain of Yale graduates turning their backs on him when he gave the commencement address at his alma mater at the height of the campus protests. In fact he had alluded to it in his inaugural address as president in January 1989, telling Congress and the country that the war 'cleaves us still' and warning that 'no great nation can long afford to be sundered by a memory'. That's why he declared with passion in a broadcast to US troops in the Gulf on 2 March 1991: 'We promised this would not be another Vietnam. And we kept that promise. The spectre of Vietnam has been buried forever in the desert sands of the Arabian Peninsula.'[193]

And the burial was truly spectacular. America's ground war in Vietnam had lasted a decade, cost 58,000 American lives and ended in failure. Driving Saddam out of Kuwait took just six weeks and only 148 American lives. The financial cost is less clear but, according to most accounts, the United States – remarkably – almost broke even. Bush and Baker had managed to secure pledges of $53.8 billion in aid, both cash and kind, against an overall US bill for Gulf operations totalling $61.1 billion. Here was further evidence of the unprecedented coalition effort. No wonder an emotional Colin Powell told Bush, 'This is historic. There's been nothing like this in history.'[194]

The victory also seemed intensely personal. Bush's approval rating soon after the end of the fighting stood at 89% – the highest opinion-poll figure for any president to that date. 'My sense is George Bush is getting close to unbeatable,' declared Jim Ruvolo, a Democrat from Ohio, as he looked ahead to the 1992 election. The media talked of the war conferring on him 'an aura of invincibility'.[195]

Yet Bush did not feel buoyed up by events. 'Still no feeling of euphoria,' he wrote on 28 February. 'I think I know why it is. After my last speech last night, Baghdad radio stated that we have been forced to capitulate.

I see on the television that public opinion in Jordan and in the streets of Baghdad is that they have won. It's such a canard, so little, but it's what concerns me. It hasn't been a clean end – there's no Battleship *Missouri* surrender.' As a veteran of the Pacific War, Bush yearned for something like that moment of ritual Japanese capitulation on a battleship in Tokyo Bay. 'This is what's missing to make this akin to WW2 – to separate Kuwait from Korea and Vietnam.'[196]

But America's mantra in 1945 had been 'unconditional surrender'. Bush's mission thirty-five years later was much more constrained. The UN resolutions authorised only the eviction of Iraq from Kuwait and the restoration of the emirate's political leaders. There was no mandate for marching on into Baghdad and toppling the Iraqi dictator. And Bush knew well that any such mission would have shattered the coalition and probably set the Arab world against him. The president was under no illusion about Saddam. 'With all of the atrocities and the damage he has done to the environment,' he told Genscher on 1 March, 'it will be impossible for us to do anything constructive with Iraq as long as he is there.' The German foreign minister was particularly concerned that 'we cannot permit Iraq to keep any weapons of mass destruction or any missiles with or without Saddam Hussein'. But the president hoped that the massive defeat in Kuwait would undermine Saddam and prompt a coup against him: Bush certainly did not want American fingerprints on this denouement. 'I hope that the Iraqi army or the Iraqi people just take matters into their own hands and put him out,' the president exclaimed.[197]

In the event, of course, Saddam stayed in power and his weapons of mass destruction became the centre of another war, waged by Bush's son a decade later. Yet in 1991 all that lay in an unimagined future. What struck contemporaries were not the limits of America's success but the magnitude. In 1989–90 bipolar rivalry and the division of Europe had given way to unprecedented cooperation between the two superpowers. But the dawning 'new world order' had then been threatened by a spectacular act of regional aggression by a Soviet client freed from Cold War constraints. Bush's line in the sand had sent the strongest possible signal that Washington would not allow the post-Cold War world to slide into anarchy – by using American power within a framework of international cooperation to maintain order and stability.

And the character of this American power proved a revelation. Kuwait was the first time that the United States had engaged in a major conflict for nearly two decades, thereby allowing the world a glimpse into its modern arsenal. Never before had precision-guided bombs and missiles played a decisive role in warfare. Pundits became obsessed by the accuracy of their lasers and miniature computers. Coalition spokesmen claimed that less than 0.1% of such weapons launched at Iraqi military targets had gone astray and hit civilian areas. The effect on Iraq's army – fourth-biggest in the world – was devastating. It had been fighting essentially a Cold War conflict, with hardware mostly from the USSR and China. Beijing paid particular attention to battlefield performance and was frankly shocked at America's technical revolution. As a result, the PRC totally overhauled China's concept of warfare, adopting the slogan 'modern local wars under high-tech conditions'. Whatever these efforts, however, it was clear that in terms of technowar, the new military world order left the United States in a league of its own.[198]

In the post-Kuwait world, declared Deputy National Security Advisor Robert Gates, 'no one questions the reality of only one superpower and its leadership'.[199] Equally, the Kuwait crisis had underlined the fading power and influence of the Soviet Union. Yet Bush's conception of the new world order depended diplomatically on the idea of two pillars. And Kohl was at pains to remind the president of this when they talked on the phone on 7 March. After appropriate words of congratulation, the German chancellor moved the conversation on to Gorbachev: 'he is pondering ways and means of how he can get into the picture. He wants to be a player.'[200]

Bush was in generous mood, glossing over the Soviet peace missions: 'I didn't worry about that ... we had no problem with his trying to make peace.' He assured Kohl: 'I will stay in touch with Gorbachev. I won't give up on him. We are very worried about what is going on in the Soviet Union, but he is president, and we will deal with him.'

This was just what Kohl wanted to hear: 'Yes, it is very important. George, it would be very good if you make this clear to him from time to time, with a remark here and a gesture there, because from a psychological viewpoint it is very important that he is confirmed in this view.'

'That is a good point,' Bush responded. 'I will accept your advice.'[201]

Taking Gorbachev seriously was also the theme of a conversation Bush had with Shevardnadze on 6 May. Although on an unofficial visit, the former Soviet foreign minister was granted a special audience at the White House because of the respect in which he was still held. He went on at length about his fears for the future of his country and for its relationship with the United States. Shevardnadze expressed alarm at what he called 'the pause in our relations' caused by the crisis in the Gulf. (That term 'pause' was, of course, an echo of the six-month hiatus after Bush's accession to the presidency, which had so unsettled the Kremlin.) 'I am afraid of the pause. We cannot allow the dynamics of this relationship to slide backwards. Mr President, no matter what happens in the Soviet Union, US–Soviet relations will determine the political climate until the end of the century.'

Shevardnadze went on to remind Bush that he and Gorbachev had not met since November 1990 – and then only briefly on the margins of the Paris CSCE. There had been plans for a summit in December, but this meeting was postponed to March 1991 and then to the summer. So Shevardnadze begged Bush to set a date. In response, the president mentioned the unresolved problems over strategic and conventional forces that stood in the way of an arms-control agreement. He also alluded to the faltering Soviet economy and the question of the Baltic independence. But, he went on, 'I want a summit … I'd like to do the summit in a way that strengthens Gorbachev.'

Bush recalled 'all the hard work we put in on this relationship', insisting 'I am anxious that it stays strong. Some criticise us for staying too close to Mikhail Gorbachev.' But he assured Shevardnadze, 'We will deal with him with respect and friendship as long as he is president.'[202]

Chapter 7

Russian Revolution

The 21st of August 1991. Vacation time. George Bush was at his holiday retreat in Kennebunkport, Maine. After a morning skippering his boat through the choppy waters of the Atlantic, he was just mooring when the head of his security detail came running down the pier, shouting 'You have a call from a chief [head] of state!'

'Who?' Bush rushed back to the house and into his bedroom, where his communications people put him through.[1]

'Oh my God, that's wonderful. Mikhail!' The president was elated.

'My dearest George. I'm so happy to hear your voice again.'

'My God I'm glad to hear you. How are you doing?'

Gorbachev was wound up with emotion. 'Mr President, the adventurers have not succeeded. I have been here four days. They tried to pressure me, using every method. They had me blocked by sea and land. My guards protected me, we withstood the challenge.'

'Where are you now?'

'I'm in the Crimea. It's only been one hour since I have assumed presidential powers. I have maintained full contact with the Republic leaders ...'[2]

On 4 August, Gorbachev had gone off for a much-needed holiday at his Black Sea villa high on the cliffs in Foros, on the southern tip of Crimea. This was some twenty-five miles west from Yalta where in 1945 the Big Three – Stalin, Churchill and Roosevelt – had conferred in the summer palace of the last Russian tsar, Nicholas II. The first two weeks had been uneventful – a mix of work, swimming, sunbathing and playing with his grandchildren. But then on 18 August, just after making arrangements over the phone with Vice President Gennady Yanaev in the Kremlin for his return to Moscow to sign the new Union Treaty on 20 August, the lines went dead. A few minutes later, Gorbachev received an unexpected visit from his chief of staff, two

Central Committee secretaries and the head of his KGB security directorate – all men he had personally appointed and in whom he had complete trust. They said they had been sent by the 'state emergency committee', who announced that Boris Yeltsin – elected the first president of the Russian Republic only in June – would be arrested that evening, and placed Gorbachev under house arrest at the dacha. On the 19th the leaders of the coup officially proclaimed that Gorbachev was ill and that his powers had been assumed by Vice President Yanaev. The junta had taken control of the country. Live CNN pictures showed tanks moving down Moscow's streets, armoured personnel carriers parked everywhere and troops guarding all major intersections.[3]

The tanks roll again: Moscow's Red Square, August 1991

But the coup was not unopposed. Yeltsin appealed for ordinary workers to go out on strike and demanded that Gorbachev be restored to power. Symbolically, Yeltsin was filmed standing on top of a tank haranguing soldiers and citizens below him. Bush was mesmerised by these TV images – one leader watching the fate of another, halfway around the world. '70% of them support him in the elections, the Russians. He's declared himself to be in charge of all functions of Russia now. How will that go down with bad guys, the coup plotters?' But the president was particularly concerned about Gorbachev, recalling the 'fantastically constructive way' the Soviet leader had led his country. 'I like you,' he mused, 'and I hope that you return to power, sceptical though I am of that.'⁴ On 19 August, nobody in America could guess who would come out on top in Moscow.

Forty-eight hours later, however, the tide began to turn in the Soviet capital. On 21 August, tens of thousands of citizens flocked to the Russian Republic's parliamentary building, 'the White House', to protect it from being stormed. Yeltsin and his team were inside. Faced with such crowds, the emergency committee lost its nerve and the storming never occurred. Several members of the so-called Gang of Eight – most notably Vladimir Kryuchkov and Dmitry Yazov – flew to Foros, with Yeltsin's men in hot pursuit, not trusting the putschists' intentions. Meanwhile, Gorbachev tried to stay calm, but his family were in a state of panic – as they watched naval vessels criss-crossing the bay and catching snippets of BBC news from the radio. Such was the stress that his wife Raisa suffered a stroke – leaving her initially unable to speak or move her left arm, and also distinctly wobbly on her legs.⁵

But when Kryuchkov and his colleagues arrived it became clear that they had come to propitiate Gorbachev and beg for forgiveness. As Gorbachev aide Anatoly Chernyaev noted, 'they looked beaten, their faces gloomy. Each one bowed to me!! I understood what was going on – they came to plead guilty ... The scum failed with their schemes.'⁶ Gorbachev had them detained. Soon afterwards, communications were suddenly restored and he immediately called Yeltsin who exclaimed: 'Dear Mikhail Sergeyevich, so you are alive! We've been ready to fight for you for forty-eight hours.' Gorbachev also spoke with the leaders of Kazakhstan and Ukraine, before ordering that the remaining plotters be barred from the Kremlin and all their communications turned off.⁷

And it was at this point that, seeking to regain his place at the helm in world affairs, Gorbachev had picked up the phone to call the president of the United States.

After their emotional exchange of greetings, Gorbachev made clear that – despite the trauma he and his family had endured – he was keen to get back to work in Moscow. His mood was upbeat: 'We want to keep going ahead with you,' he told Bush. 'We will not falter because of what happened. One thing is that this was prevented by democracy. This is a guarantee for us. We will keep working in the country and out to keep cooperation going.'

Bush laughed with relief. 'Sounds like the same old Mikhail Gorbachev, one full of life and confidence. Once you get back we'll talk about what to work on since our talks in Moscow.'

'OK, George. Please proceed on this basis. Goodbye.'[8]

Back to business as usual. Or was it? In fact, the phone call that really mattered had taken place four hours earlier on that same day, when Bush talked to the Russian president Boris Yeltsin. The tone had been equally friendly but the content very different.

'Boris, how are you doing today?'

'Well I've spent the last two days sitting in the Parliament building without leaving the premises. Mr President, I want to tell you ... This morning the Russian Supreme Soviet was in session and unanimously decided to categorically say the coup attempt is illegal and will not have any effect on Russian territory. The Supreme Soviet supported all decrees and decisions I have made as president of Russia. They also gave me additional powers to see to it that if local authorities support the junta, they can be removed from office.'[9]

Indeed, Bush and Yeltsin had already communicated the day before, 20 August, when the US president – hoping to get a 'first-hand report' – had placed a call to the Russian presidency and to his surprise actually got through to Yeltsin himself, who gave him a detailed account of what he called 'a right-wing coup' to 'take over the democratically elected leadership of Russia, Leningrad, Moscow, and other cities'. He urged Bush to 'rally world leaders to the fact that the situation here is critical'.[10]

In both phone calls, Bush was emphatic that this was what he would do. On the 20th the US president made a strong public statement against the coup.

'I thank you very much for that,' Yeltsin told him in their second conversation on the 21st. 'Please don't view this as an interference in our internal affairs, this is an important statement by the American president in support of the Soviet people ... We will try to get your statement out to the people. People understand what you are saying and are receiving it well.'

'We will keep supporting you,' Bush promised. 'People throughout the world are supporting you, except Iraq, Libya, and Cuba, crazy little renegade countries. People are supporting you more than you can understand.'

Yeltsin ended the conversation by pledging 'I will do everything I can to save democracy in Russia and throughout the USSR.'[11]

Fine words. But the situation was not so simple. The fate of Russia and that of the Soviet Union were no longer inextricably entangled. And, for all Bush's niceties over the phone to both Gorbachev and Yeltsin, it would be hard to ride two horses indefinitely. That same day the US president spoke with John Major, Thatcher's successor in London, remarking that he did not want to undermine Yeltsin or Gorbachev but wasn't sure what the events of the last few days portended. 'Out of this we may have a very different-looking Soviet Union.'[12]

*

How did Gorbachev get into this mess? Looking back, the roots of the Soviet crisis lay right back in the genesis of perestroika. He had always been more of a visionary than a practical politician and his initial ambition of going 'back to Lenin' – retrieving Marxism–Leninism in, supposedly, its pure form, before it had been polluted by Stalin – proved utterly utopian. Increasingly from 1987 he tried to move out of the command economy by incremental openings to the market while simultaneously loosening the grip of the one-party state by cautiously allowing some degree of political opposition.

The result was, however, a halfway house: leaving the USSR in an economic no man's land, amid a muddled political pluralism. This was the consequence of Gorbachev's lack of a clear strategy but it also reflected his pragmatic need to work with the old order while trying to build something new – all the while unsure of what that was. Eastern European leaders such as Jaruzelski, Németh and Havel faced similar problems but their economies were smaller and command dogma had been less entrenched. Moreover, post-1989 Poland, Hungary and Czechoslovakia undertook dramatic programmes to fully embrace the market, and they also benefited from significant Western financial packages and food. And so, by 1990, the Kremlin's half-baked reforms had left the USSR in economic chaos, at a time of escalating political turmoil. The move towards price reform had generated severe inflation, a phenomenon not experienced in the USSR since the Second World War, and Gorbachev was obliged to respond by expedients such as printing more money.[13] Data from the official Soviet price index showed that in 1990 money supply grew by 21.5%, while income and expenditure each went up by over 15%. Even in sectors completely controlled by the state, price inflation ran at 5.3% (compared to 0.6% in 1988).

Prices at the unregulated farmers' markets rose a staggering 71% during 1990. Meanwhile the rouble lost a third of its value against the dollar between 1989 and 1991.[14] 'Economic ills are deeply rooted in the system,' a CIA report noted with sublime understatement, 'and efforts to reform it will be slowed by the priority given to stabilising the economy.'[15]

Teetering on the edge

What's more, Gorbachev's hesitant reforms had exacerbated the state budget deficit, which rose from 4% of GDP in 1985 to 12% in 1989, or from some 30 billion roubles to roughly 125 billion. He had boosted imports from the West, such as machine tools, to help modernise Soviet industry. But then oil and gas prices had collapsed on the world market, further reducing national revenues. State ownership of the means of production was also dissolving, especially after the 1988 Law on Cooperatives which quickly spawned thinly disguised private enterprises – even though to Gorbachev the notion of 'private property' remained ideologically unacceptable for the world's leading socialist state. 'The attempt to restore private property means to move backwards and is a deeply erroneous decision.' So he insisted on talking about 'socialist property'. Yet that term embraced cooperative business enterprises, some of which were openly producing high-value luxury goods to make quick profits, at the same time that serious shortages were experienced in basics such as soap and matches, vegetables and fruit, bread and beef, cars and radios. Panicky consumers started hoarding.

For the third year running since 1987 the Soviet people experienced significant deterioration in indicators of consumer welfare. During 1990 alone GDP decreased by 8%.[16] Under Gorbachev, life for ordinary Soviet citizens was getting worse, not better. As he had wryly admitted to the Congress of People's Deputies, he had seen veterans on a bus in Moscow holding placards of Brezhnev festooned with medals and of Gorbachev decorated with ration cards.[17]

For 1990, the government came up with a 'stabilisation' plan but its grandiose targets – such as cutting the budget deficit in half and raising consumer-goods production by 12% – proved pie in the sky, as most people had expected. Month-on-month official statistics showed accelerating economic decline. Output down. Inflation up. Shortages rampant. Society in turmoil. The CIA warned of the 'possibility for an economic breakdown'.[18]

While the economy floundered, Soviet politics teetered precariously between party, state and democracy. In June 1988, at the 19th Party Conference, Gorbachev had embarked on a broad programme of political reform to strengthen elected legislative bodies at the expense of the party – a development that soon altered the whole political landscape. The conference endorsed principles of competitive elections and limited terms in office. At this stage the party held on to its leading role but opened up a bit, hoping to engage in public life the energies of more of the educated population. Gorbachev said he wanted to make a 'peaceful, smooth transition from one political system to another' and claimed that democratisation would be the 'principal guarantee' of the 'irreversibility of perestroika'.[19]

The year 1989 saw the peak of perestroika, and also marked the highpoint of Gorbachev's personal popularity. His push for domestic innovation also spurred East Europeans into their own transformations. He neither tried to stop their exit from communism, nor did he learn from their reforms – so distracted was he by his own battles to democratise the Soviet Union itself. Gorbachev himself later summed up his strategy for 1989 as follows: to shift power from the CPSU to the Soviet people through free elections to a new parliament and in the process compel the party, in his words, to 'voluntarily give up its own dictatorship'.[20]

Indeed, the nature of the Soviet regime changed fundamentally with the first largely free elections since the Bolshevik Revolution. Following a constitutional amendment, on 26 March 1989 a new Congress of People's Deputies with 2,250 legislators was elected – in which 13% of the seats were reserved for non-party members and the other seats were often contested by communists with differing views and policies. Gorbachev's initial reaction was ecstatic. On 28 March he informed the Politburo that the elections were a huge 'step in realising political reform and democratising our society'. Next day he told the press exultantly, 'the people have accepted perestroika in their hearts and minds'.

Overall, however, no more than one-sixth of the deputies could be described as real reformers. Party conservatives also blocked the next stage of reform. They ensured that those deputies subsequently voted from the Congress into the new 542-person Supreme Soviet were mostly compliant party faithful. And so, as his biographer William Taubman observed, whereas Gorbachev had hoped that the newly aroused 'majority of society' would put pressure on the old party apparatus, his conservative-communist critics – far from being reined in – used every opportunity to attack him with unprecedented ferocity. Rather than the new rules of electoral and parliamentary politics helping Gorbachev and uniting the party, they had instead further alienated hardliners while also giving radical liberals new platforms from which to attack him. Democratisation was necessary to foster reform but it was also weakening his power as a reformer.[21]

In fact, 1989 would mark the beginning of the end for perestroika. The political innovations Gorbachev believed to be so crucial for democ-ratisation served to cripple the essential institution that for decades had held the Soviet polity together: the CPSU. And the new forms would soon prove less effective and helpful than Gorbachev had hoped. Worse, they intensified the multitudinous crises that were already undermining his authority and the Soviet system itself. As a result, what George Bush considered the second pillar of his new world order – far from being renewed and reinforced – was disintegrating from within, due to economic freefall, national separatism and political polar-isation in and outside the Kremlin. By the year's end Gorbachev lamented that 1989 had been the 'the most difficult year' since he assumed power in 1985.[22] He predicted that '1990 will be decisive for perestroika.'[23]

Walkout from communism – Moscow on the brink

Political polarisation actually worsened dramatically in the wake of the European revolutions of 1989. In February 1990, there were mass demonstrations in Moscow, with 200,000–300,000 people in the streets, calling for 'peaceful revolution' but also warning the party leadership bluntly to 'remember Romania'. The crowds chanted and waved placards reading: 'Freedom Now!' and 'Soviet Army – Don't Shoot Your Own People'. Protestors dismissed the whole of Soviet history with banners such as 'Seventy-Two Years on the Road to Nowhere'.

At the same time, regional Communist Party leaders and other reactionary officials mounted a sustained assault on Gorbachev. There were sneers about him as the 'head German'. And at Central Committee meetings he was subjected to a battery of charges: 'converting the party into a discussion club', reducing the country to 'anarchy' and 'ruin', allowing 'the destruction of our buffer zone' in Eastern Europe, and turning a 'celebrated world power' into a state with a 'joyless present' and an 'uncertain future' out of 'incompetence, myopia and skewed priorities'. Adding to Soviet 'humiliation', said Vladimir Brovikov, Soviet ambassador to Poland, was the West's delight in 'singing our praises' while actually 'gloating over the collapse of communism and world socialism'. So Gorbachev – still leader of the party but also champion of reform – was getting it from both sides.[24]

Ironically, the Central Committee plenum of 5–7 February neverthe-less gave its approval for Gorbachev's plan to further enhance his own power while reducing that of the party. In March he was duly elected by the Congress to the newly created post of president of the Soviet Union. Although remaining the party's general secretary, he was no longer totally beholden to it. And the constitution was changed again to eliminate any reference to the 'leading and guiding role' of the CPSU. The Politburo was replaced by a Presidential Council, and consultation with the rest of the party hierarchy became largely a formality. In fact, the eighteen-member Presidential Council was a mixed bag of liberal Gorbachevites, top ministers who held a diversity of views, and assorted intellectuals. The result was an ineffectual talking shop, with which Gorbachev soon got bored. Finally, the Law on the Presidency created a second advisory body, consisting of every republic's Supreme Soviet chairman. This Federation Council was tasked with oversight of nationality and inter-republic issues and with formulating a new Union Treaty, upon which future centre-periphery relations were to be based. But in its first phase (March–November 1990), not only did the Federation Council meet infrequently but it operated most of the time without the participation of the Baltic republics, Georgia, Armenia and Moldavia – all of which were intent on independence from the union.

The failure of this latest bout of reform to provide informed and effective policymaking left Gorbachev increasingly isolated. Far from constituting the centre of power for the country, as the party had previ-ously done, his presidency just added to the organisational muddle.[25]

Gorbachev had originally rejected the idea of an 'imperial presidency'[26] as too radical a change, and one that made him uneasy: he did not want Soviet citizens to think that he had merely engaged in reform in order to promote his power.[27] But by spring 1990 his mind had changed. He saw the need for more personal power in order to advance reform. By distinguishing parliament from party and by creating the new presidency, the USSR was also moving constitutionally towards some kind of Western separation of powers. But, in this more open and fragmented system, Gorbachev found it harder to manoeuvre amid all the new political actors in Moscow.[28]

What's more, the political system had become increasingly three-dimensional – because significant power had also been devolved to the republics. In this diversified arena, non-communists and would-be nationalists were able to spread their wings. The combination of devolution and democratisation was formidably difficult to handle. And Gorbachev found playing this kind of multidimensional politics rather challenging. Particularly intractable were the Baltics, the Caucasus and above all Russia itself.

It was Baltic nationalism that really caught Western attention. By the time of the Soviet Congress elections in March 1989, the Estonian, Latvian and Lithuanian leaderships had declared their republics 'sovereign' and asserted the supremacy of their laws over those of the USSR. The Baltic republics also reserved the right to veto decisions made in Moscow, to exercise local control in all areas except military and foreign policy, and made Estonian, Latvian and Lithuanian again the state languages instead of Russian. Moreover, their Supreme Soviets proclaimed economic autonomy from the centre and embarked on a programme of rapid marketisation – which certainly paid off in Estonia,[29] as Gorbachev at times noted with approval. Less pleasing for Moscow, however, the republics also imposed limits on immigration by non-Balts, which was aimed particularly at Russians who in Estonia and Latvia comprised over 30% of the population. So far Gorbachev had been able to count on Baltic communist parties to suppress ethnic separatism but now these were moving closer to the recently formed 'popular fronts'. Indeed, in the 1989 Congress elections, the popular fronts won landslide victories.[30]

The Baltic election results shocked the Politburo. Chernyaev wrote in his diary on 2 May that he felt growing 'depression and alarm' – a 'sense of crisis of the Gorbachevian idea'. The Soviet leader's continued professions of 'socialist values' and 'the ideals of October' sounded like 'irony' to those in the know. And behind all the idealism – 'emptiness'. Chernyaev mused Gorbachev wanted to 'go far'. But was he now starting to lose control of the levers of power – probably 'irreversibly'? All around him the Soviet leader had unleashed 'processes of disintegration'. Chernyaev feared 'collapse' and 'chaos'.[31] At a Politburo meeting in Moscow on 11 May, he noted that the three Baltic communist leaders were 'put through hell'. Vadim Medvedev, the leading Kremlin ideologist, told them in no uncertain terms that now was the time for the party and state leaderships of the republics to show 'political will, determination to fulfil the course of the CPSU towards the renewal and consolidation of socialism'. Gorbachev was more emollient. 'We should look into the roots of the situation,' he said, into 'the specifics of history, in particular of the history of the 1930s and 1940s'. He added that 'in the context of perestroika, a stormy process of growing national self-consciousness emerges in those republics. And a very serious issue arises – about a more modern and complete interpretation of the notion of "sovereignty". This is a real issue.'[32]

Gorbachev was clearly trying to appease the Balts – seeking to stay in control while remaining true to his reformist outlook. After the Baltic leaders had left the meeting, the Soviet president lectured the Politburo in words that tell us a lot about his political thinking by the spring of 1989. 'We shouldn't identify the popular fronts, which are supported by 90% of the population, with extremists. We have to learn to communicate with them … We have to trust in people's common sense.' He praised the Baltic republics' drive for greater autonomy and market reforms – 'Do not be afraid of experiments with full economic self-accounting of the republics' – and he could even envisage a looser Soviet Union. 'Do not be afraid of differentiation among the republics according to the level of practised sovereignty … We have to think, think, think how in practice to transform our federation. Otherwise everything will really collapse.' Yet, he went on, even if it did come to that, 'the use of force is out of the question … We excluded it from foreign policy' and, 'especially against our people', he continued, 'it is out of the question.'[33]

Eloquent words – and very Gorbachev. The reality, however, was that the Balts were now demanding more than mere autonomy within the USSR. Their ultimate aim was the *restoration* of national independence. Only three days after the Politburo meeting, in an open declaration, the three popular-front movements spelled out their 'aspirations' for 'state sovereignty in a neutral, demilitarised Baltoscandia' while denouncing the Soviet annexations of 1940.[34] The Politburo had in any case been left unpersuaded by Gorbachev's ideas how to hold together the fraying union – not least because of what had been happening on its southern rim.

That spring secessionist agitation was a problem right across the Soviet Union. The simmering conflict between Azerbaijanis and Armenians over Nagorno-Karabakh had erupted into open fighting, and serious ethnic unrest had exploded in Tbilisi, capital of the Soviet republic of Georgia.[35] Tensions there had been building for weeks with fierce clamour for greater autonomy from Moscow. But as the tempo of strikes and demonstrations intensified, so did the Soviet troop presence on the streets. During the night of 9 April 1989, when thousands of nationalist demon-strators refused to disperse, soldiers with riot sticks and army shovels moved into the crowds. 'Their actions were savage,' Jack Matlock, US ambassador to Moscow, later wrote in his memoirs. 'Persons who had fallen on the pavement were beaten to death and gas was sprayed directly into the faces of prostrate unarmed, individuals.' In the end more than twenty were killed and hundreds injured.[36]

This was precisely the kind of bloodshed Gorbachev had feared. And yet, as leader of the USSR, he was immediately confronted with questions about whether he had authorised the crackdown and, if not, whether he had lost control. In fact, that day Gorbachev and Shevardnadze had been in London, and it was Shevardnadze – the former Georgian party leader and the only Georgian on the Politburo – who was sent to Tbilisi in an effort to restore calm.[37] In due course, an independent commission concluded that responsibility for the carnage lay with the hard-line generals in operational charge, acting at the political behest of the Georgian party leadership.[38] Even if it was the case, as Chernyaev put it graphically, that the Georgian leadership 'wet its pants and set the troops against the people' – the bloodshed proved that the Soviet system as a whole retained the will and capacity for ruthless brutality.[39]

Gorbachev sided publicly with the critics of the Tbilisi crackdown – a position that was reinforced by the shock of seeing TV images of the mass-killing of Chinese protestors that June in Beijing. He castigated Kryuchkov and the secret services for shoddy analyses of the situation, while berating Yazov for allowing Red Army deployments without an explicit order from the Politburo. Moreover, Gorbachev underlined his commitment to non-interference in the revolutions of Eastern Europe – to the West's satisfaction and the chagrin of Soviet empire-savers. In taking this stand, he would effectively circumscribe his future options to use force at home or abroad. At the same time, however, in an appeal to workers in Georgia, Gorbachev insisted: 'It is not in the interest of working people to break the existing bonds of friendship and cooperation between our peoples, to liquidate the socialist system in the republic, to push it into a tarn of national enmity ... Our common duty is to deepen and strengthen fraternal relations between peoples. But the restructuring of interethnic relations does not mean a redrawing of borders, a breakdown of the country's national and state structure.' For his part, Shevardnadze concluded that it had been wrong for him to steer clear of the nationalities issues since taking over the Foreign Ministry in 1985.[40]

Forced to respond to the domestic upheavals and show leadership, Gorbachev came to the Politburo on 14 July with a set of new policies on the 'national question'. But for the first time Shevardnadze broke ranks – dismissing Gorbachev's proposals as too vague. He demanded a much clearer statement of principles and also asked pointedly why nothing was said about Lenin's concept of the right of secession. Medvedev tried to calm the row, expressing his concern that Russia itself might soon demand the status of a sovereign republic. He therefore argued that it was essential to start serious debate about a new Union Treaty. Gorbachev agreed. Soviet prime minister Nikolai Ryzhkov, however, opposed any slide to ever greater devolution. The Politburo was out of its depth and in disarray. [41]

Two months later the party Central Committee finally held its special plenum on nationality on 19 September 1989 – one that Gorbachev had been calling for since the winter of 1988. There was lots more talk but little of substance. Gorbachev reminded his comrades about the benefits of Soviet federalism and highlighted the mutual reliance of the republics on each other. By way of example, he noted that Latvia took 96% of its fuel from other parts of the USSR; conversely, Lithuania was a significant producer of TVs and computers.[42] But rhetoric about interdependence now cut little ice. For the rest of the autumn, Kremlin discussions were plagued by endless squabbling about who was to blame for the growing national unrest, which threatened the very existence of the union. 'I smell an overall collapse,' Ryzhkov declared grimly in the Politburo the day the Wall fell. Shevardnadze – fearing a spillover from Eastern Europe – warned in mid-November that the 'destabilisation' of East Germany would 'act as a catalyst for separatist tendencies in the Baltic region' and even unsettle Ukraine and other republics. The situation, he said, was 'wholly unpredictable': might anarchy result, or even dictatorship? As for Gorbachev, he alternated between railing at Baltic separatists and cautioning against the use of force against them. He told Bush in Malta that Baltic separatism was nothing less than a 'threat to perestroika'. It was going too far: 'we lived together for fifty years, we are integrated'. In his view, the secessionists were pushing their people into a 'historical dead end'.[43]

During 1989 the main centres of nationalist unrest had been in the Baltic and the Caucasus. By the turn of the year, nothing had been resolved. Ironically, the Kremlin-directed anti-independence crackdowns had killed fewer people than interethnic violence in and between republics, several of which had by now proclaimed their own sovereignty. Tensions continued between Azerbaijan and Armenia, drawing in Soviet troops, while in Uzbekistan the government mounted bloody pogroms against Meskhetian Turks (originally deported by Stalin).[44] Energised by their mass protests for the fiftieth anniversary of the Hitler–Stalin pact of 1939, the Baltics were pressing to leave the union completely. Lithuania declared independence in March 1990, while Latvia and Estonia announced their intent to do so at a time still to be determined. Gorbachev retaliated with his economic blockade against Lithuania – causing signifi-cant friction with Western Europe and the USA. But Washington did not force the issue. Scowcroft had no doubt that the "'emotional" appeal of Baltic independence must be subordinated to the "hard-headed real-ities"' of US–Soviet relations as a whole, where there was 'a lot more at stake' for American interests.[45] The face-off continued until July 1990 when the Lithuanians agreed to freeze their declaration in return for Gorbachev opening negotiations with all three Baltic republics. This put the lid on the Baltic pressure cooker – but only for the moment.

The biggest nationality problem was not, however, on the periphery but in the metropole. The real challenge was the political emergence of Russia, because that raised the existential question of whether it was possible to have a strong Russian state without destroying the Soviet empire. The small republics could huff and puff, but Russia (RSFSR) was not only by far the biggest of the USSR's fifteen republics, it was also the pumping heart of the whole union, accounting for two-thirds of its economic activity, three-quarters of its territory, and half of the country's 290 million people.

Yet constitutionally each of the other fourteen republics was Russia's equal. To add insult to injury, the non-Russian republics had their own 'national' communist parties, albeit subservient to the CPSU, while that was never the case for Russia. That did not matter as long as Russia dominated Soviet politics, which was the case for most of Soviet history: the USSR was effectively the tsarist Russian empire under a new Bolshevik leadership. Until the ethnic revival in the 1980s, Russians had paid little attention to any distinction between Russia and the Soviet Union. For Gorbachev, too, the USSR was virtually synonymous with Russia, and his concessions to nationalism – like Lenin's – were essentially tactical: in his own mind he was pursuing the original Leninist principle of a Soviet federation.[46]

Given Russia's natural dominance of the union, nationalism there developed relatively slowly. But by the spring of 1990, nationalist senti-ment was on the rise. Pressure was growing for the republic to have its own Communist Party – a particular demand of party hardliners, while liberals wanted to turn the newly created Russian Republic's parliament into a powerhouse for rapid reform. So Gorbachev, who would have much preferred to keep the status quo with regard to Russia, was facing challenges from both sides. Moreover, this was all happening not hundreds of miles away – on the periphery of the USSR – but right on his own doorstep, in Moscow.[47]

In June 1990, the communists of the Russian Republic finally got a party of their own.[48] This new Russian Communist Party (RCP) constituted nearly 60% of the total CPSU membership. On 20 June Gorbachev addressed the RCP founding congress. He did so in two capacities – as president of the USSR, under the new constitution, and also in his old role as leader of the CPSU, to which the RCP was officially subordinate. But constitutional niceties no longer counted for much, given the mood now prevalent in Russia. Chernyaev was struck that his boss sat through the entire five-day Congress, which was broadcast live by the main Soviet television station and covered in full by the Supreme Soviet's official newspaper *Sovetskaya Rossiya*. Indeed, he was frankly shocked that the leader of the Soviet Union 'tolerated such abuse' – not just 'insults' but 'out-and-out barbarism' – from the reactionaries, many of whom simply 'loathed him'. It was Shevardnadze who, a few days later, hit back at the critics, likening the accusations by General Albert Makashov, Yegor Ligachev (second secretary of the CPSU) and others to the 'malicious witch-hunts' in the USA during the McCarthy era. 'It is time to realise that neither socialism, nor friendship, nor good-neighbourliness, nor respect can be produced by bayonets, tanks, or blood.' These exchanges revealed the rifts opening up at the top of the Soviet state.[49]

But Russian hardliners were not the only ones on the up. At the other end of the political spectrum, Russian radical reformers had capitalised on the growing surge of democratisation. On 4 March 1990, elections had been held for the 1,068-seat Congress of People's Deputies of the Russian Republic. Unlike the Soviet Congress elections of 1989, there were no reserved or uncontested seats – and this time democrats and liberals came together and mobilised as a movement-cum-party called Dem Rossiya ('Democratic Russia'). They gained 465 seats while 417 were won by the communists; 176 deputies hovered between the blocs. Among the deputies was Boris Nikolayevich Yeltsin.[50]

*

Born in 1931 in the village of Butka in the Sverdlovsk region, Yeltsin, like Gorbachev, came from a humble background: his father worked in construction, his mother was a seamstress. After studying at the Ural Polytechnic Institute in Sverdlovsk and rising through the Sverdlovsk House-Building Combine, he entered the ranks of the CPSU *nomenklatura* in 1968. By 1976 he had become party first secretary of the Sverdlovsk Oblast – a position he held for almost a decade – and was elected to the Central Committee of the CPSU in 1981.

Although actually a month older than Gorbachev, Yeltsin had always been well behind him in the party hierarchy – a source of friction between these two ambitious men, exacerbated by Yeltsin's highly competitive and rebellious nature. Nevertheless, Gorbachev recognised his talent, energy and reformist instincts. So, in December 1985, it was Gorbachev – by now leader of the Soviet Union – who appointed Yeltsin first secretary of the CPSU Moscow City Committee, making him effectively 'mayor' of the Soviet capital, and who, two months later, invited him into the Politburo as a non-voting member. Yet such patronage only intensified Yeltsin's resentment because it highlighted their difference in rank. Being given Gorbachev's former dacha on arrival in Moscow merely added insult to injury.[51]

Once in the capital, Yeltsin began to present himself as a bold populist with radical ideas – who delivered hard-hitting speeches and gained popularity among Muscovites by firing corrupt local party officials. Gorbachev was displeased by Yeltsin's demotic style and also jealous of his evident rapport with the masses. The tensions came to a head two years later, in October 1987. At a bruising plenary meeting of the Central Committee, Yeltsin openly criticised the Kremlin's reforms as too sluggish and then, in a wholly unprecedented move, requested he be allowed to resign from the Politburo. Erratic as ever in mood, he lapsed into depression and tried to commit suicide with a pair of scissors. After that episode, Yeltsin was fired from all his leadership positions in Moscow, too. So Gorbachev lost one of his Politburo's committed reformers, and gained himself a lifelong enemy.[52]

Yeltsin said he would never forgive Gorbachev for this 'immoral and inhumane' treatment inflicted by the party.[53] Perhaps regretting his harshness, Gorbachev subsequently behaved magnanimously and made Yeltsin first deputy head of the State Construction Ministry. This concession gave the humiliated Yeltsin the chance to remain active in Moscow, but he felt no gratitude to Gorbachev and began plotting his comeback and revenge. As the Soviet domestic crisis worsened, the less easy it was for Gorbachev to ignore Yeltsin. By the time Gorbachev realised that Yeltsin had grown into a truly serious rival, their relationship had been fatally poisoned.[54]

Ironically, Gorbachev's decision to establish a Soviet Congress of People's Deputies gave Yeltsin a platform for his comeback. He not only became a candidate but, thanks to his popularity, gained the backing of more than 5 million Muscovites and won the special citywide Moscow seat with a massive 89% of the vote. A little over a year later, in March 1990, he was voted into the new Russian Congress and set his eyes on becoming chairman of the Russian Supreme Soviet. Gorbachev believed he could thwart this by running alternative candidates but Yeltsin saw them all off. On 29 May 1990, he got the position he wanted and was now, in effect, leader of the Russian Republic. From the heart of the empire, he could henceforth challenge its emperor.

Some observers at the time could see the writing on the wall. 'Gorbachev is becoming a king without any subjects,' said Yuri Boldyrev, a radical representative from Leningrad on the RSFSR's Supreme Soviet. 'If he is opposed by Russia, then who is there left for him to rely on? Only the Central Asian republics, but they, too, are getting their own rulers.'[55]

Gorbachev found the Yeltsin phenomenon both infuriating and puzzling.[56] He considered his rival 'incomprehensible' and even distasteful: 'Both here and abroad he drinks like a fish,' Gorbachev sneered contemptuously at a Politburo meeting in April.[57] 'Every Monday his face doubles in size. He's inarticulate, he comes up with the devil knows what, he's like a worn-out record. But over and over the people keep repeating "He's our man" ... and they forgive him everything.' Even so, the Soviet leader had thought he could manage the man from Sverdlovsk.[58] Yeltsin's effective takeover of Russia on 29 May was therefore a real setback. Gorbachev heard the news en route to the summit with Bush at Camp David. When Jack Matlock asked Gorbachev whether he could work with Yeltsin, the Soviet leader evaded the question: 'You tell me ... You've seen more of him than I have of late.'[59]

From now on, according to diplomat Alexander Bessmertnykh, Gorbachev was 'blinded by his dislike of Yeltsin'. Gorbachev's 'sense of injury won out over the political calculation', his aide Georgy Shakhnazarov wrote later, 'and his pride took precedence over common sense'. And this at a time when what mattered was calm calculation.[60]

Because Yeltsin now had a political base that put him outside the control of Gorbachev, the Soviet leader found himself waging a two-front war – against Yeltsin, self-proclaimed Russian nationalist and committed democrat with a Russian platform in the Soviet capital and also, at the other end of the political spectrum, against the fledgling Russian Communist Party. In the end, Yeltsin would prove more dangerous for the union than the RCP.

This became apparent as early as June 1990, when Yeltsin secured the passage of legislation giving Russian laws priority over Soviet laws.[61] The move played well among ordinary Russians but, for him, ultimately nationalism and democracy were largely tactical cards. Yeltsin was essentially an old-fashioned party boss, with no dissident roots or contacts. What interested him was power: for Russia and thus for himself. On the other hand, Gorbachev was pleased with the outcome of the July Party Congress. Although sniped at by hardliners, he was re-elected leader of the CPSU and gained clear endorsement of his own policies. With a united party behind him, serving as the glue to hold the country together, he felt he could face the future with more confidence.

Yet it was Yeltsin who generated the greatest drama. With characteristic demagoguery, on 12 July he announced his resignation from the Soviet Communist Party, declared that he now answered only to the Russian people and then stormed out of the conference hall. By doing so, he presented himself as a true democrat, unlike the man he derided, 'chatterbox Gorbachev'.[62]

Political fallout: Yeltsin and Gorbachev

Meanwhile the economy had entered free fall.[63] It is easy to see why Kohl's chequebook diplomacy during the Caucasus summit and later that summer proved such an effective diplomatic tool in securing the crucial security aspects of the German unification deal. Gorbachev had few illusions left: 'If we can't come up with something to save consumers (and they are already almost destroyed), the people will explode.'[64] So far, the 'moderately radical' plan adopted during the winter by Prime Minister Ryzhkov's State Commission for Economic Reform had made little progress. The plan was a package of structural reforms and austerity measures, intended to create a 'controlled market economy' by 1995. In appearance, this was similar to the Polish 'big bang' or 'shock therapy' approach to economic transformation launched by Mazowiecki in late 1989 to achieve a market economy within one year. Although borrowing from Poland, the Soviet reform package differed in its much longer timespan and crucially because it adopted a dual-track approach. While austerity measures were imposed immediately – leading to huge price rises – the structural reforms, including anti-monopoly measures, looser controls on foreign investment and banking reforms, would not be fully implemented until 1993. As a result of this phased approach, the USSR ended up with the worst of both worlds. By mid-summer 1990 Soviet consumers were panic-buying basic foodstuffs. And several republics – Russia, Byelorussia, Ukraine and the Baltic republics – opted out of the reform programme.[65]

After the failure of the Ryzhkov plan, Gorbachev had no clear idea where to go – he had only appointed a proper economic adviser in January[66] – and the new Presidential Council (created in March) was no help. Around him, confusion reigned. The directors of state enterprises predicted disaster, if the radicals got their way. Free marketeers pressed for faster and more comprehensive liberalisation, while warning against doing too much. There was no obvious solution. The whole system was in limbo. Soviet society teetered on the edge of the abyss.[67]

It was against this grim background that, in late July 1990, Grigory Yavlinsky – Yeltsin's new deputy premier and also a pro-market economist – approached Gorbachev's neophyte economic adviser Nikolai Petrakov, proposing that they work together on a full transition to the market. Within twenty-four hours they drew up a joint paper, which was presented to Gorbachev. He embraced it and the decision was taken that all republics should be included in the plan. After much delicate diplomacy between the Gorbachev and Yeltsin camps, a new 'joint' market transition team was established in early August – consisting almost entirely of young liberal economists. It was led by Stanislav Shatalin – new head of the Academy of Sciences economics division and a member of the Presidential Council, whose career had previously been held back due to his social democratic views. Shatalin was thrilled by his appointment – likewise his new staff – and they set to work with energy and enthusiasm. But for political and practical reasons, Shatalin's team had to include the more conservative economists from Ryzhkov's State Commission who embarked on a spoiling action, refusing to provide government documents. Cooperation between the two groups was minimal.[68]

The Shatalin/Yavlinsky plan grandly promised a total economic revolution in 500 days: creating a competitive market system through large-scale privatisation and freeing prices from state control, as well as integrating the USSR in the global economic system. Even though the '500 Days Plan' set out a timetable, this was just to spur things on: it was obvious that you could not transform a system that had evolved over seven decades within a mere eighteen months. Shatalin personally had no doubt that it would take 'generations' to grow out of the Plan and into the world market. Nevertheless, this radical agenda – feasible or not – was too much for the Ryzhkovites who feared yet more chaos. As a result, they stayed in their own cocoon and worked up a rival programme.[69]

What mattered about the 500 Days Plan was the political message as much as economic doctrine. It strongly implied that socialism was dead – an idea that Gorbachev had always considered heretical. Indeed, with Chernyaev's help at this very time he was trying to write an article to prove to his critics – and perhaps to himself – that he remained ideologically sound. In the essay he advocated a 'modern socialism' – which he portrayed as 'an organic part of the march of civilisation'. Significantly, this essay was never finished.[70] But, with regard to the 500 Days Plan, Gorbachev was keenly engaged – phoning Shatalin and Petrakov several times a day for updates. So in practice – if not in theory – he appeared to fully embrace its content. Indeed, he told Chernyaev that the Shatalin plan was 'the most important thing'– nothing less than 'the final breakthrough to the new phase of perestroika'. As a political bonus, if he and Yeltsin held together on the 500 Days Plan, this might be the basis for further cooperation.[71]

In the end, however, economics could not be harmonised with politics. After many factional arguments over the summer, Yeltsin unequivocally backed the final version of the 500 Days Plan[72] – which hubristically envisaged the privatisation of 46,000 industrial enterprises and 760,000 trade enterprises – leaving under state control just a few key areas such as defence, railways, post and power. So did Gorbachev. Yeltsin then got it approved by the Russian Supreme Soviet on 11 September.[73] For Gorbachev, however, that proved too much, too fast – for both social and political reasons. In his mind, going with the 500 Days Plan would be like jumping off a cliff into the unknown. How would millions of ordinary Soviet citizens sustain the burden that 'shock therapy' would bring? Rampant inflation. Mass unemployment. Perhaps the complete breakdown of society. How could he possibly maintain order? And he could not ignore the fierce objections of Ryzhkov, who was voicing the feelings of many in the CPSU as well as the vested interests of the Soviet military-industrial complex – already inveterate critics of perestroika. Indeed, Ryzhkov threatened to resign if Gorbachev endorsed the 500 Days Plan, taking his whole government with him.[74]

But going along fully with Ryzhkov's line – and thereby leaving firmly in charge the very Moscow bureaucrats who had previously sabotaged every other Gorbachev reform – would only exacerbate the ongoing economic collapse. So Gorbachev, as ever, kept looking for a compromise. He hoped against hope that the Shatalin and Ryzhkov plans could be somehow married. Yeltsin scoffed that this was like 'trying to mate a hedgehog with a snake',[75] but Gorbachev did not give up – so much did unity matter to him. In the end, he even spent several days trying to distil the 452 pages of the Shatalin plan into an anodyne and evasive sixty-page document about a carefully graduated transition under the tellingly vague title 'Main Directions for the Stabilisation of the National Economy and the Transition to a Market Economy'. On 19 October, after launching an urgent appeal for national discipline and a scorching attack on Yeltsin, whom he portrayed as a 'destructive opportunist', he managed to gain its approval by the USSR Supreme Soviet. But this eviscerated dossier no longer embodied a clear strategy.[76]

The political fallout was quick and massive. An angry Yeltsin accused Gorbachev of reneging on a commitment to the radical reform plan. Even more dangerous, he threatened that Russia would no longer accept subordination to the central Soviet government.[77] In fact, by late autumn, the Soviet leader was under attack from all fronts. Much of the press demanded his resignation, even raising the spectre of civil war if he refused. And his power base was also eroding. On the one hand, support among the intelligentsia and reformist citizens was crumbling; on the other, KGB boss Kryuchkov was mounting a campaign to poison Gorbachev against Shevardnadze and other trusted liberals in his inner circle. In a disastrous meeting in mid-November with more than a thousand military officers, the Soviet leader was formally told that he had lost the support of the army.[78]

On 16 November, summoned by the Supreme Soviet to give an emergency report on the state of the union, Gorbachev tried to go on the offensive. In rambling remarks, he vehemently rejected demands that he form a coalition government with non-communists, while promising a shake-up of government and military leadership to win back public support. He also insisted that the constituent Soviet republics accept a new Union Treaty to preserve the country's federal structure, confirming control by the centre of the military and much of the economy. The 500 Days Plan, he asserted, was a threat to the union. As for the widespread talk of famine, that was nothing but 'vile rumours'. The country had enough food and fuel to get through the winter without calamity. The problem, he said, was not shortage but chaos in the distribution system. Hence his proposals for 'reorganisation'. Because, he warned, 'without public trust, it would be difficult if not impossible to implement a policy effectively to bring us out of this crisis'.

Gorbachev's ninety-minute speech – replete with abstractions and platitudes – received an icy reception from the deputies. The leaders of the republics, who in turn paraded up to the podium to say their bit, made it clear that the Soviet leader's blueprint for a more decentralised federation had little hope. They called for drastic measures to stop the disintegration of political authority and the slump in living standards. Their demands ranged from a countrywide food-rationing programme to an authoritarian 'committee of salvation' that would replace Gorbachev and rely on the military and police. The deputies voiced huge disappointment that Gorbachev offered no concrete new proposals to break the deadlock and just whined about ambitious rivals and their 'well-planned campaign' to discredit him. 'We wanted to hear a programme for action, not excuses and complaints about difficulties and obstacles,' said Anatoly Sobchak, mayor of Leningrad.[79]

Later that day, he got another earful from the Politburo. In a situation of total economic free fall, with crime out of control and breadlines in the streets, the new Russian Communist Party boss, Ivan Polozkov, told Gorbachev to dissolve the Presidential Council, arrest troublemakers in the mass media and take power into his own hands. He added: 'It's your fault, you began perestroika by destroying the foundation on which the party has been built.'[80]

Shaken and angry, Gorbachev stayed up all night preparing an overhaul plan, which he then unveiled to the Supreme Soviet the next morning, 17 November. This time his remarks were brief and concrete, lasting only twenty minutes, and outlined eight clear points. He proposed a complete reorganisation of the government to strengthen presidential power. He would abolish the Presidential Council and the position of prime minister, and convert the Council of Ministers appointed by the parliament into a Cabinet answerable to the president. A new Security Council, reporting to the president, would oversee the army, police and KGB. And the Federation Council, the leaders of the fifteen republics, which he chaired, would become the country's chief executive.[81]

This upgrade of the Federation Council was immediately rejected by the three Baltic republics, followed by Georgia and Armenia. 'We will not participate in any federational institution. The decision of our people is quite clear,' said Marju Lauristin, deputy chairwoman of the Estonian parliament. 'The decentralisation of power has come so far that all attempts to turn this process back will not be successful,' she added. 'It will mean that there will be a lot of conflicts.' Particularly serious for Gorbachev was Yeltsin's rejection. 'We have to speak not about a Union Treaty but about a union of sovereign states,' the Russian leader stated. 'These are two different things.'[82]

Nevertheless, the plan as a whole was accepted in the Supreme Soviet by the overwhelming margin of 316 to 19 – with thirty-one abstentions. Of course, nobody expected that his midnight magic would replenish the grocery shelves overnight, and many feared that this was all too late to halt the disintegration of the Soviet Union into warring sovereignties.[83] Still, for the first time in many months, Gorbachev seemed to have regained a foothold on the slippery terrain of Soviet domestic politics. The *Izvestiya* commentator Stanislav Kondrashev remarked that the apparent pointlessness of democracy was making the idea of a 'strong hand' attractive to the public, citing the old adage of the Roman emperors, 'bread and circuses'. But, said Kondrashev, 'when bread rations are rapidly declining, people are prepared to sacrifice parliamentary circuses'.[84]

Old-guard communists welcomed what seemed to them the strengthening of the state and a blueprint for slower, controlled reform. Conversely, Gorbachev hoped that liberals would regard his actions as a sign that he was still maintaining the momentum for reform, while seeking compromises across the political spectrum. But as Chernyaev pointed out, Gorbachev in the 'role of unifier, pacifier, and adviser' – rather than leading from the front – was 'dangerous!'[85] Indeed the rebalancing act he had announced on 17 November was itself a gamble that might in the longer term weaken his authority, because he raised unreal expectations about the use of his new powers to resolve the national crisis.

Equally, by announcing his newly configured presidential role just before the Paris CSCE summit, Gorbachev took a gamble on how it would be perceived in the West. 'No one should forget that half of the nuclear potential of the world is concentrated in this country,' declared Vladimir A. Ivashko, deputy chief of the Soviet Communist Party. 'By stabilising the situation in the Soviet Union, these proposals reduce many concerns of our neighbours abroad.' And, Gorbachev hoped, they might also strengthen his hand with the international community and loosen Western purse strings.[86]

But there was little enthusiasm in Paris. With the USSR apparently on the edge of disintegration and ethnic divisions re-emerging all over Eastern Europe, Western leaders had little appetite for pumping money into the Soviet Union. Finnish diplomat Max Jakobson discerned widespread apprehension that democracy was 'unlikely to develop in the midst of economic catastrophe'. So Gorbachev tried a different tune, using the spectre of a looming food crisis as a political lever. Although the USSR had enjoyed a bumper crop that year, much of the produce rotted in the fields because of severe problems in harvesting, storage and transport. In Paris, he handed his Western counterparts a long and urgent shopping list of basic foodstuffs: pork, beef, flour, butter, powdered milk and peanut oil.[87]

Babushkas on the breadline

Although many leaders talked about the need to reassure the famine-threatened USSR, the only serious engagement came from the Germans. Genscher told Gorbachev that the EC was considering food aid worth $1 billion.[88] Kohl had also stated in the Bundestag that Germany would increase food shipments to the Soviet Union *if* an 'acute supply crisis' developed that winter.[89] Yet, these offers did not come easily because Kohl no longer felt he had 'deep pockets'. It is noteworthy that during the Soviet leader's visit to Bonn on 9–10 November 1990 – to sign the Soviet–German cooperation treaty – the chancellor had refrained from offering him any additional direct financial injections on top of $12 billion in credits and subsidies provided in mid-1990 and the multibillion Deutschmarks package to fund the Red Army pull-out. 'We've given them all we're going to give for now,' was the line taken by one diplomat on the German negotiating team.

Bonn had two concerns on its mind. Finance Minister Theo Waigel warned that borrowing by government at all levels in the FRG would come to some $95 billion in 1991 – nearly five times the equivalent figure in 1989. Faced with such acute new financial pressures, while trying to woo voters in the December 1990 elections, Kohl was keen to shift some of the burden of backing Gorbachev to others. Hence Genscher's emphasis on the EC and G7.

The newly free nations of Eastern Europe were also clamouring for aid that winter – though they were more concerned about fuel than food. These former Soviet satellites were struggling not only with the sharp reduction in Soviet deliveries of crude but also Moscow's decision to price its oil from the New Year of 1991 in dollars rather than roubles, thereby driving up energy costs across the region. While Germany keenly supported these nations' reform efforts, it decided not to extend any specific aid and also pushed that onto the EC, which did provide several hundred million dollars of emergency assistance.[90]

In late November, however, the Bonn government decided to treat the USSR as a special case. Politics overrode economics. The chancellor did not want to see Gorbachev's position endangered. 'We know that you have supported us on our difficult path to German unity,' he told Gorbachev on 10 November. And, he added, 'We Germans, who have in this century been at the forefront of so many disastrous developments, must now rise to the challenge of setting an example.' He assured Gorbachev, 'We will help as much as we can.' Not only had Kohl found the Soviet president to be a trusted partner but he also seemed the only credible Soviet guarantor for the 2 + 4 treaty's rapid ratification and for an orderly Soviet troop withdrawal from German soil. In other words, the FRG had a basic national interest in helping to prevent Soviet economic collapse.[91]

Kohl, however, shifted responsibility to the private sector, asking business and charities to establish a programme of emergency food aid for the USSR. He even appealed to the nation in a special TV broadcast entitled *Helft Rußland!* ('Help Russia!') to offer their personal contributions. 'Now is a difficult time for the Soviet Union,' he declared on 21 November. 'Winter is at hand. Hunger threatens many cities and towns.' In addition to private donations that by mid-December amounted to a staggering DM 800 million, thousands of tons of food came from a secret network of depots in Berlin, set up in the 1950s lest the Kremlin tried to repeat its 1948 blockade of the city. In total, there was enough food to feed nearly 2 million people for six months. 'Probably everything here is going to be sent to Russia,' said Dieter Melerowicz, a warehouse manager, with cases of canned apple sauce and sliced pineapple towering behind him. 'Right now, the people there need it a lot more than we do.' An ironic end-of-the-Cold War dividend.[92]

*

While the international community debated whether to give money, a further twist occurred in Moscow. As a consequence of Gorbachev's political reorganisation and ministerial reshuffle, liberals began to disappear from his inner circle. His tightened grip on power at the end of 1990 was accomplished in close cooperation with the Communist Party, the military and the KGB.

As part of the reshuffle, and in reaction to endemic corruption and the economic malaise, Gorbachev replaced the nation's chief of police with two arch disciplinarians from the party hierarchy and the military command. He also revived the old Bolshevik practice of vigilante committees of workers to monitor food stocks and punish thieves and speculators, especially now the first planeloads of food aid and medicines from abroad were starting to arrive. The Soviet public feared these would mostly disappear into the black market.

At the very top, Vadim Bakatin, one of the more liberal members of the Soviet leadership, was obliged to surrender the Interior Ministry to Boris Pugo, a Latvian who had been the KGB boss in Riga for eight years. Making General Boris Gromov the first deputy interior minister was yet more indicative of Gorbachev's desire to satisfy public demand for a tough line. Gromov, commander of the Kiev military district, had earlier masterminded the orderly Soviet exit from Afghanistan.[93]

Some Americans speculated that Gorbachev's choice of conservative critics might signify that he was trying to reduce pressures for a coup. One could, of course, also say that by putting them so close to the seat of power, he made a coup more likely. On the whole, however, the view at the time was that the new men were being brought in as an attempt to display executive resolve.[94]

To regain the initiative against the republics, Gorbachev also submitted a fresh draft Union Treaty, which the Supreme Soviet approved on 3 December. The existing fifteen republics, it stated, should in future constitute a voluntary federation – renamed the 'Union of Sovereign Soviet Republics'. The small verbal shift indicated a crucial ideological change: 'socialist' had been replaced by 'sovereign'. Although the treaty would concede an unprecedented amount of authority to the individual republics, it also retained much power at the centre.

As a result, nobody was happy. The three Baltic republics and Georgia made clear that they had no intention of signing the treaty, while Ukraine – a republic of 53 million people – stated it would not sign until its own constitution had been rewritten. Russia's leadership dismissed the draft as totally inadequate. Gorbachev told Yeltsin and the Baltic leaders that he was ready for a fight if they rejected the new treaty out of hand. Latvia had already attempted to cut off all supplies, including food and fuel, to Soviet troops on its territory and was calling on the Kremlin to remove its military presence from the republic. Significantly Gorbachev came under attack even from party enthusiasts, who blamed him for ceding too little to the republics while seeking to accumulate greater personal power than any of his predecessors.

Gorbachev was incensed: 'On the one hand, I'm accused of a paralysis of power. So then we try to break free of this paralysis of power. Then I'm criticised for trying to create some sort of dictatorship.' On top of all this, he felt Yeltsin was trying to exploit differences between them for political ends. 'I accept the challenge of my opponents and intend to pursue a political struggle, all in the framework of the constitution,' Gorbachev declared. He insisted that the new Union Treaty was the 'key' to stabilising current conflicts over political power, halting economic disintegration and, most of all, stopping the USSR from splitting apart. The result of that, he asserted, would be 'bloodshed'.[95]

The Soviet leader was painting himself into a corner. Radical in many of his reforms, he was slow to rethink the union. As historian Archie Brown has pointed out, it was 'second nature' to Gorbachev 'to believe in a Soviet identity which transcended people's sense of belonging to particular nationalities'. Though mentally flexible in so many areas, he found the idea of republics wanting to become independent states difficult to comprehend, at least emotionally. In Robert Service's words, Gorbachev was both a 'Soviet patriot' and a 'proud Russian' – and he veered between the two. So, although appearing in mid-1990 to give Lithuania and the other Baltic republics the impression that he would eventually let them go, by the end of the year he had changed tack, using ever stronger language to deter any republic from breaking away.[96] Once the patron and spokesman of liberals, he was now openly tracking to the right, surrounding himself with men who had never been allies and, indeed, were often open critics. In turn, those who had been close to him in the Politburo since 1985 found themselves marginalised. And by bolstering his own executive powers in a belated bid to achieve stability, he increasingly seemed like a 'normal' Russian autocrat – in the tradition of past tsars and party secretaries.

The most notable liberal ally to disappear was his foreign minister, who so dramatically announced his resignation on 20 December. Shevardnadze wasn't pushed, he jumped – reiterating in his speech to the Supreme Soviet undying support for the 'ideas of perestroika' but insisting he could not reconcile himself to 'events that are taking place in our country'. Gorbachev was hurt and horrified: he told the Congress of People's Deputies afterwards that he had been about to make Shevardnadze his vice president. And he wrote a passionate letter to Bush, seeking to limit the diplomatic damage. In that, he adopted a harsh tone, denouncing Shevardnadze's 'act of disloyalty' and assuring Bush that both Kremlin policy and their bilateral relations 'remain unchanged'.[97]

Although shaken by the news, Bush was not prepared to give up on Gorbachev, especially at a time when his global coalition was on the brink of war over Kuwait. On 30 November, on the back of UN Resolution 678 which the Kremlin had carried, he had given Saddam an ultimatum to withdraw his forces by 15 January 1991. Twelve days later, on 12 December, at a press conference in the White House Rose Garden, the president announced that Moscow would receive $1 billion in agricultural aid and that he would press for rapid Soviet 'association' with the IMF and the World Bank. 'None of the measures today are in any sense payback,' Baker quickly hastened to add afterwards, but the timing spoke for itself: here was a clear example of linkage politics. Within seventy-two hours the EC followed suit, announcing an aid package amounting to $2.4 billion. So the West appeared united in its financial backing of Gorbachev's course.

Economics aside, Bush also looked forward to signing a START treaty at his planned Moscow summit with Gorbachev in February 1991. Keen on a successful face-to-face, he declared, 'I want perestroika to succeed.' There was, he said, 'good reason to act now, in order to help the Soviet Union stay the course of democratisation'. He had no doubt that the United States had an interest in a Soviet Union 'able to play a role as a full and prosperous member of the international community of states'.[98]

That's why Bush did not intend to be deflected by Shevardnadze's departure – regrettable though it was, especially given Baker's constructive partnership with the Georgian. As the president told Ambassador Alexander Bessmertnykh, proposed but not yet confirmed as Shevardnadze's successor, on 27 December, there was criticism in America that he had 'personalised' relations too much. But, he added, 'I refute that because of what Gorbachev has done in [the] past five years.' The president still placed his hope in the future of their partnership. Working together, he believed, they could truly and cleanly leave the Cold War era behind.[99]

In Moscow, Chernyaev also commented on his leader's standing: 'All the main actors on the international stage saw Gorbachev's involvement as a guarantee of the seriousness and soundness of any major decisions in world affairs.' His 'importance and irreplaceability' in world politics was underscored by what Chernyaev called 'the universal understanding (especially by the US administration) of the need for his participation in resolving the Persian Gulf crisis'.[100]

Gorbachev, of course, was engaged in a balancing act. While Bush and European leaders searched for a *common* approach with him against Iraq, Saddam Hussein at the same time appealed to Gorbachev as a mediator and sent his foreign minister Aziz to Moscow, hoping to create a split in the UN Security Council. Gorbachev's willingness to keep open the Primakov channel with Baghdad was vexing for the White House. But what worried them much more was the Baltic issue, because the new US trade sweeteners seemed no guarantee of an acceptable resolution. Increasingly Gorbachev was, like the hardliners, treating

Baltic independence as a purely 'internal' issue, which brooked no foreign interference – rather than accepting its historically international dimension.

In his post-Christmas conversation with Ambassador Bessmertnykh, Bush stressed 'I would like you to press to Gorb[achev] our concerns about use of force – it would inevitably complicate our relationship. That would be a tragedy.' Bessmertnykh retorted, 'What Gorbachev needs is one to two years of stability. Law and order is necessary.' Bush admitted that Gorbachev had told him in Paris that 'he had to go home and be tough'. But from a 'US point of view', the president observed, it was 'desirable' to find some way to 'separate out' the Baltics. Gorbachev had promised to try to do that, Bush reminded Bessmertnykh, but it had to be 'done constitutionally' – meaning, it seemed, within the laboriously constructed framework of a new Union Treaty.[101]

Bush followed up this conversation with a call from Camp David to Gorbachev on 1 January 1991. He opened on a personal note: 'we have had a quiet and peaceful Christmas and New Years. I hope everything is going well. I appreciate the message Ambassador Bessmertnykh brought the other day.' The president would not comment over an open line about the letter's substance, but wanted to assure the Soviet leader of 'our full cooperation' and of 'our keen interest in our good relationship getting better'. Gorbachev replied: 'George, I wanted despite all the things that have happened – you know we have had some hot days here recently – to write that letter to you. I am sure we will continue our good relations based on what Ambassador Bessmertnykh has told me of your conversation.' Bush agreed, 'That is true.' Then he moved on to business: 'We will want to conclude work on START and on the little discrepancies on CFE. And of course we will want to continue our total cooperation and the exchange of information on the Gulf.' He sought to reassure Gorbachev: 'We are so committed to your reforms. Any place we can help, we'll do that. Please let us know. We hope you can overcome these difficulties and continue your reforms. You still have the respect and support of the American people.' Of course there was little that was tangible on the table, but the exchange reflected the goodwill on both sides with which they looked ahead to a new year.[102]

Chernyaev was struck by the tone of the conversation: 'It seems they are great friends.' Gorbachev was 'very emotional' when talking about Bush. 'Personal affinity clearly mattered.'[103]

Bush also reflected these sentiments of friendship and goodwill in his

New Year address to Soviet people, delivered just a little later, striking an upbeat note for 1991: 'This year our two countries, as well as those around the world, have much to be grateful for – first and foremost, the improved and strengthened relations between the United States and the Soviet Union. Our countries have made great progress, particularly in important political and arms-control areas. And we've taken a common approach to a new challenge in the name of stability and peace. I applaud – the world applauds – the decisive action of the Soviet Union in strongly opposing Saddam Hussein's brutal aggression in the Gulf.'[104]

But irrespective of Bush's optimism about superpower relations, the Baltic issue could not be brushed under the carpet. Whatever Bush and Gorbachev hoped, the popular-front leaderships in Lithuania, Latvia and Estonia had no interest in letting the superpowers bury the hatchet at their expense. They wanted their independence restored. Personal relations at the highest level or the imperatives of geopolitics were, for them, of secondary consideration.

*

Gorbachev, unlike Bush, viewed 1991 with foreboding and, at times, even impotent fury. His economic adviser Nikolai Petrakov had suddenly quit, after only one year in the job. 'All these newspaper outbursts, saying that everyone is leaving Gorbachev one by one,' the Soviet leader angrily told Chernyaev, whom he summoned, with other aides, to the president's office on New Year's Day. He shuffled some papers on his desk and then jotted down various notes, fuming all the while. His embarrassed advisers sat there quietly. It seemed as if the wheels were coming off.

Gorbachev's own New Year's Day speech lacked passion and inspiration. Alexander Yakovlev, his long-term liberal aide from whom he had become increasingly estranged, told Chernyaev, 'The words aren't very banal or anything. But it's just out of steam!' Chernyaev, who momentarily contemplated resignation, felt the same: 'I also catch myself thinking that no matter what Gorbachev says now, it really is "out of steam". I felt this very acutely during the Congress. He is no longer regarded with respect or interest; at best, he is pitied. He has outlived his achievements, while disasters and chaos exacerbate the people's irritation with him. He does not see this, from this stems his even greater drama. His overconfidence is becoming absurd, laughable even.'[105]

The term 'chaos' was no exaggeration. Party organisations were in turmoil; morale was at rock bottom in the Red Army and security services; and government ministries struggled to implement the kaleidoscope of policy changes. Power at the centre was visibly weakening, amid a veritable roulette of new appointments as Gorbachev spun ever more to the right. His choice as vice president of Gennady Yanaev, head of the official trade union and formerly leader of the communist youth organisation Komsomol, was another ominous sign of the way things were going. A nervy chain-smoker and to many people frankly vulgar, Yanaev was deeply disliked by the Soviet intelligentsia. But from Gorbachev's perspective Yanaev would at least not steal the limelight from him. The Soviet leader rammed through the appointment, against the wishes of many deputies, at the Congress in late December.[106]

On top of that, Prime Minister Ryzhkov had suffered a heart attack on Christmas Day, so Gorbachev also needed to find a replacement for him. To Chernyaev's chagrin, his boss sidestepped all the names suggested by his advisers – including that of Leningrad mayor Anatoly Sobchak, an able and experienced reformist who might counterbalance Yeltsin. Instead Gorbachev plumped for Valentin Pavlov – his tubby finance minister – who was unpopular with the Soviet public and not ranked highly as an economist by foreign ambassadors. Jack Matlock considered him 'arrogant' and 'erratic'. He had 'neither the stature nor the ability to be an effective head of government, particularly at troubled times' – evident already in his poor track record when tackling the Soviet financial malaise. And now Pavlov even claimed that Soviet inflation had not been generated by the massive rouble-overhang created by his 1990 policy of printing banknotes to finance the growing budget deficit, blaming instead foreign banks for deliberately flooding the USSR with money in order to subvert its government. It was left unexplained just how this view could be married with Gorbachev's relentless policy of soliciting Western financial aid to help turn the Soviet Union into a market economy.[107] Foreign policy and domestic politics were clearly pulling in different directions. But thanks to Gorbachev, Pavlov – an arch opponent of the 500 Days Plan – now had the position and power to implement his conservative half-baked version of market reform.

In international affairs, once Gorbachev's forte, he now also seemed confused – almost adrift. On 7 January, Chernyaev noted: 'M. S. [i.e. Gorbachev] no longer seriously thinks about foreign policy issues. He is busy with "structures" and "small affairs" – talking with one person or the next, whoever is imposed on him ... He does not prepare for anything, he repeats the same thing ten times. In the meantime, a ground war in the Persian Gulf is approaching. Nothing is being done on our side.'[108]

Speculation was also mounting inside the USSR about whether the superpower summit was still on for February. And Gorbachev, increasingly tetchy, was still dragging his feet about formally appointing a new foreign minister. 'Mikhail Sergeyevich,' Chernyaev told him bluntly, 'you need to decide something about Shevardnadze. A mismanaged agency is the most dangerous kind.' But, as aide Andrei Grachev put it, Gorbachev's 'strategic reserve of optimism seemed to be on the verge of exhaustion ... it was as if everything was too much for him'.[109] Six years at the top, during the most turbulent era of post-war Soviet history, had undoubtedly taken its toll.

This was abundantly clear when Gorbachev phoned Bush on 11 January – two days after the failure of Baker's talks with Iraqi foreign minister Aziz and just four days before the UN deadline on Kuwait ran out. Yet Gorbachev was still pretending he could play peacemaker, asserting that Saddam 'is ready to listen to Moscow. He asks for my advice.' Bush simply reiterated the 15 January deadline: 'we can't let him stand up to the opinion of the rest of the world'. Nor was the US president impressed by Gorbachev's bluster about the economy: 'Well, things are moving now and we finally have a budget' and have 'adopted cuts of approximately 20%. The Supreme Soviet has reduced the military budget by 20 million roubles, so I can report that we are disarming.' Bush's response was a curt 'very interesting'.

Gorbachev also pussyfooted around the biggest issue for the White House: 'We have some problems in the Baltics,' he remarked coyly. 'We are doing all that is possible to avoid sharp turns and radical steps, but it is a difficult situation.' Bush took his usual line. 'You know our position on that; we've talked about it many times. Your relations with all of the outside world would be better if you can avoid the use of force – I think you know this.'

'George, this is what we've been trying to do,' Gorbachev protested. 'We only intervene when the situation threatens the lives of the people.' He depicted himself as the would-be moderate, 'under a lot of pressure' to introduce presidential rule because of the intransigence of the Lithuanian government and the protests on the streets. 'You know what my style is in such matters,' he assured Bush expansively: 'it is much like your style. I will do all I can to take such steps to reach a political solution.'

'I appreciate that,' Bush replied patiently. 'We look at it through the different eyes of history, but I appreciate your trying to explain it to me now.'

'Well, we will be acting in a very responsible manner. But it is not all within our control. Today there was even some shooting.'

'Oh my God.' Bush decided to shift their conversation back to the Gulf.[110]

Behind the soft soap, Gorbachev had already begun to harden his stance. On 7 January the commander of the Baltic military district, General Fyodor Kuzmin, claiming to act on orders from Soviet defence minister Yazov, informed Baltic governments that the Kremlin was immediately deploying 10,000 Soviet paratroopers on their soil. When news reached the US, Washington refrained from any official comment. Then on 10 January, Gorbachev issued an ultimatum demanding the Lithuanian Supreme Council at once 'rescind unconstitutional acts adopted previously'. Next day, as Gorbachev talked with Bush, Soviet forces started to occupy buildings in Vilnius. Little wonder that the US president was unimpressed by their conversation.[111]

It seemed, indeed, as if Gorbachev was repeating the patterns of previous Soviet leaders: surprising the world with a crackdown inside the Soviet empire when international opinion was preoccupied with other matters – in the Middle East. Was this a reprise of Khrushchev in 1956: sending the tanks into Hungary when the West was fixated on Suez? Gorbachev unmasked? The peacemaker abroad, now revealing his iron fist at home?

The Soviet president clearly did not want to openly upset his new Western allies, especially America and Germany from whom he was desperate to secure more aid. At the same time, the Gulf crisis clearly provided a good time to bury bad news. Gorbachev was determined to stop the disintegration of the union – his inheritance from Lenin and Stalin – and at least this time, it seems, he tolerated, if not ordered, the resort to military force. In Moscow, such a policy appealed to the hardliners and thereby, he hoped, it would strengthen political support for his beleaguered presidency. Among the members of NATO, only Iceland publicly called on the Soviets not to use force and urged NATO's secretary general to take action.[112]

On Sunday 13 January, tanks rolled into the streets of Vilnius and Soviet special troops stormed the TV tower, killing fifteen of several hundred Lithuanian demonstrators and wounding many more. Angry crowds gathered all over Lithuania. The pattern was repeated a week later in the Latvian capital, Riga, with four dead and mass protests.[113]

Under the tank: Vilnius, 13 January 1991

Gorbachev and the Kremlin denied complicity in the carnage,[114] but Chernyaev had no doubt where the blame lay. 'Never did I think that the inspiring processes started by Gorbachev could come to such an ignominious end,' he wrote in his diary on 13 January. 'I am worn out by the confusion, and, alas, the arbitrariness of our work; some kind of "spontaneity" in our affairs ... All of this led to the "spontaneous" actions of commandos and tanks in the Baltics and ended in bloodshed ... The Lithuanian affair has finally ruined Gorbachev's reputation and maybe his post as well.'[115]

Chernyaev was disgusted by the public charade at the Supreme Soviet next day. 'Pugo and Yazov made stupid, false, boorish speeches. Gorbachev himself spoke after the break, and his speech was pathetic, inarticulate, and full of pointless digressions. And no policy. It was sickening – plain hypocritical evasion. There was no answer to the most important question. The speech was worthy neither of the former Gorbachev, nor of the present moment, when the fate of his entire five-year cause is being decided. It was embarrassing and sad to hear.' The analysis by another veteran liberal adviser, Georgy Shakhnazarov, was both subtle and apt: Gorbachev was on the one hand a political radical and on the other a Soviet apparatchik.[116]

The evidence, though confused, strongly suggests that 'Gorbachev knew about and supported at least a limited military solution. Most likely, he did not expect numerous casualties and did not order the deaths of innocent people, but he embraced the solution that led to this outcome.'[117] In the end, however, the issue of direct responsibility is secondary: appearance counted for more than reality. The image of the bloody Baltic crackdown was a disaster for Gorbachev. His credibility as a principled political leader – the apostle of perestroika and glasnost, the man who had lectured the world at the UN on universal values – was now called into question. And even if he wasn't to blame directly, there remained perhaps a more troubling question: had he lost control of his country? Was the world's second superpower descending into anarchy?

And was a new Russia rearing its head? On the very day – 13 January – that blood was spilled in the streets of Vilnius, Boris Yeltsin was on a scheduled visit to the Estonian capital, Tallinn, in order to sign a mutual security pact between the Russian Republic and the three Baltic States. This was a calculated act: supporting Baltic independence aspirations but also defying Gorbachev and his central authority. Their 3 + 1 pact called for each of the four republics to respect the sovereignty of the others, to refrain from recognising any non-elected government among them and to come to one another's aid should the Soviet government use force against them. In addition, all four leaders issued a joint appeal to the UN for intervention in the Baltic crisis.[118]

Yeltsin's presence in Estonia probably prevented further shooting that day. He condemned the massacre in Vilnius and explicitly recognised their self-declared independence. His comments had no constitutional significance but, speaking as chairman of Russia's Supreme Soviet, they did have considerable symbolic importance and were widely noted abroad. In his personal power battle with Gorbachev, the Baltic republics now became one of Yeltsin's most significant weapons. And so, unlike Tiananmen in 1989, a crackdown by the central government did not serve to stabilise the unitary state but further undermined it.[119]

In Moscow, Leningrad and other cities the Russian democratic movement organised a demonstration, where protestors openly criticised the Soviet president. Banners read 'Gorbachev is the Saddam Hussein of the Baltics', 'Gorbachev is Today's Hitler!' and 'Give Back the Nobel Prize'.[120] The mood among his advisers was black. Chernyaev drafted a resignation letter on 15 January, confessing 'complete despair'. But he never sent it after finding Gorbachev on the 17th 'seemingly regretful' that things were turning out this way. 'Why tanks?' Chernyeaev asked. 'It is the ruin of your cause. Is Lithuania worth such stakes?'

'You do not understand,' Gorbachev replied heatedly. 'It is the army. I could not openly disassociate myself from them and condemn them after the Lithuanians humiliated them.'[121]

Grachev, equally dejected, refused to take on the job of head of the Central Committee's international department, which Gorbachev had offered him.[122]

In the liberal weekly *Moskovskie Novosti* of 17 January some thirty intellectuals, almost all of whom Gorbachev liked, including Petrakov and Shatalin, condemned the Soviet leader for 'bloody Sunday' – a reference to the notorious tsarist massacre of 1905. 'It made an impression on him,' said Chernyaev, so much so that when Gorbachev finally presented Bessmertnykh at the Foreign Ministry as Shevardnadze's successor, he referred to the article, saying: 'They are already calling me a criminal and a murderer.' Gorbachev was by now pretty much bitter at everybody, not least Yeltsin – 'that son of a bitch!' – who had not only wooed the Balts but also met with Iceland's ambassador to Moscow to discuss the situation. Over the weekend of 18–21 January, Iceland's foreign minister, Jón Baldvin Hannibalsson, pointedly visited the Baltic States, exploiting the tacit support given by Yeltsin. Gorbachev was furious with the Russian leader. 'What's to be done about him!' he exploded.[123]

For a week Gorbachev dithered. Then he made a bold and wholly unexpected declaration, claiming that the events in Vilnius did not represent his policy. In an apparent effort of damage limitation, Gorbachev appeared at the Foreign Ministry press centre with Alekander Yakovlev, who was reported to have left the president's inner circle, and Foreign Minister Bessmertnykh. There he spoke of his concern at the outcry both at home and abroad over Soviet military actions in Lithuania and Latvia and of the damage this had done to his reputation in the West. Reading out a prepared statement he claimed that the confrontations did not mark any change of policy and rejected accusations that he had abandoned his reformist course. 'The achievements of perestroika, democratisation and glasnost were and remain eternal values, which presidential power will protect.'

He blamed the deaths on the republics themselves: 'Illegal acts, violations of the constitution, crude violations of civil rights, discrimination against people of other nationalities, irresponsible behaviour in relation to the army, servicemen and their families – these have created that ground, that atmosphere, where clashes of this sort can arise very easily for the most unexpected reasons.' But he reserved his sharpest words for Yeltsin, for encouraging the separatists and calling for an independent Russian national army. 'Such irresponsible declarations are fraught with serious dangers, especially when they come from the leadership of the Russian Republic.' Through his unseemly twists and turns, Gorbachev earned himself the opprobrium of both left and right. And those who planned and executed the operation would later claim that he had authorised it.[124]

Abroad, however, he managed to wriggle out of the mess. As soon as the UN ultimatum expired and the US-led air campaign in the Gulf began at midnight on 15–16 January, the Baltics disappeared from the international radar. None of the big Western states was keen to recognise their independence amid the confusion and violence. In any case, nobody had any intention at this stage to shift the focus of their Moscow policy from Gorbachev to Yeltsin.

Iceland apart, the strongest Western response came from the European Parliament which decided to postpone debate on a $1 billion European Community aid package for the USSR. This was tantamount to a suspension. 'We cannot accept that Soviet troops attack the legally elected authorities in the Baltic States,' said Danish prime minister Poul Schlüter. 'No one knows exactly who gave the orders, but one thing is clear: the responsibility rests with the top leadership.'[125]

The Germans were certainly not keen to let the crackdown imperil their 'Moskaupolitik'. Kohl told the Lithuanian leadership patronisingly that they should take 'a hundred small steps rather than wanting to have it all with ten big steps'.[126] Germany and France then announced they were making a 'joint approach' to Gorbachev with a view to promoting a dialogue between Moscow and the republics. By eschewing the Nordic calls for sanctions, they had every intention to keep open their lines of communication to the Kremlin.[127]

In Washington, Condoleezza Rice – the NSC's Russia specialist – was the only major figure who wanted to make an issue of the Baltics. On 15 January she had warned that if yet more blood was spilled, Bush could be blamed for conniving in another 'Tiananmen'. Congress would then 'make it miserable for us' over the next couple of weeks. On the 21st, after the crackdown in Riga, she told Scowcroft that 'the Soviets have crossed our red line by using force' and that Washington had to react, at least by freezing the economic package offered on 12 December. Rice acknowledged that 'the president is hesitant to "punish" the Soviets and especially Gorbachev. But we should think of this as trying to reawaken the Gorbachev that we have come to respect and work so well with.' She asked Scowcroft to take this up with Bush. But the memo was marked 'cancelled' four days later. Deep into the air campaign against Iraq, the president had higher priorities than Baltic red lines.[128]

Representatives from Estonia, Latvia and Lithuania who were received by Baker on 22 January wanted to 'see a high-level United States delegation visit the Baltic States as soon as possible' but their plea fell on deaf ears. Apart from publicly deploring the violence, the Bush administration confined itself to requesting an 'explanation' by the USSR of its actions by reference to the principles of the 1975 Helsinki Final Act. Privately, however, in a direct letter to Gorbachev on 22 January the president stressed that over the past week he had acted 'with great restraint' following the turmoil in Lithuania because he still accepted Gorbachev's assurances made to him in person at several moments in 1990 that force would not be used as a matter of policy. But what was really going on now? he asked. Was perestroika in fact at its end? And did this also mean the end of their new phase of Soviet–American rapprochement? Bush made it clear that he was coming under increasing pressure to do some-thing from many quarters – Congress, the press and the US public as well as smaller NATO allies – especially if it looked as if Gorbachev had really changed course. Bush therefore urged the Soviet leader that there must be an unequivocal halt to the violence and a return to his concil-iatory approach. Otherwise Gorbachev ran the risk of America 'freezing many elements of our economic relationship'.

Despite the cool tone of this message, Bush's priority remained the global picture. And here what mattered was keeping Gorbachev onside as they moved towards a ground war in Kuwait. So the president didn't push the Baltic issue too hard. But Gorbachev had to pay a price. The Moscow summit, scheduled to start on 11 February, was quietly postponed. Direct superpower diplomacy would not resume in earnest until early summer.[129]

*

In the meantime, Gorbachev tried to shore up his position within the union. The economic situation had worsened dramatically, while the challenge from Yeltsin grew fiercer.

Keen to get a grip on the social unrest, in late January Gorbachev ordered the military to join local police in patrolling cities. Officially the patrols were instituted to crack down on theft and corruption, but they were widely viewed by the public as a pre-emptive move to deter likely public protest against monetary reform and the end of most government price subsidies.[130]

Pavlov's first major act as prime minister was indeed monetary reform – aiming to punish black marketeers and control inflation. On 23 January he banned 50- and 100-rouble notes, giving citizens three days to exchange them for smaller bills. Tens of thousands of people thronged banks, airports, train stations and municipal offices frantically demanding to know where and how to trade in their now useless notes. But everywhere the answer was the same, that there were no instructions save the decree published in all major newspapers. As a result, many people ended the first day of the reform strapped for cash.[131]

The *Chicago Tribune* wrote scathingly about the mess: 'Such dramatic stunts aren't those of reformers interested in introducing free markets and improving deplorable Soviet living standards, but the actions of bureaucrats desperately trying to make the central-planning system work and keep the crumbling Soviet economy from collapsing completely.' For the *Tribune* Pavlov and his cronies were merely 'caretakers' of the command system, who were 'trying some new things, but they don't add up to economic reform'.[132]

Ominously for Gorbachev, Yeltsin came out vehemently against Pavlov's measures. On 19 February the Russian leader berated Gorbachev for forty minutes on national television for an 'abrupt shift to the right, the use of the army in interethnic relations, the crash of the economy, low living standards' and a multitude of other failings. 'It is quite obvious that his intention is to keep the word perestroika, but not its essence,' Yeltsin declared. He asserted that Gorbachev had 'deceived the people' with a failed plan for national renewal and 'brought the country to dictatorship in the name of "presidential rule"'. In open defiance, Yeltsin announced, 'I separate myself from the position and policy of the president, and I stand for his immediate resignation.'[133]

As February turned to March, new crises emerged almost daily. Particularly troubling for Gorbachev was the fact that a quarter of the nation's miners had now downed tools. The strikes not only paralysed production but also had a political edge because the miners' demands extended beyond improved pay and conditions to calls for Gorbachev's resignation.[134]

In Moscow itself, Yeltsin's allies had been at the forefront of public protests. When hardline communists in the Russian parliament prepared to impeach the Russian leader, his supporters mobilised in his defence. On 25 March Gorbachev responded by banning all public rallies in the capital for three weeks and shifted control of Moscow's police from liberals in the City Hall to Pugo's Interior Ministry.[135] Two days later the centre of the city looked like an 'armed camp', according to David Remnick of the *Washington Post*. Some 50,000 Interior Ministry troops were deployed with water cannons and tear gas alongside the police. Next morning, as fresh snow began to fall, an estimated 100,000 demonstrators defied Gorbachev's ban to join a pro-Yeltsin rally. 'Not since Stalin's funeral have I seen such a shameful use of troops to control the people,' exclaimed one protestor. Chanting 'Yeltsin! Yeltsin!' and 'Gorbachev, get lost!' they marched around the centre of the city, on the edge of Red Square.

Was this Russia's Tiananmen moment? The country seemed on the brink of civil war.

But in fact both sides showed restraint and there was no violence. Indeed, the crowd behaved with remarkable serenity in the face of this massive array of force. The rally continued for the whole of the day. Cries of 'we are defenceless' gave way to contempt and then laughter as the protestors realised that the authorities would do nothing. They mocked the police power, said one journalist, 'as a burlesque of the terror' that had once made the Kremlin truly fearsome.

By the end of the day, the consensus was that the Soviet president had suffered a serious political setback. Yeltsin's supporters knew they had successfully defied Gorbachev's most aggressive effort to curb their movement and rout their leader. Yet ironically they were using the gift of public protest that Gorbachev – uniquely among Soviet leaders – had given them in the first place.[136]

Amid the turmoil, what was going on in Gorbachev's mind? Gorbachev told US ambassador Jack Matlock that he was pursuing a policy of 'zigs and zags' – trying to 'gain time by making tactical moves' and thereby 'allow the democratic process to acquire sufficient stability'. In truth, however, he was not a canny tactician and certainly no cool-headed strategist. Rather, the more Gorbachev's status declined, the more he desperately focused on political survival, which required an increasingly impossible balancing act between pursuing his ideal of reform and maintaining the CPSU – the only power base he knew and understood. Yet in a society now irreparably polarised, that meant throwing in his lot with the communist conservatives, while the radical devotees of perestroika had now found their own rival champion in Yeltsin. Not surprisingly, this was wearing him down; in fact, he was an emotional wreck. Chernyaev noted that Gorbachev had become 'more petty' and 'more irritable'. And also 'less informed': he was no longer avidly reading books and articles to 'develop himself' and gain new ideas. Like Grachev in January, Chernyaev sadly observed that Gorbachev 'has exhausted himself intellectually as a politician. He is tired. Time has passed him – his own time, created by him.'[137]

But the Soviet pillar of the new world order was not merely crumbling internally. The USSR's international standing suffered a further blow on 25 February when the Warsaw Pact agreed to dissolve itself at the end of March. Though highly symbolic, it was like burying a corpse. During 1990 the thirty-six-year-old alliance – dominated by the Red Army, which provided 3.7 million of the alliance's total troop strength of 4.8 million – had effectively ceased to function as its Eastern European members cut themselves loose from Moscow one by one.

Indeed, even before they held free elections in 1990, Hungary and

Czechoslovakia had negotiated agreements for the total withdrawal of Soviet troops from their territories by mid-1991. Although the pullout of 123,000 Soviet troops from Hungary and Czechoslovakia continued on schedule despite Gorbachev's tilt to the right, negotiations over the departure date for 50,000 Soviet soldiers in Poland had become bogged down and the Soviet parliament was not ready to ratify the 2 + 4 treaty guaranteeing German reunification until March 1991. At the same time, new security arrangements were taking shape in an East Central Europe no longer divided into blocs. That spring, Hungary, Poland and Czechoslovakia signed a mutual cooperation agreement and began to set their eyes on NATO. Economically, the same pattern was repeated. Comecon held its final meeting at the end of June 1991. Its members now looked west, seeking association with the European Community and a larger role in the CSCE.[138]

There was nothing Gorbachev could do to prevent the end of the Soviet bloc in Eastern Europe. But he was determined to move on with the renovation of the Soviet Union itself. On 17 March, he held a referendum asking Soviet citizens whether they were for or against the USSR as 'a renewed federation of equal sovereign states in which the rights and freedoms of any nationality will be fully guaranteed'. Remarkably, 76% voted in favour. Yet this headline figure was misleading. Six of the fifteen republics officially boycotted the vote – though small, mostly Russian minorities in each of them did, nevertheless, go to the polls. What's more, in the nine other republics the people showed strong majorities for anti-Kremlin local initiatives such as for a popular election of a president in Russia and greater autonomy, even independence, in Ukraine. Far from sketching a solution to the power struggle between the Kremlin and the republics, as Gorbachev had hoped, the USSR's 150 million voters only laid bare the country's passionate contradictions.[139]

The most challenging element for Gorbachev was the widespread support for a directly elected Russian president – which would launch Yeltsin into an even stronger position. It would also highlight the contrast with Gorbachev, who had sidestepped the idea of a direct election to the federal presidency in 1990, thereby denying himself the chance of a popular mandate. His sensitivity on the issue was evident on the evening of the referendum result. 'If some madman should arise to provoke a break-up of our union,' he told reporters, 'that would be a disaster for this country, for Europeans, for the entire world.' On the other side of the city, Yeltsin insisted that it would be impossible to improve people's lives as long as the centralised Kremlin system represented by Gorbachev endured: 'It should be destroyed and a new one based on democratic principles should be created.'[140]

Nobody could deny the real threat posed by Yeltsin. For now, however, Gorbachev concentrated on the referendum's positive side: the endorsement he had gained for a new Union Treaty. One month later on 23 April, at Novo-Ogarevo – the lavish government estate in the Moscow suburbs – Gorbachev, together with the nine republic presidents who had not boycotted the referendum, pledged to prepare a treaty establishing a new union of 'Sovereign States' and then to adopt a new constitution. What was variously called the '9 + 1' or Novo-Ogarevo process had been launched.[141]

The event was also political theatre for Gorbachev. Party hardliners had now been isolated and Republic leaders brought back into the fold – even Yeltsin who was forced to play second fiddle to the Soviet president, although he deliberately arrived at the meeting last. Gorbachev was firmly in the chair, with parliamentary speaker Anatoly Lukyanov and Yeltsin immediately to his right, while everyone else was seated in the alphabetical order of the territory they represented. When the business was done, there was a mood of catharsis. As they all sat down for dinner, they toasted their joint achievement, with Gorbachev and Yeltsin clinking their champagne glasses. The Russian leader even claimed that Gorbachev 'for the first time has spoken like a human being'. It seemed a moment of relief, even hope. Their plan was to sign the treaty within the next six months.[142]

But the party leadership was appalled. Next day Gorbachev had to explain himself to the Politburo and then the 410-member Central Committee of the CPSU. Some younger members, mostly Gorbachev appointees, had actually drafted a resolution demanding his resignation and spoke out forcefully. Gorbachev was furious. He stalked to the rostrum and delivered a forty-minute tirade warning that if he were forced out of office, the resulting vacuum would lead to an anti-constitutional dictatorship: 'Already, not just in words but in deeds, attempts are being made to push the country off the path of reform or to throw it into another ultra-revolutionary adventure, threatening to destroy our state or return it to the past, to a slightly dressed-up totalitarian regime.' He depicted himself in the middle of a pincer attack – on the one hand from the hard-line Soyuz ('Union') faction in the party and legislature, and on the other the opposition movement Democratic Russia who supported Yeltsin. When shouted down at one point by critics, Gorbachev exclaimed 'I'm leaving, I'm retiring,' and walked out. Pandemonium erupted in the hall and the Politburo caucus decided to take the removal resolution off the agenda. Again Gorbachev refrained from splitting the party but an eventual 322–13 majority on a vote of confidence hardly covered up the yawning cracks in his leadership.[143]

Nor was the truce with Yeltsin more than a temporary armistice. 'Now is not the time for all-out confrontation,' Yeltsin reportedly told Russian legislators when explaining why he had consented to the new Union Treaty. One of his top aides, Gennady Burbulis, said that the main virtue of the agreement was that it would enable the government of the Russian Republic to 'work in peace' without interference from the Soviet authorities.[144] Gorbachev, for his part, had no doubt that their modus vivendi was a facade. He had absolutely no respect for Yeltsin: 'The man lives for one thing only,' he told Shakhnazarov on 8 May, 'to seize power, even though he has no idea what to do with it.'[145] A month later, Yeltsin made another huge stride forward. On 12 June he was elected president of Russia, winning 59% of the votes. The man from Sverdlovsk now enjoyed the popular mandate that Gorbachev had spurned for himself, further undermining the Soviet leader.[146]

It was no accident that five days later Prime Minister Pavlov mounted his own challenge to Gorbachev, taking advantage of the Soviet leader's absence from a meeting of the Supreme Soviet. Pavlov, followed by Yazov and Kryuchkov, gave passionate speeches about the crisis facing the country and Gorbachev's failures as a leader. Pavlov went on to demand additional powers, hitherto held by Gorbachev or the parliament – for instance, to propose legislation, assume a large role in economic and social policy-making, and to take control over central banks and taxation. The liberal mayor of Moscow, Gavril Popov, privately warned Ambassador Matlock on 20 June that Pavlov's offensive was the first step towards a coup. This message was conveyed via Bush to Gorbachev, who was appreciative but dismissive, saying 'this is 1,000% impossible'. He assured the president he had the matter 'well in hand'. The following day Pavlov's demands were voted down in the Supreme Soviet by 262–24. Gorbachev scolded his ministers but chose not to sack anyone. With them standing stony-faced beside him, he told reporters with a big grin 'The "coup" is over.'[147]

A month later Gorbachev and Yeltsin managed a convivial dinner to mark approval of the draft Union Treaty. This was, nevertheless, a comprom- ise because Gorbachev wanted a strong federation with an effective central government that continued to hold substantial powers. Yeltsin preferred a much weaker union, akin to a confederation, which obviously would favour Russia as the dominant republic. The draft was more to Gorbachev's liking, because the new union state would retain responsibility for defence, diplomacy and the overall budget.[148]

Predictably this sparked another spasm of political protest from the party conservatives and the military-industrial lobby – this time very publicly in *Sovetskaya Rossiya*. 'A Word to the People', signed among others by generals Boris Gromov and Valentin Varennikov, warned that 'our motherland is dying, breaking apart and plunging into darkness and nothingness. The bones of the people and the backbone of Russia is snapped in two. How is it that we have let people come to power who do not love their country, who kowtow to foreign patrons and seek advice and blessings abroad?' But the draft Union Treaty was approved at the party plenum on 25–6 July 1991, together with a plan for a controversial new party programme – more social democrat than communist. Gorbachev seemed back in charge. He felt a sense of satisfaction about how far the country had come since the spring of 1985, when he assumed power. 'It seemed feasible that we could pull the country out of the crisis, and continue the programme of democratic changes,' he recalled. 'I left for a holiday on 4 August convinced that in sixteen days the Union Treaty would be signed in Moscow, opening a new stage of our reforms.'[149]

*

He also left with two significant, and intertwined, foreign-policy achievements during July: the USSR's participation for the first time at a G7 meeting, and Bush's first presidential visit to Moscow.

The superpower summit was supposed to have taken place much earlier in the year, but it had been deferred from February because of the Baltic crackdown and then again from March because of the Kuwait War and continuing problems over arms agreements. There were also growing doubts about Gorbachev himself. As Baker reflected later, 'Shevardnadze's resignation, the Soviet military's intransigence on arms control, and the crackdown in Lithuania in January 1991 made me all the more wary of Gorbachev's prospects.' The administration's view was to 'get as much as we could out of the Soviets before there was an even greater turn to the right or shift into disintegration'. And the way to that was to 'maintain our relations with Mikhail Gorbachev' until successfully completing at least the Gulf mission, the START treaty and ensuring that CFE did not unravel.[150]

The policy of sticking with Gorbachev was reinforced by the lack of alternatives. 'This guy Yeltsin is really a wild man, isn't he?' Bush exclaimed at the end of February.[151] Baker's experience in Moscow in March did nothing to alter this impression. On his first visit to the Soviet capital in six months he was disconcerted to find the political situation even more polarised than before. He cabled Bush that Yeltsin had stoked up public protest in order to 'declare war on the leadership of this country, which has led us into a quagmire'. At the Kremlin on 15 March, Baker encountered a 'stressed' Gorbachev who complained that the demands of the job were 'enormous'. Tinkering with the system had not worked and 'pressures for a dictator' were mounting. But he had to keep 'on the right track', 'neutralise the radical extremes' and focus on reforming 'the union' and 'the economy'. Baker agreed and sympathised with Gorbachev's 'political problems in switching to a market economy', for it effectively meant 'changing seventy years of practice'. But he did not mince his words about US dislike of the 'KGB investigating business cooperation'. Above all, he said, it was imperative for Gorbachev to get the Soviet Union to a 'price system, with convertible currency, incentive, competition, individual initiative'. On Yeltsin, Baker noted for Bush, 'Gorbachev was positively neuralgic' – calling him 'unstable', addicted to 'populist rhetoric' and full of dictatorial ambitions.

Yet Baker played down the actual danger from Yeltsin, depicting him as 'theatrical', a 'man prone to larger-than-life gestures' but above all a 'street-smart politician who sensed the democratic mood sweeping the country'. Indeed, 'anyone who could turn hundreds of thousands of people out on the street was someone the United States needed to cultivate'. And so, when Yeltsin sent Baker a note upon his arrival in Moscow, asking to talk privately, the Secretary of State – after checking with Bush – went ahead. Gorbachev got wind of this, however, and hit the roof, eventually preventing the meeting from going ahead. Baker considered the incident 'symptomatic of the complex relationship between Gorbachev and Yeltsin', but he also felt that it illustrated the 'fine balance we had to maintain between them'.[152]

The ever-cautious Bush knew which way he wanted to tilt. In the two years since his hesitant start on Governors Island, he had gradually come to develop a genuine partnership, even friendship, with the Soviet leader. And pragmatically, Gorbachev was the man who controlled 30,000 nuclear weapons; Yeltsin, democrat or not, had none. In Bush's mind, Gorbachev was still 'all we've got and all *they've* got, too'.[153] In his diary he wrote on 17 March, 'my view is, you dance with who is on the dance floor – you don't try to influence this succession'. Certainly, you don't do anything to give the 'blatant appearance' of encouraging 'destabilisation'. His precept was 'we meet with the republic leaders but we don't overdo it'.[154]

That was the basic philosophy, but the practicalities were harder to manage. Trying to decide when to give Gorbachev his much-desired boost of a Soviet–American summit, the president noted that, while needing to get arms control 'straightened out', he would 'go any minute' to Moscow if there was some way to announce that the Baltic republics were 'being set free'. He also wanted to see real progress on economic reforms. Gorbachev kept claiming that what he needed was $100 billion of Western aid. Bush, by contrast, felt it was all about developing the basics of a market economy. The chaotic lurch in 1990–1 from the aborted 500 Days Plan to the inept Pavlov reforms did not inspire confidence that the Soviet leader had a clue what to do. The chaos was repeated in the spring of 1991 when the economist Grigory Yavlinsky, acting for Gorbachev, proposed a 'grand bargain' of rapid marketisation cushioned by massive foreign aid ($30–50 billion annually until 1997), only to be stymied by Pavlov's 'anti-crisis' programme – another euphemism for minimal, state-controlled price liberalisation. It was clear to Bush that his summit meeting with Gorbachev would have to be postponed again, until after the G7 meeting that was scheduled for London in mid-July. This would be the forum to debate the vexed question of aid and also how to integrate the Soviet Union into capitalist economics and the global market.[155]

The previous year, the Houston G7 had commissioned a joint report on the Soviet economy from the IMF, the World Bank, the OECD and the EBRD. Their 2,000-page analysis – based on several 'fact-finding missions' to Moscow during the autumn of 1990 and published in January 1991 – emphatically recommended a radical approach to decontrolling prices and accelerating privatisation. The Yavlinsky plan tried to do this; indeed it drew on the help of various American advisers including two professors from the Kennedy School at Harvard, Graham Allison and Robert Blackwill. But the administration remained sceptical. Baker thought that the Russians may 'drown in the sea of Western "advice", because they don't know how to filter it and to translate it into concrete action'. Robert Zoellick, Bush's personal sherpa for the 1991 G7, warned that the 'grand bargain' was a 'dangerous illusion'. Baker's deputy, Lawrence

Eagleburger, was equally dismissive: 'An economic programme written in the Soviet Union and perfected at the Kennedy School? What could be better? At least they are ideologically compatible.' This was a bit rich, considering that in the 1988 election campaign Bush had questioned the credentials of his opponent, the Democrat Michael Dukakis, by scornfully claiming that he got his 'foreign policy from the boutique at Harvard Yard'. In any case, it was clear that Gorbachev was not firmly behind Yavlinsky's plan and preferred Pavlov's conservative approach. None of this inspired American confidence.[156]

Equally damning, Gorbachev sprayed around impossible requests for aid. In March, for instance, he floated with Mitterrand the idea of joining the IMF, backed by a five-year agreement for a loan of $15 billion a year. Then in mid-April he told Kohl he wanted DM 30 billion in bilateral aid and a German contribution to multilateral initiatives. With Bush that spring, Gorbachev's plea was $1.5 billion in grain credits, on which the White House kept stalling because of Soviet behaviour over CFE, START and the Baltics. 'The guy doesn't seem to get it,' the president told his staff. 'He seems to think that we *owe* him economic help because we support him politically. We have got to give him a lesson in basic economics. Business is business. Loans have to be made for sound financial and commercial reasons.'[157]

Begging from the old enemy

During May, Gorbachev and Bush had two long phone conversations in an effort to establish the foundations for the G7 – which Washington emphatically did not want to turn into a 'financial pledging session'[158] – and for the superpower summit. On the 11th Gorbachev was quite open in his appeal: 'When I'm looking to you, George, for assistance, it is because I am in this kind of situation. I really need it.' The president was equally direct: 'In the spirit of frankness, our experts don't believe Pavlov's anti-crisis programme will move you fast enough to market reform. If there are more steps toward a market reform effort, then we could do more and help especially with the international financial organisations.' The Soviet leader would not be put off, asking for direct discussions with the G7 and an invitation for him to participate at the London summit.[159]

On 27 May, Bush pushed on his agenda for the Moscow meeting. 'Mikhail, how are you? I am calling to say that I really would like to go to a summit if we can reach agreement on CFE and get a START agreement.' Both issues still needed substantial work by experts, and conventional forces were particularly difficult because the Americans were furious that the Soviets had backtracked on what had been signed in Paris. Bush, who blamed this on the 'shift in the political alignment of forces in the Kremlin', urged Gorbachev to break the deadlock and restore the trust needed for wrapping up START. 'That would be a historic step and I very much want to come to Moscow. Mikhail, I really want to come there.' The president was anxious to resume work on building his new world order.[160]

In June the logjam began to break. The Americans were satisfied with Soviet concessions over CFE.[161] Congress – concerned about the economic situation in the USSR – responded favourably to the Soviet request for grain credit. This was in large measure because the USSR had finally passed legislation allowing Jews to emigrate, which enabled the USA to waive the Jackson–Vanik amendment prohibiting trade relations with communist states that restricted human rights. And after Germany and France joined Italy in pressing for an invitation to Gorbachev to attend the G7 talks, British prime minister John Major, host of the summit, publicly proposed on 6 June that a formal invitation should be issued. Bush did not object. It was eventually agreed that the G7 leaders would meet Gorbachev separately in a heads-of-government discussion outside the formal session. Gorbachev was delighted.[162]

Things became more complicated, however, after Yeltsin was elected

Russia's president on 12 June. There were now two potential foci for Bush's policy towards the USSR. A week later, on 20 June, Yeltsin arrived in Washington as a guest of Congress and he was received at the White House. During a talk lasting more than an hour and a half, Yeltsin went through his own shopping list of requests – insisting that 'I want direct dealings with you' – but he was also openly supportive of the Soviet leader. 'Russia is firmly on the side of Gorbachev. I cannot act without him. We can only act together. Gorbachev's departure and the arrival of some general would be tragic. People would take to the streets and there would be civil war.' But, Yeltsin added, 'I am not that pessimistic. That is only talk.' For his part, Bush was favourably impressed by the new Russian leader. Not only was he 'well-tailored and -pressed', in contrast with previously rumpled encounters, but 'Yeltsin said everything we wanted to hear when it came to reform.'[163]

Bush was, however, at pains to brief Gorbachev on what had transpired; and they managed to connect over the phone the following day. Asked by the Soviet leader whether he was pleased with the encounter. Bush said 'Yes I am, more so than in our previous meeting.' The US president admitted that 'we worried frankly that there might be a difference so broad between you that we might be in a delicate situation. But as your ambassador undoubtedly reported, I made it very clear that you are our man. That is my obligation and I am personally pleased to work with you as president of the USSR.' Gorbachev sounded reassured: 'I think we have had a meaningful talk in the spirit of partnership and friendship.'[164]

And so Gorbachev flew to London on 16 July for a much-needed top-up of international adulation. Echoes of New York, December 1988, once again. 'As his motorcade of Zil limousines flashed across central London from one meeting to another,' reported the *New York Times*, 'he utterly dominated the scene, eclipsing and in some cases eliminating debate on other issues' as he met one-on-one with each G7 leader. He was cheered at Covent Garden Opera House, feted at a reception in Downing Street and relished a candlelit dinner in the Admiralty, where Churchill had planned the war in 1939–40. When Gorbachev met the G7 leaders as a group on the afternoon of 17 July, it seemed as if the world's leading communist state was now being brought into the inner sanctum of international capitalism.[165]

There were grand words from Kohl: 'we are experiencing an exceptional, historic moment' promising to be of 'utmost importance for Europe and the entire world'. Likewise, Mitterrand declared 'you could have behaved like your predecessors, and the result would be catastrophic. History will record this. It will note not only the fact that you are not [just] transforming a country that does not have democratic traditions, but also how its relations with other countries have changed'. Even John Major, generally more sceptical towards Moscow, felt this was a day 'history may well see as a landmark' – as 'a first step toward helping the Soviet Union become a full member of the world economic community'. Not to be outdone, Gorbachev called their four-hour session 'one of the most important meetings of our time'.[166]

But what exactly had been achieved? Before they met Gorbachev, the G7 had held extensive discussions about how to play things. On the one hand, it was vital not to snub him, given the Soviet Union's increasingly precarious situation. Kohl and Mitterrand were particularly keen to provide substantial economic support. 'We must try to influence events in the USSR,' the chancellor declared – not only because of his personal sympathy for Gorbachev but also because of the practical implications of a total Soviet collapse, jeopardising the agreement about Red Army withdrawal and possibly precipitating a major refugee crisis.[167] 'It is cheaper', one American journalist noted, 'to aid Soviet citizens in the Soviet Union than to wait until they flood into Germany.'[168]

So far Germany had carried by far the main burden of aid to Moscow – some $40 billion over the past twelve months. Everyone else was in a different league but it was striking that the next largest contribution came from Italy with $2.9 billion, followed by the USA ($2.8 billion) and then France ($1 billion).[169] Despite this, Germany and France were outvoted by the rest of the G7, led by Bush. They were singularly unimpressed by a long-winded twenty-three-page letter sent in advance by Gorbachev, or with his plea for $100–150 billion in aid – most of which he would have used simply to service the Soviet foreign debt. There was general agreement that the letter 'lacked details and credibility' and Major said bluntly, 'There can be no bag of money.' In other words, they took the consistent Bush line that effective Soviet economic reform was the essential precondition for economic aid, as it had been when dealing with Eastern Europe: 'Debt rescheduling is undesirable.' The fact that Yavlinsky had refused to accompany Gorbachev in protest at what he termed the 'foggy' nature of the Soviet leader's plans was regarded as particularly damning.[170]

Bush captured the mood of the majority. 'It is important that Gorbachev be received with respect and a sense of the honour due to him,' he stated firmly. 'We should never turn our backs on Gorbachev's achievements.' But he underlined the fact that Gorbachev was 'the leader of a country that is not a Western industrialised democracy' – and not even an 'economic superpower'; it was simply a country with 'military might'. He also insisted that they must 'do nothing with the USSR that puts Eastern Europe in a less privileged position. I don't want to send them a signal that we'll slight them.' Since 1989 the US, Western Europe and Japan had pumped about $40 billion of government money into the small states of Eastern Europe, to expedite their radical shift to market economies, and the G7 had no intention of undermining the socio-economic transformation now gathering steam. As for the USSR, Bush insisted, 'we cannot write out checks or give money until the reforms that have been talked about are implemented'.[171]

Mitterrand made the same points, framed in a larger historical context. 'It's the problem of the chicken and the egg: will the USSR establish itself first, or does it need assistance now? – recognising the risk of failure' if the Soviets were obliged to go it alone. He reminded his colleagues of the 'great problems' facing even a developed state like Germany. 'It has emerged as a great power in fifty years' and yet it 'has difficulty assimilating five states. What does this say about the USSR, without the same degree of prosperity [and] unity', and still functioning under what he called 'the system of the tsars? It will be much harder.'[172]

In consequence, what the G7 offered was symbolic more than substantive: this included what was termed 'special association' with the IMF and the World Bank; intensified 'technical assistance' both bilateral and through international organisations; and a commitment to 'continuing dialogue' between the G7 and the USSR. There was a clear consensus that no new institutions would be invented to deal with the Soviet Union. 'This is the beginning, not the end,' Major told Gorbachev on behalf of the G7. 'It's the first step towards helping the USSR become a full member of the international economic community.'

'I'll be positive,' responded Gorbachev, putting the best face on things. 'We have not yet exhausted our cooperation, but are started on it. I'd like to thank you all.'[173] But privately he was not happy with the way things had gone in London. 'What kind of Soviet Union does the US want to see?' he had asked Bush in their bilateral meeting. He stressed how far the USSR had come in a very short time towards democracy, privatisation and demilitarisation. And, as he saw it, the Soviet Union had become 'one of the solid, reliable pillars of today's world.' But what 'if that pillar disappears?' The 'consequences' were likely to be grave.'So, what is my friend George Bush going to do?' Gorbachev alluded to their recent collaboration in the Gulf, exclaiming 'it is strange to me to find $100 billion for regional war, but none to make a Soviet Union a new country. We need mutual understanding and reciprocating steps ... The world is in transition to a new order and needs US–Soviet cooperation.'[174]

The chemistry between Bush and Gorbachev had not been good. As the British interpreter noted in his strictly personal impressions for the PM penned after the summit, the main insight into Gorbachev had been his '(temporary?) irritation and coolness' towards the American president in contrast to the 'love-in' and 'chumminess' between 'Helmut' and 'Misha'. And while Gorbachev persistently talked about the '7 + 1', stressing 'John's' key role as 'coordinator', he had also played up his sense of distance from the USA by remarking over dinner that 'Europe could save the world or ruin it. "Europe had everything that we need."' What's more Europeans were content to offer their experience to the USSR, the Americans had a habit of saying, 'You Russians should do it our way!'[175]

Given these tensions, it was perhaps not surprising that a week later, on 22 July, Gorbachev abruptly submitted an application for *full* membership of both the IMF and the World Bank. To the G7 this showed up the Soviet leader's total lack of realism about what integration in the world economy actually entailed. Bush-administration insiders speculated that it may have been a politically motivated response to domestic criticism: 'Associate status has been described as second-class citizenship for a military superpower.'[176]

By contrast, the Moscow summit with Bush on 30–1 July 1991 affirmed the USSR's first-class military status. The centrepiece of his visit to the Kremlin was signing the START treaty – the first time the two superpowers agreed to reduce their arsenals of *strategic* nuclear weapons: the 1987 Washington treaty had applied only to intermediate-range nuclear forces. START I was immensely complicated, running to 700 pages, but the essential point was clear. The treaty established an aggregate limit of 1,600 delivery vehicles and 6,000 warheads for each side, to be achieved over seven years. This would entail a substantial reduction from the current levels of 10,000–12,000 warheads and therefore amounted to a cut of around a third in their strategic arsenals – returning effectively to the level of 1982, when the negotiations had started, but now framed as a clear and verifiable agreement.[177] 'It is an event of global significance,' Gorbachev declared, 'for we are imparting to the dismantling of the infrastructure of fear that has ruled the world a momentum which is so powerful that it will be hard to stop.' Bush, similarly, hailed the reversal of a half-century of arms build-ups and mistrust. 'We sign the START treaty as testament to the new relationship emerging between our two countries – in the promise of further progress toward lasting peace.'[178] Eagleburger told Bush, 'as the Paris CSCE meeting is generally seen as having sealed the end of the Cold War, this will be the first post-Cold War summit.'[179]

It was an apt comment. The arms treaty was part of a general, wide-ranging discussion in Moscow of global problems, conducted between the two cooperating superpowers. They reviewed a range of issues, including the future 'integration of Europe' through the EC and CSCE, the Middle East in the wake of the Gulf War, and the stabilisation of African hotspots such as Namibia, Angola and South Africa. The two leaders paid particular attention to China. Gorbachev assured Bush that he would not play the 'China card' or do anything to 'skew the strategic balance'. He stated categorically, 'we would welcome the return of your relationship with China back to normal'. In May Gorbachev had hosted party boss Jiang Zemin – the first visit to Moscow by a Chinese leader for thirty-four years, since the days of Nikita Khrushchev and Mao Zedong.[180] Bush reciprocated: 'There can be no question of playing the China card' and affirmed his own desire for normalisation of relations. 'I will keep contact and try to help them move forward.' But he stressed the 'bitterness' with which Americans still remembered Tiananmen Square and the continuing desire in Congress to 'punish' China. He had only been able to maintain the PRC's 'most favoured nation' status by using his presidential veto. Of course he agreed that China was 'a very important country in the global context'.[181]

They also returned to the issue of Soviet economic development, broached in London. In the opening press conference Gorbachev lauded the G7 meeting as 'the beginning of a new type of international economic relations, which will form the material foundation for world politics in the twenty-first century'. And Bush, despite his irritation in London, put a positive gloss on developments. He declared that they had now fulfilled 'our Malta goal' from the 1989 summit, namely 'normalising our economic relationship'.[182] In their first bilateral, Bush said rather patronisingly, with reference to the G7 action points, that he had 'no intention of putting you down on Burkina Faso's level', but before loans could be made it would be necessary for the Soviet Union to follow 'the rules of the game' of the international financial institutions. In Moscow, he continued, they would 'tackle the next challenge' of 'furthering economic reform in the USSR, and seeking to integrate the Soviet economy into the international system'. What, asked Bush, would you want from the IMF – 'if you could wave a magic wand'? Most critical, replied Gorbachev, was rouble convertibility and debt restructuring, and getting 'out of the transitional phase as quickly as possible' to open the country to foreign investors and trade.[183] His pleas did not fall on deaf ears. At the end of their summit Bush announced that he was sending the trade agreement signed in June 1990 to Congress for approval and to grant 'most favoured nation' status. This would fulfil a long-standing Soviet aim, dating back to 1974. Gaining MFN was, however, largely symbolic, given the small scale of trade between the two countries.[184]

Significantly, Bush did not skirt around Gorbachev's domestic problems. The previous day Yeltsin had refused to join Gorbachev in a lunch with Bush, insisting on his own one-on-one meeting to show that each republic could develop its own foreign policy. 'This was an illustration of the challenges you face,' Bush told Gorbachev. 'He always wants to get equal status with you. I want to assure you that from our side we will not take a single step that would complicate your situation. We believe in you and trust your intentions.'[185] The US president also raised again the prickly question of the Baltic States. 'I have to say that, in our opinion, it would be best if you could find a way to cut away these republics, to set them free. It would have a fantastic effect on public opinion.' But, he added, 'you know my point of view. This is your affair.' Bush made clear that he did not intend to make difficulties for Gorbachev. He had turned down an invitation to visit Lithuania on his way home. 'We certainly understood that we should not do that.'[186] But he did issue a statement deploring the 'regrettable' bloodshed during the summit, when six Lithuanian officials on the border with Byelorussia were shot dead at a customs post that the USSR considered illegal.[187]

Gorbachev made a big issue of this during the summit, reminding Bush that '70% of interstate borders in the Soviet Union are in essence not defined'. Byelorussians were demanding parts of Lithuania. Eastern Estonia was mainly populated by Russians. Moldovans wanted to join Romania. Crimea and Donetsk both sought autonomy. And in any case,

Gorbachev went on with mounting irritation, there were contested lands all over Eastern Europe, in Poland, Bulgaria, Transylvania. He asked Bush to join him in issuing a summit declaration on the principle of 'territorial integrity and the inviolability of borders'. Self-determination, he said, was only possible 'within a constitutional and legal framework. This is my position on the Baltic States as well ... For us it is a matter of principle.'[188]

Bush dodged the question of a summit declaration but he was ready to put his weight behind Gorbachev's new Union Treaty. That, he said, 'is the way to move forward'. The Novo-Ogarevo process was now delicately balanced: progress in the negotiations had been slow. Gorbachev expected that two or three republics would sign first, led by Russia and Kazakhstan. Then the rest, including Ukraine, would follow, allowing a new constitution to be adopted. But in fact, only nine of the fifteen republics had come out in favour and the position of Ukraine was particularly problematic. It was the USSR's second economic power after the Russian Republic. The situation there was volatile, with the western part of the country having voted for independence in the referendum of March 1991.[189]

To support Gorbachev, Bush had decided to visit Ukraine where he made a speech to the republic's Supreme Soviet in favour of the new Union Treaty. He flew to Kiev straight after Moscow, accompanied by Vice President Yanaev. In Scowcroft's view, this was one of Bush's most accomplished performances – a ringing affirmation of basic American principles of freedom, democracy and tolerance. The president had personally beefed up the speech draft with endorsements of what Gorbachev had achieved:[190] 'Some people have urged the United States to choose between supporting President Gorbachev and supporting independence-minded leaders throughout the USSR. I consider this a false choice. In fairness, President Gorbachev has achieved astonishing things, and his policies of glasnost, perestroika, and democratisation point toward the goals of freedom, democracy, and economic liberty.' This did not go down well with Ukrainian nationalists. Bush also used the occasion to speak more widely about the dangers of violent separatism in and around the USSR, not least in Yugoslavia. 'Yet freedom is not the same as independence. Americans will not support those who seek independence in order to replace a far-off tyranny with a local despotism. They will not aid those who promote a suicidal nationalism based upon ethnic hatred.' These words were taken by militant

Ukrainians as direct criticism of their own independence struggle. In time the Kiev speech would come back to haunt Bush.[191]

His immediate reactions to the trip were very positive. 'I am relaxed and happy because I feel the visits to Moscow and Kiev went well,' he wrote to Gorbachev on the plane home to America on 1 August. 'We had a lot of substance, and we had a few laughs along the way.' He signed off: 'These sincere best wishes come from your friend, GB.' Scowcroft was also pleased. Aside from what he called 'the black cloud over the Baltics', he felt the START treaty and their general 'rapport' were 'reason to see the glass as half full'.[192]

But other things preyed on Bush's mind. As a politician, he could never forget US domestic issues. Unburdening himself to Gorbachev during the summit, he confessed that 'I am afraid of 1992 ... You know it is an election year for us, a time when reality is replaced by rhetoric, when sides in the political struggle exchange blows.'[193] Bush found it hard to gear up for such a battle-royal. He had been depressed about it in the spring – despite the triumph of the Gulf War and the highest ever poll ratings. Admittedly his enervation was partly due to heart and thyroid conditions, which had since been successfully treated, and when he returned home from Moscow, in response to a journalist's question, he said that only bad health would prevent him running again in 1992, declaring – in case people didn't get the message – 'I feel like a million bucks.'[194] But his approval ratings were on the decline – the Gulf War spike was long gone and Americans did not seem particularly interested in the Moscow summit. With the US economy still struggling out of recession and unemployment running at nearly 7%, people were more concerned about domestic prosperity than world peace.[195] All in all, Bush said, 'it had been a long July'. He was looking for a complete rest in Maine and flew to Kennebunkport for his summer vacation on 6 August.[196]

Gorbachev, too, felt 'tired as hell' and desperate for a break, but he was also pleased overall with how things had gone. He was in a happy mood – even if the Lithuania shootings at the end had dampened the 'ebullient spirit' of the talks. For him, the summit and the START treaty had been both a 'glorious moment' personally and also a major political triumph, coming so soon after being feted in London by the inner circle of the industrialised world. What's more, just before he met Bush he had held a long and boozy dinner at Novo-Ogarevo with Yeltsin and the Kazakh president Nursultan Nazarbayev. In expansive mood, they looked ahead optimistically to signing the Union Treaty and the road beyond. Gorbachev even talked indiscreetly about replacing Kryuchkov and Pavlov – the main obstacles to reform – ignoring Yeltsin's warnings that the KGB might have bugged the room. On 2 August, after the summit, the Soviet president announced that the Union Treaty was now ready for signature, and headed off to Crimea for his vacation. He would be back, he told Kremlin aides, on 20 August for the signing ceremony.[197]

*

That's not how it worked out, however. Initially both superpower leaders enjoyed their seaside holidays, with plenty of time with the grandchildren. Bush loved the chance to sail and fish again in the Atlantic. 'On the boat, I count my blessings as I look and listen to the sea,' he noted in his diary. 'Your mind gets totally taken away from the problems at hand.' At other times, he added, 'I simply sit on the porch and watch the kids playing on the rocks.' Still, the impending election year hung over him. He felt the pressure intensely. 'The stories keep saying that I will be hard to beat. The more we hear of this, the more worried I become,' he confessed on 12 August. What kept nagging at him was the old saying 'the bigger they are, the harder they fall'.[198]

On the Black Sea, Gorbachev – never able to throw off work entirely, despite his love of long swims – put pen to paper, composing his speech for the critical ceremony on 20 August to mark his new Union Treaty. Having choreographed every detail of the event from the music to the seating plan, he was now keen to produce an appropriate valedictory for the achievements of the old Soviet Union and also an inspiring inaugural address to launch its successor. 'A voluntary federation of sovereign Soviet republics is replacing a unitary state,' he planned to begin. 'We would be poor patriots if we renounced our history, severed the life-giving roots of continuity and mutual ties.' But, the draft stated, 'we also would be poor patriots if we held on to what must die, what we cannot take into the future with us, what would interfere with rebuilding our life on a modern, democratic foundation'.

To Gorbachev – who feared Yeltsin's challenge more than the threat from the old guard whom he believed he had mollified by leaning to the right – the treaty, for all its uncertainties, offered a chance to preserve the best of the Soviet experiment. Once again, he felt like a man with a mission, but his vision of the future was not widely shared by the people at large, increasingly confused and even anxious about where things were going. Nor, more crucially, was it endorsed either by Soviet hardliners or reformers in the republics. That soon became clear.[199]

At midnight on Sunday 18 August Bush was woken by a call from Scowcroft, who said he had just seen a report that Gorbachev had resigned for health reasons. Soon it emerged there had been a coup in Moscow. Yanaev, Gorbachev's deputy – that 'friendly man' with 'a good sense of humour' as Bush had put it just a couple of weeks earlier after their trip on Air Force One to Kiev – now presented himself as president of the Soviet Union. Among the newly formed State Committee that he headed to implement emergency rule were Pavlov, Yazov, Kryuchkov and Pugo – all of whom, Bush realised, had only recently been brought by Gorbachev into his inner circle.[200]

It all looked very sinister and alarming, but in fact the 'coup' was a clumsy operation from start to finish. The plotters' motives were diffuse. They wanted to block the signing of the new Union Treaty to forestall the break-up of the Soviet Union as they knew it. And on a more mercenary level, picking up on Gorbachev's indiscretions at Novo-Ogarevo, they feared a Cabinet purge in which they would lose their jobs. But they failed to secure the key points of power – communications, transport, the media and the military – or arrest opposition leaders such as Yeltsin. They were also reluctant to use brute force in the way Deng Xiaoping had done in June 1989. At root, it seems, the conspirators had been taken in by Gorbachev's turn to the right. They assumed that their belated co-option into his Cabinet showed that the headstrong reformer had finally seen the error of his ways, and would now accept their agenda. In other words, they didn't need to take over the whole machinery of Soviet power but simply to bring the leader of the state completely onside. 'We never discussed what we'd do if Gorbachev didn't accept our proposals,' one of them admitted later. When he failed to play ball, the coup was dead in the water. That's why the television images revealed men who were uncertain, nervous, even drunk; Yanaev's hands visibly shook as he read out their declaration of a state of emergency. Watching on TV Scowcroft likened them to the Marx Brothers; Gillian Braithwaite, wife of the British ambassador, called them 'Muppets'.[201]

Tragedy or farce? For the moment nobody could be sure. And initially

Gorbachev's fate was unknown. Bush wondered whether to return to Washington,[202] but eventually decided to stay put in Maine, to avoid exacerbating the sense of crisis and even panic. Now, he noted on 20 August, the daily routine would not be 'vacation' but 'rest <u>and</u> work', backed by 'active' but not 'frantic' telephone diplomacy. The message he wanted to convey to the world was non-acceptance of the coup – but together with a shift of focus from Gorbachev to Yeltsin who ought to get 'more personal attention' as he called for the return of Gorbachev and the maintenance of democratic change. Yet Bush could not forget the American domestic angle. The final point on his note to himself was a warning that he must avoid bringing the Soviet crisis into his '92 election campaign.'[203]

And so, in this state of uncertainty, Bush placed his call to Yeltsin on 20 August – the 'wild man' who preached democracy but acted like a demagogue, whom he was now coming to accept as a serious political figure. Bush did not intend to get carried away by the emotions of the moment. 'I am determined to handle it without getting us involved in a war and, yet, standing by our principles of democracy and reform.' Yet he was fascinated by those TV images of the Russian leader on top of a tank.

On top of the tank: Yeltsin defies the coup

'This courageous man is standing by his principles,' Bush scribbled in his diary. 'Talk about being in the middle of history.' And the two phone conversations with Yeltsin on 20 and 21 August gave the president of the United States an enhanced respect for the president of the Russian Republic.[204]

This undoubtedly affected Bush's attitude when he finally managed to speak with his old friend, the president of the Soviet Union, later on the 21st. Bush's relief – evident in the transcript of their conversation – was offset by a dawning recognition that he was witnessing a transfer of power. That became public when Gorbachev was brought back to Moscow by Yeltsin's men late on 21 August.[205] Determined to reassume his full presidential powers, on the 23rd Gorbachev appeared before the Russian Supreme Soviet, trying to downplay the significance of the coup. He even claimed that the 'Pavlov Cabinet' had resisted it. Yeltsin would have none of this. Jumping to his feet, he walked onto the stage brandishing the minutes of the 19 August Cabinet meeting, which showed that all ministers were in on the plot. 'Read it now,' Yeltsin shouted, jabbing his finger in Gorbachev's face. The Soviet leader crumpled. Capitalising on the moment, Yeltsin announced with a broad grin that he would now sign a decree banning the Russian Republic's Communist Party. Ignoring Gorbachev's protestations that he hadn't read the document, Yeltsin signed it to thunderous applause – relishing every moment of Gorbachev's ritual humiliation, played out on live TV.[206]

Bush and Scowcroft were part of the global audience. 'It's all over,' Scowcroft muttered, shaking his head. Bush agreed: 'I'm afraid he may have had it.'[207] Summing up two weeks later, the US embassy in Moscow commented, 'In the aftermath of the coup Boris Yeltsin is the most powerful individual in the USSR. No decision affecting the country as a whole can be taken against his will.'[208]

Despite his personal sadness for Gorbachev, Bush felt pleased at the outcome. After all, there had not been serious bloodshed: the military had not fired on its people. This was not a repeat of Tiananmen in June 1989, or even Bucharest in December. In the event the plotters caved in – the spirit of democracy had won. Not quite a Velvet Revolution, akin to Prague, but certainly far more peaceful than anyone might have expected a few days before. Bush also felt satisfied that his habitually cautious, balanced diplomacy had again paid off, like not dancing on the Wall in November 1989. 'We could have overreacted and moved troops and scared the hell out of people. We could have under-reacted by saying, "Well we'll deal with whoever is there." But I think the advice I got was good. I think we found the proper balance, certainly in this case – we are getting enormous credit from the key players in the Soviet Union.'[209]

And there were now a lot more 'players'. In the middle of the coup, the three Baltic States took advantage of the chaos to announce the restoration of their independence, after half a century of Soviet occupation. Yeltsin quickly recognised the new states, as did many European members of NATO and Finland. Bush held back, waiting for Gorbachev's response, but by 2 September he felt he had no choice but to follow suit.[210] These small states hit the international headlines, but what mattered more were the declarations of independence on 24 August by Ukraine and then Byelorussia (now Belarus) as well as the three republics in the Caucasus – all integral members of the USSR ever since its foundation. 'Over the coming weeks and months', observed the US embassy, 'the situation in the USSR is likely to be characterised by a race between democracy and disintegration'.[211] The yawning weakness of the centre was exacerbated by Gorbachev's decision on the 23rd to abolish the Communist Party of the Soviet Union. After Yeltsin's action in Russia he had little choice, but in the process he was destroying the last political framework holding the USSR together and, with it, further undermining his fast-shrinking power base.[212]

Gorbachev still clung to his project of a new Union Treaty – his dream of the union's 'reunification', even without the Baltics, Georgia, Moldova and Armenia. But Yeltsin would not play ball, declining to ratify the agreement on a 'common economic community', and Ukraine demanded a referendum on the whole process. In a meeting at Novo-Ogarevo on 14 November, Russia and Belarus called for a 'Union of States' – whereas Gorbachev still wanted a unitary state.

'If there are no effective state structures, then what good are a president and a parliament?' Gorbachev asked heatedly. 'If that's what you decide, then I'm ready to resign.'

'You're getting carried away,' Yeltsin retorted.

'Not at all, I'm too exhausted for that.'

In the end they concocted a compromise euphemism – 'a democratic confederative state'. But at their next meeting, two weeks later, Yeltsin vetoed the whole idea – to Gorbachev's impotent fury – and on 1 December the Ukrainian referendum came out overwhelmingly for independence. It was noteworthy that not only was there almost unanimous support from Western Ukrainians, in the easternmost oblasts of Luhansk and Donetsk 85% and 77% respectively also voted to leave the union. Even in Crimea and Sevastopol, the Soviet Black Sea Fleet's main port, the figures were well above 50%. Gorbachev was shocked. Next day, Yeltsin proposed a four-member confederation, comprising Russia,

Ukraine, Belarus and Kazakhstan. 'What would be my place in it?' Gorbachev demanded angrily. 'If that's the deal, then I'm leaving. I'm not going to bobble like a piece of shit in an ice hole.'[213]

And he didn't bobble for much longer. On 8 December, Yeltsin – again behind Gorbachev's back – agreed with the leaders of Ukraine and Belarus to form what was called a 'Commonwealth of Independent States' (CIS). By doing so they effectively opted out of the Union of Soviet Socialist Republics, making it now almost an empty shell – neither socialist nor united.

The power struggle between Gorbachev and Yeltsin created a quandary for Washington. Bush had come to the conclusion in October, during his last summit with Gorbachev in Madrid, that the Soviet leader had lost the battle for power, but he refused to turn his back on a fellow head of state ('You're still the master,' he told Gorbachev while patting him on the back during their joint press conference) and a man who had become a personal friend.[214] Sticking with Gorbachev was also Scowcroft's inclination. In any case, some of those around the US president still distrusted Yeltsin whose impressive courage during the coup had been followed by his contemptuous attitude to Gorbachev after the latter's return to Moscow.

But others in the administration believed that Bush's fidelity to Gorbachev had produced a distorted policy of propping up the Soviet government beyond the point at which this was in the best interests of the United States.[215] Indeed, Cheney had urged Bush bluntly to abandon the centre and side with the republics. The problem, however, about venturing along such a path was that the republics were unknown unknowns. 'Our contacts with and understanding of the Soviet Union were Moscow-centric,' admitted Robert Hutchings of the NSC. 'One could count on one hand the number of experts within government on the non-Russian republics.'[216]

And so the White House preferred to 'step back' in the hope that Gorbachev would somehow stay at least nominally in the centre amid the key republics' renegotiations, while trying to 'manage those aspects that bore immediately on American interests'.[217] Yet Gorbachev fought back tenaciously, denouncing Yeltsin's Commonwealth as 'illegitimate and dangerous'. This conjured up a 'geopolitical nightmare' of two heavyweights slugging it out for political power, calling the army to follow them and thereby raising the spectre of civil war.[218]

As a result, the 'Gorbachev versus Yeltsin, centre versus republics', argument in Washington prevented the administration throughout the autumn from making a clear public statement of US policy. By early December (after the Ukraine referendum) Dennis Ross, director of the State Department Policy Planning Staff, warned Baker gravely that the US 'ran the risk of losing control' over the Soviet dissolution unless there was a major speech. After all, as noted in a State Department policy memo, 'the union as we've known it is not there'.[219]

Baker had been mulling over these issues for some time[220] and so he decided to speak out. In an address on 12 December at Princeton, his alma mater, he did indeed talk as if the union was no more, looking to the challenges of the future. 'If during the Cold War we faced each other as two scorpions in a bottle, now the Western nations and the former Soviet republics stand as awkward climbers on a steep mountain. Held together by a single rope, a fall toward fascism or anarchy in the former Soviet Union will pull the West down too. Yet, a strong, steady pull by the West now can help them to gain their footing.'[221]

Baker stressed that he was not offering a 'blueprint' but a set of 'principles and approaches which together define an agenda for action in a revolutionary, unpredictable situation'. His aim was to 'anchor Russia, Ukraine and other republics firmly in the Euro-Atlantic community and the democratic commonwealth of nations'. He insisted that no additional nuclear-weapons states must emerge from the Soviet ruins, that START should be ratified and implemented and that all nuclear weapons would have to be 'under single unified' authority. By way of a carrot he offered $100 million in technical assistance to promote capitalism in the republics. But, as he made clear, this was not to come from US 'domestic accounts'. Rather Baker was signalling that the post-Soviet republics would compete for the American foreign budget and that traditionally big recipients – like the Philippines, the African bloc, Israel or Egypt – would end up having their allocations cut. In any case, the 'wreckage of communism' was too large for one nation to repair and so Baker announced that the US would invite the advanced Western democracies, the Central and East European states, members of the Kuwait War coalition, and international financial institutions to meet in Washington in early January to discuss how best to meet the ongoing humanitarian needs in the former USSR over the course of the next year. The Washington Conference was clearly defined as a 'coordinating meeting with donors', not a 'pledging' one.[222]

Gorbachev was furious with Baker, as he made clear to Bush in a phone call on 13 December. 'George, I think Jim Baker's Princeton speech should not have been made, especially the point that the USSR had ceased to exist. We must all be more careful during these times. The main thing is to avoid confrontation.' Bush tried to offer soothing words: 'Let me be clear that I want to avoid confrontation. I don't want to interfere. I accept your criticism. I do not think Jim said it quite that way – he said only "the USSR as we have known it" would be very different.'[223]

It seems likely that Bush, increasingly preoccupied with the upcoming presidential elections, was quite content that Baker had taken the initiative to articulate US policy; by now Yeltsin had won the power struggle. Indeed, the Russian president had effectively gazumped Gorbachev by calling Bush earlier that morning of 13 December informing him of the ratification of 'commonwealth accords' by the 'parliaments of Ukraine, Belarus and Russia' the previous day, and explaining that the leaders of the five Central Asian republics on their part had declared their intention to join the CIS* in a signing ceremony on 21 December in Alma-Ata, Kazakhstan. Yeltsin added that he was talking to Gorbachev 'every day to carry through the transition calmly with no disturbances. What will happen by the end of December, early January is that we will have a complete commonwealth of independent states and the structures of the centre will cease to exist. We are treating Mikhail Sergeyevich Gorbachev with the greatest respect and warmly. It is up to him to decide his own fate.' Yeltsin had pronounced the political obituary of the Soviet Union and, effectively, that of Gorbachev.[224]

But how to foster the peaceful transfer of powers, to engage the newly independent republics and pre-empt the horror of what Baker called a 'Yugoslavia with nukes'?[225] And how to help the disjointed Soviet nation weather the winter and reorder its dissolving economy? Robert Strauss, US ambassador to Moscow, urged the G7 nations to grant debt assistance, warning that economic pressure was likely to generate massive social upheaval. 'It sure can blow up in our face in the next six months very

---

* The Alma-Ata Protocol expanded the CIS to include 11 members: the original three signatories of 8 December 1991 – Russia, Belarus, Ukraine – plus Armenia, Azerbaijan, Kazakhstan, Kyrgyzstan, Moldova, Turkmenistan, Tajikistan and Uzbekistan. Georgia would join two years later in December 1993, thereby bringing CIS participation to 12 out of 15 former Soviet Republics.

easily.' For this reason, he argued, it would be worth America gambling to 'risk a couple of billion bucks' in Soviet aid rather than see a 'fascist situation' if tensions exploded and people protested in the streets. Ambassador Strauss was taking a different line from the caution of the Bush administration. But, of course, he was much closer to the Russian crisis and more sensitive to it than the White House, which remained wary about committing fresh dollars, citing budget constraints, until the Soviet republics had got their house in order.[226]

To get a sense of the realities on the ground, on 15–19 December Baker followed up his Princeton speech with a brief trip to the region – meeting Gorbachev, Yeltsin and the leaders of Kyrgyzstan, Kazakhstan and Ukraine. Besides the matter of humanitarian assistance there were huge questions about the conduct of foreign and security policy. After talks in Moscow which included the post-coup Soviet defence minister, General Yevgeny Shaposhnikov, Baker felt reassured about nuclear safety and proliferation, as well as issues of arms control. He was gratified by the republics' 'intense desire to satisfy the United States', which played to Washington's perception that it had a unique chance to 'bring democracy to lands that have little knowledge of it'. The problem, of course, was that political liberalisation might allow them to embrace forms of government at odds with American values and ideas of democracy.[227]

More concretely, Baker was delighted when Yeltsin made clear his hope that the CIS military would have close ties to the USSR's former enemy, NATO. 'It would be an important part of Russia's security to associate with the only military Alliance in Europe.' Ideally, he wanted them to 'merge'. Yeltsin also requested that Russia, Belarus and Ukraine be admitted to the upcoming, inaugural ministerial meeting of the North Atlantic Cooperation Council (NACC) in Brussels on 20 December. The NACC had been launched by Baker and Genscher that October and endorsed at NATO's November summit in Rome. It was intended to reach out to the former Warsaw Pact states as well as the Baltic States as part of NATO's effort to transform itself for the post-Wall world. Indeed, it was a manifestation of the 'hand of friendship' extended at NATO's July 1990 London summit, when Allied leaders had proposed a new cooperative relationship with all countries in Central and Eastern Europe in the wake of the Cold War. But it followed also from Baker's major Berlin address in June 1991 (his second there after his 'New Atlanticism' speech of 1989), in which he proposed a

'Euro-Atlantic community that extends east from Vancouver to Vladivostok' to embrace the whole of the Soviet Union. As NATO secretary general Manfred Wörner also highlighted, at this 'decisive moment in European history' it was the United States which found itself 'in a position to lead in this endeavour'. In view of subsequent controversy, it is important to state that NATO's liaison efforts with Eastern Europe and the NACC were explicitly *not* about increasing the Alliance's membership and thereby extending NATO's security guarantee eastward. This issue together with the question mark over NATO's future mission, though hovering in the background, was being deferred to an unspecified time in the future as part of the gradually unfolding debate about a new security architecture.[228]

Yeltsin's request to Baker, asking to attend the NACC meeting, was somewhat delicate. At this stage the USSR still existed as a state entity and the new independent states had not yet been formally recognised by the international community. So it was not possible to comply with Yeltsin's request that the three key European post-Soviet republics should attend the NACC meeting. Nevertheless, given Yeltsin's vehement objections against the idea that Shevardnadze, recently reinstated as Soviet foreign minister, should represent the union and thereby speak for the republics including Russia, Gorbachev refrained from sending him to Brussels.[229]

On 20 December, when Baker found himself sitting in the first ever session of the NACC at NATO headquarters, it was a moving occasion. 'In the room where many an East–West crisis had been managed, I could look around and see foreign ministers from all the former Warsaw Pact states' – the Soviet Union, Bulgaria, Czechoslovakia, Hungary, Poland and Romania as well as newly independent Estonia, Latvia and Lithuania. 'It was quite a sight.'[230] Representing the USSR in the absence of Shevardnadze was the Soviet ambassador to Belgium, Nikolai N. Afanassievsky. And it was around him that an unforgettable drama unfolded.

Afanassievsky and the Soviet delegates were evidently in turmoil. Yeltsin had issued a decree taking over the Kremlin as well as the Foreign and Interior Ministries the night before, and so the ambassador was fully aware of the tenuousness of his position. Nervously, he began with his prepared remarks, welcoming 'this new cooperation between former foes'. Then he read out a letter from Yeltsin, by which the absent Russian president tried to stamp his mark on the session. Yeltsin called for a 'climate of mutual understanding and trust, strengthening stability and cooperation on the European continent'. He said he was keen to develop this dialogue with NATO 'in each and every direction, both on the political and military levels'. His letter even stated: 'Today we are raising a question of Russia's membership in NATO, however regarding it as a long-term political aim.' [231]

The ministers were stunned. If taken seriously, this meant that the NACC would have to accommodate the desire of Central and East European states to flee from the Russian 'Bear' and also the avowed wish of the Bear itself to become part of the disparate Western menagerie. Straddling both aspirations would be extremely hard for NATO.[232] But after a brief moment of shock, the ministers got on with the agenda and took it in turns to present their own statements.

The meeting lasted four hours, and Afanassievsky rushed out on several occasions to take phone calls from Moscow. At the end, just as the NATO secretary general was going over the final communiqué, a 'white-faced' Afanassievsky informed Wörner that he needed to take the floor immediately. The by now happy band of foreign ministers fell silent as the Soviet ambassador proceeded to announce that his country was no more. Indeed, he had received instructions from Moscow, that after consultations among the 'Sovereign States that replaced the Soviet Union' all references to the USSR had to be deleted in the final communiqué. But the document had already been distributed to the press, so Wörner would have to make an extra statement explaining the bouleversement and inserting an addendum to the communiqué at the news conference after the NACC had ended.

'It was a dramatic moment,' the Dutch foreign minister, Hans van den Broek, told reporters later. 'It shows really what a whirlwind we are in.' Another colleague added, 'We began the meeting with twenty-five nations present, and we ended with twenty-four.' So, remarked an American official, 'we got to see the Soviet Union disappear right before our eyes'.[233]

Indeed, the disappearance could be watched by the whole world, graphically captured on the international media. At 7.35 p.m. on Christmas Day 1991 the Red Flag was lowered for the last time down the flagpole of the Kremlin. Ten minutes later it was replaced by the white, blue and red tricolour of the Russian Republic.[234]

On Christmas morning the president of the United States had conversed for the last time over the phone with the leader of the Soviet

Union. Bush found it 'very moving' – there was 'a real historic note'. Though sombre, Gorbachev did not indulge in any bitterness or recrimination. He wished Bush and his family a merry Christmas and gave thanks for their friendship, but he had two fundamental points of business to convey – about what would come after the USSR and what would happen to its nuclear arsenal.

'The debate in our union on what kind of state to create took a different track from what I thought right,' he admitted. But that was now water under the bridge. 'It is necessary to move to recognise all of these countries. But I would like you to bear in mind the importance for the future of the commonwealth that the process of disintegration and destruction does not grow worse. So, helping the process of co-operation among republics is our common duty.' He asked Bush to take this seriously.

'Now, about Russia,' he continued, 'this is the second most important emphasis in our conversations.' He told Bush he would resign that evening both as president of the USSR and as its commander-in-chief, transferring authority to use its nuclear weapons to the president of the Russian Federation. 'So I am conducting affairs until the completion of the constitutional process. I can assure you that everything is under strict control.' As Gorbachev knew from other recent calls, this was an important message to get across because Bush, as ever, was concerned about the prospect of nuclear proliferation and a nightmare descent into anarchy – even Armageddon.

'I appreciate your comments on nuclear weapons,' Bush responded. 'This is of vital significance internationally and I commend you and the leaders of the republics for what has been a great process.' And, he said, 'I will, of course, deal with respect, and openly, with the leaders of the Russian Republic and the other republics. We will move forward recognition and respect for the sovereignty that each has.' He also reminisced, like Gorbachev, about how their personal relations had developed over the last few years. That contorted minuet on Governors Island in December 1988 was now a distant memory. Theirs had proved an even more creative international partnership than Gorbachev's relationship with Reagan – and one with much more far-reaching consequences.

As they closed, Bush told Gorbachev: 'We salute you and thank you for what you have done for world peace.'

'Thank you, George. I was glad to hear all of this today. I am saying goodbye and shaking your hands. You have said to me many important things and I appreciate it.'

'All the best to you, Mikhail.'

'Goodbye.'[235]

Gorbachev in the ruins

*

That evening the US president addressed his own people. 'During these last few months, you and I have witnessed one of the greatest dramas of the twentieth century, the historic and revolutionary transformation of a totalitarian dictatorship, the Soviet Union, and the liberation of its peoples.' He also noted that 'new, independent nations have emerged out of the wreckage of the Soviet empire' to form the Commonwealth of Independent States. And he promised that his administration would address these new challenges without complacency: there must be no 'retreat into isolationism'. Yet, at the end of the speech, the president turned his attention to what really mattered to most of his audience. 'These dramatic events come at a time when Americans are also facing challenges here at home. I know that for many of you these are difficult times. And I want all Americans to know that I am committed to attacking our economic problems at home with the same determination we brought to winning the Cold War.'[236]

These words had been carefully weighed. The president himself was facing 'challenges here at home' – it was now clear that his re-election in November in 1992 was far from a foregone conclusion and likely to be a dirty business. So Bush was trying to gear up for what he feared would be 'a long, cold winter'.[237] He had unburdened himself about all this in a letter written in late October. 'There are days I just hate this job – not many, but some. The articles that demean one's character sometimes get to me, too. The ugly columns don't set very well when we are trying our hardest on some project or another – but then always the sun comes up.'[238] Bush was prey to these periodic attacks of the blues, especially as he prepared for a re-election campaign that he wanted to win, but did not really have the stomach to fight.

In particular, it was worrying – and also galling – that despite having won an immensely complex coalition war in the Middle East and presided over a victory that had eluded all his twentieth-century predecessors, namely the collapse of the Soviet Union, he now faced a challenge even to his renomination as the Republican Party candidate. And this by a pain-in-the-neck columnist and former mid-level Reagan aide who had the effrontery to try to unseat him. Pat Buchanan's candidacy, announced on 11 December – two weeks before the demise of the Soviet Union – had to be taken seriously because Bush knew that the economy was his Achilles heel.

Buchanan was campaigning aggressively on the claim that Bush had abandoned conservative Republican precepts, lost touch with the nation and become consumed with world affairs, while Americans struggled with recession and increasing economic competition from abroad. 'With a $4 trillion debt, with a US budget chronically out of balance, should the United States be required to carry indefinitely the full burden of defending rich and prosperous allies who take America's generosity for granted as they invade our markets?' Buchanan asked. Bush, he said, was a man with 'globalist passions' whereas 'we are nationalists. He believes in some *pax universalis*; we believe in the old republic. He would put America's wealth and power at the service of some vague new world order; we will put America first.' Buchanan was a foreign-policy iconoclast, asserting that the United States needed to re-examine all the alliances and institutions of the Cold War, established to guard against 'communist enemies that no longer exist'. And he pointed to new economic challenges on the world stage, posed by 'the rise of a European superstate and a dynamic Asia led by Japan'. These were sharp barbs but the most painful of all was Bush's credibility problem because of his broken 1988 pledge 'Read my lips: no new taxes.' Buchanan was extreme, but the sentiments he expressed were widely, if quietly, shared among the Republican rank and file.

It would, indeed, be a long winter for the president – a struggle for political survival.[239]

Chapter 8

'Dawn of a New Era'

The 30th of December 1992. The annual letter of season's greetings from the Kremlin began in a familiar way:

> Dear George,
>
> Please accept our sincerest New Year and Christmas greetings … Looking back at the year which is about to end, I feel most profoundly gratified over the truly unprecedented level of relations between our two countries that we have been able to achieve during this period of time.
>
> History will recognise the efforts that you have been making in the name of this goal.
>
> I have no doubt that the coming year will mark further accomplishments on the path toward building the relations of strategic partnership between Russia and the United States. The work done on the START II treaty gives me reason to look forward to an early meeting with you to sign this historic instrument.[1]

But this wasn't another message from George Bush's great friend, Mikhail. It was written by his new one – Boris. And it came at the end of a year that is often overlooked in East–West relations: 1992. This was also the year in which George H. W. Bush's presidency came to an abrupt and humiliating end. The man who triumphed in the Cold War and drove Saddam Hussein out of Kuwait was toppled by a brash forty-six-year-old politico from Arkansas – young enough to be Bush's son – who had never held office in Washington.

In December 1992 – what could have been the last, forlorn weeks of Bush's one-term presidency – he was, however, no lame duck. He received Yeltsin's letter while on yet another world trip – visiting Saudi Arabia to consolidate relations after the Gulf War, and then spending New Year's Eve with US Marines in Somalia, who were trying to hold together one fragile piece of his new world order. He had sent them there three weeks before to help this fractured East African state combat famine and anarchy as part of the UN operation 'Restore Hope'. Then the president flew on to Moscow to sign the START II nuclear arms-reduction treaty with Yeltsin – pledging to cut their strategic arsenals by two-thirds. This capped a remarkable year in America's relations with post-Soviet Russia, which no one would have predicted twelve months before.[2]

Nor, more sombrely, would people have imagined the state of Europe at the end of 1992. The euphoria of 1989 and those heady hopes of a Europe free, peaceful and united – all this was a thing of the past. On New Year's Day 1993 Czechoslovakia – a country forged in the ashes of war in 1918 – divided into two separate states: the Czech Republic and Slovakia. This at least was a velvet divorce to follow Czechoslovakia's Velvet Revolution in 1989. By contrast there was nothing soft and nego- tiated about the break-up of Yugoslavia. The South Slav state – also a product of the First World War – had exploded into nationalist fragments during a series of brutal ethnic wars. Just before Christmas, Bush had issued a statement committing the United States to support UN aid and peacekeeping operations, especially in Bosnia, which had become the main war zone of the Balkans.[3]

These crises posed new challenges for Bush's rules-based diplomacy. One was the tension between respecting the territorial integrity of a state and supporting the self-determination of its people. But there was also the broader question of how to reorder the world and establish peace and stability: either through international cooperation and along universally agreed principles, or by America unilaterally using its hegemonic position.

When Bush and Yeltsin had met at Camp David in February 1992, they spoke of the 'dawn of a new era'.[4] By the end of that year it was clear that the 'new era' would be less rosy than they had hoped. And also more complex: in the post-Cold War world, Washington and Moscow would be much less in control of global developments.

Still, international stability depended to a significant extent on polit- ical leaders, especially the big two. The shift from the USSR to Russia, from Gorbachev to Yeltsin, had been accomplished with surprising smoothness, even if there were already questions about the nature of Yeltsin's rule and the direction of the new Russia's democratisation and economic reform processes. But the United States faced its own political transition – the bumpy democratic succession from one president to another, across parties and indeed generations. In fact, amid his skilful management of all this global turbulence, Bush had lost track – and eventually control – of his presidency.

*

Given the magnitude of what had happened in December 1991, one might have expected Bush to draw breath. But the pace over the next year became, if anything, more frenetic. On Christmas Day 1991 the president delivered a generous tribute to Gorbachev, declaring that he had been 'responsible for one of the most important developments of this century, the revolutionary transformation of a totalitarian dictatorship and the liberation of his people from its smothering embrace'. Bush spoke of how Gorbachev and Shevardnadze, through their 'New Thinking' in foreign affairs 'permitted the United States and the Soviet Union to move from confrontation to partnership in the search for peace across the globe'. He singled out how 'working together, we helped the people of Eastern Europe win their liberty and the German people their goal of unity in peace and freedom. Our partnership led to unprecedented cooperation in repelling Iraqi aggression in Kuwait, in bringing peace to Nicaragua and Cambodia, and independence to Namibia'. This record, declared Bush, would assure Gorbachev 'an honoured place in history and, most importantly for the future, establishes a solid basis from which the United States and the West can work in equally constructive ways with his successors'.[5]

Having penned Gorbachev's political obituary, Bush wasted no time in getting on with his successor. In his press conference next day the president made only one passing reference to Gorbachev. His comments were mainly about the big themes of nuclear security, economic instability and humanitarian aid; his central focus throughout was clearly on Russia, its new leader, and the challenges they now faced. It was no accident that the US ambassador to the USSR was immediately reclassified as Washington's envoy to the Russian Federation. The USA was clearly anxious to effect a frictionless handover in all areas sensitive for international affairs. In this vein, Bush was keen on expediting Russia's takeover of the permanent seat on the UN Security Council that had been reserved since 1945 for the Soviet Union.[6]

The Russian president was even brisker than Bush in burying Gorbachev. What appeared to be a smooth political transition was actually the final act of a long-running personal vendetta. Despite a solemn promise from Yeltsin to Bush to treat the former Soviet leader with dignity, Gorbachev had to move out of his big apartment within a day of his resignation – Yeltsin initially wanted him out in two hours. Gorbachev retained his monthly salary of 4,000 roubles – now worth about $40 – and was given a small, crumbling country dacha outside Moscow with a skeletal staff. Gorbachev agreed not to criticise his successor for the next six months and generally promised Yeltsin support as long as Russia's leader 'continued on the path of democratic reform'.[7]

But for all the humiliation and social isolation – which Gorbachev's wife Raisa in particular resented – Gorbachev's fate could have been much worse, as least by Soviet standards. He was not muzzled, being granted a sizeable building complex from which to run a think tank – what would become the Gorbachev Foundation. And although widely blamed for the country's ruination, he was not put on trial. Nor, indeed, was anyone else. There simply ensued a quasi-show trial of the Communist Party of the Soviet Union itself. Meanwhile most of its apparatchiks continued in post despite the change of systems and states – a classic case of the continuity of elites.[8]

Amid all this turmoil, both Bush and Yeltsin were anxious for a personal meeting.[9] In the New Year, plans took shape fast: the summit was eventually arranged for 1 February 1992 at Camp David. It would follow Yeltsin's attendance at a special UN Security Council meeting about the post-Cold War era in New York on 31 January, when the Russian Federation would also formally assume the permanent-member seat abruptly vacated by the demise of the Soviet Union.[10]

The summit at the UN's headquarters was intended in Bush's words as a 'history-making' event. It was not just about changing the name on one of the Big Five seats. There were now high hopes for this world body – guardian of universally agreed rights and rules – freed from the shackles of East–West conflict. The historical developments in Central and Eastern Europe, the new climate of Russo-American cooperation and the successful war in the Gulf, conducted under the aegis of the UN, created an optimistic atmosphere in which a revitalised UN was envisaged as a central ordering force of the world remade. The hope and indeed expectation was that the Security Council, in a novel spirit of unity, would come up with innovative ideas on how best to organise the international community of states so that it could respond effectively to future disputes, conflicts and crises. In fact, 'the responsibility of the Security Council in the maintenance of international peace and security' was the only agenda item.[11]

But performance did not match promise. The leaders of all fifteen members of the Security Council each gave a speech on this theme. Yet, their presentations were loose, vague and largely platitudinous – meandering around the risks and opportunities in this 'time of change'. Although the summit ended with a joint pledge to international law, collective security and the peaceful resolution of disputes, the leaders charged the new secretary general, Boutros Boutros-Ghali, with the task of making practical recommendations later in 1992. So ultimately the UN summit skirted around the crucial question – already raised by the Gulf War and the violent break-up of Yugoslavia – about whether the new order should rest on a value-based approach, aimed at conflict prevention, or a hegemonic philosophy of conflict resolution, dominated by the great powers, especially the United States.[12]

Most strikingly, no attempt was made to reform the Security Council itself, especially its permanent membership. With the end of the Cold War, and even of the whole post-war era, one might have expected a radical rethink. But here too conservatism reigned. Britain and France said nothing for they did not want to lose their permanent seats, and the related power-political status, which reflected the world of the 1940s more than of the 1990s. And among the potential rising powers, Japan and Germany did not feel ready to claim the political position to which their economic power seemed to entitle them. Scarred by the bellicose nationalism of the Second World War, neither was keen to translate its wealth into military might – as had been evident in their reticent approach to the Gulf War. And the post-Maastricht European Union – for all its rhetoric – lacked coherence and clout as an international actor.[13]

That is why, despite all the grandiloquence, the New York UN summit was notable mainly for a small but momentous name change on the place cards of the Security Council, smoothly saying farewell to the communist Soviet Union and welcoming an apparently tamed, pro-Western Russia. As John Major, acting as president of the Security Council stated: 'We celebrate … a new world power: the Russian Federation, the power which has now emerged from an aberration that lasted for seventy years.'[14]

Just beforehand, on 28 January, Bush had spelled out the nature of that 'aberration' in his third State of the Union address. Its tone was very different from his valedictory for Gorbachev on Christmas Day. Instead of all that talk about partnership, his line now was much more triumphalist – not least, of course, because 1992 for Bush was re-election year. 'The Cold War didn't end; it was won,' he told Congress and millions of Americans watching on television. In fact, 'the biggest thing that has happened in the world in my life, in our lives, is this: by the grace of God, America won the Cold War.' And he paid tribute to the 'sacrifices' made by ordinary Americans, 'all the GI Joes and Janes, all the ones who fought faithfully for freedom, who hit the ground and sucked the dust and knew their share of horror'. And he lauded the US people as a whole, because 'the American taxpayer bore the brunt of the burden and deserves a hunk of the glory'.

The president also cast his mind back to his address in January 1991, when US forces had just unleashed Desert Storm. Now, a year later, with Kuwait liberated, he proclaimed 'Our policies were vindicated,' which showed, he said, that 'much good can come from the prudent use of power. And much good can come of this: a world once divided into two armed camps now recognises one sole and pre-eminent power, the United States of America.' Bush had written his first draft of history.[15]

It was also his scenario for the future – because he was sure that America could not rest on its laurels. The transformation of Eastern Europe and the collapse of the Soviet Union had generated a wave of debate about the future global role of the United States. And this intensified in the New Year as the country geared up in earnest for the presidential election campaign, with many voices inclining towards a new isolationism. Jeane Kirkpatrick, formerly Reagan's ambassador to the UN, argued in 1990 that it was 'not within the United States' power to democratise the world', nor was it 'the American purpose to establish "universal dominance"'. Indeed, with a return to what she called 'normal times', America could again become 'a normal nation'. Similarly, commentators Robert Tucker and David Hendrickson claimed in 1992 that the current American obsession with 'the fate of free institutions and the conditions of world order' amounted to an 'imperial temptation' that had to be resisted.[16]

In his State of the Union address, Bush was determined to squash such ideas, seizing on the 'unipolar moment' as a chance to create global stability in America's image:

> There are those who say that now we can turn away from the world, that we have no special role, no special place. But we are the United States of America, the leader of the West that has become the leader of the world. And as long as I am president, I will continue to lead in support of freedom everywhere, not out of arrogance, not out of altruism, but for the safety and security of our children. This is a fact: strength in the pursuit of peace is no vice; isolationism in the pursuit of security is no virtue.[17]

With his plea for US leadership through internationalism, he effectively nailed down the foreign-policy plank for his re-election campaign.

Bush's message rang out. America had overcome the Soviet Union: its values had triumphed. This was a victory for might and right. As the unquestioned leader of the post-Cold War world, 'we were suddenly in a unique position', Scowcroft mused, 'without experience, without precedent, and standing alone at the height of power'.[18] Indeed, with the Soviet military fragmented, the USA was the only country possessing armed forces with global reach, and US defence expenditure would soon equal those of the next six countries combined (including Russia). The USA was also the world's largest and most advanced economy. The countries next on the list – Japan and Germany – each lagged far behind and were also military pygmies. Ideologically, too, with its gospel of democracy and free markets, the US model had momentum and appeal – having expanded into the Third World since the recession of the 1970s and now being in a position to advance freely into previously off-limits territory in Eastern Europe and the former Soviet Union. Yes, indeed, Congress agreed with the president: America had won.[19]

It was striking how Bush's narrative had changed over the three years of his presidency. Even as revolution spread across Eastern Europe in 1989, he had been reluctant to declare the Cold War over – evading reporters' questions in an often awkward way. It was only when he met Gorbachev for the first time as president – in Malta in December 1989 – that he stated unambiguously that the world was leaving 'the epoch of the Cold War'. But he hadn't insisted that Western values had won the day, compromising – in the face of Gorbachev's claim that both sides were now converging ideologically – on the terminology of 'common', 'democratic' and 'universal' values. In 1989–90 the evidence that the Cold War was ending lay in the continued defusing of the arms race between the superpowers, their constructive diplomacy in resolving the German question and their cooperation against Saddam's invasion of Kuwait. After the end of the Gulf War in March 1991 and with the signing of START I, Bush and Gorbachev declared their Moscow meeting of July that year to be the 'first post-Cold War summit'. But by the end of 1991 the meaning of the 'end of the Cold War' had shifted yet again. The Warsaw Pact and Comecon had dissolved, while the EU and NATO began a process of adaptation and reinvention. Then the Soviet Union had disappeared from the world map, and with it the last remnants of bipolarity. A half-century of international relations was clearly over. For most Americans the end of the Cold War now meant, simply, the demise of the Soviet Union – until so recently Reagan's 'evil empire'. QED: America *definitely* won.

Yet, as with any war – hot or cold – victory is never simple. There is always fallout to be dealt with. The threat of nuclear Armageddon might have diminished, but the nuclear hardware had not disappeared. Throughout the Cold War there had been persistent anxiety about nuclear proliferation to rogue states with maverick leaders. The Kuwait War fears of Saddam's 'weapons of mass destruction' were the most recent alarm call. And things had changed for the worse in the months after that war ended. The world's second-largest nuclear power had broken apart, and it was far from clear how the fragments would be put together. The former Soviet Union's nuclear weaponry was now in the hands of four independent states, whose mutual relations were fraught. From the Kremlin, Yeltsin claimed to be in full charge of the command and control system. But could his word be trusted? Would the leader of Russia be able to assert his power over Ukraine, Belarus and Kazakhstan?

In the Balkans, Bush could see how badly things could turn out when an apparently strong federal state fell apart: Yugoslavia was breaking up in a series of bloody wars of secession. How much worse things could be for the world if the vast area of the former Soviet empire – covering eight time zones – degenerated into war and anarchy? Was Yeltsin up to this challenge? What would happen if he, too, went the way of Gorbachev? To turn Cold War victory into post-Cold War stability, Bush needed a strong and reliable relationship with the president of the new Russia. That is why Yeltsin was being welcomed to Camp David only six weeks after he had evicted Gorbachev from the Kremlin.[20]

On 31 January, Yeltsin used his debut speech in New York at the United Nations to make a major foreign-policy statement. He was at pains to stress his identity as a Russian, rather than a Soviet, leader – in a country free from the 'yoke of communism'. He said that he represented a 'new Russia' with a 'new foreign policy'. And he spelled out what that meant in truly novel language. He told the Security Council that his Russia now 'considers the United States and the West not as mere partners but rather allies' – an assertion duly noted in the American press. Whereas Gorbachev had repudiated the idea that his country was now embracing 'Western' values – insisting on the two superpowers meeting halfway, as it were, ideologically – Yeltsin seemed to be moving completely into the Western orbit. He was emphatic about his commitment at home to political freedom and human rights and, internationally, to cooperation, disarmament and peace.[21]

The soaring rhetoric was buttressed by detail. Yeltsin proposed deep cuts in strategic and tactical nuclear weapons, further reductions in conventional arms and the creation of a global anti-missile shield, developed in tandem with the United States – another notable departure from Gorbachev's agenda. And he announced that all land-based tactical nukes had already been withdrawn from Kazakhstan and Belarus to Russia itself, only six weeks after the demise of the USSR, and stated that withdrawal from Ukraine would be completed by July. After initial storage in Russia, he promised that all these armaments would be destroyed.[22]

Having set out his shop window in Manhattan, Yeltsin flew to Camp David to sell the goods. The Russian leader seemed confident and informed, speaking without notes. Baker considered him 'relaxed', but 'in the way a championship tennis player is relaxed right before a match: on the top of his game, fully prepared and ready to go at it'.[23]

Yeltsin spent some time on the economic crisis and the prospects for reform. 'We are five years late in starting,' he said, because genuine reform 'only really became possible after the collapse of the empire and communist ideology'. Total price liberalisation on 2 January was the flagship of Yegor Gaidar's 'shock therapy'. Appointed by Yeltsin as deputy prime minister in charge of economic reform, the thirty-five-year-old Gaidar – who in 1990 had also worked on the 500 Days Plan – had pushed for an immediate end to price controls and the opening up of trade. At the same time, as part of Russia's new austerity policy, the government sought to control spending and the printing of money in order to achieve macroeconomic stabilisation.[24]

Against this backdrop, Yeltsin insisted to the Americans that Russia had a 'clear programme', even though there had been no time to implement compensatory changes in taxation and the banking system. The Russian president acknowledged the problems of soaring inflation (which currently ran at 240%) and the criticism of his economic policies from both right and left. The next couple of months would be 'critical', he said. 'We hope people can stand it.' He thanked Bush for the recent airlift of aid – almost 20,000 tons of food and medicine – but said it simply wasn't enough. And he warned of what would happen if reform failed. The hardliners, the 'hawks', would return. 'We will have a police state, repression, and the arms race will recommence. It will be a waste of billions of dollars for the US and involve the whole world.'[25]

It was a long lecture. Yeltsin promised: 'We are resolved to stay with democracy', stressing 'We need help, not aid. We need your support and cooperation.' And then, just before he finished, came a calculated aside.

'One last matter. Are we still adversaries or not?'

'No we are not,' Bush replied firmly. He handed Yeltsin the final draft of the joint declaration that he and Baker had pre-prepared in Moscow. 'This moves us away from the old era.'

The statement proclaimed a new era of American–Russian 'friendship and partnership' and declared a formal end to more than seventy years of rivalry since the Bolshevik Revolution. But Yeltsin wished to insert another, magic word. He wanted the joint communiqué to say that their relationship had moved to one of 'allies'. Bush, however, refused to go that far. 'We are using transitional language,' he countered, 'because we don't want to act like all our problems are solved.' With that, Yeltsin had to be content.[26]

After lunch the two presidents released their mutually agreed 'Declaration on New Relations' and talked to the press.[27] The language was again effusive. Yeltsin predicted a relationship in the future of 'full frankness, full openness, full honesty'. Bush said it would be based on 'trust', on 'a commitment to economic and political freedom' and, choosing his words carefully, on 'a strong hope for true partnership'. Their main substantive commitment was to hold a formal summit before the end of year.[28]

Flying back to Washington that night, Baker recalled the many superpower talks he attended over the years, and realised 'how truly special and historic' this session with Yeltsin had been. 'For the first time the elected leader of a democratic and independent Russia had sat down with an American president. Together the two had begun to chart a course of cooperation.' Sitting back in his seat, Baker thought to himself: 'Talk about "beyond containment"!'[29]

Bush was also buoyed up by the progress already made with the new Russian leader. He no longer seemed so weighed down by the re-election campaign. In mid-February he had seen off a strong challenge in the make-or-break New Hampshire primary, winning 53% of the Republican vote to Pat Buchanan's 37%. Bush wrote in his diary on 2 March, 'I have a quiet confidence that I will win. Some of it because of the opposition; some of it because I think things like world peace and experienced leadership will make a difference; and some of it because I think the economy is going to turn around.' And, despite the immense burden of navigating the last three years of world history, his appetite for the task remained keen. On 14 March at Camp David he typed up some notes for his speechwriters under the deliberately ironic heading 'The Vision Thing'. Top of the list was: 'World leadership to guarantee that our children live in peace, free from the fear of nuclear war in a world where all people know the blessings of democracy and freedom.' To achieve this vision, he added, 'we must remain as the active leader of the entire world'.[30]

A couple of days later Bush aired some of these ideas in an address at the Polish National Alliance in Chicago. It was nearly three years since the president had started to unveil his 'vision of the European future' in his Hamtramck speech in the suburbs of Detroit to another Polish–American audience. On 16 March 1992, he could look back with wonder. 'It is unbelievable. Since '88, the whole world has been transformed … Now imperial communism, the communism that always wanted to take over someone else, is dead.' But mindful of 'those who still have not won full freedom' – he spoke particularly of the peoples of the former Yugoslavia – he insisted, 'Our leadership for freedom must continue.'[31]

Baker fleshed out the nature of that leadership in a major speech of his own in Chicago on 22 April.[32] Like Bush, he rejected those who advocated isolationist, 'America first' patriotism – 'avoiding the challenges of our times by pretending they do not exist'. Instead, he claimed, 'our idea is to replace the dangerous period of the Cold War with a democratic peace – a peace built on the twin pillars of political and economic freedom. By supporting democracy and free markets in Russia and Eurasia, we can extend the "zone of peace and prosperity".' That, he said, was 'good for American interests and values'. But the Secretary of State eschewed Kennedyesque talk of paying any price and bearing any burden. Emphasising the limits of America's resources, he said that 'the community of democratic nations is larger and more vigorous than at the end of World War Two'. That is why the Bush administration pursued a policy of 'American leadership' which it called 'collective engagement'. He reminded his audience that Germany, Italy and Japan – wartime enemies – were now 'strong and prosperous allies'. By working with them and with America's other partners, as well as the key post-war international institutions – the UN, World Bank and IMF – 'we need not go it alone'. Instead, 'we can build a democratic peace together'.[33]

As an example of this policy Baker cited the Gulf War coalition. He also mentioned Western aid programmes for the former Soviet republics and post-communist Eastern Europe. But this, like the war, was no simple story. Rather it illustrated the manoeuvring for position that was part of building a new international order. On 22–3 January 1992, the Coordinating Conference on Assistance to the New Independent States, involving forty-seven countries and seven global financial institutions, which Baker had first announced in his Princeton speech before Christmas, opened in Washington.

This new American desire to be seen leading on aid efforts in the Soviet successor states had annoyed the Europeans, especially the French and the Germans. Paris wanted a stronger role for its new pet institution – the European Bank for Reconstruction and Development – since most aid to the USSR had come from the EC (in fact, 90% of it from Germany). And the view in Bonn was that the US, Japan and Arab oil states were equally neighbours of the former Soviet empire.[34] Given this mood, the FRG took the opportunity to embarrass the Americans about their usual hobby horse with the Europeans: a demand for adequate burden-sharing. 'It's always painful, when you turn it around, isn't it?' joked a Bonn official to the *Washington Post*. Bush tried to make good weather of all this: 'I don't think it's a question of who's doing the most. It's a question of each country ... doing its best.'[35]

Bush's eyes were not only on the Europeans but also his home audience – especially the Pentagon, which had been sceptical about giving aid to the arch enemy. It demanded almost a leap of faith on the part of the American military to believe that peace and stability in this new world required masses of dollars for the Russian economy rather than for US weapons programmes. Bush had proposed that Congress approve $645 million in technical and humanitarian aid to the CIS states including Russia. And – for dramatic effect to galvanise public support – a massive emergency 'airlift' of food and medicine, 'Operation Provide Hope', would begin on 10 February. But when Yeltsin's ministers angled for much greater and more far-reaching economic assistance, America claimed that issues of macroeconomic stabilisation were the remit of the IMF.[36]

After the Washington Conference, Genscher was pleased that, at the very least, the leaders had been brought up to speed on the key issues. And the USA now seemed in the same boat on aid, and looking in the same direction towards a more sustained and long-term involvement with the new independent states.[37] Some Euro-Atlantic tension however lingered over how this aid should be coordinated. The US had pressed for NATO to handle the delivery, but the French rejected this as another sign of the US seeking to patronise the Europeans.[38] On 31 March the NATO coordination office was wound up, only three months after its creation, because most EU states had boycotted it and because the EU had not used it for its own 200 million ECU emergency package agreed under the Maastricht Treaty. As a senior EC official said, it had been the European Community which 'has been coordinating aid to the former Soviet republics since the beginning of last year' – not NATO. In any event, aid reached Russia and the other ex-Soviet countries more through bilateral channels, not least because different states supported different republics (e.g. Germany focused on Russia, Belarus and Ukraine, Turkey on the Central Asian republics). But what the institutional fracas revealed was how the EU and NATO, America and the Western Europeans, were all jockeying among themselves for post-Cold War roles and positions with regard to Russia and the post-Soviet space.[39]

Despite the new American interest in helping Russia, Germany remained the major player. On 1 April Bush and Kohl announced on behalf of the G7 an aid package of $24 billion – of which $4.35 billion was to come from the USA. The Americans did not, however, commit anything to Russian debt rescheduling. The US president and the German chancellor, by far the biggest bilateral donor, stressed that Russia must follow an approved economic reform programme in order to get the aid. But both expressed their conviction that this assistance package would prevent the economic collapse of Russia and stop new authoritarianism rising from the rubble of the former USSR.[40]

The timing of their announcement was no coincidence, just five days before Yeltsin would have to appear before a hostile Russian parliament to persuade over 1,000 People's Deputies that yet more bitter free-market medicine had to be swallowed. Considering this domestic political pressure, the view of economic experts in Russia and the West was that not only did the package give Yeltsin's economic policy 'respectability', but in practical terms it would make a decisive difference between unbearable misery and hard but just about tolerable times for ordinary Russians. Some old-guard politicos resented the humiliation of IMF aid. Russia is 'not Peru or Paraguay', said Ivan Polozkov, a deputy from the Smena faction of conservative centrists, who argued that Russia's problems needed Russian solutions. But, for the moment, he was in a minority given the gravity of the economic crisis.[41]

AIR DROP

No money. Just a survival kit

Gaidar certainly was excited: the West finally appeared ready to finance a balance-of-payments gap of up to $18 billion, thereby helping to close the Russian budget deficit and to begin to control inflation. Furthermore, as in the case of Poland in 1990 the West was now willing to offer Russia a stabilisation fund to support a convertible rouble. These external funds were necessary to achieve economic stabilisation in the short term, so that the momentum of reform would be maintained. But the scale, of course, had to be massively greater than what had been done in Poland. Whereas Warsaw needed $1 billion to stabilise its currency, Moscow – so Russian officials believed – needed a hard currency pot of $6–7 billion. This is now what they got.[42]

In any case, both the balance-of-payments support and the stabilisation fund were subject to a further agreement between Russia and the IMF on a detailed economic programme, with specific budgetary and financial targets. This programme still had to be hammered out. Nor was Russian progress clear-cut. Although price liberalisation on many commodities had proved fairly successful, privatisation of major state industries had so far been very slow and private investment minimal. Consequently, Gaidar had to ease both monetary and fiscal policy to maintain political stability, and to postpone the liberalisation of energy prices from April until May or June.[43]

Gaidar and his allies were virtual unknowns in the West and Yeltsin himself was still a new boy on the block.[44] Yet Western leaders, with Bush and Kohl in the vanguard, now seemed ready to put their money where their mouth was and help fund Russia's great transition. They were keen to foster stability and they were also aware that Russia's door for Western engagement was wide open. Aiding Russia was a necessity and an opportunity at the same time. But as much as there was fear of losing Yeltsin unless he got dollars – 'with us looking like we held back and were part of the problem' (Baker) – there was also a view that Russia might prove a bottomless 'rathole' (Scowcroft). What's more, Kohl's and Bush's grand announcement aside, the G7 had not been fully consulted about detailed figures. As a result, Japan called Bush's statement 'premature', while a German official saw it as 'pure campaigning' on the American side. The uncertainty and incoherence was summed up by one British Treasury official: 'If you take a snapshot, at the moment, we are in mid-air, about three-quarters through our double spin.'[45]

The magnitude of the task was now abundantly clear. As one Western diplomat commented on 1 April: 'No one has ever tried to transform a socialist command economy of this size into a free-market one, and no one knows how it's supposed to happen, even if they pretend.' He was right. The big-bang approach to the post-Soviet economic transition was probably the greatest economic reform ever undertaken. China had proceeded by small steps over a long period, introducing special economic zones – local bubbles of capitalist activity – all of which led towards a system the PRC eventually defined as a 'socialist market economy'. And unlike in the Soviet Union the political lid had been kept tightly shut: there had been no political opening at the same time towards democratisation – no trajectory of 'modernisation-as-Westernisation'. For the West, as well as for Moscow, this simultaneity of economic and political liberalisation in Russia was undoubtedly a high-risk journey into the unknown.[46]

For now, the US press billed the $24 billion announcement as a way of 'buying time for Yeltsin', suggesting that the new Russian leader had been given something that Gorbachev had 'never received: a major vote of confidence on his economic reform'. But, as Baker had noted, Gorbachev – though a reformer – had failed to shed completely his communist, Soviet skin, whereas Yeltsin was a new political animal.[47]

Or was he? The ten-day Congress of People's Deputies, due to begin on 6 April 1992, was crucial for progress in Russia's relations with the West. It was expected to push for a draft constitution giving future parliaments more power. But Yeltsin, who also held the post of prime minister, said bluntly on the eve of the Congress that Russia could not now afford a parliamentary system of government. 'In the present situation,' he asserted, 'we can talk only of presidential government for the next two or three years. In a parliamentary republic the president is no more than a decorative figure.' That would be 'suicide' for Russia in these difficult transitional times, he said, when 'we still have to deal with a seriously ill society'.[48]

On top of this, Yeltsin had to ward off a substantial challenge by the right against his government's programme of economic shock therapy. And so, as he worked to retain his room for manoeuvre between the demands of the international financial community and domestic public opinion, he undertook a Cabinet reshuffle, tightened his grip on the army, and freed 200 billion roubles ($2 billion) in loans for bankrupt state enterprises. Under the threat of government resignation, on 14 April he finally persuaded the Deputies to pass a muted declaration of support for his programme of radical economic reform. Yeltsin had therefore managed to reassert his position as boss.[49]

But was Yeltsin seeking power for reform, or power for its own sake? Did this pose a question mark about his democratic credentials? Or was it recognition that marketising a command economy, vigorous democratisation, and the achievement of political stability were simply impossible simultaneously – as the Chinese believed?

*

Like Yeltsin, Bush also seemed a politician in flux. In the spring of 1992, he was under intense pressure from ex-president Richard Nixon, Bush's former boss in the 1970s and – with Watergate long behind him – now becoming an esteemed elder statesman, at least for the right. In public and in private, Nixon castigated the president for his lack of aid to the new democratic Russia – raising the question 'Who lost Russia?', an echo of the politically devastating Republican charge against the Truman administration after 1949: 'Who lost China?' Nixon stung Bush with his comment that 'the mark of great political leadership is not simply to support what is popular, but to make what is unpopular popular if that serves America's national interest'. Nixon's former Secretary of State, Henry Kissinger, also laid into the debate from a different angle. He accused Bush of being 'remarkably slow in dealing with the new republics' and too solicitous of Russia's dignity. Kissinger, unlike Nixon, did not favour a big aid programme for Moscow – at least until Russia showed respect for the new borders of the post-Soviet space. And in any case, he argued, 'Russia is not ours to win or to lose.'[50]

Bush decided he could turn a vigorous policy of aid to Russia to his political advantage in the election year. That's why his 1 April announcement about the $24 billion, live on CNN, was deliberately timed to upstage his main Democratic challenger Governor Bill Clinton of Arkansas who was scheduled to deliver his first major foreign-policy speech, to the Council of Foreign Relations in New York, just twenty minutes later. It was also why the legislation to authorise the aid was grandly labelled the 'FREEDOM Support Act'.*

Justifying the aid package to the American people, Bush tried to play it both ways. 'It's not a tremendous amount of money,' he assured those anxious about the economy. This was true. The IMF and World

---

* 'FREEDOM' was capitalised as an acronym for 'Freedom for Russia and Emerging Eurasian Democracies and Open Markets'.

Bank, as he rightly explained, would be 'the primary source of funding'. What's more, he promised that 'significant new trade relationships can create jobs right here in this country'. But he also draped himself in the mantle of history. 'For more than forty-five years, the highest responsibility of nine American presidents, Democrats and Republicans, was to wage and win the Cold War. It was my privilege to work with Ronald Reagan on these broad programmes'. Now, he continued, it would be his privilege (implicitly for his second term) to 'lead the American people in winning the peace by embracing the people so recently freed from tyranny to welcome them into the community of democratic nations'.[51]

This was a risky strategy: 55% of Americans wanted foreign aid to be cut, another 40% believed it shouldn't be increased. But Bush and his advisers had decided to use the incontrovertible fact that he was a foreign-policy president as an electoral asset. 'To do nothing would be irresponsible,' he told sceptical pressmen. 'The United States must continue to lead.' Baker was pleased. Back in December 1991 he had insisted to Bush, 'Historically, you've passed the first two tests – liberating Eastern Europe and liberating Kuwait – but now historians will view those as footnotes to your reaction to the present crisis.'[52] A few months later, Bush was no longer operating merely in reactive mode. The opportunities opening up across the whole of the former USSR – not just in Yeltsin's Russia but in all the successor states – and, as Nixon said, the implications for the whole world if their democratic transition failed, had all hit home. Back in 1989, as a neophyte president, Bush had dithered. In 1990–1 he had mainly responded to the agendas of others, especially Kohl and Gorbachev. But by 1992, after America's victory in the Gulf and the collapse of the USSR, George H. W. Bush was ready to lead. He had found his voice as an international leader and saw his chance – and his duty – to influence the future of a new world now opening up in the post-Soviet sphere.

Yet Bush's proposed FREEDOM Support Act was still only a bill: it had to pass the two houses of Congress – both controlled by the Democrats with substantial majorities. So he and Baker began a campaign to win public and congressional support for their Russia aid policy[53] – what Bush termed 'the most important foreign-policy opportunity of our time'. On 9 April Baker testified before the Senate Foreign Relations Committee. 'Today,' he said, 'we face a wholly different and novel situation, a chance to build a genuine peace based on common democratic values, to build a democratic peace with Russia and Eurasia. A democratic peace would be a genuine peace; it would not be just the absence of war. That is a purpose that is worthy of the American people, and that is a purpose that we think all Americans will be willing to support.' On the same day Bush took a similar line with the American Society of Newspaper Editors. 'The success of reform in Russia and Ukraine, Armenia and Kazakhstan, Belarus and the Baltics will be the single best guarantee of our security, our prosperity and our values' because, he insisted, 'real democracies' do not go to war with each other. And, he warned, 'the failure of the democratic experiment could bring a dark future, a return to authoritarianism or a descent into anarchy'.[54]

Persuading Capitol Hill was no easy task given the stuttering state of the US economy and other domestic problems, such as a new surge of racial violence in Los Angeles in late April and early May. Many lawmakers who had previously urged the administration to do more for Russia were now not willing to pay the cost. On 1 May, House Democratic whip David Bonior sent the president a letter with nearly a hundred congressional signatures, stating 'We cannot support your plan for additional assistance to the former Soviet republics until you have first addressed the issue of jobs and economic growth for America.'[55] When Bush announced the bill in April, he expected to give Yeltsin a nice present when the Russian leader visited Washington in June. One month on, however, he had changed his tune, hoping that the state visit would be a foreign-policy success sufficient to loosen the domestic logjam.[56]

The State Department worked hard to do the necessary diplomatic groundwork before Yeltsin arrived at the White House. In late May, after several months of wrangling amid a tense international situation – not least the fierce Russian–Ukrainian struggle of wills as to who had the right to control the Black Sea Fleet[57] – Baker finally managed to secure a deal with Russia, Ukraine, Belarus and Kazakhstan under which they agreed to adhere to the START I treaty signed by the USA with the USSR in 1991. With the Soviet nuclear arsenals spread out across these four successor republics, the new agreement was intended to ensure that the other three states would either destroy their nuclear weapons or hand them over to Russia. As a result, there would only be one nuclear power on the territory of the former USSR. 'We have laid the foundations for further stabilising reductions in strategic offensive arms and expanded the nuclear non-proliferation regime,' Baker declared at the signing ceremony in Lisbon. He felt that the START Protocol and the fact that the four successor states had committed to the 1968 Non-Proliferation Treaty significantly lowered the risk of nuclear war.[58]

It was now possible for America and Russia to make progress on nuclear arms reduction,[59] but few observers expected the 'extraordinary agreement' that Bush and Yeltsin were able to announce in the Rose Garden on 16 June. Each nation pledged to reduce its nuclear force to 3,000–3,500 warheads no later than 2003. Between them they currently controlled about 22,500 warheads – a figure that, once START I was fully implemented, would fall to 8,500 warheads for the USA and about 6,900 for Russia. The new treaty, START II, therefore envisaged a further cut of more than a half.[60]

Right up to that very morning, nobody in Washington had been sure whether Bush would accept a deal. In the end, rather than trying to agree on an exact ceiling, the same figure for each side, the president finally acceded to Yeltsin's compromise of a numerical 'range'. This allowed the Kremlin to go to the lower limit, which it wanted for economic reasons, while granting the USA a higher number of warheads, which better suited America's force structure. That's why, in the press conference afterwards, Yeltsin called the accord 'an unparalleled and probably unexpected thing for you and the whole world'. The two leaders expressed confidence that the formal treaty would be ready for signature in just a few months. Bush was thrilled at the breakthrough. 'With this agreement,' he told reporters, 'the nuclear nightmare recedes more and more for ourselves, for our children and for our grandchildren.'[61]

The American media was surprised and impressed. 'The arms agreement allowed Mr Bush to regain the international spotlight and the political offensive,' remarked the American reporter R. W. Apple, displaying him 'in his preferred role of accomplished international negotiator and peacemaker, which since the Persian Gulf War has been gradually eclipsed, in terms of public opinion, by concerns about healthcare, jobs, education, the environment and the credibility of politicians'.[62] Bush used this opportunity to renew his pitch for aid to Russia, exploiting in turn the image of Yeltsin the peacemaker as further justification. The president spoke of economic assistance as 'an investment in a new century of peace with Russia'. Waxing lyrical, he said that 'history offers us a rare chance, a chance to achieve what twice before this century has escaped our grasp. It is the vision that perished twice in the battlefields of Europe, the vision that gave us hope through the long Cold War, the dream of a new world of freedom.'[63]

Next day, 17 June, Yeltsin repaid Bush with a barnstorming performance before a Joint Session of Congress. He strode into the packed chamber to a standing ovation that, according to some journalists, rivalled Bush's own reception in Congress after America's triumph in Kuwait. The enthusiasm was particularly surprising since, before Yeltsin arrived in Washington, few on Capitol Hill had thought he would outdo his Kremlin predecessor, still remembered for the Gorbymania that infected Americans in 1987 and 1988. But Yeltsin had real presence – a striking figure towering over the rostrum, with his swept-back silver hair and broad smile. Amid chants of 'Boris, Boris, Boris', he won no less than thirteen further standing ovations as he vowed that the 'idol of communism has collapsed, never to rise again'. Again there was no slippery talk about reformed Leninism or perestroika-style rejuvenation: 'The experience of the past decades has taught us communism has no human face. Freedom and communism are incompatible.' Switching easily between candour and humour, lecturing and lobbying, he assured American lawmakers that they could now trust Russia – 'There will be no more lies, ever' – and reminded them of the dramatic days of August 1991 when he put his own body on the line in defence of democracy and freedom. 'Today the freedom of America is being upheld in Russia,' he declared – another example of his apparent keenness, unlike Gorbachev, to openly align himself at least rhetorically with American values.[64]

Hero of democracy: Boris before Congress

Yeltsin made a particular impact on congressional Democrats, who had been highly resistant to money for Moscow. 'It's not so much that Yeltsin won them all over,' said one Senate staffer, 'as much as his appearance improved the climate in which a vote will be taken ... It's easier now for people to vote for it politically.'[65] But commentators agreed that the outcome would depend on how much arm-twisting Bush was willing to do to win over lawmakers naturally more concerned in an election year about aid to Americans rather than Russians. It helped that at the summit he had announced that they had signed agreements to grant Russia 'most favoured nation' status in trade and to liberalise rules for US investment there. This opened the door, the Administration emphasised, to American business and therefore jobs for American workers.[66]

To wrap up the summit and reinforce its impact, Bush and Yeltsin signed a grandly entitled 'Charter for American–Russian Partnership and Friendship' committing themselves jointly to defend and advance 'common democratic values and human rights and fundamental free-doms'.[67] Bush had already lauded their meeting as 'a new kind of summit, not a meeting between two powers struggling for global supremacy but between two partners striving to build a democratic peace'. After the signing ceremony, rubbing the point home, the US president declared: 'Success for Russian democracy will enhance the security of every American.' Echoing Franklin D. Roosevelt, he said 'it means a future free from fear'. And that, he added, 'is why I call upon Congress to act quickly on the FREEDOM Support Act, so that the American support reaches Russia when it is needed most, right now'.[68]

Although the White House communications office had squeezed everything possible out of the first-ever Russian–American state visit, the bill remained controversial, particularly that headline figure of nearly $1 billion in new money. This sum was divided more or less equally between Russia and eleven other former Soviet republics on the one hand, and nine Baltic and East European states on the other. The Balts had successfully argued that they were captive nations, annexed in 1939, rather than Soviet successor states. Given this position, after independence in the autumn of 1991 they naturally did not join the CIS, and the West treated the three of them in the same category as the former Warsaw Pact countries. The US aid money would be conditional on continued movement by all these former communist states towards democracy and free markets.[69]

It was not just the price tag that exercised critics. Kissinger, already a sceptic about Bush's Russia policy, questioned the basic premises of what he called the Bush–Yeltsin 'Charter of Confusion', especially the claim that the two countries were now 'sharing identical goals' and that 'no geopolitical issues remain' between them. 'Is it prudent to base policy on the assumption that an evolution barely three years old has already a pattern of centuries?' But Bush – less burdened by history than the veteran scholar-statesman – was ready to take the risk. It seems that he and Baker had fully committed themselves, at least politically, to what Kissinger called the idea that 'liberal democracy and market economics will by themselves achieve peace everywhere'.[70]

The summit enabled Bush to get the FREEDOM Support legislation through the Senate on 2 July with an overwhelming 76–20 majority – no fewer than forty-three Democrats joining thirty-three Republicans. Despite some strong criticism – one Democrat described the president as 'drunk on foreign policy' – most senators accepted the argument of Republican floor manager Richard Lugar that the aid would be 'an investment in political, economic and social reform' which would 'pay dividends many times over in new American exports and the savings generated in our defense budget'.[71]

The House, however, proved less easy to persuade. Critics asked about the 100,000 Red Army troops still in the Baltic countries, and the border skirmishes between successor states such as Armenia and Azerbaijan, as well as the Georgian civil war. Was the former Soviet Union sufficiently stable and democratic to warrant such unprecedented generosity from Uncle Sam? And, even more important to most Democrats, what about the folks back home? 'I do not know how we can do this for Russia or anybody else and continue to ignore our cities', said Congresswoman Maxine Waters whose Los Angeles district was still struggling to recover from the spring riots.[72]

The outlines of a deal emerged in early August when administration officials tentatively agreed to speed up $370 million in spending on domestic public-works programmes and to make available as much as $2 billion in new loan guarantees to local communities. This gave the impression that Americans would not be short-changed by the Russians. Four former presidents also rallied behind Bush: Ronald Reagan, Jimmy Carter, Gerald Ford and Richard Nixon wrote a public letter on 3 August stating that this could be the most important vote that members of Congress would ever cast. 'The stakes could not be higher. If we fail to seize this historic opportunity now, authoritarianism could return to Moscow and elsewhere, the anticipated peace dividend could evaporate, future markets and jobs for Americans could be lost, and nuclear weapons may again threaten the lives of our children.' In other words, gaining the anticipated 'peace dividend' required US engagement, not disengagement.

The House Democratic leadership took up the refrain. 'We cannot live safe and prosperous and free if there is turmoil and upheaval in a vast land that possesses some 30,000 nuclear warheads,' said Lee Hamilton, chairman of the Foreign Affairs Committee's Subcommittee on Europe and the Middle East. 'If their reforms fail or are derailed, all of us are worse off.'[73]

On 6 August the FREEDOM Support Act passed the House comfortably by 255–164, including ninety-five Democrats and sixty-eight Republicans against. One of those voting in favour was Representative Jamie L. Whitten, a Democrat from Mississippi, the only member of the House who had been there to vote in the spring of 1947 for the Truman Doctrine package of $400 million to bolster anti-communism in Greece and Turkey. That began forty-five years of US aid to combat the Soviet Union; now, in a historic volte-face, Congress was ready to give billions of dollars to support the new Russia and its new neighbours. Congressman Newt Gingrich, the Republican whip, compared this vote to the adoption in 1948 of the Marshall Plan for rebuilding post-war Europe and even suggested that the rise of Hitler and the Second World War might have been averted if the USA had given more help to Germany's Weimar Republic in the late 1920s.[74]

The summer recess and the necessary reconciliation between the Senate and House bills took up the best part of three months. It was not until 24 October – just two weeks before the US elections – that Bush signed the FREEDOM Support Act into law. In addition to the $1 billion of bilateral assistance, tied to the purchase of American food, the legislation endorsed a $12 billion increase in the US share of the accompanying IMF aid package. 'I am proud that the United States has this historic opportunity to support democracy and free markets in this crucially important part of the world,' the president declared. 'Once again, the American people have united to advance the cause of freedom, to win the peace, to help transform former enemies into peaceful partners.' As usual he played up the domestic benefits. 'By contributing to a more prosperous world economy, the IMF will expand markets for US exporters and increase jobs for American workers.'[75]

All in all, the FREEDOM Support Act represented a bravura effort by the administration to show that the foreign-policy president could also deliver the goods at home. Yet it was a risky strategy ahead of an election, especially with an unemployment rate of well over 7%. In mid-July, even after the US–Russian Washington summit and the Senate vote, Bush was running more or less even with Bill Clinton, by then confirmed as the Democrats' nominee. Exuding confidence and energy, the young man from Arkansas seemed in every way a big contrast with Bush, aged sixty-eight.[76] So the president took the momentous step of asking Baker to take leave of absence from the State Department and assume the post of White House chief of staff in order to galvanise his campaign. Even in mid-August, after the Republican Convention – normally a big boost – the polls remained neck and neck. Bush got frustrated and despondent – 'everything is ugly and everything is nasty' – but he could still sound notes of confidence in his diary. 'I can make it; I can out-hustle Clinton; out-work him; out-jog him; out-think him; out-campaign him; and we'll win,' he wrote with bravado on 13 September.[77]

Sustaining the new Russia was, however, not merely an American story. Even after passage of the FREEDOM Support Act, most of the aid was going to come through international institutions. Yeltsin fully understood this. Bush and the US Congress were not the only people he needed to woo. On 1 June 1992, Russia became a full member of the IMF and the World Bank, having finally fulfilled the necessary criteria. But it had yet to reach an accord with the IMF about the terms under which aid could be released. The IMF, for instance, wanted a firm commitment from Moscow to reduce its huge budget deficit to zero and curb the growth of its money supply. It was also concerned to promote a stable 'rouble zone' across the former Soviet space. Gaidar, by now Yeltsin's acting prime minister following a Cabinet reshuffle to pacify the right, considered this disastrous for Russia.[78] After the success of Yeltsin's visit to Washington, the US administration pressed urgently for some relaxation of the IMF's criteria. 'If Boris Yeltsin can't succeed on economic reform, he will have a hard time staying as leader in Russia,' a senior official warned. 'This could seriously threaten the democratic reforms that are so much in our interest. The IMF agreement is key to this.'[79] After a frantic two weeks – including a last-minute trip to Moscow by IMF director Michel Camdessus for a tête-à-tête with Yeltsin – Russia and the IMF achieved a sufficient consensus to trigger the first tranche of aid in the form of a $1 billion loan. This occurred only on the eve of the G7 meeting, which convened in Munich on 6 July.[80]

At the summit the G7 did announce the IMF aid package to Russia. There was a sense of relief, as their final economic declaration of 8 July revealed:

> We support the phased strategy of cooperation between the Russian government and the IMF. This will allow the IMF to disburse a first credit tranche in support of the most urgent stabilisation measures within the next few weeks while continuing to negotiate a comprehensive reform programme with Russia. This will pave the way for the full utilisation of the $24 billion support package announced in April.[81]

Despite relief about an agreement on the IMF package, the mood in Munich was distinctly subdued. 'There's a sense of institutional hollowness, a staleness,' one senior American official observed off the record. 'After the euphoria of the end of the Cold War, a kind of Monday-morning feeling has set in.' The Germans, who had stepped up to the plate financially so often before, were now sounding more cautious. 'We can't finance the transition in its entirety,' said Horst Köhler, state secretary in the German Finance Ministry. 'That's not feasible.'[82] Most of the G7 leaders were up against serious economic problems at home, which threatened their poll ratings. Bush's predicament might have been worst, but Kohl was now facing the bill for German unification – both financially and through a right-wing backlash in the recent *Länder* elections. Mitterrand's Socialist Party was hitting near-record lows in opinion ratings, just before the French September referendum on the Maastricht Treaty on which he staked his presidency against an unlikely but dangerous coalition of communists, Gaullists and Front National. And Kiichi Miyazawa of Japan made clear that he wanted to concentrate on stimulating his own sluggish economy. Aid to Russia was also politically unpopular among the Japanese given their long-running dispute with Moscow over the Kuril Islands that Stalin had secured at the end of the Second World War.[83]

Collectively the Big Seven found themselves confronted by what Mitterrand called the 'morose state of the world economy' – with slow growth, high interest rates, chronic budget deficits and serious unemployment levels (at 7.8% in US and 9.4% in the EC). Despite this shared malaise, they did not really work together, instead bickering about matters on which they disagreed and pulling each other down. Most striking of all was the continued failure of the G7 to conclude an updated version of the 1947 General Agreement on Tariffs and Trade – one that was suited to the challenges of the late twentieth century. While the world was moving into the post-Cold War era politically, the global economy and its governance were still stuck in the 1980s, with little sign of creative leadership.[84]

The G7 summit also highlighted the limits of Russia's westward turn. Despite Bush's efforts to transform this meeting into the start of a full-scale G8, his colleagues refused to do so.[85] Kohl was particularly sceptical, warning Bush that Yeltsin would simply use Munich to beg for money and expressing grave doubts as to the future development of the Russian economy. What's more, Germany had to weigh up help to Russia against the continuing aid requested by Poland, Czechoslovakia, Hungary, Bulgaria and Romania. And, in addition, the CIS states were competing with each other and with Russia – none of whom in Kohl's view should be a Western responsibility. He insisted that the narrow issue of aid to Russia had to be seen within this larger nexus. Widening the context further, Scowcroft warned of a likely Chinese claim for a seat at the table as well, if Russia was granted membership. It was therefore agreed to speak of the group of eight 'democratic states', so as to do nothing to 'dilute' the G7.[86]

In this crucial matter – status – there was little difference between Yeltsin in 1992 and Gorbachev a year before: these were meetings of the 7 + 1. Yeltsin was invited not because he represented a powerful or worthy state, but because he and his country were 'so weak as to pose a potential threat to global stability'. And, for all the talk about the new Russia, Yeltsin was in a more parlous position than his predecessor – who represented a recognised ideological system and unquestioned super-power, whereas Yeltsin and Russia were 'still groping for an identity and a place in the world'.[87]

His people were really struggling with their country's transition from an imperial to post-imperial state. As historian Angela Stent has explained, while many Russians had 'rejected communism, the bankrupt state-run economy and the USSR's messianic global role', they had not accepted the break-up of the Soviet Union and Russia's catastrophic loss of status. The Red Army troop withdrawal from Eastern Europe was felt as a particular humiliation – a sense that 'Russia has been betrayed', as Mitterrand warned Bush in Munich. For hundreds of years Russians dominated their neighbours, but now Russia was back to the borders of the mid-1700s, before it had taken control of Ukraine and commenced the expansion that led ultimately to the tsarist empire and its successor, the Soviet Union. Loss of territory, prestige and influence was acutely painful.[88]

Unsurprisingly, then, Yeltsin had no intention of grovelling. In Munich, as in Washington, he made clear that he was not 'going down on his knees'. Ambassador Strauss tried to explain Yeltsin's mentality at length to Bush, calling the summer summits 'defining events for his leadership, his policies, and for Russia as a member of the Western community'. That is why in Washington, he wanted to be received by Bush 'not like Gorbachev in his heyday – the exotic visitor from a different world – but accepted as an established friend like Kohl and Major'.

Yet, 'no longer capable of unilateral action on the world scene', Yeltsin's Russia – according to Strauss – was effectively forced to look to a 'special bilateral relationship with the United States' in order to secure its 'continued place at the big table'. And 'while alignment with the US is a policy of choice and a practical necessity, lockstep with us stimulates concerns that Russia may no longer be a great power'. That, Strauss highlighted, was 'politically inadmissible in Moscow'. After all, Russia was driven by an 'abiding determination that it remain a great power which other great powers must respect as a co-equal'.[89]

At both summits Yeltsin had been at pains to present his country as a proud nation with a great imperial past. Indeed, in a particularly revealing moment, he told an interviewer just prior to Washington that Russia was 'a great power if only by virtue of its history'. Nor was he entirely convinced that the West had moved on from its past. 'The Cold War has ended', he said in Munich, 'but so far our economic relations have not become a partnership. The East–West divide is still there.'[90]

Seen in hindsight, the first half year or so of the Yeltsin era marked a brief honeymoon with the West in international relations – character-ised by Russian illusions about how much help it would get from the West and by Western unrealism about how speedily Russia would become a democracy and turn the tide economically, enabling it to join the GATT. In this early period, the aim of Yeltsin's government, as stated by his foreign minister Andrei Kozyrev, was to 'enter the community of civilised countries of the northern hemisphere'.[91] According to him, Russia had the opportunity now to 'progress according to generally accepted rules' which were invented by the West. What's more the West was 'rich' and Russia needed to 'be friends with it'. Eventually, Russia would become a 'serious economic rival' but, at the same time, an 'honest partner, adhering to the rules of the game on the world markets'. So joining the 'club of first-rate states' was for Kozyrev not a humiliation; it was a chance at last to enter Europe as a 'normal, democratic power' that could exert influence through cooperation not military domination.[92]

But there had to be question marks over the rhetoric of 'normal' and democractic'. After all, while apparently seeking integration, Russia did also not want to be gobbled up or dictated to by the West. And relations with the former Soviet republics that were part of the CIS were not so much about equality and cooperation within a new 'organisation' (that lacked any treaty framework), but a matter of Russian-dominated bilateral ties. This was certainly resented by Ukraine which from the outset had sought total independence from Moscow and kept insisting on 'equal relations'. The threat of Russian intervention was evident in the comments of even the Western-minded Kozyrev who talked as Yeltsin's spokesman about 'a zone of good neighbourly relations' all along Russia's borders, qualified, however, by the insistence that the successor states had to be mindful of 'rights, lives and dignity of ethnic Russians in the states of the former USSR'. In fact, the Russian deputy defence minister even declared that the Kremlin had the 'duty to protect all Russians with military means if necessary'. In the Baltic States there were mutterings about a 'new Brezhnev Doctrine'.[93]

Yeltsin would always hover between a Western and a Russian identity. The growing tilt towards reasserting Russia's right to great-power status did not simply reflect a foreign-policy imperative. He was battling with a Congress no longer representative of the country, having been elected while the Soviet Union still existed. He therefore came under fierce attack from various directions – ex-communists who had hardly changed their skin,[94] radicals in the Democratic Russia movement, and nationalist reactionaries, all of whom opposed both his rule and his policies. Throughout 1992 he had managed to fend off proposed constitutional changes that would have clipped his presidential powers. But when Congress reconvened from 1 to 14 December, he was bound to lose his extraordinary authority to choose members of the government at his own volition. [95]

The great transition?

Worse still for Yeltsin, by then the programme of economic reform was faltering, with inflation, though massively reduced, still running at an appalling 25–30% a month (equivalent to an annual rate of 2,200%). Industrial output and trade were also down by more than 25% from 1991, and the budget deficit was running at 20% of GDP.[96] As a result, Yeltsin was forced by an angry Congress to surrender Gaidar – the architect and symbol of Russia's economic change. In his stead, Victor Chernomyrdin – an experienced Soviet apparatchik, who had run the gas industry during the Gorbachev years before becoming deputy premier for fuel – was confirmed by the Congress as Russia's prime minister on 14 December 1992.

Chernomyrdin was a vocal critic of Gaidar. 'I am for reforms and for deepening them,' he declared in his first public comment, 'but without leaving people impoverished.' He loathed the idea of creating 'a nation of shopkeepers' and was keen instead to resume subsidies to state-run industries and to reassert a measure of government control over the economy. The fact that he announced efforts to strengthen the social safety net and to raise pensions and salaries in line with inflation was a clear signal of his conservative priorities. Yet such policies were inevitably going to create a bigger deficit which, when added to new credits, further dashed already fading Western hopes for economic stabilisation.[97]

Just like Gorbachev before him, Yeltsin had felt forced to bring some reactionaries into his government, to appease them while constantly bullying those around him in order to stay on top. In the bigger scheme of things his foreign policy became a struggle for personal power as much as for Russia's international status.

Given this volatility in Russia and the country's identity crisis – wanting to project strength despite growing weakness – Kohl as well as Bush stayed focused on Yeltsin as the devil they knew. And Kohl on his first visit (15–16 December) to Russia since the collapse of the USSR opened his purse once more, hoping that the Kremlin would stay the course. He announced $11.2 billion of debt relief for Moscow until the year 2000 while expressing confidence that Yeltsin would resolve the country's problems. The two leaders also agreed to speed up the withdrawal of former Soviet troops from Germany by four months, to 31 August 1994. In return, Germany would spend an extra $318 million to build housing in Russia for the returnees. 'It was necessary and right to come to Moscow now, at this hour,' Kohl said, 'because our friends face difficulties and will overcome them with great vigour.' Yet the Foreign Ministry warned: the change in Russia 'carries with it no small degree of uncertainty'.[98]

And it was always clear that no new security institutions had emerged in post-Cold War Europe to cope with that sense of uncertainty. The special 'Helsinki II' CSCE summit which convened on 9–10 July 1992 totally failed to fill this need. Billed as one of the world's biggest ever summits, it was the culminating bridge-building moment of which Gorbachev had dreamed ever since he and Bush met in Malta in December 1989. For the CSCE was the one pan-European structure offering a place for both Russia and the USA as co-equals. But this gathering of no less than fifty-two[99] states – now including not only the countries of Eastern Europe but also the Soviet and Yugoslav successor states – was an impossibly unwieldy forum within which to take serious decisions, especially when every leader felt obliged for domestic purposes to speak for the record.[100]

The meeting's only significant achievement was to confirm the 1990 pledge about the scaling down of conventional forces in Europe that had been agreed at the Paris CSCE. In fact, twenty-nine countries now signed a treaty setting limits on the size of their armed forces stationed on European soil.[101] Under the accord, which entailed sizeable reductions of tanks, artillery and combat aircraft, Germany could have 345,000 troops, down from more than 500,000 two years before. The ceilings were 325,000 for France, 260,000 for Britain, and 250,000 for the USA, though there were plans to reduce the actual number possibly to 150,000. The Russian ceiling was 1,450,000 and Ukraine's 450,000.

With Helsinki II proving a damp squib,[102] the problems of the new Europe were mounting inexorably. 'All the ancient conflicts, wrongs, injustices and animosities are suddenly coming back to life and back to mind,' President Havel warned. 'The sudden outburst of freedom has thus not only untied the straitjacket made by communism, it has also unveiled the centuries-old, often thorny history of nations.' His own country, Czechoslovakia, was now coming apart at the seams. The following week would see the independence declaration by the Slovak parliament, leading to negotiations which paved the way for the velvet divorce at the New Year.[103]

Worse still, Yugoslavia had descended into brutal ethnic wars which could not be handled by such peaceful bilateral diplomacy. Indeed, Bush spent most of the CSCE in meetings about former Yugoslavia. At the end of the gathering, all fifty-two states formally ascribed 'prime responsibility' for the violence to Belgrade – which had been suspended from the summit. But the commitment to tighter sanctions, backed by naval surveillance, came from NATO and the EU core states.[104] To be sure, at Helsinki II the members declared the security conference a regional organisation under the UN Charter (which gave the forum authority – in coordination with the UN to call on NATO, WEU and forces of individual countries to provide peacekeepers). But this demonstrated that the CSCE itself could not provide hard security and 'follow-through capability'. It was shown up yet again as largely a talking shop.[105] The so-called 'conscience of the continent' (Baker) lacked real political clout in the international arena. It simply was 'not a security organisation'.[106]

So over Yugoslavia, too, policing the new world order would have to depend on the instruments of the old. And the implosion of the Balkans into genocidal war proved a tougher and much more complex challenge than evicting Saddam from Kuwait – indeed from anything that Bush and his partners had been confronted with over the last three years.

*

Yugoslavia had erupted on 25 June 1991 when the Croatian and Slovenian parliaments declared independence. Next day, fighting began in earnest, as Slovenes battled the Yugoslav National Army (JNA) for control of their country's twenty-seven border crossings. On 29 June, after EC mediation (which led to the Brioni Accords), the rebellious republics agreed to suspend their declarations for three months on condition that the federal troops returned to their barracks. But this respite would be only temporary.[107]

Why had the exit from communism and the territorial transition in Yugoslavia turned so explosive?[108] The South Slav federation was a twice-invented state: like Czechoslovakia it had come into existence after the First World War in 1918 as the Kingdom of Serbs, Croats and Slovenes. Then in 1946, after the communist takeover, it was renamed the Federal People's Republic of Yugoslavia. But this putative national statehood offered only a thin veneer of unity over enmities and religious tensions that dated back centuries. Indeed, Yugoslavia was fundamentally fractured by the fact that it spanned the fault line of Roman Catholicism, Greek Orthodoxy and Islam. What's more the Serbs were the dominant political nationality, but they struggled against their cohabitants, all with their divergent, often hostile pasts – especially the Muslims (descendants of the old Ottoman ruling elite) who were most prominent in Kosovo and Bosnia, but also the Catholic Croats who were not forgiven for their role as client rulers on behalf of the Nazis during the Second World War.[109]

The vital force holding this fractious multi-ethnic state together had been veteran communist leader Josip Tito. Unity was in his blood – his father was Croat and mother Slovene – and he enjoyed a special charisma as the Partisan leader who had gained independence from the Germans in 1944–5 and then successfully slipped out of Stalin's bloc in 1948. Tito's death in 1980 removed the main unifying element, and also the figure who patched over Serbia's dominance within the Union. Yet the bloody disintegration that would ensue a decade later was by no means inevitable.

Like the Soviet-dominated states of Eastern Europe, in the 1980s Yugoslavia entered a phase of dramatic economic deterioration. And the erosion of communist authority amid the Gorbachev revolution destroyed the ideological glue that held the Balkan federation together. It was in this context that latent tensions between and within Yugoslavia's constituent republics reasserted themselves, intensifying rapidly at the end of the decade. Not least because, akin to developments in Moscow, the collapse of the communist regime led in Belgrade to a rise in nationalist agitation. Among numerous opportunistic politicians, Slobodan Milošević stood out – a communist apparatchik who now seized the chance to rebrand himself as an extreme Serbian nationalist, exploiting this rising nationalism for his own ends. His main target was Kosovo, one of Serbia's two autonomous provinces, where the population comprised predominantly Albanian Muslims. He used the 600th anniversary of the battle of Kosovo Polje – in which Prince Lazar of Serbia had been vanquished and killed by the Ottoman Turks in 1389 – to whip up anti-Muslim feeling, parading Lazar's remains throughout the country. Subsequently, a new Serbian constitution annulled Kosovo's autonomy, and the province was incorporated entirely into Serbia.[110]

Nationalism rears its ugly head

The post-communist liberalisation of Eastern Europe also played into Milošević's hands. In 1990, Yugoslavia underwent its own democratic transition and each of the provinces decided to hold multiparty elections. Crucially no all-Yugoslav movement emerged as a serious political force. And now across the country, the new non-communist governments proved much less willing to buckle down under Serbia's pressure. So the 1990 elections did not secure unity or, even less, peace. In fact, Milošević's rapacious power grab for control of the whole federation, underpinned by his hold of the Serbian-dominated federal army, provoked countervailing reactions across Yugoslavia.[111]

The richer north-western republics, Slovenia and Croatia, pressed for a looser confederation of sovereign states, but Milošević – claiming to act as protector of Yugoslavian unity – pushed for increased centralisation. Worse, he soon called for a 'greater Serbia' – one that would include those parts of the neighbouring republics that were inhabited by Serbs

– and thereby spread insecurity among the other nations of Yugoslavia. Consequently, the Belgrade-instigated armed rebellion of the Croatian Serbs in the Krajina region, to bring them into Serbia's fold, and Milošević's violent subjugation of the Kosovo province, further deepened the intra-Yugoslav conflict.

By spring 1991, any hope for agreement on new Yugoslav confederal structures had evaporated after the Serbian walkout from the Yugoslav Presidential Council in March. At the same time the economy collapsed: the central government's attempt at a policy of shock therapy was impossible to implement among the clashing provinces, and in such circumstances no Western aid was forthcoming. The simmering crisis came to the boil. Croats, Slovenes and Serbs had effectively given up on coexistence; and the growing ethnic polarisation within Bosnia–Herzegovina foreshadowed the most bitter and protracted conflict of all the Balkan wars.[112]

Why was international management of the crisis so ineffectual?[113] Why was a Czechoslovak-style velvet divorce not possible in the Balkans? After all, the CSCE's Paris Charter for a new Europe, signed in November 1990 with Yugoslavia as one of the signatories, stated a commitment to 'human rights and fundamental freedoms, including those related to national minorities'.[114] But the CSCE had no capacity – military or even political – for effective action. And the only country with real power, the United States, had been cautious all through 1989–91 about engaging with any secessionist movements in the case of the USSR – its main geopolitical concern – lest this be a recipe for anarchy. Gorbachev told Bush in July 1991, 'Even a partial break-up of Yugoslavia could create a chain reaction that will be worse than a nuclear reaction.' He was especially concerned about the USSR and Eastern Europe, warning that 'if we do not keep the issue of territorial integrity and inviolability of borders under control, chaos will break out from which we will never extricate ourselves'.[115] Bush needed little persuasion. And as Baker later explained, 'we preferred to maintain our focus on that challenge, which had global ramifications for us, in particular with regard to nuclear weapons'.[116] For Washington, therefore, independence movements in the Balkans were viewed with the same circumspection as in the Baltic region and the Caucasus – at least until the USSR disintegrated in December. And by then, Yugoslavia was far down the road to break-up and civil war. So, in 1991, US intervention in the Balkans was almost inconceivable.

Of course, the United States had mounted a major campaign in Kuwait earlier that year. But there the issues were very different. A big country, Iraq, had invaded its much smaller neighbour, violating Kuwait's territorial integrity and state sovereignty in an egregious breach of international law and a blatant challenge to Bush's new world order. The Bush administration, covered by multiple UN Security Council resolutions, decided to take the high moral ground that Iraq must be pushed back, if necessary by military means; otherwise international norms would have no authority and the world would return to the law of the jungle. In any case, the United States had clear national interests at stake: concern for the secure flow of Middle Eastern oil and the haunting analogy of Hitler in the 1930s. If aggression were not nipped in the bud, its success would encourage other aggressors.[117]

The hope was, of course, that the operation should uphold the new world order and deter other would-be challengers: the US had no desire to be the world's perennial firefighter. Yet Bush's periodic indulgence in heady language created a different impression. On 6 March 1991, for instance, in the post-victory euphoria, he told Congress that this would be 'a world in which freedom and respect for human rights find a home among all nations'.[118] A month later, he declared that the new world order defined 'a responsibility imposed by our successes' to 'deter aggression and to achieve stability' because 'what makes us American is our allegiance to an idea that all peoples elsewhere must be free'.[119] Not surprisingly, many Croats, Slovenes and Albanians took such rhetoric at face value. But, for the USA and the West, the brewing Balkan conflict was ultimately an intra-Yugoslav affair – not a breach of international law – and did not constitute a reason for outside interference, certainly not by military means and without Soviet support.[120]

This did not, of course, rule out diplomacy. In a last-ditch effort to keep Yugoslavia together, Baker travelled to Belgrade on 21 June 1991 for a twelve-hour marathon with all six parties involved. He strongly endorsed a declaration adopted two days earlier by CSCE's first Council of Ministers' meeting in Berlin, in which they expressed 'friendly concern and support for the democratic development, unity and territorial integrity of Yugoslavia' and called for continued dialogue among all parties 'without recourse to the use of force'. Baker then made clear to Slovenes and Croats that their declarations of independence would not be recognised by the US and they would be held responsible if violence broke out. He even indicated privately to Yugoslav prime minister Ante Marković that using the JNA to forcefully prevent Slovenia from controlling its border posts might be a logical decision. There was no talk of any US reprisals, military or otherwise, in the event of violent suppression of independence movements, though Baker did warn Milošević of pariah status if he persisted with his Serbian expansionist agenda.[121]

Unsurprisingly, none of this had much effect on the protagonists: the Slovenian and Croatian leaders remained set on declaring independence and Milošević was not deterred from trying to stop them. Indeed, Baker's apparent fence-sitting concealed an effective bias towards Milošević. As Robert Hutchings, the National Security Council's director for European Affairs, noted: 'By warning equally against unilateral declarations of independence and the use of force to hold the federation together, we seemed to be sanctioning the latter if the Slovenes and Croats resorted to the former.'[122] Milošević now also knew – not least because NATO's SACEUR (Supreme Allied Commander, Europe) had openly stated in June that the Alliance would 'not intervene in Yugoslavia' – that America had no intention of using force itself to stop him.[123]

Bush's diary entries made his own feelings quite clear. He was sure that national interest did not require America, after two world wars and the Cold War, to fight another, albeit regional, war in Europe at the end of the twentieth century – especially one in an area of marginal economic or strategic value which was likely to cost many lives. This also tallied with domestic pressure, especially from Democrats, that it was time to cash in on the post-Cold War 'peace dividend' by conducting a more restrained foreign policy. The president wrote on 2 July 1991 'Yugoslavia is poised on the brink of civil war ... This is one where I've told top people, "We don't want to put a dog in this fight" ... This concept that we have to work out every problem, everywhere in the world, is crazy. I think the American people understand it. I don't want to look isolationistic; I don't want to turn my back on the desires of many ethnic Americans that come from that part of the world; but I don't think that we can be looked to for solving every problem every place in the world.'[124]

While Washington was happy to keep out of Yugoslavia, Europe was ready to answer the call. After Desert Storm, many EC leaders felt the need to be more assertive about international affairs. And the negotiations on economic, monetary and political union leading up to the Maastricht summit of December 1991 raised expectations of a European superpower. Formal transformation of the looser European Community into the closer European Union – i.e. 'EC 92' – was less than a year away. Here, it seemed, was a chance to display 'Europe' as an independent force, speaking and acting with one voice, especially in a crisis affecting a European country.[125] 'This is the hour of Europe – not the hour of the Americans,' Jacques Poos, foreign minister of tiny Luxembourg, declared bombastically on 28 June 1991 in his capacity as chair of the EC foreign-affairs council. 'If one problem can be solved by the Europeans, it is the Yugoslav problem. This is a European country and it is not up to the Americans. It is not up to anyone else.'[126]

The problem was that the EC's policy – like that of the CSCE – reflected its own past and was trapped in those historic limitations. The Community originated as a peace project erected on the ruins of the two world wars in an attempt to tame aggressive nationalism. This remained its goal. The Yugoslav crisis must not be allowed to spoil the prospect of a stable and peaceful united Europe after the Cold War. Indeed, there were fears that the conflict might prove a replay of the early twentieth century when the Balkans were the powder keg of the Great War, which American diplomat George Kennan characterised in 1979 as '*the* great seminal catastrophe of this century'.[127] Totally misreading the situation on the ground, Western leaders hoped that if the Yugoslavs could be persuaded to embrace this European vision for themselves, they would surely abandon their primeval bellicosity.

There was also a more practical consideration. With regard to EC enlargement a single Yugoslavia was easier to integrate than six small separate countries. So the EC had dangled Community membership as a carrot for the Yugoslavs to alter their behaviour during spring 1991.[128] On behalf of the EC, in May Jacques Delors and Jacques Santer offered $4–5 billion economic assistance – but on condition that Yugoslavia remained a single market, with a single army and a joint foreign policy, underpinned by common systems for upholding human and minority rights. The EC's illusory policy only encouraged Milošević to continue his expansionist campaign against Croatia and Bosnia–Herzegovina by cloaking the construction of a Greater Serbia as the defence of Yugoslavia – albeit now effectively shorn of Slovenia. The EC's realpolitik attempt to conserve the broken Yugoslav federal state served to exacerbate the violence.[129]

This was not, however, how Western policymakers generally saw it at the time. On the contrary, the predominant view was that the independence declarations were 'threats to the stability and well-being of the peoples of Yugoslavia'.[130] In other words, the rebellious north-western provinces were to blame for the troubles, not Milošević's rampaging aggression. Roland Dumas, the French foreign minister, warned that the actions of Slovenia and Croatia 'could cause an explosion of Yugoslavia'. Of course, he added, 'they aspire to more liberty' and 'it is the right of a people to determine its destiny. But we are constrained by international order.' He expressed the hope that 'the Yugoslav nations will find a new solution for joint life' and insisted: 'It's not the role of the EC to promote the independence of peoples.'[131] Likewise the British FCO declared: 'We and our Western partners have a clear preference for the continuation of a single Yugoslav entity.' With history in mind, as Foreign Secretary Douglas Hurd put it, 'Yugoslavia was invented in 1919 to solve the problem of different peoples living in the same part of the Balkans with a long history of peoples fighting each other.'[132]

The French, so keen on a united European Union, had a further historic worry. President Mitterrand had warned against a Europe of 'tribes',[133] fearing that fragmentation in the Balkans and across Eastern Europe might stoke Germany's old *Drang nach Osten* ('drive to the East')[134] and create a 'Teutonic bloc' in Central Europe. This would not only destabilise the European balance of power, but could even loosen Germany's ties to the EC. The dark spectre of the past was ever present in French thinking, and the distrust that had marred Mitterrand's relationship with Kohl in the course of German unification came back to the surface – especially at a time when the US was standing back from this latest European crisis.[135]

It must be said, however, that French fears were not wholly unreasonable because, given the bankruptcy of EC and CSCE policy, Germany was about to strike out on its own – albeit not in the way the French had imagined. Throughout the spring of 1991, the Germans had stayed with the US and their European partners, culminating in the Berlin CSCE Council of Ministers' statement on Yugoslavia of 20 June. But after the independence declarations, Bonn jumped ship. Not only did Germany have unmatched commercial interests in the region – it was Yugoslavia's main trading partner, with half of its Yugoslav investments in Croatia and Slovenia – but it also had its own unique recent experience of applying the principle of self-determination in the cause of German reunification. Economically and, one might say, in terms of its mental map, Germany therefore occupied a pivotal position between the two halves of the continent.[136]

At the EC Council in Luxembourg on 28 June Kohl openly argued on behalf of the Slovenes and Croats: 'It is unacceptable that today in Europe, people are being shot, and that suddenly the right of self-determination should play no role.' Mitterrand countered, 'The European Community should not be opposed to self-determination, but it should also not be accused of treating territorial integrity lightly.' The French were supported, among others, by the Spanish who were worried about the implications of Yugoslavia for their own minority problems with separatist Basques and Catalans, and by the Italians who were afraid that the crisis would spill over their own borders. They were pitted against the German camp which included the Danes who were as supportive of the Slovenes and Croats as they had been of the Baltic cause. Meanwhile America remained on the sidelines – unwilling to break the deadlock.[137]

As Baker later noted, there was a view in Washington that Europeans should prove they were capable of dealing with European security challenges on their own or – alternatively and, some felt, even better – demonstrate that they were incapable of doing so. In Lawrence Eagleburger's words: 'Europe's bluff should be called ... They will screw it up, and this will teach them a lesson' and 'teach them to burden-share'. This snide remark followed a rift with some West Europeans (notably the French) over the relationship between NATO (US-led, and from whose command structure de Gaulle's France had resigned) and the Western European Union (WEU) – a group of nine EC states dominated by France, which insisted that WEU was the embryo of the separate defence identity Europe needed in the post-Cold War world, independent from the United States. To Washington critics like Eagleburger, Europe seemed to be wanting it both ways – having America 'in' but trying to run its own affairs. In any case, the US had no desire to get drawn into what could easily become a 'European Vietnam'.[138]

The Americans therefore left the Europeans to muddle on as Serbia's 'war of aggression' claimed thousands of lives during 1991 – right on the borders of the European Community. Germany got its way that 'action' be largely left to the EC, rather than the CSCE, with Genscher pushing the argument on his allies that 'Serbian responsibility' should be explicitly acknowledged. Subsequently, the EC condemned the 'illegal' use of force, threatened further sanctions, invoked an 'arbitration procedure' and convened a peace conference in The Hague on 7 September. But these efforts were largely hot air.[139]

The issue was then taken up by the UN Security Council in New York,[140] which had so far deferred to the EC and CSCE. But any hope of rallying support for international military intervention under UN Chapter

VII soon evaporated. Not only was it obvious that there would be no US military engagement but, furthermore, the coalition of staunch 'defenders of sovereignty' on the Security Council (such as China, India and various Asian, African and Latin American states) called the shots. They opposed any interference in what they saw as internal matters of a recognised state – indeed a leading member of the non-aligned movement. And so, in late September the Security Council adopted Resolution 713 calling upon all states to 'refrain from any action which might contribute to increasing tension and to impeding or delaying a peaceful and negotiated outcome of the conflict'. The resolution also proclaimed a 'general and complete arms embargo on all deliveries of weapons and military equipment to Yugoslavia'.[141] But by doing so the UN was effectively leaving the JNA and the Serbian bloc in pole position. The UN's principal message – far from action – was in fact non-involvement. The appointment of Cyrus Vance, formerly Jimmy Carter's Secretary of State, as the UN secretary general's personal envoy in the region in early October, gave the US some indirect influence, but his mission to Croatia in November 1991 failed to broker peace.[142]

And so it was Germany – in its first independent diplomatic démarche as a unified state – which stepped onto the stage. Genscher took the initiative to internationalise the conflict, both as German foreign minister and also under the aegis of the CSCE. In his capacity as chairman of its newly established Council of Ministers, Genscher flew to Belgrade at the end of June 1991. His encounter with Milošević was frosty. Serbia's leader clearly intended to have everything his own way. This face-to-face experience of total Serbian intransigence was Genscher's epiphany. Holding on to the CSCE's 'inviolability of borders' principle was clearly pointless, and the CSCE's new mechanism for conflict management had proved a paper tiger: nothing could be accomplished by mere statements condemning the use of force or by sending out limited monitoring missions. Genscher was now absolutely sure that policy had to change and that Germany should take the initiative itself.[143]

His decision also reflected immense pressure at home. In the Bundestag disapproval about EC policy had been mounting within all the political parties, with the CDU, SPD and Greens all now demanding diplomatic recognition of Slovenian and Croatian independence. There was general consensus that the approach adopted by the government and the EC during the first half of 1991 had failed and that it was time for a fundamental change of course. 'Recognition fever' spread through the German

political elite, infecting even Genscher's own FDP. In mid-July the representatives of the sixteen German *Länder* requested that the EC recognise
the two republics if the Yugoslav army continued its assault.[144]

Germany's internal domestic consensus for action strengthened with
every broken ceasefire, every lapsed ultimatum, and every failed multilateral effort to bring peace.[145] Throughout the autumn of 1991, Serb
aggression not only intensified across the Croatian battlefield, it expanded
into Bosnia–Herzegovina. In his drive for an ethnically homogeneous
Serbian space, Milošević displayed scant regard for human life or for
the cultural heritage of such historic sites as Dubrovnik, Zadar and
Vukovar.[146]

Western European diplomacy remained incoherent. And because of
French and British ambivalence – in their different ways – about the
future of 'Europe' itself, the EC procrastinated about giving up on the
failed Yugoslavian federation. In the run-up to the Maastricht summit,
France was coupling the issue of how the EC was managing the
Yugoslavian crisis with overall policy on where European integration was
and should be going. And Britain, which had qualms about any further
development of the European project, did not want Yugoslavia to become
an argument for deepening EC/EU foreign and security policy. The
Community's position on Yugoslavia therefore became hostage to Franco-
British attitudes towards the development of the EC itself, which only
added to German annoyance.

At the beginning of October the EC seemed to be loosening up. It
announced on the 4th an outline agreement with the warring parties
about jointly formulating 'a political solution on the basis of the perspective of recognition of the independence of those republics wishing it'. For
the first time, therefore, the EC was formally embracing recognition, and
thereby the break-up of the Yugoslav federation as the basis for a political solution to the Balkan conflict. However, the agreement also contained
an important qualifier: recognition was to be granted 'at the end of the
negotiating process conducted in good faith [and] in the framework of
a general settlement'. In other words, the EC would only recognise sepa-
rating states after a constitutional settlement had been reached which
was acceptable to all six republics.[147]

Next day, at their meeting in the Dutch castle of Haarzuilens, the EC
foreign ministers underwrote the agreement. According to Genscher this
was a turning point: 'Hereby the EC affirmed the rights of the republics
to independence if they wished it.' But what mattered equally to Genscher

was the time limit placed on that process. In a newspaper interview published on 18 October, Hans van den Broek, the chair of the EC Council of Ministers, set a deadline of no more than two months for achieving this political solution and for the JNA's complete withdrawal from Croatia. If this had not happened by 10 December, he said, 'we can no longer deny the right to independence if individual republics have expressed it in a democratic way'. Unlike France and Britain, still trying to kick the ball into the long grass, the Germans took the two-month deadline seriously – as a firm promise that by the end of the year, the policy of recognition would be followed through.[148]

Milošević's apparent cooperation with the EC lasted only a few days,[149] prompting Bonn to accelerate matters. On 27 November Kohl and Genscher confirmed in the Bundestag that Germany was ready before Christmas to recognise those Yugoslav republics which had genuinely tried their best to fulfil the conditions for a comprehensive political settlement. The chancellor categorically ruled out any use of German armed forces in the Balkans under the aegis of the UN or any peace-keeping organisation, and he also denied any wish for Germany to go it alone. But, he said, given the gravity of the crisis, Bonn was ready to proceed without complete EC consensus – though he expressed vehement opposition to 'unilateral recognition'. He would not want to go back to '1941'. Genscher, fiercely critical of Serbia's land-grabbing, warned against any forced change of borders between the republics.[150]

Kohl's willingness to step out on a limb reflected the fact that he had drawn five other Christian democratic leaders into a diplomatic coalition: Belgium, Netherlands, Luxembourg, Greece and Italy. With Denmark joining within days, the German movement toward recognition now had real momentum. By 5 December, the British were forced to admit that recognition of Slovenia and Croatia was imminent and 'unstoppable'.[151] Yeltsin's announcement on the 8th, together with his Ukrainian and Belarus counterparts, that the USSR would be dissolved and succeeded by the CIS eased persistent fears about the dissolution of Yugoslavia setting a precedent for the USSR. There was also an evident contrast between Moscow and Belgrade: unlike Milošević in Yugoslavia, Yeltsin's response to the disintegration of his country was orderly and above all peaceful. He had also previously applauded the 'parade of sovereignties' within the USSR and openly backed the drive for independence by the Baltic States. And he sought to cultivate good relations with the Western powers; Milošević did not. This underlined Kohl's and Genscher's argument that the problem was the Serbs not the Croats.[152] With the JNA launching a massive artillery bombardment of Croatia's main cities, the EC's arbitration commission now finally deemed that Yugoslavia was in the process of dissolution: federal institutions no longer met the key criteria of participation and representation.

The last legal obstacle to recognising Yugoslavia's break-up had gone. But a formal decision would not be taken until the completion of the Maastricht Treaty on 9–10 December.[153]

Europe's grand progress to 'ever closer union' had taken years to accomplish. Delors and his colleagues had no intention of letting its triumphant realisation be overshadowed by trouble in the Balkans. And so Maastricht came and went with barely a mention of Yugoslavia. The European Community was magically transformed into the European Union, comprising three pillars: the European Communities, a Common Foreign and Security Policy, and Cooperation in Justice and Home Affairs.

France was delighted because Maastricht sealed the move to economic and monetary union and the establishment of a common currency, which would finally supplant the long-dominant Deutschmark. Mitterrand jubilantly stated 'a great power is born, one at least as strong commercially, industrially and financially as the United States and Japan'. Britain was satisfied that future foreign policy would still have to be forged by consensus and also relieved at securing its opt-outs from the social charter and the single currency. And Kohl, despite the concessions he had made, particularly on the Deutschmark, took comfort from the creation of a more federally structured Europe, whose union was as much political as it was economic.[154]

EC leaders had therefore fulfilled their long-term mission: managing the exit from the Cold War, while never losing track of their plan for closer European integration in the post-Cold War world. They had avoided being sidetracked by infighting over Yugoslavia and the fallout from the Soviet Union's dissolution. Despite the EU's evident imperfections, it seemed that Europe was entering a new era of cooperation, unity and enlargement to embrace the continent as a whole.

But any hopes that the Yugoslavian break-up could now be quickly resolved were soon dashed. One complication was the sudden interference by the United States. All through the autumn the principal goals of the US and NATO had been to contain the crisis through European efforts and to preserve as large and unified a Yugoslav state as possible – which effectively meant looking for a settlement built around Milošević.

Washington objected to 'uncoordinated, ad hoc declarations and recognitions' of the sort that seemed to be the consequences of Europe's policy, or lack of it. Aware that America had little leverage available over the warring parties, Baker considered the power of withholding or conferring statehood to be the 'most powerful diplomatic tool available'. He espoused the idea of 'earned recognition'[155] – to be granted to individual republics *after* a comprehensive peace settlement had been negotiated and was ready for implementation. For this reason he saw Germany's pro-recognition efforts as premature, indeed counterproductive, and regarded the Genscher–Kohl tandem as a disruptive factor, undermining what Baker liked to believe was otherwise an EC and NATO consensus on non-recognition.

Accordingly, after agreement of the final draft of the Maastricht Treaty in December, Washington leaned on EC capitals not to proceed with recognition, arguing that this would only bring more war. Baker also pushed the issue via Vance onto UN secretary general Javier Pérez de Cuéllar, who – also under pressure from the British and French – formally warned the EC of the 'explosive consequences' of recognising Slovenian and Croatian independence. Pérez de Cuéllar also appealed to the Bonn government not to start recognising breakaway Yugoslav republics in 'a selective and uncoordinated' manner.[156]

In addition, the British and French ambassadors to the UN, backed by their US colleague, floated a draft UN Security Council resolution to deter Germany from going ahead with its plan to recognise the two republics – an action, they said, that would only further inflame ethnic passions and reduce the chances of peace. These Anglo-French machinations were clearly directed against Genscher personally, and also made a mockery of the whole spirit of European unity – so exuberantly proclaimed just days earlier at Maastricht. Britain and France even made much of Germany's unusual assertiveness, insinuating parallels with the Second World War when Nazi Germany had dominated the two Yugoslav regions, absorbing Slovenia into the Third Reich and creating a puppet regime in Croatia.[157]

Genscher brushed all this aside. He was absolutely certain that non-recognition of the republics' independence – in other words conserving the status quo – had not only failed to defuse the fighting, but had actually made it worse. In fact, Germany's resolve to press ahead reflected mounting concern that, combined with the deteriorating socio-economic situation across the post-Soviet sphere, sustained warfare in Yugoslavia could destabilise a shaky Eastern Europe by heightening ethnic tensions and drive a huge wave of refugees toward Germany and the West.

German policy was therefore not deflected by the spoiling tactics of its allies. As one government official told the world media, 'We will move ahead whether any, all, or none of the European states join us.' Nevertheless, given the EC consensus reached in Haarzuilens, Genscher fully expected backing from the rest of Community. But instead, with Britain and France stabbing him in the back, he could rely only on Italy, Belgium and Denmark among EC members, plus a few non-Community states, including Austria (which was cosying up to the FRG because it wanted EC membership), Iceland, Hungary and newly independent Ukraine.[158]

Paradoxically Genscher was helped by new fighting in Croatia. This stymied attempts to derail his policy both at the UN and in the EC. Indeed, as it became increasingly unlikely that the United Nations could press ahead with their plan to send in peacekeepers to enforce a truce, the British and French backed down. The UN resolution was diluted and on 15 December the Security Council voted unanimously to send only a token force of no more than twenty military, police and political 'observers' to Yugoslavia. It dropped the idea of statements condemning recognition of the breakaway republics.[159]

But it was not merely the worsening conflict that prompted the Franco-British retreat. They changed their tack also for fear of a rift with Germany ahead of the EC Council meeting on 16 December that was to deal with Yugoslavia. As Dumas wrote to Mitterrand just before the talks: 'For the twelve, and especially for France and Germany, to split over the Balkans seems to me to be much more dangerous than the risk of hastening the conflagration in former Yugoslavia. For Yugoslavia to split up is tragic; for the Community to do so would be catastrophic.'[160]

Despite this Franco-British climbdown, the whole business left a very sour taste in Bonn. It had damaged German trust in its two closest European allies and narrowed Genscher's options when Germany – for the first time since unification – was taking the risk of sticking its neck out in international diplomacy. What made it worse was that Germany also felt betrayed by Washington, with whom it had worked so closely on most key issues in recent years.

On the one hand, the United States had recognised the independence of the Baltic republics and was now moving towards acceptance of the USSR's break-up into Russia and the newly independent CIS states. On the other, it remained adamantly opposed to the 'selective recognition' of the two Balkan republics. In Bonn's eyes, Yugoslavia looked as dead as the Soviet Union. Yet, Bush said that he strongly disagreed with the German decision because the Yugoslav situation was 'fraught with danger'. America, he declared, wanted to see 'a peaceful evolution ... We've been strongly supportive of the EC. We've been strongly supportive of what the UN has tried to do. Their advice has been to go slow on recognition, and I think they're right.'[161]

Undeterred, the Germans kept up the momentum. At the 16 December EC meeting, when Lord Carrington (British former NATO secretary general), Douglas Hurd, Dumas and van den Broek tried more delaying tactics – pleading that the EC should make one last try – Genscher held his course. The chance for negotiation had come to an end, he insisted, with the expiration of van den Broek's own two-months deadline. Now it was time to accept hard realities. Not only had Serbia used the past month to bomb Croatian cities and massacre people, on top of that his country, Germany, had 'accommodated others at Maastricht'. Furthermore, his government could not renege on its public commitment of recognition before Christmas, unless it was prepared to lose credibility.[162]

Germany was 'calling in her Maastricht debts' and Genscher's hardball worked. Ten hours of fierce debate resulted in a deal, albeit in the form of an awkward compromise.[163] The foreign ministers agreed on two declarations. The first outlined a list of conditions all Yugoslav and Soviet republics would have to satisfy in order to gain recognition, including respect for the UN Charter (1945), the Helsinki Final Act (1975), Charter of Paris (1990) and nuclear non-proliferation. The second declaration invited all Yugoslav republics to announce by 23 December whether they wished to be recognised as independent states, whether they accepted the conditions and whether they supported the UN and EC peace efforts and the continuation thereof. After Christmas the arbitration commission would adjudicate any applications and the EC member states would implement recognition if all conditions were fulfilled on 15 January.[164]

In Croatia and Slovenia, the EC's decision was warmly welcomed, but Serbia issued vehement denunciations. 'This is a direct attack on Yugoslavia,' Dobrosav Vezović, the deputy foreign minister, told journalists. The decision, he claimed, 'erases Yugoslavia from the map of the world'. Particularly significant was the knock-on effect.[165] The ethnically mixed, centrally situated republic of Bosnia–Herzegovina indicated that it would secede from what was left of Yugoslavia if Croatia won international recognition. Since Milošević was bound to resist, this move would make it almost inevitable that the war would spill over from neighbouring Croatia. And probably in an even more lethal form: in Bosnia ethnic Serbians, Croatians and Muslims had long been training and stockpiling arms.[166]

Nonetheless, on 18 December, Kohl announced that his government would move to recognise Croatia and Slovenia the next day. Germany's decision, he stressed, 'sends a clear warning to the Serbian leadership and the Serbian-led Yugoslav army to "end the bloodshed in Yugoslavia and pave the way for United Nations peacekeeping forces"'. To slightly sugar the pill for the rest of the EC, Genscher added that Bonn would wait until January to convert its consulates in Dubrovnik and Ljubliana into embassies – in other words, delaying the formal establishment of diplomatic relations for a month. The Germans clearly sought to reconcile the Community's action with the chancellor's earlier promise to accept Croatia and Slovenia as independent nations before Christmas. These small Balkan states certainly appreciated the timely present. A cartoon in the Slovenian youth weekly *Mladina* depicted Kohl as Santa Claus with the country's leader Milan Kučan seated on his knee. The glove on Santa's hand, which extended a lollipop to little Kučan, was adorned with the German eagle.[167]

The 'chancellor of unity' also played to the domestic gallery. Between 15 and 17 December, Kohl, who had been leader of the Christian Democratic Union for eighteen years, presided over the CDU Party Congress in Dresden, the first time this annual gathering was held in the former GDR. He used the occasion to declare that 'the Croats will not be left alone' and received a standing ovation.[168] Buried in the small print about the Party Congress was a press report that the CDU, 'seeking to bridge an East–West gap in their ranks, chose a woman from Eastern Germany today as Chancellor Helmut Kohl's deputy party leader'. And thus Angela Merkel, aged thirty-seven, took her next step to the top of national politics and onto the historical stage.[169]

Germany's official statement of recognition on 19 December did not stand alone. The FRG was soon joined by Italy, Iceland, Sweden, Austria, Poland, Hungary and Czechoslovakia, each with slightly different announcements on the date and form of implementation.[170] And on the 20th, Yugoslavia slid further toward complete disintegration when Bosnia–Herzegovina (after Macedonia) also applied to the EC for recognition as an independent state – even though one of the key criteria, the expression of popular will in a referendum, was so far conspicuously absent. This step was bound to enrage the 1.4 million Serbs, who made up more than a third of Bosnia's population, and it clearly presaged open warfare because the republic's two other main ethnic groups – 1.7 million Muslims and 800,000 Croats – did not want to live under the domination of Serbia and Serbs.[171]

On 23 December, the first day when according to the Brussels EC resolution a member state could declare that a Yugoslav republic had met the conditions for recognition, Germany announced that Bonn stood behind Slovenia and Croatia, irrespective of what the arbitration commission might 'advise' in the New Year. This prompted a new furore about whether or not Germany had acted precipitately and broken the spirit of the EC's 16 December decision, with Britain and France predictably the most critical. 'Kohl hijacks Brussels Policy', proclaimed *The Times*, which blamed Germany for 'steamrollering' the other eleven EC members. Mitterrand, in another of his anti-German spasms, even claimed that 'the days of the "good Germans" are almost over and ... the world must brace itself for the worst'.[172]

Most of the criticism had little do with the consequences of German policy for Yugoslavia per se and was much more about the changing role of Germany in European affairs since the bouleversements of 1989. But while there were many reasons for Kohl's and Genscher's assertive policy line since July 1991, at root they simply believed they were right – both in their perception of what was happening on the ground and in their policy prescription.[173]

Without a military alternative to contain Serbia, which Bush ruled out, neither the US nor the EC had offered any plausible response to the German argument that in the face of brutal Serbian aggression and continuous failures to broker a comprehensive peace settlement, invoking the right to self-determination and offering recognition to the seceding states was preferable to passivity. Nobody expected fighting to end in the Balkans – the situation in Bosnia was acknowledged to be highly combustible – but Genscher believed that the two new states could at least be insulated from Serbia's war of conquest. As he would later forcefully argue, Germany had certainly not been the cause of the violent wars of secession and the break-up of Yugoslavia. In fact, he said, 'it was the other way round'. By Germany internationalising the conflict through recognition of Slovenia and Croatia, 'Milošević was forced to end his warfare against these two states.' It was a decision which in Genscher's view 'brought peace' – at least for these two ravaged countries. 'Is that nothing?' he asked.[174]

Kohl hailed his foreign minister's diplomacy as 'a great victory for German foreign policy'.[175] Yet he faced a barrage of criticism, from Belgrade to Westminster, that Germany was now trying to build a sphere of influence, embracing 'all the countries that were once under the Prussian empire and under the Hapsburg empire', as the basis of nothing less than a 'Fourth Reich'.[176] But although Genscher's démarche suggested to some that Germany's moment had come again, in fact December 1991 did not represent a new departure, either for the FRG's international posture in general or for its policy in the Balkans. Ultimately Germany remained the loyal supporter of its superpower protector, which – as ever – saw regional problems in a global perspective.

Throughout Kohl was at pains to rebut charges of German expansionism. On the contrary, he claimed, unified Germany – a Central European nation that was geographically close to the conflict zone and that had itself benefited from the protection of foreign democracies – was in a special position to understand the yearnings of isolated republics. 'We Germans are concerned about the fate of these people and about their future in democracy – nothing else,' Kohl said. He hoped that recognition would bring peace especially to Croatia. And so Germany pledged not to send military aid to Croatia, but stated it was ready to begin a civilian aid programme that would include reconstruction of war-damaged cities. The chancellor also expressed hope that the recognition would signal to Yugoslavia's Serbian leaders that their country was doomed to break apart, and perhaps therefore persuade them to accept a peace settlement.[177]

For Kohl and Genscher 'victory' had come through a mix of principle and assertiveness. Instead of remaining conservative in its diplomacy – wedded to the geopolitical orthodoxy of preserving bigger entities at a time of upheaval – Germany had taken the bold step of unlocking the door on self-determination in Yugoslavia. Consequently, this prepared the ground for Bosnia–Herzegovina and others who sought to secede. But, Bonn stressed, the fact that Germany had taken such an assertive line only after trying as far as possible to act through multilateral channels (EC and CSCE) demonstrated that its diplomatic agenda remained solely 'civilian' and its horizons primarily European. Germany was essentially a regional power. And its engagement with the Yugoslavian crisis was consequent upon its own European experience. For Germans since 1989 the peaceful application of the right to self-determination had been liberating and galvanising. Indeed, in their view, it offered a guiding light for the conduct of international relations in the post-Wall world.[178]

*

Bush, however, saw things very differently. He was not particularly interested in a regional problem on Europe's margins – certainly not one with such horrendously complex historical baggage. To him Yugoslavia was an issue from the past, not a guide for the future. In any case, his administration was always preoccupied with order on the global plane and this had been particularly true in the second half of 1991, when the president's approach to Yugoslavia was a subset of his policy towards the USSR. By inclination careful, especially amid such international turmoil, he clung to potential sources of stability. One of these was Gorbachev – representing a strong centre – whose authority should not be eroded. And, given Bush's concerns about post-Soviet nuclear proliferation, under no circumstances did he want to be seen as trying to encourage the break-up of the other nuclear superpower. In so far as the US president thought hard about Yugoslavia, it was within this paradigm.[179]

Not all his advisers agreed, however. Secretary of Defense Dick Cheney was urging a more 'aggressive' approach towards the Soviet denouement – 'we ought to lead and shape events'. Instead he said, 'we are reacting'. Scowcroft too was in favour of the break-up of the Soviet Union, and Baker actually used the Balkan card to push that point further: 'The *peaceful* break-up of the Soviet Union is in our interest. We don't want another Yugoslavia.' Bush for a long time had taken a middle position – like Colin Powell – hoping that there would be managed diffusion within the post-Soviet space – producing a confederal structure of several weaker states, which cooperated via a 'centre' to ensure economic interdependence, promote political reform and to control the nuclear weapons. But that all went up in smoke on 25 December 1991.[180]

It is therefore important to stress that the break-up of the Soviet Union forced Bush to rethink his whole approach to global as well as regional order. With regard to the world at large, he could no longer assume a two-pillar approach. At this stage he was ambivalent about Yeltsin and the new Russia; indeed, the future of the whole post-Soviet space was totally unclear. Compounding the fragmentation of the USSR was the violent disintegration of Yugoslavia – which, by January 1992, Bush could not deny. Nor had he reason to do so, because his obsession with Soviet unity was now irrelevant. In consequence of these two developments the president was confronted by a mosaic of disorder right across Eurasia and the Balkans. The collapse of state structures on this scale triggered not only a revival of long-standing ethnic disputes but also massive migratory movements and a xenophobic backlash in Western countries that felt threatened. All this was the stimulus for a profound reappraisal of US foreign policy in a situation that his 'new world order' rhetoric of 1990–1 had never envisaged.

In these novel circumstances Bush also had to recognise that he could no longer rely on the degree of help that he had received in 1989–90 from Kohl and the German government. Bonn was paying a high diplomatic price for its assertive Yugoslavia policy in 1991. And the barrage of criticism that had rained down on Kohl and Genscher after the Brussels meeting did not abate. Indeed, it got even more malicious – a savage reminder that Germany's past had neither been forgotten nor forgiven.[181]

But there were also other – domestic – reasons for Bonn pulling back on the foreign-policy front.[182] And the chancellor made those pressures clear to the president in a long conversation on 21 March 1992 at Camp David. 'Our economy is difficult now,' Kohl confessed. Inflation was running at 4% and unemployment at more than 8% (double the figure for the previous year). In the new *Länder* things looked worse, with 15% of the workforce jobless. Kohl was also engaged in a massive fight about pay with the trade unions. 'This is the toughest battle in ten years,' he told Bush. 'We may have big strikes in store. With people out in the streets, the question is who is in charge? Will it be the will of the streets that prevails, or is it the government?' But, he assured Bush, 'I won't retreat.'

In addition, voters were angry that taxes had risen despite Kohl's pledge in the 1990 election campaign that they would not – just the same problem that Bush had got himself into at home. In Germany the furore helped far-right political parties. In the *Länder* elections on 5 April 1992 the Republicans in Baden-Württemberg and the Deutsche Volksunion (DVU) in Schleswig-Holstein crossed the 5% threshold that entitled them to entry to the regional *Landtage* (legislative assemblies). Alarm bells started ringing that such rightist parties might become strong enough to win seats at the national level in Bundestag elections of 1994.[183]

Bush alluded to this issue in a conversation with federal president Richard von Weizsäcker later in April, asking whether it signified a 'return of the Nazis'. Weizsäcker hotly contested this: 'It has nothing to do with the rebirth of the Nazis. It is asylum-seekers that are at the root of it. There are so many that they threaten to overwhelm us. We are the one open country. We want to make asylum a European problem, but so far it is mostly ours.' This was fair comment. Not only was the Federal Republic still confronting the challenge of absorbing 16.5 million East Germans, it also faced mass-migration of several hundred thousand ethnic Germans from the Russian Volga region. On top came the tidal wave of foreign refugees and political asylum-seekers from Yugoslavia, Poland, Romania, Ukraine and Russia – amounting to almost half a million people in 1992 alone.[184]

The German president then told Bush that the other big problem was right-wing protest 'about national identity, in the context of EC integration'. For Germans a particular anxiety was abandoning their cherished Deutschmark, for what they feared would be a weaker European common currency. But as Weizsäcker underlined, there were similar nationalist movements in France (Le Pen), Italy and elsewhere. Yet 'none of this', he stated adamantly, had 'anything to do with fascism'.[185]

The larger point was that, whereas for the West in 1989 Eastern Europe had been a symbol of hope, by 1992 it had become an arena of anxiety. Simone Veil, a member of the European Parliament, made the point graphically: 'In the past, we lived between the Atlantic and the Wall. We would shed a tear for the misery of those in the East, but the situation was frozen. Now we have uncertainty and we don't know where we're going.' Indeed, there were mounting fears that chaos in the former Soviet empire might bring a flood of immigrants and that Yugoslav-style civil wars with their ensuing refugee crises could be repeated elsewhere. The rise of right-wing populism aroused fears of a return of the ferocities of nineteenth-century nationalism.

'We knew the transition would be difficult,' said Simon Lunn of the North Atlantic Assembly. 'What we didn't see was that as soon as communism disappeared, old resentments would bubble up.' And former French president Valéry Giscard d'Estaing summed up the Western ennui, stating: 'There's a sort of unexpressed feeling that we'd be better off if we could ignore Eastern Europe's problems.' Some West Berliners even seemed to think that life would be a lot easier if the Wall was still in place. Instead, replacing it was what the German writer Günter Grass called a 'social abyss' – or what Weizsäcker termed 'rich versus poor' in a united Europe as much as a unified Germany.[186]

Overall, however – despite its mounting problems – the Bonn government struck a positive note. Ever the optimist, Kohl assured Bush: 'I think that in another three to four years everything will be OK.' After all, 'We are seeing incredible changes taking place in Germany. We've already privatised 3,000 of 6,000 of the East German state firms from the communist system. This has been an enormous undertaking. From 1949, when we launched the Marshall Plan, to 1953 before we landed on our feet, it took a good four years. Then, the only support we got was the money from you. So in a way, the East Germans have it easier. We are giving enormous support. Psychologically, however, it's different. After the war, all of us Germans were in a bad situation. Today, we have a sharp contrast between wealth on one side of the street and poverty on the other.'[187]

Yet, Kohl did not spell out to Bush just how 'enormous' Bonn's support for the former GDR really was. The federal government was granting the new *Länder* a net transfer of well over DM 100 billion to demonstrate willingness to support the *Aufbau Ost* ('construction of the East'). But he now had to acknowledge in public that Germany no longer had the resources to continue pouring massive aid into Eastern Europe and the former USSR, while at the same time rebuilding its own eastern states. Germany's national debt had risen steeply since 1989, standing in 1992 at DM 706 billion, compared with DM 474 billion in the year when the Wall came down. The Federal Republic had used its 'deep pockets' in the reshaping of Europe in 1989–91; Kohl was now saying that America and Japan must dig deeper themselves.[188]

As if all of this was not enough to keep Kohl absorbed in domestic affairs in 1992, he also faced serious problems within his own coalition. That spring two key figures at the heart of Germany's foreign policy announced their resignations. One was Defence Minister Gerhard Stoltenberg, who departed at the end of March 1992 after a scandal broke about the illegal delivery of Leopard tanks to Turkey. The timing was particularly unfortunate because, more importantly, Hans-Dietrich Genscher had decided he would resign on 18 May 1992, exactly eighteen years after he had first taken on the post of foreign minister under SPD chancellor Helmut Schmidt in 1974.[189]

Genscher wanted to choose for himself the date of his departure. He had told Kohl in early 1992 that he would not go on his sixty-fifth birthday (21 March) nor as merely a part of the Cabinet reshuffle that Kohl had been considering for the autumn of that year. Neither moment would adequately reflect his long 'history-making' tenure of the office. Instead he selected a date that highlighted his service, across party lines, in helping to transform Germany's place in Europe and Europe's place in the world.

By this time Genscher had accomplished much of what he considered critical. The refugee from Halle in the 1950s had wanted to epitomise continuity from the divided Germany to unified Germany and see through ratification by the USSR of the 2 + 4 treaty. The man who stood on the Prague balcony on that delirious night in September 1989 was determined to be part of Germany's commitment to European integration as underwritten by the Maastricht Treaty. And, with Ostpolitik almost in his DNA, Genscher wanted to play a pivotal role in Germany's affirmation of peaceful relations with its Eastern neighbours, as evidenced in the German–Polish border treaty of November 1990 which bore his signature alone on behalf of Germany.[190]

That EC summit in Brussels on 16 December 1991 – the month of the final draft of the Maastricht Treaty and the collapse of the USSR – was in many ways his apotheosis and his farewell. Not only had he stood firm for the CSCE principle of the right to self-determination in war-torn Yugoslavia, demanding recognition of the independence of Slovenia and Croatia. That same day the European Council had also signed agreements with representatives of Czechoslovakia, Hungary and Poland – making those formerly communist countries associate members of the EC.[191] This was a step toward full membership and toward the long-held dream of Genscher's of the reunification of Europe – albeit not within a strengthened pan-European CSCE, as he had once hoped, but under the umbrella of the EC. In short, he had done enough. It was time to leave the diplomatic stage.[192]

Certainly Germany's international position had been transformed since the 1970s, but the change should not be exaggerated. This was evident in the development of Germany's Balkan policy in 1992. After the EC recognised Slovenia and Croatia on 15 January and established diplomatic relations, it left Macedonia and Bosnia–Herzegovina hanging, unrecognised. Bonn did not make an issue of this, being careful not to overreach itself. So the EC opted for a policy of placating Milošević and his proxies among Bosnian Serbs. And it approved the UN sending a so-called United Nations Protection Force (UNPROFOR) to Croatia – some 15,000 soldiers and civilian personnel who were meant to ensure the maintenance of a lasting ceasefire, protecting local Serbian populations while overseeing full demilitarisation of designated United Nations Protected Areas. With the EC standing back, Bosnia steadily slid into war. The EC's 15 February proposal of a confederalisation of Bosnia–Herzegovina into three constituent (not necessarily contiguous) ethnically defined states only played into the hands of the Serbs – they took this as a licence for ethnic cleansing.[193]

Keeping peace, shopping in a warzone

Of course, Bosnia was an intractable situation. Serbs, Croats and Muslims all had different aims for what they claimed as their territories and peoples. In turbulent referenda on 29 February and 1 March, the inhabitants of Bosnia voted overwhelmingly for independence, thereby officially fulfilling a key requirement for recognition by EC states. Germany was a lone voice in favour. The rest of the Community did not listen – 'not every village can be a state' observed Mitterrand sarcastically – even when Baker told his EC counterparts that the US had changed its view and that Bosnia should be recognised 'as a way to reinforce stability'. The predominant view was that the situation was 'confusing' and that 'Bosnia–Herzegovina could be real mess ... a real snarl-up which would keep UN troops tied up for a long time'. As Major put it to Bush: 'We are very chary.'[194] Only on 6 April 1992 after further escalation, with the JNA effectively holding all the cities of Bosnia at gunpoint, did the EC foreign ministers declare this republic to be an independent state. Next day, America followed suit, finally recognising the three breakaway republics. Meanwhile the UN Security Council cautiously approved deployment of a hundred unarmed 'observers' to Bosnia. This was hardly impressive at a time when the NSC was receiving reports on 'Serbian atrocities – death camps, torture and gang rape'. The ethnic cleansing being practised in Bosnia was nothing less than the war crime of genocide.[195]

The Bush administration now decided to press the Security Council to impose tough economic sanctions on the Yugoslav government in an effort to force Belgrade to bring peace to Bosnia and Herzegovina. On 30 May – in what was only the second time, apart from the Gulf War, that the Security Council took punitive action against an aggressor nation since the end of the Cold War – it voted 13–0 in favour of UN Resolution 757. This established a trade embargo on Serbia (including oil), the freezing of foreign assets, and the suspension of air-traffic links to Serbia and Montenegro, all the while calling for the establishment of a 'security zone' around Sarajevo airport in order to allow emergency supplies to be flown into the Bosnian capital.[196]

It was noteworthy that although China abstained, it did so without threatening to block sanctions. What's more, Russia was fully on board. A strong statement from the Kremlin held that Belgrade had 'brought upon itself the United Nations sanctions by failing to heed the demands of the international community'. Significantly, there was no specific reference to using force, though some Council members were known to be informally discussing a possible naval blockade of the Adriatic ports and the closing of Bosnian air space to Serbian war planes.[197]

The UN Security Council had spoken but the actual monitoring of compliance with Resolution 757 – in the form of surveillance, identification and reporting of maritime traffic in the Adriatic – was only implemented after the North Atlantic Council on 4 June 1992 expressed its willingness to support the UN under a mandate from the CSCE, thereby allowing NATO to mount its first post-Cold War 'out of area' peacekeeping activity. In the event, NATO and WEU states did not agree to undertake a coordinated operation until the Helsinki II summit in July 1992.

The chronic sluggishness of the international community about Bosnia was due to its larger paralytic debate about how to guarantee European security, despite the crisis on its periphery, and, longer term, how to define America's role within it. The US – aware that 'how the West responds to the crisis in Bosnia will set a precedent for the future' – was torn between 'reluctance to engage in Yugoslavia' and a 'desire to maintain NATO's primacy'.[198] And European disunity gave Mitterrand's France a chance to try to carve out a new leadership role within the EC and specifically its military arm, the WEU. Combined with France's push for a Franco-German army corps, Mitterrand's bid for a French-led European activism threatened to sideline the United States. Yet the French president was not merely exploiting France's new room for manoeuvre in the post-Cold War world for power-political advantage. France's behaviour was also a reaction to a fear of US disengagement in Europe after the Soviet foe had disappeared.

The Americans viewed French diplomacy with suspicion. They worried that France's self-assertion in the Balkans would become a 'self-fulfilling prophecy' through its impact on American opinion. Bush – who definitely did not want Bonn to prioritise the Franco-German corps over NATO – sought to reassure the FRG (and the French) that, despite the isolationist noises emanating from the other side of the Atlantic, there would be no American 'pullback' from Europe.[199]

Although anxious about French muscle-flexing, Bush did not modify his 'cautious' approach to Bosnia, even as the reports of 'atrocities' mounted in the summer of 1992. In a discussion with NATO secretary general Manfred Wörner on the margins of the Helsinki summit, Baker said that Washington believed that it might become necessary to use 'all means necessary' in such a humanitarian mission, and that America would not fail to play its part. But he also stressed that the United States had no intention of getting involved in an 'intervention' to solve Bosnia's 'political problems'. For the moment, America was willing to 'cooperate' with the Europeans on one 'discrete problem', the monitoring of the Adriatic under the WEU–NATO joint venture, by offering to commit 'air and naval forces'. But there would be no US ground combat troops. Bush was acutely conscious that boots on the ground would find themselves on a slippery slope from humanitarian support to peace enforcement. That's why he did not want NATO to be 'in the lead'. After all, he worried, 'I don't see how we can say that NATO is in and the US is out.'[200]

Scowcroft saw things the other way round. During Baker's meeting with Wörner, he warned of the 'precedent-setting' nature of any decision to stay in 'the background'. Then France would 'say that such conflicts are to be managed by Europeans'.[201] This reflected the deeper American fear that France might push NATO aside and usurp its role, as the WEU and CSCE metamorphosed by default into fully-fledged security alliances. Washington had not forgotten France's vehement opposition to America's initiatives both during and after the Cold War to 'revitalise' the transatlantic alliance. French allusions to WEU, CSCE and the Franco-German corps rang alarm bells in the White House. Western efforts should be focused – not duplicated – and thereby reduced. France, like the Germans, should convey the message that its European military efforts were 'complementary' to those of the Atlantic Alliance. Anything, Bush told Mitterrand firmly, that sent 'the clock back to the '30s' had to be avoided. 'Our objective is to achieve stability', and so 'the best signal to all' was simply 'a strong Western alliance'.[202]

Before he left office, Genscher had tried to alleviate US concerns about France's machinations and Europe's future security architecture. He had explained to Bush that France remained 'very much occupied by the Yalta system' – the Gaullist shibboleth of a continent split in two by the superpowers in 1945. That's why Paris wanted to hold on to its strong position, in comparison with Germany – as a 'nuclear power, not integrated into NATO, and having a seat on the Security Council'. French thinking was frankly geared toward certain structures that could 'constrain Germany'. Germany's position was that Bonn could 'meet their concerns, but not at the price of relations with the US'. The transatlantic relationship remained key. Giving the American presence on the old continent 'a new justification' had been central to Germany's post-Wall thinking. As a potential West–East bridge the German Foreign Ministry placed particular emphasis on the newly formed North Atlantic Cooperation Council (NACC). This, it was felt, would give NATO a novel and 'maybe more important role' than the CSCE as a device to truly bring the states of the former Warsaw Pact in from the cold.[203]

Eastern Europe certainly placed its hopes in the NACC and even eventual NATO enlargement. Hungarian prime minister József Antall told Bush in Helsinki: 'The Atlantic idea is paramount to us. The presence of the US in Europe is the only [option] ... Among Europeans conflicts are quite easy and whether you like it or not, America will have to make an appearance, so it's better to just stay on.' Rejecting any US pull-out, he implored the president 'American–West European solidarity must remain.' Nor did he seem to have much faith in the French connection: 'sometimes they say paradoxical things'.[204]

These underlying debates about the framework for European security – about the roles of America and France, NATO and WEU – vitiated every attempt at joint Western action over Bosnia. Even the very limited WEU–NATO operation to police the Adriatic as punishment for Serbia took months to put in place. Yet again it was too little, too late.[205]

And so, in 1992 – seventy-four years after its creation in the wake of Europe's Great War – the Yugoslav federation fell apart with genocidal violence – a sobering contrast to the peaceful transition of most of Europe from the Cold War.[206]

DAILY Mirror

Friday, August 7, 1992   NEWSPAPER FOR THE NINETIES   Last month's daily sale: 3,596,544 INCORPORATING THE DAILY RECORD   27p

THE PICTURE THAT SHAMES THE WORLD

STARVING AND DESPAIRING: Bosnian prisoners at the Omarska concentration camp run by Serbs dedicated to their barbaric policy of "ethnic cleansing"   Picture: ITN

BELSEN 92

HOLLOW-EYED and haggard, row upon row of men without hope stare out from a barbed wire cage.

The haunting picture of these skeletal captives evokes the ghosts of the Nazis' Belsen concentration camp during the Second World War.

But this is European bar-

By MARK DOWDNEY
Foreign Editor

barism in 1992, filmed at one of the Serbian "detention" centres in northern Bosnia.

The picture was part of a harrowing ITN report by newsgirl Penny Marshall, screened last night. Many

prisoners at the Omarska camp are thought to have futures no brighter than an executioner's bullet.

Others face the agony of slow death by starvation.

And as the men die, world leaders dither about what – if anything – they will do to halt the unspeakable atrocities which shame humanity.

HORROR OF THE NEW HOLOCAUST   PAGE 2 AND CENTRE PAGES

Prime responsibility lay with Serbia, but EC and UN diplomacy did nothing to stop the aggression and little to mitigate it. And America and NATO were also not ready to engage militarily in a conflict that was 'out of area'. While Baker complained about the EC 12 having a 'lowest-common denominator operation', and doing a 'bunch of talk ... mumbo-jumbo', the British Foreign Office minister Douglas Hogg pointed his finger across the Atlantic: 'There is no cavalry over the hill. There is no international force coming to stop this.' Ultimately, as had become clear, the Germans and the Europeans always deferred to the Americans when it came to firepower and using arms. And, in hard reality Bush was not going to alter the US policy on Yugoslavia in an election year.[207]

Asked by a reporter whether the Bosnians 'deserve some kind of protection' given that 'there is a new world order which has been declared by the president of the United States', State Department spokesperson Margaret D. Tutweiler replied: 'Where is it written that the United States government is the military policeman of the world?' As tragic as the situation in Yugoslavia was, the US had no 'national security interests' at stake there. The defence of human rights alone was not enough reason. As another official snorted: 'Do you really think the American people want to spill their blood for Bosnia?'[208]

That was also Bush's position. He was sure that age-old ethnic hatreds could not be fixed by a quick flurry of outside intervention. As he said in St Louis on 11 October 1992, during the first presidential campaign debate, 'You have ancient rivalries that have cropped up as Yugoslavia is dissolved ... It isn't going to be solved by sending in the 82nd Airborne and I'm not going to do that as commander-in-chief.' He insisted that he was concerned about 'ethnic cleansing'. But in that televised presidential debate Bush added another point that he knew would resonate with his domestic audience: 'I vowed something because I learned something from Vietnam. I am not going to commit US forces until I know what the mission is, till the military tell me that it can be completed, and till I know how they can come out.'[209]

Bush was treading a fine line. Contrary to Margaret Tutweiler, he was ready to say – even a month before the election – 'We are the sole remaining superpower, and we should be that. And we have a certain disproportionate responsibility.' In similar vein, seeking to reassure Hungary's premier József Antall about Eastern Europe's stability after the Red Army withdrawal and the potential spillover from the Yugoslav crisis, Bush had stated firmly in Helsinki that summer 'We do have a responsibility to be a stabilising force in Europe, also with Russia. In that respect we have unique responsibilities.' Equally, he insisted against those advocating troop cuts, 'I think it is important that the United States stay in Europe and continue to guarantee the peace. We simply cannot pull back.'[210]

As the president's comments in the St Louis debate made clear, he remained immensely proud of the Gulf War coalition, considering it a model for how the new world order should be sustained. That, however, had been a clear-cut mission, in the national strategic interest; a UN-authorised military operation to reinstate one country's territorial integrity and sovereignty after unlawful invasion by another. The mission was also undertaken with full international approval (including the USSR and PRC) in the middle of his first term. The Balkans, by contrast, were a nightmare of history, in which the US had no key interests and no clear game plan. What's more, the Bosnian crisis had blown up at the same time as the Soviet Union fell apart and when Bush was sucked ever deeper into an increasingly problematic campaign for re-election. Hence his obduracy about getting involved in what seemed like another Vietnam.

*

In trying to understand Bush's rethink of global order and America's leadership role after 1991, a further episode is important. It is instructive, briefly, to compare his unwavering opposition to intervention in Bosnia with his decision – after he had lost the presidential election – for a military humanitarian mission in Somalia.

Somalia had been engulfed in civil war months before the actual overthrow by General Mohamed Farrah Hassan Aidid of the country's long-time dictator, President Mohamed Siad Barre, in January 1991 – just around the time that America started its campaign against Saddam and the Soviets cracked down in Lithuania. Twelve months later, the Somali state had disintegrated into feuding tribal fiefdoms, all governmental authority and normal economic activity had collapsed and the country was ravaged by drought. Amid the anarchy, armed bands looted food stocks and the rival clans seized international aid as a means of controlling the civilian population. Periodic bloodbaths in the capital Mogadishu meant that by the spring of 1992 foreign embassies and international agencies, including the UN, had pulled out – abandoning Somalia to its grisly fate.[211]

Somalia: The poor people's war

Some 300,000 Somalis had already died from malnutrition and the Office of US Disaster Assistance estimated that two-thirds of Somalia's population of 6.5 million were facing 'the threat of starvation due to the effects of civil strife'.[212] But the international community took little action. It was only after the Organisation of African Unity, the Arab League and the Islamic Conference negotiated a ceasefire in Mogadishu in February 1992 that the UN Security Council under Resolution 751 agreed to send in fifty observers to monitor it. This token operation – UNOSOM I – was approved on 24 April.[213] Meanwhile, that summer 15,000 *armed* peace-keepers were sent to Bosnia, making it look, said Pérez de Cuéllar's successor as UN secretary general, Boutros Boutros-Ghali (an Egyptian), as if the West only cared about the 'rich man's war' while far-off Africa was left to its own devices. In similar vein, a senior US aid administrator noted: 'The number of people who perish in Yugoslavia each month equals the number of people who die in Somalia each day. Yet there is little international concern, and no outrage.' It was only in midsummer, when the UN observers finally arrived in Mogadishu, that the interna-tional media finally picked up the story, with images of dying children flickering across the First World's TV screens and front-page headlines. The *New York Times* entitled one of its editorials 'The Hell Called Somalia'.[214]

Pressure mounted from Congress and the State Department's Africa desk for the US to deploy forces to protect international aid, which was finally beginning to flow. But the State Department's Bureau of International Organisation Affairs, headed by John Bolton, saw Somalia as a food not a security problem and hence opposed anything more than UN relief and reconciliation attempts. In the same vein, and much more significantly, the Joint Chiefs of Staff considered Somalia 'a bottomless pit' – advice that any president would have to take seriously, especially when facing a re-election year.[215]

Crucially, however, the humanitarian crisis got to Bush himself, mainly because of a cable from the US ambassador to Kenya, Smith Hempstone Jr, a former journalist with a feel for words. Dated 10 July and entitled 'A Day in Hell', it declared sarcastically 'if you liked Beirut, you'll love Mogadishu'. (Beirut had been an early-1980s byword for anarchy.) Hempstone predicted 'it will take five years to get Somalia not on its feet but just on its knees'. And in the absence of fundamental change in the country, US intervention would only 'keep tens of thousands of Somali kids from starving to death in 1993 who, in all probability, will starve to death in 1994'. Hempstone called Somalia a 'tar baby', the military referred to it as a 'quagmire' and the analogy with Beirut was hardly comforting: the Reagan administration had been thrown into crisis in 1983 when 241 US Marines, sent in as peacekeepers, had been blown up in their barracks by suicide bombers. But Bush scribbled on the margins of Hempstone's telegram: 'This is a terribly moving situation. Let's do everything we can to help.'[216]

The 'Day in Hell' cable arrived just as Bush was moving Baker from the State Department to run his election campaign, but the president asked Eagleburger to be 'forward-leaning' on Somalia. And as Eagleburger recalled, this was easier to do because 'in Somalia, it was humanitarian aid' whereas 'in Bosnia, there was really a call for military intervention'.[217] A few days before the Republican National Convention opened on 17 August, Bush announced several initiatives on Somalia. First, America would provide all-important 'lift' capacity for the humanitarian mission. It was decided that US aircraft would transport to Mogadishu the 500 UN peacekeepers approved at the 28 July meeting of the Security Council. A similar offer was made when the UN subsequently announced 3,000 extra men for UNOSOM I to protect relief supplies. In addition, on 14 August the White House stated that the 'starvation in Somalia is a human tragedy' and declared that the USA would 'take a leading role with other nations and organisations' by initiating a 145,000-ton emergency food airlift. The peacekeepers were intended to protect relief convoys and 'ensure that food reaches those who so desperately need it'.[218] With the election looming, and Bush under attack from Clinton for not showing 'real leadership' and for failing to act forcefully against perpetrators of 'crimes against humanity under international law', the president was desperate to position himself as an experienced, assertive but compassionate leader. The Pentagon's 'slippery slope' warnings were brushed aside.[219]

After the shop-window moment of the party convention, Somalia slid off the front pages. The election campaign was in full swing and furthermore the White House got totally absorbed by the clean-up after Hurricane Andrew wreaked havoc in Florida and Louisiana at the end of August.[220] Meanwhile on the Horn of Africa, the aid programme faltered. The first contingent of Pakistani UN 'Blue Helmets' did not arrive until mid-September and Mogadishu airport was not secured for another two months. A major reason for these delays was the lack of precedents for deploying UN forces on a humanitarian rather than a peacekeeping mission – let alone in a situation where there were was no government with which to negotiate. In this power vacuum, clan warlords and gangs of armed thugs took a growing share of the food aid through 'protection' blackmail and outright theft. Attacks on relief workers escalated and some airports had to be closed.[221]

The UN's 500 lightly armed Pakistani guards now found themselves isolated in a corner of the capital's airport by clan warriors. On 12 November, after General Aidid told the UN guards to withdraw and they refused, he put them under fire and then organised a demonstration against foreign intervention outside UNOSOM's Mogadishu headquarters. Combined with increased violence against unarmed NGO personnel, the Somali warlord was escalating his 'anti-UN campaign'. It was obvious that the deployment of the 3,000 additional peacekeepers was now impossible. Given the anarchy, it even looked as if the US might have to mount a dangerous evacuation of the UN battalion and other staff. Lack of security was now more of a problem than lack of food.[222]

It was ironic that in Bush's new guide for US foreign policy on 'peacekeeping and emergency humanitarian relief' activities – NSD-74 of November 1992 – the focus remained on America providing 'unique' contributions in the form of 'lift, logistics, communications and intelligence capabilities'. Given what was happening in Somalia, it was clear that this new National Security directive could not serve as a template for action there because the reality on the ground demanded a military intervention.[223]

Yet the Pentagon still seemed categorically against filling this security vacuum. To do so would require 'muscular military power' which in their estimation meant some 30,000 heavily armed troops on the ground. The US military considered this would be intolerable: the risk of casualties simply too great. Throughout the autumn the Pentagon continued to insist that American power should not be used to try to resolve, or even mitigate, a humanitarian crisis. And so, with effectively impotent peace-keepers who operated under a feeble UN mandate, UNOSOM looked on the verge of collapse.[224]

By this point Bush had lost the presidential election of 3 November to Bill Clinton. His whole campaign had been complicated by the strong showing by the isolationist independent Ross Perot – a business tycoon from Texas. As a result, Bush always had to look two ways in terms of his political targeting and message.

Clinton, however, was the man who had really got under the president's skin. His mantra 'It's the economy, stupid' was a constant reminder to Bush of his broken tax pledge from 1988. And in the later stages of the campaign Clinton's pressure for an American foreign policy that was openly 'humanitarian' and also more 'aggressive' – one in which power was driven by values – had touched another nerve with the public. Despite Bush's determination to look presidential, he felt constantly pummelled and had even done an interview with Barbara Walters on ABC's *20/20* show, during which he admitted that reversing his 'no new taxes' pledge was the biggest mistake of his presidency 'because it undermined to some degree my credibility with the American people'. Throughout the campaign the president who had won the Cold War seemed perpetually on the defensive.[225]

Yet, paradoxically, in defeat Bush was freer. It was easier for a lame-duck president to keep his footing. About to leave office on 20 January, he was no longer constrained by all those domestic pressures and felt ready to take vigorous action in Somalia. In any case, America's existing involvement in UNOSOM – air transportation of food and UN troops – made it difficult for Washington to wash its hands of the situation when things got messy. And it was obviously no longer viable to act simply as logistical facilitator when the UN was so clearly failing to cope on the ground and when Boutros-Ghali was pleading for American help.

The big push for US military humanitarian intervention did not, however, come from the White House but from the State Department and, more surprisingly, from the Pentagon. On 12 November, the day the UN peacekeepers were shelled at Mogadishu airport, Assistant Secretary of State Robert L. Gallucci, in charge of politico-military affairs, recommended to Eagleburger that the United States lead a coalition to save Somalia from starvation under a Security Council authorisation to use 'all necessary means' including force. Eagleburger, convinced by Gallucci's arguments, became an advocate of more forceful US action.[226]

A week later the NSC Deputies Committee met no less than four times.[227] They discussed various options for greater US involvement in the UN's operation.[228] Undersecretary of Defense Paul Wolfowitz certainly did not believe that a bigger UN peacekeeping mission would work. He favoured using American ground combat forces. The Joint Chiefs of Staff representatives on the committee agreed and subsequently General Colin Powell himself recommended full-scale US intervention, with the support of Defense Secretary Dick Cheney who told the *Washington Post* that the US military was willing to 'do more than put a Band-Aid on the problem' because the situation in Somalia was so dire and 'what we do can make a big difference'. The Pentagon's volte-face astounded the State Department, but it was delighted. Essentially, the military had come to the conclusion that it was better for America to take the initiative rather than intervening reactively – forced into making piecemeal efforts to defend or extract beleaguered UN personnel. Instead, a strong and substantial 'US-led military coalition' – operating 'under UN authority but not UN command' – should seek to control Somali events.[229]

The 'decisive force' approach that had been vindicated in the Gulf War in 1991 and subsequently enshrined in the 1992 US National Military Strategy, drafted under Powell's guidance, was thus to be applied in Somalia – albeit as a mission inside a state, with armed forces on a smaller scale and deployed for a different – expressly humanitarian – purpose.[230]

Bush and Scowcroft were convinced by the Pentagon consensus and, on Powell's advice, decided to deploy some 28,000 US troops. On 3 December 1992, the UN Security Council adopted Resolution 794, which welcomed the US offer to help create 'as soon as possible a secure environment' for the delivery of humanitarian aid in Somalia, and authorised the use of 'all necessary means' to do so under Chapter VII of the Charter. The resolution also asked other states to provide military forces and to make contributions in cash or kind towards the operation. The unanimous vote of the Council, including traditional sceptics about the 'use of force' such as India, African members and China (which emphasised the 'exceptional nature' of the resolution given the 'chaotic conditions' in Somalia), represented a landmark in the development of international humanitarian law after the Cold War. It showed that the international community and America believed in the enforceable right to assistance for suffering people. And for the UN secretary general Boutros-Ghali, this marked a moment of personal triumph. Having taken up his post only at the beginning of the year, he had managed to convince the world to engage in a mercy mission for an impoverished part of Africa.[231]

Next day, Bush announced his decision to initiate Operation Restore Hope (of which the US would assume the unified command) in a televised address from the Oval Office. In this speech, delivered six weeks before the end of his presidency, he referred to the 'shocking images from Somalia' – the 'tragedy' and 'suffering' and the possibility that in the months ahead '1.5 million people could starve'. The mission, he said, was to 'help them live', to 'save thousands of innocents from death'. Of course, he emphasised, 'the United States alone cannot right the world's wrongs. But we also know that some crises in the world cannot be resolved without American involvement.' The president explained that only the United States had the 'global reach' to deploy a large number of troops quickly enough to make sure the food got through before many more people died.

As with Kuwait, he took pains to make clear to his fellow Americans that 'we will not, however, be acting alone'. Having in the run-up to his public announcement undertaken an intense bout of telephone diplomacy – from Tokyo to Paris and from Rome to Riyadh – Bush could say with confidence that a dozen other nations would join the UN-sanctioned effort with hardware, men and money: the Unified Task Force in Somalia (UNITAF) would definitely be multilateral, not unilateral.[232] And he was also careful to highlight the operation's 'limited objective' as a 'humanitarian' mission, stressing that it was not 'open-ended'. UNITAF, the 'coalition of peacemaking forces', would pave the way for a follow-up, 'regular UN peacekeeping' mission (UNOSOM II) and so was effectively a 'bridging operation' – limited in time as well as scope. Bush declared: 'We will not stay one day longer than is absolutely necessary.'[233]

The president made his private anxieties about the operation very clear to Boutros-Ghali. 'We have quite a big force going in there. I don't want any of them to be killed,' he explained over the phone on 8 December. 'I worry that a hopped-up kid with one of these Toyotas may shoot at the Marines, and there will be consequences.' The UN secretary general quickly responded, keen to draw the US into a military presence on the ground by disarming the gangs. But Bush saw the dangers of 'mission creep'. He agreed that disarming was important but insisted 'we have not made it part of our mission statement ... We need peacekeepers coming in quickly behind us.'[234]

Bush stuck to his guns. He had told the NSC on 3 December 'I expect that within forty days troops can start coming out,' and that remained his firm goal. The first elements of UNITAF hit the beaches of Mogadishu on 9 December, soon augmented by 17,000 additional troops from over twenty countries. Restore Hope had been sold as a 'doable mission' in which overwhelming force would ensure success with limited casualties, and that was pretty much how it played out. America's first humanitarian intervention mission in Somalia was reported as complete by March 1993, and its commander General Robert B. Johnston recommended the transition to UNOSOM II. No American lives had been lost.[235]

It is significant that UNITAF had been bipartisan – surprisingly so, given the acrimony of the election campaign. Clinton was briefed on plans for the operation[236] and gave an emphatic public endorsement of Bush's decision: 'Impediments to delivery of relief supplies and particularly looting of life-saving food supplies simply must not be allowed to continue,' the president-elect declared. 'The mandate our armed forces and our partners in the coalition will fulfil is to create a secure environment to save lives, and I commend President Bush for his leadership on this important humanitarian effort.'[237] Indeed, after he became president, Clinton embraced UNITAF as almost a joint operation. 'Our consciences said, enough,' he declared in a speech in October 1993. 'In our nation's best tradition, we took action with bipartisan support. President Bush sent in 28,000 American troops as part of a United Nations humanitarian mission. Our troops created a secure environment so that food and medicine could get through. We saved close to 1 million lives. And throughout most of Somalia, everywhere but in Mogadishu, life began returning to normal ... and none of this would have happened without American leadership and America's troops.'[238]

*

The last months of Bush's presidency had shown the limits and problems of the 'new world order' he had so boldly proclaimed in 1990–1. To be sure, in the narrow military sense UNITAF proved a success – just like the first Gulf War. Yet, longer term, neither did much to resolve the deeper problems of both Somalia and Iraq, or of their respective regions. After Saddam's defeat in Kuwait, he had begun to repress the Kurdish population of Iraq, leading to a string of ineffectual UN-sanctioned military-humanitarian operations. In Somalia the ceasefire broke almost as soon as UNITAF left and UNOSOM II did not manage to make progress on reconciliation, demilitarisation and state-building.

What the conflicts in the Middle East, the Balkans and East Africa all exposed was the true messiness of the 'messy world' – Scowcroft's phrase in August 1990 after Iraq invaded Kuwait and just two weeks before Bush first outlined his vision of 'a world where the rule of law supplants the law of the jungle', where 'nations recognise the shared responsibility for freedom and justice', and where 'the strong respect the right of the weak'.[239]

This was, however, rhetoric. Despite the globalism of Bush's vision of order, it became clear in 1991–2 that it was no definitive road map for the new era post-Wall. As Bush himself finally admitted in a big-picture wrap-up speech at Texas A&M University five weeks before he left the White House: 'There can be no single or simple guidelines for foreign policy'.[240]

In part, this was because the 'new world' was less orderly than that of the Cold War. In the heyday of bipolarity, virtually every local conflict – from Vietnam to Israel/Palestine, from Chile to Afghanistan, from Namibia to Nicaragua – engaged American interests and prompted some level of US military involvement because the Soviets were backing one side or another. Yet, the fear of precipitating nuclear war had helped maintain the principle of non-intervention in internal affairs. And the prevalence of totalitarian or authoritarian regimes in the Third World often kept the lid on civil strife. So, Western idealists advocating human rights tried mainly to make such regimes less brutal by demanding freedom of speech, rights of travel and emigration, and an end to torture and arbitrary imprisonment.[241]

The war to drive Iraq out of Kuwait – demanding as it had been logistically and diplomatically – was in some ways both a simple case and a transitional moment. The invasion had been a flagrant act of aggression by one state against another. The Soviet Union was now working in tandem with the USA, and Gorbachev was aligning himself with the principles of international law and order. The USSR, although weakened, was at this stage still the second pillar of the global system. And there was hope that the UN Security Council – no longer paralysed by Cold War ideological antagonisms – could play a rejuvenated role as guardian of the peace. In this propitious situation, the US would act as the leader of multilateral international action. As Scowcroft put it in the autumn of 1990, 'the United States henceforth would be obligated to lead the world community to an unprecedented degree, as demonstrated by the Iraqi crisis, and that we should attempt to pursue our national interests, wherever possible, within a framework of concert with our friends and the international community'.[242] The White House's big point was that 'morally, we must act so that international law, not international outlaws, governs the post-Cold War world'.[243] And so in Desert Shield and Desert Storm – the first practical implementation of this grand design – a US-led coalition under UN authority forced Iraq to abide by international law and pushed it out of Kuwait – being careful, however, not to engage in any serious breach of Iraq's own sovereignty.

At the end of 1991, however, the Soviet pillar crumbled. Suddenly the US felt itself in the position of supreme hegemon – alone and unrivalled. This was the 'unipolar' moment. 'We were suddenly in a unique position, without experience, without precedent and standing alone at the height of power,' Scowcroft later wrote, 'an unparalleled situation in history' – and one that presented America with the 'rarest opportunity to shape the world and the deeper responsibility to do so wisely not just for the benefit of the United States but all nations'.[244]

So how should the United States try to secure peace and stability in this new environment? Under its Charter, the United Nations could be used for 'peacekeeping operations' – defined as those having the consent of the parties, being based on impartiality, and ruling out the use of force except in self-defence or to sustain a specific mandate under UN Charter Chapter VII. But the UN had never developed its own 'peacemaking' capacity: the Security Council's Military Staff Committee, established under Article 47 of the UN Charter, had been dormant almost from its inception because of Cold War rivalries. The unipolar moment offered the possibility of US-led military action, supported by the rest of the Security Council under Chapter VII, but the operation undertaken in Kuwait did not prove any real precedent. With the demise of the USSR and the end of many repressive but stable regimes, local conflicts and ethno-religious rivalries that had been frozen by the Cold War were thawed out. Whether, where and how to get involved posed huge challenges for the White House.

On the one hand there was a keen sense that America had to lead. 'We can hardly entrust democracy or American interest exclusively to multilateral institutions,' Baker declared in April 1992. Bush insisted that 'Anyone who says we should retreat into an isolationist cocoon is living in the last century.' The administration's 1991 National Security Strategy had warned of how in the 1920s, when the Great War was over and 'no comparable threat was evident, the nation turned inward. That course had near disastrous consequences then and it would be even more dangerous now ...'

Yet the president had no intention of assuming for America the role of global peace*maker* and even less of global peace-*enforcer*. 'We should consider using military force only in those situations where the stakes warrant, where it can be effective and its application limited in scope and time,' he reaffirmed in his Texas A&M speech. The 'Powell Doctrine' of winnable missions and calculable risks remained fundamental to his national security policy. And he added a further qualification: 'As we seek to save lives, we must always be mindful of the lives that we may have to put at risk.'[245] No American leader who had lived through the Vietnam War could ignore the domestic cost of foreign wars. And certainly not anyone running a presidential election campaign. The Kuwait War in February was, roughly speaking, a midterm operation; whereas the break-up of Yugoslavia in 1991–2 occurred as the election campaign was hotting up and turning nasty for Bush; while the UNITAF intervention in Somalia came after his electoral defeat, when the president had nothing politically to lose.

After reeling at the shock of defeat and moaning about 'referring all calls' to Clinton and having no real responsibilities except 'walking the dogs', Bush rebounded in what presidential aides considered an attempt to 'establish a legacy for his presidency'.[246] On a personal level, perhaps, Bush saw his carefully calibrated, short-term operation on the Horn of Africa as a way to leave office on a high, rather than exiting with a whimper – as many perceived to have been the fate of Jimmy Carter in January 1980, unable to effect the release of the US hostages in Iran.

The timings of the Kuwait, Yugoslavia and Somalia operations were therefore important. Yet the cases themselves were also different. Whereas the Iraq–Kuwait crisis had been an instance of inter-state aggression, the crises in Yugoslavia and Somalia were seen – at least initially – as purely internal affairs. The former grew out of the violent break-up of a state; the latter out of anarchy-induced famine. Over the Balkan wars of secession the Bush administration decided from the start to stand on the sidelines – not just because the US military regarded the region as a quagmire but also because there were regional powers and institutions which he expected to maintain peace and order: the EC, CSCE and WEU as well as the UN.

There was also little American desire to engage NATO in the Balkans because the Alliance – as the only politico-military institution that integrated the armed forces of one half of Europe and provided the United States and its allies with a unique capacity to influence each other's policies – was in the midst of readjusting to the post-Wall world. The historical reasons for NATO had been to hedge against any Russian threat while enveloping Germany and forging a durable transatlantic bond between the US and Europe. This rationale was now imported into the post-Cold War era. But in addition, NATO was under pressure from Moscow to redefine relations and from the new democracies in Eastern Europe to open its door, which would lead to enlarging its territory. So the Alliance had to consider its future identity: should it become a larger collective 'defence community' or perhaps one more focused on 'collective security'? But as the Balkans went up in flames, there was also a pressing need to redefine NATO's mission if it wanted to stay at the leading edge of change in Europe. Gradually in 1992 the pressure mounted on Bush's America as the principal 'ordering power' for NATO to engage militarily 'out of area', to consider peacekeeping and peace-enforcement operations, and even undertake humanitarian interventions. Yet neither Bush nor the American public, preoccupied with domestic issues, were keen to embark on a US-led military intervention in Yugoslavia, and the military top brass could not identify any clear objectives for US forces or indeed which parties in the Balkan imbroglio they would fight. Bush – like Baker, Cheney and Powell – was a staunch believer in having clear war aims, conducting short operations and keeping casualties to a minimum. As a result, when it came to NATO and the explosive Balkan powder keg in 1992, he stuck to prudent pragmatism by choosing to stay out. Indeed he regarded Clinton's passionate rhetoric about refugees, human rights and limited use of force in Bosnia as largely electioneering.[247]

At the same time, however, Bush did let himself be drawn into the apparently worse mess of Somalia. There the 'CNN effect',[248] strong pressure from the Egyptian UN secretary general, Bush's post-election sense of liberation and above all the sudden endorsement of the US military combined to make the White House change tack and turn a failing UN peacekeeping mission into a US-led peace-enforcement operation – *for a deliberately brief period.*

Commander-in-Chief: Bush in Mogadishu

What Bosnia and Somalia showed was how difficult peacekeeping proved to be for smaller powers, regional organisations and the UN itself, as soon as violence erupted. And once it was agreed that in such a situation force was needed to make or keep peace, effective operations depended on America's overwhelming firepower and equally its unrivalled 'lift' capacity to move troops and supplies around the world.

Considered as a whole, the period 1991–3 revealed Bush's cautious and conservative approach, in spite of the optimistic and universalist rhetoric of America exporting and defending democratic peace all over the world. And even with the UN-authorised and US-led military operations that he did adopt, short-term success did not guarantee sustained peace. In Somalia, for instance, the predictable failure of UNOSOM II once the majority of US troops were withdrawn led Clinton to ratchet up force levels again and to expand the mission to one restoring a government – until the shooting down of two Black Hawk helicopters and the death of nineteen US service personnel in early October 1993, some of whose bodies were dragged through the streets of Mogadishu. Clinton – badly stung – promptly pulled back. He was learning the hard way the truth of Bush's sobering dictum about taking account of the American lives that may have to be put at risk when seeking to save the lives of others. As leaders of the 'sole superpower' they had to recognise that the 'new world' was suffering from chronic and endemic 'disorders'.

In practice, then, the 'new world order' required flexible response rather than rigid blueprints. What was becoming increasingly clear amid this confusion was the extent to which the supposedly 'new' world was being improvised on the basis of mostly Western concepts, structures and institutions derived from the immediate post-war era and the longer Cold War. And also that Bush's vision – which featured ideals as much as power politics – was not universally shared.

Aware of this, the Pentagon's 'Defense Planning Guidance' statement for the rest of the century explicitly argued in spring 1992 that the US must 'prevent the re-emergence of a new rival' akin to the Soviet Union and stop 'any hostile power from dominating a region whose resources would, under consolidated control, be sufficient to generate global power'. With these aims in mind the United States should strengthen its key alliances in Europe and Asia ('the US-led system of collective security') and push to expand the 'democratic "zone of peace"'. The document emphasised 'one of the primary tasks we face today in shaping the future is carrying long-standing alliances into the new era, and turning old enmities into new cooperative relationships'.[249]

The most striking example of 'turning old enmities into new cooperative relationships' was, of course, the whole Washington–Moscow transformation. Reagan had missed out on what was supposed to be the crowning achievement of his presidency: signing a strategic arms-reduction treaty during his last big summit with Gorbachev in Moscow in June 1988. The unfinished business of START hung over his successor's presidency, its realisation impeded by the momentous upheavals in Europe in 1989 and 1990. Yet, Bush kept his eye on the ball, concluding START I with Gorbachev in July 1991, and capitalising on Yeltsin's pro-Western phase to consummate START II as a last hurrah in the dying days of his presidency, in the new year of 1993. Together, implementation of the two treaties would reduce American and Soviet strategic arsenals by more than two-thirds.

In the Kremlin press conference on 3 January 1993, Bush welcomed what he called 'a new era for our two nations and for the world' after half a century in which 'the Soviet Union and the United States stood locked in a nuclear stand-off' and when 'the constant threat of war seemed imminent', indeed, at times inevitable. Likewise, Yeltsin declared that the treaty went 'further than all other treaties ever signed in the field of disarmament' and thereby represented 'a major step towards fulfilling mankind's centuries-old dream'. He predicted that START II would become 'the core of the system of global security guarantees'.[250]

On the way out. On the way up – START II in Moscow

The START treaties did indeed draw a line under the Cold War, alleviating the existential threat of global nuclear war. But, despite its awesome weaponry of mass destruction, post-Soviet Russia was no longer the force it had been in the bipolar era. START II was in truth an asymmetric deal – between two countries that were in no sense equals. With Russia suddenly stripped of its empire, during 1992 Yeltsin sounded embarrassingly eager for partnership, even integration, with the West.

But by the time he signed the START II treaty, Yeltsin was also making noises about reviving Russia as a great power and cultivating new opportunities in the Far East. In the Asia-Pacific region as a whole, in fact, the end of the Cold War had not witnessed a break-up in the manner of post-1989 Europe; yet here too, the early 1990s were a moment of flux. Divided Korea now seemed the great anomaly of the post-Cold War world – and an increasingly alarming one, given North Korea's evident aspirations to become a nuclear power. And Japan – America's staunchest Cold War Asian ally, with its boom economy once hailed as the rising sun of a dawning Pacific century – was after Tiananmen beginning to be overshadowed by the much bigger and increasingly dynamic People's Republic of China. These issues – encompassing regional security, commercial rivalry and nuclear proliferation – also preoccupied Bush in the last year of his presidency.

Chapter 9
Glimpsing a 'Pacific Century'

New Year's Day 1992. A president on the run. Running – reluctantly – for re-election, but also still running happily around the globe. On 30 December 1991 George Bush had left Washington for a 26,000-mile tour of the Pacific that lasted until 10 January 1992. While the plane refuelled at Hickam Air Force Base in Hawaii on New Year's Eve he ran two miles around the athletic field. In Sydney next morning he conducted a press conference while jogging through the grounds of Scots College. Asked if he had 'any personal New Year's resolutions' he responded 'Oh, yes.' What he wanted was to jog 'a little speedier', so the Secret Service would credit their boss with 'a little more proficiency'.[1] Even in odd spare moments at hotels or state guest houses, he would jump on an exercise bike or a Stairmaster. One perceptive reporter noted, 'Mr Bush clearly loves being president, flying around the world, tackling problems and schmoozing with fellow statesmen. Just as clearly, he dislikes and is somewhat daunted by the prospect of going back before the voters this year and asking for another four years on the job as he is beset by an endless recession and plummeting ratings in opinion polls.'[2]

Considering all the air miles that George H. W. Bush accumulated during his four years in office, it is revealing to look back to his initial six months in the White House.[3] The forty-first president had started very slowly. And his first trip outside North America (at the end of February 1989) had been to Asia not Europe – to Japan, China and South Korea. Bush did not venture across the Atlantic until the end of May, and then only to see Western European allies. It was not until July – with those revelatory visits to Poland and Hungary – that his eyes were belatedly opened to the momentous changes then engulfing Eastern Europe. Henceforth, Europe – including Soviet Russia – became his main orbit, with periodic excursions to Latin America. Finally, in January 1992, just after the USSR had collapsed, Bush ventured back to the Asia-Pacific region. And this, like so much of his globe-trotting, was an intense burst of activity rather than an extended tour: the president was away from home for less than two weeks. Yet that whistlestop New Year trip to Australia, Singapore, South Korea and Japan provides a useful lens through which to appreciate the often dizzying kaleidoscope of issues that he had to address as a global leader in 1992, during that last neglected year of his presidency, and to glimpse a region in ascent – one whose power plays and values did not fit easily into an American new world order.

When accepting his party's nomination in 1988 at the Republican Convention, Bush had asserted 'The spirit of democracy is sweeping the Pacific Rim. China feels the winds of change.' And, he added, 'one by one, the unfree places fall, not to the force of arms but to the force of an idea: freedom works'.[4]

Perhaps – or perhaps not. Unlike the whirlwind of revolutionary change in Europe in 1989–91, Asia exited the Cold War relatively quietly, and without major changes in regimes or geopolitics. To be sure, authoritarian states in America's Pacific orbit – South Korea, the Philippines and Taiwan – had opened up to democratisation and economic liberalisation in the late 1980s. But the big Cold War domino had not fallen. The People's Republic of China – having ruthlessly clamped down on democratisation and savagely crushed the protests in June 1989 in Tiananmen Square – remained wedded to its version of communism and its one-party state, even if the hardline ruling elite was pursuing a gradual entry into world capitalism. But, despite the appearance of continuities, it was here in the Asia-Pacific region that a seismic shift was getting under way. It presaged a transformation in the regional order and global balance of both economic and political power that would have long-term implications for America's position, place and self-assurance in world politics.[5]

*

Particularly problematic within the region was Korea – divided since 1945 and an Asian symbol of the persisting Cold War. On 23 December 1991 – a week before Bush's Pacific tour and two days before the Soviet Union disintegrated – the *New York Times* published a front-page story headlined 'In North Korea, the 1990s have not arrived'. Kim Il-sung's dynastic dictatorship appeared immune to the historic forces that had undermined communist states across much of the world. North Korea remained fully absorbed in the idolatry of its 'Great Leader' and the elevation of his nationalist version of Marxism–Leninism known as *juche* (self-reliance). Outsiders looked on, baffled. Since taking power in 1948, Kim had managed to create one of the most closed and warped societies on earth – crippled by a stricken economy, meagre harvests, food and fuel shortages, a decaying heavy-industrial base and a megalomaniac version of totalitarianism that, in Eastern Europe, had been swept away with the demise of Ceauşescu.[6]

Kim Jong-Il and friends

Adding to North Korea's pariah status was the symbolic slap by the global community when it chose the South Korean capital to host the 1988 summer Olympics. A gleaming, modern Seoul had relished the chance to welcome the world.[7] Yet Pyongyang was utterly defiant. Officials derided capitalism and contemptuously dismissed the 'mistakes' made by defective communist rulers elsewhere.[8] Often cited was the Soviet Union's decision in the autumn of 1990 to establish diplomatic relations with South Korea from 1 January 1991. The lure of desperately needed economic aid from Seoul (some $3 billion) had proved stronger for Gorbachev than ideological fidelity to Pyongyang.[9] Not only did Kim accuse the USSR of joining ranks with America and South Korea by selling out to capitalism, while dumping his country like 'worn-out-shoes', he even depicted this as a deliberate attempt to 'overthrow the socialist regime in our country'. North Korea, he fumed, would never capitulate like Eastern Europe, and never be annexed by South Korea in the way the GDR had been absorbed by West Germany.[10]

Relations with Moscow hit their lowest point ever. Now that Kim was unable to count on Soviet support, 'self-reliance' took on a new urgency and even flexibility. In a move that seemed intended to stem the country's growing isolation, on 29 May 1991 North Korea announced that it would apply for separate membership of the United Nations.[11] This amounted to a major policy reversal. Ever since the end of the Korean War in 1953, the North had insisted that it was the true government of the whole peninsula. But faced now with Moscow's warnings that the USSR would no longer use its permanent seat on the Security Council to veto Seoul's application for separate, independent membership, Kim had apparently been forced to follow suit. For South Korea's president Roh Tae-woo the removal of the Soviet veto represented a major victory in his aggressive courtship of Moscow, using the prospect of Korean credits, trade and investments as bait. This was part of what Roh called his wider 'nord-politik' – including improved relations with old enemies Japan and China – all of which increased the pressure on Pyongyang.[12]

South Korean diplomacy was warmly supported by Bush who promised in July 1991, 'We intend to be vigorous participants in matters of the Pacific' – engaging with China, Russia and Japan. But, he assured Roh, 'the US–Korea relationship will never be a pawn to any other relations. It will stand on its own feet.'[13] The South Korean leader was pleased to hear this but reminded Bush that 'in the Asia-Pacific region we do not have a new international order yet'. He even had the temerity to add 'I will take this opportunity to urge that the president refrain from frequent trips to Europe and come to the Asia-Pacific region.'[14]

With Pyongyang increasingly ostracised by the great powers, relations between the two Koreas started to thaw. Both countries were admitted to the UN on 17 September 1991. Three months later, on 13 December 1991 Kim and Roh signed an Agreement on Reconciliation, Non-Aggression, Exchange and Cooperation, with both sides promising to renounce the use of armed force against each other and stating that they would bring the Korean War formally to an end. They stopped short, however, of calling the accord a peace treaty: the South Korean press speaking instead of a 'peace regime' that would replace the 1953 armistice. Although the agreement stipulated talks about 'phased reductions in armaments, including the elimination of weapons of mass destruction and surprise-attack capabilities', it was clear that most real problems between the North and the South had not been put to rest by this piece of paper. But, as an American diplomat stated, 'It might make people feel better. And it is something that they can point to as progress, after a year of serious talks.'[15] The same day the two Koreas further announced that they would conduct a separate set of negotiations over nuclear issues later that month. And so, on New Year's Eve they initialled a Joint Declaration for a Non-Nuclear Korean Peninsula, banning the manufacturing, possession, storage, deployment and use of nuclear weapons.[16]

The backdrop to these dramatic moves was Bush's unilateral announcement on 27 September 1991 inviting Gorbachev to join him in eliminating all land and sea-based tactical nuclear weapons and getting rid of multiple warheads on intercontinental ballistic missiles. Bush's nuclear disarmament proposal – part of his security agenda after the Soviet coup – had been agreed in the NSC three weeks earlier. The reduction of arsenals would not only save money (to placate US tax payers and voters) but was also hoped to enhance global stability as a peace-insurance policy when the USSR was unravelling fast. In late September, with the core of the Soviet Union just about hanging together, Bush believed that Gorbachev was still in a position to ride the tide and to deliver. 'We now have an unparalleled opportunity to change the nuclear posture of both the United States and the Soviet Union.' The president added that 'America must lead again as it always has, as only it can.' America must 'provide the inspiration for lasting peace.'[17]

Gorbachev warmly reciprocated on 6 October. He could do so, after his new military chiefs turned out to be much more amenable than their pro-putschist predecessors. Bush, he said, had made an 'important initiative' that 'worthily continues the cause begun in Reykjavik' at the 1986 summit. By acting in this way 'we are resolutely advancing the process of disarmament, thereby moving close to the goal that was proclaimed in early 1986 – that of a non-nuclear world, a safer and more stable world'. Bush was pleased with what he called this 'good news for the whole world'. In consequence, the US promptly started removing its (already obsolete) warheads from post-Wall Germany and its still fully operational nuclear missiles from South Korea. The global nature of the superpowers' agreement provided convenient cover, preventing Pyongyang from claiming that the US had embarked on a withdrawal from South Korea in response to North Korean pressure.[18] More generally, it was good news for the cause of non-proliferation that Bush's arms reduction gamble with Gorbachev had worked. Indeed, their accord on the removal and destruction of hundreds of their battlefield nuclear weapons also created a basis for the START II treaty that Yeltsin and Bush would come to sign in January 1993.[19]

Taking his cue from Bush, on 8 November 1991 Roh formally proposed the denuclearisation of the whole peninsula. If implemented, South Korea would no longer possess or store nuclear weapons on its soil, although, he stressed, Seoul would remain ultimately protected by the US nuclear umbrella. The denuclearisation declaration would also prohibit Seoul from having nuclear reprocessing or uranium enrichment facilities. In this light Roh called on North Korea to abandon any plans it might harbour to develop and build its own nuclear bomb.[20]

The North Korean nuclear programme was, and remains, a tangled story.[21] Since the 1950s Kim had legitimately acquired from the Soviet Union at least two small nuclear reactors for purely research purposes, of which the most recent known example had come on stream in 1987 at the Yongbyon site about ninety kilometres north of Pyongyang. These test facilities had been placed under International Atomic Energy Agency (IAEA) safeguards. Most recently, Kim had managed in 1985 to secure a contract for a new, much bigger electric power reactor from Gorbachev on condition that he would honour the Non-Proliferation Treaty (NPT), to which Pyongyang acceded the same year. Yet it never completed the NPT's safeguarding or inspections agreements; and refused to do so again in early September 1991 when Kim sought to link acceptance of the inspection regime to US missile withdrawal from South Korea. But Bush was not to be blackmailed. As he told Roh in July: 'The big thing is not to link US presence with the illegal things they are doing.' By now US satellite surveillance had identified a previously undisclosed home-made reactor being constructed on the Yongbyon site, together with another new building that appeared to be a plutonium-reprocessing facility, essential for developing nuclear weaponry. Indeed by late 1991 there were persistent and apparently 'incontrovertible' Western intelligence reports that Kim was only one to five years away from completing an atomic bomb.[22]

Pushed into a corner, on 26 December 1991 Kim flatly denied that his country had nuclear weapons or intended to build them. And he defiantly listed a new set of conditions that would have to be fulfilled before he would allow inspection of the Yongbyon site. One of these was his demand that any talks about inspections would be conducted with the USA, not the government in Seoul. But Bush's America had no intention of engaging with North Korea. As the president once told Roh, 'Your having met with Gorbachev in no way implies that at this point I'll sit down with Kim.'[23]

The Bush administration's calculatingly hands-off approach to the Korean question – encouraging North and South along the path of détente, while hoping that the Pyongyang regime might crumble like the small communist states in Europe – did not mean that it ignored the nuclear-proliferation issue. In fact, Washington's concerns had been heightened in the spring of 1991 after the Kuwait War – when the question of Saddam Hussein's weapons of mass destruction (especially nuclear and chemical) became a matter of intense public debate.

Hitherto, both Iraq and North Korea had been Soviet client states. And the USSR had closely policed its sphere, preventing for a long time several Third World states from developing nuclear military capabilities. China had managed to emerge from the Soviet shadow, becoming a nuclear power in 1964, but otherwise Moscow's alternative to the Western regime of international control had successfully limited nuclear proliferation. With the Soviet collapse, however, things had begun to unravel.[24]

As US–Russian relations turned cooperative in the new world order of 1991–2, relations between the Kremlin and the North Korean regime fell apart. While from the Soviet perspective, Gorbachev had been extremely frustrated by Kim's unwillingness to reform, Yeltsin, as leader of Russia, was angry at Pyongyang's reluctance to open up and to fully adhere to the NPT. And, with both eager to get their hands on Roh's credits, the Kremlin was willing to cut North Korea loose: threatening Kim with the freezing of military contracts, squeezing fuel supplies and halting construction of the new nuclear plant, if they continued to 'refuse to immediately join the IAEA regime'.[25]

Crucially, just as Russia turned the screws on Pyongyang, so did China. Not only had Yeltsin's Russia approached the Chinese about an assumed 'common interest', urging them to push North Korea to comply with the NPT on inspections for 'quickest attainment of stability on the Korean peninsula',[26] Beijing also cold-shouldered Kim by beginning to shift its own economic interests to the North's booming rival, South Korea; in the autumn of 1992 China officially recognised the Seoul government – one of its last Cold War enemies. And there were even signs of Japanese rapprochement with the PRC and South Korea for Pyongyang to worry about. Beijing – post-Tiananmen – was desperate for Japan to resume the flow of aid and investment, Tokyo kept hoping its yen would 'help the modernisation of China', and Seoul was pushing its particular agenda of building 'trilateral US–Korea–Japan relations'. Nevertheless, second only to China, Japan was North Korea's largest trading partner and also a G7 member; Kim therefore hoped that Tokyo would offer help with loans and food. But the Japanese too played tough, making aid dependent on North Korean compliance with the NPT as well as dangling the threat of trade sanctions. Fenced in, Kim went on the offensive, playing a dual game of engagement with Seoul while pursuing the quest for his own 'bomb'.[27]

The dramatic reduction of Moscow's influence in the Pacific region was part of a larger geopolitical problem. In the absence of the Soviet 'policeman', America, now the sole superpower, faced the prospect of having to maintain order worldwide at a time of greatly increased instability. Washington found itself confronted with numerous unruly and dysfunctional developing countries – in Latin America, Africa, the Middle East and South East Asia. The threats to stability ranged from narcotics-trafficking and civil war to military coups and mass famine. Top of the list, however, was the danger of post-Cold War nuclear proliferation, of which North Korea seemed the most alarming example.[28]

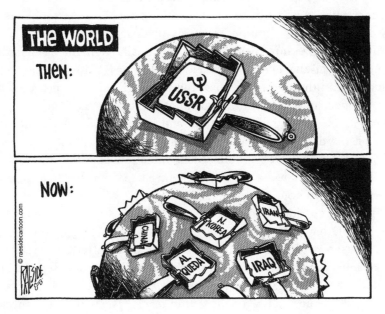

Order and orders

In March 1991, after Saddam's humiliation in Kuwait, the spotlight swung from the Middle East to Asia. Stanley Spector and Jacqueline Smith published an article in the journal *Arms Control Today* entitled, 'North Korea: The Next Nuclear Nightmare'. And on 10 April, Pulitzer Prize-winning journalist Leslie H. Gelb followed with a blistering *New York Times* op-ed entitled 'The Next Renegade State' – 'Run by a vicious dictator', with Scud missiles (that it sold to Syria and probably Iran), 'a million men under arms', and likely to possess nuclear weapons – North Korea, according to Gelb, was perhaps the most dangerous state in the world. The concept of a 'renegade' or 'rogue' state entered international parlance.[29]

Relations between the United States and North Korea[30] became a cat-and-mouse game, with Kim alternating between brinkmanship and reconciliation. Bush's response was typically cautious. On his two-day stopover in Seoul on 6–7 January 1992 – hardly the kind of sustained visit that Roh had urged – the president quietly warned the South Korean leader against moving too fast in dealing with Kim. He praised the 'positive developments' in efforts to halt North Korea's nuclear weapons programme and stressed the 'prospects for real peace' that he believed were now 'brighter than at any point in the past four decades'; 'and yet', Bush insisted, 'paper promises won't keep the peace'. Pyongyang had to 'demonstrate its sincerity, to meet the obligations it undertook when it signed the Non-Proliferation Treaty six years ago'.[31]

Under US pressure, North Korea did finally sign the safeguarding agreements at the end of January. And so IAEA inspections could commence in the summer of 1992. But the North Koreans proved reluctant to open up some facilities, fuelling suspicions that Pyongyang was hiding its weapons-grade plutonium and its missile development. With Kim on the defensive, in March 1993, less than two months after Bush left office, North Korea announced its intention to withdraw from the NPT. What ensued was a cyclical ratcheting-up of tensions to crisis point alternating with bouts of reconciliation.[32]

This game of hide and seek has continued ever since. Rogue states with WMD have been on the radar of every US president after George H. W. Bush – with North Korea proving the most intractable case of all. On 6 January 1992, in front of the South Korean National Assembly, Bush grandiloquently declared that an end to the forty-year-old division of the Korean peninsula was finally within reach. 'The winds of change are with us now. My friends, the day will inevitably come when this last wound of the Cold War struggle will heal. Korea will be whole again. I am absolutely convinced of it.'[33]

The world is still waiting.

So there was no easy exit from the Cold War on the Korean peninsula. And the other two major Pacific powers – Japan and China – were also caught in limbo between past and future while vying for position in a world that was being remade.

*

In 1989 Bush had made China his personal priority on taking office, while Baker focused on Japan. Tokyo had absorbed much of his attention when Reagan's Treasury Secretary in 1985–8, especially on the issues of market opening and exchange rates. He had called for a 'global partner-ship', and was keen to develop this when Secretary of State. His aim was to wean Japan from its introverted, mercantilist mentality and turn it into an outward-looking economic and political power, not only with strong ties to the USA but also engaged in a broader pan-Pacific commu-nity including the smaller but powerful Asian 'tigers': South Korea, Singapore, Taiwan, Hong Kong, Thailand, Malaysia and Indonesia.[34]

America's post-war relationship with Japan was complex. In 1945 Japan's bid for Pacific domination had ended in total defeat and the mushroom cloud of the atomic bomb. Occupied and demilitarised by the United States, it became an American client during the Cold War. Yet that allowed Tokyo to concentrate on economic recovery, aided by its strong techno-logical base and its remarkably rapid transition from a rural to an industrial economy. Highly protectionist at home, Japan became a major exporting nation from the 1970s – able to undercut the West in areas such as cars, computers and machine tools because of its low labour costs and superior production methods. By 1985 Japan, with its GDP second only to that of the much more populous USA, had become the world's leading creditor nation, while Reagan's America was the globe's top debtor. Two years later Tokyo overtook New York as the leading stock market in terms of the volume of equities. By now talk of 'Japan as Number One' – after the title of historian Ezra Vogel's 1979 bestseller – had become part of America's public discourse. *Newsweek* ran a cover story in February 1988 entitled 'The Pacific Century: Is America in Decline?'[35]

In other words, Baker's concern about Japan was understandable and it did not abate even when he was preoccupied as Secretary of State in

1989–91 with Europe's great transition from the Cold War. If economics is the basis of power – as a 1987 global bestseller by historian Paul Kennedy emphasised – then the United States could not afford to ignore economic rivals. What's more Japan was being emulated and chased by the other high-productivity, low-cost Asian economies whose cumulative success reinforced a sense that the transatlantic relationship might no longer be the axis that mattered.[36] The dissolution of bipolarity only accentuated the perception of an emerging regional constellation in the Far East, revolving around Japan. In fact, related to the powerful influence of Japanese trade, aid and investment linkages in the Asia-Pacific area, there were also signs in Tokyo of a desire to promote narrower, East Asian institutions explicitly aimed at excluding the West and particularly the USA. Indeed, the possibility of an emerging 'yen bloc' was a threat to America's dollar hegemony and its push for a truly global free-trade organisation post-GATT – a goal avidly pursued by Washington throughout the Uruguay Round of multilateral tariff negotiations since 1986.[37]

Alarm about the yen was the thin end of a big wedge. What if, propelled by Japan's economic power, broader political and cultural challenges might arise from Asia? These would call into question assumptions in the West and especially Washington that the end of the Cold War repre-sented another 'end of ideology' (like the vanquishing of fascism in 1945), when claims about the universality of Western values, and an international community based upon them, could be made real. The spread of Japan's 'economic miracle' to the developing countries of East Asia implied a successful formula of development different to that promulgated by the West – one based on distinctly 'Asian values'. And the rapidity of economic growth in the Asia-Pacific region, led by what Henry Kissinger already in 1973 had called the 'economic superpower' of Japan, was thought by some to signal a challenge to the key norms of the post-war international order that had been defined by the United States.[38]

American anxiety about a Japanese sphere of influence in the Pacific was exacerbated by the evident failure of the 'western hemisphere', trad-itionally the USA's own backyard by the late 1980s. Most of the developing world had ended the decade massively debt-ridden, but Latin America was an exceptionally bad case after what was called its 'lost decade'. Narcotics became the main source of employment and export earnings, with the Colombian drug cartels of Medellin and Cali providing all the USA's cocaine and 80% of its marijuana. In Bush's eyes the drug problem

amounted to a 'modern plague'. And economic failure spawned the continuance of military rule or the entrenchment of one-party states.

Central America, in particular, was the cockpit of civil wars in the
1980s backed by the two superpowers. While the Soviets, and their Cuban
proxies, provided finance, arms and ideological support for revolutionary
fronts, particularly in Nicaragua and El Salvador, Reagan had hit back
by sending the Marines into the Caribbean island of Grenada in October
1983 to put down a Marxist coup. In December 1989 Bush sent US troops
into Panama in a operation that toppled the country's drug-baron dictator,
Manuel Noriega, and led to his extradition for trial in the USA. One of
the legacies of such instability was a flood of migrants and refugees to
'El Norte' – Uncle Sam's promised land. The decade 1981–90 saw 7.3
million official migrants entering the USA, nearly a quarter of them from
Mexico, as well as millions more 'illegals'. By 1990 'Hispanics' amounted
to 9% of the official US population.[39]

Whatever the apparent appeal of Western-style democracy in post-
Soviet Europe, fostering it in parts of the American sphere of influence
was clearly a struggle – not least because the White House believed firmly
that democratic institutions would only be viable if rooted in liberal
economics. So in Baker's words, it was 'common sense for the United
States to lead alliances of free-market democracies in Asia, Europe and
the Americas in support of democracy and economic liberty'. The White
House was especially energetic in pushing free trade and open markets.[40]
One can see this in a variety of ways. On the global level, the Bush
administration played a pivotal role in the Uruguay Round, even though
the deal that finally led to the creation of the World Trade Organisation
was not sewn up until 1994, and Treasury Secretary Nicholas Brady's
dollar-denominated 'Brady Bonds' in 1989[41] were a novel way to facilitate
debt restructuring in developing countries. On the regional level, the
administration promoted the Enterprise for the Americas Initiative (EAI),
supporting economic reform from Tierra del Fuego to the Rio Grande
on the motto of 'trade, not aid'. In this area Japan was particularly
supportive through its own debt initiative, the 1988 'Miyazawa Plan' which
subsequently fed into the Brady Bonds programme, helping among others
Mexico, Brazil, Costa Rica, Nicaragua and Venezuela clear up their debt
arrears, and through cooperation in the Multilateral Investment Fund
(providing technical assistance to Latin America and the Caribbean).
These actions, implemented in close collaboration with Washington,
earned Tokyo Bush's genuine gratitude.[42]

On the institutional level Washington's priorities were the North American Free Trade Area (NAFTA) and the Asia-Pacific Economic Cooperation (APEC) forum. Washington worked intensively with Canada and Mexico to create NAFTA. The negotiations were largely thrashed out in the Bush era, with the agreement eventually signed on 17 December 1992.[43] The APEC forum, founded in November 1989, was an Australian initiative, but it was warmly supported by Bush who considered it 'the best vehicle for cooperation in Asia'.[44] NAFTA and APEC were meant to institutionalise – and secure US influence in – the ongoing liberalisation of regional economies in Latin America and East Asia. (These were the initiatives that ran in parallel to US steps to formalise relations with the EC 92 – first through a 'Transatlantic Declaration' in 1990, then in 1995 and 1998 via the New Transatlantic Agenda and the Transatlantic Economic Partnership.) As Baker asserted in a speech in New York entitled 'A New Pacific Partnership' on 26 June 1989: 'By furthering the development and integration of market economies within the international system, we strengthen the collective force of those who share our principles.'[45]

For Baker, Japan was essential to realising this vision. 'Economic achievements carry new responsibilities,' he insisted. With Japan now a 'world power', the two of them had to 'build a new and truly *global partnership*' – one based on 'creative sharing of global responsibilities' and on a 'new mechanism to increase economic cooperation'.[46] A foundation had been laid in June 1989, when Bush and Japan's prime minister Sosuke Uno had launched the joint Structural Impediments Initiative (SII) – an attempt to rectify the seriously asymmetrical trade and payments situation between the two countries. This agreement was signed twelve months later in June 1990 but, as Tokyo made clear, the figures would not change overnight. Essentially Japan remained reluctant to lift barriers against foreign goods. The Japanese justified such protectionism euphemistically as their long struggle to become an 'import superpower'. In short, SII and trade talks did not resolve the more fundamental problems of US–Japanese relations.[47]

Beneath the surface Japan was increasingly worried about the resilience of its own economy. Success in the manufacturing sectors was masking serious weaknesses in banking and real estate. And we now know that the halving of the Nikkei stock index in 1990 was an early sign that Japan's bubble was about to burst.[48] But that was not apparent at the time to Americans obsessed with Tokyo's export dominance, financial penetration and trade imbalances. What if, during a crisis, Tokyo gained leverage over Washington by threatening to withdraw its investments from the USA? And if Japan was such an economic power-house, why did the United States so heavily subsidise its defence? As Bush faced re-election amid public gloom about the United States falling into recession, the friction in Japanese–American relations over 'protec-tionism' and 'burden-sharing' suddenly surfaced as a major matter of public and political concern – all the worse, because these issues had been sidelined from the American agenda by the sustained crisis in Europe.[49]

At the start of his presidency, Bush – on his first foreign trip – had, en route to Beijing and Seoul, briefly stopped over in Tokyo to attend the funeral of Emperor Hirohito. In September 1989 he received an invitation to pay a full state visit,[50] the first since Reagan in November 1983.[51] The visit, which kept being postponed, was intended to lead to general agreement among key US allies in the Pacific on how best to foster stability and security in the region in the post-Cold War world. But the contentious issues of US–Japanese relations kept getting in the way: Bush told the Japanese prime minister Toshiki Kaifu frankly in April 1991 that he worried about 'anti-Japanese feeling in the Congress', a hangover from the Second World War.[52]

In any case, Japan was itself seriously grappling with its own history. The experience of wartime defeat and post-war occupation had left an enduring antipathy to militarism among the Japanese population and political elites, evident in Tokyo's refusal to send troops and warships to the Gulf in 1991. Japanese participation in UN peacekeeping operations required new legislation to be passed by the Diet, which meant over-coming both historical qualms and also anti-American sentiment. The leader of the Japanese governing Liberal Party, Ichiro Ozawa, told Bush in late March 1991 that Tokyo was fully aware of America's 'dissatisfac-tion and frustration' in relation to its Gulf participation. He agreed Japan needed to prove its readiness to play a new international role commen-surate with its status as an economic superpower. Only then could it be 'a true ally of the United States' and 'a true member of the international community'. This was also the prerequisite for achieving Japan's much-coveted goal – a seat on the UN Security Council.[53]

A second legacy of history was the unresolved business with the USSR over the Northern Territories. These were the four Kuril Islands of Habomai, Shikotan, Kunashiri and Etorofu located off the coast of

Hokkaido, which had belonged to Japan since 1855 but were seized and incorporated into the Soviet Union in September 1945, with all Japanese residents deported by 1949.[54] In 1986 Gorbachev had announced a new approach to Soviet interests in Asia – withdrawing troops from Afghanistan, encouraging Vietnamese restraint in Cambodia, easing tensions with China and proposing special economic zones in the Soviet Far East including making Vladivostok an open port. He had subsequently visited Deng in Beijing in May 1989 and began normalising its relations with US client South Korea through a meeting with Roh in San Francisco in June 1990 – the first time that the heads of state of the Soviet Union and South Korea had held formal discussions. Gorbachev declared that the Pacific would become 'the Mediterranean of the future', as he celebrated a new era in which the superpowers were no longer 'on opposite sides of the barricades of Asian revolutions' but instead shared in 'new standards of economic efficiency set by Asian nations'.[55]

In spite of Moscow's 'peace offensive' and the 'new breeze' that seemed to be blowing,[56] Soviet–Japanese relations remained fraught because of their territorial dispute – which Tokyo saw as a 'residue of Stalinist expansionism'. This dispute was the reason why the two countries had so far been unable to sign a Second World War peace treaty. It also explained why Japan throughout 1990 had resisted offering financial assistance to the Soviet Union – though it theoretically had the yen as a lever. To be sure, Japan was very keen to resolve this issue.[57] And, watching Bonn's adroit use of chequebook diplomacy in settling the German question in 1990, Tokyo believed that an overt bribe of credits and aid in return for the islands might have some effect on a financially desperate Gorbachev. But Japan was grossly overestimating its coercive power and underestimating the significance of Kohl's cultivation of political friendships. The Kaifu government also ignored the weight of history, prestige consciousness and nationalist sentiment prevailing in Moscow, irrespective of Russia's socio-economic malaise. For Gorbachev Japan simply was not important enough to warrant the risk of a nationalist backlash at home by making a pre-emptive territorial concession to a former foe and now rival. In his view, the Soviet superpower could proudly prevail without falling for the yen of upstart Japan.[58]

Anyhow, by the spring of 1991 the situation in Moscow was no longer conducive to any deal. The communist old guard (Kryuchkov and Yazov) had successfully pressured Gorbachev not to take the Japanese financial bait. And Yeltsin, after initially leaning to a negotiated solution with

Japan, increasingly challenged Gorbachev in nationalistic language and also came out hard on the side of those who repudiated any idea of giving up the islands. Indeed, after a visit to Kunashir in August 1990, the Russian president had declared that he considered the place so beautiful that it must not be abandoned but developed into a resort. With Yeltsin emerging as protector of the motherland, Gorbachev could not afford to look like a man selling out in some kind of grubby land-for-cash deal. So Tokyo concluded that the Soviet leader did 'not seem to be in a position to make a decision on any issue'. Though Gorbachev became the first ever Soviet leader to visit Japan in April 1991, this long-awaited summit was largely a non-event because it yielded no breakthrough on the Kuril Islands.[59]

Tokyo was, however, pleased that Washington (and Beijing) were on its side. A few days ahead of the London G7 + 1 meeting in July 1991, Bush and Kaifu coordinated their positions. The president did not believe that they would be asked by Gorbachev for 'a check', but, he told his Japanese counterpart categorically, 'if we are, we do not have one'. This was not about snubbing Gorbachev, but 'before there is real money', Bush declared, 'there must be real progress' and that included a Soviet opening to Japan on the Kuril Islands. The USA 'support you on the Northern Territories', Bush promised Kaifu.[60]

Confident about US backing, Kaifu addressed Gorbachev directly when the Soviet leader attended the later G7 sessions. 'New thinking needs to involve the Asia-Pacific region. We have seen some progress with China and Korea; this is positive. Japan is your neighbour in the Pacific.' He added: 'improvement in our relations is important beyond the bilateral context. We met and talked about the Peace Treaty. This would be significant for world peace and prosperity.'[61]

Gorbachev avoided engaging the Japanese premier. Instead, he warned Bush at their summit session in Novo-Ogarevo in late July that the Japanese would not be content with their economic expansionism, because Tokyo would want to be a 'military power' as well – taking advantage of its defence alliance with America 'for its own purposes'. But the US president was unfazed. Unconcerned about alleged 'Japanese imperialism', he instead pressed Gorbachev on the Kuril Islands issue: 'it would help if you could work out the Northern Territories', adding 'if you engage with their economy, it would discourage militarism'.[62]

Their discussion was, however, inconclusive, and after the coup and subsequent break-up of the Soviet Union, the issue fizzled out. Yet it reappeared in the run-up to the Munich G7 summit of July 1992, when the Americans toyed with the idea of dangling before Yeltsin the expansion of the G7 into a G8 once Russia was 'in a state of peace with all the Seven, i.e., Russia concludes a peace treaty with Japan that resolves the Northern Territories'.[63] But, again, there were no breakthroughs in Munich. Russia's economy remained dire and Bush's position was clear: 'Yeltsin is trying hard and we have to bet on him' but 'we don't want to pour money down a rathole'.[64] The IMF and EC were equally frustrated[65] and it was clear that with no Russian flexibility on the Kuril Islands, Japan was determined to keep its purse strings tight. In the autumn, confronted with ever growing anti-reformist factions at home, Yeltsin unsurprisingly pulled out at the last minute from planned summit talks in Tokyo, complaining that Japan was trying to take advantage of Russia's economic problems to pressure it into returning the four disputed islands.[66]

This ended any hopes for a conciliatory resolution. The islands obviously had national(ist) meaning for Russia, while Japan stubbornly tied any offer of economic assistance to the return of those Northern Territories. With neither side willing to compromise and move on from their historical antagonisms, Russo-Japanese relations had reached an impasse. And so the territorial legacy from the Second World War proved a major obstacle to forging a new world order in Asia.[67]

Similarly, creating détente between Japan and China proved difficult, even though Deng Xiaoping, who himself had fought against Japanese imperialism in China, attached huge importance to improving bilateral relations with Japan. This followed diplomatic normalisation in 1972, which in principle made possible a strategic alignment with Tokyo and therefore Washington against a common Soviet enemy. From the late 1970s Deng had embarked on a charm offensive with Japanese politicians – touring factories and wooing Japan's government and business to invest in China. From the other side, Tokyo took a clear strategic decision to engage and work with the PRC. During the 1980s, 70% of total Japanese foreign aid went to China. And as a major technology and knowledge partner, Japan clearly proved crucial to China's modernisation. Chinese economic reform and market-opening would not have succeeded so quickly and so fully without this assistance.[68]

But politics remained intractable. In 1989, after the Tiananmen Square massacre, Japan joined in Western sanctions against China. Tokyo was keen to restore relations as soon as possible – doing so with a green light from Bush, whose own hands were tied.[69] But the resumption in November 1990 of Japan's development loan programme to the PRC,[70] as well as Kaifu's trip to Beijing in 1991 and the exchange of visits in 1992 between President Jiang Zemin and Emperor Akihito, did not fundamentally change the situation. Despite all these efforts, the Sino-Japanese relationship remained edgy. To Tokyo, the supplicant for Japanese aid and investment was beginning to look more like a regional rival to Japan's own interests. Indeed China, while seeking Japanese help in securing finance and technology from industrialised nations, was increasingly determined to achieve its goals free from political dependency. And the Chinese had not forgotten or forgiven Japan for its aggression and atrocities in China in the war of 1937–45.[71] The burden of history, and the fact that Japan had done little to confront its own past openly, was a black mark against the country in Beijing and throughout Asia.[72]

Consequently China, as much as Russia, was cool towards Japan's quest for a permanent seat on the UN Security Council. And as the PRC looked warily for any signs of a reawakened Japanese imperialism, it became especially uneasy about Tokyo's proposed legislation in 1991 on UN peacekeeping operations, which would authorise for the first time since the Second World War the dispatch of up to 2,000 Japanese troops overseas. To the relief of China – and that of South Korea and Singapore, also former victims of Japan – the bill was not approved by the upper house on 10 December 1991, revealing deep fissures in Japan's society and the political establishment. Indeed, in the run-up to the vote, Japan found itself engulfed in a tide of anxiety that this legislation would be a first step on the road to rearmament. The timing of the debate was particularly sensitive. On the one hand, Pacific-region fears of Japanese militarism had reached a peak a week before with the fiftieth anniversary of the attack on Pearl Harbor. On the other hand, partisan squabbling in the Diet, with strong rightist undertones, prevented passage of a proposal for Japan to express regret over the Second World War and to apologise to the USA.[73]

As the world entered the post-Cold War era, Japan clearly was neither ready to face up to its wartime past nor prepared to assume a leading role globally commensurate with its economic might. Both votes in the Diet doomed Tokyo's hopes of using the occasion of Bush's visit – now rescheduled for early January 1992 – to really deliver on burden-sharing. Adding to the problem, by the end of 1991 Japan's economy was seriously sagging. The budget deficit had grown and the government vacillated about whether to borrow, raise taxes or both. In so many ways Japan seemed paralysed and unable to use the exit from the Cold War as an opening into its much-touted Pacific century. This was hardly an auspicious time for Bush's presidential tour of the region.

Nor were the auguries particularly favourable on the American side. The country was stuck in what some were calling the longest recession since the 1930s, with unemployment at 7.1%, up from 5.6% twelve months earlier. In fact, since May 1990, 2.3 million American jobs had been lost: a staggering number. With his popularity plummeting Bush needed to be seen taking serious steps to revive the economy and give his election campaign a boost. So the twelve-day trip had been recalibrated from its original character as a goodwill mission by overlaying it with a strong business agenda. To flag this up Bush travelled with an entourage of twenty-one corporate chiefs including the bosses of Detroit's Big Three automakers.[74]

Trade proved a central theme at every place Bush visited. He left none of his hosts in any doubt that the Pacific nations' desire for a continued American security presence would have to be tied to a better two-way economic relationship. Following his promise to Americans to 'relentlessly pursue our mission' to create 'jobs, jobs, jobs' and to 'restore prosperity', Bush kept pressing his allies to lower their trade barriers, buy more American goods and thereby generate domestic growth, claiming that each $1 billion in exports sustained almost 20,000 US jobs. That message was especially geared to Japan, which by the start of 1992 had experienced a new surge of its trade surplus – now an astronomical $45 billion with the US, three-quarters of which comprised automobiles and auto parts – while only contributing about 40% of the cost of the large American military presence. But he took the same line everywhere else.[75]

His stop in Singapore, the first by an American president, worked well in terms of this agenda. Bush announced an agreement to shift the US Navy's 7th Fleet logistics operations from Subic Bay in the Philippines to Singapore harbour as part of the US effort to create a 'security network and fabric' woven among several Pacific nations. And he also unveiled an 'environmental partnership' with Asia to share research and technologies. 'This will be good – good for Asia's environment, good for American jobs,' he said. At the same time, he could be sure that Singapore's leaders, products of a political culture that frowned on dissent, were not likely to accuse Bush of double standards – preaching free trade but not practising it, even if they were privately battling their own issues with

Washington over stiff US duties on their textiles, electronics and pharmaceuticals. In sum, Singapore was a welcome pitstop and breather on Bush's four-nation odyssey.[76]

By contrast in Australia, Bush encountered hundreds of farmers protesting 'New Wheat Orders not New World Order'. They argued that American subsidies (under the Export Enhancement programme) were undercutting their country's exports, just as Washington complained the Europeans were doing to the United States. The Australian prime minister, Paul Keating, warned that US commercial policies could polarise the world into competing trade blocs.[77]

In South Korea too, although there was consensus of the North Korean threat and the importance of nuclear non-proliferation, Bush was met with street protests over what was perceived as heavy-handed American pressure to force Seoul to 'fully open' its agricultural markets. Likewise, in the days before Bush's arrival, his Japanese hosts did not contain their anger at Bush's blatant trade imperialism, with Japan's leading newspaper *Asahi Shimbun* blaming the White House for conducting 'gunboat diplomacy in economic areas'. Bush brushed off this criticism: 'We've never said we're totally pure. We're working for freer and fairer trade.' And so, he believed, should the others.[78]

The crunch discussions unfolded in Japan between 7 and 10 January. Behind the scenes Japanese and American negotiators worked desperately hard to hammer out two key documents during the president's four-day stay: the Tokyo Declaration on the Japan–US Global Partnership and the consequent Action Plan. The latter was supposed to include Japan's responses to American complaints about trade, especially relating to the car industry, and on this issue negotiations were particularly testy.[79] Japan bought more than 130,000 German-made automobiles in 1990 (mostly luxury cars by Mercedes and BMW) but purchased only about 30,000 American-made cars – of which 9,500 were Hondas assembled in the United States. The Big Three automobile execs who stepped off Air Force One in Tokyo were contemptuous of suggestions that the inferior quality of American cars, not Japanese trade barriers, were at the root of Chrysler's, Ford's and GM's poor sales: 'They don't have to preach to us,' said Chrysler boss Lee Iacocca. It didn't help that the prime minister Kiichi Miyazawa, although treating the Americans with studied politeness, at one point expressed 'compassion' for the state of the US economy.

Given the chilly atmosphere, the president's aides decided to bury any expectations of a major trade breakthrough from the talks. Instead, they played up the international-security aspects of the visit: 'You've got to look at this in the broader historical perspective of what just happened to the Soviet Union, and the end of the Cold War.' So they pointed to the signing of the other document, the Tokyo Declaration, which was to acknowledge the growing global influence of Japan and reiterate the shared responsibility of the two countries for world peace and prosperity also in the post-Cold War era. In Bush's staccato phrase: 'world leadership is at stake.'[80]

In the end, the symbolic declaration was issued, but no agreement could be reached to lower global trade barriers, nor any joint position formulated for the GATT negotiations. The spin on the meagre accord between the Big Eight car manufacturers (three American, five from Japan), to promote the purchases of American cars, amounted to no more than a 'promising step' toward opening Japan's huge markets to foreign companies. In truth, any real 'plan' had been shot down.[81]

The president put an optimistic gloss on the whole business, calling his trip to Japan 'highly productive' and praising the industry bosses who had accompanied him. But some in Bush's entourage were not so sanguine. Indeed, upon his return Chrysler chairman Iacocca unleashed a vitriolic attack on Japan, while Democratic congressmen denigrated the president's visit as a 'photo opportunity' gone wrong. For their part, Republicans kept low, with one congressional strategist quietly stating: 'The themes just didn't sell. The whole rearrangement was for political reasons, and it was transparent, and it didn't work.' In fact, 'the feeling up here', said an adviser to a leading Republican senator, was that the visit 'is best put behind us'.[82]

Playing ball? Bush in Tokyo

For Bush himself, the trip was 'the worst of times'.[83] It ended not only in political failure but also in a moment of personal humiliation, broadcast in embarrassingly graphic detail on NHK, Japan's state TV.[84]

On the evening of 8 January 1992 – the president's second full day in Japan, and day ten of his Pacific tour – Bush was guest of honour at a state dinner in the dining room of the Japanese prime minister's residence.

He sat in the centre of the top table with Miyazawa on his left and the premier's wife on his right. At 8.20 p.m. the president suddenly 'turned white as a sheet', closed his eyes, rolled his head to the left, vomited all over his host and slumped in his chair. 'He flopped backward like a falling curtain,' one of the dinner guests recounted. As seen on Japanese television, Barbara Bush leapt up horrified, put her arms around her husband, with a napkin wiped some vomit off his mouth, before moving away, saying 'Give him room.' Miyazawa and Secret Service agents gently lowered him to the floor. The president's face was immobile, his gaze distorted and distressed. It all happened very fast; those watching were in shock. But after a few seconds Bush's 'eyes fluttered open', said Commerce Secretary Robert Mosbacher, also a head-table guest and long-time friend: 'That was scary.'

A doctor checked Bush's heartbeat and blood pressure. He remained on the floor for nearly five minutes, before managing to quip to Miyazawa: 'Why don't you just roll me under the table and let me sleep it off while you finish the dinner.' Eventually he rose, to general applause. The soiled jacket of his blue suit had been removed. Bush smiled gamely, flashed his left thumb up in the air, hitched up his trousers, pumped Miyazawa's hand and then waved both his hands to the crowd, palms outstretched, as if to say that nothing was wrong. A Secret Service agent helped Bush don an olive drab overcoat as another smoothed the hair on the back of his head.

'I just wanted to get some attention,' Bush said to the diners as he walked steadily out of the room unaided at 8.31 p.m., joking and shaking hands, telling people to go on and have a good time. Shielded from photographers and television cameras by Japanese security agents holding up white sheets, he told reporters: 'I feel good.' And with that he climbed into his limousine and was driven, sitting up, to the state guest house about ten minutes away.

Barbara Bush stayed at the dinner which continued with the president's chair empty. Miyazawa appeared grim and shaken as he delivered his toast. Then Mrs Bush handed him a note. The prime minister nodded to the first lady, who smiled broadly and announced 'The Foreign Ministry called: the president's fine. He's resting at the Akasaka Palace.' After the premier's toast, Barbara Bush rose to speak. 'I can't explain what happened to George because it never happened before,' she said. 'But I'm beginning to think it's the ambassador's fault. He and George played the emperor and the crown prince in tennis today – and they were badly beaten. And we Bushes aren't used to that. So he felt worse than I thought.' Laughter all round, before Scowcroft delivered the president's toast.[85]

The whole incident stunned the 135 VIPs who were at the banquet as well as a global audience of millions, as the Japanese TV pictures were relayed around the world. The dinner images came to define the whole visit.[86]

What exactly had happened? Speculation was rife. Was it the food that Bush had eaten that had made him so ill? Or perhaps the sixteen-time-zone odyssey had been too much for him? It had been noted that Bush had looked fatigued throughout the tour and was visibly fighting off sleep during a state dinner in Singapore. The White House naturally brushed aside any imputation that he was no longer up to the job. According to press spokesperson Marlin Fitzwater: 'The president's schedule is one that he has carried out in similar fashion for more than three years, one that he enjoys' – frequently beginning with meetings shortly after sunrise and ending with big banquets that stretch well into the night. 'He has a very rigorous schedule. He is a very physical and able man, and', Fitzwater added forcefully, 'I don't expect any changes.' Still, at this moment in his presidency, Bush was obviously totally worn out – physically and mentally.[87]

What seems a more likely explanation for Bush's 'barfing' episode[88] was that the president was actually a victim of his own entourage. White House medical officers could not remember a trip when so many people – staffers, reporters and Secret Service agents – became ill. Doctors blamed it on a passing stomach flu that the travelling party had carried with them from the United States. Bush probably picked up the bug from those with him in the confined space of Air Force One.[89] Yet the president had doggedly continued with his duties, confessing in his diary: 'I felt very, very weak. I should have gone home, but I didn't.' At least it had not been another heart-skipping atrial fibrillation of the kind that had struck him eight months earlier as he jogged at Camp David. In Tokyo, he was given an electrocardiogram and it showed his heart rhythm to be 'perfect, absolutely perfect' as he was at pains to tell the world media next day. But the damage had been done.[90]

While it was almost a miracle that in his extraordinarily hectic thirty-six months in office something similar had not happened before, the timing of the incident was disastrous for a president fighting for re-election. Democrats, naturally, were eager to make the most of the videotape of Bush's Tokyo collapse. 'He's almost a metaphor for a sick, wobbly economy looking for a Japanese pill to make him recover,' said Mike McCurry, an adviser to presidential candidate Senator Bob Kerrey. Bush was furious about the whole business. 'That was the damnedest experience,' he jotted down, and it haunted the rest of his presidency.[91] What one journalist called the 'hopscotch' tour through two continents and two archipelagos had turned into what the German magazine *Der Spiegel* dubbed a 'descent into hell'.[92]

So Bush's visit made no significant difference to the state of the US–Japanese relationship. If anything, it served to spotlight all the difficulties. In truth, Japan's foreign relations were still stuck in the past. The Japanese had been unable or unwilling to overcome their historical guilt with regard to their great power rivals – Russia and China – in marked contrast to Germany's post-war policy. To be sure, Japan had renounced militaristic nationalism after 1945, but, paradoxically, that made it harder to assume international burden-sharing in the post-Cold War world.

Furthermore, the image of the 'new' Japan as an economic superpower proved to be a chimera. The country's prodigious economic growth was never translated into substantive political and military power. In fact, Premier Miyazawa readily let Washington take 'the leadership role in the post-Cold War world'.[93] And in 1992, the Japanese asset price bubble burst, leading to long-term stagnation. Japan's economic strength had rested on a policy of aggressive export promotion and a determinedly protectionist economy. The country was unwilling to open up and this was symptomatic of its inability to exercise broader influence in international affairs.[94]

Nor did Japan build effective bridges, politically as much as economically, with any of its meaningful neighbours: South Korea, Russia and China. Across the Pacific, there was certainly nothing similar to the process of regional integration accomplished by the EC in post-war Western Europe and then in post-Wall Europe as a whole. Japan's foreign-policy project seemed to assume that its geo-economic predominance as a creditor nation and export economy would be sufficient to hold the balance of power. Yet America's unipolar moment – despite the country's economic problems – showed that geopolitics remained essential for effective international leadership. Japan's Pacific century never dawned.

*

The US president's Asian hopscotch in January 1992 did not land on the country that really mattered for the Pacific future: the People's Republic of China. Bush, of course, remained eager to visit the PRC, just as at the very start of his presidency. But China was now in the post-Square era and this walled him in. Because of the Western sanctions regime against Beijing's human-rights violations, the White House could not openly conduct relations with Beijing, so any contacts had to be cultivated surreptitiously, away from the public eye.

Tiananmen was indeed an enormous setback for Sino-American relations – one from which they have arguably never fully recovered. What had seemed in early 1989 to be a blossoming 'friendship' became set, after the events of 4 June, on a much more contentious course.[95] According to sociologist Richard Madsen, Tiananmen 'troubled Americans far out of proportion to its direct cost in human life and suffering ... The tragedy in China was so upsetting for many Americans because it contradicted widely cherished American understandings about the meanings of their democratic values.' It was a 'drama' with a bad ending, when idealistic students – the voice of individualism, goodness and justice – did not triumph; instead democracy was crushed by a dictatorship in a brutal military crackdown. Worse still, this vicious act had been ordered by a leader whom the United States had come to admire and court – a human being whom *TIME* magazine had twice voted 'Man of the Year' (in 1978 and 1985) and who treated the US president as a *lao pengyou*. China had not walked through the 'door to freedom', a step that Bush believed would ensure peace and prosperity. Instead the door had been slammed in his face.[96]

Yet Bush was resolute in ensuring that relations with China did not go into another deep freeze, as during the Cultural Revolution. And he did so in two main ways. First, he tried to maintain backchannel contacts. To this end, he had sent his national security adviser Brent Scowcroft on two secret missions to Beijing in July and December 1989, and he also welcomed private visits to Beijing in the autumn of 1989 paid by ex-president Richard Nixon and former Secretary of State Henry Kissinger. Second, he was determined to ring-fence China policy by full use of his constitutional executive powers as president and commander-in-chief. In the aftermath of Tiananmen, with Congress and the press baying for retaliation, Bush pre-empted them by imposing moderate sanctions – including suspension of military cooperation and of high-level exchanges and curbs on international loans. But he did not recall the US ambassador. Bush had decided to play a long, pragmatic game, managed by him personally. Thus, the stage was set for a serious battle of wills between the White House and Capitol Hill on how to deal with Beijing in the future. Both House and Senate voted by overwhelming majorities that the sanctions enacted by Bush could not be lifted until there were assurances that China was making 'progress' on human rights. And Congress also imposed additional restrictions: suspending talks and funds for the expansion of US–Chinese trade and banning shipment of police equipment. Given the size of the majorities, Bush could not veto them: these were now red lines that he had to live with.[97]

The president favoured what one might call prudent pragmatism, not high-octane idealism, but he had to tread a fine line. 'How to handle this relationship', he noted in his diary on 24 June, was a 'very delicate matter'. On the one hand, he had to express some of the outrage felt by millions of Americans, and also by Washington's European allies. On the other, Bush was sure China's prickly leaders must not be humiliated or isolated: 'I am determined to try to preserve this relationship.' Cutting them off from the West and moving 'unilaterally' against them was dangerous because 'China is back on track a little with the Soviets, and they could indeed come back in much stronger'. So the president was ready to accept plenty of brickbats for appeasing a callous dictatorship: he had no doubt that China was there to stay and would do things its own way.[98]

Bush was right. Beijing would not be deflected from its version of state authoritarianism, directed by the CCP and guided by Chinese values. Deng had made that abundantly clear to Scowcroft during their July meeting. A further consequence of Tiananmen was that Sino-Soviet normalisation was put on the back burner for a while. Determined to stamp on all talk of political liberalisation, the PRC condemned perestroika and glasnost, accusing Gorbachev of the 'subversion of socialism'.[99] In fact, they utterly despised Gorbachev for destroying communist rule and the Soviet empire.

For Deng, 'unity and stability' were essential for China as a society and a state. But, as he made clear only five days after Tiananmen when he addressed the units enforcing martial law, he remained passionately committed to economic reform, combining Plan and market in what he would later call an 'organic synthesis' of 'socialist market economy' while 'opening our country to the outside world'.[100] Nevertheless, his politico-economic project faltered in 1989–90. Having crushed the student revolution, the ageing Deng, now eighty-five, pulled back from public gaze after Tiananmen and the forceful, conservative Premier Li Peng emerged as the dominant figure in the post-Square party reshuffle. Thereafter China turned in on itself, during a period marked by political consolidation and economic retrenchment. Li together with conservative party elder Yao Yilin (backed by Deng's rival Chen Yun) followed their programme of 'curing and rectification' – their euphemism for recentralising the economy, reviving the primacy of the Plan over markets and minimising foreign involvement. The intention was to get a grip on rampant inflation and balance the country's finances through militarily enforced austerity (reducing the resources consumed by the population), in the hope that low inflation and rapid growth would also cool the lingering fever for democratisation. Yet the immediate consequence of this policy reversal was a sharp recession as both output and demand fell.[101]

Despite this, Bush explored ways of trying to inject 'new impetus and vigour' into Sino-American relations. He was, however, always mindful that it had to be done in a triangular context. Scowcroft's second mission to Beijing in early December – straight after the president's Malta summit with Gorbachev – was intended to make sure that the Chinese did not feel out of the loop. What's more, this mission was not concealed because Bush hoped that the publicity could help break the congressional veto over US China policy.[102]

Arriving in Beijing on 9 December 1989 Scowcroft spoke to the press. 'I would not be honest if I did not acknowledge that we have profound areas of disagreement – on the events at Tiananmen, on the sweeping changes in Eastern Europe.' But, he added, in the forthcoming meetings, 'we seek to outline broad areas where agreement is possible and to isolate for another time those areas of disagreement'.[103]

This was also the line Scowcroft took in private. He told the new CCP general secretary Jiang Zemin of Gorbachev's view that 'the world was becoming a multipolar one with a rapidly unifying Europe, a strengthening Japan, China and potentially India as great powers of the world'. Scowcroft suggested the need for a 'US–Soviet cooperative approach to this new multipolar world'. He made clear that the US had no particular interest in such an approach but did not deny that the world was 'changing rapidly' and that 'a different coalition of forces and powers' was possible. In that context he stressed the value of maintaining the 'strategic relationship' that had developed over the years between the USA and the PRC who, he stressed, had 'no points of direct conflict with each other

in strategic matters'. Scowcroft pointed particularly to their close cooperation on Afghanistan and Cambodia, where the results had been 'very
positive, both for the two countries and for the world as a whole'.
Regardless of how Soviet–American relations developed in the future,
he assured Jiang that the US looked forward to 'resolving the current
problems' between the two of them in order to 'continue and accelerate
such a relationship'.[104]

Side-by-side, trying to keep in step: Brent Scowcroft and
Jiang Zemin in Beijing

While Scowcroft sketched the architecture in cooperative terms, his
companion Lawrence Eagleburger was much blunter. 'As the diplomat of
this trip,' he told Foreign Minister Qian Qichen, 'let me be undiplomatic.
My impression is that we are engaged in a kabuki dance. You say, and we
accept, that there has to be movement on our side before you can move.
We say to you, and are sincere, that there has to be movement on your
side. We are now circling each other, each waiting for the other to move.'[105]
    To remain in dialogue, movement was needed on four central issues.
These were the lifting of martial law, the release of dissident Fang Lizhi,
World Bank loans and the removal of sanctions. In the first few weeks
some progress seemed to be made. In fact, Beijing made its first move
straight after the Scowcroft–Eagleburger visit on 12 December. Responding
to US concerns over Chinese missile sales to Syria and Libya, the PRC's
Foreign Ministry declared that, except for the ICBM sale to Saudi Arabia

in 1987, 'China has never sold, nor is planning to sell, missiles to any Middle East country.'[106] A week later, on 19 December 1989, Bush lifted a congressional ban on loans to companies doing business with China and also approved – on grounds of US 'national interest' – the export of three communications satellites to be launched by Chinese carrier rockets in 1991 and 1992.[107] On 10 January 1990 China lifted martial law in Beijing. Within hours the United States announced that it was easing its blanket opposition to World Bank loans to China, supporting lending on a case-by-case basis for humanitarian loans.

Yet the kabuki dance did not always proceed smoothly. On 18 January Beijing announced the release of 573 persons detained after the Tiananmen Square crackdown, but Bush concluded that this was essentially window dressing intended to influence American opinion. There was no general amnesty; and the strict laws banning dissent remained in force in China. So he took no steps in response. Instead, in early February, in order to get the State Department budget approved, Bush signed the Foreign Relations Authorisation bill. This included clauses enacting in legislation the economic sanctions and the restrictions on arms sales which he had applied to the PRC in an executive order right after Tiananmen. And, in another effort to propitiate Congress, when Bush offered his regular annual extension of 'most favoured nation' status to China, he used this as a lever to extract the release of Fang Lizhi and his wife to the United States.[108]

The administration's efforts to keep engaged with China[109] were proving hard going. Testifying to the fiercely hostile Senate Foreign Relations Committee, Eagleburger argued that 'contacts and relationships could only help promote reform within China and enhance respect for human rights'. Such contacts, he added, 'also help shorten the periods of tension' between the PRC and the USA. But he admitted that overall 'not enough' had been done by China in improving its human-rights record to be able to move on in any meaningful way. The White House was well aware that China depended 'almost entirely on export revenues for the hard currency needed to service its foreign debt of nearly $40 billion' and was therefore 'desperately trying to increase exports'. But since Beijing could not be bought on human rights, 'any significant overtures to thaw the Sino-American relationship', as Baker saw it, 'were neither justified nor possible'.[110]

So at the G7 summit in Houston in July 1990 Bush was happy to back the two proposals presented by Japanese prime minister Toshiki Kaifu. First, to keep the sanctions regime 'under review' in order that the West could respond to 'positive developments' in China, and, second, for Tokyo to proceed with a large yen loan to the PRC. On the latter point, Kaifu and Bush clashed with Kohl, who was supported by Mitterrand. Though ultimately unsuccessful, the Europeans' objections were revealing, namely that the G7 did too much for China and too little for the Soviet Union: 'We act as if reforms were taking place in China, and none in the Soviet Union,' complained Kohl. 'Think of the butchery in China last year. This sort of thing is not happening in the USSR now. We need a yardstick that applies uniformly both to China and the USSR.' Bush disagreed: 'There are differences between China and the USSR. The export of revolution from China has stopped or at least improved.' And, he added, 'China does not target US cities with nuclear weapons.' For him the die had been cast. If necessary, 'the US would be prepared to stand alone', he stated. There would be no US aid to the USSR, but he would support Japan's overture to China. Clearly, then, safeguarding the relationship with Beijing was of major significance for Bush – even at the expense of annoying his European allies who were fixated on Gorbachev.[111]

Nevertheless, despite Bush's statement of priorities, after Tiananmen events in Europe and the USSR increasingly absorbed his administration's attention. And by the autumn of 1990, China was little more than a political headache for Washington – its strategic capacity diminished by its stagnation at home and its unwillingness to tango. Indeed, with Li in the lead, he and Foreign Minister Qian became more involved in repairing relations with other non-Western countries whose support might ease China's international isolation. Qian travelled widely, promoting the PRC's visibility and taking the initiative to resolve long-standing disputes with its immediate neighbours. And so China went on a charm offensive with Vietnam, South Korea, India, the USSR and Japan. It even managed to establish formal diplomatic relations during 1990 with Saudi Arabia, Indonesia and Singapore.[112]

Consequently, as Baker recalled, the emphasis in US China policy 'shifted towards multilateral opportunities, where we could deal with the Chinese in a larger less controversial context on issues of mutual interest'. And as historian Jeffrey Engel has explained, 'the ties to Beijing proved useful when Bush needed China's acquiescence in United Nations sanctions against Iraq' in the autumn of 1990 and the subsequent Kuwait War in early 1991. A Chinese veto on the Security Council could have imperilled the US bid for an international mandate to force Saddam Hussein out of Kuwait. By having kept the channels to Beijing open – at

considerable political cost at home – Bush could now harvest the benefits during the unexpected crisis in the Persian Gulf.[113]

The same pattern of multilateral cooperation was evident over ending
the war in Cambodia. This had raged since 1978 – with the Cambodian
Khmer Rouge and their PRC ally pitted against the Vietnamese invader,
backed by the USSR. The Cambodia–Vietnam War ended only in 1989.
US diplomatic persistence in 1990 pushed the Chinese into joining UN
efforts to reach a negotiated settlement, particularly getting Beijing to
put pressure on the Khmer Rouge to participate in peace talks. These
culminated in the October 1991 Paris Peace Agreement, out of which
came a UN mission to promote reconstruction of the ravaged Cambodian
state after the deadly civil war.[114]

The United Nations Transitional Authority in Cambodia (UNTAC),
which started work in March 1992, was the first post-Cold War peacekeeping operation – or, more exactly, a state-building operation involving
22,000 UN peacekeepers from twenty-two countries. These included,
significantly, Japan after its Diet approved the necessary legislation on
participation in peacekeeping operations; indeed UNTAC was overseen
by Yasushi Akashi, a Japanese official who was appointed the UN special
representative. In all UNTAC also involved 6,000 officials, 3,500 police
and 1,700 civilian employees, and 56,000 electoral volunteers to register
voters and monitor elections. Though China traditionally opposed peacekeeping resolutions that authorised the use of force, in this case Beijing
made an exception – evidently keen to improve its international reputation and regain the trust of its regional neighbours, both of which had
been damaged by the Tiananmen massacre.[115]

As another example of the US multilateral approach, Washington also
worked to engineer the admission of China, Taiwan and Hong Kong into
the APEC regional economic forum in mid-November 1991.[116] On human
rights, admittedly, progress remained negligible: China had refused to
reduce the sentences of most dissidents, rebuffed US efforts to obtain a
list of the victims of Tiananmen, and rejected Western pleas to allow the
International Red Cross to inspect their prisons. But Beijing was now
desperate for American sanctions to be lifted and very keen to have a
high-profile visit from the United States. Washington, in turn, recognised
that Chinese cooperation with the UN over Iraq and Cambodia had been
hugely beneficial.[117]

The growing power imbalances and volatility of international affairs
served as another push factor that convinced Bush and Baker (and quietly

even some of their most vociferous congressional critics) of the need to deal directly with the Chinese. 'The simple truth', wrote Baker later, was that 'China was too important to our global interest to try to isolate'. No matter how big the gulf between the two systems, 'China is not Cuba'.[118] Bush told President Roh of South Korea, 'My engagement with China now is because we want relations in the future'.[119] With fears mounting of possible anarchy in the post-Soviet space, at a time when the Balkans were imploding and NATO was recalibrating, Bush and Baker considered it essential to foster stability in Asia. South Korea and Japan were in strategic terms relatively small players: the big question was how China would react to the end of bipolarity and what role the PRC would play in the emerging new order?

Given the continuing sensitivity of China at home, however, Bush found it useful that his allies could act as frontmen. Prime Minister Kaifu of Japan was the first G7 statesman after 1989 to travel to Beijing, in an effort to re-establish normal relations with its neighbour. His three-day visit on 10–12 August 1991 underscored the fact that Japan was much less constrained than the USA by a domestic human-rights lobby. Keen to resume its trade and aid relations with the PRC, Kaifu told fellow G7 leaders: 'It is important for China to develop, too.' He believed there were 'new signs of political reform' in the CCP, and said that Japan would 'work' to 'encourage' that process.[120]

British prime minister John Major's journey to Beijing in September 1991 had even greater impact in ending China's isolation from the West. As was necessary, Major began with some stinging criticism of the PRC's human-rights record, to which Li Peng replied caustically that Britain had ignored such issues during its long imperialist relationship with China. Having got that out of the way, Major and Li signed a previously announced memo on a massive $16 billion airport and port project for Hong Kong. Stating that 'we do not share common values', but 'we do have shared interests – Hong Kong foremost among them', Major reached agreement also on other aspects of the colony's 1997 reversion to Chinese sovereignty. The sun was setting on British influence in China but Major, like Kaifu, recognised the need to do business with Beijing, despite Tiananmen.[121]

Although Bush was by now increasingly preoccupied with his re-election campaign, he had no intention of leaving relations with China entirely to his allies. Japan, after all, was a trade competitor of the USA, Britain was focused on Hong Kong, and there were also issues of special interest to America, particularly nuclear proliferation. China in 1991 was the single most important influence over Kim Il-sung and North Korea's burgeoning nuclear programme. More generally, Washington was concerned about what intelligence data strongly suggested was an aggressive and secret Chinese campaign to export technology and weaponry to less developed countries in Asia, North Africa and the Middle East and to circumvent patchy Western efforts to restrict the spread of weapons of mass destruction.[122]

To advance its agenda, America certainly had potential leverage over China, including dollars, high technology and the PRC's keenness for talks. Indeed, Beijing had been pressing the USA hard for almost a year to resume official high-level contacts. But the US administration had to find a low-profile opportunity that would not attract too much comment at home. This occurred on 27 September 1991, when Baker had a chance to talk with his Chinese counterpart, Foreign Minister Qian, on the margins of the UN General Assembly in New York.[123]

Baker began by sternly reminding Qian just how devastating the PRC's crackdown in Tiananmen Square had been for Sino-American relations and for public attitudes to China. What the Chinese euphemistically called the 'Tiananmen Incident' could not simply be brushed under the carpet. 'I want to come to China,' Baker stressed. But he could not afford the mission to fail, because a largely hostile Congress would then take over US–China policy from Bush. After all, Congress was angling to 'override the president on MFN' at the first opportunity. Qian's response was inscrutably vague, much to Baker's frustration. So the Secretary of State kept pressing. 'What I need to know is what I can accomplish by a visit. Can we talk specifics? Eyeball to eyeball?' He emphasised that 'I want to leave China with something on human rights and proliferation.' This, he insisted, was Beijing's 'last, best chance'. Qian's responses were polite and soothing, but ultimately imprecise. Baker decided to trust that his message had been 'absorbed'.[124]

Six weeks later, on 15 November 1991, the US Secretary of State returned to the Forbidden City – which he had not visited since February 1989 – for three days of talks. His opening round – a four-and-a half-hour meeting and working dinner with Qian at the plush Diaoyutai state guest house, favoured centuries before by Chinese royalty – simply allowed the two sides to set out their stalls. Qian boldly presented what Baker called his 'laundry list' of concessions that the PRC desired from the USA, with the lifting of sanctions at the top. Baker answered in kind with a forty-five-minute lecture on human rights and all the other problematic bilateral and multilateral issues that troubled Washington. He concluded with the blunt message: 'now it's time to be practical, I am not expecting miracles. But I *do* expect you to recognise your own self-interest. I need concrete results – not promises, not meetings, not delays'. Each side acted as if it was in the box seat, and the other just had to back down.[125]

Next morning, having posed grim-faced for the cameras, Baker sat down in the first of six meetings with the hardline technocrat Li Peng. As expected, the Chinese premier was totally intransigent on human rights. 'Because we have different values and [a] different ideology we can only make a commitment to discussion,' Li said coldly. His main agenda item was China's entry into the GATT world trading system ahead of Taiwan: the PRC deserved to be treated like other world powers, he insisted. When Baker stressed that China would have to liberalise first and to conform to international standards before the US would endorse Beijing's GATT membership, Li grew irritated – repeating his demands several times. And when Baker steered the conversation back to human rights, this only made the atmosphere worse. 'The actions in Tiananmen Square were a good thing,' Li declared. 'We do not regard them as a tragedy. Look at Central and Eastern Europe and the Soviet Union today.' If those countries had dealt with dissent as the Chinese communist leadership had, he said, they would be in much less of a mess now. Moreover, he added, 'our people support what we did during that time'.

Baker was appalled and warned that under these circumstances Bush would not be able to 'sustain' the relationship with China. Li, not merely unrepentant, turned condescending – in his most arch Central Kingdom manner. 'You should be happy that I am even seeing you.' Baker felt like walking out. He bit his lip, deciding to stay the course until all the items on his agenda had been ticked off, but his mood was fatalistic. 'I thought this meeting was a disaster,' he scribbled down later. Only Deng's successor as party secretary, Jiang Zemin, appeared the 'slightest bit reasonable', when he claimed that while Tiananmen was no tragedy, it was no 'blessing', either. Day two finished, from Baker's perspective, with still nothing achieved.

The Chinese leaders saw things somewhat differently, having clearly intended to teach Baker a sustained lesson about how the PRC should be dealt with. They emphasised that they would not respond to any pressure from Washington, and certainly not moralistic lectures. The

United States should engage pragmatically and face to face with China, despite differences in the relationship, and it should take more account of the strategic value of Chinese–American ties. As President Yang Shankun put it to the world media: 'The practice of exerting pressure can only lead to tension in the bilateral relations, and is of no use in solving problems ... Some problems can be solved through discussions, while others need several rounds of discussion. Those which cannot be solved for the time being can be shelved. We call this "seeking common ground while reserving difference".'[126]

Only on the last day, during another meeting between Baker and Qian did things begin to move – not on human rights but on the issue of arms control and nuclear non-proliferation. Baker had gone out of his way to praise the Chinese for their recent participation in review talks of the NPT, and for starting to press Pyongyang into halting its nuclear weapons programmes on the Korean peninsula. At the same time, he did criticise Beijing for nuclear sharing with Algeria and Iran, missile transfers to Pakistan and Syria, and a variety of other global proliferation initiatives of which Washington disapproved.[127]

Qian now chose to ignore the brickbats and make some positive gestures. China, he said, would support a denuclearised Korean peninsula (as recently called for by Roh) and would ask the CCP Congress to ratify the NPT.[128] China was also prepared to observe the guidelines of the Missile Technology Control Regime (MTCR) – but only if the US lifted the recent sanctions imposed on two Chinese companies that owned the licensing of American high-speed computers and satellites. He and Baker also reached agreements on US access to Chinese markets and the protection of American intellectual property, specifically regarding computer software, patents and publications. On human rights, too, Qian was willing to make some concessions. These included promises that two leading critics of the regime would be released and that dissidents who had served jail sentences could travel to America. In addition, US diplomats would be allowed to visit China's prisons. Evidently, none of this amounted to a major breakthrough.

The outcome of eighteen hours of gruelling negotiations was what Baker considered the bare minimum. Nevertheless, the slight easing of China's suppression of human rights, combined with the limited Chinese gesture of a verbal pledge that Beijing 'intended to observe' the MTCR convention, thereby curbing missiles sales, was just about enough to maintain bilateral relations and ward off any subsequent congressional attempts to strip China of its 'most favoured nation' trading benefits. Baker was philosophical: 'unless we were to keep US–China relations in the deep freeze forever, we had to start talking'. For his part, Bush was satisfied with the visit and his administration's policy of 'constructive engagement', as he liked to call it. 'I think it was worthwhile.' And 'now we sit down and figure out what's the next step'.[129]

Both sides were operating pragmatically, but on very different time-scales. Baker, working within the rigid schedule of an American electoral cycle, was under intense domestic pressure to justify his trip to Beijing, and US China policy more generally, by winning immediate concessions. The Bush administration also thought the time was ripe because it saw the PRC as a 'weakened regime that could be pushed into more humane treatment of its citizens and along a path of democratic change'. As China expert David Lampton put it, 'the superiority of American values (evidenced in Cold War victory), America's military and technological might (demonstrated by the Gulf War)' and China's need for trade with America and other Western nations appeared to offer plenty of leverage.[130]

The PRC leadership, while also seeking results, did not share Washington's perception of Beijing's own weakness. It would not be rushed – and certainly not succumb to what it considered either bribery or blackmail: hence its treatment of Baker on the first two days. The PRC was always mindful of its long-term power, standing, and ideological identity in the post-Cold War world – looking far beyond the unipolar moment that appeared to dazzle the Americans. That's why Jiang reminded Baker of two lines of an ancient Chinese poem. 'It says that if you want to have a longer vision you should move to a higher level. We should look further by moving to a higher point, and have our eyes on the future.' The restoration of Sino-American relations would take time and patience. It would also become a step along the way in China's ascent to world-power status.[131]

Chinese self-confidence was only boosted by the breathtaking speed with which the Soviet Union fell apart in the last months of 1991, culminating in Gorbachev's dramatic declaration on Christmas Day. This seemed to vindicate Li Peng's words to Baker in September about Tiananmen being a 'good thing'. And in classic 'triangular' dynamics, Beijing saw relations with a weakened Moscow as a way to put pressure on an arrogant Washington.

The Chinese leadership had long been contemptuous of Moscow, taking the view that 'the Soviets did not grasp the economy well' and that Gorbachev was incapable of 'taking any measures'.[132] But when he asked them out of the blue for 'commodity loans', Beijing seized the opportunity to 'support' him with two loans ($333 million in spring 1990, and $730 million in March 1991) to buy Chinese grain, meat, peanuts, tea, textiles and light consumer goods. 'The loan is part of the effort to bolster the relationship,' said a foreign diplomat. 'They want to see Gorbachev maintain socialism.'[133] In addition, China had seen Gorbachev as a useful player in the strategic-triangle game. Since the US could put China under pressure 'after taking Eastern Europe', as Li Peng put it, China needed to play its Moscow card. 'Different kinds of international contradictions', he said, 'give us room for manoeuvre.'[134]

The leaders in Beijing were quite satisfied with how things had evolved since June 1989. Regardless of the resentment of many in the party and in the population at large against the CCP's iron grip, the regime was proud that it had succeeded in keeping the military, the party and the country united. Ever wary of 'separatist activities' by ethnic minorities, particularly in Tibet, Xinjian and Inner Mongolia, the leadership also made sure it kept a tight lid on all pro-independence protests. The revolutionary and nationalist contagion in Eastern Europe – most vividly dramatised by the execution of the Ceauşescus in Romania – had gravely alarmed the Beijing elite in 1989–90. But this mood had now passed. Despite the dissolution of the USSR and the collapse of Soviet communism, in 1992 Beijing felt secure in and of itself.[135]

A few weeks after the Soviet demise, Li Peng took full advantage of China's status as one of the five permanent members of the UN Security Council when the current chairman, British prime minister John Major, convened a special UN summit in New York on 1–2 February 1992. This brought together all Security Council heads of state to welcome Russia as the USSR's successor, to develop a more effective policy against nuclear proliferation and to discuss the UN's role in a post-Cold War future. In these circumstances, Bush found it hard to deny Li's request for a private conversation on the margins of the summit. Ignoring letters by nearly thirty members of the US Congress urging him not to sit down with the Chinese, Bush presented his encounter with Li as a 'courtesy' – the first tête-à-tête between US and PRC leaders since their meeting in Beijing in February 1989. For Li this proved a real coup.[136]

It was presumably not accidental that, barely an hour before Bush met Li, the State Department had issued its annual worldwide human-rights report, in which China was described as a repressive regime 'falling far short of internationally accepted norms'. Asia Watch – a US human-rights monitoring group – even called the PRC's record 'an anachronism in the new world order'.[137] But Li, as usual, had no intention of being pilloried by the Americans. In his address to the Security Council, he stated coolly that China 'values human rights' but that the issue 'falls within the sovereignty' of each state. Beijing would discuss and cooperate on this only from a position of 'equal footing'. Furthermore, 'a country's human-rights situation should not be judged in total disregard of its history and national conditions'. Li was adamant that 'it is neither appropriate nor workable that all countries measure up to the human-rights criteria or models of one of a small number of countries'. He sat expressionless as Yeltsin declared that there were 'no more any prisoners of conscience in free Russia' and that now there was a 'real chance to put an end to despotism and to dismantle the totalitarian order'. Nor did he blink when the new Russian leader called the Western countries his 'allies'.[138]

Li's talk with Bush after the summit plenary was especially formalised. Meeting in a small conference room, Bush went out of his way to avoid any display of personal warmth. He and Baker looked deliberately sombre, in contrast to Li's smiles, when pool reporters were allowed to enter the room for a photo session. The president also chose to sit across a table from Li, instead of in the side-by-side armchairs used for his meetings with other leaders in New York. They spoke for only twenty minutes.[139] Bush told Li that he found China's record on human rights inadequate. The Chinese premier responded with his stock statement – that it was an internal affair for the PRC, not fit for discussion by outsiders. Baker stressed to the media afterwards, 'This is not acceptable under our standards.' There was also no progress on non-proliferation.[140]

Yet Li Peng's visit to New York seemed like a personal and national triumph. He had used the trip for maximum visual effect – holding bilaterals with Security Council colleagues, Yeltsin, Major, Miyazawa, capped by the encounter with a grudging Bush. The only big player he did not meet was Mitterrand, whose US trip was very short and whose government had openly supported Chinese dissidents in exile. Despite vocal protests by several hundred Chinese students and pro-democracy advocates outside the UN headquarters, nobody doubted that the Chinese premier would depart New York with China's position, and his own, enhanced. 'When he returns to Beijing, he will go down as a victor for demonstrating his ability to bring China back into the world community,' said Haiching Zhao, organiser of the protest, sadly: he had hoped for 10,000 demonstrators. Chai Ling, a student leader, added: 'I don't think this is a good beginning for the new world order.'[141]

In the event, Li's moment of dominance in Chinese politics proved brief – a three-year post-Tiananmen intermezzo before the economic reformers within the CCP leadership once again began to call the tune.[142] Criticism had grown of Li's regressive turn to recentralisation and structural adjustments under strict administrative controls. One leading economist sent a strongly worded letter to the State Planning Commission stating that, whether the economy is capitalist or socialist, the strategy of 'controlling money and freeing prices is an objective law for the smooth functioning of the market mechanism that must be observed'. More important was the political backlash by 1992. Deng was not prepared to merely look on and see his practical achievements and doctrinal legacies being rolled back by Li. 'We can no longer afford a wait-and-see attitude,' Deng declared. The time had come to 'advance' again with renewed reforms. Gathering his failing strength one last time, the Paramount Leader made a brief return to the front line of politics – almost two years after he had retired from the chairmanship of the all-important military commission in November 1989, and after being forced by the conservative Party Elders, including Li, to oust the liberal Party secretary Zhao Ziyang in the wake of Tiananmen.[143]

The successor to both positions – Jiang Zemin – was a compromise candidate, but he would stay at the helm of national politics into the new millennium. Initially, however – to Deng's annoyance – Jiang had rallied his comrades around anti-Western policies and the mantra of political 'stability' built on the CCP, while allowing economic change just to take place in small ways behind the scenes. He also trod carefully among the ideological tensions between Deng and Li as the CCP commemorated its seventieth anniversary in July 1991. What emboldened Jiang to press anew for economic modernisation was Deng's vocal return to the political stage in early 1992 – following his 'southern tour' to Guangzhou, Shenzhen, and Zhuhai as well as to Shanghai, during which he tirelessly advocated a faster shift to the market. Showing that he had lost none of his political cunning, Deng managed to curtail the influence of the party elders and the military's influence in the CCP leadership – in the process boosting Jiang's position as Deng's heir apparent and giving the latter more room for manoeuvre. When Jiang resumed economic liberalisation, the results were almost instantaneous. Within a year growth tripled, foreign-exchange reserves doubled to $21.76 billion, foreign direct investment quadrupled and total foreign trade quintupled. And so China's economy was back to boom conditions by the end of 1992.[144]

Reinventing communism: Jiang and Deng

At the 14th Party Congress of the CCP in October of that year the goal of economic reform was redefined as the transition to a 'socialist market economy'. The concept then became enshrined in the Chinese constitution, together with the amendment that the PRC had entered the 'initial state of socialism' in March 1993. It was also stated that China represented a special brand of 'socialism' – one with distinctly 'Chinese characteristics'. But this 'socialist' reinvention à la chinoise should not develop in isolation. Referring to one of the classic Chinese expressions, 'stones from other hills can be used to carve jade', Jiang believed that lessons from the West and from the East European transformation processes were crucial. 'To accelerate economic growth,' he said, 'we must further emancipate our minds' and 'speed up the process of reform and opening up to the outside world.' Only by 'learning' from others' mistakes as much as success stories, could one 'achieve superiority over capitalist countries'. But while foreign investment and economic know-how were to be welcomed, Jiang 'absolutely' rejected a 'Western, multiparty, parliamentary system for China'. Economic change would not go hand in hand with a political transformation. Still, Jiang personally consolidated his position in a re-formed post-Congress party leadership; and along the way he made sure to improve his ties with the military, too. Li Peng, though defeated in the ideological power struggle by Jiang, would stay premier till 1998 – which sent a clear message to the world that the CCP leadership remained united irrespective of the factional jockeying.[145]

Jiang's sharp demarcation between economic Westernisation and political Westernisation stood at odds with Bush's typically American assumption that the first would lead almost seamlessly to the second. He revealed this in a conversation with PRC ambassador Zhu Qizhen in August 1992. The president noted candidly that 'we have our problems with human rights', especially when 'locked in a tough election fight' which meant that he had to show himself 'strongly committed' to those rights – as, he added firmly, 'truly I am'. But Bush did not press the issue in view of Chinese sensitivities, looking instead to the processes of history. 'I have to say there has been a lot of change in the world. Of course, we are champions for democracy. I believe economic change helps produce these results.' Underpinning this statement was the classic Cobdenite assumption that prosperity fostered peace – which Bush naturally defined as acceptance of America's conception of a liberal international order.

Yet in his direct dealings with Beijing he tended to be more solicitous of China's feelings, playing up his personal friendship and sense of empathy. So he tempered his warning to Ambassador Zhu on human rights by adding 'I remember well your leaders who said that we should remember that the Chinese must feed 1 billion people every day. I will never forget that'. And he happily conceded that democratisation of the PRC American-style would be long-shot. 'We don't ask that you establish a two-party system, with Republicans and Democrats in downtown

Beijing,' he said. The president wished to register American values while making clear he had no intention of interfering in China's internal politics. Much had changed in Sino-American relations since January 1989, but – at the end of his presidency as at the beginning – George Bush was determined to remain a real *lao pengyou* of China.[146]

Combining in this way the administration's strategic assumptions with his personal take on political friendship, the president remained unrepentant during the election debate of 12 October 1992 after Clinton had announced that he would not 'coddle dictators from Baghdad to Beijing'. Bush said that he had stuck with the 'most favoured nation' policy 'because you see China moving towards a free-market economy'. But, he added, if 'you isolate China and turn them inward', then 'we've made a tremendous mistake. And I'm not going to do it.' Tiananmen, he believed, had not been a dead end, but merely a setback on the world's road to Americanised modernity.[147]

By contrast, even those in the vanguard of the CCP's reform programme – Deng and Jiang – had no truck with such conceptions of the future. For them, the pro-democracy movement had been a temporary aberration from the Chinese way, and its suppression in Tiananmen Square had been a necessity of state. Their lodestar was not Bush's vision of a new world order, but the national interests of the Central Kingdom as defined by the CCP, bolstering its security, prosperity and great-power status. These interests were asserted with vigour in 1992 – landing troops at key points on the tiny uninhabited Spratly archipelago in the South China Sea to advance Beijing's territorial claims some 1,000 miles south of the nearest populated Chinese island of Hainan. Not only did the PRC set up 'sovereignty posts' on the reefs claimed also by Vietnam, to show that China was taking control of these strategically significant but highly disputed waters – through which passes over half the world's trade and most of the fuel for Japan, Taiwan and Korea – they signed oil-exploration contracts with a US company on this stretch of the seabed. The Central Kingdom's challenge to America's values and its Pacific reach was relatively minor in the early 1990s, but it would expand enormously in the twenty-first century.[148]

It is also instructive to reflect on contrasts between China and Soviet Russia. Both countries experienced a lurch to the right, but the outcomes were very different. The PRC's three-year conservative turn under Li Peng served, it transpired, to consolidate both communist ideology and the CCP, before Jiang Zemin and his more progressive Shanghai clique resumed controlled economic reform and moved China toward party-led authoritarian state capitalism. By contrast the rightist turn in the USSR that began in late 1990, provoking Shevardnadze's resignation and culminating in the attempted coup of August 1991, had ended in double failure: first, because the putschists failed to gain power, and, second, because they precipitated the collapse of the Soviet state that they were trying to preserve.

The differences go deeper still. The Soviet plotters had sought to forcefully 'stop the chaos in the country'.[149] To do so by following the Chinese model would have meant combining military repression of the pro-democracy movement with general, if temporary, austerity measures. But the Soviet putschists were not willing to accept the social costs that such a strategy would have entailed. Calling for 'labour discipline' was one thing; using the army to discipline the people and drive down consumption would have been more than the Soviet Gang of Eight, and indeed the military, could stomach. Times had moved on from the 1930s when Stalin considered mass famine an acceptable price for agricultural modernisation – that, at least, was a positive Gorbachev legacy. And the putschists failed to grasp that the institutions they strove to protect were the ones whose feather-bedding by the state was bankrupting the Soviet government – especially the Red Army and its allies in the military-industrial sector. In the USSR, military spending exceeded 15% of GDP; in China it was probably half that figure – around 8.5%. What's more, PRC reformers did not face equivalent powerful interest groups: there was no farm lobby trying to block decollectivisation, and manufacturing played a smaller role in China's economy. Furthermore, the Chinese leadership had the party and the security services firmly on board – unlike Gorbachev in 1991. In short, whereas the Soviet conservative moment served to destroy the state and its leader, China's conservative moment embodied reinvention. It represented a relatively brief period of state consolidation before economic reform resumed – according to Chinese models rather than Western values.[150]

This did not mean that China declined to engage with Yeltsin's Russia. Although relations were on hold for several weeks after the demise of the USSR because of the general disarray, the PRC recognised the Russian Federation on 27 December 1991, alongside the other remaining eleven ex-Soviet republics. And despite grave reservations about Yeltsin's talk of democratisation and economic shock therapy, China began to court the Russian leader. After all, said China's chargé d'affaires Zhang Zheng, in

Moscow to Mikhail Titarenko, director of the Far East Institute of the Russian Academy of Sciences, 'We are against the ideologisation of inter-state relations. Everyone has the right to have their own assessment of the changes which are taking place in your country.'[151]

Sino-Russian relations were certainly affected by Yeltsin's brief honey-moon with the West in the first half of 1992. Initially, Soviet collapse meant that Moscow pulled back its political feelers in the Pacific, as Yeltsin concentrated on trying to build democracy and a full market economy in what he hoped would be 'equal partnership' with the USA. But given his domestic political woes and his own appetite for power, he was eventually forced into appeasing conservatives and Eurasianists scep-tical of 'Westernisation'. As a result, the Kremlin's 'friendship' talk about being 'allies' with the West soon became muted, and the brief 'embrace' as Russia basked in the idea of being 'fully part of the democratic world' receded.[152] In its place one heard proclamations of a distinct Russian identity, rooted in its glorious history and 'great power' rhetoric, together with talk about the significance of its 'near abroad'[153] and of states in Asia and the Middle East. In other words, after a brief flirtation with the USA, Russian foreign policy moved during 1992 towards a more 'geographically balanced' approach. Coming with that was growing appreciation of the value of a mutually beneficial relationship with Beijing.[154]

Even so, the Kremlin did not abandon a fundamentally Western-centred world view – not just America and NATO, dollars and Deutschmarks but also that vexed issue of 'Western values'. Russia's 'Atlanticist' foreign minister Andrei Kozyrev highlighted the difference between Russia and China on human rights. Speaking at the UN session of the Human Rights Commission in Geneva in March 1992, Kozyrev voted in favour of placing the issue of human-rights violations in Tibet on the agenda – a direct affront to Beijing. He even proclaimed: 'The creation of civilised society in the Russian Federation is impossible without full protection of human rights. With this in view, we try to use international mechanisms and promote, to a certain extent, interference into internal affairs.'[155]

The omens were therefore not propitious for Kozyrev's visit to Beijing a few days later. This thirty-hour stopover en route to Seoul and Tokyo proved dicey as well as short. There was ratification of the Sino-Russian border agreement and attempts to 'lend additional dynamism' to talks on arms reduction and confidence-building measures in the region. And there was an accord signed on 'trade and economic ties' to replace the old treaties of 1958 and 1990, as well as discussions on opening closed border towns for trans-border trade and creating a zone of free entrepreneurship in the Tumen River region – at the point where China, Russia and North Korea meet. But otherwise little was achieved. Indeed, as their official conclusions highlighted, 'elements of considerable agreement coexist with different approaches to some quite significant questions'. Kozyrev further stated in the press conference: 'One can't pick one's neighbours. Whether we like the current Chinese leadership or not, we must cooperate with them. There is no other way.'[156]

These tensions did not, however, prevent practical military cooperation with Russia: the PRC purchased twenty-four Russian fighter aircraft which were shipped to China in mid-1992. Nor did it get in the way of inviting Yeltsin for a state visit to Beijing. Eager to escape the political turmoil at home, the Russian leader hoped to bask in the glow of an Asian summit and dreamed of reshaping the international balance of power. In late November, just before his trip, he grandly announced the beginning of a 'new and historic era' in Sino-Russian relations. China, 'a great power', he said, would now 'take priority in Russian foreign policy – not only in Asia but the world as well.'[157]

Russo-Chinese friendship? New beginnings

In Beijing, on 17 December the joint declaration signed by Yeltsin and Chinese president Yang Shangkun espoused the policy of 'constructive cooperation'. It stated that Russia and China viewed each other as 'friendly states' who would 'develop relations of good-neighbourliness, friendship, and mutually beneficial cooperation' in accordance with the UN Charter, based on the principles of 'mutual respect and territorial integrity, non-aggression, non-interference in each other's internal affairs, equality and mutual benefit, peaceful coexistence, and other universally recognised norms of international rights'. It further acknowledged the two countries' divergent political paths but also asserted that 'differences in social systems and ideologies should not impede normal development of state-to-state relations'.[158]

The language in the joint communiqué about Sino-Russian relations within the international system had changed markedly from the phrasing in 1989 and 1991. It stressed the need for the UN to play a greater role and have more authority and noted the 'surfacing of a multipolar world' – condemning any form of 'hegemonism' and 'power politics'. In offering this description of the global order, rooted effectively in realpolitik assumptions, the declaration presented a view of global politics at odds with Kozyrev's Atlanticist line. Indeed, it was a return to the time-honoured conception of Soviet foreign policy, which had viewed international relations in geostrategic as much as geo-ideological terms. The United States was the primary, if unidentified, reference point, when the document criticised 'hegemony' and 'power politics'. Here in short was a definite return to the politics of triangularity. What many had believed to be a Cold War conceptual relic was gaining new relevance as a framework for understanding great-power relations at the end of the twentieth century and into the twenty-first.[159]

Yeltsin's readiness to sign the declaration clearly signalled Russia's early desire to free itself from being America's junior partner and deepen a relationship with Beijing to gain some leverage over Washington. The Chinese leadership was equally pleased. Their vision of a multipolar world order offered an escape from diplomatic isolation after Tiananmen sanctions, the collapse of Soviet communism and the tough American line on human rights. Moreover, the burgeoning partnership with Russia gave Beijing support in their quest to constrain the virtually unipolar predominance of the United States in the post-Cold War era.[160]

Of course, while strategic and political concerns were bringing the two neighbours together – creating the foundations for an incipient alliance – nevertheless, divergent interests on issues such as Asian security, economic development and regional cooperation would soon exert countervailing pressures and set limits to the partnership. This left plenty of space for American diplomatic manoeuvring, especially where the US could exploit its financial and military superiority. In any case the power dynamics were complex and fluctuating. Russia – always obsessed about its identity as a European power and inclined to measure its military stature in relation to the USA – could never be comfortable with a full turn to the Far East. At the same time, post-Cold War America kept a foot not only in Europe via NATO but also in Asia, through its position in Japan and South Korea, thereby ensuring that the United States remained a Pacific power. In short, for Moscow and Beijing as much as for Washington the dynamics of trans-Pacific relations were truly triangular. And for all of the Pacific Big Three the line between being partners and competitors was thin and ever-changing. At the end of the Bush presidency the United States was by all measures of hard and soft power the trio's most powerful actor, both regionally and globally. But this triangularity was no guarantee of a long-term stable international order.

Epilogue

Post Wall, Post Square: A World Remade?

'Destiny, it has been said, is not a matter of chance; it's a matter of choice. It's not a thing to be waited for; it's a thing to be achieved. And we can never safely assume that our future will be an improvement over the past. Our choice as a people is simple: We can either shape our times, or we can let the times shape us. And shape us they will, at a price frightening to contemplate, morally, economically and strategically.'[1]

These were George H. W. Bush's words on 15 December 1992 in a speech at Texas A&M University, five weeks before he left office, when he was coming to terms with political defeat and trying to get a perspective on the events of his presidency. The astonishing upheavals of 1988–92 stemmed both from structural shifts in the global system and from the rising transnational salience of people power – expressed through mass protest and electoral revolution.[2] But Bush was not alone in believing that it was leaders who mattered – especially at such moments of world-historical transition.

Helmut Kohl, the impresario of German unification, articulated a similar view. 'These are historically significant years,' he told Mikhail Gorbachev during their Moscow summit in July 1990. 'Such years come and go. The opportunities have to be used. If one does not act, they will pass by.' Citing the famous phrase of Otto von Bismarck, he told the Soviet leader, 'you have to grab the mantle of history'. Gorbachev agreed: he too was anxious to seize 'the great opportunities that had opened up' after the fall of the Berlin Wall.[3]

Bush, Kohl and Gorbachev were just three among a cohort of historical actors who navigated the drama of 1988–92 together, each seeking to influence and shape events. All of these leaders had to make choices. In doing so, they contributed to outcomes that none of them had planned or foreseen, and under domestic constraints whose compass varied from case to case. Each was improvising, responding to surges of popular will, while striving to keep his own agenda in view – trying to channel the turmoil, crafting agreements to restore stability, helping to consolidate new democracies, and adapting old institutions or designing new ones. They acted individually and in concert – and cumulatively helped remake the world after the old order had shattered.[4]

During these tumultuous years, the decision-makers experienced dramatic changes in their standing. In December 1988, when Gorbachev spoke to the UN in New York he was at the height of his powers, while Bush – preparing to step into Reagan's shoes – still seemed the tongue-tied apprentice, overshadowed by the Soviet leader, a global cult figure. By the end of December 1991, however, Mikhail Gorbachev's political career was over and his country no longer existed, while George Bush appeared the arbiter of the world's fortunes.

In three short years, the map of Europe was completely redrawn. Two centuries after the French Revolution of 1789 an equally momentous revolutionary surge swept away the *ancien régime* of communist dicta-torship and command economics and eroded the Soviet security glacis that had been in place since the 1940s. Over the following year, divided Germany became one; by the time the Soviet Union disintegrated, the European Community was metamorphosing into the European Union and NATO had established a 'Cooperation Council' so that 'West' could embrace 'East' in what was billed as a new community of 'free nations' extending from Vancouver to Vladivostok. Meanwhile, the GATT – forged after the Great Depression and the Second World War – was transmuted under US pressure into a more open World Trade Organi-sation – a body that would eventually include a communist-capitalist PRC and a post-Soviet Russia. To some, it seemed that 'the West' and its way of doing things had triumphed. In a famous and widely misunder-stood book, the political scientist Francis Fukuyama spoke of 'the universalization of Western liberal democracy as the final form of human government' – in short 'the end of history'.[5]

Yet, it was people on the streets who drove the revolutionary wave of 1989. From Tallinn to Tirana, from Berlin to Bucharest, they marched, demonstrated and rebelled. East Germans travelled hundreds of miles in their Trabants, rushed border checkpoints and ran across fields hoping that no one would open fire, to pierce the Iron Curtain in a myriad of places. Political activists demanded and gained admission to the chambers of power. They bargained with the regimes that had so recently oppressed them. Excited electors crowded the polling stations, casting their votes for fresh leaders and new visions. The power of fear – of the tank and of the secret police – appeared to be broken. The image of people flooding through openings in the Berlin Wall – though a quintessentially German moment – captured the sense of breathtaking historical change throughout Eastern Europe.

The currents of revolution also swirled on the other side of the world, in China. Here the camera's eye fell upon students packed into Tiananmen Square, at the heart of the Forbidden City. Defying the police, they clamoured for democracy. And like the Germans, they adored Gorbachev, communism's alchemist of reform. But Beijing was not Berlin. Here there was to be no 'non-violent revolution'. Soldiers did shoot into the crowds; tanks rolled down boulevards and into the Square, crushing demonstrators under their tracks. Deng Xiaoping was no Mikhail Gorbachev. He had no compunction about using force to keep communism in power in China. And so 4 June 1989 came to mark a historic divide – a fundamental divergence in exiting the Cold War. Post Square would not be Post Wall.

The contrast between Deng and Gorbachev bears out the importance of leaders. Each unleashed reform without appreciating the possible consequences but when the political process got out of control, the Chinese leader applied devastating force. His Soviet counterpart allowed reform to escalate into revolution, and then refrained from using the tank in order to contain it. People power was not an irresistible force; it could be smashed by the military or channelled by politicians.

Deng's decision to crack down was a relatively simple choice for an authoritarian ruler who, despite splits in his party, was firmly in command of the army and the security forces. He operated within a state that was both vast and insular, intensely nationalist and tightly controlled. It was also a state with a deep memory of popular tumult and its calamitous effects: the Taiping rebellion that engulfed China in the mid-nineteenth century had killed between twenty and thirty million. Triggered in part by Western incursions into China, Taiping, whose instigators are commemorated on Tiananmen Square, undermined the power of the old imperial state and deepened its economic and political inferiority to the West. The imposition of international sanctions after the crackdown of 1989 caused serious inconvenience, to be sure. But Deng was adamant that he would 'never allow any people to interfere in China's internal affairs' no matter the consequences – so bitter were the memories of historic subordination to the West.[6]

The situation was more complicated in Europe. Given the new ethos in the Kremlin, by 1989 the use of force on a large scale within the Soviet bloc no longer constituted a viable option. In any case no national leader in the Warsaw Pact still exercised complete authority over his military and security services. Moreover, the impact of political change could not be contained within the bloc itself because of the German question: any transformation of East Germany had implications for neighbouring communist countries and even more for the Federal Republic because the Cold War had coalesced around the decision to divide the German polity. So, any discussion of unification affected West German allies, especially France and Britain with their painful memories of two world wars. And on a global plane, it drew in the two superpowers, pitted against each other for over forty years along the inner German border and in the city of Berlin, with each acting as security protector of its German client state. The European revolution of 1989, therefore, was nothing less than a challenge to the existing global order. And managing it required cooperation between leaders with disparate ideological outlooks, historical baggage and domestic constraints.

Such a challenge was, of course, not unique in modern history. In 1814–15 in Vienna and again in 1919 in Paris, leaders had met en masse in an effort to manage historical change. But these were gatherings of victors to make peace after hugely destructive wars. After the Second World War, no general peace treaty was ever negotiated and the summit of victors at Potsdam in 1945 prefigured a shift from wartime cooperation to Cold War confrontation. In the wake of 1989 there was neither an international conference, nor a conclave of the victorious. Post-Wall was a *process*, involving a plethora of summits, discussions and phone calls over the next two years that cumulatively negotiated the exit from the Cold War and the coming together of former enemies.

The results were indeed astonishing. By the end of 1990, communist ideology and the command economy had been buried throughout Eastern Europe. Even more notable, divided Germany had become a sovereign, unified state within both EU and NATO. Although these were talked up as victories for the West, they had been accomplished without a war and with minimal civic strife. This remarkably peaceful transition distinguishes 1989–90 from other periods of historical transformation.

A key part of the explanation for this lack of conflict was that process of cooperative international management that I have charted in these pages. First and foremost, Gorbachev defused Cold War tensions through his nuclear arms reduction talks with Ronald Reagan in 1985–8. In 1989, he inadvertently triggered a revolution through his policies of perestroika and glasnost at home and throughout the Soviet bloc. But whereas Gorbachev and Reagan had co-managed the 'de-demonisation' of relations between their two countries, Bush – whose outlook on the world was less ideological and more geopolitical than Reagan's when it came to the Soviet Union – executed a westward turn. In 1989 he looked principally to his West European NATO allies as he sought to coordinate a restrained response to the transformation under way across Eastern Europe and in the USSR.

Bush was well acquainted with the veterans of the European scene: Thatcher, Mitterrand, Delors and Kohl. The president's most constructive relationship was with the German chancellor. Bush, unlike Mitterrand and especially Thatcher, had no historical anxieties about the German question. For him Germany was, as he declared in May 1989, a 'Partner in Leadership'. He broadly supported Kohl's strategy for unification, consulting regularly on its implementation, and was ready to let West Germany take the lead in haggling with Gorbachev, particularly at the Caucasus summit of July 1990. Consequently, the year after the fall of the Wall saw the emancipation of Germany as an international actor. Bush's hallmark was his belief in the importance of regular personal contact with his fellow leaders, both face to face and over the telephone – to a degree unprecedented among US presidents.

This style of diplomacy was applied to adversaries as much as allies. After a hesitant start in the early months of his presidency, Bush also developed a cordial relationship with his Soviet opposite number: 'I liked the personal contact with Mikhail Gorbachev,' he later wrote, 'I *liked* him.'[7] As a result, a degree of genuine trust was fostered and this laid the basis for productive statecraft. Bush showed great sensitivity to Gorbachev's growing political difficulties at home, famously insisting that he would not 'jump on the Wall', and treated him as an equal at all their summits. In 1991, the G7 even made Gorbachev an honorary member, as the Soviet economy began in earnest its transition from Plan to market and its opening up to global trade. The US president also consistently tried his best to facilitate 'most favoured nation' trading status for the USSR but, when his hands were tied by Congress over the Soviet blockade of the Baltics, he was happy for Kohl to provide financial aid. This was an example of Bush's policy of working with and through allies.

The combination of direct personal contact reinforced by Alliance collaboration was equally evident in Bush's handling of America's other great communist adversary: China. The president's oldest and closest foreign contacts were with the PRC leadership, especially Deng Xiaoping, going back to his days in Beijing as America's envoy in 1974–5. The regard Deng had for him as a *lao pengyou* was a considerable asset which Bush tried to exploit right at the start of his presidency by visiting Beijing in February 1989. This policy was stymied by the Tiananmen crackdown, and Bush joined in the almost worldwide condemnation of China's violations of human rights. But, seeing China always as a potential strategic partner in triangulating the great power system, he sustained relations through the secret Scowcroft missions, and also through more public trips by Nixon and Kissinger. He did his best to minimise the effects of congressional sanctions and, although politically unable to visit China again during the rest of his presidency, used Japanese premier Toshiki Kaifu to reopen public contact and economic engagement with the PRC post-Square.

The style of management these leaders adopted could be termed 'conservative', in the literal sense of the word. Politicians like 'known knowns'. Because novelties entail risks, they usually prefer for the sake of stability and predictability to cling to what already exists and has been shown to work, making adjustments and adaptations as the need arises. This was certainly true in 1989–91. The leaders of the transition years did ultimately embrace transformative change but, at least initially, they tried to cloak it in garments from the past.

Gorbachev set out to preserve the Union and to make it more viable. He sought to reform and revitalise the USSR and thereby reposition it for continued competition with the West – albeit now peaceful in nature. He had clear, broad goals, but little idea how to achieve them. He started with partial economic reform but quickly became more radical – persuaded that true restructuring could work only if combined with political liberalisation. But the more he modified, the more he lost control – on the periphery and in the heartland. Then, losing his nerve, he swung right to the hardliners in the winter of 1990–1. As he zigged and zagged, Gorbachev undermined the command economy and the communist monopoly on power, without creating stable alternatives. And thus he wound up presiding over the destruction of the Soviet multinational state.

In the People's Republic of China, by contrast, Deng and the party leadership had embarked from the outset on a path of deliberately gradual economic reform. Even so, they could not prevent soaring inflation, which by the late 1980s triggered political protest and demands to change the system. Faced with an escalating domestic crisis and sobered by the erosion of communist authority in Eastern Europe, the CCP regime cracked down vigorously in June 1989 and reasserted its control. After a brief reactionary phase imposed by Premier Li, the process of liberalisation resumed in 1992 under reformist party boss Jiang, but he confined it strictly to the economy. China's leaders fixated on maintaining one-party rule and stamping out secessionist nationalism. So the Chinese, as they saw it, had learned lessons from what they regarded as Gorbachev's mistakes. The legacies of China's cautiously managed long-term transformation – from an insular Maoist state into an authoritarian communist-capitalist power-house with global reach – are still being played out in the twenty-first century. Whereas Gorbachev failed in remaking his Union, Deng succeeded. His PRC was remade and China's communism reinvented.

The management of change through the conservation and adaptation of existing frameworks was particularly evident in the case of the German question. Kohl facilitated unification by using Article 23 of West Germany's 1949 Basic Law to incorporate the Eastern *Länder* in the Federal Republic. Likewise, he brought them into the Deutschmark zone on the grounds that if the Deutschmark did not come to the East Germans, they would soon come to the Deutschmark. The March 1990 East German election result confirmed that the GDR would effectively be absorbed into the old West German structures. The next institutional step was that, once part of the FRG, the former GDR would automatically become part of the European Community – avoiding the danger of endless haggling with Germany's European partners about admitting a new, socio-economically weak state and, potentially setting a precedent for admitting others from the former Soviet bloc. Equally, the DM – cornerstone of the German 'economic miracle' since the late 1940s – would be subsumed into a common European currency and EMU. Kohl's European solution to the German question, though not quite sufficient to quell dyspeptic mutter-ings in London about the 'Fourth Reich', placated French fears about German revanchism and continental dominance. The trio – Kohl, Mitterrand and Delors – put their collective weight behind the reinvig-oration of the European integration project and its consummation in the Maastricht Treaty. For his part, Bush was not only supportive of unified Germany's place in a more integrated 'EC 92', but keen for America to establish a tight partnership with the reinvented Europe.

In regard to the emerging post-Cold War European security order, Bush was quick to insist that a unified Germany must remain a member of NATO. Kohl fully agreed. This ensured both the persistence of the Alliance after the Cold War and also a continued American presence in post-Wall Europe. And it went some way to reassure Gorbachev that united Germany would be kept under international control. By contrast, the Warsaw Pact withered away as the Eastern European states rejected communism and emancipated themselves from Soviet control. Indeed they, together with the USSR itself, accepted the invitation to join NATO's new North Atlantic Cooperation Council (NACC). And so it was that Germany was unified and Europe transformed on essentially Western terms. The post-Wall architecture in Europe incorporated the central features of the post-war liberal international order.

Yet that was not sufficient. As Eastern European states struggled to turn themselves into viable capitalist democracies and claim their place as equals in post-Wall Europe, they also began to press for membership of the Western 'institutional' bodies. But accommodating new members, with very different political cultures and strategic perspectives inevitably meant that the old forms could not simply be conserved. 'Building a Europe whole and free' ultimately meant that the surviving Western organisations, as they opened up to the East, would have to be remade.

This 'catalytic moment' in history also revealed other limits to what conservative management could achieve. Building on the United Nations Charter, its guiding principles in the face of territorial change were sovereignty and self-determination under international law. These were exemplified by the UN-sanctioned Kuwait War which was intended to liberate the small sovereign emirate from occupation by Iraq, not to take the war all the way to Baghdad and overthrow the internationally recognised government of Saddam Hussein. Nor could there be any question of direct Western intervention on behalf of the pro-democracy movement in China, once the PRC government had decided to send in the troops to restore internal order for the future.

The same principles also applied in Eastern Europe, where sovereign states recovered full independence in 1989–90 from Soviet clientage. And while the dismantling of the USSR in 1991 was messier, most of the successor republics already had clearly defined boundaries; so the border wars that ensued were confined to historically fractious regions such as the Caucasus.

On the other hand, conservative management completely failed in the face of the unexpected implosion of Yugoslavia. Leaders were caught between the conflicting imperatives of order and self-determination. Gorbachev, no less than Bush and most of NATO, wanted to preserve the territorial integrity of the Yugoslav federation for fear that its 'Balkanisation' would infect the USSR and other parts of South-Eastern Europe. It was Kohl and Genscher who wished to extend the principle of national self-determination from its successful application in Germany and the Baltic states to Slovenia and Croatia, which sought to secede from Serb-dominated Yugoslavia. But Milošević's bitter defence of the Yugolsav Federation as an instrument of Serbian security and the region's deeply embedded ethno-religious divisions – straddling the fault lines between Roman Catholicism, Greek Orthodoxy and Islam – made orderly self-determination impossible, especially in the case of multinational Bosnia. Indeed, a new Balkan order was only to be brought about through external military intervention and peace-enforcement after UN peace-keeping failed.

The new European Union – despite its assertive rhetoric – was never up to that peace-enforcing task. It stuck to the EC's 'civilian' tradition[8] of trying to mediate and help to keep the peace, without developing a European military capability. Progress was only achieved when America from 1995 began to engage by undertaking NATO bombing campaigns, after the Alliance post-1992 shifted its focus from 'collective defence' to 'collective security' to justify and allow NATO 'out of area' operations.[9] This Alliance intervention led to the Dayton Peace Accords. But these proved only a partial solution to the deep and wide-ranging problems of the Balkans. And this US spasm of peace-enforcement laid bare the power asymmetries between America and the Europeans, who continued to wrestle against the dark historical ghosts of their twentieth century. It also cast a harsh light on a European Union whose views on international policy were poorly coordinated and unbacked by any form of military sanction.

During the Bush presidency the US-led UN operation in Somalia at the end of 1992 was the one real exception to these principles of conservative management, and it was a relatively brief incursion lasting some four months. But it did constitute outside interference in a formally sovereign state and a member of the UN. Operation Restore Hope was justified on the grounds that Somalia's government had disintegrated so completely that the state could no longer protect the lives, liberties and survival of its people. The campaign in the Horn of Africa proved the first of many 'armed humanitarian interventions'[10] that came to characterise the post-Cold War era.

Conservative management also struggled to bridge the East–West divide. The idea of a truly integrated Europe, whole and free, proved an illusion. The NACC, though a powerful symbolic statement of East–West liaison, was little more than a talking shop and its first meeting in December 1991 virtually coincided with the disintegration of the USSR. This meant that the NACC became a collection of disparate and often fragile states extending from the Atlantic area through Central Asia to the Pacific, which made a mockery of any concept of a coherent Euro-Atlantic identity. Equally hollow and inadequate was the CSCE. This thirty-five-nation forum had helped to promote European détente in the mid-1970s, with Russia sitting as a co-equal of America. The 'conscience of the continent' covered human rights and economic issues and supposedly could serve as an instrument for 'building democratic institutions'. And it was seen by Washington as a vital tool for crisis prevention and conflict resolution (e.g. over border disputes or minority-rights issues) before force might have to be used.[11] But the CSCE had no military capability and lacked political clout. Expanded by 1992 to a membership of fifty-three, it proved – like the NACC – to be unwieldy and vacuous, and crucially failed to develop into a security organisation that could handle the Yugoslav wars. Like the vision of a Common European Home that so entranced Gorbachev, it represented another pan-European dream that could not be used to construct an overarching post-Wall framework for the continent's security.

As it turned out, there was 'no place for Russia' in the revivified core organisations of the new Europe – the EU and especially NATO.[12] The emergence of NATO as the only serious security institution both in Europe and 'out of area' made the Alliance in the long run more problematic for the Kremlin. Its enlargement to Russia's borders generated a sense of alienation later exploited by the government of Vladimir Putin. But this was neither the intention nor the fault of the conservative managers of 1989–91: all the key leaders of NATO – Bush, Kohl, Thatcher, Mitterrand – were solicitous of Gorbachev and of his country's status in public, even though in private they were playing a strong hand. They hoped that the Soviet Union – when fully reformed – would have a central place within the international system, as a stable core and cooperative partner or, as Gorbachev put it, a 'solid' and 'reliable' pillar. They neither expected nor desired the USSR to fragment at the end of 1991.

And, when it did, they adapted their policy in an effort to sustain Yeltsin's post-Soviet Russia in a comparable relationship. As a result, the West became deeply involved in helping Russia in its transition to a market democracy. Yet despite America's and Germany's conscious efforts not to 'isolate Russia' or turn it 'from potential friend to potential adversary', the handling of Moscow proved immensely complex and fraught.[13]

What ultimately happened in Russia during the 1990s was beyond Western control. Under Yeltsin, democracy was stillborn. Corruption ran rampant, the rule of law never took root. And Western leaders could not avert the country's cataclysmic economic collapse. This generated a fierce backlash from Russian nationalists humiliated by their country's chaotic impoverishment and by the sudden loss of its European empire. Growing rhetoric about reclaiming Russia's 'near-abroad' aggravated the insecurities of the newly free neighbouring states and encouraged their demands for incorporation in the 'institutional West'. By acquiescing in this, NATO not only enlarged as an organisation but projected America's military reach deep into Eastern Europe. This, coupled with the EU's parallel opening eastward, intensified Russian feelings of estrangement and heightened nostalgia for the country's great-power past, harking back especially to the defeat of Napoleon after 1812 and victory over Hitler in the Great Patriotic War. In any case, Russia had always been Janus-faced – a continent-wide Eurasian empire looking east as well as west – and a country so historically jealous of its sovereignty that it was unlikely ever to cede a scintilla of it to NATO or the EU. The prospect of being merely the eastern appendage of a Euro-Atlantic club was bound to be an affront both to the power pretensions of Russia and to its sense of identity. These issues could probably never have been resolved, even by the most sensitive diplomacy.

Even so, the achievements of the architects of the post-Wall world were historically unprecedented both in process and in outcome. The verdict of Philip Zelikow and Condoleezza Rice in their 1995 book on Europe and statecraft still stands: 'The leaders who saw their chance acted with skill, speed, and regard for the dignity of the Soviet Union. As a result, Europe bears scars but no open wounds from German unification. That is a testimony to statecraft.' In essence, 'Europe had been transformed by a general acceptance of the Western status quo.'[14]

*

What followed this Cold War transition is often described as an era of unipolarity. As we have seen, however, this is too simplistic a view. After German unification had been peacefully accomplished, the assumption of both Bush and Gorbachev had been that the international order remained bipolar, though it was now cooperative rather than confrontational in nature. On 11 September 1990, in an address to Congress, Bush spoke of the 'opportunity to move toward an historic period of cooperation', one he believed would be 'freer from the threat of terror, stronger in the pursuit of justice, and more secure in the quest for peace' – 'a world quite different than the one we've known'.[15] This was the premise of Bush's new world order and of the truly remarkable multinational coalition – from Syria to Senegal, from Britain to Bangladesh – that he mustered to drive Saddam Hussein out of Kuwait, a war effort built around the US and Soviet pillars and on the foundations of international law. But, as Kuwait amply demonstrated, Washington was the dominant force: Bush made the decision for war, and America provided the manpower, logistics and technology essential for the hundred-hour victory. So in Bush's new world order, the Soviet Union was in reality America's junior partner, and the UN – though liberated from its Cold War paralysis – could only function as a peacemaker when energised by American power.

The notion of cooperative bipolarity was therefore somewhat fictive, but in 1990–1 it was an essential fig leaf to mask Soviet decline and to facilitate the USSR's transition towards capitalism and democracy. Bush was desperate to maintain the working relationship he had developed with Gorbachev. Arguably this dependence on a single relationship was one of the drawbacks of his highly personalised and conservative approach to international relations. And perhaps Bush was undersensitised to risk, having successfully handled the apparently insuperable task of bringing the two Germanies together without a conflict. Given that the Soviet Union had been around for over seven decades it was difficult to imagine that it would fall apart in less than six months. Bush was slower than some of his Soviet specialists, and indeed his own Secretary of State, to appreciate how precarious the condition of America's historic antagonist had become.[16] Nevertheless, he persevered with the fig-leaf approach to create a new post-Soviet partnership with Boris Yeltsin in the first half of 1992 – welcoming Russia onto the UN Security Council as the Soviet successor state and perpetuating the G7 + 1 relationship.[17] Resisting the triumphalist rhetoric of unipolarity emanating from champions of neoconservatism such as columnist Charles Krauthammer, Bush was also determined to see the strategic arms reduction negotiations through to completion, culminating in the signing of the START II treaty in January 1993. Of course, these initiatives were offered from a position of strength: Russia might still be a nuclear superpower, but it was hard to imagine that this truncated country begging America for humanitarian and financial aid would ever again be seen as an equal partner of the United States.

It was during the summer of 1990 when the USSR capitulated over Germany's NATO membership that commentators had started to speculate about a 'unipolar moment'[18] or an 'emerging unipolar world'. But, as the academic Richard Spielman argued, a single 'pole', exercising a pre-eminent magnetic attraction was not the same as a sole 'hegemon' – 'a hierarchical system dominated by a single power that creates the rules as well as enforces them'. He observed that 'the European values that the US endorses predate our existence and limit our imperial ambitions'. Those European values included an underlying respect for state sovereignty, irrespective of the type of government and the values it espoused. The UN justification for the Gulf War in 1991 was indeed Iraq's violation of Kuwait's territorial integrity, not the nature of Saddam Hussein's regime – or, for that matter, the emir of Kuwait's attitude to human rights.[19]

There was also talk in the summer of 1990 of budding 'multipolarity'. According to Charles Krauthammer, 'Germany is emerging as the regional superpower in Europe, as is Japan in Asia.' And the transformation of the EC into the EU suggested that 'Europe' would also become a major international strategic actor. None of these scenarios came to pass. America remained what Krauthammer called the 'babysitter' of both Germany and Japan, neither of whom participated militarily in the Gulf or gained a permanent seat on the UN Security Council. As for the EU's pretensions as a foreign-policy actor and security provider, these were exposed as preposterous during the Yugoslav tragedy. 'The center of world power', so Krauthammer wrote in the winter 1991 issue of *Foreign Affairs*, 'is the unchallenged superpower, the United States, attended by its Western allies.'[20]

But even a unipolar world could – in theory at least – be cooperatively managed. The EU, Bonn and Tokyo embraced the identity of 'civilian powers' operating in a rules-bound environment. As the Gulf War showed, Bush's America too was pushing forward what German political scientist

Hanns Maull called the process of 'civilising' international politics in an increasingly interdependent world.[21] This idea picked up some of the grand Western ambitions at the end of the Second World War – about living as a world community of nations, adhering to international law, liberal values, limited use of force and a legitimate authority as arbiter. Bush highlighted these ideals when he announced the start of Operation Desert Storm in January 1991, declaring that the 'rule of law' should govern the 'conduct of nations', rather than 'the law of the jungle'. A multilateralist, he did not see America's future role as a perennial world policeman. But a cooperative US-led *Weltinnenpolitik* did not materialise and the UN never lived up to the high post-Wall expectations regarding its role as international arbiter.[22]

Unipolarity proved the best, or least inadequate, term for a post-Cold War era that still has no name. It was a long, lingering 'moment' – but, like every historical phase of international relations, not indefinitely sustainable. By the 2010s, challenges from Russia and China were all too real – in terms of power, influence and values. Putin's adventurism in Crimea, Ukraine and Syria and his geostrategic project to control the Arctic were flanked by campaigns to manipulate the inner life of liberal democracies through social media – all to regain what he considered Russia's rightful status as a great power and its legitimate hold over the Eurasian sphere. More significant though less visibly provocative was Xi Jinping's single-minded translation of China's demographic and economic power into military might, elbowing out challengers in the South China Sea and embarking on a grandiose project to make China a global super-power by 2050.[23] Dubbed, with innocuous opacity, 'One Belt, One Road',[24] this policy was coyly presented as Chinese 'multilateralism'.[25] Here were two powers engaged in competitive triangularity, focusing for the moment on unsettling the global leadership of the United States with their talk of multipolarity and polycentrism.[26]

The seeds of this fundamental geopolitical revision were already present in the early post-Wall, post-Square era.[27] America and its Western partners were slow to appreciate this. They held on to the belief that the embrace of capitalism would inexorably lead to the flowering of democracy, and that ideological foes would become cooperative partners. This was why both the Bush and Clinton administrations expended great energy in creating what was truly a World Trade Organisation. Ultimately, however, the United States, even in its unipolar moment, could not deny long-term the ambitions of other countries, especially states with less liberal forms of governance, such as the communist regimes it had apparently bested at the end of the Cold War.

The Russian and Chinese desire for world-power status developed in different ways. During the Yeltsin years of the 1990s, Russia tumbled into the abyss of failed democratisation and oligarchic capitalism; it was Putin who re-established stability, reasserted Russian identity, and restored the country's status in the world. But Yeltsin had already begun to talk in this way by the end of 1992, as disillusion mounted in Russia with his heady rhetoric about partnership with America and integration into the West. Western attempts to integrate Russia – through the CSCE, NACC, Partnership for Peace, the NATO–Russia Council as well as in the G8 – all proved ineffectual or problematic.

China's distinctive revisionist road was the logical consequence of 4 June 1989. As Deng lectured Scowcroft in December, there would be no compromise 'when China's sovereignty, dignity and independence are in question'.[28] Once the party recovered its grip, economic reform resumed under the banner of a 'socialist market economy'. Jiang Zemin emerged as the guardian of the Deng legacy for the next decade; his successor from 2002 to 2012, Hu Jintao, presided over steady and prodigious growth that was spectacular by Western standards and which laid firm foundations for Xi's geostrategic ambitions. And whereas Putin was operating within an economy that remained, as ever, dependent on energy and raw materials, Xi's base was the world's second largest economy and the hub of global manufacturing.

The United States, the third point of the triangle and the power that Russia and China were challenging, remained the world's largest economy and the most technologically sophisticated.[29] Its 2018 defence budget of some $700 billion was roughly triple that of China and Russia combined.[30] And despite closing dozens of installations in Iraq and Afghanistan, the United States still maintained globally some 500 military bases – compared to about twenty in the case of Russia, and China's sole foreign base at Djibouti.[31] America also had an unrivalled logistics capacity for lift-and-strike operations, ensuring that it fitted the classic definition of superpower status: 'great power plus great mobility of power'.[32]

But by the twenty-first century the nature of international affairs was in flux. Already in the Bush era, there had been challenges by 'renegade states' like Iraq and North Korea, in the form of military aggression and secret nuclear programmes. And the collapse of the USSR raised questions about the security of arms stockpiles and the danger of nuclear weapons finding their way into the hands of non-state actors. Since 2001 much of America's political energies and defence resources have been focused on 'the war on terror', especially in Afghanistan and Iraq, but also involving in some way more than seventy countries around the world.[33] This was a direct consequence of 9/11 – the terrorist attacks on the World Trade Center in New York and the Pentagon in Washington DC. America's obsession with this 'war', which has now lasted for almost two decades, reflects the uniqueness of the country's earlier twentieth-century experience – namely that throughout two world wars and the Cold War the continental United States escaped any direct attack, let alone invasion or occupation, in a way that differentiated it profoundly from Russia, China, Japan and most of Europe. What's more, 9/11 was not the consequence of a state-steered military assault, but a rather low-key operation involving four civilian airplanes and a small group of suicide bombers. Since that traumatic moment, US forces have been committed to 'numerous low-intensity, long-lasting engagements' against so-called non-state actors 'with no clear parameters for victory and no plan of exit'.[34]

America's 'counter-terror war' was an essentially reactive measure, responding to a diffuse array of threats across many locations. But the unipolar moment also breathed new life into an older geopolitical project that had envisioned America as the guardian of freedom and democracy worldwide, a project whose most celebrated exemplars had been Woodrow Wilson and Franklin D. Roosevelt. As Bush declared when championing his new world order, 'only the United States of America has both the moral standing and the means to back it up'.[35] It was the president's firm belief that the US had a unique responsibility to foster a new post-Cold War order organised around the twin principles of democratisation and market economics, but also around strengthened international institutions and universally agreed rules of international behaviour. Under Bill Clinton 'democratic enlargement' and international 'engagement' became the official American foreign-policy objective. Indeed, the Kosovo intervention in 1999 could be seen, observes historian John A. Thompson, as the 'first occasion since the Second World War on which the United States had sought by force to extend democracy (or at least self-determination)'. From 2001, President George W. Bush made democracy promotion a centrepiece of his own presidency, but he was more ideologically driven, unilateralist and military-minded in his approach than his predecessors, particularly after 9/11. And he was also less interested than his father had been in exploiting the potential of a universal collective security organisation such as the UN to re-establish order and peace.[36]

In November 2003, Bush Jr unveiled his 'new policy' – the 'Forward Strategy of Freedom' – declaring that 'the advance of freedom is the calling of our time; it is the calling of our country'. Although Bush focused particularly on the Middle East, his field of vision was global, ranging from North Korea to Zimbabwe. He even threw down the gauntlet to the leadership in Beijing:

> Our commitment to democracy is tested in China. That nation now has a sliver, a fragment of liberty. Yet, China's people will eventually want their liberty pure and whole. China has discovered that economic freedom leads to national wealth. China's leaders will also discover that freedom is indivisible – that social and religious freedom is also essential to national greatness and national dignity. Eventually, men and women who are allowed to control their own wealth will insist on controlling their own lives and their own country.[37]

As a principle around which to organise American interventions worldwide, democratisation had wide bipartisan support in Washington. Eight years later in November 2011, Barack Obama's Secretary of State, Hillary Clinton, articulated her own mission statement, which commentators called 'Bush Freedom Agenda 2.0'.[38] Reflecting on the Arab Spring – the growing demands for liberty from Tunis to Cairo, from Tripoli to Damascus that began in late 2010 – she insisted that 'real democratic change in the Middle East and North Africa is in the national interest of the United States'. Clinton rejected what she called the 'false choice between progress and stability', insisting that 'the greatest single source of instability in today's Middle East is not the demand for change. It is the refusal to change.' Clinton acknowledged that 'these revolutions are not ours. They are not by us, for us, or against us'. Nevertheless, she argued, 'we do have a role' – through 'our presence, influence, and global leadership' and because 'we have the resources, capabilities, and expertise to support those who seek peaceful, meaningful, democratic reform'. America's interest in democratisation was in the process, not the product. 'The United States does not fund political candidates or political parties. We do offer training to parties and candidates committed to democracy. We do not try to shift outcomes or impose an American model.'[39]

Yet Clinton believed that democratisation was likely to work in

America's favour: 'democracies do not always agree with us, and in the Middle East and North Africa they may disagree strongly with some of our policies. But at the end of the day, it is no coincidence that our closest allies – from Britain to South Korea – are democracies.' The unipolar world seemed to accentuate the magnetic attraction of American values. And she made clear that the Obama administration's freedom agenda was global in scope: it was a challenge to 'autocrats around the world' who might be wondering 'if the next Tahrir Square' would be in their own capital city. Clinton did not suggest that Moscow's Red Square would be next. But Putin considered the speech a direct challenge, especially when America provided 'resources, capabilities, and expertise' to Russian opposition groups in the 2012 presidential election and during the 2013–14 Euromaidan revolt which brought down Ukraine's pro-Russian president Viktor Yanukovych. On this basis, Putin was able to claim that it was Washington that had pioneered 'hybrid warfare' and that Moscow's own campaign to undermine or even roll back democratisation was simply a response to US provocations in Russia and Russia's near-abroad.[40]

The project of 'democratisation', invigorated by the 'war on terror', became a hallmark of US foreign policy in the first decade of the twenty-first century.[41] It was as if the awareness of unipolarity had diverted American leaders from traditional strategic thinking about the balance of power. Instead, they concentrated not on the big powers but on small fragile states or regional rogue actors with WMD whose problems could supposedly be solved either by military action to topple tyrants and crush terrorists or by soft-power programmes to mobilise democratic change. In the process, American policymakers tended to take their eyes off the incremental shifts in the global balance provoked by Russia and China since the 1990s. Although unipolarity could never be permanent, this loss of focus by American leaders contributed to its erosion.

By contrast Bush and his fellow managers of the 1989–91 post-Cold War transition had kept their eyes on the global balance – tempered by hopes of building a freer, more prosperous and more open post-Wall world. They also understood that US power had to be exercised within a framework of political alliances and economic interdependence. This had been characteristic of the Western alliance since its inception in the 1940s and was extended to former communist adversaries during the Cold War endgame. Bush Sr's three successors as president – Clinton, Bush Jr and Obama – for all the differences in their conduct of foreign policy – displayed a similar attention to alliance relationships and co-operative diplomacy. But America's forty-fifth president was different.

In a *Playboy* interview in March 1990, as Bush was grappling with the challenges of German unification and the deepening Soviet crisis, Donald J. Trump already hinted at the line he would take if he ever occupied the Oval Office. How would 'President Trump' conduct himself? he was asked. The answer came back: 'He would believe very strongly in extreme military strength. He wouldn't trust anyone. He wouldn't trust the Russians; he wouldn't trust our allies; he'd have a huge military arsenal, perfect it, understand it. Part of the problem is that we're defending some of the wealthiest countries in the world for nothing ...'[42]

So why not run? he was asked.

'I'd do the job as well as or better than anyone,' Trump responded, but 'I don't want to be president. I'm 100% sure. I'd change my mind only if I saw this country continue to go down the tubes.'

When Trump did become president in 2017, he started to act on these precepts. There was no announcement of a grand strategy, just a general pledge to put 'America First' and 'Make America Great Again'. The time had come, Trump declared on 27 April 2018, to 'shake the rust off America's foreign policy' because it was 'a complete and total disaster'. 'We're getting out of the nation-building business', he announced, in an unmistakable repudiation of his predecessors' passion for democratisation. And this was followed by a mystifying injunction that would become a central theme of his administration's policy: 'we must as a nation be more unpredictable'.[43]

Adopting unpredictability as a principle of action in international relations means hazarding your stake and taking chances when you believe the odds are in your favour. As gambler-in-chief, Trump believed that the combination of unpredictability and American power would give him the leverage to negotiate anything with anyone at any time.[44] This approach entailed taking risks with national security – straining or even shredding the fabric of partnerships and networks that had been an integral part of America's power and status for almost seven decades. Trump did not hesitate to insult fellow statesmen and women; he attacked painstakingly built post-war alliances like NATO, and declared as enemies the EU and longstanding European partners, including Germany. He played footsie with Russia and North Korea and walked away from arms-control deals. His policy of aggressive economic nationalism provoked a full-scale trade war with China, in response to Beijing's predatory economic policies, and led him to pull apart NAFTA (a legacy of the Bush era).

But the domain of foreign policy is not a poker room at a Trump casino; nor are tweets and tantrums the recipe for sustainable relationships with allies or adversaries. The needling of partners and the undercutting of alliances only emboldens adversaries to chance their arm, weakening regional stability in Europe and the Asia-Pacific region. In general, Trump reduced diplomacy and statecraft to a chaotic succession of purely trans-actional encounters – of deals to be won or lost. This was hardly the best response to confront the systemic, global challenges from Beijing and Moscow – expressed by the Russian foreign minister Sergey Lavrov's slogan about establishing a 'post-West world order'. Or as Vladimir Putin asserted in June 2019: 'The liberal idea' that underpinned Western democracy for decades had 'outlived its purpose' and 'become obsolete'.[45]

And so the world Post Wall Post Square has come a long way from the days of George H. W. Bush. But some of his words now look strikingly prescient. In his farewell speech in Texas, Bush warned that 'economically, a world of escalating instability and hostile nationalism will disrupt global markets, set off trade wars, set us on a path of economic decline'. And despite all the rhetoric about a rules-based future order (hopefully more peaceful and democratic), he admonished his audience: 'The new world could, in time, be as menacing as the old. And let me be blunt: A retreat from American leadership, from American involvement, would be a mistake for which future generations, indeed our own children, would pay dearly'.[46]

Abbreviations

AFP	*Agence France-Presse*
AP	*Associated Press*
APEC	Asia-Pacific Economic Cooperation
APP	American Presidency Project
AWP	Alan Whittome Papers
BATUN	Baltic Appeal to the United Nations
CCP	Chinese Communist Party
CdMDA	Chronik der Mauer Digital Archiv
CDU	Christlich Demokratische Union Deutschlands (Christian Democratic Union)
CFE	Conventional Armed Forces in Europe (Treaty)
CFSP	Common Foreign and Security Policy
CIA	Central Intelligence Agency
CIS	Commonwealth of Independent States
CPSU	Communist Party of the Soviet Union
CQ Almanac	*Congressional Quarterly Almanac*
CSCE	Conference on Security and Cooperation in Europe
CSM	*Christian Science Monitor*
CSU	Christlich-Soziale Union in Bayern (Christian Social Union in Bavaria)
CT	*Chicago Tribune*
CWH	*Cold War History*
CWIHP	Cold War International History Project, Washington DC
DDE	*Diplomatie für die deutsche Einheit* (transcripts and documents)
DDR	Deutsche Demokratische Republik
DE	*Die Einheit* (transcripts and documents)
DESE	*Deutsche Einheit Sonderedition* (transcripts and documents)

DILA	Direction de l'Information Légale et Administrative
DM	Deutschmark
DVP	Discours – Vie Publique
DW	*Deutsche Welle*
EBRD	European Bank for Reconstruction and Development
EC	European Community
ECU	European Currency Unit
ECWF	End of the Cold War Forum, Moscow (transcripts and documents)
EFTA	European Free Trade Area
EMU	Economic and Monetary Union
EPU	European Political Union
ESSG	European Strategy Steering Group
EU	European Union
FAZ	*Frankfurter Allgemeine Zeitung*
FBIS	*Foreign Broadcasting Information Service*
FCO	Foreign and Commonwealth Office
FDP	Freie Demokraten / Freie Demokratische Partei (Free Democratic Party)
FRC	Foreign Relations Committee, US Senate
FRG	Federal Republic of Germany
FT	*Financial Times*
G7	Group of Seven
G24	Group of 24 (set up in 1989, to coordinate aid to Central and Eastern Europe)
GDR	German Democratic Republic
GHDI	German History in Documents and Images
GHIDC	German Historical Institute, Washington DC
IAEA	International Atomic Energy Agency
IBRD	International Bank for Reconstruction and Development
ICBMs	intercontinental ballistic missiles
IGC	Intergovernmental Conference
INFs	intermediate-range nuclear forces
IS	*International Security*
ITAR-TASS	*Informatsionnye Telegrafnoye Agentstvto Rossii – Telegrafnoe Agentstvo Sovetskovo Soyuza*
JCWS	*Journal of Cold War Studies*
JSSE	Joint Study of the Soviet Economy
LAT	*Los Angeles Times*

LRB	*London Review of Books*
MEP	Member of European Parliament
MFN	Most Favoured Nation trade status
MGDF	*Michael Gorbatschow und die deutsche Frage* (transcripts and documents)
MoH	*Masterpieces of History* (transcripts and documents)
MTCR	Missile Technology Control Regime
NAC	North Atlantic Council
NACC	North Atlantic Cooperation Council
NAFTA	North American Free Trade Agreement
NATO	North Atlantic Treaty Organisation
ND	*Neues Deutschland*
NPT	Non-Proliferation of Nuclear Weapons Treaty
NSAEBB	National Security Archive Electronic Briefing Book
NSC	National Security Council (US)
NSDD	National Security Decision Directive
NSR	National Security Review
NVA	National People's Army of the GDR (Nationale Volksarmee)
NYRB	*New York Review of Books*
NYT	*New York Times*
NZZ	*Neue Zürcher Zeitung*
OECD	Organisation for Economic Co-operation and Development
PDS	Partei des Demokratischen Sozialismus (Party of Democratic Socialism)
PHP	Parallel History Project on Cooperative Security, Zurich
PRC	People's Republic of China
PREM	Prime Minister's Office files
RCP	Russian Communist Party
RSFSR	Russian Soviet Federative Socialist Republic
SALT	Strategic Arms Limitation Talks / Treaty
SD	*Sowjetische Dokumente*
SDP	Social Democratic Party in the GDR (SozialDemokratische Partei in der DDR)
SED	Sozialistische Einheitspartei Deutschlands (Socialist Unity Party of Germany)
SII	Structural Impediments Initiative
SNFs	short-range nuclear forces
SPD	Sozialdemokratische Partei Deutschlands (Social Democratic Party of Germany)

START	Strategic Arms Reduction Treaty
SZ	*Süddeutsche Zeitung*
TASS	*Telegrafnoye agentstvo Sovetskovo Soyuza*
taz	*Die Tageszeitung*
TLSS	*The Last Superpower Summits* (transcripts and documents)
TSMP	Teimuraz Stepanov-Mamaladze Papers
UN	United Nations
UNITAF	Unified Task Force (US-led, UN sanctioned multinational force which operated in Somalia)
UNOSOM	United Nations Operation in Somalia
UNSC	United Nations Security Council
UNTAC	United Nations Transitional Authority in Cambodia
UPI	*United Press International*
USAF	United States Airforce
USSR	Union of Soviet Socialist Republics
VM	Valutamark
WP	*Washington Post*
WSJ	*Wall Street Journal*
WSJE	*Wall Street Journal Europe*
ZA	Zwischenarchiv
ZRP	Zelikow and Rice Papers

Notes

Archives

Estonia
Välisministeerium arhiiv (EST VM), Tallinn
Rahvusarhiiv eraarhiiviosakond – endine Parteiarhiiv, Tallinn

France
Ministère des Affaires Etrangères (MAE), Archives Diplomatiques (AD), Paris

Germany
Bundesarchiv (BArch) and Stiftung Archiv der Parteien und Massenorganisationen der DDR (SAPMO), Berlin-Lichterfelde
Bundesarchiv (BA), Koblenz
Politisches Archiv des Auswärtigen Amts (PAAA), Berlin
Behörde des Bundesbeauftragten für die Stasi-Unterlagen (BStU), Stasi Records Agency, Berlin

Iceland
Ministry of Foreign Affairs Archive (ICE MFA), Reykjavik

Russia
Arkhiv Gorbachev–Fonda (AGF), Moscow
Rossiiskii Gosudarstvennyi Arkhiv Noveishei Istorii (RGANI), Moscow
State Archive of the Russian Federation (GARF), Moscow

United Kingdom
Churchill Archives Centre (CAC) and (Digital) Margaret Thatcher Foundation (MTF), Cambridge
The National Archives (TNA), Kew, Surrey

United States
George H. W. Bush Presidential Library (GHWBPL), College Station, TX
Hoover Institution Archives (HIA), Stanford, CA
International Monetary Fund Archives (IMFA), Washington, DC
National Security Archive (NSA), George Washington University (GWU), Washington, DC
Seeley G. Mudd Library (SML), Princeton, NJ
Wilson Center (Digital) Archives (DAWC), Washington, DC

Interviews and Witness Seminars
Egon Bahr, 19 May 1998, Bonn
Joachim Bitterlich, 6 September 1999, Brussels, and 9 May 2019, Washington, DC
Lothar de Mazière, 17 April 1998, Berlin
Hans-Dietrich Genscher, 26 March 1998 and 14 April 1999, Bonn
Michael Mertes, 8 September 1999, Bonn
Ulrich Weisser, 26 March 1999, Düsseldorf
Richard von Weizsäcker, 14 April 1998 and 29 April 1999, Berlin

'FCO Witness Seminar: Berlin in the Cold War 1949–1990 & German Unification 1989–1990'. Lancaster House (16 October 2009).

'Mikhail Gorbachev's 1988 Address to the UN: 30 Years Later'. SAIS – Johns Hopkins University, Washington DC (6 December 2018). Panel Discussion with Andrei Kozyrev, Pavel Palazhchenko, Thomas W. Simons Jr, and Kristina Spohr. Video available at: youtube.com/watch?v=Mi6NkWIJuzo

'Open Door: NATO and Euro-Atlantic Security in the 1990s'. SAIS – Johns Hopkins University, Washington DC (12 March 2019). Closed Oral History Workshop by Kristina Spohr and Daniel S. Hamilton with policymakers: Andrei Kozyrev, Andrei Zagorski, Sir Malcolm Rifkind, Volker Rühe, Karsten Voigt, Benoît d'Aboville, Strobe Talbott, Robert E. Hunter, Alexander Vershbow, Jenonne Walker, John Kornblum, Jeremy Rosner, Stephen J. Flanagan, General Wesley K. Clark, Mircea Geonană, Géza Jeszensky, András Simonyi, Jan Havránek, Jan Jireš.

'Exiting the Cold War, Entering a New World'. SAIS – Johns Hopkins University, Washington DC (8 May 2019). Closed Oral History Workshop by Kristina Spohr and Daniel S. Hamilton with policymakers: Anatoly Adamishin, Pavel Palazhchenko, Joachim Bitterlich, Markus Meckel, Horst Teltschik, Sir Rodric Braithwaite, Sir Roderic Lyne, Jón Baldvin Hannibalsson, Mart Laar, Adam Michnik, Avis Bohlen, David Gompert, Thomas W. Simons, Philip Zelikow.

For a full bibliography, see kristina-spohr.com/books/post-wall-post-square

Introduction

1 'Atomares Wintex' *Der Spiegel* 8/1989 20.2.1989; 'NATO-ÜBUNG: Schlag Zuviel' *Der Spiegel* 11/1989 13.3.1989; 'Der Iwan kommt – und feste druff' *Der Spiegel* 18/1989 1.5.1989; 'Schlacht von gestern' *Der Spiegel* 29/1989 17.7.1989

2 A good deal has been written about the dramatic, revolutionary upheavals of 1989. See for example Victor Sebestyen *Revolution 1989: The Fall of the Soviet Empire* Pantheon 2009; Michael Meyer *1989: The Year That Changed the World – The Untold Story Behind the Fall of the Berlin Wall* Simon & Schuster 2009; Ludger Kühnhardt *Revolutionszeiten: Das Umbruchsjahr 1989 im geschichtlichen Zusammenhang* Olzog 1995. For '1989' as the product of social revolution and 'people power' from below, see for example Padraic Kenney *A Carnival of Revolution: Central Europe 1989* Princeton UP 2003; Charles A. Maier *Dissolution: The Crisis of Communism and the End of East Germany* Princeton UP 1997; Konrad H. Jarausch & Martin Sabrow (eds) *Weg in den Untergang: Der innere Zerfall der DDR* Vandenhoeck & Ruprecht 1999. Cf. Adam Roberts & Timothy Garton Ash (eds) *Civil Resistance and Power Politics: The Experience of Non-Violent Action from Gandhi to the Present* Oxford UP 2009; April Carter *People Power and Political Change: Key Issues and Concepts* Routledge 2012. For '1989' as the result of 'reform from above' by national communist elites sanctioned by Mikhail Gorbachev, see for example Stephen Kotkin with Jan T. Gross *Uncivil Society: 1989 and the Implosion of the Communist Establishment* Modern Library 2009; Constantine Pleshakov *There Is No Freedom without Bread: 1989*

and the Civil War that Brought Down Communism Farrar, Straus & Giroux 2009; Gordon M. Hahn *Russia's Revolution from Above, 1985–2000: Reform, Transition and Revolution in the Fall of the Soviet Communist Regime* Taylor & Francis 2002; Jacques Lévesque *The Enigma of 1989: The USSR and the Liberation of Eastern Europe* Univ. of California Press 1997

3 Francis Fukuyama 'The End of History?' *The National Interest* no. 16 (Summer 1989) pp. 3–18; idem, *The End of History and the Last Man* Hamilton 1992. On 'post 1989-optimism', see Thomas Bagger 'The World According to Germany: Reassessing 1989' *Washington Quarterly* 41, 4 (Winter 2019) pp. 53–63

4 Cf. for example George Lawson et al. (eds) *The Global 1989: Continuity and Change in World Politics* Cambridge UP 2010; Richard K. Herrmann & Richard Ned Lebow (eds) *Ending the Cold War: Interpretations, Causation and the Study of International Relations* Palgrave Macmillan 2004; Bernhard Blumenau et al. (eds) *New Perspectives on the End of the Cold War: Unexpected Transformations?* Routledge 2018

5 For their memoirs and autobiographies as well as key biographies, see for example Mikhail S. Gorbachev *Memoirs* Bantam 1997; idem, *Wie es war* Ullstein 1999; William Taubman *Gorbachev: His Life and Times* W. W. Norton 2017; Archie Brown *The Gorbachev Factor* Oxford UP 1996; George Bush & Brent Scowcroft *A World Transformed* Vintage Books 1998; George Bush *All the Best, George Bush: My Life in Letters and Other Writings* Scribner 2013; Jon Meacham *Destiny and Power: The American Odyssey of George Herbert*

Walker Bush Random House 2015; Timothy Naftali *George H. W. Bush* Times Books 2007; Helmut Kohl with Kai Diekmann *Ich wollte Deutschlands Einheit* Ullstein 1996; idem, *Vom Mauerfall zur Wiedervereinigung: Meine Erinnerungen* Knaur-Taschenbuch 2009; idem, *Erinnerungen 1982–1990* Droemer 2005; idem, *Erinnerungen 1990–1994* Droemer 2007; Hans-Peter Schwarz *Helmut Kohl: Eine politische Biographie* Pantheon 2014

6 Eduard Shevardnadze *The Future Belongs to Freedom* Sinclair-Stevenson 1991; James A. Baker with Thomas M. DeFrank *The Politics of Diplomacy: Revolution, War and Peace, 1989–1992* G. P. Putnam's Sons 1995; Hans-Dietrich Genscher *Erinnerungen* Siedler 1995; idem, *Unterwegs zur Einheit: Reden und Dokumente aus bewegter Zeit* Siedler 1991; Gerhard A. Ritter *Hans-Dietrich Genscher, das Auswärtige Amt und die deutsche Vereinigung* Beck 2013

7 Margaret Thatcher *The Downing Street Years* HarperCollins 1993; George R. Urban *Diplomacy and Disillusion at the Court of Margaret Thatcher: An Insider's View* I. B. Tauris 1995; François Mitterrand *Über Deutschland* Insel 1996; Pierre Favier & Michel Martin-Roland *La Décennie Mitterrand, vol. iv: Les Déchirements (1992–1995)* Seuil 1999

8 See for example Frédéric Bozo et al. (eds) *Europe and the End of the Cold War: A Reappraisal* Routledge 2008; Harold James *Making the European Monetary Union* Harvard UP 2012; Kenneth Dyson & Kevin Featherstone *The Road to Maastricht: Negotiating Economic and Monetary Union* Oxford UP 1999; Werner Rouget & Joachim

Bitterlich *Schwierige Nachbarschaft am Rhein: Frankreich-Deutschland* Bouvier 1998

9 For released Chinese documents on Beijing's decision-making surrounding protest and crackdown in May and June 1989, which however have courted much controversy as regards 'verifiablity', see Zhang Liang et al. (eds) *The Tiananmen Papers: The Chinese Leadership's Decision to Use Force against Their Own People – In Their Own Words* Little, Brown 2001; and Andrew J. Nathan 'The Tiananmen Papers' *Foreign Affairs* 80, 1 (January/February 2001) pp. 2–50. For commentary on these sources, see Lowell Dittmer 'Review of The Tiananmen Papers' *China Quarterly* 166 (June 2001) pp. 476–83; Alfred L. Chan 'The Tiananmen Papers Revisited' *China Quarterly* 177 (March 2004) pp. 190–205; Andrew J. Nathan 'A Rejoinder to Alfred L. Chan' *China Quarterly* 177 (March 2004) pp. 206–14; Richard Baum 'Tiananmen – The Inside Story?' *China Journal* 46 (July 2001) pp. 119–23. See also Andrew J. Nathan 'The New Tiananmen Papers: Inside the Secret Meeting That Changed China' *Foreign Affairs* (May 2019) online; Bao Pu (ed.) *The Last Secret: The Final Documents from the June Fourth Crackdown* New Centrury Press 2019

10 See for example Robert L. Suettinger *Beyond Tiananmen: The Politics of US–China Relations 1989–2000* Brookings Institution Press 2003; David M. Lampton *Same Bed, Different Dreams* Univ. of California Press 2002; Ezra F. Vogel *Deng Xiaoping and the Transformation of China* Harvard UP 2013; Sergey Radchenko *Unwanted Visionaries: The Soviet Failure in Asia at*

the End of the Cold War Oxford UP
2014. For a comparison of Soviet and
Chinese economic reforms, see Chris
Miller *The Struggle to Save the Soviet
Economy: Mikhail Gorbachev the
Collapse of the USSR* Univ. of North
Carolina Press 2016; Stephen Kotkin
'Review Essay – The Unbalanced
Triangle: What Chinese–Russian
Relations Mean for the United States'
Foreign Affairs 88, 5 (September/
October 2009) pp. 130–8

11 See for example Timothy Garton Ash
*The Magic Lantern: The Revolution of
'89 Witnessed in Warsaw, Budapest,
Berlin, and Prague* Vintage Books 1999;
Michael Dobbs *Down with Big Brother:
The Fall of the Soviet Empire* Bloomsbury
1996; Gale Stokes, *The Walls Came
Tumbling Down: Collapse and Rebirth
in Eastern Europe* Oxford UP 2011;
Mark Kramer 'The Collapse of East
European Communism and the
Repercussions within the Soviet Union
(Parts 1–3)' *Journal of Cold War Studies*
(hereafter *JCWS*) 5, 4 (2003) pp.
178–256 and 6, 4 (2004) pp. 3–64 as
well as 7, 1 (2005) pp. 3–96; *idem* 'The
Demise of the Soviet Bloc' *Journal of
Modern History* 83 (December 2011) pp.
788–854; Craig Calhoun *Neither Gods
nor Emperors: Students and the Struggle
for Democracy in China* Univ. of
California Press 1997; M. E. Sarotte
'China's Fear of Contagion: Tiananmen
Square and the Power of the European
Example' *International Security* 37, 2
(Fall 2012) pp. 156–82

12 See for example Robert Service *The End
of the Cold War, 1985–1991* Pan Books
2015; James Graham Wilson *The
Triumph of Improvisation: Gorbachev's
Adaptability, Reagan's Engagement, and
the End of the Cold War* Cornell UP

2013; Raymond L. Garthoff *The Great
Transition: American–Soviet Relations
and the End of the Cold War* Brookings
Institution Press 1994

13 See for example Hal Brands *From Berlin
to Baghdad: America's Search for
Purpose in the Post-Cold War World*
Univ. Press of Kentucky 2008; Jeffrey
A. Engel (ed.) *Into the Desert: Reflections
on the Gulf War* Oxford UP 2013;
Lawrence Freedman and Efraim Karsh
The Gulf Conflict, 1990–1991 Princeton
UP 1995. See also Marc Weller *Iraq and
the Use of Force in International Law*
Oxford UP 2010

14 See for example Serhii Plokhy *The Last
Empire: The Final Days of the Soviet
Union* Oneworld 2014; Vladislav M.
Zubok *A Failed Empire: The Soviet
Union in the Cold War from Stalin to
Gorbachev* Univ. of North Carolina
Press 2009. See also Stephen Kotkin
*Armageddon Averted: The Soviet
Collapse, 1970–2000* Oxford UP 2008;
Stephan G. Bierling *Wirtschaftshilfe für
Moskau: Motive und Strategien der
Bundesrepublik Deutschland und der
USA 1990–1996* Schöningh 1998; Peter
Rutland 'Mission Impossible? The IMF
and the Failure of the Market Transition
in Russia' *Review of International
Studies* 25 (December 1999) [The
Interregnum: Controversies in World
Politics 1989–1999] pp. 183–200; Angela
Stent *The Limits of Partnership: US–
Russian Relations in the Twenty-First
Century* Princeton UP 2015

15 On Japan, see for example Ezra Vogel
*Japan as Number One: Lessons for
America* Harvard UP 1979; James
Fallows *Looking at the Sun: The Rise of
the New East Asian Economic and
Political System* Pantheon 1995;
Rosemary Foot 'Power Transitions and

Great Power Management: Three Decades of China–Japan–US Relations' *Pacific Review* 30, 6 (2017) pp. 829–42

16 See for example Josip Glaurdic *The Hour of Europe: Western Powers and the Break-up of Yugoslavia* Yale UP 2011; Richard Caplan *Europe and the Recognition of New States in Yugoslavia* Cambridge UP 2005; James Gow *Triumph of the Lack of Will: International Diplomacy and the Yugoslav War* Columbia UP 1997. On China, see for example Odd Arne Westad *Restless Empire: China and the World Since 1750* Vintage 2013 for a long-term perspective; and Julian Gewirtz *Unlikely Partners, Chinese Reformers, Western Economists and the Making of Global China* Harvard UP 2017

17 Jason Burke 'Signs of "Balkanisation" seen in Soviet Union' *Christian Science Monitor* (hereafter *CSM*) 8.10.1991; see ch. 5, p. 317

18 See for example Bruce Cumings *North Korea: Another Country* New Press 2004; Nicholas L. Miller & Vipin Narang 'North Korea Defied the Theoretical Odds: What Can We Learn from its Successful Nuclearisation?' *Texas National Security Review* 1, 2 (February 2018)

19 Cf. for example Hal Brands *Making the Unipolar Moment: US Foreign Policy and the Rise of the Post-Cold War Order* Cornell UP 2016; *idem* 'Choosing Primacy: US Strategy and Global Order at the Dawn of the Post-Cold War Era' *Texas National Security Review* 1, 2 (2018) pp. 8–33; Jeffrey A. Engel *When the World Seemed New: George H. W. Bush and the End of the Cold War* Houghton Mifflin Harcourt 2017. See also Charles Krauthammer 'The Unipolar Moment' *Foreign Affairs* 70, 1

(1990/1991) [America and the World 1990/91] pp. 23–33; *idem* 'The Unipolar Moment Revisited' *The National Interest* 70 (Winter 2002/3) pp. 5–18. Cf. Odd Arne Westad *The Global Cold War: Third World Interventions and the Making of Our Times* Cambridge UP 2007 conclusions; *idem* 'The Cold War and America's Delusion of Victory' *New York Times* (hereafter *NYT*) 28.8.2017

20 For seminal studies, see for example Mary Sarotte *1989: The Struggle to Create Post-Cold War Europe* Princeton UP 2009; Andreas Rödder *Deutschland einig Vaterland: Die Geschichte der Wiedervereinigung* Beck 2009; Frédéric Bozo *Mitterrand, la fin de la guerre froide et l'unification allemande: De Yalta à Maastricht* Odile Jacob 2005; Philip Zelikow & Condoleezza Rice *Germany Unified and Europe Transformed: A Study in Statecraft* Harvard UP 1995; *idem, To Build a Better World: Choices to End the Cold War and Create a Global Commonwealth* Twelve 2019; Alexander von Plato *Die Vereinigung Deutschlands – Ein weltpolitisches Machtspiel: Bush, Kohl, Gorbatschow und die internen Gesprächsprotokolle* Ch. Links 2009; Vladislav Zubok 'With His Back Against the Wall: Gorbachev, Soviet Demise, and German Unification' *Cold War History* (hereafter *CWH*) 14, 4 (November 2014) pp. 619–45; Mark Kramer 'The Myth of a no-NATO Enlargement Pledge to Russia' *The Washington Quarterly* 32, 2 (2009) pp. 39–61; Ron Asmus *Opening NATO's Door: How the Alliance Remade Itself for a New Era* Columbia UP 2002; James Goldgeier 'Bill and Boris: A Window Into a Most Important Post-Cold War Relationship' *Texas National*

Security Review 1, 4 (August 2018); Kristina Spohr 'Precluded or Precedent-setting? The "NATO Enlargement Question" in the Triangular Bonn–Washington–Moscow Diplomacy of 1990/1991 and Beyond' *JCWS* 14, 4 (2012) pp. 4–54; *idem, Germany and the Baltic Problem After the Cold War: The Development of a New Ostpolitik 1989–2000* Routledge 2004

21   See chs. 4 and 5 for: Gorbachev's idea of a 'Common European Home', Genscher's proposal for a CSCE-based 'pan-European Security Architecture', and Mitterrand's vision of a 'European Confederation' model built around the EC at its core

22   Kristina Spohr & David Reynolds 'Putin's Revenge' *New Statesman* 17.1.2017

23   See bibliography for a full list of 'Primary Sources'

24   Ansprache von Bundespräsident Roman Herzog bei der Deutschen Gesellschaft für Auswärtige Politik in Bonn 13.3.1995 bundespraesident.de/ SharedDocs /Reden/DE/Roman-Herzog/Reden/1995/03/19950313_Rede. html

25   Cf. Adam Tooze *Crashed: How a Decade of Financial Crises Changed the World* Viking 2018

26   Cf. Stephen Kotkin 'Russia's Perpetual Geopolitics: Putin Returns to the Historical Pattern' *Foreign Affairs* (May/June 2016) online

27   Cf. Robert D. Blackwill & Jennifer M. Harris *War by Other Means: Geoeconomics and Statecraft* Belknap Press 2018

28   Cf. Bobo Lo *Axis of Convenience: Moscow, Beijing, and the New Geopolitics* Brookings Institution Press 2008; Graham Allison *Destined for War: Can America and China Escape Thucydides's Trap?* Houghton Mifflin Harcourt 2017

29   Cf. Hanns W. Maull 'Germany and Japan: The New Civilian Powers' *Foreign Affairs* 69, 5 (Winter 1990) pp. 91–106; *idem* and Sebastian Harnisch (eds) *Germany as a Civilian Power? The Foreign Policy of the Berlin Republic* Manchester UP 2001; Jan Orbie 'Civilian Power Europe – Review of the Original and Current Debates' *Cooperation and Conflict* 41, 1 (2006) pp. 123–8 Karen E. Smith 'Beyond the Civilian Power EU Debate' *Politique européenne* 17, 3 (2005) pp. 63–82

30   Under the rubrique *Weltinnenpolitik* the Germans had espoused a similar vision since the 1960s. See Carl Friedrich von Weizsäcker 'Schachpartie der Großmächte' *Die Zeit* 7.1.1966; Ulrich Bartosch *Weltinnenpolitik: Zur Theorie des Friedens von Carl Friedrich von Weizsäcker* [Beiträge zur politischen Wissenschaft, Vol. 86] Duncker & Humblot 1995

31   Cf. Hillary Rodham Clinton 'Leading Through Civilian Power: Redefining American Diplomacy and Development' *Foreign Affairs* 89, 6 (November/December 2010) [The World Ahead] pp. 13–24

32   Cf. Henry Kissinger *World Order* Penguin Books 2015

Chapter 1

1   Maureen Dowd 'Soviet Star Is a Smash In Broadway Showing' *NYT* 8.12.1988.

2   James Barron 'For Gorbachev, Met Museum and Trump Tower Visits Due' *NYT* 1.12.1988; Howard Kurtz 'Gorbachev on the Road to New Soviet Frontiers' *Washington Post* (hereafter *WP*) 4.12.1988; Maureen Dowd 'Manhattan Goes Gorbachev – From Fish to Oreo Cookies' *NYT* 7.12.1988

3   'Excerpts From Speech to UN on Major Soviet Military Cuts' *NYT* 7.12.1988

4   George Bush & Brent Scowcroft *A World Transformed* Vintage Books 1998 p. 26. Jeffrey Engel highlights James Baker's role in Bush taking a different direction from Reagan and in the 'purge' of the White House to send the political message that 'a new man was in charge'. See Engel *When the World Seemed New* pp. 86–9; Jon Meacham *Destiny and Power: The American Odyssey of George Herbert Walker Bush* Random House 2015 p. 368; Derek H. Chollet & James M. Goldgeier 'Once Burned, Twice Shy? The Pause of 1989?' in William C. Wohlforth *Cold War Endgame: Oral History, Analysis, Debates* Penn State UP 2010 ch. 5. See also James A. Baker III Papers, Seeley G. Mudd Library, Princeton (hereafter JAB-SML), Box 96, Folder 6 (hereafter B96/F6), Meeting with President Richard Nixon 10.12.1988

5   William Taubman *Gorbachev: His Life and Times* W. W. Norton 2017 chs. 1–5; Sebestyen *Revolution 1989* p. 116; see also Don Oberdorfer *From the Cold War to a New Era: The United States and the Soviet Union, 1983–1991* Johns Hopkins UP 1998 ch. 4 esp. pp. 107–11

6   Raisa Gorbacheva *I Hope* Fontana 1991 p. 5

7   Archie Brown *Seven Years that Changed the World: Perestroika in Perspective* Oxford UP 2007 pp. 284–94; Antony D'Agostino 'How the Soviet Union Thought itself to Death' *The National Interest* (May–June 2017)

8   'The Soviet Economy in 1988: Gorbachev Changes Course' CIA/DIA April 1989; David Reynolds *One World Divisible: A Global History since 1945*

    W. W. Norton 2000 p. 540. See also IMF Archives, Office of the Managing Director Alan Whittome Papers – Joint Study of the Soviet Economy (hereafter IMFA-AWP JSSE) Box 1 Folder 7 (hereafter B1/F7) NATO – Long Term Projections for the Soviet Economy, Note by the Secretary General (C-M(89)18), pp. 1–6; and Office Memorandum Christensen to Whittome 4.10.1990 pp. 1–2

9   Geir Lundestad '"Imperial Overstretch", Mikhail Gorbachev and the End of the Cold War' *CWH* 1, 1 (2000) pp. 1–20; Arne Westad *The Global Cold War* p. 379

10 Reagan's Remarks at the Annual Convention of the National Association of Evangelicals in Orlando Florida 8.3.1983 The American Presidency Project website (hereafter APP); Reagan's Address to Members of the UK Parliament 8.6.1982 APP

11 Reagan's Address to the Nation on Defense and National Security 23.3.1983 APP

12 On the superpower summits, see for example Jack F. Matlock Jr *Reagan and Gorbachev: How the Cold War Ended* Random House 2004; James Graham Wilson *The Triumph of Improvisation: Gorbachev's Adaptability, Reagan's Engagement, and the End of the Cold War* Cornell UP 2014; Svetlana Savranskaya & Thomas Blanton (eds) *The Last Superpower Summits: Gorbachev, Reagan and Bush – Conversations that Ended the Cold War* CEU Press 2016 (hereafter *TLSS*); Jonathan Hunt & David Reynolds 'Geneva, Reykjavik, Washington, and Moscow, 1985–1991' in Kristina Spohr & David Reynolds (eds) *Transcending the Cold War: Summits, Statecraft and*

the Dissolution of Bipolarity in Europe, 1970–1990 Oxford UP 2016 pp. 151–79. On the Doomsday clock, see Bulletin of the Atomic Scientists thebulletin.org/timeline

13 Anatoly Chernyaev – Notes from a Meeting of the Politburo 31.10.1988 Archive of the Gorbachev Foundation Moscow (hereafter AGF) Digital Archive Wilson Center (hereafter DAWC); Mikhail Gorbachev Memoirs Bantam 1997 p. 459; Politburo meeting 24.11.1988, printed in V Politbyuro TsK KPSS. Po zapisyam Anatoliya Chernyaeva, Vadima Medvedeva, Georgiya Shakhnazarova, 1985–1991 Gorbachev Foundation 2008 pp. 432–6 esp. p. 433

14 See video of UN speech c-span.org/video/?5292-1/gorbachev-united-nations

15 Address by Mikhail Gorbachev at the UN General Assembly Session (Excerpts) 7.12.1988 CWIHP Archive. See also video of UN speech c-span.org/video/?5292-1/gorbachev-united-nations; and video of 'Mikhail Gorbachev's 1988 Address to the UN: 30 Years Later', Panel Discussion with Andrei Kozyrev, Pavel Palazhchenko, Thomas W. Simons Jr, and Kristina Spohr at SAIS – Johns Hopkins University (Washington DC) 6.12.2018 youtube.com/watch?v=Mi6NkWIJuzo

16 Ibid.

17 Ibid. For slightly different translations of the speech, see also astro.temple.edu/~rimmerma/gorbachev_speech_to_UN.htm; and 'Excerpts From Speech to UN on Major Soviet Military Cuts' NYT 8.12.1988 p. 16

18 Politburo meeting 24.11.1988, printed in V Politbyuro TsK KPSS p. 433

19 Entry 17.12.1988 The Diary of Anatoly S.

Chernyaev 1988 National Security Archive Electronic Briefing Book (hereafter NSAEBB) No. 250

20 'Gambler, Showman, Statesman' NYT 8.12.1988

21 Richard C. Hottelet 'The Enigmatic Gaps in Gorbachev's UN Speech' CSM 15.12.1988

22 It is noteworthy that as Gorbachev made his speech, the Soviet Foreign Ministry spokesman, Gennady I. Gerasimov, announced that Sergey F. Akhromeyev, the chief of staff of the Soviet armed forces, had retired for health reasons. As recently as July Marshal Akhromeyev had appeared to reject Soviet troop cuts without reciprocal reductions by NATO, even though he had been enthusiastic about Gorbachev's arms-control initiatives, including the INF treaty. Indeed, Soviet officials now denied that his departure reflected unhappiness in the military over the cutbacks.

23 See video of 'Mikhail Gorbachev's 1988 Address to the UN: 30 Years Later' youtube.com/watch?v=Mi6NkWIJuzo Cf. Pavel Palazhchenko My Years with Gorbachev and Shevardnadze: The Memoir of a Soviet Interpreter Pennsylvania UP 1997 pp. 105–8

24 Gorbachev Memoirs p. 463; Entry 17.12.1988 The Diary of Anatoly S. Chernyaev 1988 NSAEBB No. 250

25 Bush & Scowcroft A World Transformed p. 3

26 Ibid. pp. 6–7; Memcon of Reagan–Gorbachev meeting 7.12.1988, printed in TLSS doc. 69 p. 470

27 Ibid. pp. 472–4

28 Ibid. pp. 471–2. Gorbachev's Letter to Reagan 28.10.1987 NSAEBB No. 238

29 TLSS doc. 69 pp. 472–4

30 Memcon of Reagan–Gorbachev

luncheon 7.12.1988, printed in *TLSS* doc. 70 p. 476

31 Ibid. pp. 477–8

32 Steven V. Roberts 'Table for Three, With Talk of Bygones and Best Hopes' *NYT* 8.12.1988. See also Bill Keller 'Gorbachev pledges major troop cutback, then ends trip, citing vast Soviet quake' *NYT* 8.12.1988

33 See Engel *When the World Seemed New* ch. 2; Meacham, *Destiny and Power* parts IV and V. 'Bush Conjures Up Voodoo Economics' *Chicago Tribune* (hereafter *CT*) 13.3.1988. Just what is voodoo economics? Since George Bush first uttered the phrase in 1980, many people have sought an acceptable definition

34 Richard V. Allen 'George Herbert Walker Bush; The Accidental Vice President' *NYT Magazine* 30.7.2000; Herbert S. Parmet *George Bush: The Life of a Lone Star Yankee* Transaction 1997 p. 257. Bush's diary entry of 21.11.1986, printed in 'Was Vice President Bush in the Loop? You Make The Call' *WP* 31.1.1993

35 On loyalty, see Engel *When the World Seemed New* p. 22

36 Robert Ajemian 'Where is the Real George Bush? The Vice President must now step out from Reagan's shadow' *TIME* 26.1.1987

37 See Margaret Garrer Warner 'Bush Battles the "Wimp Factor"' *Newsweek* 19.10.1987

38 Bush's Address Accepting the Presidential Nomination at the Republican National Convention in New Orleans 18.8.1988 APP; Mark J. Rozell *The Press and the Bush Presidency* Praeger 1996 pp. 73–7; Meacham *Destiny and Power* p. 339; 'The Problem with Read My Lips' *NYT* 15.10.1992

39 Timothy Naftali *George H. W. Bush – The American Presidents Series: The 41st President, 1989–1993* Times Books 2007 pp. 61–3; Meacham *Destiny and Power* pp. 335–49. Cf. John Sides 'It's time to stop the endless hype of the "Willie Horton" ad' *WP* 6.1.2016

40 Bartholomew Sparrow, *The Strategist: Brent Scowcroft and the Call of National Security* Public Affairs 2015 p. 265. See also Russell L. Riley 'History and George Bush' in Michael Nelson & Barbara A. Perry *41: Inside the Bush Presidency of George H. W. Bush* Cornell UP 2014 pp. 7–11. Cf. David Hoffman 'How Bush Has Altered Views' *WP* 18.8.1988

41 Sparrow *The Strategist* pp. 265–7

42 Ibid. pp. 266–7. Bush & Scowcroft *A World Transformed* p. 18. James A. Baker with Thomas M. DeFrank *The Politics of Diplomacy: Revolution, War and Peace, 1989–1992* G. P. Putnam's Sons 1995 pp. 17–36. See also Maureen Dowd and Thomas L. Friedman 'The Fabulous Bush & Baker Boys' *NYT Magazine* 6.5.1990

43 Bush & Scowcroft *A World Transformed* pp. 13–14, 46

44 Sparrow *The Strategist* p. 271

45 Bush & Scowcroft *A World Transformed* pp. 19–20

46 Andrew Rosenthal 'Differing Views of America's Global Role' *NYT* 2.11.1988. See also Bush's Address Accepting the Presidential Nomination at the Republican National Convention in New Orleans 18.8.1988 APP; Hal Brands *Making the Unipolar Moment: US Foreign Policy and the Rise of the Post Cold War Order* Cornell UP 2016 pp. 276–9; and Jeffrey Engel 'A Better World … But Don't Get Carried Away: The Foreign Policy of Geroge H. W.

Bush Twenty Years On' *Diplomatic History* 34, 1 (2010) p. 29; Zelikow & Rice *To Build a Better World* introduction

47 Bush's Inaugural Address 20.1.1990 APP

48 Sparrow *The Strategist* p. 296. Cf. M. J. Heale who writes that Deputy National Security Adviser Robert Gates referred to a 'conscious pause'. See Heale *Contemporary America: Power, Dependency, and Globalisation since 1980* Wiley-Blackwell 2011 p. 134. JAB-SML B96/F6 10.12.1988. Baker's notes included the points: '** Make Gorby wait a while for a Summit. GB should do Europe, Japan, China – before any Summit w/USSR. Try to have first meeting in 1990 – not 1989! DON'T GO TO GORBACHEV TOO SOON! It's important for GB. Will enhance his stature. (RN thinks this will be brilliant) Back off the February 15 resumption of START.'

49 Bush & Scowcroft *A World Transformed* pp. 36, 40–1. According to Thomas Simons the NSRs, which he oversaw, were a 'stalling exercise' by the Bush administration vis-à-vis the Kremlin. See his commentry on the video of 'Mikhail Gorbachev's 1988 Address to the UN: 30 Years Later' youtube.com/watch?v=Mi6NkWIJuzo. See for NSR 3, NSR 4, NSR 5 fas.org/irp/offdocs / nsr/

50 JAB-SML B108/F2 JAB notes – Trip w/ GB to Japan China and Korea 21/2/– 27/2/89: JAB briefing p. 1. Going to China was, Baker noted, a 'Homecoming' – but 'also will exchange strategic views of the world'

51 Bush's Letter to Brzezinski 21.11.1988, printed in Bush *All the Best* p. 405

52 See Jeffrey A. Engel (ed.) *The China Diary of George H. W. Bush: The Making of a Global President* Princeton UP 2008; Mark S. del Vecchio 'China's "old friend" may call on old friends' *United Press International* (hereafter *UPI*) 22.2.1989

53 For China's GDP figures, see data. worldbank.org/country/china. On China's reorientation of the economy, see Barry Naughton *Growing out of the Plan: Chinese Economic Reform* Cambridge UP 1995 pp. 38–55, 59–96

54 On Deng's reform course, see Ezra F. Vogel *Deng Xiaoping and the Transformation of China* Harvard UP 2013 pp. 377–476

55 Arne Westad 'The Great Transformation: China in the Long 1970s' in Niall Ferguson et al. (eds) *The Shock of the Global: The 1970s in Perspective* Belknap Press 2011 p. 77; see also Vogel *Deng Xiaoping* pp. 333–48

56 United States–People's Republic of China Agreements Remarks at the Signing Ceremony 17.9.1980 APP. See also Dong Wang 'US–China Trade, 1971–2012' *Asia-Pacific Journal* 11, 24 (June 2013)

57 Meeting with Deng Xiaoping US Embassy Secret – Cable 16.6.1981 pp. 1–5, DNSA collection: China, 1960–1998; Arne Westad *Restless Empire* pp. 372–80. See also Henry S. Rowen 'China and the World Economy: The Short March from Isolation to Major Player' in Shuxun Chen and Charles Wolf Jr (eds) *China, the United States, and the Global Economy* Rand 2001 pp. 211–25

58 John F. Burns 'Bush Ends China Visit on High Note' *NYT* 16.10.1985

59 By way of comparison, US exports to the Soviet Union declined from $2.3 billion in 1982 to $1.6 billion in 1986.

60   Wang 'US–China Trade, 1971–2012' pp. 1–15 esp. p. 4. On US–Soviet trade, see Abraham Becker *A Rand-Note N-2682-RC: US-Soviet Trade in the 1980s* Rand 1987 pp. 1–2; and Rowen 'China and the World Economy' p. 214

61   See Nicholas R. Lardy 'Chinese Foreign Trade' *The China Quarterly* no. 131 (September 1992) [The Chinese Economy in the 1990s] pp. 691–720; Wang 'US–China Trade, 1971–2012' p. 4; Brands *Making the Unipolar Moment* p. 220; see also 'Trade in Goods with China (1989)' United States Census Bureau

62   George P. Shultz 'Shaping American Foreign Policy: New Realities and New Ways of Thinking' *Foreign Affairs* 63, 4 (Spring 1985) p. 711; Magdaleine D. Kalb 'Foreign Policy: Where Consensus Ends' *NYT Magazine* 27.10.1985 pp. 103–5

63   On inflation, Li Yunqi 'China's Inflation: Causes, Effects, and Solutions' *Asian Survey* 29, 7 (July 1989) pp. 655–68 esp. p. 658. On political liberalisation, see Peter R. Moody Jr 'Political Liberalisation in China: A Struggle Between Two Lines' *Pacific Affairs* 57, 1 (Spring, 1984) pp. 26–44; Nathan Gardels 'The Price China Has Paid: An Interview with Liu Binyan' *New York Review of Books* (hereafter *NYRB*) 19.1.1989

64   Charles Krauthammer 'A Tale of Two Revolutions' *WP* 23.1.1987. Jim Mann 'China Halts Experiment in Liberalisation: Student Unrest Blamed on "Bourgeois Thought"' *Los Angeles Times* (hereafter *LAT*) 7.1.1987. The 1987 anti-bourgeois liberalisation campaign was called *fandui zichanjieji ziyouhua yundong*, see entry in Henry Yuhuai He *Dictionary of the Political Thought of the People's Republic of China* Routledge 2001

65   Reynolds *One World Divisible* pp. 578–9; Robert L. Suettinger *Beyond Tiananmen: The Politics of US–China Relations 1989–2000* Brookings Institution Press 2003 pp. 20–3; Jeffrey A. Engel & Sergey Radchenko 'Beijing and Malta, 1989' in Spohr & Reynolds (eds) *Transcending the Cold War* p. 185

66   Yunqi 'China's Inflation' p. 655; Naughton *Growing out of the Plan* pp. 268–70

67   M. E. Sarotte 'China's Fear of Contagion: Tiananmen Square and the Power of the European Example' *International Security* (hereafter *IS*) 37, 2 (Fall 2012) p. 159. Cf. David L. Shambaugh *China's Communist Party: Atrophy and Adaptation* Woodrow Wilson Center Press 2008 pp. 43–5

68   See Deng Xiaoping [and Chong-Pin Lin] 'Deng's 25 April Speech: "This is not an Ordinary Student Movement but Turmoil"' *World Affairs* 152, 3 (Winter 1989–90) [China's 1989 Upheaval] pp. 138–40. As historian Merle Goldman noted, Deng appeared to console himself with the thought that, unlike Poland, China did not have to worry about the church and the workers, and he had no doubts that China's intellectuals and students could be handled relatively easily. See Merle Goldman 'Vengeance in China' *NYRB* 9.11.1989

69   Philip Taubman 'Chinese Visit Aims to Break the Soviet Ice' *NYT* 1.12.1988; Engel & Radchenko 'Beijing and Malta, 1989' p. 186

70   Deng's younger son quoting his father, in Ezra Vogel *Deng Xiaoping* p. 423

71   Politburo meeting 16.7.1987 'Following the trip of the delegation of the Supreme Council to China', printed in

V. Politbyuro TsK KPSS p. 207. Mikhail Gorbachev *Perestroika: New Thinking for Our Country and the World* Collins 1987

72 Shakhnazarov quoted in Sergey Radchenko *Unwanted Visionaries: The Sovet Failure in Asia at the End of the Cold War* Oxford UP 2014 pp. 179–80

73 Radchenko *Unwanted Visionaries* p. 160

74 Bush & Scowcroft *A World Transformed* p. 91

75 Bush & Scowcroft *A World Transformed* p. 91; Sparrow *The Strategist* pp. 314–16. See also the Memcons of the various bilaterals Bush held on the margins of the funeral ceremonies in Tokyo (23–5 February 1989), ranging from talks with leaders from Belgium to Zaire, from Egypt to Singapore, bush41library.tamu.edu/archives/memcons-telcons. These are held by the George H. W. Bush Presidential Library in College Station, Texas (hereafter GHWBPL)

76 Bush & Scowcroft *A World Transformed* p. 91

77 GHWBPL Memcon of Bush–Takeshita talks 23.2.1989 Tokyo

78 GHWBPL Memcon of Yang–Bush talks 25.2.1989 Beijing, pp. 2–5. Winston Lord was still in post as Reagan's ambassador to Beijing (6.11.1985–23.4.1989)

79 Ibid. p. 5

80 Bush was 6 ft 2, and Deng 4 ft 11

81 GHWBPL Memcon of Deng–Bush talks with delegations, 26.2.1989 Beijing pp. 2, 5

82 Ibid. pp. 8–9

83 Ibid. p. 9. It is noteworthy that concerning the PRC's critical view of the evolution in the USSR Li Peng was even more direct in his discussion with Bush than Deng, stating: 'For a time, the Soviets emphasised economic reform, but now they are emphasising political reform and the process of democratisation. This latter emphasis may suit the taste of the US. However, the effect of the latter approach may be rather limited and may provoke ethnic problems in the Soviet Union. At best it may only arouse the enthusiasm of the intellectuals for perestroika. In my view, the Soviet Union should mainly concentrate on the economic problems of the country.' GHWBPL Memcon of Bush–Li talks 26.2.1989 Beijing p. 10

84 Bush met not only with Deng Xiaoping and Yang Shangkun, but also twice with Premier Li Peng and once with Zhao Ziyang, general secretary of the CCP. See GHWBPL Memcon of Bush–Li talks 25.2.1989 Beijing; Memcon of Bush–Li talks 26.2.1989 Beijing; Memcon of Bush–Zhao talks 26.2.1989 Beijing

85 Bush & Scowcroft *A World Transformed* p. 97

86 Bush's Remarks Upon Returning From a Trip to the Far East 27.2.1989 APP

87 GHWBPL Memcon of Bush–Weizsäcker talks 24.2.1989 Tokyo p. 2

88 GHWBPL Memcon of Bush–Wörner talks 12.4.1989 Washington DC pp. 1–4

89 Bush's Remarks to Citizens in Hamtramck, Michigan 17.4.1989 APP

90 Bush & Scowcroft *A World Transformed* pp. 52–3

91 Bush's Remarks at the Texas A&M University Commencement Ceremony in College Station 12.5.1989 APP

92 Bush's Remarks at the United States Coast Guard Academy Commencement Ceremony in New London, Connecticut 24.5.1989 APP

93 JAB-SML B108/F5 RBZ (Zoellick) draft – NATO Summit-Possible Initiatives

15.5.1989. This five-page document stressed 'Common Values of the West' as the underpinnings of NATO historically and as 'also the source of recent success' – which should be contrasted with 'Gorbachev's more narrow, territorial Common European Home concept'. Moreover, the values served as principles for NATO 'as we draw Eastern Europe and the USSR into the "community of nations". Ends the division of Europe on our terms.' The document further insisted: 'Need to communicate the theme through speeches, initiatives, and symbolic communication (e.g. photo events). Theme should carry over to both the NATO and Economic Summits.'

94 Ann Devroy 'From Promise to Performance: The Nation Changed – but Bush did Not' *WP* 17.1.1993. On prudence, see also Engel 'A Better World' pp. 38–41; and Ryan Barilleaux and Mark Rozell *Power and Prudence: The Presidency of George H. W. Bush* Texas A&M University Press 2004; JAB-SML B108/F5 RBZ draft 15.5.1989

95 See Genscher *Erinnerungen* pp. 611–12. See also JAB-SML B108/F5 Note for Baker's Meeting with Stoltenberg 19.5.1989

96 Bush & Scowcroft *A World Transformed* pp. 57–60, 64–5, 67–77. See also Hans Peter Schwarz *Helmut Kohl: Eine politische Biographie* Pantheon 2014 pp. 508–11

97 Taubman *Gorbachev* pp. 201, 475; cf. Charles Moore *Margaret Thatcher: The Authorised Biography, vol. 2* Allen Lane 2015 pp. 240–1

98 Record of Conversation between Mikhail Gorbachev and Margaret Thatcher, 6.4.1989, printed in Svetlana Savranskaya et al. (eds) *Masterpieces of History: The Peaceful End of the Cold War in Europe, 1989* CEU Press 2011 (hereafter *MoH:1989*) doc. 56 pp. 438–41 esp. p. 440; Dan Fisher 'Thatcher Hears Gorbachev Complaint: No US Action on Arms' *LAT* 7.4.1989

99 On the complex undercurrents, see Richard Aldous *Reagan and Thatcher: The Difficult Relationship* W. W. Norton 2012

100 Margaret Thatcher *The Downing Street Years* HarperCollins 1993 p. 783

101 Bush & Scowcroft *A World Transformed* pp. 64–7

102 GHWBPL Telcon of Kohl–Bush call 5.5.1989 Oval Office p. 2

103 GHWBPL Telcon of Kohl–Bush call 21.4.1989 Oval Office p. 2

104 James M. Markham 'Bush Arrives for Talks with a Divided NATO' *NYT* 29.5.1989

105 Ibid.

106 James M. Markham 'NATO Chiefs Agree to a Compromise in Missile Dispute' *NYT* 31.5.1989

107 Bernard Weinraub 'Buoyed by Agreement, Bush Visits Bonn' *NYT* 31.5.1989

108 Bush & Scowcroft *A World Transformed* p. 83

109 Ibid.

110 Serge Schmemann 'Bush's Hour: Taking Control, He Placates the Germans and Impresses British; Kohl Gets Respite From Political Ills' *NYT* 1.6.1989

111 Weinraub 'Buoyed by Agreement'

112 Bush's Toast at a Dinner Hosted by Chancellor Helmut Kohl in Bonn, Federal Republic of Germany 30.5.1989 APP

113 Weinraub 'Buoyed by Agreement'

114 Bush's Remarks to the Citizens in Mainz, Federal Republic of Germany 31.5.1989 APP

115 Thatcher *The Downing Street Years* p. 789

116 Bush's Remarks to the Citizens in Mainz 31.5.1989

117 Reagan's Remarks on East–West Relations at the Brandenburg Gate in West Berlin 12.6.1987 APP

118 Bush's Remarks to the Citizens in Mainz 31.5.1989

119 Vincent J. Schodolski & Uli Schmetzer 'Gorbachev arrives in China: Beijing talks 1st summit in 30 years' *CT* 15.5.1989 pp. 1–2; Jim Hoagl & Daniel Southerl 'Gorbachev arrives in Beijing' *WP* 15.5.1989

120 Andrew J. Nathan 'The Tiananmen Papers' *Foreign Affairs* 80, 1 (January/February 2001) pp. 11, 15–18. See also GHWBPL NSC – SitRoom Tiananmen Square Crisis File (TSCF) China (OA/ID CF01722–002) Lilley to Baker Cable – Re: Chinese Economists support students 19.5.1989 p. 5; CIA research paper 'The Road to the Tiananmen Crackdown – An Analytic Chronology of Chinese Leadership Decision-Making' EA 89–10030 (Confidential/No Foreign Distribution) September 1989 Margaret Thatcher Foundation (hereafter MTF)

121 CIA research paper 'The Road to the Tiananmen Crackdown' p. 5; Adi Ignatius & Peter Gumbel 'Gorbachev Arrives In China as Protests Continue in Beijing' *Wall Street Journal* (hereafter *WSJ*) 15.5.1989; Udo Schmetzer 'Ceremonies moved to foil protestors' *CT* 15.5.1989 pp. 1–2. It is noteworthy that in mid-May mass demonstrations were also taking place elsewhere, especially in the north-eastern cities of Shenyang, Harbin, Dalian and Chanchun, with some 200,000 students, teachers, media personnel

and governmement cadres protesting for several consecutive days, and more than 1,000 on hunger strike. See GHWBPL NSC – SitRoom TSCF China (OA/ID CF01722–002) American Consul in Shenyang to Baker 19.5.1989 pp. 1–2

122 Radchenko *Unwanted Visionaries* p. 162

123 Notepad of Teimuraz Stepanov-Mamaladze, 15.5.1989 Hoover Institution Archive, Teimuraz Stepanov-Mamaladze Papers (hereafter HIA-TSMP): Notepad 15.5.1989 DAWC

124 Nathan 'The Tiananmen Papers' p. 14

125 Schmetzer 'Ceremonies moved to foil protestors'

126 Nicholas D. Kristof 'Gorbachev Meets Deng in Beijing; Protest Goes On' *NYT* 16.5.1989; David Helley 'Gorbachev in China: The Communist Summit; Protestors Force Summit Change – China Moves Ceremony From Square' *LAT* 15.5.1989

127 See Notepad Entry of Teimuraz Stepanov-Mamaladze 17.5.1989 HIA-TSMP: Notepad 15.5.1989 DAWC; and Excerpts from the Conversation between Mikhail Gorbachev and Rajiv Gandhi 15.7.1989 AGF DAWC

128 '1,000,000 Protestors Force Gorbachev to Cut Itinerary: The Center of Beijing Is Paralyzed' *LAT* 17.5.1989; Notepad Entry of Teimuraz Stepanov-Mamaladze 17.5.1989 HIA-TSMP: Notepad 15.5.1989 DAWC

129 Mark Kramer 'The Demise of the Soviet Bloc' in Terry Cox (ed.) *Reflections on 1989 in Eastern Europe* Routledge 2013, p. 35; Radchenko *Unwanted Visionaries* p. 163. See also Diary of Teimuraz Stepanov-Mamaladze 17.5.1989 HIA-TSMP: Diary No. 9 DAWC. Pointing to China, Gorbachev of course could argue for the home audience that

attempts to suppress the craving for political freedom will produce only disorder in the streets. Indeed, as one member of the Soviet delegation told the *New York Times* in view of the mass protests in the PRC: 'This shows what can happen if a government does not keep up with its people.' Bill Keller 'Gorbachev Praises the Students and Declares Reform Is Necessary' *NYT* 18.5.1989

130 Nathan 'The Tiananmen Papers' p. 14

131 Li's diary entry quoted in Engel & Radchenko 'Beijing and Malta, 1989' pp. 192–3

132 Radchenko *Unwanted Visionaries* p. 166; Robert Service *The End of the Cold War 1985–1991* Pan Books 2015 p. 385. On Gorbachev–Deng '58–85', see also Excerpts from the Conversation between Mikhail Gorbachev and Rajiv Gandhi 15.7.1989 AGF DAWC

133 Michael Parks & David Holley '30-Year Feud Ended by Gorbachev, Deng: Leaders Declare China–Soviet Ties Are Normalised' *LAT* 16.5.1989

134 Soviet transcript of meeting between Mikhail Gorbachev and Deng Xiaoping (Excerpts), 16.5.1989 DAWC. For a Chinese version of the record of conversation see also DAWC

135 Ibid.

136 Ibid.

137 HIA-TSMP Notepad 16.5.1989 Gorbachev Talks with Li Peng 16.5.1989 DAWC; Vladislav Zubok 'The Soviet Union and China in the 1980s: Reconciliation and Divorce' *CWH* 17, 2 (2017) pp. 121–41 esp. p. 138

138 Daniel Southerl 'Leaders Fail to Sway Chinese Protestors' *WP* 19.5.1989; '1,000,000 Protestors Force Gorbachev to Cut Itinerary' *LAT* 17.5.1989. On the trip to Shanghai and Soviet foreign

minister Eduard Shevardnadze's view that the 'normalisation of Soviet–Chinese relations is a historic event', see also HIA-TSMP: Diary No. 9 Teimuraz Stepanov-Mamaladze – Entry 18.5.1989 DAWC. For China's assessment that the summit's 'most important result' was the 'normalisation of relations', see GHWBPL NSC – SitRoom TSCF China – part 1 of 5 [2] (OA/ID CF01722–002) Am. Embassy Beijing to Baker – Re: MFA Briefing on Sino-Soviet Summit 20.5.1989 pp. 1–4

139 '1,000,000 Protestors Force Gorbachev to Cut Itinerary' *LAT* 17.5.1989; GHWBPL NSC – SitRoom TSCF China (OA/ID CF01722–002) US amb. in Beijing to Baker, Cable – Subj: Beijing at Crisis, 20.5.1989 p. 1

140 GHWBPL NSC – SitRoom TSCF China (OA/ID CF01722–002) From SSO DIA, Cable – Re: China, Beijing, 20.5.1989 p. 1; US amb. in Beijing to Baker Cable – PRC State Council declares martial law 20.5.1989 p. 1

141 Vogel *Deng Xiaoping* pp. 616–24. See also Adi Ignatius & Julia Leung 'Beijings Bind' *WSJ* 22.5.1989. On Zhao's ousting and the link between inflationary crisis and the rise of unacceptable political demands in the eyes of party elders, see also Naughton *Growing out of the Plan* pp. 269–70. It is noteworthy that protests also kept spreading to Chengdu, Chonquing and Guangzhou. GHWBPL, NSC – SitRoom TSCF China (OA/IA CF01722–002) Am. embassy Beijing to Baker Telex – Student Hunger Strikes in Chengdu, 19.5.1989; and American Consul Guangzhou to Baker, Re: Guangzhou students on the march in defiance of Li Peng (Guangzhou report no. 9),

20.5.1989; and Am. embassy Beijing to Baker, Cable – Subj: Sitrep. No. 5, 0600 – The Scene from Tiananmen Square 21.5.1989. GHWBPL NSC – SitRoom TSCF China – part 1 of 5 [3] (OA/ID CF01722–003) From SSO DIA – China: Situation report 22.5.1989

142 Claudia Rosett 'Miss Liberty Lights Her Lamp in Beijing' *WSJ* 31.5.1989

143 GHWBPL NSC – SitRoom TSCF China – part 2 of 5 [2] (OA/ID CF01722–007) Am. embassy Beijing to Baker Cable – Subj: Sitrep. No. 18 Central party organs endorse Deng line 27.5.1989 pp. 1–2; Vogel *Deng Xiaoping* pp. 625–7

144 Nicholas D. Kristof 'Troops Attack and Crush Beijing Protest – Thousands Fight Back, Scores Are Killed, Square Is Cleared' *NYT* 4.6.1989

145 Ibid.; Vogel *Deng Xiaoping* pp. 625–32; Heather Saul 'Tiananmen Square: What happened to tank man? What became of the unknown rebel who defied a column of tanks?' *Independent* 4.6.2014. See also GHWBPL NSC – SitRoom TSCF China – part 3 of 5 [1] (OA/ID CF01722–011) Am. embassy Beijing to Baker Cable – Subj: Siterep No. 32 The morning of 6.4.1989, 4.6.1989 pp. 1–4; and Am. embassy Beijing to Baker Cable – Subj: Chaos within China 4.6.1989 pp. 1–5; Baker to Am. embassy Beijing Cable – Subj: SSO TF3–3: China Task Force Situation 4.6.1989 p. 1. Cf. Am. embassy Beijing to DoS Cable – What Happened on the Night of June 3/4? 22.6.1989 NSAEBB No. 16 which stated that 'civilian deaths probably did not reach the figure of 3,000 used in some press reports'. Yet, the figure put forward by the Chinese Red Cross of 2,600 military and civilian deaths with 7,000 wounded did not seem 'an unreason-

able estimate'. By comparison the British ambassador to China, Sir Alan Donald, wrote in his situation report of 5 June: 'Minimum estimate of civilian dead 10,000.' TNA FCO 21/4181 UK emb. Beijing to FCO Cable – China: Background to Military Situation 6.6.1989 p. 3

146 State Department Bureau of Intelligence and Research 'China: Aftermath of the Crisis' 27.7.1989 NSAEBB No. 16; 'Kremlin Dismayed, Aide Says' *NYT*/ AP 10.6.1989

147 GHWBPL Telcon of Kohl–Bush talks 15.6.1989 Oval Office p. 1

148 See Excerpts from the Conversation between Mikhail Gorbachev and Rajiv Gandhi 15.7.1989 AGF DAWC

149 State Department Bureau of Intelligence and Research 'China: Aftermath of the Crisis' 27.7.1989 NSAEBB No. 16

150 See US Embassy (Lilley) Beijing Cable 'PLA Ready to Strike' (CONFIDENTIAL) 21.5.1989 NSAEBB No. 47

151 The President's News Conference Following the North Atlantic Treaty Organisation Summit Meeting in Brussels 30.5.1989 APP

152 GHWBPL NSC – SitRoom TSCF China (OA/ID CF01722–007) Sec State WashDC to US amb. in Beijing Cable RE: China matters – Letter from President to Deng Xiaoping 27.5.1989 pp. 1–2

153 Engel & Radchenko 'Beijing and Malta, 1989' p. 195

154 James R. Lilley & Jeffrey Lilley *China Hands: Nine Decades of Adventure, Espionage, and Diplomacy in Asia* Public Affairs 2004 p. 309; Kristof 'Crackdown in Beijing'

155 Vogel *Deng Xiaoping* pp. 648–52; David M. Lampton *Same Bed, Different*

Dreams Univ. of California Press 2002 pp. 21–2; Engel *When the World Seemed New* pp. 175–81. See also Bush & Scowcroft *A World Transformed* pp. 98–103; GHWBPL NSC – SitRoom TSCF China (OA/ID CF01722–011) Am. embassy Beijing to Baker Cable – Subj: Chaos in China 4.6.1989 pp. 1–5. See also JAB-SML B108/F6 RBZ draft 5.6.1989 – Response to PRC events pp. 1–2

156 Bush's Letter to Deng, 29.6.1989, printed in Bush *All the Best* pp. 428–31

157 GHWBPL Scowcroft – Special Separate China Notes Files – China Files (hereafter SSCNF-CF) China 1989 (sensitive) (OA/ID 91136–001) Handwritten notes on the flight 30 June–1 July 1989. Cf. Bush & Scowcroft *A World Transformed* pp. 105–6

158 GHWBPL Scowcroft SSCNF-CF China 1989 (sensitive) (OA/ID 91136–001) Memcon of Deng–Scowcroft talks 2.7.1989 Beijing pp. 1–14

159 Ibid. pp. 1–3

160 Ibid. p. 4

161 Ibid. pp. 7–9

162 Ibid. pp. 10–12

163 Ibid. pp. 13–14

164 Bush & Scowcroft *A World Transformed* p. 110

165 Bush *All the Best* p. 431

166 See Richard Baum *Burying Mao: Chinese Politics in the Age of Deng Xiaoping* Princeton UP 1996 pp. 18–20

167 Excerpts from the Conversation between Mikhail Gorbachev and Rajiv Gandhi 15.7.1989 AGF DAWC

168 Note by Vladimir Lukin regarding Soviet–Chinese Relations 22.8.1989 GARF f. 10026 op. 4 d. 2870 l. 75–78 DAWC

Chapter 2

1 John Tagliabue 'Poland Flirts with Pluralism Today' *NYT* 4.6.1989

2 On Poland's 'semi-competitive elections', see Marjorie Castle *Triggering Communism's Collapse: Perceptions and Power in Poland's Transition* Rowman & Littlefield 2003 ch. 6. See also Tagliabue 'Poland' *NYT* 4.6.1989

3 Timothy Garton Ash 'Revolution in Poland and Hungary' *London Review of Books* (hereafter *LRB*) 17.8.1989. Cf. *idem, The Magic Lantern* pp. 25–46 esp. p. 32

4 Kristof 'Troops Attack and Crush Beijing Protest'

5 John Daniszewski 'Communist Party Declares Solidarity Landslide Winner' AP 5.6.1989; John Tagliabue 'Stunning Vote Casts Poles into Uncharted Waters' *NYT* 6.6. 1989

6 Garton Ash *The Magic Lantern* p. 32

7 Tyler Marshall 'Russian Troops Remain in Ex-Satellite States – Military: Of an estimated 600,000 in Eastern Europe in the late 1980s, only about 113,000 haven't gone home' *LAT* 1.4.1993

8 Andrei Grachev *Gorbachev's Gamble: Soviet Foreign Policy and the End of the Cold War* Polity 2008 p. 172

9 Ibid. pp. 171–2

10 See Geir Lundestad '*Empire by Invitation*? The United States and Western Europe 1945–52' *Journal of Peace Research* 23, 3 (1986) pp. 263–77; *idem* '"Empire by Invitation" in the American Century' *Diplomatic History* 23, 2 (Spring 1999) pp. 189–217; *idem, Empire by Integration: The United States and European Integration, 1945–1997* Oxford UP 1997; and John Lewis Gaddis *We Now Know* Clarendon Press 1997 pp. 284–6

11 Useful overviews include Geoffrey

Swain & Nigel Swain *Eastern Europe since 1945* Macmillan 1993; Judy Batt *East Central Europe from Reform to Transformation* Pinter 1991

12 On IR theorists' predictions, or rather the lack thereof, see George Lawson et al. (eds) *The Global 1989: Continuity and Change in World Politics* Cambridge UP 2010 introduction esp. p. 4; or Michael Cox 'Why Did We Get the End of the Cold War Wrong?' *The British Journal of Politics and International Relations* 11, 2 (2009), pp. 161–76; John Lewis Gaddis 'International Relations Theory and the End of the Cold War' *International Security* 17, 3 (1992–3) pp. 5–58. For CIA analyses, see for example Gerald K. Haines & Robert E. Leggett (eds) *CIA's Analysis of the Soviet Union, 1947–1991* Ross & Perry 2001; Benjamin B. Fischer & Gerald K. Haines (eds) *At Cold War's End: US Intelligence on the Soviet Union and Eastern Europe, 1989–1991* Ross & Perry 2001

13 Andrzej Paczkowski *The Spring Will Be Ours: Poland and the Poles from Occupation to Freedom* Pennsylvania UP 2003

14 Andrej Paczkowski & Malcolm Byrne (eds) *From Solidarity to Martial Law: The Polish Crisis of 1980–1981 – A Documentary History* CEU Press 2007 pp. 4–5; Marcin Zaremba 'Karol Wojtyła the Pope: Complications for Comrades of the Polish United Workers' Party' *CWH* 5, 3 (2005) pp. 317–36

15 For a detailed study on 1980–1, see Timothy Garton Ash *The Polish Revolution: Solidarity* Yale UP 2002; Paczkowski & Byrne (eds) *From Solidarity to Martial Law*

16 John Tagliabue 'Thousands at Gdansk Shipyard Join Polish Strike' *NYT*

3.5.1988; see also Grzegorz W. Kołodko 'Polish Hyperinflation and Stabilization 1989–1990' *Economic Journal on Eastern Europe and the Soviet Union* (1/1991) pp. 9–36

17 Andrew A. Michta *Red Eagle: The Army in Polish Politics, 1944–1989* Hoover Institution Press 1990 p. 200; Taubman *Gorbachev* pp. 480–3; Paula Butturini 'Polish Strike "Broke the Barrier of Fear": Militant Steelworkers Sense Victory' *CT* 18.9.1989

18 For the Polish round-table talks, see Wiktor Osyatinski 'The Round-Table Talks in Poland' in Jon Elster (ed.) *Round-Table Talks and the Breakdown of Communism* Univ. of Chicago Press 1996

19 John Tagliabue 'Appeal by Wałęsa Fails to Resolve All Polish Strikes' *NYT* 2.9.1988

20 Castle *Triggering Communism's Collapse* p. 47

21 Garton Ash *The Magic Lantern* p. 14

22 Rudolf L. Tőkés *Hungary's Negotiated Revolution: Economic Reform, Social Change and Political Succession* Cambridge UP 1996 ch. 6

23 Bridget Kendall *The Cold War: A New Oral History of Life between East and West* BBC Books 2017 p. 180. On the legacy of 1956, see Karen Dawisha *Eastern Europe, Gorbachev and Reform: The Great Challenge* Cambridge UP 1990 pp. 136–9

24 Odd Arne Westad *The Cold War: A World History* Penguin Books 2017 pp. 202–6. On 'counter-revolution' vs popular insurrection, see also 'Minutes of the Meeting of the HSWP CC Political Committee' 31.1.1989, printed in *Cold War International History Bulletin* Issue 12/13 (section by Békés & Melinda Kalmár Csaba, 'The Political

Transition in Hungary') doc. 1 pp. 73–5 CWIHP

25 Nigel Swain *Collective Farms Which Work?* Cambridge UP 1985 p. 26

26 Ibid. pp. 134–5

27 Roger Gough *A Good Comrade: János Kádár, Communism and Hungary* I. B. Tauris 2006 pp. 142, 150; see also Michael Getler '"Goulash Communism" Savoured' *WP* 14.9.1977

28 Tőkés *Hungary's Negotiated Revolution* pp. 274–7

29 Ibid. ch. 7; András Bozóki *The Round-Table Talks of 1989: The Genesis of Hungarian Democracy* CEU Press 2002 pp. 98–101

30 On 1848, see Alice Freifeld *Nationalism and the Crowd in Liberal Hungary, 1848-1914* Woodrow Wilson Center Press 2000 pp. 309–16; Tamás Hofer 'The Demonstration of March 15, 1989, in Budapest: A Struggle for Pubilc Memory' *Program on Central and Eastern Europe, Working Paper Series #16* Cambridge MA 1991 pp. 6–8

31 Nigel Swain *Hungary: The Rise and Fall of Feasible Socialism* Verso 1992 pp. 18–26. See also Bozóki *The Round-Table Talks of 1989*; idem 'The Round-Table Talks of 1989: Participants, Political Visions, and Historical References' *Hungarian Studies* 14, 2 (2000) pp. 241–57

32 Henry Kamm 'Hungarian Who Led '56 Revolt Is Buried as a Hero' *NYT* 17.6.1989. On Hungary's 'political' transition more genrally, see also László Bruszt & David Stark 'Remaking the Political Field in Hungary: From the Politics of Confrontation to the Politics of Competition' *Journal of International Affairs* 45, 1 [East Central Europe: After the Revolutions] (Summer 1991) pp. 201–45

33 On the idea of diffusion, see Mark R. Beissinger 'Structure and Example in Modular Political Phenomena: The Diffusion of Bulldozer/Rose/Orange/ Tulip Revolutions' *Perspectives on Politics* 5, 2 (June 2007) pp. 259–76 at p. 259; idem 'An Interrelated Wave' *Journal of Democracy* 20, 1 (January 2009) pp. 74–7; Leeson & Dean 'The Democratic Domino Theory: An Empirical Investigation' *American Journal of Political Science* 53, 3 (July 2009) pp. 533–51. For more on 'contagion' and 'diffusion', see Valerie Bunce & Sharon Wolchik 'Getting Real about "Real Causes"' *Journal of Democracy* 20, 1 (January 2009) pp. 69–73; Kristian Skrede Gleditsch & Michael D. Ward 'Diffusion and the International Context of Democratisation' *International Organisation* 60, 4 (Fall 2006) pp. 911–33

34 On the Eastern European 'contagion' reaching China, see Vogel *Deng Xiaoping* p. 626; James Miles *The Legacy of Tiananmen: China in Disarray* Univ. of Michigan Press 1996 pp. 42–3; Baum *Burying Mao* pp. 250, 275–80; Shambaugh *China's Communist Party* pp. 43–6; Sarotte 'China's Fear of Contagion' pp. 156–82. On the contagion spreading inside the USSR, see Esther B. Fein 'Moscow Condemns Nationalist "Virus" in 3 Baltic Lands' *NYT* 27.8.1989

35 Cf. Krishan Kumar 'The Revolutions of 1989: Socialism, Capitalism, and Democracy' *Theory and Society* 21, 3 (June 1992) pp. 309–56

36 Németh quoted in Walter Mayr 'Hungary's Peaceful Revolution: Cutting the Fence and Changing History' *Spiegel-Online* 29.5.2009

37 Sebestyen *Revolution 1989* p. 259; Mayr 'Hungary's Peaceful Revolution'

38   For the Memcon extract of the Gorbachev–Németh talks in Moscow on 3.3.1989, see *MoH:1989* doc. 59 pp. 412–13. For an insight into the dynamic between Gorbachev and Németh, see a different extract of the same talk's Memcon printed in *CWIHP Bulletin* 12/13 pp. 76–7

39   Sebestyen *Revolution 1989* p. 261; Michael Meyer *1989: The Year that Changed the World* Simon & Schuster 2009 pp. 68–70. BA-MA Strausberg AZN 32665 Bl. 78/79 'Schreiben von DDR-Verteidigungsminister Heinz Keßler an Erich Honecker zur Demontage des Grenzsignalzaunes zwischen Ungarn und Österreich' 6.5.1989 pp. 1–2 Chronik der Mauer Digital Archive (CdMDA)

40   Sebestyen *Revolution 1989* p. 261

41   Gary Bruce *The Firm: The Inside Story of the Stasi* Oxford UP 2010 p. 165

42   Helmut Kohl *Ich wollte Deutschlands Einheit* Ullstein 1996 pp. 35–51

43   Record of Conversation between Gorbachev and Kohl 12.6.1989 p. 2 AGF Notes of A. S. Chernyaev DAWC. Cf. Record of Conversation between Gorbachev and Kohl 12.6.1989, printed in *MoH:1989* doc. 63 pp. 463–7. For the German Memcon of the Kohl–Gorbachev talks on 12.6.1989, see Hanns Jürgen Küsters & Daniel Hoffmann (eds) *Deutsche Einheit: Sonderedition aus den Akten des Bundeskanzleramtes, 1989/90* (hereafter *DESE*) [Dokumente zur Deutschlandpolitik] Oldenbourg 1998 doc. 2 pp. 276–87 esp. pp. 283–4

44   Kohl *Ich wollte* pp. 47–9; *Bulletin der Bundesregierung* no. 61 15.6.1989 pp. 542–4; cf. Memcon of Kohl–Gorbachev talks with delegations 13.6.1989, printed in *DESE* doc. 4 pp. 295–9. On the making of the declaration and linguistic haggling, esp. from the West German perspective, see also Hannes Adomeit *Imperial Overstretch: Germany in Soviet Policy from Stalin to Gorbachev* Nomos 1998 pp. 398–9

45   Serge Schmemann 'Bonn Declaration: "Heal the Wounds"' *NYT* 14.6.1989

46   Record of Third Conversation between Gorbachev and Kohl 14.6.1989, printed in *MoH:1989* doc. 67 pp. 477–8. There is no German Memcon of the 14 June meeting available.

47   Memcon of Kohl–Gorbachev talks 13.6.1989 (full transcript) *DESE* doc. 3 pp. 287–92 esp. p. 292; for a shorter Russian extract, see Record of Second Conversation between Gorbachev and Kohl 13.6.1989 *MoH:1989* doc. 66 p. 475

48   *MoH:1989* doc. 67 p. 476 and doc. 66 p. 475

49   See Hannes Adomeit *Imperial Overstretch* pp. 398–9

50   Kohl *Ich wollte* pp. 43–4. On the significance that bilateral relations with Bonn had for Moscow and the FRG's global role, see *DESE* doc. 2 p. 280

51   Schmemann 'Bonn Declaration' p. 12

52   Serge Schmemann 'A Gorbachev Hint for Berlin Wall' *NYT* 16.6.1989; Ferdinand Protzman 'Gorbachev Urges Greater Trade and Much Closer Ties with Bonn' *NYT* 14.6.1989

53   James M. Markham 'Gorbachev Says Change Will Sweep Bloc' *NYT* 6.7.1989; cf. Taubman *Gorbachev* p. 478

54   Record of Conversation between Gorbachev and Kohl 12.6. 1989 AGF Notes of A. S. Chernyaev DAWC. See also *MoH:1989 doc.* 63 pp. 464–5; *DESE* doc. 2 p. 282

55   For a partial Soviet Record of the Mitterrand–Gorbachev talks 5.7.1989 *MoH:1989* doc. 72 pp. 490–1. James M.

Markham 'Gorbachev Likens Soviets to French' *NYT* 5.7.1989. On the French perspective of Gorbachev's Paris visit, see Bozo *Mitterrand* pp. 60–3

56 Speech by Mikhail Gorbachev to the Council of Europe in Strasbourg – 'Europe as a Common Home' 6.7.1989 Council of Europe – Parliamentary Assembly *Official Report* 41st ordinary session 8–12.5.1989 and 3–7.7.1989 Volume I Sittings 1–9 Strasbourg 1990 pp. 197–205 DAWC

57 Mark Kramer 'The Demise of the Soviet Bloc' *Journal of Modern History* 83 (December 2011) pp. 788–854 here pp. 806–9. And US National Intelligence Council 'Status of Soviet Unilateral Withdrawals' 1.9.1989, Memorandum NIC M 89–10003 (Secret), printed in Fischer (ed.) *At Cold War's End* doc. 19 pp. 304–13. 'Warsaw Pact Warms to NATO Plan' *CT* 9.7.1989

58 The Bucharest Declaration stated as 'the vital requirements of the policy of security, mutual understanding, and cooperation between states: strict respect for the national independence, sovereignty, and equality of rights of all states, the equality of rights of peoples, and the right of each people to self-determination and a free choice of ways for their own sociopolitical development; non-interference in internal affairs … observance of all the principles and goals of the UN Charter, the principles of the Helsinki Final Act, and other universally recognised norms of international relations'. See 'For a Stable and Secure Europe Free of Nuclear and Chemical Weapons and for a Substantial Reduction in Armed Forces, Armaments, and Military Spending' Bucharest, 8.7.1989 Parallel History Project-ETH Zürich (PHP-ETHZ). For

the records of the Bucharest meeting, see PHP-ETHZ

59 Notes on the Meeting of the Warsaw Treaty Member States 8.7.1989, printed in *MoH:1989* doc. 75 pp. 499–502 esp. p. 502

60 Bush & Scowcroft *A World Transformed* p. 115. For Bush's plans to visit to Poland 'Bush to Visit Hungary, Poland in July to Show US Support for Their Reforms' *LAT* 6.5.1989. See also GHWBPL Telcon of Kohl–Bush call 5.5.1989 Oval Office p. 2

61 Maureen Dowd 'Bush Rebuffs Gorbachev's Move for Swifter Cuts in Nuclear Arms' *NYT* 7.7.1989; Bush & Scowcroft *A World Transformed* p. 115. Kevin McDermott & Matthew Stibbe (eds) *The 1989 Revolutions in Central and Eastern Europe: From Communism to Pluralism* Manchester UP 2015 p. 127

62 Bush & Scowcroft *A World Transformed* pp. 115–16

63 Ibid. p. 116; Maureen Dowd 'Bush in Warsaw on Delicate Visit to Push Changes' *NYT* 10.7.1989

64 Maureen Dowd 'For Bush, A Polish Welcome without Fervor' *NYT* 11.7.1989

65 GHWBPL Memcon of Jaruzelski–Bush and Scowcroft meeting 10.7.1989 Belvedere Palace (Poland). Bush himself later claimed the meeting lasted 'two hours', Bush & Scowcroft *A World Transformed* p. 117. For the Polish record see Information Note Regarding George H. W. Bush's Visit to Poland (July 9–11) 18.7.1989, printed in *MoH:1989* doc. 76 pp. 503–5

66 GHWBPL Memcon of Rakowski–Bush meeting 10.7.1989 Council of Ministers (Poland) pp. 2–3

67 Bush's Remarks to the Polish National Assembly in Warsaw 10.7.1989 APP

68 Gregory F. Domber 'Skepticism and

Stability: Re-evaluating US Policy during Poland's Democratic Transformation in 1989' *JCWS* 13, 3 (Summer 2011) pp. 52–82 esp. p. 62

69 Marshall Robinson 'America's Not-So-Troubling Debts and Deficits' *Harvard Business Review* (July–August 1989). Bush himself had mentioned the figure of $150 billion budget deficit to Rakowski on 10 July 1989, which indeed had doubled from $79 billion in 1981 to $153 billion in 1989 according to 'Statistical Comparison of US presidential Terms, 1981–2009' at reagan.procon.org/view.resource.php?resourceID=004090

70 R. W. Apple Jr 'Bush, in Warsaw, Unveils Proposal for Aid to Poland' *NYT* 11.7.1989. For the economic figures, see table entitled 'Political Openings, Economic Straits' *NYT* 12.7.1989. On US financial aid: Bush wanted to assist Eastern Europe, but 'we do not want to pour money in until economic reforms are in place. We must be prudent', he told EC Commission president Jacques Delors on 14 June. See GHWBPL Memcon of Bush's Luncheon Meeting with Jacques Delors 14.6.1989 White House

71 Maureen Dowd 'Bush urges Poles to pull together' *NYT* 12.7.1989; R. W. Apple Jr 'A Polish Journey; Bush Escapes Pitfalls in Weathering Tough Economic and Political Climate' *NYT* 12.7.1989; David Hoffman 'Wałęsa Pleads with Bush for Money to Spare Poland the Fate of Beijing' *WP* 12.7.1989; Bush & Scowcroft *A World Transformed* pp. 120–1. See also Bush's Question-and-Answer Session With Reporters Following a Luncheon With Solidarity Leader Lech Wałęsa in Gdansk 11.7.1989 APP; and Bush's Remarks at the

Solidarity Workers' Monument in Gdansk 11.7.1989 APP

72 Apple Jr 'A Polish Journey'

73 Bush & Scowcroft *A World Transformed* p. 124. Jack Nelson 'Bush Hailed in Hungary, Lauds Reforms' *LAT* 12 July 1989; Terry Atlas & Timothy J. McNulty 'Cheers Greet Bush Call For Reform' *CT* 12.7.1989

74 Bush & Scowcroft *A World Transformed* p. 124; George H. W. Bush *Speaking of Freedom: The Collected Speeches* Scribner 2009 pp. 79–80

75 Domber 'Skepticism and Stability' pp. 72–3; Paczkowski *The Spring Will Be Ours* p. 507; R. W. Apple Jr 'In Hungary, The Ideas for Change Are Selling Themselves' *NYT* 13.7.1989

76 GHWBPL Memcon of Bush–Németh Meeting 12.7.1989 Parliament Building (Hungary) pp. 2–4

77 GHWBPL Memcon of Bush–Pozsgay meeting 12.7. 1989 US Ambassador's Residence (Hungary) pp. 2–3

78 Bush's Remarks to Students and Faculty at Karl Marx University in Budapest 12.7.1989 APP; Apple Jr 'In Hungary, The Ideas for Change are Selling Themselves'

79 Ibid. See also Bush & Scowcroft *A World Transformed* p. 126

80 Apple Jr 'In Hungary, The Ideas for Change are Selling Themselves'

81 Bush & Scowcroft *A World Transformed* p. 126; Bush's Interview with Members of the White House Press Corps 13.7.1989 APP

82 Robert M. Gates *From the Shadows: The Ultimate Insider's Story of Five Presidents and How They Won the Cold War* Simon & Schuster 2006 p. 466

83 Bush's Interview With Members of the White House Press Corps 13.7.1989 APP. See also Maureen Dowd 'Bush

Credits Moscow with Change in East Bloc' *NYT* 14.7.1989

84 Bush & Scowcroft *A World Transformed* p. 127; James M. Markham 'France Celebrates a Day of History' *NYT* 14.7.1989; R. W. Apple Jr 'Day of Wines and Bunting: 200th Anniversary for France' *NYT* 15.7.1989; 'Bush Joins in *Joie de Vivre* in Paris: Dozens of World Leaders Help Mark French Revolution' *LAT*/AP 13.7.1989; Pleshakov *There Is No Freedom Without Bread!* p. 173

85 Peter T. Kilborn 'US Prepares Loan to Enable Mexico to Meet Payments' *NYT* 14.7.1989; Bush & Scowcroft, *A World Transformed* p. 127. On US Economic Summit priorities, see also GHWBPL Telcon of Bush–Kohl call 23.6.1989 Oval Office p. 2. Bush had told Kohl: 'US priorities would be to discuss the international debt situation and macroeconomic policy coordination. The Summit Seven need to get back to the level of policy coordination they had in the past.' Cf. for the German Telcon of Bush–Kohl call 23.6.1989, printed in *DESE* doc. 10 p. 315

86 Serge Schmemann 'Poland's Leader Asks West for Aid' *NYT* 14.7. 1989; *idem* 'Walesa to Back a Communist Chief' *NYT* 15.7.1989

87 See TNA UK PREM 19/2597 Charles Powell's notes on Bush–Thatcher Telcon 5.6.1989 MTF

88 Ezra F. Vogel, Ming Yuan, Akihiko Tanaka (eds) *The Golden Age of the US–China–Japan Triangle, 1972–1989* Harvard Univ. Asia Center 2002 pp. 105–6; Mary Nolan *The Transatlantic Century: Europe and the United States, 1890–2010* Cambridge UP 2012 p. 327; R. W. Apple Jr 'Leaders in Paris Argue over China' *NYT* 14.7.1989

89 For the declaration, see g8.utoronto.ca/summit/1989paris/east.html

90 Maureen Dowd 'Leaders at Summit Back Financial Aid For East Europe' *NYT* 16.7.1989

91 Ibid.; Robert L. Hutchings *American Diplomacy and the End of the Cold War: An Insider's Account of US Policy in Europe, 1989–1992* Woodrow Wilson Center Press 1997 pp. 67–9; R. W. Apple Jr 'Mission for Europeans Signals Growing Power' *NYT* 16.7.1989

92 D. Hodson 'Jacques Delors: Vision, Revisionism, and the Design of EMU' in Kenneth Dyson & Ivo Maes (eds) *Architects of the Euro: Intellectuals in the Making of European Monetary Union* Oxford UP 2016 pp. 212–32

93 On 'EC 92' see JAB-SML B108/F1 Talking points – Cabinet Meeting (first meeting of Bush administration) WDC 23.1.1989 p. 2; Robert B. Zoellick 'Bush 41 and Gorbachev' *Diplomatic History* 42, 4 (2018) p. 561

94 For the Madrid Declaration, see europarl.europa.eu/summits/madrid/mad1_de.pdf. For Bush's luncheon meeting with Delors, see GHWBPL Memcon of Bush–Delors talks 14.6.1989 White House pp. 2–3

95 Kohl's Letter to Bush 28.6.1989, printed in *DESE* doc. 12 pp. 320–3. On the Poland visit, see Serge Schmemann 'Old Prejudices and Hostilities Stall Effort by Bonn and Warsaw to Reconcile' *NYT* 23.6.1989; Hutchings *American Diplomacy* pp. 67–8. See also Christoph Gunkel 'Helmut Kohls Polen-Reise 1989: Problemfall Mauerfall' *Spiegel-Online*, 6.11.2009

96 'W. Europe to Start Giving Food Products to Poland' *LAT* 18.8.1989; 'Food Aid to Poland Linked to Free

Markets' *NYT* 2.8.1989. Cf. Domber 'Skepticism and Stability' p. 65; and the files in: NS Archive Washington DC End of the Cold War – Poland 1989 Cables

97 Cf. Engel 'A Better World' p. 27; Steven Hurst *The Foreign Policy of the Bush Administration: In Search of a New World Order* Cambridge UP 2009 p. 11; Meyer *1989* pp. 212–17; Melvyn Leffler 'Dreams of Freedom, Temptation of Power' in Jeffrey A. Engel (ed.) *The Fall of the Berlin Wall: The Revolutionary Legacy of 1989* Oxford UP 2009 pp. 132–69

98 Letter extracts in Steven Greenhouse 'Gorbachev Urges Economic Accords' *NYT* 16.7.1989

99 Bush & Scowcroft *A World Transformed* p. 129

100 Ibid.

101 GHWBPL Memcon of Bush–Weizsäcker meeting 6.6.1989 Oval Office p. 2

102 GHWBPL Telcon of Kohl–Bush call 15.6.1989 Oval Office pp. 1–3; for the German transcript, see *DESE* doc. 5 pp. 299–301 esp. p. 300. See also Diary Entry 15.6.1989, printed in Bush *All the Best* p. 428. Bush was happy: Kohl's 'debriefing on Gorbachev' had been good and the chancellor 'upbeat'. Generally, the 'long phone call' had been 'very personal, very friendly'. Bush further noted: 'On a personal note, Helmut mentioned a special sausage he was going to send me three or four different times, so I've got to talk to the Secret Service about getting it. They will be uncomfortable, but here's one where we need to bend the rules a little simply because it means so much to Kohl, and, besides, I like wurst.'

103 Diary Entry 18.6.1989, printed in Bush

& Scowcroft *A World Transformed* p. 130

104 Bush & Scowcroft *A World Transformed* pp. 39, 130

105 GHWBPL Memcon of Mitterrand–Bush meeting 13.7.1989 Palais de l'Elysée p. 2

106 Engel *When the World Seemed New* p. 6; James M. Markham 'The President Tours a New Europe That Calls Its Own Shots' *NYT* 16.7.1989; Dowd 'Leaders at Summit Back Financial Aid For East Europe'. On Bush's ideas on 'personal diplomacy', see Bush & Scowcroft *A World Transformed* pp. 60–1. On 'tango-ing', see Memcon of Reagan–Gorbachev talks 11.10.1986 Reykjavik p. 11 thereaganfiles.com/reykjavik-summit-transcript.pdf

107 Bush's Letter to Gorbachev 21.7.1989, printed in Bush *All the Best* pp. 433–4. Cf. Bush & Scowcroft *A World Transformed* pp. 132–3

108 John Tagliabue 'Jaruzelski Wins Polish Presidency by Minimum Votes' *NYT* 20.7.1989; Domber 'Skepticism and Stability' p. 74

109 Garton Ash *The Magic Lantern* pp. 39–40. NSArchive, End of the Cold War – Poland 1989 Cables 'US embassy Warsaw to Sec State – Coversation with Gen. Kiszczak' 11.8.1989; and 'New Prime Minister May Fail to Form a Government, Will Wałęsa Try Next?' 14.8.1989

110 John Tagliabue 'Senior Solidarity Aide Says He Is Being Named Premier; Post-War Milestone In Bloc' *NYT* 19.8.1989. On Gorbachev's pressure, see From Rakowski's polit-diary – Gorbatschow zu Mieczysław Rakowski: 'Den Weg der Verständigung gehen' 22.8.1989, printed in Stefan Karner et al. (eds) *Der Kreml und die 'Wende'*

1989: Interne Analysen der sowjetischen Führung zum Fall der kommunistischen Regime - Dokumente Studienverlag 2014 pp. 434-6; Francis X. Clines 'Gorbachev Calls, Then Polish Party Drops Its Demands' *NYT* 23.8.1989; Castle *Triggering Communism's Collapse* pp. 204-10

111 Quote from Castle *Triggering Communism's Collapse* p. 207. John Tagliabue 'Man in the News: Tadeusz Mazowiecki - A Catholic at the Helm' *NYT* 19.8.1989

112 John Tagliabue 'Jaruzelski, Moved by "Needs and Aspirations" of Poland, Names Wałęsa Aide Premier' *NYT* 20.8.1989

113 *Idem* 'Wider Capitalism to Be Encouraged by Polish Leaders' *NYT* 24.8.1989

114 *Idem* 'Poles Approve Solidarity-Led Cabinet' *NYT* 13.9.1989

115 Scowcroft quoted in Thomas L. Friedman 'The Challenge of Poland' *NYT* 25.8.1989. Bush quoted in GHWBPL Telcon Bush–Kohl call 23.6.1989 Oval Office p. 2

116 Taubman *Gorbachev* pp. 481-3, 428

117 On the Baltic question, see Kristina Spohr *Germany and the Baltic Problem after the Cold War: The Development of a New Ostpolitik, 1989–2000* Routledge 2004 pp. 20-2; Graham Smith (ed.) *The Baltic States: The National Self-Determination of Estonia, Latvia and Lithuania* St Martin's Press 1996 pp. 132-3. For contemporary reporting on the Baltic Chain, see Michael Dobbs 'Baltic States Link In Protest "So Our Children Can Be"' *WP* 24.8.1989; Francis X. Clines 'Poland Condemns Nazi–Soviet Pact' *NYT* 24.8.1989. Cf. Esther B. Fein 'Moscow Condemns Nationalist "Virus" in 3 Baltic Lands'

NYT 27.8.1989; Michael Dobbs 'Independence Fever Sets Up Confrontation' *WP* 27.8.1989

118 Garton Ash *The Magic Lantern* pp. 56-9

119 Mary Elise Sarotte *The Collapse: The Accidental Opening of the Berlin Wall* Basic Books 2014 p. 24. For the Stasi document, see BStU Sekretariat Mittig 27 Blatt 120-130 'STRENG GEHEIM! Zentrale Auswertungs- und Informationsgruppe: "Hinweise auf wesentliche motivbildende Faktoren im Zusammenhang mit Anträgen auf ständige Ausreise nach dem nichtsozialistischen Ausland und dem ungesetzlichen Verlassen der DDR"' Berlin 9.9.1989 esp. p. 3

120 David Childs *The Fall of the GDR* Longman 2001 p. 66. Serge Schmemann 'Sour German Birthday; Humiliation of Exodus to West Overwhelms East Berlin's Celebration of First 40 Years' *NYT* 6.10.1989

121 Hans Michel Kloth *Vom 'Zettelfalten' zum freien Wählen: Die Demokratisierung der DDR 1989/90 und die 'Wahlfrage'* Ch. Links 2000 p. 295; 'DDR: Zeugnis der Reife' *Der Spiegel* 20/1989 15.5.1989 pp. 24-5; Schmemann 'Sour German Birthday'

122 Politisches Archiv des Auswärtigen Amts Berlin (hereafter PAAA) Zwischen-Archiv (ZA) 139.798E Dr. Mulack an Bundesminister - Betr.: Vorsprache und Zufluchtnahme von Deutschen aus der DDR in unseren osteuropäischen Vertretungen 20.6.1989 p. 3

123 BStU ZA ZAIG 5352 Blatt 124-134 'Zentrale Auswertungs- und Informationsgruppe: "Hinweise zum verstärkten Missbrauch des Territoriums der Ungarischen Volksrepublik durch Bürger der DDR zum Verlassen

der DDR sowie zum Reiseverkehr nach der UVR'" 14.7.1989. This document includes the 1969 treaty. See also Memcon of Fischer–Horn talks in East Berlin 31.8.1989, printed in Horst Möller et al. (eds) *Die Einheit: Das Auswärtige Amt, das DDR-Außenministerium und der Zwei-plus-Vier-Vertrag* (hereafter *DE*) Vandenhoeck & Ruprecht 2015 doc. 2 p. 76 fn. 4

124 Vermerk des stellv. Referatsleiters 513, Mulack – Ausreisewillige DDR-Bürger in Ungarn, printed in *DE* doc. 1 pp. 73–4 and fn. 2; BStU ZA ZAIG 4021 Blatt 1–192 hier Blatt 79–89 'MfS – Der Minister: Referat auf der Sitzung der Kreisleitung der SED im MfS zur Auswertung der 8. Tagung des ZK [Auszug]' 29.6.1989

125 Charles S. Maier *Dissolution: The Crisis of Communism and the End of East Germany* Princeton UP 1997 pp. 125–6; PAAA ZA 178.925E StS Dr. Sudhoff (Bonn) 'Mein Gespräch mit dem ungarischen AM Horn am 14.8.1989' 18.8.1989 p. 7. See also Ferdinand Protzman 'Westward Tide of East Germans Is a Popular No-Confidence Vote' *NYT* 22.8.1989. For more on the refugee problem in Hungary generally, see Andreas Oplatka *Der erste Riß in der Mauer* Zsolnay 2009 and the files PAAA ZA 139.918E, ZA 139.946–8E, ZA 140.734E and B 85 2.338–43E

126 Sebestyen *Revolution 1989* p. 311

127 Ibid. pp. 312–13; Meyer *1989* pp. 98–102

128 Meyer *1989* p. 102; Richard A. Leiby *The Unification of Germany, 1989–1990* Greenwood Press 1999 pp. 10–11; Protzman 'Westward Tide of East Germans Is a Popular No-Confidence Vote'

129 See *DE* doc. 1 p. 74

130 *DE* doc. 2 p. 78 fn. 5; Kunzmann to StS

Lautenschlager – Betr.: Versorgung der Deutschen aus der DDR in den Botschaften Prag, Warschau und in Ungarn 5.9.1989, printed in *DE* doc. 3 pp. 79–81

131 BStU ZA ZAIG 4021 Blatt 1–192 hier Blatt 79–89 'MfS – Der Minister: Referat auf der Sitzung der Kreisleitung der SED im MfS zur Auswertung der 8. Tagung des ZK [Auszug]' 29.6.1989; *DE* doc. 2 p. 75

132 Protzman 'Westward Tide'

133 Sarotte *The Collapse* p. 25

134 Memo by Stern to Seiters 8.8.1989 and Memcon of Duisberg–Nier talks 11.8.1989, printed in *DESE* docs 20 and 21 pp. 351–5. Serge Schmemann 'Illness Sparks Succession Watch in East Germany' *NYT* 24.7.1989 p. 3; Robert J. McCartney 'East Germany "Paralysed"' *WP* 14.9.1989

135 PAAA ZA 178.925E StS Dr. Sudhoff (Bonn) – Mein Gespräch mit dem ungarischen AM Horn (14.8.1989) 18.8.1989 p. 4.

136 For the German versions of the Memcons of the two meetings between Kohl and Genscher with Németh and Horn – both on 25.8.1989 – see *DESE* docs 28–9 pp. 377–82. For an English translation, see NSAEBB No. 490

137 Memcon by Genscher on Kohl's meeting with Németh and Horn, Schloss Gymnich, printed in *DESE* doc. 28 p. 380; Kohl *Ich wollte* pp. 71–4 here esp. p. 74

138 *DESE* doc. 28 pp. 378–9 and NSAEBB No. 490; Letter from Kohl to Németh 4.10.1989 and Memcon of Kohl–Delors talks 5.10. 1989, printed in *DESE* docs 57, 58 pp. 442–3; Kohl *Ich wollte* p. 74

139 Kramer 'The Demise' p. 834

140 Kohl *Ich wollte* p. 75

141 On the Horn–Fischer conversation of

31.8.1989, see *DE* doc. 2 pp. 75–9 and Cable from Bertele to BK Chef 1.9. 1989, printed in *DESE* doc. 34 p. 391; SAPMO ZPA J IV 212/039/77 Verlauf der SED Politbürositzung am 5. September 1989 (Streng geheim!) 5.9.1989; sections of transcript of the SED Politburo session also printed in *MoH:1989* doc. 79 pp. 515–16

142 Gyula Horn *Freiheit, die ich meine*: *Erinnerungen des ungarischen Außenministers, der den eisernen Vorhang öffnete* Hoffmann & Campe 1991 pp. 327–8; Serge Schmemann 'Hungary Allows 7,000 East Germans to Emigrate West' *NYT* 11.9.1989; Henry Kamm 'Hungary's Motive: Earning Western Goodwill' *NYT* 15.9.1989

143 Ferdinand Protzman 'Thousands Swell Trek to the West by East Germans' *NYT* 12.9.1989; Craig R. Whitney 'The Dream of Reunion; Idea of One Germany Gains New Currency' *NYT* 12.9.1989

144 Telegram Kohl to Németh 12.9.1989, printed in *DESE* doc. 40 p. 404; Helmut Kohl *Vom Mauerfall zur Wiedervereinigung: Meine Erinnerungen* Knaur-Taschenbuch 2009 pp. 51–8; Protzman 'Thousands Swell Trek'

145 Zelikow & Rice *Germany Unified* p. 68; Memcon of Seiters–Horváth talks in Bonn 19.9.1989, printed in *DESE* doc. 41 p. 405; John Tagliabue 'East Germans Get Permission To Quit Prague For West' *NYT* 1.10.1989

146 On the GDR regime's fury, see 'Letter from GDR Ambassador to Hungary, Gerd Vehres, to Foreign Minister Oskar Fischer' 10.9.1989 DAWC or printed in *MoH:1989* doc. 81 pp. 518–20; On the Kremlin's perspective, see Jonathan Steele *Eternal Russia: Yeltsin, Gorbachev, and the Mirage of Democracy* Harvard

UP 1994 pp. 184–5; Kramer 'The Demise' pp. 836–7; Taubman *Gorbachev* p. 484; *MoH:1989* doc. 90 p. 548; Zelikow & Rice *Germany Unified* p. 68; Memcon of Gorbachev–Honecker Meeting in Moscow 28.6.1989, printed in Daniel Küchenmeister (ed.) *Honecker – Gorbatschow: Vieraugengespräche* (hereafter *Vieraugengespräche*) Dietz 1993 p. 209. On the discussions between Kohl and Gorbachev in Bonn on bilateral economic relations and German assistance on 13 June 1989, see Memcon of Kohl–Gorbachev Talks with Delegations in Bonn 13.6.1989, printed in *DESE* doc. 4 pp. 294–9

147 PAAA ZA 139.798E BStSL 'Betr.: Aktuelle Zahl der Zufluchtssuchenden' 27.9.1989

148 Tagliabue 'East Germans Get Permission to Quit Prague for West'

149 Memcon of Genscher talks with CSSR FM Johanes talks on 25.9.1989 in New York, printed in *DE* doc. 7 pp. 97–9; Memcon of Genscher's conversations with foreign ministers Shevardnadze (USSR), Johanes (CSSR), Fischer (GDR), Dumas (FRA), and Baker (USA) on 28.9.1989, in *DE* doc. 8 pp. 100–1 and fns 2, 4; and Letter Fischer to Honecker 29.9.1989, printed in *DE* doc. 10 pp. 106–7. See also PAAA ZA 178.931E Vermerk, Betr.: Gespräch BM mit AM Schewardnadze am 27.9.1989 in New York (Kleiner Kreis), 27.9.1989; and PAAA ZA 178.924E Note from Genscher to Shevardnadze 29.9.1989; Genscher *Erinnerungen* pp. 14–19

150 SAPMO DY 30/ J IV 2/2A/3243 Protokoll der Sitzung des Politbüros 29.9.1989. On property questions, see SAPMO DY 30/ J IV 2/2A/3245; Genscher *Erinnerungen* pp. 19–21

151 Genscher *Erinnerungen* pp. 21–2;

Richard Kiessler & Frank Elbe *Ein runder Tisch mit scharfen Ecken: der diplomatische Weg zur deutschen Einheit* Nomos 1993 pp. 33–8; *DESE* docs 51–7 pp. 429–42; Diary entry of Prague embassy staffer Thomas Strieder 30.9–1.10.1989, printed in *DE* doc. 12 pp. 110–11 fn. 3

152 *DE* doc. 12 pp. 110–14; Genscher *Erinnerungen* pp. 22–4

153 Tagliabue 'East Germans Get Permission To Quit Prague For West'

154 Genscher *Erinnerungen* part 1 pp. 27–204

155 Ibid. pp. 13–14. Genscher quoted in Serge Schmemann 'More Than 6,000 East Germans Swell Tide of Emigrés to the West' *NYT* 2.10.1989; cf. Kohl *Meine Erinnerungen* pp. 60–1

156 *DE* doc. 12 pp. 110–14; Tagliabue 'East Germans Get Permission To Quit Prague For West'; A similar scene was enacted that night in Warsaw, where more than 800 East Germans camped out at the FRG embassy were allowed to leave by train for the West German border city of Helmsted. See Cable by Bertele to Chef BK 2.10.1989, printed in *DESE* doc. 52 pp. 430–2. For the memories of Ambassador Huber, see prag.diplo.de/cz-de/botschaft/-/2176350

157 Memo by Duisberg to Klein, 2.10.1989, printed in *DESE* doc. 54 pp. 435–6; Kiessler & Elbe *Ein runder Tisch* pp. 42–4; Sarotte *1989* pp. 31–3. For the atmosphere on the trains from Poland via the GDR to the FRG, cf. *DESE* doc. 52 p. 432

158 Genscher quoted in Schmemann 'More Than 6,000 East Germans'

159 Schmemann 'Sour German Birthday'

160 BStU MfS Rechtsstelle 100 HA Konsularische Angelegenheiten 'Reiseverkehr DDR-CSSR' (not dated, but around 3.10.1989). See also Paula Butturini 'East Germany Closes Its Border After 10,000 More Flee To West' *CT* 4.10.1989

161 Cf. BStU MfS ZAIG 3804 Blatt 1–6 'Ministerium für Staatssicherheit: Information no. 438/89 'über erste Hinweise auf Reaktionen und Verhaltensweisen von Personen der DDR im Zusammenhang mit der zeitweiligen Aussetzung des pass- und visafreien Reiseverkehrs' 4.10.1989

162 Telcon of Kohl–Adameč call 3.10.1989 and Seiters–Duisberg talks and contacts 3–4.10.1989, printed in *DESE* docs 55–6 pp. 437–41; *DE* docs. 14–15 pp. 115–20. East German sources on organising trains in SAPMO DY 30/ J IV 2/2A/3245 and DY 30/IV 2/2.039/342.

163 Sarotte *The Collapse* pp. 30–1. 'Freedom Train' *TIME* 16.10.1989; Serge Schmemann 'East Germans Line Emigré Routes, Some in Hope of Their Own Exit' *NYT* 5.10.1989

164 BStU Außenstelle Dresden BV Dresden LBV 10167 Blatt 1–5 'Schilderung der Ereignisse in Dresden zwischen dem 3. und dem 8.10.1989 durch den Leiter der BVfS Dresden, Böhm' 9.10.1989; Patrick Salmon et al. (eds) *Documents on British Policy Overseas, Series III, Volume VII, German Unification, 1989–1990* (hereafter *DBPO III VII GU 1989–90*) Routledge 2010 doc. 14 p. 34. See also Ferdinand Protzman 'Jubilant East Germans Cross to West in Sealed Trains' *NYT* 6.10.1989

165 On Putin, see Vladimir Putin et al., *First Person: An Astonishingly Frank Self-Portrait by Russia's President Putin* Public Affairs 2000 pp. 69–81; Fiona Gill & Clifford G. Gaddy 'How the 1980s Explains Vladimir Putin' *The*

Atlantic 14.2.2013; Entry 5.10.1989 *The Diary of Anatoly S.Chernyaev* 1989 NSAEBB No. 275

166 Erklärung der DDR-Volkskammer zu den aktuellen Ereignissen in der Volksrepublik China, 8.6.1989, printed in *Neues Deutschland* 8.6.1989; On Honecker's thoughts on China as expressed to Yao Yilin, Serge Schmemann 'East Germans Let Largest Protest Proceed In Peace' *NYT* 10.10.1989

167 East Berlin was particularly interested in the CCP's conclusions as to the causes of the protest movement. See SAPMO ZPA IV 2/2.035/33 Bericht für das Politbüro über die Lage in der VR China (III. Quartal 1989), printed in Werner Meißner (ed.) *Die DDR und China 1945–1990: Politik – Wirtschaft – Kultur. Eine* Quellensammlung (hereafter *DDR-CHINA:PWK*) Akademie Verlag 1995 doc. 201 pp. 406–7

168 SAPMO ZPA JIV 2/2A/3247 Memcon of Jian–Krenz talks in Beijing 26.9.1989, printed in *DDR-CHINA:PWK*, doc. 204 pp. 412–14 esp. p. 413

169 SAPMO ZPA JIV 2/2A/3247 Memcon of Qiao–Krenz talks in Beijing, 25.9.1989, printed in *DDR–CHINA:PWK* doc. 203 pp. 409–11 esp. p. 410

170 SAPMO DY 30/ J IV 2/2A/3247 'Protocol #43 of the Meeting of the Politburo of the Central Committee of the SED' 17.10.1989 p. 5 DAWC

171 'How "Gorbi" Spoiled East Germany's 40th Birthday Party' *Spiegel-Online* 7.10.1989

172 David Holley 'Under Tight Wraps, China Marks 40th Anniversary of Communist Rule' *LAT* 2.10.1989. It is noteworthy that there was one American present on the rostrum in Beijing – former Secretary of State Alexander Haig who, the newspapers wrote, was on a private business visit to China. Nothing is mentioned about this in the memoirs by Bush & Scowcroft or Baker. But it seems inconceivable that Haig's public presence at the festivities did not have Bush's blessing. See Lee Feigon 'Bush and China: What's a Massacre Between Friends?' *CT* 12.12.1989

173 Nicholas D. Kristof '"People's China" Celebrates, but without the People' *NYT* 2.10.1989; Li quoted in '40 Years of Communism – China to Celebrate Loudly' *The Baltimore Sun* 16.8.1989

174 *DBPO III VII GU 1989–90* doc. 17 p. 42; Sebestyen *Revolution 1989* pp. 332–4; BStU MfS ZAIG 7314 Blatt 1–30 'Plan der Maßnahmen zur Gewährleistung der Sicherheit während des 40. Jahrestages der Gründung der Deutschen Demokratischen Republik – 6–8.10.1989' 27.9.1989; BStU MfS ZAIG 8680 Blatt 1 15–21 'Hinweise für Kollegiumssitzung 3.10.1989 Hinweise zur Aktion "Jubiläum 40"' 3.10.1989. For Honecker's speech on 6.10.1989, available at Deutsche Geschichte in Dokumenten und Bildern – German Historical Institute – Washington DC (hereafter DGDB-GHIDC)

175 Taubman *Gorbachev* pp. 484–5. Serge Schmemann 'Gorbachev Lends Honecker a Hand' *NYT* 7.10.1989. Cf. Maier *Dissolution* p. 148

176 Serge Schmemann 'Police and Protestors Clash Amid East Berlin Festivity' *NYT* 8.10.1989

177 SAPMO ZPA J IV 2/2.035/60 Memcon of Honecker–Gorbachev meeting 7.10.1989 and SAPMO ZPA J IV 2/2.035/60 Memcon of SED Politburo meeting with Gorbachev 7.10.1989,

printed in *Vieraugengespräche* docs 20–1 pp. 240–66 esp. pp. 241, 243, 256; Schmemann 'Gorbachev Lends Honecker a Hand'

178   SAPMO ZPA J IV 2/2.035/60 Memcon of SED Politburo meeting with Gorbachev 7.10.1989, printed in *Vieraugengespräche* doc. 21 p. 256. For the Soviet version of the Memcon, see *MoH:1989* doc. 88 p. 545; Schmemann 'Gorbachev Lends Honecker a Hand'

179   Gorbachevs 'Festansprache zum 40. Jahrestag der DDR (7.10.1989)' *Neues Deutschland* 9.10.1989; Gorbachev quoted in Schmemann 'Gorbachev Lends Honecker a Hand'

Chapter 3

1   Christoph Gunkel 'Helmut Kohls Polen-Reise 1989 – Problemfall Mauerfall' *Spiegel-Online* 6.11.2009; Werner A. Perger 'Friedliche Revolution: Als Kohl einmal am falschen Platz war' *Zeit Online* 9.11.2009. Kohl *Meine Erinnerungen* pp. 84–6; Horst Teltschik *329 Tage: Innenansichten der Einigung* Siedler 1991 pp. 11–14 esp. p. 14

2   Kohl *Meine Erinnerungen* p. 83; Teltschik *329 Tage* pp. 11, 13–14

3   Kohl *Meine Erinnerungen* pp. 102–3; Teltschik *329 Tage* p. 14; Andreas Rödder *Deutschland einig Vaterland: Die Geschichte der Wiedervereinigung* Beck 2009 pp. 133–4; cf. despite his historical sensitivity and political ambitions as regards German–Polish reconciliation fifty years after 1939, the symbolic gestures and locations of his Poland trip were all laced with controversy. Each choice had been rather fraught and caused planners on both sides significant headaches in the run-up to the visit. 'Weit weg von

Aussöhnung' *Der Spiegel* 45/1989 6.11.1989 pp. 18–19; 'Helmut Kohl als Symbol der Geschichte' *Der Spiegel* 47/1989 20.11.1989 pp. 130, 132–3 esp. p. 132

4   Kohl *Meine Erinnerungen* pp. 86–7; Teltschik *329 Tage* p. 15; cf. Gunkel 'Helmut Kohls Polen-Reise 1989'

5   Kohl *Meine Erinnerungen* pp. 87–8; Teltschik *329 Tage* pp. 16–19; Genscher *Erinnerungen* pp. 655, 657; Gunkel 'Helmut Kohls Polen-Reise 1989'. See also Perger 'Friedliche Revolution'

6   Serge Schmemann 'Joyous East Germans Pour Through Wall; Party Pledges Freedoms, and City Exults – Berlin a Festival' *NYT* 11.11.1989; Genscher *Unterwegs zur Einheit* pp. 228–9; idem, *Erinnerungen* pp. 657–61; cf. Teltschik *329 Tage* p. 20 who claims that Genscher at all costs tried to avoid the topic of unity in his speech; and that Brandt in his address had uttered the famous words: 'now what belongs together grows together' – he had not. See also Kohl *Meine Erinnerungen* p. 94 and 'Willy Brandt: "Now what belongs together will grow together"' *Deutsche Welle* 13.12.2012

7   Schmemann 'Joyous East Germans Pour Through Wall'. Kohl *Meine Erinnerungen* pp. 88–93; Teltschik *329 Tage* p. 20. See also 'Helmut Kohl als Symbol' pp. 130, 132–3

8   Oral Message from Gorbachev to Kohl 10.11.1989, printed in *DESE* doc. 80 pp. 504–5; Kohl *Meine Erinnerungen* pp. 89–90

9   Ibid.

10   Kohl *Meine Erinnerungen* p. 94

11   Letter by Charles Powell (No. 10) to Stephen Wall (FCO) 10.11.1989, printed in *DBPO III VII GU 1989–90* doc. 37 p. 102; Telcon of Kohl–Thatcher call

10.11.1989, printed in *DESE* doc. 81 pp. 506–7; Kohl *Meine Erinnerungen* pp. 94–5

12 Telcon of Kohl–Bush call 10.11.1989, printed in *DESE* doc. 82 pp. 507–9; for the US version see GHWBPL Telcon of Kohl–Bush call 10.11.1989 Oval Office pp. 1–3; Kohl *Meine Erinnerungen* p. 95

13 Telcon of Kohl–Mitterrand call 11.11.1989, printed in *DESE* doc. 85 p. 512; Kohl *Meine Erinnerungen* pp. 95–6

14 Telcon of Kohl–Krenz call 11.11.1989, printed in *DESE* doc. 86 pp. 513–15; Kohl *Meine Erinnerungen* pp. 96–7

15 Telcon of Kohl–Gorbachev call 11.11.1989, printed in *DESE* doc. 87 pp. 515–17; Kohl *Meine Erinnerungen* pp. 97–9; Teltschik *329 Tage* pp. 27–9

16 Letter from Waigel to Kohl 10.11.1989, printed in *DESE* doc. 84; Kohl *Meine Erinnerungen* p. 97. On West German annual support to the GDR economy, see also Christian Joppke *East German Dissidents and the Revolution of 1989: Social Movement in a Leninist Regime* Macmillan 1995 p. 82; Ian Jeffries *Socialist Economies and the Transition to the Market: A Guide* Routledge 2002 p. 313. On issues related to economic unification, see Gerlinde Sinn & Hans-Werner Sinn *Kaltstart: Volkswirtschaftliche Aspekte der deutschen Vereinigung* DTV 1993. Craig R. Whitney 'Bonn's Politicians Appear Dismayed by Cost of Influx' *NYT* 7.11.1989

17 Whitney 'Bonn's Politicians Appear Dismayed by Cost of Influx'

18 Cf. Kohl *Meine Erinnerungen* pp. 100–1. Teltschik *329 Tage* p. 29

19 Ilko-Sascha Kowalczuk *Endspiel: Die Revolution von 1989 in der DDR* Beck 2009 p. 387; Detlef Pollack 'Der Zusammenbruch der DDR als Verkettung getrennter Handlungslinien' in Konrad H. Jarausch & Martin Sabrow (eds) *Weg in den Untergang: Der innere Zerfall der DDR* Vandenhoeck & Ruprecht 1999 pp. 43–4, 51

20 See BStU MfS ZAIG 7314 Blatt 1–30 'Plan der Maßnahmen zur Gewährleistung der Sicherheit während des 40. Jahrestages der Gründung der Deutschen Demokratischen Republik – 6–8.10.1989' 27.9.1989; BStU MfS ZAIG 8680 Blatt 1 15–21 'Hinweise für Kollegiumssitzung 3.10.1989. Hinweise zur Aktion "Jubiläum 40"' 3.10.1989. See also Kowalczuk *Endspiel* pp. 389–91

21 Dieter Krüger & Armin Wagner (eds) *Konspiration als Beruf: Deutsche Geheimdienstchefs im Kalten Krieg* Ch. Links 1999 p. 260; Sebestyen *Revolution 1989* p. 335

22 Kowalczuk *Endspiel* pp. 392–3

23 Serge Schmemann 'Police and Protestors Clash Amid East Berlin Festivity' *NYT* 8.10.1989 p. 18; idem 'Security Forces Storm Protestors in East Germany' *NYT* 9.10.1989; Stefan Wolle *Die heile Welt der Diktatur: Alltag und Herrschaft in der DDR 1971–1989* Ch. Links 2013 pp. 320–2. The biggest 7 October demonstration relative to the city's size – with 76,000 inhabitants – was in Plauen, where 20,000 took to the streets to protest against the regime; but Western media did not pick up on events in this small provincial town near the inner-German border and the much bigger Karl-Marx-Stadt. See Kowalczuk *Endspiel* pp. 396–9

24 See 'Die Geduld ist zu Ende' *Der Spiegel* 41/1989 9.10.1989. Pollack 'Der Zusammenbruch' pp. 44, 52

25 Serge Schmemann 'East Germans Let Largest Protest Proceed in Peace' *NYT* 10.10.1989; 'Wir bitten Sie um Besonnenheit – Roland Wötzel über den Aufruf der Leipziger Sechs am 9. Oktober 1989 in der Messemetropole' *Neues Deutschland* 8.10.2014. See also Sarotte *The Collapse* pp. 55–6, 69

26 BStU MfS BdL/Dok 006921 Fernschreiben des SED-Generalsekretärs Honecker an die 1. Sekretäre der SED-Bezirksleitungen, von Mielke mit Begleitschreiben weitergeleitet an die Leiter der Stasi-Bezirksverwaltungen 8.10.1989. Tobias Hollitzer 'Der friedliche Verlauf des 9. Oktober in Leipzig – Kapitulation oder Reformbereitschaft?' in Günther Heydemann et al. (eds) *Revolution und Transformation in der DDR 1989/1990* Duncker & Humblot 1999 pp. 247–88 here p. 261; Sarotte *The Collapse* pp. 43–4. For fear of the 'Chinese solution' in Leipzig, see diary page of Superintendent Dr Johannes Richter 9.10.1989, printed in Tobias Hollitzer & Sven Sachenbacher (eds) *Die friedliche Revolution in Leipzig* Leipziger Uni-Vlg 2012 p. 409

27 Honecker quoted in Schmemann 'East Germans Let Largest Protest Proceed In Peace'; 'Chinesische Lehre und westliche "Hetzballons"' *taz* 11.10.1989

28 BStU MfS BdL/Dok 006921 Fernschreiben des SED-Generalsekretärs Honecker an die 1. Sekretäre der SED-Bezirksleitungen, von Mielke mit Begleitschreiben weitergeleitet an die Leiter der Stasi-Bezirksverwaltungen 8.10.1989; BStU MfS BdL/Dok 006920 Telegrafische Weisung Mielkes an die Leiter der Diensteinheiten 8.10.1989. See also Hans-Hermann Hertle *Der Fall der Mauer: Die unbeabsichtigte Selbstauflösung des SED-Staates* Westdeutscher Verlag 1999 pp. 114–15; Rödder *Deutschland* p. 88; Sarotte *The Collapse* p. 52

29 Rödder *Deutschland* p. 88; Sarotte *The Collapse* pp. 43, 53–4; Hollitzer 'Der friedliche Verlauf' pp. 268–80

30 Sarotte *The Collapse* pp. 69–77; Pollack 'Der Zusammenbruch der DDR' pp. 55–64; Rödder *Deutschland* pp. 81–2

31 BArch/P E-1– 56321 Persönliche Aufzeichnungen Schürers über die Politbürositzung am 17. Oktober 1989, printed in Hertle *Der Fall der Mauer* doc. 4 p. 431

32 SAPMO-BArch SED ZK J IV 2/2A/3247 Protokoll des Politbüros der SED vom 17.10.1989 (Auszug) printed in Gerd-Rüdiger Stephan (ed.) *'Vorwärts immer, rückwärts nimmer!' Interne Dokumente zum Zerfall von SED und DDR 1988/89* Dietz 1994 doc. 35 p. 166. Erklärung des Genossen Erich Honecker (Letter of resignation from Erich Honecker) Berlin 18.10.1989 CVCE.EU

33 Pollack 'Der Zusammenbruch der DDR' pp. 65–6. On Honecker's illness, see Sarotte *The Collapse* pp. 26, 28

34 SAPMO-BArch Ton Y 1/TD 737 Krenz's speech before the Central Committee, 18.10.1989, printed in Hans-Hermann Hertle & Gerd-Rüdiger Stephan (eds) *Das Ende der SED: Die letzen Tage des Zentralkommittees* Ch. Links 2013 doc. 9 pp. 103–33 esp. p. 112. It is ironic that it was Honecker who asked: 'Was ist Erneuerung? Welche Richtung <soll eingeschlagen werden>? Bisher <gibt es> keine Linie.' BArch/P, E-1– 56321, Persönliche Aufzeichnungen Schürers über die Politbürositzung am 17.10.1989, printed in Hertle *Der Fall*

der Mauer doc. 4 p. 437. Vorlage von Duisberg an Kohl 19.10.1989; and Telcon of Kohl–Krenz call 26.10.1989, both printed in *DESE* docs 63, 68 pp. 455–8 and p. 468

35 Pollack 'Der Zusammenbruch der DDR' p. 59; SHStA Dresden SED 13218 Modrow's manuscript for his speech in the discussions between Erich Honecker and the first SED secretaries of the regions (1. Bezirkssekretäre der SED) on 12.10.1989 in Berlin, printed in Stephan (ed.) *Interne Dokumente* doc. 33 pp. 157–161 and SAPMO-BArch Ton Y 1/TD 737 Modrow's speech before the Central Committee 18.10.1989, printed in Hertle & Stephan (eds) *Das Ende der SED* doc. 9 p. 124; Rödder *Deutschland* pp. 93–4

36 Telex von Bertele an Chef BK 22.9.1989, printed in *DESE* doc. 45 pp. 413–16 esp. p. 414; Gerhard Wettig 'Niedergang, Krise und Zusammenbruch der DDR – Ursachen und Vorgänge' in Eberhard Kuhrt et al. (eds) *Die SED-Herrschaft und ihr Zusammenbruch* Leske & Budrich 1996 p. 418; Pollack 'Der Zusammenbruch der DDR' pp. 65–7. See also Niall Ferguson *The Square and the Tower: Networks, Hierarchies and the Struggle for Global Power* Allen Lane 2017

37 Pollack 'Der Zusammenbruch der DDR' pp. 66–8; Rödder *Deutschland* pp. 98–102; Wolle *Die heile Welt der Diktatur* pp. 440–1

38 See Serge Schmemann 'East Germany's Cabinet Resigns, Bowing to Protest and Mass Flight' *NYT* 8.11.1989

39 Rödder *Deutschland* p. 95

40 SAPMO-BArch DY 30/5195 Gerhard Schürer, Gerhard Beil, Alexander Schalck, Ernst Höfner und Arno Donda: 'Vorlage für das Politbüro des ZK der SED – Analyse der ökonomischen Lage der DDR mit Schlußfolgerungen', 30.10.1989; Hertle *Der Fall der Mauer* docs 7–8 pp. 448–60 and p. 461; and for Krenz's statements in May 1989, see Rödder *Deutschland* p. 73. See also Gerhard Heske 'Die gesamtwirtschaftliche Entwicklung in Ostdeutschland 1970 bis 2000 – Neue Ergebnisse einer volkswirtschaftlichen Gesamtrechnung' *Historical Social Research* (2005) p. 238; 'Die Entwicklung der Staatsverschuldung seit der deutschen Wiedervereinigung' *Deutsche Bundesbank Monatsbericht* (March 1997)

41 SAPMO-Barch, ZPA-SED, J IV 2/2A.3255, Memo of Gorbachev–Krenz talks on 1.11.1989 in Moscow, printed in Hertle *Der Fall der Mauer* doc. 9 pp. 462–82

42 Bill Keller 'New East German Chief Hints at Election Changes' *NYT* 2.11.1989

43 Drahtbericht, Hiller (Prag) an AA 4.11.1989, printed in *DE* doc. 18 esp. fns 1, 2, 6. Telegramm des tschechoslowakischen DDR-Botschafters über die Grenzschließung 3.10.1989; Beschluss des Politbüros der SED zum visafreien Verkehr 24.10.1989, both printed in Karel Vodička *Die Prager Botschaftsflüchtlinge 1989* V&R Unipress 2014 docs 38, 55 pp. 380, 407–8. For further telegrams on the Prague refugee crisis, docs 57–67 pp. 414–28; John Tagliabue 'Travel Ban Lifted and East Germans Swarm to Prague' *NYT* 2.11.1989; idem 'More East Germans Seek Passage through Prague' *NYT* 3.11.1989

44 Serge Schmemann 'East Germans' New Leader Vows Far-Reaching Reform and Urges End to Flight' *NYT* 4.11.1989;

idem 'East Germany Opens Frontier to the West for Migration or Travel; Thousands Cross' *NYT* 10.11.1989

45 *Idem* 'East Germany's Cabinet Resigns, Bowing to Protest and Mass Flight' *NYT* 8.11.1989

46 *Idem* '500,000 in East Berlin Rally for Change; Emigres Are Given Passage to West' *NYT* 5.11.1989

47 *Idem* '10,000 More Flee as East Germany Vows Easy Travel' *NYT* 6.11.1989; *idem* 'East Germany's Cabinet Resigns, Bowing to Protest and Mass Flight' *NYT* 8.11.1989; *idem* 'East Germany Opens Frontier to the West For Migration or Travel'. See also Peter Brinkmann *Zeuge vor Ort: Korrespondent in der DDR '89/90* Edition Ost 2014 pp. 8–9

48 Kowalczuk *Endspiel* p. 454; Rödder *Deutschland* p. 106; Serge Schmemann 'Bonn Ties More Aid for East Germany to Free Elections; Politburo Ranks are Shaken up by New Leader' *NYT* 9.11.1989

49 Hertle *Der Fall der Mauer* pp. 163–76; Sarotte *The Collapse* pp. 93–119; Rödder *Deutschland* pp. 106–8

50 Günter Schabowski's Press Conference in the GDR International Press Centre 6.53–7.01 p.m. 9.11.1989 DAWC. For other versions of transcripts, see also Hertle *Der Fall der Mauer* pp. 168–72; Brinkmann *Zeuge vor Ort* pp. 23–5; Albrecht Hinze 'Versehentliche Zündung mit verzögerter Sprengkraft' *SZ* 9.11.1989 p. 17

51 *Reuters* 9.11.1989 7.02 Uhr: Ausreisewillige DDR-Bürger können ab sofort über alle Grenzübergänge der DDR in die Bundesrepublik ausreisen; AP 9.11.1989 7.05 p.m.; *ARD Tagesschau* 8.00 p.m. 9.11.1989 youtube.com/watch?v=llE7tCeNbro. Cf. Brinkmann

Zeuge vor Ort pp. 19–27; Hertle *Der Fall der Mauer* pp. 172–4

52 Hertle *Der Fall der Mauer* pp. 180–7, 380–9; Gerhard Haase-Hindenberg *Der Mann, der die Mauer öffnete: Warum Oberstleutnant Harald Jäger den Befehl verweigerte und damit Weltgeschichte schrieb* Heyne 2007 pp. 194–201. See also Sarotte *1989* pp. 41–2; *idem, The Collapse* pp. 127–50

53 Stefan Kornelius *Angela Merkel: The Chancellor and Her World* Alma Books 2014 p. 32

54 Hertle *Der Fall der Mauer* pp. 188–92; Ferdinand Protzman 'East Berliners Explore Land Long Forbidden' *NYT* 10.11.1989

55 Protzman 'East Berliners Explore Land Long Forbidden' *NYT* 10.11.1989

56 Serge Schmemann 'Joyous East Germans Pour Through Wall; Party Pledges Freedoms, And City Exults' *NYT* 11.11.1989; 'Einmal Ku'damm und zurück' *Der Morgen* 11–12.11.1989; 'DDR Reisebüro beklagt Mangel an Devisen' *Frankfurter Allgemeine Zeitung (FAZ)* 10.11.1989; 'Eine friedliche Revolution' *Der Spiegel* 46/1989 13.11.1989. Cf. Garton Ash *The Magic Lantern* p. 62

57 On 10 November, at a rally after the conclusion of the three-day Central Committee marathon meeting, Egon Krenz was still rabbiting on about an SED 'action programme' and wanting 'better socialism'. He declared: 'We plan a great work … a revolution on German soil that will bring us a socialism that is economically effective, politically democratic, morally clean and will turn to the people in everything.' Krenz quoted in Schmemann 'The Border Is Open'. Cf. *Neues Deutschland* 10.11.1989

58 Hannes Bahrmann & Christoph Links

Wir sind das Volk: Die DDR im Aufbruch – Eine Chronik Aufbau 1990 p. 99; 'Hurra - wir kaufen die DDR' *taz* 24.11.1989

59 See Christof Geisel *Auf der Suche nach einem dritten Weg: Das politische Selbstverständnis der DDR-Opposition in den 8oer Jahren* Ch. Links 2005 pp. 107–24; Karsten Timmer *Vom Aufbuch zu Umbruch: Die Bürgerbewegung in der DDR 1989* Vandenhoeck & Ruprecht 2000 p. 341

60 Hans-Hermann Hertle *Die Berliner Mauer: Biografie eines Bauwerkes* Ch. Links 2015 p. 102; Garton Ash *Magic Lantern* pp. 69, 74

61 'Die DDR öffnet ihre Grenzen zum Westen' *Tagesspiegel* 10.11.1989; 'Mauer und Stacheldraht trennen nicht mehr' *FAZ* 11.11.1989. On TV transforming reality, see Sarotte *1989* pp. 38–39, 41, 44, 46. See also Julia Sonnevend *Stories Without Borders: The Berlin Wall and the Making of a Global Iconic Event* Oxford UP 2016 pp. 89–90

62 John Tagliabue 'A Goodwill Trip Ends; Kohl Recalls Auschwitz and Agrees to Aid Poles' *NYT* 15.11.1989. See also GHWBPL WHORM Files CO054-02 FRG Letter from Kohl to Bush 6.11.1989 pp. 2–3

63 Craig R. Whitney 'Bonn Ties More Aid for East Germany to Free Elections: Kohl Says There is Less Reason Now to Accept Division of Nation' *NYT* 9.11.1989; Deutscher Bundestag *Stenographische Berichte* 11. Wahlperiode 176. Sitzung p. 13335; Serge Schmemann 'Kohl Says Bonn Will Not Press East Germany on Reunification' *NYT* 17.11.1989; Rödder *Deutschland* p. 137

64 Alan Riding 'Western Europe Pledges to Aid East' *NYT* 19.11.1989

65 The 'dual track' decision taken by NATO in December 1979 balanced deterrence with a readiness to negotiate and disarm: 'track one' committed the Alliance to stationing a new generation of American Pershing II and Cruise missiles in Europe after 1982, unless 'track two' – comprehensive arms-reduction negotiations with the Soviet Union – culminated in success. This complex and hard-won compromise had been hammered out by Chancellor Helmut Schmidt in Guadeloupe with the leaders of United States, Britain and France as NATO's three nuclear powers in January 1979. This decision was essential in holding the Alliance together at a time when it seemed in danger of falling apart. Even more important, the dual-track negotiations allowed West Germany to take a seat with other nuclear states at the top table of international politics. In the short term, the dual track was a disaster for Schmidt. Indeed, it precipitated his fall from office. His party was split over the deployment of new missiles and Kohl was able to bring Schmidt down in a vote of no-confidence. Pivotal in all this was the defection of his coalition partner and foreign minister: Hans-Dietrich Genscher, the leader of the Free Democrats, who went on to serve Kohl. And Kohl subsequently pocketed the credit for implementing the deployment of the Pershing II and Cruise missiles in 1983 which he and Schmidt believed led to the INF Treaty of 1987 – the triumphant culmination of 'track two' following the implementation of 'track one'.

66 Kohl *Meine Erinnerungen* pp. 108–9. There is no Memcon of this tête-à-tête

to be found, either in *DESE* or French papers

67   The accounts on the Elysée dinner vary. See Kohl *Meine Erinnerungen* pp. 110–11; Thatcher *The Downing Street Years* pp. 793–4; Jacques Attali *Verbatim III: Première partie, 1988–1989* Fayard 1995 pp. 431–3. Cf. Tilo Schabert *Wie Weltgeschichte gemacht wird: Frankreich und die deutsche Einheit* Klett-Cotta 2002 pp. 411–15; Bozo *Mitterrand* pp. 135–7; Sarotte *1989* p. 64

68   Kohl *Meine Erinnerungen* pp. 110–11; Sarotte *1989* p. 64; Bozo *Mitterrand* pp. 135–8. On Bush's support for Kohl, see GHWBPL Telcon of Bush's call to Kohl 17.11.1989 Oval Office pp. 1–4. For the German version of the telcon, see *DESE* doc. 93, pp. 538–40. On Bush's publicly made comments on German unity that were supportive, see also R. W. Apple Jr 'Possibility of a Reunited Germany Is No Cause for Alarm, Bush Says' *NYT* 25.10.1989

69   Bozo *Mitterrand* p. 138 – based on Mitterrand's interviews with *Paris Match* (23.11.1989) and the *WSJ* (22.11.1989)

70   Kohl's speech at the European Parliament, 22.11.1989, video at my-european-history.ep. eu/myhouse/story/921

71   Kohl *Meine Erinnerungen* p. 113; Teltschik *329 Tage* pp. 46–7

72   Rudolf Augstein 'Sagen, was ist' *Der Spiegel* 47/1989 20.11.1989

73   '"Die DDR ist am Zuge" – Spiegel-Gespräch mit Deutsche-Bank-Chef Alfred Herrhausen über die ostdeutsche Wirtschaftsmisere' *Der Spiegel* 47/1989 20.11.1989

74   Grass said: '*Da hält sich die eine Seite faul an den Status quo und sagt: Aus Gründen der Sicherheit in Mitteleuropa muß es bei der Zweistaatlichkeit bleiben. Dann gibt es die andere Liga, die sich immer zur Zeit oder zur Unzeit auf Wiedervereinigung verständigt. Dazwischen aber liegt die Möglichkeit, eine Einigung zwischen den beiden deutschen Staaten herbeizuführen. Das käme dem deutschen Bedürfnis und Selbstverständnis entgegen, und auch unsere Nachbarn könnten es akzeptieren. Also keine Machtballung im Sinne von Wiedervereinigung, keine weitere Unsicherheit im Sinne von Zweistaatlichkeit, Ausland zu Ausland, sondern vielmehr eine Konföderation zweier Staaten, die sich neu definieren müßte. Da hilft kein Rückblick auf das Deutsche Reich, sei es in den Grenzen von 1945, sei es in den Grenzen von 1937; das ist alles weg. Wir müssen uns neu definieren.*' See 'Viel Gefühl, wenig Bewußtsein – Spiegel-Gespräch mit dem Schriftsteller Günter Graß über eine mögliche Wiedervereinigung Deutschlands' *Der Spiegel* 47/1989 20.11.1989

75   '"Das Gespenst des Vierten Reiches" – Der stellvertretende SPD-Vorsitzende Oskar Lafontaine über die Politik seiner Partei' *Der Spiegel* 39/1989 25.9.1989

76   Oskar Lafontaine in the Deutschland-political debate of the Saarland Landtag, 8 November 1989: '*Es gibt bei uns die Auffassung – wir haben sie auch heute im Bundestag wieder gehört –, daß die NATO zur Staatsräson der Bundesrepublik gehöre. Ich möchte ganz klar sagen, daß ich diese Auffassung respektieren kann, daß ich sie aber genauso wie das Ziel der Wiedervereinigung des Nationalstaates für falsch und anachronistisch halte.*'

77   'Man muß auch anstößig sein' *Der Spiegel* 52/1989 25.12.1989

78 Egon *Bahr, SPD-Präsidium 'Laßt uns um alles in der Welt aufhören, von der Einheit zu träumen oder zu schwätzen' Bild am Sonntag* 1.10.1989. *Cf. Bernt Conrad, '"Ich habe nichts zu korrigieren" – Egon Bahr wird 75 – Unbeirrte Rückschau eines Vordenkers' Die Welt* 18.3.1997

79 Egon Bahr 'Nachdenken über das eigene Land' *Frankfurter Rundschau* 13.12.1988. '*Unerträglich für die Glaubwürdigkeit unserer Republik wäre die Fortsetzung Sonntagsrederei, wonach die Wiedervereinigung vordringlichste Aufgabe bleibt. Das ist objektiv und subjektiv Lüge, Heuchelei, die uns vergiftet und politische Umweltverschmutzung.*' See Margit Roth *Innerdeutsche Bestandsaufnahme der Bundesrepublik 1969–1989: Neue Deutung* Springer VS 2014 pp. 148–9

80 Rede von Willy Brandt auf dem SPD-Parteitag, Berlin, 18.12.1989 CVCE.EU. '*Es kann keine Rede davon sein, im Westen die Schotten dicht zu machen.*'

81 Brandt said '*Denn nirgends steht auch geschrieben, daß sie, die Deutschen, auf einem Abstellgleis zu verharren haben, bis irgendwann ein gesamteuropäischer Zug den Bahnhof erreicht hat.*' See 'Man muß auch anstößig sein' *Der Spiegel* 52/1989 25.12.1989 and 'In Angst vor der Einheit' *Der Spiegel* 51/1989 18.12.1989

82 'Die Geduld ist zu Ende' *Der Spiegel* 41/1989 9.10.1989

83 Rödder *Deutschland* pp. 118–24. For the quotation from the appeal 'Für unser Land' on 26.11.1989, see Matthias Judt (ed.) *DDR-Geschichte in Dokumenten: Beschlüsse, Berichte, interne Materialien und Alltagszeugnisse* Ch. Links 1998 p. 544

84 Craig R. Whitney 'New Ties to Bonn Sought by Premier of East Germany' *NYT* 18.11.1989

85 Herbert Kremp 'Lassen wir uns die Einheit vom anderen vorformulieren?' *Die Welt* 19.11.1989

86 Bahrmann & Links *Wir sind das Volk* p. 146. See also 'Republikaner – Mit Freude einschlürfen: Mit "intellektualisiertem" Programm wollen die Republikaner den Einzug in den Bundestag schaffen' *Der Spiegel* 48/1989 27.11.1989

87 Teltschik *329 Tage* p. 41

88 Ibid. pp. 42, 40

89 Vorlage von Teltschik für Kohl 6.12.1989 and Memo 'SU und "deutsche Frage"' (undated), both printed in *DESE* docs 112 and 112A pp. 616–17. Teltschik, *329 Tage* pp. 43–4. On the Portugalov mission, see also 'The Soviet Origins of Helmut Kohl's 10 Points' NSAEBB No. 296; Grachev *Gorbachev's Gamble* pp. 143–7 esp. pp. 146–7; Alexander von Plato *Die Vereinigung Deutschlands – ein weltpolitisches Machtspiel: Bush, Kohl, Gorbatschow und die internen Gesprächsprotokolle* Ch. Links 2009 pp. 115–21; Zelikow & Rice *Germany Unified* p. 118

90 Teltschik *329 Tage* p. 45

91 *DESE* doc. 112A pp. 616–18; Teltschik *329 Tage* pp. 43–4

92 Teltschik *329 Tage* pp. 44–5

93 Ibid. pp. 47–9

94 Ibid. pp. 44–5, 49

95 Kohl *Meine Erinnerungen* pp. 113–15; Teltschik *329 Tage* pp. 50–1

96 Kohl *Meine Erinnerungen* pp. 114–15

97 The resolution stated 'their right to live in secure borders will not be questioned now or in the future by territorial claims by us Germans'. See Whitney 'Bonn Ties More Aid For East Germany To Free Elections'

98 'Ein Staatenbund? Ein Bundesstaat?' *Der Spiegel* 49/1989 4.12.1989

99 Kohl *Meine Erinnerungen* p. 115

100 Helmut Kohl's Ten-Point Plan for German Unity (28.11.1989) DGDB-GHIDC. In German: Rede von Bundeskanzler Helmut Kohl im Bundestag ('10-Punkte-Programm') 28.11.1989 CdMDA

101 Teltschik *329 Tage* p. 58

102 AmEmb Bonn to Sec State Washdc Cable – Subject: Kohl's Ten-Point-Program – Silence on the Role of the Four Powers 1.12.1989, reprinted in CWIHP Paris Conference 2006

103 R. W. Apple Jr 'Millions of Czechoslovaks Increase Pressure on Party with 2-Hour General Strike' *NYT* 28.11.1989; Ferdinand Protzman 'Kohl to Outline Plan for German Unity' *NYT* 28.11.1989

104 R. W. Apple Jr 'Prague Party to Yield Some Cabinet Posts and Drop Insistence on Primacy in Society' *NYT* 29.11.1989; Ferdinand Protzman 'Kohl Offers an Outline to Create Confederation of the 2 Germanys' *NYT* 29.11.1989; 'Excerpts from Kohl Speech on Reunification of Germany' *NYT* 29.11.1989. The *Washington Post*, by contrast, had Kohl's Ten Points as its headline story: Mark Fisher 'Kohl Proposes Broad Program for Reunification' *WP* 29.11.1989. Otherwise CIA activities in Angola, the coup in the Philippines and Latin American drug-war and civil-war issues dominated the front pages

105 Ferdinand Protzman 'Head of Top West German Bank Is Killed in Bombing by Terrorists' *NYT* 1.12.1989; see article 'Wir können jeden erledigen' and cover of *Der Spiegel* 49/1989 4.12.1989

106 AmEmb Bonn to Sec State Washdc Cable – Subject: Kohl's Ten-Point-Program – Silence on the Role of the Four Powers 1.12.1989, reprinted in CWIHP Paris Conference 2006

107 Letter from Kohl to Bush 28.11.1989, printed in *DESE* doc. 101 pp. 567–73; Zelikow & Rice *Germany Unified* p. 122; Jason De Parle 'THE WORLD – The Bitter Legacy of Yalta: Four Decades of What-Ifs' *NYT* 26.11.1989

108 Letter from Krenz to Bush 28.11.1989, quoted in Zelikow & Rice *Germany Unified* p. 122

109 Bush & Scowcroft *A World Transformed* p. 194

110 GHWBPL Telcon of Bush's call to Kohl 29.11.1989 Oval Office pp. 1, 4. There is no German version declassified or in *DESE*. Kohl quoted in Zelikow & Rice *Germany Unified* p. 123

111 The 'vision thing' was a phrase that *Bush* himself inadvertently coined early on in his own administration as a self-acknowledged problem of articulating a clear vision for the country; Martin J. Medhurst (ed.) *The Rhetorical Presidency of George H. W. Bush* College Station, TX 2006 ch. 2. See also Thomas Singer (ed.) *The Vision Thing: Myth, Politics and Psyche in the World* Taylor & Francis 2014. In fact, the president may have indulged in some self-mockery with the reference to the 'vision thing' in January 1987 in an unfortunate answer to the criticism for his lack of ability to clearly articulate his fundamental beliefs and policies in comparison to Ronald Reagan. His derisory rebuff 'Oh, the vision thing' had backfired and in October 1987 *Newsweek* had featured a cover with the headline 'George Bush: Fighting The "Wimp Factor"'. Even after winning the 1988 election, Bush was never able to shake off the image of the overly pragmatist steward who reacted

mostly to events and merely managed crises. The idea that there were limits to his presidency stuck and he was seen as a president who fell short of certain leadership qualities such as long-range planning and creative thinking. It clearly bothered him. So in his remarks on 29 November he was serious too. As he made clear, he had tentatively but with unusual directness and clarity spelled out between April and June 1989 his views on the major bouleversement in Europe and where he hoped this might lead. So maybe he was not that visionless after all

112 Bush's Interview with White House Press Corps 29.11.1989 APP

113 Vorlage von Lambach für Sudhoff, 1.12.1989, printed in *DE* doc. 25 p. 152; Memcon of Andreotti–Gorbachev talks in Rome 29.11.1989, printed in *MGDF:SD* doc. 57 pp. 245–6; Zelikow & Rice *Germany Unified* p. 124; Kiessler & Elbe *Ein runder Tisch* pp. 52–4; Vorlage von Hartmann an Kohl 1.12.1989, printed in *DESE* doc. 107 pp. 595–6

114 Kiessler & Elbe *Ein runder Tisch* pp. 51–2

115 Five years later, in his memoirs, Genscher was still disparaging Kohl's Ten Point package as being too hesitant and slow-moving, with no clear time-table in a very urgent situation. 'Unity had to be completed as soon as possible.' Genscher *Erinnerungen* p. 673

116 Ibid. p. 682; see also Ritter *Hans-Dietrich Genscher* pp. 39–40

117 Werner Weidenfeld et al. *Außenpolitik für die deutsche Einheit: Die Entscheidungsjahre 1989/90* [Geschichte der deutschen Einheit, Band 4] DVA 1998 p. 646

118 Genscher *Erinnerungen* pp. 683–4. For Gorbachev's rather brief recollections by comparison, see Gorbachev *Memoirs* pp. 527–8

119 For the sanitised German Memcon, see PAAA ZA 178.931E Vermerk – Memcon of Gorbachev–Genscher talks in Moscow on 5.12.1989 by Kastrup D2 6.12.1989. For the Soviet minutes (extract), see *MGDF:SD* doc. 61 pp. 254–65

120 Minute from Sir Patrick Wright (FCO) to Wall 30.10.1989, printed in *DBPO III VII GU 1989/90* doc. 26 fn. 3 p. 79. Cf. Elisabth Guigou *Une femme au coeur de l'Etat. Entretiens avec Pierre Favier et Michel Martin-Roland* Fayard 2000 pp. 75–7. See also TNA UK PREM 19/2691 Charles Powell's 'Memo for Thatcher: Meeting with President Mitterrand' 29.8.1989

121 *DBPO III VII GU 1989/90* doc. 26 fn. 4 p. 69. Cf. Record of Conversation between Gorbachev and Thatcher 23.9.1989, printed in *MoH:1989* doc. 85 pp. 530–2; Thatcher *The Downing Street Years* p. 792; Rodric Braithwaite *Across the Moscow River: The World Turned Upside Down* Yale UP 2002 pp. 135–6. Vermerk by Hartmann on London talks 13.10.1989, printed in *DESE* doc. 61 pp. 450–1

122 G. R. Urban *Diplomacy and Disillusion at the Court of Margaret Thatcher: An Insider's View* I. B. Tauris 2006 p. 100. After the fall of the Wall, on 24 November at Camp David Thatcher told Bush that 'now was not the time to open the question of borders in Europe. To do so would undermine Mr Gorbachev's position ... So German reunification was not just a matter of self-determination'. TNA UK PREM 19/2892 Charles Powell's 'Letter to Wall: Prime Minister's Meeting with

President Bush at Camp David' 25.11.1989

123 PAAA ZA 178.931E 'Vermerk; by Amb. von Richthofen on the Thatcher–Genscher talks in London, 1710–1805hrs (29.11.1989)' 30.11.1989. This is also printed in Andreas Hilger (ed.) *Diplomatie für die deutsche Einheit: Dokumente des Auswärtigen Amts zu den deutsch-sowjetischen Beziehungen 1989/90* Oldenbourg 2011 (hereafter *DDE*) doc. 10 pp. 49–55

124 Indeed, Sir Patrick Wright had arranged for inflammatory remarks made by PM Thatcher during the Commonwealth Heads of Government Meeting in Kuala Lumpur on 19–24.10.1989, to be removed from the record produced by the Commonwealth Secretariat. 'But', he noted, 'it cannot be long before it becomes more widely known what the prime minister's views on this subject are.' *DBPO III VII GU 1989/90* doc. 26 p. 80 fn. 6

125 Minute, Sir John Fretwell to Wall 29.11.1989, printed in *DBPO III VII GU 1989/90* doc. 62 pp. 143–4

126 Cf. Diary Entry 19.12.1989 and Diary Entry 25.3.1990, both printed in *Urban Diplomacy* pp. 104–16, 131 ('wurst-eating, corpulent, plodding Teuton'), 133

127 *DE* doc. 25 p. 151. Letter from Kohl to Mitterrand 27.11.1989, printed in *DESE* doc. 100 pp. 565–6

128 Niederschrift (Memcon) by Amb. Pfeffer of Mitterrand–Genscher talks Paris 30.11.1989, printed in *DDE* doc. 11 pp. 56–7

129 On the special Franco-German relations as Mitterrand put it, see Memcon of Gorbachev–Mitterrand talks, Kiev, 6.12.1989, printed in *MGDF:SD* doc. 62 p. 268

130 *DDE* doc. 11 p. 58

131 *DBPO III VII GU 1989/90* doc. 26 fn. 3 p. 79

132 *DDE* doc. 11 pp. 56–61. See also Patrick Wright, *Behind Diplomatic Lines: Relations with Ministers* Biteback Publ. 2017 p. 52; Malcolm Rifkind, *Power and Pragmatism* Biteback Publ. 2016 p. 255; Robin Renwick *A Journey With Margaret Thatcher: Foreign Policy Under the Iron Lady* Biteback Publ. 2014 pp. xviii–xxi

133 Kohl *Meine Erinnerungen* p. 136

134 Ibid. p. 138

135 Kohl *Erinnerungen 1982–1990* pp. 1012–13

136 Mitterrand and Thatcher on German Unification (December 1989) 8.12.1989, printed in Jussi Hanhimäki & Odd Arne Westad (eds) *The Cold War – A History in Documents and Eyewitness Accounts* Oxford UP 2003 pp. 609–12

137 Alan Riding 'European Leaders Give Their Backing to Monetary Plan' *NYT* 9.12.1989. For an expression of Thatcher's views that EMU and the Social Charter were 'dirigiste, bureaucratic, centralised' and their effect 'protectionist' and that 'we are fighting this approach', see TNA UK PREM 19/3981 Charles Powell to Prime Minister (Secret) – Meeting with Secretary Baker 9.12.1989 pp. 1–3

138 'Excerpts from Statement by European Community' *NYT* 10.12.1989; Alan Riding 'Europe Backs Idea of One Germany' *NYT* 10.10.1989

139 Number 10 Downing Street, by contrast, was 'a bit vexed about America's attitude to Europe' and to Germany. TNA UK PREM 19/3981 Charles Powell to Prime Minister (Secret) – Meeting with Secretary Baker 9.12.1989 pp. 1–2

140 Teltschik *329 Tage* pp. 47, 60–1; see also

Bozo *Mitterrand* pp. 156–60, 163–7, 419–20 esp. fns 160–1, 167–8. Kiev is not mentioned in the Memcon of Working Breakfast Kohl–Mitterrand talks in Strasbourg 9.12.1989, printed in *DESE* doc. 117 pp. 628–31. For the Memcon of the Gorbachev–Mitterrand talks in Kiev on 6.12.1989, see *MoH:1989* doc. 114 pp. 657–9

141 Zelikow & Rice *Germany Unified* p. 140 (quotation); Telegraphic from Mallaby to UK Delegation Strasbourg 9.12.1989; and Telegraphic from Mallaby to Hurd 10.12.1989, both printed in *DBPO III VII GU 1989/90* docs 72–3 pp. 166–9

142 Letter from Kohl to Gorbachev 14.12.1989, printed in *DESE* doc. 123, pp. 645–50; Teltschik *329 Tage* pp. 80–1; Kohl *Meine Erinnerungen* pp. 142–4

143 Letter from Gorbachev to Kohl (undated, mid-December 1989), printed in *DESE* doc. 126 pp. 658–9; Kohl *Meine Erinnerungen* pp. 143–4; Teltschik *329 Tage* pp. 85–6. It was ironic when Soviet ambassador Kvitsinsky called Teltschik to ask whether Gorbachev's letter had arrived and to ask whether Kohl's letter was the answer to Gorbachev's lines. He had not realised that Kohl's letter had been written several days before and had been sent prior to the arrival of Gorbachev's penned thoughts. But Teltschik made the best of it by suggesting Kohl's letter would surely clarify some of the concerns raised so sharply by Gorbachev

144 Vorlage von Hartmann an Kohl (re: Gorbachev's letter) 18.12.1989, printed in *DESE* doc. 127 p. 660

145 Ibid. 127 pp. 661

146 Kohl *Erinnerungen 1982–1990* p. 1020

147 Teltschik *329 Tage* p. 87

148 Ibid. pp. 87–8, 90; Memcon of Kohl–Modrow plenary talks in Dresden 19.12.1989, printed in *DESE* doc. 129 pp. 668–73. See also Vorschlag für Gesprächslinie (for the talks in Dresden – undated, mid-December), printed in *DESE* doc. 128A p. 665

149 Teltschik *329 Tage* p. 86; Serge Schmemann 'Leaders of the 2 Germanys Meet – Symbolic Reconciliation Cheered' *NYT* 20.12.1989

150 Rede des Bundeskanzlers auf der Kundgebung vor der Frauenkirche in Dresden am 19.12.1989, printed in *Bulletin* no. 150 22.12.1989; Schmemann 'Leaders of the 2 Germanys Meet'

151 Memcon of Kohl's talks with GDR Opposition groups in Dresden 20.12.1989, printed in *DESE* doc. 130 pp. 673–5; Teltschik *329 Tage* p. 93

152 Kohl *Meine Erinnerungen* pp. 156–67

153 Teltschik *329 Tage* p. 92

154 Schmemann 'Leaders of the 2 Germanys Meet'. See also Rödder *Deutschland* pp. 144–5. Hans Modrow was rather bitter about Kohl's effect on the crowd and the visit as a whole. See Hans Modrow *Ich wollte eine neues Deutschland* Dietz 1998 pp. 391–2

155 Michael Richter *Die Friedliche Revolution: Aufbruch zur Demokratie in Sachsen 1989/90* Vandenhoeck & Ruprecht 2009 p. 1094; Genscher *Erinnerungen* pp. 697–702; idem, *Unterwegs zur Einheit* pp. 232–8. Cf. Modrow *Ich wollte eine neues Deutschland* pp. 393–4

156 '"Cold War Is Over" Says Shevardnadze at NATO' *LAT* 19.12.1989

157 Bozo *Mitterrand* pp. 163–7

158 Teltschik *329 Tage* p. 95

159 Ibid. p. 96; Kohl *Meine Erinnerungen* pp. 158–9

160 Peter Siani-Davies *The Romanian*

Revolution of December 1989 Cornell UP 2007 p. 97

161 McDermott & Stibbe (eds) *The 1989 Revolutions* pp. 18–19; Sebestyen *Revolution 1989* pp. 380–6; Thomas L. Friedman 'Casualties Reported in Rumania Protest Spawned by a Clash' *NYT* 19.12.1989

162 Friedman, 'Rumania's Suppression of Protest Condemned by the US as "Brutal"' *NYT* 20.12.1989

163 Sebestyen *Revolution 1989* pp. 386–98; David Binder 'At Least 13 Are Reported Killed at Protest in Rumania's Capital' *NYT* 22.12.1989; *idem* 'Ceauşescu Flees a Revolt in Rumania but Divided Security Forces Fight On' *NYT* 23.12.1989

164 Sebestyen *Revolution 1989* pp. 361–6; Jordan Baev '1989: Bulgarian Transition to Pluralist Democracy & Documents' *CWIHP Bulletin* 12/13 pp. 165–80. Cf. On 'the change', Maria Todorova 'Daring to remember Bulgaria, pre-1989' *Guardian* 9.11.2009

165 Oldrich Tuma 'Czechoslovak November 1989 & Documents' *CWIHP Bulletin* 12/13 pp. 181–216. Sebestyen *Revolution 1989* pp. 367–9; Garton Ash *The Magic Lantern* pp. 78–130. Cf. Michael Pullmann 'The Demise of the Communist Regime in Czechoslovakia, 1987–89: A Socio-Economic Perspective' in McDermott & Stibbe (eds) *The 1989 Revolutions* pp. 136–53

166 Garton Ash *The Magic Lantern* p. 78

167 Craig R. Whitney 'Czech Parliament Unanimously Picks Dubček as Leader' *NYT* 29.12.1989; *idem* 'Havel, Long Prague's Prisoner, Elected President' *NYT* 30.12.1989

168 For Kohl's New Year speech 31.12.1989, Bundesregierung website

Chapter 4

1 Remarks of the President and Soviet Chairman Gorbachev and a Q&A Session with Reporters in Malta 3.12.1989 APP

2 Ibid.

3 GHWBPL Memcon of President's Private Meeting with Gorbachev 1.05–1.30 p.m. Governors Island NYC 7.12.1988 pp. 4–5 NSAEBB No. 261; and Bush & Scowcroft *A World Transformed* pp. 6–7

4 GHWBPL NSC Files – Condoleezza Rice Files, Soviet Union/USSR Subject Files Folder: Summit at Malta December 1989, Malta Memcons (hereafter NSC-CRF-MM1989) First expanded bilateral session with Gorbachev on the *Maxim Gorky* 10.00–11.55 a.m. 2.12.1989 p. 2 DAWC

5 Letter from Bush to Gorbachev 22.11.1989, printed in Bush *All the Best* p. 444

6 Ibid.

7 Bush & Scowcroft *A World Transformed* p. 160; Letter from Baker to Bush 29.12.1989 pp. 1–4 End of the Cold War Forum ECWF-STY-1989-11-29. Cf. Baker *The Politics* p. 168

8 Diary Entry 2.12.1989, printed in Bush *All the Best* pp. 446–8; Scowcroft quoted in Bush & Scowcroft *A World Transformed* p. 168

9 Diary Entry 2.12.1989, printed in Bush *All the Best* p. 447. See also Baker *The Politics* pp. 169–70

10 GHWBPL NSC-CRF-MM1989 First expanded bilateral session on the *Maxim Gorky* 2.12.1989 pp. 2–3 DAWC

11 Ibid.

12 Ibid. pp. 3–4

13 Ibid. p. 10

14 Ibid. pp. 4–6

15 Ibid. pp. 6–9

16 Ibid. p. 9

17 Ibid. p. 8

18 Excerpt from Politburo discussions 26.2.1987 p. 2 NSAEBB no. 238

19 GHWBPL NSC-CRF-MM1989 First restricted bilateral session on the *Maxim Gorky* 12.00–1.00 a.m. 2.12.1989 DAWC

20 Ibid. pp. 4–5

21 Ibid. p. 5

22 Ibid. p. 4

23 Bush & Scowcroft *A World Transformed* p. 169

24 GHWBPL NSC-CRF-MM1989 Second restricted bilateral session on the *Maxim Gorky* 11.44 a.m.–12.45 p.m. 3.12.1989 p. 1 DAWC

25 GHWBPL NSC-CRF-MM1989 Second expanded bilateral session on the *Maxim Gorky* 4.35–6.45 p.m. 3.12.1989 p. 2 DAWC

26 Ibid. pp. 6–7

27 Ibid. p. 8

28 Ibid. pp. 6, 9

29 Remarks of the President and Soviet Chairman Gorbachev and a Q&A Session with Reporters in Malta 3.12.1989 APP

30 Entry 2.1.1990 *Anatoly S. Chernyaev Diary 1990* NSAEBB No. 317

31 Teltschik *329 Tage* p. 62

32 GHWBPL Memcon of Bush–Kohl talks 3.12.1989 Château Stuyvenberg nr Brussels pp. 1–2. For the German transcript, see *DESE* doc. 109 pp. 600–9 esp. pp. 600, 604

33 Memcon of Bush–Kohl talks in Laeken 3.12.1989, printed in *DESE* doc. 109 pp. 602–3. GHWBPL Memcon of Bush–Kohl talks 3.12.1989 Château Stuyvenberg nr Brussels pp. 2–3

34 Bush & Scowcroft *A World Transformed* pp. 197–9. *DESE* doc. 109 pp. 602–4; cf. Memcon of Kohl–Baker talks in West Berlin 12.12.1989, printed in *DESE* doc. 120 p. 639 for the border issue – meaning more the inner German border than the Oder–Neisse line – and the Helsinki principle on the inviolability / peaceful changeability of boundaries and Kohl's thinking

35 Outline of Remarks at the North Atlantic Treaty Organisation Headquarters in Brussels 4.12.1989 APP

36 The President's News Conference in Brussels 4.12.1989 APP

37 Ibid.

38 Ibid.

39 Pressekonferenz von US Aussenminister Baker am 29.11.1989 in Washington, printed in Karl Kaiser *Deutschlands Vereinigung: Die internationalen Askpekte* Bastei Lübbe 1993 doc. 14 p. 169

40 JAB-SML B108/F10 US-USSR (undated, sometime in mid-October)

41 JAB-SML B108/F10 Zoellick (RBZ) draft – Foreign Policy View Points: Managing Change 17.10.1989

42 JAB-SML B108/F11 Zoellick notes for Baker – Points for Consultations with European Leaders 27.11.1989

43 Ibid.

44 JAB-SML B108/F11 Germany-Kohl's speech (no author [possibly Zoellick]; undated, sometime after 28 November 1989 with JAB's annotations)

45 Baker *The Politics* pp. 171–2

46 Speech by Secretary of State James Baker to the Berlin Press Club (Extracts) 13.12.2015, printed in Lawrence Freedman (ed.) *Europe Transformed: Documents on the End of the Cold War* Tri-Service Press 1990 pp. 397–8. Cf. Baker *The Politics* pp. 172–3; JAB-SML B108/F12 Berlin Speech Initiatives 12.12.1989

47 Thomas L. Friedman 'Baker in Berlin,

Outlines Plan to Make NATO a Political Group' *NYT* 13.12.1989

48   Ibid.

49   JAB-SML B108/F12 JAB notes from 12/12/89 visit to Potsdam (GDR). On Baker's senior thesis, see Baker *The Politics* p. 174; cf. blogs.princeton.edu/ reelmudd/2011/03/james-baker-about-post-soviet-policy-1991/

50   Baker *The Politics* p. 173

51   Ibid. p. 174

52   JAB-SML B108/F12 JAB notes from 12/12/89 visit to Potsdam (GDR)

53   Weidenfeld et al. *Außenpolitik für die deutsche Einheit* pp. 179–87. See also Craig R. Whitney '4 Powers to Meet on German Issues – Bonn–East Berlin Ties Prompt First Such Talks Since '72' *NYT* 11.12.1989

54   Craig R. Whitney 'Bonn Leader Softens his Plan for German Unity' *NYT* 12.12.1989; cf. Teltschik *329 Tage* pp. 74–5

55   JAB-SML B104/F1 Letter from Baker to Kohl 17.12.1989

56   Baker *The Politics* p. 175; Bush & Scowcroft *A World Transformed* p. 201; GHWBPL Memcon of Bush–Mitterrand talks 16.12.1989 St Martin. Maureen Dowd 'Upheaval in the East: Bush Defends China Visit; Is Open to East Berlin Aid' *NYT* 17.12.1989

57   Kohl quote from GHWBPL Memcon of Bush–Kohl talks at Château Stuyvenberg nr Brussels 3.12.1989 p. 3

58   Jacques Attali's Notes on Conversation between Mitterrand and Thatcher on German Unification (December 1989), printed in Hanhimäki & Westad (eds) *The Cold War* doc. 18.9 pp. 610–11; cf. Letter from Powell (Strasbourg) to Wall 8.12.1989, printed in *DBPO III VII GU 1989/90* doc. 71 pp. 164–5

59   GHWBPL Memcon of Bush–

Mitterrand talks 16.12.1989 St Martin p. 9

60   Bush and Mitterrand – Joint News Conference at St Martin in the French West Indies 16.12.1989 APP

61   Bush & Scowcroft *A World Transformed* pp. 205, 203

62   HIA-TSMP T. G. Stepanov-Mamaladze diary 4.12.1989 box 5; and T. G. Stepanov-Mamaladze working notes 4.12.1989 box 2

63   Service *The End* pp. 425–6

64   Kohl *Ich wollte* pp. 223, 227; Adomeit *Imperial Overstretch* p. 473; Elizabeth Pond *Beyond the Wall: Germany's Road to Unification* Brookings Institution Press 1993 pp. 170–1; cf. Zelikow & Rice *Germany Unified* p. 159

65   Memcon of the Mitterrand–Kohl talks at Latché 4.1.1989, printed in *DESE* doc. 135 pp. 682–90; Kohl *Meine Erinnerungen* pp. 169–72; Bozo *Mitterrand* pp. 178–9; Rödder *Deutschland* pp. 193–5; Sarotte *1989* pp. 95–6; Adomeit *Imperial Overstretch* p. 473 fn. 304

66   *DESE* doc. 135 pp. 685–7. See also Kohl *Meine Erinnerungen* pp. 170–2

67   Sarotte *1989* pp. 96–9, 103–4; Rödder *Deutschland* pp. 178–93, 206–25. See also Teltschik *329 Tage* pp. 107–33

68   Memcon – Diskussion zur Deutschen Frage im Beraterstab von Gorbatschow 26.1.1989, printed in Aleksandr Galkin & Anatolij Tschernjajew (eds) *Michail Gorbatschow und die deutsche Frage: Sowjetische Dokumente 1986–1991* Oldenbourg 2011 (hereafter *MGDF:SD*) doc. 66 pp. 286–9; Politburo discussion on 26.1.1990 of the German issue at an intimate meeting with Gorbachev, printed in *V Politbyuro TsK KPSS* pp. 579–83 esp. pp. 579–80. See also Kramer 'The Myth of a No-NATO-Enlargement Pledge to Russia'

Washington Quarterly 39, 2 (2009) pp. 39–61 esp. p. 46 who puts the emphasis on Soviet optimism and Gorbachev's continued belief that he could slow down unification. Cf. NSAEBB No. 613 – NATO Expansion: What Gorbachev Heard

69 Vojtech Mastny 'German Unification, Its Eastern Neighbours, and European Security' in Frédéric Bozo et al. (eds) *German Reunification: A Multinational History* Routledge 2016 p. 208. On Central–Eastern European (Hungarian and Czechoslovakian) demands for Soviet troop withdrawal, see Telegraphic – Hurd to Mallaby (Bonn) 6.2.1990, printed in *DBPO III VII GU 1989/90* doc. 129 p. 263

70 Bush & Scowcroft *A World Transformed* pp. 210–11

71 Ibid. p. 211

72 Memcon of Kohl–Eagleburger talks in Bonn 30.1.1990, printed in *DESE* doc. 153 p. 741. See also Teltschik *329 Tage* p. 123. On Kohl's caution and uncertainties regarding how German unity could be reconciled with NATO, see Telegraphic – Mallaby to Hurd 25.1.1990; and Telegraphic – Aceland (Washington) to FCO 30.1.1990, printed in *DBPO III VII GU 1989/90* docs 105, 109 pp. 223, 231

73 Address before a Joint Session of Congress 31.1.1990 APP

74 Genscher's 'Tutzing speech' 31.1.1990, printed in Freedman (ed.) *Europe Transformed* pp. 436–45. Genscher *Erinnerungen* pp. 299–323. For an evolution of Genscher's CSCE ideas in his public speeches, see *idem*, *Unterwegs zur Einheit*. Cf. Confidential Cable – US Embassy (Bonn) to Secretary of State on the Speech of the German Foreign Minister: Genscher Outlines His Vision of a New European Architecture NSAEBB No. 613

75 Baker's quote was a subheading in his memoirs *The Politics of Diplomacy* p. 171. Genscher's memoirs in English were entitled: *Rebuilding a House Divided – A Memoir by the Architect of Germany's Reunification* Broadway Books 1998

76 See Kiessler & Elbe *Ein runder Tisch* pp. 78–80. See also Hutchings *American Diplomacy* pp. 111, 120–1; and Zelikow & Rice *Germany Unified* p. 177

77 Quoted from the 'Tutzing speech' as printed in Freedman (ed.) *Europe Transformed* pp. 440–1. See also Kaiser *Deutschlands Vereinigung* doc. 23 p. 191

78 GHWBPL NSC-CRF-MM1989 Second expanded bilateral session on the *Maxim Gorky* 4.35–6.45 p.m. 3.12.1989 p. 7 DAWC

79 GHWBPL Arnold Kanter Files – Germany March 1990 Cable (drafted by Dobbins) – Baker to Amb. Walters in Bonn: Baker/Genscher Meeting (2.2.1990) 3.2.1990 pp. 1–3. I am grateful to Philip Zelikow for sharing this document with me

80 Quote from Zelikow & Rice *Germany Unified* p. 176

81 For further detail and the scholarly debate about supposed 'pledges' or rather, as I argue, 'no pledges' having been made to Moscow regarding NATO's future extension to the East, see for example Kristina Spohr 'Precluded or Precedent-Setting? The "NATO Enlargement Question" in the Triangular Bonn–Washington–Moscow Diplomacy of 1990–1991' *JCWS* 14, 4 (2012) pp. 18–32. See also Hannes Adomeit 'Nato-Osterweiterung

– gab es gegenüber der UdSSR Garantien?' *NZZ* 30.12.2017 and Zelikow & Rice *To Build a Better World* pp. 225–39 fns 131–7 and pp. 281–8 esp. fn. 50 where they debunk Josh Shifrinson's recent argument of supposed 'informal [US] assurances' not to extend NATO and the 'false promise of accommodation' of Soviet interests given his 'insights from international relations theory'. Shifrinson 'Deal or No Deal? The End of the Cold War and the US Offer to Limit NATO Expansion' *IS* 40, 4 (2016) pp. 34, 38, 40

82 See Memcon of Teltschik–Walters talks in Bonn 4.2.1990, printed in *DESE* doc. 159 p. 756; JAB-SML B108/F14 JAB notes from 2.2.90 press briefing following mtg w/FRG FM Genscher, WDC—Handwritten note

83 *DESE* doc. 159 pp. 756–7. See also Teltschik *329 Tage* pp. 128–9. GHWBPL Arnold Kanter Files – Germany: March 1990 Cable (drafted by Dobbins) – Baker to Amb. Walters in Bonn: Baker/Genscher Meeting (2.2.1990) 3.2.1990 p. 3

84 Baker *The Politics* p. 205; Memcon of Gorbachev–Baker talks (extracts from Soviet transcricpt) 9.2.1990, printed in *MGDF:SD* doc. 71 p. 311

85 *MGDF:SD* doc. 71 p. 312. This is the official German translation of the Soviet minutes of the Gorbachev–Baker meeting (for which no American transcript has so far been found): 'daß die Vereinigten Staaten ihre Anwesenheit in Deutschland im Rahmen der NATO aufrecht erhalten—die Jurisdiktion oder militärische Präsenz der NATO in östlicher Richtung um keinen einzigen Zoll ausgedehnt wird'

86 Zelikow & Rice *Germany Unified* pp. 180–3; *MGDF:SD* doc. 71 pp. 313, 315–16

87 Memcon of Gorbachev–Kohl talks 'Vieraugengespräch' (extracts from Soviet minutes) 10.2.1990, printed in *MGDF:SD* doc. 72 pp. 317–33 here p. 326. The German Chancellery's version of the minutes is essentially the same. *DESE* doc. 174 pp. 795–807 here p. 801

88 Ibid. and Memcon of Gorbachev–Kohl talks 'second round' (extracts from Soviet minutes) 10.2.1990, printed in *MGDF:SD* doc. 73 pp. 333–40; and for the German version, see *DESE* doc. 175 pp. 808–11; Teltschik *329 Tage* pp. 137–43

89 Press declaration facsimile, printed in *DESE* pp. 812–13

90 Teltschik *329 Tage* p. 143

91 Letter from Bush to Kohl 9.2.1990, printed in *DESE* doc. 170 pp. 784–5

92 Ibid. p. 785. Bush & Scowcroft *A World Transformed* p. 241

93 GHWBPL Memcon of Bush–Wörner talks 24.2.1990 Camp David pp. 1–2. See also Diary Entry 24.2.1990, printed in Bush *All the Best* pp. 460–1. See also Frank Costigliola 'An "Arm Around the Shoulder": The United States, NATO and German Reunification, 1989–90' *Contemporary European History* 3, 1 (March 1994) pp. 101–2. According to Costigliola, citing US House of Representatives, Committee of Armed Services meetings in February, March and April 1990, the Bush administration also believed that a 'robust US military role through NATO, particularly with nuclear weapons, helped counter any German temptations to develop a full panopoly of modern armaments'. Wörner quoted in Bush &

Scowcroft *A World Transformed* pp. 242–3

94 JAB-SML B108/F14 JAB notes 2/20/90 MTG w/GB, Czech. Pres. Havel at WH

95 JAB-SML B108/F14 JAB notes from 2/6/90 MTG w/Czech. Pres. Havel at Hradčany Castle in Prague (Czechoslovakia)

96 JAB-SML B108/F14 Talking Points for Cabinet Meeting 15.2.1990 p. 2; Telegraphic – Fall (Ottawa) to FCO 14.2. 1990, printed in *DBPO III VII GU 1989/90* doc. 145 pp. 291–3. See also Telegraphic – Hurd to Acland 14.2.1990, printed in *DBPO III VII GU 1989/90* doc. 146 pp. 293–4. Genscher *Erinnerungen* p. 729. See also Ritter *Hans-Dietrich Genscher* pp. 185–6

97 Telcon of Kohl–Bush call 13.2.1990, printed in *DESE* doc. 180 pp. 826–8. For the American version see GHWBPL Telcon of Kohl–Bush call 13.2.1990 Oval Office

98 Telegraphic – Acland to FCO 24.2.1990 and Letter from Powell to Wall 24.2. 1990, both printed in *DBPO III VII GU 1989/90* docs 154, 155 pp. 307–8, 311

99 GHWBPL Telcon of Bush to Mulroney call 24.2.1990 Camp David p. 2. In the version of the conversation in Bush & Scowcroft *A World Transformed* p. 250, the president's disagreement with Baker is not mentioned

100 Diary Entry 24.2.1990, printed in Bush *All the Best* pp. 460–1. GHWBPL Memcon of Bush–Wörner talks 24.2.1990 Camp David, pp. 2–3 (italics are the author's)

101 Bush & Scowcroft *A World Transformed* p. 250

102 GHWBPL Memcon of Bush and Kohl talks 24.2.1990 Camp David – First Meeting pp. 8–10. See also German Memcon of Bush–Kohl talks Camp David 24.2.1990, printed in *DESE* doc. 192 p. 869. 'Präsident Bush wirft scherzhaft ein, der Bundeskanzler habe große Taschen!'

103 Kohl and Bush Joint News Conference 25.2.1990 APP

104 PAAA ZA 178.928E Vermerk—Betr: Gespräch BM mit AM Baker am 21.3.1990 in Windhuk 28.3.1990 p. 3 Cf. HIA Zelikow–Rice Papers 1989–1995 (ZRP) Box 1 Letter from Zelikow to Genscher 24.1.1995 p. 5

105 HIA-ZRP Box 1 Letter from Zelikow to Genscher 24.1.1995 p. 5

106 Regarding central Europeans' NATO desires, Genscher said, '*Dies sei eine Frage, an der wir gegenwärtig nicht rühren sollten.*' See PAAA ZA 178.928E Vermerk–Betr: Gespräch BM mit AM Baker am 21.3.1990 in Windhuk p. 6. Cf. Memcon by Elbe of Genscher–Baker talks 21.3.1990 Windhoek, printed in *DDE* doc. 22 pp. 109–13. For the Russian version from the Stepanov-Mamaladze Diaries: *Friedensvertrag mit Deutschland oder '2 + 4' – Tagebucheintrag über Genscher-Schewardnadze Unterredung in Windhoek*, printed in Stefan Karner et al. (eds) *Der Kreml und die deutsche Wiedervereinigung 1990 – Interne sowjetische Analysen* Metropol Verlag 2015 doc. 18 p. 230

107 PAAA ZA 178.928E Vermerk–Betr: Gespräch BM mit AM Baker am 21.3.1990 in Windhuk pp. 4–6

108 Genscher *Unterwegs* pp. 258–68, esp. p. 265. See also HIA-ZRP Box 1 Letter from Zelikow to Genscher 24.1.1995 p. 5; Teltschik *329 Tage* pp. 182–3, 186. Telegraphic – Mallaby to Hurd 28.3.1990, printed in *DBPO III VII GU 1989/90* doc. 184 pp. 360–1. Interestingly a sentence with a similar statement on

the two alliances' dissolution into new structures was excised from the AA record of the Genscher–Shevardnadze talks in Windhoek

109 Letter from Kohl to Genscher 23.3.1990 (facsimile), printed in Karner et al. (eds) *Der Kreml und die deutsche Wiedervereinigung 1990* p. 231. See also Teltschik *329 Tage* pp. 182–3

110 See for example Telegraphic – Braithwaite (Moscow) to FCO 26.2.1990 and Letter from Powell to Wall 1.3.1990 and Minute from Weston to Wall 7.3.1990, all printed in *DBPO III VII GU 1989/90* docs 156, 162, 165 (p. 328). See also PAAA ZA 178.054E Bonn AA to London embassy – Fernschreiben No. 1002 Betr: Gespräche AM Douglas Hurd mit BK und BM am 15.5.1990 (14.5.1990)

111 SPD in Moskau: Keine NATO-Mitgliedschaft des vereienten Deutschland – Protokoll des Gesprächs von Alksandr N. Jakovlev and Valentin M. Falin mit Egon Bahr und Karsten Voigt 27.2.1989, printed in Karner et al. (eds) *Der Kreml und die deutsche Wiedervereningung 1990* doc. 13 pp. 195–203

112 Spohr *Germany and the Baltic Problem* pp. 9–11

113 Kohl *Meine Erinnerungen* p. 208

114 Karner et al. (eds) *Der Kreml und die deutsche Wiedervereinigung 1990* doc. 18 p. 228

115 Mark Kramer 'The Collapse of East European Communism and the Repercussions within the Soviet Union (Part 3)' *JCWS* 7, 1 (2004–5) pp. 3–96 here pp. 17–19

116 Ibid. See also PAAA ZA 140.728E Fernschreiben no. 1042: Betr: Erklärung des SAM zur sowjetischen Deutschlandpolitik vom 13.3.1990 from FRG embassy in Moscow 14.3.1990; and Rödder *Deutschland* p. 230

117 See for example PAAA ZA 140.728E, Betr: Sowj. Sicherheitsinteressen, gez. Neubert 14.3.1990 pp. 4, 7. Telegraphic – Braithwaite to FCO 11.4.1990; Minute – Weston to Wall 11.4.1990; Telegraphic – Hurd to Mallaby 6.5.1990; Telegraphic – Hurd to Acland 9.5.1990; Minute – Butcher to Synnott 14.5.1990; and Telegraphic – Hurd to Mallaby; 23.5.1990, all printed in *DBPO III VII GU 1989/90* docs 191, 192, 196 (p. 385), 197 (p. 202), 198, 202; and Teltschik *329 Tage* pp. 155, 165, 184, 186–7, 194–5, 201

118 Urban *Diplomacy* pp. 128–9; Bush & Scowcroft *A World Transformed* p. 218

119 GHWBPL Memcon of Bush–Kohl meeting incl. delegations 17.5.1990 The Cabinet Room p. 6; cf. the German version of the transcript, see *DESE* doc. 278 pp. 1126–32 here p. 1130; Karner et al. (eds) *Der Kreml und die deutsche Wiedervereinigung 1990* doc. 18 p. 229

120 GHWBPL Memcon of Bush–Kohl meeting incl. delegations 17.5.1990 The Cabinet Room p. 7

121 Kohl quoted in Ferdinand Protzman 'German Leaders Agree on a July 2 Unification Date' *NYT* 25.4.1990. For the German economic figures, see Memcon of Kohl–Bush talks Washington 8.6.1990, printed in *DESE* doc. 305 pp. 1191–9 and esp. p. 1198 fn. 25. For US economic figures, see fred. stlouisfed.org/series/NETEXP. The West German economy actually grew by 4.6% GDP in 1990. Data from the 1991 World Fact Book of the United States Central Intelligence Agency

122 GHWBPL Memcon of Bush–Kohl meeting 17.5.1990 Oval Office pp. 2, 3. There is no German Memcon of the tête-à-tête between Bush and Kohl

available, only an American transcript. See also Memcon of Bush–Kohl meeting incl. delegations 17.5.1990 The Cabinet Room. For the somewhat fuller German pendant to the American transcript, see *DESE* doc. 281 pp. 1126–32

123 *DESE* doc. 281 p. 1130. Cf. GHWBPL Memcon of Bush–Kohl meeting incl. delegations 17.5.1990 Cabinet Room p. 4

124 As suggested by Taubman *Gorbachev* p. 550. For the Soviet Memcom of the Gorbachev–Mitterrand talks on 25.5.1989, see *MGDF:SD* doc. 95 pp. 420–31

125 GHWBPL Telcon Kohl to Bush 30.5.1990 Oval Office pp. 1–2

126 Ibid.

127 Zelikow & Rice *Germany Unified* p. 277; Soviet Record of Conversation between Bush and Gorbachev in Washington 4.00–6.00 p.m. 31.5.1990, printed in *TLSS* doc. 99 pp. 664–76 esp. p. 674

128 *TLSS* doc. 99 p. 672

129 Ibid. pp. 673–5

130 Ibid.; Bush & Scowcroft *A World Transformed* p. 282; Zelikow & Rice *Germany Unified* p. 277

131 *TLSS* doc. 99 p. 675

132 Bush & Scowcroft *A World Transformed* p. 281

133 On 1 June, while the summit was in full swing, Bush took time to call Kohl for twenty minutes and give him an upbeat account of progress. GHWBPL Telcon Bush to Kohl 1.6.1989 Oval Office. There is no German record currently declassified or printed in *DESE*

134 News Conference of Bush and Gorbachev 3.6.1990 APP

135 Bush knew this. 'We still have a lot of work to do,' he told Kohl on 3 June during his post-summit phone call. GHWBPL Telcon Bush to Kohl 3.6.1990 Oval Office. There is no German record

currently declassified or printed in *DESE*

136 For troop data, see Celeste A. Wallander *Mortal Friends, Best Enemies: German–Russian Cooperation after the Cold War* Cornell UP 1999 p. 71. On Soviet bankruptcy and the lever of Western (esp. German) economic assistance, see also GHWBPL Telcon of Bush to Kohl call 3.6.1990 Oval Office p. 2

137 GHWBPL Memcon of Bush–Kohl talks 8.6. Oval Office/Old Family Dining Room p. 3

138 Ibid. p. 3. *DESE* doc. 305 pp. 1191–9 and esp. pp. 1194, 1197–8. (NB The German version of the memcon is much longer.) Bush & Scowcroft *A World Transformed* pp. 276, 290

139 Alan Riding 'Europe Hastening Integration Pace' *NYT* 26.6.1990; Craig R. Whitney 'European Leaders Back Kohl's Plea to Aid Soviets' *NYT* 27.6.1990. See also Kohl's letter to EC and G7 leaders about offering the Soviet Union economic aid (13.6.1990) and a Federal Finance Ministry's memo on the subject of economic and financial assistance to the USSR (27.6.1990), printed in *DESE* docs 312, 344B pp. 1211–12, 1313–14. Cf. GHWBPL Memcon of Bush–Delors talks 8.7.1990 AstroArena Houston p. 2

140 Sarotte *1989* p. 160

141 Teltschik *329 Tage* p. 265

142 Telegraphic – Mallaby to Hurd 12.7.1990, printed in *DBPO III VII GU 1989/90* doc. 215 pp. 429–30. Cf. Vorlage von Teltschik an Kohl 19.6.1990 and Vorlage von Teltschik an Kohl 27.6.1990, both printed in *DESE* docs 320, 329 pp. 1232–4, 1275–6

143 Grachev *Gorbachev's Gamble* pp. 185, 189–90; JAB-SML B109/F2 copy of

6/23/90 send to POTUS re: mtg w/ USSR FM Shev. See also TNA UK PREM 19/3466 Letter from Gorbachev to Thatcher 4.7.1990 pp. 1–2

144 See for example TNA UK PREM 19/3466 Cable Telno 2032 Hannay (FM UK rep Brussels) to FCO – Baker's talks with Hurd re 4 July: NATO summit declaration 4.7.1990 pp. 1–2

145 For the London Declaration, see nato.int/docu/comm/49-95/c900706a.htm

146 Manfred Wörner's opening statement to NATO summit meeting in London 5.5.1990 nato.int/cps/en/natohq/opinions_23718.htm?selectedLocale=en

147 Ortez – Trautwein's Memo on the London NATO summit 5–6.7.1990 (11.7.1990), printed in DE doc. 128, pp. 609–13. Cf. Notes for Kohl ahead of NATO Summit 5–6.7.1990 (undated), printed in DESE doc. 344 p. 1309 incl. annexes docs 344A–344I pp. 1309–23

148 Teltschik 329 Tage p. 313. Cf. Telegraphic, Mallaby to Hurd, 12 July 1990, printed in DBPO III VII GU 1989/90 doc. 215 fn. 2 pp. 429–30. Amb. Sir C. Mallaby relayed to FM Douglas Hurd that Peter Hartmann of the German Chancellery 'was at pains to play down any expectations that Kohl's visit itself would bring big developments'

149 DBPO III VII GU 1989/90 doc. 215 pp. 429–30. Teltschik 329 Tage at p. 310. Kohl Meine Erinnerungen p. 327

150 Serge Schmemann 'Gorbachev Meets with NATO's Chief' NYT 15.7.1990

151 Memcon of Gorbachev–Kohl talks in Moscow 15.7.1990, printed in DESE doc. 350 p. 1340; Hans Klein Es begann im Kaukasus Ullstein 1991 p. 64

152 DESE doc. 350 p. 1340

153 Serge Schmemann 'Kohl Sees Soviets Amid Upbeat Mood' NYT 16.7.1990

154 Kohl Meine Erinnerungen pp. 337–8

155 Schmemann 'Kohl Sees Soviets Amid Upbeat Mood'

156 Klein Es begann im Kaukasus pp. 203–8

157 Ibid. pp. 216–18

158 Memcon of Gorbachev–Kohl talks – plenary in Arkhyz (Stavropol) 16.7.1990, printed in DESE doc. 353 pp. 1355–67. For the Soviet transcript of this 16 July meeting (extracts), printed in MGDF:SD doc. 104 pp. 470–88

159 DESE doc. 353 pp. 1355–7 and MGDF:SD doc. 104 pp. 470–7

160 There was speculation, according to the Auswärtiges Amt, that up to 1.2 million Soviets citizens might be living in the GDR; other government agencies spoke of 600,000 men and 300,000 women. It all depended how the soldiers' dependants were defined. In the end, Moscow and Bonn agreed on the overall figure of 600,000. See Vorlage von Westdickenberg an Teltschik 3.9.1990, printed in DESE doc. 410 pp. 1518–19

161 DESE doc. 353 pp. 1361–5; MGDF:SD doc. 104 pp. 479–88. On issues related to the Überleitungsvertrag, cf. PAAA ZA 178.928E Vermerk – Betr.: Konsultationen BM-AM Schewardnadse in Moskau am 17.8.1990 gez. Neubert 20.8.1990

162 Ibid.

163 DESE doc. 353 p. 1363, 1365; MGDF:SD doc. 104 pp. 483–8. In the event these German troop reductions were codified in an annex to the CFE Treaty which was signed in November 1990 at the Paris CSCE. See ch. 5 pp. 314–15. See David Cox Retreating from the Cold War: Germany, Russia and the Withdrawal of the Western Group Forces Macmillan 1996 pp. 91–2. Cf. Frederick Zilian Jr From Confrontation to Cooperation: The Takeover of the

National People's (East German) Army by the Bundeswehr Praeger 1999

164 *DESE* doc. 353 pp. 1357–64

165 Modified Brussels Treaty signed in Paris 23.10.1954 CVCE.EU. Cf. NSAEBB No. 617 – The Nuclear Non-Proliferation Treaty and the German Nuclear Question (Part 1) 1954–1964

166 *DESE* doc. 353 pp. 1358–60, 1366. See also Stefan G. Bierling *Wirtschaftshilfe für Moskau: Motive und Startegien der Bundesrepublik Deutschland und der USA 1990–1996* Schöningh 1998 p. 333; Vladislav Zubok 'With His Back Against the Wall: Gorbachev, Soviet Demise, and German Unification' *CWH* 14, 4 (November 2014) pp. 641–3

167 See Joint Press Conference by Gorbachev and Kohl 16.7.1990, printed in *MGDF:SD* doc. 105 pp. 488–503; Klein *Es begann im Kaukasus* pp. 274–7

168 Erklärung des BK vor der Bundespressekonferenz in Bonn 17.7.1990, printed in *Bulletin* no. 93 18.7.1990; Carl-Christian Kaiser 'Helmut im Glück' *Die Zeit* 20.7.1990; Craig R. Whitney 'Kohl Outlines a Vision: A Neighborly Vision' *NYT* 18.7.1990

169 R. W. Apple Jr 'Bush Hails Soviet Decision' *NYT* 17.7.1990; Andrew Rosenthal 'Bush Declares He Does Not Feel Left Out by Gorbachev and Kohl' *NYT* 18.7.1990. On American surprise, see also Zelikow & Rice *Germany Unified* pp. 342–3

170 Apple Jr 'Bush Hails Soviet Decision'

171 See Teltschik *329 Tage* p. 345

172 Valentin Falin *Konflikte im Kreml: Zur Vorgeschicht der Deutschen Einheit und Auflösung der Sowjetunion* Gebundenes Buch 1997 pp. 188–9, 200–4; Weidenfeld et al. *Außenpolitik für die deutsche Einheit* pp. 615–20

173 Cf. Memcon of Kohl–Gorbachev talks in Moscow 15.7.1990, printed in *DESE* doc. 350 p. 1344. Gorbachev: 'Some military, who took their interests as the starting point, and journalists were crying that they were now selling the fruits of the great victory in World War Two for German marks.'

174 See cover of *Der Spiegel* 'Allianz Bonn / Moskau: Der Krieg ist zu Ende' *Der Spiegel* 30/1990 23.7.1990

175 For the Nobel Peace Prize 1990 – press releases and award speeches, see nobel-prise.org/nobel_prises/peace/laureates/1990/press.html; Sheila Rule 'Gorbachev Gets Nobel Peace Prize for Foreign Policy Achievements' *NYT* 16.10.1990

176 See Teltschik *329 Tage* pp. 345–6

177 Drittes Treffen der AMs der 2 + 4 unter zeitweiliger Beteiligung Polens in Paris 17.7.1990, printed in *DESE* doc. 354 pp. 1367–8 plus docs 354A, 354B; Vermerk von Höynck (2 + 4 + 1 talks) 18.7.1990, printed in *DE* doc. 130 pp. 615–20

178 Letter from Bergmann-Pohl to Kohl 25.8.1990 and Decision of GDR Volkskammer to join FRG 23.8.1990, both printed in *DESE* doc. 397, 397A pp. 1497–8; Einigungsvertrag 31.8.1990, printed in Kaiser *Deutschlands Vereinigung* doc. 48 pp. 256–7; Letter from Kohl to Mazowiecki 6.9.1990, printed in *DESE* doc. 412 pp. 1523–4. Cf. Letter from Mazowiecki to Kohl 25.7.1990, printed in *DESE* doc. 371 pp. 1418–21

179 Letter from Ryzhkov to Kohl 18.7.1990, printed in *DESE* doc. 360 pp. 1400–1

180 Letter from Gorbachev to Kohl 25.7.1990, printed in *MGDF:SD* doc. 107 pp. 506–7

181 Letter from Kohl to Ryzhkov 22.8.1990, printed in *DESE* doc. 392 p. 1488

182 Telcon of Kohl–Delors call, 20.8.1990, printed in *DESE* doc. 388 pp. 1479–81

183 See Memcon of Kohl–Hurd talks in Bonn 15.5.1990, printed in *DESE* doc. 278 pp. 1119–20; Secretary of State's call on Chancellor Kohl 15.5.1990, released by the FCO via FOI. See Telcon between Kohl and Gorbachev 7.9.1990, printed in *DESE* doc. 415 p. 1528, where Gorbachev in his conversation with Kohl on 7 September 1990 referred to German experts' estimates of annual costs for the GDR's integration into the FRG at DM 50 billion per year for a decade (amounting in total to DM 500 billion). Note: Official estimates of net fiscal transfers from western to eastern Germany by the German Finance Ministry amounted to some DM 120–140 billion per year in the 1990s, then some 70–80 billion euros during the 2000s, amounting to an estimated 1.3 trillion euros over the first two decades after unification. 'Eastern Germany Is Western Germany's Trillion Euro Bet' *DW* 24.9.2010; Jörg Bibow 'The Economic Consequences of German Unification: The Impact of Misguided Macroeconomic Policies' *The Levy Economics Institute Public Policy Brief* no. 67A (2001)

184 Memcon of Teltschik–Kvitsinsky talks in Bonn 28.8.1990, printed in *DESE* doc. 402 pp. 1505–7

185 Letter from Waigel to Kohl 6.9.1990, printed in *DESE* doc. 413 pp. 1524–5. Cf. Notiz von Westerhoff an Seiters 6.9.1990, printed in *DESE* doc. 414 p. 1526

186 *DESE* doc. 415 pp. 1527–8. For the Soviet transcript of the Telcon between Kohl and Gorbachev 7.9.1990, see *MGDF:SD* doc. 110 pp. 513–17

187 *DESE* doc. 415 pp. 1528–30

188 Cover Letter from Köhler to Kohl 9.9.1990; together with Argumentation für Überleitungsvertrag (undated) and Finanztableau (undated), all printed in *DESE* docs 418–418B pp. 1534–6

189 Telcon between Gorbachev and Kohl 10.9.1990, printed in *MGDF:SD* doc. 114 pp. 520–3 esp. p. 23; Teltschik *329 Tage* pp. 361–3. Cf. Memcon of Teltschik–Terechov talks in Bonn 15.9.1990, printed in *DESE* doc. 422 pp. 1541–2.

190 Two-Plus-Four Ministerial in Moscow: Detailed account [includes text of the Treaty on the Final Settlement with Respect to Germany and Agreed Minute to the Treaty on the special military status of the GDR after unification] 12.9.1990 pp. 1–21 NSAEBB No. 613

191 Genscher *Erinnerungen* pp. 875–6; Serge Schmemann 'Moscow and Bonn in a "Good Neighbor" Pact' *NYT* 14.9.1990 p. 3

192 Drahtbericht des Botschafters zur besonderen Verwendung, Graf zu Rantzau, NY (UN), 2.10.1990, printed in *DE* doc. 164 pp. 743–5. Thomas L. Friedman 'Allies Waive Occupation Rights, Clearing Way for German Unity' *NYT* 2.10.1990

193 See Telcon of Gorbachev–Kohl 7.9.1990 and Memcon of Gorbachev–Bush talks in Helsinki 9.9.1990, both printed in *MGDF:SD* docs 110 and 111 p. 517 and p. 519

194 On the unity celebrations, see Kohl *Ich wollte* pp. 475–83; idem, *Meine Erinnerungen* pp. 394–408; Genscher *Erinnerungen* pp. 886–7. Cf. Richard von Weizsäcker *Von Deutschland nach Europa: Die bewegende Kraft der Geschichte* Siedler 1991 pp. 193–212. Serge Schmemann 'Two Germanys

Unite after 45 Years with Jubilation and a Vow of Peace' *NYT* 3.10.1990

195 Both treaties are printed in Kaiser *Deutschlands Vereinigung* docs 67–8 pp. 318–33. See also Ortez – Bettzuege on the Troop Withdrawal Treaty of 12.10.1990 (18.10.1990), printed in *DE* doc. 168 pp. 759–62

196 Helmut Kohl *Erinnerungen 1990–1994* Droemer 2007 pp. 254–6. John Tagliabue 'Germans and Poles Agree to Pact on Oder Border' *NYT* 9.11.1990

197 Genscher *Erinnerungen* pp. 890–5. Stephen Engelberg 'Poland and Germany Sign Border Guarantee Pact' *NYT* 15.11.1990. Cf. Kohl *Erinnerungen 1990–1994* p. 256. See also Tischvorlage Genschers für die Kabinettssitzung am 14.11.1990 (13.11.1990), printed in *DE* doc. 169 pp. 763–5

198 Mazowiecki quoted in Engelberg 'Poland and Germany Sign Border Guarantee Pact'

199 Genscher quoted in Engelberg 'Poland and Germany Sign Border Guarantee Pact'

200 Genscher *Erinnerungen* pp. 890–5

201 Vertrag über gute Nachbarschaft, Partnerschaft und Zusammenarbeit zwischen der BRD und der UdSSR 9.11.1990, printed in *Bulletin* no. 133 15.11.1990 pp. 1379–82. On 9 and 10 November 1990 Gorbachev held talks with President Richard von Weizsäcker, Kohl, Genscher and Waigel as well as SPD chancellor candidate Oskar Lafontaine in Bonn. For the Soviet Memcons, see *MGDF:SD* docs 122–8 pp. 551–79

202 Serge Schmemann 'Gorbachev Signs Treaty in Bonn and Is Hailed for His Unity Role' *NYT* 10.11.1990. See also Bundeskanzler Kohl – Ansprache bei einem Abendessen zu Ehren Gorbatschows auf dem Petersberg 9.11.1990, printed in *Bulletin* no. 133 15.11.1990 pp. 1375–77; Festansprachen von Gorbatschow und Kohl anlässlich der Unterzeichnung des deutsch-sowjetischen Partnerschaftsvertrags 9.11.1990, printed in *MGDF:SD* doc. 125 pp. 568–71. Cf. Bierling *Wirtschaftshilfe* pp. 98–100

203 Serge Schmemann 'Kohl's Coalition Elected to Lead Unified Germany' *NYT* 3.12.1990; Stephen Kinzer '4 New Women Named to Kohl's New Cabinet of 20' *NYT* 17.1.1991

Chapter 5

1 R. W. Apple Jr 'East and West Sign Pact to Shed Arms in Europe' *NYT* 20.11.1990

2 Cf. JAB-SML B115/F7 CSCE Summit 22.1.1990

3 For Kohl's Ten-Point Plan, see Deutscher Bundestag *Stenographischer Bericht* 177. Sitzung 28.11.1989 pp. 13510–14 and see also DGBD-GHIDC

4 James A. Baker III 'From Revolution to Democracy: Central and Eastern Europe in the New Europe' Address at Charles University Prague 7.2.1990 *Current Policy* No. 1248 United States Department of State (hereafter US DoS); JAB-SML B108/F14 Talking Points for Cabinet Meeting 15.2.1990 p. 1; Baker 'A New Europe, a New Atlanticism: Architecture for a New Era' Speech to the Berlin Press Club 12.12.1989 *Current Policy* No. 1233 US DoS

5 Mark Webber *Inclusion, Exclusion and the Governance of European Security* Manchester UP 2007 p. 38; Shevardnadze quoted in Neil Malcolm *Russia and Europe: An End to Confrontation* Pinter 1994 p. 160. Cf.

'Excerpts from the Speech by Shevardnadze Before the General Assembly' *NYT* 27.9.1989 p. 12

6   See Webber *Inclusion* p. 39. Cf. ch. 5, fns 2 and 194; and Eduard Shevardnadze's speech to the Polititical Committee of the European Parliament, Brussels, 19 December 1989, in which he not only proposed an all-European summit in order to consult on the new European political and security order, but also the creation of permanent institutional structures. This is printed in Auswärtiges Amt (ed.) *Umbruch in Europa* Das Amt 1991 pp. 146–53 esp. p. 150

7   'Gorbachev Pushes "Collective Security"' *WP/Orlando Sentinel* 16.3.1990

8   For an evolution of Genscher's CSCE ideas in his public speeches, see his *Unterwegs zur Einheit* – Potsdam Speech (9.2.1990) pp. 242–56; WEU speech (23.3.1990) pp. 258–68. Genscher's Tutzing speech (31.1.1990) is printed in Freedman (ed.) *Europe Transformed* pp. 436–45. See also Genscher *Erinnerungen* pp. 99–32. Cf. HIA-ZRP Box 1 Letter from Zelikow to Genscher 24.1.1995 p. 5; Teltschik *329 Tage* pp. 182–3, 186. Telegraphic – Mallaby to Hurd 28.3.1990, printed in *DBPO III VII GU 1989/90* doc. 184 pp. 360–1

9   See ch. 4, pp. 227–8

10   Allocution prononcée par M. François Mitterrand (Président de la République) lors de la présentation de ses vœux Paris 31.12.1989 Direction de l'Information Légale et Administrative – Discours-Vie Publique (hereafter DILA-DVP)

11   On Mitterrand's 'European Confederation' project and its failure, see Frédéric Bozo 'The Failure of a

Grand Design: Mitterrand's European Confederation, 1989–1991' *Contemporary European History* 17, 3 (2008) pp. 391–412; idem, *Mitterrand* pp. 344–61; Philip Short *Mitterrand: A Study in Ambiguity* Bodley Head 2013 pp. 482–3; Thilo Schabert *Wie Weltgeschichte gemacht wird: Frankreich und die deutsche Einheit* Klett-Cotta 2002 pp. 447–50; Pierre Favier & Michel Martin-Roland *La Décennie Mitterrand, vol. iv: Les Déchirements 1991–1995* Seuil 1999 pp. 170–7. For testimonies by former political actors, see Roland Dumas 'Un projet mort-né: la Confédération européenne' *Politique étrangère* 3 (2001) pp. 687–703; Jean Musitelli 'François Mitterrand, architecte de la Grande Europe: le projet de Confédération européenne (1990–1991)' *Revue internationale et stratégique* 82 (2011/2) pp. 18–28; Andrei Grachev 'From the Common European Home to European Confederation: François Mitterrand and Mikhail Gorbachev in Search of a Road to a Greater Europe' in Bozo et al. (eds) *Europe and the End of the Cold War*. For an external view, cf. Hutchings *American Diplomacy* p. 172

12   Allocution prononcée par M. François Mitterrand lors de la présentation de ses vœux Paris 31.12.1989 DILA-DVP

13   Ibid.

14   Bozo 'The Failure of a Grand Design' p. 392

15   On the 'acceleration of history', see Address given by Jacques Delors to the College of Europe Bruges 17.10.1989 CVCE.EU

16   Record of Conversation between Gorbachev and Mitterrand 6.12.1989, printed in *MoH:1989* doc. 114 pp. 657–8; 'Mitterrand in Kiev, Warns Bonn not

to Press Reunification Issue' *NYT* 7.12.1989

17 Cf. Short *Mitterrand* pp. 473–81; AD MAE CDP Europe 1986–1990 ALL 1–2 Unification Allemande (L'Europe entre Malte et Strasbourg) N/89/134 Note: Construction européenne et boule-versements à l'Est 29.11.1989

18 For the seventh point in Kohl's Ten-Point Plan, see his speech in DGBD-GHIDC

19 See Bozo 'The Failure of a Grand Design' p. 398

20 For Delors' concentric circles and his speech on EC Ostpolitik at the Paris special summit 18.11.1989, see Karen E. Smith *The Making of EU Foreign Policy: The Case of Eastern Europe* Palgrave Macmillan 2004 pp. 90–1

21 Julie M. Newton 'Gorbachev, Mitterrand, and the Emergence of the Post-Cold War Order in Europe' *Europe-Asia Studies* 65, 2 (March 2013) pp. 290–320 esp. pp. 313–14. Cf. Bozo 'The Failure of a Grand Design' p. 397

22 Julie M. Newton *Russia, France and the Idea of Europe* Palgrave Macmillan 2003 pp. 177–9; Marie-Pierre Rey 'Gorbatchev et la "Maison Commune Européenne"' *Institut François Mitterrand Lettre* no. 19 12.3.2007; Newton 'Gorbachev' pp. 294, 314. It is striking that William H. Hill's *No Place for Russia* Columbia UP 2018 – in which he traces the development of the post–Cold War European security – had no place for Mitterrand's Confederation model. This is all the more surprising because his study is above all focused on showing how and why attempts to integrate the Soviet Union (later Russia) into a unified Euro-Atlantic security order – not least

via the CSCE/OSCE – were gradually overshadowed by NATO and the EU

23 Ibid.; Anatoly S. Chernyaev *My Six Years with Gorbachev* Penn State UP 2000 p. 75

24 Bozo *Mitterrand* p. 170; Newton 'Gorbachev' pp. 297, 299–300

25 Mitterrand suggested this idea during his visit in East Berlin on 20–22 December 1989. Mitterrand's dinner speech in East Berlin 20.12.1989, printed in Auswärtiges Amt (ed.) *Umbruch in Europa* pp. 158–61 esp. p. 160. See Michael Sutton *France and the Construction of Europe, 1944–2007: The Geopolitical Imperative* Berghahn Books 2007 p. 254

26 See for example Mitterrand's meetings with Genscher (30.11.1989), Gorbachev (6.12.1989), Thatcher (8.12.1989), Bush (16.12.1989) and Kohl (4.1.1990)

27 Bozo 'France, "Gaullism", and the Cold War' in Melvyn P. Leffler & Odd Arne Westad (eds) *Cambridge History of the Cold War, Vol. 2: Crisis and Detente* Cambridge UP 2010 pp. 158–78. For de Gaulle's vision of a 'European Europe' set out in a speech on 4 February 1965 given exactly twenty years since the beginning of the Yalta Conference, see Charles de Gaulle *Discours et messages IV* Plon 1970 pp. 325–42. See also Short *Mitterrand* pp. 481–3

28 Memcon of Mitterrand–Kohl talks in Latché 4.1.1990, printed in *DESE* doc. 135 pp. 682–90

29 *DESE* doc. 135 pp. 685–7

30 Ibid. pp. 683–4

31 Ibid. pp. 684, 687

32 Ibid. pp. 689–90. See also 'MM. Kohl et Mitterrand sont d'accord sur l'idée de confédération européenne' *Le Monde* 6.1.1990

33 See Bozo 'The Failure of a Grand

Design' p. 400; cf. Vojtech Mastny 'Germany's unification, its eastern neighbours, and European security' in Bozo et al. (eds) *German Reunification* pp. 210–11

34 For Chancellery documents on the German economic and currency union, see *DESE* docs 163, 165–165b, 168, 169, 169a

35 Memcon of Gorbachev–Kohl talks with delegations in Moscow 10.2.1990, printed in *DESE* doc. 175 pp. 809–10, doc. 192 p. 869. Cf. Thomas L. Friedman & Michael R. Gordon 'Steps to German Unity: Bonn as a Power' *NYT* 16.2.1990. On the issue of a peace conference and peace treaty versus the 2 + 4 process and a 'Treaty on the Final Settlement with Respect to Germany', see Christoph-Matthias Brand *Souveräni-tät für Deutschland: Grundlage, Entstehungsgeschichte und Bedeutung des Zwei-plus-Vier-Vertrages vom 12. September 1990* Vlg. Wissenschaft und Politik 1993 pp. 243–69. On the CSCE, cf. Vorlage von Teltschik an Kohl (undated), printed in *DESE* doc. 166 pp. 771–6

36 *DESE* doc. 175 p. 810 fns 5, 6

37 Serge Schmemann 'Billions In Help For East Germany Approved By Bonn' *NYT* 15.2.1990. See also Mastny 'Germany's unification' pp. 208–11; Barbara Donovan 'Eastern Europe and German Unity' *Report on Eastern Europe* 2.3.1990 pp. 48–51

38 Memcon of Mitterrand–Kohl talks in Paris 15.2.1990, printed in *DESE* doc. 187 pp. 842–52

39 Ibid. pp. 849–50

40 Ibid. pp. 851–2

41 Entry 17.8.1988, printed in Jacques Attali *Verbatim Tome III: Chronique des années 1988–1991* Fayard 1995 p. 92

42 See Harold James *Making the European Monetary Union* Harvard UP 2012 ch. 7; Dyson & Maes (eds) *Architects* ch. 8 (on Pöhl) ch. 10 (on Delors); Jonathan Story & Ingo Walter *Political Economy of Financial Integration in Europe: The Battle of the Systems* MIT 1997 ch. 1

43 James *Making the European Monetary Union* pp. 235–6

44 Kenneth Dyson & Kevin Featherstone *The Road to Maastricht: Negotiating Economic and Monetary Union* Oxford UP 1999 pp. 29–30

45 Harold James 'Karl-Otto Pöhl: The Pole Position' in Dyson & Maes (eds) *Architects* p. 186

46 'Pöhl Doubts Need for EC Bank' *Financial Times* (hereafter *FT*) 1–2.7.1989

47 Cf. Memcon of 54th Franco-German consultations in Bonn 2–3.11.1989 and Vorlage von Bitterlich an Kohl 2–3.12.1989, both printed in *DESE* docs 70, 108 pp. 472–3, 596–8

48 Letter from Kohl to Mitterrand 27.11.1989 and Memo – EC summit Strasbourg 8–9.12.1989: work calendar for future steps until 1993, both printed in *DESE* docs 100, 100a pp. 565–6, 566–7. See also *DESE* doc. 108 pp. 596–8

49 Memcon by Amb. Pfeffer on Mitterrand–Genscher talks in Paris 30.11.1989, printed in *DDE* doc. 11 p. 59

50 Letter from Mitterrand to Kohl 1.12.1989, printed in *DESE* doc. 108a pp. 599–600

51 *DESE* doc. 108 p. 598

52 For background see Dyson & Featherstone *The Road* pp. 46–7. For a study of different scenarios by the French MFA on how to take the European project forward in the context of daily upheaval in late

November 1989, see AD MAE CDP Europe 1986–1990 ALL 1–2 Unification Allemande (L'Europe entre Malte et Strasbourg) N/89/133 Note – Faut-il réformer les institutions communautaires? 29.11.1989 pp. 1–16. In the same file on moving forward with EMU, see N/89/131 Note – Faciliter la mise en place de L'UEM 29.11.1989; C/89–34 Note pour le Ministre d'Etat – L'Europe entre Malte et Strasbourg: quatre propositions 29.11.1989 pp. 4–5 *'Les allemands doivent donc comprendre que l'union européenne commence par l'union monétaire. Cet objectif est fondamental pour nous, et nous devons le faire savoir aux allemands: leur engagement est un test décisif de leur volonté de concilier identité allemande et identité européenne'.*

53 Teltschik *329 Tage* p. 61; Bozo *Mitterrand* p. 145

54 Letter from Kohl to Mitterrand 5.12.1989, printed in *DESE* doc. 111 pp. 614–15

55 Bozo *Mitterrand* p. 151; For the Communiqué of the EC Strasbourg Council meeting 8–9.12.1990, see *Bulletin of the European Communities* No. 12/1989. See also 'EC Leaders Firmly Support Monetary Union, the Social Charter and Creation of European Development Bank' *European Community News* No. 41/1989 11.12.1989

56 'Excerpts From Statement By European Community' *NYT* 10.12.1989 p. 32. See also Alan Riding 'European Leaders Give Their Backing to Monetary Plan' *NYT* 9.12.1989

57 Memcon of Kohl–Baker talks in West Berlin 12.12.1989, printed in *DESE* doc. 120 p. 638

58 GHWBPL Memcon of Mitterrand–

Bush talks (incl. Baker) 16.12.1989 St Martin p. 7

59 Stanley Hoffmann 'French Dilemmas and Strategies in the New Europe' in Robert O. Keohane et al. (eds) *After the Cold War: International Institutions and State Strategies in Europe, 1989–1991* Harvard UP 1993 pp. 127–35; Bozo *Mitterrand* pp. 196–7

60 Kohl's speech on 'Die deutsche Frage und die europäische Verantwortung' delivered at a conference held by the Bureau international de liaison et de documentation and the Institut français des relations internationales, Centre de conférences internationales Paris 17.1.1990, printed in *Bulletin* no. 9 19.1.1990

61 TNA UK PREM 19/3346 Letter from Powell to Wall (FCO) – Prime Minister's Meeting with President Mitterrand at the Elysée Palace in Paris 20.1.1990 pp. 1–5. Also printed in *DBPO III VII GU 1989/90* doc. 103 pp. 215–19 esp. pp. 216, 218

62 'The Commission's programme for 1990' Address by Jacques Delors, President of the Commission, to the European Parliament and his reply to the debate Strasbourg 17.1.1990 and 13.2.1990, printed in *Bulletin of the European Communities Supplement* 1/90

63 Frédéric Bozo *Mitterrand, the End of the Cold War, and German Unification* Berghahn Books 2009 pp. 186–8; *idem* 'France, German Unification and European Integration' in *idem* et al. (eds) *Europe and the End of the Cold War: A Reappraisal* Routledge 2008 pp. 155–6

64 'The Commission's programme for 1990' Address by Jacques Delors, President of the Commission, to the

European Parliament and his reply to the debate Strasbourg 17.1.1990 and 13.2. 1990, printed in *Bulletin of the European Communities Supplement* 1/90 p. 60

65   Ibid.

66   Memcon of Mitterrand–Kohl talks in Paris 15.2.1990, printed in *DESE* doc. 187 p. 851

67   *DESE* doc. 187 pp. 849, 851. For the press conference that followed the dinner, see AD MAE CDP Europe 1986–1990 ALL 1–2 Unification Allemande (L'Europe entre Malte et Strasbourg) Conférence de presse conjointe entre M. Le Président de la République et M. Kohl Chancelier de la RFA 15.2.1990 pp. 1–6

68   Mitterrand's fears of Germany remained neurotic. He and Kohl had another 'stormy' conversation over the phone on 14 March, this time concerning the president's obsession with the Oder–Neisse line. Once again Mitterrand was pulling at loose ends that, from Kohl's perspective, could not be tied up until Germany had been unified. The chancellor repeated his previous statements that only the parliament of a unified Germany could formally ratify the German–Polish border. Undeterred, the French president continued to play his game of standing up for his 'Little Entente' friends in the East. Kohl, in turn, fumed at all the talk in France of the FRG as a budding 'Fourth Reich' and complained sarcastically about all the 'top tips' he was getting from Paris. Kohl felt he had clearly explained his true intentions (as well as his domestic party political constraints ahead of the December federal elections). Telcon between Kohl and Mitterrand 14.3.1990, printed in *DESE* doc. 218 pp. 943–7; Bozo *Mitterrand, the End of the Cold*

War pp. 228–41 esp. pp. 234–6. Cf. Federal Chancellor Helmut Kohl on the 'German Question and European Responsibility' 17.1.1989 pp. 416–17

69   Bozo *Mitterrand, the End of the Cold War* p. 236

70   Ibid. p. 237 fn. 135

71   Interview de M. François Mitterrand accordée à TF1 lors de l'émission *Sept sur Sept* 25.3.1990 DILA-DVP

72   Letter from Kohl to Delors 13.3.1990, printed in *DESE* doc. 215 pp. 935–6; Hanns Jürgen Küsters 'Deutsch-französiche Europapolitik in der Phase der Wiedervereinigung' in Günter Buchstab et al. (eds) *Die Ära Kohl im Gespräch: eine Zwischenbilanz* Böhlau 2010 pp. 153–67 esp. p. 163

73   Message conjoint de François Mitterrand et Helmut Kohl adressé à M. Haughey sur la nécessité d'accélérer la construction de l'Europe politique 18.4.1990 Paris DILA-DVP

74   Alan Riding 'Europe United?' *NYT* 28.4.1990

75   See Teltschik *329 Tage* pp. 207–9; cf. 55th Franco-German consultations in Paris 26.4.1990, printed in *DESE* doc. 257 pp. 1056–9. Kohl quoted in Craig R. Whitney 'Europe's Alliance Seeks Closer Ties' *NYT* 29.4.1990 Mitterrand quoted from the French transcript in Bozo *Mitterrand, the End of the Cold War* p. 239

76   See for example TNA UK PREM 19/3344 Letter from Charles Powell to Stephen Wall (FCO) – re: Prime Minister's Meeting with Monsieur Giscard d'Estaing 19.2.1990 pp. 1–2

77   Quote from TNA UK PREM 19/3344 Letter from Powell to Thatcher – Meeting with former President Giscard d'Estaing 16.2.1990 p. 1

78   Special Meeting of the European

Council in Dublin 28.4.1990 – Presidency Conclusions consilium. europa.eu/media/20571/1990_april_-_dublin_eng_.pdf

79 Whitney 'Europe's Alliance Seeks Closer Ties'. Thatcher was obsessed with the view that 'an integrated Europe would be a German Europe'. In this vein, there had been grave concerns in Downing Street throughout the winter that the FRG would simply 'bring East Germany into the European Community' (or as Douglas Hurd put it, that the GDR might join the EC by 'osmosis' via reunification) – something that to British chagrin Delors had appeared to 'endorse'. Furthermore, it was imperative that East Germany's absorption into the Community would not occur 'at the expense of others'. In terms of slowing-down tactics, London hoped to use the 'Community angle' as a way to constrain 'the pace of *de jure* German integration and reunification'. See TNA UK PREM 19/3344 Letter from Powell to Thatcher – Meeting with former President Giscard d'Estaing, 16.2.1990 p. 1; PREM 19/3346 Memorandum – Douglas Hurd for Thatcher on 'the German Question' 16.1.1990 p. 4; PREM 19/3346 Letter from Powell to Wall (FCO) – Prime Minister's Meeting with President Mitterrand at the Elysée Palace Paris 20.1.1990 pp. 1, 4

80 Ibid.; Special Meeting of the European Council in Dublin 28.4.1990 – Presidency Conclusions pp. 2–3; Wilfried Loth *Building Europe: A History of European Unification* De Gruyter Oldenbourg 2015 pp. 312–13; Mark Gilbert *Cold War Europe: The Politics of a Contested Continent* Rowman & Littlefield 2015 p. 277

81 Alan Riding 'Europe Hastening Integration Pace' *NYT* 26.6.1990

82 See Roland Vogt *Personal Diplomacy in the EU: Political Leadership and Critical Junctures of* European Integration Routledge 2016 pp. 154ff.

83 Schwarz *Helmut Kohl* p. 142; Manfred Görtemaker *Geschichte der Bundesrepublik Deutschland: Von der Gründung bis zur Gegenwart* Beck 1999 p. 688; Kohl *Ich wollte* pp. 13, 15–18

84 Vogt *Personal Diplomacy in the EU* pp. 154–7

85 Zelikow & Rice *Germany Unified* p. 365

86 See Ilaria Poggiolini 'Thatcher's Double-Track to the end of the Cold War: The Irreconcilability of Liberalisation and Preservation' in Frédéric Bozo et al. (eds) *Visions of the End of the Cold War in Europe, 1945–1990* Berghahn Books 2012 pp. 266ff.

87 Urban *Diplomacy* pp. 104–5

88 See Patrick Salmon 'The United Kingdom: Divided Counsels, Global Concerns' in Bozo et al. (eds) *Europe and the End of the Cold War* pp. 153ff. Cf. Sir Julian Bullard 'Great Britain and German Unification' in Jeremy Noakes et al. (eds) *Britain and Germany in Europe 1949–1990* Oxford UP 2002 pp. 219–29

89 Telegraphic – Mallaby to Hurd 5.1.1990, printed in *DBPO III VII GU 1989/90* doc. 85 p. 190

90 *DBPO III VII GU 1989/90* doc. 103 p. 217

91 Bush & Scowcroft *A World Transformed* p. 84; TNA UK PREM 19/3346 Letter from Powell to Thatcher – Meeting with President Mitterrand 16.1.1990 p. 1

92 See Chapter 3. Cf. Minute by Hurd 27.1.1990; Telegraphic – Mallaby to Hurd 1.2.1990; and Submission from

Synnott to Weston with Minute by Weston 1.2.1990, all printed in *DBPO III VII GU 1989/90* docs 108, 115 and 116 pp. 229–30, 238–43. Thatcher's inflammatory remarks on Germany in an interview for the *Wall Street Journal* on 24.1.1990 MTF

93 *DBPO III VII GU 1989/90* doc. 103 p. 217

94 *DBPO III VII GU 1989/90* doc. 85 pp. 190–1

95 See Stephen Wall *A Stranger in Europe: Britain and the EU from Thatcher to Blair* Oxford UP 2008 p. 85. For the French embassy report that includes Thatcher's statement to Mitterrand over dinner in London (March 1990) see AD MAE ASD 1985–1990 Box 16 TD Londres 370–72 DSL Secret Amb. Luc de Barre to Roland Dumas – Dîner avec Mme Thatcher: Réunification allemande et contruction européenne 13.3.1990

96 TNA UK PREM 19/3347 Letter from Powell to Wall (FCO) – Thatcher's Meeting with the Prime Minister of France in London 26.3.1990 pp. 1, 4

97 Margaret Thatcher's Speech to the College of Europe ('The Bruges Speech') 20.9.1988 MTF

98 Whitney 'Europe's Alliance Seeks Closer Ties'; Margaret Thatcher, HC Statement – Dublin European Council 1.5.1990 MTF. See also Alan Riding 'Britain 'Deeply Skeptical' of Plan by France and Germany on Unity' *NYT* 25.4.1990

99 Alan Riding 'Europe Hastening Integration Pace' *NYT* 26.6.1990; Craig R. Whitney 'Europeans Meeting Today on Unity *NYT* 25.6.1990

100 See Michael J. Turner, *Britain's International Role, 1970–1991* Palgrave Macmillan 2010 ch. 6 (last two pages);

'A Europe Whole and Free' Remarks to the Citizens at the Rheingoldhalle in Mainz (Germany) 31.5.1989 usa.usembassy.de/etexts/ga6-890531.htm. Cf. Andrew P. Hogue 'George H. W. Bush, "A Whole Europe, A Free Europe"' *Voices of Democracy* 3 (2008) pp. 205–21

101 Thomas L. Friedman 'US Ties with West Germany Begin to Eclipse Relationship with Britain' *NYT* 10.12.1989. On the decisions taken at Dublin I as regards Eastern Europe, the summit communiqué stated: 'The European Council agrees that the action within the framework of G24 should be extended to the GDR, Czechoslovakia, Yugoslavia, Bulgaria and Romania. The Community will work actively for the adoption of an action plan for assistance to these countries at the forthcoming G24 ministerial meeting. Discussions will start forthwith in the Council, on the basis of the Commission's communication, on Association Agreements with each of the countries of Central and Eastern Europe which include an institutional framework for political dialogue. The Community will work to complete Association negotiations with these countries as soon as possible on the understanding that the basic conditions with regard to democratic principles and transition towards a market economy are fulfilled. See p. 5 of the communiqué at consilium.europa.eu/media/20571/1990_april_-_dublin_eng_.pdf. Cf. GHWBPL Memcon of Bush–Delors talks 24.4.1990 The Cabinet Room/White House

102 Friedman 'US Ties with West Germany Begin to Eclipse Relationship with Britain'

103 Short *Mitterrand* p. 474

104 On Thatcher's view of 'binding Germany in' to NATO, see for example Draft Paper by Policy Planning Staff (FCO), 15.6.1990; Telegraphic – Mallaby to Hurd 20.6.1990; Budd (Bonn) to Powell (Policy Planning Staff) 22.6.1990, printed in *DBPO III VII GU 1989/90* docs 210, 212 and 213 pp. 418–22, 424–6

105 Zelikow & Rice *Germany Unified* p. 236; Kohl *Ich wollte* pp. 340–1. See also Sir Christopher Mallaby recollections of the dinner printed in 'FCO Witness Seminar: Berlin in the Cold War 1949–1990 & German Unification 1989–1990' Lancaster House 16.10.2009 pp. 82–3 issuu.com/fcohistorians/docs /full_ transcript_germany. For Thatcher's interview with *Der Spiegel*, see '"Alle gegen Deutschland – nein!" Die britische Premierministerin Margaret Thatcher über Europa und die deutsche Einheit' *Der Spiegel* 13/1990 26.3.1990 pp. 182–7. Cf. Memcon of the 20th Anglo-German consultations in London 30.3.1990, printed in *DESE* doc. 238 pp. 996–1001

106 GHWBPL Memcon of Thatcher–Bush talks 13.4.1990 Bermuda pp. 1–2

107 Ibid. p. 6

108 Ibid. pp. 3, 8

109 Ibid. pp. 5, 14

110 News Conference of the President and Prime Minister Margaret Thatcher of the United Kingdom in Hamilton Bermuda 13.4.1990 APP

111 Ibid.

112 Teltschik *329 Tage* p. 196

113 GHWBPL Memcon of Thatcher–Bush talks 13.4.1990 Bermuda p. 4; Letter from Powell to Wall 24.2.1990, printed in *DBPO III VII GU 1989/90* doc. 155 pp. 310–14 esp. p. 311

114 Paul Lewis 'Shevardnadze Calls for Meeting This Year on German Unification' *NYT* 16.2.1990

115 GHWBPL Memcon of Thatcher–Bush talks 13.4.1990 Bermuda pp. 7, 11

116 Ibid. pp. 4, 11

117 Bush told Thatcher in Bermuda: 'We need to think about how the US should interact with the CSCE. We need good solid thinking on this, with the East Europeans as players in Europe's future. It would be good to get a common NATO approach before a CSCE Summit.' Ibid. p. 3. On the history of NATO summit meetings (27 summits between 1949 and 2017), see nato.int/ cps/ua/natohq/topics_50115.htm

118 GHWBPL Memcon of Bush–Mitterrand talks (private) 19.4.1990 Key Largo Florida p. 2; Memcon of Bush–Delors talks 24.4.1990 The Cabinet Room/White House p. 2; Memcon of Bush–Mitterrand talks (full delegation) 19.4.1990 Key Largo Florida p. 2

119 GHWBPL Memcon of Bush–Delors talks 24.4.1990 The Cabinet Room/ White House p. 2

120 GHWBPL Memcon of Bush–Mitterrand talks (private) 19.4.1990 Key Largo Florida p. 2

121 GHWBPL Memcon of Bush–Delors talks 24.4.1990 The Cabinet Room/ White House p. 3

122 Ibid., p. 3; Memcon of Bush–Mitterrand talks (full delegation) 19.4.1990 Key Largo Florida p. 3

123 R. W. Apple Jr 'Bush and Mitterrand Are Putting Moscow Ties Ahead of Lithuania' *NYT* 20.4.1990

124 GHWBPL Memcon of Bush–Mitterrand talks (full delegation) 19.4.1990 Key Largo Florida p. 3; Memcon of Bush–Mitterrand talks (private) 19.4.1990 Key Largo Florida pp. 3–4

125 GHWBPL Memcon of Bush–Wörner talks 7.5.1990 Oval Office pp. 2–3

126 Whitney 'Europe's Alliance Seeks Closer Ties'

127 GHWBPL Memcon of Bush–Mitterrand talks (full delegation) 19.4.1990 Key Largo Florida p. 4

128 Zelikow & Rice *Germany Unified* pp. 238–40. See also 'Excerpts from Session by Bush on Arms Talks' *NYT* 4.5.1990; Andrew Rosenthal 'Bush, Europe and NATO: Bowing to the Inevitable as a New Germany Rises' *NYT* 4.5.1990

129 Thomas L. Friedman 'NATO Adopts Plan to Revamp Itself for German Unity' *NYT* 4.5.1990

130 Bush's Remarks at the Oklahoma State University Commencement Ceremony in Stillwater 4.5.1990 APP

131 Ibid.; Andrew Rosenthal 'Bush Sees Revamped NATO as Core of Europe's Power' *NYT* 5.5.1990

132 'Excerpts From Session by Bush on Arms Talks' *NYT* 4.5.1990; Andrew Rosenthal 'Bush, Europe and NATO: Bowing to the Inevitable as a New Germany Rises' *NYT* 4.5.1990

133 GHWBPL Memcon of Bush–Wörner talks 7.5.1990 Oval Office pp. 2–4. See also TNA UK PREM 19/4329 Memo from Douglas Hurd to Thatcher – NATO Strategy Review 4.6.1990 pp. 1–5. Teasing out Bush's Oklahoma speech for the PM, Hurd said that the term 'strategy review' meant two things: a 'fresh look at NATO's overall political objectives' and a 'narrower review of military strategy'. Both, he underlined, were 'necessary', but they were not to be confused. Hurd also wanted to involve the French in the Alliance's reviewing process 'as far as possible'; a process Mitterrand had called one 'common reflection about

the future of NATO'. But Hurd was clear that the French – though among the 'staunchest' allies – should not be allowed to 'remake the Alliance to their own specification'. Overall, the problem was the 'deep divisions just below the surface within the Alliance'. So London was inclined to stay close to Washington

134 News Conference of President Bush and President François Mitterrand of France in Key Largo Florida 19.4.1990 APP

135 Diary Entry 18.4.1990, printed in Bush & Scowcroft *A World Transformed* p. 223

136 See Andrew Rosenthal 'Bush Delays Action on Lithuania, Not Wanting to Harm Gorbachev' *NYT* 25.4.1990

137 Letter printed in *Bulletin* no. 48 28.4.1990 p. 384. See also *DESE* doc. 257 pp. 1056–9; Teltschik *329 Tage* p. 209; Bozo *Mitterrand, the End of the Cold War* pp. 240–1. See also Alan Riding 'Lithuania Is Asked by Paris and Bonn to Halt Decisions' *NYT* 27.4. 1990; Bill Keller 'Lithuania Reports Promising Contact with Soviet Aides' *NYT* 28.4.1990

138 Richard L. Berke '9 G.O.P. Senators Attack Bush on Lithuania' *NYT* 28.4.1990; Alan Riding 'US Reaches Trade Deal with Moscow' *NYT* 27.4.1990

139 For Bush's diary entries (20.4.1990 and 24.4.1990) and later reflections on the Lithuania crisis, see Bush & Scowcroft *A World Transformed* pp. 224–7. Letter from Bush to Gorbachev 29.4.1990, printed in Bush *All the Best* pp. 467–9

140 Bush & Scowcroft *A World Transformed* pp. 226–7

141 GHWBPL Memcon of Bush–Kohl meeting 17.5.1990 Oval Office pp. 3–4.

There is no German Memcon of the tête-à-tête between Bush and Kohl available, only an American transcript

142 Ibid. pp. 4–5

143 Ibid. p. 5. GHWBPL Memcon of Bush–Kohl meeting incl. delegations 17.5.1990 The Cabinet Room/White House p. 7

144 GHWBPL Memcon of Bush–Kohl meeting incl. delegations 17.5.1990 The Cabinet Room/White House p. 5. For the significantly longer German pendant to this second, plenary meeting's US transcript, see *DESE* doc. 281 pp. 1126–32

145 Bush & Scowcroft *A World Transformed* pp. 283–4

146 Robert Shepard 'Gorbachev Details Soviet Changes' *UPI* 1.6.1990; William J. Easton 'Gorbachev Chides US Over Trade: Economy: He tells congressmen of Soviet problems and presses for most-favored-nation status enjoyed by China' *LAT* 2.6.1990. Cf. Hearing Before the Committee on Finance – US Senate 101st Congress 2nd Session 20.6.1990 'Extending Most-Favored-Nation Status to China' US Govt Printing Office 1991, 169pp.

147 Bush & Scowcroft *A World Transformed* pp. 284–6; Andrew Rosenthal 'Bush and Gorbachev Sign Major Accords on Missiles, Chemical Weapons and Trade' *NYT* 2.6.1990; Clyde H. Farnsworth 'Trade Accord Holds Many Prizes, But Obstacles to Passage Remain' *NYT* 2.6.1990. Cable – US Department of State to US Embassies in NATO Capitals, Tokyo, Seoul, Canberra [and info to Moscow]: 'Briefing Allies on Washington Summit' 15.6.1990 p. 9 NSAEBB No. 320

148 GHWBPL Telcon Bush to Kohl 1.6.1989 Oval Office pp. 2–3. See also GHWBPL Telcon between Bush and Kohl 3.6.1990

Oval Office. There are no German transcripts released for these phone calls, only Bush's letter to Kohl of 4 June 1990 referring to them. See Telex from Bush to Kohl 4.6.1990, printed in *DESE* doc. 299 pp. 1178–80; Bush & Scowcroft *A World Transformed* pp. 279–89 esp. p. 287

149 Michael Dobbs 'Warsaw Pact Summit Urges Transformation' *WP* 8.6.1990. Cf. BA SAPMO DC/20/I/3/3000, Record of the Political Consultative Committee Meeting in Moscow 7.6.1990, printed in Vojtech Mastny et al. (eds) *A Cardboard Castle? An Inside History of the Warsaw Pact, 1955–1991* CEU Press 2005 doc. 153 pp. 674–7

150 GHWBPL Memcon of Bush–de Maizière talks 11.6.1990 The Cabinet Room/White House pp. 2–3

151 Bush & Scowcroft *A World Transformed* pp. 292–4. For Bush's letter to Kohl (21.6.1990), the US NATO summit declaration draft and Germany's counter-draft, see *DESE* docs 321–321A, 326, 330–330A pp. 1234–41, 1256–61 and 1276–80. See also Letter from Scowcroft to Teltschik 30.6.1990 and Memos for Kohl ahead of the NATO summit 5–6.7.1990, all printed in *DESE* docs 335, 344–344I pp. 1285–6, 1309–23. Cf. TNA UK PREM 19/3466 Cable – Hannay (FM UK REP Brussels) to FCO (and advanced to PS): Hurd's talks with Baker in Brussels, 4 July: NATO summit declaration 4.7.1990 pp. 1–2. TNA UK PREM 19/3102 Powell to 10 Downing Street – PM's meeting with NATO SG 29.6.1990; Revised Annotated Conclusions on London Declaration 20.6.1990; Appleyard (Cabinet Office) to Powell – Memo: NATO Summit – Key Issues (secret) 29.6.1990

152 GHWBPL Telcon of Bush with PM

Ruud Lubbers (NED) 3.7.1990 Kennebunkport p. 1. See also GHWBPL Telcon of Bush with PM Wilfried Martens (BEL) 3.7.1990 Kennebunkport; Telcon of Bush with PM Poul Schlueter (DK) 3.7.1990 Kennebunkport. See also JAB-SML B109/ F3 Briefing of President on NATO summit 2.7.1990 Walker's Point p. 1

153 GHWBPL Memcon of Bush–Wörner talks 5.7.1990 Lancaster House England pp. 2–3

154 'Declaration on a Transformed North Atlantic Alliance' – Issued by the Heads of State and Government participating in the meeting of the North Atlantic Council ('The London Declaration') 5–6.7.1990 nato.int/cps/en/natohq/official_texts_23693.htm

155 Craig R. Whitney 'NATO Allies, After 40 Years, Proclaim End Of Cold War; Invite Gorbachev To Speak' NYT 7.7.1990; Sarah Helm, Isabel Hilton and Christopher Bellamy 'Nato Declares Peace on the Warsaw Pact' Independent 7.7.1990

156 See Entwurf: Gipfelerklärung (undated), printed in DESE doc. 321A pp. 1237–41 (for the US draft of summit declaration); Vorlage von Ludwig and Westdickenberg an Teltschik 25.6.1990 – Entwurf: NATO-Gipfelerklärung (undated), both printed in DESE doc. 326 pp. 1256–61 (for the German analysis of US draft) and doc. 330A pp. 1276–80 (for the German counter draft-proposal)

157 London Declaration on a Transformed North Atlantic Alliance 6.7.1990 APP

158 Ibid.

159 Ibid. See also R. W. Apple Jr 'An Alliance for a New Age: Has NATO Donned a Velvet Glove?' NYT 7.7.1990

160 The President's News Conference Following the North Atlantic Treaty Organisation Summit in London 6.7.1990 APP

161 Whitney 'NATO Allies, After 40 Years, Proclaim End of Cold War; Invite Gorbachev to Speak'

162 Ibid.; Ann Devroy 'Allies Ask Gorbachev to NATO' WP 6.7.1990

163 TNA UK PREM 19/3466 Letter from Gorbachev to Thatcher 4.7.1990 pp. 1–2

164 The President's News Conference Following the North Atlantic Treaty Organisation Summit in London 6.7.1990 APP

165 Maureen Dowd 'Bush Accepts Japanese Aid to China, With Limits' NYT 8.7.1990

166 Diary Entry 24.6.1990, printed in Bush All the Best p. 475

167 Bush's written statement on Federal Budget Negotiations 26.6.1990 APP

168 Andrew Rosenthal 'Bush Now Concedes a Need for "Tax Revenue Increases" To Reduce Deficit In Budget' NYT 27.6.1990

169 Zelikow & Rice Germany Unified pp. 324–5; Bush & Scowcroft A World Transformed p. 295

170 Maureen Dowd 'Reporter's Notebook; The Welcome by Bush Is as Big as All Texas' NYT 9.7.1990

171 TNA UK PREM 19/2945 TNA UK PREM 19/2945 cover note – Powell to Wicks (Treasury) 31.7.1990: Houston Economic Summit + Record of the Heads Discussion (Monday 9.7.1990) pp. 1–34 here esp. p. 19

172 Roberto Suro 'Summit Is Divided On Aid To Moscow' NYT 11.7.1990

173 Ibid. For the IMF and EC Commission 'studies' on the Soviet Union's economy and its financial needs, see IMFA-AWP JSSE Boxes 1–3; IMFA Office of Managing Director Michel Camdessus

Papers – Chronological Files 1990 & 1992 Boxes 5–7. Note: The IMF Archives have not released the Michel Camdessus Papers – Chronological Files for 1991

174 GHWBPL Memcon of Opening Session of the 16th Economic Summit of Industrialised Nations (G7), Monday 9.7.1990 Founders Room Rice University Houston p. 2. TNA UK PREM 19/2945 cover note – Powell to Wicks (Treasury) 31.7.1990: Houston Economic Summit + Record of the Heads Discussion (Monday 9.7.1990) pp. 1–34 here esp. pp. 1–3

175 R. W. Apple Jr 'US Pushes to End Farming Subsidies' *NYT* 10.7.1990. See GHWBPL Memcon of Bush–Delors talks 8.7.1990 Astro-Arena Houston pp. 1–5 esp p. 4. Bush and Delors (as well as the European G4) also quibbled over the role of the EBRD in the assessment of the Soviet economic reform programme before offering any further financial assistance. Generally while in Bush's words 'it is impossible for the US to loan money to USSR at this time', the Europeans were much less reluctant to refuse aid. As Mitterrand put it 'The EC, which is not unanimous, wants to contribute aid to the USSR.' See also GHWBPL Memcon of First Main Plenary Session of the 16th Economic Summit of Industrialised Nations (G7) Tuesday 10.7.1990 O'Conner Room – Herring Hall Rice University Houston pp. 4–5; and Memcon of Second Main Plenary Session of the 16th Economic Summit of Industrialised Nations (G7) Tuesday 10.7.1990 O'Conner Room – Herring Hall Rice University Houston pp. 10–13

176 Hutchings *American Diplomacy* pp. 159–60

177 R. W. Apple Jr 'The Houston Summit – A New Balance of Power: Compromise is the Theme as Kohl Breaks Washington's Domination' *NYT* 12.7.1990; Bush's Remarks at the Welcoming Ceremony for the Houston Economic Summit 9.7.1990 APP

178 Bush & Scowcroft *A World Transformed* pp. 299–300

179 Tőkes *Hungary's Negotiated Revolution* pp. 361–98; Paczkowski *The Spring Will Be Ours* pp. 511–18; GHWBPL Memcon of Bush–Havel talks 30.9.1990 Waldorf Astoria Hotel New York p. 1

180 Steven Greenhouse, 'Poland's Foreign Lenders Accept Unusual Extension of Payments' *NYT* 17.2.1990; Clyde H. Farnsworth 'Poland – World Bank Approves Its First Loans to Warsaw, in Support of Economic Reforms' *NYT* 7.2.1990; GHWBPL Memcon of Bush–Mazowiecki talks 29.9.1990 Waldorf Astoria Hotel New York pp. 3–4

181 Steven Greenhouse 'Hungary Confident on Debt Payment' *NYT* 6.3.1990; Celestine Bohlen 'Democratic Hungary Nibbles on Political Fringes' *NYT* 9.7.1990

182 GHWBPL Memcon of Bush–Antall talks (expanded) 18.10.1990 The Cabinet Room/White House pp. 2–3; Bohlen 'Democratic Hungary Nibbles on Political Fringes'

183 Craig R. Whitney 'East Europe Joins the Market and Gets a Preview of the Pain' *NYT* 7.1.1990

184 GHWBPL Memcon of Havel–Bush talks 18.11.1990 Hradčany Castle Prague pp. 1–2; Memcon of Bush–Antall talks (expanded) 18.10.1990 The Cabinet Room/White House p. 2

185 Hutchings *American Diplomacy* pp. 165–7; Baker 'From Revolution to Democracy' 7.2.1990 Prague. At

Charles University Baker offered Czechoslovakia a package of economic assistance similar to that provided by Washington to Poland and Hungary in the autumn of 1989, consisting of technical aid and initiatives such as the immediate waiver of the Jackson–Vanik amendment as well as support for Czechoslovakia's bid to join the IMF and moves to make Prague eligible for export-import bank lending programmes. But beyond this – bar the notification that Eastern Europe at large could tap into the $300 million pool of new funds the White House had budgeted for Eastern Europe for 1990, if sufficient economic progress was made – there was nothing new. See also Thomas L. Friedman 'Upheaval in the East; Baker Offers Prague Economic Aid' *NYT* 7.2.1990. Cf. JAB-SML B108/F14 Talking Points for Cabinet Meeting 15.2.1990 p. 1

186 See Smith *The Making of EU Foreign Policy* pp. 66–70, 80–82. See also Ronald Tiersky 'The Rise and Fall of Attali' *French Politics and Society* 11, 4 (Fall 1993) [Etats de la corruption: Politics, Morals, and Corruption in France] pp. 105–16

187 Bozo 'The Failure of a Grand Design' pp. 404–12

188 GHWBPL Memcon of Bush–Antall talks (expanded) 18.10.1990 The Cabinet Room/White House p. 3

189 GHWBPL Memcon of Havel–Bush talks 18.11.1990 Hradčany Castle Prague p. 3. See also Henry Kamm 'Czechoslovakia – Prague Reclaiming Its Position at Center of Europe' *NYT* 8.2.1990

190 GHWBPL Memcon of Bush–Mazowiecki talks 29.9.1990 Waldorf Astoria Hotel New York pp. 2–3

191 'Soviets Ask Czechs to Extend the Time to Pull Out Troops' *NYT*/Reuters 8.2.1990

192 GHWBPL Memcon of Bush–Antall talks (private) 18.10.1990 Oval Office p. 2

193 See Vojtech Mastny *The Helsinki Process and the Reintegration of Europe, 1986–1991: Analysis and Documentation* Pinter 1992 p. 222; Hutchings *American Diplomacy* p. 192

194 Baker's Speech 'CSCE: The Conscience of the Continent' in front of CSCE Conference on the human dimension Copenhagen 6.6.1990 *Current Policy* No. 1280 US DoS

195 Andrew Rosenthal 'Bush Gives Czechs a Copy of Liberty Bell' *NYT* 18.11.1990. Bush's Remarks in Prague (Czechoslovakia) at a Ceremony Commemorating the End of Communist Rule 17.11.1990 APP

196 Bush & Scowcroft *A World Transformed* p. 404. GHWBPL Memcon of Havel–Bush talks 17.11.1990 Hradčany Castle Prague p. 1

197 GHWBPL Memcon of Havel–Bush talks (expanded) 18.11.1990 Hradčany Castle Prague pp. 3–4

198 R. W. Apple Jr 'East and West Sign Pact to Shed Arms in Europe – For 2 Blocs, Old Enemies, An Era Ends' *NYT* 20.11.1990; 'Will Europe Spell Peace CSCE?' *NYT* 19.11.1990

199 Apple Jr 'East and West Sign Pact to Shed Arms in Europe'. William Drozdiak 'Arms Treaty, Paris Meeting Seal Conclusion of Cold War' *WP* 20.11.1990

200 Charter of Paris for a New Europe 21.11.1990 state.gov/t/isn/4721.htm

201 Kohl cited in Apple Jr 'East and West Sign Pact to Shed Arms in Europe'

202 Speech by Soviet President Mikhail

Gorbachev to the Second Summit of CSCE Heads of State or Government in Paris 19.11.1990 osce.org/mc/16155?download=true

203 'Excerpts From the Charter of Paris for a New Europe as Signed Yesterday' *NYT* 22.11.1990

204 Alan Riding 'The Question That Lingers on Europe: How Will Goals Be Achieved?' *NYT* 22.11.1990

205 Bozo *Mitterrand, the End of the Cold War* pp. 299–300

206 Steven Prokesch 'Thatcher Unable to Eliminate Foe by Party Elections' *NYT* 21.11.1990; Craig R. Whitney 'Change In Britain; Thatcher Says She'll Quit; 11½ Years As Prime Minister Ended By Party Challenge' *NYT* 23.11.1990; *idem* 'Persuasion and Rigidity: How Her Chief Tool Became a Fatal Flaw' *NYT* 23.11.1990; Thatcher's Press Conference at Paris CSCE Summit in the Ballroom of the British Embassy Paris 19.11.1990 MTF. See also for the PM's off the record briefings in Paris on 20–1.11.1990 MTF margaretthatcher.org/archive/1990Novingham.asp

207 Alan Travis 'Margaret Thatcher's resignation shocked politicians in US and USSR, files show' *Guardian* 30.12.2016

208 See for example Eesti Välisministeerium (hereafter Est VM) Poliitika V Prantsusmaa Juuni 1990–Märts 1993 Üleskirjutus vestlusest prantsuse välisminister Alexandre [sic! It should be Roland] Dumas'ga 19.11.1990; Letter from Michel Pelchat [president of Baltic study group of parliamentarians] to Gorbachev 21.11.1990; Letter from Claude Huriet [senator] to Gorbachev 21.11.1990; Republic of Estonia: Paris Declaration 19.11.1990

209 Gorbachev cited in Apple Jr 'East and West Sign Pact to Shed Arms in Europe'

210 Record of Bush–Gorbachev Conversation (Main Content) in Paris 19.11.1990, printed in *TLSS* doc. 116 pp. 773–80 quoting p. 777

Chapter 6

1   Bush's Address before a Joint Session of the Congress on the State of the Union 29.1.1991 APP

2   Ibid.

3   Kennedy's Inaugural Address 20.1.1961 APP

4   Maureen Dowd 'President, in State of Union Talk, Dwells on War and the Economy' *NYT* 30.1.1991

5   Bush's Address before a Joint Session of the Congress on the State of the Union 29.1.1991 APP

6   Cf. Cecil V. Crabb & Kevin V. Mulcahy 'George Bush's Management Style and Operation Desert Storm' *Presidential Studies Quarterly* 25, 2 (Spring 1995) [Leadership, Organisation, and Security] pp. 251–65; Engel 'A Better World' pp. 40–6

7   Bush & Scowcroft *A World Transformed* p. 302

8   Mark Fineman 'Iraq Remaps Kuwait as Province 19' *LAT* 29.8.1990

9   R. W. Apple Jr 'Invading Iraqis Seize Kuwait And Its Oil; Us Condems Attack, Urges United Action' *NYT* 3.8.1990. For the oil price hike and fall of the Dow Jones, see Richard N. Haass *War of Necessity, War of Choice: A Memoir of Two Iraq Wars* Simon & Schuster 2009 p. 85. See also GHWBPL NSC Richard Haass Files – Working Files Iraq 2/8/90–12/90 [8] (OA/ID CF01478) NSC minutes 6.8.1990, Cabinet Room pp. 1–6 MTF

10   Diary Entry 4.5.1990, printed in Bush *All the Best* p. 470

11   Bush's Remarks and a Question-and-Answer Session with the Magazine Publishers of America 17.7.1990 APP

12   Diary Entry 4.5.1990, printed in Bush *All the Best* p. 470

13   Bush & Scowcroft *A World Transformed* p. 303

14   Engel *When the World Seemed New* pp. 378–85; Brands *Making the Unipolar Moment* ch. 5

15   Engel *When the World Seemed New* p. 380; 'Saddam Speech Marks Revolution's 22nd Anniversary' 17.7.1990 Daily Report – Near East & South Asia FBIS-NES-90-137

16   Haass *War of Necessity* p. 60

17   Ibid. p. 62. 'People matter. It was anything but axiomatic that the United States would decide to deploy half a million troops halfway around the world to rescue a country few Americans could find on a map. A different president and set of advisers might have tolerated Iraqi control of Kuwait and limited the US response to sanctions so long as Saddam did not go on to attack Saudi Arabia.'

18   GHWBPL NSC Richard Haass Files (OA/ID CF01479) Haass Memo to Scowcroft for Bush 6.8.1990. See also Haass *War of Necessity* p. 62

19   See Brands *Making the Unipolar Moment* pp. 301–2; idem, *From Berlin to Baghdad: America's Search for Purpose in the Post-Cold War World* Univ. Press of Kentucky 2008 pp. 49–52. See also Vladimir Nosenko 'Soviet Policy in the Conflict' in Alex Danchev & Dan Keohane (eds) *International Perspectives on the Gulf Conflict, 1990–91* Macmillan 1994 pp. 136–44 esp. p. 136

20   Bush & Scowcroft *A World Transformed* p. 303

21   Ibid. p. 304

22   Ibid. p. 314; Clyde H. Farnsworth 'The Iraqi Invasion: Holding on to the Money-Bush, in Freezing Assets, Bars $30 Billion to Hussein' *NYT* 3.8.1990

23   Paul Lewis 'The Iraqi Invasion; UN Condemns the Invasion with Threat to Punish Iraq' *NYT* 3.8.1990. See also Haass *War of Necessity* pp. 60–1

24   Bush & Scowcroft *A World Transformed* p. 314. Baker *The Politics* pp. 1–16. See also Eduard Shevardnadze *The Future Belongs to Freedom* Sinclair-Stevenson 1991 pp. 98–101. For Baker's talks with Shevardnadze, see JAB-SML B109/F4 JAB notes from 8/1–2/90 meetings w/ USSR FM Shevardnadze in Irkutsk (USSR)

25   Bush's Remarks and an Exchange with Reporters on the Iraqi Invasion of Kuwait 2.8.1990 APP

26   Cf. Grachev *Gorbachev's Gamble* pp. 192–4; Taubman *Gorbachev* p. 567

27   Baker *The Politics* pp. 13–16

28   Bill Keller 'Moscow Joins Us In Criticising Iraq' *NYT* 4.8.1990; Baker *The Politics* p. 16. Cf. Shevardnadze *The Future* pp. 101–2

29   James A. Baker III 'My friend, Eduard Shevardnadze' *WP* 8.7.2014. See also Palazchenko *My Years* pp. 209–10

30   Baker *The Politics* pp. 15, 331. See also Andrew Rosenthal 'Strategy: Embargo – US Bets Its Troops Will Deter Iraq While Sanctions Do the Real Fighting' *NYT* 9.8.1990

31   Meacham *Destiny and Power* pp. 426–7; Bush & Scowcroft *A World Transformed* pp. 319–20. Cf. Thatcher *The Downing Street Years* pp. 816–20. Remarks and a Question-and-Answer Session with

Reporters in Aspen (Colorado) – Following a Meeting with Prime Minister Margaret Thatcher of the United Kingdom 2.2.1990 APP. Maureen Dowd 'The Longest Week: How President Decided to Draw the Line' *NYT* 9.8.1990. See also Haass *War of Necessity* pp. 61–2

32 GHWBPL Telcon of Bush to King Hussein and President Mubarak call 2.8.1990 aboard Air Force One en route Aspen Colorado p. 2; Bush & Scowcroft *A World Transformed* pp. 318–19

33 GHWBPL Telcon of Bush to King Fahd call 2.8.1990 Oval Office pp. 1, 3; Bush & Scowcroft *A World Transformed* pp. 320–1; Meacham *Destiny and Power* pp. 427–8. Note: Bush recalls (and Meacham equally recounts) that he made the call from Aspen not the Oval Office

34 GHWBPL NSC Richard Haass Files – Working Files Iraq 2/8/90–12/90 (OA/ID CF01478) Minutes of the NSC Meeting 3.8.1990 The Cabinet Room pp. 1–12 esp. pp. 3–4 MTF; Christopher Maynard *Out of the Shadow: George H. W. Bush and the End of the Cold War* Texas A&M UP 2008 pp. 76–7

35 GHWBPL Telcon of Bush to Mitterrand call 3.8.1990 Oval Office p. 3

36 GHWBPL Telcon of Bush to Özal call 3.8.1990 Oval Office pp. 1–2

37 GHWBPL Telcon of Bush to Kaifu call 3.8.1990 Camp David pp. 1–3

38 Bush's diary entries of 3.8.1990 and 4.8.1990, quoted in Meacham *Destiny and Power* pp. 428–31. See also GHWBPL Richard Haass Files – Working Files Iraq 2/8/90–12/90 [8] (OA/ID CF01478) NSC minutes 4.8.1990

39 GHWBPL Telcon Bush to Fahd 4.8.1990 Camp David p. 5; John Kifner 'Arabs'

Summit Meeting Off; Iraqi Units In Kuwait Dig In; Europe Bars Baghdad's Oil' *NYT* 5.8.1990

40 GHWBPL Telcon of Bush to Mulroney call 4.8.1990 Camp David p. 2. Cf. GHWBPL Telcon of Bush to Özal call 4.8.1990 Camp David

41 Meacham *Destiny and Power* p. 431. Cf. Haass *War of Necessity* p. 70; Dick Cheney with Liz Cheney *In My Time: A Personal and Political Memoir* Threshold Editions 2011 pp. 189–91

42 Maureen Dowd 'The Longest Week' *NYT* 9.8.1990 p. 17; Youssef M. Ibrahim 'Bush Sends US Force to Saudi Arabia as Kingdom Agrees to Confront Iraq; Saudis Make a Stand: Fear of Iraq Ends Their Long Reluctance to Acknowledge Interests Lie with West' *NYT* 8.8.1990; Michael E. Gordon 'Bush Aims: Deter Attack, Send a Signal' *NYT* 8.8.1990. See also Colin Powell with Joseph E. Persico *My American Journey* Ballantine 1996 p. 453. Between 2–6.8.1990, Bush called the leaders of Jordan and Egypt, Saudi Arabia, Yemen, Japan, Germany, France, Turkey, Britain, Kuwait, Canada, as well as Italy – some of them several times. Cf. GHWBPL NSC Richard Haass Files – Working Files Iraq 2/8/90–12/90 (OA/ID CF01478) NSC meeting minutes 5.8.1990 The Cabinet Room MTF

43 Diary Entry 5.8.1990, printed in Bush *All the Best* p. 476; Meacham *Destiny and Power* pp. 431–2

44 Bush's Remarks and an Exchange with Reporters on the Iraqi Invasion of Kuwait 5.8.1990 APP; Powell *My American Journey* p. 453

45 See Paul Lewis 'Washington Calls on UN to Impose Boycott on Iraq' *NYT* 4.8.1990 p. 6

46 GHWBPL Telcon Bush to Andreotti

call 6.8.1990 Oval Office p. 2

47 JAB-SML B109/F4 Telcon of Baker–Shevardnadze call 6.8.1990 pp. 1–4

48 Remarks and an Exchange with Reporters Following Bush's Meeting with Prime Minister Margaret Thatcher of the United Kingdom and Secretary General Manfred Wörner of the North Atlantic Treaty Organisation 6.8.1990 APP. Thomas L. Friedman 'Security Council Votes 13 to 0 to Block Trade with Baghdad; Facing Boycott, Iraq Slows Oil: The Iraqi Invasion; Blockade Is Hinted' NYT 7.8.1990. On Thatcher see also Haass War of Necessity pp. 71–2; and Thatcher The Downing Street Years pp. 820–2; Thatcher Archive COI transcript, Press Conference ending visit to US 6.8.1990 MTF

49 For the drafting and presentation of the Oval Office speech, see Haass War of Necessity pp. 73–5

50 Bush's Address to the Nation Announcing the Deployment of United States Armed Forces to Saudi Arabia 8.8.1990 APP; The President's News Conference 8.8.1990 noon APP; Friedman 'Security Council Votes 13 to 0 to Block Trade with Baghdad'

51 GHWBPL Telcon of Özal to Bush call 8.8.1990 Oval Office p. 1

52 GHWBPL Telcon of Thatcher to Bush call 9.8.1990 Oval Office pp. 1, 4

53 John Kifner 'Arab Vote to Send Troops to Help Saudis: Boycott of Iraqi Oil is Reported Near 100%' NYT 1.8.1990; 'How the Arab League Voted in Cairo' NYT 11.8.1990; 'Excerpts from Hussein's Statement Declaring a Holy War' NYT 11.8.1990

54 On the atrocities, see GHWBPL Telcon of Bush to Sheikh Zayyid of UAE call 8.8.1990 Oval Office p. 2; Michael Wines 'Largest Force since Vietnam Committed in 15-Day Flurry' NYT 19.8.1990

55 Max Boot War Made New: Technology, Warfare, and the Course of History, 1500 to Today Gotham Books 2006 pp. 337–8. For figures of US deployments to the Gulf in autumn 1990, see also 'Defense Spending Held to $288 Billion' CQ Almanac 1990 pp. 812–26 esp. pp. 812, 814

56 Powell My American Journey p. 474; see also Roy Allison (ed.) Radical Reform in Soviet Defence Policy St Martin's Press 1992 p. 173; Tim Kane 'The Decline of American Engagement: Patterns of US Troop Deployments' Hoover Institution Economics Working Paper #16101 11.1.2016. Susan F. Rasky 'New Deployment in the Gulf May Slow Drive for Deep Cuts in Military Budget' NYT 12.8.1990. Cf. 'Defense Spending Held to $288 Billion' CQ Almanac 1990 p. 819; Bryan T. van Sweringen 'Variable Architectures for War and Peace: US Force Structure and Basing in Germany, 1945–1990' in Detlef Junker et al. (eds) The United States and Germany in the Era of the Cold War, 1945–68, vol. 1 Cambridge UP 2004 pp. 223–4; Steve Vogel 'US VII Corps Bids Goodbye to Germany After Four Decades' WP 19.3.1992

57 GHWBPL National Security Directive 45 – US Policy in Response to the Iraqi Invasion of Kuwait 20.8.1990

58 Wines 'Largest Force Since Vietnam Committed in 15-Day Flurry' NYT 19.8.1990; idem 'US Aid Helped Hussein's Climb; Now, Critics Say, the Bill Is Due' NYT 13.8.1990; Thomas L. Friedman 'US Gulf Policy: Vague "Vital Interest"' NYT 12.8.1990; Michael Oreskes 'Poll on Troop Move Shows Support (and Anxiety)' NYT 12.8.1990

59 See Powell *My American Journey* pp. 456–7

60 Bush & Scowcroft *A World Transformed* pp. 490–1

61 Friedman 'US Gulf Policy: Vague "Vital Interest"'. Quotes from Alan Riding 'Allies Reminded of Need for US Shield' *NYT* 12.8.1990

62 David Evans 'US Finds $50 Billion "Surplus": Agencies Put Unspent Cash in Accounts' *CT* 22.5.1990; R. W. Apple Jr 'Bush Briefs Legislators on Crisis and They Back His Gulf Strategy' *NYT* 29.8.1990; Wines 'Largest Force Since Vietnam Committed in 15-Day Flurry'. See also Powell *My American Journey* pp. 456, 459

63 The president's News Conference on the Persian Gulf Crisis 30.8.1990 APP. See also Andrea K. Grove *Political Leadership in Foreign Policy: Manipulating Support Across Borders* Palgrave Macmillan 2007 pp. 53–4; 'Defense Spending Held to $288 Billion' *CQ Almanac 1990* p. 818

64 GHWBPL Telcon of Bush to Kaifu call 13.8.1990 Kennebunkport pp. 1–3

65 GHWBPL Telcon of Bush to Kaifu call 29.8.1990 6:55–7:15 p.m. Oval Office, pp. 1–2; Telcon Kaifu to Bush call 29.8.1990 8:39–8:44 p.m. Oval Office p. 1. Cf. Steven R. Weisman 'Japan Promises Grants and Food, But Lack of Arms Aid Nettles US' *NYT* 30.8.1990

66 GHWBPL Telcon of Bush to Kohl call 22.8.1990 Kennebunkport p. 1. See also GHWBPL Telcon of Bush to Kohl call 30.8.1990 White House Situation Room pp. 1–2; Teltschik *329 Tage* pp. 350, 354

67 Memcon of Kohl–Baker talks in Ludwigshafen 15.9.1990, printed in *DESE* doc. 423 pp. 1542–4. Baker *The Politics* pp. 298–9; Teltschik *329 Tage* p. 366

68 Baker *The Politics* pp. 287–91. See for example Peter Grier 'US Begins Mission of Pressing Allies to Help Pay for Gulf Costs' *CMS* 6.9.1990 Cf. Brands *Making the Unipolar Moment* p. 304; *idem, From Berlin to Baghdad* pp. 52–3

69 On the USSR and China voting in the UN, see also Elaine Sciolino with Eric Pace 'Putting Teeth in an Embargo: How US Convinced the UN' *NYT* 30.8.1990

70 US Telcon of Baker to Shevardnadze call at 1.29 p.m. 7.8.1990, printed in *TLSS* doc. 105 pp. 723–4

71 'Where we'll be a year or two from now, I wouldn't want to speculate' Defense Secretary Dick Cheney told Congress on Friday, 17.8.1990. Quoted in Wines 'Largest Force Since Vietnam Committed in 15-Day Flurry'

72 *TLSS* doc. 105 p. 724

73 Chernyaev *My Six Years* p. 334. See also Grachev *Gorbachev's Gamble* pp. 192–3; Taubman *Gorbachev* p. 567

74 Baker *The Politics* p. 313

75 E. M. Primakov *Minnoe Pole Politiki* Molodaia Gvardiia 2007 pp. 61–86. Cf. Baker *The Politics* pp. 396–402; Palazchenko *My Years with Gorbachev and Shevardnadze* pp. 211–12. See also Service *The End* p. 464

76 Bush & Scowcroft *A World Transformed* pp. 352–3. Cf. Thatcher *The Downing Street Years* pp. 823–4

77 Baker *The Politics* pp. 396–402; Sciolino 'Putting Teeth in an Embargo' pp. 1, 15. GHWBPL NSC Richard Haass Files (OA/ID CF01937 to CF01478) Presidential Remarks to Congressional Leaders (White House) 29.8.1990

78 Letter from Bush to Gorbachev 29.8.1990, printed in *TLSS* doc. 107 pp. 727–8

79 Memorandum from Scowcroft for the President: Your Meeting with Gorbachev in Helsinki (*circa* early September 1990), printed in *TLSS* doc. 108 pp. 729–31

80 Ibid; Blanton & Savranskaya (eds) *The Last Superpower Summits* p. 713

81 Bill Keller 'Bush and Gorbachev, in Helsinki, Face the Gulf Crisis' *NYT* 9.9.1990

82 Bush's Remarks at the Arrival Ceremony in Helsinki Finland 8.9.1990 APP

83 Baker *The Policy* p. 291. See Soviet Memcon of Bush–Gorbachev Private Meeting (morning session) in Helsinki 9.9.1990, printed in *TLSS* doc. 109 pp. 732–47. For the US record, see GHWBPL Scowcroft Collection Separate USSR Notes Files – Gorbachev Files: Gorbachev (Dorbynin) sensitive 7–12/1990 (OA/ID 91128-003) Memcon of Bush–Gorbachev talks 9.9.1990 10.00 a.m.–12.45 p.m. Helsinki Finland pp. 1–11

84 Diary Entry 7.9.1990, printed in Bush & Scowcroft *A World Transformed* p. 363 an also p. 364; GHWBPL Memcon of Bush–Gorbachev talks (morning session) 9.9.1990 pp. 1–2. Cf. *TLSS* doc. 109 pp. 732–3

85 *TLSS* doc. 109 pp. 732–4; GHWBPL Memcon of Bush–Gorbachev talks (morning session) 9.9.1990 pp. 1–2; Bush & Scowcroft *A World Transformed* p. 364

86 Bush & Scowcroft *A World Transformed* p. 264. Cf. Carl P. Leubsdorf 'Bush, Gorbachev – such good friends; Past meetings stand leaders in good stead' *The Baltimore Sun* 10.9.1990

87 *TLSS* doc. 109 pp. 735–6. Cf. GHWBPL Memcon of Bush–Gorbachev talks (morning session) 9.9.1990 pp. 2–3

88 *TLSS* doc. 109 pp. 736–8. GHWBPL Memcon of Bush–Gorbachev talks (morning session) 9.9.1990 pp. 3–5

89 *TLSS* doc. 109 pp. 739, 741. GHWBPL Memcon of Bush–Gorbachev talks (morning session) 9.9.1990 pp. 5–6.

90 *TLSS* doc. 109 p. 737. GHWBPL Memcon of Bush–Gorbachev talks (morning session) 9.9.1990 p. 4

91 *TLSS* doc. 109 p. 741. GHWBPL Memcon of Bush–Gorbachev talks (morning session) 9.9.1990 p. 6

92 *TLSS* doc. 109 p. 744. GHWBPL Memcon of Bush–Gorbachev talks (morning session) 9.9.1990 p. 8

93 *TLSS* doc. 109 pp. 744–5. There is no reference to the 1930s in the US minutes

94 Bush & Scowcroft *A World Transformed* p. 366

95 Baker *The Politics* p. 294, Bush & Scowcroft *A World Transformed* pp. 366–8. See also GHWBPL Memcon of Bush–Gorbachev talks (plenary meeting) 9.9.1990 Presidential Palace Helsinki pp. 1–3. For the Soviet minutes of the afternoon talks, see *TLSS* doc. 110 pp. 748–55; Soviet Union–United States Joint Statement on the Persian Gulf Crisis 9.9.1990 APP

96 Baker *The Politics* pp. 293–4

97 GHWBPL Memcon of Bush–Gorbachev talks (plenary meeting) 9.9.1990 Presidential Palace Helsinki pp. 4–5

98 Maureen Dowd 'Reporter's Notebook: The Two New Friends Come Smiling Through' *NYT* 10.9.1990; Andrew Rosenthal 'Bush, Reversing Us Policy, Won't Oppose a Soviet Role in Middle East Peace Talks' *NYT* 11.9.1990

99 'Joint News Conference of President Bush and Soviet President Mikhail Gorbachev in Helsinki, Finland' 9.9.1990 APP. See also Bill Keller 'Junior Partner No More, Gorbachev Raises

Role to Major Player in Crisis' *NYT* 11.9.1990. Cf. *idem* 'Bush and Gorbachev Say Iraqis Must Obey UN and Quit Kuwait' *NYT* 10.9.1990

100 Dowd 'The Two New Friends Come Smiling Through'

101 See Presidential Job Approval – F. Roosevelt (1941)–Trump: George Bush (24.1.989–11.1.1993) APP

102 R. W. Apple Jr 'Bush & Gorbachev Inc.' *NYT* 11.9.1990

103 GHWBPL Telcon of Bush to Fahd call 10.9.1990 Oval Office pp. 1–2

104 GHWBPL Telcon of Kohl to Bush call 11.9.1990 Oval Office p. 1

105 Bush's Address Before a Joint Session of the Congress on the Persian Gulf Crisis and the Federal Budget Deficit 11.9.1990 APP. For Wilson's Fourteen Points Speech (1918), see usa. usembassy.de/ etexts/democrac/51.htm. See also Erez Manela *The Wilsonian Moment: Self-Determination and the International Origins of Anticolonial Nationalism* Oxford UP 2007

106 'A Gulf Pep Rally' *NYT* 13.9.1990; R. W. Apple Jr 'Bush's Two Audiences' *NYT* 12.9.1990; Mortimer B. Zuckerman 'Are We Willing Act Alone?' *US News and World Report* 24.9.1990 p. 100; Bruce W. Nelan 'Call to Arms' *TIME* 24.9.1990. See also Mark J. Rozell *The Press and the Bush Presidency* Praeger 1996 p. 71

107 Bush & Scowcroft *A World Transformed* pp. 370–1

108 Bush's Address Before a Joint Session of the Congress on the Persian Gulf Crisis and the Federal Budget Deficit 11.9.1990 APP

109 Diary Entry 4.5.1990, printed in Bush *All the Best* p. 470

110 Ann McDaniel & Evan Thomas 'The First Test of Our Mettle' *Newsweek* 24.9.1990 p. 27; Paul A. Gigot 'Two-Faced Bush – Tough Abroad, Squishy at Home' *WSJ* 14.9.1990

111 Diary Entries 25.9.1990 and 6.10.1990, printed in Bush *All the Best* pp. 480–1. See also Andrew Rosenthal 'Pivotal Moment for Bush' *NYT* 3.10.1990; Michael Oreskes 'Budget Boomerang' *NYT* 6.10.1990; David E. Rosenbaum 'Bush Rejects Stopgap Bill after Budget Pact Defeat; Federal Shutdown Begins, Congress is Pushed' *NYT* 6.10.1990; 'Countdown to Crisis: Reaching a 1991 Budget Agreement' *NYT* 9.10.1990

112 Bush *All the Best* pp. 482–3

113 David E. Rosenbaum 'Leaders Reach a Tax Deal and Predict Its Approval; Bush Awaits Final Details' *NYT* 25.10.1990; Susan F. Rasky 'Aides Say Bush Faced Choice: A Deal on Taxes, or a Fiasco' *NYT* 25.10.1990; David E. Rosenbaum 'Budget Passed By Congress, Ending a 3-Month Struggle Bush Says He's Pleased' *NYT* 28.10.1990

114 See Rosenbaum 'Leaders Reach a Tax Deal'; R. W. Apple Jr 'Much Ventured, for Little' *NYT* 7.11.1990. See also Presidential Job Approval – F. Roosevelt (1941)–Trump, George Bush (24.1.989– 11.1.1993) APP. On the budget saga see also, Barbara Sinclair 'The Offered Hand and the Veto Fist: George Bush, Congress and Domestic Policymaking' in Nelson & Perry *41* pp. 143–66 esp. pp. 160–5

115 Michael R. Gordon 'Bush Sends New Units to Gulf to Provide "Offensive Option"; US Force Could Reach 380,000' *NYT* 9.11.1990; *idem* 'US Says its Troops Won't Be Rotated Until Crisis is Over' *NYT* 10.11.1990. See also Powell *My American Journey* pp. 474–6; Baker *The Politics* p. 303

116 Diary Entry 22.9.1990, printed in Bush

& Scowcroft *A World Transformed* p. 374. Cf. On Iraqi atrocities an eighty-two-page Amnesty International Report – which Bush had widely circulated – issued in December 1990 entitled: 'Iraq/Occupied Kuwait – Human Rights Violations Since 2 August (AI Index: MDE 14/16/90)'; Bush & Scowcroft *A World Transformed* p. 427

117 Bush & Scowcroft *A World Transformed* pp. 374–5, 385

118 Ibid. p. 376. See also Nora Boustany 'Mitterrand, Soviet Envoy to the Gulf' *WP* 4.10.1990

119 Bush & Scowcroft *A World Transformed* p. 383; GHWBPL Memcon of Bush–Shevardnadze talks 1.10.1990 Waldorf Astoria Hotel New York p. 2

120 See Boustany 'Mitterrand, Soviet Envoy to the Gulf'. Cf. Blanton and Savranskaya (eds) *The Last Superpower Summits* pp. 717–18; Service *The End* pp. 70–1; Baker *The Politics* pp. 397–400. Cf. Primakov *Missions à Bagdad*, pp. 45–55

121 Soviet Record of a Conversation between Gorbachev and Mitterrand at Rambouillet 29.10.1990 NSArchive DAWC. Diary Entry and personal minutes of Mitterrand–Gorbachev talks 29.10.1990, printed in Attali *Verbatim III: Deuxième partie, 1990–1991* pp. 781–91

122 Alan Riding 'Gulf Talk: Gorbachev and Mitterrand' *NYT* 29.10.1990; *idem*, 'Gorbachev, in France, Says His Envoy Found Signs of Shift by Iraq' *NYT* 30.10.1990. For another Primakov mission ahead of the Mitterrand–Gorbachev talks, cf. Paul Lewis 'Kremlin Signals Hope in Stand-off by Sending an Envoy to Baghdad' *NYT* 28.10.1990. See also Letter from Gorbachev to Bush 6.11.1990 and Letter

from Bush to Gorbachev 20.10.1990, both printed in *TLSS* docs 114 and 113 pp. 764–7 and pp. 762–3

123 Diary Entry 17.10.1990, printed in Bush & Scowcroft *A World Transformed* pp. 383 and see also pp. 384–5. Baker *The Politics* pp. 303–4. Cf. Thatcher *The Downing Street Years* pp. 823–4, 826

124 Baker *The Politics* p. 304

125 Thomas L. Friedman 'Bush and Baker Explicit in Threat to Use Force' *NYT* 30.10.1990; Baker's Address before the Los Angeles World Affairs Council *Dispatch* [Why America Is in the Gulf] vol.1 no.10 5.11.1990 US DoS

126 Thomas L. Friedman 'Baker Seen as a Balance to Bush on Crisis in Gulf' *NYT* 3.11.1990; Baker *The Politics* p. 303

127 Baker *The Politics* pp. 303–5

128 See Gordon 'Bush Sends New Units to Gulf to Provide "Offensive Option"'

129 Baker *The Politics* pp. 305–6. Friedman 'Baker Seen as a Balance to Bush on Crisis in Gulf'; Bush & Scowcroft *A World Transformed* pp. 392–3

130 GHWBPL NSC Richard Haass Files – Working Files Iraq November 1990 (OA/ID CF01584) Memorandum for the president: Gulf Trip 6.11.1990 MTF

131 GHWBPL NSC Richard Haass Files – Working Files Iraq November 1990 (OA/ID CF01584) Memorandum for the President: Cairo Meetings 6.11.1990

132 Baker *The Politics* pp. 305–8

133 Suettinger *Beyond Tiananmen* p. 112. See also Lena H. Sun 'Chinese Foreign Minister Will Visit Middle East; Beijing Using Gulf Crisis to End Isolation' *WP* 4.11.1990; Michael Pillsbury *China Debates the Future Security Environment* National Defense UP 2000 pp. xxxv–xxxvi

134 Baker *The Politics* p. 309; Suettinger *Beyond Tiananmen* p. 113; David Hoffman 'China Signals Assent to UN Vote on Force' *WP* 7.11.1990; Thomas L. Friedman 'Baker Gets Help From China on Gulf' *NYT* 7.11.1990

135 GHWBPL NSC, Richard Haass Files – Working Files Iraq November 1990 (OA/ID CF01584) Baker's Memorandum for the President: My Day in Moscow 8.11.1990 pp. 1–7 esp. pp. 3–5 MTF. Cf. Baker *The Politics* pp. 309–13; Thomas L. Friedman 'Moscow Refuses to Rule Out Force' *NYT* 11.11.1990

136 GHWBPL NSC Richard Haass Files – Working Files Iraq November 1990 (OA/ID CF01584) Baker's Memorandum for the president: London Meetings – top secret 10.11.1990 pp. 1–2 MTF

137 GHWBPL NSC Richard Haass Files – Working Files Iraq November 1990 (OA/ID CF01584) Baker's Memorandum for the president: Paris Meetings – top secret 10.11.1990 pp. 1–2 MTF

138 GHWBPL Memcon of Bush–Thatcher Talks 19.11.1990 Ambassador Curley's Residence Paris pp. 1–3 esp. p. 1; Bush & Scowcroft *A World Transformed* p. 407; Baker *The Politics* pp. 316–17; Soviet Record of the Main Content of Gorbachev–Bush talks Paris 19.11.1990, printed in *TLSS* doc. 116 pp. 777–8. No US record of this meeting has been released.

139 *TLSS* doc. 116 pp. 777–8

140 Baker *The Politics of Diplomacy* p. 316; Suettinger *Beyond Tiananmen* p. 113

141 *TLSS* doc. 116 p. 779

142 Brands *Making the Unipolar Moment* p. 307; Suettinger *Beyond Tiananmen* p. 113; Baker *The Politics* p. 588

143 GHWBPL Scowcroft Collection SSCNF File: China 1990 (sensitive) (OA/ID 91137–004) Letter from Bush to Deng 30.8.1990 p. 2. The letter was hand-delivered in an 'EYES ONLY' sealed envelope, with 'no other distribution made' and 'no copies retained by the President's Office'. In the same folder, see Note for file re Deng letter by Wilma 30.8.1990. Baker *The Politics* p. 588

144 Suettinger *Beyond Tiananmen* pp. 117–19. See also Clifford Krauss 'Democratic Leaders Divided on China Trade' *NYT* 9.10.1990

145 GHWBPL Scowcroft Collection SSCNF File: China 1990 (sensitive) (OA/ID 91137–004) Note from Bush to Scowcroft – SUBJECT CHINA (ramblings from the Oval Office) 13.9.1990 p. 1

146 Bush & Scowcroft *A World Transformed* pp. 414–15; Paul Lewis 'UN Gives Iraq Until Jan. 15 to Retreat or Face Force Hussein Says He Will Fight' *NYT* 30.11.1990. See also 'Gulf Crisis Grows into War with Iraq' *CQ Almanac 1990* pp. 717–56.

147 Lewis 'UN Gives Iraq Until Jan. 15 to Retreat'. For Baker's statement, 'Excerpts from US, Kuwaiti, Iraqi and Chinese Remarks on the Resolution' *NYT* 30.11.1990; 'Text of UN Resolution on Using Force in the Gulf' *NYT* 30.11.1990

148 Bush & Scowcroft *A World Transformed* pp. 414–15. For Qian Qichen's statement 'Excerpts from US, Kuwaiti, Iraqi and Chinese Remarks on the Resolution'; Suettinger *Beyond Tiananmen* p. 114. Cf. Baker *The Politics* pp. 323–4

149 GHWBPL Memcon of Bush–Qian talks 30.11.1990 The Cabinet Room pp. 1–5. See also Robert Pear 'Bush, Meeting Foreign Minister, Lauds Beijing Stand Against Iraq' *NYT* 1.12.1990

150 Ambassador Lilley quote in Sparrow *The Strategist* p. 472. See also Suettinger *Beyond Tiananmen* pp. 114–15; Engel *When the World Seemed New* p. 411

151 Quotes in Brands *From Berlin to Baghdad* p. 56

152 GHWBPL NSC Richard Haass Files – Working Files Iraq 2/8/90–12/90 (OA/ID CF01478) Meeting of NSC: Minutes 6.8.1990 The Cabinet Room/White House pp. 1–6 esp. p. 4 MTF

153 Thomas L. Friedman 'Lighting the Fuse? Will UN Action Make a War Likely or Add to Diplomatic Maneuvering?' *NYT* 30.11.1990. See also Andrew Rosenthal 'Neutralising Iraq's Threat – For Bush, Toppling Hussein Isn't Required' *NYT* 29.8.1990. Brands *From Berlin to Baghdad* p. 57

154 GHWBPL NSC Richard Haass Files – Working Files Iraq January 1991 (OA/ID CF01584) Responding to Saddam's pre-January 15 Initiatives – Deputies Committee Top Secret Working Paper 31.12.1990

155 Baker *The Politics* p. 320

156 GHWBPL NSC Richard Haass Files – Working Files December 1990 (OA/ID CF01584) Memcon of One-on-One Meeting Bush–Shamir 11.12.1990 Oval Office pp. 1–2 MTF. Cf. GHWBPL Telcon of Bush–Shamir call 7.1.1991 The White House pp. 1–3. Haass *War of Necessity* p. 104

157 Service *The End* pp. 475–9, Shevardnadze quoted on p. 477. See also Shevardnadze *The Future* pp. 197–9, 201–4; Palazchenko *My Years* pp. 237–44

158 Bush & Scowcroft *A World Transformed* pp. 430–1; Blanton & Savranskaya (eds) *The Last Superpower Summits* p. 721

159 Cf. Engel *When the World Seemed New* pp. 420–1, 428–9. Service *The End* pp. 475–9; Bush & Scowcroft *A World Transformed* pp. 430–1

160 Bush's diary entry 28.11.1990, quoted in Meacham *Destiny and Power* p. 451

161 Maureen Dowd 'US Weighs Timing of Attack Against Iraq as Deadline Passes and Diplomacy Fails' *NYT* 16.1.1991. Cf. Col. Kenneth Ervin King 'Operation Desert Shield: Thunder Storms of Logistics: Did We Do Any Better During Post-Cold War Interventions?' US Army War College STRATEGY RESEARCH PROJECT (30 March 2007) pp. 6–7; Meacham *Destiny and Power* p. 450; Brands *Making the Unipolar Moment* p. 304; *idem, From Berlin to Baghdad* p. 53; Engel *When the World Seemed New* p. 417

162 Meacham *Destiny and Power* pp. 450–1; Haass *War of Necessity* pp. 96–7; Steven Casey *When Soldiers Fall: How Americans Have Confronted Combat Losses from World War I to Afghanistan* Oxford UP 2014 p. 207. Cf. Walter LaFeber 'The Rise and Fall of Colin Powell and the Powell Doctrine' *Political Science Quarterly* 124, 1 (Spring 2009) pp. 71–93

163 See David W. Moore 'Americans Believe US Participation in Gulf War a Decade Ago Worthwhile' *Gallup News Service* 26.2.2001

164 The President's News Conference 30.11.1990 11 a.m. Briefing Room White House APP; Baker *The Politics* pp. 346–55; Bob Woodward *The Commanders* Simon & Schuster 1991 pp. 335–6; Richard Morin 'Public Supports Move for Talks' *WP* 4.12.1990; Haass *War of Necessity* p. 103; Bush & Scowcroft *A World Transformed* pp. 419–21. See also Cheney *In My Time* p. 205

165 Gordon S. Black *USA Today* Poll 2.12.1990

166 Bush & Scowcroft *A World Transformed* p. 425

167 Casey *When Soldiers Fall* pp. 206–7. See also Benjamin Weiser 'Computer Simulations: Attempting to Predict the Price of Victory' *WP* 20.1.1991; Michael Oreskes 'A Debate Unfolds about Going to War against the Iraqis' *NYT* 12.11.1990; Richard Morin 'How Much War Will Americans Support?' *WP* 2.9.1990

168 Bush & Scowcroft *A World Transformed* pp. 417–18; Woodward *The Commanders* pp. 331–3

169 R. W. Apple Jr 'Washington Talk; Presidency on the Brink of a Make or Break Year' *NYT* 1.1.1991

170 *TIME* magazine cover stories on President Bush as 'Man of the Year 1990': George J. Church, 'Cover Stories: A Tale of Two Bushes' *TIME* 7.1.1991; Dan Goodgame 'In The Gulf: Bold Vision – What If We Do Nothing?' *TIME* 7.1.1991; Michael Duffy 'At Home: No Vision – A Case of Doing Nothing' *TIME* 7.1.1991

171 'Gulf Crisis Grows into War with Iraq' *CQ Almanac 1990* pp. 717–56. Cf. Haass *War of Necessity* pp. 110–13; Bush & Scowcroft *A World Transformed* pp. 438–41

172 Bush and Scowcroft *A World Transformed* pp. 440–2; 'Gulf Crisis Grows into War with Iraq' *CQ Almanac 1990*; Baker *The Politics* pp. 355–65

173 Michael Wines 'Bush Deplores Soviet Crackdown But Takes No Steps in Response' *NYT* 14.1.1991; Bill Keller 'Soviet Loyalists in Charge After Attack in Lithuania; 13 Dead – Curfew is Imposed' *NYT* 14.1.1991; 'Europeans issue Warning' *NYT* 14.1.1991;

GHWBPL Telcon of Bush–Gorbachev call 18.1.1991 Oval Office pp. 1–6 esp. p. 6; Bush & Scowcroft *A World Transformed* p. 444. Cf. GHWBPL Telcon of Bush–Gorbachev call 11.1.1991 Oval Office pp. 1–3 esp. p. 2; Service *The End* p. 483

174 'Gulf Crisis Grows into War with Iraq' *CQ Almanac 1990*; Bush & Scowcroft *A World Transformed* pp. 443–6

175 Bush's diary entry 4.1.1991, quoted in Meacham *Destiny and Power* p. 453. See also Bush & Scowcroft *A World Transformed* p. 446; Haass *War of Necessity* pp. 113–15. Note: Defense Secretary Cheney, though once a congressman himself, had never been keen on Bush going to Congress. He opposed it. Cheney *In My Time* pp. 205, 207–9; Haass *War of Necessity* pp. 109–10

176 GHWBPL NSD 54 – Responding to Iraqi Aggression in the Gulf 15.1.1991. For the president's notes on 'Themes for Pre H-Hour Calls to Foreign Leaders and Congressional Leadership 11am 16.1.1991' see GHWBPL NSC Richard Haass Files – Working Files Iraq January 1991 (OA/ID CF01584) MTF

177 Bush's Address to the Nation Announcing Allied Military Action in the Persian Gulf 16.1.1991 APP; Haass *War of Necessity* pp. 116–17

178 James Barron 'US and Allies Open Air War on Iraq; Bomb Baghdad and Kuwaiti Targets; "No Choice" But Force, Bush Declares – A Tense Wait Ends' *NYT* 17.1.1991; Philip Shenon 'Rumble in the Sky Ends a 5-Month Wait' *NYT* 17.1.1991

179 Michael R. Gordon 'Raids, on a Huge Scale, Seek to Destroy Iraqi Missiles' *NYT* 17.1.1991. For a CIA assessment on

Iraq's chemical and biological weapons, see GHWBPL NSC Richard Haass Files – Working Files Iraq January 1991 (OA/ID CF01584) Robert L. Foord to Director of CIA: Response to Questions Concerning Iraqi CBW (undated; response to 22.1.1991 questions) MTF

180 Thomas L. Friedman 'The US and Israel – Barrage of Iraqi Missiles on Israel Complicates US Strategy in Gulf' *NYT* 18.1.1991; Joel Brinkley 'Israel Says it Must Strike at Iraqis but Indicates Willingness to Wait' *NYT* 20.1.1991; Thomas L. Friedman 'Hard Times, Better Allies' *NYT* 21.1.1991

181 Bush told Mitterrand over the phone on 20 January 1991: 'Our people tell us our Air Force totally dominates the skies. The count is 11–0 when we have engaged them in the air'. GHWBPL Telcon between Bush and Mitterrand 20.1.1991 Camp David pp. 1–4 esp. p. 3

182 Philip Shenon 'Iraq Sets Oil Refineries Afire as Allies Step Up Air Attacks; Missile Pierces Tel Aviv Shield' *NYT* 23.1.1991; Brands *Making the Unipolar Moment* p. 310

183 Haass *War of Necessity* p. 117. R. W. Apple Jr 'Reporter's Notebook – Hueys and Scuds: Vietnam And Gulf Are Wars Apart' *NYT* 23.1.1991

184 Alan Riding 'French Defense Chief Quits, Opposing Allied War Goals' *NYT* 30.1.1991; see also Baker *The Politics* pp. 370–1

185 On Gorbachev's calls, see Service *The End* pp. 480; Baker *The Politics* p. 402. Cf. Entry 18.1.1991 *The Diary of Anatoly S. Chernyaev 1991* NSAEBB No. 345. On the German contribution to the war effort (financial and military), see GHWBPL Telcon of Bush's call to Kohl (11.50–11.57 a.m.) 28.1.1991 Oval Office

pp. 1–2; Ferdinand Protzman 'Kohl Says Gulf War May Bring Tax Rises' *NYT* 24.1.1991; Stephen Kinzer 'Genscher At Eye of Policy Debate' *NYT* 22.3.1991; John M. Goshko 'Germany to Complete Contribution Toward Gulf War Costs Thursday' *WP* 27.3.1991

186 Bush & Scowcroft *A World Transformed* pp. 460–1; Baker *The Politics* pp. 391–5. For the joint statement, see mfa.gov.il/MFA/ForeignPolicy/MFADocuments/Yearbook8/Pages/182%20Statement%20on%20the%20Gulf%20War%20and%20the%20Middle%20East.aspx

187 Bush wrote two letters to Gorbachev. GHWBPL NSC Richard Haass Files – Working Files, Iraq February 1991 (OA/ID CF01584) Bush's letter to Gorbachev 18.2.1991 MTF; and Bush's letter to Gorbachev (further reservations) 19.2.1991 MTF. In the same file, see also Bush's letter to coalition leaders (Gorbachev's negotiations with Saddam) 19.2.1991 MTF

188 GHWBPL Telcon of Bush–Gorbachev call 23.2.1991 Camp David pp. 1–4. See also GHWBPL Telcons of Bush–Gorbachev calls of 21.2.1991 and 22.2.1991

189 Chernyaev *My Six Years* pp. 331–2. Cf. Entry 25.2.1991 *The Diary of Anatoly S. Chernyaev 1991* NSAEBB No. 345

190 R. W. Apple Jr 'Allied Units Surge Through Kuwait; Troops Confront Elite Force in Iraq; Bush Spurns Hussein's Pullout Move, American and British Troops Gird For an Iraqi Last Stand' *NYT* 27.2.1991; *idem*, 'The Battleground: Death Stalks Desert Despite Ceasefire' *NYT* 2.3.1991

191 Bush & Scowcroft *A World Transformed* pp. 485–6; Meacham *Power and Destiny* p. 465

192 Bush's Address to the Nation on the Suspension of Allied Offensive Combat Operations in the Persian Gulf 27.2.1991 9.02 a.m. Oval Office APP

193 Diary Entry 26.2.1991, printed in Bush & Scowcroft *A World Transformed* p. 484; Inaugural Address, 20.1.1989 APP; Remarks to the American Legislative Exchange Council 1.3.1991 APP; and Radio Address to United States Armed Forces Stationed in the Persian Gulf Region 2.3.1991 APP. For a contemporary reflection on the Vietnam syndrome, see George C. Herring 'America and Vietnam: The Unending War' *Foreign Affairs* 70, 5 (Winter 1991/2) pp. 104–19

194 Bush & Scowcroft *A World Transformed* p. 487; Meacham *Power and Destiny* p. 466; Brands *Making the Unipolar Moment* p. 304

195 Jim Meyers 'George H. W. Bush Poll Numbers Swung Wildly During Presidency' *Newsmax* 12.8.2014. On the 4 March ABC Poll, see David S. Broder & Richard Morin 'Bush Popularity Surges With Gulf Victory' *WP* 6.3.1991; Robin Toner 'Political Memo; Bush's War Success Confers an Aura of Invincibility in '92' *NYT* 27.2.1991

196 Diary Entry 28.2.1991, printed in Bush & Scowcroft *A World Transformed* pp. 486–7

197 GHWBPL Memcon of Genscher–Bush talks 1.3.1991 Oval Office p. 1. See also Meacham *Destiny and Power* pp. 464–7; Palazchenko *My Years* pp. 268–9

198 Malcolm W. Browne 'Invention That Shaped the Gulf War: The Laser-Guided Bomb' *NYT* 6.2.1991; Suettinger *Beyond Tiananmen* p. 116. On the USSR supplying military equipment to Iraq, see also HIA-TSMP box 5 Stepanov-Mamaladze Diary 17.12.1990

199 'Gates Tells Canada US is No. 1' *Washington Times* 8.5.1991. GHWBPL NSC Nancy Bearg Dyke files (OA/ID CF01473) Gates – 'American Leadership in a New World Order' 7.5.1991

200 GHWBPL Telcon of Kohl to Bush call 7.3.1991 Oval Office p. 2

201 Ibid. pp. 2–3

202 GHWBPL Memcon of Bush–Baker talks with Shevardnadze 6.5.1991 Oval Office pp. 1–7 esp. pp. 1, 3–4

Chapter 7

1 Diary Entry 21.8.1990, printed in Bush & Scowcroft *A World Transformed* p. 531

2 GHWBPL Telcon of Gorbachev to Bush call 21.8.1991 Kennebunkport pp. 1–3; Bush & Scowcroft *A World Transformed* pp. 531–2

3 See Taubman *Gorbachev* pp. 600–10

4 Diary Entry 19.8.1991, printed in Bush & Scowcroft *A World Transformed* pp. 526–7

5 Taubman *Gorbachev* pp. 611–12

6 Entry of 'Three Days in Foros – August 21, 1991, Crimea, Dacha "Zarya"' *The Diary of Anatoly S. Chernyaev* 1991 NSAEBB No. 345

7 Taubman *Gorbachev* pp. 611–13

8 GHWBPL Telcon of Gorbachev–Bush call 21.8.1991 Kennebunkport p. 3

9 GHWBPL Telcon of Bush–Yeltsin call (8.30–9.05 a.m.) 21.8.1991 Kennebunkport pp. 1–4

10 GHWBPL Telcon of Bush–Yeltsin call 20.8.1991 Oval Office pp. 1–3

11 GHWBPL Telcon of Bush–Yeltsin call (8.30–9.05 a.m.) 21.8.1991 Kennebunkport pp. 1–4. Bush & Scowcroft *A World Transformed* pp. 528–30

12 Ibid. p. 531. Cf. the heavily redacted record of conversation, GHWBPL Telcon of Bush–Major call 21.8.1991 Kennebunkport

13 Brown *Seven Years* pp. 197–9; Reynolds *One World Divisible* p. 569

14 Andrei Shleifer & Robert W. Vishny 'Reversing the Soviet Economic Collapse' *Brookings Papers on Economic Activity* 2 (1991) pp. 340–60 esp. pp. 344–7. See also IMFA-AWP JSSE B3/F1 USSR: August 1990 Fact-Finding Staff Visit – Minutes of Real Sector Meeting R-4, 14.8.1990 Gosplan Moscow pp. 1–3; Minutes of Monetary Policy M1 14.8.1990 Gosbank Moscow pp. 1–4; and Minutes of Real Sector Meeting R-6 14.8.1990 & 15.8.1990 Goskomtsen Moscow pp. 1–4

15 NIE 11–18–89 November 1989 'The Soviet System in Crisis: Prospects for the Next Two Years' in Benjamin B. Fischer (ed.) *At Cold War's End: US Intelligence on the Soviet Union and Eastern Europe, 1989–1991* Ross & Perry 2001 p. 53

16 On the 'budget deficit' in 1985 and 1989, see IMFA-AWP JSSE B3/F1 USSR: August 1990 Fact-Finding Staff Visit – Minutes of Fiscal Meeting F-1 14.8.1990 Ministry of Finance Moscow p. 3; and Minutes of Real Sector Meeting R-22 20.8.1990 Council of Ministers Moscow pp. 1–3. For 1990 & 1991 figures and predictions, see IMFA-AWP JSSE B1/F6 IMF-IBRD-OECD-EBRD-USSR-Meeting with EC Delegation 8.12.1990 IMF Paris Office 1 p. 2. See also NIE 11–18–89 'The Soviet System in Crisis' pp. 50–81 esp. pp. 68–70; Shleifer & Vishny 'Reversing the Soviet Economic Collapse' p. 342. Cf. 'Soviets Foresee Budget Deficit of $162 Billion' *NYT*/AP 22.1.1991. On Gorbachev's notions of 'private property' and 'socialist property', see Michael Dobbs 'Gorbachev Rebukes Estonia on Soviet "Crisis"' *WP* 28.11.1988. See also Brown *Seven Years* p. 203

17 Mikhail Gorbachev *Sobranie Sochinenii* vol. 14 (April–June 1989) Ves' Mir 2009 p. 295

18 See IMFA-AWP JSSE B3/F3 Teresa Ter-Minassian to IMF Managing Director: Missions to Moscow – Back-to-office Report 8.9.1990 pp. 2–3; Memo: Soviet Union – Real Sector Prospects for 1990 8.9.1990 p. 4; and Memo: Soviet Union – Meeting with Academician Aganbegyan 7.9.1990 pp. 1–2 (on the 'stabilisation: plan and the 'Shatalin programme'). See also IMFA-AWP JSSE B3/F5 IMF – USSR: Staff Visit (3–7.12.1990) Minutes of Meeting No. 2 3.12.1990 Ministry of Finance Moscow pp. 1–2. Shleifer & Vishny 'Reversing the Soviet Economic Collapse' p. 343; NIE 11–18–1990 November 1990 'The Deepening Crisis in the USSR: Prospects for the Next Year, November 1990' in Fischer *At Cold War's End* pp. 101–3

19 Brown *Seven Years* p. 202; Gorbachev *Perestroika* p. 63; Ha-Joon Chang & Peter Nolan (eds) *The Transformation of the Communist Economies: Against the Mainstream* Macmillan 1995 p. 34

20 Gorbachev *Memoirs* p. 278

21 Ibid. pp. 280–2; Transcript of CC CPSU Politburo Session 'Outcome of the USSR People's Deputies Elections' 28.3.1989, printed in *MoH:1989* doc. 5 pp. 420–31; Taubman *Gorbachev* pp. 428–34. Gorbachev *Sobranie Sochinenii* vol. 13 (December 1988–March 1989) Ves' Mir 2009 pp. 426–8, 431, 444–5

22 Quote from Taubman *Gorbachev* p. 428; cf. ch. 6 'The Lost Year' in Chernyaev *My Six Years* and esp. pp. 201–3

23 Gorbachev *Sobranie Sochinenii* vol. 18 (December 1989–March 1990) Ves' Mir 2011 p. 63. Cf. Entry 2.1.1990 *The Diary*

of Anatoly S. Chernyaev 1990 NSAEBB No. 317

24 David Remnick 'Protestors Throng Moscow Streets to Demand Democracy' *WP* 5.2.1990; *idem, Lenin's Tomb* p. 302; Boris Yeltsin *Zapiski Prezidenta* Rosspen 2008 p. 39; Gorbachev *Sobranie Sochinenii* vol. 14 pp. 116–17; Mark Kramer 'The Collapse' (Part 3) pp. 3–96 esp. p. 10. Note: the complete transcripts and associated documents from this plenum are available in 'Plenum Tsentral'nogo Komiteta Kommunisticheskoi Partii Sovetskogo Soyuza: Materialy Plenuma Tsentral'nogo Komiteta KPSS, 5–7 fevralya 1990 goda', 5–7.2.1990 (Top Secret), in Rossiiskii Gosudarstvennyi Arkhiv Noveishei Istorii (RGANI) f. 2 op. 5 d. 395–451 militera.lib.ru/docs /o/ pdf/plenum1990–02.pdf

25 Richard Sakwa *Russian Politics and Society* Routledge 2002 p. 13. See also Brenda Horrigan & Theodore Karasik 'The Rise of Presidential Power under Gorbachev' in Eugene Huskey (ed.) *Executive Power and Soviet Politics: The Rise and Decline of the Soviet State* Sharpe 1992 ch. 4

26 The term was popularised for the USA by Arthur M. Schlesinger Jr *The Imperial Presidency* Houghton Mifflin 1973. See also Richard Aldous *Schlesinger: The Imperial Historian* W. W. Norton 2017 pp. 353–7; Paul Quinn-Judge 'Imperial Presidency for Gorbachev: Soviet Vote Radically Reforms Power Structure' *CSM* 2.12.1988

27 See also William Zimmerman, *Ruling Russia: Authoritarianism from the Revolution to Putin* Princeton UP 2014 pp. 174–8 esp. pp. 176, 178

28 Reynolds *One World Divisible* pp. 549–50. Cf. Brown *Seven Years* pp. 142–5, 203–8.

Cf. Richard Sakwa *Soviet Politics in Perspective* Routledge 1998 pp. 154–5

29 See Lars Fredrik Stöcker 'Paths of economic "Westernisation" in the late Soviet Union: Estonian market pioneers and their Nordic partners' *Ajalooline Ajakiri* 157/158, 3/4 (2016) [Balti riikide iseseisvus 20. Sajandil] pp. 447–76. See also Michael Parks 'Parliament in Estonia Declares "Sovereignty"' *LAT* 17.11.1988. Cf. EST Rahvusarhiiv 1-43-153 IME Probleemn[otilde]ukogu - märts 1989; and 1-44-90 Arvamusi poliitilise situatsiooni kujunemise kohta peala EKP KK xiv pleenumit 4.5.1989

30 See Gorbachev *Sobranie Sochinenii* vol. 14 pp. 151, 157, 194–5. Cf. HIA Russian Archives Collection – Fond 89 Decision of the Politburo of the CPSU CC – On anti-democratic acts and human-rights violations in the Lithuanian SSR 16.11.1990; Annex to the Decree of the Secretariat of the Central Committee of the CPSU 7.2. 1991; 'A Statement' by the Council of Secretaries of the CPSU CC of Lithuania, Latvia and Estonia to members of the Politburo in Moscow 19.1.1991 Riga. See also Dobbs 'Gorbachev Rebukes Estonia on Soviet "Crisis"' *WP* 28.11.1988. Ben Fowkes *The Disintegration of the Soviet Union: A Study in the Rise and Triumph of Nationalism* Macmillan 1996 ch. 6. For the Baltic results in the 1989 Congress of People's Deputies elections, see Roger East & Jolyon Pontin *Revolution and Change in Central and Eastern Europe* Bloomsbury 2016 p. 313

31 Entry 2.5.1989, published in Anatoly Chernyaev *1991 God: Dnevnik pomoshchnika prezidenta SSSR* Terra 1997 pp. 9–10 and an excerpt in English at DAWC. For a different translation, see Entry 2.5.1989 *The Diary of Anatoly*

S. Chernyaev 1989 NSAEBB No. 275. 'Overall I am anxious and troubled. I feel a sense of crisis of the Gorbachev period ... The invocations of "socialist values" and "the ideals of October" ... as soon as he starts reciting them they sound ironic in knowing ears – there is no substance behind them.'

32 CPSU Politburo Discussion of the Memorandum of Six Politburo members on the Situation in the Baltic Republics 11.5.1989 AGF f. 4 op. 1 DAWC. See also Gorbachev *Sobranie Sochinenii* vol. 14 pp. 194–5

33 Ibid.

34 'Declaration of the Rights of the Baltic Nations' Tallinn 14.5.1989 letton.ch/lvx_tall1.htm. See also Mall Laur & Riina Löhmus 'The May 1989 Baltic Assembly' *Nationalities Papers – Journal of Nationalism and Ethnicity* 16, 2 (1988) pp. 242–58

35 Demands for greater autonomy from Georgia had also grown louder among Abkhazians and South Ossetians. As Serhii Plokhy pointed out almost three decades later: 'the frozen or semi-frozen conflicts in Transnistria, Abkhazia, South Ossetia, Nagorno-Karabakh, and the semi-independent state of Chechnya' as well as the 'ongoing war in Eastern Ukraine' serve as a reminder that the process of Soviet disintegration is still incomplete. Plokhy 'The Soviet Union is still Collapsing' *Foreign Policy* 22.12.2016

36 Jack Matlock Jr *Autopsy on an Empire: The American Ambassador's Account of the Collapse of the Soviet Union* Random House 1997 pp. 238; Service *The End* pp. 370–1. See also Concept protocol of Georgian SSR Defence Council 8.4.1989 – 'Antisowjetische Demonstrationen in Tiflis: Schickte Gorbacev die Sondertruppen nach Georgien?'; and Concept protocol of Georgian SSR Defence Council 8.4.1989 – 'Der Gewalteinsatz von Tiflis wird vor Ort entschieden', both printed in Karner et al. (eds) *Der Kreml und die Wende 1989* docs 46–7 pp. 320–9

37 Diary Entry of T. Stepanov-Mamaladze 10.4.1989 'Schock in der sowjetischen Führung: In Tiflis wird auf Demonstranten geschossen; Krisensitzung am Tag danach: Wer trägt die Verantwortung?', printed in Karner et al. (eds) *Der Kreml und die Wende 1989* doc. 48 pp. 329–32

38 'Findings of the Commission of the USSR Congress of People's Deputies to Investigate the Events which Occurred in the City of Tbilisi on 9.4.1989' May 1989 TsKhSD f. 89 Collection of documents (Xerox copy) published in *Istoricheskii Arkhiv* 3 (1993) pp. 102–20 DAWC

39 Entry 16.4.1989 *The Diary of Anatoly S. Chernyaev 1989* NSAEBB No. 275

40 Gorbachev *Sobranie Sochinenii* vol. 14 pp. 116–17, 97–8. Cf. CPSU Politburo Discussion on the Report of Eduard Shevardnadze Regarding the Use of Violence in Tbilisi 20.4.1989 AGF f. 2 op. 3 Notes of A.S. Chernyaev DAWC

41 Mark Kramer & Vit Smetana (eds) *Imposing, Maintaining, and Tearing Open the Iron Curtain: The Cold War and East-Central Europe, 1945–1989* Lexington Books 2014 pp. 466–7; Service *The End* p. 371. Politburo Meeting 14.7.1989, printed in *V Politbyuro TsK KPSS* pp. 510–18

42 From the Plenum of the Central Committee of the CPSU on national policy 19–20.9.1989, printed in *V Politbyuro TsK KPSS* pp. 525–33. See also Service *The End* p. 458

43 Session of the CC CPSU Politburo 9.11.1989 AGF f. 2 op. 2 NSAEBB No. 293; Diary Entry by T. Stepanov-Mamaladze 18.11.1990 'Wir haben den deutschen Nationalismus unterschätzt' printed in Karner et al. (eds) *Der Kreml und die Wende 1989* doc. 84 pp. 514–15; GHWBPL Memcon of Bush–Gorbachev talks (second restricted bilateral meeting) 1989 on the *Maxim Gorky* Malta 3.12.1989 p. 1

44 Cf. Astrid S. Tuminez 'The Soviet Union's "Small" Dictators' *CSM* 3.5.1991

45 Scowcroft quoted in Michael R. Beschloss & Strobe Talbott *At the Highest Levels: The Inside Story of the End of the Cold War* Little Brown 1994 p. 201

46 Reynolds *One World Divisible* p. 571; Taubman *Gorbachev* pp. 500–1. See also Stephen Lovell *Destination in Doubt: Russia since 1989* Zed Books 2006 pp. 22–3

47 Ibid. On nationalism and Russia, cf. Stephen Lovell *Shadow of War: Russia and the USSR, 1941 to the Present* Wiley-Blackwell 2010 ch. 7 esp. pp. 221–3

48 See Kevin O'Connor *Intellectuals and Apparatchiks: Russian Nationalism and the Gorbachev Revolution* Lexington Books 2008 pp. 186–91

49 Chernyaev *My Six Years* pp. 275–6; Entry 24.6.1990 *The Diary of Anatoly S. Chernyaev 1990* NSAEBB No. 317. See also 'O vneshnei politike' *Pravda* (Moscow) 26.6.1990 p. 3

50 Taubman *Gorbachev* p. 509. See also Yitzhak M. Brudny 'The Dynamics of "Democratic" Russia, 1990–1993' *Post-Soviet Affairs* 9, 2 (1993) pp. 141–70

51 Timothy J. Colton *Yeltsin: A Life* Basic Books 2008 pp. 129–32; Marc Zlotnik 'Yeltsin and Gorbachev: The Politics of Confrontation' *JCWS* 5, 1 (Winter 2003) pp. 128–64, 130

52 Zlotnik 'Yeltsin and Gorbachev' pp. 131–8; John Dunlop 'One of a Kind: The Gorbachev-to-Yeltsin Transition' in Uri Ra'naan *Flawed Succession: Russia's Power Transfer Crises* Lexington Books 2006 pp. 103ff. Service *The End* p. 322. See also 'Excerpts from TASS Account of Gorbachev Talk on Yeltsin' *NYT* 13.11.1987; Francis X. Clines 'Moscow Talk: Leader's Fall from Heights' *NYT* 13.11.1987

53 See Boris Yeltsin *Against the Grain: An Autobiography* Summit Book 1990 pp. 199–200

54 Andrei S. Grachev *Final Days: The Inside Story of the Collapse of the Soviet Union* Westview Press 1995 p. 72; Zlotnik 'Yeltsin and Gorbachev' p. 138. Cf. Yeltsin *The Struggle for Russia* p. 16; *idem Zapiski Prezidenta* p. 32

55 David Remnick 'Yeltsin Wins Landslide Victory in Moscow' *WP* 28.3.1989; Michael Dobbs 'Yeltsin Wins Presidency of Russia' *WP* 30.5.1990. Taubman *Gorbachev* pp. 432–3, 513–16

56 Leon Aron 'Yeltsin Russia's Rogue Populist' *WP* 3.6.1990

57 Georgy Shakhnazarov's notes of the Politburo meeting of 20 April 1990, printed in his *S vozhdiami i bez nikh* Vagrius 2001 p. 383

58 Shakhnazarov quoted in Taubman *Gorbachev* pp. 514–15

59 Gorbachev *Sobranie Sochinenii* vol. 20 [May–June 1990] Ves' Mir 2011 pp. 166–7. Matlock *Autopsy* pp. 367–8

60 Bessmertnykh quoted in David Pryce-Jones

61 Service *The End* p. 435

62 Colton *Yeltsin* p. 184; Michael Dobbs 'Yeltsin Quits Communist Party' *WP* 13.7.1990; Yeltsin *Zapiski Prezidenta* p. 50

63 On the situation of the Soviet economy and Deutsche Bank estimates in July/

August 1990, see IMFA-AWP JSSE B2/
F42 Memo: Whittome's meeting with
Dr Storf (Deutsche Bank) 7.8.1990 pp.
1–3

64 Gorbachev *Sobranie Sochinenii* vol. 20
p. 62. This quote is from Gorbachev's
concluding remarks during a joint
meeting of the Presidential Council and
the Federation Council on 22 May
1990.

65 IMFA-AWP JSSE B3/F1 USSR: August
1990 Fact-Finding Staff Visit – Minutes
of Real Sector Meeting R-4 14.8.1990
Gosplan Moscow pp. 3–4. Brian G.
Martin *The Soviet Union at the
Crossroads: Gorbachev's Reform
Program* [Foreign Affairs Research
Group, Parliamentary Research Service,
Australian Parliament] 7.8.1990 pp. 6–7.
Cf. Taubman *Gorbachev* pp. 521–2

66 Taubman *Gorbachev* pp. 450–1

67 Bobo Lo *Soviet Labour Ideology and the
Collapse of the State* Macmillan 2000
p. 142

68 Petrakov *Russkaya ruletka* pp. 133–9

69 On the 'Shatalin Plan', see IMFA-AWP
JSSE B3/F3 Memo: Soviet Union –
Meeting with Academician Aganbegyan
7.9.1990 pp. 1–3. Taubman *Gorbachev*
pp. 521–4; Remnick *Lenin's Tomb* p. 359

70 Chernyaev *My Six Years* pp. 284–5.
IMFA-AWP JSSE B3/F1 IMF – USSR:
August 1990 Fact-Finding Staff Visit,
Minutes of Meeting F-21 21.8.1990
Ministry of Finances of the RSFSR pp.
1–2

71 Taubman *Gorbachev* pp. 524–6;
Chernyaev *My Six Years* p. 286. See also
Michael McFaul *Russia's Unfinished
Revolution: Political Change from
Gorbachev to Putin* Cornell UP 2001
pp. 98–100

72 For Shatalin's 500 Days Plan, as printed
in *Izvestiya* on 4.9.1990 and subse-

quently in English in *Current Digest of
the Soviet Press*, XLII, 35 (31.10.1990)
pp. 4–7. See also G. Yavlinsky et al. *500
Days: Transition to the Market* St
Martin's Press 1991

73 Michael Dobbs 'A Plan for a Two-Year
Revolution' *WP* 14.9.1990. See also
David Remnick 'Gorbachev Shits on
Economy' *WP* 13.9.1990

74 On the 'Shatalin Plan', see IMFA-AWP
JSSE B3/F3 Ter-Minassian to the IMF
Managing Director: Missions to
Moscow – Back-to-office Report
8.9.1990 pp. 3–6. Michael Dobbs
'Gorbachev's Middle Way' *WP*
20.9.1990. See also Service *The End* p.
469

75 'Flying Blind in the Kremlin' *NYT*
30.9.1990.

76 Taubman *Gorbachev* pp. 526–30; Dobbs
'A Plan for a Two-Year Revolution'. See
also Bill Keller 'Gorbachev's Economic
Plan Approved' *NYT* 20.10.1990 and
'Excerpts from Gorbachev's Speech on
His Plan for a Market Economy' *NYT*
20.10.1990

77 Taubman *Gorbachev* pp. 530–1

78 Ibid. pp. 531–3

79 Bill Keller 'Conceding a Crisis,
Gorbachev Vows to Shift Leaders' *NYT*
17.11.1990; *idem* 'Gaining Some Vital
Time: Gorbachev Takes Charge to Win
Respite from Talk of Coup and
Investor's Fears' *NYT* 18.11.1990

80 Brown *Seven Years* p. 255; Taubman
Gorbachev p. 533

81 On the '8 points' speech, see
IMFA-AWP JSSE B3/F5 IMF – USSR:
Staff Visit 3.-7.12.1990 Minutes of
Meeting No. 1 3.12.1990 Gosplan
Moscow p. 3. For the Constitution of
the USSR, as amended in December
1990, see David Lane *Soviet Society
Under Perestroika* Taylor & Francis

2002 pp. 393–432 (appendix). Bill Keller 'Soviets Adopt Emergency Plan to Center Power in Gorbachev and Leaders of the Republics' *NYT* 18.11.1990

82 Keller 'Gaining Some Vital Time'; Francis X. Clines 'Yeltsin Rejects Gorbachev's Reorganisation Plan' *NYT* 18.11.1990

83 Keller 'Gaining Some Vital Time'; *idem* 'Soviets Adopt Emergency Plan'; Clines 'Yeltsin Rejects Gorbachev's Reorganisation Plan'

84 Keller 'Gaining Some Vital Time'; Taubman *Gorbachev* p. 534

85 Entry 2.1.1990 *The Diary of Anatoly S. Chernyaev 1990* NSAEBB No. 317

86 Keller 'Gaining Some Vital Time'

87 R. W. Apple Jr '34 Leaders Adopt Pact Proclaiming a United Europe' *NYT* 22.11.1990

88 Ibid.; and IMFA-AWP JSSE B1/F6 IMF-IBRD-OECD-EBRD – USSR – Meeting with EC Delegation 8.12.1990 IMF Paris Office 1 p. 3. The EC saw a 'strong and increasing political case for emergency assistance (the economic case … was not very evident)'. Moscow had asked for ECU 2 billion emergency aid and food imports for about ECU 3–4 billion. But aid on such a huge scale as the USSR requested was clearly not going to be granted

89 Kohl quoted in Ferdinand Protzman 'Kohl Pledges Help in Soviet Food Crisis' *NYT* 16.11.1990

90 Helmut Kohl *Erinnerungen 1990–1994* pp. 258–66; Protzman 'Kohl Pledges Help in Soviet Food Crisis' p. 17; Clyde Haberman 'Europe Supports $2.4 Billion Plan to Assist Kremlin' *NYT* 15.12.1990; David Remnick 'Kohl, Gorbachev Sign Historic Treaty of Non-aggression' *WP* 10.11.1990. On the

sharp decline in Soviet crude deliveries to the CMEA, see IMFA-AWP JSSE B3/F3 Vibe Christensen's Memo: USSR – CMEA Systems 10.9.1990 pp. 1–4; and B3/B5 IMF – USSR: Staff Visit 3–7.12.1990 Minutes of Meeting No. 4 4.12.1990 Goskomstat Moscow p. 1

91 Bierling *Wirtschaftshilfe* pp. 107–10 quote on p. 107. See also Remnick 'Kohl, Gorbachev Sign Historic Treaty of Non-aggression'

92 '800 Million Mark für Sowjetbürger gespendet' *SZ* 20.12.1990; 'Spendenrekord bei "Rußland-Hilfe"' *FAZ* 9.1.1991; 'Hilfsaktionen: Von Mensch zu Mensch – Winterhilfe für Gorbatschow: Eine Welle der Hilfsbereitschaft hat die Deutschen erfaßt' *Der Spiegel* 48/1990 26.11.1990; Stephen Kinzer 'Germans Mobilise to Feed Russians' *NYT* 29.11.1990.

93 See generally Service *The End* pp. 475–6

94 Francis X. Clines 'Getting Tougher, Gorbachev Shakes Up the Soviet Police' *NYT* 3.12.1990; see also Anthony Lewis 'Abroad At Home; Politics by Command' *NYT* 28.12.1990. Cf. Yeltsin *Zapiski Prezidenta* p. 33. IMFA-AWP JSSE B1/F2 Decree of the USSR Supreme Soviet on the Situation in the Country signed A. Lukyanov (Chair) 23.11.1990 pp. 1–4.

95 David Remnick 'Gorbachev Unveils His New Union Treaty' *WP* 24.11.1990

96 Brown *Seven Years* p. 295. Remnick 'Gorbachev Unveils His New Union Treaty'. Cf. Service *The End* p. 462; Entry 19.12.1990, Braithwaite *Moscow Diary 1988–1992*.

97 Taubman *Gorbachev* pp. 535–6; GHWBPL Scowcroft Special Separate USSR Notes Files – Gorbachev Files: Gorbachev (Dobrynin) sensitive – July–December 1990 (OA/ID91128–

005) Letter from Gorbachev to Bush 27.12.1990. See also Entry of 21.12.1990 *The Diary of Anatoly S. Chernyaev 1990* NSAEBB No. 317. See also entries 20.12.1990 and 21.12.1990 Braithwaite *Moscow Diary 1988–1992*

98 Remarks on the Waiver of the Jackson-Vanik Amendment and on Economic Assistance to the Soviet Union 12.12.1990 APP. Andrew Rosenthal 'Bush Lifting 15-Year-Old Ban, Approves Loans for Kremlin to Help Ease Food Shortages' *NYT* 13.12.1990; Haberman 'Europe Supports $2.4 Billion Plan to Assist Kremlin'

99 GHWBPL Scowcroft Special Separate USSR Notes Files – Gorbachev Files: Gorbachev (Dobrynin) sensitive – July–December 1990 (OA/ID91128–005) Handwritten notes on yellow pad by Scowcroft on Bessmertnykh's delivery of Gorbachev's letter (of 27.12.1990) to Bush 3pp. 27.12.1990

100 Chernyaev *My Six Years* p. 304

101 GHWBPL Scowcroft Special Separate USSR Notes Files – Gorbachev Files: Gorbachev (Dobrynin) sensitive – July–December 1990 (OA/ID91128–005) Handwritten notes on yellow pad by Scowcroft on Bessmertnykh's delivery of Gorbachev's letter (of 27.12.1990) to Bush 3pp. 27.12.1990

102 GHWBPL Telcon of Bush to Gorbachev call 1.1.1991 Camp David pp. 1–2

103 Entry 2.1.1991 *The Diary of Anatoly S. Chernyaev 1991* NSAEBB No. 345

104 Bush's New Year's Message to the People of the Soviet Union 1.1.1991 APP

105 Entry 2.1.1991 *The Diary of Anatoly S. Chernyaev 1991* NSAEBB No. 345

106 Matlock *Autopsy* pp. 434, 453

107 Michael Dobbs, 'Soviet Premier's Heart Attack Symbolises Changing of the Guard', *WP* 27.12 1990; Entry 2.1.1991 *The Diary of Anatoly S. Chernyaev 1991* NSAEBB No. 345. For Pavlov and his policies, see IMFA-AWP JSSE B1/F2 Memo: Ter-Minassian to Whittome re USSR – Mr Pavlov's Interview 13.2.1991 pp. 1–2; Matlock *Autopsy* pp. 463–5; 'Soviet Economic Change Isn't Reform', *CT* 19.2.1991; Quentin Peel 'Pavlov Accuses Western Banks of anti-Soviet Plot' *FT* 13.2.1991

108 Entry 7.1.1991 *The Diary of Anatoly S. Chernyaev 1991* NSAEBB No. 345

109 Entry 4.1.1991 *The Diary of Anatoly S. Chernyaev 1991* NSAEBB No. 345; Andrei S. Grachev *Gorbachev* Vagrius 2001 p. 339

110 GHWBPL Telcon of Gorbachev–Bush talks 11.1.1991 Oval Office pp. 1–3

111 HIA Estonian Subject Collection Box 1 BATUN (Baltic Appeal to the United Nations) – Baltic Chronology, January 1991. See also Matlock *Autopsy* pp. 449–50; Bush & Scowcroft *A World Transformed* p. 444; EST-VM USA I 1990–1991 'Text from the White House spokesman Marlin Fitzwater's statement on the use of Soviet troops to enforces the draft' 8.1.1991

112 Spohr *Germany and the Baltic Problem* pp. 32–3; EST-VM Islandi 1990–1992 Meetings with Baltic representatives (undated)

113 See Vytautas Landsbergis *Lithuania Independent Again* Univ. of Washington Press 2000 pp. 244–62; William E. Odom *The Collapse of the Soviet Military* Yale UP 1998 pp. 268–71; Anatol Lieven *The Baltic Revolution: Estonia, Latvia and Lithuania and the Path to Independence* Yale UP 1993 pp. 244–55. See also Andrejs Vaisbergs, Jonathon Steele and John Rettie 'Latvia's Interior Ministry Seized by Soviet Forces' *Guardian* 21.1.1991; Francis X.

Clines 'Latvia to Create Self-Defense Unit' *NYT* 22.1.1991

114 Ainius Lasas 'Bloody Sunday: What Did Gorbachev Know About the January 1991 Events in Vilnius and Riga?' *Journal of Baltic Studies* 38, 2 (2007) pp. 179–94. Cf. Matlock *Autopsy* pp. 454–63. Baker thought Gorbachev – in desperation – had made a 'calculated gamble' to tack in the direction of his conservative critics, see Baker *The Politics* pp. 380–1

115 Entry 13.1.1991 *The Diary of Anatoly S. Chernyaev 1991* NSAEBB No. 345

116 Entry 14.1.1991 *The Diary of Anatoly S. Chernyaev 1991* NSAEBB No. 345; Service *The End* p. 483

117 See Lasas 'Bloody Sunday' p. 190; Brian D. Taylor 'The Soviet Military and the Disintegration of the USSR' *JCWS* 5, 1 (January 2003) pp. 40–3; Anthony D'Agostino, *Gorbachev's Revolution* New York UP 1998 pp. 289–92; Edward W. Walker *Dissolution: Sovereignty and the Break-up of the Soviet Union* Rowman & Littlefield 2003 pp. 77; Kramer 'The Collapse' (Part 2) p. 40. Cf. Brown *The Gorbachev Factor* p. 280; Amy Knight 'The KGB, Perestroika, and the Collapse of the Soviet Union' *JCWS* 5, 1 (January 2003) p. 81. See also Una Bergmane 'French and US reactions facing the disintegration of the USSR: The case of the Baltic States (1989–91)' unpubl. PhD thesis Sciences Po 2016 pp. 242–3

118 Andreas Oplatka *Lennart Meri: Ein Leben für Estland – Dialog mit dem Präsidenten* Verl. Neue Zürcher Zeitung 1999 pp. 324–7; for the Estonian version of the 3 + 1 Pact, see EST-VM USA I 1990–1991 Treaty on Inter-State Relations between RSFSR and the Republic of Estonia 13.1.1991

119 Spohr *Germany and the Baltic Problem* p. 33. See also Entries of 13.1.1991 and 14.1.1991, Braithwaite *Moscow Diary 1988–1992*. See also Edijs Bošs 'The Baltic-American Alliance: The Evolving Post-Cold War Security Policies of Estonia, Latvia and Lithuania, 1988–1998' unpubl. PhD thesis Cambridge University July 2009 pp. 76–8

120 See HIA Russian Archives Project – Fond 1989 Pronouncement – 'About the events in the Republic of Lithuania' by the Presidium of the Kiev District Council of People's Deputies 15.1.1991; statement in connection with the events in Vilnius on 13.1.1991 by the Krasnogvardeysky District Council of People's Deputies 15.1.1991; Telegram to Gorbacchev – 'A Declaration' by Presidium of Sosnovsky City Council of People's Deputies of 15.1.1991, supported at a city rally on 16.1.1991. See also Elizabeth Shogren 'Soviets Angry, Fearful Over Lithuania Clash: Protests: Thousands rally against what they say is a threat of dictatorship. More disapproval pours in from across Europe' *LAT* 14.1.1991; Michael Dobbs *Down with Big Brother: The Fall of the Soviet Empire* Bloomsbury 1997 p. 345

121 Entries of 15.1.1991 and 17.1.1991 *The Diary of Anatoly S. Chernyaev 1991* NSAEBB No. 345

122 Taubman *Gorbachev* p. 576. Grachev *Final Days* pp. xvii–xviii

123 On Iceland's actions, see EST-VM Islandi 1990–1992 Meetings with Baltic Representatives; Iceland's PM's Letter to Gorbachev 13.11.1991; Althingi's Resolution Condemning the Soviet Forces' Acts of Violence in Lithuania 14.1.1991; Joint Statement by the FMs of Iceland and Estonia 21.1.1991. Entry

17.1.1991 *The Diary of Anatoly S. Chernyaev 1991* NSAEBB No. 345; Taubman *Gorbachev* p. 576. Beschloss & Talbott *At the Highest Levels* p. 307. See also Jón Baldvin Hannibalsson's memoir-essay entitled 'The Baltic Road to Freedom and the Fall of the Soviet Union' in Daniel S. Hamilton & Kristina Spohr (eds) *Exiting the Cold War, Entering a New World* Brookings Institution Press 2019

124 Serge Schmemann 'Gorbachev Denies Any Shift Away from Liberalisation' *NYT* 23.1.1991. See also Francis X. Clines 'Lithuania Feels Betrayed by "Bad King" Gorbachev' *NYT* 23.1.1991. Cf. HIA Russian Archives Project, Fond 89, 'An Appeal to the Supreme Soviet of the RSFSR, People's Deputies of Russia' by Baltic conservative Communist leaders 19.1.1991 Riga; 'Secret Annex' by the Department of National Policies of the CPSU CC – 'On the situation in the Baltic Republics' belonging to the 'Decree of the Secretariat of the CPSU CC' 7.2.1991. Matlock *Autopsy* pp. 454–63. See also Taubman *Gorbachev* pp. 576–7

125 Alan Riding 'Baltic Assaults Lead Europeans to Hold Off Aid' *NYT* 23.1.1991

126 Quote in: ICE-MFA Iceland 8.G.2–6 Icelandic embassy Bonn Bad-Goderberg to MFA Reykjavik 17.1.1991 – according to Gudni Johannesson's notes given to the author, and also in the *Diary of Michael Mertes* – official from chancellor's office – shown to the author

127 Ibid.; Spohr *Germany and the Baltic Problem* p. 34. EST-VM Prantsusmaa 1991.a–1993.a Kohli ja Mitterrandi kohtumine (Lille) 29.-30.3.1991

128 GHWBPL NSC Condoleezza Rice papers: SU/USSR Subject Files – Baltics (CFO0718–009) Memos from Rice to Scowcroft 15.1.1991 and 21.1.1991

129 David Binder 'Washington: Baltic Officials Meet with Baker and Congressional Panel on Crisis' *NYT* 23.1.1991. Bush had clearly been relatively lenient with Gorbachev over the Baltic crackdown in January. As Baker pithily put it in his memoirs: 'While we couldn't ignore Soviet behavior [in the Baltics], neither could we afford to lose the Soviet Union on the eve of the Gulf War. This was one of many instances where we juggled principle and interest, realism and idealism, in the pursuit of creative diplomacy.' Baker *The Politics* p. 381. See also Matlock *Autopsy* pp. 469–73. For Bush's letter see GHWBPL NSC Nicholas Burns Files – Subject Files Bush Gorbachev Correspondence [3] Rice to Scowcroft 'Letter to Gorbachev Regarding the Baltic Situation' 22.1.1991. See also Bošs 'The Baltic-American Alliance' pp. 78–80

130 Francis X. Clines 'Gorbachev Bans Moscow Rallies' *NYT* 26.3.1991

131 See the section 'Pavlov's Fog' in Matlock *Autopsy* pp. 473–5. Serge Schmemann 'Ruble Recall Deepens Soviet Hardships' *NYT* 24.1.1991

132 'Soviet Economic Change Isn't Reform' *CT* 19.2.1991. See also IMFA-AWP JSSE B1/F4 Memo: USSR – Meeting of Soviet Delegation with Whittome 7.2.1991 (confidential) pp. 1–3; Memo: Whittome to Managing Director 6.2.1991. Whittome also wondered what the Pavlovites meant in practice when they spoke of 'moving to a market economy in a state guided manner'.

133 Entry 19.1.1991 *The Diary of Anatoly S. Chernyaev 1991* NSAEBB No. 345; Francis X. Clines 'Yeltsin, Criticising

Failures, Insists That Gorbachev Quit' *NYT* 20.2.1991

134 Serge Schmemann 'Strike by Soviet Miners Spreads in Rising Challenge to Kremlin' *NYT* 28.3.1991

135 Clines 'Gorbachev Bans Moscow Rallies'

136 David Remnick *Lenin's Tomb* pp. 420–2; Serge Schmemann '100,000 Join Moscow Rally, Defying Ban By Gorbachev to Show Support For Rival' *NYT* 29.3.1991; Francis X. Clines 'Rally Takes Kremlin Terror and Turns It into Burlesque' *NYT* 29.3.1991

137 Matlock *Autopsy* p. 471; Mikhail Gorbachev *The August Coup: The Truth and the Lessons* HarperCollins 1991 p. 13; Entries 14.3.1991 and 20.3.1991 *The Diary of Anatoly S. Chernyaev 1991* NSAEBB No. 345

138 Celestine Bohlen 'Warsaw Pact Agrees to Dissolve Its Military Alliance by March 31' *NYT* 26.2.1991. The last Russian combat troops would not leave Poland until the end of October 1992, finally confirming Polish sovereignty and, as Poland's Deputy Defence Minister stated, 'closing an important chapter of history of central Europe'. See 'Last Russian Combat Troops Are Withdrawn from Poland' *Reuters* 29.10.1992

139 Matlock *Autopsy* pp. 492–4; Francis X. Clines 'Gorbachev Given a Partial Victory in Voting on Unity' *NYT* 19.3.1991

140 Francis X. Clines 'Soviets in Millions Deciding on Unity' *NYT* 18.3.1991

141 Zbigniew Brzezinski & Paige Sullivan (eds) *Russia and the Commonwealth of Independent States: Documents, Data, and Analysis* M. E. Sharpe 1997 ch. 1 esp. pp. 13–14. Gorbachev's own favoured variant was 1 + 9 rather than 9 + 1, indicating where for him the power was still supposed to lie – in the centre and with him, rather than the remaining republics. Cf. Brown *Seven Years* p. 305

142 Taubman *Gorbachev* pp. 580–1; Boris Yeltsin *The Struggle for Russia* Times Books 1994 p. 27

143 Taubman *Gorbachev* pp. 582–3; Grachev *Gorbachev* pp. 358–9; Entry 27.4.1991 *The Diary of Anatoly S. Chernyaev 1991* NSAEBB No. 345; David Remnick 'Gorbachev, Yeltsin Sign Crisis Pact' *WP* 25.4.991; Serge Schmemann 'Gorbachev Offers to Resign as Party's Chief, but Is Given a Vote of Support' *NYT* 26.4.1991

144 Michael Dobbs 'Gorbachev Escapes Again, But Economy's Grip May Be Tightening' *WP* 28.4.1991

145 Shakhnazarov quoted in Taubman *Gorbachev* p. 581

146 Colton *Yeltsin* pp. 193–4. See also Brown *Seven Years* p. 204

147 Beschloss & Talbott *At the Highest Levels* p. 400; Remnick *Lenin's Tomb* pp. 428–9; Taubman *Gorbachev* pp. 584–6; Service *The End* p. 487; Matlock *Autopsy* pp. 539–46. See also GHWBPL Telcon of Bush–Gorbachev talks 21.6.1991 The Oval Office. Cf. Serge Schmemann 'Gorbachev to Mix Plans on Economy of Left and Right' *NYT* 22.6.1991

148 Taubman *Gorbachev* p. 581; Remnick *Lenin's Tomb* pp. 439–40

149 Remnick *Lenin's Tomb* pp. 438–9; Entry 23.7.1991 *The Diary of Anatoly S. Chernyaev 1991* NSAEBB No. 345; Gorbachev *Memoirs* p. 628. On the new party programme, see Serge Schmemann 'Gorbachev Offers Party a Charter That Drops Icons' *NYT* 26.7.1991; *idem* 'Leadership of

Communists Approves Gorbachev Plan' *NYT* 27.7.1991

150 Baker *The Politics* p. 475

151 Beschloss & Talbott *At the Highest Levels* p. 349

152 Baker *The Politics* pp. 475–7; Bush & Scowcroft *A World Transformed* p. 500. Cf. Soviet Record of Conversation between Gorbachev and Baker in Moscow (excerpt) 15.3.1991, printed in *TLSS* doc. 122 pp. 814–19. See also JAB-SML B110/F2 JAB notes from 3/15/91 meeting with USSR Pres. Gorbachev in the Kremlin pp. 1–2

153 Baker *The Politics* p. 477; Beschloss & Talbott *At the Highest Levels* p. 346

154 Diary Entry 17.3.1991, printed in Bush & Scowcroft *A World Transformed* p. 500

155 Ibid. p. 501; Service *The End* pp. 485–6. On economic reforms, see Peter Reddaway & Dmitri Glinski *The Tragedy of Russia's Reforms: Market Bolshevism Against Democracy* US Institute of Peace Press 2001 pp. 178–80; Matlock *Autopsy* pp. 534–9, 547–51

156 On the IMF–World Bank–OECD–EBRD 'joint-report', see IMFA-AWP JSSE B3/F5 and B1/F2. See also IMFA Michel Camdessus Papers – Chronological Files Boxes 5 and 6 January–September 1990 and October–December 1990. Drafts of the joint-report itself have not been released by the IMF. JAB-SML B115/F7 Proposed Agenda for Meeting with the president 19.12.1990 1.30 p.m. pp. 1–3. GHWBPL Council of Economic Advisers – Michael Boskin Files: Interagency Meeting on IMF-led Study (CF01113–023) 9.8.1990. Walter S. Mossberg & Gerald F. Seib 'White House Intends to Aid Kremlin if it Follows US Advice on Reforms' *WSJE*

3.6.1991; Felicity Barringer 'Fiscal Epic by Moscow and Harvard Gets Skeptical Reviews' *NYT* 3.6.1991; Lloyd Grove 'The Professor's Soviet Solution' *WP* 26.8.1991. See also Bierling *Wirtschaftshilfe* p. 122

157 '30 Milliarden mehr' *Wirtschaftswoche* 17.5.1991; Beschloss & Talbott *At the Highest Levels* pp. 377–8. See also John T. Dahlburg 'Gorbachev Urges World to Help Save Perestroika' *LAT* 18.4.1991

158 JAB-SML B115/F8 Proposed Agenda for Meeting with the president 26.6.1991 p. 1

159 GHWBPL Telcon of Bush–Gorbachev call 11.5.1991 Camp David pp. 1–6 esp. pp. 2, 4. See also TNA UK PREM 19/3279 Memorandum by Wicks to PM – London Economic Summit: Soviet Union and Associating President Gorbachev 7.6.1991 pp. 1–3

160 GHWBPL Telcon of Bush–Gorbachev call 27.5.1991 Kennebunkport pp. 1–3

161 Thomas L. Friedman 'Us and Soviets Bridge Gap on Conventional Weapons and Plan for Summit Soon – Soviets' Real Issue: Aid' *NYT* 2.6.1991; Alan Riding 'Bush Hails Accord' *NYT* 2.6.1991

162 Thomas L. Friedman 'Bush Clears Soviet Trade Benefits and Weighs Role in London Talks' *NYT* 4.6.1991; William E. Schmidt 'Europeans Want Gorbachev at Talks' *NYT* 2.6.1991; *idem* 'Britain Is Proposing to Invite Gorbachev to London Talks' *NYT* 7.6.1991. Bush & Scowcroft *A World Transformed* p. 502. See also TNA UK PREM 19/3279 Memorandum by Wicks to Bayne – London Economic Summit: Possible Association of President Gorbachev 30.5.1991 pp. 1–2; Letter from Cradock to Wall (confidential) – 'Soviet Union: A Grand Bargain with the G7?' 31.5.1991

pp. 1–4. Letter from Wall to Gozney (restricted) – Telephone Call from Bush: Gorbachev's Attendance at the G7 summit – and other issues 4.6.1991 pp. 1–2; Note from Wicks to Wall (confidential) – Sherpas: Gorbachev and the Economic Summit 8.6.1991 pp. 1–2 incl. chairman's non-paper – Gorbachev and the summit (confidential, undated) pp. 1–3

163 GHWBPL Memcon of Bush–Yeltsin talks 20.6.1991 The Cabinet Room pp. 1–9 esp. pp. 4, 6; Bush & Scowcroft *A World Transformed* pp. 504–5

164 GHWBPL Telcon of Bush–Gorbachev call 21.6.1991 Oval Office pp. 1–4 esp. pp. 1, 4

165 TNA UK PREM 19/3283 Letter from Bishop to Wall (confidential) – Gorbachev Visit 16–19 July: Some Interpreter's-eye Impressions 22.7.1991 p. 6. R. W. Apple Jr 'Pact Is Reached to Reduce Nuclear Arms; Bush and Gorbachev to Meet This Month; 7 Powers Give Soviets New Economic Role' *NYT* 18.7.1991; Francis X. Clines 'Gorbachev's Big Gamble' *NYT* 17.7.1991

166 GHWBPL G7 Meeting with President Gorbachev 17.7.1991 Music Room Lancaster House London pp. 1–13 here esp. p. 13; Gorbachev *Memoirs* pp. 613–16. Cf. TNA UK PREM 19/3284 Meeting of Heads of States and President Gorbachev 17.7.1991 pp. 1–15

167 GHWBPL Memcon of Second Plenary – London Economic Summit 16.7.1991 Long Gallery Lancaster House London pp. 1–8 esp. p. 3

168 Stephen Kinzer 'Weakened Kohl Frustrated by Summit Colleagues' *NYT* 19.7.1991

169 Bierling *Wirtschaftshilfe* p. 127

170 GHWBPL Memcon of Second Plenary 16.7.1991 Long Gallery Lancaster House London; Memcon of Opening Session of the London Economic Summit 15.7.1991 Music Room Lancaster House London p. 3; Bush & Scowcroft *A World Transformed* p. 503; Serge Schmemann 'Soviet Economist Who Urged Change Calls Gorbachev and West "Foggy"' *NYT* 19.7.1991 p. 6. Cf. Letter from Bush to Gorbachev, *circa* early July 1990, printed in *TLSS* doc. 130 pp. 845–8. TNA UK PREM 19/3282–1 Memo from Wicks to PM – Heads of Delegation Lunch 16.7.1991 pp. 1–2 incl. Memo on Economic Summit: Handling of Gorbachev – Point to Make [at Lunch] (undated) pp. 1–4

171 GHWBPL Memcon of the Opening Session of the London Economic Summit 15.7.1991 Music Room Lancaster House London pp. 1–11 here p. 3; Craig R. Whitney 'Toward a Smaller World' *NYT* 18.7.1991

172 GHWBPL Memcon of G7 Meeting with President Gorbachev 17.7.1991 Music Room Lancaster House London p. 8

173 Ibid. pp. 12–13

174 GHWBPL Memcon of Bush–Gorbachev talks 17.7.1991 Winfield House London pp. 1–4 esp. pp. 1–2; Francis X. Clines 'Gorbachev Pleads for $100 Billion in Aid from West' *NYT* 23.5.1991

175 TNA UK PREM 19/3283 Letter from Bishop to Wall (confidential) – Gorbachev Visit 16–19 July: Some Interpreter's-eye Impressions 22.7.1991 pp. 1–6

176 TNA UK PREM 19/3283 Letter from Heywood to Wall (confidential) – The Economic Summit and the Soviet Union 22.7.1991 pp. 1–2. Keith Bradsher 'Soviets, in Surprise, Apply for Full World Bank Status' *NYT* 24.7.1991; *idem* 'Soviet Bid to Join IMF Still a Puzzle' *NYT* 29.7.1991 p. 6

177 For START I, see armscontrol.org/fact-sheets/start1

178 Remarks by President Gorbachev and President Bush at the Signing Ceremony for the Strategic Arms Reduction Talks Treaty in Moscow 31.7.1991 APP. See also TNA UK PREM 19/3760 Letter from Gorbachev to Major 7.8.1991 p. 4 where Gorbachev wrote: 'I can state with confidence that the Soviet–US summit at Moscow has started a new phase in the interaction and cooperation between our two nations ... Judging from experience ... what is good for Soviet–US relations, is also good for the international community and will serve the process of forming a new peaceful world order in the interest of all countries.'

179 Memorandum from Eagleburger for the president: 'Your Visit to the USSR' 25.7.1991, printed in TLSS doc.134 pp. 864–7 here p. 865

180 Francis X. Clines 'Chinese Party Chief Mending Relations in Moscow' NYT 16.5.1991

181 Soviet Record of Main Content of Conversation between Bush and Gorbachev in Novo-Ogarevo 31.7.1991 printed in TLSS doc. 139 p. 893; for US transcript, see GHWBPL Memcon of Gorbachev–Bush talks 31.7. Novo-Ogarevo pp. 1–8

182 Remarks at the Arrival Ceremony in Moscow 30.7.1991 APP; The President's News Conference with Soviet President Mikhail Gorbachev in Moscow 31.7.1991 APP

183 Soviet Record of Main Content of Conversation between Gorbachev and Bush, First Private Meeting, Moscow 30.7.1991 doc. 135 pp. 868–79 here pp. 876–7. No US transcript of this discussion has been released

184 The President's News Conference with Soviet President Mikhail Gorbachev in Moscow 31.7.1991 APP. Cf. Keith Badger 'Soviet Trade Favor Costs US Little' NYT 31.7.1991

185 TLSS doc. 139 p. 893. For a US transcript, see GHWBPL Memcon of Gorbachev–Bush talks 31.7.1991 Novo-Ogarevo pp. 1–8

186 TLSS doc. 135 p. 874

187 Bill Keller 'Gunmen Kill 6 Lithuania Border guards' NYT 1.8.1991. See also Bush & Scowcroft A World Transformed pp. 513–14

188 TLSS doc. 139 pp. 900–1. Cf. the much less detailed US transcript on this point: GHWBPL Memcon of Gorbachev–Bush talks 31.7.1991 Novo-Ogarevo p. 8

189 TLSS doc. 135 pp. 869–70, 874

190 Bush & Scowcroft A World Transformed pp. 515–16; Beschloss & Talbott At the Highest Levels p. 417

191 Bush's Remarks to the Supreme Soviet of the Republic of the Ukraine in Kiev, Soviet Union 1.8.1991 APP. The US press verdict was lukewarm, and the Ukrainian–American pro-independence lobby vehemently rejected what they saw as Bush's toadying to Gorbachev. See for example Francis X. Clines 'Bush, in Ukraine, Walks Fine Line on Sovereignty' NYT 2.8.1991. A few weeks later New York Times columnist and former Nixon speechwriter William Safire would slam Bush in an essay entitled 'After the Fall' and refer to his address as the 'dismaying "chicken Kiev" speech'. Whatever Safire's intention, the metaphor would stick to Bush like tar. And it caught the Americans' imagination – reflecting Bush's indecisiveness and lack of own vision in foreign affairs. After all Safire

claimed Bush had 'lectured the Ukrainians against self-determination, foolishly placing Washington on the side of Moscow'. William Safire 'Essay – After the Fall' *NYT* 29.8.1991

192 Letter from Bush to Gorbachev 1.8.1991, printed in Bush *All the Best* p. 530; Bush & Scowcroft *A World Transformed* pp. 514–15

193 *TLSS* doc. 135 p. 879

194 Michael Wines 'Bush Says Only Bad Health Would Bar Candidacy in '92' *NYT* 3.8.1991; The president's News Conference 2.8.1991 APP; Diary Entries 28.2.1991, 15.4.1991, 4.5.1991, 5.5.1991, 10.6.1991 June (Burial instructions), 27.6.1991, 7.7.1991, and 25.7.1991, all printed in Bush *All the Best* pp. 514–18, 525–6, 528–9

195 Adam Clymer 'President Is Sent Measure to Widen Jobless Benefits' *NYT* 3.8.1991; Robert D. Hershey Jr 'Economy Turns Up With Gain of 0.4% in the 2nd Quarter' *NYT* 27.7.1991; Michael deCourcy Hinds 'States and Cities Fight Recession with New Taxes' *NYT* 27.7.1991. See also Presidential Job Approval, George Bush 1989–1993 APP

196 Bush & Scowcroft *A World Transformed* p. 517

197 Entry 3.8.1991 *The Diary of Anatoly S. Chernyaev 1991* NSAEBB No. 345; Bush & Scowcroft *A World Transformed* pp. 511, 514, 517; Gorbachev *Memoirs* pp. 623–4; Francis X. Clines 'Economy Sulks as Gorbachev Enjoys His Encore' *NYT* 28.7.1991; Taubman *Gorbachev* p. 582

198 Diary Entry 12.8.1991, printed in Bush *All the Best* pp. 532–3

199 Chernyaev *My Six Years* pp. 372–3. See also Engel *When the World Seemed New* pp. 453–4 and Taubman *Gorbachev* pp. 602–6

200 Diary Entries, 1.8.1991 and 19.8.1991, printed in Bush *All the Best* pp. 529–30 and p. 533. See also Letter from Bush to Gorbachev 1.8.1991, printed in Bush *All the Best* p. 530 and Bush & Scowcroft *A World Transformed* pp. 519–20

201 Taubman *Gorbachev* pp. 618–19; Entry 19.8.1991 Braithwaite *Diary 1988–1992*. Cf. Plokhy *The Last Empire* pp. 87–90

202 Diary Entry 19.8.1991, printed in Bush & Scowcroft *A World Transformed* p. 519. This is different from the longer section of the Diary Entry 19.8.1991 printed in Bush *All the Best* pp. 533–4

203 Note – Matters to address today 20.8.1991, printed in Bush *All the Best* p. 534. Bush & Scowcroft *A World Transformed* pp. 518–19

204 Diary Entries 20.8.1991 and 21.8.1991, printed in Bush *All the Best* pp. 534–6. GHWBPL Telcon of Bush–Yeltsin call 20.8.1991 Oval Office; Telcon of Bush–Yeltsin call (8.30–9.05 a.m.) 21.8.1991 Kennebunkport

205 See GHWBPL Telcon of Yeltsin–Bush talks (9.20–9.31 p.m.) 21.8.1991 Kennebunkport

206 Remnick *Lenin's Tomb* pp. 494–5; Taubman *Gorbachev* pp. 620–3; Francis X. Clines 'After The Coup: Yeltsin is Routing Communist Party From Key Roles Throughout Russia – He Forces Vast Gorbachev Shake-Up; Soviet President is Heckled by the Republic's Parliament' *NYT* 24.8.1991. For a transcript of the 23.8.1991 Russian parliamentary session, 'Gorbachev's Speech to Russians: "A Major Regrouping of Political Forces"' *NYT* 24.8.1991

207 Beschloss & Talbott *At the Highest Levels* p. 438

208 GHWBPL NSC Susan Koch Files – Subject Files Folder: After the [Soviet]

Coup – AmEmbassy Moscow to State: 'The USSR Two Weeks After the Failed Coup' 6.9.1991

209 Diary Entry 2.9.1991, printed in Bush *All the Best* p. 536

210 David Binder 'Baltics' Campaign is Gaining in West' *NYT* 23.8.1991. See also Diary Entry, 2.9.1991 printed in Bush *All the Best* pp. 536–7. For a longer version of Diary Entry 2.9.1991, see Bush & Scowcroft *A World Transformed* p. 539 and more generally pp. 537–40

211 GHWBPL NSC Susan Koch Files – Subject Files Folder: After the [Soviet] Coup – AmEmbassy Moscow to State: 'The USSR Two Weeks After the Failed Coup' 6.9.1991

212 Remnick *Lenin's Tomb* p. 495. See also Diary Entry 2.9.1991, printed in Bush & Scowcroft *A World Transformed* p. 539

213 Ibid. pp. 498–9; Taubman *Gorbachev* p. 625; Entry 1.12.1991 *The Diary of Anatoly S. Chernyaev 1991* NSAEBB No. 345; Grachev *Final Days* pp. 106–11 esp. pp. 108, and 119–26; Plokhy *The Last Empire* pp. 293–4

214 Beschloss & Talbott *At the Highest Levels* p. 447; Palazchenko *My Years* p. 339. Cf. Soviet Record of Dinner Conversation between Gorbachev, Bush, Gonzalez and King Juan Carlos of Spain 29.10.1991, printed in *TLSS* doc. 150 p. 953

215 'For a long time, the solution to concerns about Yeltsin and security-related fears about the Soviet Union falling apart was to prop up Gorbachev', a US official told the *New York Times*. Andrew Rosenthal 'Bush Reluctantly Concludes Gorbachev Tried to Cling to Power Too Long' *NYT* 25.12.1991. See also Goldgeier & McFaul *Power and Purpose* p. 73

216 Hutchings *American Diplomacy* pp. 331, 335

217 Ibid. p. 331

218 Baker *The Politics* p. 563

219 Ibid. p. 558. See also David Hoffman 'Baker: US Must Resist Temptation to Move Toward Isolationism' *WP* 8.12.1991

220 JAB-SML B115/F8 Soviet Points for Meeting with the President 10.12.1991 pp. 1–2

221 Thomas L. Friedman 'Baker Presents Steps to Aid Transition by Soviets' *NYT* 13.12.1991; Baker *The Politics* pp. 562–4

222 'Baker Sees Opportunities and Risks as Soviet Republics Grope for Stability – Excerpts from Baker's Princeton speech' *NYT* 13.12.1991; cf. GHWBPL Telcon of Bush–Yeltsin call 13.12.1991 Oval Office p. 3. Technical assistance came on top of the $100 million approved by Congress to support 'humanitarian assistance' for the Soviet Republics, see GHWBPL NSC Nicholas Burns Files – Subject File: USSR Food Grant Aid (CF01498–002) Options for Use of the $100 million to support humanitarian assistance for the Soviet Union and the republics 8.12.1991 pp. 1–5

223 GHWBPL Telcon of Bush–Gorbachev call 13.12.1991 Oval Office p. 4

224 GHWBPL Telcon of Bush–Yeltsin call 13.12.1991 Oval Office p. 1

225 Baker *The Politics* p. 562

226 Francis X. Clines 'US Envoy Urges Debt Relief for Soviets' *NYT* 19.11.1991. Cf. GHWBPL NSC Burns–Hewett Files – Subject File: POTUS Meetings November 1991 – POTUS Meeting on Debt Situation in the USSR 11/5/91 (OA/ID CF01422–039) Scowcroft Memo to Bush on 'Meeting on Soviet Debt'

5.11.1991 Cabinet Room pp. 1–3 + attachments. As Scowcroft wrote to Bush 'In short, it appears the Soviets are on the verge of serious financial crisis ... we are being asked now to provide exceptional balance of payments support for November and December and possibly for all of 1992. I had hoped we could avoid getting involved in large financial transfers to the Soviets, but given the likelihood of a Soviet default in the absence of any Western action, we face some unpleasant choices.'

227 Goldgeier & McFaul *Power and Purpose* pp. 48–9; Baker *The Politics* pp. 564–83. For the 'chance' of exporting democracy, see also 'Baker Sees Opportunities and Risks as Soviet Republics Grope for Stability – Excerpts from Baker's Princeton speech' p. 24

228 Baker *The Politics* pp. 571–2; GHWBPL NSC Craig Chellis Files – (59) NATO-EE/Soviet Liaison [1] (CF01436–009) Cable from Sec State to European Pol. Collective – Genscher–Baker Statement 2.10.1991 pp. 1–3; TNA UK PREM 19/3760 Memo & Letter from Gass to Wall – The Baker–Genscher Declaration 5.11.1992 pp. 1–2; JAB-SML B115/F8 Proposed Agenda for Meeting with the president 31.12.1991 11.00 a.m. pp. 1–2; GHWBPL NSC Barry Lowenkron Files – NATO: Wörner (CF01526–021) Memo by Scowcroft for Bush re: President's 11 October Meeting with Wörner 9.10.1991 p. 2; Memcon of Bush–Wörner talks 11.10.1991 Oval Office pp. 1–5. GHWBPL NSC Barry Lowenkron Files European Strategy Steering Group: ESSG Meeting – 3 February 1992, NATO and the East: Key Issues, no author (likely NSC) undated. TNA UK PREM 19/4329 Memo from

Weston to Goulden (confidential) – The Future of NATO: The Question of Enlargement 3.3.1992 pp. 1–7. Hutchings *American Diplomacy* pp. 290–1; Genscher *Erinnerungen* p. 978; Norman Kempster 'Baker Proposes New Partnership for East, West' *LAT* 19.6.1991; Liz Sly 'Baker Wants Soviets in US–Europe Alliance' *CT* 19.6.1991

229 Baker *The Politics* pp. 572, 584. Cf. GHWBPL NSC Barry Lowenkron Files NATO: Wörner (CF01526–021) Memcon of Bush–Wörner talks 11.10.1991 Oval Office pp. 4–5

230 Baker *The Politics* p. 584. Cf. Genscher *Erinnerungen* p. 978

231 Thomas L. Friedman 'Yeltsin Says Russia Seeks to Join NATO' *NYT* 21.12.1991

232 Hutchings *American Diplomacy* p. 292

233 GHWBPL NSC Barry Lowenkron Files – NATO Files, NATO: NAC/NACC Ministerials – December 1991 Brussels, Cable from US Mission NATO to Sec State – NATO: NACC Ministerial Summary Report 20.12.1991 pp. 1–3 + NACC Ministerial Declaration – Soviet Union ends as Meeting Ends 4pp. 'Dissolution of the Soviet Union Announced at Nato Meeting' 1.1.1992 NATO. Friedman 'Yeltsin Says Russia Seeks to Join NATO'. For the 'North Atlantic Cooperation Council Statement on Dialogue, Partnership and Cooperation', Press Communiqué M-NACC-1(91)111 NAC 20.12.1991 NATO

234 Plokhy *The Last Empire* pp. 295–316; Reynolds *One World Divisible* p. 575

235 GHWBPL Telcon of Bush–Gorbachev talks 25.12.1991 Camp David pp. 1–3. Bush & Scowcroft *A World Transformed* pp. 559–61

236 Bush's Address to the Nation on the

Commonwealth of Independent States 25.12.1991 APP

237 Diary Entry 2.9.1991, printed in Bush *All the Best* p. 537

238 Letter from Bush to Senator Al Simpson 21.10.1991, printed in Bush *All the Best* p. 539

239 Robin Toner 'Buchanan, Urging New Nationalism, Joins '92 Race' *NYT* 11.12.1992

Chapter 8

1 GHWBPL Scowcroft Special Separate USSR Notes Files – Yeltsin Files: Yeltsin (January–December 1992) (OA/ID 91131–008) Letter from Yeltsin to Bush 30.12.1992

2 Michael Wines 'Bush Off on Foreign Trip, With Russia on Agenda' *NYT* 31.12.1992. In the event, a heavy snowstorm forced Bush and Yeltsin to abandon at the last minute their original plan to meet in the Black Sea resort of Sochi to sign START II. The abrupt shift back to Moscow contributed to the low-key air of the summit. See GHWBPL NSC Burns–Hewett Files – Subject Files: POTUS Telcons CIS Leaders 1992 (OA/ID CF01421–037) Telcon of Bush–Yeltsin call 20.12.1992 Camp David pp. 1–4; Serge Schmemann 'Bush's Last Hurrah in Cold, Wintry Moscow' *NYT* 3.1.1993; The President's News Conference with President Boris Yeltsin of Russia in Moscow 3.1.1993 APP

3 Hutchings *American Diplomacy* pp. 236–8. Mary Battita 'Czech, Slovak Leaders Agree on Plan to Split their Federation' *WP* 24.7.1992; Peter Maas 'After Their Civil Divorce, Czechs and Slovaks are Still Friends' *WP* 10.8.1993. Bush's Joint Statement with Prime Minister John Major of the United Kingdom on the Former Yugoslavia 20.12.1992 APP

4 'Dawn of a New Era' *NYT* 2.2.1992

5 Bush's Statement on the Resignation of Mikhail Gorbachev as President of the Soviet Union 25.12.1991 APP

6 The President's News Conference 26.12.1991 APP

7 Taubman *Gorbachev* pp. 639–40, 653–5

8 Ibid. pp. 652–4; Olga Kryshtanovskaya & Stephen White 'From Soviet Nomenklatura to Russian Elite' *Europe-Asia Studies* 48, 5 (July 1996) pp. 711–33

9 Indeed, during Bush's Christmas call on 23 December Yeltsin had proposed to meet soon, and the US president was responsive: 'That would be very constructive, to answer in principle. Of course we would want to do that.' GHWBPL Telcon of Bush–Yeltsin call 23.12.1991 Oval Office

10 GHWBPL NSC Burns Files – Subject Files: Yeltsin (OA/ID CF01487–006) Note from Burns to Scowcroft re: letter from Yeltsin regarding proposed Washington DC summit 31.12.1991. 'Bush to meet with Yeltsin at Camp David' *UPI* 23.1.1992; Paul Lewis 'Security Council to Chart Post-Cold War Path' *NYT* 8.1.1992

11 Dimitris Bourantonis & Georgios Kostakos 'Diplomacy at the United Nations: The Dual Agenda of the 1992 Security Council Summit' *Diplomacy and Statecraft* 11, 3 (2000) pp. 212–26 quoting p. 213

12 United Nations: Security Council Summit Statement Concerning the Council's Responsibility in the Maintenance of International Peace and Security' *International Legal Materials* 31, 3 (May 1992) pp. 758–62 esp. pp. 760, 762. Paul Lewis 'Leaders

Want to Enhance UN's Role' *NYT* 31.1.1992

13   Annika Savill 'UK Finds a Way to Hold on to the Mother of all Seats' *Independent* 7.1.1992

14   Major quoted in Bourantonis & Kostakos 'Diplomacy at the United Nations' p. 216. See also Stavros Blavoukos & Dimitris Bourantonis 'Pursuing National Interests: The 1992 British Presidency of the UN Security Council and the Soviet Permanent Seat' *British Journal of Politics and International Relations* 16, 2 (2014) pp. 349–65 esp. pp. 356–60

15   Bush's Address Before a Joint Session of the Congress on the State of the Union 28.1.1992 APP

16   Jeane Kirkpatrick 'A Normal Country in a Normal Time' *The National Interest* (Fall 1990) pp. 40–3; Robert W. Tucker & David C. Hendrickson *The Imperial Temptation: The New World Order and America's Purpose* CFR Press 1992 pp. 15, 205

17   Bush's Address Before a Joint Session of the Congress on the State of the Union 28.1.1992 APP

18   Bush & Scowcroft *A World Transformed* p. 564

19   On America's power as the sole hegemon and its military expenditure (100%) in comparison with Russia (26%), Japan (17%), France (17%), Germany (14%), Britain (13%) and China (13%) as the next six countries, see William Wohlforth 'The Stability of a Unipolar World' *International Security* 24, 1 (Summer 1999) pp. 5–41 esp. the tables on p. 12 (figures for 1996). See also Bush's Address before a Joint Session of the Congress on the State of the Union 28.1.1992. Note that in 1989 the US military expenditure was $427

billion, then $379 billion in 1992, and $358 billion the following year. In other words, it had been reduced under the Bush presidency by some $50 billion. There were further reductions until 1999 ($298 billion) after which military expenditure increased again inexorably for the next decade. See infoplease. com/us/military-personnel/us-military-spending-1946–2009 and 'Trends in US Military Spending' *Council on Foreign Relations* 15.7.2014 cfr.org/ report/trends-us-military-spending

20   Cf. GHWBPL NSC Burns–Hewett Files – Subject Files: Yeltsin [Meeting with President] – Camp David February [1] 1992 (OA/ID CF01408–019) Scowcroft's Note to President – Key Objectives for the Yeltsin Visit 1.2.1992 10.00 a.m. Camp David [One-on-One Meeting] pp. 1–5 + annexes; and Warning Report and Forecast: From Robert Blackwell to Director of CIA – Subj.: Russian Foreign Policy and Economic Reform 23.1.1992 pp. 1–4

21   Allison Mitchell 'Yeltsin, on Summit's Stage, Stresses His Russian Identity' *NYT* 1.2.1992; Paul Lewis 'World Leaders, at the UN, Pledge to Expand Its Role to Achieve Lasting Peace' *NYT* 1.2.1992; Terry Atlas 'Yeltsin's Troubled Debut' *CT* 6.4.1992

22   Boris Yeltsin in 'Excerpts from Speeches by Leaders of Permanent Members of the UN Security Council' *NYT* 1.2.1992

23   Baker *The Politics* p. 623

24   GHWBPL NSC Burns–Hewett Files – Subject Files: POTUS Meetings February 1992–April 1992 (OA/ID CF 01421–009) Memcon of Bush–Yeltsin talks 1.2.1992 Camp David pp. 2–3; Goldgeier & McFaul *Power and Purpose* pp. 65–6. Cf. Yegor Gaidar *Days of*

Defeat and Victory Univ. of Washington Press 1999. See also GHWBPL NSC Burns–Hewett Files – Subject Files: Yeltsin [Meeting with President] [1] (OA/ID CF 01408–019) Economic reform in the Former Soviet Union 24.1.1992 pp. 1–2; NSC Burns–Hewett Files – Subject File: Russia – IMF #1 [2] (OA/ID CF 01408–005) Memorandum of Economic Policies (Document of IMF – not for public use) 11.3.1992 pp. 1–3. Fred Hiatt 'Russia's Controversial Course: Economic Reforms Face Critical Test of the People' *WP* 12.1.1992

25   GHWBPL NSC Burns–Hewett Files – Subject Files: POTUS Meetings February 1992–April 1992 (OA/ID CF01421–009) Memcon of Bush–Yeltsin talks 1.2.1992 Camp David p. 2. On Soviet economic performance, see also GHWBPL NSC Burns–Hewett Files – Subject Files: Yeltsin [Meeting with President] – Camp David February [1] 1992 (OA/ID CF 01408–019) Economic Reform in the Former Soviet Union 24.1.1992 p. 2

26   Ibid. p. 10; see also Baker *The Politics* p. 625

27   Ibid.; GHWBPL NSC Burns–Hewett Files – Subject Files: POTUS Meetings February 1992–April 1992 (CF 01421–009) Camp David Declaration on New Relations by President Bush and President Yeltsin pp. 1–3. See also Joint Declaration (AP) in 'Presidents Bush and Yeltsin: "Dawn of a New Era"' *NYT* 2.2.1992; The President's News Conference with President Boris Yeltsin of Russia 1.2.1992 APP

28   Michael Wines 'Bush and Yeltsin Declare Formal End to Cold War; Agree to Exchange Visits' *NYT* 2.2.1992

29   Baker *The Politics* pp. 623–5

30   Diary Entry 2.3.1992 and Notes for Speechwriters 14.3.1992, printed in Bush *All the Best* pp. 549, 551

31   Bush's Remarks to the Polish National Alliance in Chicago (Illinois) 16.3.1992 APP

32   Baker, after a trip to the Former Soviet Union (FSU) in late February, had noted in an aide-memoire for himself ahead of a meeting with the president: 'I think I need to give a speech on the relationship of all this [US assistance efforts to FSU and arms-control issues] to our domestic well-being.' JAB-SML B115/F9 Key Impressions from the Trip [to FSU] 18.2.1992 p. 3

33   Thomas L. Friedman 'Baker Spells Out US Approach: Alliances and "Democratic Peace"' *NYT* 22.4.1992

34   JAB-SML B115/F9 Proposed Agenda for Meeting with the President 14.1.1992 (Coordinating Conference, Soviet Debt) pp. 1–3; Proposed Agenda for Meeting with the President 24.1.1992 (Coordinating Conference, Econ. Reform in Russia & the Other Republics) pp. 1–2. See also Baker *The Politics* pp. 616–19; Bierling *Wirtschaftshilfe* pp. 196–201; Thomas L. Friedman 'US Is Criticised on Aid to Russia' *NYT* 22.1.1992

35   Marc Fisher 'Bonn on Russian Aid: Put Up or Shut up' *WP* 16.1.1992. See also 'Ein feiner Geruch von deutscher Arroganz' *SZ* 25.1.1992. Cf. GHWBPL NSC Burns–Hewett Files – Subject Files: Yeltsin [Meeting with President] – Camp David February [1] 1992 (OA/ID CF 01408–019) Memorandum from Hewett to Scowcroft and Howe – Subj.: Results of the Coordinating Conference 24.1.1992

36   GHWBPL NSC Burns–Hewett Files – Subject Files: Yeltsin [Meeting with

President] – Camp David February [1] 1992 (OA/ID CF 01408–019) Note from Scowcroft to Bush – Points to be made re: meeting with Yeltsin on 1 February 1991 Tab A pp. 2–3 29.1.1992; and Coordinating Conference – Technical Assistance Fact Sheet 23.1.1992 pp. 1–3; US Department of State – OAS/ Spokesman: Fact Sheet – Operation Provide Hope 23.1, 1992; United States Government Initiatives – Medicine 23.1.1992. GHWBPL NSC Burns–Hewett Files – Subject Files: POTUS Meetings February 1992–April 1992 (OA/ID CF01421–009) US Technical Assistance for the Russian Federation (undated, late January 1992) pp. 1–4. See also Thomas L Friedman 'Ex-Soviet Lands To Get Swift Aid' *NYT* 24.1.1992; Yegor Gaidar 'Russia Needs Three Kinds of Economic aid – and Quickly' *FT* 22.1.1992; Gennady Burbulis 'Come, Make Goods and Sell Them' *WP* 23.1.1992. Baker *The Politics* p. 618. Cf. 'Unmut bei der "Operation Hoffnung"' *Der Spiegel* 8/1992 17.2.1992. On IMF action, GHWBPL NSC Burns–Hewett Files – Subject Files: Yeltsin [Meeting with President] – Camp David February [1] 1992 (OA/ID CF 01408–019) Jeff Sachs to Ed Hewitt 21.1.1992; and Fund Activities in the Former USSR Republics, November/December 1991

37   JAB-SML B115/F9 Proposed Agenda for Meeting with the President 19.2.1992 (Trip to FSU – Note on CCC credits) p. 1; 'Operation Hoffnung' *Der Spiegel* 5/1992 27.1.1992

38   See GHWBPL NSC Holl Files – Subject File: NATO and European Security January–June 1992 (CF01398–018) US Mission at NATO Amb. Taft to Sec State: Coordinating Conference – Time to Decide NATO's Role 10.1.1992; 'Unmut bei der "Operation Hoffnung"' *Der Spiegel* 8/1992 17.2.1992

39   Ian Mather 'Supplies Rot as NATO and EC Wrangle' *The European* 27.2.-4.3.1992; Sarah Lambert 'NATO Disbands Unit That Sent Aid to Its Old Foe' *Independent* 1.4.1992

40   Washington pledged $1.5 billion towards the $6 billion rouble-stabilisation fund, a $2 billion share of the $11 billion in bilateral aid, and more than half a billion towards the $4.5 billion pot of IMF and World Bank loans. Andrew Rosenthal 'Bush and Kohl Unveil Plan for 7 Nations to Contribute $24 Billion in Aid for Russia' *NYT* 2.4.1992; Steven Greenhouse 'Buying Time for Yeltsin' *NYT* 2.4.1992. Cf. JAB-SML B115/F9 Proposed Agenda for Meeting with the President 20.3.1992 (Follow-Up on FSU; Kohl Visit: Russian Economic Reform) pp. 1–2. GHWBPL NSC Burns–Hewett Files – Subject Files: Working Papers for June Summit 1992 (Bush–Yeltsin) [2] (OA/ID CF01408–018) G7 Financial Support for Russia 29.5.1992 pp. 1–3. For Bush's statement, see: The President's News Conference on Aid to the States of the Former Soviet Union 1.4.1992 APP

41   Celestine Bohlen 'The Pain's Good for Russia, Parliament is Told' *NYT* 9.4.1992. GHWBPL NSC Burns Files –Subject Files: Yeltsin (OA/ID CF01487–006) Telcon of Bush–Yeltsin call 1.4.1992 Oval Office p. 1. Cf. GHWBPL NSC Burns–Hewett Files – POTUS Telcon CIS Leaders 1992: Yeltsin 3/19/1992 (OA/ID CF01421–052) Memorandum from Howe to Bush – Subj: Phone call from Yeltsin (undated, March 1992) + talking points p. 1 (cover note) and p. 2 (talking points

doc.). The Bush administration was very aware of the pressure Yeltsin was under from the Russian Congress. Given this 'severe test for Yeltsin' it was calculated that 'he will appreciate our support at this crucial time'. The US were keen to reassure Yeltsin: 'we will endeavor to get you the resources' from the IMF, 'whatever your quota'. In the same Burns–Hewett File as above ('POTUS Telcon CIS Leaders 1992: Yeltsin 3/19/1992') Telcon of Bush to Yeltsin call 19.3.1992 Oval Office p. 2.

42   Goldgeier & McFaul *Power and Purpose* pp. 66–7, 81–2. Cf. Stephen Engelberg '21 months of "Shock Therapy" Resuscitates Polish Economy' *NYT* 17.12.1992. See also TNA UK PREM 19/3922–2 Memo from Barder (Treasury) to Wall – Financial Assistance to Russia: Proposal for a G7 Announcement for a Rouble Stabilisation Fund 31.3.1992 5pp.

43   GHWBPL NSC Burns–Hewett Files – Subject File: Russia IMF #2 (OA/ID CF01408–006) Cable from US Emb. Moscow to Baker re: Russia's negotiations with IMF on Economic Programme 26.2.1992 5pp.; NSC Burns–Hewett Files – Subject File: Russia IMF #1 [2] (CF01408–005) Memo of Econ. Policies (between IMF and Russia) 11.3.1992 16pp. On the diplomacy surrounding the G7 and IMF/World Bank assistance to Russia in January–March 1992, see also TNA UK PREM 19/3670 and 19/3672–1. Steven Erlanger 'Aid to Russia – Thankful Russia Still Wary of Daunting Tasks Ahead' *NYT* 2.4.1992

44   Margaret Shapiro 'Yeltsin's Inner Circle of "Young Turks"' *WP* 9.4.1992

45   Baker quoted in JAB-SML B115/F9 Key Impressions from the Trip [to the FSU]

18.2.1992 p. 2; Scowcroft quoted in Brands *Making the Unipolar Moment* p. 320. The German finance minister Theo Waigel believed that Moscow should only get financial aid for 'self help' (*Hilfe zur Selbtshilfe*), not as part of a never-ending bailout. Waigel quoted in his speech 'Wir müssen einen Pakt der Vernunft und der Solidarität abschließen'. Rede des Bundesministers der Finanzen anläßlich der ersten Beratung des Bundeshaushalts 1993 am 8.9.1992 im Deutschen Bundestag *CDU Dokumentation* 26/1992 p. 20; Steven Greenhouse with Thomas L. Friedman 'Aid for Yeltsin and Russians: A Package with Loose Ends' *NYT* 9.4.1992

46   Erlanger 'Aid to Russia'; Steven Greenhouse with Thomas L. Friedman 'Aid for Yeltsin and Russians'; Gewirtz *Unlikely Partners* pp. 1–10

47   Greenhouse 'Buying Time for Yeltsin'

48   'Yeltsin Calls For Strong Authority' *CT* 6.4.1992. On Russia's Congresses, see Jeffrey Gleisner et al. 'The Parliament and the Cabinet: Parties, Factions and Parliamentary Control in Russia (1900– 93)' *Journal of Contemporary History* 31, 3 (July 1996) pp. 427–61 here pp. 435–9

49   Michael Dobbs 'Yeltsin Shifts Aides on Eve of Congress – Russian Leader tightens Control on Troops' *WP* 4.4.1992; *idem* 'Russians Reach Compromise on Reform Dispute' *WP* 15.4.1992; Serge Schmemann 'Russian Cabinet Wins Shaky Support of Assembly' *NYT* 16.4.1992. Cf. GHWBPL Memcon of Bush's talks with Gaidar 28.4.1992 Oval Office.

50   Letter from Bush to Nixon 5.3.1992, printed in Bush *All the Best* p. 549; Thomas L. Friedman 'Nixon's "Save Russia" Memo: Bush Feels the Sting' *NYT* 11.3.1992 p. 12; *idem* 'Nixon Scoffs

at Level of Support for Russian Democracy by Bush' *NYT* 10.3.1992; Henry Kissinger 'Proposals, Like Nixon's, to Send Money to Save Democracy in Russia Won't Work' *LAT* 30.3.1992. Carroll Bogert 'The "Who Lost Russia" Debate' *Newsweek* 22.3.1992. See also Marvin Kalb *The Nixon Memo: Political Respectability, Russia, and the Press* pp. 80–2

51 The President's News Conference on Aid to the States of the Former Soviet Union 1.4.1992 APP

52 Ibid. JAB-SM B115/F8 Soviet Points for Meeting with the President 10.12.1991

53 See JAB-SM B115/F9 Proposed Agenda for Meeting with the President (FSU-Freedom Bill) 31.3.1992 p. 1; and Proposed Agenda for Meetings with the President (Aid to the FSU) 8.4.1992, 10.4.1992 and 15.4.1992 p. 1 respectively

54 Thomas L. Friedman 'Bush and Baker Press Aid to Russia but Meet Worries About Costs' *NYT* 10.4.1992; Remarks to the American Society of Newspaper Editors 9.4.1992 APP

55 Seth Mydans '23 Dead After 2nd Day of Los Angeles Riots; Fires and Looting Persist Despite Curfew – 900 Reported Hurt' *NYT* 1.5.1992; Leslie Berger 'A City in Crisis' *LAT* 3.5.1992. Thomas L. Friedman 'Baker on Hill, Passes Hat for Russia' *NYT* 1.5.1992

56 Friedman 'Bush and Baker Press Aid to Russia but Meet Worries About Costs'

57 For Ukraine's complaints about Russian 'aggression' placing the Black Sea Fleet under its jurisdiction by Yeltsin's decree of 7 April, see Bohlen 'The Pain's Good for Russia'; GHWBPL Telcon of Bush and Ukrainian President Leonid Kravchuk call 10.4.1992 Oval Office pp.

1–2. See also Eleanor Randolph 'Yeltsin Challenges Ukraine on Fleet: Kiev Postpones Its Demand of Allegiance from Crews of Black Sea Vessels' *WP* 10.1.1992. For Yeltsin's nationalist vice president Rutskoi's statements on Russia's claims on Crimea (and Sevastopol, the home port of the Fleet), see Bohlen 'Russian Vice President Wants to Redraw Borders' *NYT* 31.1.1992

58 Baker *The Politics* pp. 658–65. Baker quoted in Barbara Crossette '4 Ex-Soviet States And US in Accord on 1991 Arms Pact' *NYT* 24.5.1992. Cf. GHWBPL NSC Burns–Hewett Files – POTUS Telcon CIS 1992: Yeltsin (OA/ID CF01421–050) Telcon of Bush to Yeltsin call 23.3.1992 Oval Office

59 On US and Russian proposals during winter and spring to reduce nuclear weapons, especially the 'nuclear initiatives' by Bush and Yeltsin in late January 1992, see GHWBPL NSC Davis Files – Subject Files: Yeltsin /Bush – January 1992 (OA/ID CF01589–009)

60 GHWBPL NSC Susan Koch Files [Bush/Yeltsin Washington] Summit [June 15–18] 1992 [2] (OA/ID CF01339–002) Joint Understanding 16.6.1992

61 Bush's Remarks with President Boris Yeltsin of Russia Announcing Strategic Arms Reductions and an Exchange with Reporters 16.6.1992 APP; Joint Understanding on Reductions in Strategic Offensive Arms 17.6.1992 APP. Baker *The Politics* pp. 670–1; Michael Wines 'Bush and Yeltsin Agree to Cut Long-Range Atomic Warheads; Scrap Key Land-Based Missiles' *NYT* 17.7.1992. Cf. on US doubts up to the last minute to be able to conclude START II at the Washington summit, GHWBPL NSC Susan Koch Files [Bush/Yeltsin

Washington] Summit [June 15–18] 1992 [3] (OA/ID CF01339–003) Scowcroft to Bush: Overview for Your Upcoming Meetings with Boris Yeltsin 16–17.6.1992 (undated, early June 1992) pp. 1–2; Burns to Gordon, Koch and Gompert – Points to Be Made: Military and Security Issues 11.6.1992 p. 1

62 R. W. Apple Jr 'And Now, the Political Plowshares; Boost for Bush Campaign, but Will It Last?' *NYT* 17.6.1992

63 Remarks at the Arrival Ceremony for President Boris Yeltsin of Russia 16.6.1992 APP

64 Andrew Rosenthal 'Yeltsin Cheered at Capitol as he Pledges Era of Trust and Asks for Action on Aid' *NYT* 18.6.1992; and 'Excerpts from Yeltsin's Speech: "There Will Be No More Lies"' *NYT* 18.6.1992

65 'Bush Signs Freedom Support Act' *CQ Almanac 1992* pp. 523–32; Thomas L. Friedman 'Shaping a New Agenda' *NYT* 18.6.1992; Clifford Krauss 'Yeltsin Speaks, Congressional Wall Tumbles' *NYT* 18.6.1992

66 Rosenthal 'Yeltsin Cheered at Capitol'; Steven Greenhouse 'Russia Is Given Most-Favored Status' *NYT* 18.6.1992

67 For 'A Charter for American–Russian Partnership and Friendship' *The White House Press Release* 17.6.1992. Cf. On the Charter, see also GHWBPL NSC Burns–Hewett Files – Subject Files: Working Papers for June Summit 1992 (Bush–Yeltsin) [1] (OA/ID CF01408–017) Baker to Bush Subj: Your Meetings with Boris Yeltsin (undated, June 1992) p. 1

68 Bush's Remarks at the Arrival Ceremony for President Boris Yeltsin of Russia 16.6.1992 APP; The President's News Conference with President Boris Yeltsin of Russia 17.6.1992 APP

69 See also 'Senate Votes $981 Million in Aid for Ex-Soviet Bloc' *NYT* 3.7.1992 p. 3. Note that the 'Munich G7 – Economic Declaration' of 8 July 1992, for example, referred explicitly to the category 'Central and Eastern European Europe including the Baltic States' – a group of countries which, unlike the New Independent States of the former Soviet Union (including Russia), were receiving significant financing through the EBRD and G24 and were in the process of developing formal ties with EC and EFTA; see worldjpn.grips.ac.jp/documents/texts/summit/19920708.D1E.html

70 Henry Kissinger 'Charter of Confusion' *WP* 5.7.1992. On the White House perspective ('What is at stake for us') as regards the Bush–Yeltsin summit and that Yeltsin was 'the very best we can hope for', see GHWBPL NSC Burns–Hewett Files – Subject Files: Working Papers for June Summit 1992 (Bush–Yeltsin) [1] (OA/ID CF01408–017) Draft Outline for Scowcroft Memo (undated) pp. 1–5

71 See US Senate 'Floor Action' on 2 July 1992, printed in 'Bush Signs Freedom Support Act' *CQ Almanac 1992*. See also 'Senate Votes $981 Million in Aid for Ex-Soviet Bloc'. Bush had informed Yeltsin on 27 June that the decks were cleared to get a vote on the Freedom Support Act. GHWBPL NSC Burns–Hewett Files – Subject Files: POTUS Telcons CIS Leaders 1992 (OA/ID CF01421–045) Memcon of Bush–Yeltsin call 27.6.1992 Camp David p. 2

72 See House 'Floor Action' on 6 August 1992, printed in 'Bush Signs Freedom Support Act' *CQ Almanac 1992*. Cf. GHWBPL NSC Burns Files – Subject

Files: Yeltsin (OA/ID CF01487–006) Memcon of Bush–Yeltsin talks (expanded meeting) 16.6.1992 4.10 p.m. Cabinet Room p. 5. As Bush told Yeltsin on 16 June, 'It is in our interest to get this legislation through, to see you succeed. We are not doing this just because we are nice guys. It is in the interest of the US too. We have a $400 billion deficit. People criticise and ask why I've lost it. Why give money to Russia, they ask, why not to Los Angeles?'

73 See House 'Floor Action' on 6 August 1992, printed in 'Bush Signs Freedom Support Act' *CQ Almanac 1992*.

74 GHWBPL NSC Burns Files – Subject Files, Yeltsin (OA/ID CF01487–006) Message [incl. presidential statement praising Congress for its vote] from Bush to Yeltsin (sent via privacy channels) 6.8.1992. See also Adam Clymer 'House Votes Billions in Aid to Ex-Soviet Republics' *NYT* 7.8.1992; *idem* 'House Democrats Agree to a Vote on Russian Aid' *NYT* 6.8.1992

75 Statement on Signing the FREEDOM Support Act 24.10.1992 APP. See also GHWBPL NSC Burns–Hewett Files – Subject Files: POTUS Telcons with CIS Leaders 1992 (OA/ID CF01421–041) Telcon of Bush–Yeltsin call 29.10.1992 Detroit (Michigan) p. 1

76 Steven Greenhouse 'Unemployment Up Sharply, Prompting Federal Reserve to Cut Its Key Lending Rate' *NYT* 3.7.1992; Robin Toner 'Democrats Display a New Optimism, Reflected in Poll' *NYT* 13.7.1992

77 Baker *The Politics* p. 671; Andrew Rosenthal 'Baker Leaving State Dept. to Head White House Staff and Guide Bush's Campaign' *NYT* 14.8.1992. R. W Apple Jr 'Friend in a Time of Need'

NYT 14.8.1992; Andrew Rosenthal 'Pressure Is Growing on President to Bring Baker in for Campaign' *NYT* 31.5.1992; Diary Entry 13.9.1992, printed in Bush *All the Best* p. 567. Cf. his Diary Entry 3.9.1992, printed in ibid. on p. 566

78 On the Russian government reshuffle, see GHWBPL NSC Burns–Hewett Files – Subject Files: Working Papers for June Summit 1992 (Bush–Yeltsin) [1] (OA/ID CF01408–017) AmEmb Moscow (Amb. Strauss) to White House: NSC – Subj: Power and Palace Politics in the Renewed Russian Government – A Profile 8.6.1992 pp. 1–6. Strauss wrote that 'With the new government appointments of June 1–5, Yeltsin has added a third axis of power to the previous delicate balance inside the Kremlin and Staraya Ploshad between energetic, younger reformer and more seasoned, conservative apparatschiks. Industrial technocrats are coming to power, with equities and influence previously absent from the Russian policy mix.'

79 See JAB-SML B115/F9 Note from Zoellick to Baker – Russia Economic Reform and the IMF 2.6.1992 pp. 1–3; Steven Greenhouse 'US Backs Easier Terms for Russian Aid' *NYT* 19.6.1992

80 Louis Uchitelle 'IMF and Russia Reach Accord on Loan Aid and Spending Limits' *NYT* 6.7.1992. Note: the $1 billion IMF loan was ratified by the Fund's board on 5 August 1992 – incidentally the day before the House voted in favour of the Freedom Support Act. For an overview of Russia–IMF developments, see IMFA Accession 1996-0187-0006 – OMD-AD Box 9110 Russia (3) 1992, Memo by Odling-Smee to the Managing Director – Russian

Federation: Back-To-Office Report 8.7.1992; TNA UK PREM 19/3923 and 19/3924; and GHWBPL NSC Burns–Hewett Files – Subject File: Russia – IMF #2 (OA/ID CF01408–006). Cf. James M. Boughton *Tearing Down Walls: The International Monetary Fund 1990–1999* IMF 2012 chs. 6–8

81   For the Munich G7 Economic Declaration 8.7.1992, see worldjpn. grips.ac.jp/documents/texts/summit/ 19920708.D1E.html. For the Bush–Miyazawa agreement forged on 1 July to support the IMF in releasing the $1 billion as a first tranche to Russia, see GHWBPL Memcon of Bush–Miyazawa talks 1.7.1992 The Cabinet Room p. 5. See also GHWBP NSC H-Files – NSC/ DC Meeting Files: NSC/DC 389 6.11.1992 – NSC/DC Meeting on US Policy toward Russia (OA/ID 90023– 034) The IMF and Russian Reform (undated; probably November 1992) pp. 1–3; and Russia – Rescheduling the USSR Debt 4.11.1992 pp. 1–4

82   On the German economy, see also TNA UK PREM 19/4500 Memo by Wall – Visit by Alan Greenspan 12.5.1992 pp. 2–3. 'Mr Greenspan thought the situation in Germany would get quite nasty for the next two years.' The PM agreed: 'There was no doubt the East German adjustment process was a real albatross around Kohl's neck ... East Germany would go on being a huge drain ... If East Germany could not succeed, what hope did Russia have?'; JAB-SML B115/ F9 Agenda for Meeting with the president (German economy) 22.4.1992 Craig R. Whitney 'Economic Powers Facing Their Limits at Munich Summit' *NYT* 5.7.1992.

83   Ibid.; Don Oberdorfer 'Face of Doubts, Bush Defends Role as Low-Key Summit

Leader' *WP* 9.7.1992. For British and US problems, see also GHWBPL Telcon between Bush and Major 6.3.1992 White House p. 1. On Kohl's economic and political woes, see Memcon of Bush–Weizsäcker talks (10.30–10.55 a.m.) 29.4.1992 Oval Office pp. 1–3. On Japan, see GHWBPL Memcon of Bush–Miyazawa talks 1.7.1992 The Cabinet Room pp. 1–6. Cf. Telcon of Bush–Miyazawa call 28.6.1992 The Residence pp. 1–2. On the Kuril Islands issue, see also Mark Kramer & Gareth Cook 'The Last Russo-Japanese War: Should America Encourage a Kuril Islands Settlement?' *WP* 13.9.1992; Steven R. Weisman 'Dispute Over Seized Islands Delays Tokyo Aid to Russia' *NYT* 7.2.1992

84   Roger Cohen 'Industrial Nations Fighting Deadlock on Farm Subsidies' *NYT* 7.7.1992. Marc Fisher & Stuart Auerbach '7 Leaders Pledge Aid for Yeltsin: Support Promised for Debt, A-Plants' *WP* 9.7.1992; Tom Redburn 'Unpopular G7 Leaders Keep Bickering on Issues – Discord is Theme of Annual Summit' *International Herald Tribune* 6.7.1992

85   JAB-SML B115/F9 Proposed Agenda for Meeting with the president (Miyazawa Visit ['G8']) 26.6.1992 p. 3; Cohen 'Industrial Nations Fighting Deadlock on Farm Subsidies'

86   GHWBPL Memcon of Bush–Kohl talks 21.3.1992 Camp David pp. 1–17 quoting pp. 13, 15

87   Serge Schmemann 'Yeltsin's Song: Summit Blues; 7 Pats on the Back – and Some Token Aid' *NYT* 9.7.1992. Cf. GHWBPL NSC Burns–Hewett Files – POTUS Telcon CIS 1992: Yeltsin (OA/ ID CF01421–050) Telcon of Bush to Yeltsin call 23.3.1992 Oval Office pp.

2–3. For Yeltsin's aspirations to be invited to the G7, see GHWBPL NSC Burns–Hewett Files – POTUS Telcon CIS 1992: Yeltsin (OA/ID CF01421–052) Telcon of Bush to Yeltsin call 19.3.1992 Oval Office pp. 3–4

88 See Angela Stent *Russia and Germany Reborn: Unification, the Soviet Collapse and the New Europe* Princeton UP 2000 pp. 186–7; GHWBPL Memcon of Bush–Mitterrand talks 5.7.1992 Munich Germany pp. 1–9 here p. 6

89 GHWBPL NSC Burns–Hewett Files – Subject Files: Working Papers for June Summit 1992 (Bush–Yeltsin) [1] (OA/ID CF01408–017) AmEmb Moscow (Amb. Strauss) to White House: NSC – Subj: Yeltsin's world 9.6.1992 pp. 1–7 esp. pp. 2–3

90 Apple Jr 'And Now, the Political Plowshares' p. 11; Schmemann 'Yeltsin's Song' p. 12

91 Interview with Andrei Kozyrev in *Novye Vremena* (*New Times*) no. 3 (1992) pp. 20–4. It must be noted that Russia would not apply to the GATT until 1993 and it would not join the new WTO until December 2011 – after eighteen years of membership negotiations – which was ten years later than the PRC.

92 Interview with Andrei Kozyrev in *Moscow News* 7–14.6.1992 p. 14; Kozyrev quoted in *Moscow Interfax* 2.11.1992 Daily Report – Central Eurasia FBIS-SOV-92-229, and in 'Kozyrev Article in US Journal Reported' Itar-TASS 9.4.1992 p. 16 FBIS-SOV-92-070; Andrei Kozyrev *Preobrazhenie Mezhdunar. otnosheniia* 1995 p. 230. See also David McDonald 'Domestic Conjectures, the Russian State, and the World Outside, 1700–2006' in Robert Legvold (ed.) *Russian Foreign Policy in*

the Twenty-First Century and the Shadow of the Past Columbia UP 2007 p. 179

93 Kozyrev quoted in Stent *Russia and Germany Reborn* p. 189. For Ukrainian president Kravchuk's views of 'equal relations' and his plea with Bush that 'any assistance by the US to Russia should not go to support imperialism', see GHWBPL Memcon of Bush–Kravchuk talks 6.5.1992 Old Family Dining Room pp. 2, 4, 6; Memcon of Bush's meeting with presidents Rüütel (EST), Gorbunovs (LAT) and Landsbergis (LIT) 10.7.1992 Helsinki Fair Center Finland pp. 1–5 here p. 4

94 Cf. Michael Dobbs 'Russia Redux: What Yeltsin's Revolution Didn't Change' *WP* 4.6.1992; Hannes Adomeit 'Russia as a "Great Power" in World Affairs: Images and Reality' *International Affairs* 71, 1 (January 1995) pp. 35–68

95 Cf. TNA UK PREM 19/3924 Memo from Braithwaite to Butler – Russia: Internal 28.10.1992 p. 1; GHWBPL NSC H-Files – MSC/DC Meeting Files: NSC/DC 389 6.11.1992 (OA/ID 90023–034) US Response to Situation in Russia 2.11.1992 pp. 1–9

96 TNA UK PREM 19/3927 Memo from N.L. (Treasury) to Prime Minister – The State of Economic Reform in Russia 26.10.1992 10pp. esp. pp. 1–3

97 Matlock *Autopsy* pp. 680–3, 734–5; Michael Dobbs 'Yeltsin, Congress Reach Power-Sharing Compromise – Status Quo Frozen Until New Constitution Adopted' *WP* 13.12.1992; *idem* 'Russian Leader's Public Appeal is Age-old Gambit' *WP* 13.12.1992; Steven Erlanger 'Kremlin's Technocrat: Viktor Stepanovich Chernomyrdin' *NYT* 15.12.1992; Serge Schmemann

'Yeltsin Abandons His Principal Aide to Placate Rivals' *NYT* 15.12.1992

98   'Kohl Grants Debt Relief to Russia And Offers Confidence in Yeltsin' *NYT* 17.12.1992. See also Kohl *Erinnerungen 1990–1994* pp. 511–15. According to Kohl's memoirs these were tough negotiations – a real marathon. Yeltsin demanded DM 850 million for Red Army returnees, Kohl conceded an extra DM 550 million ($318 million) in addition to the DM 7.8 billion for housing that had already been agreed in 1990. Cf. ch. 4 pp. 248–9. It is noteworthy that following his 29 October phone conversation with Yeltsin, Bush too was looking into supporting concerted efforts by the G7 to reschedule the former Soviet Union's debt. He insisted at the same time that a legal framework be worked out which would accommodate the interest of both Russia and Ukraine. GHWBPL NSC Burns Files – Subject Files: Yeltsin (OA/ID CF01487–006) Letter from Bush to Yeltsin (via privacy channels) 11.11.1992 pp. 1–2

99   Ordinarily the number of CSCE member states would have been fifty-three, but Belgrade had been suspended in May and was to remain excluded for a further 3 months after Helsinki II had ended

100   As Bush told Georgia's chairman, Eduard Shevardnadze, when they met on the margins of the summit: 'We've been through a lot together including the fifty-five speeches we are hearing together here in Helsinki but at least everybody is keeping it short. Castro came to Rio and everyone expected a two-hour speech but give the man credit he finished in the allotted seven minutes.' GHWBPL Memcon of Bush–

Shevardnadze talks 9.7.1992 Guest House Helsinki p. 1

101   See 'NATO and Eastern Lands Initial Troop Pact' *NYT* 7.7.1992

102   Cf. GHWBPL NSC Holl Files – Subject File: NATO and European Security January-June 1992 (OA/ID CF01398–018) 984 – Secret – Continuing Momentum for European Security Identity (undated, ca early 1992). The paper suggested that 'The Europeans'' desire to tinker with security architecture – including CSCE, NATO and the NACC – is likely to decline sharply after the July CSCE summit, and they will increasingly focus on how to use the institutions to cope with specific sources of instability.' What's more, in Washington's view, 'for the foreseeable future' Europeans would 'depend on US support via NATO structures for any significant military undertaking'.

103   CFE figures and Havel quote from Craig R. Whitney 'NATO and Europe Tighten Sanctions Against Yugoslavs' *NYT* 11.7.1992. Cf. GHWBPL Memcon of Bush–Havel talks 9.7.1992 Helsinki Fair Center pp. 1–3

104   Ibid.; Craig R. Whitney 'Belgrade Suspended by European Security Group' *NYT* 9.7.1992; and Andrew Rosenthal 'Bush Vows to Get Supplies to Bosnia' *NYT* 10.7.1992

105   Note: The CSCE had originally of course not been conceived as a classic international 'organisation', but rather as a 'dynamic process'. At Helsinki II the members approved an eighty-page declaration entitled 'The Challenges of Change' to underpin the CSCE's new role as a regional organisation under the UN Charter. What's more, as a more permanent forum, the CSCE had already established a permanent

Council of (Foreign) Ministers which met for the first time on 19–20 June 1991 in Berlin. See Uwe Andersen & Wichard Woyke (eds) *Handwörterbuch Internationale Organisationen* VS Verlag für Sozialwissenschaften 1995 p. 267. See also Th. J. W. Sneek 'The CSCE in the new Europe: From Process to Regional Arrangement' *Indiana International & Comparative Law Review* 5, 1 (1994) pp. 1–73. On the CSCE NATO/NACC relationship and NATO's unique capacity to provide security see GHWBPL NSC John Gordon Files – Subject Files: NACC – November 1991 (OA/ID CF01652–021) AmEmb Warsaw (Amb. Hornblow) to Sec State: Note – Giving Life to the NACC – Some Thoughts from Warsaw 22.11.1991 pp. 1–7

106 Baker quoted in GHWBPL Memcon of Bush–Weizsäcker plenary talks (10.58–11.40 a.m.) 29.4.1992 The Cabinet Room p. 4. See also GHWBPL NSC Gompert Files – European Strategy [Steering] Group (ESSG) (CF01301–009) NACC-CSCE relationship – drafted by S. McGinnis 4pp. n.d. *circa* Feb. 1992. The paper held that 'in the interlocking set of organisations developing in the post-Cold War era' – NATO, EC and the CSCE – the latter's 'specific functions' and 'overlapping responsibilities' could be defined as: 'inclusive; provides a sense of direction and values – a set of standard – by which to judge European developments: "Conscience of the Continent"' p. 1

107 Blaine Harden 'Slovenia, Belgrade Declare Ceasefire' *WP* 29.6.1991. Chuck Sudetic '2 Yugoslav States Agree to Suspend Secession Process' *NYT* 29.6.1991. See also GHWBPL NSC Chellis Files – Subject File: CSCE –

Yugoslavia Crisis (OA/ID CF01441–002) AmEmb Luxembourg to Sec State: Note – EC Strategy – Position at August 8 CSCE Meeting 7.8.1991 pp. 1–3

108 On the early, emotive and tangled historiography of Yugoslavia, see Gale Stokes et al. 'Instant History: Understanding the Wars of Yugoslav Succession' *Slavic Review* 55, 1 (Spring 1996) pp. 136–60. Cf. Florian Bieber et al. (eds) *Debating the End of Yugoslavia* Ashgate 2014. For useful accounts of the succession wars, see also Laura Silber & Alan Little *Yugoslavia: Death of a Nation* Penguin Books 1997; Misha Glenny *The Fall of Yugoslavia: The Third Balkan War* Penguin Books 1996. See also Marc Weller 'The International Response to the Dissolution of the Socialist Federal Republic of Yugoslavia' *The American Journal of International Law* 86, 3 (Jul. 1992) pp. 569–607

109 See John R. Lampe *Twice There Was a Country* Cambridge UP 2000; Reynolds *One World Divisible* p. 621

110 See for example Igor Štiks *Nations and Citizens in Yugoslavia and the Post-Yugoslav States: One Hundred Years of Citizenship* Bloomsbury 2015; Dejan Jović *Yugoslavia: A State that Withered Away* Purdue UP 2009; Susan L. Woodward *Balkan Tragedy: Chaos and Dissolution after the Cold War* Brookings Institution Press 1995

111 Human Rights Watch *Human Rights Watch World Report 1990 – Yugoslavia* 1.1.1991 refworld.org/docid/467fca3a1d. html. See also Josip Glaurdic *The Hour of Europe: Western Powers and the Break-up of Yugoslavia* Yale UP 2011 pp. 69–118

112 Glaurdic *The Hour* pp. 119–43, 148–57

113 For attempted explanations, see for

example James *Gow Triumph of the Lack of Will: International Diplomacy and the Yugoslav War* Columbia UP 1997; Brendan Simms *Unfinest Hour: Britain and the Destruction of Bosnia* Allen Lane 2001. Cf. Michael Rose *Fighting for Peace: Bosnia 1994* Harvill Press 1998; Susan L. Woodward 'Costly Disinterest: Missed Opportunities for Preventive Diplomacy in Croatia and Bosnia Herzegovina, 1985–1991' in Bruce W. Jentleson (ed.) *Opportunities Missed, Opportunities Seized: Preventive Diplomacy in the Post-Cold War World* Rowman & Littlefield 2000

114 Charter of Paris for a New Europe 21.11.1990 state.gov/t/isn/4721.htm

115 Soviet Record of Main Content of Conversation between Bush and Gorbachev in Novo-Ogarevo 31.7.1991 *TLSS* doc. 139 pp. 900–1. For the US transcript, see GHWBPL Memcon of Gorbachev–Bush talks (10.55 a.m.–2.55 p.m. three-on-three mtg) 31.7.1991 Novo-Ogarevo pp. 1–8

116 Baker *The Politics* p. 636

117 See ch. 6.

118 Bush's Address Before a Joint Session of the Congress on the Cessation of the Persian Gulf Conflict 6.3.1991 APP

119 Bush's Remarks at Maxwell Air Force Base War College in Montgomery Alabama 13.4.1991 APP

120 See for example Bush's comment on 11 April 1991 when he insisted on the 'common interest' of the US with the EC 'in seeing Yugoslavia held together without violence and with reform'. GHWBPL Memcon of Bush's meeting with PM Jacques Santer and EC President Jacques Delors 11.4.1991 Cabinet Room and Old Family Room pp. 1–10 esp. p. 4. See also Norbert Both *From Indifference to Entrapment:*

The Netherlands and the Yugoslav Crisis 1990–1995 Amsterdam UP 2000 p. 95

121 Baker *The Politics* pp. 478–83, 634–5; Hutchings *American Diplomacy* pp. 309–12; William Zimmermann *Origins of a Catastrophe: Yugoslavia and Its Destroyers – America's Last Ambassador Tells What Happened and Why* Times Books 1996 pp. 133–7

122 Hutchings *American Diplomacy* p. 310

123 Zimmermann *Origins* p. 137. Note: NATO commander-in-chief General John Galvin explained that 'Yugoslavia is not within NATO's defense zone', specifying that in military operations 'the operative zone of the forces extends within the boundaries of the NATO member countries'. See 'NATO Will Not Intervene in Country' Belgrade *TANJUG* in English 1.6.1991 FBIS Daily Report – East Europe FBIS-EEU-91–106 (3.6.1991)

124 Diary Entry 2.7.1991, printed in Bush *All the Best* pp. 527–8

125 Robert Dover 'The EU and the Bosnian Civil War 1992–95: The Capabilities–Expectations Gap at the Heart of EU Foreign Policy' *European Security* 14, 3 (2005) pp. 297–318

126 Alan Riding 'Conflict in Yugoslavia; Europeans Send High-Level Team' *NYT* 29.6.1991. The full quote can be found in Mark Wintz *Transatlantic Diplomacy and the Use of Military Force in the Post-Cold War Era* Palgrave Macmillan 2010 p. 33

127 George F. Kennan *The Decline of Bismarck's European Order: Franco-Russian Relations, 1875–1890* Princeton UP 1979 p. 3

128 On 26 March 1991, for instance, the EC foreign ministers declared that 'a united and democratic Yugoslavia stands

the best chance to integrate itself harmoniously in the new Europe'. See Both *From Indifference* p. 95; Glaurdic *The Hour* p. 145

129 Glaurdic *The Hour* pp. 165–6

130 Lawrence Eagleburger quoted in David Binder 'Europeans Warn on Yugoslav Split: US Deplores Moves' *NYT* 26.6.1991; Alan Riding 'Europeans Warn on Yugoslav Split' *NYT* 26.6.1991. See also Joshua Muravchik *The Imperative of American Leadership: A Challenge to Neo-isolationism* AEI Press 1996 p. 89

131 Dumas' quotes from Glaurdic *The Hour* p. 174; Riding 'Europeans Warn on Yugoslav Split'; and Mark Almond *Europe's Backyard War: The War in the Balkans* Mandarin 1994 p. 237

132 Mark Lennox-Boyd, Parliamentary Undersecretary for Foreign and Commonwealth Affairs, quoted in the Common's debate on 'Yugoslavia' in *Hansard* (vol. 193 cols. 1137–8) 27.6.1991; Hurd quoted in Noel Malcolm 'Bosnia and the West: A Study in Failure' *National Interest* 1.3.1995

133 Mitterrand feared tribal wars: 'la guerre des tribus'

134 The French spoke of 'la dérive vers l'Est de l'Allemagne'

135 See ch. 5; Hans Stark 'La Yougoslavie et les dissonances franco-allemandes' in Henri Ménudier (ed.) *Le couple franco-allemand en Europe* L'Harmattan 1993 pp. 197–205; Hanns W. Maull & Bernhard Stahl 'Durch den Balkan nach Europa? Deutschland und Frankreich in den Jugoslawienkriegen' *Politische Vierteljahresschrift* 43, 1 (March 2002) pp. 82–111 esp. p. 85; William Dorzdiak 'Conflicts over Yugoslav Crisis Surface in Europe' *WP* 5.7.1991

136 See Stephen Kinzer 'Germans in Warning on Yugoslav Economy' *NYT* 28.6.1991

137 William Dorzdiak 'West Europeans Send Envoys, Debate Yugoslav Crisis' *WP* 29.6.1991. For America's perspective, see also GHWBPL Memcon of Gorbachev–Bush talks (10.55 a.m.–2.55 p.m. three-on-three mtg) 31.7.1991 Novo-Ogarevo pp. 7–8

138 Baker *The Politics* p. 636. Eagleburger quoted in Simms *Unfinest Hour* p. 54. GHWBPL NSC Holl Files – Subject Files: Yugoslavia – EC [2] (OA/ID CF01476–016) Sensitive (need to know basis) AmEmb Belgrade (Amb. Warren Zimmermann) to Baker (as well as Eagleburger, Zoellick and Scowcroft): Note – A Plan for Yugoslavia 30.9.1991 pp. 1–9 esp. p. 2. Cf. on US doubts regarding France's position, see GHWBPL NSC Barry Lowenkron Files – NATO File: NATO – Wörner (OA/ID CF01526–021) Memcon of Bush–Wörner talks 25.6.1992 Oval Office pp. 1–3. See also GHWBPL Memcon of Bush–Mitterrand talks 5.7.1992 Munich pp. 1–9

139 Hutchings *American Diplomacy* p. 313. See also GHWBPL NSC Chellis Files – Subject File: CSCE – Yugoslavia Crisis (OA/ID CF01441–002) AmEmb Bonn (Amb. Walters) to Sec State: Note – Germans want Prague COSO to endorse continued EC/WEU roles 7.8.1991 pp. 1–2

140 On bringing the Yugoslav crisis before the UN Security Council, see GHWPL NSC Holl Files – Subject Files: Yugoslavia – EC [3] (CF01476–017) AmEmb The Hague (Amb. Wilkins) to Sec State: Note – EC/Yugoslavia: EC/ WEU Ministerials (9.9.1991) 20.9.1991 pp. 1–7; US Mission New York (amb.

Pickering) to Sec State: Note – European Security Council Initiative 22.9.1991 pp. 1–4

141 For Resolution 713, see Daniel Bethlehem & Marc Weller (eds) *The Yugoslav Crisis in International Law, General Issues – Part 1* Cambridge UP 1997 pp. 1–2. Weller 'The International Response' pp. 578–81

142 Weller 'The International Response' pp. 581ff.; and Hutchings *American Diplomacy* p. 313

143 Glaurdic *The Hour* pp. 185–7. Cf. Genscher *Erinnerungen* pp. 938–9. On Germany's policies, see also Michael Libal *Limits of Persuasion: Germany and the Yugoslav Crisis, 1991–1992* Praeger 1997; Hanns W. Maull 'Germany in the Yugoslav Crisis' *Survival* 37, 4 (1995) pp. 99–130

144 Beverly Crawford 'German Foreign Policy and European Political Cooperation: The Diplomatic Recognition of Croatia in 1991' *German Politics & Society* 13, 2 (Summer 1995) pp. 1–34 here esp. pp. 6–7, 16–17; William Drozdiak 'Germany Criticises European Community Policy on Yugoslavia' *WP* 2.7.1991

145 Crawford 'German Foreign Policy' pp. 16–23

146 GHWBPL NSC Holl Files – Subject Files: Yugoslavia – EC [2] (OA/ID CF 01476–016) AmEmb The Hague (Amb. Wilkins) to Sec State: Note – EC Monitors' 10/24 updated on Yugoslav situation 24.10.1991 pp. 1–5; and in the same file Cable: no subj. 12.11.1991 p. 1. Glaurdic *The Hour* p. 215

147 Richard Caplan *Europe and the Recognition of New States in Yugoslavia* Cambridge UP 1995 pp. 19–20. See also GHWBPL NSC Holl Files – Subject Files: Yugoslavia – EC [2] (OA/ID

CF01476–016) AmEmb The Hague (Amb. Wilkins) to WH router: Note – EC/Yugoslavia: Yugoslav Leaders agree on one month JNA Withdrawal / Talks timetable 11.10.1990 pp. 1–7. See also GHWBPL NSC Holl Files – Subject Files: Yugoslavia – EC [2] (OA/ID CF01476–016) AmEmb Belgrade (Amb. Zimmermann) to Sec State: Note – EC-proposed compromise on Yugoslavia's future: The devil's in the details 18.10.1991, pp. 1–7

148 Genscher *Erinnerungen* pp. 951–4; 'In zwei Monaten entscheiden wir über die Anerkennung' *Die Presse* 18.10.1991. See also 'Declaration on Yugoslavia' Extraordinary EPC Ministerial Meeting (Rome) *EPC Press Release* 09/91 8.11.1991. The EC Council of Ministers' Meeting on the margins of the Rome NATO summit reinforced the French and British in their view that 'the prospect of recognition of the independence of those republics wishing it can only be envisaged in the framework of an overall settlement'. There was no mention of the 10 December deadline; in fact, the majority of the ministers cautioned against 'premature recognition' of Slovenia and Croatia. See also Henry Wynaendts *L'engrenage: Chroniques yougoslaves, juillet 1991– août 1992* Editions Denoël 1993 pp. 132–3; Glaurdic *The Hour* p. 233

149 GHWBPL NSC Holl Files – Subject Files: Yugoslavia – EC [2] (OA/ID CF 01476–016) AmEmb Belgrade (Amb. Zimmermann) to Sec State: Note – Serbian Reactions to EC Hague Proposal 22.10.1991 pp. 1–7

150 For Kohl's and Genscher's Bundestag speeches, printed in Deutscher Bundestag *Stenographischer Bericht* 60. Sitzung Plenarprotokoll 27.11.1991 pp.

5007–17C esp. pp. 5014–15C and 5056Bff. See also TNA UK PREM 19/3353 Memo from Wall to Gozney – PM's meeting with Chancellor Kohl 27.11.1991 pp. 1–2; Glaurdic *The Hour* pp. 234–5. Libal *Limits* pp. 78–9; Genscher *Erinnerungen* p. 958

151 Both *From Indifference* pp. 131–2 Hella Pick 'Early Recognition "Is Unstoppable"' *Guardian* 5.12.1991

152 Serge Schmemann 'Declaring Death of Soviet Union, Russia and 2 Republics Form New Commonwealth' *NYT* 9.12.1991; Celestine Bohlen 'The Union is Buried: What's Being Born?' *NYT* 9.12.1991. See also David C. Gompert 'Bonfire of the Vanities: An American Insider's Take on the Collapse of the Soviet Union and Yugoslavia' in Hamilton & Spohr (eds) *Exiting the Cold War, Entering a New World*

153 Glaurdic *The Hour* pp. 259–60

154 Kohl *Erinnerungen 1990–1994* pp. 385–90; Favier & Martin-Roland *La Décennie Mitterrand iv* pp. 227–33. Cf. Alan Riding 'West Europeans Gather to Seek a Tighter Union' *NYT* 9.12.1991; *idem* 'Europeans Accept a Single Currency and Bank by 1999' *NYT* 10.12.1991; *idem* 'Europe at Crossroads – Leaders Return from Meetings Confident That Region Will Move Onward to Union' *NYT* 12.12.1991. See also Craig R. Whitney 'British Bend on Single Currency but Resist Full European Unity' *NYT* 14.11.1991

155 On 'earned recognition', see GHWBPL NSC H-Files – NSC/DC Meetings Files: NSC/DC 325 13.12.1991 – NSC/DC Meeting re: Yugoslavia (OA/ID 90021–013) Summary of Conclusions for Meeting of Deputies Committee 13.12.1991 White House Situation Room pp. 1–2. GHWBPL Rostow Files –

Subject Files: Yugoslavia (UN) (OA/ID CF-1320–024) Deputies Meeting 23.12.1991 10:30 a.m. White House Situation Room – Attachment: Yugoslavia Policy Paper pp. 1–5

156 Baker *The Politics* pp. 638–9; Bethlehem & Weller (eds) *The Yugoslav Crisis* p. 481. For an extensive extract of Pérez de Cuéllar's letter of 10.12.1991 to van den Broek, see Steven L. Burg & Paul S. Shoup *The War in Bosnia-Herzegovina: Ethnic Conflict and International Intervention* M. E. Sharpe 1999 p. 94; John Tagliabue 'Germany Insists It Will Recognise Yugoslav Republics' Sovereignty' *NYT* 15.12.1991. Cf. GHWBPL NSC H-Files – NSC/DC Meetings Files: NSC/DC 325 – 13.12.1991 (OA/ID 90021–013) Director of Intelligence Report – Yugoslavia: Implications of International Recognition 11.12.1991 pp. 1–3; Background Paper (undated, early December 1991) pp. 1–3; Director of Intelligence Report – The Yugoslav Crisis: Where Does It Go from Here? 10.12.1991 pp. 1–4. The US worried about conflict, its need to engage militarily – and, if it would not do so, the loss of US influence in Europe and the dangers of a spreading Yugoslav conflict for European cohesion.

157 For the UK–FR–US machinations at the UN, see also Glaurdic *The Hour* p. 266. Tagliabue 'Germany Insists It Will Recognise Yugoslav Republics' Sovereignty'

158 Tagliabue 'Germany Insists It Will Recognise Yugoslav Republics' Sovereignty'. See also *idem* 'European Ties for Slovenia and Croatia' *NYT* 17.12.1991

159 Paul Lewis 'UN Yields to Plans by Germany to Recognise Yugoslav

Republics' *NYT* 16.12.1991. See also Resolution 724 (1991) adopted by the Security Council at its 3023rd meeting 15.12.1991, printed in Snežana Trifunovska *Yugoslavia Through Documents: From Its Creation to Its Dissolution* Martinus Nijhoff 1994 pp. 429–30

160 Favier & Martin-Roland *La Décennie Mitterrand iv* p. 244

161 Lewis 'UN Yields to Plans by Germany to Recognise Yugoslav Republics'

162 For Genscher's glossed-over version, see his *Erinnerungen* pp. 659–62; Both *From Indifference* pp. 134–5; Douglas Hurd *Memoirs* Abacus 2004 pp. 450–1. On the two-month deadline, cf. Ian Traynor 'Bonn Launches Campaign to Isolate Serbia' *Guardian* 5.12.1991

163 Both *From Indifference* p. 135; Tagliabue 'European Ties for Slovenia and Croatia'

164 'EC Declaration concerning the conditions for recognition of new states' adopted at the Extraordinary EPC Ministerial Meeting in Brussels 16.12.1991, printed in Trifunovska *Yugoslavia Through Documents* pp. 431–2

165 John Tagliabue 'Kohl to Compromise on Yugoslavia' *NYT* 18.12.1991

166 *Idem* 'European Ties for Slovenia and Croatia'; and 'Kohl to Compromise on Yugoslavia'

167 Ibid.

168 Ibid. See also Kohl *Erinnerungen 1990–1994* pp. 391–7

169 'Woman from East Elected as Kohl's Deputy' *NYT* 16.12.1991

170 Glaurdic *The Hour* p. 269

171 Note: only Serbia and Montenegro decided not to apply for recognition from the Community by the 23 December deadline. Macedonia had voted on 19 December to seek EC recognition after it had also overwhelmingly approved a September referendum on seceding from Yugoslavia. Macedonia's case, however, was, like Bosnia's, not straightforward, because of its complex historical relationship with Greece. Athens wanted to ensure that Macedonia pledge formally that it did not harbour any territorial claims against its 'neighbouring Community state'. See Chuck Sudetic 'Yugoslav Break-up Gains Momentum' *NYT* 21.12.1991; Caplan *Europe* p. 24

172 Georg Brock 'Kohl Hijacks Brussels Policy' *Times* 18.12.1991; Hella Pick 'A Master Germany Wants to Lose' *Guardian* 10.1.1992. See also Caplan *Europe* pp. 24–5; *idem* 'Conditional Recognition as an Instrument of Ethnic Conflict Regulation: The European Community and Yugoslavia' *Nations and Nationalism* 8, 2 (2002) pp. 157–77 here p. 171

173 See Richard Holbrooke *To End a War* Random House 1998 pp. 31–2. Cf. Wolfgang Krieger 'Toward a Gaullist Germany? Some Lessons from the Yugoslav Crisis' *World Policy Journal* 11, 1 (Spring 1994) pp. 26–38. John Tagliabue 'Bold New Germany: No Longer a Political "Dwarf"' *NYT* 16.12.1991

174 Hutchings *American Diplomacy* pp. 314–15; Daniel Brössler 'Genschers Alleingang' *SZ* 23.11.2011. See also Caplan quoting from a Memorandum of the Auswärtiges Amt 'Recognition of the Yugoslav Successor States (10 March 1993)', which implied that Germany saw only two options for the international community in the face of what Bonn regarded not as a civil war

but as war of conquest by Serbia: either military containment of Serbia or the 'internationalisation of the conflict by political means through formal recognition of the threatened republics in order to thwart any hopes Belgrade might have of faits accomplis achieved through the use of force being tolerated'. Caplan *Europe* p. 28. See also Stephen Engelberg 'Yugoslav Ethnic Hatreds Raise Fears of a War without End' *NYT* 23.12.1991

175 'Ein großer Erfolg für uns' *Der Spiegel* no. 51/1991 23.12.1991. See also Stephen Kinzer 'Slovenia and Croatia Get Bonn's Nod' *NYT* 24.12.1991

176 UK House of Commons 'Supplementary Estimates 1991–1992: Class II, Vote 2: Yugoslavia' in Hansard (vol. 205 col. 470) 5.3.1992

177 Kinzer 'Slovenia and Croatia Get Bonn's Nod'

178 Glaurdic *The Hour* pp. 270–5. See also Kohl *Erinnerungen 1990–1994* p. 407; Genscher *Erinnerungen* pp. 960–8

179 See ch. 7. See also Keith Bradsher 'Noting Soviet Eclipse, Baker Sees Arms Risk' *NYT* 9.12.1991. Cf. Andrew Rosenthal 'Bush Reluctantly Concludes Gorbachev Tried to Cling to Power Too Long' *NYT* 25.12.1991. See also GHWBPL Rostow Files – Subject Files: Yugoslavia (UN) (OA/ID CF01320–024) Hutchings to Howe: Note – DC Meeting on Yugoslavia 21.12.1991 pp. 1–2

180 Bush & Scowcroft *A World Transformed* pp. 541, 544

181 Daniele Conversi *German-Bashing and the Break-up of Yugoslavia* Univ. of Washington 1998. Kohl *Erinnerungen 1990–1994* p. 407

182 See TNA UK PREM 19/4164–2 Memo from Mallaby to Hurd – Germany: United but Troubled 18.12.1992 pp. 1–8

183 GHWBPL Memcon of Bush–Kohl talks 21.3.1992 Camp David pp. 1, 3–4; Kohl *Erinnerungen 1990–1994* pp. 428–9, 440. See also *Arbeitsmarkt – Registrierte Arbeitslose, Arbeitslosenquote nach Gebietsstand* Statistik der Bundesagentur für Arbeit, Arbeitslosigkeit im Zeitverlauf (1950–2017) Statistisches Bundesamt; *Arbeitsmarkt in Zahlen – Entwicklung der Arbeitslosenquote für Deutschland, West- und Ostdeutschland von 1991 bis heute* Statistik der Bundesagentur für Arbeit 2008

184 GHWBPL Memcon of Bush–Weizsäcker talks (10.30–10.55 a.m.) 29.4.1992 Oval Office p. 2; Craig R. Whitney '50,000 In Germany Protest Violence Against Migrants' *NYT* 9.11.1992; Stephen Kinzer 'Germany Agrees on Law to Curb Refugees and Seekers of Asylum' *NYT* 8.12.1992. Cf. Steven Erlanger 'Germany Pays to Keep Ethnic Germans in Russia' *NYT* 9.5.1993. On the refugee and minorities problem in Central Europe (esp. the borderlands of Yugoslavia, here Hungary), see also GHWBPL Telcon of Bush–Antall call 20.9.1991 aboard Air Force One pp. 1–3

185 GHWBPL Memcon of Bush–Weizsäcker talks (10.30–10.55 a.m.) 29.4.1992 Oval Office p. 2. It is noteworthy that in contrast to Germany, France, Italy and Spain were mostly worried about immigration from North Africa

186 Alan Riding 'At East–West Crossroads, Western Europe Hesitates' *NYT* 25.3.1992

187 GHWBPL Memcon of Bush–Kohl talks 21.3.1992 Camp David p. 3

188 See 'Entwurf des Bundeshaushalts 1993

und Finanzplan 1992 bis 1996' *Bulletin* No.72 2.7.1992; Wissenschaftlicher Dienst *Entwicklung der Staatsverschuldung von 1970 bis 2013* Deutscher Bundestag 2009; Germany's National Debt countryeconomy.com/national-debt/germany. See also Oliver Schwinn *Die Finanzierung der deutschen Einheit: Eine Untersuchung aus politisch-institutionalistischer Perspektive* VS Verlag für Sozialwissenschaften 1997 ch. 4; 'Ein schwerer Fehler' *Der Spiegel* 10/1991 4.3.1991

189 Kohl *Erinnerungen 1990–1994* pp. 414–21. Benjamin Stahl 'Türkei-Panzer-Affäre' *Das Parlament* 31.3.1992. See also Stephen Kinzer 'The Costs of Unification; For Kohl Ending the Strike was Just the First Step' *NYT* 10.5.1992

190 Genscher *Erinnerungen* pp. 999–1007 esp. pp. 1002–3. See also 'As Goes Germany' *NYT* 30.4.1992

191 Estonia, Latvia and Lithuania were expected to be the next signatories. On 1 January 1992 they were included in the EC's PHARE (originally created in 1989 as the 'Poland and Hungary: Assistance for Restructuring their Economies') programme. On 12 June 1995 they signed the Association Agreements with the EU – europa.eu/rapid/press-release_PRES-95-173_en.htm

192 Genscher *Erinnerungen* pp. 1003–9; John Tagliabue 'European Ties for Slovenia and Croatia' *NYT* 17.12.1991; Riding 'At East–West Crossroads'

193 Glaurdic *The Hour* pp. 279–91. See also GHWBPL NSC Gompert Files – Subject Files: Bosnia I [4] (OA/ID CF01301–004) AmEmb Belgrade to Baker: Note – Concentration Camps in Bosnia–Herzegovina 4.8.1992 pp. 1–4

194 Glaurdic *The Hour* pp. 281, 292–3, 397;

Baker *The Politics* pp. 639–41; GHWBPL Telcon of Bush–Major call 6.3.1992 White House p. 4. GHWBPL NSC Chellis Files – Subject File: CSCE – Yugoslavia Crisis (OA/ID CF01441–002) Yugoslavia political situation (undated, early 1992)

195 Bush's Statement on United States Recognition of the Former Yugoslav Republics 7.4.1992 APP. Hutchings *American Diplomacy* p. 316; 'Bosnia: All Fall Down' *WhiteHall Papers* 19, 1 (1993) pp. 61–73. The Helsinki Human Rights Watch report of August 1992 made clear also that serious war crimes were being committed in the Balkans. Indeed, it asked the Security Council to urgently 'exercise under its authority under the 1951 Convention on the Prevention and Punishment of the Crime of Genocide to intervene in Bosnia–Herzegovina to prevent and suppress genocide'. Helsinki Watch *War Crimes in Bosnia–Hercegovina* (August 1992) pp. 1–2. Baker also alluded to US intent to recognise Macedonia – but the territorial disputes with Greece made the Macedonian case more complex. In fact, formal recognition did not occur until 1994 and the countries only established full diplomatic relations in 1995

196 On UN Resolution 757 on 30.5.1992, see GHWBPL Rostow Files – Subject Files: Yugoslavia (UN) (OA/ID CF01320–024) UN SC Resolution 757 pp. 1–6. On UN SC Res. 757 and humanitarian assistance, see GHWBPL NSC Gompert Files: Subject Files – Bosnia I [4] (OA/ID CF01301–004) Humanitarian Aid to Bosnia Hercegovina 2.6.1992 pp. 1–4

197 Baker *The Politics* pp. 646–8; Paul Lewis 'UN Votes 13–0 For Embargo On Trade With Yugoslavia Air Travel And Oil

Curbed' *NYT* 31.5.1992; 'Excerpts From UN Resolution: "Deny Permission"' *NYT* 31.5.1992. On Russian support of the US position, see GHWBPL NSC Burns Files – Subject Files – Yeltsin (OA/ID CF01487-006) Telcon of Bush–Yeltsin call 27.6.1992 Camp David pp. 2–3. Bush told Yeltsin: 'we're all beginning to think that military action may be needed for a humanitarian effort' though he made clear he did not seek a change to the UN resolution in order to 'change or sort out the political situation in Bosnia'. His sole focus was 'to make sure the relief effort' was no longer blocked. 'If we go to the UN, I hope you will be able to help us in preventing mass starvation in Sarajevo'. Yeltsin reassured Bush 'we are not going to back out. We will support any additional moves and measures. Both in the humanitarian and in the military'.

198 GHWBPL NSC H-Files – NSC-DC Meeting Files: NSC/DC 363 10.7.1992 – NSC/DC Meeting on NATO Role in Assistance to Bosnia (OA/ID 90023-001) DC Meeting on NATO – Bosnia 10.7.1992 pp. 1–2

199 GHWBPL Memcon of Bush–Weizsäcker plenary talks (10.58–11.40 a.m.) 29.4.1992 The Cabinet Room pp. 3–5; Memcon of Bush–Mitterrand talks 5.7.1992 Munich pp. 1–9. See also GHWBPL NSC Gompert Files – Subject Files: Bosnia I [4] (OA/ID CF01301-004) Lowenkron/Holl to Scowcroft: Memorandum – NATO and the Bosnian Crisis 2.7.1992 pp. 1–3

200 GHWBPL Memcon of Bush–Wörner talks (11:00–11:30 a.m.) 9.7.1992 Helsinki Fair Center pp. 2–3. See also Bush's comment to Kohl on 28 June concerning the option of 'air support & cover' and a 'sea blockade', if the UN thought it

would be useful: 'My instinct is that neither side will welcome US ground troops' but 'we might have to pitch in and help resolve this … We are not enthusiastic about military support, but we have to act'. GHWBPL Telcon of Bush with Kohl 28.6.1992 Camp David p. 2

201 GHWBPL Memcon of Bush–Wörner talks 9.7.1992 Helsinki Fair Center p. 3

202 GHWBPL Memcon of Bush–Weizsäcker plenary talks (10.58–11.40 a.m.) 29.4.1992 The Cabinet Room pp. 3–5; Memcon of Bush–Mitterrand talks 5.7.1992 Munich pp. 1–9 esp. pp. 5–6

203 Genscher quoted in GHWBPL Memcon of Bush–Weizsäcker plenary talks (10.58–11.40 a.m.) 29.4.1992 The Cabinet Room pp. 4–5. On Genscher's role in the creation of the NACC in 1991, see also his *Erinnerungen* p. 978 and op-ed 'Neue Ordnung in Europa muß einen Rückfall in Zeit vor 1914 verhindern' *Welt am Sonntag* 13.10.1991; and ch. 7, p. 448

204 GHWBPL Memcon of Bush–Antall talks 10.7.1992 Helsinki Fair Center pp. 1–2, 4. Cf. Helmut Kohl's comment to John Major as early as 10 November 1991, who stated that 'it was extraordinary how forcefully Prime Minister Antall of Hungary was seeking to join NATO. That alone showed how completely the world had changed.' TNA UK PREM 19/3353 Memo from Wall to Gozney – PM's talks with Kohl in Bonn 10.11.1991 p. 2

205 NAC Statement on NATO Maritime Operations – Helsinki 10.7.1992 NATO website; WEU Council of Ministers 'Extraordinary Meeting on the Situation in Yugoslavia' Helsinki 10.7.1992 WEU website. See also Tarcisio Gazzini, 'NATO Coercive Military Activities in

the Yugoslav Crisis (1992–1999)'
European Journal of International Law
12, 3 (2001) pp. 391–435, esp. pp. 392–3
See also Whitney 'NATO and Europe
Tighten Sanctions Against Yugoslavs'

206 Cf. on problems regarding information
flow on war crimes, see GHWBPL NSC
Rostow Files – Subject Files: Yugoslavia
(War Crimes) (OA/ID CF1320–026)
NSC Cable – UN Secretariat
Responsibility for Disseminating
Information on War Crimes in the
Former Yugoslavia 23.10.1992 pp. 1–3

207 Baker *The Politics* p. 646; Kurt Schoker
'American Killed as Snipers Attack Panic
Convoy' *Independent* 14.8.1992. See also
GHWBPL NSC Gompert Files – Subject
Files: Bosnia I [2] (OA/ID CF01301–002)
Assessment of Humanitarian Situation
in Bosnia and Herzegovina 9.9.1992 pp.
1–3; US Actions in the Yugoslav Crisis
Checklist (undated, sent as a fax on
6.8.1992) pp. 1–3

208 Thomas L. Friedman '"Realists" vs.
"Idealists" – It's Harder Now to Figure
Out Compelling National Interests'
NYT 31.5.1992

209 'Campaign '92: Transcript of the First
Presidential Debate' *WP* 12.10.1992. Cf.
GHWBPL NSC Gompert Files –
Subject Files: Bosnia I [4] (OA/ID
01301–004) Remarks by the President
upon Departure, Peterson Air Force
Base, Colorado Springs 6.8.1992 pp.
1–2. Bush was keen on 'defusing and
containing' the conflict through 'international cooperation (UN, NATO, EC,
CSCE)'.

210 Ibid.; GHWBPL Memcon of Bush–
Antall talks 10.7.1992 Helsinki Fair
Center pp. 1–2, 4. Cf. GHWBPL Telcon
of Bush–Antall call 20.9.1991 aboard
Air Force One pp. 1–5. Note that
Hungary was concerned about Russia

flexing its muscles once more as much
as ethnic rivalries erupting within the
New Independent States. Equally,
Budapest worried about the Hungarian
minorities' rights in the former
Yugoslav republics, the spread of
violence from Croatia and Bosnia, and
the floods of refugees pouring from the
Balkans into the neighbouring states
(Hungary, Austria and Germany).

211 Ioan Lewis & James Mayall 'Somalia' in
Mats Berdal & Spyros Economides (eds)
*United Nations Interventionism, 1991–
2004* Cambridge UP 2009 pp. 118–21

212 Boutros Boutros-Ghali *The United
Nations and Somalia, 1992–1996* Dept
of Public Information UN 1996 p. 5;
Don Oberdorfer 'US Took Slow
Approach to Somali Crisis' *WP* 24.8.1992

213 Lewis & Mayall 'Somalia' p. 121

214 UN Secretary General Boutros Boutros-
Ghali quoted in Trevor Rowe 'Aid to
Somalia Stymied' *WP* 29.7.1992; For the
SG's concern generally 'the perception'
pervaded that the UN was 'acting in
Yugoslavia/Europe at the expense of the
south', see GHWBPL Memcon of
Working Lunch between Bush and
Boutros-Ghali 12.5.1992 Old Family
Dining Room; Written Statement by
Andrew S. Natsios (Assistant
Administrator for Food and
Humanitarian Assistance) 'Somalia:
The Case for Action' Select Committee
on Hunger – House of Representatives
22.7.1992 Serial No. 102–35 p. 100; 'The
Hell Called Somalia' *NYT* 23.7.1992

215 See Kenneth R. Rutherford
*Humanitarianism Under Fire: The US
and UN Intervention in Somalia*
Kumarian Press 2008 p. 43; Don
Oberdorfer 'The Path to Intervention'
WP 6.12.1992

216 Oberdorfer 'US Took Slow Approach

to Somali Crisis'. See also Walter H. Kanstiner 'US Policy in Africa in the 1990s' in Jeremy R. Azrael & Emil A. Payin (eds) *US and Russian Policymaking with Respect to the Use of Force* Rand 1996 p. 107. Cf. Oberdorfer 'The Path to Intervention'. Cf. Smith Hempstone 'Dispatch from a Place Near Hell; The Killing Drought in Kenya, As Witnessed by the US Ambassador' *WP* 23.8.1992

217 See Rutherford *Humanitarianism under Fire* pp. 43–4

218 Stefano Recchia 'Pragmatism over Principle: US Intervention and Burden Shifting in Somalia, 1992–1993' *Journal of Strategic Studies* (February 2018, online) pp. 5–6; Rowe 'Aid to Somalia Stymied'. UN Security Council Resolution 775 28.8.1992 – authorising 3,000 additional peacekeepers – UN website; 'Statement by Press Secretary Fitzwater on Additional Humanitarian Aid for Somalia' 14.8.1992 APP

219 Andrew Rosenthal 'Clinton Attacked On Foreign Policy' *NYT* 28.7.1992; Walter S. Poole *The Effort to Save Somalia: August 1992 – March 1994* Joint History Office 2005 pp. 8–9; Michael R. Gordon 'With UN's Help, US Will Airlift Food to Somalia' *NYT* 15.8.1992

220 Jane Perlez 'As Much of a Nation Starves, A Young Somali Grasps Life' *NYT* 17.8.1992. Between 17–23 August 1992 the newspaper front pages were dominated by election campaign headlines. From 24 August to 2 September Hurricane Andrew dominated the US news.

221 Holly Burkhalter 'What Took Us So Long in Somalia?' *WP* 6.9.1992. See also Lewis & Mayall 'Somalia' p. 122; Glenn M. Harned *Stability Operations in Somalia 1992–1993: A Case Study*

[PKSOI paper] US Army War College Press, 2016 p. xi

222 GHWBPL NSC H-Files – NSC/DC Meeting Files: NSC/DC 395 20.11.1992 – NSC/DC Meeting on Somalia (OA/ID 90024–004) Memo – Somalia: The Threat to the UN's Pakistani Battalion in Mogadishu 18.11.1992 pp. 1–4; and John M. Ordway to Jonathan T. Howe: Memo – DC Meeting on Somalia (on 20.11.1992) 19.11.1992 pp. 1–4; and CIA: NSC Memorandum – Can the United Nations Successfully Carry Out Their Mission in Somalia? pp. 1–4. Cf. Oberdorfer 'The Path to Intervention'. Cf. GHWBPL NSC H-Files – NSC/DC Meetings Files: NSC/DC 385 21.10.1991 – NSC/DC Meeting on Somalia (OA/ID 90023–029) Interagency Planning Group Status Report by Vincent D. Kern (Africa Region OSD/ISA) 15.10.1992 p. 1

223 National Security Directive 74 24.11.1992 fas.org/irp/offdocs /nsd/nsd74.pdf

224 Lewis & Mayall 'Somalia' p. 123; Quote from Recchia 'Pragmatism over Principle' p. 6. See also GHWBPL NSC H-Files – NSC/DC Meeting Files: NSC/DC 395 20.11.1992 (OA/ID 90024–004) State Discussion Paper for the DC – The Need for Action in Somalia (undated) pp. 1–5 esp. p. 4

225 On Bush's early views of Perot, see Diary Entry 31.3.1992 printed in Bush *All the Best* p. 555. Cf. Timothy J. McNulty 'Bush Focuses Attack on Perot' *CT* 26.6.1992. ABC TV's *20/20* show with the interview of George and Barbara Bush was aired on Friday 26.6.1992.

226 Oberdorfer 'The Path to Intervention'. See also Robert G. Patman *Strategic Shortfall: The Somalia Syndrome and the March to 9/11* Praeger Security Intl

2010 pp. 32–3. See also David Jeremiah Oral History (Commander of the Pacific Fleet, Vice Chairman and Acting Chairman of the Joint Chiefs of Staff) Transcript 15.11.2000. On the question whether 'the president was driving policy' regarding a US intervention in Somalia, Jeremiah was clear: 'He was not.'

227   The National Security Council Deputies Committee (DC) is a committee of the NSC and the senior sub-Cabinet interagency forum for consideration of national security policy issues by the US government. The committee was established in 1989 by incoming president George H. W. Bush, and has been retained in each reorganisation of the National Security Council.

228   For the options, see GHWBPL NSC H-Files – NSC/DC Meeting Files: NSC/DC 396 23.11.1992 – Small Group Meeting on Somalia (OA/ID 90024–005) Next Steps in Somalia (undated) pp. 1–4

229   Ibid., esp. p. 3; and GHWBPL NSC H-Files – NSC/DC Meeting Files: NSC/DC 395 20.11.1992 (OA/ID 90024–004) Minutes for the DC Meeting on Somalia 20.11.1990 pp. 1–6; Oberdorfer 'The Path to Intervention'; Patman *Strategic Shortfall* pp. 32–4. For different arguments why the US decided to get militarily involved in Somalia, cf. for example Brands *From Berlin to Baghdad* p. 94 who suggests Somalia was a preferable mission to Bosnia (because it was 'easier'), and Recchia who in his essay 'Pragmatism over Principle' presents UNITAF as a pragmatic response by the US military to fill the vacuum of a collapsing UN peacekeeping mission. See also Lidwie Kapteijns 'Test-firing the "New World

Order" in Somalia: The US/UN Military Humanitarian Intervention of 1992–1995' *Journal of Genocide Research* 15, 4 (2013) pp. 421–44

230   See Frank G. Hoffman *Decisive Force* Praeger 1996 pp. 100–1; *idem* 'A Second Look at the Powell Doctrine' *War on the Rocks* 20.2.2014. For *The National Military Strategy of the United States 1992*, see history.defense.gov/Portals/70/Documents/nms/nms1992.pdf?ver=2014-06-25-123420-723

231   Michael R. Gordon 'UN Backs A Somalia Force as Bush Vows a Swift Exit; Pentagon Sees Longer Stay' *NYT* 4.12.1992; Paul Lewis 'First UN Goal is Security; Political Outlook is Murky' *NYT* 4.12.1992; 'Excerpts from a Resolution on Delivering Somalia Aid' *NYT* 4.12.1992. See also Bush's letter to Boutros-Ghali 4.12.1992, printed in Bush *All the Best* pp. 579–80

232   See for example GHWBPL Telcon of Bush–Miyazawa call 2.12.1992 White House pp. 1–3; Telcon of Bush with Mulroney 2.12.1992 Oval Office pp. 1–2; Telcon of Bush–Amato call 3.12.1992 Oval Office pp. 1–2; Telcon of Bush–King Fahd call 3.12.1992 Oval Office pp. 1–3; Telcon of Bush–Mitterrand call 3.12.1992 Oval Office pp. 1–3

233   Bush's Address to the Nation on the Situation in Somalia 4.12.1992 APP; David Halberstam *War in a Time of Peace: Bush, Clinton and the Generals* Scribner 2001 pp. 251–2. See also Michael Wines 'Bush Declares Goal in Somalia to "Save Thousands" – Force to Remain into Clinton Presidency' *NYT* 5.12.1992; Michael R. Gordon, 'US Is Sending Large Force as Warning to Somali Clans' *NYT* 5.12.1992; Don Oberdorfer 'Bush Sends Forces to Help Somalia' *WP* 5.12.1992. For the quotes

on peacemaking and peacekeeping, see GHWBPL NSC Burns–Hewett Files – Subject Files: POTUS Telcons with CIS Leaders 1992 – Telcon with Yeltsin 12/6/1992 (OA/ID CF01421–038) Points to be made – telephone call with President Boris Yeltsin 4.12.1992

234 GHWBPL Telcon of Bush–Boutros call 8.12.1992 Oval Office pp. 1–3 here p. 2; cf. GHWBPL Telcon of Bush–Boutros call 4.12.1992 Oval Office pp. 1–2. See also John S. Brown *The United States Army in Somalia 1992–1994* US Army Center of Military History 2003 p. 14. See also GWHBPL NSC H-Files – NSC/DC Meetings Files: NSC/DC 403A 3.12.1992 – Small Group Meeting on Somalia (OA/ID 90024–013) Minutes – Meeting of the NSC Deputies Small Group 3.12.1992 SVTS Room p. 9. As Admiral Jeremiah put it in the meeting: 'If we believe in the hundred-day programme, there is no reason to believe there is any humanitarian disaster in the north ... Boutros-Ghali is keen for us to go north for disarming and de-mining operations. That's scary. If there's a reason to go to Hargeisa, that's OK but we need to have it defined.'

235 'Minutes of the NSC Meeting on Somalia 3.12.1992' p. 1 as quoted in Recchia 'Pragmatism over Principle' p. 16. 'Doable mission' quoted in GHWBPL NSC H-Files – NSC/DC Meeting Files: NSC/DC 395 20.11.1992 (OA/ID 90024–004) Minutes for the DC Meeting on Somalia 20.11.1992 p. 6. See also 'Somalia: Transition from US to United Nations Command – Statement by Deputy Assistant Secretary of State for African Affairs Robert Houdek 17.2.1993' *Foreign Policy Bulletin* 3, 6 (May 1993) pp. 44–8. For

UNOSOM I and UNITAF see UN website. Note: UNITAF was officially dissolved on 4 May 1993. The transition to UNOSOM II was set in motion following UNSC Resolution 814 of 26 March 1993 and the Clinton administration's fulfilment of his predecessors' commitment to leave after the hand-off of a quick-reaction force (2,500 men) off the coast of Somalia. On top, Boutros-Ghali only agreed to the transfer to UNOSOM II after Washington offered another 4,000 US troops for logistical support inland.

236 See for example Bush's comment on briefing Clinton in GHWBPL Telcon of Bush–Mulroney call 2.12.1992 Oval Office p. 2

237 Michael Wines 'Bush Declares Goal in Somalia to Save Thousands' *NYT* 4.12.1992 p. 4

238 Clinton's Address to the Nation on Somalia 7.10.1993 APP

239 Bush & Scowcroft *A World Transformed* p. 355; Address Before a Joint Session of the Congress on the Persian Gulf Crisis and the Federal Budget Deficit 11.9.1990 APP

240 Remarks at Texas A&M University in College Station Texas 15.12.1992 APP

241 See Thomas L. Friedman 'It's Harder Now to Figure Out Compelling National Interests' *NYT* 31.5.1992

242 Bush & Scowcroft *A World Transformed* p. 400

243 GHWBPL White House Office of Communications Paul McNeill Files – Persian Gulf Working Group: Notebooks of David Demarest [6] (OA/ID 03195) Gulf Policy Themes revised 14.12.1990

244 Bush & Scowcroft *A World Transformed* p. 564

245 Remarks at Texas A&M University in College Station Texas 15.12.1992 APP

246 Michael Wines 'Bush Rebounds to Center of the World Stage' *NYT* 4.12.1992

247 GHWBPL NSC Holl Files – Subject Files: NATO and European Security (General 1991) (CF01397–005) The Rome Summit and NATO's Mission (undated, *circa* October/November 1991) pp. 1–5. GHWBP NSC Gompert Files – European Strategy [Steering] Group (ESSG) (CF01301–009) The NACC in the New Europe 7pp. + cover note Gompert to Tim Niles et al. 31.3.1992; Memorandum from Lowenkron to Howe 26.3.1992; Memorandum from Gompert to Zoellick et al. – US National Security Interests in Europe Beyond the NATO Area 7.2.1992; NATO and the East: Key issues (Secret) 7pp. (undated [early 1992] – no author). See also Daniel Hamilton & Kristina Spohr (eds) *Open Door: NATO and Euro-Atlantic Security after the Cold War* Brookings Institution Press 2019 pp. viii–xx; Gompert 'Bonfire of the Vanities'

248 Cf. Piers Robinson *The CNN Effect: The Myth of News, Foreign Policy and Intervention* Routledge 2002; *idem* 'The CNN Effect: Can the News Media Drive Foreign Policy?' *Review of International Studies* 25, 2 (April 1999) pp. 301–9; Jonathan Mermin 'Myth of Media-Driven Foreign Policy' *Political Science Quarterly* 112, 3 (autumn 1997) pp. 385–403; Steven Livingston & Todd Eachus 'Humanitarian Crises and US Foreign Policy: Somalia and the CNN Effect Reconsidered' *Political Communication* 12, 4 (1995) pp. 413–29; Bernard C. Cohen 'A View from the Academy' in W. Lance Bennett & David L. Paletz (eds) *Taken By Storm: The Media, Public Opinion, and US Foreign*

Policy in the Gulf War Univ. of Chicago Press 1994 pp. 9–10; Michael Mandelbaum 'The Reluctance to Intervene' *Foreign Policy* 95 (Summer 1994) pp. 3–18; Adam Roberts 'Humanitarian War: Military Intervention and Human Rights' *International Affairs* 69, 3 (July 1993) pp. 429–49; George F. Kennan 'Somalia, Through a Glass Darkly' *NYT* 30.9.1993

249 Excerpts from 1992 Draft 'Defense Planning Guidance; for the fiscal years 1994–1999' PBS; 'Excerpts from Pentagon's Plan: "Prevent the Re-Emergence of a New Rival" (18.2.1992 draft)' *NYT* 8.3.1992; cf. Patrick E. Tyler 'US Strategy Plan Calls for Insuring No Rivals Develop' *NYT* 8.3.1992. A later April 1992 'DPG, FY 1994–1999' draft can be found at: archives.gov/files/declassification/iscap/pdf/2008-003-docs-1–12.pdf. See also 'Prevent the Reemergence of a New Rival' – The Making of the Cheney Regional Defense Strategy, 1991–1992 NSAEBB No. 245

250 Bush's News Conference with President Boris Yeltsin of Russia in Moscow 3.1.1993 APP

Chapter 9

1 Bush's Exchange with Reporters in Sydney Australia 1.1.1992 APP

2 Michael Wines 'Reporter's Notebook; For Bush, Jog Overseas Beats Running at Home' *NYT* 5.1.1992; John E. Yang 'Bush Discounts Fears About Collapse' *WP* 9.1.1992

3 For a full list of Bush's foreign travels, see US DoS Office of the Historian website

4 Bush's Address Accepting the Presidential Nomination at the Republican National Convention in New Orleans 18.8.1988 APP

5 Engel *When the World Seemed New* pp. 104–5. Cf. Stephen W. Bosworth 'The United States and Asia' *Foreign Affairs* 71, 1 (1991/1992) [America and the World 1991/92] pp. 113–29

6 See GHWBPL NSC H-Files – NSC/DC Meeting Files: NSC/DC 221 13.11.1990 – NSC/DC Meeting on Korea (OA/ID 90017–017) US Policy Toward North Korea (undated) p. 1; Steve R. Weisman 'In North Korea, the 1990s Have Not Arrived' *NYT* 23.12.1991

7 On the various attempts by North Korea to obstruct the games, including unsuccessfully trying to get China and the Soviet Union to boycott them, see Olivia B. Waxman 'How Drama Between North and South Korea Threatened the Olympics 30 Years Ago' *TIME* 8.2.2018

8 Weisman 'In North Korea, the 1990s Have Not Arrived'

9 Sergey Radchenko 'Russia's Policy in the Run-Up to the First North Korean Nuclear Crisis 1991–1993' *NPIHP Working Paper #4* 2/2015 p. 8

10 Radchenko *Unwanted Visionaries* p. 244

11 Until then North and South Korea only had observer status at the United Nations, with no voting power

12 David E. Sanger 'North Korea Reluctantly Seeks UN Seat' *NYT* 29.5.1991; GHWBPL Memcon of Bush–Roh talks 17.10.1989 Oval Office/ Cabinet Room/Old Family Dining Room p. 3. See also GHWBPL NSC H-Files – NSC/DC Meeting Files: NSC/ DC 221 13.11.1990 – NSC/DC Meeting on Korea (OA/ID 90017–017) US Policy Toward North Korea (undated) p. 1

13 GHWBPL Memcom of Bush–Roh talks 2.7.1991 Oval Office and Cabinet Room p. 2

14 Ibid. p. 4

15 David E. Sanger 'Koreas Sign Pact Renouncing Force in a Step to Unity' *NYT* 13.12.1991

16 Bruce Cumings 'Spring Thaw for Korea's Cold War?' *The Bulletin of Atomic Scientists* (April 1992) p. 14; '2 Koreas Agree on Nuclear Ban, But Not on Method of Inspections' *NYT* 2.12.1991

17 Bush's Address to the Nation on Reducing United States and Soviet Nuclear Weapons 27.9.1991 APP; GHWBPL Telcon of Bush–Gorbachev call 27.9.1991 Oval Office pp. 1–3. See also DoD Secretary of Defense – Memorandum for Secretaries of the Military Departments: Reducing the US Nuclear Arsenal (Secret) 28.9.1991 NSAEBB No. 561; Andrew Rosenthal 'US to Give Up Short-Range Nuclear Arms – Bush Seeks Soviet Cuts and Further Talks' *NYT* 28.9.1991; Michael R. Gordon 'Bush's Arms Plan; Why US Was Worried' *NYT* 28.12.1991

18 GHWBPL Telcon of Bush–Gorbachev call 5.10.1991 Camp David pp. 1–3. Bush & Scowcroft *A World Transformed* pp. 542, 544–7; Plokhy *The Last Empire* pp. 201, 209–11. Serge Schmemann 'Gorbachev Matches US on Nuclear Cuts and Goes Further on Strategic Warheads' *NYT* 6.10.1991; Michael R. Gordon 'Room for Differences – Amid Accord over Tactical Nuclear Arms, Less Progress to Cut Long-Range Weapons' *NYT* 7.10.1991; Don Oberdorfer 'US Decides to Withdraw A-Weapons from S. Korea' *WP* 19.10.1991

19 On the link between the SNF disarmament initiatives and moving to START II, see GHWBPL NSC Burns Files – Subject Files: Yeltsin (OA/ID

CF01487–006) Cable by Scowcroft to Amb. Strauss at AmEmb Moscow incl. cover note and letter from Bush to Yeltsin 14.2.1992 pp. 1–2 and pp. 1–4. See also Susan J. Koch *The Presidential Nuclear Initiatives of 1991–1992* Center for the Study of Weapons of Mass Destruction Case Study #5 National Defense Univ. Press (September 2012) NSAEBB No. 561

20 Steven R. Weisman 'South Korea to Keep Out All Atom Arms' *NYT* 9.11.1991. See also Terence Roehrig 'The US Nuclear Umbrella over South Korea: Nuclear Weapons and Extended Deterrence' *Political Science Quarterly* 132, 4 (2017–18) pp. 667–8

21 See 'North Korea and Nuclear Weapons: The Declassified US Record' NSAEBB No. 87

22 Markku Anttila 'Pohjois-Korean ydinaseohjelma ja sen taustaa' October 2018 pp. 1–3 (paper given to the author); Bruce Cumings *Korea's Place in the Sun: A Modern History* W. W. Norton 1997 pp. 465–6, 469; Peter Hayes & Young Whan Kihl (eds) *Peace and Security in Northeast Asia: Nuclear Issue and the Korean Peninsula* M. E. Sharpe 1996 ch. 2; CIA *East Asia Brief* 27.12.1985 NSAEBB No. 87. GHWBPL Memcom of Bush–Roh talks 2.7.1991 Oval Office and Cabinet Room p. 3

23 Steven R. Weisman 'Leader of North Korea Denies Atom Arms Plan' *NYT* 20.12.1991. GHWBPL Memcon of Bush–Roh talks 6.6.1990 Oval Office p. 2. As Bush had told Kaifu two days before meeting Roh: 'We still do not want to have direct consultations with them. We want to make clear to North Korea that signing an IAEA agreement is absolutely essential before we begin to normalise in any way.' See GHWBPL

Telcon between Bush and Kaifu 4.6.1990 Oval Office p. 3

24 Cumings *Korea's Place in the Sun* pp. 466–7

25 Radchenko *Unwanted Visionaries* pp. 225, 244–5. 'Letter from G. F. Kunadze to R. I. Khazbulatov' 15.11.1991 State Archive of the Russian Federation (GARF) f. 10026 op. 5 d. 157 l. 17–19 DAWC. See also GHWBPL NSC H-Files – NSC/DC Meeting Files NSC/DC 221 13.11.1990 – NSC/DC Meeting on Korea (OA/ID 90017–017) US Policy Toward North Korea (undated) p. 3. Cf. Baker, who presents Russia's and China's pressure on their North Korean client state simply as the result of a policy masterminded by the USA, in his *The Politics* p. 595

26 'Record of Conversation between G. F. Kunadze and Yu Hongliang', 8.10.1991 (GARF) f. 10026 op. 1 d. 2290 l. 36–8 DAWC. See also Cable from Baker (DoS) to Cheney Subject: Dealing with the North Korean Nuclear Problem; Impressions from My Asia Trip 18.11.1991 NSAEBB No. 87

27 Taik-young Hamm 'North-South Korean Reconciliation and Security on the Korean Peninsula' *Asian Perspective* 25, 2 (2001) pp. 130–1; Clayton Jones 'China to Recognise South Korea' *CT* 24.8.1992; GHWBPL Memcon of Roh–Bush talks (one-on-one) 27.2.1989 Ching Wa Dae (Blue House) Seoul p. 3. Cf. Emma Chanlett-Avery et al. 'Sino-Japanese Relations: Issues for US Policy' *CRS report for Congress* 19.12.2008 pp. 5–6; Seongho Sheen 'Japan–South Korea Relations: Slowly Lifting the Burden of History?' *Occasional Papers – Asia-Pacific Center for Security Studies* (October 2003). On 'entering a new era' between

Japan and South Korea, see also GHWBPL Telcon of Bush–Kaifu talks 10.1.1991 Oval Office p. 2; Memcom of Bush–Roh talks 6.6.1990 Oval Office pp. 4–5. See also Memcon of Bush's talks with Prime Minister Noboru Takeshita of Japan 23.2.1989 Akasaka Palace Tokyo

28   Cumings *Korea's Place in the Sun* p. 466. On how the Bush administration sought to confront the nuclear programme of North Korea, see Briefing Book for NSC/DC 327 – Meeting on Korea Nuclear Program (to be held on 17.12.1991) 13.12.1991 (Secret) 34pp. NSAEBB 610

29   Leonard S. Spector & Jacqueline R. Smith 'North Korea: The Next Nuclear Nightmare?' *Arms Control Today* 21, 2 (March 1991) pp. 8–13; Leslie H. Gelb 'The Next Renegade State' *NYT* 10.4.1991. President Bush highlighted the danger of so-called 'renegade regimes' when he gave a speech in Aspen, Colorado on 2 August 1990. Then he had in mind the regime of Saddam Hussein in Iraq which had just invaded Kuwait. See Remarks at the Aspen Institute Symposium in Aspen Colorado 2.8.1990 APP. President Clinton in turn spoke in the July 1994 and subsequent 1995 version of his *National Security Strategy of Engagement and Enlargement* of 'rogue states' that 'pose a serious danger to regional stability in many corners of the globe'. Generally, American commentators and policymakers also referred to 'outlaw', 'pariah' or 'backlash' states. In their eyes, this 'distinct category' of states consisted – according to Robert Litwak – of North Korea, Iran, Iraq and Libya. See President William J. Clinton *National Security Strategy of Engagement*

and Enlargement White House July 1994; and Robert Litwak *Rogue States and US Foreign Policy* Woodrow Wilson Center Press 2000 esp. p. xiii and introduction. Cf. Michael Klare *Rogue States and Nuclear Outlaws: America's Search for a New Foreign Policy* Hill & Wang 1995; Anthony Lake 'Confronting Backlash States' *Foreign Affairs* 73, 2 (March/April 1994) pp. 45–55

30   See for example 'Engaging North Korea: Evidence from the Bush I Administration' NSAEBB No. 610

31   Bush's Remarks to the Korean National Assembly in Seoul 6.1.1992 APP

32   Memorandum by Pendley to Undersecretary of Defense for Policy – Subject: North Korea Nuclear Issue – Where are We Now? (Secret) 27.10.1992 NSAEBB No. 610; Anon. 'North Korea's Nuclear Power Programme Revealed' *Nuclear Engineering International* 37, 456 (1992) pp. 2–3; Duk-ho Moon 'North Korea's Nuclear Weapons Program: Verification Priorities and New Challenges' *Cooperative Monitoring Center Occasional Paper* no. 32 (2003) p. 7; J. B. Wolfsthal 'North Korea threatens withdrawal from Non-Proliferation Treaty' *Arms Control Today* 23, 3 (1993) p. 22; 'KCNA "Detailed Report" Explains NPT Withdrawal' Pyongyang KCNA 22.1.2003. See also GHWBPL NSC H-Files – NSC/DC Meeting Files: NSC/DC 341 20.3.1992 – NSC/DC Meeting on Korean Nuclear Programme (OA/ID 90021–029) Illustrative Timeline – DPRK could 'plausibly' delay IAEA inspections (undated, perhaps March 1992) pp. 1–2

33   Bush's Remarks to the Korean National Assembly in Seoul 6.1.1992 APP

34 Baker *The Politics* p. 44. Cf. *idem* 'America in Asia: Emerging Architecture for Pacific Community' *Foreign Affairs* 70, 5 (Winter 1991) [America and the Pacific, 1941–1991] pp. 1–18

35 Reynolds *One World Divisible* pp. 411–20. See also Ezra Vogel *Japan as Number One* Harvard UP 1979. Also index under Paul Kennedy *The Rise and Fall of Great Powers* Random House 1987 ch. 8. See the cover page 'Special Report – The Pacific Century: Is America In Decline?' *Newsweek* 22.2.1988

36 Kennedy *The Rise and Fall of Great Powers* ch. 8 ('The Japanese Dilemma')

37 Rosemary Foot & Andrew Walter 'Whatever happened to the Pacific Century?' *Review of International Studies* 25, 5 (1999) pp. 245–69; Jeffrey A. Frankel & Miles Kahler (eds) *Regionalism and Rivalry: Japan and the US in Pacific Asia* Univ. of Chicago Press 1993; Rüdiger Dornbusch 'The Dollar in the 1990s: Competitiveness and the Challenges of New Economic Blocs' in *Monetary Policy Issues in the 1990s* Federal Reserve Bank of Kansas City 1989 pp. 245–90

38 Foot & Walter 'Whatever happened to the Pacific Century?' p. 251

39 Saori N. Katada *Banking on Stability: Japan and the Cross-Pacific Dynamics of International Financial Crisis Management* Univ. of Michigan Press 2001 ch. 5; cf. Barbara Stallings 'The Reluctant Giant: Japan and the Latin American Debt Crisis' *Journal of Latin American Studies* 22, 1 (February 1990) pp. 1–30; Reynolds *One World Divisible* pp. 459–71. On the drug cartels, see Eugene Robinson 'The Other Cartel in Colombia' *WP* 28.1.1990. For the drug problem seen by Bush as a 'modern plague', see GHWBPL Memcon of Plenary Meeting of Bush–Kaifu talks (plenary) 1.9.1989 Oval Office p. 4

40 Brands *Making the Unipolar Moment* p. 325. Baker's Address 'Building a Newly Democratic International Society' at the World Affairs Council Dallas 30.3.1990 in *American Foreign Policy Current Documents 1990* Washington DC 1991 pp. 12–17 US DoS

41 'Brady Bonds' were introduced in 1989. The programme known as the Brady Plan called for the US and multilateral lending agencies, such as the IMF and the World Bank, to cooperate with commercial bank creditors in restructuring and reducing the debt of those developing countries that were pursuing structural adjustments and economic programmes supported by these agencies. The process of creating Brady Bonds involved converting defaulted loans into bonds with US Treasury zero-coupon bonds as collateral. On Brady Bonds, see investopedia.com/terms/b/bradybonds.asp#ixz-z5W5P74xLQ

42 Katada *Banking on Stability* pp. 127–30; *idem* 'Japan's Two-Track Aid Approach: The Forces behind Competing Triads' *Asian Survey* 42, 2 (March/April 2002) pp. 320–42; Erik Lundsgaarde et al. 'Trade Versus Aid: Donor Generosity in an Era of Globalisation' *Policy Sciences* 40, 2 (2007) pp. 157–8. See also GHWBPL Memcon of Bush–Kaifu talks 11.7.1991 Walker's Point p. 3; Memcon of Plenary Meeting of Bush–Kaifu talks (plenary) 1.9.1989 Oval Office p. 5; Memcon of Bush–Takeshita talks 23.2.1989 Akasaka Palace Tokyo pp. 3–5. On the US view 'trade is better than aid', see GHWBPL Memcon of

Bush–Miyazawa talks 1.7.1992 Cabinet Room p. 2

43 Bush's Remarks on Signing the North American Free Trade Agreement 17.12.1992 APP

44 GHWBPL Memcon of Bush–Kaifu talks 11.7.1991 Walker's Point p. 4.

45 James A. Baker 'A New Pacific Partnership: Framework for the Future' Asia Society New York 26.6.1989 p. 2 *Current Policy* No. 1185 US DoS

46 Ibid. pp. 1, 4. Note: Reagan in 1983 had lobbied for Japan to join the US in 'a powerful partnership for good'. Francis X. Clines 'Reagan Urges Japan to Join US in a Global "Partnership For Good"' *NYT* 11.11.1983. See also Hyung-Kook Kim 'US–JAPAN Relations: A Global Partnership "in Preparation"' *Asian Perspective* 23, 2 (1999) [Special Issue on the Dynamics of Northeast Asia and the Korean Peninsula] pp. 143–62 here esp. p. 145; and Warren S. Hunsberger (ed.) *Japan's Quest: The Search for International Role, Recognition, and Respect* Routledge 2015

47 See GHWBPL Memcon of Plenary Meeting of Bush–Kaifu talks 1.9.1989 Oval Office pp. 2–3; Memcon of Bush/Scowcroft talks with Matsunaga 11.1.1990 Brent Scowcroft's Office pp. 3–4. On SII, see Mitsuo Matsushita 'The Structural Impediments Initiative: An Example of Bilateral Trade Negotiation' *Michigan Journal of International Law* 12, 2 (1991) pp. 436–49; Michael Mastanduno 'Framing the Japan problem: The Bush Administration and the Structural Impediments Initiative' *International Journal* XLVll (Spring 1992) pp. 235–6

48 Foot & Walter 'Whatever happened to the Pacific Century?' p. 263

49 GHWBPL Memcon of plenary meeting between Bush and Takeshita 2.2.1989 Cabinet Room p. 3; Telcon of Bush–Miyazawa call 20.12.1991 Oval Office p. 1

50 GHWBPL Memcon of Bush–Kaifu meeting 1.9.1991 Oval Office p. 3

51 Clines 'Reagan Urges Japan to Join US in a Global "Partnership For Good"'

52 GHWBPL Telcon of Kaifu–Bush talks (one-on-one) 28.2.1991 Oval Office pp. 1–2; Memcon of one-on-one Bush–Kaifu talks 4.4.1991 Newport Beach California pp. 1, 4

53 GHWBPL Memcon of Bush–Ozawa talks 28.3.1991 Brent Scowcroft's Office p. 2

54 GHWBPL Memcon of Bush–Takeshita talks (Luncheon) 2.2.1989 Family Dining Room/The Residence pp. 2–4.

55 James A. Baker 'A New Pacific Partnership: Framework for the Future' p. 3; Cynthia Gorney 'Gorbachev Meets With Roh' *WP* 5.6.1990; Jim Mann 'Gorbachev, Roh Hold Historic Post-war Talks' *LAT* 5.6.1990

56 GHWBPL Memcon of plenary meeting between Bush and Takeshita 2.2.1989 Cabinet Room p. 4; Memcon of Bush–Takeshita talks (Luncheon) 2.2.1989 Family Dining Room/The Residence p. 2

57 GHWBPL Memcon of Working Lunch with Japanese Prime Minister Toshiki Kaifu 7.7.1990 Manor House Hotel Houston pp. 4–5. Kaifu had offered two further reasons why Japan was not keen at this stage to offer the Soviets aid: first, he said, 'we must see whether Soviet reform efforts are genuine or not'; second, he argued 'we take account of Soviet assistance to Cuba and Vietnam. We would like to see the Soviets withhold assistance to such countries. That's a great concern to us.'

58 Radchenko *Unwanted Visionaries* ch. 8 and pp. 309–10; Tuomas Forsberg 'Explaining Territorial Disputes: From Power Politics to Normative Reasons' *Journal of Peace Research* 33, 4 (November 1996) pp. 440–5; and *idem* 'Economic Incentives, Ideas, and the End of the Cold War: Gorbachev and German Unification' *JCWS* 7, 2 (Spring 2005) pp. 158–64

59 Radchenko *Unwanted Visionaries* pp. 274–5, 292–5; Tsuyoshi Hasegawa 'Gorbachev's Visit to Japan and Soviet–Japanese relations' *Acta Slavica Iaponica* 10 (1992) pp. 65–91; GHWBPL Memcon of Bush–Ozawa talks 28.3.1991 Brent Scowcroft's Office p. 5

60 GHWBPL Memcon of Bush–Kaifu talks 11.7.1991 Walker's Point p. 1

61 GHWBPL Memcon of G7 Meeting with President Gorbachev 17.7.1991 Music Room Lancaster House London p. 9

62 GHWBPL Memcon of Gorbachev–Bush talks (three-on-three meeting) 31.7.1991 Novo-Ogarevo pp. 2–3

63 JAB-SML B115/F9 Proposed Agenda for Meeting with the President 26.6.1992 p. 3. Baker further elaborated on US calculations as follows: 'A G8 including Russia might actually help us; the G7 is too EC-dominated; getting Russia in would break that. – It might help get a breakthrough on the Northern Territories.'

64 GHWBPL Memcon of Bush–Giuliano Amato (PM of Italy) talks 6.7.1992 Munich p. 3. Cf. TNA UK PREM 19/3924 Memo – Braithwaite to Prime Minister: Russia (restricted) pp. 1–3

65 GHWBPL Memcon of Bush–Delors talks 7.7.1992 Munich pp. 3–4; TNA UK PREM 10/3924 Memo – Heywood to Wall, Russia and the IMF 31.7.1992 pp. 1–3

66 Eleanor Randolph 'Yeltsin Scraps Japan Trip; Tokyo Irked' *WP* 10.9.1992; Peter Pringle 'Yeltsin Cancels visit to Japan' *Independent* 10.9.1992; Jim Hoagland 'The Yen for Small Islands' *WP* 17.9.1992. See also GHWBPL Memcon of Bush's talks with Deputy Foreign Minister Kunihiko Saito of Japan 9.6.1992 Brent Scowcroft's Office p. 3; Memcon of Bush–Miyazawa talks 1.7.1992 Cabinet Room p. 3. Cf. Peggy Falkenheim Meyer 'Moscow's Relations with Tokyo: Domestic Obstacles to a Territorial Agreement' *Asian Survey* 33, 10 (October 1993) pp. 953–67

67 Duckjoon Chang 'Breaking Through Stalemate? A Study Focusing on the Kuril Islands Issue in Russo-Japanese Relations' *Asian Perspective* 22, 3 (1998) pp. 177–83. Cf. Peter Berton 'A New Russo-Japanese Alliance? Diplomacy in the Far East during World War I' *Acta Slavica Iaponica* 11 (1993) p. 57; Harry Gelman 'Russo-Japanese Relations and the Future of the US Japanese Alliance' *Rand – Project AIR FORCE* Rand 1993 pp. i–xxv; GHWBPL Telcon of Bush and Yeltsin 10.9.1992 Oval Office pp. 1–2

68 June Teufel Dreyer *Middle Kingdom and Empire of the Rising Sun: Sino-Japanese Relations Past and Present* Oxford UP 2016 pp. 263–6, 292; Kerry Brown 'The Most Dangerous Problem in Asia: China–Japan Relations' *The Diplomat* 31.8.2016; Radchenko *Unwanted Visionaries* p. 310

69 GHWBPL Memcon of Bush–Mitsuzuka talks 26.6.1989 Oval Office p. 2; Memcon of Plenary Meeting of Bush–Kaifu talks 1.9.1989 Oval Office p. 2; Memcon of Working Lunch with Kaifu 7.7.1990 Manor House Hotel Houston p. 4. For Japan's continuous keenness

to help China 'modernise', see also GHWBPL Memcon of Bush–Takeshita talks 23.2.1989 Akasaka Palace Tokyo p. 5

70 This was a five-year package of some $6.28 billion. 'Japan Loans to China' *NYT* 5.11.1990

71 Furthermore, there was the renewed Chinese claim in the East China Sea to the Senkaku islands – known in the PRC as Diaoyutai Archipelago – which Tokyo considered its own. On 25 February 1992 Beijing had passed a law stipulating the islands as indigenous territory. See 'Foreign Minister on Disputes with PRC, Russia' Tokyo KYODO 28.3.1992 Daily Report – East Asia FBIS-EAS-92–061 30.3.1992 p. 4

72 Teufel *Middle Kingdom and Empire of the Rising Sun* pp. 190–1; Emma Chanlett-Avery et al. 'Sino-Japanese Relations: Issues for US Policy' *CRS Report for Congress* 19.12.2008 p. 6. For Japan's difficult history with China, see also GHWBPL Memcon of Bush–Deng talks 26.2.1989 Great Hall of the People Beijing pp. 2, 5; and Ezra F. Vogel's and Gilbert Rozman's contributions in 'The US–Japan–China Triangle: Who's the Odd Man Out?' *Asia Program Special Report* no. 113 (July 2003) pp. 5–6, 9–10. On exchange of visits between Jiang and the Japanese emperor, see Nicholas D. Kristof 'China's Party Chief Plans Trip to Japan' *NYT* 5.1.1992

73 Jian Yang 'Sino-Japanese Relations: Implications for Southeast Asia' *Contemporary Southeast Asia* 25, 2 (August 2003) p. 311; Steven R. Weisman 'Japan Leaders Are in Disarray on Troop Role' *NYT* 11.12.1991

74 It is noteworthy that in each capital Bush visited – Canberra, Singapore, Seoul and Tokyo – he underlined the enduring American commitment as well as his personal ties to the region. 'Let me put it plainly: I have served in Asia personally in time of war and in time of peace … Our role and our purpose as a Pacific power will remain constant … We will remain engaged.' See Michel Wines 'Bush Assures Australians of His Support' *NYT* 2.1.1992. On Japan's economic problems, see Mariko Fujii and Masahiro Kawa 'Lessons from Japan's Banking Crisis, 1991–2005' *ADBI (Asian Development Bank Institute) Working Paper Series* no. 222 (June 2010) pp. 2–3; Mitsuhiro Fukao 'Financial Crisis and Long-term Stagnation in Japan: Fiscal Consolidation under Deflationary Pressures' Paper for New York University Workshop 7–8.10.2010 pp. 1–23. On the US perspective, see Steven R. Weisman 'Japan's Chief Regrets Scrapping of Bush Trip' *NYT* 7.11.1991; *idem* 'Japan Irked as Bush Visit Turns into a Trade Quest' *NYT* 22.12.1991; Michael Wines 'Bush's Asian Trip Recast to Stress Jobs and Exports' *NYT* 29.12.1991. Cf. Michael Wines 'Bush Returns, Hailing Gains in Japan Agreement' *NYT* 11.1.1992 and Ezra F. Vogel 'Japanese–American Relations after the Cold War' *Daedalus* 121, 4 (Fall, 1992) [Immobile Democracy?] pp. 43–4

75 Timothy J. McNulty 'Bush Ups Price Of Pacific Security' *CT* 5.1.1992; Wines 'Bush's Asian Trip Recast'; James Sterngold 'The Quandary in Japan' *NYT* 6.1.1992

76 Michael Wines 'Bush Opens Singapore Trip with Announcements' *NYT* 4.1.1992; *idem* 'Reporter's Notebook; For Bush, Jog Overseas Beats Running at Home' *NYT* 5.1.1992

77   Bush was only the second US president to visit the country since Lyndon B. Johnson in 1967. Timothy J. McNulty 'Australians Rail at Bush Over Farm Subsidies' *CT* 2.1.1992

78   John E. Yang 'Bush Discounts Fears About Collapse' *WP* 9.1.1992; David E. Sanger 'Nuclear Deal, Seoul Halts War Game with US' *NYT* 7.1.1992; McNulty 'Australians Rail at Bush'; Wines 'Bush's Asian Trip Recast'

79   Sterngold 'The Quandary in Japan'

80   Michael Wines 'Japanese Visit, on the Surface: Jovial Bush, Friendly Crowds' *NYT* 8.1.1992; Rowland Evans & Robert Novak 'Bush's Tokyo Fall' *WP* 10.1.1992

81   See GHWBPL NSC Patterson Files – Subject File [President Pacific Trip 30 December 1991–10 January 1992] (OA/ ID CF01492–009) The White House – Press Release Fact Sheet: US–Japan Achievements on Economic issues 9.1.1992; The Tokyo Declaration on the US–Japan Global Partnership pp. 1–4; Global Partnership Plan of Action (Part I) and (Part II) pp. 1–11 and pp. 1–7; and 'Action by the Japanese and US Sides plus Joint Action' pp. 1–7. See also David E. Sanger 'A Trade Mission Ends in Tension as the "Big Eight" of Autos Meet' *NYT* 10.1.1992; Michael Wines 'Bush Reaches Pact with Japan, But Auto Makers Denounce It – Export Goal Unmet' *NYT* 10.12.1992

82   Wines 'Bush Reaches Pact With Japan'; *idem* 'Bush Returns, Hailing Gains in Japan Agreement'

83   Diary Entry 9.1.1992, printed in Bush *All the Best* p. 545

84   Ibid. p. 546

85   For a graphic description of the dinner, see John E. Yang 'Bush Discounts Fears About Collapse' *WP* 9.1.1992; Michael Wines 'Bush Collapses at State Dinner with the Japanese' *NYT* 9.1.1992; T. R. Reid 'New Tape Shows Bush's Dinner Fall; Media: Dramatic footage was shot by Japanese network that defied a ban and left cameras running – Film has not been broadcast' *LAT* 11.1.1992

86   Wines 'Bush Collapses at State Dinner with the Japanese'

87   Yang 'Bush Discounts Fears About Collapse'

88   Letter from Bush to Ellis 12.1.1992, printed in Bush *All the Best* p. 547

89   Ibid.; Wines 'Bush Collapses at State Dinner with the Japanese'

90   Yang 'Bush Discounts Fears about Collapse'; Diary Entry 9.1.1992, printed in Bush *All the Best* pp. 545–6

91   Anne McDaniel '25 Years Ago Today, George H. W. Bush Vomited on the Prime Minister of Japan' *Newsweek* 8.1.2017; Diary Entry 9.1.1992, printed in Bush *All the Best* p. 546

92   For 'hopscotch', see Wines 'Bush's Asian Trip Recast'. For 'descent into hell', see 'Die Höllenfahrt des Präsidenten' *Der Spiegel* 3/1992 13.1.1992

93   GHWBPL Memcon of Bush–Miyazawa talks 1.7.1992 Cabinet Room p. 3

94   Fukao 'Financial Crisis and Long-term Stagnation in Japan'

95   GHWBPL Memcon of Bush with Wan Li (Chairman of the Standing Committee of the National People's Congress and Member of the Politburo) talks 23.5.1989 Oval Office/Cabinet Room/Residence p. 2

96   Richard Madsen *China and the American Dream: A Moral Inquiry* Univ. of California Press 1995 pp. xvi, 4; Suettinger *Beyond Tiananmen* p. 85; UPI 'China's Deng is chosen *TIME*'s Man of the Year' *CT* 30.12.1985; Bush's Inaugural Address 20.1.1989 APP

97 Lampton *Same Bed* pp. 21–3. Bush & Scowcroft *A World Transformed* pp. 98–105. Regarding 'progress' on human rights, see Martin Tolchin 'House, Breaking With Bush, Votes China Sanctions' *NYT* 30.6.1989. Andrew Glass 'House Sanctions Post-Tiananmen China 29.6.1989' *Politico* 28.6.2011. Cf. Thomas Lum 'Human Rights in China and US Policy' *CPS Report for Congress* 18.7.2011

98 Bush's diary entry 24.6.1989, printed in Bush & Scowcroft *A World Transformed* pp. 104–5; David Skidmore & William Gates 'After Tiananmen: The Struggle over US Policy toward China in the Bush Administration' *Presidential Studies Quarterly* 27, 3 (Summer 1997) [The Presidency in the World] pp. 514–39

99 'Worried Chinese Leadership Says Gorbachev Subverts Communism' *NYT* 28.12.1989

100 Willy Wo-Lap Lam *China After Deng Xiaoping: The Power Struggle in Beijing Since Tiananmen* John Wiley & Sons 1995 p. 54; see also Suettinger *Beyond Tiananmen* pp. 93, 124

101 Suettinger *Beyond Tiananmen* pp. 92–3; Lam *China* pp. 62–4; Chris Miller *The Struggle to Save the Soviet Economy* Univ. of North Carolina Press 2016 pp. 164, 170. See also David Shambaugh 'China in 1990: The Year of Damage Control' *Asian Survey* 31, 1 (January 1991) [A Survey of Asia in 1990: Part I] pp. 36–49 here esp. p. 37

102 Steven Erlanger 'Top Aides to Bush are Visiting China to Mend Relations' *NYT* 10.12.1989

103 Ibid.

104 GHWBPL Scowcroft Collection SSCNF-CF China 1989 (sensitive) (OA/ID 91136–003) Memcon of Jiang–Scowcroft talks 10.12.1989 9:45–10:47 a.m. Beijing p. 8

105 GHWBPL Scowcroft Collection SSCNF-CF China 1989 (sensitive) (OA/ID 91136–003) Memcon of Private Meeting between Scowcroft and Qian 10.12.1989 2.13–2.50 p.m. Diaoyutai Guest House No. 9 Beijing p. 1

106 'Yang Says China Will Sell Saudi Arabia Missiles' *UPI* 27.12.1989; Kenneth Kaplan 'Syria China Sign Missile Deal' *Jerusalem Post* 12.12.1989 Lexis-Nexis

107 Andrew Rosenthal 'President Waives Some China Curbs' *NYT* 20.12.1989

108 Suettinger *Beyond Tiananmen* pp. 100–3. Robert Pear 'US Easing Curbs as China Declares Martial Law Over' *NYT* 11.1.1990; Daniel Southerland 'China Announces Release of 573 Detainees' *WP* 19.1.1990. Cf. GHWBPL Memcon of Bush–Qian talks 30.11.1990 Cabinet Room p. 4

109 See GHWBPL Scowcroft Collection SSCNF – CF China 1989 (sensitive) (OA/ID 91137–003) Talk by Douglas H. Paal (NSC) 'An Update on US Policy Toward China' at the Asia Society Washington DC 19.1.1990

110 Robert Pear 'US Official Urges "Real World" View of China' *NYT* 8.2.1990; John M. Goshko 'Eagleburger Defends China Policy, Senators Unconvinced' *WP* 8.2.1990; Robert Pear 'Bush Distressed as Policy Fails to Move China' *NYT* 11.3.1990; Baker *The Politics* p. 588. Cf. Steven Erlanger 'China Line: No Thawing' *NYT* 29.12.1989; GHWBPL Memcon of Bush–Qian talks 30.11.1990 Cabinet Room p. 5

111 GHWBPL First Main Plenary Session of the 16th Economic Summit of Industrialised Nations (G7) 10.7.1990 O'Conner Room – Herring Hall Rice University Houston pp. 2, 6. There has

so far been no German transcript released. For the British transcript, see TNA PREM 10/2945

112 Suettinger *Beyond Tiananmen*, p. 111

113 Baker *The Politics* p. 588; Engel *When the World Seemed New* pp. 197–8. See also GHWBPL Memcon of Bush's talks with Former Chinese Foreign Minister Huang Hua 23.1.1991 West Wing and Oval Office pp. 1–6

114 Frank Frost 'The Peace Process in Cambodia: The First Stage' *Background Paper* #14 (1992) Parliamentary Research Service Canberra Australia p. 2

115 Frost 'The Peace Process in Cambodia' pp. 3–4. M. Taylor Fravel 'China's Attitude toward UN Peacekeeping Operations since 1989' *Asian Survey* 36, 11 (November 1996) pp. 1102–21 esp. 1109–10. On the USSR and China holding the 'keys to peace in Cambodia' because 'They are waging a proxy war' see Mitterrand's comments at the Houston G7 summit in July 1990. Mitterrand held: 'China is the main culprit, helping the Khmer Rouge. It used to be the USSR that was the main problem, but now it is China. How do we put pressure on China?' See GHWBPL First Main Plenary Session of the 16th Economic Summit of Industrialised Nations (G7) 10.7.1990 Rice University Houston p. 14

116 Chien-peng Chung 'Designing Asia–Pacific Economic Cooperation' *Centre for Asian and Pacific Studies* Working Paper No. 189 (October 2007) pp. 5–6

117 Baker *The Politics* pp. 588–90

118 Ibid. p. 594

119 GHWBPL Memcon of Bush–Roh talks 2.7.1991 Oval Office and Cabinet Room p. 2

120 GHWBPL Telcon of Bush–Kaifu call 19.8.1991 Kennebunkport p. 2; Opening Session of the London Economic Summit (G7) 15.7.1991 Music Room Lancaster House London p. 7. See also Robert Benjamin 'Kaifu Visit Highlights China's Rebound, Ties Restored in Wake of 1989 Massacre' *Baltimore Sun* 9.8.1991

121 David Holley 'British Leader Visits Beijing, Easing Sanctions' *LAT* 3.9.1991; *idem* 'Britain and China Clash Over Rights' *LAT* 4.9.1991

122 Thomas L. Friedman 'US Calls North Korea Atom Plan a Global Concern' *NYT* 14.11.1991. See also Elaine Sciolino with Eric Schmitt 'Algerian Reactor Came From China' *NYT* 15.11.1991. See also David R. Schweisberg 'China vows to join Nuclear Non-Proliferation Treaty' *UPI* 10.8.1991.

123 Baker *The Politics* pp. 588, 590

124 Ibid. p. 590

125 Ibid.; Thomas L. Friedman 'Baker Asks China to Free Prisoners' *NYT* 16.11.1991 p. 3

126 Baker *The Politics* pp. 591–2; Thomas L. Friedman 'Baker Fails to Win Any Commitments in Talks in Beijing' *NYT* 17.11.1991. On China's desire to resume its status as a contracting party to GATT and to continue retaining MFN with the US, see GHWBPL Memcon of Scowcroft–Zhu Qizhen talks 25.6.1991 West Wing pp. 1–3

127 Baker *The Politics* p. 593; Thomas L. Friedman 'Baker's China Trip Fails to Produce Pledge on Rights' *NYT* 18.11.1991. China's global proliferation initiatives included: shipments of nuclear-related technology and the sale of nuclear weapons designs to Argentina, Brazil, India, South Africa, as well as selling weapons-grade uranium to Johannesburg and Islamabad (which passed the weapons' designs later to

Libya). See Gary Milhollin & Gerard White 'A New China Syndrome: Beijing's Atomic Bazaar' *WP* 12.5.1991; Sciolino with Schmitt 'Algerian Reactor Came From China'

128 China's ratification of the NPT occurred in March 1992 with the PRC being the last of the acknowledged nuclear powers to sign up to the pact. See also Haotan Wu 'China's Non-proliferation Policy and the Implementation of WMD Regimes in the Middle East' *Asian Journal of Middle Eastern and Islamic Studies* 11, 1 (2017) pp. 65–82

129 Baker *The Politics* pp. 592–4; Friedman 'Baker's China Trip Fails To Produce Pledge On Rights'; Adam Clymer 'China Rebuff Seems Unlikely to Hurt Trade Status' *NYT* 19.11.1991

130 Lampton *Same Bed* p. 31

131 Ibid.; Friedman 'Baker Fails To Win Any Commitments In Talks In Beijing'. See also Nicholas D. Kristof 'Visit to China: Vexing Ritual' *NYT* 19.11.1991

132 Qian Qichen quoted in Bush & Scowcroft *A World Transformed* p. 177

133 'China Extends a Friendly Loan to Moscow' *NYT* 16.3.1991

134 Li Peng quoted in Radchenko *Unwanted Visionaries* p. 183

135 See Radchenko *Unwanted Visionaries* pp. 181, 183–4; Lampton *Same Bed* pp. 30–1. See also Nicholas D. Kristof 'Chinese Premier Defends '89 Crackdown on Protestors' *NYT* 10.4.1991

136 Jim Mann, 'Official Dilemma: Should Bush Meet China's Li?' *LAT* 25.1.1992; Barbara Crossette 'Despite Criticism, Bush Will Meet Chinese Premier' *NYT*, 30.1.1992; 'Mr Bush Meets Mr Li' *WP* 31.1.1992; Robert D. McFadden 'Leaders Gather in New York to Chart a World Order' *NYT* 31.1.1992

137 Barbara Crossette 'State Department Cites China and Other Nations for Human Rights Abuses' *NYT* 1.2.1992

138 'Excerpts from Speeches by Leaders of Permanent Members of UN Council' *NYT* 1.2.1992

139 There is no Memcon released or currently to be found at the GHWBPL.

140 Seth Faison Jr 'Bush and Chinese Prime Minister Meet Briefly at UN Amid Protests' *NYT* 1.2.1992. See also Elaine Sciolino 'US Lifts Its Sanctions on China over High-Technology Transfers' *NYT* 2.2.1992

141 Ibid.

142 Suettinger in his book *Beyond Tiananmen* dedicated his fourth chapter to this period 1989–1992 which he entitled 'The Slow Road to Recovery'

143 Julian Gewirtz *Unlikely Partners: Chinese Reformers, Western Economists, and the Making of Global China* Harvard UP 2017 pp. 236–9; Baum *Burying Mao* p. 321

144 Suettinger *Beyond Tiananmen* pp. 122–9, 134–8; Lampton *Same Bed* p. 31; Gewirtz *Unlikely Partners* pp. 241, 243, 245–50. See also Lyman Miller 'Overlapping Transitions in China's Leadership' *SAIS Review* 16, 2 (Summer/ Fall 1996) pp. 21–42

145 Suettinger *Beyond Tiananmen* pp. 136–8; Gerwitz *Unlikely Partners* pp. 241, 251–2, 136–8. See also 'Full Text of Jiang Zemin's Report at 14th Party Congress' bjreview.com.cn/document/ txt/2011–03/29/content_363504.htm

146 GHWBPL Memcon of Bush–Zhu Qizhen talks 3.8.1992 Residence p. 2; Peter Mattis 'From Engagement to Rivalry: Tools to Compete with China' *Texas National Security Review* 21.8.2018

147 Nicholas D. Kristof 'China Worried by Clinton's Linking of Trade to Human

Rights' *NYT* 9.10.1992; C-Span's presidential debate 12 October 1992 (video and transcript) c-span.org/video/?33071–1/1992–presidential-candidates-debate

148 Nicholas D. Kristof 'China Signs US Oil Deal for Disputed Waters' *NYT* 18.6.1992; Marc J. Valencia 'The Spratly Imbroglio in the Post-Cold War Era' in Bruce Burton & David Wurfel (eds) *Southeast Asia in the New World Order: The Political Economy of a Dynamic Region* St Martin's Press 1996 p. 248; Sanqiang Jian 'Multinational oil companies and the Spratly Dispute' *Journal of Contemporary China* 6, 16 (1997) pp. 591–601. See also Christopher Helman 'Whatever Is Behind China's Spratly Island Showdown, It Isn't Drilling for Oil' *Forbes* 27.5.2015

149 This is what Defence Minister Yazov and General Staff Mikhail Moiseyev told a Chinese military delegation a week *before* the coup! Quote from Radchenko *Unwanted Visionaries* p. 185

150 Miller *The Struggle* pp. 168–71. On the figures regarding military expenditure for the Soviet Union (based on Soviet sources not CIA estimates which were a few per cent higher), see Mark Harrison 'A No-Longer-Useful Lie' *Hoover Digest* no. 1 (2009); *idem* 'Secrets, Lies, and Half Truths: the Decision to Disclose Soviet Defense Outlays' *PERSA Working Paper* no. 55 (September 2008). For Chinese figures and problems with PRC data (the official PRC figure for defence spending was 2.5%), see Shaoguang Wang 'Estimating China's Defence Expenditure: Some Evidence from Chinese Sources' *The China Quarterly* 147 (September 1996) pp. 889–911, here esp. pp. 895–6. Cf. *idem* 'The Military

Expenditure of China, 1989–98' p. 15 web.duke.edu/pass/pdf/warpeaceconf/p-wangs.pdf; Richard A. Bitzinger & Chong-Pin Lin 'The Defense Budget of the People's Republic of China' *The Defense Budget Project* Washington November 1994 p. 2

151 Zhang Zhen quoted in Radchenko *Unwanted Visionaries* p. 188

152 See ch. 8 pp. 462–4; Alison Mitchell 'Yeltsin, on Summit's Stage, Stresses his Russian Identity' *NYT* 1.2.1992; Paul Lewis 'World Leaders, at the UN, Pledge to Expand Its Role to Achieve a Lasting Peace' *NYT* 1.2.1992

153 William Safire 'On Language; The Near Abroad' *NYT Magazine* 22.5.1994

154 Bobo Lo 'China and Russia: Common Interests, Contrasting Perceptions' *CLSA-Asia Pacific Markets – Asian geopolitics: special report* (May 1996) pp. 1–31 here p. 8

155 Kozyrev quoted in Jeanne L. Wilson *Strategic Partners: Russian–Chinese Relations in the Post-Soviet Era* M. E. Sharpe 2004 p. 145

156 Yuri Davenkov 'Foreign Ministry on Kozyrev's Asia Trip Result' *Moscow Rossiyskaya Gazeta* 27.3.1992 Daily Report – Central Eurasia FBIS-SOV-92–228 (31.3.1992); 'Moscow Plans on Expanding Trade With PRC' *Moscow INTERFAX* 2.4.1992 Daily Report – Central Eurasia FBIS-SOV-92–228 (3.4.1992); Helen Belopolsky *Russia and the Challengers: Russian Alignment with China, Iran and Iraq in the Unipolar Era* Palgrave Macmillan 2009 p. 66

157 Mette Skak 'Post-Soviet Foreign Policy: The Emerging Relationship Between Russia and North East Asia' *Journal of East Asian Affairs* 7, 1 (Winter/Spring 1993) pp. 137–85 esp. p. 164; 'Yeltsin

Hails New Era in Relations with China' Daily Report – Central Eurasia FBIS-SOV-92-228 (25.11.1992). NOTE: in the FBIS the translation of *Itar-TASS* into English says 'a new and historical era'.

158 Alexander Lukin *China and Russia: The New Rapprochement* Polity Press 2018 ch. 4

159 Wilson *Strategic Partners* p. 146

160 Elizabeth Wishnick 'Russia and China: Brothers Again?' *Asian Survey* 41, 5 (September/October 2001) pp. 797–821 esp. pp. 799–800; Gilbert Rozman 'China's Quest for Great Power Identity' *Orbis* 43, 3 (Summer 1999) pp. 383–402. See also Martin A. Smith 'Russia and multipolarity since the end of the Cold War' *East European Politics* 29, 1 (2013) pp. 36–51. See also Pierre Lagayette *Exchange: Practices and Representations* Univ. of Paris-Sorbonne Press 2005 p. 46; and Bobo Lo *Axis of Convenience: Moscow, Beijing, and the New Geopolitics* Brookings Institution Press 2008

Epilogue

1 Bush's Remarks at Texas A&M University in College Station Texas 15.12.1992 APP

2 On the concepts of 'electoral revolution' and cross-national or transnational 'diffusion', see Valerie Bunce & Sharon L. Wolchik 'Transnational Networks, Diffusion Dynamics, and Electoral Revolutions in the Postcommunist World' *Physica A* 378 (2007) pp. 92–9; Padraic Kenney 'Opposition Networks and Transnational Diffusion in the Revolutions of 1989' in Gerd-Rainer Horn & Padraic Kenney *Transnational Moments of Change: Europe 1945, 1968, 1989* Rowman & Littlefield 2004 pp. 207–23

3 Memcon of Kohl–Gorbachev talks in Moscow 15.7.1990, printed in *DESE* doc. 350 pp. 1340–1. Cf. Memcon of Kohl–Gorbachev plenary talks in Moscow 15.7.1990, printed in *DESE* doc. 352 p. 1354

4 On leaders making choices in 1989–92, see Zelikow & Rice *To Build a Better World*

5 Russia joined the WTO (previously GATT) in 2012 after nineteen years of 'tortuous negotiations', China in 2001 after fifteen years of talks. Catherine Belton 'Russia joins WTO after nineteen years of talks' *FT* 22.8.2012; 'China Joins WTO Ranks' *NYT* 12.12.2001. Fukuyama 'The End of History?' p. 4 and *idem*, *The End of History* p. 330

6 GHWBPL Scowcroft SSCNF-CF China 1989 (sensitive) (OA/ID 91136-001) Memcon of Deng–Scowcroft talks 2.7.1989 10:00 a.m. Great Hall of the People Beijing p. 5

7 Bush & Scowcroft *A World Transformed* p. 9

8 Jan Orbie 'Civilian Power Europe – Review of the Original and Current Debates' *Cooperation and Conflict* 41, 1 (2006) pp. 123–8; Smith 'Beyond the Civilian Power EU Debate' pp. 63–82

9 See David S. Yost 'The New NATO and Collective Security' *Survival* 40, 2 (Summer 1998) pp. 135–60; Hamilton & Spohr (eds) *Open Door* p. xv. See also Tarcisio Gazzini 'NATO's Role in the Collective Security System' *Journal of Conflict & Security Law* 8, 2 (October 2003) pp. 231–63

10 Walter Clarke & Jeffrey Herbst 'Somalia and the Future of Humanitarian Intervention' *Foreign Affairs* 76, 2, (March/April 1996) pp. 70–1.

11 GHWBP NSC Gompert Files ESSG (CF01301-009) US Security and Institutional Interest in Europe and

Eurasia in the post-Cold War era (undated, *circa* February 1992) p. 2 [with cover note from Gompert to Zoellick et al. 19.2.1992]; US National Security Interest in Europe and Beyond the NATO Area (undated, *circa* February 1992) pp. 1–4 [with cover note from Gompert to Zoellick et al. 7.2.1992]; NACC – CSCE Relationship (undated, early 1992 by EUR/RPM: SMcGinnis) pp. 1–4

12   William H. Hill *No Place for Russia: European Security and Institutions Since 1989* Columbia UP 2018

13   GBWPL NSC Gompert Files ESSG (CF01301–009) Memorandum from Lowenkron to Howe – Subj.: ESSG Mtg 30.3.1992 SitRoom 26.3.1992 p. 2 ('Handling Russia'). Francis X. Clines 'Gorbachev Pleads for $100 Billion in Aid from West' *NYT* 23.5.1991

14   Zelikow & Rice *Germany Unified* pp. 370, 368. Cf. Mary Elise Sarotte 'Mourning a President, and Much Else Besides: George H. W. Bush and the Lost Art of Transatlantic Statecraft' *Foreign Affairs* (5 December 2018) online

15   Bush's Address Before a Joint Session of the Congress on the Persian Gulf Crisis and the Federal Budget Deficit 11.9.1990 APP

16   See Andrew Rosenthal 'Bush Reluctantly Concludes Gorbachev Tried to Cling to Power Too Long' *NYT* 25.12.1991

17   Russia's participation at the G7 in the 7 + 1 format, and from 1997 Russia's formal admission to what became the G8, was based on the premise that Russia was democratising. As had been agreed in at the Munich G7 in 1992, the club was defined as one consisting of the eight largest 'democratic states',

which thus allowed for the inclusion of Russia and the exclusion of China. In March 2014 after Russia's annexation of Crimea, Russian membership was suspended and in 2017 Russia announced its withdrawal from the forum which reverted back to its G7 name. As the G20 (founded in 1999 to promote international financial stability) has meanwhile grown in stature, the G7 retains its relevance as the steering group for the West with special significance appointed to Japan.

18   Charles Krauthammer 'The Unipolar Moment' *WP* 20.7.1990

19   Richard Spielman 'The Emerging Unipolar World' *NYT* 21.8.1990

20   For Krauthammer's revised view in winter 1991 – that the summer 1990 'myth' had exploded and that the 'new rivals, the great pillars of the new multipolar world, would be Japan and Germany (and/or Europe)', because, so Krauthammer thought, 'the notion that economic power inevitably translates into geopolitical influence is a materialist illusion' – see his article 'The Unipolar Moment' *Foreign Affairs* 70, 1 (1990/1) [America and the World 1990/91] pp. 23–33. For a critique on Krauthammer's Unipolar Moment linked to unilateral US actions, see for example Barbara J. Falk '1989 and Post-Cold War Policymaking: Were the "Wrong" Lessons Learned from the Fall of Communism?' *International Journal of Politics, Culture, and Society* 22, 3 (September 2009) pp. 293–5. Cf. Charles Krauthammer 'The Unipolar Moment Revisited' *The National Interest* 70 (Winter 2002/03) pp. 5–17 and Brands *Making the Unipolar Moment*

21   Maull 'Germany and Japan' p. 106

22 Bush's Address to the Nation Announcing Allied Military Action in the Persian Gulf 16.1.1991 APP. Bagger 'The World According to Germany' p. 57

23 Tong Shi 'Xi Jinping Lays Out Blueprint to Make China a Global Superpower by 2050' *National Post* 18.10.2017

24 John Movroydis 'Synopsis: The Rise of Xi Jinping and China as Global Player' 26.6.2018 Richard Nixon Presidential Library and Museum website

25 Jonathan Hillman 'A Chinese World Order' *WP* 23.7.2018

26 Cf. Odd Arne Westad 'The Cold War and America's Delusion of Victory' *NYT* 28.8.2017

27 In view of Europe, this era has also been coined an epoch of 'cold peace' – a time when a peace system marked by the tension between cooperative and competitive behaviour of Russia and the Atlantic community – which lasted from 1992 until the crisis exploded in Ukraine in 2014 provoking what some have called a 'new Cold War'. See Richard Sakwa *Russia Against the Rest: The Post-Cold War Crisis of World Order* Cambridge UP 2017. Cf. Horst Teltschik *Russisches Roulette: Vom Kalten Krieg zum Kalten Frieden* Beck 2019

28 GHWBPL, Scowcroft SSCNF-CF China 1989 (sensitive) (OA/ID 91136–001) Memcon of Deng–Scowcroft talks 2.7.1989 10.00 a.m. Great Hall of the People Beijing p. 5

29 'The World's top 10 Largest Economies 2018' focus-economics.com/blog/the-largest-economies-in-the-world

30 Jeff Stein 'US Military Budget Inches Closer to $1 Trillion Mark, as Concerns over Federal Deficit Grow' *WP* 19.6.2018; 'China raises 2018 military budget by 8.1%' *Reuters* 4.3.2018; Craig Caffrey 'Russia Adjusts Defence Spending Upward' *Jane's Defence Weekly* 21.3.2018

31 David Vine lists 516 US bases and 271 US lily pads (plus fifty-six US-funded host nation bases) – overall almost 800 US-controlled base sites – overseas. See David Vine, 'List of US Military Bases Abroad, 2017, derived from research for *Base Nation: How US Military Bases Abroad Harm America and the World* [Metropolitan Books 2015]'; *idem* 'Where in the World Is the US Military?' *POLITICO Magazine* July/August 2015; Damien Sharkov 'Russia's Military Compared to the US: Which Country Has More Military Bases across the World?' *Newsweek* 3.6.2018

32 William T. R. Fox *The Super-Powers: The United States, Britain, and the Soviet Union – Their Responsibility for Peace* Harcourt Brace 1944 p. 21

33 'Current United States Counterterror War Locations Map' *Costs of War Project* Watson Institute for International and Public Affairs website; Tom Engelhardt 'Mapping a World From Hell: 76 Countries Are Now Involved in Washington's War on Terror' *TomDispatch & Watson Institute* 4.1.2018

34 David Brennan '9/11 Anniversary: How Safe Is America after 17 Years of War on Terror?' *Newsweek* 11.9.2018

35 Bush's Address Before a Joint Session of the Congress on the State of the Union 29.1.1991 APP

36 John A. Thompson 'Wilsonianism: The Dynamics of a Conflicted Concept' *International Affairs* 86, 1 (2010) pp. 27–48 esp. pp. 27–30, 44–5

37 Remarks by President George W. Bush at the 20th Anniversary of the National Endowment for Democracy at the US

Chamber of Commerce in Washington DC 6.11.2003 GWB WHArchives website

38 Hillary Clinton's Keynote Address for the National Democratic Institute's 2011 Democracy Awards Dinner at the Andrew W. Mellon Auditorium in Washington DC 7.11.2011 USDoS 2009–2017 archived content website; Clinton embraces the freedom agenda 7.11.2011 Freedom House website

39 Clinton's Keynote at the National Democratic Institute's 2011 Democracy Awards Dinner 6.11.2003

40 Ibid.; Mark Galeotti '(Mis)Understanding Russia's Two "Hybrid Wars"' *Critique & Humanism* 49, 1 (2018) [Media, Conspiracies and Propaganda in the post-Cold War World] 29.11.2018. The Euromaidan revolt in Ukraine revived the 'colour revolutions' a decade earlier. Cf. Tristan Landry 'The Colour Revolutions in the Rear-view Mirror: Closer Than They Appear' *Canadian Slavonic Papers / Revue Canadienne des Slavistes* 53, 1 (March 2011) pp. 1–24; Melinda Haring & Michael Cecire 'Why the Colour Revolutions Failed' *Foreign Policy* (18 March 2013) online

41 Cf. Brian Grodsky 'Trump, Clinton and the Future of Global Democracy' *The Conversation* (25 September 2016) online

42 Glenn Plaskin 'The 1990 *Playboy* Interview with Donald Trump' *Playboy* 1.3.1990

43 'Transcript: Donald Trump's Foreign Policy Speech' *NYT* 27.4.2016

44 Michael H. Fuchs 'Donald Trump's doctrine of Unpredictability has the World on Edge' *Guardian* 13.2.2017

45 Nicole Gaouette 'Russia, China Use UN Stage to Push Back on a US-led World Order' *CNN* 21.9.2017; Joel Gehrke 'Russia: "We Are in the post-West World Order"' *Washington Examiner* 29.6.2018; *idem* 'Russia Calls for "post-West World Order"' *Washington Examiner* 18.2.2017; 'Vladimir Putin Says Liberalism Has "Become Obsolete"' *FT* 27.6.2019; '"Liberalism Is Obsolete," Russian President Vladimir Putin Says Amid G20 Summit' *TIME* 28.6.2019

46 Bush's Remarks at Texas A&M University in College Station Texas 15.12.1992 APP

Acknowledgements

This book could not have been written without the assistance, encouragement and advice of numerous individuals and organisations.

On the business side Andrew Gordon (of David Higham Associates) and his team have been great champions – without them there would be no *Post Wall, Post Square* in its various incarnations. My editor Arabella Pike (at HarperCollins) took a keen and constructive interest in the project from the beginning. My copyeditor David Milner was wonderfully precise, while on the production side Heike Schüssler, Jo Thompson and Iain Hunt turned this book into a piece of art.

For primary sources and images, I would like to thank the helpful archivists and staff of the Bundesarchiv, Bundesbildstelle, Politisches Archiv des Auswärtigen Amts (PAAA), Deutsche Presse-Agentur (DPA), George H. W. Bush Presidential Library (GHWBPL), Seeley Mudd Library (SML), National Security Archive at George Washington University (NSA-GWU), Wilson Center (WC), The UK National Archives (TNA), Churchill Archives (CHU), Margaret Thatcher Foundation, Foreign and Commonwealth Office (FCO), Centre des Archives diplomatiques du ministère des Affaires étrangères (MAE), Eesti Välisministeerium (ESTVM). I am especially grateful to Cody McMilian and Cori Conrad (GHWBPL), Knut Piening (PAAA), Alan Packwood and Andrew Riley (CHU), Daniel S. Linke and Christa Cleeton (SML), Kadri Linnas (EST VM), Charles Kraus (WC) and Peter Stroh (DPA) for help with declassification requests or special searches. I am also indebted to Meelis Maripuu and Indrek Elling (in Estonia) for helping me take notes in Tallinn's archives; to Olga Kucherenko (in France) for translating a mountain of Soviet sources and chasing Quai d'Orsay memos; to Mary Sarotte, Stephan Kieninger and Liviu Horowitz (at SAIS), Stefano Recchia (at Cambridge), Patrick Salmon (at the FCO), Ilse Dorothee Pautsch (in Berlin) as well as Gudni Johannesson and Jón Baldvin Hannibalsson (in Iceland) for sharing documents; to Zhong Zhong Chen (at LSE) and Julian Gewirtz (at Harvard) for pointing me to Chinese materials; to Matthew Wilson (at SAIS/USAF) for helping me compile the bibliography; to Sir Rodric Braithwaite for letting me read his 'Moscow Diary'; to James A. Baker III for granting me access to his papers; and among many other policymakers especially to several late German statesmen who offered up their time for interviews: Hans-Dietrich Genscher, Egon Bahr, Richard von Weizsäcker and Ulrich Weisser.

The following institutions and grant-awarding bodies have generously facilitated the researching and writing of this book: the Henry A. Kissinger Center for Global Affairs at Johns Hopkins University's School of Advanced International Studies (SAIS) in Washington DC which – under the directorship of Francis Gavin – is hosting me as Helmut Schmidt Distinguished Chair, a transatlantic initiative supported by the German Academic Exchange Service (DAAD) and funded by the Federal Foreign Ministry (AA); the Leverhulme Foundation with a Fellowship for 2017–18 (grant RF-2016-318); Churchill College Cambridge which elected me as an Archives By-Fellow; Christ's College Cambridge with its perpetual hospitality towards its former fellows; and the London School of Economics and Political Science (LSE) and my home department of International History, which under the headship of Janet Hartley and Matthew Jones has tolerated my absence, while Robert Brier and Una Bergmane have splendidly covered my teaching and Keri Rowsell together with Demetra Frini and Nayna Bhatti managed the research grants. Special thanks to Andreas Görgen (AA), Margret Wintermantel (DAAD), Vali Nasr and Eliot Cohen (SAIS), as well as Christopher Crosbie, Diane Bernabei, Mary Gronkiewicz, Robin Forsberg and last but not least Jason Moyer (HKC and FPI, SAIS) for all their support along the way.

The book benefited from three AA/DAAD-sponsored author-witness workshops on East–West relations in the 1980s and 1990s that I co-organised – whose topics and participating policymakers are listed in the Notes. These projects would not have been possible without the stimulating input and congeniality of 'my' postdocs: John-Michael Arnold, Elias Götz, Wencke Meteling, Cengiz Günay as well as Liviu and Stephan (mentioned above). I am also lucky for the many illuminating conversations with several generations of LSE and SAIS students and fellow historians Gundula Bavendamm, Frédéric Bozo, Stefan Forss, Tuomas Fosberg, Bridget Kendall, Mark Kramer, Jaakko Lehtovirta, Vojtech Mastny, Sönke Neitzel, Andreas Rödder, Jyrki Vesikansa and Arne Westad.

Over the past years, I have accumulated huge debts with friends, colleagues, practitioners and loved ones – without whose support such an international venture and global book project would be impossible.

I thank David Reynolds who, between the composition of *The Kremlin Letters* and *Island Stories*, still found the time to tirelessly read drafts and debate the political ventures of Mrs T. or Frau M. in their attempts to cope with Helmut or Donald. I am also very grateful to Zara Steiner, David Stevenson, Sirpa Nyberg, Steve Casey, Philip Zelikow, Robert Blackwill and Dan Hamilton for their immensely insightful comments on all or parts of the first draft.

On this journey, from Wintex 89 (via Taiping and 1848) to Washington, Christopher Clark has been a wonderfully inquisitive and inspiring companion. Thanks to him, this has become a much richer book.

Beyond all things history, I wish to thank my parents: 'Tehtävä on suoritettu.' With this story, I want to remind them of moments in their lives when they were beyond the Iron Curtain (in Kiev, Warsaw and Murmansk) as funny historical coincidences of global import. Thanks also to my cousins Kalle and Teemu Kinnari (plus extended family) who have reminded me of the beauty of Finnish summers on the family farm and by the lakeside; and to Sanna Vesikansa, Dorle Sanwald, Lizzie Watson, Gavin Hyman, Sarah Windheuser, Uli Volp, Alexia Holstein-Volp, Torsten Krude, Astrid Langer, Jochen Starke and Jakob von Weizsäcker for great friendship.

As I have written this book and travelled between continents, I have kept thinking of several people full of joie de vivre and drive with striking life stories that have spurred me on to persist and dig deeper. *In memoriam* Kyllikki and Toivo Anttila (Hollola), Ilse Kempgen, Hatto Küffner (Düsseldorf) and Anna Skinnari (Coral Gables). Equally crucial on my personal path out of the Cold War era – letting me glimpse that world through the artistic and the scientific eye – have been my violin teacher Rosa Fain (a concert musician originally from Odessa) and my Finnish uncle Markku Anttila (a nuclear physicist).

From all these individuals, I have learned many different things.

This book is dedicated to my four lovely godchildren – with whom I always share such happy and enriching times. I thank their parents Dagmar and Gene Schäfer-Gehrau, Kathryn and Antony Rix as well as Ariel and Peter Speicher for all the trust they placed in me many years ago. Anna Lisa, Daniel, James and Clio were born into the post-Wall world. As they set out amid today's unsettled times to shape their future and chase their dreams, I hope they sense from the following pages how their world first came to be – through cooperation not conflagration, through peace not war.

ARKS

17.6.2019 in Washington DC

List of Illustrations

p. 468 IMF 'Air Drop' cartoon by Herb Block, 23 December 1993 *(© The Herb Block Foundation)*

p. 475 Yeltsin before the US Congress, 16 June 1992 *(ITAR-TASS/Alexander Chumichev and Alexander Sentsov/Getty Images)*

p. 484 Communism/Capitalism Bakery cartoon by Dan Wasserman, *Boston Globe*, 1992 *(© 1992 Dan Wasserman. All rights reserved. Distributed by Tribune Content Agency)*

p. 488 Slobodan Milošević, Belgrade, 28 February 1989 *(Martin Cleaver/AP/Shutterstock)*

p. 510 United Nations Protection Force (UNPROFOR), soldiers of the British battalion monitor the movement of Bosnian Muslims at a United Nations checkpoint, 1 May 1994, Stari Vitez, Bosnia and Herzegovina *(UN Photo/John Isaac)*

p. 514 *Daily Mirror* front page, 7 August 1992 *(Mirrorpix)*

p. 517 Famine in Somalia, August 1992 *(Gysembergh Benoit/Paris Match via Getty Images)*

p. 528 Bush in Mogadishu, 1 January 1993 *(Larry Downing/Sygma/Sygma via Getty Images)*

p. 530 Bush and Yeltsin toast START II, Moscow, 3 January 1993 *(David Ake/AFP/Getty Images)*

p. 532 Bush jogging in Sydney, 1 January 1992 *(Craig Golding/Fairfax Media via Getty Images)*

p. 534 Kim Jong-Il with North Korean top brass, September 1988 *(AFP/Getty Images)*

p. 539 World (dis-)order cartoon by Adrian Raeside *(© raesidecartoon.com)*

p. 551 Farmers' protest, Sydney, 5 January 1992 *(Philip Wayne Lock/Fairfax Media via Getty Images)*

p. 553 Bush in Tokyo, 7 January 1992 *(Dennis Cook/AP/Shutterstock)*

p. 560 Brent Scowcroft and Jiang Zemin, Beijing, 10 December 1989 *(Forrest Anderson/The LIFE Images Collection via Getty Images/Getty Images)*

p. 572 Jiang and Deng at the 14th CCP Party Congress, Beijing, October 1992 *(top: Mike Fiala/AFP/Getty Images; bottom: AFP/Getty Images)*

p. 577 Yeltsin and Yang Shangkun sign the joint declaration, Beijing, 17 December 1992 *(ITAR-TASS/Alexander Chumichev and Alexander Sentsov/Getty Images)*

Index